Introductory Maths for Physicists and Astronomers

PEARSON
Custom Publishing

We work with leading authors to develop the strongest educational materials bringing cutting-edge thinking and best learning practice to a global market.

Under a range of well-known imprints, including Financial Times/Prentice Hall, Addison Wesley and Longman, we craft high quality print and electronic publications which help readers to understand and apply their content, whether studying or at work.

Pearson Custom Publishing enables our customers to access a wide and expanding range of market-leading content from world-renowned authors and develop their own tailor-made book. You choose the content that meets your needs and Pearson Custom Publishing produces a high-quality printed book.

To find out more about custom publishing, visit www.pearsoncustom.co.uk

A Pearson Custom Publication

Introductory Maths for Physicists and Astronomers

Compiled from:

Mathematics for Engineers: A Modern Interactive Approach Third Edition
by Anthony Croft and Robert Davison

Advanced Modern Engineering Mathematics
Third Edition
by Glyn James

PEARSON
Custom Publishing

Pearson Education Limited
Edinburgh Gate
Harlow
Essex CM20 2JE

And associated companies throughout the world

Visit us on the World Wide Web at:
www.pearsoned.co.uk

First published 2011

Compiled from:

Mathematics for Engineers: A Modern Interactive Approach Third Edition
by Anthony Croft and Robert Davison
ISBN 978 0 13 205156 9

Advanced Modern Engineering Mathematics Third Edition
by Glyn James
ISBN 978 0 13 045425 6

ISBN 978 0 85776 015 9

Printed and bound in Great Britain by Ashford Colour Press, Gosport, Hampshire.

Contents

Logarithms and exponentials

Chapter 8

This chapter examines two important functions: the exponential function and the logarithmic function. Each function is the inverse of the other.

The **exponential function** has been found to have widespread application in many areas of science and engineering, whereas the gain of an amplifier can be modelled using the logarithmic function. **Logarithms** are used extensively in the study of sound, and the decibel, used in defining the intensity of sound, is based on a logarithmic scale.

The properties and laws of both functions are covered in this chapter, and methods of solving equations involving exponentials and logarithms are explained.

Chapter 8 contents

BLOCK 1

The exponential function

1.1 Introduction

The exponential function has widespread application in many areas of science and engineering. Areas that utilise the exponential function include expansion of materials, laws of cooling, radioactive decay, and the discharge of a capacitor. This block details some properties of the exponential function and includes some of its applications.

The hyperbolic functions are also introduced. These functions are defined in terms of the exponential function. Identities involving the hyperbolic functions are tabulated.

1.2 Exponential expressions

An **exponent** is another name for a power or index. Expressions involving exponents are called **exponential expressions**. For example, 3^4 and a^b are exponential expressions. In the exponential expression a^x, a is called the **base** and x is the exponent. Exponential expressions can be simplified and manipulated using the laws of indices. These laws were given in Chapter 5, Block 2 but are stated again here for reference.

Laws of indices

$$a^m a^n = a^{m+n}, \quad \frac{a^m}{a^n} = a^{m-n}, \quad (a^m)^n = a^{mn}$$

In this chapter we shall be dealing with exponential expressions in which the base will always be a particular constant called the **exponential constant**. This has the symbol e and is approximately equal to 2.718. Exponential expressions with this base dominate engineering applications.

Example 1.1

Most calculators have powers of the exponential constant preprogrammed; these can be calculated, probably with a button marked e^x. Check that you can use your calculator by calculating the following:

(a) $e^{3.7}$ (b) $e^{-1.6}$ (c) $2e^{1.5}$

Solution

(a) $e^{3.7} =$ 40.4473

(b) $e^{-1.6} =$ 0.2019

(c) $2e^{1.5} =$ 8.9634

1.3 Simplifying exponential expressions

The laws of indices and the rules of algebra apply to exponential expressions. The following examples illustrate this.

Example 1.2

Simplify (a) $e^{2x}e^{3x}$, (b) $\dfrac{e^{4x}}{e^{7x}}$, (c) $(e^{2x})^3$.

Solution

(a) $e^{2x}e^{3x} = e^{2x+3x} = e^{5x}$.

(b) $\dfrac{e^{4x}}{e^{7x}} = e^{4x-7x} = e^{-3x}$. This may be written as $\dfrac{1}{e^{3x}}$.

(c) $(e^{2x})^3 = e^{2x\times 3} = e^{6x}$.

Example 1.3

Expand the brackets and simplify where possible:

(a) $e^x(e^{-x} + 1)$

(b) $(e^x + 1)^2 - 1$

(c) $(e^x + e^{-x})^2 - 2$

Solution

(a) $e^x(e^{-x} + 1) = e^x e^{-x} + e^x$
$= e^0 + e^x$
$= 1 + e^x$

(b) $(e^x + 1)^2 - 1 =$ $e^x e^x + 2e^x + 1 - 1$
$= e^{2x} + 2e^x$

(c) $(e^x + e^{-x})^2 - 2 =$ $e^x e^x + 2e^x e^{-x} + e^{-x}e^{-x} - 2$
$=$ $e^{2x} + 2 + e^{-2x} - 2$
$= e^{2x} + e^{-2x}$

Exercises

1 Simplify each expression as far as possible:

(a) $e^{2x}e^{7x}$
(b) $(3e^{x})(2e^{-x})$
(c) $e^{2x}(e^{-2x} + e^{-x} + 1) - e^{x}(1 + e^{x})$
(d) $\dfrac{e^{-3x}}{2e^{-x}}$

2 Expand the brackets of the following expressions:

(a) $(e^{x} + 2)^2$
(b) $(e^{x} + 1)(e^{-x} - 1)$
(c) $(e^{2x} + e^{x})(e^{-2x} + e^{-x})$
(d) $(1 + e^{2x} + e^{-2x})(1 - e^{x})$

3 Simplify as far as possible:

(a) $\dfrac{e^{x} + e^{-x}}{2} + \dfrac{e^{x} - e^{-x}}{2}$
(b) $e^{x} + \dfrac{1}{e^{x}} - e^{-x}$
(c) $\dfrac{e^{2x} + e^{x}}{e^{x}} - 1$
(d) $e^{3x}(e^{-2x} - e^{-3x}) + 1$

Solutions to exercises

1 (a) e^{9x} (b) 6 (c) 1 (d) $\dfrac{e^{-2x}}{2}$

2 (a) $e^{2x} + 4e^{x} + 4$ (b) $e^{-x} - e^{x}$
(c) $2 + e^{x} + e^{-x}$
(d) $1 - e^{x} + e^{2x} - e^{3x} + e^{-2x} - e^{-x}$

3 (a) e^{x} (b) e^{x} (c) e^{x} (d) e^{x}

1.4 The exponential function and its graph

Key point

An exponential function has the form

$$y = a^{x}$$

where a is a positive constant called the **base**.

Hence $y = (0.4)^{x}$, $y = 2.5^{x}$ and $y = 10^{x}$ are all exponential functions. Note that, in an exponential function, the independent variable appears as a power.

Key point

The most commonly used exponential function, commonly called the **exponential function**, is

$$y = e^{x}$$

where the base e is the exponential constant whose value is e = 2.71828182 . . .

Table 1.1 gives values of the exponential function e^{x} for various x values and Figure 1.1 illustrates a graph of $y = e^{x}$ for $-3 \le x \le 3$.

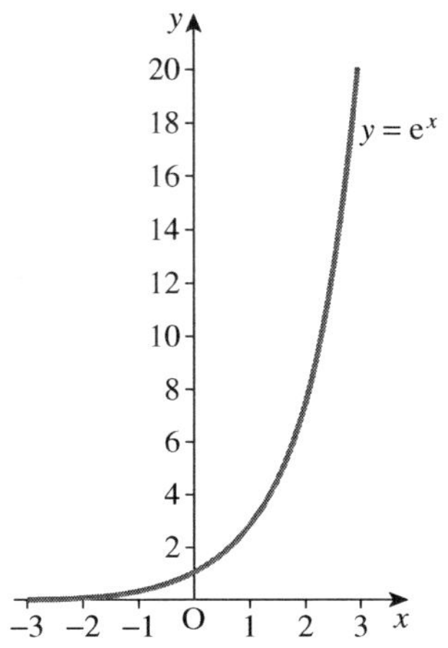

Figure 1.1
The exponential function, $y = e^x$.

Table 1.1
Values of e^x.

x	e^x	x	e^x
−3	0.05	0.5	1.65
−2.5	0.08	1.0	2.72
−2.0	0.14	1.5	4.48
−1.5	0.22	2.0	7.39
−1.0	0.37	2.5	12.18
−0.5	0.61	3.0	20.09
0	1.00		

From Figure 1.1 we note some properties of the exponential function:

1 As x becomes large and positive, e^x increases without bound. We express this mathematically as $e^x \to \infty$ as $x \to \infty$.
2 As x becomes large and negative, e^x approaches 0. We write $e^x \to 0$ as $x \to -\infty$.
3 e^x is never negative.

The property that e^x increases as x increases is referred to as **exponential growth**.

Figure 1.2 shows a graph of the related function $y = e^{-x}$ for $-3 \le x \le 3$ and Table 1.2 lists appropriate values of e^{-x}.

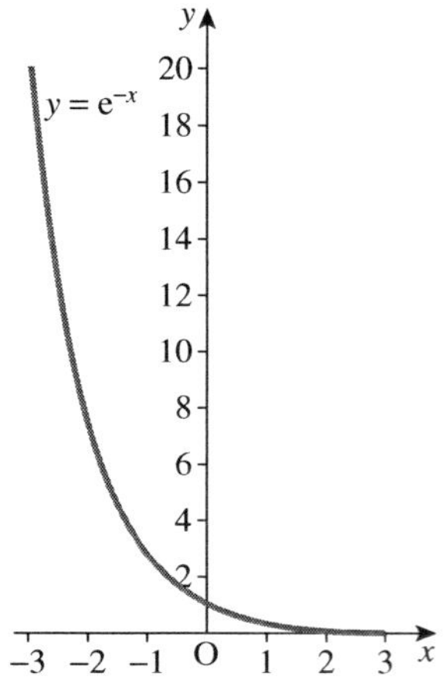

Figure 1.2
The function $y = e^{-x}$ exhibits exponential decay.

Table 1.2
Values of e^{-x}.

x	e^{-x}	x	e^{-x}
−3	20.09	0.5	0.61
−2.5	12.18	1.0	0.37
−2.0	7.39	1.5	0.22
−1.5	4.48	2.0	0.14
−1.0	2.72	2.5	0.08
−0.5	1.65	3.0	0.05
0	1.00		

From Figure 1.2 we see that e^{-x} decreases as x increases: this is referred to as **exponential decay**.

Example 1.4

Plot $y = e^{0.5x}$ and $y = e^{0.7x}$ for $0 \le x \le 3$. Comment on your graphs.

Solution

Table 1.3 shows values of $e^{0.5x}$ and $e^{0.7x}$ for $0 \le x \le 3$. Figure 1.3 illustrates the graphs.

From Figure 1.3 we see that $y = e^{0.7x}$ grows more rapidly than $y = e^{0.5x}$.

Table 1.3 Values of $e^{0.5x}$ and $e^{0.7x}$.

x	$e^{0.5x}$	$e^{0.7x}$
0	1.00	1.00
0.5	1.28	1.42
1.0	1.65	2.01
1.5	2.12	2.86
2.0	2.72	4.06
2.5	3.49	5.75
3.0	4.48	8.17

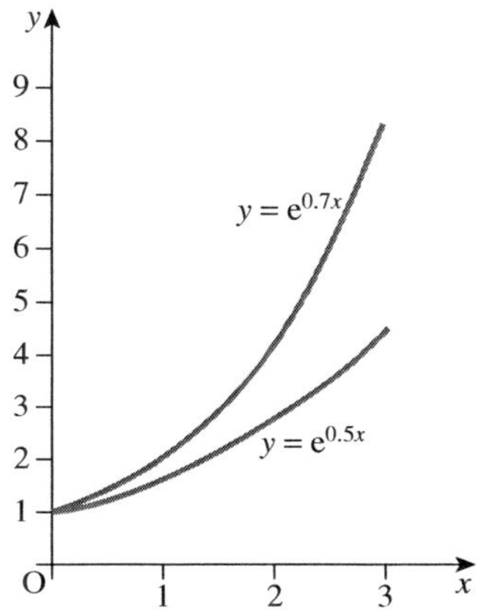

Figure 1.3 $y = e^{0.7x}$ grows more rapidly than $y = e^{0.5x}$.

Exercises

1. Evaluate (a) $e^{2.7}$, (b) $e^{-1.6}$, (c) $3e^{0.7}$, (d) $-1.9e^{0.5}$.

2. Plot

$$x = 3 + 2e^{-t} \quad 0 \le t \le 4$$

Which value does x approach as t increases?

3. Plot

$$R(t) = 4 - 2e^{-1.5t} \quad 0 \le t \le 3$$

Which value does R approach as t increases?

4. State the domain and range of (a) $y = e^x$, (b) $y = e^{-x}$.

Solutions to exercises

1. (a) 14.8797 (b) 0.2019 (c) 6.0413 (d) -3.1326

2. See Figure 1.4. As t increases, x approaches 3.

3. See Figure 1.5. As t increases R approaches 4.

4. (a) $(-\infty, \infty)$, $(0, \infty)$ (b) $(-\infty, \infty)$, $(0, \infty)$

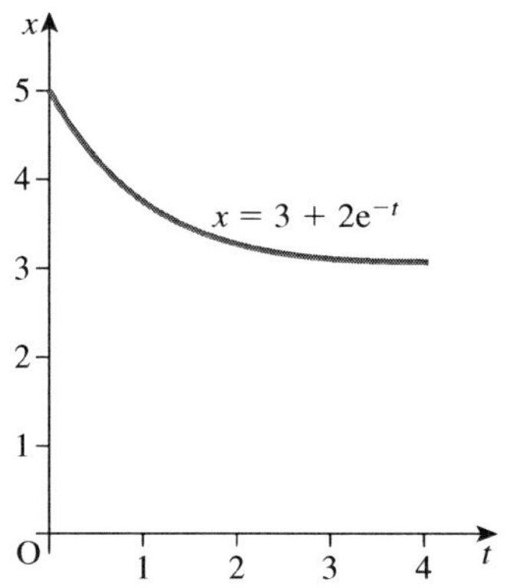

Figure 1.4

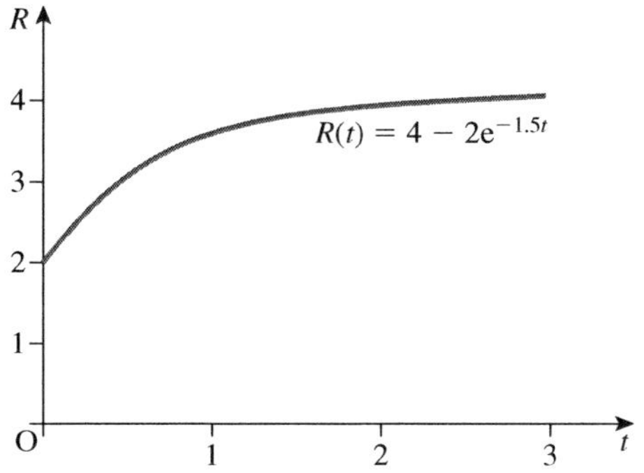

Figure 1.5

1.5 Applications of the exponential function

The following examples illustrate some of the applications of the exponential function.

Example 1.5 Electrical Engineering – Discharge of a capacitor

The charge, $q(t)$, stored on a capacitor having a capacitance C, discharging through a resistor of resistance R, is given by

$$q(t) = Qe^{-\frac{t}{CR}}$$

where Q is the initial charge.

(a) Find the value of the charge when $t = 1$ given $Q = 50$, $C = 0.25$ and $R = 2$.

(b) If the value of R is doubled calculate the new value of the charge when $t = 1$.

Solution

(a)

$$\begin{aligned} q(1) &= 50e^{-\frac{1}{(0.25)(2)}} \\ &= 50e^{-2} \\ &= 6.77 \end{aligned}$$

(b)

$$\begin{aligned} q(1) &= 50e^{-\frac{1}{(0.25)(4)}} \\ &= 50e^{-1} \\ &= 18.39 \end{aligned}$$

Example 1.6 Electrical Engineering – Decay of a current in a circuit
Consider a circuit with resistance R, inductance L and an initial current of i_0. The current $i(t)$ will decay with time, t, according to the law

$$i(t) = i_0 e^{-\frac{Rt}{L}}$$

(a) Calculate the current when $t = 1.5$ given $i_0 = 12$, $R = 2$ and $L = 6$.
(b) If L is increased from 6 to 9 calculate the new value of $i(1.5)$.

Solution

(a) $i(1.5) = 12e^{-\frac{2(1.5)}{6}}$
$= 12e^{-0.5}$
$= 7.28$

(b) $i(1.5) = 12e^{-\frac{2(1.5)}{9}} = 12e^{-\frac{1}{3}} = 8.60$

Example 1.7 Chemical Engineering – Newton's law of cooling
Newton's law of cooling states that the rate at which a body cools is proportional to the excess of its temperature above the temperature of the environment in which it is placed. Let $\Theta(t)$ be the temperature of a body at time t, Θ_0 its initial temperature and Θ_e the temperature of the environment. Newton's law of cooling can be stated mathematically as

$$\Theta(t) = \Theta_e + (\Theta_0 - \Theta_e)e^{-kt}$$

where k is a positive constant that depends upon the material of the body. From this equation we see that the temperature is dropping exponentially owing to the term e^{-kt}: that is, the temperature follows an exponential decay curve. In this example we take $k = 1$, $\Theta_e = 20$ and $\Theta_0 = 120$, so

$$\Theta(t) = 20 + 100e^{-t}$$

(a) Plot $\Theta(t)$ for $t = 0$ to $t = 6$.
(b) Use your graph to find the temperature that the body approaches as t increases.

Solution

(a) Table 1.4 gives values of $\Theta(t)$ for various values of t from 0 to 6. Figure 1.6 shows the graph of $\Theta(t)$.

Table 1.4

t	$\Theta(t) = 20 + 100e^{-t}$	t	$\Theta(t) = 20 + 100e^{-t}$
0	120.0	3.5	23.0
0.5	80.7	4.0	21.8
1.0	56.8	4.5	21.1
1.5	42.3	5.0	20.7
2.0	33.5	5.5	20.4
2.5	28.2	6.0	20.2
3.0	25.0		

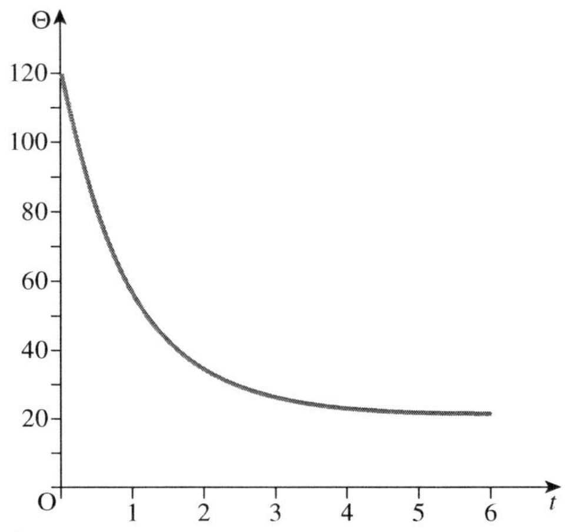

Figure 1.6 Temperature decays exponentially with time.

(b) From Figure 1.6 we see that the temperature, $\Theta(t)$, approaches 20 as t increases. This is to be expected: the temperature of the body approaches the temperature of the environment.

The result stated in Example 1.7(b) can be seen for the general case by considering the equation

$$\Theta(t) = \Theta_e + (\Theta_0 - \Theta_e)e^{-kt}$$

We have already noted that e^{-x} approaches 0 as x increases; clearly e^{-t} and e^{-kt} approach 0 as t increases since k is positive. Hence $(\Theta_0 - \Theta_e)e^{-kt}$ approaches 0 as t increases. Finally $\Theta_e + (\Theta_0 - \Theta_e)e^{-kt}$ approaches Θ_e as t increases.

Exercises

1 The number of particles, $N(t)$, emitted by a radioactive substance varies with time, t, according to the law

$$N(t) = 9.63 \times 10^{17}e^{-0.6t} \quad t \geq 0$$

(a) Calculate the number of particles emitted when $t = 0$.
(b) Calculate the number of particles emitted when $t = 2$.

2 The length, $l(T)$, of a bar depends upon the temperature, T, according to the law

$$l(T) = l_0 e^{\alpha T}$$

where l_0 is the length of the bar when $T = 0$, and α is a positive constant.

(a) Calculate the percentage change in length when T increases from $T = 20$ to $T = 100$, given $\alpha = 0.001$.
(b) Calculate the percentage change in length when T decreases from $T = 150$ to $T = 50$.

3 Atmospheric pressure, $P(h)$ atmospheres, varies according to the height, h metres, above the surface of the Earth. Given

$$P(h) = e^{-0.000016h}$$

calculate the pressure at a height of
(a) 2 km
(b) 10 km
above the Earth.

Solutions to exercises

1 (a) 9.63×10^{17} (b) 2.90×10^{17}

2 (a) 8.33% increase (b) 9.52% decrease

3 (a) 0.9685 atmospheres
(b) 0.8521 atmospheres

1.6 Hyperbolic functions

Closely associated to the exponential function are the **hyperbolic functions**. The hyperbolic functions are defined as follows:

Key point

$$\text{hyperbolic sine: } \sinh x = \frac{e^x - e^{-x}}{2}$$

$$\text{hyperbolic cosine: } \cosh x = \frac{e^x + e^{-x}}{2}$$

$$\text{hyperbolic tangent: } \tanh x = \frac{\sinh x}{\cosh x} = \frac{e^x - e^{-x}}{e^x + e^{-x}}$$

$$\operatorname{cosech} x = \frac{1}{\sinh x} = \frac{2}{e^x - e^{-x}}$$

$$\operatorname{sech} x = \frac{1}{\cosh x} = \frac{2}{e^x + e^{-x}}$$

$$\coth x = \frac{1}{\tanh x} = \frac{e^x + e^{-x}}{e^x - e^{-x}}$$

Readers already familiar with the trigonometrical functions will note the similarity of the names. Most scientific calculators have values of the hyperbolic functions pre-programmed. Use Example 1.8 to check that you can use your calculator to find the values of the hyperbolic functions.

Example 1.8

Use a calculator to evaluate
(a) $\sinh 2.1$ (b) $\cosh(-1.3)$ (c) $\tanh 1.4$
(d) $\operatorname{cosech} 2.2$ (e) $\operatorname{sech}(-1.6)$ (f) $\coth(-2)$

Solution

(a) $\sinh 2.1 = 4.0219$
(b) $\cosh(-1.3) = 1.9709$
(c) $\tanh 1.4 = 0.8854$
(d) $\operatorname{cosech} 2.2 = \dfrac{1}{\sinh 2.2} = 0.2244$

(e) $\operatorname{sech}(-1.6) = \dfrac{1}{\cosh(-1.6)} = 0.3880$

(f) $\coth(-2) = \dfrac{1}{\tanh(-2)} = -1.0373$

Figure 1.7 illustrates graphs of $y = \sinh x$, $y = \cosh x$ and $y = \tanh x$.

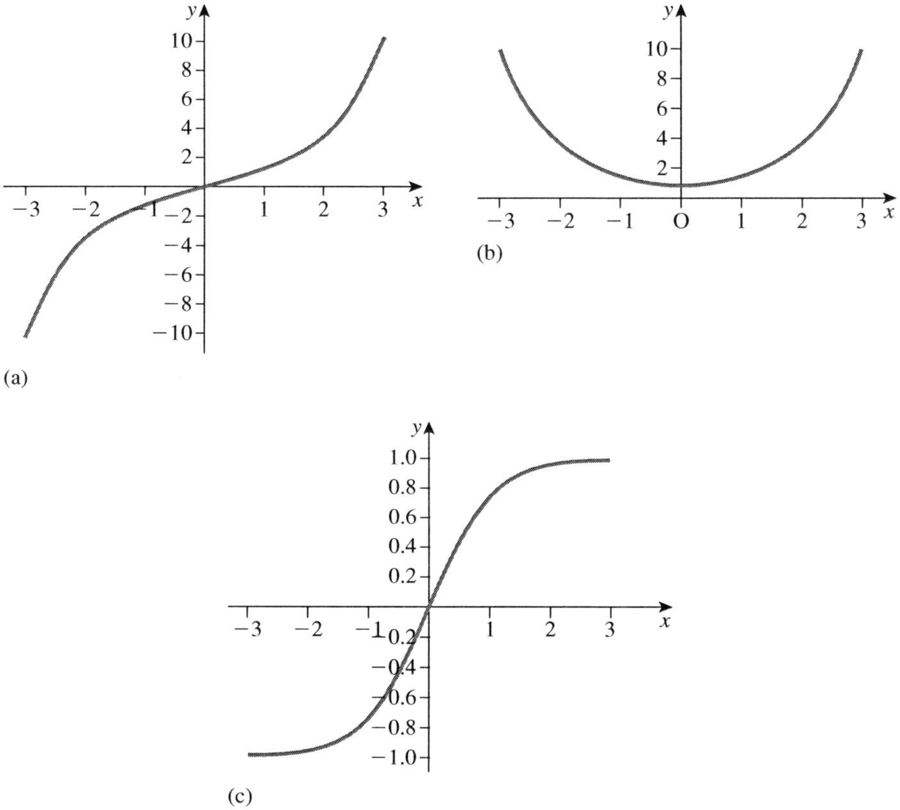

Figure 1.7
(a) $y = \sinh x$,
(b) $y = \cosh x$,
(c) $y = \tanh x$.

Example 1.9

Express $7e^x + 3e^{-x}$ in terms of sinh x and cosh x.

Solution

We note that

$$\cosh x + \sinh x = \frac{e^x + e^{-x}}{2} + \frac{e^x - e^{-x}}{2}$$
$$= e^x$$

$$\cosh x - \sinh x = \frac{e^x + e^{-x}}{2} - \frac{e^x - e^{-x}}{2}$$
$$= e^{-x}$$

So

$$7e^x + 3e^{-x} = 7(\cosh x + \sinh x) + 3(\cosh x - \sinh x)$$
$$= 10\cosh x + 4\sinh x$$

Example 1.10 Mechanical Engineering – The catenary

A heavy chain, suspended at both ends, hangs in the shape defined by

$$y = a\cosh\left(\frac{x}{b}\right)$$

Note that when $x = 0$ we have

$$y(0) = a\cosh 0$$
$$= a$$

and that when $x = b$ we have

$$y(b) = a\cosh\left(\frac{b}{b}\right)$$
$$= a\cosh 1$$
$$= 1.54a$$

The points $(0, a)$ and $(b, 1.54a)$ are marked on Figure 1.8.

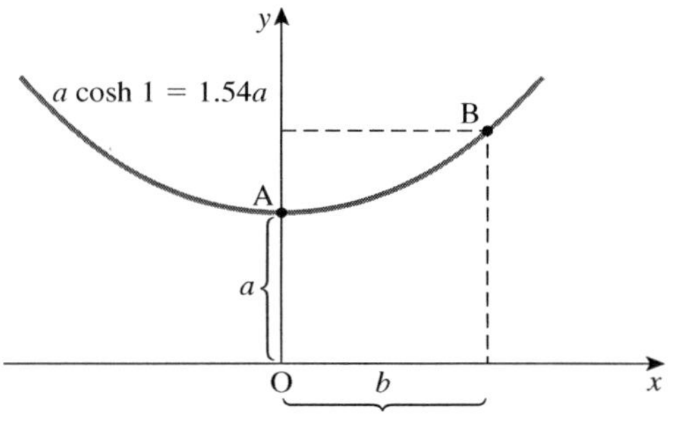

Figure 1.8 A catenary is defined by $y = a\cosh\left(\frac{x}{b}\right)$.

Such a curve is known as a **catenary**.

1.7 Hyperbolic identities

If two expressions have the same value for all values of x, we say that they are identical. For example, e^x and $\cosh x + \sinh x$ have the same value for any value of x. A statement of the form $e^x = \cosh x + \sinh x$ is called an **identity**. There are many identities that relate different hyperbolic functions. Table 1.5 lists some of the common hyperbolic identities.

Table 1.5 Hyperbolic identities.

$$
\begin{aligned}
e^x &= \cosh x + \sinh x \\
e^{-x} &= \cosh x - \sinh x \\
\cosh^2 x - \sinh^2 x &= 1 \\
1 - \tanh^2 x &= \operatorname{sech}^2 x \\
\coth^2 x - 1 &= \operatorname{cosech}^2 x \\
\sinh(x \pm y) &= \sinh x \cosh y \pm \cosh x \sinh y \\
\cosh(x \pm y) &= \cosh x \cosh y \pm \sinh x \sinh y \\
\sinh 2x &= 2 \sinh x \cosh x \\
\cosh 2x &= \cosh^2 x + \sinh^2 x \\
\cosh^2 x &= \frac{\cosh 2x + 1}{2} \\
\sinh^2 x &= \frac{\cosh 2x - 1}{2}
\end{aligned}
$$

Note that $\cosh^2 x$ means $(\cosh x)^2$ and $\sinh^2 x$ means $(\sinh x)^2$.

Example 1.11

Prove the following identities:
(a) $\cosh^2 x - \sinh^2 x = 1$
(b) $\sinh 2x = 2 \sinh x \cosh x$

Solution

(a) Note that from Example 1.9

$$\cosh x + \sinh x = e^x, \cosh x - \sinh x = e^{-x}$$

Now

$$
\begin{aligned}
\cosh^2 x - \sinh^2 x &= (\cosh x + \sinh x)(\cosh x - \sinh x) \\
&= (e^x)(e^{-x}) \\
&= 1
\end{aligned}
$$

(b) We have

$$\sinh 2x = \frac{e^{2x} - e^{-2x}}{2}$$

Also

$$
\begin{aligned}
2 \sinh x \cosh x &= 2\left(\frac{e^x - e^{-x}}{2}\right)\left(\frac{e^x + e^{-x}}{2}\right) \\
&= \frac{(e^x - e^{-x})(e^x + e^{-x})}{2} \\
&= \frac{(e^x)^2 + e^x e^{-x} - e^{-x} e^x - (e^{-x})^2}{2} \\
&= \frac{e^{2x} + 1 - 1 - e^{-2x}}{2} \\
&= \frac{e^{2x} - e^{-2x}}{2}
\end{aligned}
$$

Hence

$$\sinh 2x = 2 \sinh x \cosh x$$

Example 1.12 Electrical Engineering – Voltage in a transmission line

A transmission line is an arrangement of electrical conductors for transporting electromagnetic waves. The coaxial cable used to carry a signal from a TV aerial to a TV set is a common example.

The voltage in a line depends upon both distance along the line, z, and time, t. For any fixed time, the voltage at distance z along the line has the form

$$v(z) = Ae^{-\alpha z} + Be^{\alpha z}$$

where A and B are constants. For a particular transmission line $A = 1$ and $B = 4$ giving

$$v = e^{-\alpha z} + 4e^{\alpha z}$$

Show that v may be written as

$$v = 3 \sinh \alpha z + 5 \cosh \alpha z$$

Solution

$$\begin{aligned} v &= e^{-\alpha z} + 4e^{\alpha z} \\ &= (\cosh \alpha z - \sinh \alpha z) + 4(\cosh \alpha z + \sinh \alpha z) \quad \text{(using Table 1.5)} \\ &= 5 \cosh \alpha z + 3 \sinh \alpha z \end{aligned}$$

Exercises

1 Evaluate
(a) $\sinh(-3)$ (b) $\cosh 1.9$ (c) $\tanh(-3.2)$
(d) $\operatorname{cosech} 2$ (e) $\operatorname{sech}(-2.5)$ (f) $\coth 0.6$

2 Sketch $y = \operatorname{cosech} x$ for $-3 \le x \le 3$.

3 Sketch $y = \operatorname{sech} x$ for $-3 \le x \le 3$.

4 Prove the identities
(a) $1 - \tanh^2 x = \operatorname{sech}^2 x$
(b) $\sinh^2 x = \dfrac{\cosh 2x - 1}{2}$

5 Express $4e^{2x} - 6e^{-2x}$ in terms of $\sinh 2x$ and $\cosh 2x$.

6 **Electrical Engineering – Transmission line.** The voltage in a transmission line, v, is given by

$$v = 7e^{-\alpha z} + 3e^{\alpha z}$$

Express the voltage, v, using hyperbolic functions.

Solutions to exercises

1 (a) -10.02 (b) 3.42 (c) -1.00 (d) 0.28 (e) 0.16 (f) 1.86

2 See Figure 1.9.

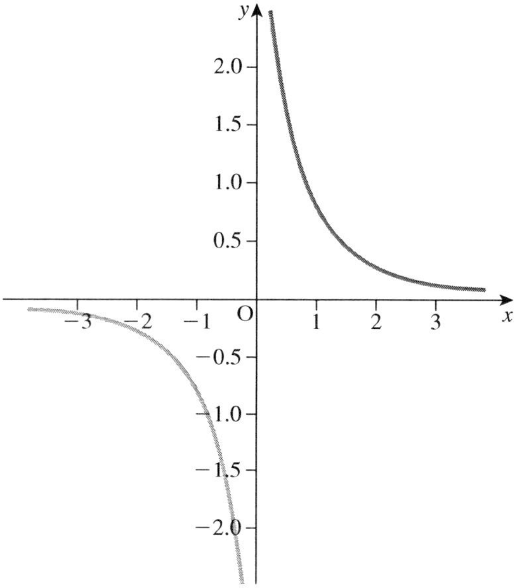

Figure 1.9
$y = \text{cosech}\, x$.

3 See Figure 1.10.

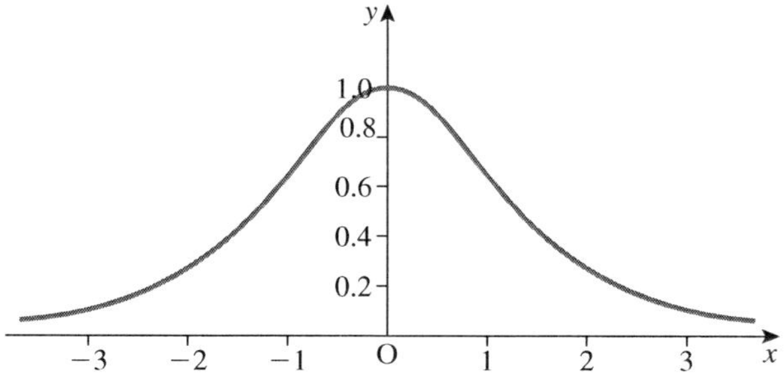

Figure 1.10
$y = \text{sech}\, x$.

5 $10 \sinh 2x - 2 \cosh 2x$

6 $10 \cosh \alpha z - 4 \sinh \alpha z$

End of block exercises

1 Sketch $y = \coth x$ for $-3 \leq x \leq 3$.

2 Simplify each of the following as much as possible:
(a) $e^{-7x}e^{4x}$ (b) $2e^{3x}e^{5x}$ (c) $(3e^{3x})(2e^{2x})(-e^{-x})$
(d) $\dfrac{8e^{6x}}{2e^{-2x}}$

3 Prove the identities
(a) $\cosh 2x = \cosh^2 x + \sinh^2 x$
(b) $\sinh(x + y) = \sinh x \cosh y + \cosh x \sinh y$

4 The charge on a capacitor, $C(t)$, decays according to the law

$$C(t) = 100e^{-0.2t} \quad t \geq 0$$

(a) Calculate the charge when $t = 3$.
(b) Calculate the charge when $t = 5$.

5 (a) Plot $y = 6 + 4e^{-2t}$, for $0 \leq t \leq 3$.
(b) What value does y approach as t increases?

6 Given

$$y = a + be^{-t}$$

where a and b are constants, state the value that y approaches as t increases.

7 (a) Show that

$$\frac{e^x + 6}{2e^x + 5}$$

may be expressed as

$$\frac{1 + 6e^{-x}}{2 + 5e^{-x}}$$

(b) What value does

$$\frac{e^x + 6}{2e^x + 5}$$

approach as x becomes large and positive?

8 **Electrical Engineering – Decay of a current in a circuit.** The current, $i(t)$, in a circuit changes with time, t, according to

$$i(t) = i_0 e^{-\frac{Rt}{L}}$$

(a) Calculate the current when $t = 0.5$ given $i_0 = 10$, $R = 3$ and $L = 5$.
(b) Describe the effect on $i(t)$ if the value of R is increased, all other values remaining constant.
(c) Describe the effect on $i(t)$ if the value of L is increased, all other values remaining constant.

Solutions to exercises

1 See Figure 1.11.

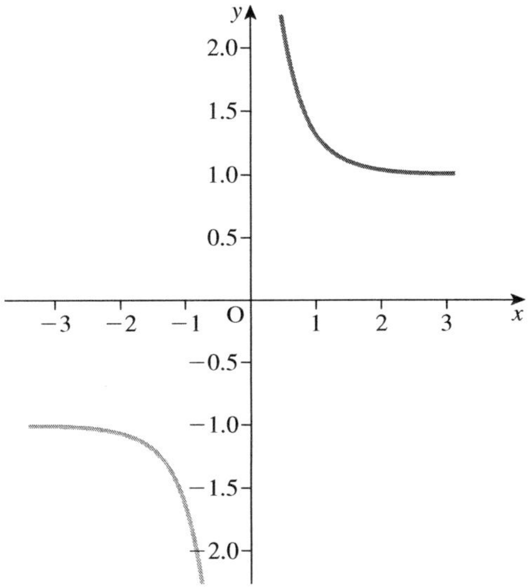

Figure 1.11
$y = \coth x$.

2 (a) e^{-3x} (b) $2e^{8x}$ (c) $-6e^{4x}$ (d) $4e^{8x}$

4 (a) 54.88 (b) 36.79

5 (a) See Figure 1.12 (b) 6

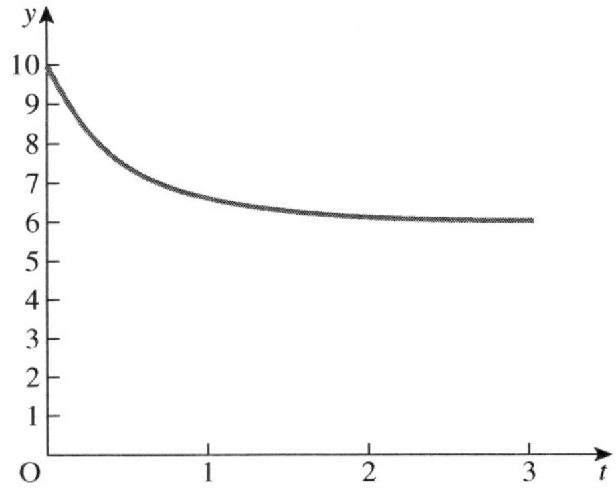

Figure 1.12
$y = 6 + 4e^{-2t}$.

6 a

7 (b) 0.5

8 (a) 7.41
(b) The current decreases as R increases.
(c) The current increases as L increases.

BLOCK 2

Logarithms and their laws

2.1 Introduction

Logarithms are an alternative way of writing expressions that involve powers, or indices. They are used extensively in the study of sound. The decibel, used in defining the intensity of sound, is based on a logarithmic scale. In this block we define the logarithm and give the laws that are used to simplify and manipulate expressions involving logarithms.

2.2 Definition of the logarithm

Consider the statement that

$$16 = 2^4$$

Here 2 is the base and 4 is the power. This may be expressed in an alternative way using logarithms as

$$\log_2 16 = 4$$

We read this as 'log 16, to the base 2, equals 4'. Some more examples follow:

$8 = 2^3$ may be written as $\log_2 8 = 3$

$25 = 5^2$ may be written as $\log_5 25 = 2$

$81 = 3^4$ may be written as ______ $\log_3 81 = 4$

$0.125 = (0.5)^3$ may be written as ______ $\log_{0.5} 0.125 = 3$

$10000 = 10^4$ may be written as $\log_{10} 10000 = 4$

$10^{-1} = 0.1$ may be written as ______ $\log_{10} 0.1 = -1$

In general we have

Key point

If a is a positive constant and

$$N = a^x$$

then

$$\log_a N = x$$

The number a is called the **base** of the logarithm. In practice, most logarithms are to the base 10 or e. Logarithms to base e are called **natural logarithms**. Natural logarithms are often denoted by ln rather than $\log_e$, whereas logarithms to base 10 are denoted simply by log rather than $\log_{10}$.

Key point

If $N = 10^x$ then $x = \log_{10} N = \log N$.
If $N = e^x$ then $x = \log_e N = \ln N$.

Scientific calculators are preprogrammed with both natural logarithms and logarithms to base 10. Use Example 2.1 to check that you can use your calculator.

Example 2.1

Use a scientific calculator to find:
(a) log 79 (b) ln 79 (c) log 0.21 (d) ln 0.036

Solution

(a) log 79 = 1.8976
(b) ln 79 = 4.3694
(c) log 0.21 = −0.6778
(d) ln 0.036 = −3.3242

Example 2.2

Express each of the following statements using logarithms:
(a) $10^3 = 1000$ (b) $10^{-2} = 0.01$ (c) $12.1825 = e^{2.5}$ (d) $e^{-2.3026} = 0.1$

Solution

(a) log 1000 = 3 (b) log 0.01 = −2 (c) ln 12.1825 = 2.5
(d) ln 0.1 = −2.3026

Exercises

1 Write the following using logarithms:
(a) $32 = 2^5$ (b) $125 = 5^3$ (c) $243 = 3^5$
(d) $4^3 = 64$ (e) $6^2 = 36$

2 Write the following using logarithms:
(a) $10^2 = 100$ (b) $0.001 = 10^{-3}$
(c) $e^{-1.3} = 0.2725$ (d) $e^{1.5} = 4.4817$

3 Evaluate
(a) log 250 (b) ln 250 (c) log 0.46
(d) ln 0.46

4 Write the following using indices:
(a) $\log_5 625 = 4$
(b) $\log_2 256 = 8$
(c) $\log 0.0251 = -1.6$
(d) $\ln 17 = 2.8332$

Solutions to exercises

1 (a) $\log_2 32 = 5$ (b) $\log_5 125 = 3$
(c) $\log_3 243 = 5$ (d) $\log_4 64 = 3$
(e) $\log_6 36 = 2$

2 (a) $\log 100 = 2$ (b) $\log 0.001 = -3$
(c) $\ln 0.2725 = -1.3$ (d) $\ln 4.4817 = 1.5$

3 (a) 2.3979 (b) 5.5215
(c) −0.3372 (d) −0.7765

4 (a) $5^4 = 625$ (b) $2^8 = 256$
(c) $10^{-1.6} = 0.0251$ (d) $e^{2.8332} = 17$

2.3 Logarithms to any base

To calculate a logarithm to base a, knowing logarithms to base b, we use

Key point

$$\log_a N = \frac{\log_b N}{\log_b a}$$

Example 2.3
Evaluate $\log_3 40$.

Solution

$$\log_3 40 = \frac{\log 40}{\log 3} = \frac{1.6021}{0.4771} = 3.358$$

Example 2.4
Evaluate $\log_7 36$.

Solution

$$\log_7 36 = \frac{\log 36}{\log 7} = 1.842$$

Exercises

1 Evaluate
(a) $\log_4 36$ (b) $\log_2 9$ (c) $\log_{12} 10$

Solutions to exercises

1 (a) 2.585 (b) 3.170 (c) 0.927

2.4 Laws of logarithms

Just as expressions involving indices can be simplified using appropriate laws, so expressions involving logarithms can be simplified using the laws of logarithms. The laws of logarithms hold true for any base. However, it is essential that the same base is used throughout an expression before the laws can be applied.

The first law of logarithms is

Key point

$$\log A + \log B = \log AB$$

Example 2.5

Simplify each of the following to a single logarithmic expression:

(a) $\log 7 + \log 2$
(b) $\ln 9 + \ln 10$
(c) $\log x + \log x^2$
(d) $\ln 2y + \ln 3y$

Solution

(a) $\log 7 + \log 2 = \log(7 \times 2) = \log 14$
(b) $\ln 9 + \ln 10 = \ln 90$
(c) $\log x + \log x^2 =$ $\log(xx^2) = \log x^3$
(d) $\ln 2y + \ln 3y =$ $\ln(2y3y) = \ln 6y^2$

The second law of logarithms states

Key point

$$\log A - \log B = \log\left(\frac{A}{B}\right)$$

Example 2.6

Express as a single logarithm:

(a) $\log 15 - \log 3$
(b) $\ln 6 - \ln(0.5)$
(c) $\ln 6x^2 - \ln 2x$
(d) $\log 1 - \log x$

Solution

(a) $\log 15 - \log 3 = \log\left(\frac{15}{3}\right) = \log 5$

(b) $\ln 6 - \ln(0.5) = \ln\left(\frac{6}{0.5}\right) = \ln 12$

(c) $\ln 6x^2 - \ln 2x =$ $\ln\left(\frac{6x^2}{2x}\right) = \ln 3x$

(d) $\log 1 - \log x =$ $\log\frac{1}{x}$

We use the second law of logarithms to develop another result. Clearly $\log A - \log A = 0$. Using the second law we may also write

$$\begin{aligned}\log A - \log A &= \log\left(\frac{A}{A}\right)\\ &= \log 1\end{aligned}$$

Hence we see that

Key point

$$\log 1 = 0$$

The third law of logarithms states

Key point

$$\log A^n = n \log A$$

Example 2.7

Rewrite the following in an alternative form without using a power:
(a) $\log 2^3$ (b) $\log 2^2$ (c) $\log x^2$ (d) $\ln t^5$

Solution

(a) $\log 2^3 =$ $3 \log 2$

(b) $\log 2^2 =$ $2 \log 2$

(c) $\log x^2 =$ $2 \log x$

(d) $\ln t^5 =$ $5 \ln t$

Example 2.8

Simplify each of the following as much as possible:

(a) $3 \log 2 - \log 6$
(b) $\ln 250 + 2 \ln 2$
(c) $\log 3x^3 + 2 \log x$
(d) $\ln t^5 - 3 \ln t^2$

Solution

(a)

$$\begin{aligned}3 \log 2 - \log 6 &= \log 2^3 - \log 6\\ &= \log 8 - \log 6\\ &= \log\left(\frac{8}{6}\right)\\ &= \log\left(\frac{4}{3}\right)\end{aligned}$$

(b)
$$\begin{aligned}\ln 250 + 2\ln 2 &= \ln 250 + \ln 2^2\\ &= \ln 250 + \ln 4\\ &= \ln(250\times 4)\\ &= \ln 1000\end{aligned}$$

(c)
$$\begin{aligned}\log 3x^3 + 2\log x &= \log 3x^3 + \log x^2\\ &= \log 3x^5\end{aligned}$$

(d)
$$\begin{aligned}\ln t^5 - 3\ln t^2 &= \ln t^5 - \ln(t^2)^3\\ &= \ln t^5 - \ln t^6\\ &= \ln\frac{t^5}{t^6}\\ &= \ln\frac{1}{t}\end{aligned}$$

Note that

$$\begin{aligned}\ln\frac{1}{t} &= \ln t^{-1}\\ &= -\ln t\end{aligned}$$

Example 2.9
Simplify

(a) $\frac{1}{2}\log 25$ (b) $\frac{1}{3}\log 8$ (c) $\frac{1}{2}\log x^2$ (d) $\frac{1}{2}\ln 9t^2$

Solution

(a) $\frac{1}{2}\log 25 = \log 25^{1/2} = \log 5$

(b) $\frac{1}{3}\log 8 = \log 8^{1/3} = \log 2$

(c) $\frac{1}{2}\log x^2 =$ $\log(x^2)^{1/2} = \log x$

(d) $\frac{1}{2}\ln 9t^2 =$ $\ln(9t^2)^{1/2} = \ln 3t$

Example 2.10
Simplify

(a) $3\log x - 2\log\left(\frac{1}{x}\right) - \frac{1}{2}\log 9$

(b) $4\log t^2 - 2\log t^3 + \log\left(\frac{1}{t^2}\right)$

Solution

(a) $3\log x = \log x^3$, $2\log\frac{1}{x} = \log\frac{1}{x^2} = \log x^{-2}$, and $\frac{1}{2}\log 9 = \log 9^{1/2} = \log 3$, so

$$3\log x - 2\log\left(\frac{1}{x}\right) - \frac{1}{2}\log 9 = \log x^3 - \log x^{-2} - \log 3$$
$$= \log\left(\frac{x^3}{3x^{-2}}\right)$$
$$= \log\left(\frac{x^5}{3}\right)$$

(b) $4\log t^2 = \log (t^2)^4 = \log t^8$

$2\log t^3 =$ $\log(t^3)^2 = \log t^6$

$\log\frac{1}{t^2} = \log t^{-2}$

So

$$4\log t^2 - 2\log t^3 + \log\frac{1}{t^2} = \log t^8 - \log t^6 + \log t^{-2}$$
$$= \log\left(\frac{t^8\,t^{-2}}{t^6}\right)$$
$$= \log 1$$
$$= 0$$

Exercises

1 Simplify to a single log term:
(a) $\log 10 + \log 20$
(b) $\log 30 - \log 6$
(c) $\log 1 + \log 2 + \log 3 + \log 4$
(d) $\log 4 - \log 3$
(e) $\log 6 - \log 5 + \log 4 - \log 3$

2 Simplify to a single log term:
(a) $2\log 3 + 3\log 2$
(b) $4\log 3 - \log 27$
(c) $2\log 8 - 4\log 2 + \log 3$
(d) $2\log 12 - 3\log 6 + 2\log 2$
(e) $5\log 3 - 2\log 9 + 2\log 6 - 3\log 2$

3 Simplify to a single log term:
(a) $\frac{1}{2}\log 16 + \frac{1}{3}\log 8$
(b) $\frac{2}{3}\log 27 - 2\log 3$
(c) $\frac{1}{4}\log 1 + \frac{3}{4}\log 16 + \frac{1}{2}\log 9 - 2\log 2$
(d) $\frac{3}{2}\log 4 - \frac{2}{3}\log 8$
(e) $\frac{4}{3}\log 64 + \frac{2}{3}\log 27 - \log 24$

4 Simplify to a single log term:
(a) $\log x + \log 2x$
(b) $\log x + \log 3x + \log 5x$
(c) $\log x^2y - \log y^2$
(d) $\log x^2 + \log y^2 - \log z^2$
(e) $\log A + \log B - \log\frac{1}{C}$

5 Simplify to a single log term:
(a) $2\log x^2 - 3\log x$
(b) $3\log x^2y + 2\log xy$
(c) $4\log AB^2 - 3\log A^2B$
(d) $2\log rs + 3\log rs^2 - 4\log r^2s$
(e) $4\log abc - 2\log a^2b - 3\log bc$

6 Simplify to a single log term:

(a) $2 \log \frac{x}{y} + 3 \log \frac{y}{x}$

(b) $2 \log \frac{x^2}{y} - 3 \log \frac{y^2}{x}$

(c) $4 \log rs^2 t - 2 \log r^2 st^2 + 3 \log \frac{r^2}{st}$

(d) $\frac{1}{2} \log \frac{x^2}{y^2} - \frac{1}{3} \log \frac{x^3}{y^6}$

(e) $\frac{2}{3} \log \frac{a^2 b}{c^2} + \frac{3}{2} \log \frac{c}{ab} - \frac{1}{2} \log abc$

Solutions to exercises

1 (a) log 200 (b) log 5 (c) log 24
(d) $\log \frac{4}{3}$ (e) $\log \frac{8}{5}$

2 (a) log 72 (b) log 3 (c) log 12
(d) $\log \frac{8}{3}$ (e) $\log \frac{27}{2}$

3 (a) log 8 (b) log 1 = 0 (c) log 6
(d) log 2 (e) log 96

4 (a) $\log 2x^2$ (b) $\log 15x^3$ (c) $\log \frac{x^2}{y}$
(d) $\log \frac{x^2 y^2}{z^2}$ (e) $\log ABC$

5 (a) $\log x$ (b) $\log x^8 y^5$ (c) $\log \frac{B^5}{A^2}$
(d) $\log \frac{s^4}{r^3}$ (e) $\log \frac{c}{b}$

6 (a) $\log \frac{y}{x}$ (b) $\log \frac{x^7}{y^8}$ (c) $\log \frac{r^6 s^3}{t^3}$
(d) $\log y$ (e) $\log \frac{1}{a^{2/3} b^{4/3} c^{1/3}}$

2.5 The logarithmic functions

We are now ready to introduce the logarithmic functions. They are defined as follows:

Key point

$$y = \log x \text{ and } y = \ln x \text{ for } x > 0$$

Table 2.1 shows values of x, $\log x$ and $\ln x$. Their graphs are shown in Figure 2.1.

We note the following common properties:

1 As x increases, both $\log x$ and $\ln x$ increase indefinitely. We write this mathematically as $\log x \to \infty$ as $x \to \infty$, $\ln x \to \infty$ as $x \to \infty$.
2 As x approaches 0 both $\log x$ and $\ln x$ approach minus infinity. We express this as $\log x \to -\infty$ as $x \to 0$, $\ln x \to -\infty$ as $x \to 0$.
3 $\log 1 = \ln 1 = 0$.

4 $\log x$ and $\ln x$ are not defined when x is negative or zero. Thus the domain of the logarithm functions is $x > 0$. The range of these functions is $(-\infty, \infty)$.

Table 2.1

x	$\log x$	$\ln x$
0.1	−1	−2.30
0.2	−0.70	−1.61
0.5	−0.30	−0.69
1	0	0
2	0.30	0.69
3	0.48	1.10
4	0.60	1.39
5	0.70	1.61
6	0.78	1.79
7	0.85	1.95
8	0.90	2.08
9	0.95	2.20
10	1	2.30

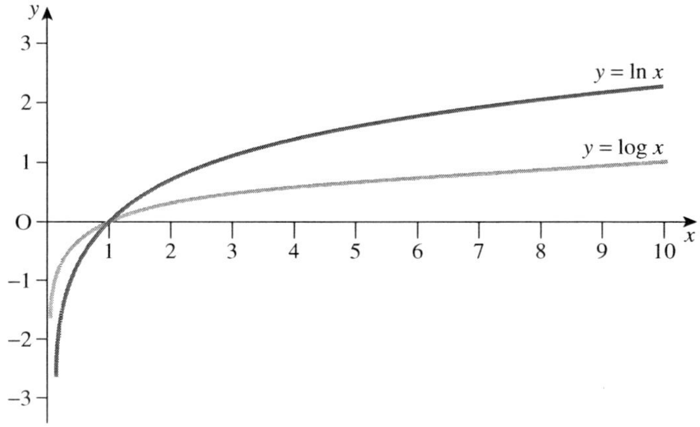

Figure 2.1 The graphs of $y = \log x$ and $y = \ln x$.

End of block exercises

1 Express the following statements using logarithms:
(a) $2^7 = 128$
(b) $4^5 = 1024$
(c) $243 = 3^5$
(d) $0.125 = 2^{-3}$
(e) $4^{-1/2} = 0.5$

2 Express the following using indices:
(a) $\log_3 81 = 4$
(b) $\log_{10} 0.0001 = -4$
(c) $\log_{16} 8 = 0.75$
(d) $\log_4 8 = 1.5$
(e) $\log_4 0.125 = -1.5$

3 Express as a single log term in its simplest form:
(a) $2 \log y + 3 \log x$
(b) $3 \log AB - 2 \log B - \log A$
(c) $\frac{1}{2} \log 4x^2 - \frac{1}{3} \log x$
(d) $\frac{1}{2} \log 8x + \frac{3}{2} \log 2x$
(e) $\log 2x - 2 \log x + x \log 2$

4 Simplify as far as possible
(a) $\log(x^2 + 4x + 3) - \log(x + 1)$
(b) $2 \log(x - 1) - \log(x^2 - 1)$

5 Evaluate (a) $\log_4 9$, (b) $\log_{12} 6$.

Solutions to exercises

1 (a) $\log_2 128 = 7$ (b) $\log_4 1024 = 5$
(c) $\log_3 243 = 5$ (d) $\log_2 0.125 = -3$
(e) $\log_4 0.5 = -0.5$

2 (a) $3^4 = 81$ (b) $10^{-4} = 0.0001$
(c) $16^{0.75} = 8$ (d) $4^{1.5} = 8$
(e) $4^{-1.5} = 0.125$

3 (a) $\log x^3y^2$ (b) $\log A^2B$ (c) $\log 2x^{2/3}$
(d) $\log 8x^2$ (e) $\log\left(\frac{2^{x+1}}{x}\right)$

4 (a) $\log(x + 3)$ (b) $\log\left(\frac{x - 1}{x + 1}\right)$

5 (a) 1.585 (b) 0.721

BLOCK 3 Solving equations involving logarithms and exponentials

3.1 Introduction

In this block we examine the techniques used in solving equations involving logarithmic and exponential terms. We recall the connection between logarithmic and exponential expressions:

Key point

if $N = a^x$ then $x = \log_a N$

In particular,

Key point

if $N = 10^x$ then $x = \log N$

and

Key point

if $N = e^x$ then $x = \ln N$

The process of finding x, having been given 10^x or e^x, is known as **taking logs**.

The following examples illustrate the technique for solution.

Example 3.1

Solve

(a) $10^x = 17.4$ (b) $e^x = 5.25$

Solution

(a) We have

$$10^x = 17.4$$

so taking logs gives

$$\begin{aligned} x &= \log 17.4 \\ &= 1.2405 \end{aligned}$$

(b) We have $e^x = 5.25$. Taking logs gives

$$\begin{aligned} x &= \ln 5.25 \\ &= 1.6582 \end{aligned}$$

Example 3.2

Solve

(a) $10^{2x} = 39$ (b) $e^{3x-1} = 75$

Solution

(a) We have $10^{2x} = 39$. Taking logs gives

$$\begin{aligned} 2x &= \log 39 \\ x &= \frac{\log 39}{2} \\ &= 0.7955 \end{aligned}$$

(b)

$$\begin{aligned} e^{3x-1} &= 75 \\ 3x - 1 &= \ln 75 \\ 3x &= \ln 75 + 1 \\ x &= \frac{\ln 75 + 1}{3} \\ &= 1.7725 \end{aligned}$$

Example 3.3

Solve $3(10^{0.5x-2}) = 96$.

Solution

$$\begin{aligned} 3(10^{0.5x-2}) &= 96 \\ 10^{0.5x-2} &= \frac{96}{3} \\ &= 32 \end{aligned}$$

$0.5x - 2 =$ ______ $\quad \log 32$

$0.5x =$ ______ $\quad \log 32 + 2$

$x =$ ______ $\quad 2(\log 32 + 2)$

$= 7.0103$

Example 3.4

Solve

(a) $\log x = 1.4$ (b) $\ln x = -0.5$

Solution

(a)

$$\begin{aligned} \log x &= 1.4 \\ x &= 10^{1.4} \\ &= 25.12 \end{aligned}$$

(b)

$$\begin{aligned} \ln x &= -0.5 \\ x &= e^{-0.5} \\ &= 0.61 \end{aligned}$$

Example 3.5
Solve
(a) $\log(x^2 + 2) = 2.6$ (b) $3 \ln(5x + 1) = 9.3$

Solution
(a) $\log(x^2 + 2) = 2.6$

$$x^2 + 2 = 10^{2.6}$$
$$x^2 = 10^{2.6} - 2$$
$$x = \sqrt{10^{2.6} - 2}$$
$$= \pm 19.90$$

(b) $3 \ln(5x + 1) = 9.3$

$$\ln(5x + 1) = \frac{9.3}{3}$$
$$= 3.1$$
$$5x + 1 = e^{3.1}$$
$$5x = e^{3.1} - 1$$
$$x = \frac{e^{3.1} - 1}{5}$$
$$= 4.24$$

Example 3.6 Electronic Engineering – Current through a diode
The current through a diode, I, is given by

$$I = I_s(e^{40V} - 1)$$

where I_s is the reverse saturation current and V is the voltage across the diode.
(a) Express V as the subject of the equation.
(b) Evaluate V when $I = 3 \times 10^{-2}$, $I_s = 1.5 \times 10^{-4}$.

Solution
(a)

$$I = I_s(e^{40V} - 1)$$
$$e^{40V} - 1 = \frac{I}{I_s}$$
$$e^{40V} = \frac{I}{I_s} + 1$$

Now, taking logs,

$$40V = \ln\left(\frac{I}{I_s} + 1\right)$$
$$V = \frac{1}{40} \ln\left(\frac{I}{I_s} + 1\right)$$

(b) Substituting the given values of I and I_s into the expression for V results in

$$V = \frac{1}{40} \ln\left(\frac{3 \times 10^{-2}}{1.5 \times 10^{-4}} + 1\right)$$

$$= \frac{1}{40} \ln (200 + 1)$$
$$= \frac{1}{40} \ln 201$$
$$= 0.133$$

Example 3.7 Electronic Engineering – Gain of an amplifier

The voltage gain of an amplifier is given by

$$\text{gain} = 20 \log \left(\frac{V_o}{V_i} \right)$$

where V_i is the input voltage and V_o is the output voltage.

The output voltage from an amplifier is 250 mV. If the amplifier has a gain of 17 dB calculate the input voltage.

Solution

We have

$$\text{gain} = 20 \log \left(\frac{V_o}{V_i} \right)$$

where the gain is 17 dB and $V_o = 250$ mV. So

$$17 = 20 \log \left(\frac{250}{V_i} \right)$$
$$\log \left(\frac{250}{V_i} \right) = \frac{17}{20}$$
$$= 0.85$$
$$\frac{250}{V_i} = 10^{0.85}$$
$$V_i = \frac{250}{10^{0.85}}$$
$$= 35.31$$

The input voltage is 35.3 mV.

Exercises

1 Solve the following equations:
(a) $\log x = 0.7531$
(b) $\log x = 1.6431$
(c) $\log x = -0.4213$
(d) $\log x = -2.3500$

2 Solve
(a) $\ln x = 2.4050$
(b) $\ln x = 0.9611$
(c) $\ln x = -0.9611$
(d) $\ln x = -2.0000$

3 Solve
(a) $10^x = 7$
(b) $10^x = 70$
(c) $10^x = 17$
(d) $10^x = 0.7000$

4 Solve
(a) $e^x = 5$
(b) $e^x = 0.5$
(c) $e^x = 25$
(d) $e^x = 0.001761$

5 Solve
(a) $\log 2x = 1.5$
(b) $\log (3x + 1) = 2.1500$
(c) $\log (x^2 + 3) = 2.3671$
(d) $4 \log (5x - 6) = -0.8000$

6 Solve
(a) $\ln (2x^2) = 3$
(b) $2 \ln (x^2) = 3$
(c) $\ln (x^2 + 2) = 1.3$
(d) $3 \ln (x^2 + 1) = 3.9$

7 An amplifier has a gain of 25 dB. If the input voltage is 15 mV calculate the output voltage.

8 The current, I, through a diode is given by

$$I = I_s(e^{40V} - 1)$$

where I_s is the reverse saturation current and V is the voltage across the diode. If the current is 300 times greater than the reverse saturation current, calculate the voltage across the diode.

Solutions to exercises

1 (a) 5.6637 (b) 43.9643 (c) 0.3791 (d) 0.004467

2 (a) 11.0784 (b) 2.6146 (c) 0.3825 (d) 0.1353

3 (a) 0.8451 (b) 1.8451 (c) 1.2304 (d) −0.1549

4 (a) 1.6094 (b) −0.6931 (c) 3.2189 (d) −6.3419

5 (a) 15.8114 (b) 46.7513 (c) ±15.1612 (d) 1.3262

6 (a) ±3.1690 (b) ±2.1170 (c) ±1.2920 (d) ±1.6338

7 267 mV

8 143 mV

End of block exercises

1 Solve
(a) $\log (3x - 7) = 2.6500$
(b) $2 \ln (x^2 + 4) = 3.9$

2 Solve
(a) $e^{-2x} = 4$ (b) $10^{3-x} = 20$

3 Solve
(a) $\dfrac{10^{3x}}{10^x} = 30$ (b) $\log x + \log (2x) = 3$

4 Solve
(a) $3e^{4x} = 2.7$ (b) $3 \ln 4x = -2.7$

5 Solve
(a) $\log (5 - x^2) = \dfrac{1}{2}$ (b) $e^{\frac{3}{x}} = \dfrac{1}{3}$

Solutions to exercises

1 (a) 151.2 (b) ±1.7403

2 (a) −0.6931 (b) 1.6990

3 (a) 0.7386 (b) 22.36

4 (a) −0.02634 (b) 0.1016

5 (a) ±1.3556 (b) −2.7307

BLOCK 4 Applications of logarithms

4.1 Introduction

Block 2 looked at the definition and laws of logarithms. This block concentrates on some of the applications of logarithms.

4.2 Signal ratio and decibels

The ratio between two signal levels is often of interest to engineers. For example, the output and input signals of an electronic system can be compared to see whether the system has increased the level of a signal. A common case is an amplifier, where the output signal is usually much larger than the input signal. This signal ratio is often expressed in decibels (dB), given by

$$\text{power gain (dB)} = 10 \log\left(\frac{P_o}{P_i}\right)$$

where P_o is the power of the output signal and P_i is the power of the input signal. The term **gain** is used because if $P_o > P_i$ then the logarithm function is positive, corresponding to an increase in power. If $P_o < P_i$ then the gain is negative, corresponding to a decrease in power. A negative gain is often termed an **attenuation**.

The advantage of using decibels as a measure of gain is that if several electronic systems are connected together then it is possible to obtain the overall system gain in decibels by adding together the individual system gains. We shall show this for three systems connected together, but the development is easily generalised to more systems. Let the power input to the first system be P_{i1}, and the power output from the third system be P_{o3}. Suppose the three are connected so that the power output from system 1, P_{o1}, is used as input to system 2: that is, $P_{i2} = P_{o1}$. The power output from system 2, P_{o2}, is then used as input to system 3: that is, $P_{i3} = P_{o2}$. We wish to find the overall power gain, $10 \log\left(\frac{P_{o3}}{P_{i1}}\right)$. Now

$$\frac{P_{o3}}{P_{i1}} = \frac{P_{o3}P_{o2}P_{o1}}{P_{i3}P_{i2}P_{i1}}$$

because $P_{i3} = P_{o2}$ and $P_{i2} = P_{o1}$. Therefore

$$10 \log\left(\frac{P_{o3}}{P_{i1}}\right) = 10 \log\left(\frac{P_{o3}P_{o2}P_{o1}}{P_{i3}P_{i2}P_{i1}}\right)$$

That is,

$$10\log\left(\frac{P_{o3}}{P_{i1}}\right) = 10\log\left(\frac{P_{o3}}{P_{i3}}\right) + 10\log\left(\frac{P_{o2}}{P_{i2}}\right) + 10\log\left(\frac{P_{o1}}{P_{i1}}\right)$$

using the laws of logarithms.

It follows that the overall power gain is equal to the sum of the individual power gains. Often engineers are more interested in voltage gain rather than power gain. The power of a signal is proportional to the square of its voltage. We define **voltage gain** (dB) by

$$\text{voltage gain (dB)} = 10\log\left(\frac{V_o^2}{V_i^2}\right) = 20\log\left(\frac{V_o}{V_i}\right)$$

Example 4.1

Calculate the voltage gain in decibels of an amplifier where the input signal is 0.8 V and the output signal is 1.2 V.

Solution

We have $V_o = 1.2$ and $V_i = 0.8$. Then

$$\begin{aligned}\text{voltage gain (dB)} &= 20\log\frac{V_o}{V_i}\\ &= 20\log\frac{1.2}{0.8}\\ &= 3.52\end{aligned}$$

The voltage gain is 3.52 decibels.

Exercises

1. Calculate the voltage gain in decibels of an amplifier where the input signal is 0.5 V and the output signal is 2.2 V.

2. Calculate the voltage gain in decibels of an amplifier where the input signal is 0.15 V and the output signal is 1.9 V.

Solutions to exercises

1. 12.87 dB

2. 22.05 dB

4.3 Use of log-linear and log-log scales

We look at each kind of scale separately.

Log–linear scales

Suppose we wish to plot

$$y(x) = x^6 \quad 1 \leq x \leq 10$$

This may appear a straightforward exercise, but consider the variation in the x and y values. As x varies from 1 to 10, then y varies from 1 to 1000000, as tabulated in Figure 4.1.

x	y
1	1
2	64
3	729
4	4096
5	15625
6	46656
7	117649
8	262144
9	531441
10	1000000

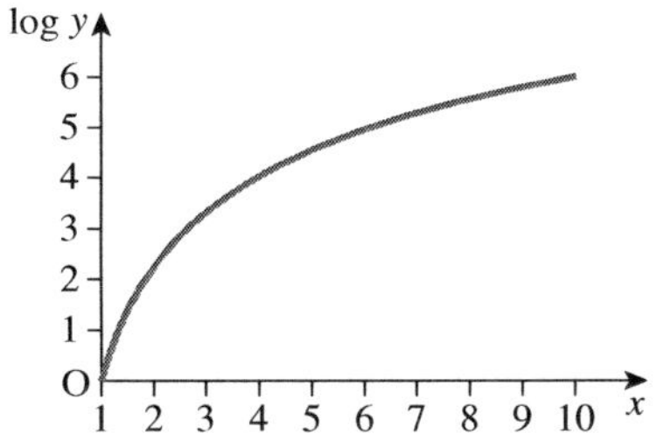

Figure 4.1 The function $y = x^6$ plotted on a log–linear graph.

Several of these points would not be discernible on a graph, and so information would be lost. This can be overcome by using a **log scale**, which accommodates the large variation in y. Thus $\log y$ is plotted against x, rather than y against x. Note that in this example

$$\begin{aligned} \log y &= \log x^6 \\ &= 6 \log x \end{aligned}$$

so as x varies from 1 to 10, $\log y$ varies from 0 to 6. A plot in which one scale is logarithmic and the other is linear is known as a **log–linear** graph. Figure 4.1 shows $\log y$ plotted against x. In effect, use of the log scale has compressed a large variation into one that is much smaller and easier to observe.

Example 4.2

Consider $y = 7^x$ for $-3 \leq x \leq 3$. Plot a log–linear graph of this function.

Solution

We have

$$y = 7^x$$

and so

$$\begin{aligned}\log y &= \log (7^x) \\ &= x \log 7 \\ &= 0.8451x\end{aligned}$$

Putting $Y = \log y$ we have $Y = 0.8451x$, which is the equation of a straight line passing through the origin with gradient log 7. Hence when log y is plotted against x a straight line graph is produced. This is shown in Figure 4.2. Note that, by taking logs, the range on the vertical axis has been greatly reduced.

Figure 4.2
A log–linear plot of $y = 7^x$ produces a straight line graph.

x	y	$Y = \log y$
−3	0.003	−2.54
−2	0.020	−1.69
−1	0.143	−0.85
0	1	0
1	7	0.85
2	49	1.69
3	343	2.54

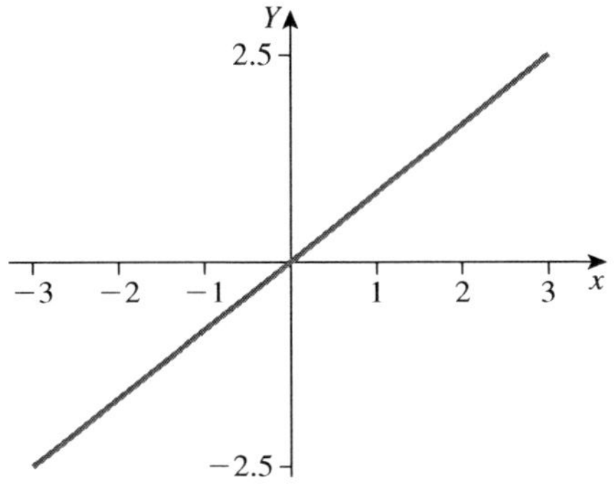

Log–log scales

A plot in which both scales are logarithmic is known as a **log–log plot**. Here log y is plotted against log x.

Example 4.3

Consider $y = x^7$ for $1 \leq x \leq 10$. Plot a log–log graph of this function.

Solution

We have

$$y = x^7$$

and so

$$\begin{aligned}\log y &= \log (x^7) \\ &= 7 \log x\end{aligned}$$

We plot log y against log x for a log–log plot. Putting $Y = \log y$ and $X = \log x$ we have $Y = 7X$, which is a straight line through the origin with gradient 7, as shown in Figure 4.3.

x	y	$X = \log x$	$Y = \log y$
1	1	0	0
2	128	0.301	2.107
3	2187	0.477	3.340
4	16384	0.602	4.214
5	78125	0.699	4.893
6	279936	0.778	5.447
7	823543	0.845	5.916
8	2097152	0.903	6.322
9	4782969	0.954	6.680
10	10000000	1	7

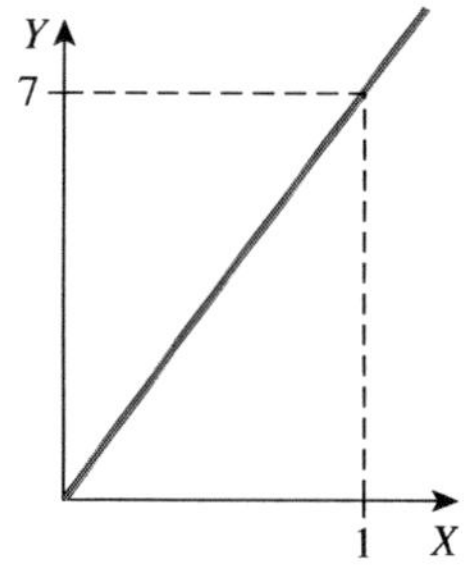

Figure 4.3
A log–log plot of $y = x^7$ produces a straight line graph.

We have seen how a log scale has the effect of compressing a very large range of values into a more meaningful size. Similarly a log scale expands a very small range into a more meaningful size. Consider the following example.

Example 4.4

Plot a log–log graph of

$$y = x^3 \quad 10^{-6} \leq x \leq 10^{-1}$$

Solution

The small range of x values would almost be impossible to plot. The plot is more meaningful when a log–log scale is used. Table 4.1 shows values of x, y, log x and log y.

Table 4.1

x	y	$\log x$	$\log y$
10^{-6}	10^{-18}	-6	-18
10^{-5}	10^{-15}	-5	-15
10^{-4}	10^{-12}	-4	-12
10^{-3}	10^{-9}	-3	-9
10^{-2}	10^{-6}	-2	-6
10^{-1}	10^{-3}	-1	-3

From Table 4.1 we see that both x and y have a very small range but that log x and log y have a much more meaningful range. Figure 4.4 shows a plot of log y against log x.

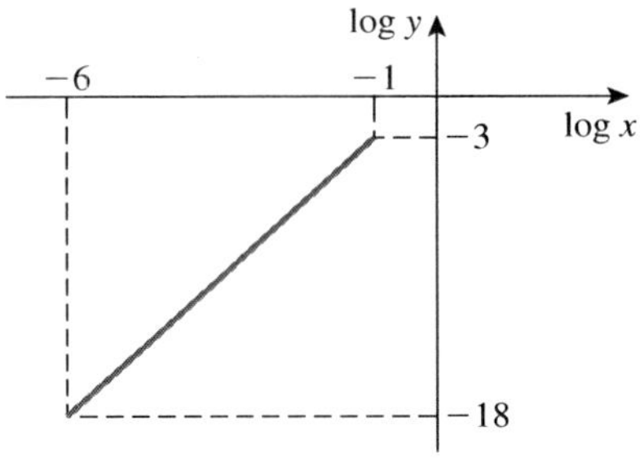

Figure 4.4
A plot of log y against log x.

Figure 4.4 shows a straight line graph with gradient 3. This can be seen from

$$\begin{aligned} y &= x^3 \\ \log y &= \log x^3 \\ &= 3 \log x \end{aligned}$$

4.4 Use of log–linear and log–log paper

The requirement to take logarithms is a tedious process, which can be avoided by using special graph papers called log–linear graph paper and log–log graph paper. An example of log–linear graph paper is shown in Figure 4.5.

Note that on one axis the scale is uniform; this is the linear scale. On the other, the scale is not uniform and is marked in **cycles** from 1 to 9. This is the logarithmic scale. On this scale values of y are plotted directly, without first taking logarithms. On the graph paper shown in Figure 4.5 there are two cycles but papers are also available with three or more cycles. To decide which sort of graph paper is appropriate it is necessary to examine the variation in size of the variable to be plotted measured in powers of 10. If, for example, y varies from 1 to 10, then paper with one cycle is appropriate. If y varies from 1 to 10^2, two-cycle paper is necessary. If y varies from 10^{-1} to 10^4, then paper with $4 - (-1) = 5$ cycles would be appropriate. To see how log–linear paper is used in practice, consider the following example.

Example 4.5
Following an experiment the following pairs of data values were recorded:

	A	B	C	D
x	0	1	5	12
y	4.00	5.20	14.85	93.19

It is believed that y and x are related by the equation $y = ab^x$. By plotting a log–linear graph verify the relationship is of this form and determine a and b.

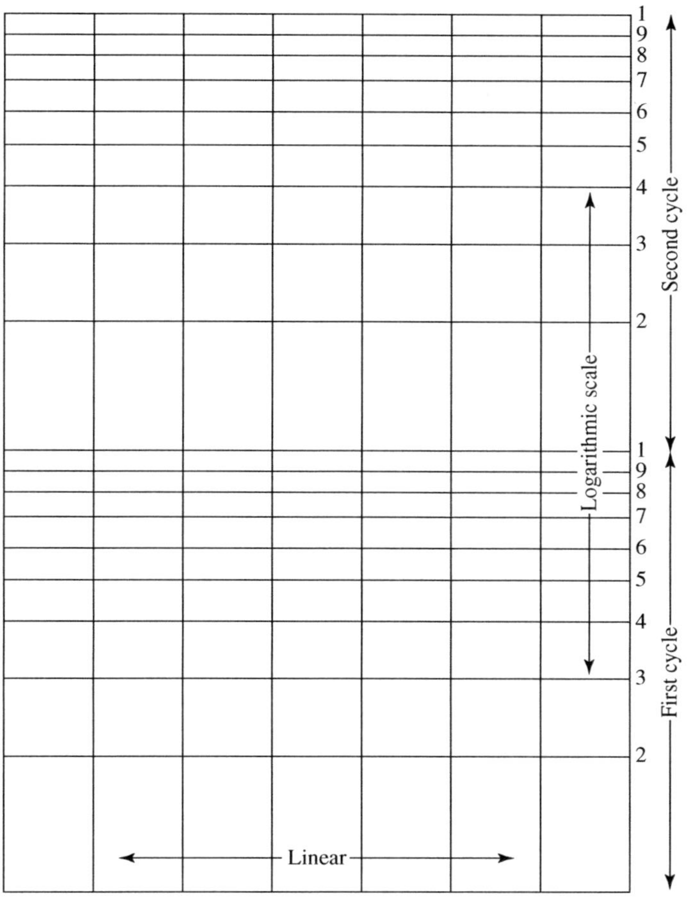

Figure 4.5 Two-cycle log–linear graph paper.

Solution

If the relationship is given by $y = ab^x$, then taking logarithms yields

$$\log y = \log a + x \log b$$

So, plotting log y against x should produce a straight line graph with gradient log b and vertical intercept log a. The need to find log y is eliminated by plotting the y values directly on a logarithmic scale. Examining the table of data we see that y varies from approximately 10^0 to 10^2 so that two-cycle paper is appropriate. Values of y between 1 and 10 are plotted on the first cycle, and those between 10 and 100 are plotted on the second. The points are plotted in Figure 4.6. Note in particular that in this example the '1' at the start of the second cycle represents the value 10, the '2' represents the value 20, and so on. From the graph, the straight line relationship between log y and x is evident. It is therefore reasonable to assume that the relationship between y and x is of the form $y = ab^x$.

Figure 4.6
The log–linear graph is a straight line.

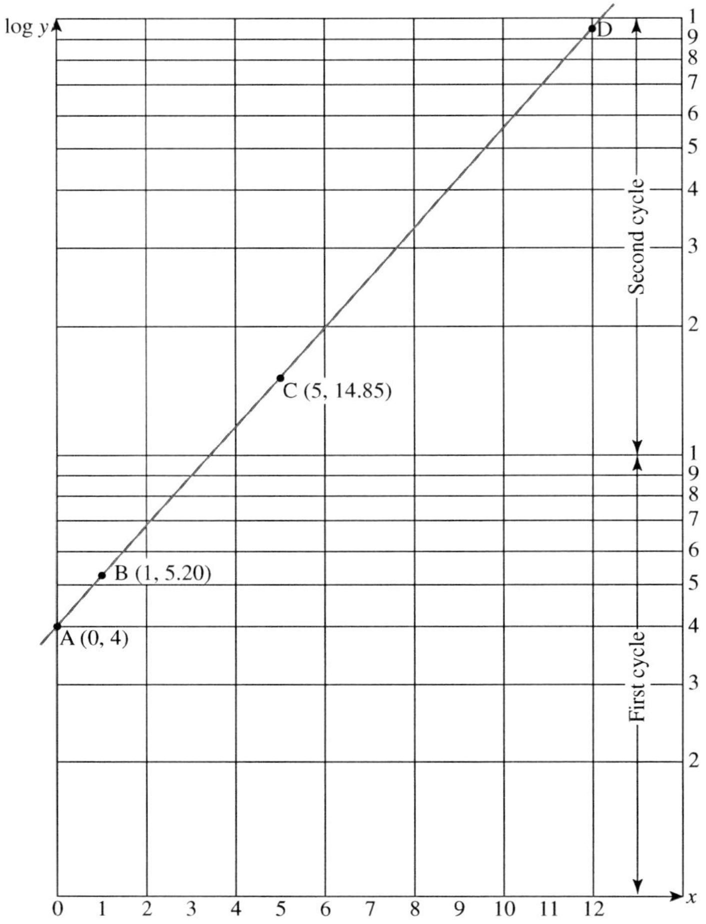

To find the gradient of the graph we can choose any two points on the line, for example C and B. The gradient is then

$$\frac{\log 14.85 - \log 5.20}{5 - 1} = \frac{\log\left(\dfrac{14.85}{5.20}\right)}{4}$$
$$= 0.1139$$

Recall that $\log b$ is the gradient of the line and so

$$\log b = 0.1139$$

that is

$$b = 10^{0.1139}$$
$$= 1.2999$$

The vertical intercept is log a. From the graph the vertical intercept is log 4 so that

$$\log a = \log 4$$

that is

$$a = 4$$

We conclude that the relationship between y and x is given by $y = 4\,(1.3)^x$.

Example 4.6

The variables x and y are thought to be connected by an equation of the form

$$y = ax^n$$

Some experimental values are tabulated below:

	A	B	C	D
x	1	3	7	9
y	2	31	255	500

By plotting the data on appropriate graph paper, determine the law connecting x and y.

Solution

If $y = ax^n$ then

$$\log y = \log (ax^n)$$
$$= \log a + n \log x$$

Letting $Y = \log y$ and $X = \log x$ we have

$$Y = nX + \log a$$

This is a straight line equation with gradient n and vertical intercept log a. Since both log x and log y are used then a log scale on both axes is needed: that is, log–log paper is used. One cycle is needed to accommodate the x variation; three cycles are needed to accommodate the y variation. Log–log paper comes in 1 cycle × 1 cycle, 2 cycle × 2 cycle and 3 cycle × 3 cycle. Consequently, for the example in question, 3 cycle × 3 cycle paper is needed. Figure 4.7 shows the log–log paper with the data points plotted. The straight line fit tells us that x and y are connected by a law of the form $y = ax^n$.

Using points A and D to calculate the gradient we have

$$\text{gradient} = \frac{\log 500 - \log 2}{\log 9 - \log 1} = \frac{\log 250}{\log 9} = 2.5$$

Hence we see that $n = 2.5$.

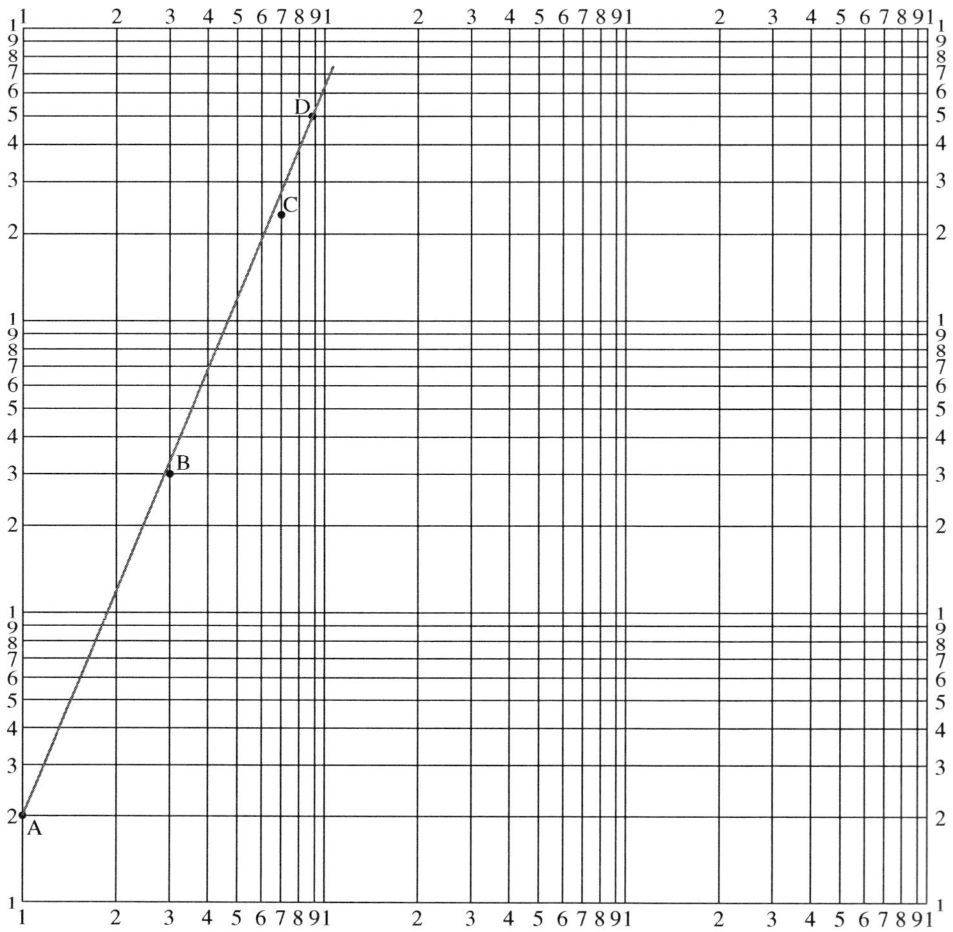

Figure 4.7 If $y = ax^n$, then log–log paper produces a straight line.

From the graph the vertical intercept is log 2 and so

$$\log a = \log 2$$
$$a = 2$$

Hence x and y are connected by $y = 2x^{2.5}$.

Examples 4.5 and 4.6 illustrate the following points.

Key point

If $y = ax^n$ then a log–log plot produces a straight line with gradient $= n$ and vertical intercept $= \log a$.

If $y = ab^x$, then a log–linear plot produces a straight line with gradient $= \log b$ and vertical intercept $= \log a$.

Example 4.7 Electrical Engineering – Bode plot of a linear circuit
Engineers are often interested in how a circuit will respond to a sinusoidal signal. A Bode plot helps in the analysis.

A **Bode plot** consists of two components:

1 The ratio of the amplitudes of the output signal and the input signal is plotted against frequency.
2 The phase shift between the input and output signals is plotted against frequency.

A log scale is used for the frequency in order to compress its length: for example, a typical frequency range is 0.1 Hz to 10^6 Hz, which corresponds to a range of -1 to 6 on a log scale. A log scale is also used for the ratio of the signal amplitudes as this is calculated in decibels. Phase shift is plotted on a linear scale. So the signal amplitude ratio against frequency is a log–log graph and the phase shift against frequency is a linear–log graph.

Exercises

1 It is thought that x and y are connected by a law of the form $y = ax^n$.
Measurements of x and y are

x	1.5	3	5	10	20	25
y	7.2	23	55	180	600	860

(a) By using appropriate paper find the law connecting x and y.
(b) Predict the y measurement when $x = 30$.

2 It is thought that x and y are connected by a law of the form $y = ax^n$.
Measurements of x and y are

x	0.25	0.5	0.8	1.3	4	7
y	0.18	0.30	0.42	0.61	1.41	2.2

(a) By using appropriate paper find the law connecting x and y.
(b) Predict the y measurement when $x = 10$.

3 It is thought that x and y are connected by a law of the form $y = ab^x$.
Measurements of x and y are

x	2	3	4	4.5	5	5.5
y	18	54	160	280	500	840

(a) By using appropriate paper find the law connecting x and y.
(b) Predict the y measurement when $x = 6$.

4 It is thought that x and y are connected by a law of the form $y = ab^x$.
Measurements of x and y are

x	2	5	10	20	30	35	38
y	1	1.75	4.33	27	170	400	700

(a) By using appropriate paper find the law connecting x and y.
(b) Predict the y measurement when $x = 40$.

5 The time of swing of a pendulum, T seconds, is measured for different lengths of the pendulum, l metres. The results are

l	0.2	0.4	0.6	0.8	1.0	1.2
T	0.9	1.3	1.5	1.8	2.0	2.2

If $T = kl^n$ use appropriate graph paper to find the values of k and n.

Solutions to exercises

1 (a) $y = 3.6x^{1.7}$ (b) 1168

2 (a) $y = 0.5x^{0.75}$ (b) 2.81

3 (a) $y = 2(3^x)$ (b) 1458

4 (a) $y = 0.7(1.2^x)$ (b) 1029

5 $k = 2,\ n = 0.5$

End of block exercises

1 Measurements of the variables x and y are recorded as follows

x	1.5	2.0	2.5	3.0	3.5
y	1.76	1.47	1.23	1.03	0.86

(a) Given $y = ab^x$, use appropriate graph paper to find a and b.
(b) Predict y when $x = 4$.

2 It is believed that in a particular circuit the power, P, and voltage, V, are related by a law of the form $P = kV^n$. Measurements of P and V are

P	11	45	125	245	405
V	1.5	3	5	7	9

(a) By plotting the data on appropriate paper, find the values of k and n.
(b) If the voltage is increased to 12 V, calculate the power.
(c) Calculate the minimum voltage required if the power must exceed 1000 W.

3 Calculate the voltage gain (dB) of an amplifier that produces an output signal of 2.35 V when the input signal is 40 mV.

4 An amplifier consists of a preamplifier and a main amplifier. The input signal to the preamplifier is 5 mV and the output signal is 80 mV. The input to the main amplifier is 80 mV and the output signal is 3 V.
(a) Calculate the voltage gain of the preamplifier.
(b) Calculate the voltage gain of the main amplifier.
(c) Calculate the overall gain of the amplifier.

Solutions to exercises

1 (a) $a = 3,\ b = 0.7$ (b) 0.72

2 (a) $k = 5,\ n = 2$ (b) 720 (c) 14.2

3 35.4

4 (a) 24.08 (b) 31.48 (c) 55.6

End of chapter exercises

1 Evaluate (a) $e^{1.6}$, (b) $e^{-1.6}$, (c) $\frac{1}{e^{1.6}}$.

2 The current in a circuit, $i(t)$, is given by

$$i(t) = 25e^{-0.2t} \quad t \geq 0$$

(a) State the current when $t = 0$.
(b) Calculate the value of the current when $t = 2$.
(c) Calculate the time when the value of the current is 12.5.

3 Simplify as far as possible:
(a) $\dfrac{e^{2x}e^{x}}{e^{-3x}}$ (b) $(4e^{2x})(3e^{-x})$
(c) $\dfrac{2e^{x}+1}{2}+\dfrac{2-e^{x}}{3}$ (d) $e^{4x}-(e^{2x}+1)^2$

4 Simplify as far as possible:
(a) $e^{2t}e^{3t}$ (b) $3e^{2t}e^{-t}$ (c) $\dfrac{(e^{x})^2}{e^{2x}}$ (d) $\sqrt{\dfrac{e^{4x}}{9}}$

5 Evaluate (a) sinh 4.7, (b) cosh (−1.6), (c) tanh 1.2.

6 Express $6e^{x}+3e^{-x}$ in terms of the hyperbolic functions sinh x and cosh x.

7 Prove the hyperbolic identity

$$\cosh 2x = \sinh^2 x + \cosh^2 x$$

8 Express the following statements using logarithms:
(a) $8^2 = 64$ (b) $4^3 = 64$ (c) $2^6 = 64$

9 Express the following using indices:
(a) $\log 35 = 1.5441$ (b) $\log_6 1296 = 4$
(c) $\ln 50 = 3.9120$ (d) $\log_9 3 = 0.5$

10 Evaluate (a) $\log_2 20$, (b) $\log_7 2$

11 Simplify to a single logarithmic expression:
(a) $\ln 4y + \ln x$
(b) $3\ln t^2 - 2\ln t$
(c) $3\log t - \log 3t$
(d) $\log 2x + \log 5x - 1$

12 Solve
(a) $2\ln(3x-10) = 8.5$
(b) $\log(x^3+1) = 2.4$
(c) $3\log 4x - 8 = 0$
(d) $\dfrac{\ln 5x}{2} = 1.6$

13 Solve
(a) $e^{4x} = 90$
(b) $10^{x/2} - 20 = 0$
(c) $3e^{-x} = 20$
(d) $10^{3x-6} = 40$

14 Solve
(a) $10^{\log x} = 17$
(b) $10^{2\log x} = 17$
(c) $10^{x}10^{2x} = 90$
(d) $10^{2x} = 30(10^{x})$

15 Solve
(a) $\ln(e^{x}) = 5000$
(b) $\ln(e^{x}+10) = 5$
(c) $\dfrac{2}{3}\ln(x^2+9) = 3$
(d) $\log\left(\dfrac{x}{2}+1\right) = 1.5$

16 Simplify (a) $\sqrt{e^{2\ln x}}$, (b) $\log(100^{x})$.

17 The temperature, T, of a chemical reaction is given by

$$T = 120e^{0.02t} \quad t \geq 0$$

Calculate the time needed for the temperature to (a) double its initial value, (b) treble its initial value.

18 Calculate the voltage gain in decibels of an amplifier where the input voltage is 17 mV and the output voltage is 300 mV.

19 The voltage input to an amplifier is 30 mV.
(a) Calculate the output voltage if the amplifier has a gain of 16 dB.
(b) Calculate the output voltage if the amplifier has a gain of 32 dB.

20 The variables x and y are believed to be connected by a law of the form $y = ax^n$. Measurements of x and y are

x	2	5	7	10	15	20
y	7.9	28.6	46.0	74.7	134.1	200.0

(a) By drawing an appropriate graph, find the law connecting x and y.
(b) Predict y when $x = 17$.

21 Variables y and t are thought to be connected by a law of the form

$$y = \frac{a^t}{k}$$

Measurements of t and y are

t	2	4	6	8	10
y	0.80	2.62	8.50	27.8	90.0

(a) By using appropriate graph paper find the law connecting y and t.
(b) Predict y when $t = 12$.
(c) Predict the value of t when y first exceeds 1000.

Solutions to exercises

1 (a) 4.9530 (b) 0.2019 (c) 0.2019

2 (a) 25 (b) 16.76 (c) 3.4657

3 (a) e^{6x} (b) $12e^x$ (c) $\frac{2e^x}{3} + \frac{7}{6}$ (d) $-(2e^{2x} + 1)$

4 (a) e^{5t} (b) $3e^t$ (c) 1 (d) $\frac{e^{2x}}{3}$

5 (a) 54.9690 (b) 2.5775 (c) 0.8337

6 $9 \cosh x + 3 \sinh x$

8 (a) $\log_8 64 = 2$ (b) $\log_4 64 = 3$ (c) $\log_2 64 = 6$

9 (a) $10^{1.5441} = 35$ (b) $6^4 = 1296$ (c) $e^{3.9120} = 50$ (d) $9^{0.5} = 3$

10 (a) 4.3219 (b) 0.3562

11 (a) $\ln 4xy$ (b) $\ln t^4$ (c) $\log\left(\frac{t^2}{3}\right)$ (d) $\log x^2$

12 (a) 26.7018 (b) 6.3012 (c) 116.0397 (d) 4.9065

13 (a) 1.1250 (b) 2.6021 (c) −1.8971 (d) 2.5340

14 (a) 17 (b) $\sqrt{17}$ (c) 0.6514 (d) 1.4771

15 (a) 5000 (b) 4.9302 (c) 9.0010 (d) 61.2456

16 (a) x (b) $2x$

17 (a) 34.66 (b) 54.93

18 24.93 dB

19 (a) 189.3 (b) 1194.3

20 (a) $y = 3x^{1.4}$ (b) 158

21 (a) $y = \frac{1.8^t}{4}$ (b) 289 (c) 14.11

Trigonometry

Chapter 9

This chapter opens with a treatment of the two common units used for measuring angles: degrees and radians. The trigonometrical ratios of sine, cosine and tangent are then introduced. Initially the ratios of angles between 0° and 90° are dealt with and then the ratios of angles of any size are incorporated. The common identities involving trigonometrical ratios are studied together with the solution of trigonometrical equations. The application of trigonometry to combining two waves into a single wave concludes the chapter.

Chapter 9 contents

BLOCK 1

Angles

1.1 Introduction

Angles measure the amount through which a line or object has been turned. The Greek letters α, θ and ϕ are commonly used to denote angles. In Figure 1.1 the angle between lines AB and AC is θ.

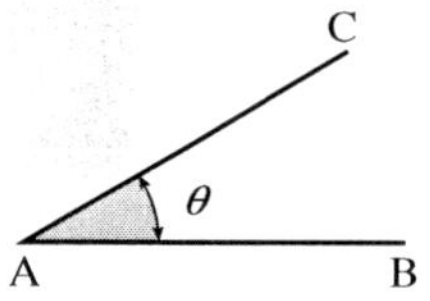

Figure 1.1
The angle between AB and AC is θ.

We can think of the line AB as being turned through or rotated an angle θ to the new position AC.

1.2 Units

There are two main units used to measure angles: the **degree** and the **radian**. Both units are defined with reference to a circle.

Degree

Consider a circle, centre O, as shown in Figure 1.2.

A typical radius, OA, is shown. If the radius OA is rotated as indicated so that it ends up in its original position we say it has been turned through a complete revolution. The angle that is equivalent to a complete revolution is 360 degrees, denoted 360°.

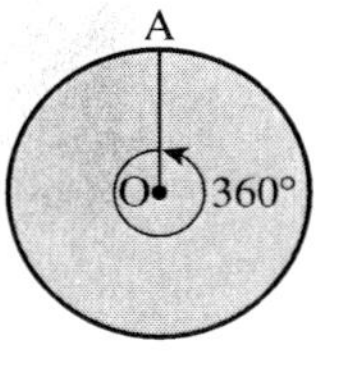

Figure 1.2
One complete revolution is 360°.

Key point

1 complete revolution = $360°$

Radian

Consider a circle of radius r, centre O. An arc AB of length r is shown. We say that the arc AB **subtends** an angle at the centre O. This is angle AOB. The situation is illustrated in Figure 1.3.

Then the angle AOB is defined to be 1 radian.

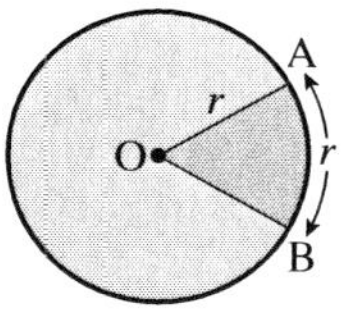

Figure 1.3 The arc AB has length r.

Key point

1 radian = angle subtended at centre by an arc whose length is one radius

An arc length r subtends an angle of 1 radian. Then an arc of length $2r$ subtends an angle of 2 radians and in general an arc of length αr subtends an angle of α radians. Let us examine the case where $\alpha = 2\pi$. An arc length of $2\pi r$ is the entire circumference of the circle, and this subtends an angle of 2π radians. But the circumference subtends a complete revolution at the centre, that is $360°$, and so

$$2\pi \text{ radians} = 360°$$

Hence we have

Key point

π radians = $180°$

Some common angles, marked in both degrees and radians, are shown in Figure 1.4.

Example 1.1
Convert $37°$ to radians.

Solution
We have

$$180° = \pi \text{ radians}$$

and so

$$\begin{aligned} 1° &= \frac{\pi}{180} \text{ radians} \\ 37° &= 37 \times \frac{\pi}{180} \text{ radians} \\ &= 0.6458 \text{ radians} \end{aligned}$$

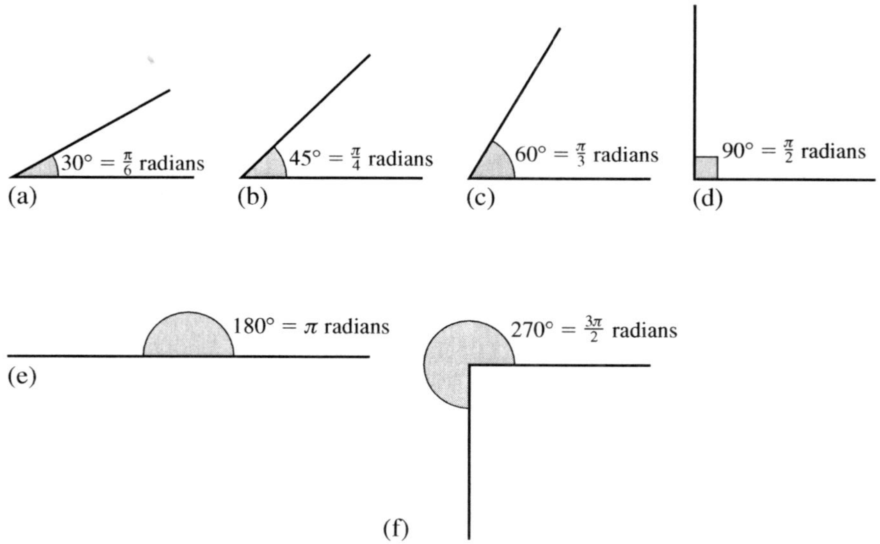

Figure 1.4 Some common angles.

Example 1.2
Convert 1.2 radians to degrees.

Solution

$$\begin{aligned} \pi \text{ radians} &= 180^\circ \\ 1 \text{ radian} &= \frac{180^\circ}{\pi} \\ 1.2 \text{ radians} &= 1.2 \times \frac{180^\circ}{\pi} \\ &= 68.75^\circ \end{aligned}$$

Commonly, angles measured in radians are expressed as multiples of π: for example, 3π radians, $\frac{\pi}{2}$ radians and $\frac{2\pi}{3}$ radians.

Example 1.3
Express 72° in the form $\alpha\pi$ radians.

Solution
We have

$$\begin{aligned} 180^\circ &= \pi \text{ radians} \\ 1^\circ &= \frac{1}{180} \times \pi \text{ radians} \\ 72^\circ &= \frac{72}{180} \times \pi \text{ radians} \\ &= \frac{2\pi}{5} \text{ radians} \end{aligned}$$

Example 1.4
Express 117° in radians.

Solution
We have

$$180^\circ = \pi \text{ radians}$$

$$1^\circ = \frac{\pi}{180} \text{ radians}$$

$$117^\circ = 117 \times \frac{\pi}{180} = 2.0420 \text{ radians}$$

Example 1.5
Express 3.12 radians in degrees.

Solution

$$\pi \text{ radians} = 180^\circ$$

$$1 \text{ radian} = \frac{180^\circ}{\pi}$$

$$3.12 \text{ radians} = 3.12 \times \frac{180^\circ}{\pi} = 178.8^\circ$$

End of block exercises

1 Convert the following angles in radians to degrees:
(a) 0.3609 (b) 0.4771 (c) 1.3692 (d) $\frac{\pi}{3}$
(e) $\frac{2\pi}{3}$ (f) 6π (g) $\frac{\pi}{5}$ (h) $\frac{3\pi}{2}$

2 Convert the following angles in degrees to radians:
(a) 12° (b) 65° (c) 200° (d) 340° (e) 1000°

3 Express the following angles in the form $\alpha\pi$ radians:
(a) 90° (b) 45° (c) 60° (d) 120° (e) 240°
(f) 72° (g) 216° (h) 135° (i) 108° (j) 270°

Solutions to exercises

1 (a) 20.68° (b) 27.34° (c) 78.45° (d) 60°
(e) 120° (f) 1080° (g) 36° (h) 270°

2 (a) 0.2094 (b) 1.1345 (c) 3.4907 (d) 5.9341
(e) 17.4533

3 (a) $\frac{\pi}{2}$ (b) $\frac{\pi}{4}$ (c) $\frac{\pi}{3}$ (d) $\frac{2\pi}{3}$ (e) $\frac{4\pi}{3}$ (f) $\frac{2\pi}{5}$
(g) $\frac{6\pi}{5}$ (h) $\frac{3\pi}{4}$ (i) $\frac{3\pi}{5}$ (j) $\frac{3\pi}{2}$

BLOCK 2

The trigonometrical ratios

2.1 Introduction

The three common trigonometrical ratios of sine, cosine and tangent are defined with reference to a right-angled triangle. Some simple properties of the ratios are developed. The use of scientific calculators to find the trigonometrical ratios and their inverses is explained.

2.2 Some terms associated with a right-angled triangle

A **right angle** is an angle of 90°. In Figure 2.1, $\triangle$ABC has a right angle at C. The side opposite a right angle is called the **hypotenuse**. In Figure 2.1, AB is the hypotenuse.

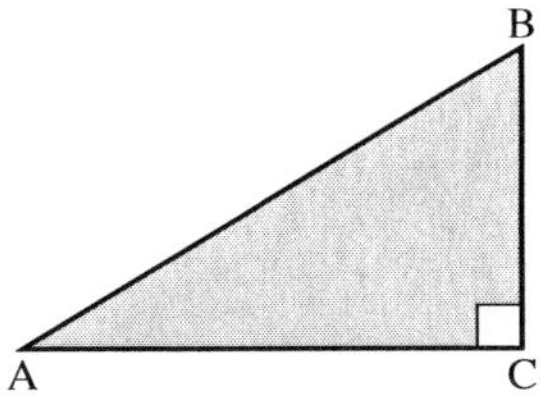

Figure 2.1
The hypotenuse is *AB*. The hypotenuse is always opposite the right angle.

Consider now the angle at A. We often write just *A* when referring to the angle at A; similarly with B. The **side opposite** *A* is BC. The **side adjacent** to *A* is AC. Similarly the side opposite *B* is AC; the side adjacent to *B* is BC.

2.3 Definition of the trigonometrical ratios

We refer to the right-angled triangle in Figure 2.1 to define the trigonometrical ratios, sine, cosine and tangent. The sine of *A* is written sin *A*, the cosine of *A* is written cos *A*, and the tangent of *A* is written tan *A*. We define:

Key point

$$\sin A = \frac{\text{length of side opposite}}{\text{length of hypotenuse}} = \frac{\text{BC}}{\text{AB}}$$

$$\cos A = \frac{\text{length of side adjacent}}{\text{length of hypotenuse}} = \frac{\text{AC}}{\text{AB}}$$

$$\tan A = \frac{\text{length of side opposite}}{\text{length of side adjacent}} = \frac{\text{BC}}{\text{AC}}$$

The sine, cosine and tangent of B are defined in exactly the same way, leading to

$$\sin B = \frac{\text{AC}}{\text{AB}}, \quad \cos B = \frac{\text{BC}}{\text{AB}}, \quad \tan B = \frac{\text{AC}}{\text{BC}}$$

2.4 Properties of the trigonometrical ratios

We note some properties of the trigonometrical ratios:

1 Since all are defined as the ratio of two lengths, none of the trigonometrical ratios has any units.
2 Since the hypotenuse is always the longest side of a right-angled triangle, the sine and cosine ratios can never be greater than 1.
3 The tangent ratio does not involve the hypotenuse and so this ratio can be greater than 1.
4
$$\begin{aligned}\tan A &= \frac{\text{BC}}{\text{AC}} \\ &= \frac{\text{BC}}{\text{AB}}\frac{\text{AB}}{\text{AC}} \\ &= \frac{\text{BC}/\text{AB}}{\text{AC}/\text{AB}} \\ &= \frac{\sin A}{\cos A}\end{aligned}$$

Similarly we see that

$$\tan B = \frac{\sin B}{\cos B}$$

Indeed, for any angle, θ, we have

Key point

$$\tan\theta = \frac{\sin\theta}{\cos\theta}$$

5
$$\begin{aligned}\sin A &= \frac{\text{BC}}{\text{AB}} \\ &= \cos B\end{aligned}$$

$$\cos A = \frac{AC}{AB} = \sin B$$

We note that $B = 90° - A$. Hence we have for any angle A

Key point

$$\sin A = \cos(90° - A)$$
$$\cos A = \sin(90° - A)$$

6 We have

$$\tan A = \frac{BC}{AC} = \frac{1}{AC/BC} = \frac{1}{\tan B}$$

We also note that $B = 90° - A$ and so

Key point

$$\tan A = \frac{1}{\tan(90° - A)}$$

We now look at some examples.

Example 2.1

Figure 2.2 shows a right-angled triangle with the lengths of the sides labelled. Calculate
(a) $\sin A$ (b) $\cos A$ (c) $\tan A$ (d) $\sin B$ (e) $\cos B$ (f) $\tan B$

Figure 2.2

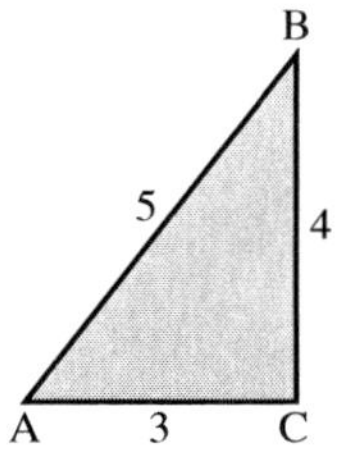

Solution

(a) $\sin A = \frac{BC}{AB} = \frac{4}{5} = 0.8$

(b) $\cos A = \dfrac{AC}{AB} = \dfrac{3}{5} = 0.6$

(c) $\tan A = \dfrac{BC}{AC} = \dfrac{4}{3} = 1.3333$

(d) $\sin B = \dfrac{AC}{AB} = 0.6$

(e) $\cos B = \dfrac{BC}{AB} = 0.8$

(f) $\tan B = \dfrac{AC}{BC} = \dfrac{3}{4} = 0.75$

Example 2.2

Figure 2.3 shows $\triangle XYZ$. The angle at X is 90°. Calculate
(a) $\sin Y$ (b) $\cos Y$ (c) $\sin Z$ (d) $\tan Y$ (e) $\tan Z$ (f) $\cos Z$

Figure 2.3

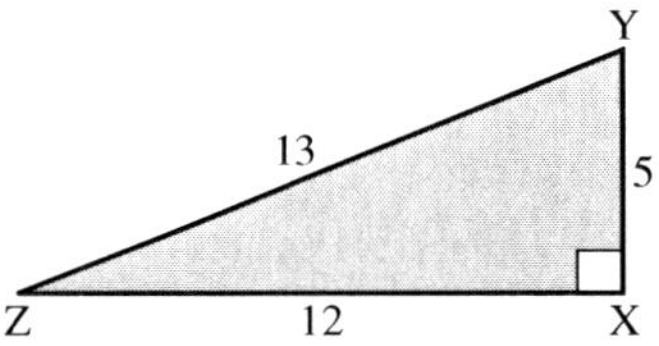

Solution

(a) $\sin Y = \dfrac{\text{opposite}}{\text{hypotenuse}} =$ $\dfrac{XZ}{YZ} = \dfrac{12}{13}$

(b) $\cos Y = \dfrac{\text{adjacent}}{\text{hypotenuse}} =$ $\dfrac{XY}{YZ} = \dfrac{5}{13}$

(c) $\sin Z =$ $\dfrac{XY}{YZ} = \dfrac{5}{13}$

(d) $\tan Y = \dfrac{\text{opposite}}{\text{adjacent}} =$ $\dfrac{XZ}{XY} = \dfrac{12}{5}$

(e) $\tan Z =$ $\dfrac{XY}{XZ} = \dfrac{5}{12}$

(f) $\cos Z =$ $\dfrac{XZ}{YZ} = \dfrac{12}{13}$

When an angle is known, a scientific calculator can be used to find its trigonometrical ratios. The angle may be expressed in degrees or radians.

Example 2.3

Use a scientific calculator to evaluate the following:
(a) $\sin 37°$ (b) $\cos 80°$ (c) $\tan 53°$ (d) $\sin 1.1$ (e) $\cos 0.6321$ (f) $\tan 0.5016$

Solution

Using a scientific calculator we find:

(a) $\sin 37° = 0.6018$
(b) $\cos 80° = 0.1736$
(c) $\tan 53° =$ 1.3270

For (d), (e) and (f) the angles are given in radians. Make sure your calculator is set to RADIAN mode.

(d) $\sin 1.1 = 0.8912$
(e) $\cos 0.6321 =$ 0.8068
(f) $\tan 0.5016 = 0.5484$

Exercises

1 In $\triangle$CDE, D is a right angle. The lengths of CD, DE and CE are α, β and γ respectively. State
(a) $\sin C$ (b) $\cos C$ (c) $\tan C$ (d) $\sin E$
(e) $\tan E$ (f) $\cos E$

2 Use a scientific calculator to evaluate
(a) $\cos 61°$ (b) $\tan 0.4$ (c) $\sin 70°$
(d) $\cos 0.7613$ (e) $\tan 51°$ (f) $\sin 1.2$

Solutions to exercises

1 (a) $\dfrac{\beta}{\gamma}$ (b) $\dfrac{\alpha}{\gamma}$ (c) $\dfrac{\beta}{\alpha}$ (d) $\dfrac{\alpha}{\gamma}$ (e) $\dfrac{\alpha}{\beta}$ (f) $\dfrac{\beta}{\gamma}$

2 (a) 0.4848 (b) 0.4228 (c) 0.9397 (d) 0.7239
(e) 1.2349 (f) 0.9320

2.5 Secant, cosecant and cotangent ratios

These ratios are the reciprocals of the cosine, sine and tangent ratios. Secant, cosecant and cotangent are usually abbreviated to sec, cosec and cot, respectively.

Key point

$$\sec A = \frac{1}{\cos A}$$

$$\text{cosec}\, A = \frac{1}{\sin A}$$

$$\cot A = \frac{1}{\tan A}$$

Example 2.4
Evaluate
(a) cosec 50° (b) cot 20° (c) sec 70° (d) cot 0.7

Solution

(a)
$$\operatorname{cosec} 50° = \frac{1}{\sin 50°} = 1.3054$$

(b)
$$\cot 20° = \frac{1}{\tan 20°} = 2.7475$$

(c) $\sec 70° = \dfrac{1}{\cos 70°} = 2.9238$

(d) Note that the angle is in radians.

$$\cot 0.7 = \frac{1}{\tan 0.7} = 1.1872$$

Exercises

1 Evaluate the following:
(a) cot 1.2 (b) sec 45° (c) cosec 0.6391
(d) cot 57° (e) sec 0.9600

Solutions to exercises

1 (a) 0.3888 (b) 1.4142 (c) 1.6765 (d) 0.6494
(e) 1.7436

2.6 The inverse trigonometrical ratios

Suppose we know the value of sin A, but not the value of A. For example, let $\sin A = 0.6513$, and we wish to find the value of A. Given

$$\sin A = 0.6513$$

we write

$$A = \sin^{-1}(0.6513)$$

This states that A is the angle whose sine is 0.6513. We read this as A is the **inverse sine** of 0.6513. So the notation $\sin^{-1}$ means 'the angle whose sine is . . .'. The -1 should not be interpreted as a power. Other notations are sometimes used, namely

$$A = \text{inv}\,\sin(0.6513) \quad \text{and} \quad A = \arcsin(0.6513)$$

Similarly if $\cos B = 0.3619$ we write $B = \cos^{-1}(0.3619)$; if $\tan C = 1.4703$ then $C = \tan^{-1}(1.4703)$.

Key point

$\sin^{-1}$ means 'the angle whose sine is . . .'
$\cos^{-1}$ means 'the angle whose cosine is . . .'
$\tan^{-1}$ means 'the angle whose tangent is . . .'

We use a scientific calculator to find the inverse sine, inverse cosine and inverse tangent of a number.

Example 2.5

Find A given
(a) $\sin A = 0.4213$ (b) $\cos A = 0.5316$ (c) $\tan A = 1.7503$

Solution

(a) We have

$$\sin A = 0.4213$$

and so

$$A = \sin^{-1}(0.4213)$$

Using a scientific calculator we see

$$A = 24.92°$$

If your calculator is in radian mode you will obtain the equivalent answer in radians, that is 0.4349 radians.

(b)

$$\begin{aligned} \cos A &= 0.5316 \\ A &= \cos^{-1}(0.5316) \\ &= 57.89° \end{aligned}$$

(c)

$$\begin{aligned} \tan A &= 1.7503 \\ A &= \tan^{-1}(1.7503) \\ &= 60.26° \end{aligned}$$

Example 2.6

Find B given

(a) $\cos B = 0.8061$ (b) $\sin B = 0.4611$ (c) $\tan B = 1.2500$

Solution

(a) $\cos B = 0.8061$

$B = \cos^{-1}(0.8061)$

$=$ 36.28°

(b) $\sin B = 0.4611$

$B =$ 27.46°

(c) $\tan B = 1.2500$

$B =$ 51.34°

End of block exercises

1 θ is an angle between 0° and 90°. In each case find θ given:
(a) $\sin\theta = 0.3467$
(b) $\cos\theta = 0.6419$
(c) $\tan\theta = 1.7500$
(d) $\sin\theta = 0.7396$
(e) $\tan\theta = 0.5050$
(f) $\cos\theta = 0.3507$

2 Evaluate sec 37°.

3 Evaluate cot 75°.

4 Evaluate cosec 17°.

5 Evaluate cosec 1.

6 θ is an angle between 0° and 90°. In each case, find θ.
(a) $\sin\theta = \cos\theta$
(b) $\sin\theta = 2\cos\theta$

7 △ABC has a right angle at C, AC = 6 cm, BC = 10 cm and AB = 11.66 cm. Find
(a) $\sin A$
(b) $\cos A$
(c) $\tan A$
(d) $\sin B$
(e) $\cos B$
(f) $\tan B$
(g) A
(h) B

8 We have seen that $\sin^{-1} x$ means 'the angle whose sine is x' and not the reciprocal $\frac{1}{\sin x}$. How would you write the reciprocal using a negative power?

Solutions to exercises

1 (a) 20.29° (b) 50.07° (c) 60.26° (d) 47.70° (e) 26.79° (f) 69.47°

2 1.2521

3 0.2679

4 3.4203

5 1.1884

6 (a) 45° (b) 63.43°

7 (a) 0.8576 (b) 0.5146 (c) 1.6667 (d) 0.5146 (e) 0.8576 (f) 0.6 (g) 59.04° (h) 30.96°

8 Brackets would be inserted to show the intention, that is

$$\frac{1}{\sin x} = (\sin x)^{-1}$$

BLOCK 3 The trigonometrical ratios in all quadrants

3.1 Introduction

Block 2 defined the trigonometrical ratios sine, cosine and tangent with reference to the sides of a right-angled triangle. No angle in a right-angled triangle is greater than 90°. So, if we wish to define the trigonometrical ratios of angles greater than 90° we need a method that does not use right-angled triangles. This block looks at how this is achieved.

3.2 The four quadrants

Figure 3.1 shows the x and y axes intersecting at the origin O. The axes divide the x−y plane into four sections, called **quadrants**. These are numbered 1 to 4 as indicated in Figure 3.1.

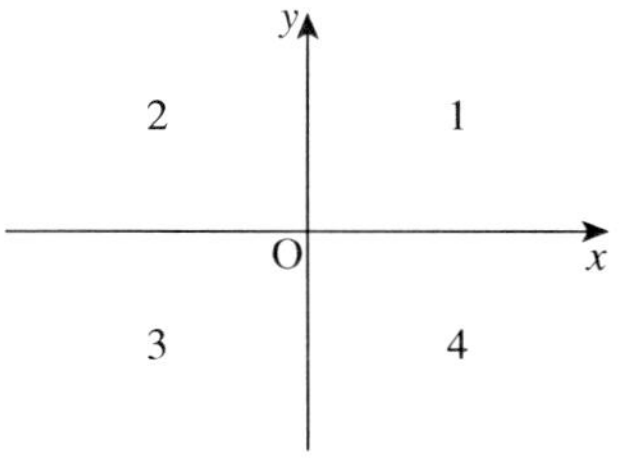

Figure 3.1
The x and y axes divide the plane into four quadrants.

We now consider a rotating arm, OC. The arm is fixed at the origin, O. We measure the angle θ from the positive x axis to the arm, measuring in an anticlockwise direction. Figure 3.2 shows the arm in each of the four quadrants.

Note that in quadrant 1, θ lies between 0° and 90°; in quadrant 2, θ is between 90° and 180°; in quadrant 3, θ is between 180° and 270°; and in quadrant 4, θ is between 270° and 360°. Figure 3.3 illustrates this.

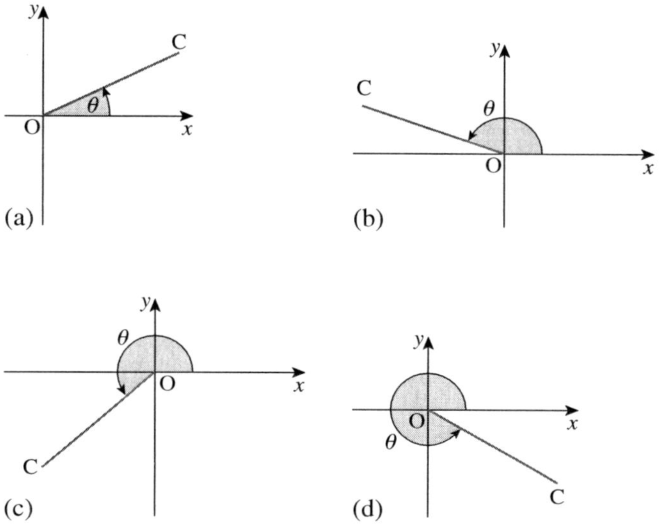

Figure 3.2
The arm OC rotates anticlockwise into each of the four quadrants.

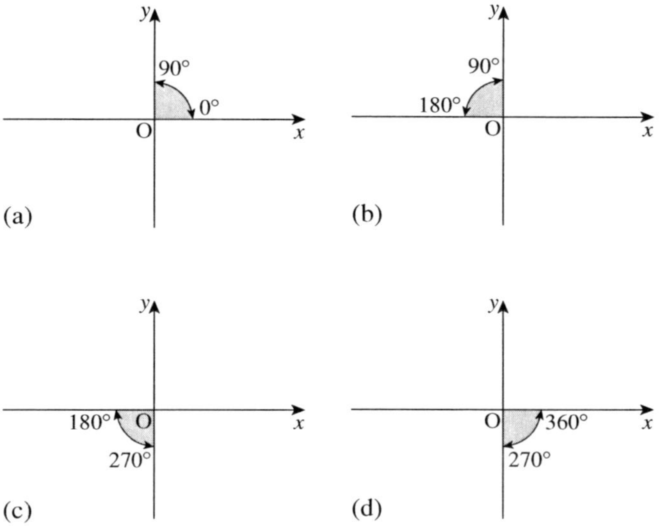

Figure 3.3
(a) In quadrant 1, θ lies between 0° and 90°; (b) in quadrant 2, θ lies between 90° and 180°; (c) in quadrant 3, θ lies between 180° and 270°; (d) in quadrant 4, θ lies between 270° and 360°.

3.3 Projections onto the x and y axes

We now introduce **projections** of the arm OC onto the x and y axes. The projection of OC onto the x axis is OA; the projection onto the y axis is OB. Figure 3.4 shows the x and y projections as the arm rotates into the four quadrants.

Note that the projections may be positive or negative. For example, when OC is in the second quadrant, the x projection, OA, is on the negative x axis and so is

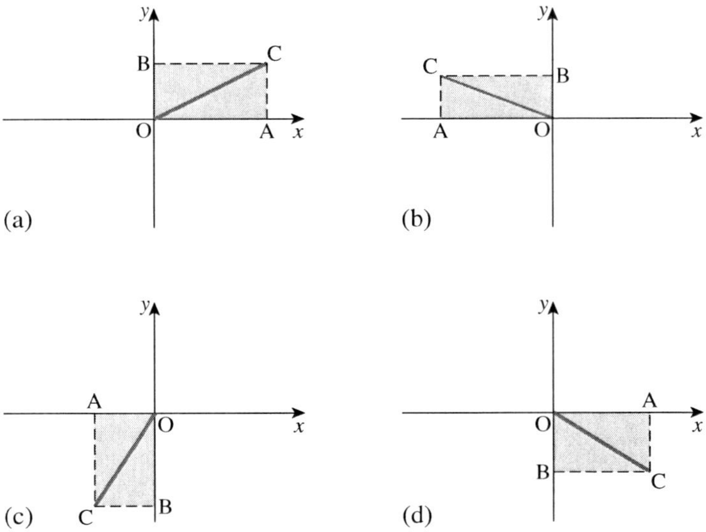

Figure 3.4 The x projection is OA, the y projection is OB.

negative. The y projection, OB, is on the positive y axis and so is positive. The arm OC is considered to be always positive.

Table 3.1 gives the signs of the x and y projections of OC as it rotates through the four quadrants.

Table 3.1

	First quadrant	Second quadrant	Third quadrant	Fourth quadrant
x projection	+	−	−	+
y projection	+	+	−	−

3.4 Extended definition of the trigonometrical ratios

We define the trigonometrical ratios in terms of the x and y projections of a rotating arm, OC.

Key point

$$\sin\theta = \frac{y \text{ projection of OC}}{\text{OC}}$$

$$\cos\theta = \frac{x \text{ projection of OC}}{\text{OC}}$$

$$\tan\theta = \frac{y \text{ projection of OC}}{x \text{ projection of OC}}$$

By examining the signs of the x and y projections in Table 3.1 it is easy to determine the signs of $\sin\theta$, $\cos\theta$ and $\tan\theta$ for the four quadrants. For example, consider θ in the second quadrant. Since the y projection is positive, then $\sin\theta$ is positive. Similarly, as the x projection is negative, then $\cos\theta$ is negative. The sign of $\tan\theta$ is negative since it is given by the ratio of a positive number and a negative number. Table 3.2 shows the sign of $\sin\theta$, $\cos\theta$ and $\tan\theta$ for θ in the four quadrants.

Table 3.2

	First quadrant	Second quadrant	Third quadrant	Fourth quadrant
$\sin\theta$	+	+	−	−
$\cos\theta$	+	−	−	+
$\tan\theta$	+	−	+	−

Example 3.1

An angle θ is such that $\sin\theta < 0$ and $\cos\theta > 0$. In which quadrant does θ lie?

Solution

Referring to Table 3.2 we see that $\sin\theta < 0$ when θ lies in the third or fourth quadrants. When $\cos\theta > 0$, θ lies in the first or fourth quadrants. Hence for both conditions to be satisfied simultaneously θ must be in the fourth quadrant.

Example 3.2

Show $\sin 17° = \sin 163°$.

Solution

Although $\sin 17°$ and $\sin 163°$ can easily be evaluated using a calculator and hence shown to be equal, it is instructive to show their equality using the definition of $\sin\theta$.

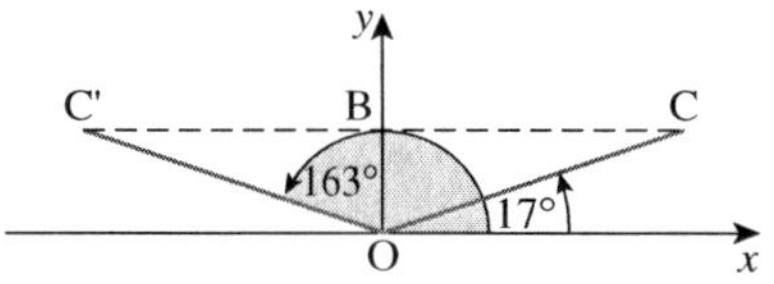

Figure 3.5
OC and OC′ have the same y projection and so $\sin 17° = \sin 163°$.

Consider two arms, OC and OC′, of equal length. Figure 3.5 shows the arm OC forming an angle of 17° with the positive x axis, and the arm OC′ forming an angle of 163° with the positive x axis. Noting that $163° = 180° - 17°$, we can see that OC′ is the reflection of OC in the y axis. By symmetry both the y projections of OC and OC′ will be OB. Since the y projections are equal and the arms are of equal length, then from the definition of $\sin\theta$ we have $\sin 17° = \sin 163°$.

Example 3.2 illustrates a general rule that is true for any value of θ:

Key point

$$\sin(180° - \theta) = \sin\theta$$

Example 3.3

An angle θ is such that $\tan\theta > 0$ and $\sin\theta < 0$. In which quadrant does θ lie?

Solution

Using Table 3.2, we see that $\tan\theta > 0$ when θ lies in the

______ and ______ quadrants — first and third

Also, $\sin\theta < 0$ when θ lies in the

______ and ______ quadrants — third and fourth

Hence θ lies in the ______ quadrant. — third

Exercises

1 An angle θ is such that $\sin\theta < 0$ and $\cos\theta < 0$. In which quadrant does θ lie?

2 An angle β is such that $\cos\beta > 0$ and $\tan\beta < 0$. State the range of possible values of β.

Solutions to exercises

1 third

2 $270° < \beta < 360°$

3.5 Adding and subtracting multiples of 360°

The sine of an angle is governed by the position of the rotating arm, OC. We note that 360° corresponds to exactly one complete revolution. Thus rotating the arm, either clockwise or anticlockwise, through multiples of 360° will leave it in exactly the same position, and consequently the value of the sine remains unchanged. This may be stated mathematically as:

$$\begin{aligned}\sin\theta &= \sin(\theta + 360°)\\ &= \sin(\theta + 720°)\\ &= \sin(\theta + 1080°)\\ &= \cdots\end{aligned}$$

and also

$$\begin{aligned}\sin\theta &= \sin(\theta - 360°)\\ &= \sin(\theta - 720°)\end{aligned}$$

$$= \sin(\theta - 1080°)$$
$$= \cdots$$

Written compactly we have

Key point

$$\sin\theta = \sin(\theta \pm n\,360°) \quad n = 1, 2, 3, \ldots$$

An exactly similar argument can be applied to $\cos\theta$. Thus

Key point

$$\cos\theta = \cos(\theta \pm n\,360°) \quad n = 1, 2, 3, \ldots$$

We now consider $\tan\theta$. Recall that $\tan\theta$ is defined by

$$\tan\theta = \frac{y \text{ projection}}{x \text{ projection}}$$

The corresponding result for $\tan\theta$ is

Key point

$$\tan\theta = \tan(\theta \pm n\,180°) \quad n = 1, 2, 3, \ldots$$

Hence, adding 180° to, or subtracting 180° from, an angle leaves the tangent unaltered. Note that with sine and cosine we can add or subtract multiples of 360°, but with the tangent we can add and subtract multiples of 180°.

Expressions that repeat their values at regular intervals are called **periodic**. Hence $\sin\theta$, $\cos\theta$ and $\tan\theta$ are all periodic.

Example 3.4
Simplify $\sin(\theta + 1000°)$.

Solution
Subtracting multiples of 360° from $\theta + 1000°$ leaves the sine unchanged. Hence

$$\begin{aligned}\sin(\theta + 1000°) &= \sin[\theta + 1000° - 2(360°)] \\ &= \sin(\theta + 280°)\end{aligned}$$

Example 3.5
Simplify $\cos(x - 900°)$.

Solution
Adding multiples of 360° to $x - 900°$ leaves the cosine unchanged. Hence

$$\begin{aligned}\cos(x - 900°) &= \cos[x - 900° + 3(360°)] \\ &= \cos(x + 180°)\end{aligned}$$

Example 3.6
Simplify $\tan(z - 540^\circ)$.

Solution
Adding multiples of 180° to $z - 540^\circ$ leaves the tangent unchanged. So we have

$$\begin{aligned}\tan(z - 540^\circ) &= \tan[z - 540^\circ + 3(180^\circ)] \\ &= \tan z\end{aligned}$$

Example 3.7
Simplify $\sin(-180^\circ - \theta)$.

Solution
Adding 360° to an angle leaves the sine unchanged. Hence
$\sin(-180^\circ - \theta) = \sin(-180^\circ - \theta + 360^\circ)$

$=$ $\sin(180^\circ - \theta)$

Using the result following Example 3.2, we can further simplify this to

$\sin\theta$

Hence

$$\sin(-180^\circ - \theta) = \sin\theta$$

Exercises

1 Simplify
(a) $\sin(\alpha + 400^\circ)$
(b) $\sin(\beta - 500^\circ)$
(c) $\sin(\alpha - 450^\circ)$
(d) $\sin(\theta + 1000^\circ)$
(e) $\sin(2\theta + 1080^\circ)$

2 Simplify
(a) $\cos(x - 300^\circ)$
(b) $\cos(\theta - 810^\circ)$
(c) $\tan(x + 200^\circ)$
(d) $\tan(x - 540^\circ)$
(e) $\cos(\beta + 500^\circ)$

Solutions to exercises

1 (a) $\sin(\alpha + 40^\circ)$ (b) $\sin(\beta - 140^\circ)$
(c) $\sin(\alpha - 90^\circ)$ (d) $\sin(\theta - 80^\circ)$
(e) $\sin 2\theta$

2 (a) $\cos(x + 60^\circ)$ (b) $\cos(\theta - 90^\circ) = \sin\theta$
(c) $\tan(x + 20^\circ)$ (d) $\tan x$ (e) $\cos(\beta + 140^\circ)$

End of block exercises

1 The angles are given in radians. Evaluate the following:
(a) $\sin 30$
(b) $\cos 27$
(c) $\tan 31$

2 An angle α is such that $\sin\alpha < 0$ and $\cos\alpha > 0$. In which quadrant does α lie?

3 Simplify $\cos(450° - \theta)$.

4 Simplify $\tan(y + 1260°)$.

5 Simplify $\sin(-1260° - \theta)$.

6 An angle β is such that $\tan\beta > 0$ and $\sin\beta < 0$. In which quadrant does β lie?

7 An angle α is such that $\sin\alpha \geq 0$ and $\sin 2\alpha \geq 0$. State the range of possible values of α.

8 An angle θ is such that $\cos\theta < 0$ and $\cos 2\theta > 0$. State the range of possible values for θ.

9 An angle θ is such that $\tan\theta > 0$ and $\tan\frac{\theta}{2} < 0$. State the range of possible values of θ.

10 An angle ϕ is such that $\sin\phi > 0$ and $\cos 2\phi < 0$. State the range of possible values of ϕ.

Solutions to exercises

1 (a) -0.9880 (b) -0.2921 (c) -0.4417

2 fourth quadrant

3 $\sin\theta$

4 $\tan y$

5 $\sin\theta$

6 third quadrant

7 $0° \leq \alpha \leq 90°$

8 $135° < \theta < 180°$

9 $180° < \theta < 270°$

10 $45° < \phi < 135°$

BLOCK 4 Trigonometrical functions and their graphs

4.1 Introduction

Having introduced the trigonometrical ratios of sine, cosine and tangent we are ready to consider the three trigonometrical functions $y = \sin x$, $y = \cos x$ and $y = \tan x$. A number of properties and graphs of these functions are considered. Extensions are made to include the functions $y = \sin kx$, $y = \cos kx$ and $y = \tan kx$ for various values of k.

4.2 The function $y = \sin x$

Table 4.1 gives values of x and the corresponding values of $\sin x$ found using a scientific calculator.

Table 4.1

x	0	30	60	90	120	150	180
$\sin x$	0	0.500	0.866	1	0.866	0.500	0

x	210	240	270	300	330	360
$\sin x$	−0.500	−0.866	−1	−0.866	−0.500	0

Plotting these values produces the graph shown in Figure 4.1.
Note that the maximum value of $\sin x$ is 1; the minimum value of $\sin x$ is −1.

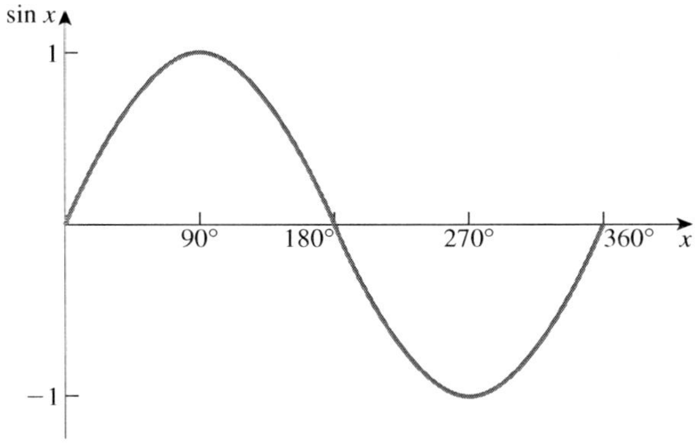

Figure 4.1 A graph of $y = \sin x$ for $0° \leq x \leq 360°$.

If we had been working in radians, then $0° \le x \le 360°$ would be replaced by $0 \le x \le 2\pi$. The shape of the sine function is often referred to as a **sine wave** or a **cycle**.

We saw in Block 3 that $\sin x = \sin(x + 360°) = \sin(x + 720°)$ and $\sin x = \sin(x - 360°) = \sin(x - 720°)$ and so on. In other words, adding or subtracting multiples of 360° to an angle does not alter the sine of the angle. Hence the graph in Figure 4.1 can be extended to the left and to the right by repeating cycles of the same shape every 360°. Figure 4.2 illustrates this.

Figure 4.2
Cycles are repeated every 360°.

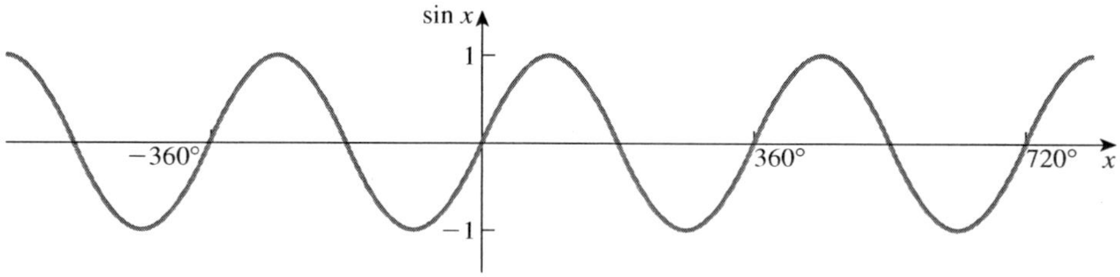

When using radian measure, cycles are repeated every 2π radians.

Exercises

Use the graphs in Figures 4.1 and 4.2 to answer the following questions:

1 What is the maximum possible domain of the function $y = \sin x$?

2 What is the range of $y = \sin x$?

3 Is the function $y = \sin x$ one-to-one or many-to-one?

Solutions to exercises

1 all x

2 $[-1, 1]$

3 many-to-one

4.3 The function $y = \cos x$

Using a scientific calculator values of $\cos x$ are found for various values of x. These are recorded in Table 4.2.

Table 4.2

x	0	30	60	90	120	150	180
$\cos x$	1	0.866	0.500	0	−0.500	−0.866	−1

x	210	240	270	300	330	360
$\cos x$	−0.866	−0.500	0	0.500	0.866	1

The values are graphed in Figure 4.3.

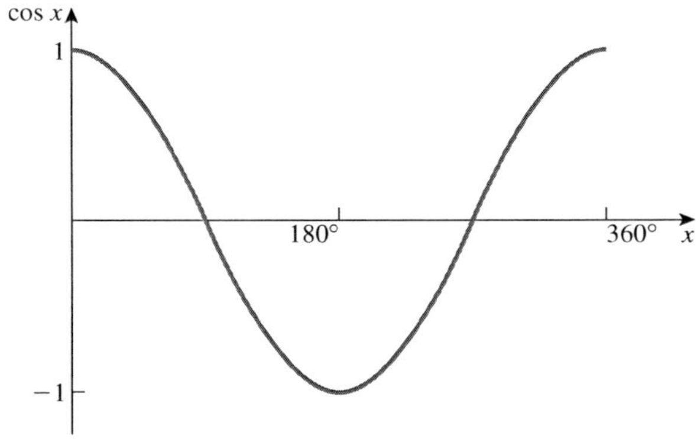

Figure 4.3 The function $y = \cos x$ for $0° \le x \le 360°$.

As with $y = \sin x$, the function $y = \cos x$ may be extended to the left and to the right. Since adding or subtracting multiples of 360° to an angle leaves its cosine unchanged, then full cycles will be repeated every 360°. Figure 4.4 illustrates this.

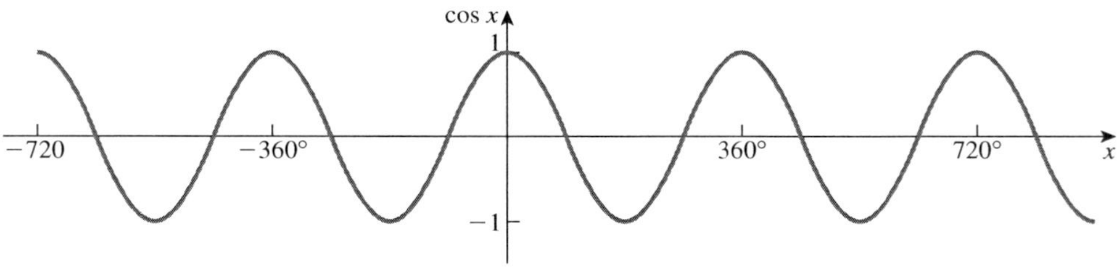

Figure 4.4 The function $y = \cos x$ completes a full cycle every 360°.

Note that $y = \cos x$ completes a full cycle every 360° or 2π radians. The maximum value of $\cos x$ is 1; the minimum value is -1.

Exercises

Use the graphs in Figures 4.3 and 4.4 to answer the following questions:

1 What is the maximum possible domain of the function $y = \cos x$?

2 What is the range of $y = \cos x$?

3 Is the function $y = \cos x$ one-to-one or many-to-one?

Solutions to exercises

1 all x

2 $[-1, 1]$

3 many-to-one

4.4 The function $y = \tan x$

Table 4.3 gives values of x and corresponding values of $\tan x$.

Table 4.3

x	0	30	60	90	120	150	180
$\tan x$	0	0.577	1.732	–	−1.732	−0.577	0

x	210	240	270	300	330	360
$\tan x$	0.577	1.732	–	−1.732	−0.577	0

Figure 4.5 shows a graph of $y = \tan x$ for $0° \le x \le 360°$.

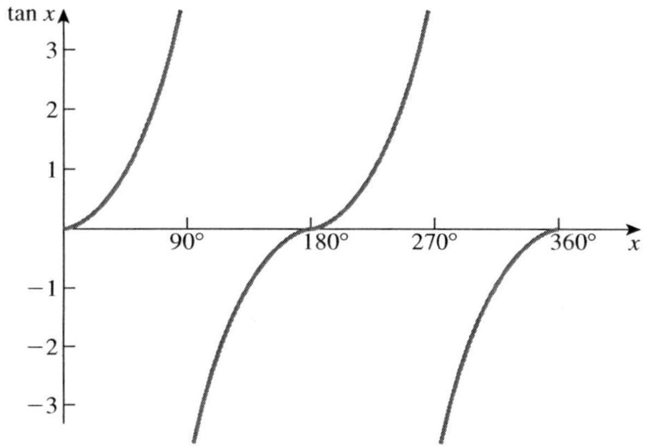

Figure 4.5 The function $y = \tan x$ for $0° \le x \le 360°$.

Note that the graph is radically different from those of $y = \sin x$ and $y = \cos x$. The function $y = \tan x$ has no maximum or minimum value.

Recalling from Block 3 that adding or subtracting multiples of 180° to an angle leaves its tangent unchanged, we see that extending the graph in Figure 4.5 to the left and right produces that shown in Figure 4.6.

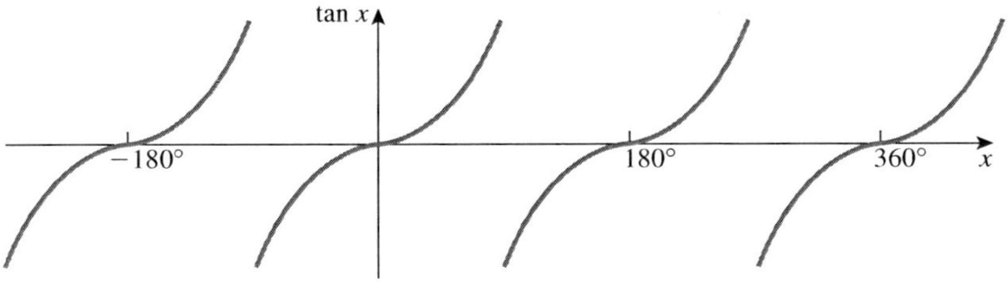

Figure 4.6 For $y = \tan x$, cycles are repeated every 180° or π radians.

Note that the function is discontinuous at $x = \cdots -270°, -90°, 90°, 270°, \ldots$.

Exercises

Use the graphs in Figures 4.5 and 4.6 to answer the following questions:

1 What is the maximum possible domain of the function $y = \tan x$?

2 What is the range of $y = \tan x$?

3 Is the function $y = \tan x$ one-to-one or many-to-one?

Solutions to exercises

1 All values except $x = \cdots -270°, -90°, 90°, 270°, \ldots$. These values must be excluded from the domain.

2 $(-\infty, \infty)$

3 many-to-one

4.5 The amplitude of $y = A \sin x$ and $y = A \cos x$

Consider the function $y = A \sin x$, where A is a positive constant, that is $A > 0$. The number A is called the **amplitude**. It is the maximum value of y. The minimum value of y is $-A$. Thus $y = 3 \sin x$ has an amplitude of 3. The maximum value of $3 \sin x$ is 3; the minimum value is -3. Note that the amplitude of $y = \sin x$ is 1. Figure 4.7 shows graphs of $y = \sin x$ and $y = 3 \sin x$ for $0° \leq x \leq 360°$.

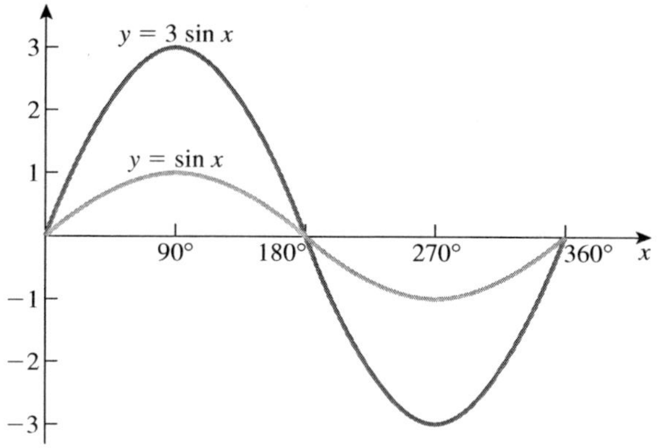

Figure 4.7
The amplitude of $y = \sin x$ is 1; the amplitude of $y = 3 \sin x$ is 3.

Note that a full cycle of $y = 3 \sin x$ is completed in 360°. The amplitude does not affect the periodic properties of $\sin x$: that is, it takes 360° for both $y = \sin x$ and $y = 3 \sin x$ to complete a full cycle. In general, $y = A \sin x$ completes a cycle every 360°.

Similar comments apply to $y = A \cos x$. The amplitude of $A \cos x$ is A. It takes 360° for a full cycle of $A \cos x$ to be completed.

Key point

The amplitude of $y = A \sin x$ and $y = A \cos x$ is A.

Example 4.1

State the amplitude of each of the following functions:

(a) $y = 2 \sin x$
(b) $y = 4.7 \cos x$
(c) $y = \dfrac{2 \sin x}{3}$
(d) $y = 0.8 \cos x$

Solution

(a) 2 (b) 4.7 (c) $\frac{2}{3}$ (d) 0.8

Exercises

1 State the amplitude of
(a) $10 \sin x$ (b) $7.3 \cos x$ (c) $0.01 \sin t$
(d) $1.2 \cos \theta$

Solutions to exercises

1 (a) 10 (b) 7.3 (c) 0.01 (d) 1.2

4.6 The functions $y = A \sin kx$ and $y = A \cos kx$

We have already seen that A is the amplitude and this is the maximum value of y. We now consider the effect of the parameter k in $A \sin kx$. To allow us to focus on k we take A to be 1. Thus we examine the function $y = \sin kx$ for various values of k, for example $y = \sin 2x$, $y = \sin 3x$, $y = \sin \frac{x}{2}$ and $y = \sin \frac{3}{2}x$. We can deduce the graphs of these functions by reference to the graph of $y = \sin x$.

We begin by looking at $y = \sin 2x$. Recall that $y = \sin x$ completes one full cycle as x varies from 0° to 360°. Then $y = \sin 2x$ completes one full cycle as $2x$ varies from 0° to 360°, that is as x varies from 0° to $\frac{360°}{2} = 180°$. If x is measured in radians then $y = \sin 2x$ completes a full cycle as x varies from 0 to π radians. A graph of the function is illustrated in Figure 4.8.

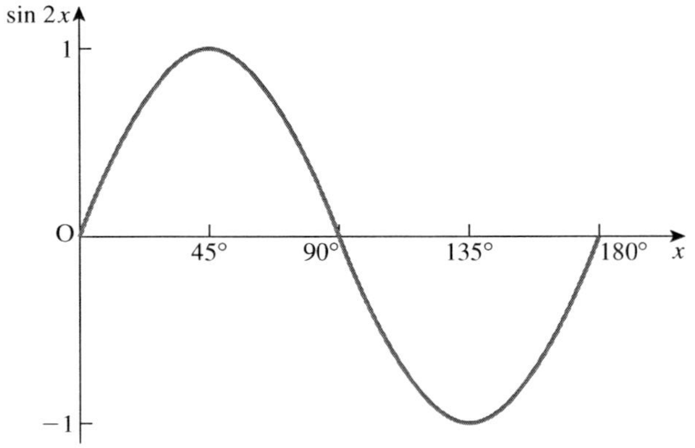

Figure 4.8 The function $y = \sin 2x$ completes a full cycle every 180° or π radians.

We have noted previously that the amplitude does not affect the periodic property of $y = \sin x$. Since $y = \sin 2x$ completes a cycle every 180°, then in general $y = A \sin 2x$ completes a cycle every 180° also. Note that the amplitude of $y = \sin 2x$ is 1.

As another example consider $y = \sin \frac{3x}{2}$. A full cycle is completed as $\frac{3x}{2}$ varies from 0° to 360°: that is, as x varies from 0° to $\frac{360°}{3/2} = 240°$. A graph of $y = \sin \frac{3x}{2}$ is illustrated in Figure 4.9.

Similarly, $y = A \sin \frac{3x}{2}$ completes a cycle every 240°.

In general, $y = A \sin kx$ completes a full cycle in $\frac{360°}{k}$ or $\frac{2\pi}{k}$ radians.

The function $y = A \cos kx$ also has these properties. We have

Key point

The functions $y = A \sin kx$ and $y = A \cos kx$ complete a cycle every $\dfrac{360°}{k}$ or $\dfrac{2\pi}{k}$ radians.

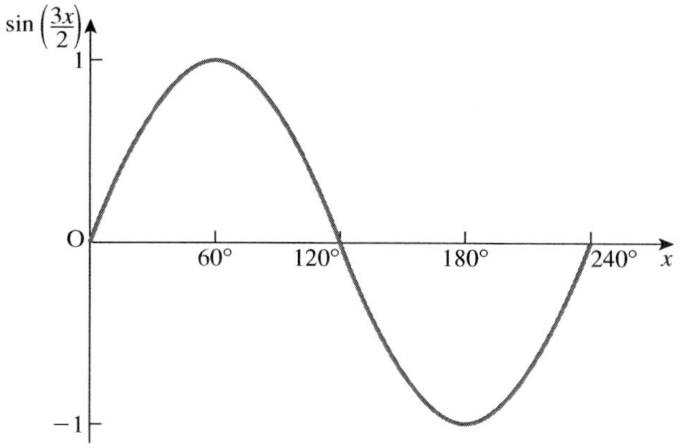

Figure 4.9 $y = \sin\frac{3x}{2}$ completes a cycle every 240° or $\frac{4\pi}{3}$ radians.

Example 4.2

State the number of cycles of y in 360° given

(a) $y = 3\sin 4x$
(b) $y = 4\cos 3x$
(c) $y = \frac{1}{2}\cos\frac{x}{2}$
(d) $y = 5\sin\frac{3x}{4}$

Solution

(a) $y = 3\sin 4x$ completes a cycle every $\frac{360^\circ}{4} = 90^\circ$. In 360°, four cycles are completed.
(b) $y = 4\cos 3x$ completes a cycle every $\frac{360^\circ}{3} = 120^\circ$. In 360° three cycles are completed.
(c) $y = \frac{1}{2}\cos\frac{x}{2}$ completes a cycle every $\frac{360^\circ}{1/2} = 720^\circ$. In 360°, 0.5 of a cycle is completed.
(d) $y = 5\sin\frac{3x}{4}$ completes a cycle every $\frac{360^\circ}{3/4} = 480^\circ$. In 360°, 0.75 of a cycle is completed.

Example 4.2 illustrates the following general statement.

Key point

The functions $y = A\sin kx$ and $y = A\cos kx$ complete k cycles every 360° or every 2π radians.

Example 4.3

For each function, state (i) the minimum value (ii) the increase in x required for y to complete a full cycle.

(a) $y = 3 \sin 5x$

(b) $y = 0.65 \cos 6x$

(c) $y = \dfrac{4}{5} \sin \dfrac{x}{3}$

(d) $y = -2 \cos \dfrac{5x}{3}$

Solution

(a) The amplitude is 3 and so the minimum value is -3. A full cycle requires x to increase by $\dfrac{360^\circ}{5} = 72^\circ$.

(b) The minimum value is -0.65. A full cycle requires x to increase by $\dfrac{360^\circ}{6} = 60^\circ$.

(c) The minimum value is $-\dfrac{4}{5}$. A full cycle requires x to increase by $\dfrac{360^\circ}{1/3} = 1080^\circ$.

(d) The minimum value is -2. A full cycle requires x to increase by $\dfrac{360^\circ}{5/3} = 216^\circ$.

Example 4.4

State the maximum value, the minimum value and the number of cycles completed in 720° for the function $y = \dfrac{3}{2} \cos \dfrac{5x}{2}$.

Solution

The amplitude of $y = \dfrac{3}{2} \cos \dfrac{5x}{2}$ is $\dfrac{3}{2}$. Hence the maximum value is ____ [$\dfrac{3}{2}$]

and the minimum value is ____ [$-\dfrac{3}{2}$]

The function $y = \dfrac{3}{2} \cos \dfrac{5x}{2}$ completes ____ cycles every 360°. [$\dfrac{5}{2}$]

Hence in 720° the function completes ____ cycles. [5]

4.7 The function $y = A \tan kx$

We consider the function $y = A \tan kx$. As with $y = A \sin kx$ and $y = A \cos kx$, the factor A does not affect the periodic properties of the tangent function. Recall that $y = \tan x$ completes a cycle as x increases by 180° or π radians. Hence $\tan kx$

completes a cycle as kx increases through 180°, that is as x increases through $\frac{180°}{k}$. So, for example, $y = A \tan 2x$ completes a cycle every $\frac{180°}{2} = 90°$, $y = A \tan 3x$ completes a cycle every $\frac{180°}{3} = 60°$, and $y = A \tan \frac{2x}{3}$ completes a cycle every $\frac{180°}{2/3} = 270°$. A graph of $y = 2 \tan 3x$ for $-30° \le x \le 150°$ is shown in Figure 4.10.

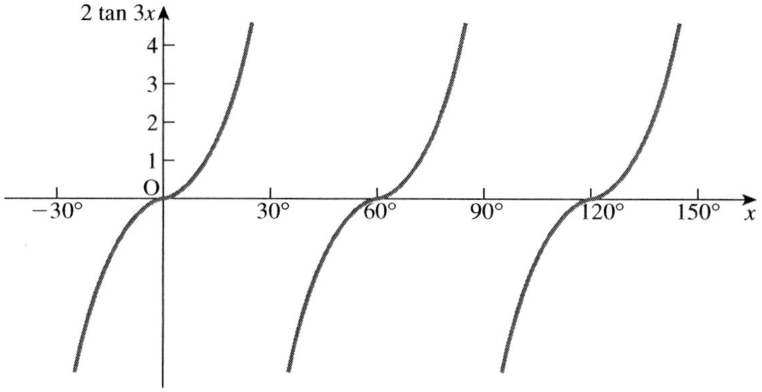

Figure 4.10 $y = 2 \tan 3x$ completes a cycle every 60°.

In general $y = A \tan kx$ completes a cycle every $\dfrac{180°}{k}$. In other words, k cycles are completed every 180°.

Example 4.5

State the number of cycles completed every 360° for

(a) $y = 3 \tan x$

(b) $y = 7 \tan 2x$

(c) $y = -\dfrac{1}{2} \tan \dfrac{3x}{2}$

Solution

(a) For $y = 3 \tan x$, the '3' does not affect the periodic properties.

Now $y = 3 \tan x$ completes ▢ cycles every 180° and so in 360°, 1

▢ cycles are completed. 2

(b) $y = 7 \tan 2x$ completes ▢ cycles every 180° and hence completes 2

▢ cycles every 360°. 4

(c) $y = -\dfrac{1}{2} \tan \dfrac{3x}{2}$ completes ▢ cycles every 180° and so completes $\dfrac{3}{2}$

▢ cycles every 360°. 3

End of block exercises

State the amplitude of the functions given in questions 1–6.

1 $y = 3 \sin 4x$

2 $y = \frac{3}{7} \cos 2x$

3 $y = 0.96 \sin x$

4 $y = -2 \cos 7x$

5 $y = -0.6 \sin 3x$

6 $y = \dfrac{4 \cos x}{7}$

State the number of cycles completed every 360° for the functions given in questions 7–12.

7 $y = 2 \sin 3x$

8 $y = -2 \sin 3x$

9 $y = 4 \cos \dfrac{5x}{6}$

10 $y = 0.5 \cos 0.5x$

11 $y = 6 \tan 6x$

12 $y = -3 \tan 9x$

13 Sketch $y = \sin(-x)$ for $0° \le x \le 360°$.

14 Sketch $y = \tan\dfrac{x}{2}$ for $0° \le x \le 360°$

15 State two properties that are common to both $y = A \sin kx$ and $y = A \cos kx$.

Solutions to exercises

1 3

2 $\frac{3}{7}$

3 0.96

4 2

5 0.6

6 $\frac{4}{7}$

7 3

8 3

9 $\frac{5}{6}$

10 0.5

11 12

12 18

BLOCK 5 Trigonometrical identities

5.1 Introduction

Consider the two expressions $\sin 2x$ and $2 \sin x \cos x$. These two expressions have the same value for every value of x. Try evaluating the expressions for, say, $x = 25°$, $60°$, 1.2 radians.

If two expressions are equal for all values of the variables used, then we say the expressions are **identical**. Hence $\sin 2x$ and $2 \sin x \cos x$ are identical, that is equal for all values of x. A statement such as $\sin 2x = 2 \sin x \cos x$ is known as an **identity**. In this block we provide a table of important identities and show how expressions involving the trigonometrical ratios can be simplified using them.

5.2 Common trigonometrical identities

There are several commonly used trigonometrical identities. These are listed in Table 5.1.

Table 5.1

$$\sin^2 A + \cos^2 A = 1$$

$$\frac{\sin A}{\cos A} = \tan A$$

$$\sin(A + B) = \sin A \cos B + \sin B \cos A$$

$$\sin(A - B) = \sin A \cos B - \sin B \cos A$$

$$\cos(A + B) = \cos A \cos B - \sin A \sin B$$

$$\cos(A - B) = \cos A \cos B + \sin A \sin B$$

$$\sin 2A = 2 \sin A \cos A$$

$$\cos 2A = 1 - 2\sin^2 A = 2\cos^2 A - 1 = \cos^2 A - \sin^2 A$$

$$\tan(A + B) = \frac{\tan A + \tan B}{1 - \tan A \tan B}$$

$$\tan(A - B) = \frac{\tan A - \tan B}{1 + \tan A \tan B}$$

$$2 \sin A \cos B = \sin(A + B) + \sin(A - B)$$

$$2 \cos A \cos B = \cos(A + B) + \cos(A - B)$$

$$2 \sin A \sin B = \cos(A - B) - \cos(A + B)$$

$$\sin^2 A = \tfrac{1}{2}(1 - \cos 2A)$$

$$\cos^2 A = \tfrac{1}{2}(1 + \cos 2A)$$

Note that we write $\sin^2 A$ to mean $(\sin A)^2$. Similarly, $\cos^2 A$ is the accepted notation for $(\cos A)^2$. The identities can be used to simplify trigonometrical expressions.

The first entry in the table is particularly important and should be remembered.

Key point

$$\sin^2 A + \cos^2 A = 1$$

Choose any angle A for yourself and verify that this identity is true.

Example 5.1

Use trigonometrical identities to simplify $\cos A \tan A$.

Solution

We note that $\tan A = \dfrac{\sin A}{\cos A}$ and so

$$\begin{aligned}\cos A \tan A &= \cos A \frac{\sin A}{\cos A}\\ &= \sin A\end{aligned}$$

Hence $\cos A \tan A$ is identical to $\sin A$.

Example 5.2

(a) Show that $\sin 2A = 2\sin A \cos A$.
(b) Show that $\cos 2A = \cos^2 A - \sin^2 A$.

Solution

(a) We use the identity

$$\sin(A + B) = \sin A \cos B + \sin B \cos A$$

A special case of this identity occurs when $B = A$. We then have

$$\sin 2A = \sin A \cos A + \sin A \cos A$$

that is

$$\sin 2A = 2 \sin A \cos A$$

(b) We use the identity

$$\cos(A + B) = \cos A \cos B - \sin A \sin B$$

A special case of this identity occurs when $B = A$. We then have

$$\cos 2A = \cos A \cos A - \sin A \sin A$$

that is

$$\cos 2A = \cos^2 A - \sin^2 A$$

Example 5.3

Show that $\cos(-\theta) = \cos\theta$.

Solution

We use the identity for $\cos(A - B)$ with $A = 0$ and $B = \theta$.
Now from Table 5.1

$$\cos(A - B) = \cos A \cos B + \sin A \sin B$$

With $A = 0$ and $B = \theta$ this becomes

$\cos(-\theta) =$ $\cos 0 \cos\theta + \sin 0 \sin\theta$

Noting that $\sin 0 = 0$ and $\cos 0 = 1$ this simplifies to

$\cos\theta$

Hence $\cos(-\theta) = \cos\theta$ as required.

Example 5.4

Show that

$$\tan(\theta + 45°) = \frac{1 + \tan\theta}{1 - \tan\theta}$$

Solution

We use the identity

$$\tan(A + B) = \frac{\tan A + \tan B}{1 - \tan A \tan B}$$

Putting $A = \theta$ and $B = 45°$ gives

$$\tan(\theta + 45°) = \frac{\tan\theta + \tan 45°}{1 - \tan\theta \tan 45°}$$

Now $\tan 45° = 1$ and so

$$\tan(\theta + 45°) = \frac{\tan\theta + 1}{1 - \tan\theta} = \frac{1 + \tan\theta}{1 - \tan\theta}$$

Example 5.5

Simplify

$$\frac{\sin^3 A}{\cos A} + \sin A \cos A$$

Solution

We write the expression with a common denominator of $\cos A$:

$$\frac{\sin^3 A}{\cos A} + \sin A \cos A = \frac{\sin^3 A + \sin A \cos^2 A}{\cos A}$$

Now

$$\frac{\sin^3 A + \sin A \cos^2 A}{\cos A} = \frac{\sin A(\sin^2 A + \cos^2 A)}{\cos A}$$
$$= \frac{\sin A}{\cos A} \quad \text{since } \sin^2 A + \cos^2 A = 1$$
$$= \tan A$$

Hence $\dfrac{\sin^3 A}{\cos A} + \sin A \cos A$ simplifies to $\tan A$.

Example 5.6
Simplify

$$\frac{\sin 2A \sin A}{2 \cos A} + \cos 2A$$

Solution
From Example 5.2, $\sin 2A = 2 \sin A \cos A$ and so

$$\frac{\sin 2A \sin A}{2 \cos A} = \qquad \frac{2 \sin A \cos A \sin A}{2 \cos A} = \sin^2 A$$

Also from Example 5.2, $\cos 2A = \cos^2 A - \sin^2 A$. Hence

$$\frac{\sin 2A \sin A}{2 \cos A} + \cos 2A$$

$$= \qquad \sin^2 A + \cos^2 A - \sin^2 A = \cos^2 A$$

Example 5.7 Electrical Engineering – Amplitude modulation
Amplitude modulation is a technique which allows a signal of a certain frequency (the signal frequency) to be transmitted at a different frequency (the carrier frequency). (Note that the term **frequency** is explained in Block 7.)

The signal can be represented by the cosine wave $y_s = S \cos \omega_s t$. The carrier can be represented by $y_c = C \cos \omega_c t$. The modulated signal is given by the product $y_c y_s$. Use a trigonometrical identity to show that the modulated signal can be written as the sum of two cosine waves.

Solution
The modulated signal is

$$y_c y_s = (C \cos \omega_c t) \times (S \cos \omega_s t)$$
$$= CS(\cos \omega_c t \cos \omega_s t)$$

Using the identity $2 \cos A \cos B = \cos(A + B) + \cos(A - B)$ (Table 5.1), we can write

$$y_c y_s = \frac{1}{2} CS(\cos(\omega_c + \omega_s)t + \cos(\omega_c - \omega_s)t)$$

which is the sum of two cosine waves, oscillating at different frequencies from the original signal. This result enables the design of an antenna which can be used to transmit the original signal efficiently.

End of block exercises

1 From Table 5.1 we have

$\cos(A - B) = \cos A \cos B + \sin A \sin B$

Verify this identity when $A = 80°$ and $B = 30°$.

2 Verify the identity

$2 \sin A \sin B = \cos(A - B) - \cos(A + B)$

with $A = 50°$ and $B = 15°$.

3 Verify

$$\tan(A - B) = \frac{\tan A - \tan B}{1 + \tan A \tan B}$$

with $A = 65°$ and $B = 30°$.

4 Show $\sin(-\theta) = -\sin\theta$.

5 Show $\sin\left(\frac{\pi}{2} - \theta\right) = \cos\theta$.

6 Show $\cos\left(\frac{\pi}{2} - \theta\right) = \sin\theta$.

7 Show $\sin\left(\theta + \frac{\pi}{2}\right) = \cos\theta$.

8 Show $\cos\left(\theta + \frac{\pi}{2}\right) = -\sin\theta$.

9 Show $\sin(180° - \theta) = \sin\theta$.

10 Show $\cos(180° - \theta) = -\cos\theta$.

11 Show $\tan(180° - \theta) = -\tan\theta$.

12 Show $\sin(180° + \theta) = -\sin\theta$.

13 Show $\cos(180° + \theta) = -\cos\theta$.

14 Show $\tan(180° + \theta) = \tan\theta$.

15 Show $\sin(360° - \theta) = -\sin\theta$.

16 Show $\cos(360° - \theta) = \cos\theta$.

17 Show $\tan(360° - \theta) = -\tan\theta$.

18 Show $\sin 3A = 3 \sin A \cos^2 A - \sin^3 A$.

19 Show $\cos 3A = 4 \cos^3 A - 3 \cos A$.

20 Show $\sin 4A = 4 \sin A \cos A(\cos^2 A - \sin^2 A)$.

21 Show $\cos 4A = 8 \cos^4 A - 8 \cos^2 A + 1$.

22 Simplify

$$\sin A \cos A \tan A + \frac{2 \sin A \cos^3 A}{\sin 2A}$$

23 Simplify

$$\tan A + \frac{1}{\tan A}$$

24 Show

$$\frac{\sin 3A}{\sin 2A} = 2\cos A - \frac{1}{2\cos A}$$

Solutions to exercises

22 1

23 $\frac{1}{\cos A \sin A}$ which may be written as $\frac{2}{\sin 2A}$

BLOCK 6 Trigonometrical equations

6.1 Introduction

We examine the method of solving equations of the form $\sin\theta = k$, $\cos\theta = k$ and $\tan\theta = k$, where k is a constant. Because $\sin\theta$, $\cos\theta$ and $\tan\theta$ are periodic functions, then there is an infinite number of solutions of trigonometrical equations. Often the values of θ are restricted to a limited range. This restriction means there is then only a finite number of solutions.

6.2 Notation

If

$$\sin\theta = k$$

then we write

$$\theta = \sin^{-1} k$$

This is read as 'θ equals the inverse sine of k'. Similarly if $\cos\theta = k$ then $\theta = \cos^{-1} k$ and if $\tan\theta = k$ then $\theta = \tan^{-1} k$. The inverse functions $\sin^{-1}$, $\cos^{-1}$ and $\tan^{-1}$ are available on scientific calculators. Sometimes $\sin^{-1}$ is written as 'inv sin' or 'arcsin'.

Example 6.1
Given $\sin\theta = 0.3214$ find θ using a scientific calculator.

Solution

$$\sin\theta = 0.3214$$

and so

$$\begin{aligned}\theta &= \sin^{-1}(0.3214)\\ &= 18.75^\circ\end{aligned}$$

using a scientific calculator.

Example 6.2
Given $\sin\theta = -0.2000$ find θ using a scientific calculator.

Solution
$\sin\theta = -0.2000$

$\theta =$ $\sin^{-1}(-0.2000) = -11.54^\circ$

Example 6.3
Given $\cos\theta = -0.6132$ find θ using a scientific calculator.

Solution

$\cos\theta = -0.6132$

$\theta = \cos^{-1}(-0.6132) = 127.82°$

A scientific calculator returns only one solution to a trigonometrical equation. As $\sin\theta$, $\cos\theta$ and $\tan\theta$ are periodic functions, then trigonometrical equations involving these functions have many solutions. The following section illustrates how these equations are solved.

6.3 Solving trigonometrical equations

The method of solution is illustrated by examples.

Example 6.4
Solve

$$\sin\theta = 0.7215 \quad 0° \leq \theta \leq 360°$$

Solution

Figure 6.1 illustrates a graph of $y = \sin\theta$ for $0° \leq \theta \leq 360°$. We require solutions between 0° and 360°. The values of θ such that $\sin\theta = 0.7215$ are marked as A and B.

From Figure 6.1 we see there are two solutions, one between 0° and 90°, that is the first quadrant, and one between 90° and 180°, that is the second quadrant. Using a scientific calculator gives

$$\theta = \sin^{-1}(0.7215) = 46.18°$$

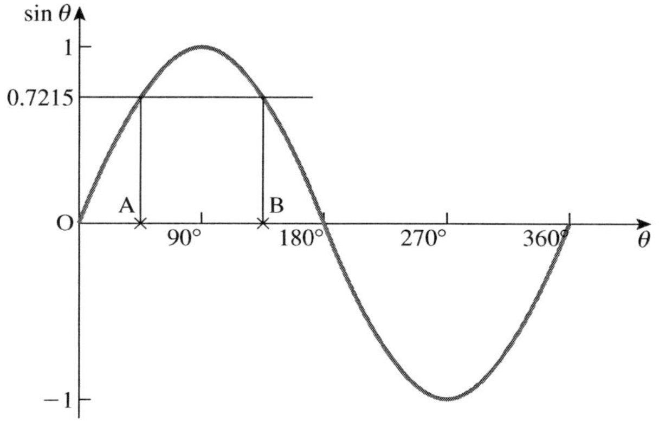

Figure 6.1 $\sin\theta = 0.7215$ has a solution in the first quadrant and a solution in the second quadrant.

This is the solution represented by point A. By symmetry, the solution at B is given by

$$\theta = 180^\circ - 46.18^\circ = 133.82^\circ$$

The required solutions are $\theta = 46.18^\circ, 133.82^\circ$.

Example 6.5
Solve

$$\cos x = 0.3456 \quad 0 \le x \le 2\pi$$

Solution
A graph of $y = \cos x$ for $0 \le x \le 2\pi$ is shown in Figure 6.2. Note that in this example angles are measured in radians.

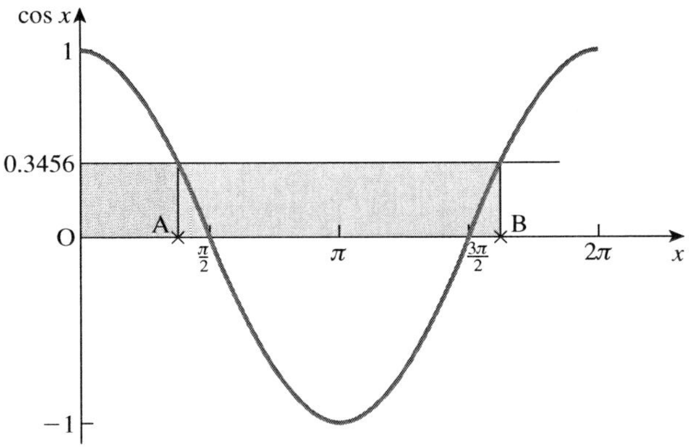

Figure 6.2
$\cos x = 0.3456$ has a solution in the first quadrant and a solution in the fourth quadrant.

From Figure 6.2 there are two solutions, A and B. Solution A is in the first quadrant, that is between 0 and $\frac{\pi}{2}$, and solution B is in the fourth quadrant, that is between $\frac{3\pi}{2}$ and 2π.

We have

$$\cos x = 0.3456$$

Using a scientific calculator we find

$$x = \cos^{-1}(0.3456) = 1.2179$$

This is the solution represented by A. Using symmetry the solution in the fourth quadrant is found from

$$x = 2\pi - 1.2179 = 5.0653$$

The required solutions are $x = 1.2179, 5.0653$.

Example 6.6
Solve

$$\tan t = -1.3000 \quad 0 \le t \le 2\pi$$

Solution

Figure 6.3 illustrates $y = \tan t$ and marks the solution points A and B.

Point A lies between $\frac{\pi}{2}$ and π

Point B lies between $\frac{3\pi}{2}$ and 2π

Using a scientific calculator we have

$\tan t = -1.3000$

$t = \tan^{-1}(-1.3000) = -0.9151$

Clearly the value of t returned by a calculator is not within the range of values of interest, namely 0 to 2π.

Recall from Block 3 that adding π radians to an angle does not change its tangent, and so another solution is given by $-0.9151 + \pi = 2.2265$. This is the solution represented in the second quadrant by point A.

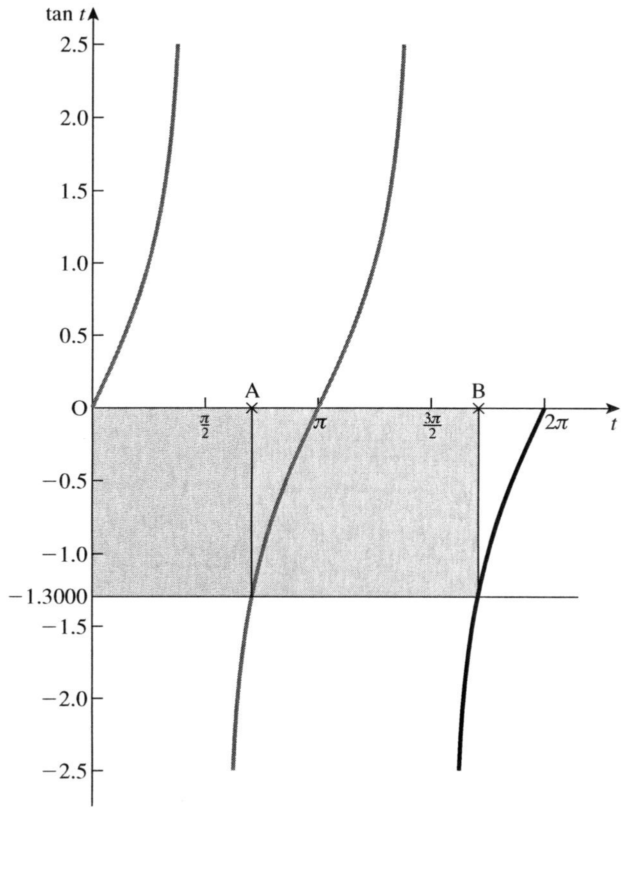

Figure 6.3 $\tan t = -1.3000$ has solutions at A and B.

By examining the graph in Figure 6.3, we see the solution at point B is π radians above point A. So the solution at point B is given by $2.2265 + \pi = 5.3681$.

The required solutions are $t = 2.2265, 5.3681$.

Example 6.7

Solve

$$\sin\theta = -0.6500 \quad 0 \leq \theta \leq 2\pi$$

Solution

From Figure 6.4, $\sin\theta = -0.6500$ has solutions at A and B.

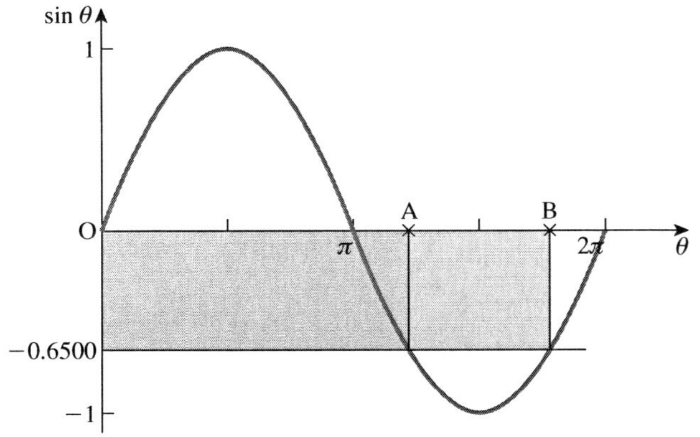

Figure 6.4 $\sin\theta = -0.6500$ has solutions at A and B.

Point A is between π and $\dfrac{3\pi}{2}$

Point B is between $\dfrac{3\pi}{2}$ and 2π

We have

$$\sin\theta = -0.6500$$

and so

$\theta =$ $\sin^{-1}(-0.6500) = -0.7076$

Clearly this solution is not within the range of interest.

Recall from Block 3 that adding $2\pi(360°)$ to an angle does not change its sine. Hence $-0.7076 + 2\pi = 5.5756$ is a solution.

This solution is represented by point B

Using the symmetry of Figure 6.4 we see that point A is above π by the same amount that B is below 2π.

Hence the solution at point A is given by $\pi + 0.7076 = 3.8492$

The required solutions are $\theta = 3.8492, 5.5756$.

Example 6.8
Solve

$$\cos\theta = -0.4215 \quad 0^\circ \leq \theta \leq 360^\circ$$

Solution
Sketch $y = \cos\theta$ and mark the points where $\cos\theta = -0.4215$.

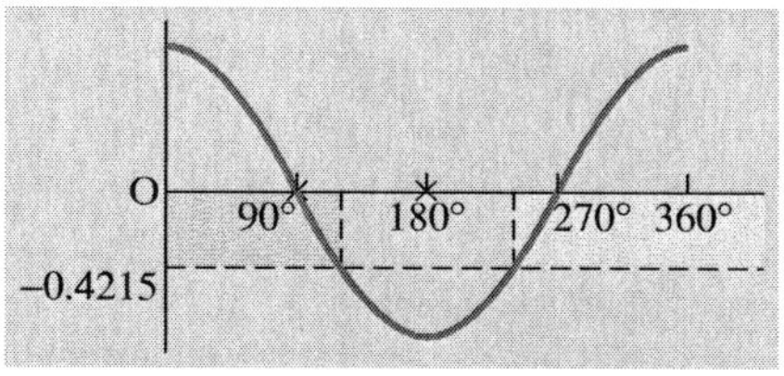

There are two solutions.

One is between and the other is between

90° and 180°

180° and 270°

We have

$$\cos\theta = -0.4215$$

and so

$\theta =$

$\cos^{-1}(-0.4215) = 114.93^\circ$

Using the symmetry of the cosine curve, the other solution is

$\theta =$

$360^\circ - 114.93^\circ = 245.07^\circ$

Exercises

1 Solve

(a) $\sin\theta = 0.3510, 0^\circ \leq \theta \leq 360^\circ$
(b) $\sin\theta = 0.4161, 0 \leq \theta \leq 2\pi$
(c) $\cos t = -0.3778, 0 \leq t \leq 2\pi$
(d) $\cos x = 0.7654, 0^\circ \leq x \leq 360^\circ$
(e) $\tan y = 1.7136, 0^\circ \leq y \leq 360^\circ$
(f) $\tan y = -0.3006, 0^\circ \leq y \leq 360^\circ$

Solutions to exercises

1 (a) 20.55°, 159.45° (b) 3.5707, 5.8540
(c) 1.9582, 4.3250 (d) 40.06°, 319.94°
(e) 59.73°, 239.73° (f) 163.27°, 343.27°

6.4 Further trigonometrical equations

We now consider more complex trigonometrical equations.

Example 6.9
Solve

$$\sin 3\theta = 0.7215 \qquad 0^\circ \le \theta \le 360^\circ$$

Solution
We introduce a new variable, z, defined by $z = 3\theta$. As θ moves from 0° to 360° then z moves through 0° to 1080°. Hence the problem may be written as one of finding z given

$$\sin z = 0.7215 \qquad 0^\circ \le z \le 1080^\circ$$

Using Example 6.4, the solutions between 0° and 360° are

$$z = 46.18^\circ, 133.82^\circ$$

Recognising that adding 360° to an angle does not change its sine, we see that the solutions between 360° and 720° are

$$\begin{aligned} z &= 46.18^\circ + 360^\circ, 133.82^\circ + 360^\circ \\ &= 406.18^\circ, 493.82^\circ \end{aligned}$$

Similarly the solutions between 720° and 1080° are

$$\begin{aligned} z &= 406.18^\circ + 360^\circ, 493.82^\circ + 360^\circ \\ &= 766.18^\circ, 853.82^\circ \end{aligned}$$

Hence

$$z = 46.18^\circ, 133.82^\circ, 406.18^\circ, 493.82^\circ, 766.18^\circ, 853.82^\circ$$

Recall that $z = 3\theta$, that is $\theta = \frac{z}{3}$, and so

$$\theta = 15.39^\circ, 44.61^\circ, 135.39^\circ, 164.61^\circ, 255.39^\circ, 284.61^\circ$$

Example 6.10
Solve

$$\cos\frac{\theta}{2} = -0.4215 \qquad 0^\circ \le \theta \le 360^\circ$$

Solution

We define $z = \frac{\theta}{2}$

As θ moves from 0° to 360°, then z moves from 0° to 180°. Hence the problem may be recast as one of finding z given

$$\cos z = -0.4215 \qquad 0^\circ \le z \le 180^\circ$$

In Example 6.8 we solved

$$\cos\theta = -0.4215 \qquad 0° \le \theta \le 360°$$

and found $\theta = 114.93°, 245.07°$. Since z is restricted to 0° to 180°, then the only solution is $z = 114.93°$. Recall that $z = \frac{\theta}{2}$, that is $\theta = 2z$, and so

$$\theta = 2 \times 114.93° = 229.86°$$

Example 6.11
Solve

$$\tan 2\theta = -1.4213 \qquad 0° \le \theta \le 360°$$

Solution
We define $z =$ 2θ

As θ ranges through 0° to 360° then z ranges through 0° to 720°
Hence the problem becomes one of solving

$$\tan z = -1.4213 \qquad 0° \le z \le 720°$$

Using a scientific calculator we see

$z =$ $\tan^{-1}(-1.4213) = -54.87°$

This is outside the range of interest.
Adding 180° to an angle does not change the value of its tangent.
Hence the required solutions are

$z =$ $125.13°, 305.13°, 485.13°, 665.13°$

Recall that $z = 2\theta$, that is $\theta = \frac{z}{2}$, and so

$\theta =$ $62.57°, 152.57°, 242.57°, 332.57°$

Exercises

1 Solve the following:
(a) $\sin 3\theta = 0.7614, 0° \le \theta \le 360°$
(b) $\tan\dfrac{\theta}{2} = 1.0137, 0° \le \theta \le 360°$
(c) $\cos 2\theta = -0.8314, 0° \le \theta \le 360°$
(d) $\sin\dfrac{2\theta}{3} = -0.5000, 0° \le \theta \le 360°$
(e) $\cos\dfrac{\theta}{3} = 0.4162, 0° \le \theta \le 360°$
(f) $\tan\dfrac{4\theta}{3} = -1, 0° \le \theta \le 360°$

Solutions to exercises

1 (a) 16.53°, 43.47°, 136.53°, 163.47°, 256.53°, 283.47°
(b) 90.78°
(c) 73.12°, 106.88°, 253.12°, 286.88°
(d) 315° (e) 196.22° (f) 101.25°, 236.25°

End of block exercises

Solve the following trigonometrical equations:

1. $\sin\theta = 0.7506, 0° \le \theta \le 360°$
2. $\sin x = 0.2913, 0 \le x \le 2\pi$
3. $3\sin\theta = 2, 0° \le \theta \le 360°$
4. $\sin t = -0.3490, 0 \le t \le 2\pi$
5. $2\sin x = -1.4600, 0 \le x \le 2\pi$
6. $3\sin\theta + 1.5 = 0, 0 \le \theta \le 2\pi$
7. $\cos t = 0.4500, 0 \le t \le 2\pi$
8. $\cos t = 0.8020 = 0, 0 \le t \le 2\pi$
9. $3\cos\theta - 1.4216 = 0, 0° \le \theta \le 360°$
10. $5\cos x + 3 = 0, 0 \le x \le 2\pi$
11. $\tan\theta = 0.4906, 0° \le \theta \le 360°$
12. $\tan t = 2.1630, 0 \le t \le 4\pi$
13. $\tan z = -0.1421, 0 \le z \le 4\pi$
14. $4\tan\phi + 2.5 = 0, 0° \le \phi \le 540°$
15. $\sin 4\theta = 0.6000, 0° \le \theta \le 180°$
16. $\sin 3\theta = -0.2556, 0° \le \theta \le 180°$
17. $\cos\dfrac{t}{3} = -0.4000, 0 \le t \le 3\pi$
18. $2\cos 2\theta = -1.3146, 0° \le \theta \le 360°$
19. $\tan\dfrac{2\theta}{3} = -1, -180° \le \theta \le 180°$
20. $\tan(\theta - 20°) = 0.5614, 0° \le \theta \le 360°$
21. $\sin(2\theta + 10°) = 0.7516, 0° \le \theta \le 360°$
22. $\cos\left(\dfrac{\theta}{2} - 20°\right) = -0.5516, 0° \le \theta \le 360°$
23. $\tan\left(\dfrac{\theta + 30°}{4}\right) = -1.6319, -270° \le \theta \le 270°$

Solutions to exercises

1. 48.64°, 131.36°
2. 0.2956, 2.8460
3. 41.81°, 138.19°
4. 3.4981, 5.9267
5. 3.9599, 5.4649
6. 3.6652, 5.7596
7. 1.1040, 5.1792
8. 2.5014, 3.7818
9. 61.71°, 298.29°
10. 2.2143, 4.0689
11. 26.13°, 206.13°
12. 1.1377, 4.2793, 7.4209, 10.5625
13. 3.0004, 6.1420, 9.2836, 12.4252
14. 147.99°, 327.99°, 507.99°
15. 9.22°, 35.78°, 99.22°, 125.78°
16. 64.94°, 115.06°
17. 5.9469°
18. 65.55°, 114.45°, 245.55°, 294.45°
19. −67.5°
20. 49.31°, 229.31°
21. 19.36°, 60.64°, 199.36°, 240.64°
22. 286.95°
23. −264.00°

BLOCK 7

Engineering waves

7.1 Introduction

Often voltages and currents vary with time, and can be modelled by sine and cosine functions. Important parameters such as amplitude, frequency, period and phase are used in the description of these waves. These terms are described in the following sections.

Two or more waves may be added together, producing a new single wave. The method of doing this is explained and illustrated.

7.2 Time-varying waves

The functions $y = \sin\theta$ and $y = \cos\theta$ were described in Block 4. There we saw that the graphs of these functions look like waves. The angle θ may be measured in degrees or radians.

Voltages and currents encountered in electrical circuits usually vary with time, t. Hence we consider sine and cosine waves in which the independent variable is t. For example, consider $y = \sin t$. As t increases from 0 seconds to 2π seconds, one complete cycle is produced. This is illustrated in Figure 7.1.

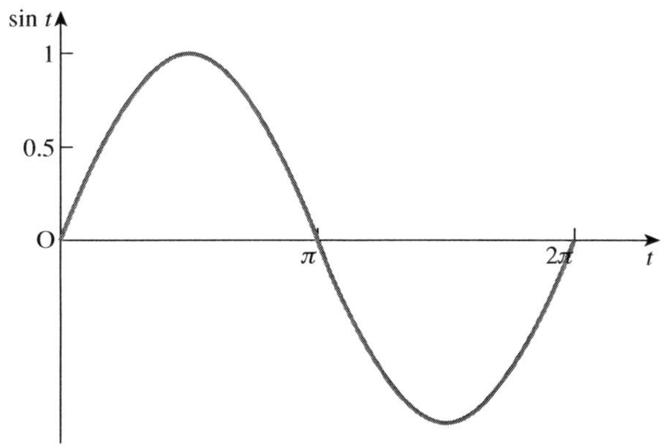

Figure 7.1 As time t varies from 0 to 2π seconds one complete cycle is produced.

7.3 Amplitude of a wave

We introduced the amplitude in Block 4 and simply recap here. Consider the function $y = A \sin t$ for $A > 0$. Then A is the amplitude of the wave. This is the highest value attained by the wave. Similarly the amplitude of $y = A \cos t$ is A.

Key point

The **amplitude** of both $y = A \sin t$ and $y = A \cos t$ is A.

Example 7.1

State the amplitude of each of the following functions:

(a) $y = 3 \sin t$

(b) $y = \frac{2}{3} \cos t$

(c) $y = -\sin t$

Solution

(a) amplitude $= 3$

(b) amplitude $= \frac{2}{3}$

(c) Noting that the amplitude of a wave is the largest value attained, the amplitude of $-\sin t$ is 1.

7.4 Angular frequency of a wave

Consider the wave $y = A \sin \omega t$. We call ω the **angular frequency** of the wave. The units of ω are radians per second. Noting that t is measured in seconds, then ωt has units of radians. For example, $y = \sin 4t$ has an angular frequency of 4 radians per second. Note that $y = \sin t$ has an angular frequency of 1 radian per second. In like manner the angular frequency of $y = A \cos \omega t$ is ω radians per second.

Key point

The **angular frequency** of $y = A \sin \omega t$ and $y = A \cos \omega t$ is ω radians per second.

Note that the amplitude, A, has no effect upon the angular frequency of a function.

Example 7.2

State the angular frequency of each of the following waves:

(a) $y = 5 \sin 3t$

(b) $y = 7 \cos \dfrac{t}{2}$

(c) $y = \cos \dfrac{2t}{3}$

Solution

(a) Comparing 5 sin $3t$ with $A \sin \omega t$, we see that $\omega = 3$: that is, the angular frequency is 3 radians per second.

(b) angular frequency = $\frac{1}{2}$ radian per second

(c) angular frequency = $\frac{2}{3}$ radians per second

Exercises

1 State (i) the amplitude and (ii) the angular frequency of the following waves:
(a) $y = 2 \sin 5t$ (b) $y = 3 \cos 6t$ (c) $y = \sin \frac{t}{2}$ (d) $y = \cos \frac{4t}{3}$ (e) $y = \frac{3}{2} \sin \frac{2t}{3}$ (f) $y = -4 \sin \pi t$

Solutions to exercises

1 (a) 2, 5 (b) 3, 6 (c) 1, $\frac{1}{2}$ (d) 1, $\frac{4}{3}$ (e) $\frac{3}{2}$, $\frac{2}{3}$ (f) 4, π

7.5 Period of a wave

The time taken to complete one full cycle is called the **period** of the wave. It is closely connected to the angular frequency of the wave.

Consider $y = A \sin \omega t$. When $t = 0$ seconds, then $\omega t = 0$ radians. When $t = \frac{2\pi}{\omega}$ seconds, then $\omega t = \omega(\frac{2\pi}{\omega}) = 2\pi$ radians. Hence as t increases by $\frac{2\pi}{\omega}$ seconds, the angle, ωt, increases by 2π radians. Recall from Block 4 that a sine function completes one full cycle as the angle increases by 2π radians. Hence $y = A \sin \omega t$ completes a full cycle as t increases by $\frac{2\pi}{\omega}$ seconds: that is, the period of y is $\frac{2\pi}{\omega}$ seconds. Similarly the period of $y = A \cos \omega t$ is also $\frac{2\pi}{\omega}$ seconds. The period is denoted by T.

Key point

The **period** of both $y = A \sin \omega t$ and $y = A \cos \omega t$ is given by $T = \frac{2\pi}{\omega}$.

Example 7.3

State the period of each of the following functions:
(a) $y = 3 \sin 6t$
(b) $y = 5.6 \cos \pi t$
(c) $y = 50 \sin 100\pi t$

Solution

(a) Here $\omega = 6$ and so

$$T = \frac{2\pi}{6} = \frac{\pi}{3}$$

The period is $\frac{\pi}{3}$ seconds.

(b) Here $\omega = \pi$ and so

$T =$ $\frac{2\pi}{\pi} = 2$

The period is 2 seconds.

(c) Here $\omega =$ 100π and so

$T =$ $\frac{2\pi}{100\pi} = 0.02$

The period is 0.02 seconds.

Example 7.4 Electrical Engineering – Oscilloscope trace

Figure 7.2 shows an oscilloscope trace of a sine wave. State the equation of the wave.

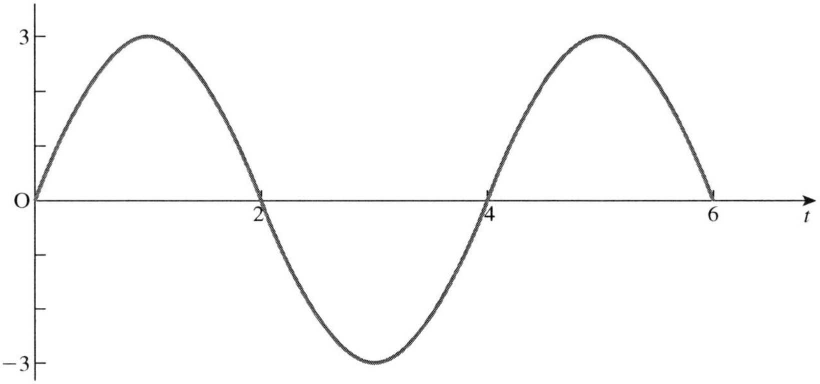

Figure 7.2 Oscilloscope trace.

Solution

The wave has an equation of the form

$$y = A \sin \omega t$$

The maximum value of the wave is 3: that is, the amplitude, A, is 3. A full cycle is completed in 4 seconds: that is, $T = 4$. So

$$T = \frac{2\pi}{\omega} = 4$$

from which

$$\omega = \frac{\pi}{2}$$

The equation of the wave is $y = 3 \sin \frac{\pi t}{2}$.

Example 7.5 Electrical Engineering – Oscilloscope trace

Figure 7.3 shows an oscilloscope trace of a cosine wave. State the equation of the wave.

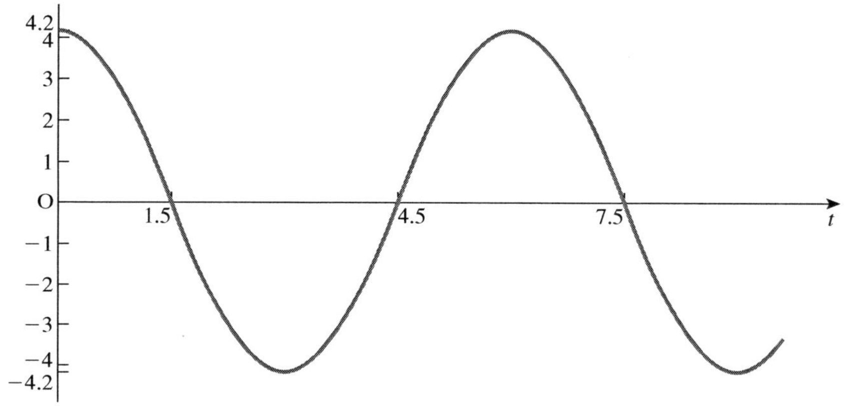

Figure 7.3 Oscilloscope trace of a cosine wave.

Solution

The wave has an equation of the form

$$y = A \cos \omega t$$

The highest value of the wave is ______ 4.2

Hence the value of the amplitude is 4.2.

A cycle is completed in ______ seconds, and so 6

$$T = \frac{2\pi}{\omega} = 6$$

Hence

$\omega =$ ______ $\frac{2\pi}{6} = \frac{\pi}{3}$

The equation of the wave is therefore ______ $4.2 \cos \frac{\pi t}{3}$

7.6 The frequency of a wave

The **frequency**, f, of a wave is the number of cycles completed in 1 second. It is measured in hertz (Hz). One hertz is one cycle per second.

Consider again the function $y = A \sin \omega t$. The period is $\frac{2\pi}{\omega}$ seconds: that is, one cycle is completed in $\frac{2\pi}{\omega}$ seconds. Hence ω cycles are completed in 2π seconds and $\frac{\omega}{2\pi}$ cycles are completed in 1 second. Thus we have

Key point

$$\text{frequency } f = \frac{\omega}{2\pi}$$

We note that

$$\text{period } T = \frac{2\pi}{\omega}, \text{ frequency } f = \frac{\omega}{2\pi}$$

and so

Key point

$$T = \frac{1}{f}$$

Example 7.6

State the period and frequency of the following waves:

(a) $y = 2 \sin 4t$
(b) $y = 3 \cos 2t$
(c) $y = \sin \pi t$

Solution

(a) Comparing $2 \sin 4t$ with $A \sin \omega t$ we see that $\omega = 4$. Hence the frequency, f, is found from

$$\begin{aligned} f &= \frac{\omega}{2\pi} \\ &= \frac{4}{2\pi} \\ &= \frac{2}{\pi} \\ &= 0.6366 \text{ Hz} \end{aligned}$$

So 0.6366 cycles are completed every second. The period, T, is found from

$$\begin{aligned} T &= \frac{1}{f} \\ &= \frac{\pi}{2} \\ &= 1.5708 \end{aligned}$$

It takes 1.5708 seconds to complete one cycle.

(b) Here $\omega = 2$ and so

$$f = \frac{\omega}{2\pi} = \frac{2}{2\pi} = \frac{1}{\pi} = 0.3183 \text{ Hz}$$

Thus, 0.3183 of a cycle is completed every second.
The period, T, is found using

$$T = \frac{1}{f} = \pi = 3.1416$$

It takes π seconds to complete one cycle.

(c) Here $\omega = \pi$ and so

$$f = \frac{\omega}{2\pi} = \frac{\pi}{2\pi} = \frac{1}{2} \text{ Hz}$$

and

$$T = \frac{1}{f} = 2$$

Thus, 0.5 of a cycle is completed each second. It takes 2 seconds to complete one full cycle.

Exercises

1 State (i) the period and (ii) the frequency of the following waves:
(a) $y = 6 \sin 4t$ (b) $y = \cos 3t$ (c) $y = -4 \sin t$ (d) $y = \frac{1}{2} \cos 100\pi t$
(e) $y = \pi \sin 1.5t$

Solutions to exercises

1 (a) $\frac{\pi}{2}, \frac{2}{\pi}$ (b) $\frac{2\pi}{3}, \frac{3}{2\pi}$ (c) $2\pi, \frac{1}{2\pi}$ (d) 0.02, 50 (e) $\frac{4\pi}{3}, \frac{3}{4\pi}$

7.7 Phase and time displacement of a wave

We now introduce waves of the form $y = A \sin(\omega t + \alpha)$ and $y = A \cos(\omega t + \alpha)$. Introducing α has the effect of moving the wave to either the left or the right. Figure 7.4 shows graphs of $y = \sin 2t$ and $y = \sin(2t + 1)$.

From Figure 7.4 we note that the peak of $y = \sin(2t + 1)$ occurs 0.5 seconds before the peak of $y = \sin 2t$. We say $\sin(2t + 1)$ **leads** $\sin 2t$ by 0.5 seconds. The quantity, 0.5 seconds, is known as the **time displacement** of $y = \sin(2t + 1)$.

Figure 7.4
The waves
$y = \sin 2t$ and
$y = \sin(2t + 1)$.

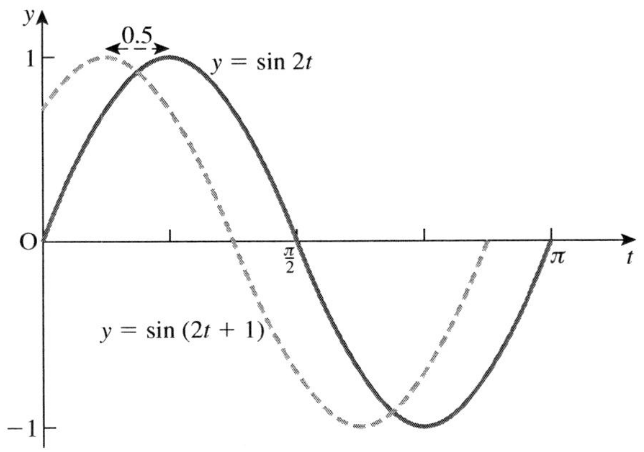

Figure 7.5
The waves
$y = \sin 2t$ and
$y = \sin(2t - 1)$.

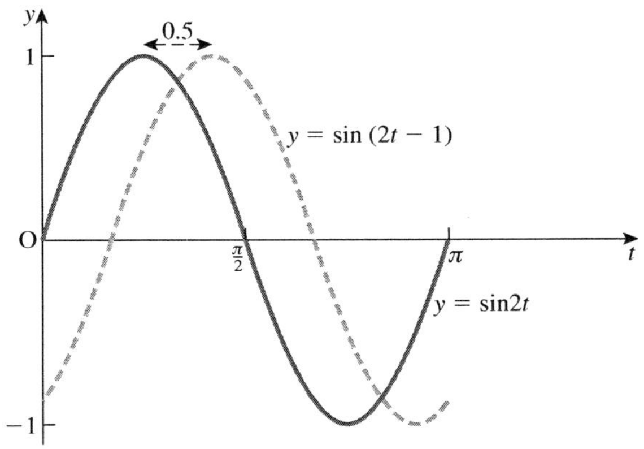

Figure 7.5 shows graphs of $y = \sin 2t$ and $y = \sin(2t - 1)$.

The peak of $y = \sin(2t - 1)$ is reached 0.5 seconds after the peak of $y = \sin 2t$. We say $\sin(2t - 1)$ **lags** $\sin 2t$ by 0.5 seconds. The time displacement of $\sin(2t - 1)$ is -0.5 seconds.

These examples lead us to the following general treatment.

Consider the wave $y = A\sin(\omega t + \alpha)$. The angle α is called the **phase angle**, or simply the **phase**. We note that y may be written as

$$y = A\sin\left[\omega\left(t + \frac{\alpha}{\omega}\right)\right]$$

We call $\frac{\alpha}{\omega}$ the **time displacement** of the wave.

Key point

The **phase** of $y = A\sin(\omega t + \alpha)$ is α radians.

The **time displacement** of $y = A\sin(\omega t + \alpha)$ is $\frac{\alpha}{\omega}$ seconds.

In similar manner the phase and time displacement of $y = A\cos(\omega t + \alpha)$ are α radians and $\frac{\alpha}{\omega}$ seconds.

Example 7.7

State the phase and time displacement of each of the following waves:

(a) $y = \sin(2t + 1)$

(b) $y = \sin(2t - 1)$

(c) $y = 3\cos\left(\frac{t}{2} + 3\right)$

Solution

(a) Here $\omega = 2$, $\alpha = 1$ and so the phase is 1 radian and the time displacement is

$$\frac{\alpha}{\omega} = \frac{1}{2} = 0.5 \text{ seconds}$$

This wave is illustrated in Figure 7.4.

(b) Here $\omega = 2$, $\alpha = -1$ and so the phase is -1 radian and the time displacement is

$$\frac{\alpha}{\omega} = \frac{-1}{2} = -0.5 \text{ seconds}$$

This wave is illustrated in Figure 7.5.

(c) Here $\omega =$ ______ and $\alpha =$ ______ 0.5, 3

and so the phase is 3 radians and the time displacement is $\dfrac{3}{(0.5)} = 6$ seconds.

Exercises

1 State (i) the phase and (ii) the time displacement of the following waves:

(a) $y = 4\sin(3t + 12)$

(b) $y = \sin(4t - 6)$

(c) $y = 2\cos(t + 0.5)$

(d) $y = \sin(0.5t - 2)$

(e) $y = 3\cos\left(\frac{t + 4}{3}\right)$

Solutions to exercises

1 (a) 12, 4 (b) -6, -1.5 (c) 0.5, 0.5 (d) -2, -4 (e) $\frac{4}{3}$, 4

7.8 Adding waves of the same frequency

Waves of the same angular frequency may be added together to form a new wave. The new wave has the same angular frequency as the original waves. The trigonometrical identities (see Block 5) are used, especially the formulae for $\sin(A \pm B)$ and $\cos(A \pm B)$. The following examples illustrate the technique.

Example 7.8
Express $2 \sin 3t + 6 \cos 3t$ in the form $A \cos(\omega t + \alpha)$, $\alpha \geq 0$.

Solution
The angular frequency of both $2 \sin 3t$ and $6 \cos 3t$ is 3 radians per second. Hence, on adding the waves, the angular frequency of the sum is also 3 radians per second and so $\omega = 3$. Recall the trigonometrical identity from Block 5:

$$\cos(A + B) = \cos A \cos B - \sin A \sin B$$

and so

$$\begin{aligned} 2 \sin 3t + 6 \cos 3t &= A \cos(\omega t + \alpha) \\ &= A \cos(3t + \alpha) \\ &= A(\cos 3t \cos \alpha - \sin 3t \sin \alpha) \\ &= (A \cos \alpha) \cos 3t - (A \sin \alpha) \sin 3t \\ &= -(A \sin \alpha) \sin 3t + (A \cos \alpha) \cos 3t \end{aligned}$$

We now compare the coefficients of $\sin 3t$ and $\cos 3t$ on the left-hand and right-hand sides.
Comparing the $\sin 3t$ coefficients we have

$$2 = -A \sin \alpha \qquad (1)$$

Comparing the $\cos 3t$ coefficients we have

$$6 = A \cos \alpha \qquad (2)$$

Equations (1) and (2) must be solved for A and α. To find A, α is eliminated. This is accomplished by squaring equations (1) and (2) and then adding the results.
Squaring equation (1) gives

$$4 = A^2 \sin^2 \alpha \qquad (3)$$

Squaring equation (2) gives

$$36 = A^2 \cos^2 \alpha \qquad (4)$$

Adding equations (3) and (4) gives

$$\begin{aligned} 40 &= A^2 \sin^2 \alpha + A^2 \cos^2 \alpha \\ &= A^2(\sin^2 \alpha + \cos^2 \alpha) \\ &= A^2 \text{ using } \sin^2 \alpha + \cos^2 \alpha = 1 \end{aligned}$$

Hence $A = \sqrt{40}$.

To find α, A is eliminated from equations (1) and (2). This is achieved by dividing equation (1) by equation (2) and using the identity $\dfrac{\sin \alpha}{\cos \alpha} = \tan \alpha$.
Dividing equation (1) by equation (2) gives

$$\frac{2}{6} = -\frac{A \sin \alpha}{A \cos \alpha} = -\tan \alpha$$

Hence

$$\tan \alpha = -\frac{1}{3}$$

Since $\tan\alpha < 0$, then α lies in either the second quadrant or the fourth quadrant. Noting from equation (1) that $\sin\alpha < 0$, then α must be in the fourth quadrant.

Solving $\tan\alpha = -\frac{1}{3}$ with α in the fourth quadrant gives $\alpha = 5.9614$. So finally

$$2\sin 3t + 6\cos 3t = \sqrt{40}\cos(3t + 5.9614)$$

The resulting wave has an amplitude of $\sqrt{40}$, an angular frequency of 3 radians per second and a phase of 5.9614 radians.

Example 7.9

Express $2\sin 5t - 5\cos 5t$ in the form $A\sin(\omega t - \alpha)$, $\alpha \geq 0$.

Solution

The angular frequency of both $2\sin 5t$ and $5\cos 5t$ is 5, and so the resultant wave has an angular frequency of 5, that is $\omega = 5$.

Recall the trigonometrical identity for $\sin(A - B)$:

$$\sin(A - B) = \sin A\cos B - \sin B\cos A$$

Hence

$$\begin{aligned} 2\sin 5t - 5\cos 5t &= A\sin(\omega t - \alpha) \\ &= A\sin(5t - \alpha) \\ &= A(\sin 5t\cos\alpha - \sin\alpha\cos 5t) \\ &= (A\cos\alpha)\sin 5t - (A\sin\alpha)\cos 5t \end{aligned}$$

Comparing the $\sin 5t$ terms on both sides gives

$$2 = A\cos\alpha \quad (5)$$

Comparing the $\cos 5t$ terms on both sides gives

$$5 = A\sin\alpha \quad (6)$$

To eliminate α from equations (5) and (6), the equations are squared and then added. Squaring the equations gives

$$\begin{aligned} 4 &= A^2\cos^2\alpha \\ 25 &= A^2\sin^2\alpha \end{aligned}$$

and then adding gives

$$\begin{aligned} 29 &= A^2\cos^2\alpha + A^2\sin^2\alpha \\ &= A^2(\cos^2\alpha + \sin^2\alpha) \\ &= A^2 \end{aligned}$$

Hence $A = \sqrt{29}$.

To eliminate A, equation (6) is divided by equation (5) to give

$$\begin{aligned} \frac{5}{2} &= \frac{A\sin\alpha}{A\cos\alpha} \\ &= \tan\alpha \\ \tan\alpha &= 2.5 \end{aligned}$$

We note that $\tan\alpha > 0$ and from equation (5) that $\cos\alpha > 0$ and so α must be in the first quadrant.

$$\alpha = \tan^{-1} 2.5 = 1.1903$$

So

$$2\sin 5t - 5\cos 5t = \sqrt{29}\sin(5t - 1.1903)$$

Example 7.10

Express $\cos 2t - 2\sin 2t$ in the form $A\sin(\omega t + \alpha)$, $\alpha \geq 0$.

Solution

The angular frequency of both $\cos 2t$ and $2\sin 2t$ is

2

Hence the angular frequency of the resulting wave is also 2, that is $\omega = 2$.

Recall from Block 5 the trigonometrical identity

$\sin(A + B) =$ $\sin A\cos B + \sin B\cos A$

Hence

$$\begin{aligned}\cos 2t - 2\sin 2t &= A\sin(\omega t + \alpha)\\ &= A\sin(2t + \alpha)\\ &= A(\sin 2t\cos\alpha + \sin\alpha\cos 2t)\\ &= A\cos\alpha\,\sin 2t + A\sin\alpha\,\cos 2t\end{aligned}$$

So we have

$$\cos 2t - 2\sin 2t = A\cos\alpha\sin 2t + A\sin\alpha\cos 2t$$

Comparing the $\sin 2t$ terms on both sides of the equation gives

$$-2 = A\cos\alpha \qquad (7)$$

Comparing the $\cos 2t$ terms on both sides of the equation gives

$$1 = A\sin\alpha \qquad (8)$$

Squaring equations (7) and (8) and then adding gives

$A^2 =$ 5

and so $A = \sqrt{5}$.

To determine α, equation (8) is divided by equation (7). This gives

$\tan\alpha =$ -0.5

Recognising that α is in the second quadrant we see that

$\alpha =$ $\tan^{-1}(-0.5) = 2.6779$

Hence

$\cos 2t - 2\sin 2t =$ $\sqrt{5}\sin(2t + 2.6779)$

Exercises

1. Express $6 \sin 3t - 7 \cos 3t$ in the form $A \cos(\omega t + \alpha)$, $\alpha \geq 0$.

2. Express $2 \cos t + 6 \sin t$ in the form $A \sin(\omega t - \alpha)$, $\alpha \geq 0$. State the maximum value of $2 \cos t + 6 \sin t$.

3. Express $5 \sin 2t + \cos 2t$ in the form $A \cos(\omega t - \alpha)$, $\alpha \geq 0$.

4. Show that the maximum value of

   $a \sin \omega t + b \cos \omega t$ is $\sqrt{a^2 + b^2}$.

Solutions to exercises

1. $\sqrt{85} \cos(3t + 3.8502)$

2. $\sqrt{40} \sin(t - 5.9614), \sqrt{40}$

3. $\sqrt{26} \cos(2t - 1.3734)$

End of block exercises

State the amplitude of the functions in questions 1–5.

1. $y = 3 \sin 2t$

2. $y = 2 \cos 3t$

3. $y = \dfrac{4}{3} \sin\left(\dfrac{t}{2}\right)$

4. $y = \cos\left(\dfrac{2t}{3}\right)$

5. $y = \dfrac{5 \cos 3t}{3}$

For questions 6–10 state the angular frequency of the functions given in questions 1–5.

For questions 11–15 state the period of the functions in questions 1–5.

For questions 16–20 state the frequency of the functions in questions 1–5.

State the phase of the functions in questions 21–25.

21. $y = 3 \sin(t + 2)$

22. $y = 2.3 \cos(4t - 2)$

23. $y = \cos\left(\dfrac{3t - 1}{2}\right)$

24. $y = \sin(0.5t + 3)$

25. $y = \sin\left(\dfrac{2t}{3} - \dfrac{\pi}{2}\right)$

For questions 26–30 state the time displacement of the functions in questions 21–25.

31. Express $3 \sin 5t + 6 \cos 5t$ in the form $A \sin(\omega t + \alpha)$, $\alpha \geq 0$.

32. Express $2 \cos 3t - \sin 3t$ in the form $A \sin(\omega t + \phi)$, $\phi \geq 0$.

33. Express $\sin 4t + 3 \cos 4t$ in the form $A \cos(\omega t + \phi)$, $\phi \geq 0$.

34. Express $\cos t - 7 \sin t$ in the form $A \cos(\omega t + \alpha)$, $\alpha \geq 0$.

35. Express $4 \sin 2t + 5 \cos 2t$ in the form $A \sin(\omega t - \phi)$, $\phi \geq 0$.

36. Express $5 \sin 3t - 3 \cos 3t$ in the form $A \sin(\omega t - \alpha)$, $\alpha \geq 0$.

37. Express $\sin t - 3 \cos t$ in the form $A \cos(\omega t - \phi)$, $\phi \geq 0$.

38. Express $-2 \sin 2t + 4 \cos 2t$ in the form $A \cos(\omega t - \alpha)$, $\alpha \geq 0$.

Solutions to exercises

1 3

2 2

3 $\frac{4}{3}$

4 1

5 $\frac{5}{3}$

6 2

7 3

8 $\frac{1}{2}$

9 $\frac{2}{3}$

10 3

11 π

12 $\frac{2\pi}{3}$

13 4π

14 3π

15 $\frac{2\pi}{3}$

16 $\frac{1}{\pi}$

17 $\frac{3}{2\pi}$

18 $\frac{1}{4\pi}$

19 $\frac{1}{3\pi}$

20 $\frac{3}{2\pi}$

21 2

22 -2

23 $-\frac{1}{2}$

24 3

25 $-\frac{\pi}{2}$

26 2

27 $-\frac{1}{2}$

28 $-\frac{1}{3}$

29 6

30 $-\frac{3\pi}{4}$

31 $\sqrt{45}\sin(5t + 1.1071)$

32 $\sqrt{5}\sin(3t + 2.0344)$

33 $\sqrt{10}\cos(4t + 5.9614)$

34 $\sqrt{50}\cos(t + 1.4289)$

35 $\sqrt{41}\sin(2t - 5.3871)$

36 $\sqrt{34}\sin(3t - 0.5404)$

37 $\sqrt{10}\cos(t - 2.8198)$

38 $\sqrt{20}\cos(2t - 5.8195)$

End of chapter exercises

1 Convert the following angles to radians, giving your answer to 4 d.p:
(a) 40° (b) 100° (c) 527° (d) −200°

2 Convert the following angles in radians to degrees:
(a) $\frac{\pi}{2}$ (b) $\frac{\pi}{3}$ (c) $\frac{4\pi}{3}$ (d) 1.25π (e) 1.25
(f) 9.6314 (g) 3

3 Evaluate
(a) cosec 37° (b) cot 1.3 (c) sec 40°

4 An arc of a circle, radius 5cm, subtends an angle of $\frac{3\pi}{4}$ radians at the centre. Calculate the length of the arc.

5 A sector of a circle, radius 9 cm, has an area of 100 cm^2. Calculate the angle subtended at the centre by the sector.

6 Express $6\sin 2t - 3\cos 2t$ in the form $A\cos(\omega t - \alpha)$, $\alpha \geq 0$.

7 If $\sin\phi < 0$ and $\cos\phi > 0$, state the quadrant in which ϕ lies.

8 If $\tan\phi < 0$ and $\sin\phi > 0$, state the quadrant in which ϕ lies.

9 Express $\frac{1}{2}\cos t + \sin t$ in the form $A\sin(\omega t - \alpha)$, $\alpha \geq 0$.

10 A voltage source, $v(t)$, varies with time, t, according to

$$v(t) = 50\sin(\pi t + 10)$$

State (a) the angular frequency, (b) the phase, (c) the amplitude, (d) the period, (e) the time displacement, (f) the frequency of the voltage.

11 Solve

$$3\cos\theta = 1.2 \quad 0 \leq \theta \leq 2\pi$$

12 Solve

$$\sin 2\theta = -0.4010 \quad 0 \leq \theta \leq 2\pi$$

13 Simplify $\sin\theta\cos\theta\tan\theta + \cos^2\theta$.

14 Express $5\cos 3t + 2\sin 3t$ in the form $A\cos(\omega t + \alpha)$, $\alpha \geq 0$.

15 Show that
(a) $\tan^2\theta + 1 = \sec^2\theta$
(b) $1 + \cot^2\theta = \operatorname{cosec}^2\theta$

16 (a) Sketch $y = \cos(x - 20°)$, $0° \leq x \leq 360°$.
(b) On the same axes, sketch $y = \sin x$.
(c) Use your graphs to obtain approximate solutions of

$$\sin x = \cos(x - 20°)$$

17 A current, $i(t)$, varies with time, t, and is given by

$$i(t) = 30\cos(t - 0.4) \quad t \geq 0$$

(a) Find the time when the current is first zero.
(b) Find the time when the current reaches its first peak.

18 Solve

$$\sin\theta\cos 41° + \sin 41°\cos\theta = 0.6100$$
$$0° \leq \theta \leq 360°$$

19 If $0 \leq \theta \leq 2\pi$ and $\cos 2\theta < 0$, state the range of possible values for θ.

20 Simplify

$$(\sin\theta + \cos\theta)^2 - \sin 2\theta$$

21 Solve

$$\tan\left(\frac{2x}{3}\right) = 0.7 \quad 0 \leq x \leq 2\pi$$

22 Solve

$$\cos\left(\frac{\theta - 30°}{3}\right) = -0.6010 \quad 0 \leq \theta \leq 720°$$

23 A voltage, $v(t)$, has the form

$$2\sin t + \cos t \quad t \geq 0.$$

(a) Calculate the maximum value of v.
(b) Calculate the first time that this maximum value occurs.

Solutions to exercises

1 (a) 0.6981 (b) 1.7453 (c) 9.1979 (d) -3.4907

2 (a) 90° (b) 60° (c) 240° (d) 225° (e) 71.62° (f) 551.84° (g) 171.89°

3 (a) 1.6616 (b) 0.2776 (c) 1.3054

4 11.78 cm

5 2.4691 radians

6 $\sqrt{45}\cos(2t - 2.0344)$

7 fourth quadrant

8 second quadrant

9 $1.1180 \sin(t - 5.8195)$

10 (a) π (b) 10 (c) 50 (d) 2 (e) $\frac{10}{\pi}$ (f) 0.5

11 1.1593, 5.1239

12 1.7771, 2.9353, 4.9187, 6.0769

13 1

14 $\sqrt{29}\cos(3t + 5.9027)$

16 (c) 55°, 235°

17 (a) 1.9708 (b) 0.4

18 101.41°, 356.59°

19 $\frac{\pi}{4} < \theta < \frac{3\pi}{4}, \frac{5\pi}{4} < \theta < \frac{7\pi}{4}$

20 1

21 0.9161, 5.6285

22 410.82°

23 (a) $\sqrt{5}$ (b) 1.1071

Further trigonometry

Chapter 10

The chapter opens with a statement of **Pythagoras's theorem.** This famous theorem relates the lengths of the sides of a right-angled triangle. A triangle is solved when all its angles and the lengths of all its sides have been found. Methods are covered for solving right-angled triangles.

Blocks 2 and 3 deal with the **sine** and **cosine rules.** These are used to solve any triangle. Conditions under which the rules can be applied are clearly stated.

The application of the **solution of triangles** in surveying is covered in Block 4. Finally trigonometry is applied to the resolution and addition of **forces.**

Chapter 10 contents

BLOCK 1 Pythagoras's theorem and the solution of right-angled triangles

1.1 Introduction

We introduce some common terms and notation used for right-angled triangles. Consider a right-angled $\triangle$ABC as shown in Figure 1.1.

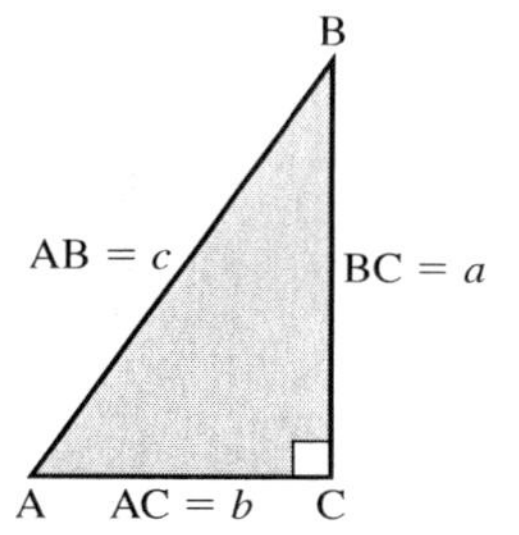

Figure 1.1 A right-angled $\triangle$ABC.

There is a right angle at C; the hypotenuse is AB. The side AC is opposite B. A common notation is to refer to the length of AC as b. Similarly, BC is opposite A and so the length of BC is written as a. Finally, the hypotenuse AB is opposite C and so is labelled c. In summary we have

$$a = \text{BC}, \quad b = \text{AC}, \quad c = \text{AB}$$

The convention of referring to sides of a triangle in such a way is not restricted to right-angled triangles. It is used for any triangle.

1.2 Pythagoras's theorem

Pythagoras's theorem can only be applied to right-angled triangles. Consider the right-angled $\triangle$ABC in Figure 1.1. Then Pythagoras's theorem states

Key point

$$c^2 = a^2 + b^2$$

Thus the square of the hypotenuse equals the sum of the squares of the other two sides.

Example 1.1
In $\triangle$ABC in Figure 1.1, AC = 9 cm and BC = 14 cm. Calculate AB.

Solution
We have b = AC = 9 and a = BC = 14. We need to find AB, that is c. By Pythagoras's theorem we know

$$\begin{aligned} c^2 &= a^2 + b^2 \\ &= 14^2 + 9^2 \\ &= 277 \\ c &= \sqrt{277} = 16.64 \end{aligned}$$

The hypotenuse, AB, is 16.64 cm.

Example 1.2
Consider $\triangle$ABC in Figure 1.1. Given AB = 19 cm and AC = 12.5 cm calculate BC.

Solution
We have c = AB = 19 and b = 12.5
We seek BC, that is a. Using Pythagoras's theorem

$$\begin{aligned} c^2 &= a^2 + b^2 \\ 19^2 &= a^2 + 12.5^2 \\ a^2 &= 19^2 - 12.5^2 = 204.75 \\ a &= \sqrt{204.75} = 14.31 \end{aligned}$$

The length of BC is 14.31 cm.

Exercises

1. $\triangle$ABC has a right angle at B. Given AB = 7 cm, BC = 12 cm, calculate the length of AC.
2. $\triangle$PQR has a right angle at P. If PR = 3.2 m, QR = 4.9 m, calculate the length of PQ.
3. $\triangle$CDE has a right angle at E. Given CD = 55 mm and DE = 37 mm, calculate the length of CE.

Solutions to exercises

1. 13.89 cm
2. 3.71 m
3. 40.69 mm

1.3 Solving right-angled triangles

When asked to solve a triangle we need to calculate all the unknown angles and all the unknown sides. Sometimes we are asked to calculate only specified angle(s) and/or side(s). The following examples illustrate the method. You should be aware that the sum of the angles in any triangle is 180°.

Example 1.3

As shown in Figure 1.2, △ABC has a right angle at C, $A = 53°$ and BC = 9 cm. Calculate (a) AC and (b) AB.

Figure 1.2

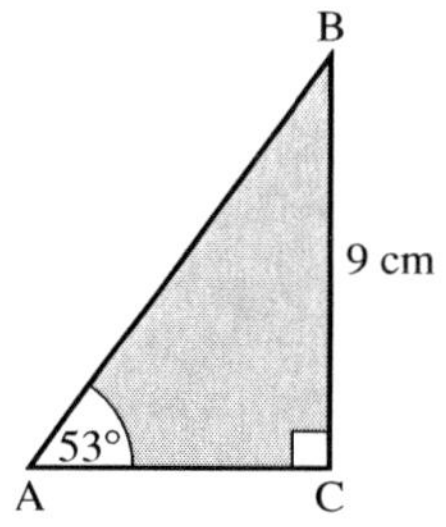

Solution

(a)
$$\begin{aligned} \tan A &= \frac{BC}{AC} \\ \tan 53° &= \frac{9}{AC} \\ AC &= \frac{9}{\tan 53°} \\ &= 6.7820 \end{aligned}$$

(b)
$$\begin{aligned} \sin A &= \frac{BC}{AB} \\ \sin 53° &= \frac{9}{AB} \\ AB &= \frac{9}{\sin 53°} \\ &= 11.2692 \end{aligned}$$

Example 1.4

△XYZ has a right angle at Y, $X = 26°$ and XZ = 12 cm.

(a) Sketch △XYZ.
(b) Calculate XY.
(c) Calculate YZ.

Solution

(a) △XYZ is illustrated in Figure 1.3.

Figure 1.3

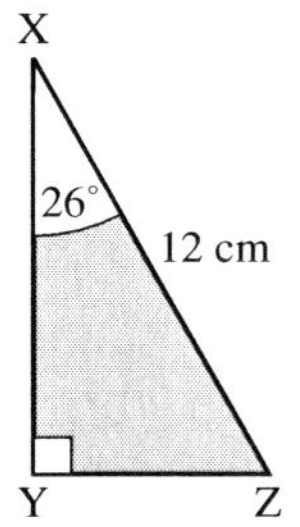

(b) $$\cos X = \frac{XY}{XZ}$$

$$\cos 26^\circ = \frac{XY}{12}$$

$$XY = \qquad 12\cos 26^\circ = 10.7855$$

(c) $$\sin X = \frac{YZ}{XZ}$$

$$\sin 26^\circ = \qquad \frac{YZ}{12}$$

$$YZ = \qquad 12\sin 26^\circ = 5.2605$$

Example 1.5

△KLM has a right angle at L, $M = 25^\circ$ and ML = 14 cm. It is illustrated in Figure 1.4. Calculate (a) KL and (b) KM.

Figure 1.4

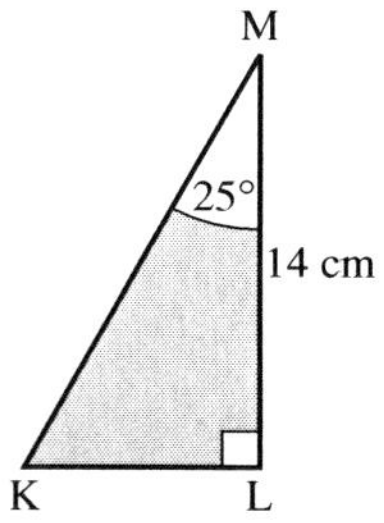

Solution

(a) $$\tan M = \frac{KL}{ML}$$

$$\tan 25^\circ = \frac{KL}{14}$$

$$KL = \qquad 6.5283$$

(b) $\cos M = \frac{ML}{KM} = \frac{14}{KM}$

$KM = \frac{14}{\cos 25^\circ} = 15.4473$

Example 1.6

$\triangle PQR$ has a right angle at P, $Q = 39^\circ$ and QR = 18 cm.

(a) Sketch $\triangle PQR$.
(b) Calculate PQ.
(c) Calculate PR.

Solution

(a) $\triangle PQR$ is illustrated in Figure 1.5.

Figure 1.5

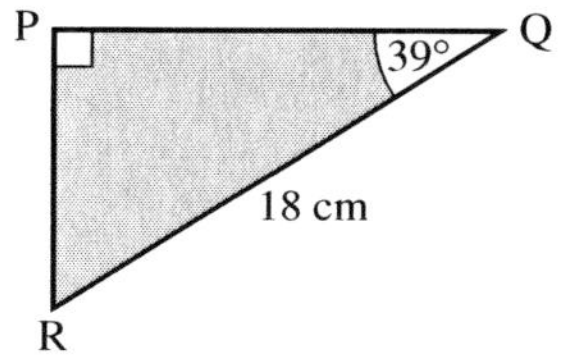

(b) $\cos 39^\circ = \frac{PQ}{QR} = \frac{PQ}{18}$

$PQ = 18 \cos 39^\circ = 13.9886$

(c) $\sin 39^\circ = \frac{PR}{QR} = \frac{PR}{18}$

$PR = 18 \sin 39^\circ = 11.3278$

Example 1.7

$\triangle ABC$ has $C = 90^\circ$, AC = 14 cm and BC = 9 cm.

(a) Sketch $\triangle ABC$.
(b) Solve $\triangle ABC$.

Solution

(a) $\triangle ABC$ is illustrated in Figure 1.6.

Figure 1.6

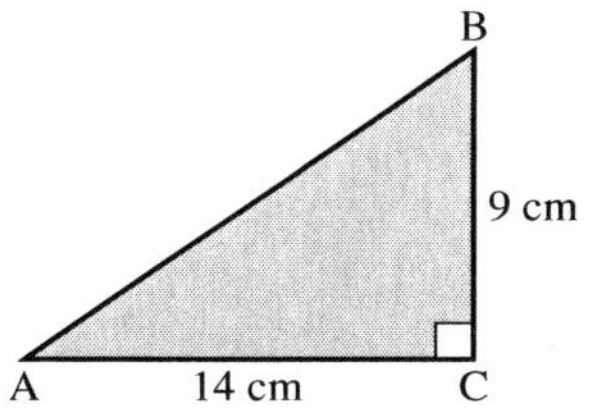

(b) We need to find A, B and AB. First we find A.

$$\begin{aligned}\tan A &= \frac{\mathrm{BC}}{\mathrm{AC}}\\ &= \frac{9}{14}\\ A &= \tan^{-1}\left(\frac{9}{14}\right)\\ &= 32.74^\circ\end{aligned}$$

B may now be found. The sum of the angles in any triangle is 180° and so

$$\begin{aligned}A + B + C &= 180^\circ\\ B &= 180^\circ - A - C\\ &= 180^\circ - 32.74^\circ - 90^\circ\\ B &= 57.26^\circ\end{aligned}$$

Finally using Pythagoras's theorem we have

$$\begin{aligned}(\mathrm{AB})^2 &= (\mathrm{BC})^2 + (\mathrm{AC})^2\\ &= 9^2 + 14^2\\ &= 277\\ \mathrm{AB} &= \sqrt{277}\\ &= 16.64\end{aligned}$$

Example 1.8

XYZ is a right-angled triangle as shown in Figure 1.7, with XY = 23 cm and YZ = 14 cm. Solve △XYZ.

Figure 1.7

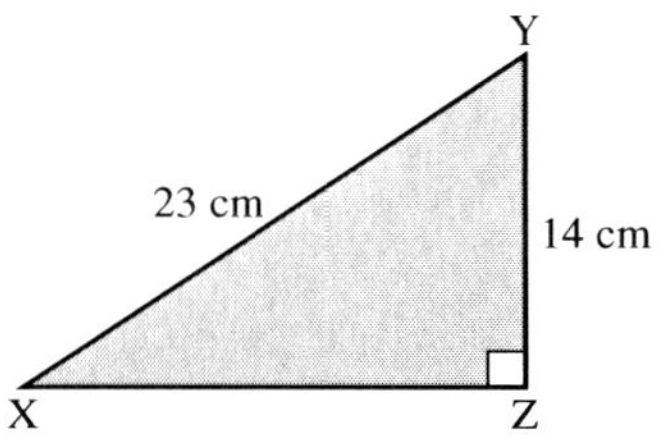

Solution

We need to find X, Y and XZ. We find X first.

$$\sin X = \frac{14}{23}$$

$$X = \sin^{-1}\left(\frac{14}{23}\right) = 37.50^\circ$$

Y may now be found.

$X + Y + Z =$ 180°

$Y =$ 52.50°

Using Pythagoras's theorem we can find XZ.

$(XY)^2 = (XZ)^2 + (YZ)^2$

$(XZ)^2 =$ $(XY)^2 - (YZ)^2 = 333$

$XZ =$ $\sqrt{333} = 18.25$

Exercises

Questions 1–3 refer to △ABC in Figure 1.1.

1 Find A given BC = 13 cm and AB = 19 cm.

2 Find B given BC = 14 cm and AB = 21 cm.

3 Find A given AC = 10 cm and BC = 12 cm.

4 △PQR has a right angle at R, $P = 62°$ and PR = 11 cm. Calculate (a) PQ, (b) QR, (c) Q.

5 △ABC has a right angle at A, $B = 25°$ and AC = 17.2 cm. Solve △ABC.

Solutions to exercises

1 43.17°

2 48.19°

3 50.19°

4 (a) 23.43 cm (b) 20.69 cm (c) 28°

5 AB = 36.89 cm BC = 40.70 cm C = 65°

End of block exercises

Questions 1–3 refer to △ABC in Figure 1.1.

1 Find AB given AC = 3 cm and BC = 6 cm.

2 Find AC given AB = 12.3 cm and BC = 9.6 cm.

3 Find BC given AB = 190 cm and AC = 142 cm.

4 △ABC has a right angle at C, AB = 21 cm and AC = 17 cm. Calculate the length of BC.

5 △XYZ has a right angle at Z, $Y = 47°$ and XY = 17 cm. Calculate (a) XZ, (b) YZ, (c) X.

6 △CDE has a right angle at D, CD = 17 cm and DE = 19 cm. Solve △CDE.

7 $\triangle$KLM has a right angle at M, KL = 14 cm. and KM = 10 cm. Calculate (a) K, (b) L, (c) LM.

8 $\triangle$RST has a right angle at T, $S = 36°$ and ST = 15 cm. Solve $\triangle$RST.

9 $\triangle$UVW has a right angle at V, UV = 15 cm and VW = 6 cm. Solve $\triangle$UVW.

10 $\triangle$CDE has a right angle at E, CE = 19 cm and DE = 14 cm. Calculate (a) CD, (b) C, (c) D.

11 $\triangle$KLM has a right angle at K, $L = 51°$ and ML = 10 cm. Calculate (a) KL, (b) KM, (c) M.

12 $\triangle$XYZ has a right angle at Y, $X = 42°$ and YZ = 13 cm. Calculate (a) XY, (b) XZ, (c) Z.

13 Figure 1.8 illustrates $\triangle$ABC and $\triangle$BDC, where C is a right angle, AC = 17 cm and DC = 6 cm. Given $\angle$BDC = 2θ and $\angle$BAD = θ, find θ.

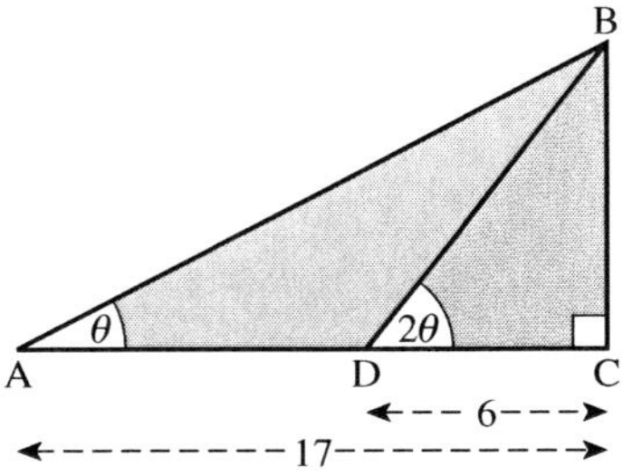

Figure 1.8

14 $\triangle$DEF has a right angle at F, $E = 38°$ and DF = 14 cm. Solve $\triangle$DEF.

15 $\triangle$XYZ has a right angle at Y, XY = 40 cm and YZ = 57 cm. Solve $\triangle$XYZ.

16 $\triangle$ABC has a right angle at C, AB = 30 cm and AC = 2BC. Solve $\triangle$ABC.

Solutions to exercises

1 6.71 cm

2 7.69 cm

3 126.24 cm

4 12.33 cm

5 (a) 12.43 cm (b) 11.59 cm (c) 43°

6 $E = 41.82°$, $C = 48.18°$, CE = 25.50 cm

7 (a) 44.42° (b) 45.58° (c) 9.80

8 $R = 54°$, RT = 10.90 cm, RS = 18.54 cm

9 $W = 68.20°$, $U = 21.80°$, UW = 16.16 cm

10 (a) 23.60 cm (b) 36.38° (c) 53.62°

11 (a) 6.29 cm (b) 7.77 cm (c) 39°

12 (a) 14.44 cm (b) 19.43 cm (c) 48°

13 28.47°

14 EF = 17.92 cm, DE = 22.74 cm, $D = 52°$

15 $X = 54.94°$, $Z = 35.06°$, XZ = 69.63 cm

16 $A = 26.57°$, $B = 63.43°$, BC = 13.42 cm, AC = 26.83 cm

BLOCK 2

Solving triangles using the sine rule

2.1 Introduction

Recall that by solving a triangle we mean calculating all the unknown angles and sides. In Block 1 we solved right-angled triangles. In this block and the next we solve triangles where there is no right angle. This is done by using either the sine rule or the cosine rule. This block focuses on the sine rule.

2.2 The sine rule

Consider any $\triangle ABC$ as shown in Figure 2.1.

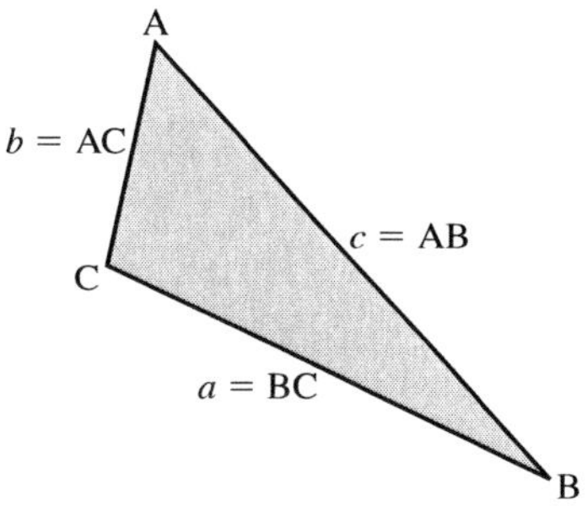

Figure 2.1
a = BC, b = AC, c = AB.

We have used the convention that the side opposite A is labelled a, and so on. The sine rule states:

Key point

$$\frac{a}{\sin A} = \frac{b}{\sin B} = \frac{c}{\sin C}$$

The rule can be used to solve a triangle when we are given either (a) one side and two angles or (b) two sides and one angle that is not included by the given sides. The two cases are illustrated by the following examples.

Example 2.1
Solve $\triangle$ABC given $A = 46°$, $B = 32°$ and $BC = 13$ cm.

Solution
We are given two angles and a side and so the triangle can be solved using the sine rule. We have $A = 46°$, $B = 32°$ and $a =$ BC $= 13$ cm, and need to find C, AB and AC.
First we calculate C.

$$\begin{aligned} A + B + C &= 180° \\ C &= 180° - A - B \\ &= 180° - 46° - 32° \\ &= 102° \end{aligned}$$

We now apply the sine rule.

$$\frac{a}{\sin A} = \frac{b}{\sin B} = \frac{c}{\sin C}$$

$$\frac{13}{\sin 46°} = \frac{b}{\sin 32°} = \frac{c}{\sin 102°}$$

so

$$b = \frac{13 \sin 32°}{\sin 46°} \quad \text{and} \quad c = \frac{13 \sin 102°}{\sin 46°}$$

that is

$$b = 9.58 \text{ and } c = 17.68$$

Hence $C = 102°$, $b =$ AC $= 9.58$ cm, $c =$ AB $= 17.68$ cm.

It is worth noting that the largest angle is always opposite the longest side, and the smallest angle is opposite the shortest side.

Example 2.2
In $\triangle$ABC, $A = 21°$, AC $= 17$ cm and BC $= 14$ cm. Solve $\triangle$ABC.

Solution
Figure 2.2 illustrates the situation.

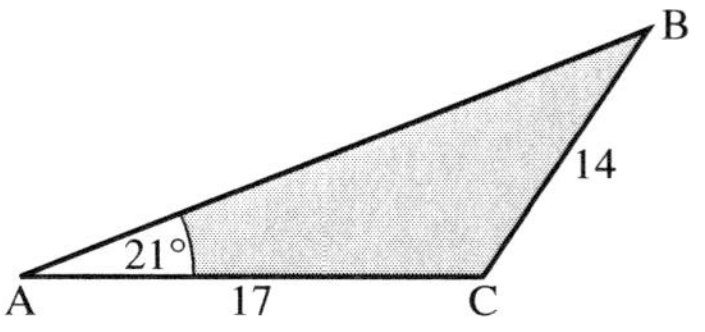

Figure 2.2
Two sides and a non-included angle are known.

We know $A = 21°$, $a = \text{BC} = 14$ and $b = \text{AC} = 17$. Since two sides and a non-included angle are given the sine rule can be applied. We need to calculate B, C and AB. The sine rule states

$$\frac{a}{\sin A} = \frac{b}{\sin B} = \frac{c}{\sin C}$$

so

$$\frac{14}{\sin 21°} = \frac{17}{\sin B} = \frac{c}{\sin C}$$

Hence

$$\sin B = \frac{17 \sin 21°}{14} = 0.4352$$

So

$$\begin{aligned} B &= \sin^{-1}(0.4352) \\ &= 25.80° \text{ and } 154.20° \end{aligned}$$

Note that there are two possible solutions for B. Both are acceptable.

Case 1: $B = 25.80°$

We calculate C.

$$\begin{aligned} C &= 180° - A - B \\ &= 133.2° \end{aligned}$$

Applying the sine rule gives

$$\frac{a}{\sin A} = \frac{b}{\sin B} = \frac{c}{\sin C}$$

$$\frac{14}{\sin 21°} = \frac{17}{\sin 25.8°} = \frac{c}{\sin 133.2°}$$

So

$$c = \frac{17 \sin 133.2°}{\sin 25.8°} = 28.47$$

Solution 1 is $B = 25.8°$, $C = 133.2°$, $c = \text{AB} = 28.47$ cm.

Case 2: $B = 154.20°$

Here $C = 180° - A - B = 4.80°$.
Applying the sine rule gives

$$\frac{a}{\sin A} = \frac{b}{\sin B} = \frac{c}{\sin C}$$

and so

$$\frac{14}{\sin 21°} = \frac{17}{\sin 154.20°} = \frac{c}{\sin 4.8°}$$

Hence

$$c = \qquad \frac{17 \sin 4.8^\circ}{\sin 154.20^\circ} = 3.27$$

Solution 2 is $B = 154.20^\circ$, $C = 4.80^\circ$, $c = \text{AB} = 3.27$ cm.

Example 2.3

In $\triangle$ABC, $C = 42^\circ$, AB $= 15$ cm and AC $= 11$ cm. Solve $\triangle$ABC.

Solution

We are given two sides and a non-included angle and so the sine rule can be applied. We have $C = 42^\circ$, $b = \text{AC} = 11$ and $c = \text{AB} = 15$. We need to calculate A, B and BC. Using the sine rule,

$$\frac{a}{\sin A} = \frac{b}{\sin B} = \frac{c}{\sin C}$$

and so

$$\frac{a}{\sin A} = \frac{11}{\sin B} = \frac{15}{\sin 42^\circ}$$

Hence

$$\begin{aligned} \sin B &= \frac{11 \sin 42^\circ}{15} \\ &= 0.4907 \\ B &= \sin^{-1}(0.4907) \\ &= 29.39^\circ \text{ and } 150.61^\circ \end{aligned}$$

The solution $B = 150.61^\circ$ is rejected because we are given $C = 42^\circ$ and the sum of the angles in a triangle must equal 180°. We now calculate A.

$$\begin{aligned} A &= 180^\circ - B - C \\ &= 108.61^\circ \end{aligned}$$

Finally

$$\begin{aligned} a &= \frac{15 \sin A}{\sin 42^\circ} \\ &= \frac{15 \sin 108.61^\circ}{\sin 42^\circ} \\ &= 21.25 \end{aligned}$$

Thus we have $A = 108.61^\circ$, $B = 29.39^\circ$, $a = \text{BC} = 21.25$ cm.

Example 2.4

Solve $\triangle$XYZ given $X = 63^\circ$, $Z = 42^\circ$ and YZ $= 11.3$ cm.

Solution

We are given two angles and a side, so the sine rule can be applied. We have $X = 63^\circ$, $Z = 42^\circ$ and $x = \text{YZ} = 11.3$. We need to calculate Y, XZ $= y$ and XY $= z$. First we calculate Y.

$$Y = \qquad 75^\circ$$

The sine rule states

$$\frac{x}{\sin X} = \frac{y}{\sin Y} = \frac{z}{\sin Z}$$

and so

$$\frac{11.3}{\sin 63^\circ} = \frac{y}{\sin 75^\circ} = \frac{z}{\sin 42^\circ}$$

Hence

$$y = \frac{11.3 \sin 75^\circ}{\sin 63^\circ} = 12.25$$

$$z = \frac{11.3 \sin 42^\circ}{\sin 63^\circ} = 8.49$$

Example 2.5

Solve △ABC given $C = 40^\circ$, $b = 23$ cm and $c = 19$ cm.

Solution

We are given two sides and a non-included angle and so the sine rule can be applied. We know $C = 40^\circ$, AB $= c = 19$ and AC $= b = 23$. We need to calculate A, B and a. Using the sine rule

$$\frac{a}{\sin A} = \frac{b}{\sin B} = \frac{c}{\sin C}$$

we have

$$\frac{a}{\sin A} = \frac{23}{\sin B} = \frac{19}{\sin 40^\circ}$$

Hence

$$\sin B = \frac{23 \sin 40^\circ}{19} = 0.7781$$

$$B = 51.09^\circ \text{ or } 128.91^\circ$$

Both solutions are acceptable.

Case 1: $B = 51.09^\circ$

Then $A = 180^\circ - 40^\circ - 51.09^\circ = 88.91^\circ$

and from the sine rule

$$a = \frac{19 \sin 88.91^\circ}{\sin 40^\circ} = 29.55$$

Solution 1 is: $A = 88.91^\circ$, $B = 51.09^\circ$, BC $= 29.55$ cm.

Case 2: $B = 128.91°$

Then

$A = 180° - 40° - 128.91° = 11.09°$

and

$$a = \frac{19 \sin 11.09°}{\sin 40°} = 5.69$$

Solution 1 is $A = 11.09°$, $B = 128.91°$, BC = 5.69 cm.

End of block exercises

For questions 1–10 solve △ABC given

1 $A = 36°$, $B = 79°$, AC = 11.63 cm

2 AB = 15 cm, AC = 23 cm, $B = 57°$

3 AB = 10 cm, BC = 6 cm, $A = 32°$

4 $B = 21°$, $C = 46°$, AB = 9 cm

5 $B = 18°$, $C = 110°$, BC = 12.3 cm

6 AC = 29 cm, BC = 19 cm, $B = 49°$

7 $A = 37°$, $B = 47°$, AB = 17 cm

8 BC = 14 cm, AB = 20 cm, $C = 50°$

9 AB = 27 cm, AC = 36 cm, $B = 17°$

10 $B = 42°$, $C = 93°$, BC = 13 cm

Solutions to exercises

1 $C = 65°$, BC = 6.96 cm, AB = 10.74 cm

2 $C = 33.16°$, $A = 89.84°$, BC = 27.42 cm

3 solution 1: $C = 62.03°$, $B = 85.97°$, AC = 11.29 cm; solution 2: $C = 117.97°$, $B = 30.03°$, AC = 5.67 cm

4 $A = 113°$, BC = 11.52 cm, AC = 4.48 cm

5 $A = 52°$, AC = 4.82 cm, AB = 14.67 cm

6 $A = 29.63°$, $C = 101.37°$, AB = 37.67 cm

7 $C = 96°$, AC = 12.50 cm, BC = 10.29 cm

8 $A = 32.43°$, $B = 97.57°$, AC = 25.88 cm

9 $A = 150.33°$, $C = 12.67°$, BC = 60.95 cm

10 $A = 45°$, AC = 12.30 cm, AB = 18.36 cm

BLOCK 3

Solving triangles using the cosine rule

3.1 Introduction

The cosine rule, like the sine rule, can be applied to any triangle. It is used to solve a triangle when we are given either (a) three sides or (b) two sides and the included angle.

3.2 The cosine rule

Key point

For any $\triangle$ABC the cosine rule states

$$a^2 = b^2 + c^2 - 2bc\cos A$$
$$b^2 = a^2 + c^2 - 2ac\cos B$$
$$c^2 = a^2 + b^2 - 2ab\cos C$$

Example 3.1

In $\triangle$ABC, AB = 17.3 cm, BC = 23.9 cm and $B = 71°$. Solve $\triangle$ABC.

Solution

Figure 3.1 illustrates the given information.

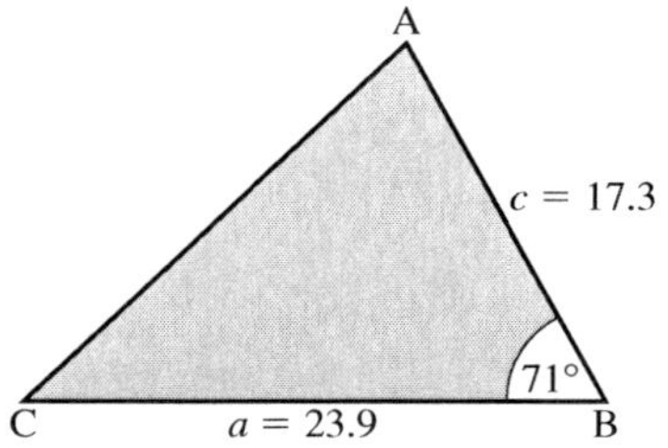

Figure 3.1 Given two sides and the included angle, the cosine rule can be applied.

We are given two sides and the included angle and so the cosine rule can be used. We have a = BC = 23.9, c = AB = 17.3 and $B = 71°$. We need to find A, C and AC: that is, b. We find b first using the cosine rule.

$$\begin{aligned} b^2 &= a^2 + c^2 - 2ac\cos B \\ &= 23.9^2 + 17.3^2 - 2(23.9)(17.3)\cos 71° \\ &= 601.27 \\ b &= 24.52 \end{aligned}$$

We now find A. We can use either the sine rule or the cosine rule to find A. Using the sine rule,

$$\frac{a}{\sin A} = \frac{b}{\sin B}$$

that is

$$\frac{23.9}{\sin A} = \frac{24.52}{\sin 71^\circ}$$
$$\sin A = \frac{23.9 \sin 71^\circ}{24.52}$$
$$= 0.9216$$
$$A = 67.16^\circ \quad \text{or} \quad 112.84^\circ$$

The solution $A = 112.84^\circ$ is rejected because we already have $B = 71^\circ$ and the sum of the angles of a triangle must be 180°. Finally

$$C = 180^\circ - A - B$$
$$= 41.84^\circ$$

Hence $A = 67.16^\circ$, $C = 41.84^\circ$, $AC = 24.52$ cm.

Example 3.2

Solve $\triangle$XYZ given XY = 18.4 cm, YZ = 19.6 cm and XZ = 29.3 cm.

Solution

Figure 3.2 illustrates the situation.

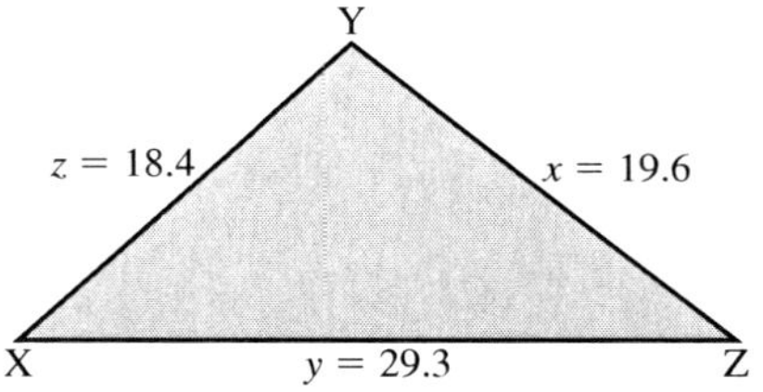

Figure 3.2 Three sides of the triangle are known and so the cosine rule can be applied.

We are given three sides and so the cosine rule can be applied. We have x = YZ = 19.6, y = XZ = 29.3 and z = XY = 18.4. Using the cosine rule we find X.

$$x^2 = y^2 + z^2 - 2yz \cos X$$

$$19.6^2 = 29.3^2 + 18.4^2 - 2(29.3)(18.4) \cos X$$

$$\cos X = \frac{29.3^2 + 18.4^2 - 19.6^2}{2(29.3)(18.4)} = 0.7539$$

$$X = 41.07^\circ$$

Now we find Y.

$$y^2 = x^2 + z^2 - 2xz \cos Y$$

$$29.3^2 = 19.6^2 + 18.4^2 - 2(19.6)(18.4) \cos Y$$

$\cos Y =$

$$\frac{19.6^2 + 18.4^2 - 29.3^2}{2(19.6)(18.4)} = -0.1882$$

$Y =$ 100.85°

Finally

$$Z = 180° - X - Y$$
$$= 38.08°$$

Hence $X = 41.07°$, $Y = 100.85°$, $Z = 38.08°$.

Example 3.3

In $\triangle$RST, RS = 85 cm, ST = 104 cm and $S = 105°$. Figure 3.3 illustrates the triangle. Solve $\triangle$RST.

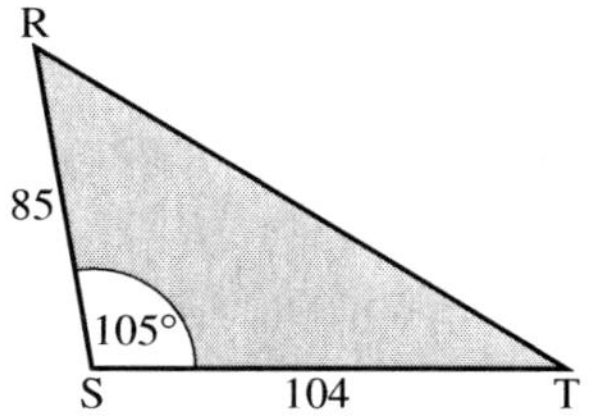

Figure 3.3 When given two sides and the included angle, the cosine rule can be applied.

Solution

We are given two sides and the included angle and so the cosine rule can be applied. We have $t = \text{RS} = 85$, $r = \text{ST} = 104$ and $S = 105°$. We need to calculate R, T and $s = \text{RT}$. First s is found using the cosine rule.

$s^2 = r^2 + t^2 -$ $2rt \cos S$

$= 104^2 + 85^2 -$ $2(104)(85) \cos 105°$

$$= 22616.92$$

$$s = 150.39$$

Using the sine rule, R is found. We have

$$\frac{r}{\sin R} = \frac{s}{\sin S}$$

from which

$$\frac{104}{\sin R} = \frac{150.39}{\sin 105°}$$

$$\sin R = \frac{104 \sin 105°}{150.39} = 0.6680$$

$$R = 41.91°$$

Finally $T = 180° - R - S = 33.09°$.

Hence RT $= 150.39$, $R = 41.91°$, $T = 33.09°$.

Example 3.4

In $\triangle$XYZ, XY $= 40$ cm, YZ $= 57$ cm and XZ $= 81$ cm. The triangle is illustrated in Figure 3.4. Solve $\triangle$XYZ.

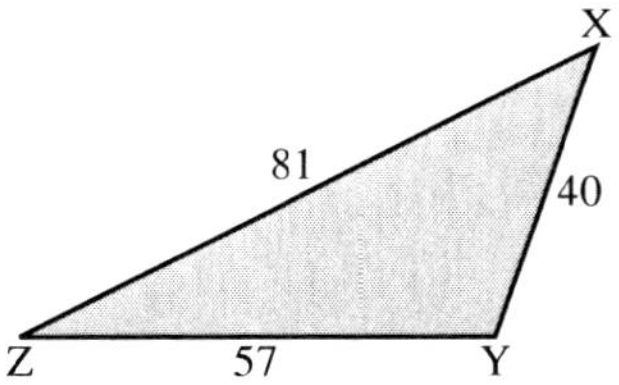

Figure 3.4 When all three sides of a triangle are known, the cosine rule can be applied.

Solution

We are given three sides and so the cosine rule can be applied. We have x = YZ = 57, y = XZ = 81 and z = XY = 40. We need to calculate X, Y and Z. First X is calculated. From the cosine rule we have

$$x^2 = y^2 + z^2 - 2yz \cos X$$

Substituting in the known values of x, y and z, and rearranging for $\cos X$, gives

$$\cos X = \frac{81^2 + 40^2 - 57^2}{2(81)(40)} = 0.7580$$

$$X = 40.71°$$

Now Y is found.

$$y^2 = x^2 + z^2 - 2xz \cos Y$$

Rearranging for cos Y yields

$$\cos Y = \frac{57^2 + 40^2 - 81^2}{2(57)(40)} = -0.3754$$

$$Y = 112.05°$$

Finally $Z = 180° - X - Y = 27.24°$.

Hence $X = 40.71°$, $Y = 112.05°$, $Z = 27.24°$.

End of block exercises

In questions 1–10 solve △ABC given

1. AB = 42 cm, BC = 37 cm, AC = 26 cm
2. AB = 29 cm, BC = 41 cm, $B = 100°$
3. AC = 105 cm, AB = 76 cm, $A = 29°$
4. BC = 36 cm, AC = 92 cm, $C = 51°$
5. AB = 69 cm, BC = 52 cm, AC = 49 cm
6. AB = 32 cm, BC = 30 cm, AC = 41 cm
7. BC = 17 cm, AC = 27 cm, $C = 45°$
8. AB = 36 cm, BC = 36 cm, $B = 60°$
9. AB = 21 cm, AC = 30 cm, $A = 42°$
10. AB = 80 cm, BC = 70 cm, AC = 62 cm

Solutions to exercises

1. $A = 60.63°$, $B = 37.76°$, $C = 81.61°$
2. AC = 54.18 cm, $A = 48.19°$, $C = 31.81°$
3. a = BC = 53.31 cm, $B = 107.28°$, $C = 43.72°$
4. AB = 74.78 cm, $B = 107.03°$, $A = 21.97°$
5. $A = 48.76°$, $B = 45.11°$, $C = 86.13°$
6. $A = 46.54°$, $B = 82.73°$, $C = 50.73°$
7. $A = 38.75°$, $B = 96.25°$, c = AB = 19.21 cm
8. AC = 36 cm, $A = 60°$, $C = 60°$
9. a = BC = 20.12 cm, $B = 93.69°$, $C = 44.31°$
10. $A = 57.40°$, $B = 48.26°$, $C = 74.33°$

BLOCK 4 Surveying

4.1 Introduction

This block considers the application of mathematics to surveying. The three areas covered are (a) units to measure angles, (b) angles of elevation and depression, and (c) bearings. Typical calculations in each area are included.

4.2 Units of angles

We have already introduced the units degree and radian in Chapter 9. Surveyors use the degree. For greater accuracy the degree is subdivided into **minutes** denoted $'$ and **seconds** denoted $''$.

Key point

$$1^\circ = 60 \text{ minutes} = 60'$$

$$1' = 60 \text{ seconds} = 60''$$

The angle 36 degrees 21 minutes and 4 seconds is written as $36^\circ 21' 04''$. Many calculations express angles in decimal format, for example 36.3511°. It is useful to be able to convert from decimal format to degrees/minutes/seconds and vice versa. To retain the accuracy required for surveying, angles in decimal format should be given to 4 decimal places.

Example 4.1

Convert $36^\circ 21' 04''$ to decimal format.

Solution

We note there are 60 minutes in 1 degree and 60 seconds in each minute. Hence there are $60 \times 60 = 3600$ seconds in 1 degree.

To write $36^\circ 21' 04''$ in decimal format we consider the fractional part, that is $21' 04''$, and express this in seconds.

$$\begin{aligned} 21' &= 21 \times 60 \\ &= 1260'' \end{aligned}$$

and so

$$21' 04'' = 1264''$$

We now express 1264″ as a decimal fraction.

$$1264'' = \frac{1264^\circ}{3600} = 0.3511^\circ$$

Hence $21'04'' = 0.3511^\circ$ and so $36^\circ21'04'' = 36.3511^\circ$.

Example 4.2

Convert 42.9614° to degree/minute/second format.

Solution

The fractional part 0.9614° needs to be converted to minutes and seconds. Each degree comprises 60 minutes and so to convert from degrees to minutes we multiply by a factor of 60.

$$\begin{aligned} 0.9614^\circ &= 0.9614 \times 60' \\ &= 57.684' \end{aligned}$$

We now look at the fractional part, 0.684, and convert this to seconds. Each minute comprises 60 seconds and so to convert from minutes to seconds we multiply by 60.

$$\begin{aligned} 0.684' &= 0.684 \times 60'' \\ &= 41.04'' \end{aligned}$$

Hence 42.9614° may be written as $42^\circ57'41''$.

Exercises

1 Express the following angles in degree/minute/second format.
(a) 11.1731° (b) 14.0017° (c) 36.9213°

2 Express the following angles in decimal format.
(a) $12^\circ17'46''$ (b) $32^\circ32'56''$ (c) $1^\circ1'40''$

Solutions to exercises

1 (a) $11^\circ10'23''$ (b) $14^\circ0'6''$ (c) $36^\circ55'17''$

2 (a) 12.2961° (b) 32.5489° (c) 1.0278°

4.3 Angles of elevation and depression

Consider a tower AB and an observer at O, as shown in Figure 4.1.

The angle e is called the **angle of elevation** of the tower from the point O. It is the angle, measured from the horizontal, through which an observer must turn his or her eyes to look at the top of the tower.

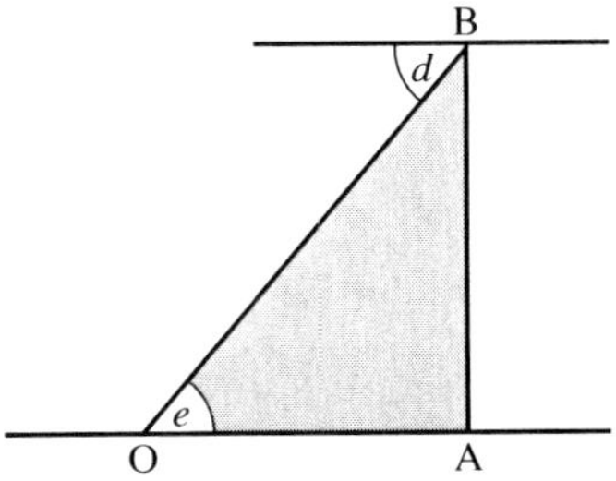

Figure 4.1 The angle of elevation is e and the angle of depression is d.

Now consider an observer at the top of the tower, B. The angle d is called the **angle of depression**. This is the angle, again measured from the horizontal, through which an observer turns his or her eyes to look at a point O. Note that e and d have equal magnitude.

Example 4.3 Civil Engineering – Height of a tower

An observer is 50 m from the base of a vertical tower. The angle of elevation is 11°3′17″. Calculate the height of the tower.

Solution

Figure 4.1 illustrates the situation, with OA = 50 m and $e = 11°3'17''$. First e is expressed in decimal format as 11.0547°. Now consider the right-angled △OAB.

$$\tan e = \tan 11.0547°$$

$$= \frac{AB}{OA} = \frac{AB}{50}$$

$$AB = 50 \tan 11.0547° = 9.77$$

The tower is 9.77 m high.

Example 4.4 Civil Engineering – Angle of Depression

An observer is on top of a vertical tower, AB, 23.7 m high. The angle of depression of a point O is 15°42′18″. Calculate the distance of O from the foot of the tower.

Solution

Figure 4.1 illustrates the problem, with AB = 23.7 m and $d = 15°42'18''$.
First d is expressed in decimal format as

$$15.705°$$

Noting that $e = d$ we consider △OBA.

$$\tan e = \tan 15.705°$$

$$= \frac{AB}{OA} = \frac{23.7}{OA}$$

$$OA = \frac{23.7}{\tan 15.705^\circ} = 84.29$$

The point O is 84.29 m from the foot of the tower.

Example 4.5 Civil Engineering – Finding the height of a tower using three angles of elevation

A, B and C are three points lying in a straight line. The distance AB is known to be x, and the distance BC is known to be y. It is required to find the height, h, of a vertical tower, DE. From A, B and C the angles of elevation to the top of the tower are α, β and γ respectively. Figure 4.2 illustrates the position.

Determine the height, h, in terms of the known quantities, x, y, α, β and γ.

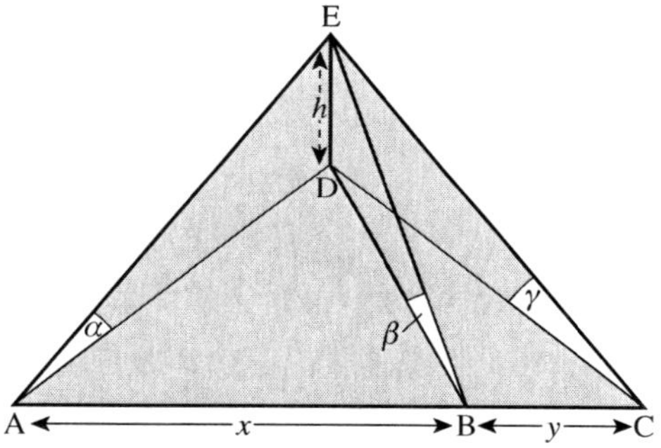

Figure 4.2 The height, h, can be expressed in terms of known distances, x and y, and known angles α, β and γ.

Solution

Consider △ADE. In this triangle, ∠ADE = 90° and so

$$\tan\alpha = \frac{\text{DE}}{\text{AD}} = \frac{h}{\text{AD}}$$

$$\text{AD} = \frac{h}{\tan\alpha} = h\cot\alpha$$

Similarly by considering △BDE and △CDE we see $\text{BD} = h\cot\beta$ and $\text{CD} = h\cot\gamma$. We now consider △ADB and let $\angle\text{DAB} = \phi$. Figure 4.3 illustrates this triangle.

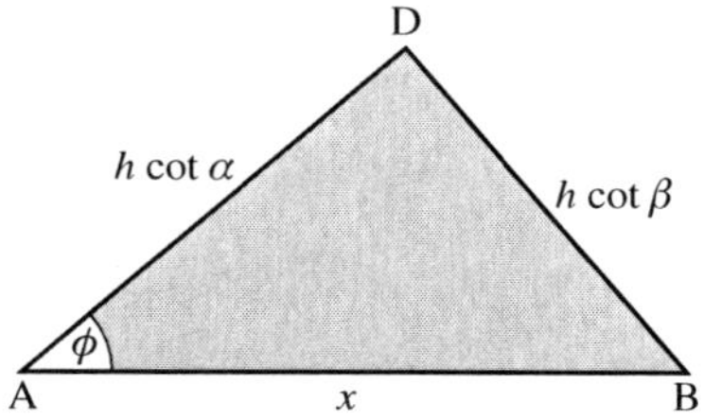

Figure 4.3 The cosine rule is applied to △ADB.

Applying the cosine rule to △ADB gives

$$(h \cot \beta)^2 = (h \cot \alpha)^2 + x^2 - 2xh \cot \alpha(\cos \phi)$$

from which

$$\cos \phi = \frac{(h \cot \alpha)^2 + x^2 - (h \cot \beta)^2}{2xh \cot \alpha} \tag{1}$$

Next we consider △ADC, as illustrated in Figure 4.4.

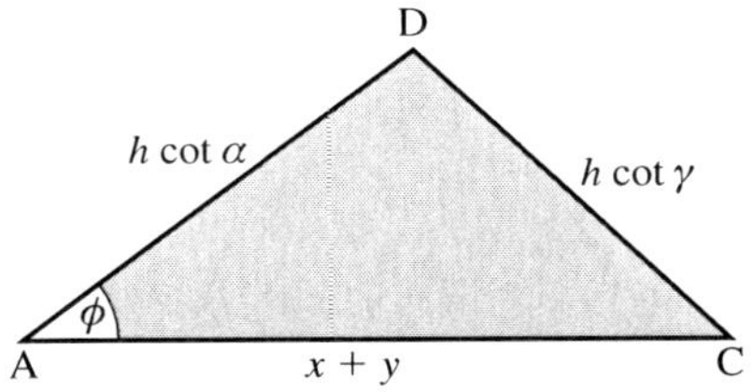

Figure 4.4
The cosine rule is applied to △ADC.

Applying the cosine rule to △ADC gives

$$(h \cot \gamma)^2 = (h \cot \alpha)^2 + (x + y)^2 - 2(x + y)h \cot \alpha (\cos \phi)$$

from which

$$\cos \phi = \frac{(h \cot \alpha)^2 + (x + y)^2 - (h \cot \gamma)^2}{2(x + y)h \cot \alpha} \tag{2}$$

We have two expressions for $\cos \phi$ given by (1) and (2). Equating these yields

$$\frac{(h \cot \alpha)^2 + x^2 - (h \cot \beta)^2}{2xh \cot \alpha} = \frac{(h \cot \alpha)^2 + (x + y)^2 - (h \cot \gamma)^2}{2(x + y)h \cot \alpha}$$

This equation is rearranged to make h the subject.

$$\frac{h^2 \cot^2 \alpha + x^2 - h^2 \cot^2 \beta}{x} = \frac{h^2 \cot^2 \alpha + x^2 + 2xy + y^2 - h^2 \cot^2 \gamma}{x + y}$$

$$(x + y)(h^2 \cot^2 \alpha + x^2 - h^2 \cot^2 \beta) = x\,(h^2 \cot^2 \alpha + x^2 + 2xy + y^2 - h^2 \cot^2 \gamma)$$

$$-xh^2 \cot^2 \beta + yh^2 \cot^2 \alpha - yh^2 \cot^2 \beta = x^2 y + xy^2 - xh^2 \cot^2 \gamma$$

$$h^2\,[x\,(\cot^2 \gamma - \cot^2 \beta) + y\,(\cot^2 \alpha - \cot^2 \beta)] = xy(x + y)$$

$$h^2 = \frac{xy\,(x + y)}{x\,(\cot^2 \gamma - \cot^2 \beta) + y\,(\cot^2 \alpha - \cot^2 \beta)}$$

$$h = \sqrt{\frac{xy\,(x + y)}{x\,(\cot^2 \gamma - \cot^2 \beta) + y\,(\cot^2 \alpha - \cot^2 \beta)}}$$

Example 4.6

A, B and C are points lying on a straight line. The distance from A to B is 40 m, the distance from B to C is 70 m. The angles of elevation to the top of a tower from A, B and C are 21°, 27° and 24° respectively. Calculate the height of the tower.

Solution

We use the notation and result of Example 4.5, that is AB $= x = 40$, BC $= y = 70$, $\alpha = 21°$, $\beta = 27°$, $\gamma = 24°$.
If h is the height of the tower then

$$h = \sqrt{\frac{40(70)(40 + 70)}{40\,(\cot^2 24° - \cot^2 27°) + 70(\cot^2 21° - \cot^2 27°)}}$$
$$= 34.88$$

The tower is 34.88 m high.

Exercises

1 From a point 26.3 m from the foot of a tower the angle of elevation to the top of the tower is 29.27°. Calculate the height of the tower.

2 A tower is 36 m high. Calculate the angle of elevation to the top of the tower from a point 50 m from the base of the tower.

3 The angle of depression to the point O from the top of a tower 17 m high is 12°17′. Calculate the distance of O from the foot of the tower.

Solutions to exercises

1 14.74 m

2 35.75°

3 78.08 m

4.4 Bearings

A bearing is the angle that a line makes with some reference direction, usually north. Bearings are measured clockwise from north. (Note the different conventions: in mathematics clockwise angles are considered negative; in surveying clockwise angles are considered positive.) In Figure 4.5, OA has a bearing of 58°31′, OB has a bearing of 100°17′ and OC has a bearing of 301°49′.

Example 4.7

A ship leaves harbour and sails for 19.1 km on a bearing of 47°17′. It then changes direction and travels for 12 km on a bearing of 100°25′. Calculate the distance from the harbour to the ship.

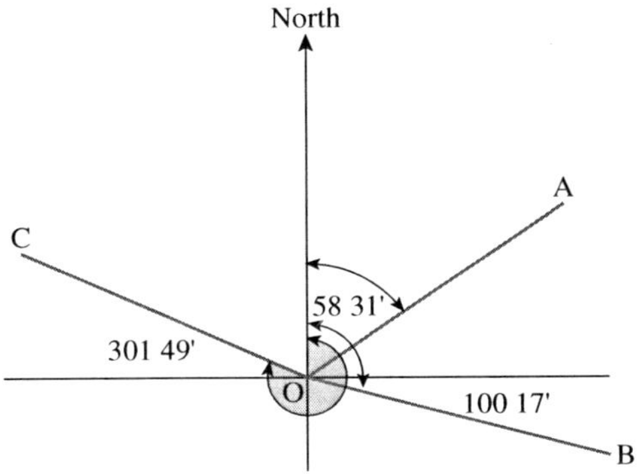

Figure 4.5
Bearings are measured clockwise from north.

Solution
Figure 4.6 illustrates the ship's movement, starting from the harbour at O.

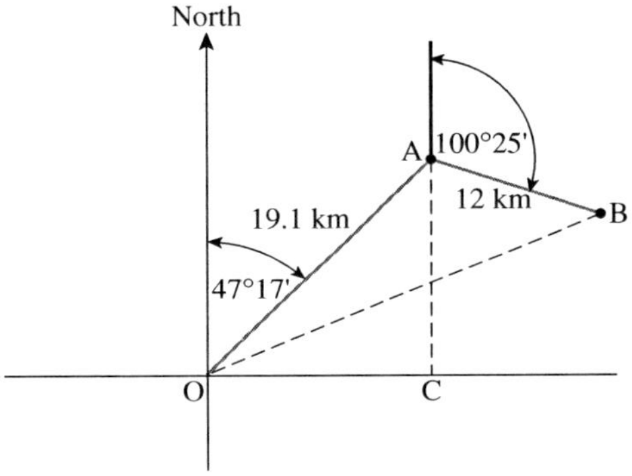

Figure 4.6
The ship moves from the harbour at O to A and then B.

The ship travels 19.1 km on a bearing of $47°17'$. This is represented by OA. It then travels 12 km on a bearing of $100°25'$: this is represented by AB. The final position of the ship is B. We seek the distance OB.

Clearly OA $= 19.1$ and AB $= 12.0$. Consider $\triangle OAC$.

$$\begin{aligned}\angle AOC &= 90° - 47°17' \\ &= 42°43' \\ \angle OAC &= 90° - \angle AOC \\ &= 90° - 42°43' \\ &= 47°17'\end{aligned}$$

Now

$$\begin{aligned}\angle BAC &= 180° - 100°25' \\ &= 79°35'\end{aligned}$$

Hence

$$\begin{aligned}\angle OAB &= \angle OAC + \angle BAC \\ &= 47°17' + 79°35' \\ &= 126°52' \\ &= 126.8667°\end{aligned}$$

We now apply the cosine rule to ΔOAB.

$$\begin{aligned} OB^2 &= OA^2 + AB^2 - 2(OA)(AB)\cos 126.8667^\circ \\ &= (19.1)^2 + 12^2 - 2(19.1)(12)\cos 126.8667^\circ \\ &= 783.83 \\ OB &= 28.00 \end{aligned}$$

The ship is 28 km from the harbour.

Example 4.8

A ship travels 17.1 km on a bearing of 120°35′. It then travels 24 km on a bearing of 275°20′.

(a) Find the distance of the ship from its starting position.

(b) Find the bearing the ship must take so that it can travel in a straight line back to its starting position.

Solution

Figure 4.7 illustrates the movement of the ship, starting at O. The final position of the ship is B.

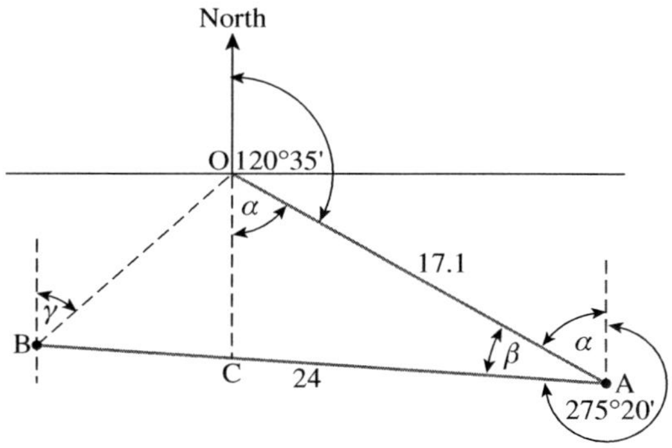

Figure 4.7 The ship travels on a bearing of 120°35′ to A, and then on a bearing of 275°20′ to B.

(a) We need to find the distance OB. The angles α and β are determined, and then the cosine rule is applied to △OAB.

$\alpha =$ ______ $180^\circ - 120^\circ 35' = 59^\circ 25'$

$$\begin{aligned} \beta &= 360^\circ - 275^\circ 20' - \alpha \\ &= 360^\circ - 275^\circ 20' - 59^\circ 25' \\ &= 25^\circ 15' \end{aligned}$$

The cosine rule is applied to △OAB.

$(OB)^2 =$ ______ 126.0332

$OB = 11.23$

The ship is 11.23 km from its starting position.

(b) The bearing that the ship must take to return to its starting point is γ. We note that

$\angle BOC = \gamma$ and $\angle BOA =$ $\alpha + \gamma$

The sine rule is applied to $\triangle OAB$.

$$\frac{24}{\sin BOA} = \frac{11.23}{\sin BAO}$$

$$\frac{24}{\sin(\alpha + \gamma)} = \frac{11.23}{\sin 25°15'}$$

$$\sin(\alpha + \gamma) = \frac{24 \sin 25°15'}{11.23} = 0.91163$$

$$\alpha + \gamma = 65.732° = 65°44'$$

$$\begin{aligned} \gamma &= 65°44' - \alpha \\ &= 65°44' - 59°25' \\ &= 6°19' \end{aligned}$$

The required bearing is 6°19′.

Exercises

1 A ship travels for 10 km on a bearing of 30°. It then follows a bearing of 60° for 20 km. Calculate the distance of the ship from the starting position.

2 An aeroplane flies 150 miles on a bearing of 105° and then 107 miles on a bearing of 217°. Find the bearing that the aeroplane must take to fly directly back to the starting position.

3 A ship travels 50 km from O on a bearing of 290° to get to position A. From A it heads directly to B. Position B is 90 km from O on a bearing of 190°.
(a) Calculate the distance AB.
(b) Calculate the bearing the ship must follow from A to arrive directly at B.

Solutions to exercises

1 29.09 km

2 327.07°

3 (a) 110.29 km (b) 163.48°

End of block exercises

1 Convert the following angles to degree/minute/second format:
(a) 39.4613° (b) 101.0913° (c) 1.0036°

2 Convert the following angles to decimal format:
(a) 21°31′46″ (b) 19°49′17″ (c) 1°1′1″

3 The angle of elevation to the top of an aerial is 21°31′2″ when measured from a point 41.6 m from the base of the aerial. Calculate the height of the aerial.

4 The angle of elevation to the top of a tower is 23°0′17″ when measured from a point 51.5 m from the base of the tower. Calculate the height of the tower.

5 A vertical tower AB is situated on a ramp, as shown in Figure 4.8.

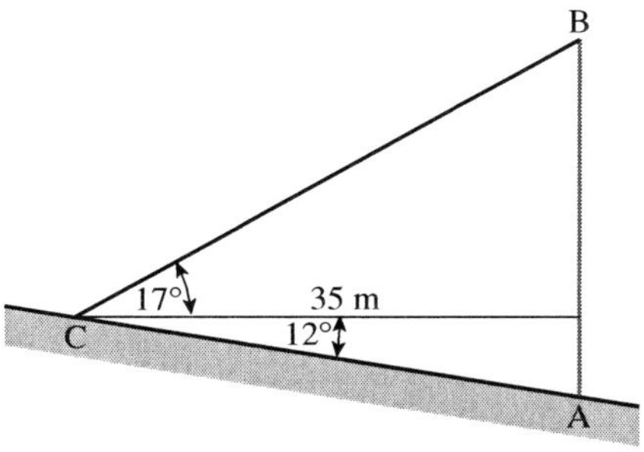

Figure 4.8

From C, the angle of elevation to the top of the tower is 17°; the angle of depression to the foot of the tower is 12°. Given that C is 35 m from the tower, calculate the height of the tower.

6 A ship travels for 9.3 km on a bearing of 36°19′. It then changes its bearing to 100°00′ and travels for 12.2 km.
(a) Find the distance of the ship from its starting point.
(b) Calculate the bearing the ship must take to go directly back to its starting point.

7 The angle of elevation to the top of a tower is 19°30′ ± 15′ when measured from a point 27.00 ± 0.5 m from the base of the tower. Calculate the maximum and minimum possible heights of the tower.

8 A tower AB leans, being 3° from the vertical position. From C the angle of elevation to the top of the tower is 42°. C is 17 m from the base of the tower. Figure 4.9 illustrates the problem.

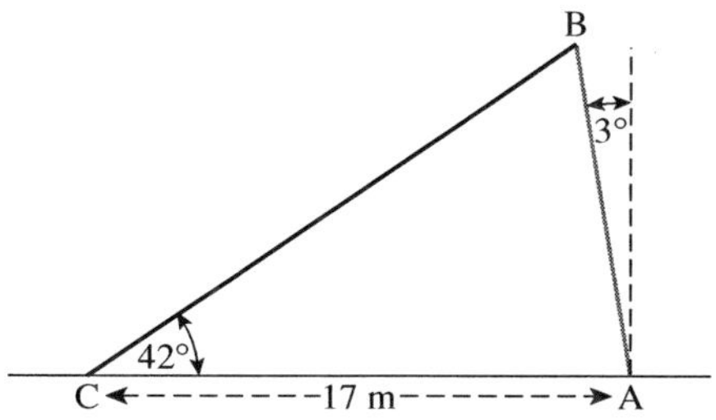

Figure 4.9

Calculate
(a) the length of the tower AB
(b) the height of B above the horizontal AC.

9 A ship starts at O and travels for 10 km on a bearing of 42°10′ to arrive at A. From O point B has a bearing of 90° (i.e. due east of O) and is distant 21 km from O. Calculate the bearing the ship must take from A so as to travel directly to B.

Solutions to exercises

1 (a) 39°27′41″ (b) 101°5′29″ (c) 1°0′13″

2 (a) 21.5294° (b) 19.8214° (c) 1.0169°

3 16.40 m

4 21.87 m

5 18.14 m

6 (a) 18.33 km (b) 252°57′12″

7 Minimum height is 9.25 m, maximum height is 9.87 m.

8 (a) 14.64 m (b) 14.62 m

9 117°25′11″

BLOCK 5 Resolution and resultant of forces

5.1 Introduction

Many engineering problems involve calculations involving forces. To specify a force both its magnitude and its direction must be known. The unit of force is the **newton**, N. For example, a force may be described as 10 N acting at 40° to the horizontal. This force is illustrated in Figure 5.1.

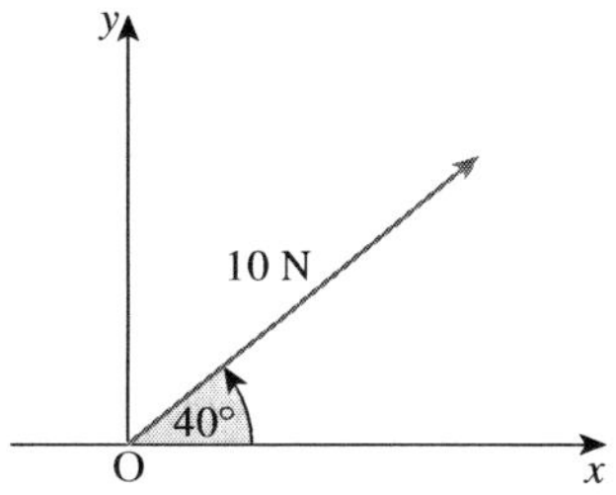

Figure 5.1 A force has magnitude and direction.

The length of the line represents the magnitude of the force and the direction of the line shows the direction of the force.

5.2 Resolution of a force

A single force may be replaced by two forces acting at right angles to each other. Together these forces are equivalent to the original single force. The process of replacing a single force by two perpendicular forces is called **resolution**. The single force is said to have been **resolved** into two forces at right angles to one another. The following example shows how to resolve a force.

Example 5.1
Resolve the force shown in Figure 5.1 into a horizontal and vertical force.

Solution
Figure 5.2 illustrates the resolution of the 10 N force.

Consider the magnitude of the horizontal component. $\triangle$OAB contains the relevant information, with OB representing the horizontal force. Then

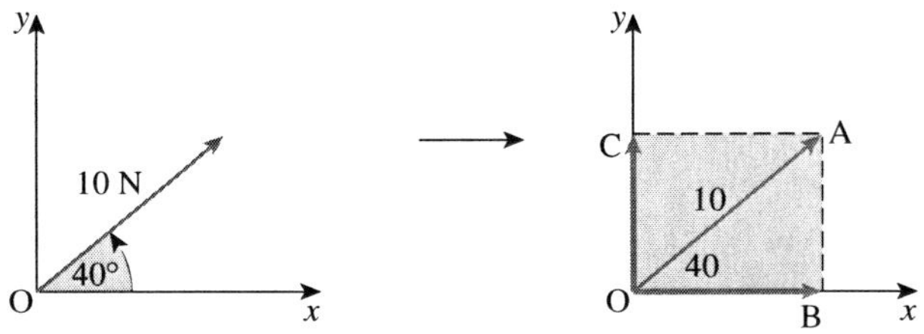

Figure 5.2
A force may be resolved into two perpendicular forces.

$$\cos 40^\circ = \frac{OB}{OA}$$
$$= \frac{OB}{10}$$
$$OB = 10 \cos 40^\circ$$
$$= 7.66$$

The horizontal force is 7.66 N.

Similarly the vertical force may be calculated using $\triangle$OCA. OC represents the vertical force. Then

$$\angle COA = 90^\circ - 40^\circ$$
$$= 50^\circ$$
$$\cos 50^\circ = \frac{OC}{OA}$$
$$= \frac{OC}{10}$$
$$OC = 10 \cos 50^\circ$$
$$= 6.43$$

The vertical force is 6.43 N. It is useful to note that the vertical force can also be found by calculating AB in $\triangle$OAB. In this triangle

$$\sin 40^\circ = \frac{AB}{OA}$$
$$= \frac{AB}{10}$$
$$AB = 10 \sin 40^\circ$$
$$= 6.43$$

The vertical force is 6.43 N.

Hence the 10 N force in Figure 5.1 may be resolved into a 7.66 N force acting horizontally and a 6.43 N force acting vertically.

Example 5.2

A force of 17 N acts at 35° to the negative x axis as shown in Figure 5.3. Resolve the force into two forces, one in the x direction and one in the y direction.

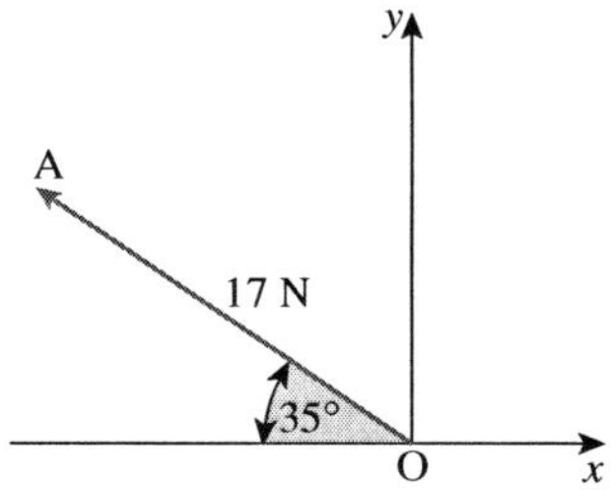

Figure 5.3 A force of 17 N acts at 35° to the negative x axis.

Solution

The horizontal force is represented by OB as shown in Figure 5.4.

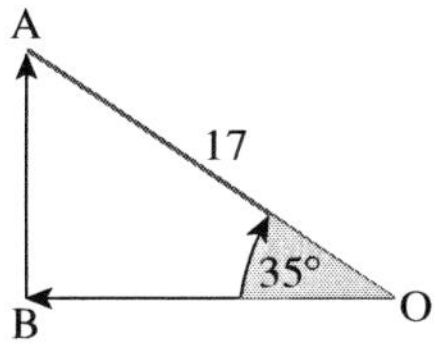

Figure 5.4 The horizontal force is represented by OB; the vertical force is represented by BA.

From △OBA

$$\cos 35^\circ = \frac{OB}{OA} = \frac{OB}{17}$$

$$OB = 17\cos 35^\circ = 13.93$$

The vertical force is represented by BA. From △OBA

$$\sin 35^\circ = \frac{AB}{OA} = \frac{AB}{17}$$

$$AB = 17\sin 35^\circ = 9.75$$

The 17 N force is equivalent to 13.93 N acting in the negative x direction and 9.75 N acting in the y direction.

Example 5.2 illustrates the general result:

Key point

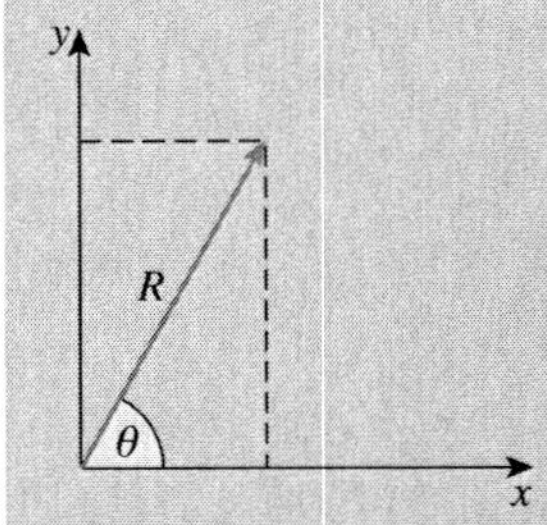

Figure 5.5

The horizontal component $= R\cos\theta$

The vertical component $= R\sin\theta$

Exercises

1 A 23 N force acts at 71° to the horizontal axis. Resolve the force into forces acting horizontally and vertically.

2 A 40 N force acts at 54° to the horizontal. Resolve the force into horizontal and vertical forces.

3 A 12 N force acts at 43° to the vertical. Resolve the force into horizontal and vertical forces.

Solutions to exercises

1 7.49 N horizontally, 21.75 N vertically

2 23.51 N horizontally, 32.36 N vertically

3 8.18 N horizontally, 8.78 N vertically

5.3 Resolving on an inclined plane

Figure 5.6 illustrates a plane inclined at angle θ to the horizontal. Resting on the plane at O is a body of mass m kg. The body experiences a vertical force mg N due to its weight, as illustrated. Here, g is a constant called the acceleration due to gravity. It is often required to resolve this force into forces that are parallel and perpendicular to the plane.

Figure 5.7 shows the force resolved into forces OA down the plane, and OB perpendicular to the plane. Note that $\angle$AOC has been labelled α and $\alpha = 90° - \theta$. Side OC is the hypotenuse of the right-angled triangle OAC. Furthermore,

$$\sin\alpha = \cos\theta \quad \text{and} \quad \cos\alpha = \sin\theta$$

Figure 5.6

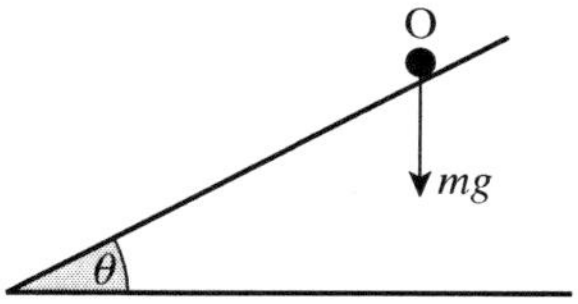

Figure 5.7

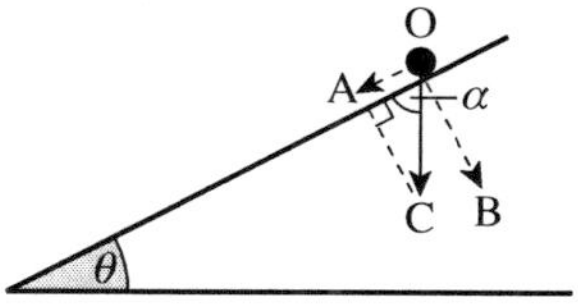

In $\triangle$AOC

$$\cos \alpha = \frac{OA}{OC}$$

so

$$OA = OC \cos \alpha$$
$$= OC \sin \theta$$

Also

$$\sin \alpha = \frac{AC}{OC}$$

so

$$AC = OC \sin \alpha$$
$$= OC \cos \theta$$

Note also that

$$OB = AC = OC \cos \theta$$

So the component parallel to the plane is

$$OA = OC \sin \theta$$
$$= mg \sin \theta$$

The component perpendicular to the plane is

$$OB = OC \cos \theta$$
$$= mg \cos \theta$$

Note the limiting case. If $\theta = 0°$ then the plane is horizontal and intuitively there is no component parallel to the plane. Evaluating the component parallel to the plane, $mg \sin \theta$ with $\theta = 0°$ agrees with the intuitive result.

Key point

For a vertical force mg N and a plane inclined at $\theta°$ to the horizontal:

- Component parallel to plane $= mg \sin \theta$
- Component perpendicular to plane $= mg \cos \theta$

Example 5.3

A body of mass 6 kg rests on a plane inclined at 15° to the horizontal. Find the component of the weight (a) perpendicular to the plane, (b) parallel to the plane.

Solution

Here $m = 6$ and $\theta = 15°$.

(a) The force perpendicular to the plane is

$$mg\cos\theta = 6g\cos 15° = 5.7956g \text{ N}$$

(b) The force parallel to the plane is

$$mg\sin\theta = 6g\sin 15° = 1.5529g \text{ N}$$

Exercises

1 A body of mass 10 kg rests on a plane inclined at 20° to the horizontal. Calculate the component of the weight
(a) perpendicular to the plane
(b) parallel to the plane.

2 A body of mass 1 kg rests on an inclined plane. The force perpendicular to the plane is 0.9g N. Calculate the angle of the inclined plane.

Solutions to exercises

1 (a) $9.3969g$ N (b) $3.420g$ N

2 25.84°

5.4 Resultant of a force

In Section 5.2 we saw how a single force can be resolved: that is, expressed as two forces acting at right angles to one another. We now examine a related problem, that of replacing two or more forces acting at a point by a single equivalent force. A single force that is equivalent to two or more forces is called the **resultant**.

Example 5.4 Mechanical Engineering – Forces in a line

A force of 6 N acts in the positive x direction and a force of 2 N acts in the negative x direction. Calculate the resultant.

Solution

The resultant force is $6 - 2 = 4$ N acting in the x direction. Figure 5.8 illustrates this.

Figure 5.8 The resultant is 4N acting in the x direction.

Example 5.5 Mechanical Engineering – Forces in a plane

A force of 7 N acts in the x direction and a force of 10 N acts in the negative y direction. Find the resultant force.

Solution

The forces are illustrated in Figure 5.9. The 7 N force is represented by OA; the 10 N force is represented by OC. Let the resultant force be R. The magnitude and direction of R must be found. $\triangle$OAB contains the relevant information. Note that AB = 10. Let $\angle$AOB = α. Using $\triangle$OAB

$$\tan\alpha = \frac{\text{AB}}{\text{OA}} = \frac{10}{7}$$

$$\alpha = \tan^{-1}\left(\tfrac{10}{7}\right) = 55.0°$$

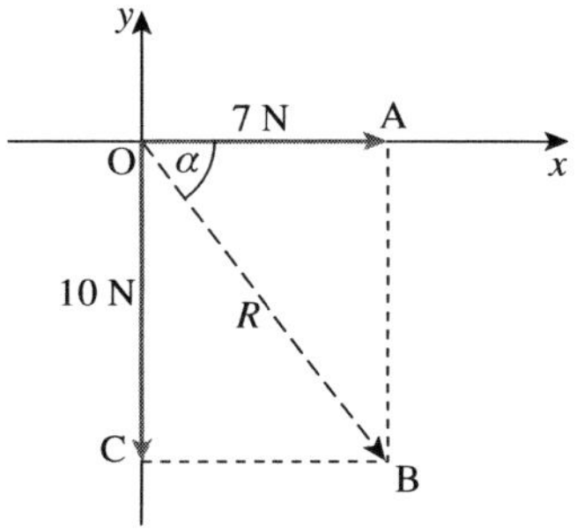

Figure 5.9 R is the resultant of the 10 N force and the 7 N force.

Using Pythagoras's theorem,

$$\begin{aligned} \text{OB}^2 &= \text{OA}^2 + \text{AB}^2 \\ R^2 &= 7^2 + 10^2 \\ &= 149 \\ R &= \sqrt{149} \\ &= 12.21 \end{aligned}$$

The resultant is 12.21 N acting at 55° below the x axis.

Example 5.6 Mechanical Engineering – Several forces acting at a point

Figure 5.10 illustrates three forces acting at the origin O.

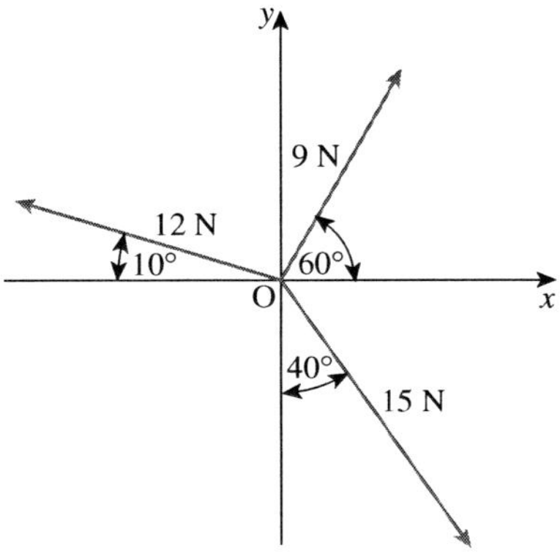

Figure 5.10 Three forces acting at the origin.

By resolving each force find the resultant.

Solution

Each force is resolved into forces in the x and y directions.

The 9 N force is resolved into ____ N acting in the x direction and ____ N acting in the y direction. — $9 \cos 60°$, $9 \sin 60°$

The 12 N force is resolved into ____ N in the negative x direction and ____ N in the y direction. — $12 \cos 10°$, $12 \sin 10°$

The 15 N force is resolved into ____ N in the x direction and ____ N in the negative y direction. — $15 \sin 40°$, $15 \cos 40°$

The net total force acting in the x direction is then

$$9 \cos 60° - 12 \cos 10° + 15 \sin 40° = 2.3241 \text{ N}$$

The net total force acting in the y direction is

$$9 \sin 60° + 12 \sin 10° - 15 \cos 40° = -1.6127 \text{ N}$$

The resultant, R, may now be found. Figure 5.11 illustrates the situation. From Figure 5.11

$\tan \theta =$ ____

$$\frac{1.6127}{2.3241}$$

$\theta =$ ____

$$34.76°$$

The magnitude of the resultant is found using Pythagoras's theorem.

$R^2 =$ ____

$$(2.3241)^2 + (1.6127)^2$$

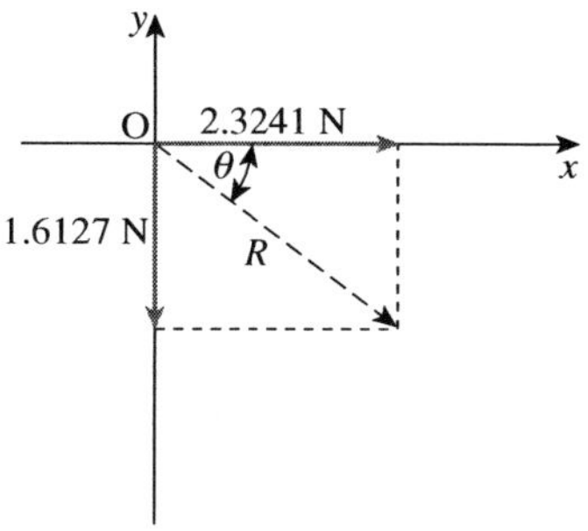

Figure 5.11 The resultant, R, is found using the net forces in the x and y directions.

$R =$ 2.83

The resultant is 2.83 N acting 34.76° below the x axis.

Example 5.7 Mechanical Engineering – Several forces acting at a point

Figure 5.12 shows three forces acting at the origin O. Calculate the resultant.

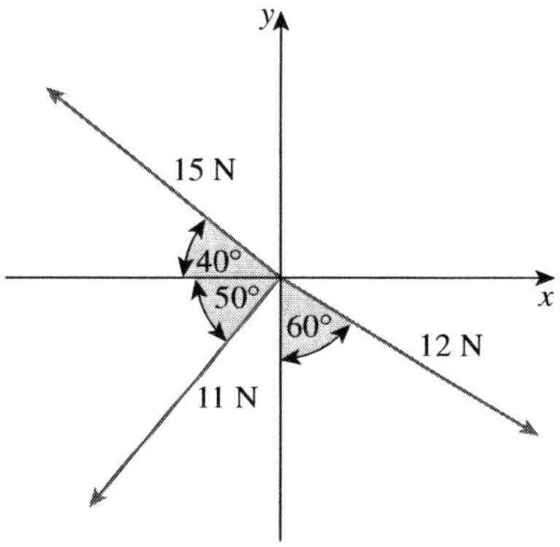

Figure 5.12 The resultant of several forces may be found.

Solution

Each force is resolved into forces along the x and y axes.

The 12 N force is resolved into N in the x direction and N in the negative y direction. 12 sin 60°, 12 cos 60°

The 11 N force is resolved into N in the negative x direction and N in the negative y direction. 11 cos 50°, 11 sin 50°

The 15 N force is resolved into N in the negative x direction and N in the y direction. 15 cos 40°, 15 sin 40°

The net total force in the x direction is −8.1690

The net total force in the y direction is −4.7847

Figure 5.13 illustrates these forces.

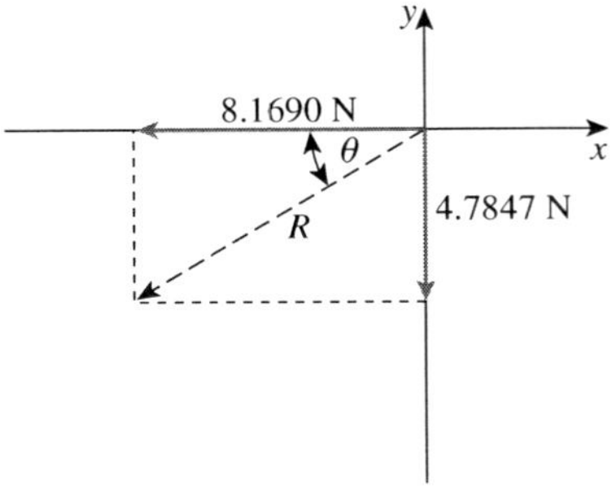

Figure 5.13 The resultant force is R.

Using Pythagoras's theorem

$$R^2 = (8.1690)^2 + (4.7847)^2$$

$$R = 9.47$$

and

$$\tan\theta = \frac{4.7847}{8.1690}$$

$$\theta = 30.36°$$

The resultant is a force of 9.47 N acting at 30.36° below the negative x axis.

Exercises

1 Find the resultant of the forces shown in Figure 5.14.

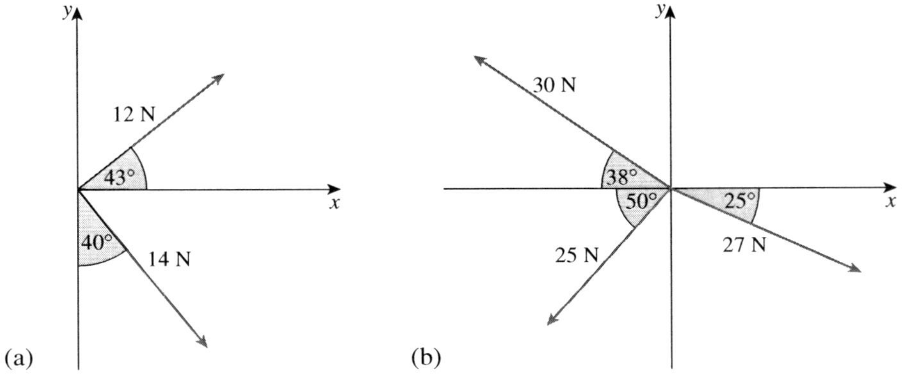

Figure 5.14

Solutions to exercises

1 (a) 17.96 N acting at 8.13° below the positive x axis;

(b) 19.45 N acting at 38.43° below the negative x axis.

End of block exercises

1 Resolve the forces shown in Figure 5.15 into forces along the x and y axes.

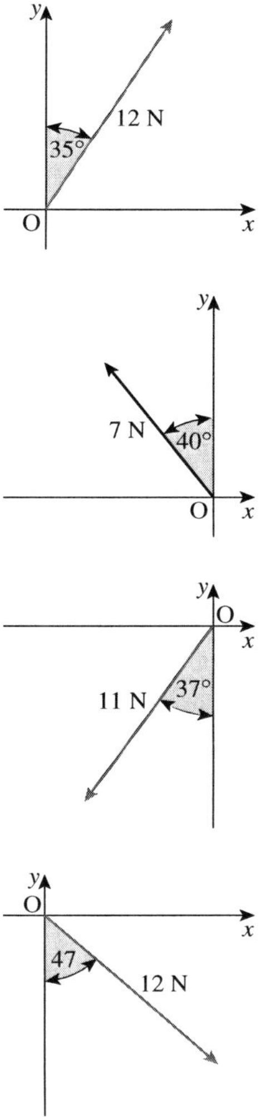

Figure 5.15

2 Find the resultant of the forces shown in Figure 5.16.

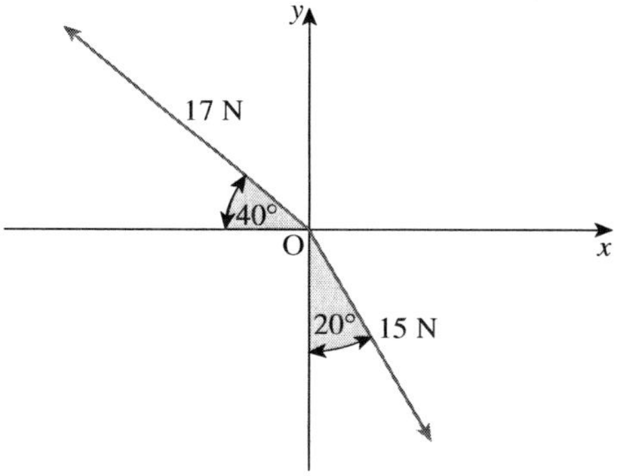

Figure 5.16

3 Find the resultant of the forces shown in Figure 5.17.

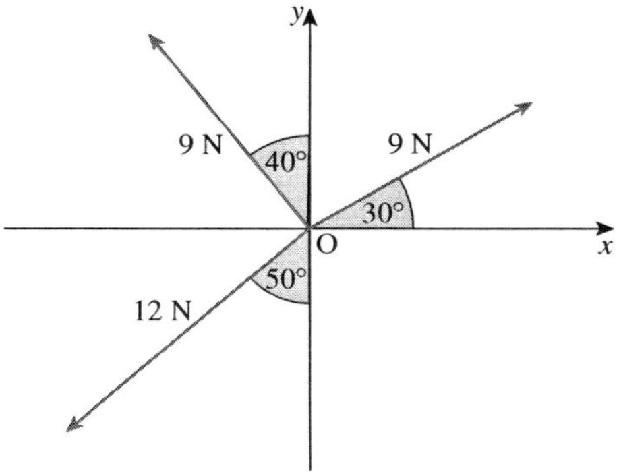

Figure 5.17

4 Find the resultant of the forces shown in Figure 5.18.

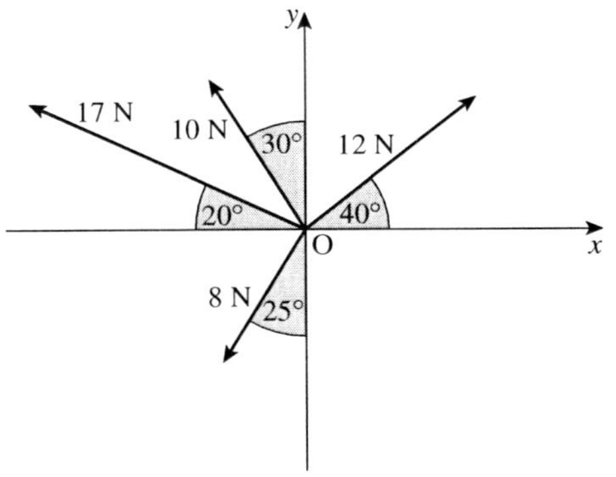

Figure 5.18

5 Forces are said to be in **equilibrium** if their resultant is zero. The forces in Figure 5.19 are in equilibrium. Find R and θ.

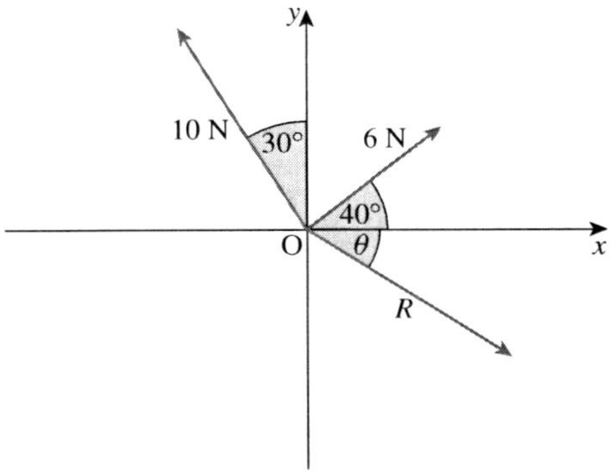

Figure 5.19

6 The forces in Figure 5.20 are in equilibrium. Find R and θ.

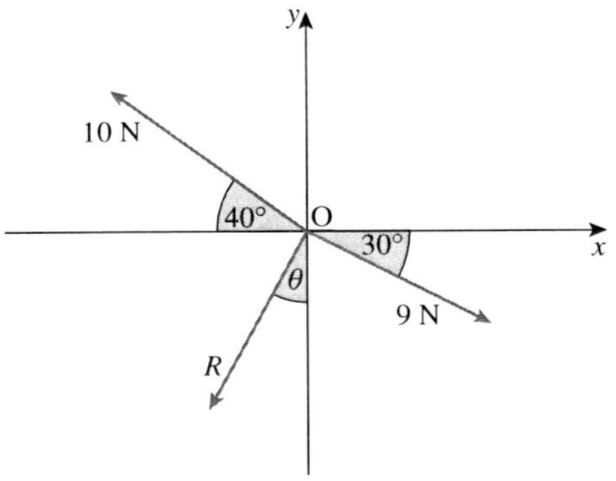

Figure 5.20

Solutions to exercises

1 (a) 6.88 N in the x direction; 9.83 N in the y direction
(b) 4.50 N in the negative x direction; 5.36 N in the y direction
(c) 6.62 N in the negative x direction; 8.78 in the negative y direction
(d) 8.78 N in the x direction; 8.18 N in the negative y direction

2 8.50 N, directed at 21.87° below the negative x axis.

3 $R = 8.07$ N, directed at 27.13° above the negative x axis.

4 21.29 N, directed at 44.57° above the negative x axis.

5 $R = 12.52$ N, $\theta = 88.15°$

6 $R = 1.93$ N, $\theta = 3.97°$

End of chapter exercises

In questions 1–11 ΔABC has a right angle at C.

1 Calculate AB given AC = 9 cm and BC = 15 cm.

2 Calculate sin A given AC = 10 cm and AB = 14 cm.

3 Calculate sin B given AC = 6 cm and BC = 9 cm.

4 Calculate A given AC = 14 cm and BC = 9 cm.

5 Calculate AC given AB = 15 cm and BC = 12 cm.

6 Calculate B given AB = 2(BC).

7 Calculate A given BC is three times AC.

8 Calculate AC given BC = 10 cm and $A = 40°$.

9 Calculate BC given AB = 27 cm and $B = 32°$.

10 Calculate AB given AC = 12 cm and $A = 57°$.

11 Calculate AC given BC = 12 cm and $B = 53°$.

12 A 15 N force acts at 35° to the x axis. Resolve the force into forces in the x and y directions.

13 A 12 N force acts at 40° to the negative y axis. Resolve the force into forces in the x and y directions.

14 Convert the following angles to decimal format: (a) 36°29′42″ (b) 1°2′41″ (c) 10°12′21″

15 Convert the following angles to degree/minute/second format: (a) 7.3614° (b) 10.0932° (c) 14.9610°

In questions 16–23 solve ΔXYZ given

16 XY = 17 cm, YZ = 23 cm and XZ = 31 cm.

17 YZ = 15 cm, $X = 39°$ and $Y = 75°$.

18 XZ = 85 cm, YZ = 70 cm and $Z = 59°$.

19 $Z = 46°$, YZ = 30 m and XY = 25 m.

20 XY = 71 cm, $Y = 110°$ and $Z = 21°$.

21 XZ = 41 cm, YZ = 29 cm and XY = 52 cm.

22 $Y = 51°$, XY = 25 cm and XZ = 22.5 cm.

23 XY = 100 cm, XZ = 73 cm and $Y = 50°$.

24 Calculate the resultant of the forces in Figure C10.1.

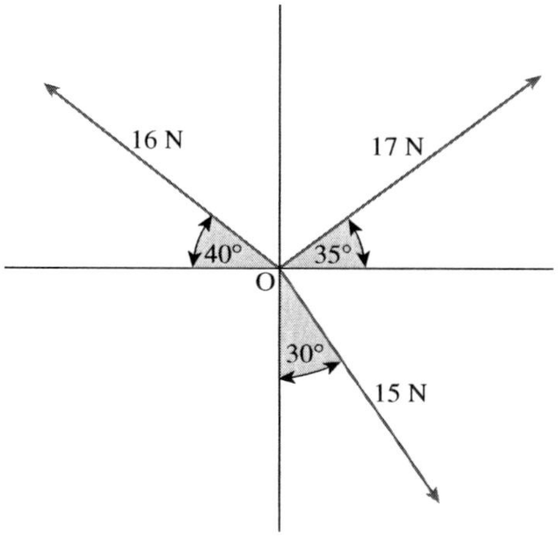

Figure C10.1

25 Calculate the resultant of the forces shown in Figure C10.2.

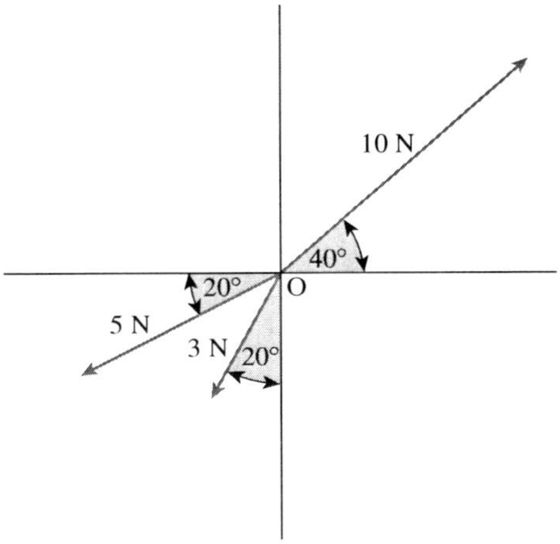

Figure C10.2

26 The angle of elevation to the top, B, of a vertical tower AB is 19°3′ when measured from a point, C, 27.3 m from the base of the tower. Calculate
(a) the height of the tower
(b) the distance BC.

27 Two vertical towers have heights 9 m and 17.2 m and are 42 m apart.
(a) Calculate the angle of elevation from the base of the shorter tower to the top of the taller tower.
(b) Calculate the angle of depression from the top of the taller tower to the top of the shorter tower.

28 A ship travels on a bearing of 40°00′ for 12 km and then changes to a bearing of 270° and travels for 30 km. Calculate
(a) the distance of the ship from its starting point
(b) the bearing the ship must take to return to its starting position.

29 The forces in Figure C10.3 are in equilibrium. Find R and θ.

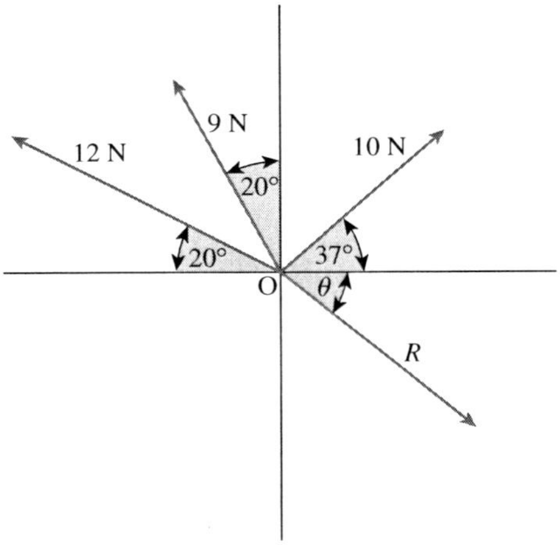

Figure C10.3

30 A tower has a bearing of 37°00′ when measured from a point O, and is 973 m distant from O. A chimney has a bearing of 100°30′ when measured from O and is 1042 m distant from O. Calculate the distance from the tower to the chimney.

31 A point, A, has a bearing of 45° and is 10 km distant from O. A point B has a bearing of 160° and is 20 km distant from O. A point C is mid-way between A and B. Calculate
(a) the bearing of C from O
(b) the distance of C from O.

Solutions to exercises

1 17.49 cm

2 0.6999

3 0.5547

4 32.74°

5 9 cm

6 60°

7 71.57°

8 11.92 cm

9 22.90 cm

10 22.03 cm

11 15.92 cm

12 12.29 N horizontally, 8.60 N vertically

13 x component is 7.71 N; y component is −9.19 N

14 (a) 36.495° (b) 1.0447° (c) 10.2058°

15 (a) 7°21′41″ (b) 10°5′35″ (c) 14°57′40″

16 $X = 46.84°$, $Y = 100.54°$, $Z = 32.63°$

17 $Z = 66°$, XZ = 23.02 cm, XY = 21.77 cm

18 XY = 77.43 cm, $X = 50.79°$, $Y = 70.21°$

19 solution 1: $X = 59.6787°$, $Y = 74.3213°$, XZ = 33.46 m; solution 2: $X = 120.3213°$, $Y = 13.6787°$, XZ = 8.22 m

20 $X = 49°$, XZ = 186.17 cm, YZ = 149.52 cm

21 $X = 33.7835°$, $Y = 51.8271°$, $Z = 94.3894°$

22 solution 1: $X = 69.29°$, $Z = 59.71°$, YZ = 27.08 cm; solution 2: $X = 8.71°$, $Z = 120.29°$, YZ = 4.38 cm

23 no triangle possible

24 11.56 N acting 37.54° above positive x axis.

25 $R = 2.87$ N, acting at 47.59° to the positive x axis.

26 (a) 9.43 m (b) 28.88 m

27 (a) 22.27° (b) 11.05°

28 (a) 24.11 km (b) 112.41°

29 $R = 19.64$, $\theta = 71.08°$

30 1062 m

31 (a) 130.1198° (b) 9.0961 km

Chapter 11

Complex numbers

Complex numbers are a generalisation of the real number system with which you have been working all your life. Whenever any real non-zero number, whether positive or negative, is squared the result is always positive. Relaxing this condition and allowing numbers that when squared result in negative numbers is the driving force behind the theory of complex numbers. These numbers seem strange when first introduced because we deal with imaginary quantities. However, by persevering a much wider variety of problems can be solved. For example, equations that have no real solutions can have complex solutions as we shall see in this chapter.

Chapter 11 contents

BLOCK 1 Arithmetic of complex numbers

1.1 Introduction

In this block we explain how the set of real numbers is extended to enable us to find solutions of a greater range of equations. This leads to a study of **complex numbers**, which are useful in a variety of applications, especially alternating current circuit analysis. Complex numbers may seem rather strange at first because you will be dealing with imaginary rather than real quantities. Nevertheless they are so useful in applications that an understanding of them is essential.

1.2 Finding the square root of a negative number

If a real number is squared the answer cannot be negative. For example, squaring both 7 and −7, the result is positive. That is,

$$7^2 = 49 \text{ and } (-7)^2 = 49$$

It is impossible to obtain a negative result by squaring a real number.

Suppose we introduce a new sort of number, called j, with the property that $j^2 = -1$. The number j cannot be a real number because its square is negative. We say it is **imaginary**. Having defined j^2 as −1 it follows that $j = \sqrt{-1}$ and we can use this to write down the square root of any negative number.

Key point

j is an imaginary number such that $j^2 = -1$

Example 1.1

Write down expressions for the square roots of (a) 9, (b) −9.

Solution

(a) $\sqrt{9} = \pm 3$

(b) Noting that $-9 = 9 \times -1$ we can write

$$\begin{aligned}\sqrt{-9} &= \sqrt{9 \times -1}\\ &= \sqrt{9} \times \sqrt{-1}\\ &= \pm 3 \times \sqrt{-1}\end{aligned}$$

Then using the fact that $\sqrt{-1} = j$ we have

$$\sqrt{-9} = \pm 3j$$

Example 1.2

Write down (a) $\sqrt{100}$, (b) $\sqrt{-100}$, (c) $\sqrt{-\omega^2}$.

Solution

(a) $\sqrt{100} =$ ± 10

(b) Write $-100 = 100 \times -1$ so that

$$\sqrt{-100} = \sqrt{100 \times (-1)}$$

$$=$$ $\pm 10\text{j}$

(c) $\sqrt{-\omega^2} = \sqrt{-1 \times \omega^2}$

$$=$$ $\pm \text{j}\omega$

Example 1.3

Using the fact that $\text{j}^2 = -1$ simplify (a) j^3, (b) j^4

Solution

(a) $\text{j}^3 = \text{j}^2 \times \text{j}$. But $\text{j}^2 = -1$ and so $\text{j}^3 = -1 \times \text{j} = -\text{j}$.

(b) $\text{j}^4 = \text{j}^2 \times \text{j}^2 = (-1) \times (-1) = 1$.

Using the imaginary number j it is possible to solve all quadratic equations.

Example 1.4

Use the formula for solving a quadratic equation to solve $2x^2 + x + 1 = 0$.

Solution

We use the formula $x = \dfrac{-b \pm \sqrt{b^2 - 4ac}}{2a}$. With $a = 2$, $b = 1$ and $c = 1$ we find

$$x = \frac{-1 \pm \sqrt{1^2 - (4)(2)(1)}}{2(2)}$$

$$= \frac{-1 \pm \sqrt{-7}}{4}$$

$$= \frac{-1 \pm \sqrt{7}\text{j}}{4}$$

$$= -\frac{1}{4} \pm \frac{\sqrt{7}}{4}\text{j}$$

Example 1.5

Use the formula for solving a quadratic equation to solve $x^2 - 10x + 29 = 0$.

Solution

Using the formula $x = \dfrac{-b \pm \sqrt{b^2 - 4ac}}{2a}$ we find

$x =$ $\dfrac{10 \pm \sqrt{-16}}{2}$

Now using j we can find the square root of -16 and write down two solutions of the equation. Finally simplifying the answers gives

$x =$ and $5 + 2\mathrm{j}$ and $5 - 2\mathrm{j}$

Exercises

1 Write down an expression for (a) $\sqrt{4}$, (b) $\sqrt{-4}$, (c) $\sqrt{81}$, (d) $\sqrt{-81}$.

2 With the help of a calculator find (a) $\sqrt{7}$, (b) $\sqrt{-7}$, (c) $\sqrt{5.32}$, (d) $\sqrt{-5.32}$

3 Simplify (a) $-\mathrm{j}^2$, (b) $(-\mathrm{j})^2$, (c) $(-\mathrm{j})^3$, (d) $-\mathrm{j}^3$.

4 Solve the following quadratic equations:
(a) $x^2 + 1 = 0$ (b) $x^2 + x + 2 = 0$
(c) $x^2 + 5x + 3 = 0$ (d) $2x^2 + 5x + 3 = 0$
(e) $2x^2 + x + 3 = 0$

5 Solve the quadratic equation $5x^2 - 11x + 13 = 0$.

Solutions to exercises

1 (a) ± 2 (b) $\pm 2\mathrm{j}$ (c) ± 9 (d) $\pm 9\mathrm{j}$

2 (a) ± 2.646 (b) $\pm 2.646\mathrm{j}$ (c) ± 2.307 (d) $\pm 2.307\mathrm{j}$

3 (a) 1 (b) -1 (c) j (d) j

4 (a) $\pm \mathrm{j}$ (b) $-\dfrac{1}{2} \pm \dfrac{\sqrt{7}}{2}\mathrm{j}$ (c) $-\dfrac{5}{2} \pm \dfrac{\sqrt{13}}{2}$ (d) $-1, -\dfrac{3}{2}$ (e) $-\dfrac{1}{4} \pm \dfrac{\sqrt{23}}{4}\mathrm{j}$

5 $\dfrac{11}{10} \pm \dfrac{\sqrt{139}}{10}\mathrm{j}$

1.3 Complex numbers

Real and imaginary parts

In Example 1.5 we found that the solutions of the equation $x^2 - 10x + 29 = 0$ are $5 \pm 2\mathrm{j}$. The solutions are known as **complex numbers**. A complex number such as $5 + 2\mathrm{j}$ is made up of two parts, a **real part** 5 and an **imaginary part** 2. The imaginary part is the multiple of j.

It is common practice to use the letter z to stand for a complex number and write $z = a + b\mathrm{j}$ where a is the real part and b is the imaginary part.

Key point

If z is a complex number then we write

$$z = a + b\text{j}$$

where a is the real part and b is the imaginary part.

Example 1.6

State the real and imaginary parts of $-11 - 19\text{j}$.

Solution

The real part is -11

The imaginary part is -19

Equal complex numbers

Two complex numbers are equal only when their real parts are equal and their imaginary parts are equal. So if $a + b\text{j}$ is equal to $3 - 2\text{j}$ it follows that a must be 3 and b must be -2.

Complex conjugate

In Example 1.5 we solved the quadratic equation $x^2 - 10x + 29 = 0$ and saw that the second solution, $5 - 2\text{j}$, is almost the same as the first, $5 + 2\text{j}$; only the sign of the imaginary part has changed. The number $5 - 2\text{j}$ is said to be the **complex conjugate** of $5 + 2\text{j}$.

In general, to find the complex conjugate of a complex number the sign of the imaginary part is changed from $+$ to $-$, or vice versa. We denote the complex conjugate of z by $\bar{z}$.

Key point

If $z = a + b\text{j}$, its **complex conjugate**, denoted by $\bar{z}$, is

$$\bar{z} = a - b\text{j}$$

When solving quadratic equations with real coefficients any complex roots occur in complex conjugate pairs just as we saw in Example 1.5.

Example 1.7

A complex number z_1 is given by $z_1 = a_1 + b_1\text{j}$.

(a) State the real and imaginary parts of z_1.

(b) Write down the complex conjugate of z_1.

Solution

(a) The real part of z_1 is a_1. The imaginary part is b_1.

(b) The complex conjugate of z_1 is found by changing the sign of the imaginary part. Thus $\overline{z_1} = a_1 - b_1\text{j}$.

Example 1.8

Write down the complex conjugates of each of the following complex numbers: (a) $z_1 = 11 + 2\text{j}$, (b) $z_2 = 7 - 3\text{j}$, (c) $z_3 = 8$, (d) $z_4 = -9\text{j}$.

Solution

In each case the sign of the imaginary part is changed. In part (c) there is no imaginary part to alter.

(a) $\overline{z_1} = 11 - 2\text{j}$

(b) $\overline{z_2} = 7 + 3\text{j}$

(c) $\overline{z_3} = 8$

(d) $\overline{z_4} = 9\text{j}$

Exercises

1. If $z = a + b\text{j}$ explain what is meant by $\bar{z}$.

2. State the real and imaginary parts of (a) $3 + 7\text{j}$ (b) $a_1 + b_1\text{j}$ (c) -0.35j (d) $\cos\theta + \text{j}\sin\theta$ (e) $\cos\omega t + \text{j}\sin\omega t$

3. Write down the complex conjugate of (a) $3 + 13\text{j}$ (b) $3 - 13\text{j}$ (c) 17j (d) 18.5 (e) $3.36 + 2.24\text{j}$

4. State the real and imaginary parts of $\text{j}V\sin(\omega t + \phi)$.

Solutions to exercises

1. $\bar{z}$ is the complex conjugate of z. That is $\bar{z} = a - b\text{j}$.

2. (a) real part 3, imaginary part 7 (b) a_1, b_1 (c) $0, -0.35$ (d) $\cos\theta$, $\sin\theta$ (e) $\cos\omega t$, $\sin\omega t$

3. (a) $3 - 13\text{j}$ (b) $3 + 13\text{j}$ (c) -17j (d) 18.5 (e) $3.36 - 2.24\text{j}$

4. Real part 0, imaginary part $V\sin(\omega t + \phi)$.

1.4 Addition and subtraction of complex numbers

Given two complex numbers we can find their sum and difference in an obvious way.

Key point

Addition and subtraction of complex numbers

If $z_1 = a_1 + b_1\text{j}$ and $z_2 = a_2 + b_2\text{j}$ then

$$z_1 + z_2 = (a_1 + a_2) + (b_1 + b_2)\text{j}$$

$$z_1 - z_2 = (a_1 - a_2) + (b_1 - b_2)\text{j}$$

Note that to add the complex numbers we simply add the real parts together and add the imaginary parts together.

Example 1.9

If $z_1 = 3 + 11j$ and $z_2 = 18 - 21j$ find (a) $z_1 + z_2$, (b) $z_2 - z_1$.

Solution

(a) $z_1 + z_2 = (3 + 11j) + (18 - 21j)$
$= 21 - 10j$

(b) $z_2 - z_1 = (18 - 21j) - (3 + 11j)$
$= 15 - 32j$

Example 1.10

If $z_1 = 3 + 4j$ and $z_2 = 8 + 11j$, find (a) $z_1 + z_2$, (b) $z_1 - z_2$.

Solution

(a) To add the complex numbers just add the real parts and then add the imaginary parts:

$z_1 + z_2 =$ $\quad$ $11 + 15j$

(b) Subtract the real parts, and then subtract the imaginary parts:

$z_1 - z_2 = (3 + 4j) - (8 + 11j)$

$=$ $\quad$ $-5 - 7j$

Exercises

1 If $z_1 = 1 + j$ and $z_2 = 3 + 2j$ find (a) $z_1 + z_2$, (b) $z_1 - z_2$, (c) $z_2 - z_1$.

2 If $z = 13 - 11j$ and $w = -2 + 5j$ find (a) $z + w$, (b) $z - w$, (c) $w - z$.

3 If $z = \alpha + j\beta$ and $w = \gamma + j\delta$ write down $z + w$.

Solutions to exercises

1 (a) $4 + 3j$ (b) $-2 - j$ (c) $2 + j$

2 (a) $11 - 6j$ (b) $15 - 16j$ (c) $-15 + 16j$

3 $\alpha + \gamma + j(\beta + \delta)$

1.5 Multiplication of complex numbers

To multiply two complex numbers we use the normal rules of algebra and also the fact that $j^2 = -1$. If z_1 and z_2 are the two complex numbers their product is written $z_1 z_2$.

Example 1.11
If $z_1 = 5 - 2j$ and $z_2 = 2 + 4j$ find $z_1 z_2$.

Solution

$$\begin{aligned} z_1 z_2 &= (5 - 2j)(2 + 4j) \\ &= 10 - 4j + 20j - 8j^2 \end{aligned}$$

Replacing j^2 by -1 we obtain

$$\begin{aligned} z_1 z_2 &= 10 + 16j - 8(-1) \\ &= 18 + 16j \end{aligned}$$

In general we have the following result:

Key point

Multiplication of two complex numbers

If $z_1 = a_1 + b_1 j$ and $z_2 = a_2 + b_2 j$ then

$$\begin{aligned} z_1 z_2 &= (a_1 + b_1 j)(a_2 + b_2 j) \\ &= a_1 a_2 + a_1 b_2 j + b_1 a_2 j + b_1 b_2 j^2 \\ &= (a_1 a_2 - b_1 b_2) + j(a_1 b_2 + a_2 b_1) \end{aligned}$$

Example 1.12
Find $z_1 z_2$ if $z_1 = 3 - 2j$ and $z_2 = 5 + 3j$.

Solution

$z_1 z_2 = (3 - 2j)(5 + 3j)$

$=$

$15 + 9j - 10j - 6j^2$

Simplify your result to obtain

$(3 - 2j)(5 + 3j) =$

$21 - j$

Example 1.13
Find $z \bar{z}$ if $z = a + bj$.

Solution
Recall that $\bar{z}$ is the complex conjugate of z.

$$\begin{aligned} z \bar{z} &= (a + bj)(a - bj) \\ &= a^2 + baj - abj - b^2 j^2 \end{aligned}$$

$$= a^2 - b^2(-1)$$
$$= a^2 + b^2$$

Note that the result is purely real: multiplying a complex number by its conjugate results in a non-negative real answer. For example, taking $a = 4$ and $b = 3$, we see that $(4 + 3j)(4 - 3j) = 4^2 + 3^2 = 25$.

The result of the previous example is particularly important.

Key point

If $z = a + bj$ then

$$z\bar{z} = a^2 + b^2$$

Exercises

1 If $z_1 = 1 + j$ and $z_2 = 3 + 2j$ find (a) $z_1 z_2$, (b) $\bar{z}_1$, (c) $\bar{z}_2$, (d) $z_1\bar{z}_1$, (e) $z_2\bar{z}_2$.

2 Express in the form $x + jy$
(a) $j(3 + 2j)$ (b) $(4 - 2j)j$ (c) $5j(1 - j)$
(d) $(1 + j)(9 + j)$

3 Find a quadratic equation whose roots are $s = -7 + 0.5j$ and $s = -7 - 0.5j$.

4 Find a cubic equation with roots $z = 2$, $z = 1 + j$ and $z = 4 + 2j$. (Note that this cubic equation will have complex coefficients.)

5 Find the real and imaginary parts of (a) $7(2 + j)$, (b) $-13(j - 1)$.

6 Find (a) $(4 - 3j)(4 + 3j)$, (b) $(5 - 2j)(5 + 2j)$.

Solutions to exercises

1 (a) $1 + 5j$ (b) $1 - j$ (c) $3 - 2j$ (d) 2 (e) 13

2 (a) $-2 + 3j$ (b) $2 + 4j$ (c) $5 + 5j$
(d) $8 + 10j$

3 For example, $4s^2 + 56s + 197 = 0$

4 For example,
$$z^3 - (7 + 3j)z^2 + (12 + 12j)z - 4 - 12j = 0$$

5 (a) real 14, imaginary 7 (b) $13, -13$

6 (a) 25 (b) 29

1.6 Division of complex numbers

Division of complex numbers requires a special technique that uses the complex conjugate. Consider the following example.

Example 1.14

Find $\dfrac{z_1}{z_2}$ when $z_1 = 3 + 2j$ and $z_2 = 4 - 3j$.

Solution

We require

$$\frac{z_1}{z_2} = \frac{3 + 2j}{4 - 3j}$$

The special technique is to multiply both numerator and denominator by the complex conjugate of the denominator. Overall, this is equivalent to multiplying by 1 and so the fraction remains unaltered. However, it has the effect of making the denominator purely real as we saw in Example 1.13.

$$\begin{aligned}
\frac{3 + 2j}{4 - 3j} &= \frac{3 + 2j}{4 - 3j} \times \frac{4 + 3j}{4 + 3j} \\
&= \frac{(3 + 2j)(4 + 3j)}{(4 - 3j)(4 + 3j)} \\
&= \frac{12 + 8j + 9j + 6j^2}{16 + 12j - 12j - 9j^2} \\
&= \frac{6 + 17j}{25} \\
&= \frac{6}{25} + \frac{17}{25}j
\end{aligned}$$

In general we have the following result:

Key point

Division of two complex numbers

$$\begin{aligned}
\frac{z_1}{z_2} &= \frac{a_1 + b_1 j}{a_2 + b_2 j} \\
&= \frac{a_1 + b_1 j}{a_2 + b_2 j} \times \frac{a_2 - b_2 j}{a_2 - b_2 j} \\
&= \frac{a_1 a_2 + b_1 b_2 + (a_2 b_1 - a_1 b_2)j}{a_2^2 + b_2^2}
\end{aligned}$$

Example 1.15

If $z_1 = 2 + 9j$ and $z_2 = 5 - 2j$ find $\dfrac{z_1}{z_2}$.

Solution

Both numerator and denominator are multiplied by the complex conjugate of the denominator.

So

$$\frac{2 + 9j}{5 - 2j} = \frac{2 + 9j}{5 - 2j} \times \frac{5 + 2j}{5 + 2j}$$

$$= \qquad \frac{10 + 45j + 4j + 18j^2}{25 + 4}$$

Simplify the result to produce

$$\frac{2+9\text{j}}{5-2\text{j}} = \qquad -\frac{8}{29}+\frac{49}{29}\text{j}$$

Exercises

1 If $z_1 = 1 + \text{j}$ and $z_2 = 3 + 2\text{j}$ find
(a) $\frac{z_1}{z_2}$ (b) $\frac{z_2}{z_1}$ (c) $\frac{z_1}{\bar{z}_1}$ (d) $\frac{z_2}{\bar{z}_2}$

2 Find (a) $\frac{7-6\text{j}}{2\text{j}}$, (b) $\frac{3+9\text{j}}{1-2\text{j}}$.

3 Express the following in the form $x + \text{j}y$:
(a) $\frac{1}{\text{j}}$ (b) $\frac{2}{\text{j}}$ (c) $\frac{3}{-\text{j}}$ (d) $\frac{1}{1+\text{j}}$ (e) $\frac{2}{1-\text{j}}$

4 If $z = \frac{3+2\text{j}}{2-\text{j}}$ express both (a) $\frac{1}{z}$ and
(b) $z + \frac{1}{z}$ in the form $x + \text{j}y$.

5 Express $\frac{1}{\cos\theta - \text{j}\sin\theta}$ in the form $a + b\text{j}$.

Solutions to exercises

1 (a) $\frac{5}{13}+\frac{\text{j}}{13}$ (b) $\frac{5}{2}-\frac{\text{j}}{2}$ (c) j (d) $\frac{5}{13}+\frac{12}{13}\text{j}$

2 (a) $-3-\frac{7}{2}\text{j}$ (b) $-3+3\text{j}$

3 (a) $-\text{j}$ (b) -2j (c) 3j (d) $\frac{1}{2}-\frac{\text{j}}{2}$ (e) $1+1\text{j}$

4 (a) $\frac{4}{13}-\frac{7}{13}\text{j}$ (b) $\frac{72}{65}+\frac{56}{65}\text{j}$

5 $\cos\theta + \text{j}\sin\theta$

Computer and calculator exercises

Computer algebra packages allow the user to input and manipulate complex numbers. Investigate how the complex number $a + b\text{j}$ is input to the package to which you have access.

1 Use a package to express each of the following numbers in the form $a + b\text{j}$:

(a) $(2-\text{j})^6$ (b) $\frac{5}{(3-2\text{j})^4}$

2 Solve the equations
(a) $x^3 + 7x^2 + 9x + 63 = 0$
(b) $2x^4 - 3x^3 + 11 = 0$

3 A common requirement in control theory is to find the poles of a rational function, $G(s)$. The poles are the values of s that make the denominator zero. Find the poles of

$$G(s) = \frac{0.25}{s^3 - 2s^2 + 0.1s + 0.006}$$

End of block exercises

1. Write down an expression for (a) $\sqrt{1}$, (b) $\sqrt{-1}$, (c) $\sqrt{49}$, (d) $\sqrt{-49}$.

2. Find $\sqrt{-9.24}$.

3. Solve the equations
(a) $x^2 + x + 1 = 0$, (b) $7s^2 + s + 1 = 0$.

4. Write down the complex conjugate of
(a) $15 + 3j$ (b) $-3j + 2$
(c) $\frac{1}{2}j + 3$ (d) $\frac{1}{2} + \frac{\sqrt{3}}{2}j$

5. Find
(a) $\frac{3 + 2j}{5 + 4j}$, (b) $\frac{5 + 4j}{3 + 2j}$.

6. Find
(a) $z_1 z_2$, (b) $\frac{z_1}{z_2}$, (c) $\frac{z_2}{z_1}$, if $z_1 = 3 + 5j$ and $z_2 = 3 - 5j$.

7. Express the following in the form $x + jy$:
(a) $\frac{5}{-j}$ (b) $\frac{2 + j}{j}$ (c) $\frac{3}{4 - j}$
(d) $\frac{j}{1 + j}$ (e) $\frac{2j}{1 - j}$

8. Write down the complex conjugate of
(a) $\alpha + j\beta$ (b) $\cos\theta + j\sin\theta$
(c) $\cos\theta - j\sin\theta$, (d) $\cos\omega t - j\sin\omega t$

9. Express in the form $x + jy$
(a) $(3 + 2j)j(4 - 3j)$
(b) $(5 + 3j)(2 + j)(2 - j)$
(c) $\frac{(2 - 3j)(6 + 7j)}{j(1 - j)}$

10. Find a quadratic equation whose roots are $x = -3 + j$ and $x = -3 - j$.

11. Find a cubic equation with roots $x = 1$, $x = 1 - j$ and $x = 1 + j$.

Solutions to exercises

1. (a) ± 1 (b) $\pm j$ (c) ± 7 (d) $\pm 7j$

2. $\pm 3.04j$

3. (a) $-\frac{1}{2} \pm \frac{\sqrt{3}j}{2}$ (b) $-\frac{1}{14} \pm \frac{3\sqrt{3}}{14}j$

4. (a) $15 - 3j$ (b) $3j + 2$
(c) $-\frac{1}{2}j + 3$ (d) $\frac{1}{2} - \frac{\sqrt{3}}{2}j$

5. (a) $\frac{23}{41} - \frac{2}{41}j$ (b) $\frac{23}{13} + \frac{2}{13}j$

6. (a) 34 (b) $-\frac{8}{17} + \frac{15}{17}j$ (c) $-\frac{8}{17} - \frac{15}{17}j$

7. (a) $5j$ (b) $1 - 2j$ (c) $\frac{12}{17} + \frac{3}{17}j$ (d) $\frac{1}{2} + \frac{1}{2}j$
(e) $-1 + j$

8. (a) $\alpha - j\beta$ (b) $\cos\theta - j\sin\theta$
(c) $\cos\theta + j\sin\theta$ (d) $\cos\omega t + j\sin\omega t$

9. (a) $1 + 18j$ (b) $25 + 15j$ (c) $\frac{29}{2} - \frac{37}{2}j$

10. $x^2 + 6x + 10 = 0$, for example

11. $x^3 - 3x^2 + 4x - 2 = 0$, for example

BLOCK 2

The Argand diagram and polar form of a complex number

2.1 Introduction

Engineers often find a graphical interpretation of complex numbers useful. This graphical interpretation is known as an Argand diagram. From the Argand diagram two other useful quantities, the modulus and the argument, can be defined. These provide an alternative way of describing complex numbers, known as the polar form.

2.2 The Argand diagram

The complex number $z = a + b\mathrm{j}$ is plotted as a point with coordinates (a, b) as shown in Figure 2.1. Because the real part of z is plotted on the horizontal axis we often refer to this as the **real axis**. The imaginary part of z is plotted on the vertical axis and so we refer to this as the **imaginary axis**. Such a diagram is called an **Argand diagram**. Engineers often refer to this diagram as the **complex plane**.

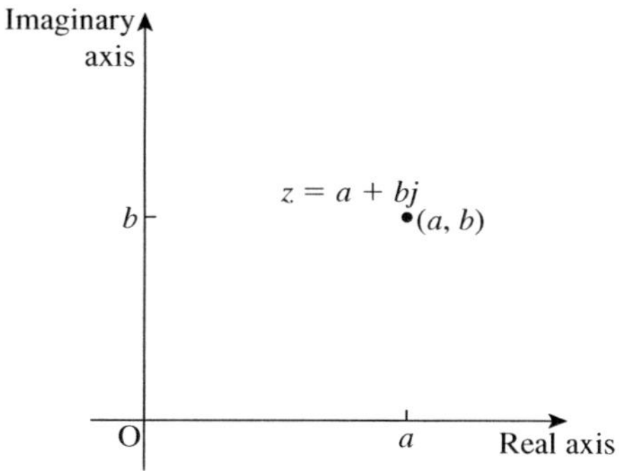

Figure 2.1 An Argand diagram in which the point with coordinates (a, b) represents the complex number $z = a + b\mathrm{j}$.

Example 2.1

Plot the complex numbers $z_1 = 2 + 3\mathrm{j}$, $z_2 = -3 + 2\mathrm{j}$, $z_3 = -3 - 2\mathrm{j}$, $z_4 = 2 - 5\mathrm{j}$, $z_5 = 6$, $z_6 = \mathrm{j}$ on an Argand diagram.

Solution

Figure 2.2 shows the Argand diagram. Note that purely real numbers lie on the real axis. Purely imaginary numbers lie on the imaginary axis. Note also that complex conjugate pairs such as $-3 \pm 2\mathrm{j}$ lie symmetrically on opposite sides of the real axis.

Figure 2.2
Argand diagram for Example 2.1.

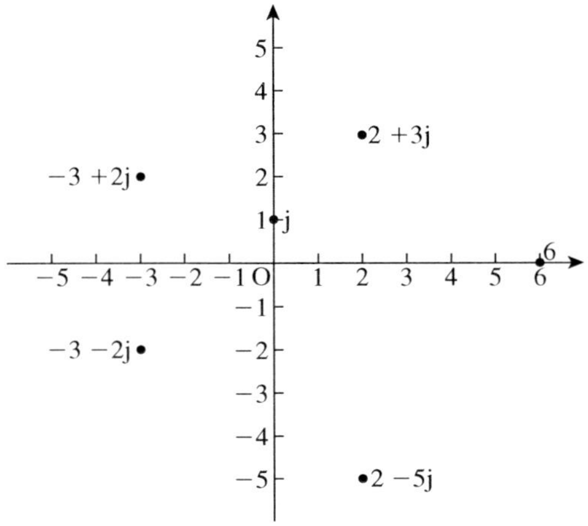

Exercises

1 Plot the following numbers on an Argand diagram:
(a) $3 + 3j$ (b) $2 - 4j$ (c) -0.5 (d) $6j$ (e) $-j$ (f) $-5 - 11j$.

2 Simplify the following complex numbers and show them on an Argand diagram:
(a) j^2 (b) $-j^2$ (c) $(-j)^2$ (d) j^3 (e) j^4

Solutions to exercises

1 See Figure 2.3.

2 See Figure 2.4.

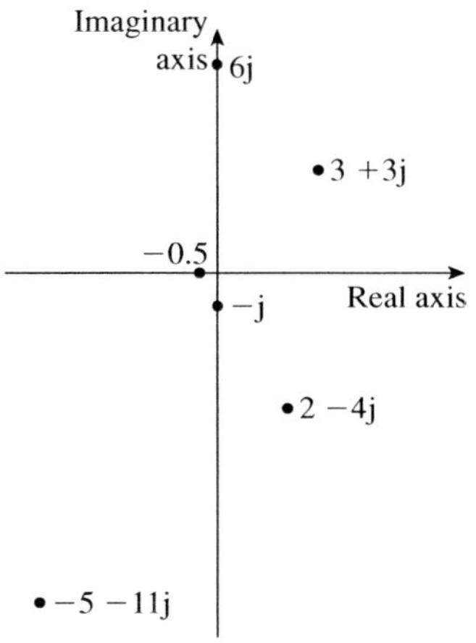

Figure 2.3

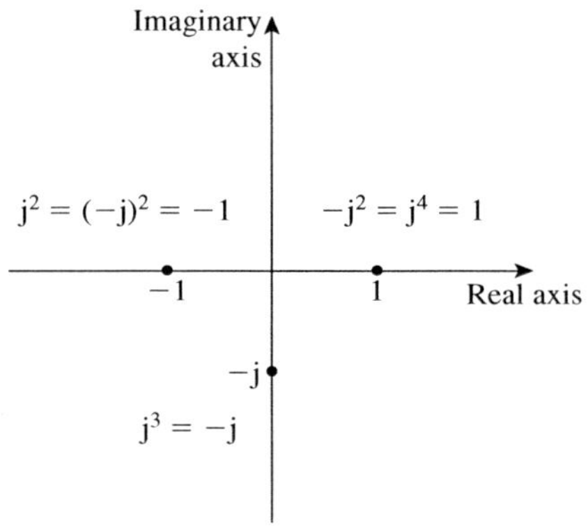

Figure 2.4

2.3 The modulus and argument of a complex number

Modulus

Consider the Argand diagram in Figure 2.5, which shows the complex number $z = a + b\mathrm{j}$. The distance of the point (a, b) from the origin is known as the **modulus**, or **magnitude**, of the complex number and is given the symbol r. Alternatively r is written as $|z|$. The plural of modulus is **moduli.** The modulus can be found using Pythagoras's theorem, that is $|z| = r = \sqrt{a^2 + b^2}$. The modulus is never negative.

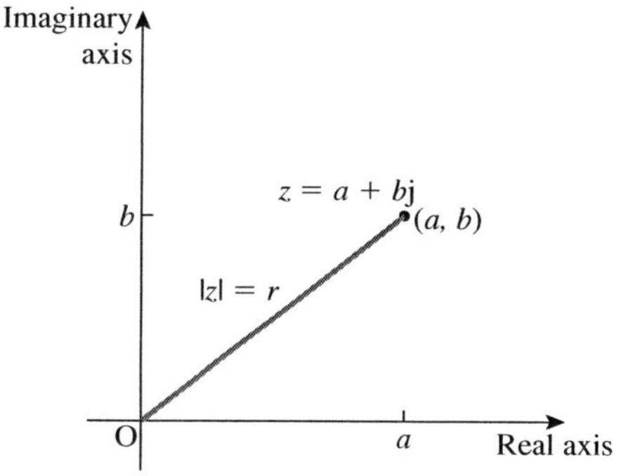

Figure 2.5
The modulus of $a + b\mathrm{j}$ is the distance of (a, b) from the origin O.

Key point

The **modulus** of the complex number $z = a + b\mathrm{j}$ is

$$r = |z| = \sqrt{a^2 + b^2}$$

Graphically, this is the distance of (a, b) from the origin.

Example 2.2

Plot the following complex numbers on an Argand diagram and find their moduli:
(a) $z_1 = 3 + 4\mathrm{j}$ (b) $z_2 = -2 + \mathrm{j}$ (c) $z_3 = 3\mathrm{j}$

Solution

The complex numbers are shown in Figure 2.6.

In each case we can use Pythagoras's theorem to find the modulus.

(a) $|z_1| = \sqrt{3^2 + 4^2} = \sqrt{25} = 5$.

(b) $|z_2| = \sqrt{(-2)^2 + 1^2} = \sqrt{5}$ or 2.236. It is usually sufficient to leave your answer in the surd form as $\sqrt{5}$.

(c) $|z_3| = \sqrt{0^2 + 3^2} = 3$.

Figure 2.6

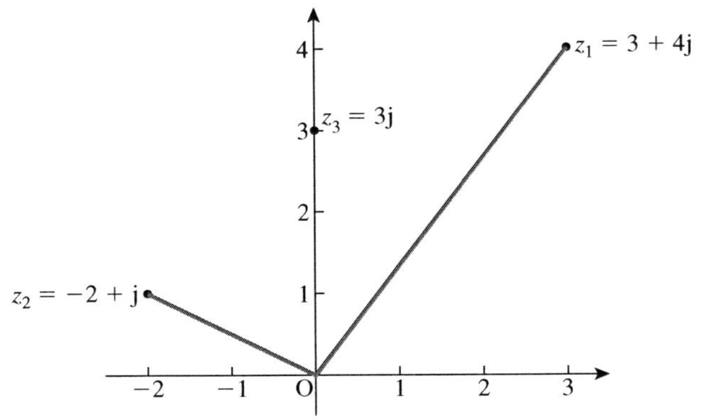

Example 2.3

Find the modulus of each of the following complex numbers:
(a) $z = 5 + 12j$ (b) $z = -6 - 8j$

Solution

(a) $|z| = |5 + 12j| = \sqrt{5^2 + 12^2} = 13$

(b) $|z| = |-6 - 8j| = \sqrt{(-6)^2 + (-8)^2} = 10$

Argument

Consider Figure 2.7. Given a complex number $z = a + bj$ we can calculate the angle between the positive x axis and a line joining (a, b) to the origin. This angle is called the **argument** of the complex number. It is abbreviated to arg(z) and often given the symbol θ.

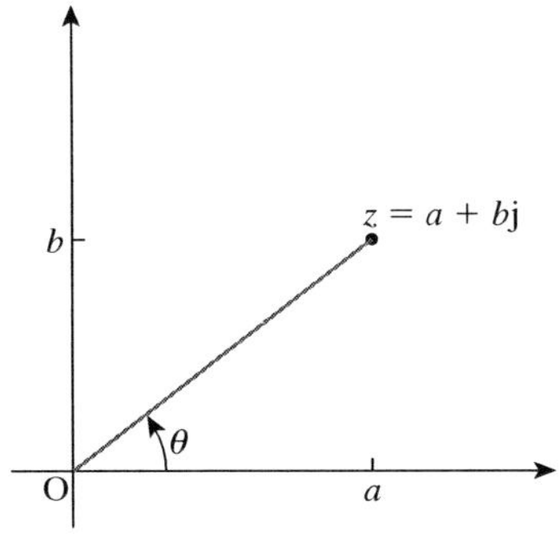

Figure 2.7
The argument of a complex number.

We usually measure this angle so that $-\pi < \theta \leq \pi$, in which case θ is called the **principal value** of the argument. Angles measured anticlockwise from the positive x axis are conventionally positive whereas angles measured clockwise are negative. Several complex numbers with positive and negative arguments are shown in Figure 2.8.

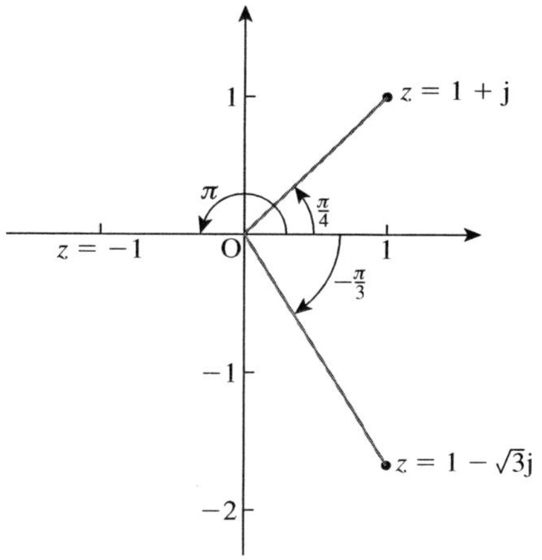

Figure 2.8 Some complex numbers with positive and negative arguments.

Because the angles in Figure 2.8 can be described in a variety of ways, the argument of a complex number is not unique. For example, the argument of $z = 1 + j$ has been labelled $\frac{\pi}{4}$. This is the principal value of the argument. However, it is important to note that we could have also stated the argument as $\frac{\pi}{4} + 2\pi = \frac{9\pi}{4}$. Repeatedly adding on 2π will produce other valid arguments. This will become important in Block 5 when we use complex numbers to solve equations.

Given $z = a + bj$, then trigonometry can be used to determine θ. Specifically, referring to Figure 2.7,

$$\tan \theta = \frac{b}{a}$$

so that

$$\theta = \tan^{-1}\left(\frac{b}{a}\right)$$

but when using a calculator to find an inverse tangent care must be taken that the solution obtained is in the correct quadrant. Drawing an Argand diagram will always help to identify the correct quadrant. At this stage you may find it helpful to refer back to Chapter 9 on trigonometry, and ensure that you are aware of the sign of the trigonometrical ratios in the four quadrants.

Key point

The argument of the complex number $z = a + bj$ is the angle between the positive x axis and the line joining (a, b) to the origin.

Polar form

The position of a complex number is uniquely determined by giving its modulus and argument. This description is known as the **polar form**. Engineers often write the polar form of a complex number as $z = r\angle\theta$.

Key point

> The **polar form** of a complex number can be written as
>
> $$z = r\angle\theta$$
>
> where r is the modulus and θ is the argument.

Example 2.4

Find the arguments of the complex numbers in Example 2.2 and pictured in Figure 2.6.

Solution

(a) $z_1 = 3 + 4\mathrm{j}$ is in the first quadrant. Its argument is given by

$$\theta = \tan^{-1}\frac{4}{3}$$

Using a calculator we find $\theta = 0.927$ radians.

(b) $z_2 = -2 + \mathrm{j}$ is in the second quadrant. To find its argument we seek an angle, θ, in the second quadrant such that $\tan\theta = \frac{1}{-2}$. To calculate this correctly it may help to refer to Figure 2.9 in which α is an acute angle with $\tan\alpha = \frac{1}{2}$. From a calculator $\alpha = 0.464$, and so $\theta = \pi - 0.464 = 2.678$ radians.

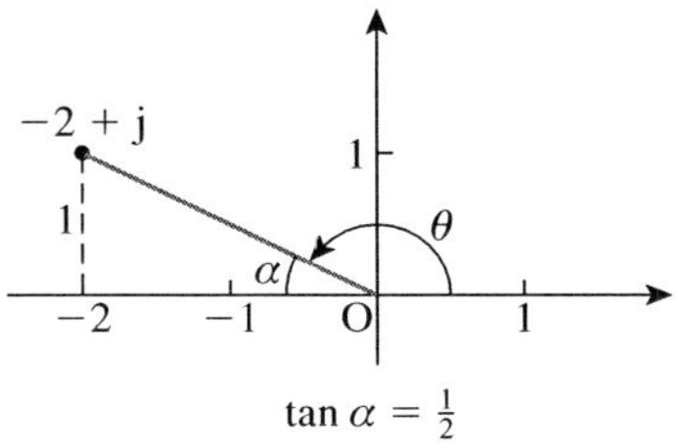

Figure 2.9
To calculate θ it is simpler to first calculate α.

(c) $z_3 = 3\mathrm{j}$ is purely imaginary. Its argument is $\frac{\pi}{2}$ radians.

Example 2.5

Sketch an Argand diagram showing the following complex numbers and in each case calculate the argument.

(a) $z = 5 + 12\mathrm{j}$ (b) $z = -\sqrt{3} + \mathrm{j}$ (c) $z = 2 - 3\mathrm{j}$

Solution

(a) Sketch $z = 5 + 12\text{j}$ and identify the quadrant in which it lies:

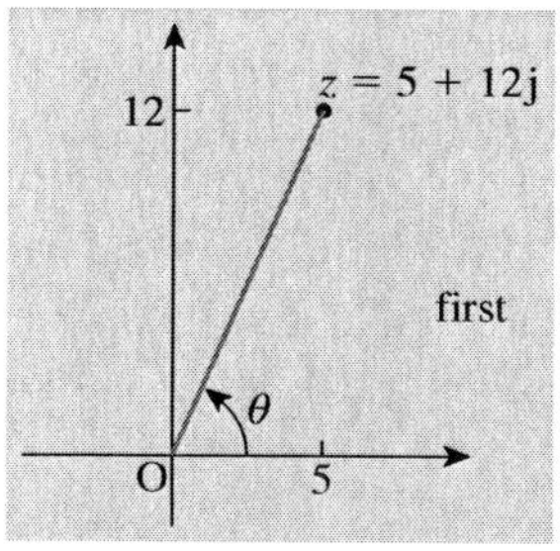

Then $\arg z = \theta =$ $\tan^{-1}\left(\frac{12}{5}\right) = 1.176$ radians

(b) Sketch $z = -\sqrt{3} + \text{j}$ and identify the quadrant in which it lies:

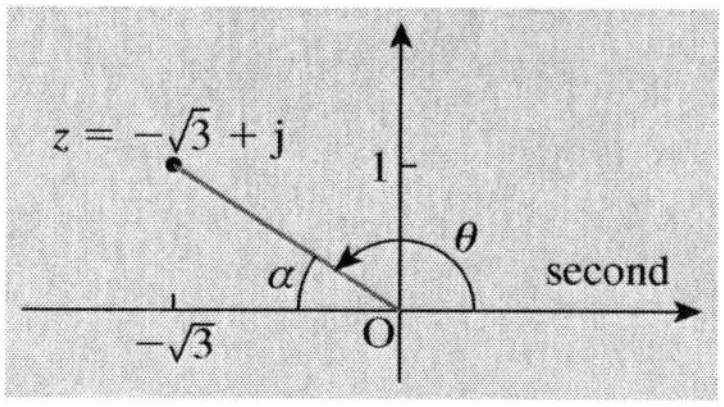

Then $\arg z = \theta =$

$$\tan^{-1}\left(-\frac{1}{\sqrt{3}}\right) = \frac{5\pi}{6} = 2.618 \text{ radians}$$

If you have difficulty calculating the correct angle it is often simpler to calculate first the related acute angle. So, in the diagram above, α is acute and $\tan \alpha = \frac{1}{\sqrt{3}}$ from which $\alpha = \frac{\pi}{6} = 0.524$ radians. It follows that $\theta = \pi - \alpha = \frac{5\pi}{6} = 2.618$ radians.

(c) Sketch $z = 2 - 3\text{j}$ and identify the quadrant in which it lies:

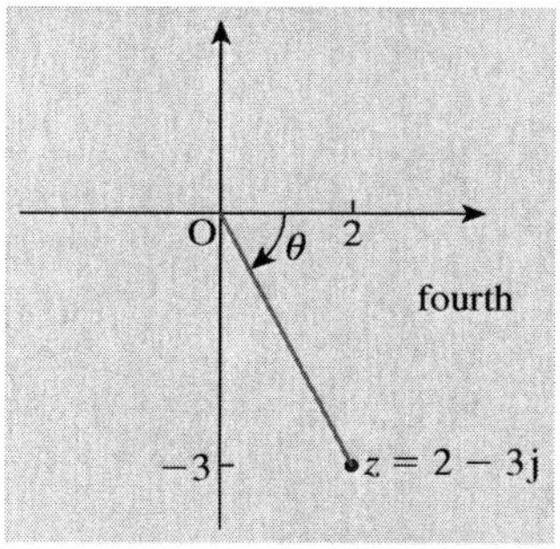

Then arg $(z) = \theta =$

$$\tan^{-1}\left(-\frac{3}{2}\right) = -0.983 \text{ radians}$$

Ensure you have located the angle in the correct quadrant. If you have difficulty calculating the correct angle use the method described in part (b).

Most scientific calculators are able to convert complex numbers given in cartesian form into polar form and vice versa. You should check your calculator to see whether you can carry out these conversions.

Exercises

1 The following complex numbers were plotted on an Argand diagram in question 1 of the previous exercises:
(a) $3 + 3j$ (b) $2 - 4j$ (c) -0.5 (d) $6j$ (e) $-j$ (f) $-5 - 11j$.
Express each one in polar form.

2 Show the following complex numbers on an Argand diagram:
(a) $5\angle 30°$ (b) $4\angle 45°$ (c) $2\angle -135°$ (d) $4\angle 270°$ (e) $17\angle 110°$ (f) $1\angle(\frac{\pi}{3})$ (g) $4\angle(\frac{\pi}{4})$ (h) $2\angle -2.3$

3 (a) If $z = 5$, plot z and jz on an Argand diagram. Deduce that multiplying z by j causes an anticlockwise rotation through 90° about the origin.
(b) If $z = 2 + 3j$, plot z and jz. Show that the same behaviour as that in part (a) occurs. Is it true in general that multiplying a complex number by j will rotate it through 90°?

4 (a) Solve the equation $z^2 - 4z + 13 = 0$ and plot your solutions on an Argand diagram.
(b) Express the solutions in polar form.

5 If $z = a + bj$ show that $|z| = |\bar{z}|$ and that $|z|^2 = z\,\bar{z}$.

Solutions to exercises

1 (a) $\sqrt{18}\angle\frac{\pi}{4} = 3\sqrt{2}\angle\frac{\pi}{4}$ (b) $2\sqrt{5}\angle -1.107$
(c) $0.5\angle\pi$ (d) $6\angle(\frac{\pi}{2})$ (e) $1\angle(-\frac{\pi}{2})$
(f) $\sqrt{146}\angle -1.997$

2 See Figure 2.10.

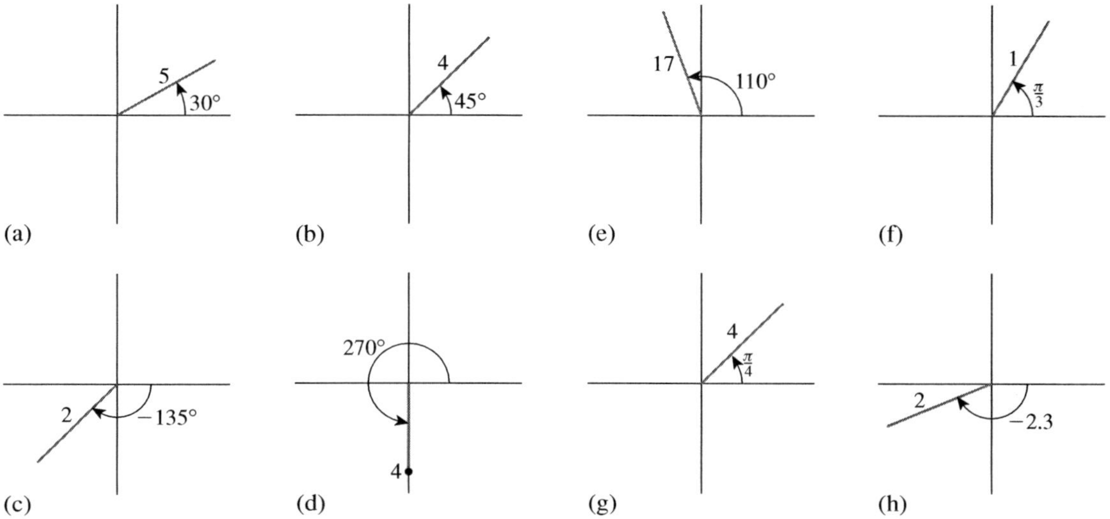

Figure 2.10

4 (a) $2 \pm 3j$ (b) $\sqrt{13}\angle 0.98$, $\sqrt{13}\angle -0.98$.

2.4 The form $r(\cos\theta + j\sin\theta)$

Consider Figure 2.11, which shows the complex number $z = a + bj = r\angle\theta$.

Figure 2.11

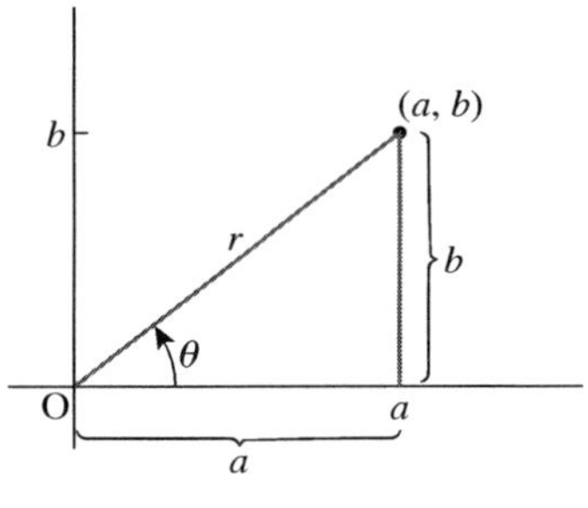

Using trigonometry we can write

$$\cos\theta = \frac{a}{r} \quad \text{and} \quad \sin\theta = \frac{b}{r}$$

so that, by rearrangement,

$$a = r\cos\theta \quad \text{and} \quad b = r\sin\theta$$

We can use these results to find the real and imaginary parts of a complex number given in polar form:

Key point

If $z = r\angle\theta$, the real and imaginary parts of z are, respectively,

$$a = r\cos\theta \quad \text{and} \quad b = r\sin\theta$$

Using these results we can then write $z = a + bj$ as

$$\begin{aligned} z = a + bj &= r\cos\theta + jr\sin\theta \\ &= r(\cos\theta + j\sin\theta) \end{aligned}$$

This is an alternative way of expressing the complex number with modulus r and argument θ.

Key point

$$\begin{aligned} z &= a + bj \\ &= r\angle\theta \\ &= r(\cos\theta + j\sin\theta) \end{aligned}$$

Recall that the complex conjugate of $z = a + bj$ is the complex number $\bar{z} = a - bj$, as shown in Figure 2.12.

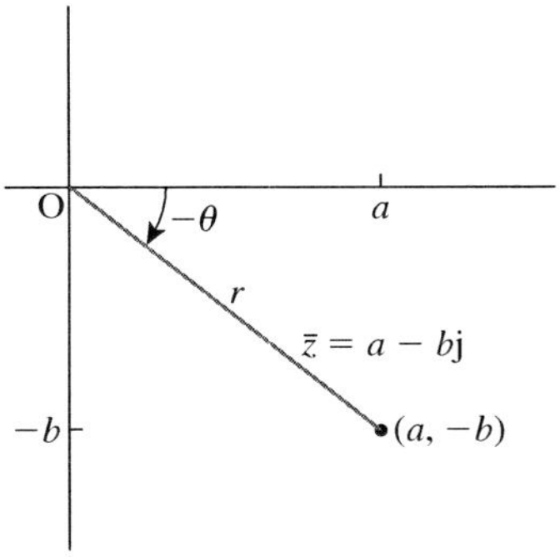

Figure 2.12 The complex conjugate of $a + bj$.

Note that $\bar{z}$ has the same real part as z but the sign of the imaginary part has changed. It follows that we can write $\bar{z} = a - bj = r(\cos\theta - j\sin\theta)$.

Key point

$$\begin{aligned} \bar{z} &= a - bj \\ &= r(\cos\theta - j\sin\theta) \end{aligned}$$

Example 2.6

State the modulus and argument of $z = 17(\cos 3.2 + j\sin 3.2)$.

Solution

Comparing the given complex number with the standard form $r(\cos\theta + j\sin\theta)$ we see that $r = 17$ and $\theta = 3.2$ radians.

Example 2.7

(a) Find the modulus and argument of the complex number $z = 5j$.
(b) Express 5j in the form $r(\cos\theta + j\sin\theta)$.

Solution

(a) On an Argand diagram the complex number 5j lies on the positive vertical axis a distance 5 from the origin. Thus 5j is a complex number with modulus 5 and argument $\frac{\pi}{2}$.

(b)
$$z = 5j = 5\left(\cos\frac{\pi}{2} + j\sin\frac{\pi}{2}\right)$$

Example 2.8

(a) Show the complex number $z = 4\angle(\frac{\pi}{3})$ on an Argand diagram.
(b) State its modulus and argument.
(c) Find the real and imaginary parts of the complex number and hence express it in the form $a + bj$.

Solution

(a) The complex number $z = 4\angle(\frac{\pi}{3})$ is shown in Figure 2.13.

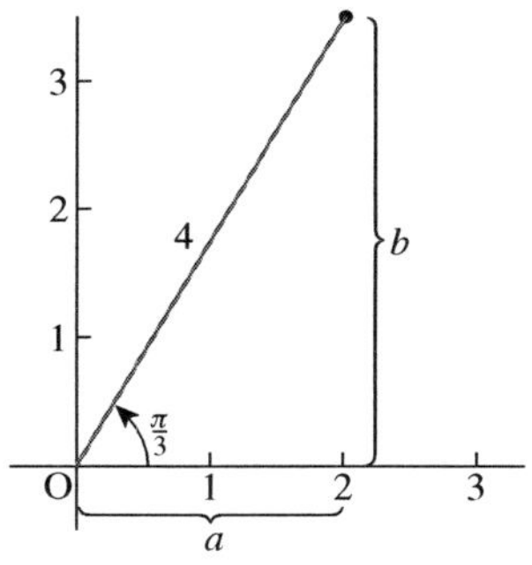

Figure 2.13 The complex number $z = 4\angle(\frac{\pi}{3})$.

(b) Its modulus is 4 and its argument is $\frac{\pi}{3}$.
(c) To find the real and imaginary parts we can use the key point on p. 444. Specifically,

$$a = r\cos\theta, \quad b = r\sin\theta$$

so that

$$a = 4\cos\frac{\pi}{3} = 2$$

and

$$b = 4\sin\frac{\pi}{3} = 3.464$$

Hence the complex number can be written $2 + 3.464j$.

Example 2.9
Find the real and imaginary parts of $z = 3\angle(\frac{\pi}{15})$.

Solution
Writing $z = a + bj$, the real part is found from $a = r\cos\theta$ and the imaginary part from $b = r\sin\theta$. Thus

$$a = 3\cos\left(\frac{\pi}{15}\right) = 2.934$$

$$b = 3\sin\left(\frac{\pi}{15}\right) = 0.624$$

Exercises

1 State the modulus and argument of z when

(a) $z = 13\left(\cos\frac{\pi}{3} + j\sin\frac{\pi}{3}\right)$,

(b) $z = 15\left(\cos\frac{\pi}{3} - j\sin\frac{\pi}{3}\right)$.

2 State the modulus and argument of
(a) $z = -13$, (b) $z = -4$, (c) $z = -2j$,
(d) $z = 3$.

Solutions to exercises

1 (a) $13, \frac{\pi}{3}$ (b) $15, -\frac{\pi}{3}$

2 (a) modulus 13, argument $-\pi$ (b) $4, -\pi$
(c) $2, -\frac{\pi}{2}$ (d) 3, 0

2.5 Multiplication and division of complex numbers in polar form

When two complex numbers are given in polar form it is particularly simple to multiply and divide them. This is an advantage of using the polar form.

Key point

If $z_1 = r_1\angle\theta_1$ and $z_2 = r_2\angle\theta_2$ then

$$z_1z_2 = r_1r_2\angle(\theta_1 + \theta_2), \quad \frac{z_1}{z_2} = \frac{r_1}{r_2}\angle(\theta_1 - \theta_2)$$

Note that to multiply the two numbers we multiply their moduli and add their arguments. To divide, we divide their moduli and subtract their arguments.

Example 2.10

If $z_1 = 5\angle(\frac{\pi}{6})$ and $z_2 = 4\angle(-\frac{\pi}{4})$ find (a) $z_1 z_2$, (b) $\dfrac{z_1}{z_2}$.

Solution

(a) To multiply the two complex numbers we multiply their moduli and add their arguments. Therefore

$$\begin{aligned} z_1 z_2 &= 20\angle\left[\frac{\pi}{6} + \left(-\frac{\pi}{4}\right)\right] \\ &= 20\angle\left(-\frac{\pi}{12}\right) \end{aligned}$$

(b) To divide the two complex numbers we divide their moduli and subtract their arguments.

$$\begin{aligned} \frac{z_1}{z_2} &= \frac{5}{4}\angle\left[\frac{\pi}{6} - \left(-\frac{\pi}{4}\right)\right] \\ &= \frac{5}{4}\angle\frac{5\pi}{12} \end{aligned}$$

Example 2.11

For z_1 and z_2 in Example 2.10 find $\dfrac{z_2}{z_1}$.

Solution

$$\frac{z_2}{z_1} = \qquad \frac{4}{5}\angle\left(-\frac{\pi}{4} - \frac{\pi}{6}\right) = \frac{4}{5}\angle\left(-\frac{5\pi}{12}\right)$$

Let us consider the important and special case of multiplication and division by the imaginary number j.

In polar form

$$\mathrm{j} = 1\angle\frac{\pi}{2}$$

If $z = r\angle\theta$, then

$$\begin{aligned} \mathrm{j}z &= \left(1\angle\frac{\pi}{2}\right)(r\angle\theta) \\ &= r\angle\left(\theta + \frac{\pi}{2}\right) \end{aligned}$$

Thus multiplying by j has left the modulus of z unchanged but increased the argument by $\frac{\pi}{2}$. This represents an anticlockwise rotation by $\frac{\pi}{2}$ on the Argand diagram.

If $z = r\angle\theta$, then

$$\begin{aligned} \frac{z}{\mathrm{j}} &= \frac{r\angle\theta}{1\angle\frac{\pi}{2}} \\ &= r\angle\left(\theta - \frac{\pi}{2}\right) \end{aligned}$$

Thus dividing by j has left the modulus unchanged but reduced the argument by $\frac{\pi}{2}$. This represents a clockwise rotation by $\frac{\pi}{2}$ on the Argand diagram.

Key point

Multiplying a complex number by j causes an anticlockwise rotation by $\frac{\pi}{2}$ on the Argand diagram.
Dividing a complex number by j causes a clockwise rotation by $\frac{\pi}{2}$ on the Argand diagram.

These results are very important in electrical engineering applications of complex numbers, in particular phasors, which are described in Block 6.

As a further special case of the multiplication rule consider what happens when both z_1 and z_2 are equal. Suppose $z = r\angle\theta$. Then it follows that $z^2 = r^2\angle 2\theta$. For example, if

$$z = 5\angle\frac{\pi}{3}, \text{ then } z^2 = 25\angle\left(\frac{2\pi}{3}\right)$$

Even more generally, we can state:

Key point

If $z = r\angle\theta$ then $z^n = r^n\angle n\,\theta$.

This is a form of De Moivre's theorem, which is studied in detail in Block 4.

Exercises

1. If $z_1 = 5\angle 20°$, $z_2 = 3\angle 35°$ find (a) $z_1 z_2$, (b) $\frac{z_1}{z_2}$, (c) $\frac{z_2}{z_1}$.

2. If $z = 3 - \text{j}$ find z^4 expressing your answer in polar form.

3. If $z = 1 + \text{j}$ find z^{10}.

4. If $z = -1 - \text{j}\sqrt{3}$ find z^5

5. Consider the complex number $z = r\angle\theta$. By multiplying this by $1\angle\alpha$ show that the result is a rotation of z through an angle α about the origin.

6. Simplify
$$\frac{\left(4\angle\left(\frac{2\pi}{3}\right)\right)^2\left(3\angle\left(\frac{\pi}{6}\right)\right)^2}{5\angle\frac{\pi}{4}}$$

Solutions to exercises

1. (a) $15\angle 55°$ (b) $\frac{5}{3}\angle -15°$ (c) $\frac{3}{5}\angle 15°$

2. $100\angle -73.72°$

3. $2^5\angle\frac{5\pi}{2} = 2^5\angle\frac{\pi}{2}$

4. $2^5\angle\frac{2\pi}{3} = -16 + 16\sqrt{3}j$

5. $\frac{144}{5}\angle\frac{17\pi}{12}$

End of block exercises

1 Plot each of the following complex numbers on an Argand diagram:
(a) $3 - 3j$ (b) $-4 - 7j$ (c) -5 (d) $4j$

2 If $z = 3 + 8j$ find $|z|$ and $\arg(z)$.

3 If $z = -3 - 6j$ find $|z|$ and $\arg(z)$.

4 Suppose $z_1 = 3 + 2j$ and $z_2 = 4 + 5j$.
(a) Find $|z_1||z_2|$ and $|z_1z_2|$. Deduce that these are equal.
(b) Find $\left|\frac{z_1}{z_2}\right|$ and $\frac{|z_1|}{|z_2|}$. Deduce that these are equal.

5 Find the modulus of the complex number $\cos\theta + j\sin\theta$.

6 Find the real and imaginary parts of each of the following complex numbers:
(a) $2\angle 70°$ (b) $4\angle\pi$ (c) $8\angle\left(-\frac{\pi}{2}\right)$
(d) $2\angle 2.306$

7 Simplify

$$\frac{\left(3\angle\left(\frac{\pi}{2}\right)\right)^4\left(5\angle\left(\frac{\pi}{6}\right)\right)^2}{\left(2\angle\frac{\pi}{4}\right)^3}$$

8 Find (a) arg 5, (b) arg -5, (c) $\arg(1 + j)$.

Solutions to exercises

2 $\sqrt{73}$, 69.4°

3 $\sqrt{45}$, $-116.6°$

4 (a) $\sqrt{13}\sqrt{41} = \sqrt{533}$ (b) $\frac{\sqrt{13}}{\sqrt{41}}$

5 1

6 (a) 0.684, 1.879 (b) -4, 0 (c) 0, -8
(d) -1.341, 1.483

7 $\frac{2025}{8}\angle -\frac{5\pi}{12}$

8 (a) 0 (b) π (c) $\frac{\pi}{4}$

BLOCK 3 The exponential form of a complex number

3.1 Introduction

In addition to the cartesian and polar forms of a complex number there is a third form in which a complex number may be written – the **exponential form**. In this block we explain the exponential form.

3.2 Some useful power series expansions and Euler's relations

To derive the exponential form we shall need to refer to the power series expansions of $\cos x$, $\sin x$ and e^x. Provided x is measured in radians, the functions $\cos x$ and $\sin x$ can be expressed in the following forms, known as **power series**:

$$\cos x = 1 - \frac{x^2}{2!} + \frac{x^4}{4!} - \cdots$$
$$\sin x = x - \frac{x^3}{3!} + \frac{x^5}{5!} - \cdots$$

Example 3.1
Write down the power series expansions for $\cos\theta$ and $\sin\theta$.

Solution
Simply replace x with θ in the given expansions:

$\cos\theta =$ $\quad 1 - \frac{\theta^2}{2!} + \frac{\theta^4}{4!} - \cdots$

$\sin\theta =$ $\quad \theta - \frac{\theta^3}{3!} + \frac{\theta^5}{5!} - \cdots$

We shall also make use of the power series expansion for e^x. The exponential function has a power series expansion given by

$$e^x = 1 + x + \frac{x^2}{2!} + \frac{x^3}{3!} + \frac{x^4}{4!} + \frac{x^5}{5!} + \cdots$$

Suppose we allow x to be an imaginary number in the expansion of e^x and write $x = j\theta$. We find

$$e^{j\theta} = 1 + j\theta + \frac{j^2\theta^2}{2!} + \frac{j^3\theta^3}{3!} + \frac{j^4\theta^4}{4!} + \frac{j^5\theta^5}{5!} + \cdots$$

$$= 1 + j\theta - \frac{\theta^2}{2!} - j\frac{\theta^3}{3!} + \frac{\theta^4}{4!} + j\frac{\theta^5}{5!} - \cdots$$

since $j^2 = -1, j^3 = -j$, etc. If we now rearrange this to separate the real and imaginary parts we can write

$$e^{j\theta} = 1 - \frac{\theta^2}{2!} + \frac{\theta^4}{4!} - \cdots + j\left(\theta - \frac{\theta^3}{3!} + \frac{\theta^5}{5!} - \cdots\right)$$

The two power series on the right we recognise, from Example 3.1, as $\cos\theta$ and $\sin\theta$, so that we have the following important result, known as **Euler's relation:**

$$e^{j\theta} = \cos\theta + j\sin\theta$$

It is straightforward, and left as an exercise, to show that

$$e^{-j\theta} = \cos\theta - j\sin\theta$$

Key point

Euler's relations

$$e^{j\theta} = \cos\theta + j\sin\theta, \quad e^{-j\theta} = \cos\theta - j\sin\theta$$

Example 3.2

Use Euler's relations to express $\cos\theta$ and $\sin\theta$ in terms of $e^{j\theta}$ and $e^{-j\theta}$.

Solution

Writing down Euler's relations we have

$$e^{j\theta} = \cos\theta + j\sin\theta$$
$$e^{-j\theta} = \cos\theta - j\sin\theta$$

First, adding, and then subtracting, these two identities give

$e^{j\theta} + e^{-j\theta} =$ $2\cos\theta$

$e^{j\theta} - e^{-j\theta} =$ $2j\sin\theta$

Rearrange your results to obtain

$\cos\theta =$ $\dfrac{e^{j\theta} + e^{-j\theta}}{2}$

$\sin\theta =$ $\dfrac{e^{j\theta} - e^{-j\theta}}{2j}$

The results obtained in Example 3.2 are important:

Key point

$$\cos\theta = \frac{e^{j\theta} + e^{-j\theta}}{2}, \quad \sin\theta = \frac{e^{j\theta} - e^{-j\theta}}{2j}$$

Exercises

1 Express each of the following in terms of trigonometrical functions:
(a) $e^{j\alpha}$ (b) $e^{j\omega t}$ (c) $e^{-j\omega t}$
where α, ω and t are real.

2 Express $\cos\omega t$ in terms of exponential functions.

3 Express $\sin\omega t$ in terms of exponential functions.

4 Show that $3\left(\frac{e^{j\omega} - e^{-j\omega}}{j\omega}\right) = \frac{6\sin\omega}{\omega}$.

Solutions to exercises

1 (a) $\cos\alpha + j\sin\alpha$ (b) $\cos\omega t + j\sin\omega t$
(c) $\cos\omega t - j\sin\omega t$

2 $\dfrac{e^{j\omega t} + e^{-j\omega t}}{2}$

3 $\dfrac{e^{j\omega t} - e^{-j\omega t}}{2j}$

3.3 The exponential form of a complex number

Using the polar form, recall that a complex number with modulus r and argument θ may be written as

$$z = r(\cos\theta + j\sin\theta)$$

It follows immediately from Euler's relations that we can also write this complex number in **exponential form** as $z = re^{j\theta}$. Further, since the complex conjugate of $\cos\theta + j\sin\theta$ is $\cos\theta - j\sin\theta$, the conjugate may be written $\bar{z} = re^{-j\theta}$.

Key point

Exponential form of a complex number

$$z = r(\cos\theta + j\sin\theta) = re^{j\theta}$$
$$\bar{z} = r(\cos\theta - j\sin\theta) = re^{-j\theta}$$

When using this form you should ensure that all angles are measured in radians and not degrees.

Example 3.3

State the modulus and argument of the following complex numbers: (a) $z = 4e^{j\pi/6}$, (b) $z = 0.01e^{0.02j}$, (c) $3e^{-j\pi/2}$.

Solution

(a) The modulus and argument of $4e^{j\pi/6}$ are 4 and $\frac{\pi}{6}$ respectively.

(b) The modulus and argument of $0.01e^{0.02j}$ are 0.01 and 0.02 respectively.

(c) The modulus and argument of $3e^{-j\pi/2}$ are 3 and $-\frac{\pi}{2}$ respectively.

Example 3.4

Express the number $z = 3 + 3j$ in exponential form.

Solution

To express a number in exponential form we must first find its modulus and argument. The modulus of $3 + 3j$ is $\sqrt{3^2 + 3^2} = \sqrt{18}$ or $3\sqrt{2}$. The complex number lies in the first quadrant of the Argand diagram and so its argument θ is given by $\theta = \tan^{-1}(\frac{3}{3}) = \frac{\pi}{4}$. Thus

$$\begin{aligned} z &= 3 + 3j \\ &= \sqrt{18}\, e^{j\pi/4} \end{aligned}$$

Example 3.5

Find the real and imaginary parts of $z = e^{j\omega t}$ where ω and t are real numbers.

Solution

Using the first of Euler's relations we can write

$e^{j\omega t} =$

$\cos \omega t + j \sin \omega t$

Write down the real and imaginary parts:

$\cos \omega t$, $\sin \omega t$

Example 3.6 Control Engineering – Stability of a system

In control theory it is often useful to work with complex numbers in the form

$$z = e^{st}$$

where s is the complex number $\sigma + j\omega$, and where t, ω and σ are real. The quantity ω is a frequency.

(a) Find the real and imaginary parts of z.

(b) Find $|z|$.

Solution

(a) Writing $s = \sigma + j\omega$ we have

$$\begin{aligned} z &= e^{st} \\ &= e^{(\sigma + j\omega)t} \\ &= e^{\sigma t + j\omega t} \end{aligned}$$

Using the first law of indices we can write this as

$$\begin{aligned} z &= e^{\sigma t}e^{j\omega t} \\ &= e^{\sigma t}(\cos \omega t + j \sin \omega t) \end{aligned}$$

Now because σ and t are real, so too is $e^{\sigma t}$. Thus the real part of z is $e^{\sigma t}\cos \omega t$ and the imaginary part of z is $e^{\sigma t}\sin \omega t$.

(b) Recall that the modulus of $re^{j\theta}$ is r. Hence the modulus of $z = e^{\sigma t}e^{j\omega t}$ is $e^{\sigma t}$, that is

$$|z| = e^{\sigma t}$$

If $\sigma > 0$ then $e^{\sigma t}$ increases as time, t, increases and the system is said to be **unstable**. If $\sigma < 0$, then $e^{\sigma t}$ decreases with t and the system is said to be **stable**.

Exercises

1 State the modulus and argument of each of the following complex numbers:
(a) $4e^{0.2j}$ (b) $3e^{2\pi j/3}$ (c) $e^{2\pi j}$ (d) $0.35e^{-0.2j}$
(e) $0.35e^{-0.2}$

2 Express each of the following in the form $re^{j\theta}$:
(a) $3\angle\left(\frac{\pi}{3}\right)$ (b) $\sqrt{2}\angle\left(\frac{\pi}{4}\right)$
(c) $3\angle\left(\frac{-\pi}{4}\right)$ (d) $5\angle 0$ (e) $17\angle\left(\frac{\pi}{2}\right)$

3 Express each of the following in the form $a + bj$:
(a) $13e^{j\pi/3}$ (b) $13e^{-j\pi/3}$ (c) $4e^{2\pi j}$

4 Show that $|e^{j\theta}| = 1$.

5 Show that $|e^{-j\theta}| = 1$.

6 Write down the complex conjugate of $e^{j\theta}$.

7 Express $z = -1 + 2j$ in the form $re^{j\theta}$.

8 Show that the real and imaginary parts of $e^{(\alpha+\beta j)t}$ are respectively $e^{\alpha t}\cos \beta t$ and $e^{\alpha t}\sin \beta t$.

9 Express each of the following in exponential form:
(a) -5 (b) $(1 + j)(1 - 2j)$ (c) $(1 + 8j)^{11}$
(d) $\dfrac{(1 + 2j)^3}{1 - j}$

Solutions to exercises

1 (a) 4, 0.2 radians (b) 3, $\frac{2\pi}{3}$ radians
(c) 1, 2π radians (d) 0.35, -0.2 radians
(e) $0.35e^{-0.2}$, 0 radians

2 (a) $3e^{j\pi/3}$ (b) $\sqrt{2}e^{j\pi/4}$ (c) $3e^{-j\pi/4}$ (d) $5e^0 = 5$
(e) $17e^{j\pi/2}$

3 (a) $6.5 + 11.3j$ (b) $6.5 - 11.3j$ (c) 4

6 $e^{-j\theta}$

7 $\sqrt{5}e^{2.03j}$

9 (a) $5e^{\pi j}$ (b) $\sqrt{10}e^{-0.32j}$ (c) $65^{11/2}e^{-2.94j}$
(d) $7.91e^{-2.18j}$

End of block exercises

1 Show the following complex numbers on an Argand diagram:
(a) $5e^{j\pi/3}$ (b) $7e^{2\pi j}$ (c) $4e^{\pi j}$ (d) $e^{j\pi/4}$

2 Find the real and imaginary parts of the following:
(a) $4e^{j\pi/3}$ (b) $5e^{-j2\pi/3}$ (c) $e^{j\pi/2}$ (d) $e^{-j\pi/2}$

3 Find the real and imaginary parts of
(a) e^{j-1} (b) $4e^{\alpha+j\beta}$ (c) $e^{-j\pi/6}$ (d) $e^{0.1}$ (e) $je^{0.1}$

4 Show that $\tan\theta = -j\left(\dfrac{e^{j\theta} - e^{-j\theta}}{e^{j\theta} + e^{-j\theta}}\right)$.

5 If $z_1 = 4e^{j\pi/4}$ and $z_2 = 5e^{-j\pi/6}$ find

(a) $z_1 z_2$ (b) $\frac{z_1}{z_2}$ (c) $z_1\overline{z_1}$ (d) $z_1 + z_2$

6 Given $z = 6e^{j0.23}$ express z^3 in exponential and polar forms.

7 If a and b are real, and

$(a + jb)e^{j\pi/3} + \sqrt{2}e^{-j\pi/4} = 5 + j$

find a and b.

Solutions to exercises

2 (a) $2, \frac{4\sqrt{3}}{2} = 3.464$ (b) $-\frac{5}{2}, -\frac{5\sqrt{3}}{2}$

(c) 0, 1 (d) 0, −1

3 (a) $e^{-1}\cos 1, e^{-1}\sin 1$ (b) $4e^{\alpha}\cos\beta, 4e^{\alpha}\sin\beta$

(c) $\frac{\sqrt{3}}{2}, \frac{-1}{2}$ (d) $e^{0.1}$, 0, (e) 0, $e^{0.1}$

5 (a) $20e^{j\pi/12}$ (b) $\frac{4}{5}e^{j5\pi/12}$ (c) 16

(d) 7.158 + 0.328j

6 $6^3e^{0.69j}, 6^3(\cos 0.69 + j\sin 0.69)$

7 $a = \sqrt{3} + 2, b = 1 - 2\sqrt{3}$

BLOCK 4 De Moivre's theorem

4.1 Introduction

De Moivre's theorem is one of the most important results in the theory of complex numbers. It can be used to find powers of complex numbers, and to prove trigonometrical identities. In this block we introduce and illustrate the use of the theorem. In Block 5 we show how the theorem can be used to solve equations. To understand this block it is essential that you are aware that a complex number can be written in polar form as $z = r(\cos\theta + \mathrm{j}\sin\theta)$ or more compactly as $z = r\angle\theta$.

4.2 De Moivre's theorem

We state and use the theorem here. The proof is left as an exercise (see question 4 in the exercises below). The theorem involves raising the complex number $\cos\theta + \mathrm{j}\sin\theta$ to the power n.

Key point

De Moivre's theorem

$$(\cos\theta + \mathrm{j}\sin\theta)^n = \cos n\theta + j\sin n\theta$$

Note that by using the theorem an expression involving powers of trigonometrical functions can be converted into one involving trigonometrical functions of multiple angles. This is useful in proving trigonometrical identities, as we shall see.

The theorem is valid when n is an integer and enables us to write, for example,

$$(\cos\theta + \mathrm{j}\sin\theta)^2 \text{ as } \cos 2\theta + \mathrm{j}\sin 2\theta$$

It is also valid if n is a fraction and in such a case can be used to find roots of complex numbers. Examples of this can be found in Block 5.

Example 4.1

Use De Moivre's theorem to write $(\cos\theta + \mathrm{j}\sin\theta)^3$ in an alternative form.

Solution

Use the theorem with $n = 3$:

$(\cos\theta + \mathrm{j}\sin\theta)^3 =$ $\cos 3\theta + \mathrm{j}\sin 3\theta$

Example 4.2

Use De Moivre's theorem to write $(\cos\theta + \mathrm{j}\sin\theta)^5$ in an alternative form.

Solution

Use the theorem with $n = 5$:

$(\cos\theta + \mathrm{j}\sin\theta)^5 =$ $\cos 5\theta + \mathrm{j}\sin 5\theta$

We can use De Moivre's theorem to obtain powers of a complex number very easily. Consider the following example.

Example 4.3

If $z = r(\cos\theta + \mathrm{j}\sin\theta)$ write down expressions for (a) z^2 and (b) z^3, and use De Moivre's theorem to write your results in an alternative form.

Solution

(a) $z^2 =$ $r^2(\cos\theta + \mathrm{j}\sin\theta)^2$

which, using De Moivre's theorem, can be written as

$r^2(\cos 2\theta + \mathrm{j}\sin 2\theta)$

(b) $z^3 =$ $r^3(\cos\theta + \mathrm{j}\sin\theta)^3$

which, using De Moivre's theorem, can be written as

$r^3(\cos 3\theta + \mathrm{j}\sin 3\theta)$

If we use the abbreviated form $r\angle\theta$ the previous example can be written much more concisely:

Key point

If $z = r\angle\theta$ then

$$z^n = r^n\angle n\theta$$

for example,

$$z^2 = r^2\angle 2\theta, \quad z^3 = r^3\angle 3\theta, \quad \text{and so on}$$

Example 4.4

(a) If $z = 3\angle\frac{\pi}{4}$ write down z^5.

(b) Express your answer in the form $r(\cos\theta + \mathrm{j}\sin\theta)$ and its cartesian form.

Solution

(a) If $z = 3\angle\frac{\pi}{4}$ then $z^5 =$

$$3^5\angle\left(5 \times \frac{\pi}{4}\right) = 243\angle\frac{5\pi}{4}$$

(b) $243\angle\frac{5\pi}{4} = 243\left(\cos\frac{5\pi}{4} + \mathrm{j}\sin\frac{5\pi}{4}\right) = -171.8 - 171.8\mathrm{j}$

Example 4.5

If $z = 7\left(\cos\frac{\pi}{4} + \mathrm{j}\sin\frac{\pi}{4}\right)$ find z^2.

Solution

Using De Moivre's theorem with $n = 2$ we can write

$$\begin{aligned} z^2 &= 7^2\left(\cos\frac{\pi}{4} + \mathrm{j}\sin\frac{\pi}{4}\right)^2 \\ &= 49\left(\cos\frac{2\pi}{4} + \mathrm{j}\sin\frac{2\pi}{4}\right) \\ &= 49\left(\cos\frac{\pi}{2} + \mathrm{j}\sin\frac{\pi}{2}\right) \\ &= 49\,\mathrm{j} \end{aligned}$$

since $\cos\frac{\pi}{2} = 0$ and $\sin\frac{\pi}{2} = 1$.

Example 4.6

(a) Express $z = 2 + 5\mathrm{j}$ in polar form.
(b) Hence find $(2 + 5\mathrm{j})^{12}$, leaving your answer in polar form.

Solution

(a) The modulus of $2 + 5\mathrm{j}$ is $\sqrt{2^2 + 5^2} = \sqrt{29}$. The number lies in the first quadrant of an Argand diagram and so its argument θ is given by $\theta = \tan^{-1}\frac{5}{2} = 1.190$. Thus $z = 2 + 5\mathrm{j} = \sqrt{29}\angle 1.190$.

(b) Using De Moivre's theorem we have

$$\begin{aligned} (\sqrt{29}\angle 1.190)^{12} &= (\sqrt{29})^{12}\angle 12 \times 1.190 \\ &= 29^6\angle 14.283 \end{aligned}$$

Example 4.7

If $z = \cos\theta + \mathrm{j}\sin\theta$ use De Moivre's theorem with $n = -1$ to obtain an expression for $\frac{1}{z}$.

Solution

With $n = -1$ we have

$$\begin{aligned} z^{-1} &= (\cos\theta + \mathrm{j}\sin\theta)^{-1} \\ &= \cos(-\theta) + \mathrm{j}\sin(-\theta) \\ &= \cos\theta - \mathrm{j}\sin\theta \end{aligned}$$

The last line follows since $\cos\theta$ is an even function and $\sin\theta$ is an odd function. Thus $\frac{1}{z} = \cos\theta - \mathrm{j}\sin\theta$.

Exercises

1. If $z = 4\angle\frac{\pi}{6}$ find z^6 in polar form.

2. Express $z = 2 + 2\mathrm{j}$ in polar form and hence find z^8, leaving your answer in polar form. Deduce that $(2 + 2\mathrm{j})^8 = 4096$.

3. Express $z = -3 + 2\mathrm{j}$ in polar form and hence find z^6, converting your answer into cartesian form.

4. Consider the complex number $z = \cos\theta + \mathrm{j}\sin\theta$.
   (a) Write down the exponential form of this number.
   (b) By raising the exponential form to the power n, and using one of the laws of indices, deduce De Moivre's theorem.

5. Use De Moivre's theorem to show that if $z = \cos\theta + \mathrm{j}\sin\theta$ then
   (a) $z^n = \cos n\theta + \mathrm{j}\sin n\theta$
   (b) $z^{-n} = \cos n\theta - \mathrm{j}\sin n\theta$
   Deduce that

$$z^n + \frac{1}{z^n} = 2\cos n\theta \text{ and}$$

$$z^n - \frac{1}{z^n} = 2\mathrm{j}\sin n\theta$$

Solutions to exercises

1. $4^6\angle\pi$

2. $\sqrt{8}\angle\frac{\pi}{4}$, $8^4\angle 2\pi$

3. $\sqrt{13}\angle 2.554$, $13^3\angle 15.322$, $-2035 + 827\mathrm{j}$

4. (a) $z = \mathrm{e}^{\mathrm{j}\theta}$ (b) $z^n = (\mathrm{e}^{\mathrm{j}\theta})^n = \mathrm{e}^{\mathrm{j}n\theta}$

4.3 Using De Moivre's theorem to prove trigonometrical identities

One of the applications of the theorem is to prove various trigonometrical identities. Consider the following example.

Example 4.8

Use De Moivre's theorem to prove that

(a) $\sin 2\theta = 2\sin\theta\cos\theta$

(b) $\cos 2\theta = \cos^2\theta - \sin^2\theta$

Solution

(a) Using De Moivre's theorem with $n = 2$ we obtain

$$(\cos\theta + \mathrm{j}\sin\theta)^2 = \cos 2\theta + \mathrm{j}\sin 2\theta$$

Expanding the left-hand side we can write

$$\cos^2\theta + 2\mathrm{j}\sin\theta\cos\theta - \sin^2\theta = \cos 2\theta + \mathrm{j}\sin 2\theta$$

Equating the imaginary parts on both sides gives the required expression for $\sin 2\theta$:

$$\sin 2\theta = 2\sin\theta\cos\theta$$

(b) Equate the real parts in part (a) to obtain an identity for $\cos 2\theta$:

$$\cos 2\theta = \cos^2\theta - \sin^2\theta$$

Example 4.9

Express $\sin 3\theta$ as powers of $\sin\theta$.

Solution

Consider De Moivre's theorem with $n = 3$:

$$(\cos\theta + \mathrm{j}\sin\theta)^3 = \cos 3\theta + \mathrm{j}\sin 3\theta$$

Expand the expression on the left-hand side:

$$\cos^3\theta + 3\mathrm{j}\cos^2\theta\sin\theta - 3\cos\theta\sin^2\theta - \mathrm{j}\sin^3\theta$$

Compare this result with the right-hand side and equate the imaginary parts:

$$\sin 3\theta = 3\cos^2\theta\sin\theta - \sin^3\theta$$

Finally, noting that $\cos^2\theta = 1 - \sin^2\theta$, you should verify that

$$\sin 3\theta = 3\sin\theta - 4\sin^3\theta$$

In the two previous examples you saw how to convert trigonometrical functions of multiple angles into powers of trigonometrical functions. In the previous set of exercises it was shown (question 5) that if $z = \cos\theta + \mathrm{j}\sin\theta$ then

$$z^n + \frac{1}{z^n} = 2\cos n\theta \quad \text{and} \quad z^n - \frac{1}{z^n} = 2\mathrm{j}\sin n\theta$$

These results allow us to obtain a further range of trigonometrical identities. In particular they allow us to convert powers of trigonometrical functions into expressions involving trigonometrical functions of multiple angles.

Key point

If $z = \cos\theta + \mathrm{j}\sin\theta$ then

$$z^n + \frac{1}{z^n} = 2\cos n\theta \quad \text{and} \quad z^n - \frac{1}{z^n} = 2\mathrm{j}\sin n\theta$$

Example 4.10

If $z = \cos\theta + \mathrm{j}\sin\theta$ write down expressions for

(a) $z + \frac{1}{z}$ (b) $z^2 + \frac{1}{z^2}$ (c) $z - \frac{1}{z}$ (d) $z^2 - \frac{1}{z^2}$

Solution

(a) $z + \dfrac{1}{z} =$ $2\cos\theta$

(b) $z^2 + \dfrac{1}{z^2} =$ $2\cos 2\theta$

(c) $z - \dfrac{1}{z} =$ $2\mathrm{j}\sin\theta$

(d) $z^2 - \dfrac{1}{z^2} =$ $2\mathrm{j}\sin 2\theta$

Example 4.11

Show that $\cos^2\theta = \frac{1}{2}\cos 2\theta + \frac{1}{2}$.

Solution

Starting with $2\cos\theta = z + \dfrac{1}{z}$ and squaring both sides we obtain

$$\begin{aligned} 4\cos^2\theta &= \left(z + \frac{1}{z}\right)^2 \\ &= z^2 + 2 + \frac{1}{z^2} \\ &= \left(z^2 + \frac{1}{z^2}\right) + 2 \text{ by rearranging} \end{aligned}$$

But $z^2 + \frac{1}{z^2} = 2\cos 2\theta$ and so

$$4\cos^2\theta = 2\cos 2\theta + 2$$

from which

$$\cos^2\theta = \tfrac{1}{2}\cos 2\theta + \tfrac{1}{2}$$

as required.

Example 4.12

By squaring the result $2j\sin\theta = z - \dfrac{1}{z}$ prove the identity $\sin^2\theta = \frac{1}{2} - \frac{1}{2}\cos 2\theta$.

Solution

Consider $2j\sin\theta = z - \dfrac{1}{z}$.

Squaring the left-hand side gives $-4\sin^2\theta$. Now square the right-hand side.

$$\left(z - \frac{1}{z}\right)^2 = \qquad z^2 - 2 + \frac{1}{z^2}$$

Rearrange this and express it in terms of $\cos 2\theta$ using the previous key point.

$$z^2 - 2 + \frac{1}{z^2} = \qquad \left(z^2 + \frac{1}{z^2}\right) - 2 = 2\cos 2\theta - 2$$

Finally we have

$$-4\sin^2\theta = 2\cos 2\theta - 2$$

from which $\sin^2\theta = \frac{1}{2} - \frac{1}{2}\cos 2\theta$ as required.

Exercises

1 Show that $\cos 4\theta = 8\cos^4\theta - 8\cos^2\theta + 1$.

2 Show that

$$\sin 4\theta = 4\cos^3\theta\sin\theta - 4\cos\theta\sin^3\theta$$

3 Use your answers from questions 1 and 2 to deduce that

$$\tan 4\theta = \frac{4\tan\theta - 4\tan^3\theta}{1 - 6\tan^2\theta + \tan^4\theta}$$

4 Show that $\cos^3\theta = \dfrac{1}{4}(\cos 3\theta + 3\cos\theta)$.

End of block exercises

1 Use De Moivre's theorem to show that $\cos 5\theta = 16\cos^5\theta - 20\cos^3\theta + 5\cos\theta$ and obtain a similar expression for $\sin 5\theta$ in powers of $\sin\theta$.

2 Show that

$$\sin^4\theta = \tfrac{1}{8}(\cos 4\theta - 4\cos 2\theta + 3)$$

Solutions to exercises

1 $\sin 5\theta = 16\sin^5\theta - 20\sin^3\theta + 5\sin\theta$

BLOCK 5 Solving equations and finding roots of complex numbers

5.1 Introduction

By using complex numbers, solutions can be obtained to a wide range of equations. There is no single appropriate method for tackling these and so experience and practice are essential. Sometimes it is convenient to work in cartesian form, but on other occasions solutions are easier to obtain in polar form. You should be aware that a polynomial equation of degree n possesses n roots, but some of these can be repeated, or equal, roots. So, when solving a quadratic equation we shall be looking for two roots, when solving a cubic equation we shall be looking for three roots, and so on.

5.2 Solving equations

Example 5.1
Solve the equation $z^3 + 5z = 0$.

Solution
This is a polynomial equation of degree 3. We seek three solutions. The equation can be factorised:

$$z^3 + 5z = z(z^2 + 5) = 0$$

so that one solution is $z = 0$, and others can be obtained by solving $z^2 + 5 = 0$.
From $z^2 + 5 = 0$ we have

$$\begin{aligned} z^2 &= -5 \\ z &= \pm\sqrt{-5} \\ &= \pm\sqrt{5}\mathrm{j} \end{aligned}$$

Thus the solutions of the given equation are $z = 0$ and $z = \pm\sqrt{5}\mathrm{j}$.

Example 5.2
Solve the equation $z^2 + 2z + 2 = 0$.

Solution
This is simply a quadratic equation. Apply the formula

$$z = \frac{-b \pm \sqrt{b^2 - 4ac}}{2a}$$

$$= \frac{-2 \pm \sqrt{4 - 4(1)(2)}}{2}$$

$$= \frac{-2 \pm \sqrt{-4}}{2}$$

$$= \quad z = -1 \pm \mathrm{j}$$

Often it is more convenient to work in polar form, and so before attempting to solve any more equations it will be useful to review how the polar form of a complex number is obtained. Consider the number 4, illustrated in Figure 5.1(a). Its modulus is 4 and its argument is 0. However, it is important to note that if we increase the argument by 360°, or 2π, we remain at the same location on the Argand diagram as shown in Figure 5.1(b). Indeed we can increase the argument by further multiples of 360° and still represent the same complex number, as shown in Figure 5.1(c).

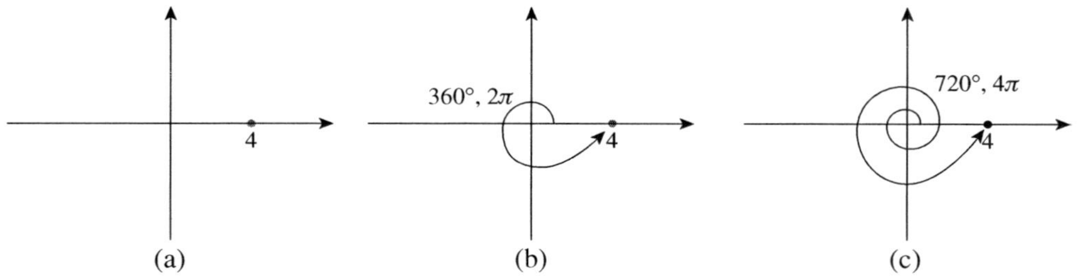

Figure 5.1
The argument of a complex number takes many values.

Thus in polar form we can write 4 as $4\angle 0$, $4\angle 2\pi$, $4\angle 4\pi$, and so on. We can generalise this as $4\angle 2k\pi$ where $k = 0, 1, 2, \ldots$. In the examples that follow you should bear this in mind when converting complex numbers to polar form.

Example 5.3

Express the number $z = 2 + \mathrm{j}$ in polar form, and include the general form for the argument.

Solution

The complex number $z = 2 + \mathrm{j}$ is shown in Figure 5.2. Its modulus is $|z| = \sqrt{2^2 + 1^2} = \sqrt{5}$. Its argument is $\tan^{-1}\frac{1}{2} = 0.464$. However, adding on multiples of 2π results in the same complex number, so we can write $\arg(z) = 0.464 + 2k\pi$. Finally the polar form is $z = \sqrt{5}\angle(0.464 + 2k\pi)$.

Figure 5.2

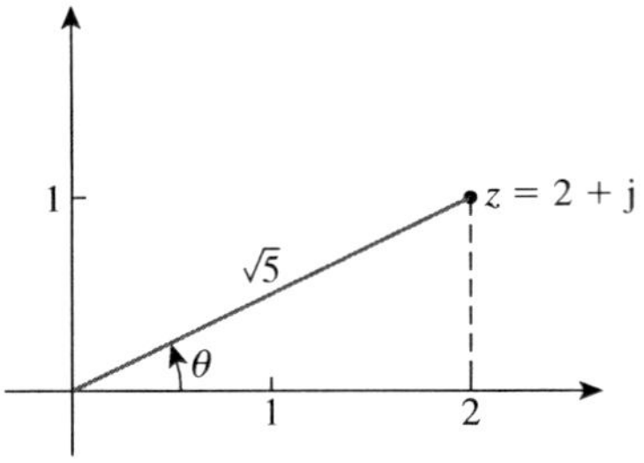

$\theta = \tan^{-1}(\frac{1}{2}) = 0.464$
$\arg(z) = 0.464 + 2k\pi$

Example 5.4

Solve the equation $z^3 - 4 = 0$.

Solution

This is a polynomial equation of degree 3. We look for three solutions. Note that this equation can be written as $z^3 = 4$. We shall show that by working in polar form it is straightforward to obtain the solutions. You should also note that the equation is equivalent to $z = 4^{1/3}$ so we are finding the cube roots of 4.

As z is a complex number, we can write it in polar form as $z = r\angle\theta$. When we have succeeded in finding r and θ, we shall know z and will have solved the problem.

Consider, first, the left-hand side of

$$z^3 = 4$$

If $z = r\angle\theta$ then write down an expression for z^3:

$z^3 =$ $\qquad$ $r^3\angle 3\theta$

Now express the right-hand side in polar form including the general term for the argument.

$4 =$ $\qquad$ $4\angle 2k\pi, k = 0, 1, 2, \ldots$

Therefore, working entirely in polar form, the equation becomes

$$r^3\angle 3\theta = 4\angle 2k\pi$$

Equating moduli on both sides gives $r^3 = 4$ so that $r = 4^{1/3}$, the real cube root of 4 since r is real.

Equating arguments,

$$3\theta = 2k\pi \text{ so that } \theta = \frac{2k\pi}{3}, \quad k = 0, 1, 2, \ldots$$

Taking $k = 0, 1, 2$ in turn gives the three solutions

$$z = 4^{1/3}\angle 0, \quad z = 4^{1/3}\angle\frac{2\pi}{3}, \quad z = 4^{1/3}\angle\frac{4\pi}{3}$$

Figure 5.3
The solutions of $z^3 - 4 = 0$.

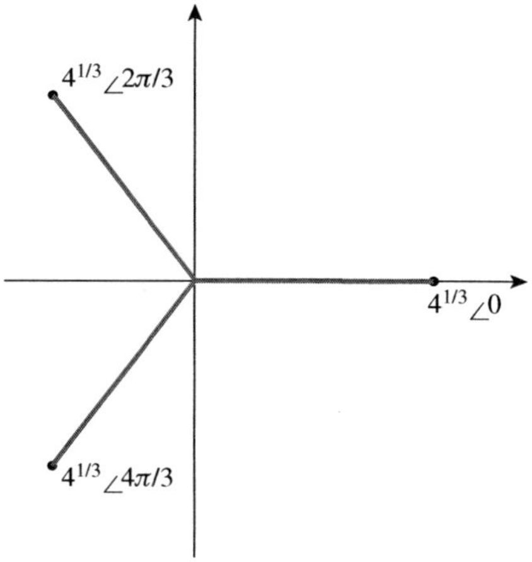

These solutions are illustrated in Figure 5.3.

Note that if k is increased beyond 2, we find the solutions already obtained.

If necessary these solutions can be expressed in cartesian form. Do this for yourself now:

$4^{1/3}\angle 0 =$ $\qquad$ $4^{1/3}$ or $\sqrt[3]{4}$

$4^{1/3}\angle\frac{2\pi}{3} =$ $\qquad$ $4^{1/3}\left(-\frac{1}{2} + \frac{\sqrt{3}}{2}\text{j}\right)$

$4^{1/3}\angle\frac{4\pi}{3} =$ $\qquad$ $4^{1/3}\left(-\frac{1}{2} - \frac{\sqrt{3}}{2}\text{j}\right)$

Example 5.5

Solve the equation $z^3 + 2 = 0$.

Solution

Note that this equation can be written $z^3 = -2$. Again we work in polar form.

Consider, first, the left-hand side of

$$z^3 = -2$$

If $z = r\angle\theta$ then $z^3 = r^3\angle 3\theta$.

Now express the right-hand side in polar form. The complex number $z = -2$ is shown in Figure 5.4 to help you do this.

Figure 5.4
The complex number $z = -2$.

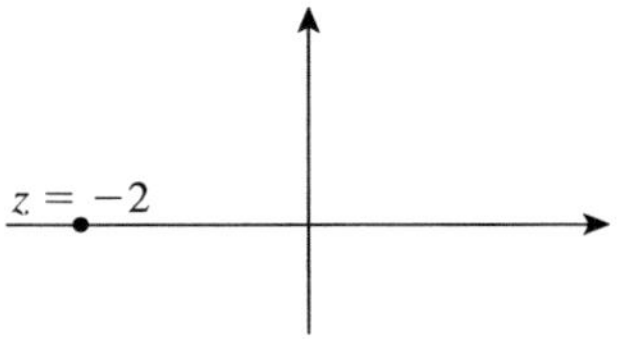

$-2 = 2\angle(\pi + 2k\pi)$ where $k = 0, 1, 2, \ldots$

Therefore, working entirely in polar form the equation becomes

$$r^3\angle 3\theta = 2\angle(\pi + 2k\pi)$$

Equate moduli on both sides to find r.

$r =$

$r = 2^{1/3}$, the real cube root of 2

Equate arguments, to find θ:

$\theta =$

$\dfrac{\pi}{3} + \dfrac{2k\pi}{3}, k = 0, 1, 2, \ldots$

Taking $k = 0, 1, 2$ in turn gives the three solutions

$z = 2^{1/3}\angle\dfrac{\pi}{3}, 2^{1/3}\angle\pi, 2^{1/3}\angle\dfrac{5\pi}{3}$

These solutions are illustrated in Figure 5.5.

Figure 5.5

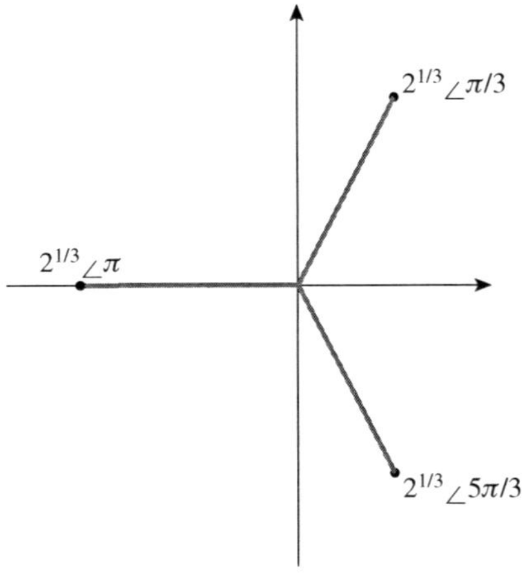

Note that if k is increased beyond 2, we find the solutions already obtained.

If necessary these solutions can be expressed in cartesian form. Do this for yourself now:

$2^{1/3}\angle\dfrac{\pi}{3} =$

$2^{1/3}\left(\dfrac{1}{2} + \dfrac{\sqrt{3}}{2}\mathrm{j}\right)$

$2^{1/3}\angle\pi =$ $-2^{1/3}$ or $-\sqrt[3]{2}$

$2^{1/3}\angle\dfrac{5\pi}{3} =$ $2^{1/3}\left(\dfrac{1}{2} - \dfrac{\sqrt{3}}{2}\mathrm{j}\right)$

Example 5.6

Solve the equation $z^6 - 2z^3 - 8 = 0$.

Solution

By careful inspection note that this equation can be factorised as

$$\begin{aligned} z^6 - 2z^3 - 8 &= (z^3 - 4)(z^3 + 2) \\ &= 0 \end{aligned}$$

(If you cannot spot this directly, try making a substitution, $w = z^3$, and obtain a quadratic equation in w.) Thus $z^3 - 4 = 0$ or $z^3 + 2 = 0$. We have already solved each of these separately in Examples 5.4 and 5.5. Thus the six solutions are those obtained in these examples.

Example 5.7

Solve the equation $z^2 = 2 + \mathrm{j}$.

Solution

In general the unknown z will be a complex number and so $z = r\angle\theta$. Then $z^2 = r^2\angle 2\theta$. Now consider the right-hand side of the given equation, $2 + \mathrm{j}$. This has been expressed in polar form in Example 5.3. Therefore

$$r^2\angle 2\theta = 5^{1/2}\angle(0.464 + 2k\pi)$$

Comparing moduli on both sides we see that

$$r^2 = 5^{1/2} \quad \text{so that} \quad r = 5^{1/4}$$

Also, comparing arguments,

$$2\theta = 0.464 + 2k\pi$$

from which

$$\begin{aligned} \theta &= \frac{0.464 + 2k\pi}{2} \\ &= 0.232 + k\pi, k = 0, 1, 2, \ldots \end{aligned}$$

The two solutions we seek are obtained by letting $k = 0$ and then $k = 1$. Increasing k further will reproduce solutions already found.

When $k = 0, \theta = 0.232$.
When $k = 1, \theta = 0.232 + \pi$.

Hence the two solutions are

$$5^{1/4}(\cos 0.232 + \mathrm{j}\sin 0.232) \quad \text{and} \quad 5^{1/4}[\cos(0.232 + \pi) + \mathrm{j}\sin(0.232 + \pi)]$$

These solutions are shown in the Argand diagram in Figure 5.6. If necessary they can be converted to cartesian form as $1.46 + 0.34\mathrm{j}$ and $-1.46 - 0.34\mathrm{j}$.

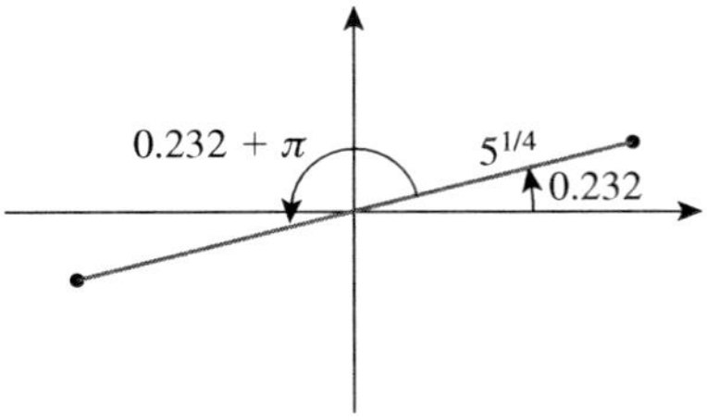

Figure 5.6
The two solutions of $z^2 = 2 + \mathrm{j}$.

The techniques used in the previous examples can be used to find roots of complex numbers. Suppose we wanted to find the cube roots of j, that is $\mathrm{j}^{1/3}$. Writing $z = \mathrm{j}^{1/3}$ and cubing both sides we obtain

$$z^3 = \mathrm{j}$$

So finding the cube roots of j is equivalent to solving the equation $z^3 = \mathrm{j}$. This can be done using the technique of Examples 5.4, 5.5 or 5.7.

Exercises

1 Solve the equation $-z^2 + 3z - 4 = 0$.

2 Solve each of the following equations leaving your answers in polar form:
(a) $z^2 = 1 + \mathrm{j}$ (b) $z^2 = 1 - \mathrm{j}$
(c) $z^3 = -2 + 3\mathrm{j}$

3 Solve the following equations converting your solutions to cartesian form:
(a) $z^3 = -1$ (b) $z^3 = 1$ (c) $z^3 - 6\mathrm{j} = 0$

Solutions to exercises

1 $z = \frac{3}{2} \pm \frac{\sqrt{7}}{2}\mathrm{j}$.

2 (a) $2^{1/4}\angle\frac{\pi}{8}, 2^{1/4}\angle\frac{9\pi}{8}$

(b) $2^{1/4}\angle -\frac{\pi}{8}, 2^{1/4}\angle\frac{7\pi}{8}$

(c) $13^{1/6}\angle 0.720, 13^{1/6}\angle 2.814, 13^{1/6}\angle 4.908$

3 (a) $z = -1, z = \frac{1}{2} + \frac{\sqrt{3}}{2}\mathrm{j}, z = \frac{1}{2} - \frac{\sqrt{3}}{2}\mathrm{j}$

(b) $z = 1, z = -\frac{1}{2} \pm \mathrm{j}\frac{\sqrt{3}}{2}$

(c) $-6^{1/3}\mathrm{j}, 6^{1/3}\left(\frac{\sqrt{3}}{2} + \mathrm{j}\frac{1}{2}\right),$
$6^{1/3}\left(-\frac{\sqrt{3}}{2} + \mathrm{j}\frac{1}{2}\right)$

End of block exercises

1 Find the three cube roots of -8.

2 Find the three cube roots of 8.

3 Find the cube roots of $z = \dfrac{(-3 + j)^4}{(2 - j)^2}$.

4 Find all complex numbers which satisfy $z^5 + 4z = 0$ and express your answers in cartesian form.

5 Solve the equation $z^4 + 25 = 0$ showing each solution on an Argand diagram.

6 Find the cube roots of $\sqrt{3} + j$.

7 Find the cube roots of $\sqrt{3} - j$.

Solutions to exercises

1 $-2, 1 \pm \sqrt{3}j$

2 $2, -1 \pm \sqrt{3}j$

3 $z = 2.695 - 0.325j$, $z = -1.066 + 2.496j$, $z = -1.629 - 2.172j$

4 $z = 0, 1 \pm j, -1 \pm j$

5 $z = \dfrac{\sqrt{10}}{2} \pm \dfrac{\sqrt{10}}{2}j$, $z = -\dfrac{\sqrt{10}}{2} \pm \dfrac{\sqrt{10}}{2}j$

6 $z = 1.241 + 0.219j$, $z = -0.431 - 1.184j$, $z = -0.810 + 0.965j$

7 $z = 1.241 - 0.219j$, $z = -0.431 + 1.184j$, $z = -0.810 - 0.965j$

BLOCK 6 Phasors

6.1 Introduction

One of the most important applications of complex numbers in engineering is in the study of alternating current (a.c.) circuits. The phase relationships between different components in a circuit can be expressed using complex numbers. A phasor is a quantity that contains information about the peak voltage or peak current in a component together with its phase.

6.2 Phase relationships in *LCR* circuits

The voltage in an a.c. circuit can be expressed in the form

$$v(t) = V\sin(\omega t + \phi)$$

where V is the peak voltage, ω is the angular frequency, ϕ is the phase relative to some reference voltage and t is time. Recall that $\omega = 2\pi f$ where f is the frequency. Similarly a current can be expressed as $i(t) = I\sin(\omega t + \phi)$ where I is the peak current.

Resistor

Consider a circuit containing a resistor of resistance R. Let $v_R(t)$ be the voltage across the resistor. The current, $i(t)$, through the resistor is in phase with this voltage. This means that both the voltage and current are zero at the same time and peak at the same time. This fact is illustrated in the graphs of $i(t)$ and $v_R(t)$ in Figure 6.1.

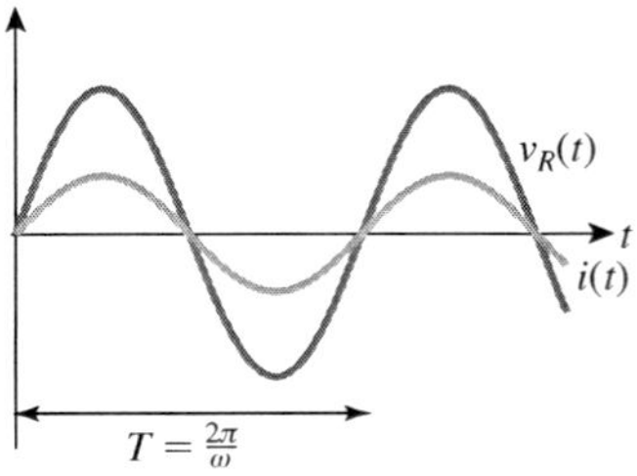

Figure 6.1 In a circuit containing a resistor, R, the current and voltage are in phase.

The current is related to the voltage by Ohm's law, which states that $v_R = Ri$. For example, if $i(t) = I \sin \omega t$, then $v_R = IR \sin \omega t$.

Inductor

Consider a circuit containing an inductor having inductance L. Experiment shows that the voltage across the inductor, v_L, leads the current by a phase of $\frac{\pi}{2}$. If $i(t) = I \sin \omega t$, then it can be shown from Faraday's law that

$$v_L = \omega LI \sin\left(\omega t + \frac{\pi}{2}\right)$$

This means that the voltage peaks earlier than the current, as illustrated in Figure 6.2.

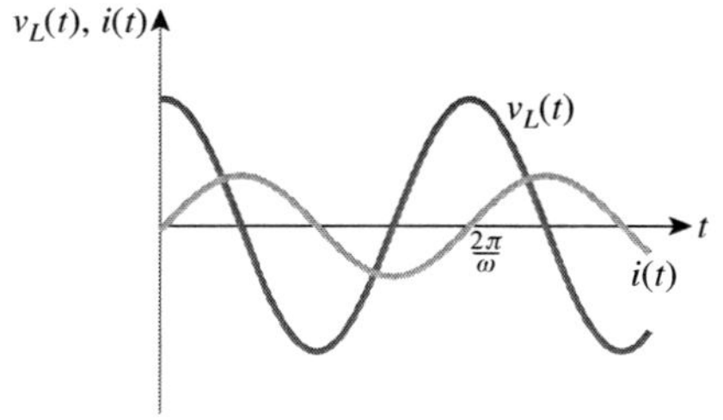

Figure 6.2 In a circuit containing an inductor, the voltage leads the current by a phase of $\frac{\pi}{2}$.

Capacitor

In a circuit containing a capacitor having capacitance C, experiment shows that the voltage across the capacitor, v_C, lags behind the current by a phase of $\frac{\pi}{2}$. It can be shown that if $i(t) = I \sin \omega t$, then

$$v_C = \frac{I}{\omega C} \sin\left(\omega t - \frac{\pi}{2}\right)$$

This means that the voltage peaks after the current, as illustrated in Figure 6.3.

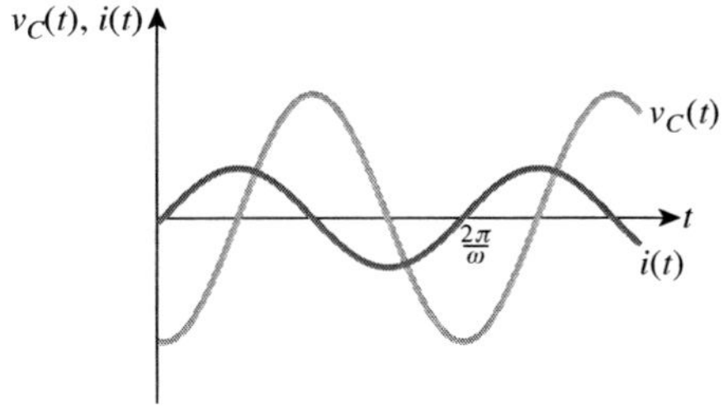

Figure 6.3 In a circuit containing a capacitor, the voltage lags behind the current by a phase of $\frac{\pi}{2}$.

6.3 Phasors

Consider the waveform in Figure 6.4(a), which might represent a voltage, $V_1 \sin \omega t$, in an a.c. circuit. The time it takes to complete one cycle, that is the period, is $\frac{2\pi}{\omega}$.

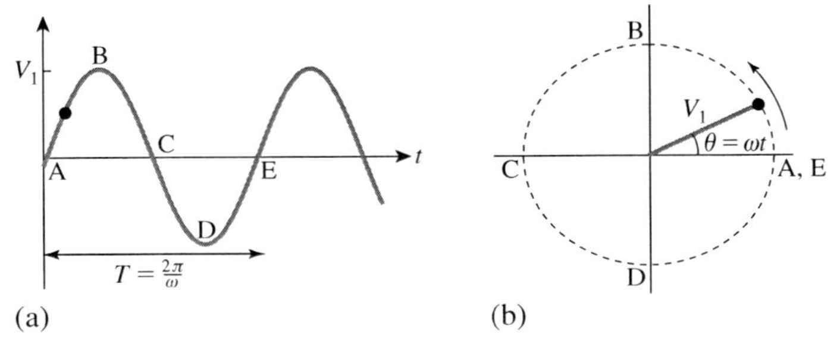

Figure 6.4 Points on a waveform and equivalent points on a rotating arm.

An alternative representation of the same physical situation is shown in Figure 6.4(b). It shows an arm rotating anticlockwise. The length of the arm is V_1 and it rotates at ω radians per second.

Moving at an angular velocity of ω radians per second means that it completes

$$1 \text{ radian in } \frac{1}{\omega} \text{ seconds}$$

$$2\pi \text{ radians in } \frac{2\pi}{\omega} \text{ seconds}$$

So it completes a full revolution in $T = \frac{2\pi}{\omega}$ seconds. The time it takes to complete a revolution is the same as the time it takes for one cycle of the waveform to be completed in Figure 6.4(a). There is an obvious correspondence between points on the sine wave and positions of the arm. Points A, B, C, D and E illustrate this. For any value of t on the waveform, the angle of the arm is ωt. Such a rotating arm is called a **phasor**.

If we have a second waveform, such as $V_2 \sin(\omega t + \frac{\pi}{2})$, which leads the first by a phase of $\frac{\pi}{2}$, then its rotating arm will lead that of $V_1 \sin \omega t$ by $\frac{\pi}{2}$, as shown in Figure 6.5.

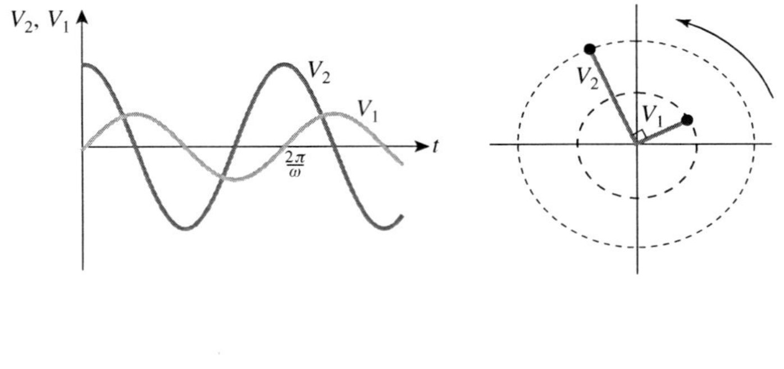

Figure 6.5 Phasor 2 leads phasor 1 by $\frac{\pi}{2}$.

Similarly, if we have a third waveform, such as $V_3\sin(\omega t - \frac{\pi}{2})$, which lags behind the first by a phase of $\frac{\pi}{2}$, then its rotating arm will lag that of $V_1 \sin \omega t$ by $\frac{\pi}{2}$ as shown in Figure 6.6.

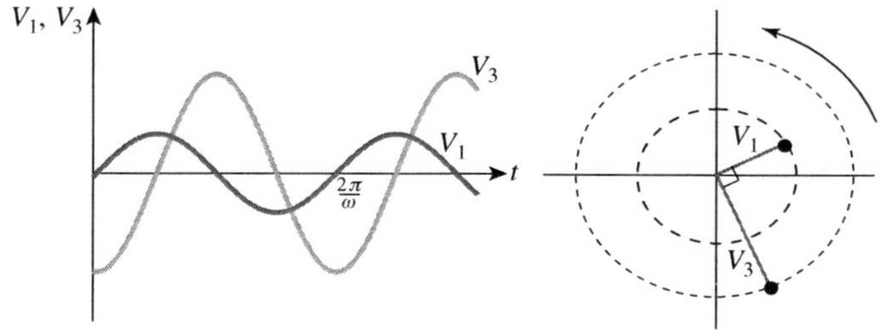

Figure 6.6
Phasor 3 lags phasor 1 by $\frac{\pi}{2}$.

Because these phasors have a length and an angle measured from the positive direction of the x axis they can be represented by complex numbers. We think of the phasor diagram as an Argand diagram. We write a typical phasor in polar form as $\widetilde{V} = V\angle\phi$, where the $\sim$ is used to distinguish the complex quantity, with magnitude V and phase ϕ, from the peak value V. Alternatively we can write $\widetilde{V}$ in cartesian form by stating its real and imaginary parts.

In Block 2 we showed that when a complex number is multiplied by j this has the effect of rotating that number anticlockwise by $\frac{\pi}{2}$ on an Argand diagram.

So, if we want to represent a phase lead of $\frac{\pi}{2}$ we multiply the corresponding phasor by j.

Similarly, dividing a complex number by j has the effect of rotating that number clockwise by $\frac{\pi}{2}$ on an Argand diagram. So, if we want to represent a phase lag of $\frac{\pi}{2}$ we divide the corresponding phasor by j.

Note that

$$\begin{aligned}\frac{1}{\mathrm{j}} &= \left(\frac{1}{\mathrm{j}}\right)\cdot\left(\frac{-\mathrm{j}}{-\mathrm{j}}\right)\\ &= \frac{-\mathrm{j}}{1}\\ &= -\mathrm{j}\end{aligned}$$

So dividing by j is equivalent to multiplying by $-$j.

If the current through a circuit is represented by $\widetilde{I}$ the voltage across a resistor will be given, from Ohm's law, by $\widetilde{V}_R = R\widetilde{I}$. The voltage across an inductor will be $\widetilde{V}_L = \mathrm{j}\omega L\widetilde{I}$ and that across a capacitor will be $\widetilde{V}_C = -\frac{\mathrm{j}}{\omega C}\widetilde{I}$. Notice the way that multiplication by j achieves the required phase differences for the inductor and capacitor.

In general we write

$$\widetilde{V} = \widetilde{I}Z \text{ where } Z = \begin{cases} R & \text{for a resistor}\\ \mathrm{j}\omega L & \text{for an inductor}\\ -\dfrac{\mathrm{j}}{\omega C} & \text{for a capacitor}\end{cases}$$

The quantity Z is called the **complex impedance**.

Key point

Complex impedances

$$\widetilde{V} = \widetilde{I}Z \text{ where } Z = \begin{cases} R & \text{for a resistor} \\ j\omega L & \text{for an inductor} \\ -\dfrac{j}{\omega C} & \text{for a capacitor} \end{cases}$$

More generally, the complex impedance is written in cartesian form as $Z = R + jX$ where R is the resistance and X is called the **reactance**. The argument of Z gives the phase of the voltage relative to the current. The complex impedance is very important because it can be used in the same way that resistance, R, is used in Ohm's law, which is clear from inspecting the two forms $V = IR$ (Ohm's law) and $\widetilde{V} = \widetilde{I}Z$.

When k circuit elements are placed in series their total impedance, Z, is found by adding the individual impedances, Z_k, that is

$$Z = \sum Z_k$$

When the elements are in parallel

$$\frac{1}{Z} = \sum \frac{1}{Z_k}$$

Example 6.1 Electrical Engineering – *LCR* series circuit

For the series *LCR* circuit shown in Figure 6.7 the total impedance is the sum of the individual impedances.

$$Z = R + j\omega L - \frac{j}{\omega C}$$

The voltage phasor is

$$\begin{aligned} \widetilde{V} &= \widetilde{I}Z \\ &= \widetilde{I}R + j\omega L\widetilde{I} - \frac{j}{\omega C}\widetilde{I} \end{aligned}$$

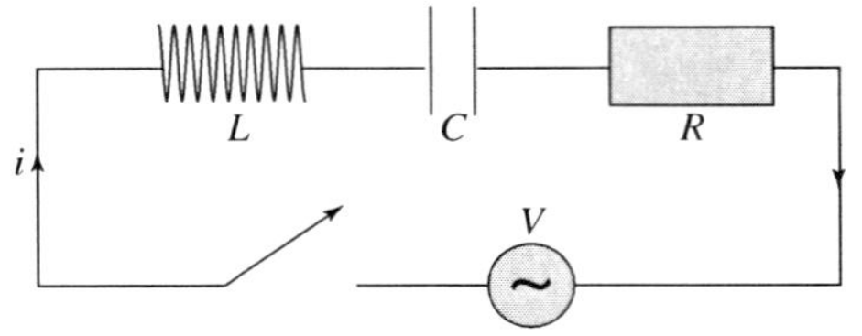

Figure 6.7
A series *LCR* circuit.

Example 6.2 Electrical Engineering – A series *RC* circuit

The circuit shown in Figure 6.8 consists of an alternating voltage source, a resistor R and a capacitor C in series. Suppose a voltage of 8 mV is applied with a frequency of 10^6 Hz to the circuit in which R is 12 Ω and $C = 100\,\text{pF}$.

(a) Find the angular frequency ω.

(b) State the supply voltage in phasor form, taking its phase to be zero. This will be the reference phasor.

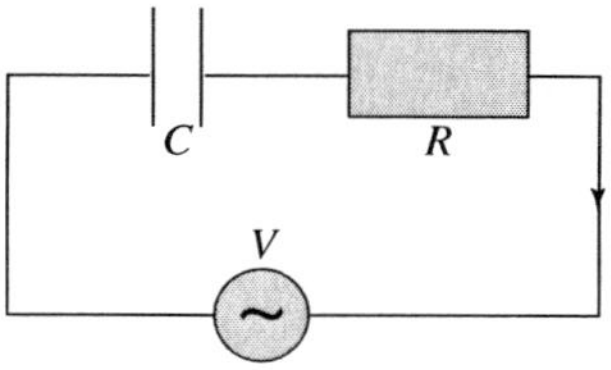

Figure 6.8 A series *RC* circuit.

(c) Find the complex impedance for this circuit.
(d) Find the current phasor $\tilde{I}$ for the circuit.
(e) Find the voltage across each component.

Solution

(a) The angular frequency $\omega = 2\pi f = 2\pi \times 10^6 = 6.2832 \times 10^6$.
(b) The voltage phasor is $\tilde{V} = 8 \times 10^{-3}\angle 0$.
(c) The complex impedance is the sum of the individual impedances:

$$\begin{aligned} Z &= R - \frac{j}{\omega C} \\ &= 12 - \frac{j}{6.2832 \times 10^6 \times 10^{-10}} \\ &= \end{aligned}$$

$12 - 1591.55j$

(d) Since $\tilde{V} = \tilde{I}Z$ it follows that $\tilde{I} = \dfrac{\tilde{V}}{Z} = \dfrac{8 \times 10^{-3}}{12 - 1591.55j}$.

Simplify this:

$\tilde{I} = 3.7897 \times 10^{-8} + 5.0263 \times 10^{-6}j$

(e) Since the current is the same through each component, we have

$$\begin{aligned} \tilde{V}_R &= \tilde{I}R \\ &= 12\tilde{I} \\ &= 4.5477 \times 10^{-7} + 6.0316 \times 10^{-5}j \end{aligned}$$

and

$$\begin{aligned} \tilde{V}_C &= -\frac{j}{\omega C}\tilde{I} \\ &= 8.000 \times 10^{-3} - 6.0316 \times 10^{-5}j \end{aligned}$$

In polar form $\tilde{V}_R = 6.0317 \times 10^{-5}\angle(1.5633)$ and $\tilde{V}_C = 0.008\angle(-0.0075)$.

We see from the polar form that the voltage across the resistor leads the voltage across the capacitor by $1.5633 + 0.0075 \approx \frac{\pi}{2}$ radians, as expected. It is easy to check from the cartesian forms that $\tilde{V}_R + \tilde{V}_C = \tilde{V}$.

End of block exercises

1 The impedance of a component is $Z = 12 - 12\text{j}$. State (a) the resistance, (b) the reactance, (c) the phase of the voltage relative to the current.

2 The **admittance** is the reciprocal of the impedance. Find the admittance of the component in question 1.

3 The impedance of an LCR circuit is

$$Z = R + \text{j}\left(\omega L - \frac{1}{\omega C}\right)$$

(a) Find $|Z|$.

(b) From the result of part (a) deduce that the impedance has minimum magnitude when

$$\omega = \sqrt{\frac{1}{(LC)}}$$

(c) Deduce that this minimum value is R.

4 A capacitor and resistor are placed in parallel. Show that the complex impedance of this combination is given by

$$\frac{1}{Z} = \frac{1}{R} + \text{j}\omega C$$

Find an expression for Z.

Solutions to exercises

1 (a) 12 (b) −12 (c) $-\frac{\pi}{4}$

2 0.0417 + 0.0417j

3 (a) $\sqrt{R^2 + \left(\omega L - \frac{1}{\omega C}\right)^2}$

4 $Z = \dfrac{R}{1 + \text{j}\omega CR}$

End of chapter exercises

1 Find the modulus and argument of (a) $-\text{j}$, (b) -3, (c) $1 + \text{j}$, (d) $\cos\theta + \text{j}\sin\theta$.

2 Represent the following numbers on an Argand diagram:
(a) 13 (b) j^2 (c) $-4 + 2\text{j}$ (d) $\pi + \pi\text{j}$

3 If $z_1 = 5 + 3\text{j}$ and $z_2 = 3 + 2\text{j}$ find $z_1 z_2$ and $\frac{z_1}{z_2}$.

4 Find the modulus and argument of $-1 + \text{j}$.

5 Express $2 + 3\text{j}$ in exponential form. Write down its complex conjugate.

6 Sketch an Argand diagram and upon it mark the poles of the rational function

$$G(s) = \frac{3(s - 3)}{(s + 1)(s + 1 + 3\text{j})(s + 1 - 3\text{j})}$$

7 Use De Moivre's theorem to simplify
(a) $(\cos 3\theta + \text{j}\sin 3\theta)(\cos 4\theta + \text{j}\sin 4\theta)$
(b) $\dfrac{\cos 8\theta + \text{j}\sin 8\theta}{\cos 2\theta - \text{j}\sin 2\theta}$

8 Express $(\cos\theta + \text{j}\sin\theta)^9$ in the form $\cos n\theta + \text{j}\sin n\theta$.

9 Use De Moivre's theorem to show that $\cos 3\theta = 4\cos^3\theta - 3\cos\theta$.

10 Solve the equation $z^2 = 4j$ expressing your solutions in cartesian form and using surds.

11 Find $\sqrt[3]{2 + 2j}$.

12 Find the fifth roots of j.

13 Solve the equation $z^4 + 1 = j\sqrt{3}$.

14 Show that

$$32 \sin^6\theta = 10 - 15 \cos 2\theta + 6 \cos 4\theta - \cos 6\theta$$

15 Let $z_1 = r_1(\cos \theta_1 + j \sin \theta_1)$ and let $z_2 = r_2(\cos \theta_2 + j \sin \theta_2)$.
Use trigonometrical identities to prove that

$$z_1 z_2 = r_1 r_2[\cos(\theta_1 + \theta_2) + j \sin(\theta_1 + \theta_2)]$$

and

$$\frac{z_1}{z_2} = \frac{r_1}{r_2}[\cos(\theta_1 - \theta_2) + j\sin(\theta_1 - \theta_2)]$$

16 The hyperbolic functions cosh x and sinh x are defined as

$$\cosh x = \frac{e^x + e^{-x}}{2}, \quad \sinh x = \frac{e^x - e^{-x}}{2}$$

Use these definitions and Euler's relations to prove (a) $\cosh jx = \cos x$, (b) $\sinh jx = j \sin x$, (c) $\cos jx = \cosh x$, (d) $\sin jx = j \sinh x$.

17 Writing $z = re^{j\theta}$ and using the laws of logarithms show that $\ln z = \ln r + j\theta$. Hence interpret $\ln(2 + 2j)$.

18 In each case, draw an Argand diagram and shade the region that satisfies
(a) $\text{Re}(z) > 0$ (b) $\text{Re}(z) \leq -2$
(c) $\text{Im}(z) < 3$ (d) $\text{Im}(z) \geq -3$

where Re(z) stands for the real part of z, and Im(z) stands for imaginary part of z.

19 Find the real and imaginary parts of

$$\frac{1}{1 + j\omega}$$

20 Find the modulus and argument of $\frac{1}{1 + j\omega}$.

21 Find $\frac{1}{1 + j\omega} + \frac{1}{2 + j\omega}$.

22 **Electrical Engineering**. The impedance, Z, of a component is given by $Z = 7 + 5j$. The admittance, Y, is given by

$$Y = \frac{1}{Z}$$

Find Y in Cartesian form.

23 **Electrical Engineering**. A resistor of resistance, R, and an inductor of inductance, L, are connected in series. If $R = 9$ and $L = 2j$ find
(a) the total impedance, Z;
(b) the admittance.

24 **Electrical Engineering**. A resistor of resistance, R, and an inductor of inductance, L, are connected in parallel. If $R = 9$ and $L = 2j$ find
(a) the total impedance, Z;
(b) the admittance.

Solutions to exercises

1 (a) $1, -\frac{\pi}{2}$ (b) $3, \pi$ (c) $\sqrt{2}, \frac{\pi}{4}$ (d) $1, \theta$

3 $9 + 19\mathrm{j}, \frac{21}{13} - \frac{1}{13}\mathrm{j}$

4 $\sqrt{2}, \frac{3\pi}{4}$

5 $\sqrt{13}\mathrm{e}^{0.983\mathrm{j}}$. The conjugate is $\sqrt{13}\mathrm{e}^{-0.983\mathrm{j}}$.

7 (a) $\cos 7\theta + \mathrm{j}\sin 7\theta$ (b) $\cos 10\theta + j\sin 10\theta$

8 $\cos 9\theta + \mathrm{j}\sin 9\theta$

10 $z = \pm\sqrt{2}(1 + \mathrm{j})$

11 $8^{1/6}\angle\left(\frac{\pi}{12} + \frac{2k\pi}{3}\right), k = 0, 1, 2$

12 $1\angle\left(\frac{\pi}{10} + \frac{2k\pi}{5}\right), k = 0, 1, 2, 3, 4$

13 $2^{1/4}\angle\left(\frac{\pi}{6} + \frac{k\pi}{2}\right), k = 0, 1, 2, 3$

17 $\ln(\sqrt{8}) + \mathrm{j}\frac{\pi}{4}$

19 real part $= \frac{1}{1 + \omega^2}$

imaginary part $-\frac{\omega}{1 + \omega^2}$

21 modulus $\frac{1}{\sqrt{1 + \omega^2}}$, argument $\tan^{-1}(-\omega)$

21 $\frac{3 + 2\mathrm{j}\omega}{2 + 3\mathrm{j}\omega - \omega^2}$

22 $\frac{7 - 5\mathrm{j}}{74}$

23 (a) $9 + 2\mathrm{j}$ (b) $\frac{9 - 2\mathrm{j}}{85}$

24 (a) $\frac{36 + 162\mathrm{j}}{85}$ (b) $\frac{1}{9} - \frac{\mathrm{j}}{2}$

Matrices and determinants

A **matrix** is a rectangular array of numbers or expressions. The plural of matrix is matrices. This chapter deals with the addition, subtraction and multiplication of matrices. Unlike numbers, the processes of addition, subtraction and multiplication can be applied to matrices only under specific conditions. Division of matrices is not defined. However, the inverse of a matrix may be found under certain conditions. The inverse matrix and its calculation are explained in Block 4.

Determinants are introduced in Block 3. A **determinant** is a number that is calculated from the elements of a matrix and is used in finding the inverse matrix.

The chapter closes with the application of matrices to **computer graphics**. Multiplication by a matrix can be interpreted as a transformation of a figure.

Chapter 12 contents

BLOCK 1 Introduction to matrices

1.1 Introduction

A **matrix** is a rectangular array of numbers or expressions usually enclosed in brackets. For example,

$$\begin{pmatrix} 3 & 1 & 9 \\ 0 & -6 & 2 \end{pmatrix}, \begin{pmatrix} \alpha & \beta \\ \gamma & \delta \end{pmatrix}, \begin{pmatrix} 3-\lambda & 4 \\ 7 & 6-\lambda \end{pmatrix}$$

are all matrices. Note that the plural of matrix is matrices.

We often denote a matrix by a capital letter, for example

$$A = \begin{pmatrix} 4 & 1 \\ 3 & 6 \\ -1 & 0 \end{pmatrix}, \quad B = \begin{pmatrix} 1 & 0 & -1 & 3 \\ 6 & 1 & 4 & 2 \end{pmatrix}$$

The **size** of a matrix is given by the number of rows and the number of columns. The matrix A has three rows and two columns and so is described as a 3×2 matrix. We say that A is a 'three by two matrix'. Matrix B has two rows and four columns and so is a 2×4 matrix. Notice that the number of rows is always stated first. An $n \times m$ matrix has n rows and m columns.

The individual numbers or expressions in a matrix are called the **elements** and are usually denoted by a small letter. For example, for A, the element in row 1, column 2 is denoted by a_{12}, the element in row 3, column 1 is denoted by a_{31}, and so on. So

$$a_{11} = 4, \quad a_{12} = 1, \quad a_{21} = 3, \quad a_{22} = 6, \quad a_{31} = -1, \quad a_{32} = 0$$

Example 1.1

Given

$$C = \begin{pmatrix} 3 & 0 & 4 & x \\ \lambda & 1 & z & -1 \end{pmatrix}$$

state (a) c_{13}, (b) c_{21}, (c) c_{22}.

Solution

(a) c_{13} is the element in row 1, column 3, and so $c_{13} = 4$.
(b) c_{21} is the element in row 2, column 1, and so $c_{21} = \lambda$.
(c) c_{22} is the element in row 2, column 2, and so $c_{22} = 1$.

Example 1.2 Matrices and digital image processing

A digital image is an image that is represented by an array of numbers. Consider, as a very simple example, the mathematical representation of the symbol π. Very crudely we can picture the symbol as in Figure 1.1.

Figure 1.1 A simple digital representation of π.

We could represent this image of π by a 3×5 matrix such as

$$B = \begin{pmatrix} 1 & 1 & 1 & 1 & 1 \\ 0 & 1 & 0 & 1 & 0 \\ 0 & 1 & 0 & 1 & 0 \end{pmatrix}$$

Note that we have divided the image into a number of areas, or fields, in this case 15 of them. We have then assigned a number to each field: 1 if the field is to be shaded, and 0 otherwise.

Images such as black and white photographs can be 'digitised' in the same way. The image is divided into $m \times n$ fields, where in practice m and n are large integers. Each field is assigned a number that represents the intensity of the image in that area. Often a 64 point grey scale is used so that a range of grey levels can be represented ranging from white at one extreme to black at the other. A digital image is then represented by an $m \times n$ matrix, B say, whose elements are numbers in the range 1–64. In image processing the matrix B is often referred to as $b[m, n]$.

Exercises

1 The matrix, H, is defined by

$$H = \begin{pmatrix} 2 & 1 \\ \alpha & 0 \\ -3 & \beta \end{pmatrix}$$

(a) State the size of H.
(b) State h_{11}, h_{21}, h_{32}.

2 State the number of elements in an $n \times m$ matrix.

Solution to exercises

1 (a) 3×2 (b) $2, \alpha, \beta$

2 nm

1.2 Some special matrices

There are a number of matrices that you will use frequently and which have special names. These are now described.

A **square matrix** has the same number of columns as rows. Both D and E are square matrices where

$$D = \begin{pmatrix} 3 & 1 \\ 4 & 2 \end{pmatrix}, \quad E = \begin{pmatrix} 1 & -1 & 3 \\ 0 & \lambda & 3 \\ -1 & y & 7 \end{pmatrix}$$

The **main diagonal** of a square matrix is the diagonal running from 'top left' to 'bottom right'. The main diagonal of D contains the elements 3 and 2. In general, if A is an $n \times n$ matrix, the main diagonal contains the elements $a_{11}, a_{22}, a_{33}, \ldots, a_{nn}$.

An **identity matrix** is a square matrix with ones on the main diagonal and zeros everywhere else. Identity matrices are usually denoted by I, with a subscript to denote its size. The 2×2 identity matrix is I_2 where

$$I_2 = \begin{pmatrix} 1 & 0 \\ 0 & 1 \end{pmatrix}$$

the 3×3 identity matrix is I_3 where

$$I_3 = \begin{pmatrix} 1 & 0 & 0 \\ 0 & 1 & 0 \\ 0 & 0 & 1 \end{pmatrix}$$

and so on.

The **transpose** of a matrix is obtained by writing rows as columns. The transpose of A is denoted A^T. For example, if

$$A = \begin{pmatrix} 6 & 1 & -3 & 0 \\ 9 & 2 & 3 & 7 \end{pmatrix}$$

then the transpose of A, A^T, is given by

$$A^T = \begin{pmatrix} 6 & 9 \\ 1 & 2 \\ -3 & 3 \\ 0 & 7 \end{pmatrix}$$

Example 1.3

Given

$$B = \begin{pmatrix} 1 & -2 & 4 \\ 3 & 1 & 0 \\ 7 & 5 & 9 \end{pmatrix}$$

state the transpose of B.

Solution
The transpose is

$$\begin{pmatrix} 1 & 3 & 7 \\ -2 & 1 & 5 \\ 4 & 0 & 9 \end{pmatrix}$$

Exercises

1 State the transpose of C where

$$C = \begin{pmatrix} 9 & 3 \\ 1 & -2 \\ \alpha & 4 \end{pmatrix}$$

2 State the transpose of I_3.

Solutions to exercises

1 $C^{\mathrm{T}} = \begin{pmatrix} 9 & 1 & \alpha \\ 3 & -2 & 4 \end{pmatrix}$

2 I_3

1.3 Addition and subtraction of matrices

Matrices of the same size may be added to and subtracted from one another. To do this, the corresponding elements are added or subtracted.

Example 1.4
Given

$$A = \begin{pmatrix} 3 & 1 & -1 \\ 0 & -2 & 4 \end{pmatrix}, \quad B = \begin{pmatrix} 2 & 6 & 1 \\ 10 & -3 & 6 \end{pmatrix}, \quad C = \begin{pmatrix} -1 & 0 \\ 3 & 2 \end{pmatrix}$$

find, if possible,
(a) $A + B$ (b) $B - C$ (c) $B - A$ (d) $A + C$

Solution

(a)

$$\begin{aligned} A + B &= \begin{pmatrix} 3 & 1 & -1 \\ 0 & -2 & 4 \end{pmatrix} + \begin{pmatrix} 2 & 6 & 1 \\ 10 & -3 & 6 \end{pmatrix} \\ &= \begin{pmatrix} 3+2 & 1+6 & -1+1 \\ 0+10 & -2-3 & 4+6 \end{pmatrix} \\ &= \begin{pmatrix} 5 & 7 & 0 \\ 10 & -5 & 10 \end{pmatrix} \end{aligned}$$

(b) B is a 2×3 matrix; C is a 2×2 matrix. Since B and C have different sizes then $B - C$ cannot be calculated.

(c)
$$B - A = \begin{pmatrix} 2 & 6 & 1 \\ 10 & -3 & 6 \end{pmatrix} - \begin{pmatrix} 3 & 1 & -1 \\ 0 & -2 & 4 \end{pmatrix}$$
$$= \begin{pmatrix} 2-3 & 6-1 & 1-(-1) \\ 10-0 & -3-(-2) & 6-4 \end{pmatrix}$$
$$= \begin{pmatrix} -1 & 5 & 2 \\ 10 & -1 & 2 \end{pmatrix}$$

(d) A and C have different sizes and so $A + C$ is not defined.

Example 1.5

If $C = \begin{pmatrix} 7 & 2 \\ -2 & 1 \\ 4 & 3 \end{pmatrix}$ and $D = \begin{pmatrix} -1 & 0 \\ 3 & 4 \\ 9 & 1 \end{pmatrix}$

calculate

(a) $C + D$ (b) $C^T + D^T$ (c) $(C + D)^T$

Solution

(a) $C + D = \begin{pmatrix} 7 & 2 \\ -2 & 1 \\ 4 & 3 \end{pmatrix} + \begin{pmatrix} -1 & 0 \\ 3 & 4 \\ 9 & 1 \end{pmatrix}$

$$= \begin{pmatrix} 6 & 2 \\ 1 & 5 \\ 13 & 4 \end{pmatrix}$$

(b) $C^T + D^T = \begin{pmatrix} 7 & -2 & 4 \\ 2 & 1 & 3 \end{pmatrix} + \begin{pmatrix} -1 & 3 & 9 \\ 0 & 4 & 1 \end{pmatrix}$

$$= \begin{pmatrix} 6 & 1 & 13 \\ 2 & 5 & 4 \end{pmatrix}$$

(c) $C + D$ has been found in (a).

$$(C + D)^T = \begin{pmatrix} 6 & 1 & 13 \\ 2 & 5 & 4 \end{pmatrix}$$

Note that $(C + D)^T = C^T + D^T$.

Example 1.5 illustrates a general rule for matrices.

Key point

The transpose of the sum of two matrices is the same as the sum of the individual matrices transposed:

$$(A + B)^T = A^T + B^T$$

Exercises

1 Given

$$R = \begin{pmatrix} 4 & 1 \\ 6 & 2 \end{pmatrix} \quad S = \begin{pmatrix} -3 & 2 \\ 7 & -4 \end{pmatrix}$$

find
(a) $R + S$ (b) $S - R$ (c) $R + R^T$
(d) $(R - S)^T$ (e) $(S^T)^T$

Solutions to exercises

1 (a) $\begin{pmatrix} 1 & 3 \\ 13 & -2 \end{pmatrix}$ (b) $\begin{pmatrix} -7 & 1 \\ 1 & -6 \end{pmatrix}$ (e) $\begin{pmatrix} -3 & 2 \\ 7 & -4 \end{pmatrix}$

(c) $\begin{pmatrix} 8 & 7 \\ 7 & 4 \end{pmatrix}$ (d) $\begin{pmatrix} 7 & -1 \\ -1 & 6 \end{pmatrix}$

1.4 Multiplication of a matrix by a number

Any matrix can be multiplied by a number. To do this, each element of the matrix is multiplied by the number.

Example 1.6
If

$$A = \begin{pmatrix} 3 & 1 & -1 \\ 0 & -2 & 4 \end{pmatrix}$$

find
(a) $2A$ (b) $\frac{1}{2}A$ (c) $-A$

Solution

(a)
$$2A = 2\begin{pmatrix} 3 & 1 & -1 \\ 0 & -2 & 4 \end{pmatrix}$$

$$= \begin{pmatrix} 2 \times 3 & 2 \times 1 & 2 \times (-1) \\ 2 \times 0 & 2 \times (-2) & 2 \times 4 \end{pmatrix}$$

$$= \begin{pmatrix} 6 & 2 & -2 \\ 0 & -4 & 8 \end{pmatrix}$$

(b)
$$\frac{1}{2}A = \frac{1}{2}\begin{pmatrix} 3 & 1 & -1 \\ 0 & -2 & 4 \end{pmatrix}$$

$$= \begin{pmatrix} 1.5 & 0.5 & -0.5 \\ 0 & -1 & 2 \end{pmatrix}$$

(c)
$$-A = (-1)A$$
$$= (-1)\begin{pmatrix} 3 & 1 & -1 \\ 0 & -2 & 4 \end{pmatrix}$$
$$= \begin{pmatrix} -3 & -1 & 1 \\ 0 & 2 & -4 \end{pmatrix}$$

Example 1.7

If

$$A = \begin{pmatrix} 3 & 1 & -1 \\ 0 & -2 & 4 \end{pmatrix} \text{ and } B = \begin{pmatrix} 2 & 6 & 1 \\ 10 & -3 & 6 \end{pmatrix}$$

find

(a) $2A + 3B$ (b) $A - 2B$ (c) $\frac{1}{2}A + \frac{1}{2}B$

Solution

(a) $$2A + 3B = \begin{pmatrix} 6 & 2 & -2 \\ 0 & -4 & 8 \end{pmatrix} + \begin{pmatrix} 6 & 18 & 3 \\ 30 & -9 & 18 \end{pmatrix}$$

$$=$$

$$\begin{pmatrix} 12 & 20 & 1 \\ 30 & -13 & 26 \end{pmatrix}$$

(b) $$A - 2B = \begin{pmatrix} 3 & 1 & -1 \\ 0 & -2 & 4 \end{pmatrix} -$$

$$\begin{pmatrix} 4 & 12 & 2 \\ 20 & -6 & 12 \end{pmatrix}$$

$$=$$

$$\begin{pmatrix} -1 & -11 & -3 \\ -20 & 4 & -8 \end{pmatrix}$$

(c) $$\frac{1}{2}A + \frac{1}{2}B = \frac{1}{2}(A + B) =$$

$$\begin{pmatrix} 2.5 & 3.5 & 0 \\ 5 & -2.5 & 5 \end{pmatrix}$$

Example 1.8

Given

$$A = \begin{pmatrix} 3 & 1 & 4 \\ 2 & 9 & 6 \end{pmatrix}$$

and k is a constant find

(a) A^{T} (b) kA^{T} (c) $(kA)^{\mathrm{T}}$

Solution

(a) $A^{\mathrm{T}} = \begin{pmatrix} 3 & 2 \\ 1 & 9 \\ 4 & 6 \end{pmatrix}$

(b) $kA^{\mathrm{T}} = k\begin{pmatrix} 3 & 2 \\ 1 & 9 \\ 4 & 6 \end{pmatrix}$

$= \begin{pmatrix} 3k & 2k \\ k & 9k \\ 4k & 6k \end{pmatrix}$

(c) $kA = \begin{pmatrix} 3k & k & 4k \\ 2k & 9k & 6k \end{pmatrix}$

Hence

$$(kA)^{\mathrm{T}} = \begin{pmatrix} 3k & 2k \\ k & 9k \\ 4k & 6k \end{pmatrix}$$

Example 1.8 illustrates a general rule:

Key point

$$(kA)^{\mathrm{T}} = kA^{\mathrm{T}}$$

Exercises

1. Given

$$A = \begin{pmatrix} 2 & 1 \\ 3 & -2 \end{pmatrix} \quad B = \begin{pmatrix} 4 & -1 \\ -2 & 6 \end{pmatrix}$$

find
(a) $3A$ (b) $2B$ (c) $4A + 3B$ (d) $B - 2A$
(e) $2A^{\mathrm{T}}$ (f) $(2A)^{\mathrm{T}}$

2. Given

$$A = \begin{pmatrix} 6 & 1 \\ 3 & 7 \end{pmatrix}$$

state
(a) $A - 2I_2$ (b) $A - \lambda I_2$ where λ is a constant.

3. Given

$$A = \begin{pmatrix} 1 & 2 & 3 \\ 4 & 5 & -1 \end{pmatrix} \quad B = \begin{pmatrix} -2 & 3 \\ 0 & 4 \\ 7 & -1 \end{pmatrix}$$

calculate
(a) $A + B^{\mathrm{T}}$ (b) $B - 2A^{\mathrm{T}}$

Solutions to exercises

1 (a) $\begin{pmatrix} 6 & 3 \\ 9 & -6 \end{pmatrix}$ (b) $\begin{pmatrix} 8 & -2 \\ -4 & 12 \end{pmatrix}$

(c) $\begin{pmatrix} 20 & 1 \\ 6 & 10 \end{pmatrix}$ (d) $\begin{pmatrix} 0 & -3 \\ -8 & 10 \end{pmatrix}$

(e) $\begin{pmatrix} 4 & 6 \\ 2 & -4 \end{pmatrix}$ (f) $\begin{pmatrix} 4 & 6 \\ 2 & -4 \end{pmatrix}$

2 (a) $\begin{pmatrix} 4 & 1 \\ 3 & 5 \end{pmatrix}$ (b) $\begin{pmatrix} 6-\lambda & 1 \\ 3 & 7-\lambda \end{pmatrix}$

3 (a) $\begin{pmatrix} -1 & 2 & 10 \\ 7 & 9 & -2 \end{pmatrix}$ (b) $\begin{pmatrix} -4 & -5 \\ -4 & -6 \\ 1 & 1 \end{pmatrix}$

End of block exercises

Questions 1–13 refer to matrices A, B and C where

$$A = \begin{pmatrix} 4 & 1 \\ 9 & -1 \\ 2 & 0 \end{pmatrix}, \quad B = \begin{pmatrix} 1 & 2 & 3 \\ 4 & 5 & -1 \end{pmatrix}, \quad C = \begin{pmatrix} -1 & 3 \\ 0 & 4 \\ 1 & 6 \end{pmatrix}$$

1 State the size of A.

2 State the size of B.

3 State a_{32}, b_{13}, c_{22}.

4 Calculate $5A$.

5 Calculate $-2C$.

6 Calculate $\frac{1}{2}C$.

7 State A^T.

8 State C^T.

9 Calculate $A + 2C$.

10 Calculate $3C - 4A$.

11 Calculate $A + 2B^T$.

12 Calculate $B - 3C^T$.

13 Calculate $\dfrac{2C + 5B^T}{3}$.

14 If D is an $n \times m$ matrix, state the size of (a) D^T, (b) $(D^T)^T$.

15 If

$$T = \begin{pmatrix} 3 & 1 & 4 \\ -1 & 2 & 6 \\ 7 & 3 & 0 \end{pmatrix}$$

state
(a) $T - 2I$
(b) $T - \lambda I$ where λ is a constant.

Solutions to exercises

1 3×2

2 2×3

3 0, 3, 4

4 $\begin{pmatrix} 20 & 5 \\ 45 & -5 \\ 10 & 0 \end{pmatrix}$

5 $\begin{pmatrix} 2 & -6 \\ 0 & -8 \\ -2 & -12 \end{pmatrix}$

6 $\begin{pmatrix} -\frac{1}{2} & \frac{3}{2} \\ 0 & 2 \\ \frac{1}{2} & 3 \end{pmatrix}$

7 $\begin{pmatrix} 4 & 9 & 2 \\ 1 & -1 & 0 \end{pmatrix}$

8 $\begin{pmatrix} -1 & 0 & 1 \\ 3 & 4 & 6 \end{pmatrix}$

9 $\begin{pmatrix} 2 & 7 \\ 9 & 7 \\ 4 & 12 \end{pmatrix}$

10 $\begin{pmatrix} -19 & 5 \\ -36 & 16 \\ -5 & 18 \end{pmatrix}$

11 $\begin{pmatrix} 6 & 9 \\ 13 & 9 \\ 8 & -2 \end{pmatrix}$

12 $\begin{pmatrix} 4 & 2 & 0 \\ -5 & -7 & -19 \end{pmatrix}$

13 $\begin{pmatrix} 1 & \frac{26}{3} \\ \frac{10}{3} & 11 \\ \frac{17}{3} & \frac{7}{3} \end{pmatrix}$

14 (a) $m \times n$ (b) $n \times m$

15 (a) $\begin{pmatrix} 1 & 1 & 4 \\ -1 & 0 & 6 \\ 7 & 3 & -2 \end{pmatrix}$

(b) $7\begin{pmatrix} 3-\lambda & 1 & 4 \\ -1 & 2-\lambda & 6 \\ 7 & 3 & -\lambda \end{pmatrix}$

BLOCK 2

Multiplication of matrices

2.1 Introduction

In Block 1 we saw how a matrix can be multiplied by a number. In this section we look at how one matrix can be multiplied by another matrix. We also specify the conditions under which such a multiplication can take place.

2.2 Conditions needed for two matrices to be multiplied together

Let A and B be two matrices. Then under certain conditions the product AB can be found. The way in which such a product is calculated is explained in the next section; for this section we focus on the conditions needed for the product to exist.

To decide whether the product AB exists we look at the size of each matrix. Suppose A is an $n \times m$ matrix and B is a $p \times q$ matrix. For the product AB to exist it must be that $m = p$: that is, the number of columns in A must be the same as the number of rows in B.

Key point

For the product AB to exist, the number of columns of A must equal the number of rows of B.

When $m = p$ the product AB can be calculated. The result is another matrix whose size is $n \times q$.

Key point

$$\underbrace{A}_{n \times m} \quad \underbrace{B}_{p \times q} = \underbrace{C}_{n \times q}$$

$$\underbrace{n \times m \quad p \times q}_{m = p}$$

If the number of columns in A differs from the number of rows in B then the product AB cannot be found. We say AB does not exist.

The product AB is distinct from the product BA. For example, if A is a 3×2 matrix and B is a 2×4 matrix then the number of columns in A equals the number of rows in B, that is 2, and so AB can be found. It is a 3×4 matrix:

$$\underbrace{A}_{3 \times 2} \; \underbrace{B}_{2 \times 4} = \underbrace{C}_{3 \times 4}$$

However, let us now consider BA. The number of columns in B is four; the number of rows of A is three and so the product BA cannot be found. Hence the order of the product is crucial, and we say that matrix multiplication is, in general, **not commutative**. In the product AB we say A **premultiplies** B. Alternatively we can say that B **postmultiplies** A.

Products involving three or more matrices are possible. If P, Q and R are three matrices then to calculate PQR we firstly calculate PQ, and then postmultiply the result by R, that is PQR is treated as $(PQ)R$. Alternatively we can calculate QR and premultiply the result by P, that is we may treat PQR as $P(QR)$. The final result in both cases is the same. This means that matrix multiplication is **associative**.

Finally we note that the product AA is written as A^2, AAA is written as A^3, and so on.

Exercises

Questions 1–3 refer to matrices P, Q and R where P is a 3×2 matrix, Q is a 3×3 matrix and R is a 2×3 matrix.

1 State the size of the following products if they can be found. If they cannot be found then state this.
(a) PQ (b) PR (c) QR (d) RQ (e) P^2 (f) Q^2 (g) RP

2 State the size of each of the following:
(a) P^T (b) Q^T (c) R^T (d) R^TP^T (e) P^TQ^T

3 State the size of the following products. If a product cannot be found then state this.
(a) PQR (b) PRQ (c) QPR (d) RQP

4 If A is a matrix, state conditions on A for A^2 to exist.

Solutions to exercises

1 (a) cannot be found (b) 3×3 (c) cannot be found (d) 2×3 (e) cannot be found (f) 3×3 (g) 2×2

2 (a) 2×3 (b) 3×3 (c) 3×2 (d) 3×3 (e) 2×3

3 (a) cannot be found (b) 3×3 (c) 3×3 (d) 2×2

4 A must be a square matrix for A^2 to exist

2.3 How to multiply two matrices

Section 2.2 stated the conditions needed for a product of matrices to exist. In this section we look at how the product is actually calculated. The method is illustrated in Example 2.1.

Example 2.1
Given

$$A = \begin{pmatrix} 3 & 1 & 4 \\ 5 & 2 & -2 \end{pmatrix} \text{ and } B = \begin{pmatrix} 1 & -1 \\ 2 & 0 \\ -6 & 4 \end{pmatrix}$$

calculate the product AB.

Solution
We note that A is a 2×3 matrix, B is a 3×2 matrix and so the product AB exists. The result is a 2×2 matrix, say C.

$$AB = C = \begin{pmatrix} c_{11} & c_{12} \\ c_{21} & c_{22} \end{pmatrix}$$

To find c_{11}, that is the element in row 1, column 1, we use row 1 from A and column 1 from B. The elements in this row and column are multiplied and added thus:

$$\begin{aligned} c_{11} &= 3(1) + 1(2) + 4(-6) \\ &= 3 + 2 - 24 \\ &= -19 \end{aligned}$$

The element c_{12} is in row 1, column 2 of C. It is calculated from row 1 of A and column 2 of B.

$$\begin{aligned} c_{12} &= 3(-1) + 1(0) + 4(4) \\ &= 13 \end{aligned}$$

The element c_{21} is in row 2, column 1 of C. It is calculated from row 2 of A and column 1 of B.

$$\begin{aligned} c_{21} &= 5(1) + 2(2) - 2(-6) \\ &= 21 \end{aligned}$$

The element c_{22} is in row 2, column 2 of C. It is calculated from row 2 of A and column 2 of B.

$$\begin{aligned} c_{22} &= 5(-1) + 2(0) - 2(4) \\ &= -13 \end{aligned}$$

Hence

$$AB = \begin{pmatrix} 3 & 1 & 4 \\ 5 & 2 & -2 \end{pmatrix} \begin{pmatrix} 1 & -1 \\ 2 & 0 \\ -6 & 4 \end{pmatrix}$$

$$= \begin{pmatrix} -19 & 13 \\ 21 & -13 \end{pmatrix}$$

Example 2.1 illustrates the following important point regarding matrix multiplication.

Key point

If $AB = C$ then the element c_{ij} is found from row i of A and column j of B.

Check the working to the following example.

Example 2.2

Given

$$A = \begin{pmatrix} 9 & -1 \\ 2 & 3 \end{pmatrix} \text{ and } B = \begin{pmatrix} 4 & 3 & 2 \\ 1 & 2 & -1 \end{pmatrix}$$

calculate AB.

Solution

Note that A has two columns, B has two rows and so the product AB can be found. The result is a 2×3 matrix, C.

$$AB = \begin{pmatrix} 9 & -1 \\ 2 & 3 \end{pmatrix} \begin{pmatrix} 4 & 3 & 2 \\ 1 & 2 & -1 \end{pmatrix}$$

$$= C = \begin{pmatrix} c_{11} & c_{12} & c_{13} \\ c_{21} & c_{22} & c_{23} \end{pmatrix}$$

Now

$$c_{11} = 9(4) - 1(1) = 35$$

$c_{12} =$ $\quad$ $9(3) - 1(2) = 25$

$$c_{13} = 9(2) - 1(-1) = 19$$

$c_{21} =$ $\quad$ $2(4) + 3(1) = 11$

$$c_{22} = 2(3) + 3(2) = 12$$

$c_{23} =$ $\quad$ $2(2) + 3(-1) = 1$

Hence

$$\begin{pmatrix} 9 & -1 \\ 2 & 3 \end{pmatrix} \begin{pmatrix} 4 & 3 & 2 \\ 1 & 2 & -1 \end{pmatrix} = \begin{pmatrix} 35 & 25 & 19 \\ 11 & 12 & 1 \end{pmatrix}$$

Recall the identity matrix, I, given by

$$I_2 = \begin{pmatrix} 1 & 0 \\ 0 & 1 \end{pmatrix}, \quad I_3 = \begin{pmatrix} 1 & 0 & 0 \\ 0 & 1 & 0 \\ 0 & 0 & 1 \end{pmatrix}$$

and so on. If no subscript is given then the size of the identity matrix is taken as that for which any stated product exists.

Example 2.3
Given

$$A = \begin{pmatrix} 3 & -2 \\ 10 & 7 \end{pmatrix}$$

calculate
(a) AI (b) IA

Solution
Since A has two columns the required identity matrix is I_2:

(a) $AI = \begin{pmatrix} 3 & -2 \\ 10 & 7 \end{pmatrix}\begin{pmatrix} 1 & 0 \\ 0 & 1 \end{pmatrix}$

$= \qquad \begin{pmatrix} 3 & -2 \\ 10 & 7 \end{pmatrix}$

(b) $IA = \begin{pmatrix} 1 & 0 \\ 0 & 1 \end{pmatrix}\begin{pmatrix} 3 & -2 \\ 10 & 7 \end{pmatrix}$

$= \qquad \begin{pmatrix} 3 & -2 \\ 10 & 7 \end{pmatrix}$

Example 2.3 illustrates a general point. For any square matrix A:

Key point

When a square matrix is post- or premultiplied by an identity matrix of the appropriate size the matrix is unchanged.

$$AI = IA = A$$

Example 2.4
Given

$$\begin{pmatrix} 4 & -1 \\ 6 & 5 \end{pmatrix}\begin{pmatrix} x \\ y \end{pmatrix} = \begin{pmatrix} -13 \\ 13 \end{pmatrix}$$

find x and y.

Solution

Multiplying out the matrices on the left-hand side of the equation yields

$$\begin{pmatrix} 4 & -1 \\ 6 & 5 \end{pmatrix}\begin{pmatrix} x \\ y \end{pmatrix} = \qquad \begin{pmatrix} 4x - y \\ 6x + 5y \end{pmatrix}$$

Hence

$$\begin{aligned} 4x - y &= -13 \\ 6x + 5y &= 13 \end{aligned}$$

Solving these equations simultaneously for x and y yields $x = -2$, $y = 5$.

Example 2.5

Given

$$A = \begin{pmatrix} 1 & 2 \\ -1 & 3 \\ 2 & 1 \end{pmatrix}$$

find

(a) A^{T}
(b) AA^{T}
(c) $A^{\mathrm{T}}A$

Solution

(a) Recall that A^{T} denotes the transpose of A.

$$A^{\mathrm{T}} = \qquad \begin{pmatrix} 1 & -1 & 2 \\ 2 & 3 & 1 \end{pmatrix}$$

(b) $$AA^{\mathrm{T}} = \begin{pmatrix} 1 & 2 \\ -1 & 3 \\ 2 & 1 \end{pmatrix}\begin{pmatrix} 1 & -1 & 2 \\ 2 & 3 & 1 \end{pmatrix}$$

$$= \qquad \begin{pmatrix} 5 & 5 & 4 \\ 5 & 10 & 1 \\ 4 & 1 & 5 \end{pmatrix}$$

(c) $$A^{\mathrm{T}}A = \begin{pmatrix} 1 & -1 & 2 \\ 2 & 3 & 1 \end{pmatrix}\begin{pmatrix} 1 & 2 \\ -1 & 3 \\ 2 & 1 \end{pmatrix}$$

$$= \qquad \begin{pmatrix} 6 & 1 \\ 1 & 14 \end{pmatrix}$$

Exercises

Questions 1–8 refer to matrices A, B and C where

$$A = \begin{pmatrix} 3 & 1 \\ -1 & 2 \end{pmatrix}, \quad B = \begin{pmatrix} 1 & 4 & 0 \\ 2 & 7 & -1 \end{pmatrix}, \quad C = \begin{pmatrix} -2 & 1 \\ 4 & -1 \\ 0 & 3 \end{pmatrix}$$

Calculate the following products.

1 AB

2 A^2

3 BC

4 CA

5 AA^{T}

6 BCA

7 ABC

8 $B^{\mathrm{T}}AC^{\mathrm{T}}$

Solutions to exercises

1 $\begin{pmatrix} 5 & 19 & -1 \\ 3 & 10 & -2 \end{pmatrix}$

2 $\begin{pmatrix} 8 & 5 \\ -5 & 3 \end{pmatrix}$

3 $\begin{pmatrix} 14 & -3 \\ 24 & -8 \end{pmatrix}$

4 $\begin{pmatrix} -7 & 0 \\ 13 & 2 \\ -3 & 6 \end{pmatrix}$

5 $\begin{pmatrix} 10 & -1 \\ -1 & 5 \end{pmatrix}$

6 $\begin{pmatrix} 45 & 8 \\ 80 & 8 \end{pmatrix}$

7 $\begin{pmatrix} 66 & -17 \\ 34 & -13 \end{pmatrix}$

8 $\begin{pmatrix} 3 & -1 & 15 \\ 8 & 2 & 54 \\ -4 & 6 & -6 \end{pmatrix}$

End of block exercises

Questions 1–6 refer to matrices A, B, C and D where

$$A = (2 \quad -1 \quad 7), \quad B = \begin{pmatrix} 9 \\ 2 \\ 0 \end{pmatrix}, \quad C = \begin{pmatrix} 3 & 6 \\ -3 & 1 \end{pmatrix}, \quad D = \begin{pmatrix} 1 & 2 & 3 \\ 4 & 5 & 6 \end{pmatrix}$$

1 State the size of each of the following products. If a product does not exist then state this.
(a) AB (b) BA (c) CD (d) DC (e) DB (f) BD (g) A^2 (h) C^2

2 State the size of each of the following products. If a product does not exist then state this.
(a) AA^T (b) D^TB (c) D^TC (d) AD^T (e) $(AD^T)^T$

3 State the size of each of the following products. If a product does not exist then state this.
(a) CDB (b) C^2D (c) DBA (d) D^TCD (e) AD^TC

4 Calculate all the products in question 1 that exist.

5 Calculate all the products in question 2 that exist.

6 Calculate all the products in question 3 that exist.

Questions 7–9 refer to matrices A, B, C, D and E. These are given by

$$A = \begin{pmatrix} 4 & -1 \\ 1 & 0 \\ -2 & 2 \end{pmatrix}, \quad B = (2 \quad 1), \quad C = (3 \quad 1 \quad -1), \quad D = \begin{pmatrix} 5 & -2 \\ 1 & 0 \end{pmatrix}, \quad E = \begin{pmatrix} 3 \\ -1 \end{pmatrix}$$

7 State the size of each of the following products if they exist. If a product does not exist then state this.
(a) DE (b) CA (c) DB (d) CA (e) AE

8 State the size of each of the following products if they exist. If a product does not exist then state this.
(a) A^TA (b) AA^T (c) CAD (d) BDE (e) CAB

9 Calculate
(a) AD (b) E^TD (c) CAE

10 If

$$\begin{pmatrix} 3 & 1 \\ 4 & 2 \end{pmatrix}\begin{pmatrix} x \\ y \end{pmatrix} = \begin{pmatrix} 9 \\ 14 \end{pmatrix}$$

calculate x and y.

11 Given

$$\begin{pmatrix} 5 & 2 \\ -3 & 4 \end{pmatrix}\begin{pmatrix} x \\ y \end{pmatrix} = \begin{pmatrix} 19 \\ -27 \end{pmatrix}$$

find x and y.

12 P is an $n \times m$ matrix. Show that the products PP^T and P^TP can always be found. State the size of each product.

13 Given

$$A = \begin{pmatrix} 4 & -2 \\ 1 & 3 \end{pmatrix}, \quad B = \begin{pmatrix} 1 & 3 & 4 \\ -1 & 2 & 0 \end{pmatrix}$$

calculate (a) AB (b) $(AB)^T$ (c) B^TA^T. What do you observe from (b) and (c)?

14 This question asks you to show that $(AB)^T = B^TA^T$. A is an $n \times m$ matrix and B is an $m \times p$ matrix given by

$$A = \begin{pmatrix} a_{11} & a_{12} & \cdots & a_{1m} \\ a_{21} & a_{22} & \cdots & a_{2m} \\ \vdots & \vdots & \ddots & \vdots \\ a_{n1} & a_{n2} & \cdots & a_{nm} \end{pmatrix}$$

$$B = \begin{pmatrix} b_{11} & b_{12} & \cdots & b_{1p} \\ b_{21} & b_{22} & \cdots & b_{2p} \\ \vdots & \vdots & \ddots & \vdots \\ b_{m1} & b_{m2} & \cdots & b_{mp} \end{pmatrix}$$

(a) State an expression for the (i, j)th element of AB, that is the element in the ith row and jth column.

(b) State an expression for the (i, j)th element of $(AB)^T$.
(c) State the ith row of B^T.
(d) State the jth column of A^T.
(e) State an expression for the (i, j)th element of B^TA^T.
(f) Hence show that $(AB)^T = B^TA^T$.

Solutions to exercises

1 (a) 1×1 (b) 3×3 (c) 2×3 (d) does not exist (e) 2×1 (f) does not exist (g) does not exist (h) 2×2

2 (a) 1×1 (b) does not exist (c) 3×2 (d) 1×2 (e) 2×1

3 (a) 2×1 (b) 2×3 (c) 2×3 (d) 3×3 (e) 1×2

4 (a) (16) (b) $\begin{pmatrix} 18 & -9 & 63 \\ 4 & -2 & 14 \\ 0 & 0 & 0 \end{pmatrix}$

(c) $\begin{pmatrix} 27 & 36 & 45 \\ 1 & -1 & -3 \end{pmatrix}$ (e) $\begin{pmatrix} 13 \\ 46 \end{pmatrix}$

(h) $\begin{pmatrix} -9 & 24 \\ -12 & -17 \end{pmatrix}$

5 (a) (54) (c) $\begin{pmatrix} -9 & 10 \\ -9 & 17 \\ -9 & 24 \end{pmatrix}$ (d) $(21 \quad 45)$

(e) $\begin{pmatrix} 21 \\ 45 \end{pmatrix}$

6 (a) $\begin{pmatrix} 315 \\ 7 \end{pmatrix}$ (b) $\begin{pmatrix} 87 & 102 & 117 \\ -80 & -109 & -138 \end{pmatrix}$

(c) $\begin{pmatrix} 26 & -13 & 91 \\ 92 & -46 & 322 \end{pmatrix}$

(d) $\begin{pmatrix} 31 & 32 & 33 \\ 59 & 67 & 75 \\ 87 & 102 & 117 \end{pmatrix}$ (e) $(-72 \quad 171)$

7 (a) 2×1 (b) 1×2 (c) does not exist (d) 1×2 (e) 3×1

8 (a) 2×2 (b) 3×3 (c) 1×2 (d) 1×1 (e) does not exist

9 (a) $\begin{pmatrix} 19 & -8 \\ 5 & -2 \\ -8 & 4 \end{pmatrix}$ (b) $(14 \quad -6)$ (c) (50)

10 $x = 2, y = 3$

11 $x = 5, y = -3$

12 PP^T is an $n \times n$ matrix; P^TP is an $m \times m$ matrix.

13 (a) $\begin{pmatrix} 6 & 8 & 16 \\ -2 & 9 & 4 \end{pmatrix}$ (b) $\begin{pmatrix} 6 & -2 \\ 8 & 9 \\ 16 & 4 \end{pmatrix}$

(c) $\begin{pmatrix} 6 & -2 \\ 8 & 9 \\ 16 & 4 \end{pmatrix}$

Conclude that $(AB)^T = B^TA^T$.

14 (a) $\sum_{k=1}^{m} a_{ik}b_{kj}$ (b) $\sum_{k=1}^{m} a_{jk}b_{ki}$

(c) $(b_{1i}\ b_{2i}\ \ldots\ b_{mi})$ (d) $(a_{j1}\ a_{j2}\ \ldots\ a_{jm})$

(e) $\sum_{k=1}^{m} a_{jk}b_{ki}$

(f) From (b) and (e), the (i, j)th elements of $(AB)^T$ and B^TA^T are identical. Since this is true for all values of i and j then the two matrices are equal.

BLOCK 3

Determinants

3.1 Introduction

We have seen how to add and subtract matrices in Block 1. Block 2 dealt with the multiplication of one matrix by another. Division of one matrix by another is not defined. However, for some matrices it is possible to calculate an inverse matrix. In some ways, use of the inverse matrix takes the place of division. To calculate an inverse matrix requires knowledge of determinants, and it is this topic that is addressed first. All square matrices possess a determinant. We begin with the simplest square matrices: 2×2 matrices.

3.2 Determinant of a 2 × 2 matrix

Consider the 2×2 matrix A where

$$A = \begin{pmatrix} a & b \\ c & d \end{pmatrix}$$

Then the **determinant** of A is $ad - bc$. The determinant of A is denoted by

$$\det(A), |A| \quad \text{or} \quad \begin{vmatrix} a & b \\ c & d \end{vmatrix}$$

When you have evaluated the determinant of a matrix you will see that the result is no longer a matrix, but a single number or expression.

Key point

If

$$A = \begin{pmatrix} a & b \\ c & d \end{pmatrix}$$

then $\det(A) = ad - bc$. Det(A) may also be written as

$$|A| \quad \text{or} \quad \begin{vmatrix} a & b \\ c & d \end{vmatrix}$$

Example 3.1
Given

$$A = \begin{pmatrix} 3 & 6 \\ -1 & 1 \end{pmatrix}$$

calculate the determinant of (a) A, (b) A^T.

Solution

(a) $$|A| = 3(1) - 6(-1) = 9$$

Note that the value of the determinant is the single number, 9.

(b) $$A^T = \begin{pmatrix} 3 & -1 \\ 6 & 1 \end{pmatrix}$$

Hence

$|A^T| =$ $3(1) - (-1)\,6 = 9$

Example 3.2
If A is a 2×2 matrix show $\det(A) = \det(A^T)$.

Solution
Let

$$A = \begin{pmatrix} a & b \\ c & d \end{pmatrix}$$

Then $|A| = ad - bc$.
Now

$A^T =$ $\begin{pmatrix} a & c \\ b & d \end{pmatrix}$

and so

$|A^T| =$ $ad - bc$

Hence $|A| = |A^T|$: that is, the determinant of a matrix and the determinant of its transpose are the same.

Example 3.3
Calculate the determinant of

$$\begin{pmatrix} 4 & 2 \\ 6 & 3 \end{pmatrix}$$

Solution

$$\begin{vmatrix} 4 & 2 \\ 6 & 3 \end{vmatrix} = \qquad 4(3) - 2(6) = 0$$

A matrix that has a zero determinant is called **singular.**

Example 3.4 Control Engineering – Stability of a system
Many engineering systems can be modelled by a set of simultaneous equations. From these equations, a **state matrix**, A, can be formed which encapsulates crucial information about the system.

The stability of a system is determined by the **poles** of the system. The systems poles, s, are determined from the equation

$$|A - sI| = 0$$

where I is the identity matrix.

Given the state matrix is

$$A = \begin{pmatrix} 3 & -2 \\ -1 & 5 \end{pmatrix}$$

determine the system poles.

Solution
The system poles are found from

$$|A - sI| = 0$$

Given

$$A = \begin{pmatrix} 3 & -2 \\ -1 & 5 \end{pmatrix} \quad \text{and} \quad I = \begin{pmatrix} 1 & 0 \\ 0 & 1 \end{pmatrix}$$

then we have

$$A - sI = \begin{pmatrix} 3 & -2 \\ -1 & 5 \end{pmatrix} - s\begin{pmatrix} 1 & 0 \\ 0 & 1 \end{pmatrix} = \begin{pmatrix} 3 - s & -2 \\ -1 & 5 - s \end{pmatrix}$$

So

$$\begin{aligned} |A - sI| &= \begin{vmatrix} 3 - s & -2 \\ -1 & 5 - s \end{vmatrix} \\ &= (3 - s)(5 - s) - 2 \\ &= s^2 - 8s + 13 \end{aligned}$$

The systems poles are solutions of $s^2 - 8s + 13 = 0$. Using the quadratic formula, values of s are obtained:

$$s = 2.268, \quad 5.732$$

A system where $s < 0$, or the $\mathrm{Re}(s) < 0$ in the case of complex poles, is said to be **stable**. If $s > 0$, or $\mathrm{Re}(s) > 0$, then the system is **unstable**. Hence the system in Example 3.4 is unstable.

Exercises

1 Calculate the determinant of each of the following matrices.

(a) $\begin{pmatrix} 8 & 3 \\ -3 & 5 \end{pmatrix}$ (b) $\begin{pmatrix} 6 & 10 \\ -3 & -5 \end{pmatrix}$

(c) $\begin{pmatrix} x & 3 \\ y & 4 \end{pmatrix}$ (d) $\begin{pmatrix} 3-\lambda & 2 \\ 8 & 1-\lambda \end{pmatrix}$

(e) $\begin{pmatrix} -\lambda & 2 \\ 1 & 1-\lambda \end{pmatrix}$

2 Calculate the determinant of each of the following matrices.

(a) $\begin{pmatrix} 3 & 6 \\ 2 & 9 \end{pmatrix}$ (b) $\begin{pmatrix} -2 & 1 \\ 1 & 4 \end{pmatrix}$

(c) $\begin{pmatrix} -1 & -1 \\ 4 & -3 \end{pmatrix}$ (d) $\begin{pmatrix} 12 & 20 \\ 6 & 10 \end{pmatrix}$

(e) $\begin{pmatrix} 1 & 0 \\ 3 & \lambda \end{pmatrix}$ (f) $\begin{pmatrix} 3-\lambda & 4 \\ 6 & 2-\lambda \end{pmatrix}$

3 Find conditions on a, b and c for

$$\begin{pmatrix} a & b \\ 0 & c \end{pmatrix}$$

to be singular.

4 Under what conditions is the matrix

$$F = \begin{pmatrix} x & 3 \\ 2x & y \end{pmatrix}$$

singular?

5 Find values of λ for

$$\begin{pmatrix} 7-\lambda & 2 \\ 12 & 5-\lambda \end{pmatrix}$$

to be singular.

6 Find

$$\begin{vmatrix} \cos\theta & \sin\theta \\ -\sin\theta & \cos\theta \end{vmatrix}$$

7 Find $|I|$ where I is a 2×2 identity matrix.

8 **Control Engineering.** Determine the system poles of the following state matrices. In each case state whether the system is stable or unstable.

(a) $\begin{pmatrix} -4 & 5 \\ -5 & 3 \end{pmatrix}$ (b) $\begin{pmatrix} -1 & -2 \\ 5 & 4 \end{pmatrix}$

Solutions to exercises

1 (a) 49 (b) 0 (c) $4x - 3y$ (d) $\lambda^2 - 4\lambda - 13$ (e) $\lambda^2 - \lambda - 2$

2 (a) 15 (b) -9 (c) 7 (d) 0 (e) λ (f) $\lambda^2 - 5\lambda - 18$

3 Either a or c is 0.

4 F is singular if $x = 0$ or $y = 6$.

5 1, 11

6 $\cos^2\theta + \sin^2\theta = 1$, using a trigonometrical identity to simplify.

7 1

8 (a) $s = \frac{-1 \pm \sqrt{-51}}{2}$. System is stable.

(b) $s = \frac{3 \pm \sqrt{-15}}{2}$. System is unstable.

3.3 Minors and cofactors of a 3 × 3 matrix

Before we can calculate the determinant of a 3 × 3 matrix it is necessary to introduce the minor of an element and the cofactor of an element. Consider a 3 × 3 matrix A where

$$A = \begin{pmatrix} a_{11} & a_{12} & a_{13} \\ a_{21} & a_{22} & a_{23} \\ a_{31} & a_{32} & a_{33} \end{pmatrix}$$

If we choose an element of A, say a_{ij}, and cross out its row and column, that is the ith row and the jth column, we are left with a 2 × 2 matrix. The determinant of this 2 × 2 matrix is called the **minor** of a_{ij}.

Example 3.5

Given

$$A = \begin{pmatrix} 3 & -1 & 6 \\ 9 & -5 & 2 \\ 0 & 4 & 7 \end{pmatrix}$$

calculate the minor of (a) 3, (b) 9, (c) 2.

Solution

(a) The element 3 occurs in row 1, column 1, that is $a_{11} = 3$. Deleting row 1 and column 1 leaves

$$\begin{pmatrix} -5 & 2 \\ 4 & 7 \end{pmatrix}$$

The determinant of this 2 × 2 matrix is $(-5)7 - 2(4) = -43$. The minor of 3 is -43.

(b) The element 9 occurs in row 2, column 1. Deleting these leaves

$$\begin{pmatrix} -1 & 6 \\ 4 & 7 \end{pmatrix}$$

The determinant of this 2 × 2 matrix is

$$(-1)7 - 6(4) = -31$$

The minor of 9 is -31.

(c) The element 2 occurs in row 2, column 3. Deleting these leaves

$$\begin{pmatrix} 3 & -1 \\ 0 & 4 \end{pmatrix}$$

whose determinant is 12. The minor of 2 is 12.

Closely related to the minor of an element is the **cofactor** of an element. The cofactor of a_{ij} is given as

$$\text{cofactor of } a_{ij} = (-1)^{i+j} \times \text{minor of } a_{ij}$$

The term $(-1)^{i+j}$ is either 1 or -1 depending upon the position of the element. The following grid of + and − is an easy way to visualise this. The + and − signs are known as the **place signs** of the elements. If the place sign is + then the cofactor and minor are identical; if the place sign is − then the cofactor is − (minor).

$$\begin{pmatrix} + & - & + \\ - & + & - \\ + & - & + \end{pmatrix}$$

Example 3.6

The matrix A is given as

$$A = \begin{pmatrix} 3 & -1 & 6 \\ 9 & -5 & 2 \\ 0 & 4 & 7 \end{pmatrix}$$

Calculate the cofactor of (a) 3, (b) 9, (c) 2.

Solution

(a) The minor of 3 is -43. Since the place sign is + then the cofactor of 3 is also -43.
(b) The minor of 9 is -31. The place sign is − and so the cofactor is 31.
(c) The minor of 2 is 12. The place sign is − and so the cofactor is -12.

Exercises

1 The matrix D is given by

$$D = \begin{pmatrix} 7 & -8 & 3 \\ 9 & 2 & -2 \\ 1 & -3 & 0 \end{pmatrix}$$

(a) Calculate the minor of (i) 7, (ii) -8, (iii) 3, (iv) 9.
(b) Calculate the cofactor of (i) 2, (ii) -2, (iii) 1, (iv) -3, (v) 0.

2 The matrix G is defined by

$$G = \begin{pmatrix} 2-\lambda & 3 & 6 \\ 9 & -\lambda & 4 \\ -1 & 0 & 1-\lambda \end{pmatrix}$$

(a) Calculate the minor of (i) $2-\lambda$, (ii) 3, (iii) 6.
(b) Calculate the cofactor of (i) 9, (ii) $-\lambda$ (iii) 4.

Solutions to exercises

1 (a) (i) -6 (ii) 2 (iii) -29 (iv) 9
(b) (i) -3 (ii) 13 (iii) 10 (iv) 41 (v) 86

2 (a) (i) $\lambda^2 - \lambda$ (ii) $13 - 9\lambda$ (iii) $-\lambda$
(b) (i) $3\lambda - 3$ (ii) $\lambda^2 - 3\lambda + 8$ (iii) -3

3.4 Determinant of a 3 × 3 matrix

Consider a general 3 × 3 matrix, A.

$$A = \begin{pmatrix} a_{11} & a_{12} & a_{13} \\ a_{21} & a_{22} & a_{23} \\ a_{31} & a_{32} & a_{33} \end{pmatrix}$$

The determinant of A is found using

$$|A| = a_{11} \times \text{(its cofactor)} + a_{12} \times \text{(its cofactor)} + a_{13} \times \text{(its cofactor)}$$

Calculation of the determinant using this expression is known as **expanding along the first row**.

Key point

$$|A| = a_{11} \times \text{(its cofactor)} + a_{12} \times \text{(its cofactor)} + a_{13} \times \text{(its cofactor)}$$

Example 3.7
Calculate $|A|$ where

$$A = \begin{pmatrix} 3 & -1 & 6 \\ 9 & -5 & 2 \\ 0 & 4 & 7 \end{pmatrix}$$

Solution
We have $a_{11} = 3$, $a_{12} = -1$ and $a_{13} = 6$. The cofactors of these elements are required. The cofactor of 3 is -43 as found in Example 3.6.

The minor of -1 is $\begin{vmatrix} 9 & 2 \\ 0 & 7 \end{vmatrix} = 63$

The place sign of -1 is $-$

and so the cofactor is -63

The minor of 6 is

$$\begin{vmatrix} 9 & -5 \\ 0 & 4 \end{vmatrix} = 36$$

The place sign is + and so the cofactor is 36. Hence

$$\begin{aligned} |A| &= 3(-43) + (-1)(-63) + 6(36) \\ &= 150 \end{aligned}$$

The determinant of a matrix can also be found by expanding along any row or column. Thus, for example, we could calculate $|A|$ by expanding along the second row thus:

$$|A| = a_{21} \times \text{(its cofactor)} + a_{22} \times \text{(its cofactor)} + a_{23} \times \text{(its cofactor)}$$

or expanding along the third column thus:

$$|A| = a_{13} \times \text{(its cofactor)} + a_{23} \times \text{(its cofactor)} + a_{33} \times \text{(its cofactor)}$$

Example 3.8

The matrix A is defined in Example 3.5 as

$$A = \begin{pmatrix} 3 & -1 & 6 \\ 9 & -5 & 2 \\ 0 & 4 & 7 \end{pmatrix}$$

Evaluate $\det(A)$ by
(a) expanding along the third row
(b) expanding along the second column.

Solution

(a) By expanding along the third row we have

$$|A| = a_{31} \times \text{(its cofactor)} + a_{32} \times \text{(its cofactor)} + a_{33} \times \text{(its cofactor)}$$

Now $a_{31} = 0$, $a_{32} = 4$, $a_{33} = 7$.
The minor of a_{31} is

$$\begin{vmatrix} -1 & 6 \\ -5 & 2 \end{vmatrix} = 28.$$

The cofactor is also 28.

The minor of a_{32} is

$$\begin{vmatrix} 3 & 6 \\ 9 & 2 \end{vmatrix} = -48$$

The cofactor is

48

The minor of a_{33} is

$$\begin{vmatrix} 3 & -1 \\ 9 & -5 \end{vmatrix} = -6$$

The cofactor is -6. Hence

$$|A| = 0(28) + 4(48) + 7(-6)$$
$$= 150$$

(b) We now expand along column 2.
The elements are

$a_{12} = -1$, $a_{22} = -5$, $a_{32} = 4$

The minor of a_{12} is

$$\begin{vmatrix} 9 & 2 \\ 0 & 7 \end{vmatrix} = 63$$

The cofactor is -63.

The minor of a_{22} is

$$\begin{vmatrix} 3 & 6 \\ 0 & 7 \end{vmatrix} = 21$$

The cofactor is 21.

The minor of a_{32} is

$$\begin{vmatrix} 3 & 6 \\ 9 & 2 \end{vmatrix} = -48$$

The cofactor is 48

Hence

$$\begin{aligned} |A| &= (-1)(-63) + (-5)(21) + 4(48) \\ &= 150 \end{aligned}$$

Exercises

1 The matrix H is defined by

$$H = \begin{pmatrix} 6 & -2 & 4 \\ 3 & -1 & 7 \\ 9 & 8 & -3 \end{pmatrix}$$

Evaluate $|H|$ by expanding
(a) along the first row
(b) along the third row
(c) along the second column.

2 The matrix K is defined by

$$K = \begin{pmatrix} 17 & 9 & -4 \\ 0 & 11 & 3 \\ 0 & 0 & -6 \end{pmatrix}$$

Calculate $|K|$.

3 Calculate the determinant of each of the following matrices:

(a) $\begin{pmatrix} -1 & 6 & 1 \\ -3 & 9 & 2 \\ 6 & 3 & 0 \end{pmatrix}$

(b) $\begin{pmatrix} 5 & 3 & 6 \\ 10 & 11 & 1 \\ -6 & 8 & -7 \end{pmatrix}$

(c) $\begin{pmatrix} 6 & 6 & 3 \\ -1 & 9 & 7 \\ 11 & 21 & 13 \end{pmatrix}$

(d) $\begin{pmatrix} 3 & -6 & 9 \\ 4 & 6 & -6 \\ 5 & 18 & -21 \end{pmatrix}$

(e) $\begin{pmatrix} 1 & 3 & 6 \\ 6 & 3 & 1 \\ 3 & 1 & 6 \end{pmatrix}$

4 Find det(B) by expanding along the second column.

$$B = \begin{pmatrix} 1 & 0 & 3 \\ 22 & -1 & 17 \\ -3 & 0 & 19 \end{pmatrix}$$

Solutions to exercises

1 -330

2 -1122

3 (a) 15 (b) 643 (c) 0 (d) 0 (e) -100

4 -28

3.5 Determinant of a 4 × 4 matrix

The determinant of a 4 × 4 matrix is found in a similar way to that for a 3 × 3 matrix. We can expand along any row or column. The minor of an element is the determinant of the 3 × 3 matrix left after deleting the row and column containing the element. The cofactor is then found by multiplying by either 1 or -1 depending upon the place sign.

The place signs for a 4 × 4 matrix are as follows:

$$\begin{pmatrix} + & - & + & - \\ - & + & - & + \\ + & - & + & - \\ - & + & - & + \end{pmatrix}$$

Expanding along the first row of a 4 × 4 matrix, A, for example, would give:

$$|A| = a_{11} \times \text{(its cofactor)} + a_{12} \times \text{(its cofactor)}$$
$$+ a_{13} \times \text{(its cofactor)} + a_{14} \times \text{(its cofactor)}$$

Example 3.9

Find $|A|$ by expanding along the first row where

$$A = \begin{pmatrix} 3 & -2 & 4 & 1 \\ 6 & 2 & 0 & 3 \\ 9 & 1 & 1 & -1 \\ 4 & 2 & -2 & 5 \end{pmatrix}$$

Solution

We have $a_{11} = 3$, $a_{12} = -2$, $a_{13} = 4$, $a_{14} = 1$. The cofactors of these elements are found by deleting the appropriate rows and columns.

The minor of a_{11} is

$$\begin{vmatrix} 2 & 0 & 3 \\ 1 & 1 & -1 \\ 2 & -2 & 5 \end{vmatrix} = -6$$

The cofactor is -6.

The minor of a_{12} is

$$\begin{vmatrix} 6 & 0 & 3 \\ 9 & 1 & -1 \\ 4 & -2 & 5 \end{vmatrix} = -48$$

The cofactor is 48.

The minor of a_{13} is

$$\begin{vmatrix} 6 & 2 & 3 \\ 9 & 1 & -1 \\ 4 & 2 & 5 \end{vmatrix} = -14$$

The cofactor is -14.

The minor of a_{14} is

$$\begin{vmatrix} 6 & 2 & 0 \\ 9 & 1 & 1 \\ 4 & 2 & -2 \end{vmatrix} = 20$$

The cofactor is -20.

Hence

$$\begin{aligned} |A| &= 3(-6) + (-2)48 + 4(-14) + 1(-20) \\ &= -190 \end{aligned}$$

The sensible choice of row or column can save work.

Example 3.10

Calculate $|T|$ where

$$T = \begin{pmatrix} 13 & 2 & 1 & -9 \\ 4 & 7 & 0 & 6 \\ -1 & 11 & -2 & 3 \\ 4 & -2 & 0 & 6 \end{pmatrix}$$

Solution

Expansion along column 3 is efficient as it contains two zeros. The cofactors of these zero elements need not be calculated. We have $t_{13} = 1$ and $t_{33} = -2$.

$$\begin{aligned} T &= t_{13} \times (\text{its cofactor}) + t_{33} \times (\text{its cofactor}) \\ &= \begin{vmatrix} 4 & 7 & 6 \\ -1 & 11 & 3 \\ 4 & -2 & 6 \end{vmatrix} + (-2) \begin{vmatrix} 13 & 2 & -9 \\ 4 & 7 & 6 \\ 4 & -2 & 6 \end{vmatrix} \\ &= 162 - 2(1026) = -1890 \end{aligned}$$

Exercises

1 Calculate the determinant of each of the following matrices by expanding along an appropriate row or column.

(a) $\begin{pmatrix} 6 & 3 & -2 & 1 \\ 4 & 0 & -2 & 0 \\ 1 & 1 & 7 & 4 \\ 6 & 3 & 0 & 2 \end{pmatrix}$

(b) $\begin{pmatrix} 3 & 17 & 7 & 2 \\ -1 & 6 & 0 & -3 \\ 9 & 6 & 0 & 5 \\ 5 & -3 & 0 & 4 \end{pmatrix}$

(c) $\begin{pmatrix} 2 & -1 & 0 & 6 \\ 6 & -5 & 2 & 1 \\ 0 & 3 & 2 & 0 \\ 1 & 2 & 4 & 5 \end{pmatrix}$

(d) $\begin{pmatrix} 9 & 3 & 5 & -2 \\ 0 & -1 & 6 & 7 \\ 0 & 4 & 9 & 11 \\ -2 & -6 & 3 & 5 \end{pmatrix}$

2 Calculate $|A|$ where

$$A = \begin{pmatrix} \alpha & 17 & 6 & 3 \\ 0 & \beta & 14 & 7 \\ 0 & 0 & \gamma & 13 \\ 0 & 0 & 0 & \delta \end{pmatrix}$$

Solutions to exercises

1 (a) 2 (b) 462 (c) −278 (d) −54

2 $\alpha\beta\gamma\delta$

3.6 Properties of determinants

There are a number of properties of determinants that can be used to simplify their evaluation. Some of these properties are given now.

Property 1

Key point

Suppose A is an $n \times n$ matrix and k a scalar. Suppose the matrix B is obtained by multiplying a *single* row or column of A by k. Then

$$\det(B) = k \det(A)$$

If the matrix A is multiplied by k, that is every element in the matrix is multiplied by k, then we obtain

$$\det(kA) = k^n \det(A)$$

Example 3.11
Suppose

$$A = \begin{pmatrix} 5 & 7 \\ -2 & 3 \end{pmatrix}$$

Obtain B from A by multiplying the second column of A by 4.
(a) Write down B.
(b) Find det(B).
(c) Find det(A).
(d) Verify that det(B) = 4 det(A) as in Property 1.

Solution

(a) $B =$ $\begin{pmatrix} 5 & 28 \\ -2 & 12 \end{pmatrix}$

(b) $|B| =$ 116

(c) $|A| =$ 29

(d) It follows that det(B) = 4 det(A).

Example 3.12
Suppose

$$A = \begin{pmatrix} 1 & 3 \\ 2 & -7 \end{pmatrix}$$

(a) Write down $5A$.
(b) Find det(A).
(c) Find det($5A$).
(d) Verify Property 1, that is det($5A$) = 5^2 det(A).

Solution

(a) $5A =$ $\begin{pmatrix} 5 & 15 \\ 10 & -35 \end{pmatrix}$

(b) det(A) = -13

(c) det($5A$) = $(5)(-35) - (15)(10) = -325$

(d) Then, since $-325 = 25 \times -13$, it follows that det($5A$) = $5^2 \times$ det(A).

Example 3.13
Find det(B) given

$$B = \begin{pmatrix} 6 & -2 & 12 \\ 27 & -15 & 6 \\ 0 & 4 & 7 \end{pmatrix}$$

and given that the determinant of

$$A = \begin{pmatrix} 3 & -1 & 6 \\ 9 & -5 & 2 \\ 0 & 4 & 7 \end{pmatrix}$$

is 150.

Solution

By careful inspection of B note that it is obtained from A by multiplying row 1 by 2 and row 2 by 3. Hence

$$\det(B) = 2 \times 3 \times \det(A) = 6 \times 150 = 900$$

Property 2

Key point

> If B is obtained from A by interchanging two rows or two columns then
>
> $$\det(B) = -\det(A)$$

In other words, interchanging two rows or two columns changes the sign of the determinant. Carrying out two interchanges introduces two sign changes and hence leaves the determinant unchanged.

Example 3.14

Given

$$A = \begin{pmatrix} 3 & -1 & 6 \\ 9 & -5 & 2 \\ 0 & 4 & 7 \end{pmatrix}$$

and $|A| = 150$, find the determinant of each of the following matrices.

(a) $\begin{pmatrix} 0 & 4 & 7 \\ 9 & -5 & 2 \\ 3 & -1 & 6 \end{pmatrix}$ (b) $\begin{pmatrix} 9 & -5 & 2 \\ 0 & 4 & 7 \\ 3 & -1 & 6 \end{pmatrix}$ (c) $\begin{pmatrix} -5 & 9 & 2 \\ -1 & 3 & 6 \\ 4 & 0 & 7 \end{pmatrix}$

Solution

(a) By interchanging row 1 and row 2 of $|A|$ we obtain

$$\begin{vmatrix} 0 & 4 & 7 \\ 9 & -5 & 2 \\ 3 & -1 & 6 \end{vmatrix} = -150$$

(b) Interchanging row 1 and row 2 of the determinant in (a) we obtain

$$\begin{vmatrix} 9 & -5 & 2 \\ 0 & 4 & 7 \\ 3 & -1 & 6 \end{vmatrix} = 150$$

(c) We begin with $|A|$. Interchanging column 1 and column 2 we obtain

$$\begin{vmatrix} -1 & 3 & 6 \\ -5 & 9 & 2 \\ 4 & 0 & 7 \end{vmatrix} = -150$$

We now interchange row 1 and row 2 to produce:

$$\begin{vmatrix} -5 & 9 & 2 \\ -1 & 3 & 6 \\ 4 & 0 & 7 \end{vmatrix} = 150$$

Property 3

Key point

Adding or subtracting a multiple of one row (or column) to another row (or column) leaves the determinant unchanged.

Example 3.15
Evaluate

$$\begin{vmatrix} 3 & -1 & 6 \\ 9 & -5 & 2 \\ 0 & 4 & 7 \end{vmatrix}$$

Solution
We use Property 3 repeatedly to simplify the determinant.

$$\begin{vmatrix} 3 & -1 & 6 \\ 9 & -5 & 2 \\ 0 & 4 & 7 \end{vmatrix} = \begin{vmatrix} 3 & -1 & 6 \\ 0 & -2 & -16 \\ 0 & 4 & 7 \end{vmatrix} \text{(subtracting } 3 \times \text{ row 1 from row 2)}$$

$$= \begin{vmatrix} 3 & 0 & 6 \\ 0 & -2 & -16 \\ 0 & 4 & 7 \end{vmatrix} \left(\text{adding } \frac{1}{3} \text{ column 1 to column 2}\right)$$

$$= \begin{vmatrix} 3 & 0 & 0 \\ 0 & -2 & -16 \\ 0 & 4 & 7 \end{vmatrix} \text{(subtracting } 2 \times \text{ column 1 from column 3)}$$

$$= \begin{vmatrix} 3 & 0 & 0 \\ 0 & -2 & -16 \\ 0 & 0 & -25 \end{vmatrix} \text{(adding } 2 \times \text{ row 2 to row 3)}$$

$$= 150 \text{ (by expanding along row 1)}$$

Property 4

Key point

If A and B are two square matrices such that AB exists then

$$\det(AB) = \det(A)\det(B)$$

Example 3.16
Given

$$A = \begin{pmatrix} 3 & 2 \\ 1 & 4 \end{pmatrix}, \quad B = \begin{pmatrix} -1 & 3 \\ 0 & 2 \end{pmatrix}$$

verify $\det(AB) = \det(A)\det(B)$.

Solution

$$|A| = 12 - 2 = 10, \quad |B| = -2, \quad |A||B| = -20$$

Now

$$AB = \begin{pmatrix} -3 & 13 \\ -1 & 11 \end{pmatrix}, \quad |AB| = -33 + 13 = -20$$

Hence $\det(AB) = \det(A)\det(B)$.

Property 5

Key point

If two rows or two columns of a matrix are equal, the determinant of the matrix is zero.

Example 3.17
Find the determinant of the matrix

$$A = \begin{pmatrix} 4 & -5 & 2 \\ 4 & -5 & 2 \\ 1 & 2 & 1 \end{pmatrix}$$

Solution
Note that the first two rows are the same. It is easy to check that $|A| = 0$.

Exercises

1 Use the properties of determinants to simplify the following determinants and then evaluate them.

(a) $\begin{vmatrix} 5 & 20 & 9 \\ 3 & 31 & 15 \\ 1 & 24 & 12 \end{vmatrix}$ (b) $\begin{vmatrix} 28 & 12 & 35 \\ 24 & 10 & 31 \\ 15 & 6 & 20 \end{vmatrix}$

(c) $\begin{vmatrix} 113 & 92 & 58 \\ 175 & 144 & 90 \\ 64 & 53 & 33 \end{vmatrix}$

(d) $\begin{vmatrix} 176 & 152 & 101 \\ 229 & 195 & 133 \\ 109 & 95 & 62 \end{vmatrix}$

(e) $\begin{vmatrix} -19 & -15 & -12 \\ -21 & -17 & -14 \\ -23 & -19 & -15 \end{vmatrix}$

2 Determine the value of:

(a) $\begin{vmatrix} 29 & 39 & -3 & 11 \\ 5 & 3 & 3 & 4 \\ 24 & 36 & -6 & 7 \\ 30 & 59 & -2 & 1 \end{vmatrix}$

(b) $\begin{vmatrix} 19 & 25 & 16 & -30 \\ 7 & 9 & 6 & -8 \\ -11 & -15 & -10 & 22 \\ 21 & 25 & 12 & -15 \end{vmatrix}$

3 Verify $\det(GH) = \det(G)\det(H)$ where

$$G = \begin{pmatrix} -3 & 1 \\ 2 & 5 \end{pmatrix} \text{ and } H = \begin{pmatrix} 2 & 4 \\ -1 & 3 \end{pmatrix}$$

Solutions to exercises

1 (a) 9 (b) 2 (c) 8 (d) 28 (e) 8

2 (a) 0 (b) 4

Computer and calculator exercises

Many computer algebra packages will calculate the determinant of a matrix. If you have access to such a package try these exercises.

1 Calculate the determinant of

(a) $\begin{pmatrix} 7 & 4 & 11 & 6 \\ 3 & 1 & 7 & -2 \\ 4 & 4 & 5 & 9 \\ 3 & 2 & 1 & 8 \end{pmatrix}$

(b) $\begin{pmatrix} 1 & 2 & 5 & 8 & 3 \\ 3 & 8 & 1 & -2 & 6 \\ 4 & 7 & 5 & -1 & 0 \\ -11 & 11 & 3 & 6 & 7 \\ -1 & 6 & 9 & 4 & 3 \end{pmatrix}$

Solutions to exercises

1 (a) 0 (b) 28118

End of block exercises

1 Find the determinant of each of the following matrices:

(a) $\begin{pmatrix} 6 & 11 \\ 2 & 4 \end{pmatrix}$ (b) $\begin{pmatrix} -1 & 6 \\ 3 & 9 \end{pmatrix}$ (c) $\begin{pmatrix} -1 & 0 \\ 2 & 3 \end{pmatrix}$ (d) $\begin{pmatrix} 3 & 4 \\ -1 & -2 \end{pmatrix}$

(e) $\begin{pmatrix} -7 & -1 \\ -2 & -3 \end{pmatrix}$

2 Find the determinant of each of the following matrices:

(a) $\begin{pmatrix} 3-\lambda & 4 \\ 2 & 1-\lambda \end{pmatrix}$ (b) $\begin{pmatrix} -\lambda & 3 \\ 1 & 2-\lambda \end{pmatrix}$

(c) $\begin{pmatrix} 7-\lambda & 2 \\ 3 & 2-\lambda \end{pmatrix}$

(d) $\begin{pmatrix} -1-\lambda & 1 \\ 6 & 4-\lambda \end{pmatrix}$

(e) $\begin{pmatrix} 4-\lambda & 2 \\ -1 & 7-\lambda \end{pmatrix}$

3 Calculate the values of λ for which each matrix in question 2 is singular.

4 Given

$$A = \begin{pmatrix} 9 & 6 & -1 \\ 3 & 5 & 7 \\ -3 & 2 & -5 \end{pmatrix}$$

calculate (a) the minor of 9, (b) the cofactor of 6, (c) the minor of 3, (d) the cofactor of -5, (e) $\det(A)$.

5 Calculate the determinant of each of the following matrices:

(a) $\begin{pmatrix} 3 & 1 & -6 \\ 4 & 2 & 0 \\ 5 & 6 & -1 \end{pmatrix}$ (b) $\begin{pmatrix} 9 & 1 & 1 \\ 4 & 2 & 3 \\ 1 & 6 & 9 \end{pmatrix}$

(c) $\begin{pmatrix} 5 & 1 & 6 \\ 9 & 3 & 2 \\ 1 & -1 & 10 \end{pmatrix}$ (d) $\begin{pmatrix} 1 & 1 & 1 \\ 2 & 2 & 3 \\ 5 & 6 & 8 \end{pmatrix}$

(e) $\begin{pmatrix} 17 & -19 & 31 \\ 18 & 21 & 30 \\ 14 & 20 & 32 \end{pmatrix}$

6 Calculate the determinant of

(a) $\begin{pmatrix} 5 & 2 & 6 & 3 \\ 3 & 9 & 12 & 1 \\ -3 & 1 & 4 & 1 \\ 4 & 1 & 5 & 3 \end{pmatrix}$

(b) $\begin{pmatrix} 6 & 7 & 10 & 1 \\ 11 & 5 & 14 & 2 \\ 12 & 9 & 21 & 3 \\ 7 & 2 & 11 & 2 \end{pmatrix}$

7 If

$$A = \begin{pmatrix} 3 & 8 \\ 2 & 6 \end{pmatrix} \text{ and } B = 3A$$

(a) find $|A|$, (b) find $|B|$,

(c) verify $\det(B) = 3^2 \det(A)$.

8 Given

$$A = \begin{pmatrix} -4 & 2 \\ 1 & 3 \end{pmatrix}, \quad B = \begin{pmatrix} 6 & -1 \\ 5 & 3 \end{pmatrix}$$

verify (a) $\det(A^2) = [\det(A)]^2$,
(b) $\det(AB) = \det(A)\det(B)$.

9 Calculate the determinant of each of the following matrices:

(a) $\begin{pmatrix} 11 & 6 \\ -3 & -1 \end{pmatrix}$ (b) $\begin{pmatrix} 300 & 170 \\ 150 & 85 \end{pmatrix}$

(c) $\begin{pmatrix} 2x & 2y \\ -x & y \end{pmatrix}$

10 Calculate the following determinants:

(a) $\begin{vmatrix} 1 & 2 & 3 \\ 1 & 3 & 2 \\ -2 & 3 & 1 \end{vmatrix}$ (b) $\begin{vmatrix} 17 & 1 & -23 \\ \lambda & 0 & 6 \\ 0 & 0 & \lambda-1 \end{vmatrix}$

11 Given

$$H = \begin{pmatrix} 3 & -2 & 1 \\ 6 & -1 & 5 \\ -3 & 0 & 9 \end{pmatrix}$$

calculate (a) the minor of -2,
(b) the cofactor of 0.

12 Calculate the values of λ for which the matrix A is singular given

$$A = \begin{pmatrix} 5-\lambda & -1 \\ 6 & -2-\lambda \end{pmatrix}$$

13 Calculate $|A|$ where

$$A = \begin{pmatrix} 6 & 19 & -36 & 0 \\ 0 & 4 & 1 & 0 \\ 0 & 2 & 1 & 0 \\ 17 & -21 & 32 & 2 \end{pmatrix}$$

14 Without explicitly evaluating the determinant find $|A|$ if

$$A = \begin{pmatrix} -1 & 3 & -1 \\ 7 & 8 & 7 \\ -15 & 1 & -15 \end{pmatrix}$$

15 **Control Engineering.** A system has a state matrix, A, given by

$$A = \begin{pmatrix} -5 & 2 \\ -11 & -2 \end{pmatrix}$$

Find the system poles and hence determine whether the system is stable or unstable.

Solutions to exercises

1 (a) 2 (b) -27 (c) -3 (d) -2 (e) 19

2 (a) $\lambda^2 - 4\lambda - 5$ (b) $\lambda^2 - 2\lambda - 3$ (c) $\lambda^2 - 9\lambda + 8$ (d) $\lambda^2 - 3\lambda - 10$ (e) $\lambda^2 - 11\lambda + 30$

3 (a) $-1, 5$ (b) $-1, 3$ (c) $1, 8$ (d) $-2, 5$ (e) $5, 6$

4 (a) -39 (b) -6 (c) -28 (d) 27 (e) -408

5 (a) -86 (b) -11 (c) 0 (d) -1 (e) 6234

6 (a) 10 (b) -9

7 (a) 2 (b) 18

9 (a) 7 (b) 0 (c) $2xy + 2xy = 4xy$

10 (a) 14 (b) $\lambda(1 - \lambda)$

11 (a) 69 (b) -9

12 $-1, 4$

13 24

14 0 since two columns are identical.

15 Poles are $s = \frac{-7 \pm \sqrt{-79}}{2}$. System is stable.

BLOCK 4 The inverse of a matrix

4.1 Introduction

This block examines the idea of an inverse matrix. Division of one matrix by another is not defined: use of an inverse matrix is the nearest equivalent of 'matrix division'.

4.2 Definition

Let A be an $n \times n$ matrix. Recall that I_n is the $n \times n$ identity matrix. Suppose that B is an $n \times n$ matrix such that

$$AB = BA = I_n$$

We say that B is the **inverse** of A. We often write A^{-1} to denote the inverse of A. It is important to realise that in this context A^{-1} does not mean $\frac{1}{A}$. Division by a matrix is not defined. In what follows we shall write the identity matrix as I, rather than I_n. Its size should be obvious from the context.

Key point

Multiplying a square matrix A by its inverse A^{-1}, if this exists, yields the identity matrix I.

$$AA^{-1} = A^{-1}A = I$$

Example 4.1

Given $A = \begin{pmatrix} 3 & 4 \\ 2 & 3 \end{pmatrix}$

show that

$$B = \begin{pmatrix} 3 & -4 \\ -2 & 3 \end{pmatrix}$$

is the inverse of A.

Solution

We calculate AB and BA.

$$AB = \begin{pmatrix} 3 & 4 \\ 2 & 3 \end{pmatrix}\begin{pmatrix} 3 & -4 \\ -2 & 3 \end{pmatrix}$$

$$= \begin{pmatrix} 1 & 0 \\ 0 & 1 \end{pmatrix}$$
$$= I$$

$$BA = \begin{pmatrix} 3 & -4 \\ -2 & 3 \end{pmatrix}\begin{pmatrix} 3 & 4 \\ 2 & 3 \end{pmatrix}$$
$$= \begin{pmatrix} 1 & 0 \\ 0 & 1 \end{pmatrix}$$
$$= I$$

Hence $AB = BA = I$ and so B is the inverse of A. Note also that A is the inverse of B.

The term 'inverse' can only be applied to square matrices. It is meaningless to talk about the inverse of a 2×3 or 3×7 matrix, for example. However, even though a matrix is square this is no guarantee that its inverse matrix exists. If the determinant of A is 0, that is A is singular, then A does not have an inverse. If the determinant is non-zero, then the inverse can be found.

Key point

If $|A| = 0$, A does not have an inverse.

If $|A| \neq 0$, A does have an inverse.

4.3 Finding the inverse of a 2 × 2 matrix

Suppose A is a 2×2 matrix and $|A| \neq 0$. Then the inverse of A can be found. If

$$A = \begin{pmatrix} a & b \\ c & d \end{pmatrix}$$

then recall $|A| = ad - bc$. Now A^{-1} is given by

$$A^{-1} = \frac{1}{|A|}\begin{pmatrix} d & -b \\ -c & a \end{pmatrix}$$

Key point

If

$$A = \begin{pmatrix} a & b \\ c & d \end{pmatrix}$$

then

$$A^{-1} = \frac{1}{|A|}\begin{pmatrix} d & -b \\ -c & a \end{pmatrix}$$

Example 4.2

Find A^{-1}, if it exists, when A is given by

(a) $\begin{pmatrix} 3 & 4 \\ 2 & 6 \end{pmatrix}$ (b) $\begin{pmatrix} -1 & 4 \\ 1 & 0 \end{pmatrix}$ (c) $\begin{pmatrix} 1 & 0 \\ 0 & 1 \end{pmatrix}$ (d) $\begin{pmatrix} 3 & -6 \\ -6 & 12 \end{pmatrix}$

Solution

(a) Here $a = 3$, $b = 4$, $c = 2$, $d = 6$ and $|A| = 10$. Then

$$A^{-1} = \frac{1}{10}\begin{pmatrix} 6 & -4 \\ -2 & 3 \end{pmatrix}$$

$$= \begin{pmatrix} 0.6 & -0.4 \\ -0.2 & 0.3 \end{pmatrix}$$

It is useful to check that $AA^{-1} = A^{-1}A = I$.

(b) Here $a =$ ___ , $b =$ ___ , $c =$ ___ , $d =$ ___ — $-1, 4, 1, 0$

and

$|A| =$ ___ — -4

Hence we have

$A^{-1} =$ ___ — $\frac{1}{-4}\begin{pmatrix} 0 & -4 \\ -1 & -1 \end{pmatrix}$

$=$ ___ — $\begin{pmatrix} 0 & 1 \\ 0.25 & 0.25 \end{pmatrix}$

(c) Here $a = 1$, $b = 0$, $c = 0$, $d = 1$ and $|A| = 1$. We have

$$A^{-1} = \begin{pmatrix} 1 & 0 \\ 0 & 1 \end{pmatrix}$$

Hence the identity matrix is its own inverse.

(d) Here $|A| = 0$. Hence the matrix is singular and does not have an inverse.

Example 4.3

Find the inverse of

$$B = \begin{pmatrix} 3 & -2 \\ 4 & -2 \end{pmatrix}$$

Solution

Here the values of a, b, c and d are given by ___ — $3, -2, 4, -2$

The determinant of B is found.

$|B| =$ ___ — 2

The inverse, B^{-1}, may now be stated.

$$B^{-1} = \qquad \begin{pmatrix} -1 & 1 \\ -2 & 1.5 \end{pmatrix}$$

Exercises

1 State the condition under which a square matrix does not have an inverse.

2 Find the inverse of the following matrices. If an inverse does not exist, state this.

(a) $\begin{pmatrix} 6 & 1 \\ 4 & 3 \end{pmatrix}$ (b) $\begin{pmatrix} -4 & -1 \\ 3 & 5 \end{pmatrix}$

(c) $\begin{pmatrix} x & -y \\ y & x \end{pmatrix}$ (d) $\begin{pmatrix} 4 & 8 \\ 5 & 10 \end{pmatrix}$

Solutions to exercises

1 If the determinant is zero, then the inverse does not exist.

2 (a) $\frac{1}{14}\begin{pmatrix} 3 & -1 \\ -4 & 6 \end{pmatrix}$ (b) $\frac{1}{17}\begin{pmatrix} -5 & -1 \\ 3 & 4 \end{pmatrix}$

(c) $\frac{1}{x^2 + y^2}\begin{pmatrix} x & y \\ -y & x \end{pmatrix}$ (d) no inverse

4.4 Finding the inverse of a matrix – the general case

We wish to find the inverse of A, an $n \times n$ matrix. We have already noted that, if $|A| = 0$, then the inverse of A does not exist. Suppose $|A| \neq 0$. To find A^{-1} we proceed thus:

1 Find the transpose of A, by interchanging the rows and columns of A.
2 Replace each element of A^{T} by its cofactor. The resulting matrix is known as the **adjoint** of A, written adj (A).
3 The inverse of A is given by

Key point

$$A^{-1} = \frac{\text{adj}\,(A)}{|A|}$$

Example 4.4

Find the inverse of

$$A = \begin{pmatrix} 3 & 1 & 0 \\ 5 & 2 & -1 \\ 1 & 4 & -2 \end{pmatrix}$$

Solution

We find the transpose, A^T, by interchanging rows and columns.

$$A^T = \begin{pmatrix} 3 & 5 & 1 \\ 1 & 2 & 4 \\ 0 & -1 & -2 \end{pmatrix}$$

Each element of A^T is replaced by its cofactor to yield the adjoint of A.

$$\text{adj}(A) = \begin{pmatrix} 0 & 2 & -1 \\ 9 & -6 & 3 \\ 18 & -11 & 1 \end{pmatrix}$$

Calculating the determinant of A gives $|A| = 9$ and so

$$A^{-1} = \frac{\text{adj}(A)}{|A|}$$

$$= \frac{1}{9}\begin{pmatrix} 0 & 2 & -1 \\ 9 & -6 & 3 \\ 18 & -11 & 1 \end{pmatrix}$$

Example 4.5

Find the inverse of

$$H = \begin{pmatrix} 4 & -2 & 1 \\ 9 & 6 & 0 \\ 3 & -4 & 5 \end{pmatrix}$$

Solution

The transpose, H^T, is found.

$H^T =$

$$\begin{pmatrix} 4 & 9 & 3 \\ -2 & 6 & -4 \\ 1 & 0 & 5 \end{pmatrix}$$

The adjoint of H is obtained by replacing each element of H^T by its cofactor.

$\text{adj}(H) =$

$$\begin{pmatrix} 30 & 6 & -6 \\ -45 & 17 & 9 \\ -54 & 10 & 42 \end{pmatrix}$$

The determinant of H is found.

$|H| =$ 156

Finally

$$H^{-1} = \frac{\operatorname{adj}(H)}{|H|}$$

$$= \frac{1}{156}\begin{pmatrix} 30 & 6 & -6 \\ -45 & 17 & 9 \\ -54 & 10 & 42 \end{pmatrix}$$

Exercises

1 Calculate, where possible, the inverse of

(a) $\begin{pmatrix} 3 & -1 & 7 \\ 2 & 0 & 1 \\ 5 & -2 & 6 \end{pmatrix}$ (b) $\begin{pmatrix} 1 & 2 & -4 \\ -1 & 3 & 6 \\ 1 & 12 & 0 \end{pmatrix}$ (c) $\begin{pmatrix} -2 & 0 & 3 \\ 4 & 4 & -1 \\ 3 & 1 & 6 \end{pmatrix}$

Solutions to exercises

1 (a) $\frac{1}{15}\begin{pmatrix} -2 & 8 & 1 \\ 7 & 17 & -11 \\ 4 & -1 & -2 \end{pmatrix}$ (b) no inverse (c) $\frac{1}{74}\begin{pmatrix} -25 & -3 & 12 \\ 27 & 21 & -10 \\ 8 & -2 & 8 \end{pmatrix}$

Computer and calculator exercises

1 Use a package to find the inverse of each of the following matrices:

(a) $\begin{pmatrix} 4 & 3 & -2 & 2 \\ 3 & -1 & 0 & 4 \\ 6 & 5 & -3 & 0 \\ 1 & 1 & 2 & 1 \end{pmatrix}$

(b) $\begin{pmatrix} -3 & 10 & 9 & 4 \\ 6 & 0 & 1 & 0 \\ 3 & 2 & -1 & 1 \\ 5 & 2 & 3 & 1 \end{pmatrix}$

(c) $\begin{pmatrix} 1 & 2 & 4 & 6 \\ -1 & -1 & 5 & 0 \\ 9 & 7 & 2 & 3 \\ 14 & 8 & 6 & 1 \end{pmatrix}$

(d) $\begin{pmatrix} 6 & 1 & 0 & 3 & 2 \\ 1 & 4 & -1 & 2 & -3 \\ 0 & 1 & -6 & 6 & 5 \\ 0 & 3 & 2 & 1 & -1 \\ 5 & 1 & -5 & 3 & 4 \end{pmatrix}$

(e) $\begin{pmatrix} -6 & 2 & 0 & 3 & 9 \\ 5 & 1 & 6 & -1 & 4 \\ 7 & 3 & 4 & -2 & 3 \\ 6 & 5 & 5 & 5 & 1 \\ 3 & -2 & -1 & 3 & 4 \end{pmatrix}$

Solutions to exercises

1 (a) $\frac{1}{91}\begin{pmatrix} -55 & 27 & 38 & 2 \\ 51 & -30 & -22 & 18 \\ -25 & 4 & 9 & 34 \\ 54 & -5 & -34 & 3 \end{pmatrix}$

(b) $\frac{1}{44}\begin{pmatrix} 0 & 8 & 2 & -2 \\ 22 & 86 & 5 & -93 \\ 0 & -4 & -12 & 12 \\ -44 & -200 & 16 & 204 \end{pmatrix}$

(c) $\frac{1}{455}\begin{pmatrix} 101 & -192 & -262 & 180 \\ -181 & 272 & 447 & -255 \\ -16 & 107 & 37 & -15 \\ 130 & -130 & -130 & 65 \end{pmatrix}$

(d) $\frac{1}{1722}\begin{pmatrix} 188 & 69 & -146 & -141 & 105 \\ -370 & -90 & -134 & 708 & 462 \\ 226 & -201 & 26 & 261 & -231 \\ 456 & 204 & 342 & -342 & -588 \\ -202 & -468 & -8 & 582 & 336 \end{pmatrix}$

(e) $\frac{1}{13400}\begin{pmatrix} -640 & -760 & 1348 & 68 & 1172 \\ 850 & -2550 & 2460 & 810 & -1410 \\ -210 & 3310 & -2468 & 462 & -1102 \\ -50 & 150 & -1800 & 1450 & 950 \\ 890 & 10 & 952 & -618 & 778 \end{pmatrix}$

End of block exercises

1 Check that

$$\begin{pmatrix} 2 & 6 \\ -1 & 4 \end{pmatrix}$$

is the inverse of

$$\begin{pmatrix} \frac{2}{7} & -\frac{3}{7} \\ \frac{1}{14} & \frac{1}{7} \end{pmatrix}$$

2 Explain why the matrix

$$\begin{pmatrix} x^2 & x \\ xy & y \end{pmatrix}$$

has no inverse.

3 Calculate, if possible, the inverse of each of the following matrices:

(a) $\begin{pmatrix} 4 & 2 \\ 8 & 5 \end{pmatrix}$ (b) $\begin{pmatrix} 6 & 10 \\ 1 & -2 \end{pmatrix}$

(c) $\begin{pmatrix} 1 & 2 \\ 2 & 1 \end{pmatrix}$ (d) $\begin{pmatrix} 5 & -5 \\ 3 & -6 \end{pmatrix}$

(e) $\begin{pmatrix} 10 & -20 \\ -2 & 4 \end{pmatrix}$ (f) $\begin{pmatrix} 0.4 & 2 \\ 0.9 & 3 \end{pmatrix}$

(g) $\begin{pmatrix} -0.5 & -1.5 \\ -2 & -1 \end{pmatrix}$

4 Find the inverse of

$$\begin{pmatrix} x & x \\ x & 2x \end{pmatrix}$$

given $x \neq 0$.

5 A is a square matrix. State a condition that ensures A does not have an inverse.

6 Find, if possible, the inverse of each of the following 2×2 matrices:

(a) $\begin{pmatrix} 3 & -6 \\ 5 & 0 \end{pmatrix}$ (b) $\begin{pmatrix} 5 & 2 \\ 6 & 10 \end{pmatrix}$

(c) $\begin{pmatrix} 1 & 1 \\ -2 & -2 \end{pmatrix}$ (d) $\begin{pmatrix} 9 & 3 \\ -2 & 1 \end{pmatrix}$

(e) $\begin{pmatrix} -3 & 1 \\ 2 & -4 \end{pmatrix}$

7 Calculate the inverse of each of the following matrices. If it is not possible to calculate the inverse then state this clearly.

(a) $\begin{pmatrix} 5 & 6 \\ 2 & 3 \end{pmatrix}$ (b) $\begin{pmatrix} -6 & 0 \\ 3 & -1 \end{pmatrix}$

(c) $\begin{pmatrix} 4 & -2 \\ -3 & 1.5 \end{pmatrix}$

8 Calculate the values of λ for which

$$\begin{pmatrix} 2-\lambda & 4 \\ 1.5 & 1-\lambda \end{pmatrix}$$

has no inverse.

9 If

$$\begin{pmatrix} 3 & x \\ 5 & y \end{pmatrix}$$

is the inverse of

$$\begin{pmatrix} 2 & -1 \\ -5 & 3 \end{pmatrix}$$

state the values of x and y.

10 Calculate the inverse of each of the following matrices:

(a) $\begin{pmatrix} 1 & 4 & 3 \\ 5 & 6 & -4 \\ 2 & 0 & 1 \end{pmatrix}$ (b) $\begin{pmatrix} 1 & 2 & 3 \\ -4 & 6 & 1 \\ 0 & 0 & 3 \end{pmatrix}$

(c) $\begin{pmatrix} -3 & -1 & 2 \\ 4 & 7 & 1 \\ 5 & 0 & 3 \end{pmatrix}$

(d) $\begin{pmatrix} 1 & 1 & -3 & 0 \\ 4 & 6 & 1 & 3 \\ 9 & -2 & 0 & 4 \\ 5 & 6 & 3 & 1 \end{pmatrix}$

(e) $\begin{pmatrix} 0 & 1 & 4 & -1 \\ 2 & 7 & 3 & 5 \\ 6 & 3 & -1 & 0 \\ 1 & 2 & 4 & 7 \end{pmatrix}$

11 Find, if possible, the inverse of each of the following matrices:

(a) $\begin{pmatrix} 5 & 2 & -1 \\ 6 & 3 & 1 \\ 5 & 9 & 6 \end{pmatrix}$ (b) $\begin{pmatrix} -4 & 3 & 0 \\ -1 & 1 & 2 \\ 4 & 0 & 1 \end{pmatrix}$

(c) $\begin{pmatrix} 9 & 6 & -9 \\ 7 & 3 & 1 \\ -6 & 4 & 8 \end{pmatrix}$ (d) $\begin{pmatrix} 4 & 2 & -3 \\ 6 & 0 & 5 \\ 2 & 4 & -11 \end{pmatrix}$

(e) $\begin{pmatrix} 4 & -3 & 6 \\ 10 & 9 & 14 \\ 3 & -6 & 0 \end{pmatrix}$

12 Find, if possible, the inverse of each of the following matrices:

(a) $\begin{pmatrix} \lambda & 3 \\ \lambda & 5 \end{pmatrix}$ (b) $\begin{pmatrix} 3 & x \\ x & x^2 \end{pmatrix}$

(c) $\begin{pmatrix} a & bc \\ ab & b^2c \end{pmatrix}$ (d) $\begin{pmatrix} \frac{2}{\lambda} & -2 \\ 4 & \lambda \end{pmatrix}$

Solutions to exercises

2 The determinant of the matrix is zero: hence no inverse exists.

3 (a) $\begin{pmatrix} 1.25 & -0.5 \\ -2 & 1 \end{pmatrix}$ (b) $\frac{1}{22}\begin{pmatrix} 2 & 10 \\ 1 & -6 \end{pmatrix}$

(c) $\frac{1}{3}\begin{pmatrix} -1 & 2 \\ 2 & -1 \end{pmatrix}$ (d) $\frac{1}{15}\begin{pmatrix} 6 & -5 \\ 3 & -5 \end{pmatrix}$

(e) no inverse (f) $\frac{1}{6}\begin{pmatrix} -30 & 20 \\ 9 & -4 \end{pmatrix}$

(g) $\frac{1}{5}\begin{pmatrix} 2 & -3 \\ -4 & 1 \end{pmatrix}$

4 $\frac{1}{x}\begin{pmatrix} 2 & -1 \\ -1 & 1 \end{pmatrix}$

5 $|A| = 0$

6 (a) $\frac{1}{30}\begin{pmatrix} 0 & 6 \\ -5 & 3 \end{pmatrix}$ (b) $\frac{1}{38}\begin{pmatrix} 10 & -2 \\ -6 & 5 \end{pmatrix}$

(c) no inverse (d) $\frac{1}{15}\begin{pmatrix} 1 & -3 \\ 2 & 9 \end{pmatrix}$

(e) $-\frac{1}{10}\begin{pmatrix} 4 & 1 \\ 2 & 3 \end{pmatrix}$

7 (a) $\frac{1}{3}\begin{pmatrix} 3 & -6 \\ -2 & 5 \end{pmatrix}$ (b) $\frac{1}{6}\begin{pmatrix} -1 & 0 \\ -3 & -6 \end{pmatrix}$

(c) no inverse

8 $-1, 4$

9 $x = 1, y = 2$

10 (a) $\frac{1}{82}\begin{pmatrix} -6 & 4 & 34 \\ 13 & 5 & -19 \\ 12 & -8 & 14 \end{pmatrix}$

(b) $\frac{1}{42}\begin{pmatrix} 18 & -6 & -16 \\ 12 & 3 & -13 \\ 0 & 0 & 14 \end{pmatrix}$

(c) $\frac{1}{126}\begin{pmatrix} -21 & -3 & 15 \\ 7 & 19 & -11 \\ 35 & 5 & 17 \end{pmatrix}$

(d) $\frac{1}{570}\begin{pmatrix} 64 & -90 & 44 & 94 \\ 44 & 45 & -41 & 29 \\ -154 & -15 & 1 & 41 \\ -122 & 225 & 23 & -197 \end{pmatrix}$

(e) $\frac{1}{933}\begin{pmatrix} 42 & -105 & 177 & 81 \\ -15 & 193 & -41 & -140 \\ 207 & -51 & 6 & 66 \\ -120 & -11 & -17 & 124 \end{pmatrix}$

11 (a) $\frac{1}{56}\begin{pmatrix} -9 & 21 & -5 \\ 31 & -35 & 11 \\ -39 & 35 & -3 \end{pmatrix}$

(b) $\frac{1}{23}\begin{pmatrix} 1 & -3 & 6 \\ 9 & -4 & 8 \\ -4 & 12 & -1 \end{pmatrix}$

(c) $\frac{1}{606}\begin{pmatrix} -20 & 84 & -33 \\ 62 & -18 & 72 \\ -46 & 72 & 15 \end{pmatrix}$

(d) no inverse

(e) $\frac{1}{312}\begin{pmatrix} -84 & 36 & 96 \\ -42 & 18 & -4 \\ 87 & -15 & -66 \end{pmatrix}$

12 (a) $\frac{1}{2\lambda}\begin{pmatrix} 5 & -3 \\ -\lambda & \lambda \end{pmatrix}$ (b) $\frac{1}{2x^2}\begin{pmatrix} x^2 & -x \\ -x & 3 \end{pmatrix}$

(c) no inverse (d) $\frac{1}{10}\begin{pmatrix} \lambda & 2 \\ -4 & \frac{2}{\lambda} \end{pmatrix}$

BLOCK 5 Computer graphics

5.1 Introduction

Many engineering components can now be represented on a computer screen. Modelling components in this way allows calculations of stresses, bending moments, pressure and so forth to be performed before the component is actually manufactured. Hence potential weaknesses and problem areas can be identified at the design stage. Fundamental to representing components is the ability to define points, lines and shapes, for example triangles and rectangles. Points, lines and shapes can be represented by matrices.

Once a component has been drawn it may be necessary to transform it. Transformation includes scaling, translation, shearing, rotation and reflection. Transformations are brought about by the use of matrices.

5.2 Representation of points using matrices

A point in two dimensions is represented by its coordinates, x and y. These values may be written as a 1×2 matrix, for example $(3 \quad -2)$, or as a 2×1 matrix, for example, $\begin{pmatrix} 3 \\ -2 \end{pmatrix}$. Such matrices are sometimes referred to as **position matrices** or **position vectors**. In this block we use 2×1 matrices to represent points.

A line can be determined by its two end-points. Hence the matrix

$$\begin{pmatrix} 1 & 3 \\ 2 & 7 \end{pmatrix}$$

represents the line joining the points $\begin{pmatrix} 1 \\ 2 \end{pmatrix}$ and $\begin{pmatrix} 3 \\ 7 \end{pmatrix}$. Similarly a triangle is defined by three points. Figure 5.1 illustrates a triangle.

The triangle can be 'stored' as a 2×3 matrix, T, where

$$T = \begin{pmatrix} 2 & 5 & 3 \\ 3 & 6 & -1 \end{pmatrix}$$

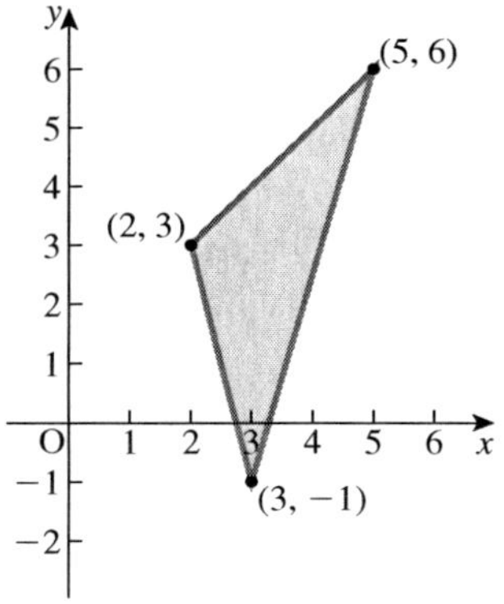

Figure 5.1
A triangle is defined by three points.

Example 5.1

Write matrices that represent the quadrilaterals shown in Figure 5.2(a), (b).

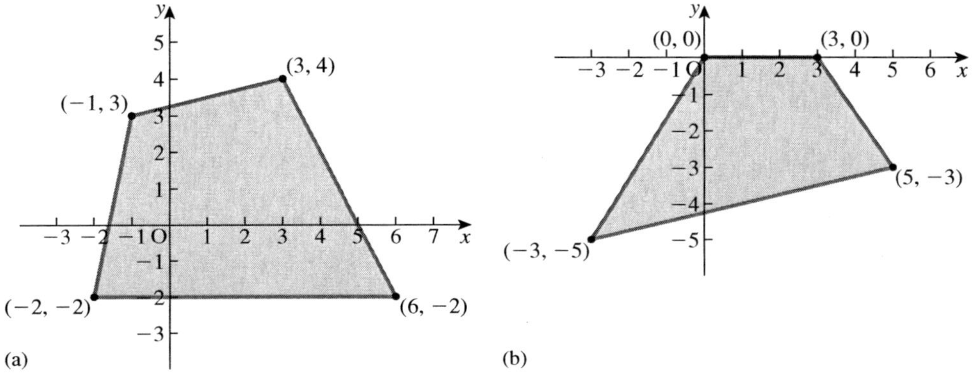

Figure 5.2

Solution

Each quadrilateral is defined by four points.

(a) The quadrilateral can be stored as

$$Q = \begin{pmatrix} -1 & 3 & 6 & -2 \\ 3 & 4 & -2 & -2 \end{pmatrix}$$

Note that other matrices would also be suitable, for example

$$\begin{pmatrix} 3 & 6 & -1 & -2 \\ 4 & -2 & 3 & -2 \end{pmatrix} \text{ and } \begin{pmatrix} -2 & 3 & -1 & 6 \\ -2 & 4 & 3 & -2 \end{pmatrix}$$

also describe the quadrilateral.

(b) A possible matrix is

$$\begin{pmatrix} 0 & 3 & 5 & -3 \\ 0 & 0 & -3 & -5 \end{pmatrix}$$

5.3 Matrices as transformations

Figures on a computer screen need to be transformed. Transformation includes scaling, translation, rotation, reflection and shearing. Mathematically, each transformation can be represented by a matrix, called a **transformation matrix**. Since every figure is made up of points we first examine the effect of a transformation matrix on a single point.

Consider the point $X = \begin{pmatrix} x \\ y \end{pmatrix}$ and a transformation matrix, T, given by

$$T = \begin{pmatrix} a & b \\ c & d \end{pmatrix}$$

The matrix T premultiplies the point X. Let the result of this calculation be X^*.

$$\begin{aligned} TX &= \begin{pmatrix} a & b \\ c & d \end{pmatrix} \begin{pmatrix} x \\ y \end{pmatrix} \\ &= \begin{pmatrix} ax + by \\ cx + dy \end{pmatrix} \\ &= X^* \end{aligned}$$

We can think of the point $\begin{pmatrix} x \\ y \end{pmatrix}$ as having been transformed into the point

$$\begin{pmatrix} ax + by \\ cx + dy \end{pmatrix}$$

by the matrix T.

Example 5.2

The point $\begin{pmatrix} -1 \\ 3 \end{pmatrix}$ is transformed by the matrix $\begin{pmatrix} 1 & 2 \\ -1 & 4 \end{pmatrix}$.

Determine the position of the transformed point.

Solution

We calculate

$$\begin{pmatrix} 1 & 2 \\ -1 & 4 \end{pmatrix} \begin{pmatrix} -1 \\ 3 \end{pmatrix} = \qquad \begin{pmatrix} 5 \\ 13 \end{pmatrix}$$

The point $\begin{pmatrix} -1 \\ 3 \end{pmatrix}$ is transformed to $\begin{pmatrix} 5 \\ 13 \end{pmatrix}$.

Exercises

1 The point $\begin{pmatrix} 3 \\ -4 \end{pmatrix}$ is transformed by the matrix

$$\begin{pmatrix} 2 & 0 \\ 3 & 1 \end{pmatrix}$$

Find the position of the transformed point.

2 The point $\begin{pmatrix} 5 \\ -1 \end{pmatrix}$ is transformed by the matrix

$$\begin{pmatrix} -1 & 3 \\ 4 & 2 \end{pmatrix}$$

Find the position of the transformed point.

Solutions to exercises

1 $\begin{pmatrix} 6 \\ 5 \end{pmatrix}$

2 $\begin{pmatrix} -8 \\ 18 \end{pmatrix}$

5.4 Transformation of lines

Consider a straight line and a transformation matrix, T, whose elements are constants. If T is applied to every point on the straight line the transformed points form a new straight line; in other words, the transformation of a straight line is another straight line provided the elements of T are constant. Thus to find the transformation of a straight line we need only find the transformation of the end-points of the line and then join these. This is illustrated in Figure 5.3.

Figure 5.3 The transformation of a straight line is another straight line.

Example 5.3

A straight line joins the points $\begin{pmatrix} 2 \\ -3 \end{pmatrix}$ and $\begin{pmatrix} 4 \\ 2 \end{pmatrix}$. It is transformed by the matrix

$$T = \begin{pmatrix} 1 & 2 \\ -1 & 3 \end{pmatrix}$$

Describe the transformed line.

Solution

The end-points $\begin{pmatrix} 2 \\ -3 \end{pmatrix}$ and $\begin{pmatrix} 4 \\ 2 \end{pmatrix}$ are transformed.

$$\begin{pmatrix} 1 & 2 \\ -1 & 3 \end{pmatrix}\begin{pmatrix} 2 \\ -3 \end{pmatrix} = \qquad \begin{pmatrix} -4 \\ -11 \end{pmatrix}$$

$$\begin{pmatrix} 1 & 2 \\ -1 & 3 \end{pmatrix}\begin{pmatrix} 4 \\ 2 \end{pmatrix} = \qquad \begin{pmatrix} 8 \\ 2 \end{pmatrix}$$

The transformed line joins $\begin{pmatrix} -4 \\ -11 \end{pmatrix}$ and $\begin{pmatrix} 8 \\ 2 \end{pmatrix}$.

5.5 Scaling

Consider a rectangle with vertices at $\begin{pmatrix} 0 \\ 0 \end{pmatrix}, \begin{pmatrix} 0 \\ 1 \end{pmatrix}, \begin{pmatrix} 1 \\ 1 \end{pmatrix}$ and $\begin{pmatrix} 1 \\ 0 \end{pmatrix}$ and a transformation matrix

$$T = \begin{pmatrix} 4 & 0 \\ 0 & 1 \end{pmatrix}$$

The points $\begin{pmatrix} 0 \\ 0 \end{pmatrix}, \begin{pmatrix} 0 \\ 1 \end{pmatrix}, \begin{pmatrix} 1 \\ 1 \end{pmatrix}$ and $\begin{pmatrix} 1 \\ 0 \end{pmatrix}$ are transformed by T to $\begin{pmatrix} 0 \\ 0 \end{pmatrix}, \begin{pmatrix} 0 \\ 1 \end{pmatrix}, \begin{pmatrix} 4 \\ 1 \end{pmatrix}$ and $\begin{pmatrix} 4 \\ 0 \end{pmatrix}$ respectively. This is illustrated in Figure 5.4.

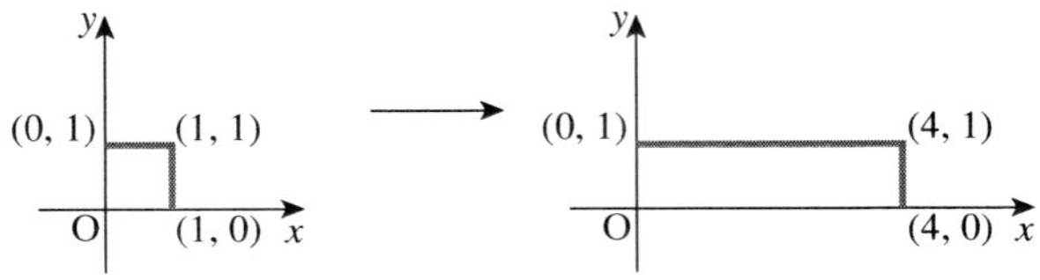

Figure 5.4
An example of horizontal scaling.

Clearly T has the effect of increasing the horizontal lengths by a factor of 4; the vertical lengths remain unchanged.

In general, scaling is brought about by a diagonal matrix. The first row determines the horizontal scaling; the second row determines the vertical scaling. The matrix

$$\begin{pmatrix} \alpha & 0 \\ 0 & \beta \end{pmatrix}$$

scales the horizontal lengths by a factor of α and the vertical lengths by a factor of β. For horizontal expansion α must be greater than 1; for horizontal compression we require α to be less than 1. Similar comments apply to vertical expansion and compression.

Example 5.4

The zoom facilities of a graphing package expand both horizontal and vertical lengths by a factor of 2.5. Determine the transformation matrix to do this.

Solution

A diagonal matrix is needed for scaling. Since both horizontal and vertical lengths are scaled by a factor of 2.5 the required matrix is

$$\begin{pmatrix} 2.5 & 0 \\ 0 & 2.5 \end{pmatrix}$$

Exercises

1 Write down the transformation matrix that
(a) scales horizontal distances by a factor of 4 and leaves vertical distances unchanged
(b) scales horizontal distances by a factor of 3 and vertical distances by a factor of 7
(c) scales horizontal distances by a factor of 0.7 and vertical distances by a factor of 1.2
(d) leaves horizontal distances unchanged and trebles vertical distances.

Solutions to exercises

1 (a) $\begin{pmatrix} 4 & 0 \\ 0 & 1 \end{pmatrix}$ (b) $\begin{pmatrix} 3 & 0 \\ 0 & 7 \end{pmatrix}$

(c) $\begin{pmatrix} 0.7 & 0 \\ 0 & 1.2 \end{pmatrix}$ (d) $\begin{pmatrix} 1 & 0 \\ 0 & 3 \end{pmatrix}$

5.6 Rotation

Rotation is an important and commonly used transformation. Components can be 'viewed' from different angles using packages with a rotation facility. By convention, anticlockwise movement is considered to be positive. Figure 5.5 illustrates the line from the origin to the point $\begin{pmatrix} x \\ y \end{pmatrix}$ being rotated through an angle θ. We say the point $\begin{pmatrix} x \\ y \end{pmatrix}$ has been rotated about the origin to the new position $\begin{pmatrix} x^* \\ y^* \end{pmatrix}$.

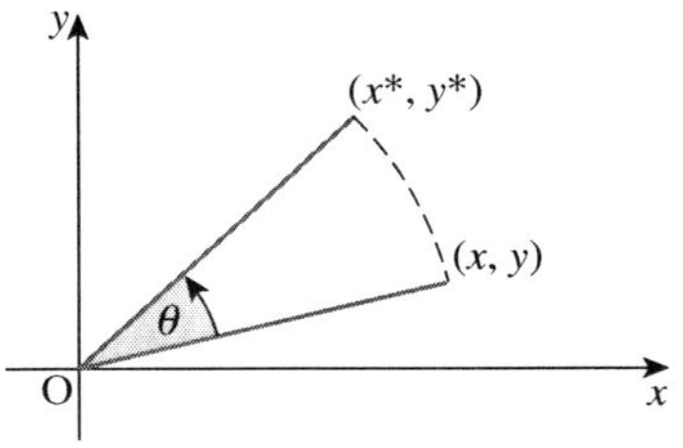

Figure 5.5 The point $\begin{pmatrix} x \\ y \end{pmatrix}$ is rotated anticlockwise through an angle θ to $\begin{pmatrix} x^* \\ y^* \end{pmatrix}$.

Key point

The transformation matrix, T, that rotates a point anticlockwise about the origin by an angle θ is given by

$$T = \begin{pmatrix} \cos\theta & -\sin\theta \\ \sin\theta & \cos\theta \end{pmatrix}$$

Example 5.5

The point $\begin{pmatrix} 2 \\ 6 \end{pmatrix}$ is rotated anticlockwise about the origin through 40°. Calculate the position of the new point.

Solution

The transformation matrix is

$$T = \begin{pmatrix} \cos 40^\circ & -\sin 40^\circ \\ \sin 40^\circ & \cos 40^\circ \end{pmatrix}$$

and hence the new point is given by

$$\begin{pmatrix} \cos 40^\circ & -\sin 40^\circ \\ \sin 40^\circ & \cos 40^\circ \end{pmatrix}\begin{pmatrix} 2 \\ 6 \end{pmatrix} = \begin{pmatrix} 2\cos 40^\circ - 6\sin 40^\circ \\ 2\sin 40^\circ + 6\cos 40^\circ \end{pmatrix}$$
$$= \begin{pmatrix} -2.3246 \\ 5.8818 \end{pmatrix}$$

Example 5.6
A triangle is defined by the matrix

$$\begin{pmatrix} 1 & 2 & 3 \\ 1 & 5 & 1 \end{pmatrix}$$

It is rotated clockwise about the origin through 120°. Determine the resulting triangle.

Solution
Clockwise angles are considered to be negative and so the transformation matrix, T, is

$$\begin{aligned} T &= \begin{pmatrix} \cos(-120^\circ) & -\sin(-120^\circ) \\ \sin(-120^\circ) & \cos(-120^\circ) \end{pmatrix} \\ &= \begin{pmatrix} -0.5 & 0.866 \\ -0.866 & -0.5 \end{pmatrix} \end{aligned}$$

The transformed triangle is then given by

$$\begin{pmatrix} -0.5 & 0.866 \\ -0.866 & -0.5 \end{pmatrix} \begin{pmatrix} 1 & 2 & 3 \\ 1 & 5 & 1 \end{pmatrix} = \begin{pmatrix} 0.366 & 3.330 & -0.634 \\ -1.366 & -4.232 & -3.098 \end{pmatrix}$$

The transformed triangle is defined by the points $\begin{pmatrix} 0.366 \\ -1.366 \end{pmatrix}$, $\begin{pmatrix} 3.330 \\ -4.232 \end{pmatrix}$ and $\begin{pmatrix} -0.634 \\ -3.098 \end{pmatrix}$.

Example 5.7
The line joining $\begin{pmatrix} -1 \\ 4 \end{pmatrix}$ and $\begin{pmatrix} 3 \\ 1 \end{pmatrix}$ is rotated through 90° anticlockwise about the origin. Determine the new line.

Solution
The transformation matrix, T, is

$$T = \begin{pmatrix} \cos 90^\circ & -\sin 90^\circ \\ \sin 90^\circ & \cos 90^\circ \end{pmatrix} = \begin{pmatrix} 0 & -1 \\ 1 & 0 \end{pmatrix}$$

The original end-points of the line are $\begin{pmatrix} -1 \\ 4 \end{pmatrix}$ and $\begin{pmatrix} 3 \\ 1 \end{pmatrix}$.

Thus the line is defined by the matrix

$$\begin{pmatrix} -1 & 3 \\ 4 & 1 \end{pmatrix}$$

The transformed end-points are thus

$$\begin{pmatrix} 0 & -1 \\ 1 & 0 \end{pmatrix}\begin{pmatrix} -1 & 3 \\ 4 & 1 \end{pmatrix} = \begin{pmatrix} -4 & -1 \\ -1 & 3 \end{pmatrix}$$

The transformed line joins the points $\begin{pmatrix} -4 \\ -1 \end{pmatrix}$ and $\begin{pmatrix} -1 \\ 3 \end{pmatrix}$.

Exercises

1. State a matrix that rotates points anticlockwise about the origin by 45°.
2. State a matrix that rotates points clockwise about the origin by 200°.
3. The point $\begin{pmatrix} 4 \\ -3 \end{pmatrix}$ is rotated 30° anticlockwise about the origin. State the coordinates of the new point.
4. The point $\begin{pmatrix} -1 \\ 2 \end{pmatrix}$ is rotated 75° clockwise about the origin. State the coordinates of the new point.

Solutions to exercises

1. $\begin{pmatrix} 0.7071 & -0.7071 \\ 0.7071 & 0.7071 \end{pmatrix}$
2. $\begin{pmatrix} -0.9397 & -0.3420 \\ 0.3420 & -0.9397 \end{pmatrix}$
3. $\begin{pmatrix} 4.9641 \\ -0.5981 \end{pmatrix}$
4. $\begin{pmatrix} 1.6730 \\ 1.4836 \end{pmatrix}$

5.7 Reflection

We now consider transformation matrices that effect reflection in the x axis, y axis, the line $y = x$ and the line $y = -x$.

Reflection in the x axis

Figure 5.6 illustrates the line AB reflected in the x axis to produce the line A*B*. Consider the coordinates of A and A*. If the coordinates of A are, say, $\begin{pmatrix} 3 \\ 2 \end{pmatrix}$, then the coordinates of A* will be $(3, -2)$. Clearly, on reflection the x coordinate remains unchanged and the y coordinate changes sign. The transformation matrix to effect this is

$$T = \begin{pmatrix} 1 & 0 \\ 0 & -1 \end{pmatrix}$$

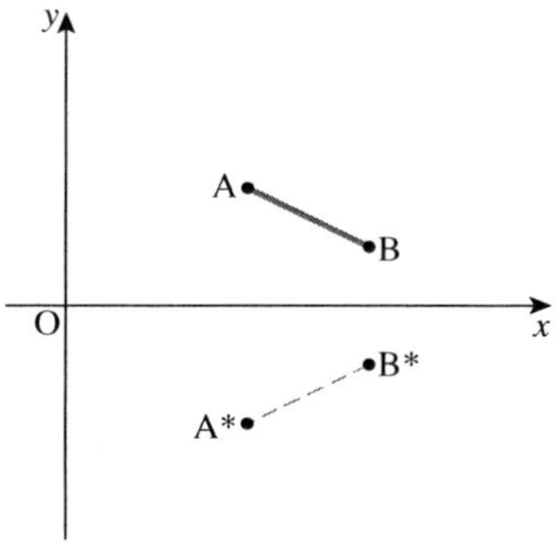

Figure 5.6
The line AB is reflected in the x axis to produce A*B*.

Key point

Reflection in the x axis is brought about by

$$T = \begin{pmatrix} 1 & 0 \\ 0 & -1 \end{pmatrix}$$

Reflection in the y axis

Figure 5.7 illustrates reflection of the line AB in the y axis. Again, considering the coordinates of A and A′, we see that on reflection the x coordinate changes sign and

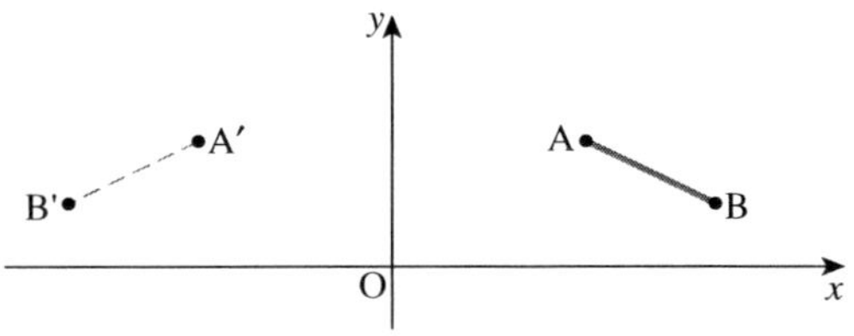

Figure 5.7
The line AB is reflected in the y axis to produce A′B′.

the y coordinate remains unchanged. The transformation matrix is

$$T = \begin{pmatrix} -1 & 0 \\ 0 & 1 \end{pmatrix}$$

Key point

Reflection in the y axis is brought about by

$$T = \begin{pmatrix} -1 & 0 \\ 0 & 1 \end{pmatrix}$$

Reflection in the line $y = x$

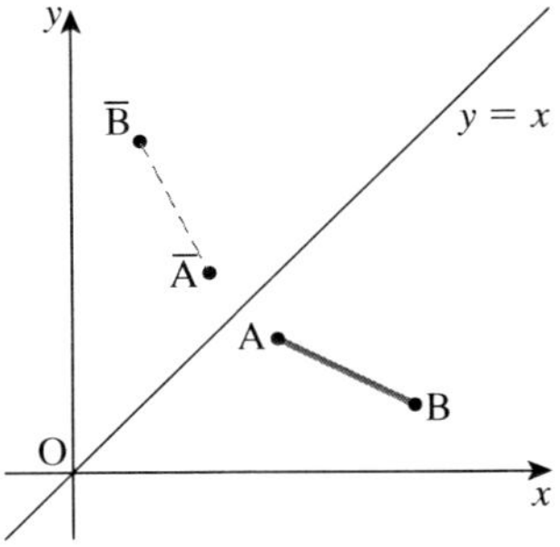

Figure 5.8
AB is reflected in the line $y = x$ to produce $\overline{A}\,\overline{B}$.

Figure 5.8 illustrates reflection about the line $y = x$. In effect, the x and y coordinates are interchanged. The required transformation matrix is

$$T = \begin{pmatrix} 0 & 1 \\ 1 & 0 \end{pmatrix}$$

Key point

Reflection in $y = x$ is brought about by

$$T = \begin{pmatrix} 0 & 1 \\ 1 & 0 \end{pmatrix}$$

Reflection in the line $y = -x$

Figure 5.9 illustrates reflection in $y = -x$. Here the x and y coordinates are interchanged and also changed in sign. The transformation matrix is

$$T = \begin{pmatrix} 0 & -1 \\ -1 & 0 \end{pmatrix}$$

Key point

Reflection in $y = -x$ is brought about by

$$T = \begin{pmatrix} 0 & -1 \\ -1 & 0 \end{pmatrix}$$

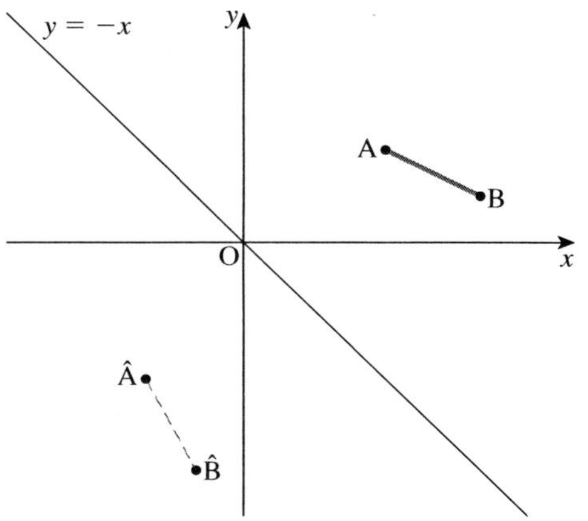

Figure 5.9
AB is reflected in $y = -x$ to produce $\hat{A}\hat{B}$.

Example 5.8

The point $A\begin{pmatrix} 3 \\ 2 \end{pmatrix}$ is reflected in the y axis and then the resulting point is reflected in the line $y = -x$. Calculate the coordinates of the final point.

Solution

Reflection in the y axis is effected by the matrix

$$\begin{pmatrix} -1 & 0 \\ 0 & 1 \end{pmatrix}$$

Hence when $A\begin{pmatrix} 3 \\ 2 \end{pmatrix}$ is reflected in the y axis the resulting point is given by

$$\begin{pmatrix} -1 & 0 \\ 0 & 1 \end{pmatrix}\begin{pmatrix} 3 \\ 2 \end{pmatrix} = \begin{pmatrix} -3 \\ 2 \end{pmatrix}$$

Reflection in $y = -x$ is effected by

$$\begin{pmatrix} 0 & -1 \\ -1 & 0 \end{pmatrix}$$

and so the final point is given by

$$\begin{pmatrix} 0 & -1 \\ -1 & 0 \end{pmatrix}\begin{pmatrix} -3 \\ 2 \end{pmatrix} = \begin{pmatrix} -2 \\ 3 \end{pmatrix}$$

The final point is $\begin{pmatrix} -2 \\ 3 \end{pmatrix}$.

Exercises

1 The point $\begin{pmatrix} 3 \\ 5 \end{pmatrix}$ is reflected in the line $y = -x$. State the coordinates of the resulting point.

2 The point $\begin{pmatrix} -1 \\ 4 \end{pmatrix}$ is reflected in the y axis and the resulting point is then reflected in the line $y = x$. State the coordinates of the final point.

3 The point $\begin{pmatrix} a \\ b \end{pmatrix}$ is reflected in the x axis. The resulting point is then reflected in the line $y = -x$. State the coordinates of the final point.

Solutions to exercises

1 $\begin{pmatrix} -5 \\ -3 \end{pmatrix}$

2 $\begin{pmatrix} 4 \\ 1 \end{pmatrix}$

3 $\begin{pmatrix} b \\ -a \end{pmatrix}$

5.8 Shearing

A shear is a distortion. Figure 5.10 illustrates an x direction shear of a square, and Figure 5.11 illustrates a y direction shear.

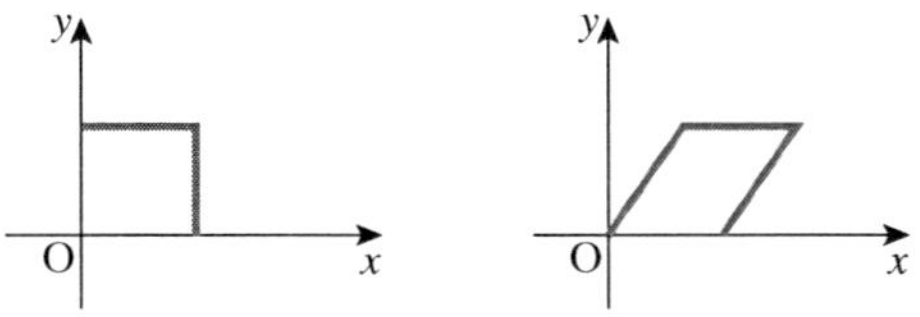

Figure 5.10
An x direction shear.

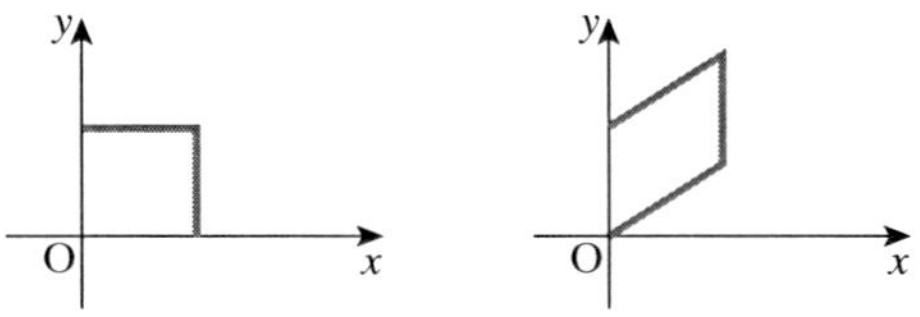

Figure 5.11
A y direction shear.

A shear can be represented by a transformation matrix,

$$\begin{pmatrix} a & b \\ c & d \end{pmatrix}$$

The off-diagonal terms, b and c, determine the kind of shear produced. The element b produces a shear in the x direction whereas c produces a shear in the y direction. As mentioned in Section 5.5, the elements a and b are scale factors for the x and y directions.

Example 5.9

A unit square with vertices at $\begin{pmatrix}0\\0\end{pmatrix}$, $\begin{pmatrix}0\\1\end{pmatrix}$, $\begin{pmatrix}1\\0\end{pmatrix}$ and $\begin{pmatrix}1\\1\end{pmatrix}$ is sheared by

$$T = \begin{pmatrix}1 & 0\\3 & 1\end{pmatrix}$$

(a) Determine the coordinates of the vertices of the figure after shearing.
(b) Sketch both figures.

Solution

(a) The unit square can be represented by

$$\begin{pmatrix}0 & 0 & 1 & 1\\0 & 1 & 0 & 1\end{pmatrix}$$

Shearing produces

$$\begin{pmatrix}1 & 0\\3 & 1\end{pmatrix}\begin{pmatrix}0 & 0 & 1 & 1\\0 & 1 & 0 & 1\end{pmatrix} = \begin{pmatrix}0 & 0 & 1 & 1\\0 & 1 & 3 & 4\end{pmatrix}$$

The resulting figure has vertices at $\begin{pmatrix}0\\0\end{pmatrix}$, $\begin{pmatrix}0\\1\end{pmatrix}$, $\begin{pmatrix}1\\3\end{pmatrix}$ and $\begin{pmatrix}1\\4\end{pmatrix}$.

(b) See Figure 5.12(a), (b).

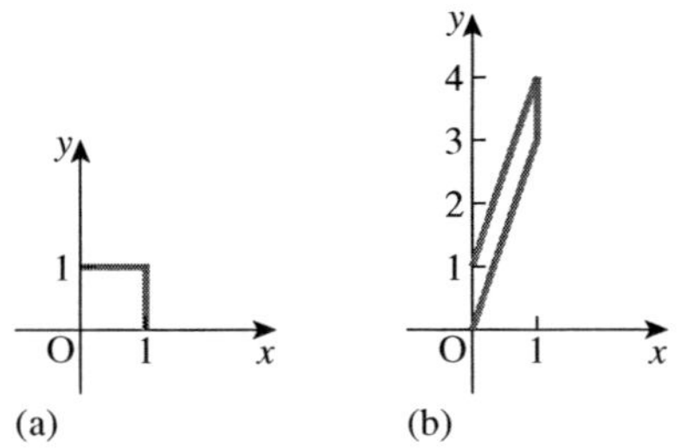

Figure 5.12 (a) The original unit square; (b) the figure after shearing.

Exercises

1. State the effect of the transformation matrix

$$\begin{pmatrix}1 & 2\\0 & 1\end{pmatrix}$$

2. The line joining $\begin{pmatrix}1\\2\end{pmatrix}$ and $\begin{pmatrix}3\\7\end{pmatrix}$ is transformed by the shearing matrix

$$\begin{pmatrix}1 & 0\\4 & 1\end{pmatrix}$$

Describe the transformed figure.

Solutions to exercises

1 A shear by a factor of 2 in the x direction.

2 Line joins $\begin{pmatrix}1\\6\end{pmatrix}$ and $\begin{pmatrix}3\\19\end{pmatrix}$.

5.9 Translation

A translation is a movement in a specific direction by a specific amount. Figure 5.13 illustrates a translation of the line AB to A*B*.

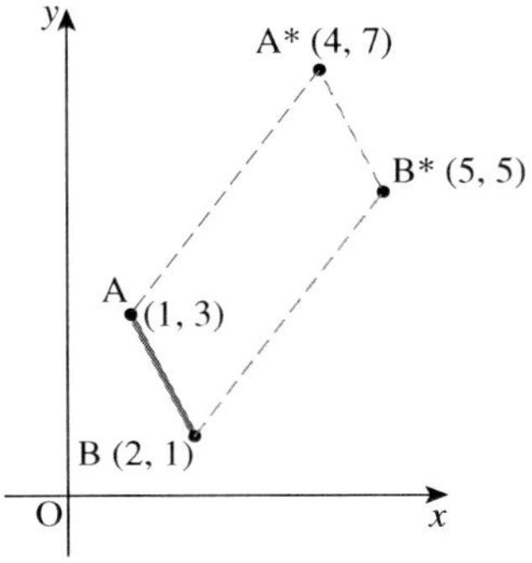

Figure 5.13
AB is translated to A*B*.

In computer graphics many figures need to be translated, for example a piston moving within a cylinder.

Consider the coordinates of A and B in Figure 5.13. The point A$\begin{pmatrix}1\\3\end{pmatrix}$ is translated to the point A*$\begin{pmatrix}4\\7\end{pmatrix}$. The translation has the effect of adding 3 to the x coordinate and adding 4 to the y coordinate. Note that the same change is encountered when B is translated to B*.

Denoting the x translation by t_x and the y translation by t_y we see that if a point $\begin{pmatrix}x\\y\end{pmatrix}$ is translated to $\begin{pmatrix}x^*\\y^*\end{pmatrix}$ then

$$\begin{aligned} x^* &= x + t_x \\ y^* &= y + t_y \end{aligned} \qquad (1)$$

Note that t_x and/or t_y may be negative.

Mathematically, translations are different from the other transformations. The previous transformations could all be represented by matrix multiplication. Equations (1) suggest that translations are represented by matrix addition.

To enable translation to be represented by matrix multiplication we introduce **homogeneous coordinates**. If the coordinates of a point are $\begin{pmatrix}x\\y\end{pmatrix}$ then the homogeneous coordinates of that point are

$$\begin{pmatrix}x\\y\\1\end{pmatrix}$$

The purpose of the extra '1' is to increase the order of the transformation matrix from 2×2 to 3×3. We now introduce a translation matrix, T, where

$$T = \begin{pmatrix} 1 & 0 & t_x \\ 0 & 1 & t_y \\ 0 & 0 & 1 \end{pmatrix}$$

Applying T to

$$X = \begin{pmatrix} x \\ y \\ 1 \end{pmatrix}$$

we have

$$TX = \begin{pmatrix} 1 & 0 & t_x \\ 0 & 1 & t_y \\ 0 & 0 & 1 \end{pmatrix} \begin{pmatrix} x \\ y \\ 1 \end{pmatrix}$$

$$= \begin{pmatrix} x + t_x \\ y + t_y \\ 1 \end{pmatrix}$$

The homogeneous coordinates

$$\begin{pmatrix} x + t_x \\ y + t_y \\ 1 \end{pmatrix}$$

represent the point

$$\begin{pmatrix} x + t_x \\ y + t_y \end{pmatrix}$$

Thus by introducing homogeneous coordinates translation can be represented by matrix multiplication.

Example 5.10

Determine the translation matrix for the translation depicted in Figure 5.13 above.

Solution

Here $t_x = 3$ and $t_y = 4$ and so

$$T = \begin{pmatrix} 1 & 0 & 3 \\ 0 & 1 & 4 \\ 0 & 0 & 1 \end{pmatrix}$$

Example 5.11

The translation matrix

$$T = \begin{pmatrix} 1 & 0 & -1 \\ 0 & 1 & 2 \\ 0 & 0 & 1 \end{pmatrix}$$

is applied to $\begin{pmatrix} 4 \\ -6 \end{pmatrix}$. Calculate the position of the translated point.

Solution

We can proceed in one of two ways. By examining T we see that $t_x = -1$ and $t_y = 2$. Hence

$$\begin{aligned} x^* &= x + t_x \\ &= 4 - 1 \\ &= 3 \\ y^* &= y + t_y \\ &= -6 + 2 \\ &= -4 \end{aligned}$$

The translated point is $\begin{pmatrix} 3 \\ -4 \end{pmatrix}$.

Alternatively we can introduce homogeneous coordinates

$$\begin{pmatrix} 4 \\ -6 \\ 1 \end{pmatrix}$$

Then

$$\begin{pmatrix} 1 & 0 & -1 \\ 0 & 1 & 2 \\ 0 & 0 & 1 \end{pmatrix}\begin{pmatrix} 4 \\ -6 \\ 1 \end{pmatrix} = \begin{pmatrix} 3 \\ -4 \\ 1 \end{pmatrix}$$

Hence the translated point is $\begin{pmatrix} 3 \\ -4 \end{pmatrix}$.

Exercises

1 A point is translated from $\begin{pmatrix} 1 \\ 6 \end{pmatrix}$ to $\begin{pmatrix} 4 \\ 8 \end{pmatrix}$. State the corresponding translation matrix.

2 A point is translated from $\begin{pmatrix} -3 \\ -1 \end{pmatrix}$ to $\begin{pmatrix} -6 \\ 0 \end{pmatrix}$. State the corresponding translation matrix.

3 State the effect of the translation matrix

$$\begin{pmatrix} 1 & 0 & 4 \\ 0 & 1 & -3 \\ 0 & 0 & 1 \end{pmatrix}$$

4 The line AB is translated 3 units in the x direction with no movement in the y direction. State the corresponding translation matrix.

Solutions to exercises

1 $\begin{pmatrix} 1 & 0 & 3 \\ 0 & 1 & 2 \\ 0 & 0 & 1 \end{pmatrix}$

2 $\begin{pmatrix} 1 & 0 & -3 \\ 0 & 1 & 1 \\ 0 & 0 & 1 \end{pmatrix}$

3 Translation of 4 units in the x direction and 3 units in the negative y direction.

4 $\begin{pmatrix} 1 & 0 & 3 \\ 0 & 1 & 0 \\ 0 & 0 & 1 \end{pmatrix}$

5.10 Composite transformations

We have represented each transformation by a matrix multiplication. Often not one but several transformations are required, and this leads to a product of matrices. Care must be taken in ensuring that the correct order of multiplication is carried out. Recall that if A and B are two matrices then AB and BA are usually not equal.

A sequence of transformations is called a **composite transformation**. Before we can proceed and examine composite transformations we must examine the transformation matrices. The translation matrix is 3×3; all other transformation matrices are 2×2. Multiplication of a 3×3 matrix with a 2×2 matrix is not defined. To overcome this, all the 2×2 matrices are extended so as to become 3×3 matrices and homogeneous coordinates are employed.

Consider any 2×2 transformation matrix

$$\begin{pmatrix} a & b \\ c & d \end{pmatrix}$$

and coordinates $\begin{pmatrix} x \\ y \end{pmatrix}$. The matrix is extended to become

$$T = \begin{pmatrix} a & b & 0 \\ c & d & 0 \\ 0 & 0 & 1 \end{pmatrix}$$

and homogeneous coordinates

$$\begin{pmatrix} x \\ y \\ 1 \end{pmatrix}$$

are used. Note that

$$\begin{pmatrix} a & b \\ c & d \end{pmatrix}\begin{pmatrix} x \\ y \end{pmatrix} = \begin{pmatrix} ax + by \\ cx + dy \end{pmatrix}$$

and

$$\begin{pmatrix} a & b & 0 \\ c & d & 0 \\ 0 & 0 & 1 \end{pmatrix}\begin{pmatrix} x \\ y \\ 1 \end{pmatrix} = \begin{pmatrix} ax + by \\ cx + dy \\ 1 \end{pmatrix}$$

Transforming a point using the extended matrix and homogeneous coordinates has exactly the same effect as using the 2×2 matrix on the coordinates $\begin{pmatrix} x \\ y \end{pmatrix}$. However, all transformation matrices are now 3×3 and so composite transformations, in the form of matrix products, can be calculated.

Example 5.12

The point $\begin{pmatrix} 4 \\ 1 \end{pmatrix}$ is reflected in the line $y = x$ and then rotated anticlockwise about the origin by 70°.

(a) Calculate the composite transformation matrix.
(b) Calculate the final position of the point.

Solution

(a) Reflection about the line $y = x$ is represented by T_{ref} where

$$T_{\text{ref}} = \begin{pmatrix} 0 & 1 & 0 \\ 1 & 0 & 0 \\ 0 & 0 & 1 \end{pmatrix}$$

Rotation about the origin by 70° is represented by T_{rot} where

$$T_{\text{rot}} = \begin{pmatrix} \cos 70° & -\sin 70° & 0 \\ \sin 70° & \cos 70° & 0 \\ 0 & 0 & 1 \end{pmatrix}$$

Hence the composite transformation is given by

$$T_{\text{rot}}\,T_{\text{ref}} = \begin{pmatrix} \cos 70° & -\sin 70° & 0 \\ \sin 70° & \cos 70° & 0 \\ 0 & 0 & 1 \end{pmatrix}\begin{pmatrix} 0 & 1 & 0 \\ 1 & 0 & 0 \\ 0 & 0 & 1 \end{pmatrix}$$

$$= \begin{pmatrix} -\sin 70° & \cos 70° & 0 \\ \cos 70° & \sin 70° & 0 \\ 0 & 0 & 1 \end{pmatrix}$$

(b) The homogeneous coordinates of the point are

$$\begin{pmatrix} 4 \\ 1 \\ 1 \end{pmatrix}$$

The transformed point is then

$$\begin{pmatrix} -\sin 70^\circ & \cos 70^\circ & 0 \\ \cos 70^\circ & \sin 70^\circ & 0 \\ 0 & 0 & 1 \end{pmatrix}\begin{pmatrix} 4 \\ 1 \\ 1 \end{pmatrix} = \begin{pmatrix} -4\sin 70^\circ + \cos 70^\circ \\ 4\cos 70^\circ + \sin 70^\circ \\ 1 \end{pmatrix}$$

$$= \begin{pmatrix} -3.417 \\ 2.308 \\ 1 \end{pmatrix}$$

The transformed point is $\begin{pmatrix} -3.417 \\ 2.308 \end{pmatrix}$.

Example 5.13

Determine a transformation matrix that rotates a point 30° anticlockwise about the point $\begin{pmatrix} 1 \\ 2 \end{pmatrix}$.

Solution

The rotation matrices so far encountered have all represented rotation about the origin. Hence to represent rotation about $\begin{pmatrix} 1 \\ 2 \end{pmatrix}$ we require three transformations (Figure 5.14):

1 translation of $\begin{pmatrix} 1 \\ 2 \end{pmatrix}$ to the origin, T_{trans}

2 rotation of 30° anticlockwise, T_{rot}

3 translation from the origin back to $\begin{pmatrix} 1 \\ 2 \end{pmatrix}$, T_{ret}.

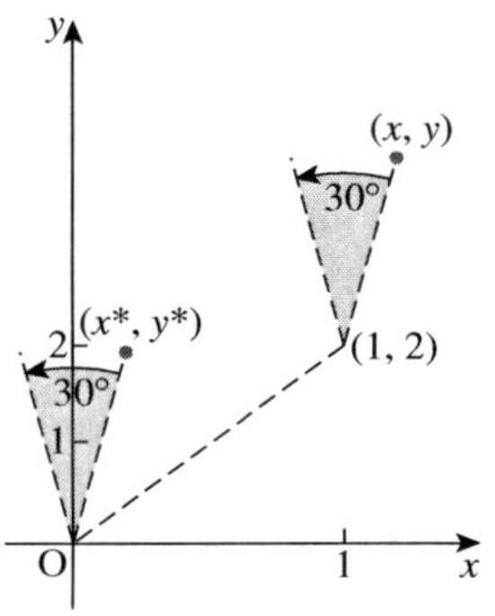

Figure 5.14 Rotation about $\begin{pmatrix} 1 \\ 2 \end{pmatrix}$ requires three basic transformations.

The required transformation matrices are

$$T_{\text{trans}} = \begin{pmatrix} 1 & 0 & -1 \\ 0 & 1 & -2 \\ 0 & 0 & 1 \end{pmatrix}$$

$$T_{\text{rot}} = \begin{pmatrix} 0.8660 & -0.5 & 0 \\ 0.5 & 0.8660 & 0 \\ 0 & 0 & 1 \end{pmatrix}$$

$$T_{\text{ret}} = \begin{pmatrix} 1 & 0 & 1 \\ 0 & 1 & 2 \\ 0 & 0 & 1 \end{pmatrix}$$

The composite transformation is then

$$T_{\text{ret}}\,T_{\text{rot}}\,T_{\text{trans}} = \begin{pmatrix} 1 & 0 & 1 \\ 0 & 1 & 2 \\ 0 & 0 & 1 \end{pmatrix}\begin{pmatrix} 0.8660 & -0.5 & 0 \\ 0.5 & 0.8660 & 0 \\ 0 & 0 & 1 \end{pmatrix}\begin{pmatrix} 1 & 0 & -1 \\ 0 & 1 & -2 \\ 0 & 0 & 1 \end{pmatrix}$$

$$= \begin{pmatrix} 0.8660 & -0.5 & 1.1340 \\ 0.5 & 0.8660 & -0.232 \\ 0 & 0 & 1 \end{pmatrix}$$

Exercises

1. Determine a matrix that shears vertically by a factor of 2 and then rotates anticlockwise about the origin by 30°.

2. Determine a matrix that rotates a figure anticlockwise through 40° about the point $\begin{pmatrix} 1 \\ 0 \end{pmatrix}$.

Solutions to exercises

1. $\begin{pmatrix} -0.1340 & -0.5 & 0 \\ 2.2321 & 0.8660 & 0 \\ 0 & 0 & 1 \end{pmatrix}$

2. $\begin{pmatrix} 0.7660 & -0.6428 & 0.2340 \\ 0.6428 & 0.7660 & -0.6428 \\ 0 & 0 & 1 \end{pmatrix}$

End of block exercises

1 Write matrices that represent the figures shown in Figure 5.15(a), (b), (c).

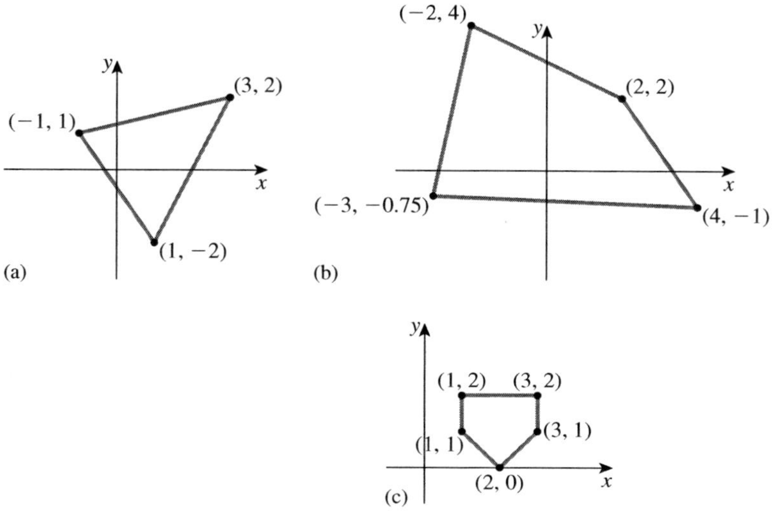

Figure 5.15

2 Draw the figures represented by each of the following matrices:

(a) $\begin{pmatrix} 2 & -1 \\ 0 & 1 \end{pmatrix}$ (b) $\begin{pmatrix} 1 & 3 & 5 \\ 2 & 4 & 6 \end{pmatrix}$

(c) $\begin{pmatrix} -1 & 2 & -4 & 3 \\ 3 & 4 & 1 & 0 \end{pmatrix}$

3 The line joining $\begin{pmatrix} 1 \\ 7 \end{pmatrix}$ and $\begin{pmatrix} -2 \\ 1 \end{pmatrix}$ is transformed by the matrix

$$\begin{pmatrix} 3 & 2 \\ -1 & 1 \end{pmatrix}$$

Describe the transformed line.

4 The triangle with vertices at $\begin{pmatrix} -1 \\ 1 \end{pmatrix}$, $\begin{pmatrix} 2 \\ 1 \end{pmatrix}$ and $\begin{pmatrix} 3 \\ 4 \end{pmatrix}$ is transformed by the matrix

$$\begin{pmatrix} 2 & 1 \\ 1 & -2 \end{pmatrix}$$

Describe the transformed triangle.

5 The zoom facility of a computer graphics package has the following options:
(a) double horizontal lengths only
(b) double vertical lengths only
(c) double both horizontal and vertical lengths
(d) halve both horizontal and vertical lengths.
Write down the transformation matrix for each option.

6 The point $\begin{pmatrix} -1 \\ 6 \end{pmatrix}$ is rotated anticlockwise about the origin through 70°. Calculate the coordinates of the resulting point.

7 The point $\begin{pmatrix} 3 \\ -2 \end{pmatrix}$ is rotated clockwise about the origin through 40°. By applying a suitable rotation matrix, determine the coordinates of the resulting point.

8 A triangle defined by

$$\begin{pmatrix} 3 & 2 & -1 \\ 1 & 7 & 6 \end{pmatrix}$$

is rotated clockwise about the origin through 90°. Calculate the matrix that defines the transformed triangle.

9 Show that for any transformation matrix, R, that represents a rotation

$$R^{T} = R^{-1}$$

that is, the transpose of a rotation matrix is equal to its inverse.

10 A rotation matrix, R, represents an anticlockwise rotation about the origin through an angle θ.
(a) State the rotation matrix, S, that represents a clockwise rotation through an angle θ.
(b) Calculate R^{-1}. (Hint: see question 9.)
(c) What do you conclude from (a) and (b)?

11 A line joins $\begin{pmatrix} 1 \\ 4 \end{pmatrix}$ and $\begin{pmatrix} -2 \\ 3 \end{pmatrix}$.
(a) The line is reflected about $y = x$. Describe the resulting line.
(b) The line found in (a) is then reflected in the x axis. Describe the resulting line.

12 Determine a matrix that increases horizontal lengths by a factor of 5, leaving vertical lengths unchanged.

13 The line joining $\begin{pmatrix} -1 \\ 1 \end{pmatrix}$ and $\begin{pmatrix} 4 \\ 2 \end{pmatrix}$ is reflected in the line $y = -x$. Determine the new line.

14 The triangle with vertices at $\begin{pmatrix} 0 \\ 0 \end{pmatrix}$, $\begin{pmatrix} 0 \\ 1 \end{pmatrix}$ and $\begin{pmatrix} 1 \\ 0 \end{pmatrix}$ is sheared by

$$\begin{pmatrix} 1 & 2 \\ 0 & 1 \end{pmatrix}$$

Sketch the resulting triangle.

15 State a matrix that will translate a figure 4 units in the x direction and 5 units in the y direction.

16 A line joins $\begin{pmatrix} 4 \\ -2 \end{pmatrix}$ and $\begin{pmatrix} 5 \\ 9 \end{pmatrix}$. It is translated using the translation matrix

$$\begin{pmatrix} 1 & 0 & 3 \\ 0 & 1 & -1 \\ 0 & 0 & 1 \end{pmatrix}$$

Describe the translated line.

17 Determine a single transformation matrix that will first reflect a figure in the y axis and then translate it 2 units in the x direction and -3 units in the y direction.

18 Determine a single transformation matrix that will first scale a figure by a factor of 2 in the horizontal and 0.5 in the vertical, and then rotate it clockwise about the origin through 90°.

19 Find a matrix that will rotate a figure anti-clockwise through 45° about the point $\begin{pmatrix} -2 \\ 1 \end{pmatrix}$.

Solutions to exercises

1 (a) $\begin{pmatrix} -1 & 3 & 1 \\ 1 & 2 & -2 \end{pmatrix}$

(b) $\begin{pmatrix} -3 & -2 & 2 & 4 \\ -0.75 & 4 & 2 & -1 \end{pmatrix}$

(c) $\begin{pmatrix} 1 & 3 & 3 & 2 & 1 \\ 2 & 2 & 1 & 0 & 1 \end{pmatrix}$

2 See Figure 5.16.
(a)

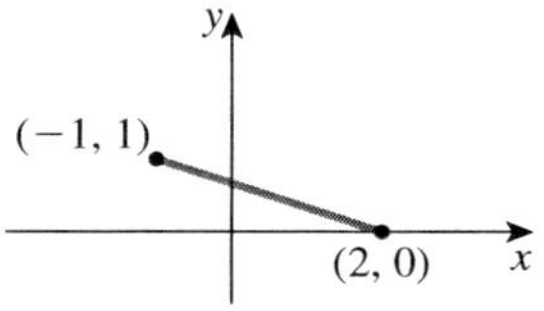

(b)

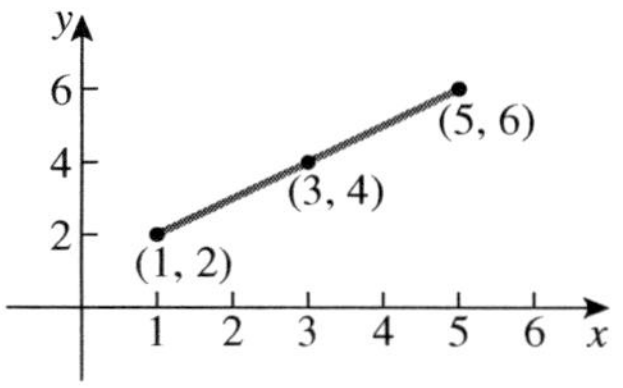

(c)

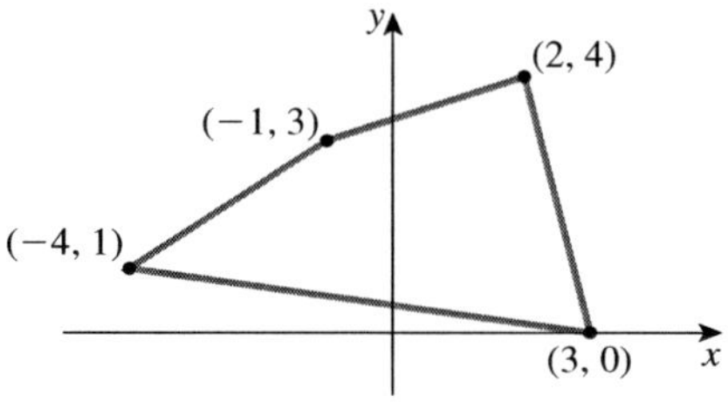

3 The transformed line joins $\begin{pmatrix} 17 \\ 6 \end{pmatrix}$ and $\begin{pmatrix} -4 \\ 3 \end{pmatrix}$.

4 The transformed triangle has vertices at $\begin{pmatrix} -1 \\ -3 \end{pmatrix}$, $\begin{pmatrix} 5 \\ 0 \end{pmatrix}$ and $\begin{pmatrix} 10 \\ -5 \end{pmatrix}$.

5 (a) $\begin{pmatrix} 2 & 0 \\ 0 & 1 \end{pmatrix}$ (b) $\begin{pmatrix} 1 & 0 \\ 0 & 2 \end{pmatrix}$

(c) $\begin{pmatrix} 2 & 0 \\ 0 & 2 \end{pmatrix}$ (d) $\begin{pmatrix} 0.5 & 0 \\ 0 & 0.5 \end{pmatrix}$

6 $\begin{pmatrix} -5.9802 \\ 1.1124 \end{pmatrix}$

7 $\begin{pmatrix} 1.0126 \\ -3.4605 \end{pmatrix}$

8 $\begin{pmatrix} 1 & 7 & 6 \\ -3 & -2 & 1 \end{pmatrix}$

10 (a) $\begin{pmatrix} \cos\theta & \sin\theta \\ -\sin\theta & \cos\theta \end{pmatrix}$

(b) $\begin{pmatrix} \cos\theta & \sin\theta \\ -\sin\theta & \cos\theta \end{pmatrix}$

(c) The inverse of R represents a clockwise rotation through θ.

11 (a) The line joins $\begin{pmatrix} 4 \\ 1 \end{pmatrix}$ and $\begin{pmatrix} 3 \\ -2 \end{pmatrix}$.

(b) The line joins $\begin{pmatrix} 4 \\ -1 \end{pmatrix}$ and $\begin{pmatrix} 3 \\ 2 \end{pmatrix}$.

12 $\begin{pmatrix} 5 & 0 \\ 0 & 1 \end{pmatrix}$

13 The new line joins $\begin{pmatrix} -1 \\ 1 \end{pmatrix}$ and $\begin{pmatrix} -2 \\ -4 \end{pmatrix}$.

15 $\begin{pmatrix} 1 & 0 & 4 \\ 0 & 1 & 5 \\ 0 & 0 & 1 \end{pmatrix}$

16 The line joins $\begin{pmatrix} 7 \\ -3 \end{pmatrix}$ and $\begin{pmatrix} 8 \\ 8 \end{pmatrix}$.

17 $\begin{pmatrix} -1 & 0 & 2 \\ 0 & 1 & -3 \\ 0 & 0 & 1 \end{pmatrix}$

18 $\begin{pmatrix} 0 & 0.5 & 0 \\ -2 & 0 & 0 \\ 0 & 0 & 1 \end{pmatrix}$

19 $\begin{pmatrix} 0.7071 & -0.7071 & 0.1213 \\ 0.7071 & 0.7071 & 1.7071 \\ 0 & 0 & 1 \end{pmatrix}$

End of chapter exercises

1 If

$$A = \begin{pmatrix} 4 & -2 \\ 1 & -3 \end{pmatrix} \quad \text{and} \quad B = \begin{pmatrix} 9 & 3 \\ -2 & 1 \end{pmatrix}$$

find (a) $A + B$, (b) $A - B$, (c) $B - A$, (d) $3A$, (e) $\frac{1}{2}B$, (f) $2A - 4B$.

2 Given

$$A = \begin{pmatrix} 2 & 1 & 3 \\ -1 & 4 & 0 \end{pmatrix} \quad \text{and}$$

$$B = \begin{pmatrix} -1 & 2 & 4 \\ -4 & 1 & 3 \end{pmatrix}$$

calculate (a) $4A$, (b) $-B$, (c) $B - 2A$, (d) $\frac{B}{4}$, (e) $A + 3B$, (f) $\alpha A + \beta B$ where α and β are constants.

3 Give an example of (a) a 2×4, (b) a 4×2 matrix.

4 Calculate the number of elements in (a) a 3×4, (b) a 7×2, (c) a $3 \times n$, (d) an $m \times n$ matrix.

5 Calculate the determinant of each of the following matrices:

(a) $\begin{pmatrix} 3 & 1 \\ 4 & 2 \end{pmatrix}$ (b) $\begin{pmatrix} -1 & 3 \\ 2 & 1 \end{pmatrix}$

(c) $\begin{pmatrix} 0 & 1 \\ 1 & 0 \end{pmatrix}$ (d) $\begin{pmatrix} 1 & 0 \\ 0 & 1 \end{pmatrix}$

(e) $\begin{pmatrix} 3 & 2 \\ x & x \end{pmatrix}$ (f) $\begin{pmatrix} \alpha & \beta \\ \beta & \alpha \end{pmatrix}$

6 Find the inverse of each of the following matrices:

(a) $\begin{pmatrix} -1 & 4 \\ 5 & 6 \end{pmatrix}$ (b) $\begin{pmatrix} 6 & -4 \\ 2 & 3 \end{pmatrix}$

(c) $\begin{pmatrix} -3 & 5 \\ 0 & 1 \end{pmatrix}$ (d) $\frac{1}{2}\begin{pmatrix} -7 & -2 \\ 4 & 3 \end{pmatrix}$

7 Calculate the determinant of each of the following matrices:

(a) $\begin{pmatrix} 1 & 2 & 1 \\ 0 & 1 & 1 \\ 1 & -1 & 0 \end{pmatrix}$ (b) $\begin{pmatrix} -1 & 3 & 2 \\ 2 & 1 & 0 \\ 1 & 3 & 0 \end{pmatrix}$

(c) $\begin{pmatrix} 3 & -2 & -1 \\ 4 & 1 & 0 \\ 3 & 2 & -1 \end{pmatrix}$ (d) $\begin{pmatrix} 2 & 2 & 1 \\ 1 & 2 & 2 \\ 2 & 1 & 2 \end{pmatrix}$

8 Calculate the inverse of each of the matrices in question 5.

9 Calculate the inverse of each of the matrices in question 7.

10 State conditions under which a square matrix does not possess an inverse.

11 Given

$$A = \begin{pmatrix} 3 & 1 & 4 \\ 0 & 2 & -1 \end{pmatrix} \quad \text{and}$$

$$B = \begin{pmatrix} 9 & -6 \\ 3 & 1 \\ 2 & 0 \end{pmatrix}$$

calculate (a) A^{T}, (b) B^{T}, (c) $A + B^{\mathrm{T}}$, (d) $A^{\mathrm{T}} + B$, (e) $2A$, (f) $(2A)^{\mathrm{T}}$, (g) $2(A^{\mathrm{T}})$.

12 Given

$$A = \begin{pmatrix} 3 \\ 1 \end{pmatrix}, \quad B = \begin{pmatrix} 1 & -3 \\ 2 & 1 \end{pmatrix} \quad \text{and}$$

$$C = (-2 \quad 3)$$

calculate, if possible, (a) AB, (b) BA, (c) AC, (d) CA, (e) BC, (f) CB.

13 Given

$$A = (1 \quad 3 \quad -2), \quad B = \begin{pmatrix} 4 & 2 \\ 1 & 3 \\ -1 & 0 \end{pmatrix}$$

$$C = \begin{pmatrix} 1 & -1 & 0 \\ 4 & 1 & 2 \end{pmatrix}$$

calculate, if possible, (a) $B + C$, (b) $B + C^T$, (c) AB, (d) BA, (e) AC^T, (f) $(AC)^T$, (g) BC, (h) CB.

14 The straight line joining $\begin{pmatrix} -6 \\ 2 \end{pmatrix}$ and $\begin{pmatrix} 1 \\ -4 \end{pmatrix}$ is rotated 50° anticlockwise about the origin. Determine the transformed line.

15 The point $\begin{pmatrix} 2 \\ -3 \end{pmatrix}$ is reflected in the line $y = x$ and then the resulting point is rotated 30° anticlockwise about the origin. Determine the coordinates of the final point.

16 A unit square has vertices at $\begin{pmatrix} 0 \\ 0 \end{pmatrix}$, $\begin{pmatrix} 0 \\ 1 \end{pmatrix}$, $\begin{pmatrix} 1 \\ 0 \end{pmatrix}$ and $\begin{pmatrix} 1 \\ 1 \end{pmatrix}$. It is subject to a shear, and this results in a figure with vertices at $\begin{pmatrix}0\\0\end{pmatrix}, \begin{pmatrix}2\\1\end{pmatrix}, \begin{pmatrix}1\\3\end{pmatrix}$ and $\begin{pmatrix}3\\4\end{pmatrix}$. Determine a transformation that effects this shear.

17 The transformation matrix

$$T = \begin{pmatrix} 1 & 0 & 4 \\ 0 & 1 & 0.5 \\ 0 & 0 & 1 \end{pmatrix}$$

is applied to the line joining $\begin{pmatrix}0\\1\end{pmatrix}$ and $\begin{pmatrix}3\\-1\end{pmatrix}$. Determine the transformed line.

18 The point $\begin{pmatrix}-1\\2\end{pmatrix}$ is rotated 90° anticlockwise about the origin and then translated 2 units in the x direction and 3 units in the y direction. Calculate
(a) the composite transformation matrix
(b) the coordinates of the transformed point.

19 The **leading diagonal** of a square matrix, A, is the diagonal running from the top left to the bottom right. The sum of the elements on the leading diagonal is called the **trace** of A.
(a) Find the trace of

$$A = \begin{pmatrix} 1 & 2 \\ 5 & -3 \end{pmatrix}$$

(b) Find the trace of

$$A = \begin{pmatrix} 4 & 1 & 3 \\ 2 & 7 & 1 \\ 0 & 0 & 12 \end{pmatrix}$$

(c) For an arbitrary 2 × 2 and 3 × 3 matrix A, show that trace(A) = trace (A^T).

20 Evaluate

$$\begin{vmatrix} 1 & 4 & 2 & 1 \\ 3 & 0 & 1 & 9 \\ 0 & -1 & 1 & 1 \\ 2 & 1 & 0 & 1 \end{vmatrix}$$

21 (a) A square matrix A is said to be **symmetric** if $A = A^T$, and **skew-symmetric** if $A = -A^T$. State which, if any, of the following matrices are symmetric and which are skew-symmetric.

$$C = \begin{pmatrix} 4 & 7 \\ 0 & -2 \end{pmatrix}$$

$$D = \begin{pmatrix} 0 & -7 & -9 \\ 7 & 0 & 8 \\ 9 & -8 & 0 \end{pmatrix}$$

$$E = \begin{pmatrix} 3 & 4 & 1 \\ 4 & 1 & 0 \\ 1 & 0 & 7 \end{pmatrix}$$

(b) Show that if A is a 2 × 2 or 3 × 3 skew-symmetric matrix then its diagonal elements must all be zero.

22 (a) A non-singular matrix A is said to be **orthogonal** if its transpose is equal to its inverse: that is, $A^T = A^{-1}$. Given that

$$A = \begin{pmatrix} \cos\theta & \sin\theta \\ -\sin\theta & \cos\theta \end{pmatrix}$$

is an orthogonal matrix, write down its inverse, and check your answer by evaluating AA^{-1}.
(b) Show that

$$\begin{pmatrix} \frac{3}{5} & -\frac{4}{5} \\ \frac{4}{5} & \frac{3}{5} \end{pmatrix}$$

is an orthogonal matrix.

23 If

$$A = \begin{pmatrix} 0 & 1 \\ -3 & -2 \end{pmatrix}$$

(a) write down the matrix $sI - A$, where s is a constant and I is the 2 × 2 identity matrix
(b) find $(sI - A)^{-1}$.

24 **Control engineering.** The state matrix of an engineering system is given by

$$A = \begin{pmatrix} -2 & -1 \\ 16 & 5 \end{pmatrix}$$

Calculate the values of the system poles. Determine whether the system is stable or unstable.

Solutions to exercises

1 (a) $\begin{pmatrix} 13 & 1 \\ -1 & -2 \end{pmatrix}$ (b) $\begin{pmatrix} -5 & -5 \\ 3 & -4 \end{pmatrix}$

(c) $\begin{pmatrix} 5 & 5 \\ -3 & 4 \end{pmatrix}$ (d) $\begin{pmatrix} 12 & -6 \\ 3 & -9 \end{pmatrix}$

(e) $\begin{pmatrix} 4.5 & 1.5 \\ -1 & 0.5 \end{pmatrix}$ (f) $\begin{pmatrix} -28 & -16 \\ 10 & -10 \end{pmatrix}$

2 (a) $\begin{pmatrix} 8 & 4 & 12 \\ -4 & 16 & 0 \end{pmatrix}$ (b) $\begin{pmatrix} 1 & -2 & -4 \\ 4 & -1 & -3 \end{pmatrix}$

(c) $\begin{pmatrix} -5 & 0 & -2 \\ -2 & -7 & 3 \end{pmatrix}$

(d) $\begin{pmatrix} -0.25 & 0.5 & 1 \\ -1 & 0.25 & 0.75 \end{pmatrix}$

(e) $\begin{pmatrix} -1 & 7 & 15 \\ -13 & 7 & 9 \end{pmatrix}$

(f) $\begin{pmatrix} 2\alpha - \beta & \alpha + 2\beta & 3\alpha + 4\beta \\ -\alpha - 4\beta & 4\alpha + \beta & 3\beta \end{pmatrix}$

3 (a) $\begin{pmatrix} 1 & 2 & 3 & 4 \\ 1 & -1 & 0 & 1 \end{pmatrix}$ (b) $\begin{pmatrix} 1 & 1 \\ 2 & 2 \\ 3 & -1 \\ 4 & 3 \end{pmatrix}$

4 (a) 12 (b) 14 (c) $3n$ (d) mn

5 (a) 2 (b) −7 (c) −1 (d) 1 (e) x (f) $\alpha^2 - \beta^2$

6 (a) $\frac{1}{26}\begin{pmatrix} -6 & 4 \\ 5 & 1 \end{pmatrix}$ (b) $\frac{1}{26}\begin{pmatrix} 3 & 4 \\ -2 & 6 \end{pmatrix}$

(c) $\frac{1}{3}\begin{pmatrix} -1 & 5 \\ 0 & 3 \end{pmatrix}$ (d) $\frac{2}{13}\begin{pmatrix} -3 & -2 \\ 4 & 7 \end{pmatrix}$

7 (a) 2 (b) 10 (c) −16 (d) 5

8 (a) $\begin{pmatrix} 1 & -0.5 \\ -2 & 1.5 \end{pmatrix}$ (b) $\frac{1}{7}\begin{pmatrix} -1 & 3 \\ 2 & 1 \end{pmatrix}$

(c) $\begin{pmatrix} 0 & 1 \\ 1 & 0 \end{pmatrix}$ (d) $\begin{pmatrix} 1 & 0 \\ 0 & 1 \end{pmatrix}$

(e) $\begin{pmatrix} 1 & -\frac{2}{x} \\ -1 & \frac{3}{x} \end{pmatrix}$ (f) $\frac{1}{\alpha^2 - \beta^2}\begin{pmatrix} \alpha & -\beta \\ -\beta & \alpha \end{pmatrix}$

9 (a) $\frac{1}{2}\begin{pmatrix} 1 & -1 & 1 \\ 1 & -1 & -1 \\ -1 & 3 & 1 \end{pmatrix}$

(b) $\frac{1}{10}\begin{pmatrix} 0 & 6 & -2 \\ 0 & -2 & 4 \\ 5 & 6 & -7 \end{pmatrix}$

(c) $\frac{1}{16}\begin{pmatrix} 1 & 4 & -1 \\ -4 & 0 & 4 \\ -5 & 12 & -11 \end{pmatrix}$

(d) $\frac{1}{5}\begin{pmatrix} 2 & -3 & 2 \\ 2 & 2 & -3 \\ -3 & 2 & 2 \end{pmatrix}$

10 If the determinant is zero, then the matrix has no inverse.

11 (a) $\begin{pmatrix} 3 & 0 \\ 1 & 2 \\ 4 & -1 \end{pmatrix}$ (b) $\begin{pmatrix} 9 & 3 & 2 \\ -6 & 1 & 0 \end{pmatrix}$

(c) $\begin{pmatrix} 12 & 4 & 6 \\ -6 & 3 & -1 \end{pmatrix}$ (d) $\begin{pmatrix} 12 & -6 \\ 4 & 3 \\ 6 & -1 \end{pmatrix}$

(e) $\begin{pmatrix} 6 & 2 & 8 \\ 0 & 4 & -2 \end{pmatrix}$ (f) $\begin{pmatrix} 6 & 0 \\ 2 & 4 \\ 8 & -2 \end{pmatrix}$

(g) $\begin{pmatrix} 6 & 0 \\ 2 & 4 \\ 8 & -2 \end{pmatrix}$

12 (a) not possible (b) $\begin{pmatrix} 0 \\ 7 \end{pmatrix}$ (c) $\begin{pmatrix} -6 & 9 \\ -2 & 3 \end{pmatrix}$

(d) -3 (e) not possible (f) $(4 \quad 9)$

13 (a) not possible (b) $\begin{pmatrix} 5 & 6 \\ 0 & 4 \\ -1 & 2 \end{pmatrix}$

(c) $(9 \quad 11)$ (d) not possible (e) $(-2 \quad 3)$

(f) not possible (g) $\begin{pmatrix} 12 & -2 & 4 \\ 13 & 2 & 6 \\ -1 & 1 & 0 \end{pmatrix}$

(h) $\begin{pmatrix} 3 & -1 \\ 15 & 11 \end{pmatrix}$

14 Line joins $\begin{pmatrix} -5.3888 \\ -3.3107 \end{pmatrix}$ to $\begin{pmatrix} 3.7070 \\ -1.8051 \end{pmatrix}$.

15 $\begin{pmatrix} -3.5981 \\ 0.2321 \end{pmatrix}$

16 $\begin{pmatrix} 1 & 2 \\ 3 & 1 \end{pmatrix}$

17 The transformed line joins the points $\begin{pmatrix} 4 \\ 1.5 \end{pmatrix}$ and $\begin{pmatrix} 7 \\ -0.5 \end{pmatrix}$.

18 (a) $\begin{pmatrix} 0 & -1 & 2 \\ 1 & 0 & 3 \\ 0 & 0 & 1 \end{pmatrix}$ (b) $\begin{pmatrix} 0 \\ 2 \end{pmatrix}$

19 (a) -2 (b) 23

20 70

21 D is skew-symmetric, E is symmetric and C is neither.

22 $A^{-1} = \begin{pmatrix} \cos\theta & -\sin\theta \\ \sin\theta & \cos\theta \end{pmatrix}$

23 (a) $\begin{pmatrix} s & -1 \\ 3 & s+2 \end{pmatrix}$

(b) $\dfrac{1}{s^2 + 2s + 3}\begin{pmatrix} s+2 & 1 \\ -3 & s \end{pmatrix}$

24 Poles are $s = \frac{3 \pm \sqrt{-15}}{2}$. System is unstable.

Using matrices and determinants to solve equations

Chapter 13

This chapter looks at some of the ways in which matrices and determinants can be used to solve linear simultaneous equations.

Block 1 introduces **Cramer's rule**, which expresses the solution to simultaneous equations as a ratio of two determinants. The next block shows how simultaneous equations may be written in matrix form. Once in this form an **inverse matrix** method can be used to solve them.

Block 3 explains the method of **Gaussian elimination**. When the simultaneous equations have been written as a matrix, the rows of the matrix are systematically manipulated to yield the solution. The block includes an explanation of the way in which the manipulation is carried out.

Matrices are sometimes used in calculations that model vibrating objects, and in particular those vibrating because of forces in stretched and compressed springs. In such applications engineers are interested in the possible frequencies of vibration. These frequencies are related to what are known as the **eigenvalues** of a matrix. The **eigenvectors** represent the various modes of vibration. Block 4 will explain how the eigenvalues and eigenvectors of a matrix are calculated. As they are usually studied in terms of linear systems, they are included here. In many practical applications, approximate solutions of linear equations are obtained using what are called **numerical methods**. These are introduced in Block 5.

The final block focuses on the application of matrices to the analysis of **electrical networks**. Engineers often need to know the currents in the various branches of a circuit. The idea of branch currents is introduced. A set of simultaneous equations can be formed that models these branch currents, and which can be solved using matrix methods.

Chapter 13 contents

BLOCK 1

Cramer's rule

1.1 Introduction

In Chapter 12 we introduced determinants. In this block we study Cramer's rule, which uses determinants to solve a set of simultaneous linear equations. Such equations are often referred to as a **system of linear equations**.

1.2 Cramer's rule

Consider a system of two linear simultaneous equations in the two unknowns x and y.

$$a_1x + b_1y = k_1$$
$$a_2x + b_2y = k_2$$

Here a_1, b_1, k_1, a_2, b_2 and k_2 are known constants and we wish to find the values of x and y.

Cramer's rule is a method of obtaining the solution of equations like these as the ratio of two determinants.

Key point

Cramer's rule states

$$x = \frac{\begin{vmatrix} k_1 & b_1 \\ k_2 & b_2 \end{vmatrix}}{\begin{vmatrix} a_1 & b_1 \\ a_2 & b_2 \end{vmatrix}}, \quad y = \frac{\begin{vmatrix} a_1 & k_1 \\ a_2 & k_2 \end{vmatrix}}{\begin{vmatrix} a_1 & b_1 \\ a_2 & b_2 \end{vmatrix}}$$

Note that the denominator is the same in each case. The denominator is simply the determinant made up of the coefficients of x and y. If the denominator is zero then Cramer's rule cannot be applied. In such a case, either a unique solution to the system does not exist or there is no solution.

Note how the numerator of each fraction is formed. To form the numerator for the x fraction we replace the column of as in

$$\begin{vmatrix} a_1 & b_1 \\ a_2 & b_2 \end{vmatrix}$$

by a column of ks. Similarly the numerator for the y fraction is formed by replacing the column of bs by a column of ks.

Example 1.1 Electrical Engineering – Currents in a circuit

The currents i_1 and i_2 in a simple circuit are connected by the equations

$$\begin{aligned} i_1 + i_2 &= 3 \\ 2i_1 + 3i_2 &= 7 \end{aligned}$$

Calculate i_1 and i_2 using Cramer's rule.

Solution

Using Cramer's rule we have

$$i_1 = \frac{\begin{vmatrix} 3 & 1 \\ 7 & 3 \end{vmatrix}}{\begin{vmatrix} 1 & 1 \\ 2 & 3 \end{vmatrix}} = \frac{2}{1} = 2, \quad i_2 = \frac{\begin{vmatrix} 1 & 3 \\ 2 & 7 \end{vmatrix}}{\begin{vmatrix} 1 & 1 \\ 2 & 3 \end{vmatrix}} = \frac{1}{1} = 1$$

The currents in the circuit are $i_1 = 2$, $i_2 = 1$.

Cramer's rule may be extended to systems of linear equations with more than two unknowns. Consider the following linear system with three unknowns, x, y and z.

$$\begin{aligned} a_1x + b_1y + c_1z &= k_1 \\ a_2x + b_2y + c_2z &= k_2 \\ a_3x + b_3y + c_3z &= k_3 \end{aligned}$$

Then Cramer's rule states

Key point

$$x = \frac{\begin{vmatrix} k_1 & b_1 & c_1 \\ k_2 & b_2 & c_2 \\ k_3 & b_3 & c_3 \end{vmatrix}}{\begin{vmatrix} a_1 & b_1 & c_1 \\ a_2 & b_2 & c_2 \\ a_3 & b_3 & c_3 \end{vmatrix}}, \quad y = \frac{\begin{vmatrix} a_1 & k_1 & c_1 \\ a_2 & k_2 & c_2 \\ a_3 & k_3 & c_3 \end{vmatrix}}{\begin{vmatrix} a_1 & b_1 & c_1 \\ a_2 & b_2 & c_2 \\ a_3 & b_3 & c_3 \end{vmatrix}}, \quad z = \frac{\begin{vmatrix} a_1 & b_1 & k_1 \\ a_2 & b_2 & k_2 \\ a_3 & b_3 & k_3 \end{vmatrix}}{\begin{vmatrix} a_1 & b_1 & c_1 \\ a_2 & b_2 & c_2 \\ a_3 & b_3 & c_3 \end{vmatrix}}$$

Note again that, in all three cases, the denominators are the same. The numerators are formed by replacing a column of as, bs or cs by a column of ks.

Example 1.2 Electrical Engineering – Circuit voltages

The voltages v_1, v_2 and v_3 in an electrical circuit are connected by the system

$$\begin{aligned} v_1 + 2v_2 + v_3 &= 2 \\ 2v_1 - v_2 - 2v_3 &= 5 \\ 2v_1 + 2v_2 + 3v_3 &= 7 \end{aligned}$$

Use Cramer's rule to determine the three voltages.

Solution

Using Cramer's rule we have:

$$v_1 = \frac{\begin{vmatrix} 2 & 2 & 1 \\ 5 & -1 & -2 \\ 7 & 2 & 3 \end{vmatrix}}{\begin{vmatrix} 1 & 2 & 1 \\ 2 & -1 & -2 \\ 2 & 2 & 3 \end{vmatrix}} = \frac{-39}{-13}$$

$$= 3$$

$$v_2 = \frac{\begin{vmatrix} 1 & 2 & 1 \\ 2 & 5 & -2 \\ 2 & 7 & 3 \end{vmatrix}}{-13}$$

$$= \frac{13}{-13} = -1$$

$$v_3 = \frac{\begin{vmatrix} 1 & 2 & 2 \\ 2 & -1 & 5 \\ 2 & 2 & 7 \end{vmatrix}}{-13}$$

$$= \frac{-13}{-13} = 1$$

The voltages are $v_1 = 3$, $v_2 = -1$ and $v_3 = 1$.

Cramer's rule can be extended to four and more unknowns in an obvious way, but the determinants become too large to make this a sensible approach. Gaussian elimination, described in Block 3, is a practical alternative.

Exercises

1 Solve the following systems of two linear equations using Cramer's rule:

(a) $2x + y = 10$
$3x - 2y = 1$

(b) $-\theta_1 - \theta_2 = 1$
$2\theta_1 + \theta_2 = 1$

(c) $2i_1 + i_2 = 9.3$
$3i_1 - 2i_2 = 5.9$

(d) $3v_1 - v_2 = 6.6$
$2v_1 - 3v_2 = -1.9$

(e) $\alpha - 3\beta = 0.5$
$\beta + 2\alpha = -3.9$

2 Solve the following systems of three linear equations using Cramer's rule:

(a) $2x - y - 2z = 1$
$x + y + 3z = 6$
$-2x + 3z = -1$

(b) $\beta - 2\gamma = -6$
$\alpha + 3\beta + \gamma = 2$
$3\alpha + 2\gamma = 3$

(c) $i_1 + i_2 - i_3 = 1$
$3i_1 - i_2 + 2i_3 = 7$
$-i_1 + 2i_2 - i_3 = -0.5$

(d) $2v_1 - v_2 + v_3 = 5.9$
$v_1 + \frac{1}{2}v_2 - v_3 = 0.7$
$-3v_1 + 2v_3 = -3.1$

(e) $\theta_1 + \theta_2 + 4\theta_3 = 0$
$2\theta_1 - \theta_2 + \theta_3 = 5.4$
$\theta_1 + 2\theta_2 - \theta_3 = 9.2$

Solutions to exercises

1 (a) $x = 3, y = 4$
(b) $\theta_1 = 2, \theta_2 = -3$
(c) $i_1 = 3.5, i_2 = 2.3$
(d) $v_1 = 3.1, v_2 = 2.7$
(e) $\alpha = -1.6, \beta = -0.7$

2 (a) $x = 2, y = 1, z = 1$
(b) $\alpha = -1, \beta = 0, \gamma = 3$
(c) $i_1 = 1.5, i_2 = 1.5, i_3 = 2$
(d) $v_1 = 2.3, v_2 = 0.6, v_3 = 1.9$
(e) $\theta_1 = 4.3, \theta_2 = 1.7, \theta_3 = -1.5$

End of block exercises

1 **Electrical Engineering**. Voltages v_1 and v_2 in a circuit are related by the system of equations

$$\begin{aligned} 3v_1 + 2v_2 &= 6 \\ -4v_1 + 10v_2 &= -27 \end{aligned}$$

Calculate v_1 and v_2 using Cramer's rule.

2 **Electrical Engineering**. The currents i_1, i_2 and i_3 of a circuit are related by

$$\begin{aligned} 2i_1 + i_2 - i_3 &= 8 \\ i_1 - i_2 + i_3 &= -5 \\ 3i_1 + 2i_2 &= 9 \end{aligned}$$

Use Cramer's rule to evaluate the three currents.

3 Explain why Cramer's rule cannot be applied to the following system of equations:

$$\begin{aligned} 3x - 2y &= 10 \\ y - 1.5x &= -5 \end{aligned}$$

4 **Mechanical Engineering**. The magnitudes of forces f and g in a mechanical system are connected by the equations

$$\begin{aligned} 3f + 5g - 16.1 &= 0 \\ 2f - g - 3.8 &= 0 \end{aligned}$$

Use Cramer's rule to determine the magnitudes of f and g.

Solutions to exercises

1 $v_1 = 3,\ v_2 = -1.5$

2 $i_1 = 1,\ i_2 = 3,\ i_3 = -3$

3 The matrix

$$\begin{pmatrix} 3 & -2 \\ -1.5 & 1 \end{pmatrix}$$

has a zero determinant.

4 $f = 2.7, g = 1.6$

BLOCK 2 Using the inverse matrix to solve simultaneous equations

2.1 Introduction

Block 1 dealt with Cramer's rule for solving a system of linear equations. The solutions were given in terms of determinants. This block shows how an inverse matrix can be used to solve a system of linear simultaneous equations. You will need to be familiar with the techniques for finding the inverses of 2×2 and 3×3 matrices as described in Chapter 12, Block 4.

2.2 Writing equations in matrix form

Consider the simultaneous equations

$$\begin{aligned} 7x + 2y &= 12 \\ 3x + y &= 5 \end{aligned}$$

Recalling how matrices are multiplied we note that the product

$$\begin{pmatrix} 7 & 2 \\ 3 & 1 \end{pmatrix} \begin{pmatrix} x \\ y \end{pmatrix}$$

is equivalent to

$$\begin{pmatrix} 7x + 2y \\ 3x + y \end{pmatrix}$$

Hence we can write the simultaneous equations as

$$\begin{pmatrix} 7 & 2 \\ 3 & 1 \end{pmatrix} \begin{pmatrix} x \\ y \end{pmatrix} = \begin{pmatrix} 12 \\ 5 \end{pmatrix}$$

This is the **matrix form** of the simultaneous equations.

Writing

$$A = \begin{pmatrix} 7 & 2 \\ 3 & 1 \end{pmatrix}, \quad X = \begin{pmatrix} x \\ y \end{pmatrix}, \quad B = \begin{pmatrix} 12 \\ 5 \end{pmatrix}$$

we have the standard form

$$AX = B$$

Note that the elements of A come from the coefficients of x and y and that the elements of B come from the right-hand sides of the equations.

Example 2.1

Write the following system of equations in the standard matrix form $AX = B$.

$$\begin{aligned} 2x + y - z &= 4 \\ x - y + 3z &= -2 \\ 2x + 2y - 3z &= 9 \end{aligned}$$

Solution

The elements of A are the coefficients of x, y and z. Hence

$$A = \begin{pmatrix} 2 & 1 & -1 \\ 1 & -1 & 3 \\ 2 & 2 & -3 \end{pmatrix}$$

and

$$X = \begin{pmatrix} x \\ y \\ z \end{pmatrix}, \quad B = \begin{pmatrix} 4 \\ -2 \\ 9 \end{pmatrix}$$

Hence in matrix form the equations are written as

$$\begin{pmatrix} 2 & 1 & -1 \\ 1 & -1 & 3 \\ 2 & 2 & -3 \end{pmatrix} \begin{pmatrix} x \\ y \\ z \end{pmatrix} = \begin{pmatrix} 4 \\ -2 \\ 9 \end{pmatrix}$$

Example 2.2

Express the following system in the form $AX = B$.

$$\begin{aligned} -x + 3y + 4z &= 7 \\ y - 4x &= 7 \\ y + 3x - z &= -9 \end{aligned}$$

Solution

The equations are rewritten so that the variables x, y and z appear in the same order.

$$\begin{aligned} -x + 3y + 4z &= 7 \\ -4x + y + 0z &= 7 \\ 3x + y - z &= -9 \end{aligned}$$

Then

$A =$

$$\begin{pmatrix} -1 & 3 & 4 \\ -4 & 1 & 0 \\ 3 & 1 & -1 \end{pmatrix}$$

$X = \begin{pmatrix} x \\ y \\ z \end{pmatrix}$, $B =$

$$\begin{pmatrix} 7 \\ 7 \\ -9 \end{pmatrix}$$

In matrix form the equations are

$$\begin{pmatrix} -1 & 3 & 4 \\ -4 & 1 & 0 \\ 3 & 1 & -1 \end{pmatrix}\begin{pmatrix} x \\ y \\ z \end{pmatrix} = \begin{pmatrix} 7 \\ 7 \\ -9 \end{pmatrix}$$

Exercises

1 Write the following simultaneous equations in matrix form:

(a) $3x - 4y = 9$
$x + 2y = 6$

(b) $\alpha - \beta = 0.5$
$3\alpha + 7\beta = 11.6$

(c) $2x - y + 3z = 0$
$3x + 4y + z = 1$
$-2x + 3z = -2$

Solutions to exercises

1 (a) $\begin{pmatrix} 3 & -4 \\ 1 & 2 \end{pmatrix}\begin{pmatrix} x \\ y \end{pmatrix} = \begin{pmatrix} 9 \\ 6 \end{pmatrix}$

(b) $\begin{pmatrix} 1 & -1 \\ 3 & 7 \end{pmatrix}\begin{pmatrix} \alpha \\ \beta \end{pmatrix} = \begin{pmatrix} 0.5 \\ 11.6 \end{pmatrix}$

(c) $\begin{pmatrix} 2 & -1 & 3 \\ 3 & 4 & 1 \\ -2 & 0 & 3 \end{pmatrix}\begin{pmatrix} x \\ y \\ z \end{pmatrix} = \begin{pmatrix} 0 \\ 1 \\ -2 \end{pmatrix}$

2.3 Solving equations using the inverse matrix method

Consider a system of equations written in matrix form, that is

$$AX = B$$

where A is a square matrix. Note that A and B are matrices with numerical elements. We wish to find an expression for the unknowns, that is the elements of X. To achieve this we premultiply both sides of the equation by the inverse of A, if it exists, to obtain

$$A^{-1}AX = A^{-1}B \qquad (1)$$

The left-hand side can be simplified by noting that multiplying a matrix by its inverse gives the identity matrix, that is $A^{-1}A = I$. Hence

$$A^{-1}AX = (A^{-1}A)X$$
$$= IX$$

Multiplying a matrix by the identity matrix has no effect and so $IX = X$. So the left-hand side of equation (1) simplifies to

$$\begin{aligned} A^{-1}AX &= IX \\ &= X \end{aligned}$$

and so, from (1),

$$X = A^{-1}B$$

Key point

Given $AX = B$, then $X = A^{-1}B$ if A^{-1} exists.

Example 2.3
Solve

$$\begin{aligned} 7x + 2y &= 12 \\ 3x + y &= 5 \end{aligned}$$

using the inverse matrix method.

Solution
Writing the equations in matrix form, $AX = B$, gives

$$\begin{pmatrix} 7 & 2 \\ 3 & 1 \end{pmatrix}\begin{pmatrix} x \\ y \end{pmatrix} = \begin{pmatrix} 12 \\ 5 \end{pmatrix}$$

Here

$$A = \begin{pmatrix} 7 & 2 \\ 3 & 1 \end{pmatrix}, \quad B = \begin{pmatrix} 12 \\ 5 \end{pmatrix}, \quad X = \begin{pmatrix} x \\ y \end{pmatrix}$$

We calculate A^{-1}.

$$A^{-1} = \begin{pmatrix} 1 & -2 \\ -3 & 7 \end{pmatrix}$$

Hence

$$\begin{aligned} X &= A^{-1}B \\ &= \begin{pmatrix} 1 & -2 \\ -3 & 7 \end{pmatrix}\begin{pmatrix} 12 \\ 5 \end{pmatrix} \\ &= \begin{pmatrix} 2 \\ -1 \end{pmatrix} \end{aligned}$$

We have

$$\begin{aligned} X &= \begin{pmatrix} x \\ y \end{pmatrix} \\ &= \begin{pmatrix} 2 \\ -1 \end{pmatrix} \end{aligned}$$

that is $x = 2$, $y = -1$.

Example 2.4 Electrical Engineering – Circuit currents

The currents i_1 and i_2 in a circuit are connected by the equations

$$2i_1 + i_2 = 8.6$$
$$3i_1 - i_2 = 9.4$$

Use the inverse matrix method to find the values of i_1 and i_2.

Solution

We have $AX = B$ where

$$A = \qquad , \qquad B = \begin{pmatrix} 8.6 \\ 9.4 \end{pmatrix} \text{ and } X = \begin{pmatrix} i_1 \\ i_2 \end{pmatrix}$$

$$\begin{pmatrix} 2 & 1 \\ 3 & -1 \end{pmatrix}$$

We calculate A^{-1}.

$$A^{-1} = $$

$$\begin{pmatrix} \frac{1}{5} & \frac{1}{5} \\ \frac{3}{5} & -\frac{2}{5} \end{pmatrix}$$

So

$$\begin{aligned} X &= A^{-1}B \\ &= \begin{pmatrix} \frac{1}{5} & \frac{1}{5} \\ \frac{3}{5} & -\frac{2}{5} \end{pmatrix} \begin{pmatrix} 8.6 \\ 9.4 \end{pmatrix} \\ &= \end{aligned}$$

$$\begin{pmatrix} 3.6 \\ 1.4 \end{pmatrix}$$

So $i_1 = 3.6$ and $i_2 = 1.4$.

Example 2.5 Mechanical Engineering – Forces in a pulley system

Forces f_1, f_2 and f_3 in a simple pulley system satisfy the equations

$$-f_1 + 3f_2 + 4f_3 = 7$$
$$f_2 - 4f_1 = 7$$
$$f_2 + 3f_1 - f_3 = -9$$

Solve the system for f_1, f_2 and f_3.

Solution

The equations are written in matrix form:

$$\begin{pmatrix} -1 & 3 & 4 \\ -4 & 1 & 0 \\ 3 & 1 & -1 \end{pmatrix} \begin{pmatrix} f_1 \\ f_2 \\ f_3 \end{pmatrix} = \begin{pmatrix} 7 \\ 7 \\ -9 \end{pmatrix}$$

Writing

$$A = \begin{pmatrix} -1 & 3 & 4 \\ -4 & 1 & 0 \\ 3 & 1 & -1 \end{pmatrix}$$

we then calculate A^{-1} as

$$A^{-1} = \frac{1}{39}\begin{pmatrix} 1 & -7 & 4 \\ 4 & 11 & 16 \\ 7 & -10 & -11 \end{pmatrix}$$

Hence

$$\begin{pmatrix} f_1 \\ f_2 \\ f_3 \end{pmatrix} = \frac{1}{39}\begin{pmatrix} 1 & -7 & 4 \\ 4 & 11 & 16 \\ 7 & -10 & -11 \end{pmatrix}\begin{pmatrix} 7 \\ 7 \\ -9 \end{pmatrix}$$
$$= \begin{pmatrix} -2 \\ -1 \\ 2 \end{pmatrix}$$

So $f_1 = -2, f_2 = -1, f_3 = 2$.

Exercises

1 Solve the following systems of linear equations using the inverse matrix method:
(a) $3x - y = 4$
$x + 2y = 13$
(b) $2\alpha - \beta = -11$
$\frac{1}{2}\alpha + \beta = 1$
(c) $v_1 - 2v_2 = -3.5$
$3v_1 + 5v_2 = 17$
(d) $2\,i_1 + i_2 = 3.5$
$-i_1 + 2i_2 = 3.5$
(e) $p - 2q = -0.7$
$2p - q = -1.1$

2 State conditions under which the inverse matrix method will fail to find a set of solutions.

3 Given that the inverse of

$$\begin{pmatrix} 2 & -1 & -1 \\ 1 & 2 & -2 \\ 2 & 3 & 1 \end{pmatrix}$$

is

$$\frac{1}{22}\begin{pmatrix} 8 & -2 & 4 \\ -5 & 4 & 3 \\ -1 & -8 & 5 \end{pmatrix}$$

solve the following system of equations:

$$2x - y - z = 7$$
$$x + 2y - 2z = 13$$
$$2x + 3y + z = 9$$

4 Given that the inverse of

$$\begin{pmatrix} 1 & -1 & 2 \\ 4 & 3 & -1 \\ 3 & -1 & 4 \end{pmatrix}$$

is

$$\frac{1}{4}\begin{pmatrix} 11 & 2 & -5 \\ -19 & -2 & 9 \\ -13 & -2 & 7 \end{pmatrix}$$

solve the system of linear equations

$$4x + 3y - z = 3$$
$$3x - y + 4z = 10$$
$$x - y + 2y = 4$$

5 **Electrical Engineering**. Resistances r_1, r_2 and r_3 in a circuit are connected by the equations

$$r_1 - 2r_2 + r_3 = -0.9$$
$$2r_1 - r_2 + r_3 = 0.8$$
$$r_1 - 2r_2 - r_3 = -2.3$$

Use the inverse matrix method to calculate r_1, r_2 and r_3.

Solutions to exercises

1 (a) $x = 3, y = 5$
(b) $\alpha = -4, \beta = 3$
(c) $v_1 = 1.5, v_2 = 2.5$
(d) $i_1 = 0.7, i_2 = 2.1$
(e) $p = -0.5, q = 0.1$

2 Given $AX = B$, the method will fail if $|A| = 0$; that is, if A^{-1} does not exist.

3 $x = 3, y = 2, z = -3$

4 $x = 0, y = 2, z = 3$

5 $r_1 = 0.6, r_2 = 1.1, r_3 = 0.7$

Computer and calculator exercises

1 Using a computer algebra package to calculate the relevant inverse matrix and perform the matrix multiplication, solve the following systems using the inverse matrix method:

(a)
$$\begin{aligned} 2x - y + z &= -7 \\ x + 2y + \tfrac{1}{2}z &= 19 \\ 4x + 3z &= 0 \end{aligned}$$

(b)
$$\begin{aligned} 2\alpha + 4\beta - \gamma &= -2 \\ \alpha + 2\beta + 3\gamma &= 20 \\ \alpha + \beta &= 0.5 \end{aligned}$$

(c)
$$\begin{aligned} i_1 + i_2 + i_3 - i_4 &= 2 \\ i_1 - i_2 + i_3 + i_4 &= 6 \\ -i_1 + i_2 + i_3 - i_4 &= 0 \\ -i_1 + i_2 - i_3 + 4i_4 &= 14 \end{aligned}$$

Solutions to exercises

1 (a) $x = 3, y = 9, z = -4$
(b) $\alpha = -1, \beta = 1.5, \gamma = 6$
(c) $i_1 = 1, i_2 = 2, i_3 = 3, i_4 = 4$

End of block exercises

1 Use the inverse matrix method to solve

(a)
$$\begin{aligned} 4x - 3y &= 6 \\ -2x + y &= -4 \end{aligned}$$

(b)
$$\begin{aligned} \alpha + 2\beta &= 2 \\ 3\alpha - 4\beta &= -9 \end{aligned}$$

2 Explain why the inverse matrix method cannot be applied to the following system:

$$\begin{aligned} 3x - y &= 7 \\ -6x + 2y &= -14 \end{aligned}$$

3 Given that the inverse of

$$\begin{pmatrix} 1 & -1 & 3 \\ 2 & 1 & 1 \\ -3 & 1 & 4 \end{pmatrix}$$

is

$$\frac{1}{29}\begin{pmatrix} 3 & 7 & -4 \\ -11 & 13 & 5 \\ 5 & 2 & 3 \end{pmatrix}$$

solve the following systems:

(a) $x - y + 3z = 3$
$2x + y + z = 7$
$-3x + y + 4z = 0$

(b) $2x + y + z = -1$
$-3x + y + 4z = -7$
$x - y + 3z = -7$

(c) $3x - 3y + 9z = 30$
$-3x + y + 4z = 20$
$4x + 2y + 2z = 6$

Solutions to exercises

1 (a) $x = 3, y = 2$
(b) $\alpha = -1, \beta = 1.5$

2 The matrix

$$\begin{pmatrix} 3 & -1 \\ -6 & 2 \end{pmatrix}$$

has no inverse.

3 (a) $x = 2, y = 2, z = 1$
(b) $x = 0, y = 1, z = -2$
(c) $x = -1, y = 1, z = 4$

BLOCK 3

Gaussian elimination

3.1 Introduction

Gaussian elimination is a systematic way of simplifying a system of equations so that a solution can easily be found. Rather than work with the actual equations, a matrix, whose elements capture all the properties of the equations, is used.

Manipulation of the matrix is carried out by performing a sequence of elementary row operations. These operations eventually bring the matrix into a form known as echelon form. Once in this form, the solution to the original equations is easily found.

3.2 The augmented matrix

Consider the system of linear equations:

$$\begin{aligned} 2x + 3y &= 16 \\ x - y &= -2 \end{aligned}$$

This system may be represented in the matrix form

$$\begin{pmatrix} 2 & 3 & 16 \\ 1 & -1 & -2 \end{pmatrix}$$

This is an example of an **augmented matrix**. Note that the elements of the augmented matrix comprise the coefficients of x and y and also the right-hand sides of the equations.

Example 3.1

State the augmented matrix for the system

$$\begin{aligned} 3x - y + 2z &= 7 \\ 4x + y &= 6 \\ x + 2y - z &= 2 \end{aligned}$$

Solution

The augmented matrix is

$$\begin{pmatrix} 3 & -1 & 2 & 7 \\ 4 & 1 & 0 & 6 \\ 1 & 2 & -1 & 2 \end{pmatrix}$$

Exercises

1 Write the augmented matrix for each of the following systems of equations:

(a) $2x - y = 8$
$x + 2y = 14$

(b) $3x + 2y = 4$
$5x + 2y = 0$

(c) $x - 3y = 10$
$2x + y = -1$

(d) $x - y = 4$
$6x + 3y = 1.5$

(e) $3x + 4y = 50$
$-5x + 2y = -1$

2 Write the augmented matrix for each of the following systems of equations:

(a) $x + y + z = 4$
$3x - 2y + 4z = 25$
$2x + 3y + 2z = 6$

(b) $x - \frac{1}{2}y + 3z = 1$
$3x + 2y + z = -5$
$5x + 2z = -8$

(c) $7x - y - z = 3$
$3x + 2y + z = 4$
$5x + 2y + 3z = 20$

(d) $x - y + z = 2$
$5x + y + 2z = 7$
$4x - 2y - z = -1$

(e) $x - 2y + z = 0$
$-4x + y = 10$
$2y - 7z = 3$

Solutions to exercises

1 (a) $\begin{pmatrix} 2 & -1 & 8 \\ 1 & 2 & 14 \end{pmatrix}$ (b) $\begin{pmatrix} 3 & 2 & 4 \\ 5 & 2 & 0 \end{pmatrix}$

(c) $\begin{pmatrix} 1 & -3 & 10 \\ 2 & 1 & -1 \end{pmatrix}$ (d) $\begin{pmatrix} 1 & -1 & 4 \\ 6 & 3 & 1.5 \end{pmatrix}$

(e) $\begin{pmatrix} 3 & 4 & 50 \\ -5 & 2 & -1 \end{pmatrix}$

2 (a) $\begin{pmatrix} 1 & 1 & 1 & 4 \\ 3 & -2 & 4 & 25 \\ 2 & 3 & 2 & 6 \end{pmatrix}$

(b) $\begin{pmatrix} 1 & -\frac{1}{2} & 3 & 1 \\ 3 & 2 & 1 & -5 \\ 5 & 0 & 2 & -8 \end{pmatrix}$

(c) $\begin{pmatrix} 7 & -1 & -1 & 3 \\ 3 & 2 & 1 & 4 \\ 5 & 2 & 3 & 20 \end{pmatrix}$

(d) $\begin{pmatrix} 1 & -1 & 1 & 2 \\ 5 & 1 & 2 & 7 \\ 4 & -2 & -1 & -1 \end{pmatrix}$

(e) $\begin{pmatrix} 1 & -2 & 1 & 0 \\ -4 & 1 & 0 & 10 \\ 0 & 2 & -7 & 3 \end{pmatrix}$

3.3 Types of solutions to systems of linear equations

When a system of linear equations is solved, there are three possible outcomes.

Key point

A system of linear equations may have

1 a unique solution
2 an infinite number of solutions
3 no solution.

These three possible outcomes were studied in Block 4 of Chapter 7. In this section we revisit these three possibilities and note the form of the augmented matrix in each case.

Case 1

For example, consider the system

$$\begin{aligned} x + 3y &= 7 \\ 0x + y &= 2 \end{aligned}$$

This system has a unique solution, $x = 1$, $y = 2$. The corresponding augmented matrix is

$$\begin{pmatrix} 1 & 3 & 7 \\ 0 & 1 & 2 \end{pmatrix}$$

Case 2

Consider the system

$$\begin{aligned} x + 3y &= 7 \\ 0x + 0y &= 0 \end{aligned}$$

There is really only one equation here because the second states that $0 = 0$. There is an infinite number of solutions of the first equation. For example, $x = 7$ and $y = 0$; $x = 10$ and $y = -1$. In general, whatever the value of y, the equation is satisfied if $x = 7 - 3y$. We write this as follows: letting $y = t$, say, then $x = 7 - 3t$. This is true for any value of t we choose, so t is called a **free variable**. The corresponding augmented matrix is

$$\begin{pmatrix} 1 & 3 & 7 \\ 0 & 0 & 0 \end{pmatrix}$$

Case 3

Finally consider the system

$$\begin{aligned} x + 3y &= 7 \\ 0x + 0y &= 2 \end{aligned}$$

The second equation seems to state that $0 = 2$. This is nonsense. There are no solutions and the augmented matrix is

$$\begin{pmatrix} 1 & 3 & 7 \\ 0 & 0 & 2 \end{pmatrix}$$

It is worthwhile rereading Block 4 in Chapter 7 before continuing.

Example 3.2

A system has augmented matrix

$$\begin{pmatrix} 1 & -4 & 13 \\ 0 & 1 & -3 \end{pmatrix}$$

State the solution of the system.

Solution

Row 2 of the augmented matrix is equivalent to the equation

$$0x + 1y = -3$$

that is

$$y = -3$$

Row 1 of the matrix is equivalent to the equation

$$x - 4y = 13$$

Substituting in $y = -3$ we can obtain x.

$$\begin{aligned} x - 4(-3) &= 13 \\ x + 12 &= 13 \\ x &= 1 \end{aligned}$$

The system has a unique solution $x = 1$, $y = -3$.

In Example 3.2 the value of y was found and substituted back into the remaining equation so that x could be found. This technique is known as **back substitution**.

Example 3.3

A system has augmented matrix

$$\begin{pmatrix} 1 & 3 & -6 \\ 0 & 0 & 4 \end{pmatrix}$$

Solve the system.

Solution

Row 2 of the augmented matrix corresponds to the equation

$$0x + 0y = 4$$

This equation has no solution and so the system has no solution.

Example 3.4
A system has augmented matrix

$$\begin{pmatrix} 1 & 3 & 17 \\ 0 & 0 & 0 \end{pmatrix}$$

Solve the system.

Solution
Row 2 of the matrix is equivalent to the equation

$$0x + 0y = 0$$

This equation is satisfied for any value of x and y. Row 1 is equivalent to

$$x + 3y = 17$$

This has an infinite number of solutions: $x = 17 - 3t$, $y = t$.

Example 3.5
A system has augmented matrix

$$\begin{pmatrix} 1 & 2 & -3 & 11 \\ 0 & 1 & -4 & 7 \\ 0 & 0 & 1 & -1 \end{pmatrix}$$

Solve the system.

Solution
From row 3, the equation is

$$0x + 0y + 1z = -1$$

that is

$$z = -1$$

From row 2 the corresponding equation is

$y - 4z = 7$

Substituting in $z = -1$ the equation can be solved for y.

$$\begin{aligned} y - 4(-1) &= 7 \\ y + 4 &= 7 \\ y &= 3 \end{aligned}$$

The equation corresponding to row 1 is

$1x + 2y - 3z = 11$

By substituting in the values already obtained for y and z, we can determine x.

$x =$ 2

The system has a unique solution: $x = 2$, $y = 3$, $z = -1$.

Exercises

1 Solve the systems whose augmented matrices are

(a) $\begin{pmatrix} 1 & 2 & 18 \\ 0 & 1 & 7 \end{pmatrix}$

(b) $\begin{pmatrix} 1 & -2 & 10 \\ 0 & 0 & 0 \end{pmatrix}$

(c) $\begin{pmatrix} 1 & 5 & 6 \\ 0 & 1 & 0 \end{pmatrix}$

(d) $\begin{pmatrix} 1 & 5 & 6 \\ 0 & 0 & 1 \end{pmatrix}$

(e) $\begin{pmatrix} 1 & -2 & -1 & 5 \\ 0 & 1 & 3 & 1 \\ 0 & 0 & 1 & 1 \end{pmatrix}$

(f) $\begin{pmatrix} 1 & 3 & 4 & 2 \\ 0 & 1 & -2 & 6 \\ 0 & 0 & 0 & 0 \end{pmatrix}$

(g) $\begin{pmatrix} 1 & 3 & 6 & 25 \\ 0 & 0 & 1 & 3 \end{pmatrix}$

Solutions to exercises

1 (a) $x = 4, y = 7$ (b) $x = 2t + 10, y = t$
(c) $x = 6, y = 0$ (d) no solution
(e) $x = 2, y = -2, z = 1$
(f) $x = -10t - 16, y = 2t + 6, z = t$
(g) $x = 7 - 3t, y = t, z = 3$

3.4 Row-echelon form of an augmented matrix

We now introduce the **row-echelon form** of an augmented matrix. All the matrices in Section 3.3 are in row-echelon form. When a matrix is in row-echelon form it is then easy to determine the solution of the system.

Key point

For a matrix to be in row-echelon form:

1 Any rows that consist entirely of zeros are the last rows of the matrix.
2 For a row that is not all zeros, the first non-zero element is a one. We call this a **leading 1**.
3 As you move down the rows of the matrix, the leading 1s move progressively to the right.

Example 3.6

Determine which of the following matrices are in row-echelon form:

(a) $\begin{pmatrix} 1 & 2 & 5 \\ 0 & 1 & 7 \end{pmatrix}$

(b) $\begin{pmatrix} 0 & 1 & 3 & 6 \\ 1 & 4 & -1 & 3 \\ 0 & 0 & 0 & 0 \end{pmatrix}$

(c) $\begin{pmatrix} 0 & 0 & 1 & 6 \\ 0 & 0 & 0 & 0 \end{pmatrix}$

(d) $\begin{pmatrix} 1 & 6 & 9 & 4 \\ 0 & 1 & -3 & 6 \\ 0 & 0 & 1 & 5 \end{pmatrix}$

Solution

(a) This is in row-echelon form. Note that the leading 1 in row 2 is further to the right than the leading 1 in row 1.
(b) This is not in row-echelon form since the leading 1 in row 1 is further to the right than the leading 1 in row 2.
(c) This is in row-echelon form.
(d) This is in row-echelon form.

Exercises

1 Explain what is meant by row-echelon form.

2 Determine which of the following matrices are in row-echelon form:

(a) $\begin{pmatrix} 1 & 4 & 3 & 9 \\ 0 & 1 & -3 & 6 \end{pmatrix}$

(b) $\begin{pmatrix} 1 & -1 & 0 \\ 0 & 1 & 0 \end{pmatrix}$

(c) $\begin{pmatrix} 1 & 2 & 5 & 6 \\ 1 & 0 & 3 & 6 \\ 0 & 0 & 1 & 4 \end{pmatrix}$

(d) $\begin{pmatrix} 1 & -1 & 3 & 7 \\ 0 & 0 & 0 & 0 \\ 0 & 1 & 5 & 6 \end{pmatrix}$

(e) $\begin{pmatrix} 1 & 0 & 0 & 2 \\ 0 & 0 & 1 & -1 \\ 0 & 1 & 0 & 3 \end{pmatrix}$

Solutions to exercises

1 (a) row-echelon form
(b) row-echelon form
(c) not row-echelon form
(d) not row-echelon form
(e) not row-echelon form

3.5 Elementary row operations

Given any augmented matrix we would like to be able to transform it into row-echelon form as the solution of the system can then easily be found. The way we effect this transformation is by using **elementary row operations**.

We define three **elementary operations** that we can apply to the equations of the system.

Key point

The elementary operations that change a system but leave the solution unaltered are as follows:

1 Interchange the order of the equations.
2 Multiply or divide an equation by a non-zero constant.
3 Add, or subtract, a multiple of one equation to, or from, another equation.

When applied to a system, elementary row operations may change the equations but the solution to the resulting system remains unchanged. We apply elementary row operations to a simple system to illustrate this.

Consider the system of linear equations

$$2x + 5y = 12 \qquad (1)$$
$$x + y = 3 \qquad (2)$$

The system has solution $x = 1$, $y = 2$.

If we interchange the order of the equations, the system becomes

$$\begin{aligned} x + y &= 3 \\ 2x + 5y &= 12 \end{aligned}$$

The solution to the system is obviously still $x = 1$, $y = 2$.

To illustrate the second of the elementary operations consider multiplying equation (1) by, say, 6 and dividing equation (2) by, say, 5. The system is then

$$\begin{aligned} 12x + 30y &= 72 \\ \frac{x}{5} + \frac{y}{5} &= \frac{3}{5} \end{aligned}$$

You can check that this system still has solution $x = 1$, $y = 2$.

Finally, to illustrate the third elementary operation, we add 3 times equation (1) to equation (2). The system becomes

$$\begin{aligned} 2x + 5y &= 12 \\ 7x + 16y &= 39 \end{aligned}$$

Check that this resulting system has solution $x = 1$, $y = 2$.

Thus elementary operations may change the system, but they do not change the solutions of a system.

We have been writing a system in the form of an augmented matrix, where each row of the matrix corresponds to an equation of the system. Thus we can apply elementary operations to the rows of an augmented matrix rather than the equations of the system. When elementary operations are applied to the rows of a matrix they are called **elementary row operations**.

Example 3.7

(a) Write down the augmented matrix of the system

$$\begin{aligned} 2x + 5y &= 12 \\ x + y &= 3 \end{aligned}$$

(b) Carry out the following elementary row operations, each time applying the operation to the most recent augmented matrix:
   (i) interchange the rows
   (ii) subtract 2 × row 1 from row 2
   (iii) divide row 2 by 3.

(c) Hence solve the system.

Solution

(a) The augmented matrix is

$$\begin{pmatrix} 2 & 5 & 12 \\ 1 & 1 & 3 \end{pmatrix}$$

(b) (i) The rows are interchanged. The augmented matrix becomes

$$\begin{pmatrix} 1 & 1 & 3 \\ 2 & 5 & 12 \end{pmatrix}$$

(ii) We now use the augmented matrix in (b) (i). Subtracting 2 × row 1 from row 2 results in

$$\begin{pmatrix} 1 & 1 & 3 \\ 0 & 3 & 6 \end{pmatrix}$$

(iii) We now use the augmented matrix in (b) (ii). Dividing row 2 by 3 gives

$$\begin{pmatrix} 1 & 1 & 3 \\ 0 & 1 & 2 \end{pmatrix}$$

(c) Note that the matrix is now in row-echelon form. From row 2 we see that $y = 2$. From row 1 we have

$$1x + 1y = 3$$

Substituting $y = 2$ into this equation we obtain $x = 1$. Thus the solution to the original system is $x = 1$, $y = 2$.

The method of solution of Example 3.7 is thus

1 Write down the augmented matrix.
2 Apply elementary row operations to obtain row-echelon form.
3 Solve the system.

This method is known as **Gaussian elimination**.

Example 3.8

Use Gaussian elimination to solve

$$3x - y = 1$$
$$2x + 3y = 19$$

Solution

The augmented matrix is

$$\begin{pmatrix} 3 & -1 & 1 \\ 2 & 3 & 19 \end{pmatrix}$$

We now apply a series of elementary row operations to transform the augmented matrix into row-echelon form.

Subtract row 2 from row 1.

$$\begin{pmatrix} 1 & -4 & -18 \\ 2 & 3 & 19 \end{pmatrix}$$

Subtract 2 × row 1 from row 2

$$\begin{pmatrix} 1 & -4 & -18 \\ 0 & 11 & 55 \end{pmatrix}$$

Divide row 2 by 11.

$$\begin{pmatrix} 1 & -4 & -18 \\ 0 & 1 & 5 \end{pmatrix}$$

The matrix is now in row-echelon form. From row 2 we see that $y = 5$. Row 1 corresponds to the equation

$$1x - 4y = -18$$

Substituting $y = 5$ into this equation allows x to be found.

$$2$$

The solution to the system is $x = 2$, $y = 5$.

Example 3.9

Use Gaussian elimination to solve

$$2x + y + 2z = 8$$
$$x - 3y + 3z = -4$$
$$4x + 2y - z = 1$$

Solution

The augmented matrix is

$$\begin{pmatrix} 2 & 1 & 2 & 8 \\ 1 & -3 & 3 & -4 \\ 4 & 2 & -1 & 1 \end{pmatrix}$$

We apply a series of elementary row operations to transform the matrix into row-echelon form.

Interchange row 1 and row 2.

$$\begin{pmatrix} 1 & -3 & 3 & -4 \\ 2 & 1 & 2 & 8 \\ 4 & 2 & -1 & 1 \end{pmatrix}$$

Subtract 2 × row 1 from row 2, subtract 4 × row 1 from row 3. This produces

$$\begin{pmatrix} 1 & -3 & 3 & -4 \\ 0 & 7 & -4 & 16 \\ 0 & 14 & -13 & 17 \end{pmatrix}$$

Subtract 2 × row 2 from row 3 to get

$$\begin{pmatrix} 1 & -3 & 3 & -4 \\ 0 & 7 & -4 & 16 \\ 0 & 0 & -5 & -15 \end{pmatrix}$$

Divide row 2 by 7, divide row 3 by −5.

$$\begin{pmatrix} 1 & -3 & 3 & -4 \\ 0 & 1 & -\frac{4}{7} & \frac{16}{7} \\ 0 & 0 & 1 & 3 \end{pmatrix}$$

The matrix is now in row-echelon form. From row 3 we see that

$z =$ 3

Row 2 is equivalent to the equation

$$1y - \frac{4}{7}z = \frac{16}{7}$$

Substituting $z = 3$ and solving for y yields

$y =$ 4

Row 1 is equivalent to the equation

$$1x - 3y + 3z = -4$$

Substituting in the values for y and z and solving for x yields

$x =$ −1

The solution to the system is $x = -1, y = 4, z = 3$.

Exercises

1 Use Gaussian elimination to solve the systems of linear equations given in question 1 of Section 3.2.

2 Use Gaussian elimination to solve the systems of linear equations given in question 2 of Section 3.2.

3 Use Gaussian elimination to solve

$$\begin{aligned} 2x + y &= 8 \\ 3x + 1.5y &= 12 \end{aligned}$$

4 Use Gaussian elimination to solve

$$\begin{aligned} 6x - 8y &= 10 \\ -3x + 4y &= 4 \end{aligned}$$

5 Use Gaussian elimination to solve

$$\begin{aligned} x + 2y + z &= 6 \\ 3x - 4y + 2z &= 1 \\ 7x - 6y + 5z &= 8 \end{aligned}$$

Solutions to exercises

1 (a) $x = 6, y = 4$ (b) $x = -2, y = 5$
(c) $x = 1, y = -3$ (d) $x = 1.5, y = -2.5$
(e) $x = 4, y = 9.5$

2 (a) $x = 3, y = -2, z = 3$
(b) $x = -2, y = 0, z = 1$
(c) $x = 1, y = -3, z = 7$
(d) $x = \frac{1}{2}, y = \frac{1}{2}, z = 2$
(e) $x = -3, y = -2, z = -1$

3 $x = 4 - \dfrac{t}{2}, y = t$

4 no solution

5 $x = \dfrac{13 - 4t}{5}, y = \dfrac{17 - t}{10}, z = t$

End of block exercises

1 State the augmented matrix of each of the following systems of equations:
(a) $3\alpha - \beta = 4$
$2\beta + 3\gamma = -7$
$\alpha - \beta + \gamma = 11$
(b) $a + b = 3$
$2a - b = 0$
$5a + 3b = 11$

2 Determine which of the following matrices are in echelon form:

(a) $\begin{pmatrix} 1 & 1 & 1 & 0 & 1 \\ 0 & 0 & 0 & 1 & 3 \\ 0 & 0 & 0 & 0 & 0 \end{pmatrix}$

(b) $\begin{pmatrix} 1 & 0 & 1 & 0 & 3 \\ 0 & 1 & 4 & 3 & 6 \\ 0 & 0 & 0 & 0 & 0 \end{pmatrix}$

(c) $\begin{pmatrix} 1 & 3 & 1 & 0 & -4 \\ 0 & 0 & 1 & 0 & 2 \\ 0 & 0 & 0 & 1 & -1 \\ 0 & 0 & 0 & 0 & 0 \end{pmatrix}$

3 Use Gaussian elimination to solve each of the following systems of equations:
(a) $x - 2y = -15$
$y + 2x = 15$
(b) $3x + 4y = 14$
$-2x + y = -24$

4 Use Gaussian elimination to solve:

$$\begin{aligned} 2x - y + z &= -2 \\ x + 2y + 3z &= -1 \\ 2x + 2y - z &= 8 \end{aligned}$$

5 Use Gaussian elimination to solve

$$\begin{aligned} 2x + y &= 10 \\ x + 0.5y &= 5 \end{aligned}$$

6 Use Gaussian elimination to solve

$$\begin{aligned} 3x + y &= -3 \\ 4x + 17y &= -4 \end{aligned}$$

7 Use Gaussian elimination to solve

$$\begin{aligned} 2x - 3y &= 12 \\ 6x - 9y &= 24 \end{aligned}$$

8 Use Gaussian elimination to solve

$$\begin{aligned} 2x + y - z &= -3 \\ 3x + 2y + z &= 6 \\ x + y + 2z &= 8 \end{aligned}$$

9 Use Gaussian elimination to solve

$$\begin{aligned} 2x + y - z &= -3 \\ 3x + 2y + z &= 6 \\ x + y + 2z &= 9 \end{aligned}$$

Solutions to exercises

1 (a) $\begin{pmatrix} 3 & -1 & 0 & 4 \\ 0 & 2 & 3 & -7 \\ 1 & -1 & 1 & 11 \end{pmatrix}$

(b) $\begin{pmatrix} 1 & 1 & 3 \\ 2 & -1 & 0 \\ 5 & 3 & 11 \end{pmatrix}$

2 (a) echelon form (b) echelon form (c) echelon form

3 (a) $x = 3, y = 9$ (b) $x = 10, y = -4$

4 $x = 1, y = 2, z = -2$

5 $x = 5 - \frac{t}{2}, y = t$

6 $x = -1, y = 0$

7 no solution

8 no solution

9 $x = 3t - 12, y = 21 - 5t, z = t$

BLOCK 4 Eigenvalues and eigenvectors

4.1 Introduction

In this block we consider the meaning and calculation of eigenvalues and eigenvectors. Although such calculations may at first sight appear abstract, eigenvalues have important applications in the area of vibration analysis. Familiarity with the evaluation of determinants and the solution of simultaneous equations by Gaussian elimination is essential.

4.2 Trivial and non-trivial solutions

Before we can discuss eigenvalues some preliminary results about determinants are required. These are now developed.

Consider the simultaneous equations

$$\begin{aligned} ax + by &= 0 \\ cx + dy &= 0 \end{aligned}$$

where a, b, c and d are constants. Clearly $x = 0$, $y = 0$ is a solution of these equations. We call this the **trivial solution**. Let us explore the relationship that must exist between a, b, c and d so that the system has **non-trivial solutions**. These are solutions other than $x = 0$, $y = 0$. For definiteness we consider two cases with values of a, b, c and d given.

Case 1:

$$\begin{aligned} 5x - 3y &= 0 \\ 10x - 2y &= 0 \end{aligned}$$

Case 2:

$$\begin{aligned} 5x - 3y &= 0 \\ 10x - 6y &= 0 \end{aligned}$$

Solving Case 1, for example, by Gaussian elimination leads to $x = 0$, $y = 0$ as the only possible solution. Thus the only solution is the trivial solution.

Looking at Case 2 we see that the second equation is simply twice the first equation. This means that the second equation can be deduced from the first equation. In essence, there is only one equation to work with. So we consider the solution of

$$5x - 3y = 0$$

Rearranging we have

$$y = \frac{5}{3}x$$

As long as the y value is $\frac{5}{3}$ of the x value the equation is satisfied. Hence, for example, $x = 1$, $y = \frac{5}{3}$; $x = 2$, $y = \frac{10}{3}$; $x = -5$, $y = -\frac{25}{3}$ are all solutions. In general, the solutions have the form $x = t$, $y = \frac{5}{3}t$ for any value of t. Thus there are an infinite number of non-trivial solutions.

We now return to the system

$$\begin{aligned} ax + by &= 0 \\ cx + dy &= 0 \end{aligned}$$

As seen, depending upon the values of a, b, c and d the system has either only the trivial solution or an infinity of non-trivial solutions. For there to be an infinity of solutions the second equation must be a multiple of the first. When this is the case then c is a multiple of a and d is the same multiple of b: that is

$$c = \alpha a,\ d = \alpha b \text{ for some value of } \alpha$$

In this case, consider the quantity $ad - bc$:

$$\begin{aligned} ad - bc &= a(\alpha b) - b(\alpha a) \\ &= \alpha ab - \alpha ab \\ &= 0 \end{aligned}$$

Hence the condition for non-trivial solutions to exist is that $ad - bc = 0$. Writing the system in matrix form gives

$$\begin{pmatrix} a & b \\ c & d \end{pmatrix}\begin{pmatrix} x \\ y \end{pmatrix} = \begin{pmatrix} 0 \\ 0 \end{pmatrix}$$

or

$$AX = \mathbf{0}$$

where

$$A = \begin{pmatrix} a & b \\ c & d \end{pmatrix},\quad X = \begin{pmatrix} x \\ y \end{pmatrix} \quad \text{and} \quad \mathbf{0} = \begin{pmatrix} 0 \\ 0 \end{pmatrix}$$

We note that $ad - bc$ is the determinant of A, so non-trivial solutions exist when the determinant of A is zero, that is when A is a singular matrix.

In summary

Key points

Consider the system

$$AX = \mathbf{0}$$

- If $|A| = 0$ the system has non-trivial solutions.
- If $|A| \neq 0$ the system has only the trivial solution.

This key point holds true for a square matrix of any size.

Example 4.1

Decide which system has non-trivial solutions.

(a) $4x - y = 0$
$2x - 3y = 0$

(b) $x + 2y = 0$
$3x + 6y = 0$

Solution

(a) We write the system as

$$\begin{pmatrix} 4 & -1 \\ 2 & -3 \end{pmatrix}\begin{pmatrix} x \\ y \end{pmatrix} = \begin{pmatrix} 0 \\ 0 \end{pmatrix}$$

Let

$$A = \begin{pmatrix} 4 & -1 \\ 2 & -3 \end{pmatrix}$$

Then

$$\det(A) = 4(-3) - (-1)(2) = -10$$

Since the determinant of A is non-zero the system has only the trivial solution.

(b) We write the system as

$$\begin{pmatrix} 1 & 2 \\ 3 & 6 \end{pmatrix}\begin{pmatrix} x \\ y \end{pmatrix} = \begin{pmatrix} 0 \\ 0 \end{pmatrix}$$

Then

$$A = \begin{pmatrix} 1 & 2 \\ 3 & 6 \end{pmatrix}$$

and $|A| = 6 - 6 = 0$. Since the determinant of A is zero the system has non-trivial solutions.

Example 4.2

Determine which system has non-trivial solutions.

(a) $3x - y + z = 0$
$x + 2y + 2z = 0$
$4x + y + 3z = 0$

(b) $3x - y + z = 0$
$x + 2y + 2z = 0$
$5x - y + 3z = 0$

Solution

(a) We have

$$AX = \mathbf{0}$$

where

$$A = \begin{pmatrix} 3 & -1 & 1 \\ 1 & 2 & 2 \\ 4 & 1 & 3 \end{pmatrix} \quad \text{and} \quad X = \begin{pmatrix} x \\ y \\ z \end{pmatrix}$$

Evaluate the determinant of A:

$|A| = 0$

Since $|A| = 0$ the system has non-trivial solutions.

(b) Here

$$A = \begin{pmatrix} 3 & -1 & 1 \\ 1 & 2 & 2 \\ 5 & -1 & 3 \end{pmatrix}$$

Evaluate the determinant of A:

$|A| = 6$

Since $|A| \neq 0$ the system has only the trivial solution.

Exercises

1. Explain what is meant by the trivial solution of a system of linear equations and what is meant by a non-trivial solution.

2. Determine which of the following systems have non-trivial solutions:

(a) $x - 2y = 0$
$3x - 6y = 0$

(b) $3x + y = 0$
$9x + 2y = 0$

(c) $4x - 3y = 0$
$-4x + 3y = 0$

(d) $6x - 2y = 0$
$2x - \frac{2}{3}y = 0$

(e) $y = 2x$
$x = 3y$

3. Determine which of the following systems have non-trivial solutions:

(a) $x + 2y - z = 0$
$3x + y + 2z = 0$
$x + y = 0$

(b) $2x - 3y - 2z = 0$
$3x + y - 3z = 0$
$x - 7y - z = 0$

(c) $x + 2y + 3z = 0$
$4x - 3y - z = 0$
$6x + y + 3z = 0$

(d) $x + 3z = 0$
$x - y = 0$
$y + 2z = 0$

Solutions to exercises

2. (a), (c) and (d) have non-trivial solutions.

3. (a) and (b) have non-trivial solutions.

4.3 Eigenvalues

We shall explain the meaning of the term eigenvalue by means of an example.
Consider the system

$$\begin{aligned} 2x + y &= \lambda x \\ 3x + 4y &= \lambda y \end{aligned}$$

where λ is some unknown constant. Clearly these equations have the trivial solution $x = 0$, $y = 0$. The equations may be written in matrix form as

$$\begin{pmatrix} 2 & 1 \\ 3 & 4 \end{pmatrix}\begin{pmatrix} x \\ y \end{pmatrix} = \lambda\begin{pmatrix} x \\ y \end{pmatrix}$$

or, using the usual notation,

$$AX = \lambda X$$

We now seek values of λ so that the system has non-trivial solutions. Although it is tempting to write $(A - \lambda)X = \mathbf{0}$ this would be incorrect since $A - \lambda$ is not defined; A is a matrix and λ is constant. Hence to progress we need to write the right-hand side in a slightly different way. To help us do this we use the 2×2 identity matrix, I. Now $\lambda\begin{pmatrix} x \\ y \end{pmatrix}$ may be expressed as

$$\lambda\begin{pmatrix} 1 & 0 \\ 0 & 1 \end{pmatrix}\begin{pmatrix} x \\ y \end{pmatrix}$$

since multiplying $\begin{pmatrix} x \\ y \end{pmatrix}$ by the identity matrix leaves it unaltered. So λX may be written as λIX. Hence we have

$$AX = \lambda IX$$

which can be written as

$$\begin{aligned} AX - \lambda IX &= \mathbf{0} \\ (A - \lambda I)X &= \mathbf{0} \end{aligned}$$

Note that the expression $(A - \lambda I)$ is defined since both A and λI are square matrices of the same size.

We have seen in Section 4.2 that for $AX = \mathbf{0}$ to have non-trivial solutions then $|A| = 0$. Hence for

$$(A - \lambda I)\,X = \mathbf{0}$$

to have non-trivial solutions then

$$|A - \lambda I| = 0$$

Now

$$A - \lambda I = \begin{pmatrix} 2 & 1 \\ 3 & 4 \end{pmatrix} - \lambda \begin{pmatrix} 1 & 0 \\ 0 & 1 \end{pmatrix}$$
$$= \begin{pmatrix} 2 & 1 \\ 3 & 4 \end{pmatrix} - \begin{pmatrix} \lambda & 0 \\ 0 & \lambda \end{pmatrix}$$
$$= \begin{pmatrix} 2 - \lambda & 1 \\ 3 & 4 - \lambda \end{pmatrix}$$

So the condition $|A - \lambda I| = 0$ gives

$$\begin{vmatrix} 2 - \lambda & 1 \\ 3 & 4 - \lambda \end{vmatrix} = 0$$

It follows that

$$(2 - \lambda)(4 - \lambda) - 3 = 0$$
$$\lambda^2 - 6\lambda + 5 = 0$$
$$(\lambda - 1)(\lambda - 5) = 0$$

so that

$$\lambda = 1 \text{ or } 5$$

These are the values of λ that cause the system $AX = \lambda X$ to have non-trivial solutions. They are called **eigenvalues**.

The equation

$$|A - \lambda I| = 0$$

which when written out explicitly is the quadratic equation in λ, is called the **characteristic equation**.

Example 4.3

Find values of λ for which

$$x + 4y = \lambda x$$
$$2x + 3y = \lambda y$$

has non-trivial solutions.

Solution

We write the system as

$$AX = \lambda X$$

where

$$A = \begin{pmatrix} 1 & 4 \\ 2 & 3 \end{pmatrix}, \quad X = \begin{pmatrix} x \\ y \end{pmatrix}$$

To have non-trivial solutions we require

$$|A - \lambda I| = 0$$

Now

$$A - \lambda I = \begin{pmatrix} 1 & 4 \\ 2 & 3 \end{pmatrix} - \lambda \begin{pmatrix} 1 & 0 \\ 0 & 1 \end{pmatrix}$$
$$= \begin{pmatrix} 1 & 4 \\ 2 & 3 \end{pmatrix} - \begin{pmatrix} \lambda & 0 \\ 0 & \lambda \end{pmatrix}$$
$$= \begin{pmatrix} 1 - \lambda & 4 \\ 2 & 3 - \lambda \end{pmatrix}$$

Hence

$$|A - \lambda I| = (1 - \lambda)(3 - \lambda) - 8$$
$$= \lambda^2 - 4\lambda - 5$$

To have non-trivial solutions we require

$$\lambda^2 - 4\lambda - 5 = 0$$
$$(\lambda + 1)(\lambda - 5) = 0$$

which yields

$$\lambda = -1 \quad \text{or} \quad \lambda = 5$$

The given system has non-trivial solutions when $\lambda = -1$ and $\lambda = 5$. These are the eigenvalues.

If A is a 2×2 matrix, the characteristic equation will be a polynomial of degree 2, that is a quadratic equation in λ, leading to two eigenvalues. If A is a 3×3 matrix, the characteristic equation will be a polynomial of degree 3, that is a cubic, leading to three eigenvalues. In general an $n \times n$ matrix gives rise to a characteristic equation of degree n and hence to n eigenvalues.

Key point

The **characteristic equation** of a square matrix A is given by

$$|A - \lambda I| = 0$$

Solutions of this equation are the **eigenvalues** of A. These are the values of λ for which $AX = \lambda X$ has non-trivial solutions.

Example 4.4

Determine the characteristic equation and eigenvalues, λ, in the system

$$\begin{pmatrix} 3 & 1 \\ -1 & 5 \end{pmatrix}\begin{pmatrix} x \\ y \end{pmatrix} = \lambda \begin{pmatrix} x \\ y \end{pmatrix}$$

Solution

In this example the equations have been written in matrix form with

$$A = \begin{pmatrix} 3 & 1 \\ -1 & 5 \end{pmatrix}$$

The characteristic equation is given by

$$|A - \lambda I| = 0$$

$$\left|\begin{pmatrix} 3 & 1 \\ -1 & 5 \end{pmatrix} - \lambda \begin{pmatrix} 1 & 0 \\ 0 & 1 \end{pmatrix}\right| = 0$$

$$\begin{vmatrix} 3 - \lambda & 1 \\ -1 & 5 - \lambda \end{vmatrix} = 0$$

$$(3 - \lambda)(5 - \lambda) + 1 = 0$$

$$\lambda^2 - 8\lambda + 16 = 0$$

The characteristic equation is $\lambda^2 - 8\lambda + 16 = 0$. Solving the characteristic equation gives

$$\lambda^2 - 8\lambda + 16 = 0$$
$$(\lambda - 4)(\lambda - 4) = 0$$
$$\lambda = 4 \text{ (twice)}$$

There is one repeated eigenvalue: $\lambda = 4$.

Example 4.5
Find the eigenvalues λ in the system

$$\begin{pmatrix} 4 & 1 \\ 3 & 2 \end{pmatrix}\begin{pmatrix} x \\ y \end{pmatrix} = \lambda \begin{pmatrix} x \\ y \end{pmatrix}$$

Solution
We form the characteristic equation, $|A - \lambda I| = 0$. Now

$A - \lambda I =$ $\begin{pmatrix} 4 - \lambda & 1 \\ 3 & 2 - \lambda \end{pmatrix}$

Then

$|A - \lambda I| =$ $\lambda^2 - 6\lambda + 5$

Solving the characteristic equation $\lambda^2 - 6\lambda + 5 = 0$ gives

$\lambda =$ 1, 5

There are two eigenvalues, $\lambda = 1$ and $\lambda = 5$.

The process of finding the characteristic equation and eigenvalues of a matrix has been illustrated using 2×2 matrices. This same process can be applied to a square matrix of any size.

Example 4.6
Find (a) the characteristic equation and (b) the eigenvalues of A where

$$A = \begin{pmatrix} 1 & 2 & 0 \\ -1 & -1 & 1 \\ 3 & 2 & -2 \end{pmatrix}$$

Solution

(a) We need to calculate $|A - \lambda I|$. Now

$$A - \lambda I = \begin{pmatrix} 1-\lambda & 2 & 0 \\ -1 & -1-\lambda & 1 \\ 3 & 2 & -2-\lambda \end{pmatrix}$$

and

$$\begin{vmatrix} 1-\lambda & 2 & 0 \\ -1 & -1-\lambda & 1 \\ 3 & 2 & -2-\lambda \end{vmatrix} = (1-\lambda)\begin{vmatrix} -1-\lambda & 1 \\ 2 & -2-\lambda \end{vmatrix} - 2\begin{vmatrix} -1 & 1 \\ 3 & -2-\lambda \end{vmatrix}$$

$$= (1-\lambda)[(-1-\lambda)(-2-\lambda) - 2] - 2[-1(-2-\lambda) - 3]$$

Upon simplification this reduces to $-\lambda^3 - 2\lambda^2 + \lambda + 2$. Hence

$$|A - \lambda I| = 0$$

yields

$$-\lambda^3 - 2\lambda^2 + \lambda + 2 = 0$$

which may be written as

$$\lambda^3 + 2\lambda^2 - \lambda - 2 = 0$$

The characteristic equation is $\lambda^3 + 2\lambda^2 - \lambda - 2 = 0$.

(b) We solve the characteristic equation to find the eigenvalues. This cubic can be factorised using the technique described in Chapter 7, Block 3, to give $(\lambda + 2)(\lambda + 1)(\lambda - 1)$ and so the characteristic equation may be written as

$$(\lambda + 2)(\lambda + 1)(\lambda - 1) = 0$$

from which

$$\lambda = -2, -1, 1$$

The eigenvalues are $\lambda = -2, -1, 1$.

Exercises

1 Calculate (i) the characteristic equation and (ii) the eigenvalues of the system $AX = \lambda X$ where A is given by

(a) $\begin{pmatrix} 5 & 6 \\ 2 & 1 \end{pmatrix}$ (b) $\begin{pmatrix} -3 & 4 \\ -4 & 5 \end{pmatrix}$

(c) $\begin{pmatrix} 7 & -2 \\ 1 & 4 \end{pmatrix}$ (d) $\begin{pmatrix} 1 & 3 \\ 4 & -1 \end{pmatrix}$

2 Calculate (i) the characteristic equation and (ii) the eigenvalues of the following 3×3 matrices:

(a) $\begin{pmatrix} 1 & -1 & 2 \\ -3 & -2 & 3 \\ 2 & -1 & 1 \end{pmatrix}$

(b) $\begin{pmatrix} 1 & 0 & -1 \\ 3 & 1 & 4 \\ 0 & 2 & 2 \end{pmatrix}$

(c) $\begin{pmatrix} 2 & 1 & 2 \\ -1 & 1 & -1 \\ 8 & 3 & 0 \end{pmatrix}$

(d) $\begin{pmatrix} -2 & 6 & 2 \\ 0 & 3 & 4 \\ 3 & -3 & 5 \end{pmatrix}$

(e) $\begin{pmatrix} 3 & -2 & 1 \\ 2 & -4 & 3 \\ 16 & -4 & 1 \end{pmatrix}$

Solutions to exercises

1 (a) (i) $\lambda^2 - 6\lambda - 7 = 0$ (ii) $\lambda = -1, 7$
(b) (i) $\lambda^2 - 2\lambda + 1 = 0$ (ii) $\lambda = 1$ (twice)
(c) (i) $\lambda^2 - 11\lambda + 30 = 0$ (ii) $\lambda = 5, 6$
(d) (i) $\lambda^2 - 13 = 0$ (ii) $\lambda = -\sqrt{13}, \sqrt{13}$

2 (a) (i) $-\lambda^3 + 7\lambda + 6 = 0$
(ii) $\lambda = -2, -1, 3$
(b) (i) $\lambda^3 - 4\lambda^2 - 3\lambda + 12 = 0$
(ii) $\lambda = -\sqrt{3}, \sqrt{3}, 4$
(c) (i) $\lambda^3 - 3\lambda^2 - 10\lambda + 24 = 0$
(ii) $\lambda = -3, 2, 4$
(d) (i) $\lambda^3 - 6\lambda^2 + 5\lambda = 0$ (ii) $\lambda = 0, 1, 5$
(e) (i) $\lambda^3 - 13\lambda + 12 = 0$ (ii) $\lambda = -4, 1, 3$

4.4 Eigenvectors

We have studied the system

$$AX = \lambda X \tag{1}$$

and determined the values of λ for which non-trivial solutions exist. These values of λ are called eigenvalues of the system or, more simply, eigenvalues of A. For each eigenvalue there is a non-trivial solution of the system. This solution is called an **eigenvector**.

Example 4.7

Find the eigenvectors of

$$AX = \lambda X$$

where

$$A = \begin{pmatrix} 4 & 1 \\ 3 & 2 \end{pmatrix} \quad \text{and} \quad X = \begin{pmatrix} x \\ y \end{pmatrix}$$

Solution

We seek solutions of $AX = \lambda X$ that may be written as

$$(A - \lambda I)X = \mathbf{0}$$

The eigenvalues were found in Example 4.5 to be $\lambda = 1, 5$.

First we consider $\lambda = 1$. The system equation becomes

$$(A - \lambda I)X = \mathbf{0}$$
$$(A - I)X = \mathbf{0}$$
$$\left[\begin{pmatrix} 4 & 1 \\ 3 & 2 \end{pmatrix} - \begin{pmatrix} 1 & 0 \\ 0 & 1 \end{pmatrix}\right]\begin{pmatrix} x \\ y \end{pmatrix} = \begin{pmatrix} 0 \\ 0 \end{pmatrix}$$
$$\begin{pmatrix} 3 & 1 \\ 3 & 1 \end{pmatrix}\begin{pmatrix} x \\ y \end{pmatrix} = \begin{pmatrix} 0 \\ 0 \end{pmatrix}$$

Written as individual equations we have

$$3x + y = 0$$
$$3x + y = 0$$

Clearly there is only one equation, which is repeated. As long as $y = -3x$ the equation is satisfied. Thus there are an infinite number of solutions such as $x = 1$, $y = -3$; $x = -5$, $y = 15$, and so on. Generally we write

$$x = t,\ y = -3t$$

for any number t. Thus the eigenvector corresponding to $\lambda = 1$ is

$$\begin{aligned} X &= \begin{pmatrix} x \\ y \end{pmatrix} \\ &= \begin{pmatrix} t \\ -3t \end{pmatrix} \\ &= t\begin{pmatrix} 1 \\ -3 \end{pmatrix} \end{aligned}$$

Note that the eigenvector has been determined to within an arbitrary scalar, t. Thus there is an infinity of solutions corresponding to $\lambda = 1$.

We now consider $\lambda = 5$ and seek solutions of the system equation

$$(A - \lambda I)X = \mathbf{0}$$
$$\left[\begin{pmatrix} 4 & 1 \\ 3 & 2 \end{pmatrix} - 5\begin{pmatrix} 1 & 0 \\ 0 & 1 \end{pmatrix}\right]\begin{pmatrix} x \\ y \end{pmatrix} = \begin{pmatrix} 0 \\ 0 \end{pmatrix}$$
$$\begin{pmatrix} -1 & 1 \\ 3 & -3 \end{pmatrix}\begin{pmatrix} x \\ y \end{pmatrix} = \begin{pmatrix} 0 \\ 0 \end{pmatrix}$$

Written as individual equations we have

$$-x + y = 0$$
$$3x - 3y = 0$$

We note that the second equation is simply a multiple of the first so that in essence there is only one equation. Solving $-x + y = 0$ gives $y = x$ for any x. So we write $x = t$, $y = t$. Hence the eigenvector corresponding to $\lambda = 5$ is

$$X = t\begin{pmatrix} 1 \\ 1 \end{pmatrix}$$

Again the eigenvector has been determined to within an arbitrary scaling constant.

Sometimes the arbitrary scaling constants are not written down; it is understood that they are there. In such a case we say the eigenvectors of the system are

$$X = \begin{pmatrix} 1 \\ -3 \end{pmatrix} \quad \text{and} \quad X = \begin{pmatrix} 1 \\ 1 \end{pmatrix}$$

Example 4.8

Determine the eigenvectors of

$$\begin{pmatrix} 3 & 1 \\ -1 & 5 \end{pmatrix}\begin{pmatrix} x \\ y \end{pmatrix} = \lambda\begin{pmatrix} x \\ y \end{pmatrix}$$

Solution

In Example 4.4 we found that there is only one eigenvalue, $\lambda = 4$. We seek the solution of $(A - \lambda I)X = 0$. Write down the equations that result from letting $\lambda = 4$, firstly in matrix form and then as a single equation.

$$\begin{pmatrix} -1 & 1 \\ -1 & 1 \end{pmatrix}\begin{pmatrix} x \\ y \end{pmatrix} = \begin{pmatrix} 0 \\ 0 \end{pmatrix}$$

$$-x + y = 0$$

Find the infinite number of solutions.

$$x = t, y = t$$

Hence there is one eigenvector:

$$X = t\begin{pmatrix} 1 \\ 1 \end{pmatrix}$$

The concept of eigenvectors is easily extended to matrices of higher order.

Example 4.9

Determine the eigenvectors of

$$\begin{pmatrix} 1 & 2 & 0 \\ -1 & -1 & 1 \\ 3 & 2 & -2 \end{pmatrix}\begin{pmatrix} x \\ y \\ z \end{pmatrix} = \lambda\begin{pmatrix} x \\ y \\ z \end{pmatrix}$$

The eigenvalues were found in Example 4.6.

Solution

From Example 4.6 the eigenvalues are $\lambda = -2, -1, 1$. We consider each eigenvalue in turn.

$\underline{\lambda = -2}$

$$\begin{pmatrix} 1 & 2 & 0 \\ -1 & -1 & 1 \\ 3 & 2 & -2 \end{pmatrix}\begin{pmatrix} x \\ y \\ z \end{pmatrix} = -2\begin{pmatrix} x \\ y \\ z \end{pmatrix}$$

$$\left[\begin{pmatrix} 1 & 2 & 0 \\ -1 & -1 & 1 \\ 3 & 2 & -2 \end{pmatrix} + 2\begin{pmatrix} 1 & 0 & 0 \\ 0 & 1 & 0 \\ 0 & 0 & 1 \end{pmatrix}\right]\begin{pmatrix} x \\ y \\ z \end{pmatrix} = \begin{pmatrix} 0 \\ 0 \\ 0 \end{pmatrix}$$

$$\begin{pmatrix} 3 & 2 & 0 \\ -1 & 1 & 1 \\ 3 & 2 & 0 \end{pmatrix}\begin{pmatrix} x \\ y \\ z \end{pmatrix} = \begin{pmatrix} 0 \\ 0 \\ 0 \end{pmatrix}$$

We note that the first and last rows are identical. So we have

$$3x + 2y = 0$$
$$-x + y + z = 0$$

Solving these equations gives

$$x = t, \quad y = -\tfrac{3}{2}t, \quad z = \tfrac{5}{2}t$$

Hence the corresponding eigenvector is

$$X = t\begin{pmatrix} 1 \\ -\dfrac{3}{2} \\ \dfrac{5}{2} \end{pmatrix}$$

$\underline{\lambda = -1}$

We have

$$\left[\begin{pmatrix} 1 & 2 & 0 \\ -1 & -1 & 1 \\ 3 & 2 & -2 \end{pmatrix} + \begin{pmatrix} 1 & 0 & 0 \\ 0 & 1 & 0 \\ 0 & 0 & 1 \end{pmatrix}\right]\begin{pmatrix} x \\ y \\ z \end{pmatrix} = \begin{pmatrix} 0 \\ 0 \\ 0 \end{pmatrix}$$

$$\begin{pmatrix} 2 & 2 & 0 \\ -1 & 0 & 1 \\ 3 & 2 & -1 \end{pmatrix}\begin{pmatrix} x \\ y \\ z \end{pmatrix} = \begin{pmatrix} 0 \\ 0 \\ 0 \end{pmatrix}$$

Thus we have

$$2x + 2y = 0$$
$$-x + z = 0$$
$$3x + 2y - z = 0$$

We note that the third equation can be derived from the first two equations: equation (1) minus equation (2) produces equation (3). If you can't spot this, the equations should be solved by Gaussian elimination. In effect we have only two equations:

$$2x + 2y = 0$$
$$-x + z = 0$$

Solving these gives $x = t, y = -t, z = t$. The eigenvector is

$$X = t\begin{pmatrix} 1 \\ -1 \\ 1 \end{pmatrix}$$

$\underline{\lambda = 1}$

We have

$$\left[\begin{pmatrix} 1 & 2 & 0 \\ -1 & -1 & 1 \\ 3 & 2 & -2 \end{pmatrix} - \begin{pmatrix} 1 & 0 & 0 \\ 0 & 1 & 0 \\ 0 & 0 & 1 \end{pmatrix}\right]\begin{pmatrix} x \\ y \\ z \end{pmatrix} = \begin{pmatrix} 0 \\ 0 \\ 0 \end{pmatrix}$$

$$\begin{pmatrix} 0 & 2 & 0 \\ -1 & -2 & 1 \\ 3 & 2 & -3 \end{pmatrix}\begin{pmatrix} x \\ y \\ z \end{pmatrix} = \begin{pmatrix} 0 \\ 0 \\ 0 \end{pmatrix}$$

Thus we have

$$\begin{aligned} 2y &= 0 \\ -x - 2y + z &= 0 \\ 3x + 2y - 3z &= 0 \end{aligned}$$

From the first equation, $y = 0$; putting $y = 0$ into the other equations yields

$$\begin{aligned} -x + z &= 0 \\ 3x - 3z &= 0 \end{aligned}$$

Here the second equation can be derived from the first by multiplying the first by -3. Solving, we have $x = t$, $z = t$. So the eigenvector is

$$X = t\begin{pmatrix} 1 \\ 0 \\ 1 \end{pmatrix}$$

Exercises

1 Calculate the eigenvectors of the matrices given in Exercise 1 of the previous section.

2 Calculate the eigenvectors of the matrices given in Exercise 2 of the previous section.

Solutions to exercises

1 (a) $t\begin{pmatrix} 1 \\ -1 \end{pmatrix}, t\begin{pmatrix} 1 \\ \frac{1}{3} \end{pmatrix}$ (b) $t\begin{pmatrix} 1 \\ 1 \end{pmatrix}$

(c) $t\begin{pmatrix} 1 \\ 1 \end{pmatrix}, t\begin{pmatrix} 1 \\ \frac{1}{2} \end{pmatrix}$

(d) $t\begin{pmatrix} 1 \\ -\frac{1 + \sqrt{13}}{3} \end{pmatrix}, t\begin{pmatrix} 1 \\ \frac{\sqrt{13} - 1}{3} \end{pmatrix}$

2 (a) $t\begin{pmatrix} 1 \\ 5 \\ 1 \end{pmatrix}, t\begin{pmatrix} 1 \\ 12 \\ 5 \end{pmatrix}, t\begin{pmatrix} 1 \\ 0 \\ 1 \end{pmatrix}$

(b) $t\begin{pmatrix} 1 \\ -5.0981 \\ 2.7321 \end{pmatrix}, t\begin{pmatrix} 1 \\ 0.0981 \\ -0.7321 \end{pmatrix}, t\begin{pmatrix} 1 \\ -3 \\ -3 \end{pmatrix}$

(c) $t\begin{pmatrix} 1 \\ -\frac{1}{3} \\ -\frac{7}{3} \end{pmatrix}$, $t\begin{pmatrix} 1 \\ -2 \\ 1 \end{pmatrix}$, $t\begin{pmatrix} 1 \\ -0.8 \\ 1.4 \end{pmatrix}$

(d) $t\begin{pmatrix} 1 \\ \frac{4}{9} \\ -\frac{1}{3} \end{pmatrix}$, $t\begin{pmatrix} 1 \\ 0.6 \\ -0.3 \end{pmatrix}$, $t\begin{pmatrix} 1 \\ 1 \\ 0.5 \end{pmatrix}$

(e) $t\begin{pmatrix} 1 \\ \frac{19}{6} \\ -\frac{2}{3} \end{pmatrix}$, $t\begin{pmatrix} 1 \\ 4 \\ 6 \end{pmatrix}$, $t\begin{pmatrix} 1 \\ 2 \\ 4 \end{pmatrix}$

End of block exercises

1 Determine which of the following systems have non-trivial solutions:

(a) $2x - y = 0$
$3x - 1.5y = 0$

(b) $6x + 5y = 0$
$5x + 6y = 0$

(c) $-x - 4y = 0$
$2x + 8y = 0$

(d) $7x - 3y = 0$
$1.4x - 0.6y = 0$

(e) $-4x + 5y = 0$
$3x - 4y = 0$

2 Determine which of the following systems have non-trivial solutions:

(a) $3x - 2y + 2z = 0$
$x - y + z = 0$
$2x + 2y - z = 0$

(b) $x + 3y - z = 0$
$4x - y + 2z = 0$
$6x + 5y = 0$

(c) $x + 2y - z = 0$
$x - 3z = 0$
$5x + 6y - 9z = 0$

3 The matrix A is defined by:

$$A = \begin{pmatrix} 3 & 2 \\ -3 & -4 \end{pmatrix}$$

(a) Determine the characteristic equation of A.
(b) Determine the eigenvalues of A.
(c) Determine the eigenvectors of A.
(d) Form a new matrix M whose columns are the two eigenvectors of A. M is called a **modal matrix**.
(e) Show that $M^{-1}AM$ is a diagonal matrix, D, with the eigenvalues of A on its leading diagonal. D is called the **spectral matrix** corresponding to the modal matrix M.

4 (a) Show that the matrix

$$A = \begin{pmatrix} 5 & 2 \\ -2 & 1 \end{pmatrix}$$

has only one eigenvalue and determine it.
(b) Calculate the eigenvector of A.

5 The matrix H is given by

$$H = \begin{pmatrix} 4 & -1 & 1 \\ -2 & 4 & 0 \\ -4 & 3 & 1 \end{pmatrix}$$

(a) Find the eigenvalues of H.
(b) Determine the eigenvectors of H.
(c) Form a new matrix M whose columns are the three eigenvectors of H. M is called a **modal matrix**.
(d) Show that $M^{-1}HM$ is a diagonal matrix, D, with the eigenvalues of H on its leading diagonal. D is called the **spectral matrix** corresponding to the modal matrix M.

Solutions to exercises

1 (a), (c) and (d) have non-trivial solutions.

2 (b) and (c) have non-trivial solutions.

3 (a) $\lambda^2 + \lambda - 6 = 0$

(b) $\lambda = -3, 2$

(c) $\begin{pmatrix} 1 \\ -3 \end{pmatrix} \begin{pmatrix} 1 \\ -0.5 \end{pmatrix}$

4 (a) $\lambda = 3$

(b) $\begin{pmatrix} 1 \\ -1 \end{pmatrix}$

5 (a) $\lambda = 2, 3, 4$

(b) $\begin{pmatrix} 1 \\ 1 \\ -1 \end{pmatrix}, \begin{pmatrix} 1 \\ 2 \\ 1 \end{pmatrix}, \begin{pmatrix} 0 \\ 1 \\ 1 \end{pmatrix}$

BLOCK 5 Iterative techniques

5.1 Introduction

So far we have met a number of techniques used for solving systems of linear equations – Cramer's rule (Block 1), the inverse matrix method (Block 2) and Gaussian elimination (Block 3) are three such methods.

We now examine two techniques that provide approximate solutions to linear systems. In these, an initial guess of the solution is repeatedly improved, generating a sequence of approximate solutions. With repeated application of the method, under certain conditions, the approximate solutions approach the exact solution. Such methods are known as **iterative methods**. The two iterative methods we look at are Jacobi's method and the Gauss–Seidel method.

5.2 Jacobi's method

We illustrate the method with examples.

Example 5.1

Solve

$$\begin{aligned} 3x - 2y &= 9 \\ x + 4y &= -11 \end{aligned}$$

using Jacobi's iterative method.

Solution

We rewrite the equations so that x and y are the subjects. This yields

$$x = \frac{2}{3}y + 3 \qquad (1)$$

$$y = -\frac{x}{4} - \frac{11}{4} \qquad (2)$$

We now guess a solution. In practice an educated guess may be possible if realistic estimates of x and y are known. Suppose we guess $x = 0$, $y = -4$. To show this is our initial guess and not the exact solution we write $x_0 = 0$, $y_0 = -4$.

We improve our initial guess by substituting $x_0 = 0$, $y_0 = -4$ into the right-hand side of equations (1) and (2). The values of x and y so obtained are labelled x_1 and y_1.

Hence

$$\begin{aligned} x_1 &= \frac{2}{3}y_0 + 3 \\ &= \frac{2}{3}(-4) + 3 \\ &= 0.3333 \\ y_1 &= -\frac{x_0}{4} - \frac{11}{4} \\ &= -\frac{0}{4} - \frac{11}{4} \\ &= -2.7500 \end{aligned}$$

At this stage we have made one application, or **iteration**, of Jacobi's method. To obtain the next approximate solution, x_2, y_2, we substitute x_1 and y_1 into the right-hand side of equations (1) and (2). This produces

$$\begin{aligned} x_2 &= \frac{2}{3}y_1 + 3 \\ &= \frac{2}{3}(-2.7500) + 3 \\ &= 1.1667 \\ y_2 &= -\frac{x_1}{4} - \frac{11}{4} \\ &= -\frac{(0.3333)}{4} - \frac{11}{4} \\ &= -2.8333 \end{aligned}$$

At this stage two iterations have been performed. We perform another iteration to obtain x_3 and y_3.

$$\begin{aligned} x_3 &= \frac{2}{3}y_2 + 3 \\ &= \frac{2}{3}(-2.8333) + 3 \\ &= 1.1111 \\ y_3 &= -\frac{x_2}{4} - \frac{11}{4} \\ &= -\frac{(1.1667)}{4} - \frac{11}{4} \\ &= -3.0417 \end{aligned}$$

Similarly

$$\begin{aligned} x_4 &= \frac{2}{3}y_3 + 3 \\ &= \frac{2}{3}(-3.0417) + 3 \\ &= 0.9722 \end{aligned}$$

$$\begin{aligned} y_4 &= -\frac{x_3}{4} - \frac{11}{4} \\ &= -\frac{(1.1111)}{4} - \frac{11}{4} \\ &= -3.0278 \end{aligned}$$

The iterations can be continued. Table 5.1 summarises the results of successive iterations.

Table 5.1

Iteration no. (n)	x_n	y_n
0	0.0000	−4.0000
1	0.3333	−2.7500
2	1.1667	−2.8333
3	1.1111	−3.0417
4	0.9722	−3.0278
5	0.9815	−2.9931
6	1.0046	−2.9954
7	1.0031	−3.0012
8	0.9992	−3.0008
9	0.9995	−2.9998
10	1.0001	−2.9999
11	1.0001	−3.0000
12	1.0000	−3.0000

The value of x_n seems to converge to 1 as n increases; the value of y_n seems to converge to -3 as n increases. It is easy to verify that the exact solution of the given equations is $x = 1$, $y = -3$. So Jacobi's method has produced a sequence of approximate solutions that has converged to the exact solution.

Example 5.2

Find an approximate solution to

$$\begin{aligned} 4x + y &= 12 \\ -2x + 5y &= 16 \end{aligned}$$

using Jacobi's method. Perform five iterations and take $x_0 = 0$, $y_0 = 3$ as your initial guess.

Solution

The equations are rearranged to make x and y the subjects.

$x = -0.25y + 3$

$y =$

$0.4x + 3.2$

The initial guess is $x_0 = 0$, $y_0 = 3$. Then

$$x_1 = -0.25y_0 + 3$$

$$= -0.25(3) + 3$$
$$= 2.25$$

$y_1 =$ $0.4x_0 + 3.2 = 3.2$

We now find x_2 and y_2.

$x_2 =$

$-0.25y_1 + 3 = -0.25(3.2) + 3 = 2.2$

$y_2 =$

$0.4x_1 + 3.2 = 0.4(2.25) + 3.2 = 4.1$

Continuing in this way we find

$x_3 =$, $y_3 =$ $1.975, 4.08$

$x_4 =$, $y_4 =$ $1.98, 3.99$

$x_5 =$, $y_5 =$ $2.003, 3.99$

If the iterations are continued then x_n approaches 2 and y_n approaches 4, the exact solution.

Clearly, this sort of approach is simple to program, and iterative techniques are best implemented on a computer. When writing a program a test is incorporated so that after each iteration a check for convergence is made by comparing successive estimates. The method may not converge, and, even if it does, convergence may be very slow. Other methods with improved rates of convergence are available such as the Gauss–Seidel method, which is covered in Section 5.3.

Exercises

1 Use five iterations of Jacobi's method to find approximate solutions of each system of equations:

(a) $3x - y = 17$
$2x - 5y = 20$
Take $x_0 = 3, y_0 = 0$.

(b) $2x + y = 11$
$x - 3y = -26$
Take $x_0 = 0, y_0 = 7$.

(c) $-3x + y = 14$
$2x - 7y = 16$
Take $x_0 = -4, y_0 = -2$.

(d) $4x + y = 19$
$-3x + 7y = 40$
Take $x_0 = 1, y_0 = 5$.

(e) $-3x + 2y = 37$
$x + 5y = 50$
Take $x_0 = -3, y_0 = 9$.

Solutions to exercises

1 (a)

Iteration no. (n)	x_n	y_n
0	3.0000	0.0000
1	5.6667	−2.8000
2	4.7333	−1.7333
3	5.0889	−2.1067
4	4.9644	−1.9644
5	5.0119	−2.0142

(b)

Iteration no. (n)	x_n	y_n
0	0.0000	7.0000
1	2.0000	8.6667
2	1.1667	9.3333
3	0.8333	9.0556
4	0.9722	8.9444
5	1.0278	8.9907

(c)

Iteration no. (n)	x_n	y_n
0	−4.0000	−2.0000
1	−5.3333	−3.4286
2	−5.8095	−3.8095
3	−5.9365	−3.9456
4	−5.9819	−3.9819
5	−5.9940	−3.9948

(d)

Iteration no. (n)	x_n	y_n
0	1.0000	5.0000
1	3.5000	6.1429
2	3.2143	7.2143
3	2.9464	7.0918
4	2.9770	6.9770
5	3.0057	6.9902

(e)

Iteration no. (n)	x_n	y_n
0	−3.0000	9.0000
1	−6.3333	10.6000
2	−5.2667	11.2667
3	−4.8222	11.0533
4	−4.9644	10.9644
5	−5.0237	10.9929

5.3 Gauss–Seidel method

The Gauss–Seidel method is very similar to Jacobi's method. The difference comes in the calculation of the y values. When calculating the y values the most recent x value is used. Example 5.3 illustrates this.

Example 5.3

Use the Gauss–Seidel method to find an approximate solution to the system given in Example 5.1. Perform five iterations and take $x_0 = 0$, $y_0 = -4$.

Solution

We arrange the equations so that x and y are the subjects:

$$x = \frac{2}{3}y + 3$$

$$y = -\frac{x}{4} - 2.75$$

We make an initial guess, say, $x_0 = 0$, $y_0 = -4$. Now we calculate x_1.

$$\begin{aligned} x_1 &= \frac{2}{3}y_0 + 3 \\ &= \frac{2}{3}(-4) + 3 \\ &= 0.3333 \end{aligned}$$

Up to this point, the method is identical to Jacobi's method.

When calculating y_1 the most recent value of x, that is x_1, is used.

$$\begin{aligned} y_1 &= -\frac{x_1}{4} - 2.75 \\ &= -\frac{(0.3333)}{4} - 2.75 \\ &= -2.8333 \end{aligned}$$

This completes the first iteration. We are now ready to calculate x_2 and y_2.

$$\begin{aligned} x_2 &= \frac{2}{3}y_1 + 3 \\ &= \frac{2}{3}(-2.8333) + 3 \\ &= 1.1111 \end{aligned}$$

When calculating y_2 we use the most recent value of x, that is x_2.

$$\begin{aligned} y_2 &= -\frac{x_2}{4} - 2.75 \\ &= -\frac{(1.1111)}{4} - 2.75 \\ &= -3.0278 \end{aligned}$$

This completes the second iteration. The process is repeated.

$$\begin{aligned} x_3 &= \frac{2}{3}y_2 + 3 \\ &= \frac{2}{3}(-3.0278) + 3 \\ &= 0.9815 \\ y_3 &= -\frac{x_3}{4} - 2.75 \\ &= -\frac{(0.9815)}{4} - 2.75 \\ &= -2.9954 \end{aligned}$$

Table 5.2 summarises some further iterations.

Table 5.2

Iteration no. (n)	x_n	y_n
0	0.0000	−4.0000
1	0.3333	−2.8333
2	1.1111	−3.0278
3	0.9815	−2.9954
4	1.0031	−3.0008
5	0.9995	−2.9999
6	1.0001	−3.0000

Note that the Gauss–Seidel method converges more rapidly than Jacobi's method (see Table 5.1). This is because the Gauss–Seidel method uses the most recent value of x in the calculation of the y values.

Example 5.4

Use the Gauss–Seidel method to find an approximate solution of

$$4x + 3y = 0.5$$
$$x - 2y = -9.5$$

Perform five iterations taking $x_0 = 0$, $y_0 = 0$.

Solution

The equations are rearranged to make x and y the subjects.

$x =$ $-0.75y + 0.125$

$y =$ $0.5x + 4.75$

The initial guess is $x_0 = 0$, $y_0 = 0$. So

$$x_1 = -0.75y_0 + 0.125 = 0.125$$

$y_1 =$ $0.5x_1 + 4.75 = 4.8125$

and

$x_2 =$ $-0.75y_1 + 0.125 = -3.4844$

$y_2 =$ $0.5x_2 + 4.75 = 3.0078$

Continuing in this way we find:

$x_3 =$, $y_3 =$ $-2.1309, 3.6846$

$x_4 =$, $y_4 =$ $-2.6384, 3.4308$

$x_5 =$, $y_5 =$ $-2.4481, 3.5260$

Unfortunately, as with all iterative methods, convergence is not guaranteed. However, it can be shown that, if the matrix of coefficients of the equations is **diagonally dominant** (i.e., the modulus of each diagonal element is greater than the sum of the moduli of the other elements in its row), then the Gauss–Seidel method will converge. For further details you should consult a text on numerical methods.

Exercises

1 Find approximate solutions to the linear systems in question 1 of Section 5.2 using five iterations of the Gauss–Seidel method.

Solutions to exercises

1 (a)

Iteration no. (n)	x_n	y_n
0	3.0000	0.0000
1	5.6667	−1.7333
2	5.0889	−1.9644
3	5.0119	−1.9953
4	5.0016	−1.9994
5	5.0002	−1.9999

(b)

Iteration no. (n)	x_n	y_n
0	0.0000	7.0000
1	2.0000	9.3333
2	0.8333	8.9444
3	1.0278	9.0093
4	0.9954	8.9985
5	1.0008	9.0003

(c)

Iteration no. (n)	x_n	y_n
0	−4.0000	−2.0000
1	−5.3333	−3.8095
2	−5.9365	−3.9819
3	−5.9940	−3.9983
4	−5.9994	−3.9998
5	−5.9999	−4.0000

(d)

Iteration no. (n)	x_n	y_n
0	1.0000	5.0000
1	3.5000	7.2143
2	2.9464	6.9770
3	3.0057	7.0025
4	2.9994	6.9997
5	3.0000	7.0000

(e)

Iteration no. (n)	x_n	y_n
0	−3.0000	9.0000
1	−6.3333	11.2667
2	−4.8222	10.9644
3	−5.0237	11.0047
4	−4.9668	10.9994
5	−5.0004	11.0001

End of block exercises

1 Use five iterations of Jacobi's method to find approximate solutions of the following system:

$$-4x + y = 17$$
$$2x + 5y = 19$$

Take $x_0 = -1$ and $y_0 = 3$.

2 Use five iterations of the Gauss–Seidel method to find approximate solutions to the system

$$4x - 3y = 25$$
$$2x + 5y = -7$$

Take $x_0 = 2$, $y_0 = -1$.

3 Consider the system

$$4x + y + z = 6$$
$$2x + 5y - z = 18$$
$$3x - y + 6z = -6$$

(a) Use three iterations of Jacobi's method to find an approximate solution to the given system. Take $x_0 = 0$, $y_0 = 2$, $z_0 = 0$.
(b) Repeat (a) using the Gauss–Seidel method.

Solutions to exercises

1

Iteration no. (n)	x_n	y_n
0	−1.0000	3.0000
1	−3.5000	4.2000
2	−3.2000	5.2000
3	−2.9500	5.0800
4	−2.9800	4.9800
5	−3.0050	4.9920

2

Iteration no. (n)	x_n	y_n
0	2.0000	−1.0000
1	5.5000	−3.6000
2	3.5500	−2.8200
3	4.1350	−3.0540
4	3.9595	−2.9838
5	4.0122	−3.0049

3 (a)

Iteration no. (n)	x_n	y_n	z_n
0	0.0000	2.0000	0.0000
1	1.0000	3.6000	−0.6667
2	0.7667	3.0667	−0.9000
3	0.9583	3.1133	−0.8722

(b)

Iteration no. (n)	x_n	y_n	z_n
0	0.0000	2.0000	0.0000
1	1.0000	3.2000	−0.9667
2	0.9417	3.0300	−0.9658
3	0.9840	3.0133	−0.9898

BLOCK 6 Electrical networks

6.1 Introduction

In this block we consider electrical networks comprising known resistors and known voltage sources. We wish to determine the current in various parts of the network.

The network can be modelled by a set of simultaneous equations, which may be solved by matrix methods. In order to formulate the simultaneous equations we introduce the idea of a mesh current and a branch current.

6.2 Mesh and branch currents

Figure 6.1 shows an example of an electrical network.

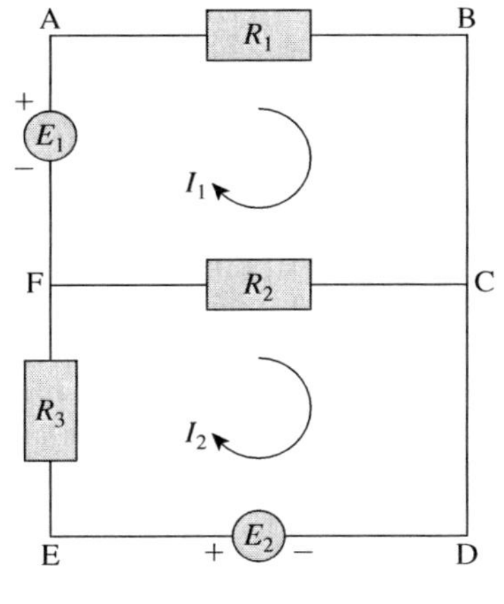

Figure 6.1 An electrical network with mesh currents marked.

A **mesh** is a loop that does not contain any smaller loops. Figure 6.1 contains two meshes: ABCF and CDEF. Note, for example, that ABCDEF is not a mesh.

We introduce **mesh currents**, I_1 and I_2, as shown in Figure 6.1. Mesh currents are usually denoted as running clockwise although in reality they may run anticlockwise. Upon calculation this would be denoted by the current being negative.

The net current in a particular branch is called the **branch current**. The branch currents are found by combining the mesh currents. For example, the current from C to F is $I_1 - I_2$.

The aim of analysing the network is to determine the mesh currents, I_1 and I_2. Once these are known the branch currents can easily be found.

Extensive use is made of **Kirchhoff's voltage law**, which states that the algebraic sum of voltages around a mesh is zero: that is, the sum of the voltage drops equals the sum of the voltage rises.

Example 6.1 Electrical Engineering – Mesh currents

Figure 6.1 shows a circuit with two meshes, ABCF and CDEF. The values of voltages E_1, E_2 and resistances R_1, R_2 and R_3 are known. The unknowns are the values of the currents I_1 and I_2.

(a) By applying Kirchhoff's voltage law to each mesh formulate two equations in the unknowns I_1 and I_2.
(b) Given $E_1 = 3$, $E_2 = 6$, $R_1 = 1$, $R_2 = 4$ and $R_3 = 2$, find I_1 and I_2.
(c) Find the branch current running from F to C.

Solution

(a) Kirchhoff's voltage law states that the algebraic sum of voltages around a mesh is zero: that is, the sum of the voltage drops equals the sum of the voltage rises. Recall that the voltage drop, V volts, across a resistor of resistance R ohms carrying I amps is given by $V = IR$.

Consider the mesh ABCF. Starting at A and working clockwise around the mesh we equate voltage drops to voltage rises.

$$R_1I_1 + (I_1 - I_2)R_2 = E_1$$

This may be written as

$$I_1(R_1 + R_2) - I_2R_2 = E_1 \qquad (1)$$

Consider now the mesh CDEF. Applying Kirchhoff's voltage law we obtain

$$(I_2 - I_1)R_2 + I_2R_3 = E_2$$

which is then written as

$$-I_1R_2 + I_2(R_2 + R_3) = E_2 \qquad (2)$$

Equations (1) and (2) are written in matrix form as

$$\begin{pmatrix} R_1 + R_2 & -R_2 \\ -R_2 & R_2 + R_3 \end{pmatrix}\begin{pmatrix} I_1 \\ I_2 \end{pmatrix} = \begin{pmatrix} E_1 \\ E_2 \end{pmatrix}$$

(b) Substituting in the values of E_1, E_2, R_1, R_2 and R_3 we get

$$\begin{pmatrix} 5 & -4 \\ -4 & 6 \end{pmatrix}\begin{pmatrix} I_1 \\ I_2 \end{pmatrix} = \begin{pmatrix} 3 \\ 6 \end{pmatrix}$$

These equations can be solved by any of the techniques described in Chapter 12. You should verify that $I_1 = 3$, $I_2 = 3$.

(c) Consider the branch FC. The net current in FC is $I_2 - I_1 = 0$.

Example 6.2 Electrical Engineering – Mesh currents

Determine the mesh currents I_1, I_2 and I_3 in Figure 6.2 given $E_1 = 5$, $E_2 = 15$, $R_1 = 3$, $R_2 = 5$, $R_3 = 1$, $R_4 = 6$ and $R_5 = 2$.

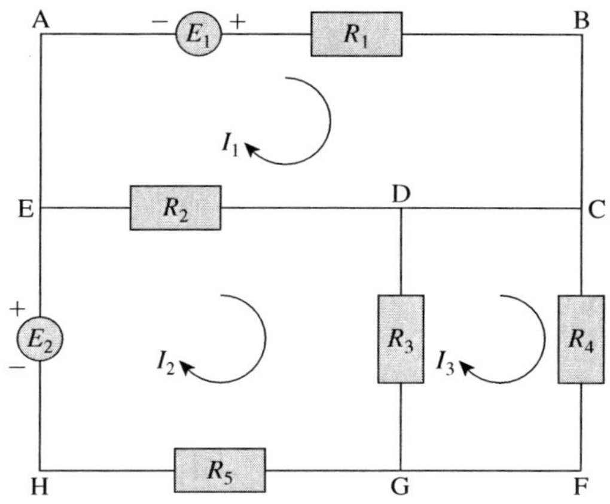

Figure 6.2 Electrical network for Example 6.2.

Solution

We use Kirchhoff's voltage law. Recall that the voltage drop, V, across a resistor of resistance R ohms carrying a current I amps is given by $V = IR$.

Consider the mesh ABCDE. For clarity this is shown in Figure 6.3.

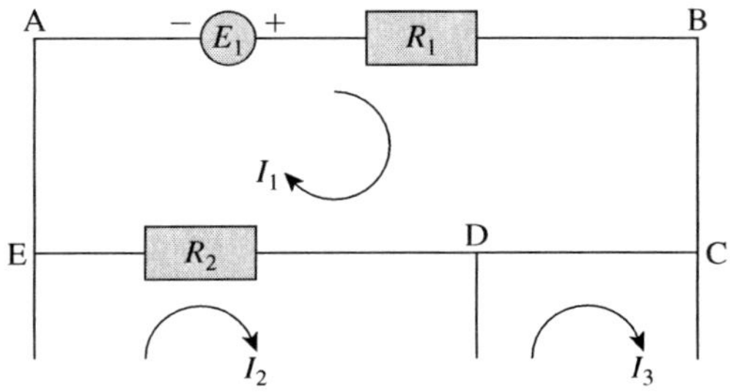

Figure 6.3 Mesh ABCDE.

Starting from A and working clockwise around the mesh we apply Kirchhoff's voltage law, equating the voltage rises to the voltage drops. We obtain

$$I_1R_1 + (I_1 - I_2)R_2 = E_1$$

This is rewritten as

$$I_1(R_1 + R_2) - I_2R_2 = E_1 \quad (3)$$

Consider the mesh EDGH, as shown in Figure 6.4.

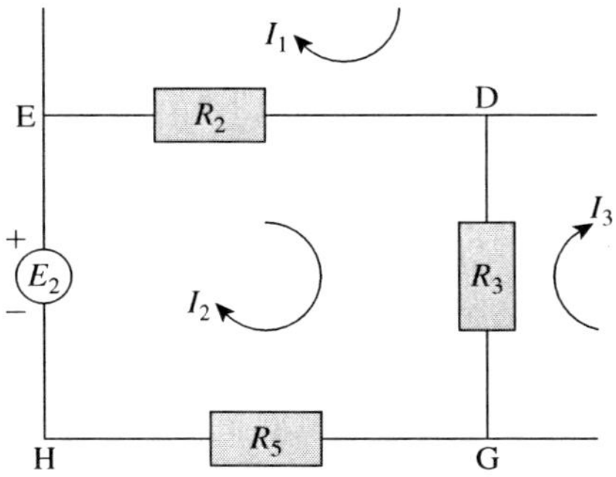

Figure 6.4
Mesh EDGH.

Starting at E and working clockwise we equate the voltage drops and the voltage rises to obtain

$$(I_2 - I_1)R_2 + (I_2 - I_3)R_3 + I_2R_5 = E_2$$

which is then rewritten as

$$-I_1R_2 + I_2(R_2 + R_3 + R_5) - I_3R_3 = E_2 \qquad (4)$$

Finally we look at mesh DCFG, as shown in Figure 6.5.

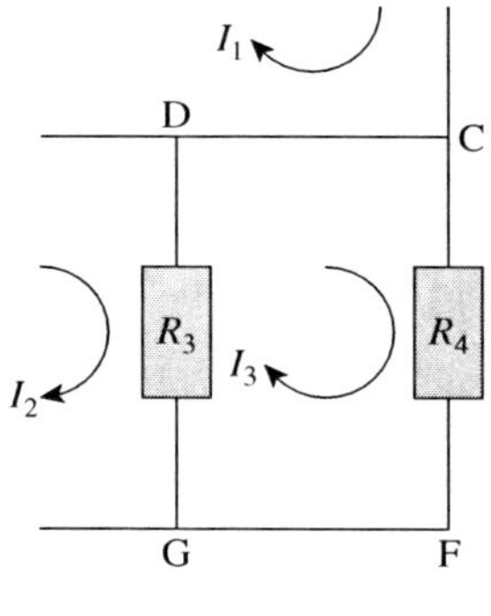

Figure 6.5
Mesh DCFG.

Starting at D and working clockwise we have

$$I_3R_4 + (I_3 - I_2)R_3 = 0$$

which is written as

$$-I_2R_3 + I_3(R_3 + R_4) = 0 \qquad (5)$$

The equations (3), (4) and (5) are written in matrix form as

$$\begin{pmatrix} R_1 + R_2 & -R_2 & 0 \\ -R_2 & R_2 + R_3 + R_5 & -R_3 \\ 0 & -R_3 & R_3 + R_4 \end{pmatrix} \begin{pmatrix} I_1 \\ I_2 \\ I_3 \end{pmatrix} = \begin{pmatrix} E_1 \\ E_2 \\ 0 \end{pmatrix}$$

Substituting in the given values we have

$$\begin{pmatrix} 8 & -5 & 0 \\ -5 & 8 & -1 \\ 0 & -1 & 7 \end{pmatrix} \begin{pmatrix} I_1 \\ I_2 \\ I_3 \end{pmatrix} = \begin{pmatrix} 5 \\ 15 \\ 0 \end{pmatrix}$$

The system may be solved using one of the methods explained in Blocks 1–4 of Chapter 12. We find

$$I_1 = 3.0189, \quad I_2 = 3.8302, \quad I_3 = 0.5472$$

Example 6.3 Electrical Engineering – Mesh currents

Figure 6.6 shows an electrical network with the mesh currents I_1, I_2, I_3 and I_4 marked in meshes 1, 2, 3 and 4 respectively. The resistances R_1, R_2, R_3, R_4 and R_5 and the voltage sources E_1, E_2, E_3 and E_4 are known.

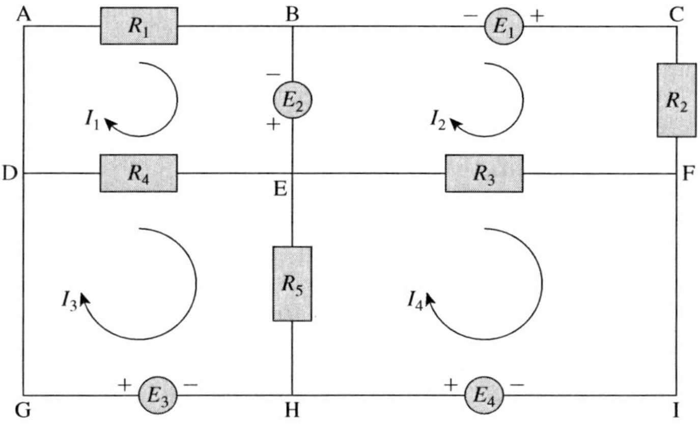

Figure 6.6 Electrical network for Example 6.3.

(a) Formulate a matrix equation for the unknowns I_1, I_2, I_3 and I_4.
(b) Given $R_1 = 3$, $R_2 = 4$, $R_3 = 1$, $R_4 = 7$, $R_5 = 4$, $E_1 = 6$, $E_2 = 10$, $E_3 = 5$ and $E_4 = 5$, solve for I_1, I_2, I_3 and I_4.
(c) State the value of the current from E to H.

Solution

(a) We apply Kirchhoff's voltage law to each of the meshes.

Mesh 1 (ABED)

We equate voltage drops to voltage rises.

$$(I_1 - I_3)R_4 + I_1R_1 = E_2$$

which is written as

$$\qquad = E_2 \qquad\qquad I_1(R_1 + R_4) - I_3R_4 \quad (6)$$

Mesh 2 (BCFE)

$= E_1$ $\qquad$ $I_2R_2 + (I_2 - I_4)R_3 + E_2$

which is written as

$$I_2(R_2 + R_3) - I_4R_3 = E_1 - E_2 \qquad (7)$$

Mesh 3 (DEHG)

$$(I_3 - I_1)R_4 + (I_3 - I_4)R_5 = E_3$$

which is written as

$$-I_1R_4 + I_3(R_4 + R_5) - I_4R_5 = E_3 \qquad (8)$$

Mesh 4 (EFIH)

$= E_4$ $\qquad$ $(I_4 - I_3)R_5 + (I_4 - I_2)R_3$

which is written as

$$-I_2R_3 - I_3R_5 + I_4(R_3 + R_5) = E_4 \qquad (9)$$

Equations (6), (7), (8) and (9) are written in matrix form as

$$\begin{pmatrix} R_1 + R_4 & 0 & -R_4 & 0 \\ 0 & R_2 + R_3 & 0 & -R_3 \\ -R_4 & 0 & R_4 + R_5 & -R_5 \\ 0 & -R_3 & -R_5 & R_3 + R_5 \end{pmatrix} \begin{pmatrix} I_1 \\ I_2 \\ I_3 \\ I_4 \end{pmatrix} = \begin{pmatrix} E_2 \\ E_1 - E_2 \\ E_3 \\ E_4 \end{pmatrix}$$

(b) Substituting in the given values, the matrix equation becomes

$$\begin{pmatrix} 10 & 0 & -7 & 0 \\ 0 & 5 & 0 & -1 \\ -7 & 0 & 11 & -4 \\ 0 & -1 & -4 & 5 \end{pmatrix} \begin{pmatrix} I_1 \\ I_2 \\ I_3 \\ I_4 \end{pmatrix} = \begin{pmatrix} 10 \\ -4 \\ 5 \\ 5 \end{pmatrix}$$

The system is solved to give

$$I_1 = 4.9217, \quad I_2 = 0.3087, \quad I_3 = 5.6024, \quad I_4 = 5.5437$$

(c) The current running from E to H is

$I_3 - I_4$

$$\begin{aligned} I_3 - I_4 &= 5.6024 - 5.5437 \\ &= 0.0587 \end{aligned}$$

Exercises

1 Figure 6.7 shows a circuit with two meshes.

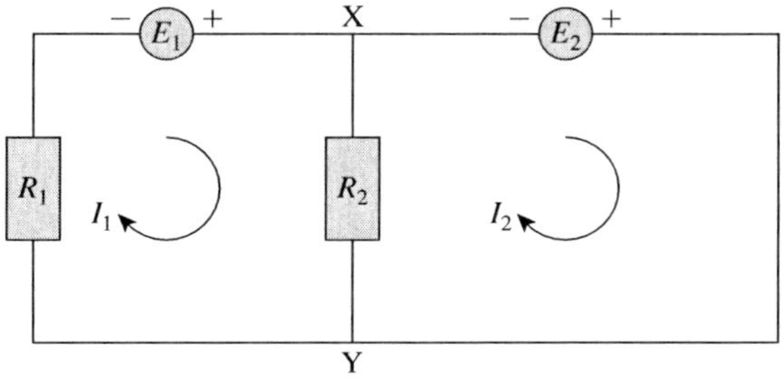

Figure 6.7

(a) Formulate a matrix equation for I_1 and I_2.
(b) Solve for I_1 and I_2 given $E_1 = 3$, $E_2 = 7$, $R_1 = 6$ and $R_2 = 10$.
(c) Calculate the current in the branch XY.

2 Figure 6.8 shows a circuit with three meshes.

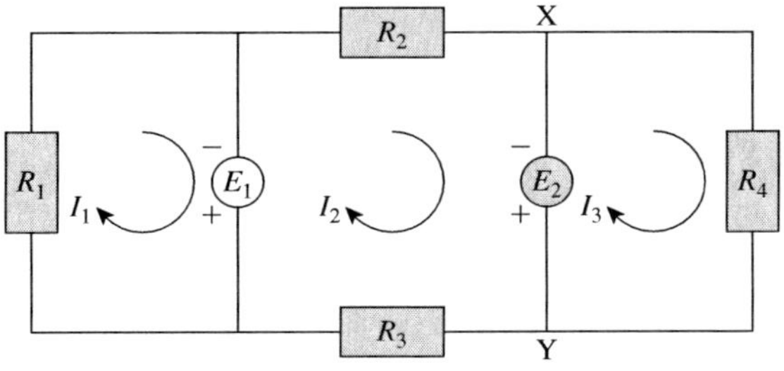

Figure 6.8

(a) Formulate a matrix equation for the mesh currents I_1, I_2 and I_3.
(b) Given $E_1 = 4$, $E_2 = 5$, $R_1 = 3$, $R_2 = 1$, $R_3 = 2$ and $R_4 = 6$, find I_1, I_2 and I_3.
(c) Calculate the current in the branch XY.

3 (a) Formulate a matrix equation for the mesh currents I_1, I_2 and I_3 as shown in Figure 6.9.

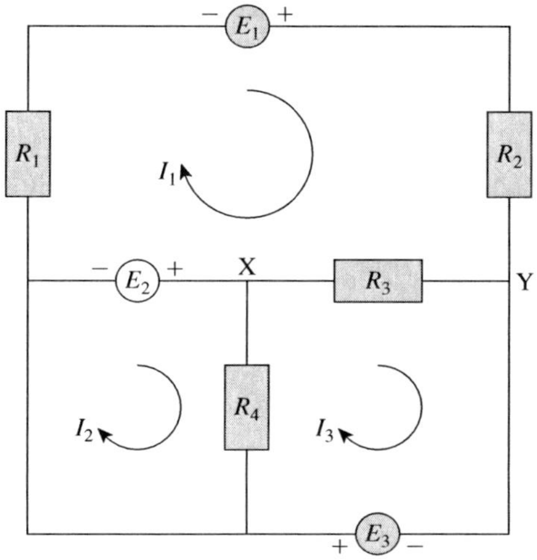

Figure 6.9

(b) Calculate the mesh currents given $E_1 = 5$, $E_2 = 4$, $E_3 = 6$, $R_1 = 5$, $R_2 = 4$, $R_3 = 2$ and $R_4 = 7$.
(c) Calculate the current in the branch XY.

4 (a) Formulate a matrix equation for the mesh currents I_1, I_2, I_3 and I_4 as shown in Figure 6.10.

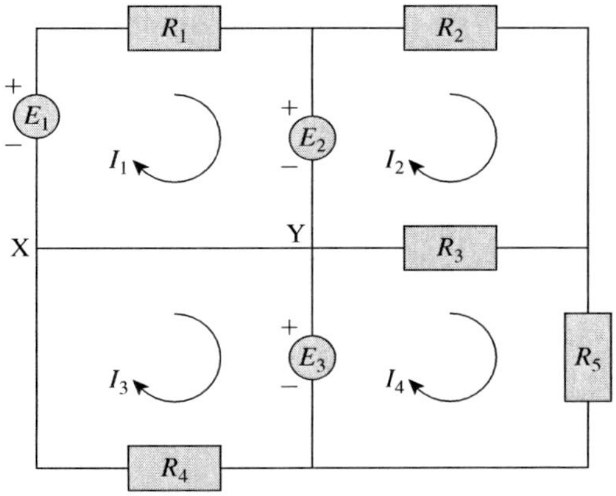

Figure 6.10

(b) Calculate the mesh currents given $E_1 = 5$, $E_2 = 2$, $E_3 = 10$, $R_1 = 6$, $R_2 = 7$, $R_3 = 10$, $R_4 = 1$ and $R_5 = 6$.
(c) Calculate the current in the branch XY.

5 Figure 6.11 shows a circuit with four meshes.

(a) Formulate a matrix equation for the mesh currents I_1, I_2, I_3 and I_4.
(b) Given $E_1 = 5$, $E_2 = 5$, $E_3 = 6$, $E_4 = 12$, $R_1 = 1$, $R_2 = 4$, $R_3 = 2$, $R_4 = 1$, $R_5 = 7$ and $R_6 = 9$, find the mesh currents.
(c) Calculate the current in the branch XY.

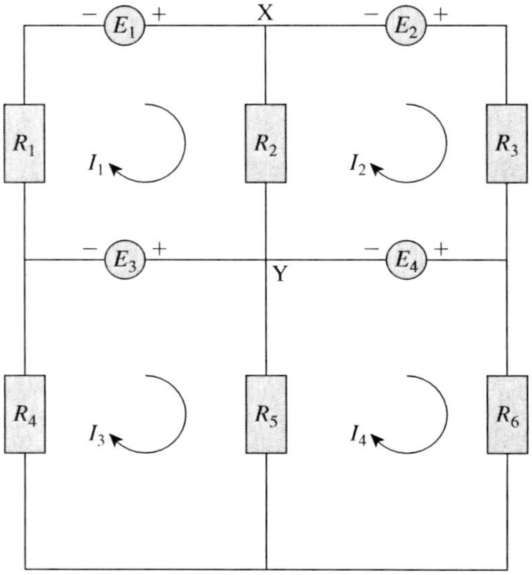

Figure 6.11

Solutions to exercises

1 (a) $$\begin{pmatrix} R_1 + R_2 & -R_2 \\ -R_2 & R_2 \end{pmatrix}\begin{pmatrix} I_1 \\ I_2 \end{pmatrix} = \begin{pmatrix} E_1 \\ E_2 \end{pmatrix}$$

(b) $I_1 = \frac{5}{3}$, $I_2 = \frac{71}{30}$

(c) $-\frac{21}{30}$, that is a current of $\frac{21}{30}$ from Y to X.

2 (a) $$\begin{pmatrix} R_1 & 0 & 0 \\ 0 & R_2 + R_3 & 0 \\ 0 & 0 & R_4 \end{pmatrix}\begin{pmatrix} I_1 \\ I_2 \\ I_3 \end{pmatrix} = \begin{pmatrix} E_1 \\ E_2 - E_1 \\ -E_2 \end{pmatrix}$$

(b) $I_1 = \frac{4}{3}$, $I_2 = \frac{1}{3}$, $I_3 = -\frac{5}{6}$

(c) $I_2 - I_3 = \frac{7}{6}$

3 (a)

$$\begin{pmatrix} R_1 + R_2 + R_3 & 0 & -R_3 \\ 0 & R_4 & -R_4 \\ -R_3 & -R_4 & R_3 + R_4 \end{pmatrix}\begin{pmatrix} I_1 \\ I_2 \\ I_3 \end{pmatrix} = \begin{pmatrix} E_1 - E_2 \\ E_2 \\ E_3 \end{pmatrix}$$

(b) $I_1 = -1.2222$, $I_2 = 6.7937$, $I_3 = 6.2222$

(c) $I_3 - I_1 = 5$

4 (a) $$\begin{pmatrix} R_1 & 0 & 0 & 0 \\ 0 & R_2+R_3 & 0 & -R_3 \\ 0 & 0 & R_4 & 0 \\ 0 & -R_3 & 0 & R_3+R_5 \end{pmatrix}\begin{pmatrix} I_1 \\ I_2 \\ I_3 \\ I_4 \end{pmatrix} = \begin{pmatrix} E_1-E_2 \\ E_2 \\ -E_3 \\ E_3 \end{pmatrix}$$

(b) $I_1 = 0.5000$, $I_2 = 0.7674$, $I_3 = -10.0000$, $I_4 = 1.1047$

(c) $I_3 - I_1 = -10.5$, that is a current of 10.5 from Y to X.

5 (a) $$\begin{pmatrix} R_1+R_2 & -R_2 & 0 & 0 \\ -R_2 & R_2+R_3 & 0 & 0 \\ 0 & 0 & R_4+R_5 & -R_5 \\ 0 & 0 & -R_5 & R_5+R_6 \end{pmatrix}\begin{pmatrix} I_1 \\ I_2 \\ I_3 \\ I_4 \end{pmatrix} = \begin{pmatrix} E_1-E_3 \\ E_2-E_4 \\ E_3 \\ E_4 \end{pmatrix}$$

(b) $I_1 = -2.4286$, $I_2 = -2.7857$, $I_3 = 2.2785$, $I_4 = 1.7468$

(c) $I_1 - I_2 = 0.3571$

End of block exercises

1 Figure 6.12 shows an electrical circuit with mesh currents I_1 and I_2 marked.
(a) Determine a matrix equation for I_1 and I_2.
(b) Solve for I_1 and I_2 given $E_1 = 12$, $R_1 = 3$ and $R_2 = 4$.
(c) Calculate the current in branch XY.

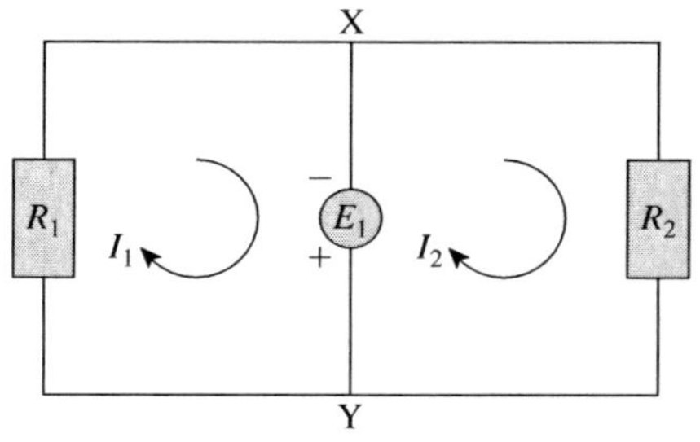

Figure 6.12

2 Figure 6.13 shows an electrical circuit with mesh currents I_1 and I_2 marked.
(a) Determine a matrix equation for I_1 and I_2.

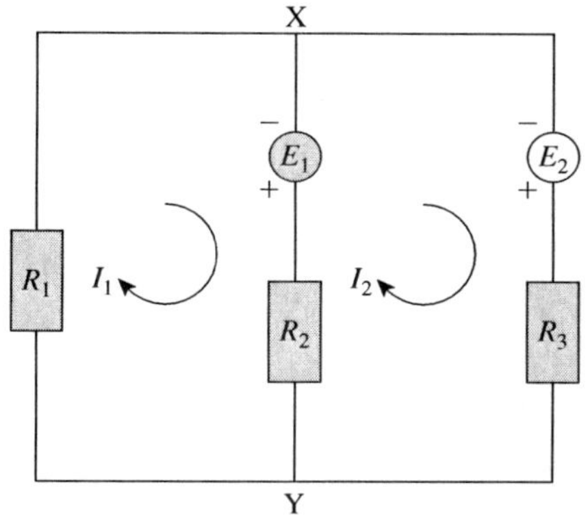

Figure 6.13

(b) Solve for I_1 and I_2 given $E_1 = 12$, $E_2 = 6$, $R_1 = 4$, $R_2 = 3$ and $R_3 = 4$.
(c) Calculate the current in branch XY.

3 Figure 6.14 shows an electrical circuit with mesh currents I_1, I_2 and I_3 marked.:
(a) Determine a matrix equation for I_1, I_2 and I_3.
(b) Solve for I_1, I_2 and I_3 given $E_1 = 6$, $E_2 = 12$, $R_1 = 2$, $R_2 = 3$, $R_3 = 2$ and $R_4 = 1$.
(c) Calculate the current in branch XY.

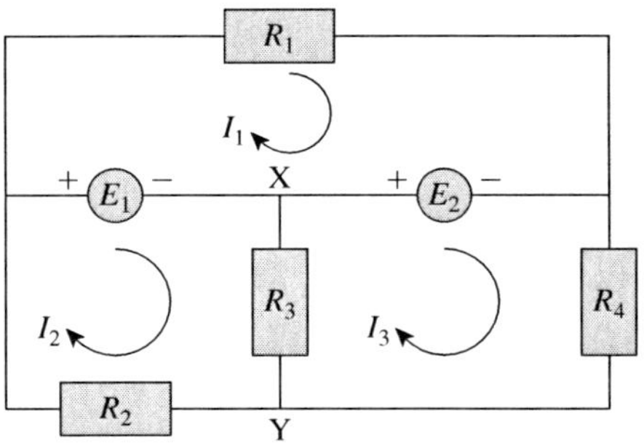

Figure 6.14

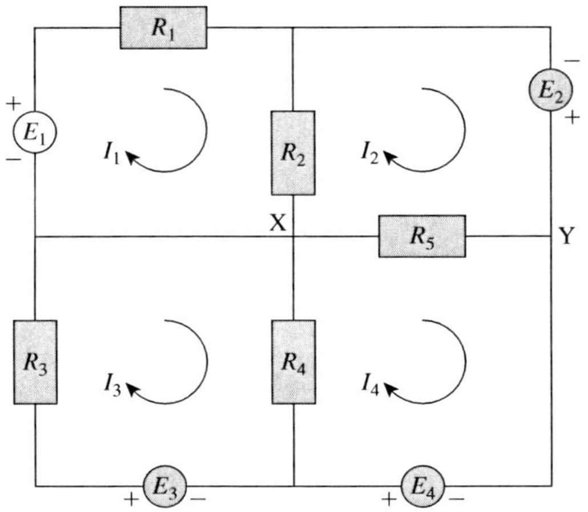

Figure 6.15

4 Figure 6.15 shows an electrical circuit with mesh currents I_1, I_2, I_3 and I_4 marked.
(a) Determine a matrix equation for I_1, I_2, I_3 and I_4.
(b) Solve for I_1, I_2, I_3 and I_4 given $E_1 = 6$, $E_2 = 12$, $E_3 = 6$, $E_4 = 10$, $R_1 = 3$, $R_2 = 5$, $R_3 = 4$, $R_4 = 5$ and $R_5 = 1$.
(c) Calculate the current in branch XY.

Solutions to exercises

1 (a) $\begin{pmatrix} R_1 & 0 \\ 0 & R_2 \end{pmatrix}\begin{pmatrix} I_1 \\ I_2 \end{pmatrix} = \begin{pmatrix} E_1 \\ -E_1 \end{pmatrix}$

(b) $I_1 = 4, I_2 = -3$

(c) $I_1 - I_2 = 7$

2 (a) $\begin{pmatrix} R_1 + R_2 & -R_2 \\ -R_2 & R_2 + R_3 \end{pmatrix}\begin{pmatrix} I_1 \\ I_2 \end{pmatrix}$
$= \begin{pmatrix} E_1 \\ E_2 - E_1 \end{pmatrix}$

(b) $I_1 = 1.65, I_2 = -0.15$

(c) $I_1 - I_2 = 1.8$

3 (a) $\begin{pmatrix} R_1 & 0 & 0 \\ 0 & R_2 + R_3 & -R_3 \\ 0 & -R_3 & R_3 + R_4 \end{pmatrix}\begin{pmatrix} I_1 \\ I_2 \\ I_3 \end{pmatrix}$
$= \begin{pmatrix} E_1 + E_2 \\ -E_1 \\ -E_2 \end{pmatrix}$

(b) $I_1 = 9, I_2 = -\frac{42}{11}, I_3 = -\frac{72}{11}$

(c) $I_2 - I_2 = \frac{30}{11}$

4 (a) $\begin{pmatrix} R_1 + R_2 & -R_2 & 0 & 0 \\ -R_2 & R_2 + R_5 & 0 & -R_5 \\ 0 & 0 & R_3 + R_4 & -R_4 \\ 0 & -R_5 & -R_4 & R_4 + R_5 \end{pmatrix}\begin{pmatrix} I_1 \\ I_2 \\ I_3 \\ I_4 \end{pmatrix}$
$= \begin{pmatrix} E_1 \\ E_2 \\ E_3 \\ E_4 \end{pmatrix}$

(b) $I_1 = 5.5966, I_2 = 7.7546, I_3 = 4.3025, I_4 = 6.5445$

(c) $I_4 - I_2 = -1.2101$, that is a current of 1.2101 from Y to X.

End of chapter exercises

1 Determine which of the following systems have a non-trivial solution:
(a) $2x + 3y = 0$
$4x + 6y = 0$
(b) $9x - y = 0$
$x + 9y = 0$
(c) $x - 3y = 0$
$-3x + 9y = 0$
(d) $\frac{x}{2} - \frac{2y}{3} = 0$
$3x - 4y = 0$
(e) $-x + 4y = 0$
$2x - 6y = 0$

2 Determine which of the following systems have a non-trivial solution:
(a) $2x - y + 3z = 0$
$x + 2y - z = 0$
$5x + 5z = 0$
(b) $3x + 2y - z = 0$
$2x - 3y + 2z = 0$
$7x - 4y + 3z = 0$
(c) $x + 4y + 3z = 0$
$9x - 10y - z = 0$
$6x - 3y + z = 0$
(d) $3x - y - z = 0$
$x + y + 2z = 0$
$2x - 2y + 3z = 0$
(e) $-x + 2y - 3z = 0$
$4x + z = 0$
$11x + 2y = 0$

3 Figure C13.1 illustrates an electrical network with two mesh currents, I_1 and I_2, shown.
(a) Determine a matrix equation for I_1 and I_2.

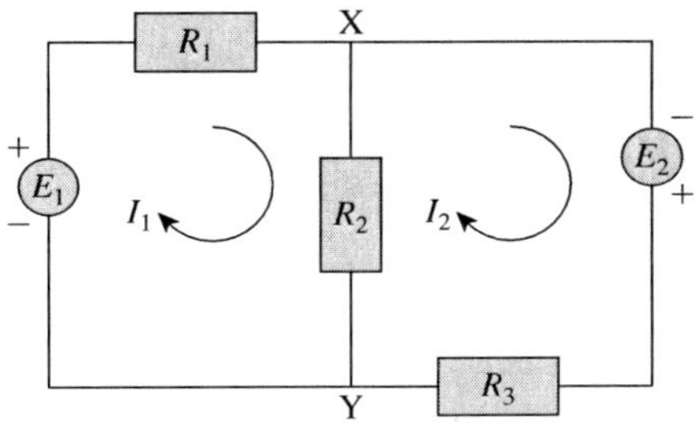

Figure C13.1

(b) Calculate I_1 and I_2 given $E_1 = 5$, $E_2 = 5$, $R_1 = 10$, $R_2 = 6$ and $R_3 = 5$.
(c) Calculate the current in the branch XY.

4 Figure C13.2 illustrates an electrical network with mesh currents I_1, I_2 and I_3 shown.
(a) Determine a matrix equation for I_1, I_2 and I_3.
(b) Calculate I_1, I_2 and I_3 given $E_1 = 5$, $E_2 = 6$, $E_3 = 12$, $R_1 = 15$, $R_2 = 5$ and $R_3 = 10$.
(c) Calculate the current in the branch XY.

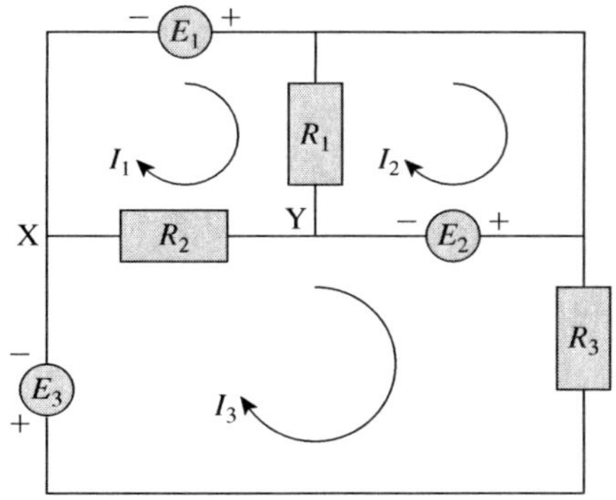

Figure C13.2

5 Figure C13.3 illustrates an electrical network with mesh currents I_1, I_2, I_3 and I_4 shown.
(a) Determine a matrix equation for I_1, I_2, I_3 and I_4.
(b) Calculate I_1, I_2, I_3 and I_4 given $E_1 = 6$, $E_2 = 12$, $R_1 = R_2 = 3$ and $R_3 = R_4 = R_5 = 2$.
(c) Calculate the current in the branch XY.

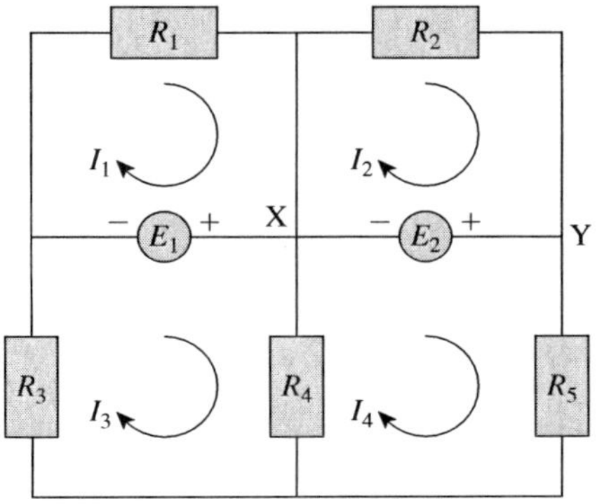

Figure C13.3

6 Solve the following simultaneous equations using Cramer's rule:

(a) $2x - y = 5$
$x + y = 1$

(b) $2x - y = 5$
$-x + 3y = 0$

(c) $x + 3y = 1$
$2x - 5y = -9$

7 Solve the following simultaneous equations using Cramer's rule:

(a) $i_1 + 2i_2 - i_3 = 7$
$i_1 + i_2 + 2i_3 = 7$
$2i_1 - i_3 = 3$

(b) $3a - b + c = 4$
$a - 2b + 3c = 2$
$a + b - 5c = 4$

(c) $\alpha + 2\beta + \gamma = 1$
$2\alpha + 3\beta + 2\gamma = 2$
$a + 4\beta - \gamma = -3$

8 Solve the following simultaneous equations using the inverse matrix method:

(a) $x + 2y = 11$
$2x - y = 7$

(b) $r_1 + 2r_2 = 13.5$
$3r_1 + r_2 = 23$

(c) $2\alpha + 3\beta = 5$
$\alpha + \dfrac{\beta}{2} = 0.5$

9 Solve the following simultaneous equations using the inverse matrix method:

(a) $x + y - z = -1$
$2x - y + 2z = 8$
$2x + 3y - z = -3$

(b) $2I_1 + I_2 - I_3 = 10$
$4I_1 + 3I_2 + 2I_3 = 18$
$3I_1 - 3I_2 + 4I_3 = 0.5$

(c) $r + s - t = 0.5$
$-2r - s + 2t = -0.2$
$r - 4s - 2t = -5$

10 Given that

$$\frac{1}{21}\begin{pmatrix} 4 & 51 & 49 & -28 \\ -9 & -57 & -63 & 42 \\ -6 & -66 & -63 & 42 \\ 4 & 9 & 7 & -7 \end{pmatrix}$$

is the inverse of

$$\begin{pmatrix} 3 & -1 & 4 & 6 \\ 1 & 2 & -1 & 2 \\ 2 & -2 & 3 & -2 \\ 5 & 0 & 4 & 1 \end{pmatrix}$$

solve the following systems of equations:

(a) $3w - x + 4y + 6z = 19$
$w + 2x - y + 2z = 11$
$2w - 2x + 3y - 2z = -11$
$5w + 4y + z = 2$

(b) $2\alpha - 2\beta + 3\gamma - 2\delta = 11$
$\alpha + 2\beta - \gamma + 2\delta = -2$
$5\alpha + 4\gamma + \delta = 15$
$3\alpha - \beta + 4\gamma + 6\delta = 1$

11 State which of the following matrices are in echelon form:

(a) $\begin{pmatrix} 1 & 0 & 1 \\ 0 & 1 & 1 \end{pmatrix}$

(b) $\begin{pmatrix} 1 & 1 & 1 & 0 \\ 0 & 0 & 0 & 1 \\ 0 & 0 & 0 & 0 \end{pmatrix}$

(c) $\begin{pmatrix} 1 & 2 & 3 & 1 & 4 \\ 0 & 0 & 1 & -1 & 0 \\ 0 & 0 & 0 & 1 & 2 \end{pmatrix}$

(d) $\begin{pmatrix} 1 & 0 & 1 & -3 \\ 0 & 0 & 0 & 0 \\ 0 & 1 & 4 & 3 \end{pmatrix}$

(e) $\begin{pmatrix} 0 & 0 & 1 & 2 & 0 & -4 \\ 0 & 0 & 0 & 0 & 1 & 3 \end{pmatrix}$

12 Use Gaussian elimination to solve the following systems of equations:

(a) $3i_1 - 2i_2 = 13$
$2i_1 - 5i_2 = 16$

(b) $4\alpha - \beta = 4$
$\dfrac{\alpha}{2} + \dfrac{\beta}{3} = 6$

(c) $-\dfrac{x}{2} + 3y = 4$
$2x - 7y = -11$

13 Use Gaussian elimination to solve the following sets of equations:

(a) $2x - y - z = 3$
$5x + 7y + 3z = 10$
$-3x - y + 4z = -17$

(b) $2\alpha - \beta + \gamma = 11$
$\dfrac{\alpha}{2} + \beta + 2\gamma = 6$
$3\beta - 7\gamma = -37$

(c) $i_1 + 2i_2 - 3i_3 = 2$
$-3i_1 + 2i_2 + i_3 = 10$
$2i_1 - 3i_3 = -9$

14 Use Jacobi's method to find the solution of

$$-2x + y = 8.5$$
$$3x + 4y = 1$$

Take $x_0 = -2$, $y_0 = 2$ and perform five iterations.

15 Solve the equations in question 14 using the Gauss–Seidel method; take $x_0 = -2$, $y_0 = 2$ and perform five iterations.

16 Use Jacobi's method to solve

$$4x - y = -9.4$$
$$3x + 5y = 7.9$$

Take $x_0 = -1$, $y_0 = 1.5$ and perform five iterations.

17 Solve the equations of question 16 using the Gauss–Seidel method. Use the same initial values and perform five iterations.

18 The matrix, A, is defined by

$$A = \begin{pmatrix} 3 & 7 \\ -1 & -5 \end{pmatrix}$$

(a) Calculate the characteristic equation of A.
(b) Calculate the eigenvalues of A.
(c) Calculate the eigenvectors of A.

19 (a) Show that the matrix

$$\begin{pmatrix} 5 & -1 \\ 4 & 1 \end{pmatrix}$$

has only one eigenvalue.
(b) Find the eigenvector of the matrix.

20 The matrix A is defined by

$$A = \begin{pmatrix} 3 & 2 & -2 \\ 0 & -4 & 4 \\ 7 & 2 & -2 \end{pmatrix}$$

(a) Calculate the eigenvalues of A.
(b) Calculate the eigenvectors of A.

21 The matrix B is defined by

$$B = \begin{pmatrix} -3 & -1 & 0 \\ 5 & 2 & 1 \\ -5 & 5 & -4 \end{pmatrix}$$

(a) Calculate the eigenvalues of B.
(b) Calculate the eigenvectors of B.

Solutions to exercises

1 (a), (c) and (d) have non-trivial solutions.

2 (a), (b) and (e) have non-trivial solutions.

3 (a) $\begin{pmatrix} R_1 + R_2 & -R_2 \\ -R_2 & R_2 + R_3 \end{pmatrix}\begin{pmatrix} I_1 \\ I_2 \end{pmatrix} = \begin{pmatrix} E_1 \\ E_2 \end{pmatrix}$

(b) $I_1 = 0.6071$, $I_2 = 0.7857$
(c) 0.1786 from Y to X

4 (a) $\begin{pmatrix} R_1 + R_2 & -R_1 & -R_2 \\ -R_1 & R_1 & 0 \\ -R_2 & 0 & R_2 + R_3 \end{pmatrix}\begin{pmatrix} I_1 \\ I_2 \\ I_3 \end{pmatrix}$
$= \begin{pmatrix} E_1 \\ -E_2 \\ E_2 + E_3 \end{pmatrix}$

(b) $I_1 = 1.5$, $I_2 = 1.1$, $I_3 = 1.7$
(c) 0.2

5 (a) $$\begin{pmatrix} R_1 & 0 & 0 & 0 \\ 0 & R_2 & 0 & 0 \\ 0 & 0 & R_3 + R_4 & -R_4 \\ 0 & 0 & -R_4 & R_4 + R_5 \end{pmatrix}\begin{pmatrix} I_1 \\ I_2 \\ I_3 \\ I_4 \end{pmatrix} = \begin{pmatrix} -E_1 \\ -E_2 \\ E_1 \\ E_2 \end{pmatrix}$$

(b) $I_1 = -2, I_2 = -4, I_3 = 4, I_4 = 5$
(c) 9

6 (a) $x = 2, y = -1$
(b) $x = 3, y = 1$
(c) $x = -2, y = 1$

7 (a) $i_1 = 2, i_2 = 3, i_3 = 1$
(b) $a = 1, b = -2, c = -1$
(c) $\alpha = -1, \beta = 0, \gamma = 2$

8 (a) $x = 5, y = 3$
(b) $r_1 = 6.5, r_2 = 3.5$
(c) $\alpha = -0.5, \beta = 2$

9 (a) $x = 2, y = -2, z = 1$
(b) $I_1 = 3.5, I_2 = 2, I_3 = -1$
(c) $r = 1.2, s = 0.8, t = 1.5$

10 (a) $w = 2, x = -1, y = -3, z = 4$
(b) $\alpha = 1, \beta = 2, \gamma = 3, \delta = -2$

11 (a), (b), (c) and (e) are in echelon form.

12 (a) $i_1 = 3, i_2 = -2$
(b) $\alpha = 4, \beta = 12$
(c) $x = -2, y = 1$

13 (a) $x = 1, y = 2, z = -3$
(b) $\alpha = 2, \beta = -3, \gamma = 4$
(c) $i_1 = 3, i_2 = 7, i_3 = 5$

14

n	x_n	y_n
0	−2	2
1	−3.25	1.75
2	−3.375	2.6875
3	−2.9063	2.7813
4	−2.8594	2.4297
5	−3.0351	2.3496

The exact answer is $x = -3, y = 2.5$.

15

n	x_n	y_n
0	−2	2
1	−3.25	2.6875
2	−2.9063	2.4297
3	−3.0352	2.5264
4	−2.9868	2.4901
5	−3.0049	2.5037

16

n	x_n	y_n
0	−1	1.5
1	−1.975	2.18
2	−1.805	2.765
3	−1.6588	2.663
4	−1.6843	2.5753
5	−1.7062	2.5906

The exact answer is $x = -1.7, y = 2.6$.

17

n	x_n	y_n
0	−1	1.5
1	−1.975	2.765
2	−1.6588	2.5753
3	−1.7062	2.6037
4	−1.6991	2.5994
5	−1.7001	2.6001

18 (a) $\lambda^2 + 2\lambda - 8 = 0$
(b) −4, 2
(c) $\begin{pmatrix} -0.7071 \\ 0.7071 \end{pmatrix}, \begin{pmatrix} 0.9899 \\ -0.1414 \end{pmatrix}$

19 (a) $\lambda = 3$
(b) $\begin{pmatrix} 1 \\ 2 \end{pmatrix}$

20 (a) −4, 0, 1
(b) $\begin{pmatrix} -0.2747 \\ 0.9615 \\ 0 \end{pmatrix}, \begin{pmatrix} 0 \\ 0.7071 \\ 0.7071 \end{pmatrix}, \begin{pmatrix} 0.1543 \\ 0.6172 \\ 0.7715 \end{pmatrix}$

21 (a) −4, −3, 2
(b) $\begin{pmatrix} -0.0902 \\ -0.0902 \\ 0.9919 \end{pmatrix}, \begin{pmatrix} -0.1961 \\ 0 \\ 0.9806 \end{pmatrix}, \begin{pmatrix} 0.1400 \\ -0.7001 \\ -0.7001 \end{pmatrix}$

Vectors

Chapter 14

In many engineering applications the direction of a physical quantity is of particular interest. **Vectors** are mathematical quantities that contain information about direction as well as magnitude and so are particularly suited to modelling physical situations where direction is important.

Special rules and methods have been developed for handling vectors, and these are described and developed in this chapter.

Chapter 14 contents

BLOCK 1 Basic concepts of vectors

1.1 Introduction

In engineering, frequent reference is made to physical quantities, such as force, speed and time. For example, we talk of the speed of a car, and the force in a compressed spring. It is useful to separate physical quantities into two types. Quantities of the first type are known as **scalars**. These can be fully described by a single number known as the **magnitude**. An example of a scalar quantity is the mass of an object, so we might state

'the mass of the stone is 3 kg'

It is important to give the units in which the quantity is measured.

Quantities of the second type are those that require the specification of a **direction**, in addition to a magnitude, before they are completely described. These are known as **vectors**. An example of a vector quantity is the force applied to an object to make it move. When the object shown in Figure 1.1 is moved by applying a force to it we can achieve different effects by applying the force in different directions.

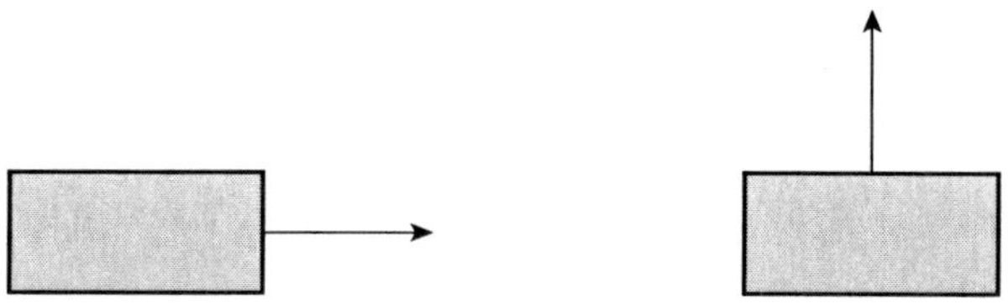

Figure 1.1 Applying the force in a different direction will achieve a different effect.

In order to specify the force completely we must state the direction in which the force acts. For example, we might state

'a force of 5 newtons is applied vertically upwards'

Clearly this would achieve a different effect from applying the force horizontally to the right. The direction in which the force acts is crucial.

Special methods have been developed for handling vectors in calculations, giving rise to subjects known as vector algebra, vector geometry and vector calculus. Quantities that are vectors must be manipulated according to certain rules, which are described in this and subsequent blocks.

Key point

Vectors are quantities that are specified by giving both their magnitudes and directions, and which are manipulated according to particular, and well-defined, rules.

There are many engineering applications in which vector and scalar quantities play an important role. For example, speed, mass, work, voltage, energy are all scalars, whereas force, acceleration, velocity, electromagnetic field strength are all vectors. Furthermore, when computer software is written to control the position of a robot, the position is described by vectors.

Sometimes confusion can arise because words used in general conversation have specific technical meanings when used in engineering calculations. An example of this ambiguity is the use of the words 'speed' and 'velocity'. In everyday conversation these words have the same meaning and can be used interchangeably. However, in engineering and science they are not the same. **Speed** is a scalar quantity described by giving a single number in appropriate units. So we can make statements such as

'the speed of the car is 40 kilometres per hour'

On the other hand **velocity** is a vector quantity and must be specified by giving a direction as well. So, for example, we can state

'the velocity of the aircraft is 200 metres per second due north'

In engineering calculations, the words 'speed' and 'velocity' should not be used interchangeably. Similar problems arise from use of the words 'mass' and 'weight'. In engineering and science these are different. **Mass** is a scalar that describes the amount of substance in an object. The unit of mass is the kilogram. **Weight** is a vector, the direction of which is vertically downwards. Weight arises through the action of gravity. The unit of weight is the newton.

Displacement and **distance** are related quantities that can cause confusion. Whereas distance is a scalar, displacement is 'directed distance': that is, distance together with a specified direction. So, referring to Figure 1.2, if an object is moved from point A to point B, we can state that the distance moved is 10 metres, but the displacement is 10 metres *in the direction from A to B*.

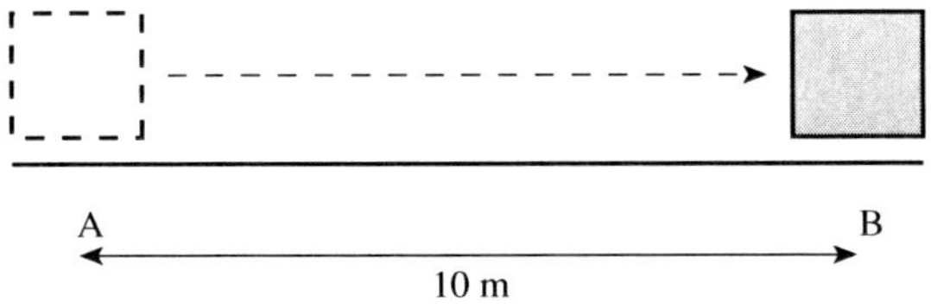

Figure 1.2 Displacement means directed distance.

You will meet many other quantities in the course of your studies, and it will be helpful to know which are vectors and which are scalars. Some common quantities and their type are listed in Table 1.1. The common units in which these are measured are also shown.

Table 1.1
Some common scalar and vector quantities.

Quantity	Type	SI unit
Distance	Scalar	metre, m
Area	Scalar	metres squared, m^2
Mass	Scalar	kilogram, kg
Temperature	Scalar	kelvin, K
Pressure	Scalar	pascal, Pa
Work	Scalar	joule, J
Energy	Scalar	joule, J
Displacement	Vector	metre, m
Force	Vector	newton, N
Velocity	Vector	metres per second, $m\ s^{-1}$
Acceleration	Vector	metres per second per second, $m\ s^{-2}$

Exercises

1 State, or find out, which of the following are scalars and which are vectors: (a) the volume of a petrol tank, (b) a length measured in metres, (c) a length measured in miles, (d) the angular velocity of a flywheel, (e) the relative velocity of two aircraft, (f) the work done by a force, (g) electrostatic potential, (h) the momentum of an atomic particle.

Solutions to exercises

1 (a), (b), (c), (f), (g) are scalars; (d), (e) and (h) are vectors.

1.2 The mathematical description of vector quantities

Because a vector has a direction as well as a magnitude we can represent a vector by drawing a line. The length of the line represents the magnitude of the vector given some appropriate scale, and the direction of the line represents the direction of the vector. We call such a representation a **directed line segment**. The length of the line is also referred to as the **modulus** of the vector.

For example, Figure 1.3 shows a vector that might represent a velocity of 3 m s^{-1} north-west. Note that the arrow on the vector indicates the direction required.

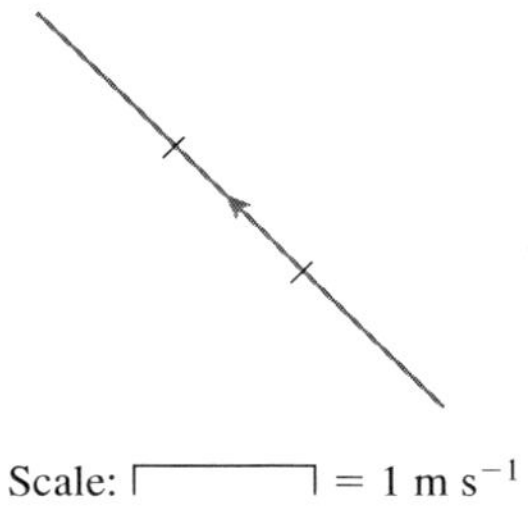

Figure 1.3
A vector quantity can be represented by drawing a line marked with an arrow.

More generally, Figure 1.4 shows an arbitrary vector quantity. It is important when writing vectors to distinguish them from scalars, and so various notations are used. In Figure 1.4 we can write the vector as $\overrightarrow{AB}$ where the arrow is used to emphasise that we mean the vector from A to B. In books and other printed work, vectors are often indicated by using a bold typeface such as $\boldsymbol{a}$. It is difficult when handwriting to reproduce the bold face and so it is conventional to underline vector quantities and write $\underline{a}$ instead. So $\overrightarrow{AB}$, $\boldsymbol{a}$ and $\underline{a}$ all represent the same vector in Figure 1.4. In Figure 1.4 the point A is the **tail** of vector $\overrightarrow{AB}$ and point B is referred to as its **head**.

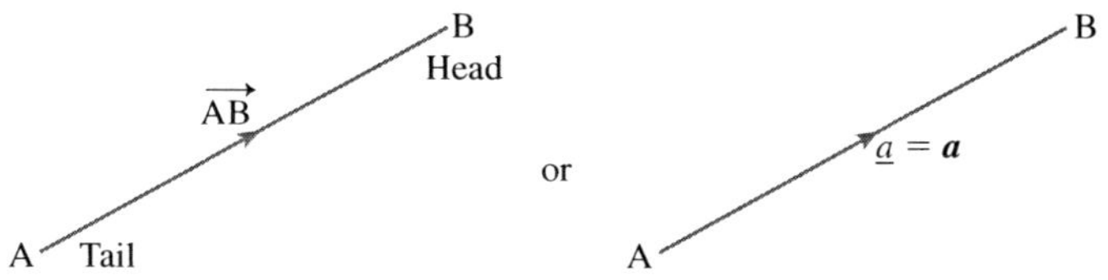

Figure 1.4
Vectors can be written in different ways:
$\overrightarrow{AB} = \boldsymbol{a} = \underline{a}$.

Example 1.1

Consider Figure 1.5, which shows an object being pulled by a force of 5N at an angle of 60° to the horizontal. Show how this force can be represented by a vector.

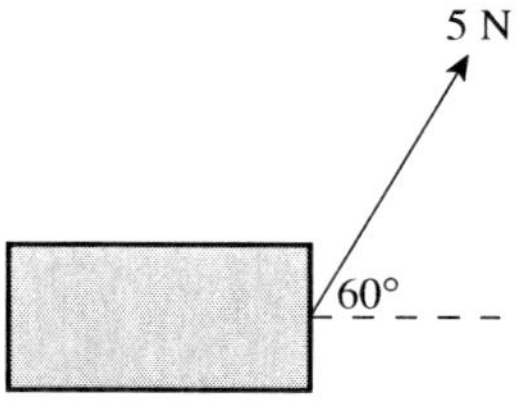

Figure 1.5
An object being pulled by a force.

Solution

The force can be represented by drawing a line of length 5 units at an angle of 60° to the horizontal, as shown in Figure 1.6. Note that we have labelled the force $\boldsymbol{F}$. The modulus of the force is 5 newtons. Whenever several forces are involved they can be labelled $\boldsymbol{F}_1$, $\boldsymbol{F}_2$ and so on.

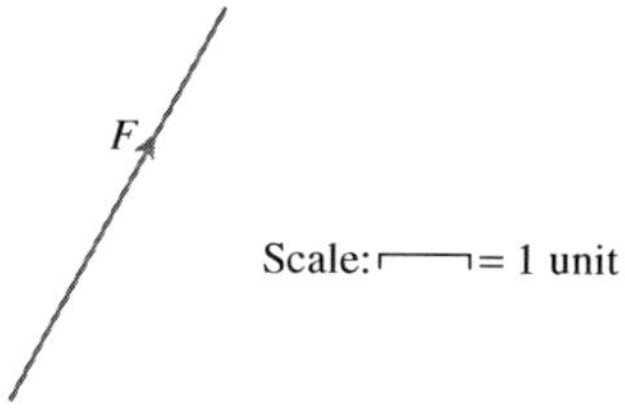

Figure 1.6 The force in Figure 1.5 represented as a vector.

When we wish to refer to just the magnitude of a vector we write this using the modulus sign as $|\overrightarrow{AB}|$, or $|\boldsymbol{a}|$, or $|\underline{a}|$. Alternatively we write simply a.

Referring to Figure 1.6, we can write the magnitude of the force $\boldsymbol{F}$ as $|\boldsymbol{F}|$ or simply F (not bold, and without the underline or modulus signs).

Key point

The magnitude, or **modulus**, of a vector $\underline{a} = \overrightarrow{AB}$ can be written as

$$|\boldsymbol{a}|, \quad |\underline{a}|, \quad \text{or} \quad |\overrightarrow{AB}|, \quad \text{or simply} \quad a$$

Equal vectors

In general two vectors are said to be **equal vectors** if they have the same magnitude and direction. So, in Figure 1.7 the vectors $\overrightarrow{CD}$ and $\overrightarrow{AB}$ are equal even though their locations differ.

This is a useful and important property of vectors: a vector can be translated maintaining the same direction and magnitude, without changing the vector itself.

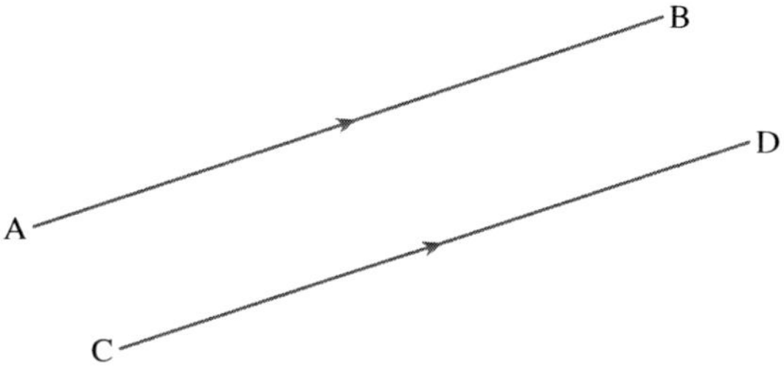

Figure 1.7 Vectors can be equal even when their locations differ.

There are exceptions to this property. For example, a vector is sometimes used to represent the position of an object that might be located at a particular point in space. Such a vector cannot be translated freely. Nevertheless most of the vectors we shall meet can be translated, and as such are called **free vectors**.

Negative vectors

The vector $-\boldsymbol{a}$ is a vector in the opposite direction to $\boldsymbol{a}$, but with the same magnitude as $\boldsymbol{a}$, as shown in Figure 1.8. Geometrically, if $\boldsymbol{a} = \overrightarrow{AB}$ then $-\boldsymbol{a} = \overrightarrow{BA}$.

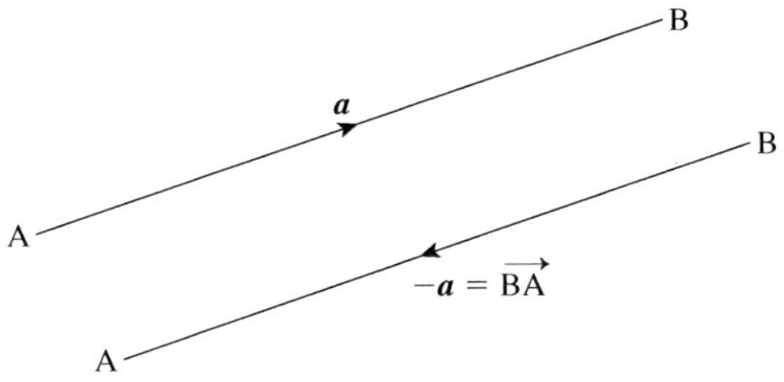

Figure 1.8
The negative vector $-\boldsymbol{a}$ has the opposite direction to $\boldsymbol{a}$.

Exercises

1 An object is subject to two forces, one of 3 N vertically downwards, and one of 8 N horizontally to the right. Draw a diagram representing these two forces as vectors.

2 Draw a diagram showing an arbitrary vector $\boldsymbol{F}$. On the diagram show the vector $-\boldsymbol{F}$.

3 Vectors $\boldsymbol{p}$ and $\boldsymbol{q}$ are equal vectors. Draw a diagram that might be used to represent $\boldsymbol{p}$ and $\boldsymbol{q}$.

Solutions to exercises

1 See Figure 1.9.

2 See Figure 1.10.

3 See Figure 1.11.

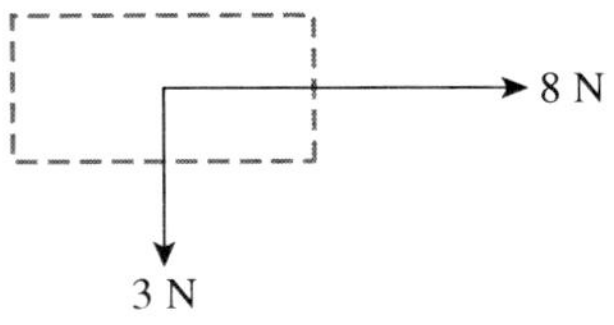

Figure 1.9

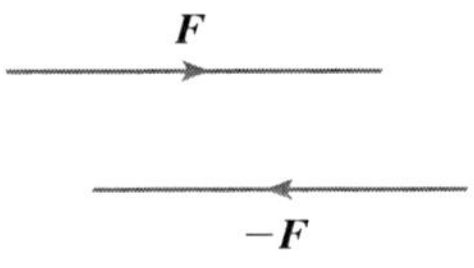

Figure 1.10

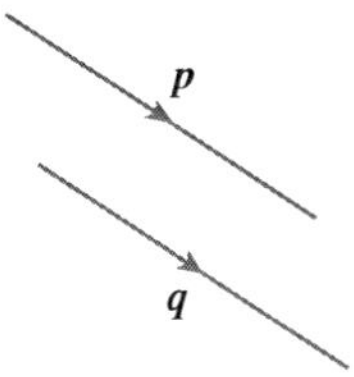

Figure 1.11

1.3 Addition and subtraction of vectors

Addition of vectors is carried out according to a rule known as the **triangle law**.

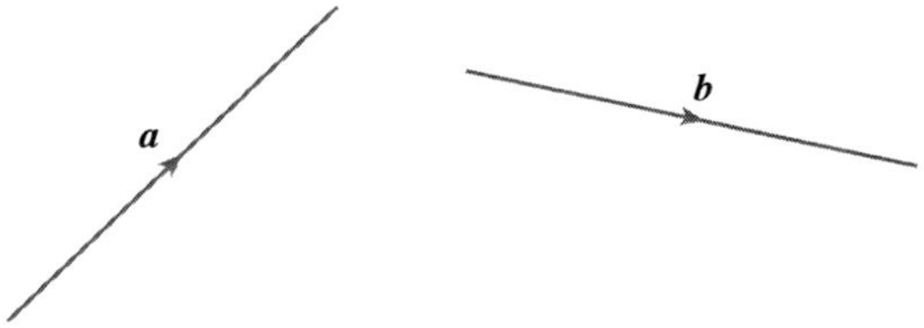

Figure 1.12 Two vectors ***a*** and ***b***.

Consider Figure 1.12. Suppose we wish to add ***b*** to ***a***. To do this ***b*** is translated, keeping its direction and length unchanged, until its tail coincides with the head of ***a***. Then the sum $\boldsymbol{a} + \boldsymbol{b}$ is defined by the vector representing the third side of the completed triangle, that is ***c*** in Figure 1.13. Note from Figure 1.13 that we can write $\boldsymbol{c} = \boldsymbol{a} + \boldsymbol{b}$.

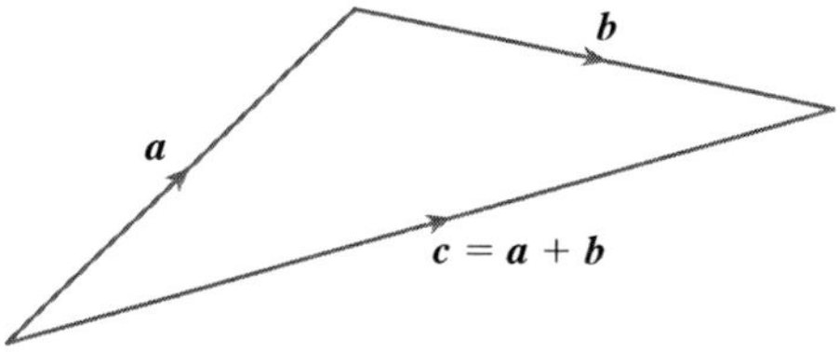

Figure 1.13 Addition of the two vectors of Figure 1.12 using the triangle law.

Key point

Vectors are added using the **triangle law**:

Example 1.2

Redraw the diagram in Figure 1.14 to show the vector sum $\boldsymbol{a} + \boldsymbol{b}$.

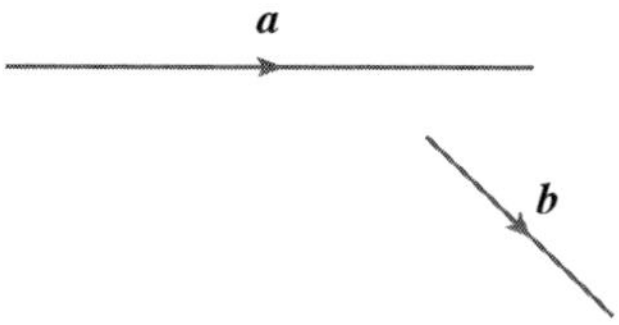

Figure 1.14

Solution

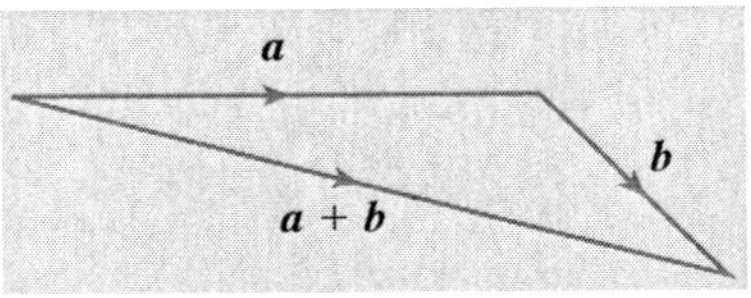

It is possible, using the triangle law, to prove the following rules, which apply to any three vectors $\boldsymbol{a}$, $\boldsymbol{b}$ and $\boldsymbol{c}$:

Key point

$\boldsymbol{a} + \boldsymbol{b} = \boldsymbol{b} + \boldsymbol{a}$ vector addition is commutative.

$\boldsymbol{a} + (\boldsymbol{b} + \boldsymbol{c}) = (\boldsymbol{a} + \boldsymbol{b}) + \boldsymbol{c}$ vector addition is associative.

To see why it is appropriate to add vectors using the triangle law consider the following examples.

Example 1.3 The route taken by an automated vehicle

An unmanned vehicle moves on tracks around a factory floor carrying components from the store at A to workers at C, as shown in Figure 1.15.

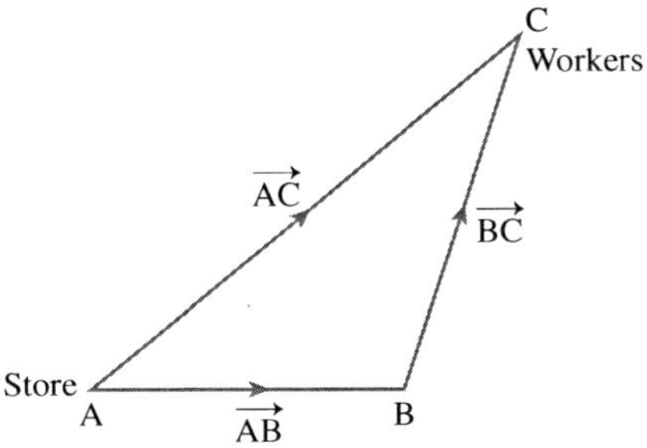

Figure 1.15
$\overrightarrow{AB} + \overrightarrow{BC} = \overrightarrow{AC}$.

The vehicle may arrive at C either directly or via a second location at B. The movement from A to B can be represented by a displacement vector $\overrightarrow{AB}$. Similarly movement from B to C can be represented by the displacement vector $\overrightarrow{BC}$, and movement from A to C can be represented by $\overrightarrow{AC}$. Since the head of vector $\overrightarrow{AB}$ touches the tail of $\overrightarrow{BC}$ the triangle law can be applied immediately to find the combined effect of the two displacements.

$$\overrightarrow{AB} + \overrightarrow{BC} = \overrightarrow{AC}$$

Example 1.4 Mechanical Engineering – Resultant of two forces acting upon a body

A force $\boldsymbol{F}_1$ of 2 N acts vertically downwards, and a force $\boldsymbol{F}_2$ of 3 N acts horizontally to the right, upon the body shown in Figure 1.16. Both forces act through the same point in the body.

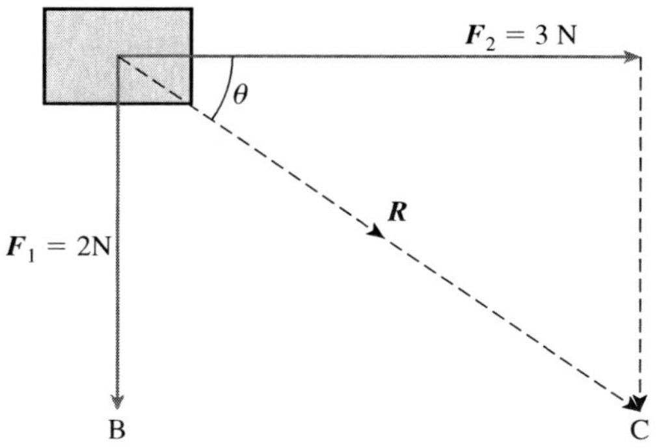

Figure 1.16
The combined effect of forces $\boldsymbol{F}_1$ and $\boldsymbol{F}_2$ is the resultant $\boldsymbol{R}$.

We can use vector addition to find the combined effect of the two forces, known as the **resultant force**. Translating $\boldsymbol{F}_1$ until its tail touches the head of $\boldsymbol{F}_2$, we complete the triangle as shown. The vector represented by the third side is the resultant, $\boldsymbol{R}$. We write

$$\boldsymbol{R} = \boldsymbol{F}_2 + \boldsymbol{F}_1$$

and say that $\boldsymbol{R}$ is the **vector sum** of $\boldsymbol{F}_2$ and $\boldsymbol{F}_1$. The resultant force acts at an angle of θ below the horizontal where $\tan\theta = \frac{2}{3}$, so that $\theta = 33.7°$, and has magnitude given by Pythagoras's theorem as $\sqrt{13}$N.

Key point

The **resultant** of two vectors $\boldsymbol{a}$ and $\boldsymbol{b}$ is their **vector sum** $\boldsymbol{a} + \boldsymbol{b}$.

Example 1.5 Mechanical Engineering – Resolving a force into two perpendicular directions

In the previous example we saw that two forces acting upon a body can be replaced by a single force which has the same effect. It is sometimes useful to consider a single force as two forces acting at right angles to each other. Consider the force $\boldsymbol{F}$ in Figure 1.17.

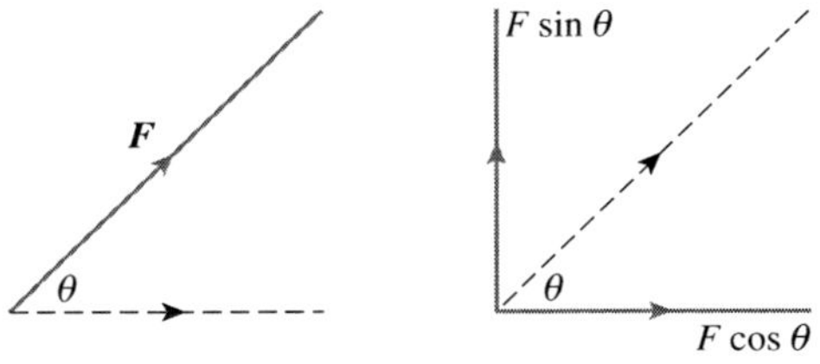

Figure 1.17
Force $\boldsymbol{F}$ has two perpendicular components.

This force can be replaced by two perpendicular forces as shown. It is a straightforward use of trigonometry to show that the horizontal force has magnitude $F\cos\theta$. The vertical force has magnitude $F\sin\theta$. We say that $\boldsymbol{F}$ has been **resolved into two perpendicular components**.

For example, Figure 1.18 shows a force of 5 N acting at an angle of 30° to the x axis. It can be resolved into two components, one directed along the x axis with magnitude 5 cos 30° and one perpendicular to this of magnitude 5 sin 30°. Together, these two components have the same effect as the original force.

Figure 1.18

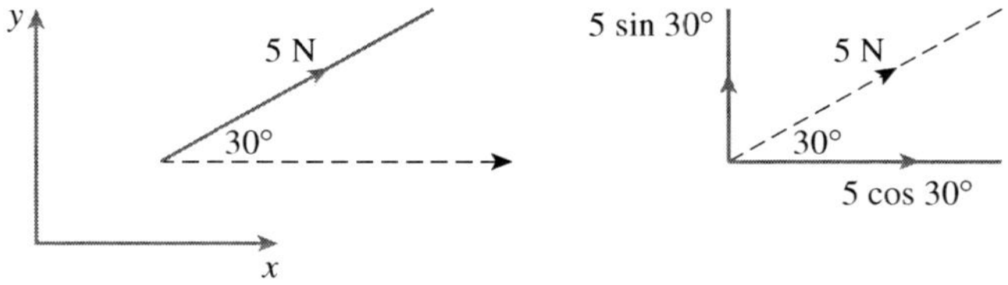

Example 1.6

Consider the force shown in Figure 1.19. Resolve this force into two perpendicular components, one horizontally to the right, and one vertically upwards.

Figure 1.19

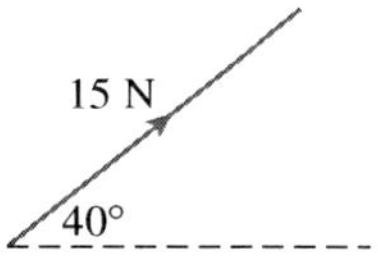

Solution

15 cos 40° = 11.49 N horiz., 15 sin 40° = 9.64 N vert.

Subtraction of one vector from another is performed by adding the corresponding negative vector. That is, if we seek $\boldsymbol{a} - \boldsymbol{b}$ we form $\boldsymbol{a} + (-\boldsymbol{b})$. This is shown geometrically in Figure 1.20.

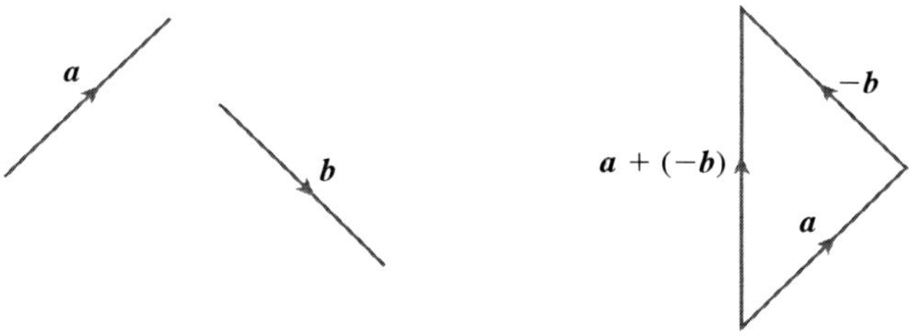

Figure 1.20 Subtraction of a vector is performed by adding a negative vector.

Example 1.7

Figure 1.21 shows vectors $\boldsymbol{p} = \overrightarrow{OP}$ and $\boldsymbol{q} = \overrightarrow{OQ}$. What is the geometrical significance of the vector $\boldsymbol{q} - \boldsymbol{p}$?

Figure 1.21

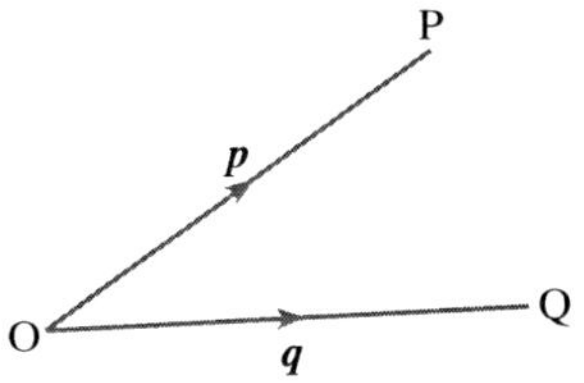

Solution

We know that $\boldsymbol{q} - \boldsymbol{p}$ is interpreted as $\boldsymbol{q} + (-\boldsymbol{p})$.

Start by drawing in the vector $-\boldsymbol{p}$. This is shown in Figure 1.22(a). It has been drawn with its tail touching the head of $\boldsymbol{q}$ so that we can apply the triangle rule for addition. Figure 1.22(b) shows the application of the triangle rule. Note that the resultant $\boldsymbol{q} + (-\boldsymbol{p})$ is the same as the vector $\overrightarrow{PQ}$. This result is very important.

Figure 1.22

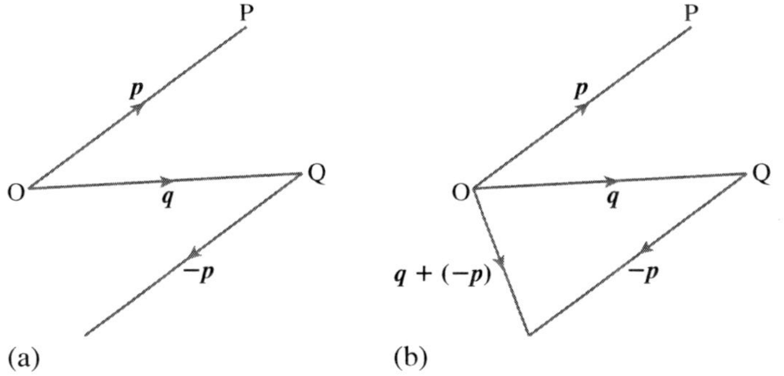

Key point

Given two vectors $\boldsymbol{p} = \overrightarrow{OP}$ and $\boldsymbol{q} = \overrightarrow{OQ}$ (Figure 1.23) the vector from P to Q is given by $\boldsymbol{q} - \boldsymbol{p}$.

Figure 1.23

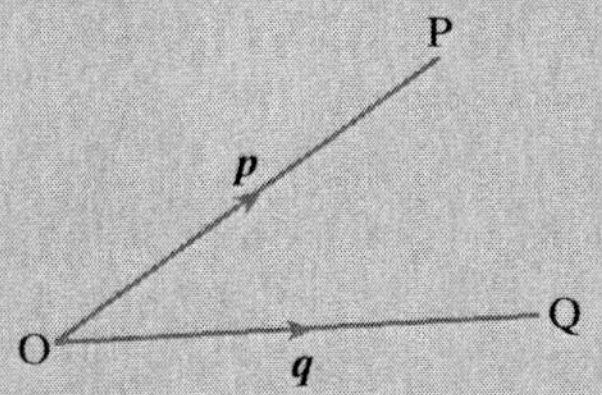

Exercises

1 Vectors $\boldsymbol{p}$ and $\boldsymbol{q}$ represent two perpendicular sides of a square ABCD with $\boldsymbol{p} = \overrightarrow{AB}$ and $\boldsymbol{q} = \overrightarrow{BC}$. Find vector expressions that represent the diagonals of the square $\overrightarrow{AC}$ and $\overrightarrow{BD}$.

2 In the rectangle ABCD, side AB is represented by the vector $\boldsymbol{p}$ and side BC is represented by the vector $\boldsymbol{q}$. State the physical significance of the vectors $\boldsymbol{p} + \boldsymbol{q}$ and $\boldsymbol{p} - \boldsymbol{q}$.

3 An object is positioned at the origin of a set of axes. Two forces act upon it. The first has magnitude 9 N and acts in the direction of the positive y axis. The second has magnitude 4 N and acts in the direction of the negative x axis. Calculate the magnitude and direction of the resultant force.

4 An object moves in the xy plane with a velocity of 15 ms^{-1} in a direction at 48° above the positive x axis. Resolve this velocity into two components, one along the x axis and one along the y axis.

5 Draw a right-angled triangle ABC with the right angle at B. Label ∠ACB as θ. Show that
(a) $BC = AC\cos\theta$
(b) $AB = AC\sin\theta$

Solutions to exercises

1 $\boldsymbol{p} + \boldsymbol{q}$, $\boldsymbol{q} - \boldsymbol{p}$.

2 $\boldsymbol{p} + \boldsymbol{q}$ is the diagonal AC, $\boldsymbol{p} - \boldsymbol{q}$ is the diagonal DB.

3 magnitude $\sqrt{97}$, at an angle 66° above the negative x axis

4 10.04 ms^{-1} along the x axis, and 11.15 ms^{-1} along the y axis

1.4 Multiplying a vector by a scalar

If k is any positive scalar and $\boldsymbol{a}$ is a vector then $k\boldsymbol{a}$ is a vector in the same direction as $\boldsymbol{a}$ but k times as long. If k is negative, $k\boldsymbol{a}$ is a vector in the opposite direction to $\boldsymbol{a}$ and k times as long. The vector $k\boldsymbol{a}$ is said to be a **scalar multiple** of $\boldsymbol{a}$. Consider the vectors shown in Figure 1.24.

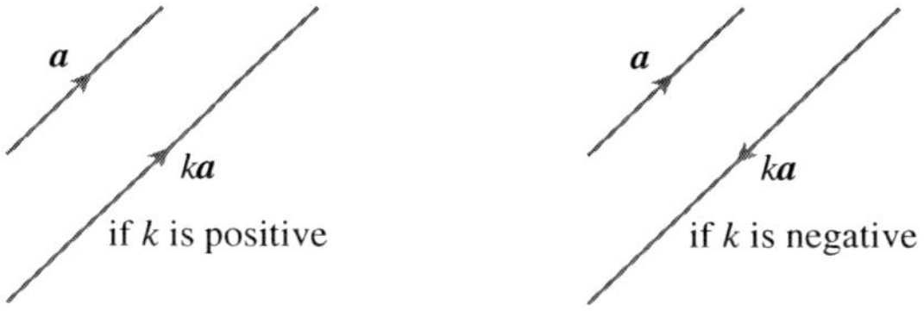

Figure 1.24 Multiplying a vector by a scalar.

The vector $3\boldsymbol{a}$ is three times as long as $\boldsymbol{a}$ and has the same direction. The vector $\frac{1}{2}\boldsymbol{r}$ is in the same direction as $\boldsymbol{r}$ but is half as long. The vector $-4\boldsymbol{b}$ is in the opposite direction to $\boldsymbol{b}$ and four times as long.

For any scalars k and l, and any vectors $\boldsymbol{a}$ and $\boldsymbol{b}$, the following rules hold:

Key point

$$k(\boldsymbol{a} + \boldsymbol{b}) = k\boldsymbol{a} + k\boldsymbol{b}$$
$$(k + l)\boldsymbol{a} = k\boldsymbol{a} + l\boldsymbol{a}$$
$$k(l)\boldsymbol{a} = (kl)\boldsymbol{a}$$

Unit vectors

A vector that has a modulus of 1 is called a **unit vector**. Unit vectors will play an important role when we come to study cartesian components in Block 2.

If $\boldsymbol{a}$ has modulus 3, say, then a unit vector in the direction of $\boldsymbol{a}$ is $\frac{1}{3}\boldsymbol{a}$, as shown in Figure 1.25.

Figure 1.25

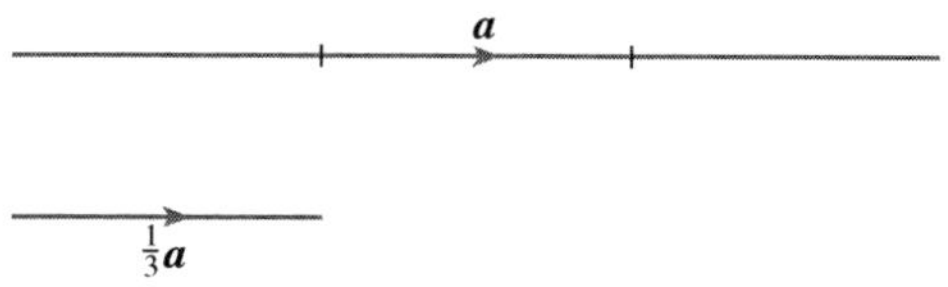

More generally, to obtain a unit vector in the direction of any vector $\boldsymbol{a}$ we divide by its modulus. A unit vector in the direction of $\boldsymbol{a}$ is given the 'hat' symbol $\hat{\boldsymbol{a}}$.

Key point

$$\hat{\boldsymbol{a}} = \frac{\boldsymbol{a}}{|\boldsymbol{a}|}$$

Exercises

1. Draw an arbitrary vector $\boldsymbol{r}$. On your diagram draw $2\boldsymbol{r}$, $4\boldsymbol{r}$, $-\boldsymbol{r}$, $-3\boldsymbol{r}$ and $\frac{1}{2}\boldsymbol{r}$.

2. In triangle OAB the point P is the midpoint of AB.
   (a) If $\overrightarrow{OA} = \boldsymbol{a}$ and $\overrightarrow{OB} = \boldsymbol{b}$ depict this on a diagram.
   (b) Write down an expression for $\overrightarrow{AB}$ in terms of $\boldsymbol{a}$ and $\boldsymbol{b}$.
   (c) Write down an expression for $\overrightarrow{AP}$ in terms of $\boldsymbol{a}$ and $\boldsymbol{b}$.
   (d) Find an expression for $\overrightarrow{OP}$ in terms of $\boldsymbol{a}$ and $\boldsymbol{b}$.

3. In triangle OAB the point P divides AB in the ratio $m{:}n$. If $\overrightarrow{OA} = \boldsymbol{a}$ and $\overrightarrow{OB} = \boldsymbol{b}$ depict this on a diagram and then find an expression for $\overrightarrow{OP}$ in terms of $\boldsymbol{a}$ and $\boldsymbol{b}$.

4. Explain what is meant by a unit vector. Given an arbitrary vector $\boldsymbol{n}$, how is a unit vector having the same direction as $\boldsymbol{n}$ found?

5. If $\hat{\boldsymbol{e}}$ is a unit vector, how would you write a vector in the same direction as $\hat{\boldsymbol{e}}$ but having modulus 8?

Solutions to exercises

2. (b) $\boldsymbol{b} - \boldsymbol{a}$ (c) $\frac{1}{2}(\boldsymbol{b} - \boldsymbol{a})$
   (d) $\boldsymbol{a} + \frac{1}{2}(\boldsymbol{b} - \boldsymbol{a}) = \frac{1}{2}\boldsymbol{a} + \frac{1}{2}\boldsymbol{b}$

3. $\overrightarrow{OP} = \boldsymbol{a} + \dfrac{m}{m + n}(\boldsymbol{b} - \boldsymbol{a})$

4. Divide $\boldsymbol{n}$ by its modulus.

5. $8\hat{\boldsymbol{e}}$

End of block exercises

1. Draw three arbitrary vectors $\boldsymbol{a}$, $\boldsymbol{b}$ and $\boldsymbol{c}$. By using the triangle law verify that vector addition is associative, that is

$$(\boldsymbol{a} + \boldsymbol{b}) + \boldsymbol{c} = \boldsymbol{a} + (\boldsymbol{b} + \boldsymbol{c})$$

2. Draw two arbitrary vectors $\boldsymbol{a}$ and $\boldsymbol{b}$. By using the triangle law verify that vector addition is commutative, that is

$$\boldsymbol{a} + \boldsymbol{b} = \boldsymbol{b} + \boldsymbol{a}$$

3 A force of 13 N acts at an angle of 62° above the x axis. Resolve this force into two components: one along the x axis and one along the y axis.

4 In the triangle ABC, M is the midpoint of BC and N is the midpoint of AC. Show that $\overrightarrow{NM} = \frac{1}{2}\overrightarrow{AB}$.

5 A particle is positioned at the origin. Two forces act on the particle. The first has magnitude 7 N and acts in the negative x direction. The second has magnitude 12 N and acts in the y direction. Calculate the magnitude and direction of the resultant force.

6 Draw two arbitrary vectors $\boldsymbol{a}$ and $\boldsymbol{b}$. Verify that

$$2(\boldsymbol{a} + \boldsymbol{b}) = 2\boldsymbol{a} + 2\boldsymbol{b}$$

(This is the first of the rules concerning scalar multiplication given on p. 638.)

Solutions to exercises

3 6.10 N along the x axis, 11.48 N along the y axis

5 13.9 N at 59.7° to the negative x axis

BLOCK 2 Cartesian components of vectors

2.1 Introduction

It is useful to be able to describe vectors with reference to various coordinate systems, such as the xy plane. So, in this block, we show how this is possible by defining unit vectors in the directions of the x and y axes. Any other vector in the xy plane can be represented as a combination of these **basis vectors**. Such a representation is called a **cartesian form**. You will learn how to calculate the modulus of a vector given in cartesian form. Then, the idea is extended to three-dimensional vectors. This is useful because most engineering problems arise in three-dimensional situations.

2.2 Two-dimensional coordinate frames and the vectors *i* and *j*

The unit vectors *i* and *j*

Figure 2.1 shows a two-dimensional coordinate frame. Any point in the plane of the figure can be defined in terms of its x and y coordinates.

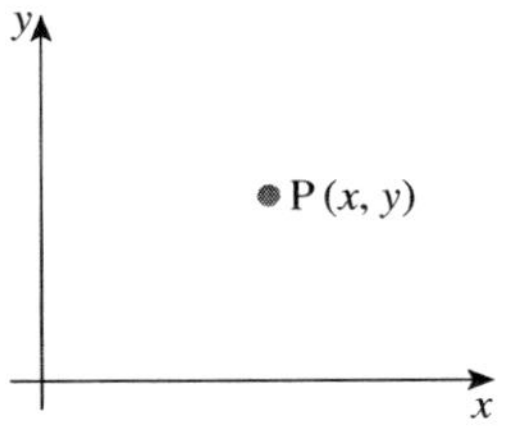

Figure 2.1 A two-dimensional coordinate frame.

A unit vector pointing in the positive direction of the x axis is denoted by $\boldsymbol{i}$. (Note that it is common practice to write this particular unit vector without the hat ^ .) It follows that any vector in the direction of the x axis will be a multiple of $\boldsymbol{i}$. Figure 2.2 shows vectors $\boldsymbol{i}$, $2\boldsymbol{i}$, $5\boldsymbol{i}$ and $-3\boldsymbol{i}$. In general a vector of length a in the direction of the x axis will be $a\boldsymbol{i}$.

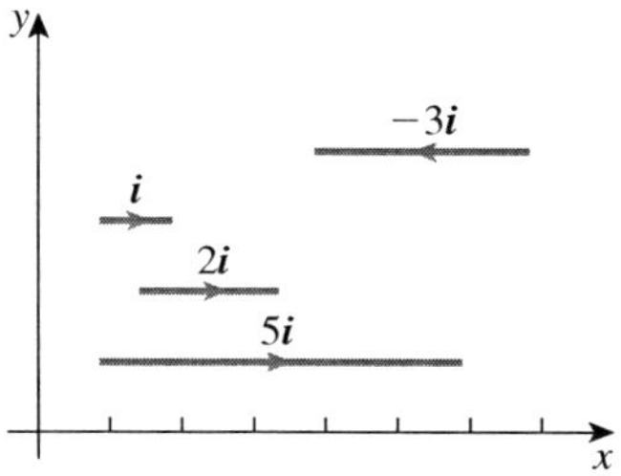

Figure 2.2
All these vectors are multiples of $\boldsymbol{i}$.

Similarly, a unit vector pointing in the positive direction of the y axis is denoted by $\boldsymbol{j}$. Any vector in the direction of the y axis will be a multiple of $\boldsymbol{j}$. Figure 2.3 shows $\boldsymbol{j}$, $4\boldsymbol{j}$ and $-2\boldsymbol{j}$. In general a vector of length b in the direction of the y axis will be $b\boldsymbol{j}$.

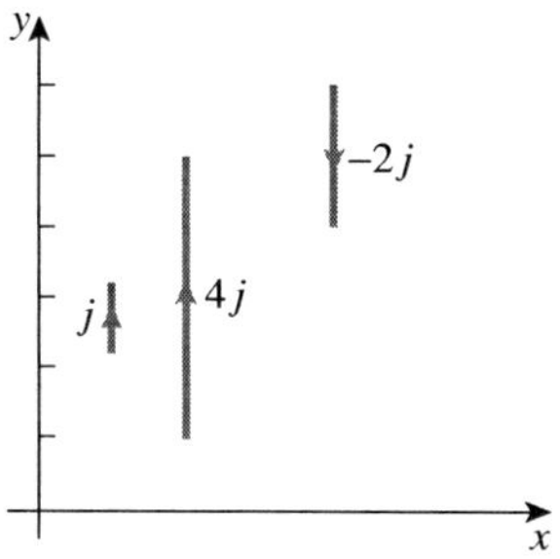

Figure 2.3
All these vectors are multiples of $\boldsymbol{j}$.

Key point

$\boldsymbol{i}$ represents a unit vector in the direction of the positive x axis.
$\boldsymbol{j}$ represents a unit vector in the direction of the positive y axis.

Example 2.1

Draw the vectors $5\boldsymbol{i}$ and $4\boldsymbol{j}$. Use your diagram and the triangle law of addition to add these two vectors together to obtain the sum $5\boldsymbol{i} + 4\boldsymbol{j}$.

Solution

First draw the vectors $5\boldsymbol{i}$ and $4\boldsymbol{j}$.

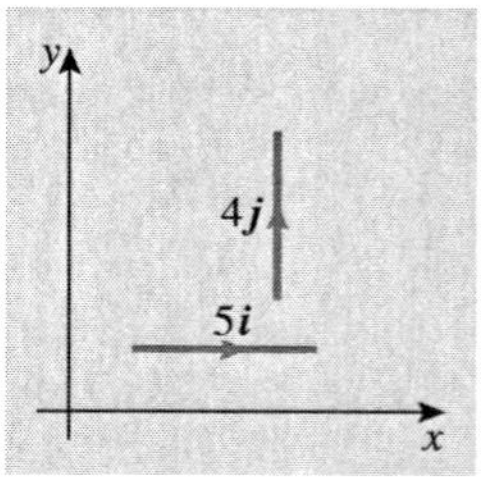

By translating the vectors so that they lie head to tail, find the vector sum $5\boldsymbol{i} + 4\boldsymbol{j}$.

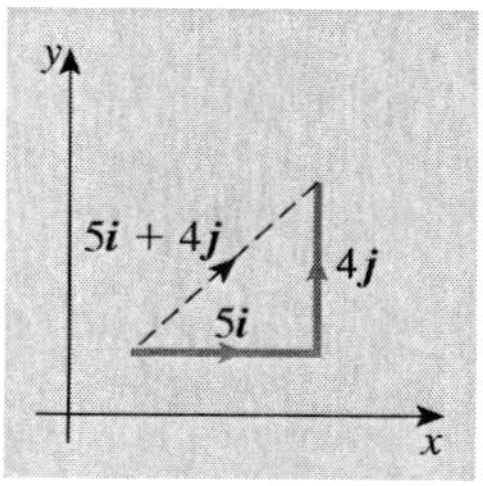

We now generalise the situation in the previous example. Consider Figure 2.4, which shows a vector $\boldsymbol{r} = \overrightarrow{AB}$.

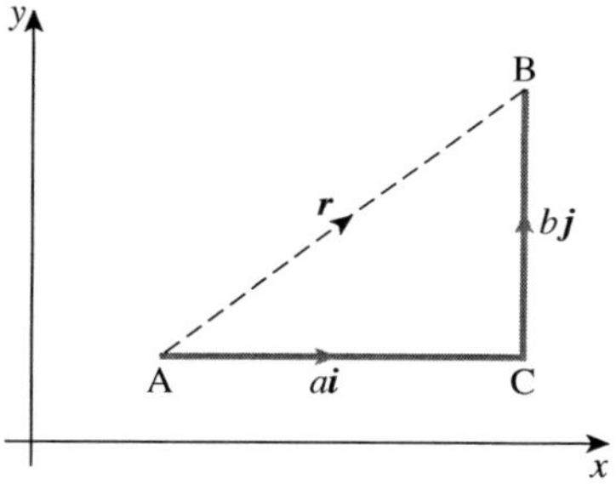

Figure 2.4
$\overrightarrow{AB} = \overrightarrow{AC} + \overrightarrow{CB}$ by the triangle law.

We can regard $\boldsymbol{r}$ as being the resultant of the two vectors $\overrightarrow{AC} = a\boldsymbol{i}$ and $\overrightarrow{CB} = b\boldsymbol{j}$. From the triangle law of vector addition

$$\boldsymbol{r} = \overrightarrow{AB} = \overrightarrow{AC} + \overrightarrow{CB} = a\boldsymbol{i} + b\boldsymbol{j}$$

We conclude that any vector in the xy plane can be expressed in the form $\boldsymbol{r} = a\boldsymbol{i} + b\boldsymbol{j}$. An alternative way of writing this vector is to use **column vector** notation. We write

$$\boldsymbol{r} = \begin{pmatrix} a \\ b \end{pmatrix}$$

A **row vector** would be written as (a, b), but care must be taken not to confuse this form with cartesian coordinates.

Key point

Any vector in the xy plane can be written $\boldsymbol{r} = a\boldsymbol{i} + b\boldsymbol{j}$ or as

$$\boldsymbol{r} = \begin{pmatrix} a \\ b \end{pmatrix}$$

The numbers a and b are called the $\boldsymbol{i}$ and $\boldsymbol{j}$ **components** of $\boldsymbol{r}$.

Addition of vectors

Example 2.2

(a) Draw an xy plane and show the vectors $\boldsymbol{a} = 2\boldsymbol{i} + 3\boldsymbol{j}$ and $\boldsymbol{b} = 5\boldsymbol{i} + \boldsymbol{j}$.
(b) By translating one of the vectors apply the triangle law to show the sum $\boldsymbol{a} + \boldsymbol{b}$.
(c) Express the resultant in terms of $\boldsymbol{i}$ and $\boldsymbol{j}$.

Solution

(a) Draw the xy plane and the required vectors. They can be drawn from any point in the plane.

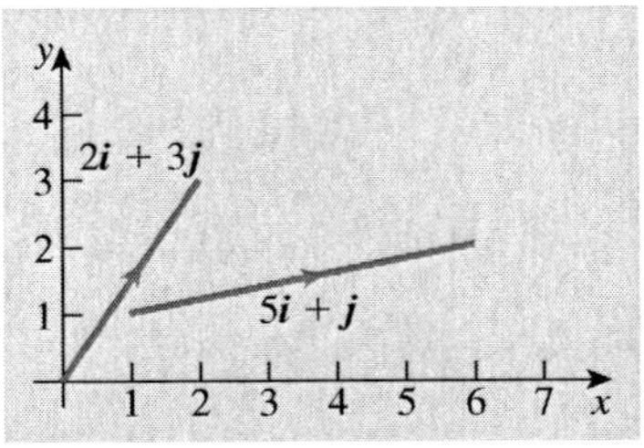

(b) Translate one of the vectors so that they lie head to tail, completing the third side of the triangle to give the resultant $\boldsymbol{a} + \boldsymbol{b}$.
(c) By studying your diagram note that the resultant consists of the two components $7\boldsymbol{i}$ horizontally, and $4\boldsymbol{j}$ vertically. Hence write down an expression for $\boldsymbol{a} + \boldsymbol{b}$.

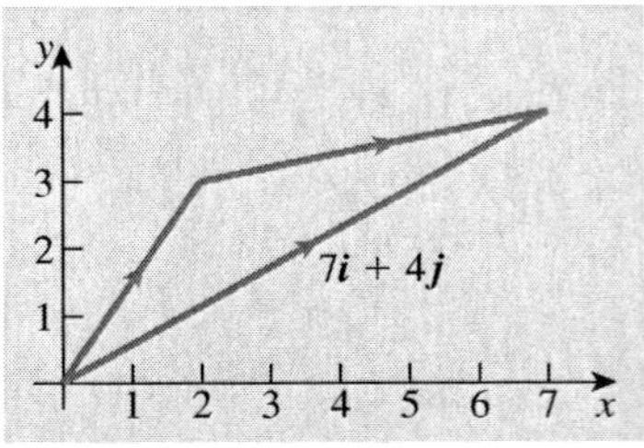

$\boldsymbol{a} + \boldsymbol{b} =$ $7\boldsymbol{i} + 4\boldsymbol{j}$

Note that this result consists of the sum of the respective components of $\boldsymbol{a}$ and $\boldsymbol{b}$. That is,

$$(2\boldsymbol{i} + 3\boldsymbol{j}) + (5\boldsymbol{i} + \boldsymbol{j}) = 7\boldsymbol{i} + 4\boldsymbol{j}$$

It is important to note from the last example that vectors in cartesian form can be added by simply adding their respective $\boldsymbol{i}$ and $\boldsymbol{j}$ components.

Key point

If $\boldsymbol{a} = a_x\boldsymbol{i} + a_y\boldsymbol{j}$ and $\boldsymbol{b} = b_x\boldsymbol{i} + b_y\boldsymbol{j}$ then

$$\boldsymbol{a} + \boldsymbol{b} = (a_x + b_x)\boldsymbol{i} + (a_y + b_y)\boldsymbol{j}$$

Example 2.3
If $\boldsymbol{a} = 9\boldsymbol{i} + 7\boldsymbol{j}$ and $\boldsymbol{b} = 8\boldsymbol{i} + 3\boldsymbol{j}$ find
(a) $\boldsymbol{a} + \boldsymbol{b}$
(b) $\boldsymbol{a} - \boldsymbol{b}$

Solution
(a) Simply add the respective components:

$\boldsymbol{a} + \boldsymbol{b} =$ $17\boldsymbol{i} + 10\boldsymbol{j}$

(b) Simply subtract the respective components:

$\boldsymbol{a} - \boldsymbol{b} =$ $\boldsymbol{i} + 4\boldsymbol{j}$

Example 2.4
If

$$\boldsymbol{r} = \begin{pmatrix} 7 \\ 11 \end{pmatrix} \quad \text{and} \quad \boldsymbol{s} = \begin{pmatrix} 3 \\ -5 \end{pmatrix}$$

find $\boldsymbol{r} + \boldsymbol{s}$.

Solution
The vectors are added by adding their respective components.

$$\begin{pmatrix} 10 \\ 6 \end{pmatrix}$$

It follows that to multiply any vector, $\boldsymbol{a}$ by a scalar k, we multiply each component of $\boldsymbol{a}$ by k.

Example 2.5
If $\boldsymbol{a} = 9\boldsymbol{i} + 3\boldsymbol{j}$ write down (a) $4\boldsymbol{a}$, (b) $-\frac{1}{3}\boldsymbol{a}$.

Solution
(a) $4\boldsymbol{a} =$ $36\boldsymbol{i} + 12\boldsymbol{j}$

(b) $-\frac{1}{3}\boldsymbol{a} =$ $-3\boldsymbol{i} - \boldsymbol{j}$

Key point

If $\boldsymbol{a} = a_x\boldsymbol{i} + a_y\boldsymbol{j}$ then $k\boldsymbol{a} = ka_x\boldsymbol{i} + ka_y\boldsymbol{j}$.

Position vectors

Now consider the special case when $\boldsymbol{r}$ represents the vector from the origin to the point P(x, y) as shown in Figure 2.5. This vector is known as the **position vector** of P.

Key point

The **position vector** of P(x, y) is $\boldsymbol{r} = \overrightarrow{OP} = x\boldsymbol{i} + y\boldsymbol{j}$.

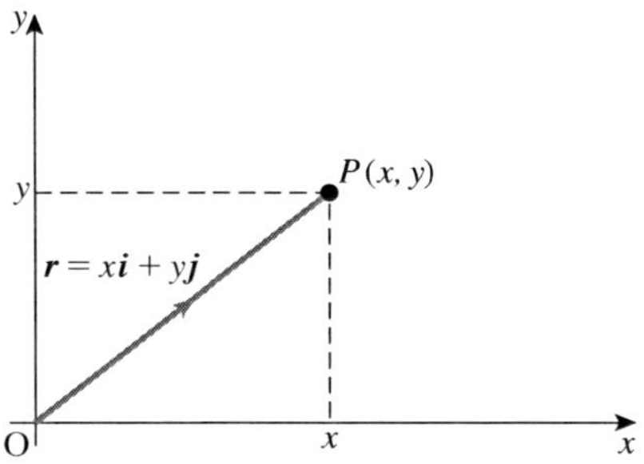

Figure 2.5
$\boldsymbol{r} = x\boldsymbol{i} + y\boldsymbol{j}$ is the position vector of the point P with coordinates (x, y).

Unlike most vectors, position vectors cannot be freely translated. Because they indicate the position of a point they are fixed vectors in the sense that the tail of a position vector is always located at the origin.

Example 2.6

State the position vectors of the points with coordinates (a) P(2, 4), (b) Q(−1, 5), (c) R(−1, −7), (d) S(8, −4).

Solution

(a) The position vector of P is $2\boldsymbol{i} + 4\boldsymbol{j}$. This could be written

$$\begin{pmatrix} 2 \\ 4 \end{pmatrix}$$

(b) The position vector of Q is $-\boldsymbol{i} + 5\boldsymbol{j}$.
(c) The position vector of R is $-\boldsymbol{i} - 7\boldsymbol{j}$.
(d) The position vector of S is $8\boldsymbol{i} - 4\boldsymbol{j}$.

Example 2.7

Sketch the position vectors $\boldsymbol{r}_1 = 3\boldsymbol{i} + 4\boldsymbol{j}$, $\boldsymbol{r}_2 = -2\boldsymbol{i} + 5\boldsymbol{j}$ and $\boldsymbol{r}_3 = -3\boldsymbol{i} - 2\boldsymbol{j}$.

Solution

The vectors are shown in Figure 2.6. Note that all position vectors start at the origin.

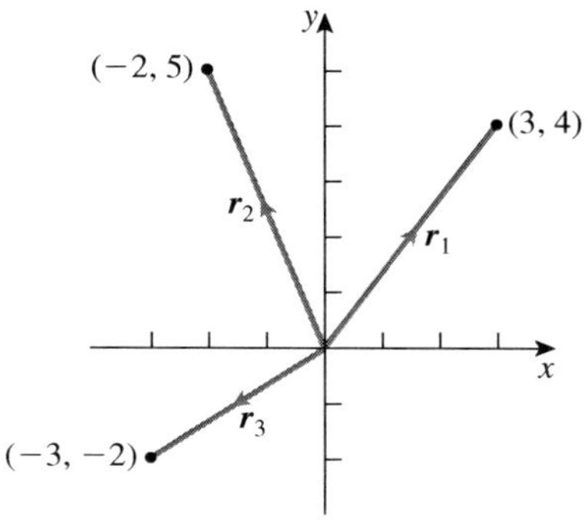

Figure 2.6
The position vectors $\boldsymbol{r}_1 = 3\boldsymbol{i} + 4\boldsymbol{j}$, $\boldsymbol{r}_2 = -2\boldsymbol{i} + 5\boldsymbol{j}$ and $\boldsymbol{r}_3 = -3\boldsymbol{i} - 2\boldsymbol{j}$.

Modulus

The **modulus** of any vector $\boldsymbol{r}$ is equal to its length. When $\boldsymbol{r} = x\boldsymbol{i} + y\boldsymbol{j}$ the modulus can be obtained by Pythagoras's theorem. Referring to Figure 2.5, if $\boldsymbol{r}$ is the position vector of point P then the modulus is clearly the distance of P from the origin.

Key point

If $\boldsymbol{r} = x\boldsymbol{i} + y\boldsymbol{j}$ then $|\boldsymbol{r}| = \sqrt{x^2 + y^2}$.

Example 2.8

Find the modulus of each of the vectors (a) $\boldsymbol{r}_1 = 3\boldsymbol{i} + 4\boldsymbol{j}$, (b) $\boldsymbol{r}_2 = -2\boldsymbol{i} + 5\boldsymbol{j}$, (c) $\boldsymbol{r}_3 = 9\boldsymbol{i} - 2\boldsymbol{j}$ and (d) $\boldsymbol{r}_4 = -5\boldsymbol{i} - 3\boldsymbol{j}$.

Solution

(a) The modulus of $\boldsymbol{r}_1 = |3\boldsymbol{i} + 4\boldsymbol{j}| = \sqrt{3^2 + 4^2} = \sqrt{25} = 5$.

(b) The modulus of $\boldsymbol{r}_2 = |-2\boldsymbol{i} + 5\boldsymbol{j}| = \sqrt{(-2)^2 + 5^2} = \sqrt{4 + 25} = \sqrt{29}$.

(c) Similarly $|\boldsymbol{r}_3| = \sqrt{9^2 + (-2)^2} = \sqrt{85}$.

(d) $|\boldsymbol{r}_4| = \sqrt{(-5)^2 + (-3)^2} = \sqrt{25 + 9} = \sqrt{34}$.

Example 2.9

Find the modulus of the vector

$$\boldsymbol{r} = \begin{pmatrix} 7 \\ -3 \end{pmatrix}$$

Solution

$\sqrt{7^2 + (-3)^2} = \sqrt{58}$

Example 2.10

Point A has coordinates (3, 5). Point B has coordinates (7, 8).

(a) Depict these points on a diagram and state their position vectors.

(b) Find an expression for $\overrightarrow{AB}$.

(c) Find $|\overrightarrow{AB}|$.

Solution

(a) Draw a diagram that shows points A and B.

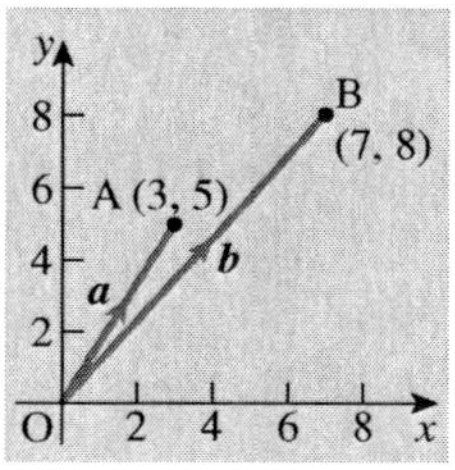

The position vector of A is then $\overrightarrow{OA} = \boldsymbol{a} = 3\boldsymbol{i} + 5\boldsymbol{j}$

The position vector of B is $\overrightarrow{OB} = \boldsymbol{b} = 7\boldsymbol{i} + 8\boldsymbol{j}$

(b) Refer to your figure and use the triangle law to write

$$\overrightarrow{OA} + \overrightarrow{AB} = \overrightarrow{OB}$$

so that

$$\overrightarrow{AB} = \overrightarrow{OB} - \overrightarrow{OA}$$
$$= \boldsymbol{b} - \boldsymbol{a}$$

Hence write down an expression for $\overrightarrow{AB}$ in terms of the unit vectors $\boldsymbol{i}$ and $\boldsymbol{j}$.

$(7\boldsymbol{i} + 8\boldsymbol{j}) - (3\boldsymbol{i} + 5\boldsymbol{j}) = 4\boldsymbol{i} + 3\boldsymbol{j}$

(c) The length of $\overrightarrow{AB} = |4\boldsymbol{i} + 3\boldsymbol{j}| =$

$\sqrt{4^2 + 3^2} = \sqrt{25} = 5$

Exercises

1 Explain the distinction between a position vector and a more general or free vector.

2 What is meant by the symbols $\boldsymbol{i}$ and $\boldsymbol{j}$?

3 State the position vectors of the points with coordinates (a) P(4, 7), (b) Q(−3, 5), (c) R(0, 3), (d) S(−1, 0).

4 State the coordinates of the point P if its position vector is given as (a) $3\boldsymbol{i} - 7\boldsymbol{j}$, (b) $-4\boldsymbol{i}$, (c) $-0.5\boldsymbol{i} + 13\boldsymbol{j}$, (d) $a\boldsymbol{i} + b\boldsymbol{j}$.

5 Find the modulus of each of the following vectors:
(a) $\boldsymbol{r} = 7\boldsymbol{i} + 3\boldsymbol{j}$ (b) $\boldsymbol{r} = 17\boldsymbol{i}$ (c) $\boldsymbol{r} = 2\boldsymbol{i} - 3\boldsymbol{j}$
(d) $\boldsymbol{r} = -3\boldsymbol{j}$ (e) $\boldsymbol{r} = a\boldsymbol{i} + b\boldsymbol{j}$ (f) $\boldsymbol{r} = a\boldsymbol{i} - b\boldsymbol{j}$

6 Point P has coordinates (7, 8). Point Q has coordinates (−2, 4).
(a) Draw a sketch showing P and Q.
(b) State the position vectors of P and Q.
(c) Find an expression for $\overrightarrow{PQ}$.
(d) Find $|\overrightarrow{PQ}|$.

Solutions to exercises

1 Free vectors can be translated keeping their direction and length the same. Position vectors must always start at the origin.

2 $\boldsymbol{i}$ is a unit vector in the direction of the positive x axis. $\boldsymbol{j}$ is a unit vector in the direction of the positive y axis.

3 (a) $4\boldsymbol{i} + 7\boldsymbol{j}$ (b) $-3\boldsymbol{i} + 5\boldsymbol{j}$ (c) $3\boldsymbol{j}$ (d) $-\boldsymbol{i}$

4 (a) (3, −7) (b) (−4, 0) (c) (−0.5, 13) (d) (a, b)

5 (a) $\sqrt{58}$ (b) 17 (c) $\sqrt{13}$ (d) 3 (e) $\sqrt{a^2 + b^2}$ (f) $\sqrt{a^2 + b^2}$

6 (b) $\boldsymbol{p} = 7\boldsymbol{i} + 8\boldsymbol{j}$, $\boldsymbol{q} = -2\boldsymbol{i} + 4\boldsymbol{j}$
(c) $\overrightarrow{PQ} = -9\boldsymbol{i} - 4\boldsymbol{j}$ (d) $|\overrightarrow{PQ}| = \sqrt{97}$

2.3 The direction ratio and direction cosines

Consider the point P(4, 5) and its position vector $4\boldsymbol{i} + 5\boldsymbol{j}$ as shown in Figure 2.7.

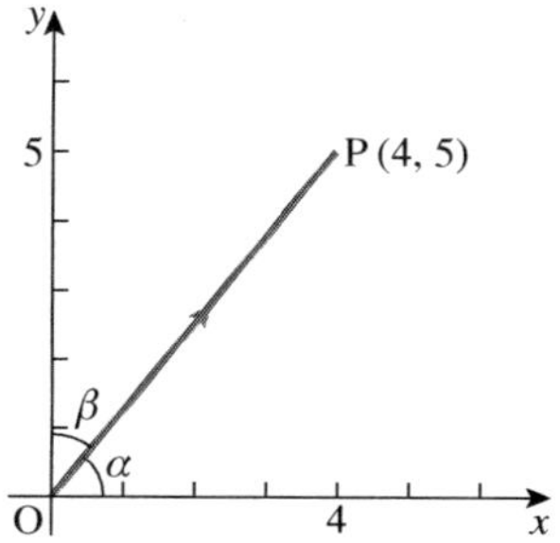

Figure 2.7 The direction cosines of $\overrightarrow{OP}$ are $\cos\alpha$ and $\cos\beta$.

The **direction ratio** of the vector $\overrightarrow{OP}$ is defined to be 4:5. We can interpret this as stating that to move in the direction of the line we must move 5 units in the y direction for every 4 units in the x direction.

The **direction cosines** of the vector $\overrightarrow{OP}$ are the cosines of the angles between the vector and each of the positive axes. Specifically, referring to Figure 2.7 these are

$$\text{direction cosines:} \quad \cos\alpha \quad \text{and} \quad \cos\beta$$

Noting that the length of $\overrightarrow{OP}$ is $\sqrt{4^2 + 5^2} = \sqrt{41}$ we can write

$$\cos\alpha = \frac{4}{\sqrt{41}}, \quad \cos\beta = \frac{5}{\sqrt{41}}$$

It is conventional to label the direction cosines as l and m so that

$$l = \frac{4}{\sqrt{41}}, \quad m = \frac{5}{\sqrt{41}}$$

More generally we have the following result:

Key point

For any vector $\boldsymbol{r} = a\boldsymbol{i} + b\boldsymbol{j}$, its direction ratio is $a{:}b$. Its direction cosines are

$$l = \frac{a}{\sqrt{a^2 + b^2}}, \quad m = \frac{b}{\sqrt{a^2 + b^2}}$$

Example 2.11

Refer back to Example 2.10, in which point A has coordinates (3, 5), and point B has coordinates (7, 8).

(a) Find the direction ratio of the vector $\overrightarrow{AB}$.
(b) Find its direction cosines, l and m.
(c) Show that $l^2 + m^2 = 1$.

Solution

From Example 2.10 we know that $\overrightarrow{AB} = 4\boldsymbol{i} + 3\boldsymbol{j}$.

(a) The direction ratio of $\overrightarrow{AB}$ is therefore 4:3.

(b) The direction cosines are

$$l = \frac{4}{\sqrt{4^2 + 3^2}} = \frac{4}{5}, \quad m = \frac{3}{\sqrt{4^2 + 3^2}} = \frac{3}{5}$$

(c)
$$\begin{aligned} l^2 + m^2 &= \left(\frac{4}{5}\right)^2 + \left(\frac{3}{5}\right)^2 \\ &= \frac{16}{25} + \frac{9}{25} \\ &= \frac{25}{25} \\ &= 1 \end{aligned}$$

The final result in the previous example is true in general:

Key point

If l and m are the direction cosines of a line lying in the xy plane, then

$$l^2 + m^2 = 1$$

Exercises

1 For the vectors in Exercise 6 of the previous section, find
(a) the direction ratio of the vector $\overrightarrow{PQ}$
(b) the direction cosines of $\overrightarrow{PQ}$.
(c) Explain why the direction cosines are both negative.

Solutions to exercises

1 (a) $-9{:}-4$ (b) $-\frac{9}{\sqrt{97}}, -\frac{4}{\sqrt{97}}$
(c) The angle between the vector and the positive direction of both axes is greater than 90° and hence each cosine is negative. (Draw the vector $\overrightarrow{PQ} = -9\boldsymbol{i} - 4\boldsymbol{j}$ to see this.)

2.4 Three-dimensional coordinate frames

The real world is three-dimensional, and in order to solve many engineering problems it is necessary to develop expertise in the mathematics of three-dimensional space. An important application of vectors is their use to locate points in three dimensions. When two distinct points are known we can draw a line between them. Three distinct points that do not lie on the same line form a plane. Vectors can be used to describe points, lines and planes in three dimensions. These mathematical foundations underpin much of the technology associated with computer graphics and the control of robots. In this section we shall introduce the vector methods that underlie these applications.

Figure 2.8 shows a three-dimensional coordinate frame. Note that the third dimension requires the addition of a third axis, the z axis. Although these three axes are drawn in the plane of the paper you should remember that we are now thinking of three-dimensional situations. Just as in two dimensions the x and y axes are perpendicular, in three dimensions the x, y and z axes are perpendicular to each other. We say they are **mutually perpendicular**. There is no reason why we could not have chosen the z axis in the opposite sense. However, it is conventional to choose the directions shown in Figure 2.8. Any point in the three dimensions can be defined in terms of its x, y and z coordinates. Consider the point P with coordinates (x, y, z) as shown. The vector from the origin to the point P is known as the **position vector** of P, $\overrightarrow{\text{OP}}$ or $\boldsymbol{r}$. To arrive at P from O we can think of moving x units in the x direction, y units in the y direction and z units in the z direction.

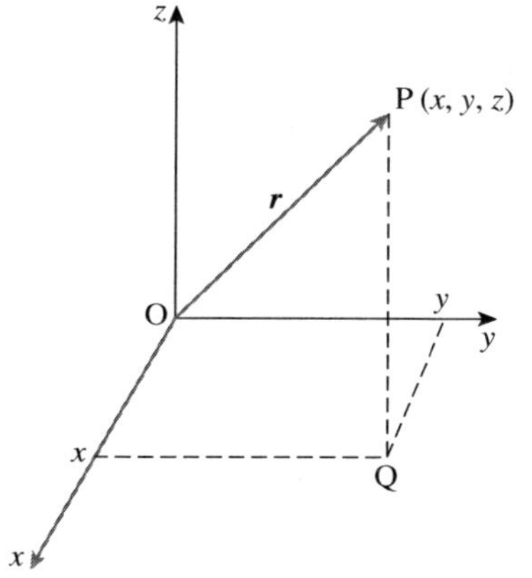

Figure 2.8
The position vector of the point with coordinates (x, y, z) is $\boldsymbol{r} = x\boldsymbol{i} + y\boldsymbol{j} + z\boldsymbol{k}$.

Extending the concept of unit vectors in the direction of each of the axes, a unit vector pointing in the positive direction of the z axis is denoted by $\boldsymbol{k}$. Noting that $\overrightarrow{\text{OQ}} = x\boldsymbol{i} + y\boldsymbol{j}$ and that $\overrightarrow{\text{QP}} = z\boldsymbol{k}$ we can state

$$\begin{aligned}\boldsymbol{r} &= \overrightarrow{\text{OP}} \\ &= \overrightarrow{\text{OQ}} + \overrightarrow{\text{QP}} \\ &= x\boldsymbol{i} + y\boldsymbol{j} + z\boldsymbol{k}\end{aligned}$$

We conclude that the position vector of the point with coordinates (x, y, z) is $\boldsymbol{r} = x\boldsymbol{i} + y\boldsymbol{j} + z\boldsymbol{k}$.

In column vector notation we would write

$$\boldsymbol{r} = \begin{pmatrix} x \\ y \\ z \end{pmatrix}$$

Key point

The position vector of $P(x, y, z)$ is $\boldsymbol{r} = \overrightarrow{OP} = x\boldsymbol{i} + y\boldsymbol{j} + z\boldsymbol{k}$ or alternatively,

$$\boldsymbol{r} = \begin{pmatrix} x \\ y \\ z \end{pmatrix}$$

Example 2.12

State the position vector of the point with coordinates $(9, -8, 6)$.

Solution

The position vector is $9\boldsymbol{i} - 8\boldsymbol{j} + 6\boldsymbol{k}$

Addition and subtraction

Addition and subtraction are carried out in an obvious way.

Example 2.13

If

$$\boldsymbol{r} = \begin{pmatrix} 1 \\ 4 \\ -2 \end{pmatrix} \quad \text{and} \quad \boldsymbol{s} = \begin{pmatrix} 4 \\ -3 \\ 2 \end{pmatrix}$$

find (a) $\boldsymbol{r} + \boldsymbol{s}$ (b) $\boldsymbol{r} - \boldsymbol{s}$.

Solution

(a) $\begin{pmatrix} 5 \\ 1 \\ 0 \end{pmatrix}$

(b) $\begin{pmatrix} -3 \\ 7 \\ -4 \end{pmatrix}$

Modulus

The modulus of the vector $\overrightarrow{OP}$ is equal to the distance OP, which can be obtained by Pythagoras's theorem.

Key point

If $\boldsymbol{r} = x\boldsymbol{i} + y\boldsymbol{j} + z\boldsymbol{k}$ then $|\boldsymbol{r}| = \sqrt{x^2 + y^2 + z^2}$.

Example 2.14

Find the modulus of the vector $\boldsymbol{r} = 4\boldsymbol{i} + 2\boldsymbol{j} + 3\boldsymbol{k}$.

Solution

$|\boldsymbol{r}| =$

$$\sqrt{4^2 + 2^2 + 3^2} = \sqrt{16 + 4 + 9} = \sqrt{29}$$

Example 2.15

Points A, B and C have coordinates (−1, 1, 4), (8, 0, 2) and (5, −2, 11) respectively.

(a) Find the position vectors of A, B and C.

(b) Find $\overrightarrow{AB}$ and $\overrightarrow{BC}$.

(c) Find $|\overrightarrow{AB}|$ and $|\overrightarrow{BC}|$.

Solution

(a) Denoting the position vectors of A, B and C by $\boldsymbol{a}$, $\boldsymbol{b}$ and $\boldsymbol{c}$ respectively, we find

$$\boldsymbol{a} = -\boldsymbol{i} + \boldsymbol{j} + 4\boldsymbol{k}, \quad \boldsymbol{b} = 8\boldsymbol{i} + 2\boldsymbol{k}, \quad \boldsymbol{c} = 5\boldsymbol{i} - 2\boldsymbol{j} + 11\boldsymbol{k}$$

(b) $\overrightarrow{AB} = \boldsymbol{b} - \boldsymbol{a} = 9\boldsymbol{i} - \boldsymbol{j} - 2\boldsymbol{k}$, $\overrightarrow{BC} = \boldsymbol{c} - \boldsymbol{b} = -3\boldsymbol{i} - 2\boldsymbol{j} + 9\boldsymbol{k}$.

(c) $|\overrightarrow{AB}| = \sqrt{9^2 + (-1)^2 + (-2)^2} = \sqrt{86}$,

$|\overrightarrow{BC}| = \sqrt{(-3)^2 + (-2)^2 + 9^2} = \sqrt{94}$

Exercises

1 State the position vector of the point with coordinates (4, −4, 3).

2 Find the modulus of each of the following vectors:
(a) $7\boldsymbol{i} + 2\boldsymbol{j} + 3\boldsymbol{k}$ (b) $7\boldsymbol{i} - 2\boldsymbol{j} + 3\boldsymbol{k}$
(c) $2\boldsymbol{j} + 8\boldsymbol{k}$ (d) $-\boldsymbol{i} - 2\boldsymbol{j} + 3\boldsymbol{k}$
(e) $a\boldsymbol{i} + b\boldsymbol{j} + c\boldsymbol{k}$

3 Points P, Q and R have coordinates (9, 1, 0), (8, −3, 5) and (5, 5, 7) respectively.
(a) Find the position vectors of P, Q and R.
(b) Find $\overrightarrow{PQ}$ and $\overrightarrow{QR}$.
(c) Find $|\overrightarrow{PQ}|$ and $|\overrightarrow{QR}|$.

4 If $\boldsymbol{a} = 5\boldsymbol{i} - 2\boldsymbol{j} + 3\boldsymbol{k}$ and $\boldsymbol{b} = 2\boldsymbol{i} + \boldsymbol{j} - 4\boldsymbol{k}$ write down $\boldsymbol{b} - \boldsymbol{a}$.

Solutions

1 $4\boldsymbol{i} - 4\boldsymbol{j} + 3\boldsymbol{k}$

2 (a) $\sqrt{62}$ (b) $\sqrt{62}$ (c) $\sqrt{68}$ (d) $\sqrt{14}$
(e) $\sqrt{a^2 + b^2 + c^2}$

3 (a) $\boldsymbol{p} = 9\boldsymbol{i} + \boldsymbol{j}, \boldsymbol{q} = 8\boldsymbol{i} - 3\boldsymbol{j} + 5\boldsymbol{k},$
$\boldsymbol{r} = 5\boldsymbol{i} + 5\boldsymbol{j} + 7\boldsymbol{k}$

(b) $\overrightarrow{PQ} = -\boldsymbol{i} - 4\boldsymbol{j} + 5\boldsymbol{k},$
$\overrightarrow{QR} = -3\boldsymbol{i} + 8\boldsymbol{j} + 2\boldsymbol{k}$

(c) $|\overrightarrow{PQ}| = \sqrt{42}, |\overrightarrow{QR}| = \sqrt{77}$

4 $-3\boldsymbol{i} + 3\boldsymbol{j} - 7\boldsymbol{k}$

2.5 Direction ratios and direction cosines in three dimensions

The concepts of direction ratio and direction cosines extend naturally to three dimensions. Consider Figure 2.9.

Consider point P with position vector

$$\boldsymbol{r} = a\boldsymbol{i} + b\boldsymbol{j} + c\boldsymbol{k}$$

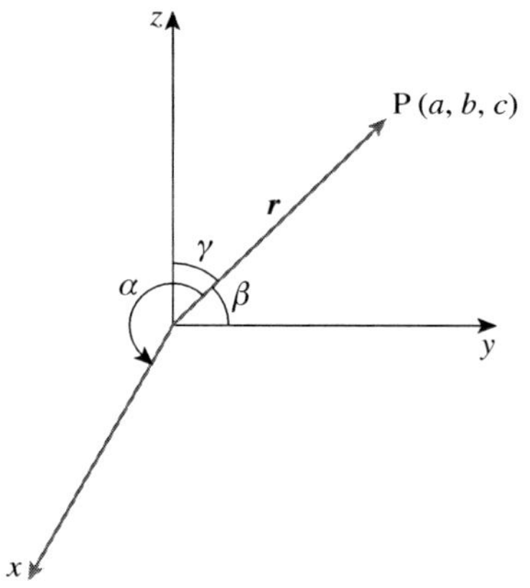

Figure 2.9 The direction cosines of $\overrightarrow{OP}$ are $\cos\alpha$, $\cos\beta$ and $\cos\gamma$.

Its direction ratio is

$$a{:}b{:}c$$

This means that to move in the direction of the vector we must must move b units in the y direction and c units in the z direction for every a units in the x direction.

The direction cosines are the cosines of the angles between the vector and each of the axes. It is conventional to label them as l, m and n, and they are given by

$$l = \cos\alpha = \frac{a}{\sqrt{a^2 + b^2 + c^2}}, \quad m = \cos\beta = \frac{b}{\sqrt{a^2 + b^2 + c^2}},$$

$$n = \cos\gamma = \frac{c}{\sqrt{a^2 + b^2 + c^2}}$$

In general we have the following result:

Key point

For any vector $\boldsymbol{r} = a\boldsymbol{i} + b\boldsymbol{j} + c\boldsymbol{k}$, its direction ratio is a:b:c. Its direction cosines are

$$l = \frac{a}{\sqrt{a^2 + b^2 + c^2}}, \quad m = \frac{b}{\sqrt{a^2 + b^2 + c^2}}, \quad n = \frac{c}{\sqrt{a^2 + b^2 + c^2}}$$

and

$$l^2 + m^2 + n^2 = 1$$

Example 2.16

(a) Calculate the direction ratio of $\boldsymbol{r} = 3\boldsymbol{i} - 2\boldsymbol{j} + \boldsymbol{k}$.
(b) Calculate its direction cosines.

Solution

(a) The direction ratio is 3:−2:1.
(b) The direction cosines are

$$l = \frac{3}{\sqrt{3^2 + (-2)^2 + 1^2}} = \frac{3}{\sqrt{14}}$$

$$m = \frac{-2}{\sqrt{3^2 + (-2)^2 + 1^2}} = -\frac{2}{\sqrt{14}}$$

$$n = \frac{1}{\sqrt{3^2 + (-2)^2 + 1^2}} = \frac{1}{\sqrt{14}}$$

Exercises

1 Points A and B have position vectors $\boldsymbol{a} = -3\boldsymbol{i} + 2\boldsymbol{j} + 7\boldsymbol{k}$ and $\boldsymbol{b} = 3\boldsymbol{i} + 4\boldsymbol{j} - 5\boldsymbol{k}$ respectively. Find

(a) $\overrightarrow{AB}$
(b) $|\overrightarrow{AB}|$
(c) the direction ratios of $\overrightarrow{AB}$
(d) the direction cosines of $\overrightarrow{AB}$.
(e) Show that the sum of the squares of the direction cosines equals 1.

2 Find the direction ratios, the direction cosines and the angles that the vector $\overrightarrow{OP}$ makes with each of the axes when P is the point with coordinates (2, 4, 3).

3 A line is inclined at 60° to the x axis and 45° to the y axis. Find its inclination to the z axis.

Solutions to exercises

1 (a) $6\boldsymbol{i} + 2\boldsymbol{j} - 12\boldsymbol{k}$ (b) $\sqrt{184}$ (c) 6:2:−12

(d) $\dfrac{6}{\sqrt{184}}, \dfrac{2}{\sqrt{184}}, \dfrac{-12}{\sqrt{184}}$

2 2:4:3; $\dfrac{2}{\sqrt{29}}, \dfrac{4}{\sqrt{29}}, \dfrac{3}{\sqrt{29}}$; 68.2°, 42.0°, 56.1°

3 60° or 120°

2.6 *N*-dimensional vectors

The vectors we have described so far have been either two- or three-dimensional. However, there are some situations when it is desirable to generalise what we have done to higher dimensions. No geometrical interpretation is then available. Nevertheless we can still refer to the components of a vector and the modulus of a vector.

Two examples of four-dimensional column vectors are

$$\boldsymbol{a} = \begin{pmatrix} 3 \\ 1 \\ 2 \\ 4 \end{pmatrix} \quad \text{and} \quad \boldsymbol{b} = \begin{pmatrix} 1 \\ 0 \\ 3 \\ 1 \end{pmatrix}$$

The modulus of a, which is generally referred to as its **norm**, is then defined as

$$\begin{aligned} |\boldsymbol{a}| &= \sqrt{3^2 + 1^2 + 2^2 + 4^2} \\ &= \sqrt{30} \end{aligned}$$

An n-dimensional vector will have n components.

Example 2.17 Vector norms and digital signal processing

Signals are quantities used to transmit information. If a signal changes, then this corresponds to information being conveyed. For example, the sequence of symbols

000000000000000000000

contains no information, whereas

000000000010000000000

contains information relating to a change occurring in the middle of the sequence. Consider a signal such as that depicted in Figure 2.10, which corresponds to the sequence of symbols 0, 0, 3, 5, 0.

Figure 2.10

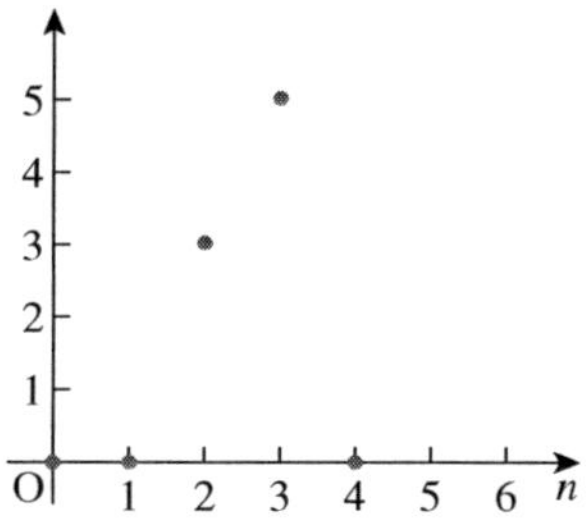

This sequence can also be represented by a vector: for example, we could write it as the **row vector**

$$\boldsymbol{f} = (0, 0, 3, 5, 0)$$

The **norm** of the signal is the modulus of the vector $\boldsymbol{f}$, defined, by generalising the two- and three-dimensional case, as

$$\begin{aligned} |\boldsymbol{f}| &= \sqrt{0^2 + 0^2 + 3^2 + 5^2 + 0^2} \\ &= \sqrt{34} \end{aligned}$$

More generally a vector, $\boldsymbol{f}$, with N components can represent a signal of length N, that is

$$\boldsymbol{f} = (f_0, f_1, \ldots, f_{N-1})$$

and its norm is given by

$$|\boldsymbol{f}| = \sqrt{\sum_{n=0}^{N-1} f_n^2}$$

A related quantity is the **power** in a signal, which is given by

$$\frac{1}{N}|\boldsymbol{f}|^2 = \frac{1}{N}\sum_{n=0}^{N-1} f_n^2$$

Therefore the power in the signal (0, 0, 3, 5, 0) is $\frac{34}{5}$.

One of the main problems in signal processing is that of representing a large amount of information by a smaller amount without significantly distorting the original signal. Very often a signal, $\boldsymbol{f}$, with a large information content is approximated by $\boldsymbol{f}'$, which is a signal with a smaller information content. Then

$$|\boldsymbol{f} - \boldsymbol{f}'|$$

is a measure of the 'distance' or difference between the two signals and is therefore a measure of the quality of the approximation.

End of block exercises

1 If

$$\boldsymbol{p} = \begin{pmatrix} 3 \\ 1 \\ 2 \end{pmatrix} \quad \text{and} \quad \boldsymbol{q} = \begin{pmatrix} 7 \\ 9 \\ 1 \end{pmatrix}$$

find (a) $3\boldsymbol{p}$, (b) $\boldsymbol{p} - \boldsymbol{q}$, (c) $-2\boldsymbol{q}$, (d) $3\boldsymbol{p} - 2\boldsymbol{q}$.

2 If

$$\boldsymbol{x}_1 = \begin{pmatrix} 1 \\ 2 \\ 3 \end{pmatrix}, \quad \boldsymbol{x}_2 = \begin{pmatrix} 1 \\ 0 \\ 1 \end{pmatrix}, \quad \boldsymbol{x}_3 = \begin{pmatrix} 2 \\ 2 \\ 4 \end{pmatrix}$$

show that $\boldsymbol{x}_1 + \boldsymbol{x}_2 - \boldsymbol{x}_3 = \boldsymbol{0}$ where $\boldsymbol{0}$ is the zero vector.

3 A triangle has vertices A, B and C with coordinates (1, 3, 2), (−1, 5, 9) and (2, 7, 1) respectively. Calculate the vectors that represent the sides of the triangle.

4 Find a unit vector in the direction of the vector $\boldsymbol{i} - \boldsymbol{j}$.

5 Find the norm of the row vector $\boldsymbol{x} = (2, 3, 6)$.

6 If

$$\boldsymbol{a} = \begin{pmatrix} 1 \\ 1 \\ 0 \\ 1 \\ 1 \end{pmatrix} \quad \text{and} \quad \boldsymbol{b} = \begin{pmatrix} 3 \\ 2 \\ 1 \\ 0 \\ 1 \end{pmatrix}$$

find the norm of $\boldsymbol{a}$, the norm of $\boldsymbol{b}$, and the norm of $\boldsymbol{a} - \boldsymbol{b}$.

Solution to exercises

1 (a) $\begin{pmatrix} 9 \\ 3 \\ 6 \end{pmatrix}$ (b) $\begin{pmatrix} -4 \\ -8 \\ 1 \end{pmatrix}$

(c) $\begin{pmatrix} -14 \\ -18 \\ -2 \end{pmatrix}$ (d) $\begin{pmatrix} -5 \\ -15 \\ 4 \end{pmatrix}$

3 $\overrightarrow{AB} = -2\boldsymbol{i} + 2\boldsymbol{j} + 7\boldsymbol{k}$,

$\overrightarrow{BC} = 3\boldsymbol{i} + 2\boldsymbol{j} - 8\boldsymbol{k}$,

$\overrightarrow{AC} = \boldsymbol{i} + 4\boldsymbol{j} - \boldsymbol{k}$

4 $\dfrac{1}{\sqrt{2}}(\boldsymbol{i} - \boldsymbol{j})$

5 7

6 $2, \sqrt{15}, \sqrt{7}$

BLOCK 3 The scalar product, or dot product

3.1 Introduction

Multiplication of two vectors is defined in two different ways. The first way is known as the **scalar product**. When the scalar product of two vectors is calculated the result is a scalar and not a vector. The second way is known as the **vector product**. When this is calculated the result is a vector. These products are summarised in Table 3.1. The ways in which these products are defined seem rather strange when first met, but the reason for this lies in their applications. In this block we consider only the scalar product.

Table 3.1 The two types of vector multiplication.

Name	Written as	Result
Scalar product	$\boldsymbol{a} \cdot \boldsymbol{b}$	Scalar
Vector product	$\boldsymbol{a} \times \boldsymbol{b}$	Vector

3.2 Definition of the scalar product

Consider the two vectors $\boldsymbol{a}$ and $\boldsymbol{b}$ shown in Figure 3.1.

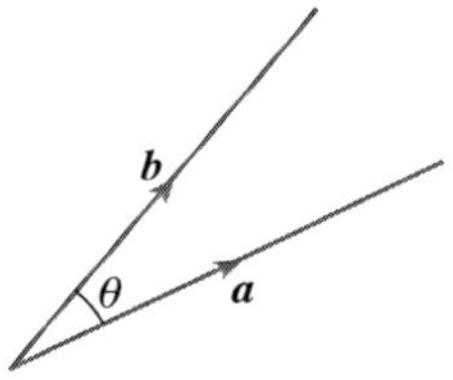

Figure 3.1 Two vectors separated by an angle θ.

Note that the tails of the two vectors coincide and that the angle between the vectors has been labelled θ. Their scalar product, denoted $\boldsymbol{a} \cdot \boldsymbol{b}$, is defined as

$$\boldsymbol{a} \cdot \boldsymbol{b} = |\boldsymbol{a}|\,|\boldsymbol{b}| \cos \theta$$

It is very important to use the dot in the formula. The dot is the symbol for the scalar product, and is the reason why the scalar product is also known as the **dot product**.

You should never use a × sign in this context because the × sign is reserved for the vector product, which is quite different.

Key point

Scalar product

$$\boldsymbol{a} \cdot \boldsymbol{b} = |\boldsymbol{a}|\,|\boldsymbol{b}| \cos\theta$$

We can remember this formula as: the length of the first vector times the length of the second times the cosine of the angle in between them.

Example 3.1

Vectors $\boldsymbol{a}$ and $\boldsymbol{b}$ are shown in Figure 3.2. The vector $\boldsymbol{a}$ has modulus 6, the vector $\boldsymbol{b}$ has modulus 7, and the angle between them is 60°. Calculate $\boldsymbol{a} \cdot \boldsymbol{b}$.

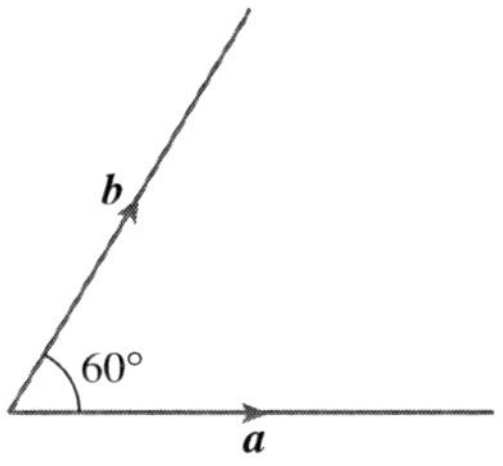

Figure 3.2 When the tails of $\boldsymbol{a}$ and $\boldsymbol{b}$ coincide the angle between them is 60°.

Solution

Identify the angle between the two vectors, and also their moduli. Then apply the formula for the dot product.

$$\boldsymbol{a} \cdot \boldsymbol{b} = |\boldsymbol{a}|\,|\boldsymbol{b}| \cos\theta = (6)(7)\cos 60° = 21$$

The scalar product of $\boldsymbol{a}$ and $\boldsymbol{b}$ is equal to 21. Note that when finding a scalar product the result is always a scalar.

Example 3.2

Find $\boldsymbol{i} \cdot \boldsymbol{i}$, where $\boldsymbol{i}$ is a unit vector in the direction of the positive x axis.

Solution

Because $\boldsymbol{i}$ is a unit vector its modulus is 1. The angle between any two parallel vectors is zero. So the angle between $\boldsymbol{i}$ and itself is zero. Therefore

$$\begin{aligned} \boldsymbol{i} \cdot \boldsymbol{i} &= (1)(1)\cos 0° \\ &= 1 \text{ since } \cos 0° = 1 \end{aligned}$$

So the scalar product of $\boldsymbol{i}$ with itself equals 1. It is easy to verify that $\boldsymbol{j} \cdot \boldsymbol{j} = 1$ and $\boldsymbol{k} \cdot \boldsymbol{k} = 1$.

Example 3.3

Find $i \cdot j$, where $\boldsymbol{i}$ and $\boldsymbol{j}$ are unit vectors in the directions of the x and y axes.

Solution

Because $\boldsymbol{i}$ and $\boldsymbol{j}$ are unit vectors they both have a modulus of 1. The angle between the two vectors is 90° as shown in Figure 3.3.

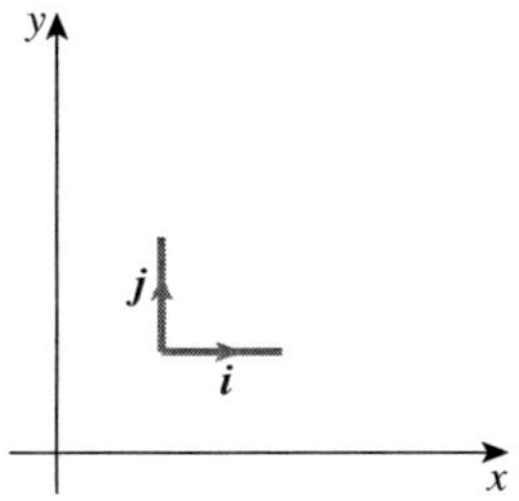

Figure 3.3 The angle between the unit vectors $\boldsymbol{i}$ and $\boldsymbol{j}$ is 90°.

Therefore

$$\begin{aligned} \boldsymbol{i} \cdot \boldsymbol{j} &= (1)(1)\cos 90^\circ \\ &= 0 \quad \text{since} \quad \cos 90^\circ = 0 \end{aligned}$$

That is $\boldsymbol{i} \cdot \boldsymbol{j} = 0$.

More generally, the following results are easily verified:

Key point

$$\boldsymbol{i} \cdot \boldsymbol{i} = \boldsymbol{j} \cdot \boldsymbol{j} = \boldsymbol{k} \cdot \boldsymbol{k} = 1$$
$$\boldsymbol{i} \cdot \boldsymbol{j} = \boldsymbol{i} \cdot \boldsymbol{k} = \boldsymbol{j} \cdot \boldsymbol{k} = 0$$

Exercises

1. Write down the definition of the scalar product of two vectors and illustrate your definition with a diagram.

2. Use the definition of the scalar product to show that, if two vectors are perpendicular, their scalar product is zero.

3. Two vectors have moduli 7 and 13 respectively. The angle between them is 45°. Evaluate their scalar product.

4. Two unit vectors are parallel. What can you deduce about their scalar product?

5. Two vectors have modulus 10 and 12. The angle between them is $\frac{\pi}{3}$. Find their scalar product.

Solutions to exercises

3 64.35

4 It equals 1.

5 60

3.3 Some properties of the scalar product

The scalar product has a number of properties that are necessary for further development.

Commutativity

If $\boldsymbol{a} \cdot \boldsymbol{b} = |\boldsymbol{a}|\,|\boldsymbol{b}| \cos\theta$ then it follows that $\boldsymbol{b} \cdot \boldsymbol{a} = |\boldsymbol{b}|\,|\boldsymbol{a}| \cos\theta$. Since $|\boldsymbol{b}|$, $|\boldsymbol{a}|$ and $\cos\theta$ are numbers, and multiplication of numbers is commutative,

$$|\boldsymbol{a}|\,|\boldsymbol{b}| \cos\theta = |\boldsymbol{b}|\,|\boldsymbol{a}| \cos\theta$$

Clearly then $\boldsymbol{a} \cdot \boldsymbol{b} = \boldsymbol{b} \cdot \boldsymbol{a}$. Thus we can evaluate a scalar product in any order – the operation is commutative.

Distributivity

For three vectors $\boldsymbol{a}$, $\boldsymbol{b}$ and $\boldsymbol{c}$

$$\boldsymbol{a} \cdot (\boldsymbol{b} + \boldsymbol{c}) = \boldsymbol{a} \cdot \boldsymbol{b} + \boldsymbol{a} \cdot \boldsymbol{c}$$

This means that the scalar product is distributive over addition.

Example 3.4
Simplify $\boldsymbol{i} \cdot (\boldsymbol{i} + \boldsymbol{j})$.

Solution
Using the distributivity property,

$$\boldsymbol{i} \cdot (\boldsymbol{i} + \boldsymbol{j}) = \boldsymbol{i} \cdot \boldsymbol{i} + \boldsymbol{i} \cdot \boldsymbol{j}$$

which simplifies to $1 + 0 = 1$.

Multiplication by a scalar

For two vectors $\boldsymbol{a}$ and $\boldsymbol{b}$, and a scalar k,

$$\begin{aligned} k(\boldsymbol{a} \cdot \boldsymbol{b}) &= (k\boldsymbol{a}) \cdot \boldsymbol{b} \\ &= \boldsymbol{a} \cdot (k\boldsymbol{b}) \end{aligned}$$

Example 3.5
Simplify $\boldsymbol{i} \cdot 7\boldsymbol{i}$.

Solution
Using this rule, with $k = 7$, $\boldsymbol{i} \cdot (7\boldsymbol{i})$ can be written $7(\boldsymbol{i} \cdot \boldsymbol{i})$. So

$$\begin{aligned} \boldsymbol{i} \cdot 7\boldsymbol{i} &= 7(\boldsymbol{i} \cdot \boldsymbol{i}) \\ &= 7(1) = 7 \end{aligned}$$

Example 3.6
Simplify $(3\boldsymbol{i} + 2\boldsymbol{j}) \cdot (7\boldsymbol{i} + 4\boldsymbol{j})$.

Solution
Using the distributivity property we can write

$$(3\boldsymbol{i} + 2\boldsymbol{j}) \cdot (7\boldsymbol{i} + 4\boldsymbol{j}) = (3\boldsymbol{i} + 2\boldsymbol{j}) \cdot (7\boldsymbol{i}) + (3\boldsymbol{i} + 2\boldsymbol{j}) \cdot (4\boldsymbol{j})$$

This can be expanded further to give

$$3\boldsymbol{i} \cdot 7\boldsymbol{i} + 2\boldsymbol{j} \cdot 7\boldsymbol{i} + 3\boldsymbol{i} \cdot 4\boldsymbol{j} + 2\boldsymbol{j} \cdot 4\boldsymbol{j}$$

This simplifies to

$$(3)(7)\boldsymbol{i} \cdot \boldsymbol{i} + (2)(7)\boldsymbol{j} \cdot \boldsymbol{i} + (3)(4)\boldsymbol{i} \cdot \boldsymbol{j} + (2)(4)\boldsymbol{j} \cdot \boldsymbol{j}$$

Finally

$$\begin{aligned} (3\boldsymbol{i} + 2\boldsymbol{j}) \cdot (7\boldsymbol{i} + 4\boldsymbol{j}) &= 21 + 0 + 0 + 8 \\ &= 29 \end{aligned}$$

Exercises

1 If $\boldsymbol{a}$ and $\boldsymbol{b}$ are perpendicular, simplify

$$(\boldsymbol{a} - 2\boldsymbol{b}) \cdot (3\boldsymbol{a} + 5\boldsymbol{b})$$

Solutions to exercises

1 $3a^2 - 10b^2$

3.4 A formula for finding the scalar product

We can use the previous results to obtain a formula for finding a scalar product when the vectors are given in cartesian form. Suppose $\boldsymbol{a} = a_1\boldsymbol{i} + a_2\boldsymbol{j}$ and $\boldsymbol{b} = b_1\boldsymbol{i} + b_2\boldsymbol{j}$. Then

$$\begin{aligned}\boldsymbol{a} \cdot \boldsymbol{b} &= (a_1\boldsymbol{i} + a_2\boldsymbol{j}) \cdot (b_1\boldsymbol{i} + b_2\boldsymbol{j}) \\ &= a_1\boldsymbol{i} \cdot (b_1\boldsymbol{i} + b_2\boldsymbol{j}) + a_2\boldsymbol{j} \cdot (b_1\boldsymbol{i} + b_2\boldsymbol{j}) \\ &= a_1b_1\boldsymbol{i} \cdot \boldsymbol{i} + a_1b_2\boldsymbol{i} \cdot \boldsymbol{j} + a_2b_1\boldsymbol{j} \cdot \boldsymbol{i} + a_2b_2\boldsymbol{j} \cdot \boldsymbol{j}\end{aligned}$$

Now, since $\boldsymbol{i} \cdot \boldsymbol{i} = \boldsymbol{j} \cdot \boldsymbol{j} = 1$, and $\boldsymbol{i} \cdot \boldsymbol{j} = \boldsymbol{j} \cdot \boldsymbol{i} = 0$, we can simplify this to give the following formula:

Key point

If $\boldsymbol{a} = a_1\boldsymbol{i} + a_2\boldsymbol{j}$ and $\boldsymbol{b} = b_1\boldsymbol{i} + b_2\boldsymbol{j}$ then

$$\boldsymbol{a} \cdot \boldsymbol{b} = a_1b_1 + a_2b_2$$

Thus to find the scalar product of two vectors their $\boldsymbol{i}$ components are multiplied together, their $\boldsymbol{j}$ components are multiplied together and the results are added.

Example 3.7

If $\boldsymbol{a} = 7\boldsymbol{i} + 8\boldsymbol{j}$ and $\boldsymbol{b} = 5\boldsymbol{i} - 2\boldsymbol{j}$, find the scalar product $\boldsymbol{a} \cdot \boldsymbol{b}$.

Solution

We use the previous key point and multiply corresponding components together, adding the results.

$$\begin{aligned}\boldsymbol{a} \cdot \boldsymbol{b} &= (7\boldsymbol{i} + 8\boldsymbol{j}) \cdot (5\boldsymbol{i} - 2\boldsymbol{j}) \\ &= (7)(5) + (8)(-2) \\ &= 35 - 16 \\ &= 19\end{aligned}$$

Note that the answer is a scalar.

Example 3.8

If $\boldsymbol{p} = 5\boldsymbol{i} - 3\boldsymbol{j}$ and $\boldsymbol{q} = 2\boldsymbol{i} + \boldsymbol{j}$, find the scalar product $\boldsymbol{p} \cdot \boldsymbol{q}$.

Solution

$(5)(2) + (-3)(1) = 7$

This result readily generalises to vectors in three dimensions as follows:

Key point

If $\boldsymbol{a} = a_1\boldsymbol{i} + a_2\boldsymbol{j} + a_3\boldsymbol{k}$ and $\boldsymbol{b} = b_1\boldsymbol{i} + b_2\boldsymbol{j} + b_3\boldsymbol{k}$ then

$$\boldsymbol{a} \cdot \boldsymbol{b} = a_1b_1 + a_2b_2 + a_3b_3$$

Example 3.9

If $\boldsymbol{a} = 5\boldsymbol{i} + 3\boldsymbol{j} - 2\boldsymbol{k}$ and $\boldsymbol{b} = 8\boldsymbol{i} - 9\boldsymbol{j} + 11\boldsymbol{k}$, find $\boldsymbol{a} \cdot \boldsymbol{b}$.

Solution

Corresponding components are multiplied together and the results are added.

$\boldsymbol{a} \cdot \boldsymbol{b} =$

$$(5)(8) + (3)(-9) + (-2)(11) = 40 - 27 - 22 = -9$$

Note again that the result is a scalar: there are no $\boldsymbol{i}$s, $\boldsymbol{j}$s or $\boldsymbol{k}$s in the answer.

Example 3.10
If $\boldsymbol{p} = 4\boldsymbol{i} - 3\boldsymbol{j} + 7\boldsymbol{k}$ and $\boldsymbol{q} = 6\boldsymbol{i} - \boldsymbol{j} + 2\boldsymbol{k}$, find $\boldsymbol{p} \cdot \boldsymbol{q}$.

Solution
Corresponding components are multiplied together and the results are added.

41

Example 3.11
If $\boldsymbol{r} = 3\boldsymbol{i} + 2\boldsymbol{j} + 9\boldsymbol{k}$ find $\boldsymbol{r} \cdot \boldsymbol{r}$. Show that this is the same as $|\boldsymbol{r}|^2$.

Solution

94

Exercises

1. If $\boldsymbol{a} = 2\boldsymbol{i} - 5\boldsymbol{j}$ and $\boldsymbol{b} = 3\boldsymbol{i} + 2\boldsymbol{j}$ find $\boldsymbol{a} \cdot \boldsymbol{b}$ and verify that $\boldsymbol{a} \cdot \boldsymbol{b} = \boldsymbol{b} \cdot \boldsymbol{a}$.

2. If $\boldsymbol{p} = \boldsymbol{i} + 8\boldsymbol{j} + 7\boldsymbol{k}$ and $\boldsymbol{q} = 3\boldsymbol{i} - 2\boldsymbol{j} + 5\boldsymbol{k}$, find $\boldsymbol{p} \cdot \boldsymbol{q}$.

3. Show that the vectors $\frac{1}{2}\boldsymbol{i} + \boldsymbol{j}$ and $2\boldsymbol{i} - \boldsymbol{j}$ are perpendicular.

4. The work done by a force $\boldsymbol{F}$ in moving a body through a displacement $\boldsymbol{r}$ is given by $\boldsymbol{F} \cdot \boldsymbol{r}$. A force $\boldsymbol{F} = 3\boldsymbol{i} + 7\boldsymbol{k}$ causes a body to move from the point with coordinates (1, 1, 2) to the point (7, 3, 5).
   (a) Find the displacement, $\boldsymbol{r}$, of the body.
   (b) Find the work done by the force.

Solutions to exercises

1. -4

2. 22

4. (a) $6\boldsymbol{i} + 2\boldsymbol{j} + 3\boldsymbol{k}$ (b) 39 units.

3.5 Using the scalar product to find the angle between two vectors

Using the scalar product we can find the angle between two vectors.

Example 3.12
Find the angle between the vectors $\boldsymbol{a} = 5\boldsymbol{i} + 3\boldsymbol{j} - 2\boldsymbol{k}$ and $\boldsymbol{b} = 8\boldsymbol{i} - 9\boldsymbol{j} + 11\boldsymbol{k}$ of Example 3.9.

Solution

Their scalar product has already been found to be -9. The modulus of $\boldsymbol{a}$ is

$$\sqrt{5^2 + 3^2 + (-2)^2} = \sqrt{38}$$

The modulus of $\boldsymbol{b}$ is

$$\sqrt{8^2 + (-9)^2 + 11^2} = \sqrt{266}$$

Substituting these into the formula for the scalar product we find

$$\boldsymbol{a} \cdot \boldsymbol{b} = |\boldsymbol{a}|\,|\boldsymbol{b}| \cos\theta$$
$$-9 = \sqrt{38}\,\sqrt{266}\cos\theta$$

from which

$$\cos\theta = \frac{-9}{\sqrt{38}\,\sqrt{266}} = -0.0895$$

so that

$$\theta = \cos^{-1}(-0.0895) = 95.14^\circ$$

In general, the angle between two vectors can be found from the following formula:

Key point

$$\cos\theta = \frac{\boldsymbol{a} \cdot \boldsymbol{b}}{|\boldsymbol{a}|\,|\boldsymbol{b}|}$$

Exercises

1. Find the angle between $\boldsymbol{p} = 3\boldsymbol{i} - \boldsymbol{j}$ and $\boldsymbol{q} = -4\boldsymbol{i} + 6\boldsymbol{j}$.
2. Find the angle between the vectors $\boldsymbol{i} - \boldsymbol{j} - \boldsymbol{k}$ and $2\boldsymbol{i} + \boldsymbol{j} + 2\boldsymbol{k}$.

Solutions to exercises

1. 142.1°
2. 101.1°

3.6 Using the scalar product to find the component of a vector in the direction of another vector

Consider Figure 3.4, which shows arbitrary vectors $\boldsymbol{a}$ and $\boldsymbol{n}$. Let $\hat{\boldsymbol{n}}$ be a **unit vector** in the direction of $\boldsymbol{n}$.

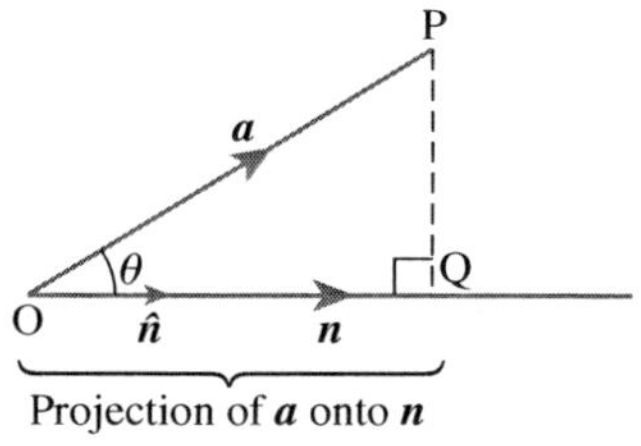

Figure 3.4 OQ is the component of $\boldsymbol{a}$ in the direction of $\boldsymbol{n}$.

Study the figure carefully and note that a line has been drawn from P to meet $\boldsymbol{n}$ at right angles. The distance OQ is called the **projection** of $\boldsymbol{a}$ onto $\boldsymbol{n}$, or alternatively 'the component of $\boldsymbol{a}$ in the direction of $\boldsymbol{n}$'. Simple trigonometry tells us that

$$\cos\theta = \frac{\text{length of projection OQ}}{|\boldsymbol{a}|}$$

so that the length of the projection is $|\boldsymbol{a}|\cos\theta$.

Now by taking the scalar product of $\boldsymbol{a}$ with the unit vector $\hat{\boldsymbol{n}}$ we find

$$\begin{aligned}\boldsymbol{a}\cdot\hat{\boldsymbol{n}} &= |\boldsymbol{a}|\,|\hat{\boldsymbol{n}}|\cos\theta \\ &= |\boldsymbol{a}|\cos\theta \quad \text{since } |\hat{\boldsymbol{n}}| = 1\end{aligned}$$

We conclude that $\boldsymbol{a}\cdot\hat{\boldsymbol{n}}$ is the length of the projection OQ.

Key point

$\boldsymbol{a}\cdot\hat{\boldsymbol{n}}$ is the length of the projection of $\boldsymbol{a}$ onto $\boldsymbol{n}$

alternatively

$\boldsymbol{a}\cdot\hat{\boldsymbol{n}}$ is the component of $\boldsymbol{a}$ in the direction of $\boldsymbol{n}$

Example 3.13

Find the component of the vector $\boldsymbol{a} = 2\boldsymbol{i} + 3\boldsymbol{j}$ in the direction of the vector $\boldsymbol{n} = \boldsymbol{i} + 5\boldsymbol{j}$.

Solution

First we need a unit vector in the direction of $\boldsymbol{n}$.

$$\begin{aligned}\hat{\boldsymbol{n}} &= \frac{\boldsymbol{n}}{|\boldsymbol{n}|} \\ &= \frac{1}{\sqrt{26}}(\boldsymbol{i} + 5\boldsymbol{j})\end{aligned}$$

Then the component of $\boldsymbol{a}$ in the direction of $\boldsymbol{n}$ is

$$\begin{aligned}\boldsymbol{a} \cdot \hat{\boldsymbol{n}} &= (2\boldsymbol{i} + 3\boldsymbol{j}) \cdot \frac{1}{\sqrt{26}}(\boldsymbol{i} + 5\boldsymbol{j}) \\ &= \frac{1}{\sqrt{26}}(2\boldsymbol{i} + 3\boldsymbol{j}) \cdot (\boldsymbol{i} + 5\boldsymbol{j}) \\ &= \frac{1}{\sqrt{26}}(2 + 15) \\ &= \frac{17}{\sqrt{26}} \\ &= 3.334\end{aligned}$$

This is illustrated in Figure 3.5.

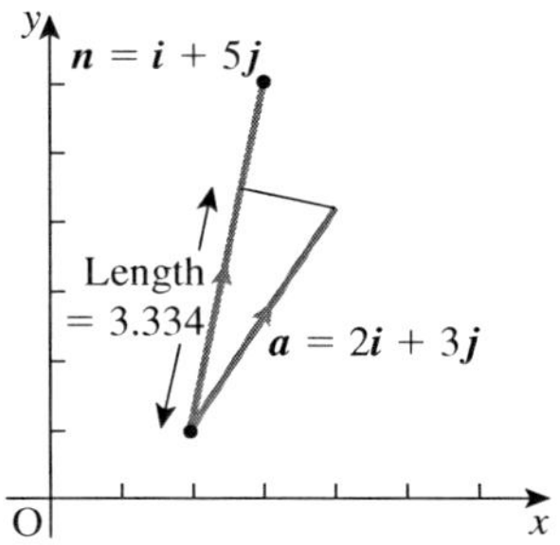

Figure 3.5
The projection of $\boldsymbol{a}$ onto $\boldsymbol{n}$ is 3.334.

Example 3.14

Figure 3.6 shows a plane containing the point A with position vector $\boldsymbol{a}$. The vector $\boldsymbol{n}$ is a perpendicular, or **normal**, to the plane. Find an expression for the perpendicular distance of the plane from the origin.

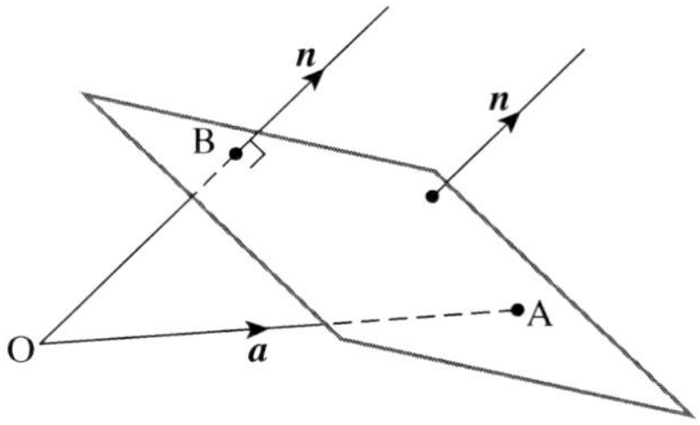

Figure 3.6
OB is the perpendicular distance of the plane from the origin.

Solution

From the figure note that the perpendicular distance of the plane from the origin, which is OB, is the projection of $\boldsymbol{a}$ onto $\boldsymbol{n}$. Thus the perpendicular distance of the plane from the origin is $\boldsymbol{a} \cdot \hat{\boldsymbol{n}}$.

Example 3.15 The scalar product and digital signal recognition and identification

A problem arising in digital signal analysis is to attempt to compare a given but unrecognised signal with a collection of known ones. Such recognition and identification problems arise for example when astronomers interpret signals received from outer space and attempt to identify the objects from which they originated, perhaps stars or galaxies.

If the unrecognised signal resembles one of the known ones sufficiently well it may be possible to identify it. To quantify this resemblance we can make use of vector methods.

Suppose that the unrecognised digital signal is represented by the vector $\boldsymbol{x}$ as shown in Figure 3.7 whereas the vectors $\boldsymbol{e}_1, \boldsymbol{e}_2, \ldots, \boldsymbol{e}_N$ represent known signals. Usually these vectors are **normalised**, that is they are unit vectors. We seek the particular unit vector that most closely resembles $\boldsymbol{x}$. The 'distance' between the unrecognised vector and any one of the known vectors, $\boldsymbol{e}$ say, is defined as

$$|\boldsymbol{x} - \boldsymbol{e}|$$

Figure 3.7

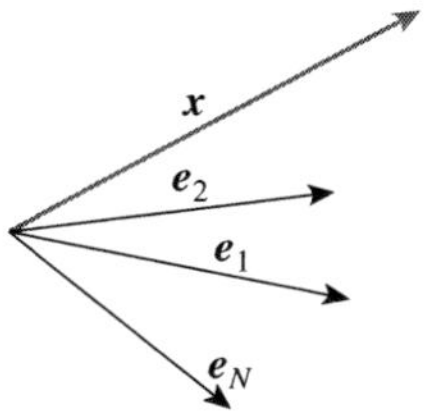

We would like to choose the particular $\boldsymbol{e}$ for which this distance is minimal. First consider the square of this distance $|\boldsymbol{x} - \boldsymbol{e}|^2$. Recall that, for any vector $\boldsymbol{a}$, then $|\boldsymbol{a}|^2 = \boldsymbol{a} \cdot \boldsymbol{a}$. So,

$$\begin{aligned} |\boldsymbol{x} - \boldsymbol{e}|^2 &= (\boldsymbol{x} - \boldsymbol{e}) \cdot (\boldsymbol{x} - \boldsymbol{e}) \\ &= \boldsymbol{x} \cdot \boldsymbol{x} + \boldsymbol{e} \cdot \boldsymbol{e} - \boldsymbol{e} \cdot \boldsymbol{x} - \boldsymbol{x} \cdot \boldsymbol{e} \\ &= |\boldsymbol{x}|^2 + 1 - 2\boldsymbol{x} \cdot \boldsymbol{e} \end{aligned}$$

since $\boldsymbol{e}$ is a unit vector and the scalar product is commutative. We see that the square distance, and hence the distance between $\boldsymbol{x}$ and $\boldsymbol{e}$, is minimal when $\boldsymbol{x} \cdot \boldsymbol{e}$ is maximal. So, the unit vector most closely resembling $\boldsymbol{x}$ is the one having the largest scalar product with $\boldsymbol{x}$.

For example, suppose an unrecognised signal is represented by

$$\boldsymbol{x} = (4, 3, 6)$$

while the known unit vectors are

$$\boldsymbol{e}_1 = (1, 0, 0), \quad \boldsymbol{e}_2 = \frac{1}{\sqrt{6}}(1, 2, 1) \quad \text{and} \quad \boldsymbol{e}_3 = \frac{1}{3}(2, 2, -1)$$

Evaluating the three scalar products in turn we find

$$\boldsymbol{x} \cdot \boldsymbol{e}_1 = 4, \quad \boldsymbol{x} \cdot \boldsymbol{e}_2 = \frac{16}{\sqrt{6}} = 6.53, \quad \boldsymbol{x} \cdot \boldsymbol{e}_3 = \frac{8}{3} = 2.67$$

We conclude that $\boldsymbol{x}$ most closely resembles $\boldsymbol{e}_2$.

Exercises

1 (a) What is the component of the vector $2\boldsymbol{i} + 7\boldsymbol{j}$ in the direction of the vector $\boldsymbol{i}$?

(b) What is the component of $2\boldsymbol{i} + 7\boldsymbol{j}$ in the direction of the vector $\boldsymbol{j}$? Interpret your results graphically.

2 Find the component of the vector

$$\begin{pmatrix} 2 \\ 1 \\ 7 \end{pmatrix}$$

in the direction of the vector

$$\begin{pmatrix} 1 \\ 1 \\ 1 \end{pmatrix}$$

3 What is the projection of the vector $2\boldsymbol{i} - \boldsymbol{j} + \boldsymbol{k}$ onto the vector $3\boldsymbol{i} - 2\boldsymbol{k}$?

Solutions to exercises

1 (a) 2 (b) 7. These are just the x and y components.

2 $\dfrac{10}{\sqrt{3}}$

3 $\dfrac{4}{\sqrt{13}}$

End of block exercises

1 If $\boldsymbol{a} = 4\boldsymbol{i} + 6\boldsymbol{j}$ and $\boldsymbol{b} = 3\boldsymbol{i} - 3\boldsymbol{j}$ find $\boldsymbol{a} \cdot \boldsymbol{b}$ and verify that $\boldsymbol{a} \cdot \boldsymbol{b} = \boldsymbol{b} \cdot \boldsymbol{a}$.

2 Find the angle between $\boldsymbol{p} = 2\boldsymbol{i} + \boldsymbol{j}$ and $\boldsymbol{q} = 5\boldsymbol{i} + 11\boldsymbol{j}$.

3 If a and b are perpendicular, simplify $(5\boldsymbol{a} + 2\boldsymbol{b}) \cdot (\boldsymbol{a} + 7\boldsymbol{b})$.

4 If $\boldsymbol{a} = 5\boldsymbol{i} + 3\boldsymbol{j} + 7\boldsymbol{k}$ and $\boldsymbol{b} = \boldsymbol{i} - 2\boldsymbol{j} - 7\boldsymbol{k}$, find $\boldsymbol{a} \cdot \boldsymbol{b}$.

5 Show that the vectors $7\boldsymbol{i} + 2\boldsymbol{j} + \boldsymbol{k}$ and $\boldsymbol{i} - 4\boldsymbol{j} + \boldsymbol{k}$ are perpendicular.

6 Find the angle between the vectors $2\boldsymbol{i} + \boldsymbol{j} - \boldsymbol{k}$ and $5\boldsymbol{i} + \boldsymbol{j} - 3\boldsymbol{k}$.

7 If

$$\boldsymbol{r} = \begin{pmatrix} x \\ y \\ z \end{pmatrix} \quad \text{and} \quad \boldsymbol{a} = \begin{pmatrix} 3 \\ 2 \\ 5 \end{pmatrix}$$

find $\boldsymbol{r} \cdot \boldsymbol{a}$.

8 Find the component of the vector $7\boldsymbol{i} + 2\boldsymbol{j} - \boldsymbol{k}$ in the direction of the vector $\boldsymbol{i} - \boldsymbol{j} + 2\boldsymbol{k}$.

9 Write down an expression for the component of $\boldsymbol{a}$ in the direction of $\boldsymbol{b}$.

10 A rhombus is a parallelogram in which all sides have equal length. Use the scalar product to show that the diagonals of a rhombus intersect at 90°.

Solutions to exercises

1 -6

2 39°

3 $5a^2 + 14b^2$

4 -50

6 15°

7 $3x + 2y + 5z$

8 $\dfrac{3}{\sqrt{6}}$

9 $\boldsymbol{a} \cdot \hat{\boldsymbol{b}}$

BLOCK 4 The vector product, or cross product

4.1 Introduction

In this block we describe how to find the **vector product** of two vectors. Like the scalar product its definition may seem strange when first met but it is defined in this way because of its many applications. When multiplying vectors using the vector product the result is always a vector. To understand how this vector is formed it is helpful to consider first the right-handed screw rule.

4.2 The right-handed screw rule

Consider the two vectors $\boldsymbol{a}$ and $\boldsymbol{b}$ shown in Figure 4.1.

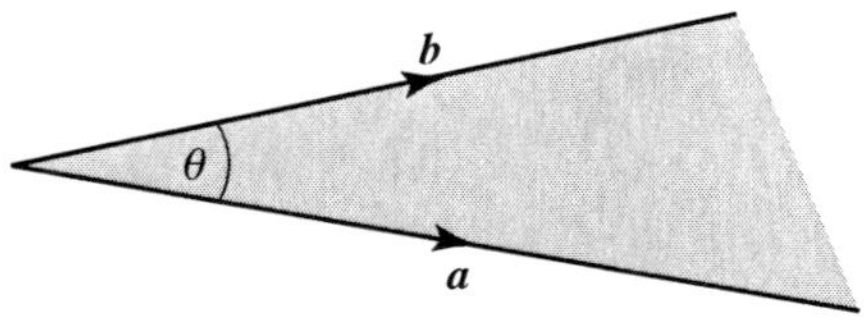

Figure 4.1 Two vectors separated by an angle θ.

The two vectors lie in a plane; this plane is shaded in Figure 4.1. Figure 4.2 shows the same two vectors and the plane in which they lie together with a unit vector, denoted $\hat{\boldsymbol{e}}$, which is perpendicular to this plane. Imagine turning a right-handed screw in the sense from $\boldsymbol{a}$ towards $\boldsymbol{b}$ as shown. A right-handed screw is one that when turned clockwise enters the material into which it is being screwed. You will see from Figure 4.2 that the screw will advance in the direction of $\hat{\boldsymbol{e}}$.

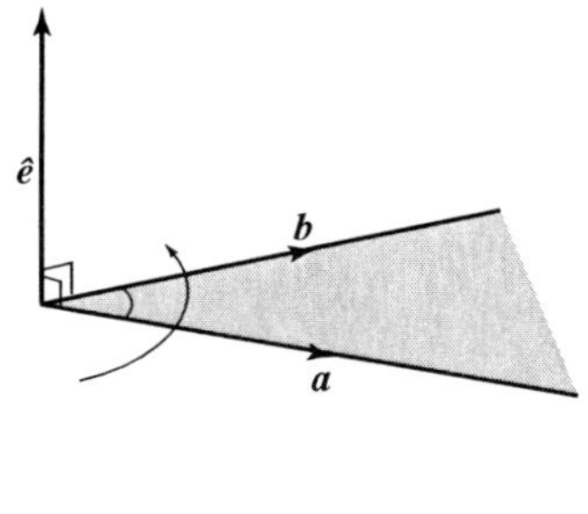

Figure 4.2 A right-handed screw turned from $\boldsymbol{a}$ towards $\boldsymbol{b}$ will advance in the direction of $\hat{\boldsymbol{e}}$.

Example 4.1

If a right-handed screw is turned from $\boldsymbol{b}$ towards $\boldsymbol{a}$, in which direction will it advance? Show this on a diagram similar to Figure 4.2.

Solution

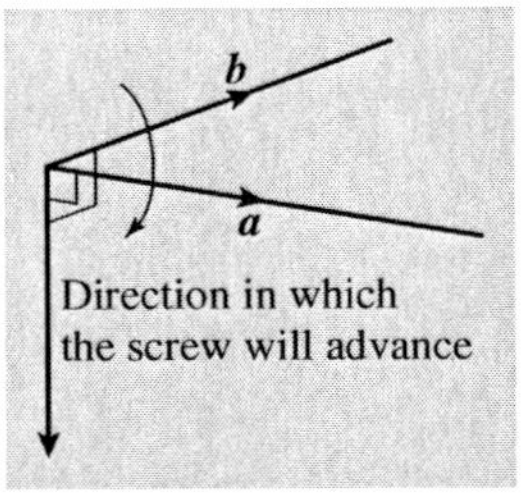

We are now in a position to describe the vector product.

4.3 Definition of the vector product

The result of finding the vector product of two vectors $\boldsymbol{a}$ and $\boldsymbol{b}$ is a vector of modulus $|\boldsymbol{a}|\,|\boldsymbol{b}|\sin\theta$ in the direction of $\hat{\boldsymbol{e}}$, where $\hat{\boldsymbol{e}}$ is a unit vector perpendicular to the plane containing $\boldsymbol{a}$ and $\boldsymbol{b}$ in a sense defined by the right-handed screw rule, as we imagine turning the screwdriver from $\boldsymbol{a}$ towards $\boldsymbol{b}$, as shown in Figure 4.3.

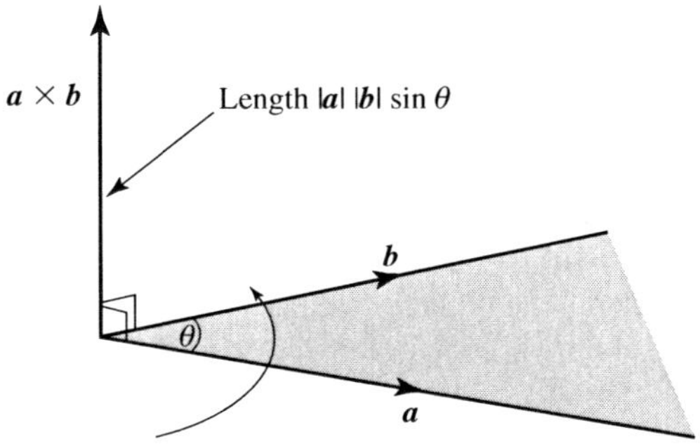

Figure 4.3 The vector $\boldsymbol{a}\times\boldsymbol{b}$ is perpendicular to the plane containing $\boldsymbol{a}$ and $\boldsymbol{b}$.

The symbol we shall use for the vector product is the times sign $\times$, which is why the vector product is also called the cross product. The quantity $\boldsymbol{a}\times\boldsymbol{b}$ is read as $\boldsymbol{a}$ cross $\boldsymbol{b}$.

Key point

Vector product

$$\boldsymbol{a}\times\boldsymbol{b} = |\boldsymbol{a}|\,|\boldsymbol{b}|\sin\theta\,\hat{\boldsymbol{e}}$$

Note that $|\boldsymbol{a}|\ |\boldsymbol{b}|\sin\theta$ is the modulus of the vector product whereas $\hat{\boldsymbol{e}}$ gives the direction.

Now study Figure 4.4, which is used to illustrate the calculation of $\boldsymbol{b} \times \boldsymbol{a}$. In particular note the direction of $\boldsymbol{b} \times \boldsymbol{a}$ arising through the application of the right-handed screw rule.

Figure 4.4 Calculation of $\boldsymbol{b} \times \boldsymbol{a}$.

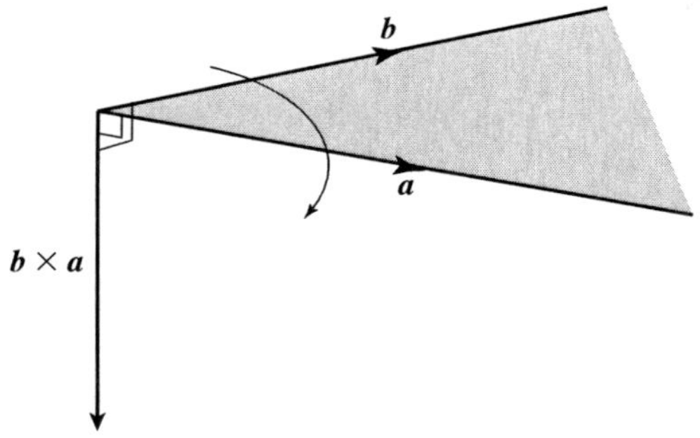

We see that $\boldsymbol{a} \times \boldsymbol{b}$ is not equal to $\boldsymbol{b} \times \boldsymbol{a}$ because their directions are different. In fact $\boldsymbol{a} \times \boldsymbol{b} = -\boldsymbol{b} \times \boldsymbol{a}$.

Example 4.2

If $\boldsymbol{a}$ and $\boldsymbol{b}$ are parallel, show that $\boldsymbol{a} \times \boldsymbol{b} = \boldsymbol{0}$, the zero vector.

Solution

Use the definition: $\boldsymbol{a} \times \boldsymbol{b} = |\boldsymbol{a}|\ |\boldsymbol{b}|\sin\theta\,\hat{\boldsymbol{e}}$. What is the angle θ given that $\boldsymbol{a}$ and $\boldsymbol{b}$ are parallel?

$\theta = 0°$

If $\boldsymbol{a}$ and $\boldsymbol{b}$ are parallel then the angle between them is zero. Consequently $\sin\theta = 0$. It follows that $\boldsymbol{a} \times \boldsymbol{b} = \boldsymbol{0}$. Note that the result, $\boldsymbol{0}$, is the zero vector.

Note in particular the following important results:

Key point

$$\boldsymbol{i} \times \boldsymbol{i} = \boldsymbol{0}, \quad \boldsymbol{j} \times \boldsymbol{j} = \boldsymbol{0}, \quad \boldsymbol{k} \times \boldsymbol{k} = \boldsymbol{0}$$

Example 4.3

Show that $\boldsymbol{i} \times \boldsymbol{j} = \boldsymbol{k}$ and find expressions for $\boldsymbol{j} \times \boldsymbol{k}$ and $\boldsymbol{k} \times \boldsymbol{i}$.

Solution

Note that $\boldsymbol{i}$ and $\boldsymbol{j}$ are perpendicular so that the angle between them is 90°. So the modulus of $\boldsymbol{i} \times \boldsymbol{j}$ is $(1)\ (1)\sin 90° = 1$. The unit vector perpendicular to $\boldsymbol{i}$ and $\boldsymbol{j}$ in the sense defined by the right-handed screw rule is $\boldsymbol{k}$ as shown in Figure 4.5. Therefore $\boldsymbol{i} \times \boldsymbol{j} = \boldsymbol{k}$ as required.

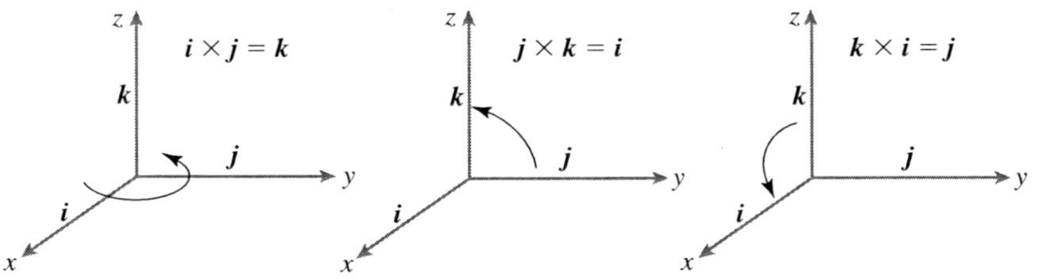

Figure 4.5 The vector $\boldsymbol{k}$ is perpendicular to both $\boldsymbol{i}$ and $\boldsymbol{j}$.

Similarly, by referring to Figure 4.5, you should verify that $\boldsymbol{j} \times \boldsymbol{k} = \boldsymbol{i}$ and $\boldsymbol{k} \times \boldsymbol{i} = \boldsymbol{j}$.

Key point

$$\boldsymbol{i} \times \boldsymbol{j} = \boldsymbol{k}, \quad \boldsymbol{j} \times \boldsymbol{k} = \boldsymbol{i}, \quad \boldsymbol{k} \times \boldsymbol{i} = \boldsymbol{j}$$
$$\boldsymbol{j} \times \boldsymbol{i} = -\boldsymbol{k}, \quad \boldsymbol{k} \times \boldsymbol{j} = -\boldsymbol{i}, \quad \boldsymbol{i} \times \boldsymbol{k} = -\boldsymbol{j}$$

Exercises

1. Write down the definition of the vector product of two vectors $\boldsymbol{p}$ and $\boldsymbol{q}$. Illustrate the definition with a diagram showing clearly the direction of $\boldsymbol{p} \times \boldsymbol{q}$.

2. Explain why, for arbitrary vectors, $\boldsymbol{p} \times \boldsymbol{q}$ is not equal to $\boldsymbol{q} \times \boldsymbol{p}$.

3. Show that if $\boldsymbol{a}$ and $\boldsymbol{b}$ are parallel vectors then their vector product is the zero vector.

4.4 Some properties of the vector product

The vector product has a number of properties that are necessary for further development.

Non-commutativity

We have already seen that $\boldsymbol{a} \times \boldsymbol{b} = -\boldsymbol{b} \times \boldsymbol{a}$.

Distributivity

For three vectors $\boldsymbol{a}$, $\boldsymbol{b}$ and $\boldsymbol{c}$

$$\boldsymbol{a} \times (\boldsymbol{b} + \boldsymbol{c}) = \boldsymbol{a} \times \boldsymbol{b} + \boldsymbol{a} \times \boldsymbol{c}$$

This means that the vector product is distributive over addition.

Example 4.4
Simplify $\boldsymbol{i} \times (\boldsymbol{i} \times \boldsymbol{j})$.

Solution
Using the distributivity property,

$$\boldsymbol{i} \times (\boldsymbol{i} + \boldsymbol{j}) = \boldsymbol{i} \times \boldsymbol{i} + \boldsymbol{i} \times \boldsymbol{j}$$

which simplifies to $\boldsymbol{k}$.

Multiplication by a scalar

For two vectors $\boldsymbol{a}$ and $\boldsymbol{b}$, and a scalar k

$$\begin{aligned} k(\boldsymbol{a} \times \boldsymbol{b}) &= (k\boldsymbol{a}) \times \boldsymbol{b} \\ &= \boldsymbol{a} \times (k\boldsymbol{b}) \end{aligned}$$

Example 4.5
Simplify $\boldsymbol{i} \times 5\boldsymbol{k}$.

Solution
Using this rule,

$$\begin{aligned} \boldsymbol{i} \times 5\boldsymbol{k} &= 5(\boldsymbol{i} \times \boldsymbol{k}) \\ &= 5(-\boldsymbol{j}) \\ &= -5\boldsymbol{j} \end{aligned}$$

4.5 A formula for finding the vector product

We can use the properties of the vector product to develop a formula for finding the vector product of two vectors given in cartesian form. Suppose $\boldsymbol{a} = a_1\boldsymbol{i} + a_2\boldsymbol{j} + a_3\boldsymbol{k}$ and $\boldsymbol{b} = b_1\boldsymbol{i} + b_2\boldsymbol{j} + b_3\boldsymbol{k}$; then

$$\begin{aligned} \boldsymbol{a} \times \boldsymbol{b} &= (a_1\boldsymbol{i} + a_2\boldsymbol{j} + a_3\boldsymbol{k}) \times (b_1\boldsymbol{i} + b_2\boldsymbol{j} + b_3\boldsymbol{k}) \\ &= a_1\boldsymbol{i} \times (b_1\boldsymbol{i} + b_2\boldsymbol{j} + b_3\boldsymbol{k}) \\ &\quad + a_2\boldsymbol{j} \times (b_1\boldsymbol{i} + b_2\boldsymbol{j} + b_3\boldsymbol{k}) \\ &\quad + a_3\boldsymbol{k} \times (b_1\boldsymbol{i} + b_2\boldsymbol{j} + b_3\boldsymbol{k}) \\ &= a_1b_1(\boldsymbol{i} \times \boldsymbol{i}) + a_1b_2(\boldsymbol{i} \times \boldsymbol{j}) + a_1b_3(\boldsymbol{i} \times \boldsymbol{k}) \\ &\quad + a_2b_1(\boldsymbol{j} \times \boldsymbol{i}) + a_2b_2(\boldsymbol{j} \times \boldsymbol{j}) + a_2b_3(\boldsymbol{j} \times \boldsymbol{k}) \\ &\quad + a_3b_1(\boldsymbol{k} \times \boldsymbol{i}) + a_3b_2(\boldsymbol{k} \times \boldsymbol{j}) + a_3b_3(\boldsymbol{k} \times \boldsymbol{k}) \end{aligned}$$

Using the key points on pages 673 and 674 this expression simplifies to

$$\boldsymbol{a} \times \boldsymbol{b} = (a_2b_3 - a_3b_2)\boldsymbol{i} - (a_1b_3 - a_3b_1)\boldsymbol{j} + (a_1b_2 - a_2b_1)\boldsymbol{k}$$

Key point

If $\boldsymbol{a} = a_1\boldsymbol{i} + a_2\boldsymbol{j} + a_3\boldsymbol{k}$ and $\boldsymbol{b} = b_1\boldsymbol{i} + b_2\boldsymbol{j} + b_3\boldsymbol{k}$ then

$$\boldsymbol{a} \times \boldsymbol{b} = (a_2b_3 - a_3b_2)\boldsymbol{i} - (a_1b_3 - a_3b_1)\boldsymbol{j} + (a_1b_2 - a_2b_1)\boldsymbol{k}$$

Example 4.6

Evaluate the vector product $\boldsymbol{a} \times \boldsymbol{b}$ if $\boldsymbol{a} = 3\boldsymbol{i} - 2\boldsymbol{j} + 5\boldsymbol{k}$ and $\boldsymbol{b} = 7\boldsymbol{i} + 4\boldsymbol{j} - 8\boldsymbol{k}$.

Solution

Identifying $a_1 = 3$, $a_2 = -2$, $a_3 = 5$, $b_1 = 7$, $b_2 = 4$, $b_3 = -8$ we find

$$\begin{aligned}\boldsymbol{a} \times \boldsymbol{b} &= [(-2)(-8) - (5)(4)]\boldsymbol{i} - [(3)(-8) - (5)(7)]\boldsymbol{j} \\ &\quad + [(3)(4) - (-2)(7)]\boldsymbol{k} \\ &= -4\boldsymbol{i} + 59\boldsymbol{j} + 26\boldsymbol{k}\end{aligned}$$

Example 4.7

Evaluate the vector product $\boldsymbol{b} \times \boldsymbol{a}$ where $\boldsymbol{a}$ and $\boldsymbol{b}$ are the vectors in Example 4.6.

Solution

$4\boldsymbol{i} - 59\boldsymbol{j} - 26\boldsymbol{k}$

Example 4.8

Use the key point to find the vector product of $\boldsymbol{p} = 3\boldsymbol{i} + 5\boldsymbol{j}$ and $\boldsymbol{q} = 2\boldsymbol{i} - \boldsymbol{j}$.

Solution

Note that in this example there are no $\boldsymbol{k}$ components so a_3 and b_3 are both zero. Apply the formula:

$\boldsymbol{p} \times \boldsymbol{q} =$

$-13\boldsymbol{k}$

Exercises

1 Find the vector product of $\boldsymbol{p} = -2\boldsymbol{i} - 3\boldsymbol{j}$ and $\boldsymbol{q} = 4\boldsymbol{i} + 7\boldsymbol{j}$.

2 (a) Find $\boldsymbol{a} \times \boldsymbol{b}$ when $\boldsymbol{a} = 13\boldsymbol{j}$ and $\boldsymbol{b} = -7\boldsymbol{i} + 2\boldsymbol{j}$.
(b) Verify that $\boldsymbol{a} \times \boldsymbol{b} = -\boldsymbol{b} \times \boldsymbol{a}$.

3 Find $|\boldsymbol{r}_1 \times \boldsymbol{r}_2|$ when $\boldsymbol{r}_1 = 2\boldsymbol{i} + 3\boldsymbol{j}$ and $\boldsymbol{r}_2 = -7\boldsymbol{i} + 2\boldsymbol{j}$.

Solutions to exercises

1 $-2\boldsymbol{k}$

2 (a) $91\boldsymbol{k}$

3 25

4.6 Using determinants to evaluate a vector product

Evaluation of a vector product using the previous formula is very cumbersome. A more convenient and easily remembered method is to use determinants.

The vector product of two vectors $\boldsymbol{a} = a_1\boldsymbol{i} + a_2\boldsymbol{j} + a_3\boldsymbol{k}$ and $\boldsymbol{b} = b_1\boldsymbol{i} + b_2\boldsymbol{j} + b_3\boldsymbol{k}$ can be found by evaluating the determinant:

$$\boldsymbol{a} \times \boldsymbol{b} = \begin{vmatrix} \boldsymbol{i} & \boldsymbol{j} & \boldsymbol{k} \\ a_1 & a_2 & a_3 \\ b_1 & b_2 & b_3 \end{vmatrix}$$

To find the $\boldsymbol{i}$ component of the vector product, imagine crossing out the row and column containing $\boldsymbol{i}$ and finding the determinant of what is left, that is

$$\begin{vmatrix} a_2 & a_3 \\ b_2 & b_3 \end{vmatrix} = a_2b_3 - a_3b_2$$

The resulting number is the $\boldsymbol{i}$ component of the vector product. The $\boldsymbol{j}$ component is found by crossing out the row and column containing $\boldsymbol{j}$ and evaluating

$$\begin{vmatrix} a_1 & a_3 \\ b_1 & b_3 \end{vmatrix} = a_1b_3 - a_3b_1$$

and then changing the sign of the result. Finally the $\boldsymbol{k}$ component is found by crossing out the row and column containing $\boldsymbol{k}$ and evaluating

$$\begin{vmatrix} a_1 & a_2 \\ b_1 & b_2 \end{vmatrix} = a_1b_2 = a_2b_1$$

Key point

If $\boldsymbol{a} = a_1\boldsymbol{i} + a_2\boldsymbol{j} + a_3\boldsymbol{k}$ and $\boldsymbol{b} = b_1\boldsymbol{i} + b_2\boldsymbol{j} + b_3\boldsymbol{k}$ then

$$\boldsymbol{a} \times \boldsymbol{b} = \begin{vmatrix} \boldsymbol{i} & \boldsymbol{j} & \boldsymbol{k} \\ a_1 & a_2 & a_3 \\ b_1 & b_2 & b_3 \end{vmatrix}$$
$$= (a_2b_3 - a_3b_2)\boldsymbol{i} - (a_1b_3 - a_3b_1)\boldsymbol{j} + (a_1b_2 - a_2b_1)\boldsymbol{k}$$

Example 4.9

Find the vector product of $\boldsymbol{a} = 3\boldsymbol{i} - 4\boldsymbol{j} + 2\boldsymbol{k}$ and $\boldsymbol{b} = 9\boldsymbol{i} - 6\boldsymbol{j} + 2\boldsymbol{k}$.

Solution

The two given vectors are represented in the determinant

$$\begin{vmatrix} \boldsymbol{i} & \boldsymbol{j} & \boldsymbol{k} \\ 3 & -4 & 2 \\ 9 & -6 & 2 \end{vmatrix}$$

Evaluating this determinant we obtain

$$\boldsymbol{a} \times \boldsymbol{b} = [-8 - (-12)]\boldsymbol{i} - (6 - 18)\boldsymbol{j} + [-18 - (-36)]\boldsymbol{k}$$
$$= 4\boldsymbol{i} + 12\boldsymbol{j} + 18\boldsymbol{k}$$

Example 4.10

Find the vector product of $\boldsymbol{a} = 7\boldsymbol{i} + \boldsymbol{j} + 2\boldsymbol{k}$ and $\boldsymbol{b} = \boldsymbol{i} + 3\boldsymbol{j} - 2\boldsymbol{k}$.

Solution

$$\begin{vmatrix} \boldsymbol{i} & \boldsymbol{j} & \boldsymbol{k} \\ & & \\ & & \end{vmatrix} = \qquad\qquad -8\boldsymbol{i} + 16\boldsymbol{j} + 20\boldsymbol{k}$$

Example 4.11 Mechanical Engineering – The moment of a force

Figure 4.6 shows a force $\boldsymbol{F}$ applied to an object causing the object to rotate around a fixed axis. The force is applied at a point with position vector $\boldsymbol{r}$. The moment of the force about O is defined to be the vector $\boldsymbol{M}_{\mathrm{O}}$ given by

$$\boldsymbol{M}_{\mathrm{O}} = \boldsymbol{r} \times \boldsymbol{F}$$

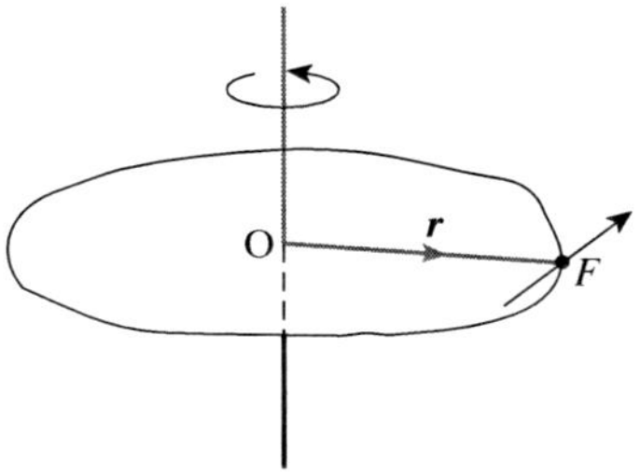

Figure 4.6 The moment of a force is found by evaluating a vector product.

The magnitude of $\boldsymbol{M}_{\mathrm{O}}$ is a measure of the turning effect of the force.

(a) Calculate the moment about O of the force $\boldsymbol{F} = 2\boldsymbol{i} + 3\boldsymbol{j} + \boldsymbol{k}$ newtons applied at the point with position vector $3\boldsymbol{j}$.

(b) Calculate its magnitude.

Solution

(a)

$$\boldsymbol{M}_{\mathrm{O}} = \begin{vmatrix} \boldsymbol{i} & \boldsymbol{j} & \boldsymbol{k} \\ 0 & 3 & 0 \\ 2 & 3 & 1 \end{vmatrix}$$

$$= 3\boldsymbol{i} - 6\boldsymbol{k}$$

(b) The magnitude of this moment is $\sqrt{3^2 + (-6)^2} = \sqrt{45}$ Nm.

Example 4.12 The area of a triangle

The area of the triangle shown in Figure 4.7 is given by the formula area $= \frac{1}{2}bc\sin A$. Show that an equivalent formula is

$$\text{area} = \tfrac{1}{2}|\overrightarrow{\mathrm{AB}} \times \overrightarrow{\mathrm{AC}}|$$

Figure 4.7
The area of a triangle can be found by evaluating a vector product.

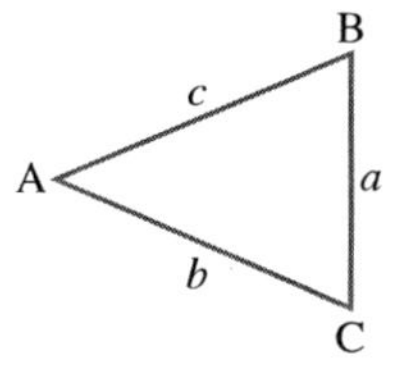

Solution

From the definition of the vector product

$$|\overrightarrow{AB} \times \overrightarrow{AC}| = |\overrightarrow{AB}||\overrightarrow{AC}|\sin A$$

since A is the angle between $\overrightarrow{AB}$ and $\overrightarrow{AC}$. Furthermore $|\overrightarrow{AB}| = c$ and $|\overrightarrow{AC}| = b$. Therefore

$$\begin{aligned} \text{area} &= \tfrac{1}{2} bc \sin A \\ &= \tfrac{1}{2} |\overrightarrow{AB} \times \overrightarrow{AC}| \end{aligned}$$

as required.

Example 4.13

Find the area of the triangle that has vertices at the following points: A(0, 7, 1), B(1, 3, 2) and C(−2, 0, 3).

Solution

To apply the result of Example 4.12 we need to find the vectors $\overrightarrow{AB}$ and $\overrightarrow{AC}$.

We are given the coordinates of the vertices. Write down the position vectors of these points.

$\overrightarrow{OA} = 7\boldsymbol{j} + \boldsymbol{k}$, $\overrightarrow{OB} = \boldsymbol{i} + 3\boldsymbol{j} + 2\boldsymbol{k}$ and $\overrightarrow{OC} = -2\boldsymbol{i} + 3\boldsymbol{k}$

Hence find vectors $\overrightarrow{AB}$ and $\overrightarrow{AC}$.

$\overrightarrow{AB} = \boldsymbol{i} - 4\boldsymbol{j} + \boldsymbol{k}$ and $\overrightarrow{AC} = -2\boldsymbol{i} - 7\boldsymbol{j} + 2\boldsymbol{k}$

Now find $\overrightarrow{AB} \times \overrightarrow{AC}$ and apply the formula of Example 4.12.

$\overrightarrow{AB} \times \overrightarrow{AC} =$ $-\boldsymbol{i} - 4\boldsymbol{j} - 15\boldsymbol{k}$

area $=$ $\frac{11}{2}\sqrt{2}$

Exercises

1. If $\boldsymbol{p} = 3\boldsymbol{i} + 2\boldsymbol{j} - \boldsymbol{k}$ and $\boldsymbol{q} = 5\boldsymbol{i} - \boldsymbol{j} - \boldsymbol{k}$ find $\boldsymbol{p} \times \boldsymbol{q}$.

2. If $\boldsymbol{a} = 12\boldsymbol{i} + 13\boldsymbol{j}$ and $\boldsymbol{b} = 7\boldsymbol{i} + 3\boldsymbol{j}$ find $\boldsymbol{a} \times \boldsymbol{b}$.

3. If $\boldsymbol{a} = \boldsymbol{i} + 2\boldsymbol{j} + 3\boldsymbol{k}$ and $\boldsymbol{b} = 4\boldsymbol{i} + 3\boldsymbol{j} + 2\boldsymbol{k}$ find $\boldsymbol{a} \times \boldsymbol{b}$. Show that $\boldsymbol{a} \times \boldsymbol{b} \neq \boldsymbol{b} \times \boldsymbol{a}$.

4. Points A, B and C have coordinates $(9, 1, -2)$, $(3, 1, 3)$ and $(1, 0, -1)$ respectively. Find the vector product $\overrightarrow{AB} \times \overrightarrow{AC}$.

5. Find a vector that is perpendicular to both of the vectors $\boldsymbol{a} = \boldsymbol{i} + 2\boldsymbol{j} + 7\boldsymbol{k}$ and $\boldsymbol{b} = \boldsymbol{i} + \boldsymbol{j} - 2\boldsymbol{k}$. Hence find a unit vector that is perpendicular to both $\boldsymbol{a}$ and $\boldsymbol{b}$.

6. Find a vector that is perpendicular to the plane containing $6\boldsymbol{i} + \boldsymbol{k}$ and $2\boldsymbol{i} + \boldsymbol{j}$.

7. For the vectors $\boldsymbol{a} = 4\boldsymbol{i} + 2\boldsymbol{j} + \boldsymbol{k}$, $\boldsymbol{b} = \boldsymbol{i} - 2\boldsymbol{j} + \boldsymbol{k}$ and $\boldsymbol{c} = 3\boldsymbol{i} - 3\boldsymbol{j} + 4\boldsymbol{k}$, evaluate $\boldsymbol{a} \times (\boldsymbol{b} \times \boldsymbol{c})$ and $(\boldsymbol{a} \times \boldsymbol{b}) \times \boldsymbol{c}$.
Deduce that, in general, the vector product is not associative.

8. A force of magnitude 3 units acts at the point with coordinates $(1, 2, 3)$. The force is applied in the direction of the vector $3\boldsymbol{i} - \boldsymbol{j} + 4\boldsymbol{k}$. Find the moment of the force about 0. What is the moment of the force about the point with coordinates $(1, 2, 3)$?

9. Find the area of the triangle with vertices at the points with coordinates $(1, 2, 3)$, $(4, -3, 2)$ and $(8, 1, 1)$.

10. For the vectors $\boldsymbol{a} = \boldsymbol{i} + 2\boldsymbol{j} + 3\boldsymbol{k}$, $\boldsymbol{b} = 2\boldsymbol{i} - 2\boldsymbol{j} - 5\boldsymbol{k}$ and $\boldsymbol{c} = \boldsymbol{i} - 3\boldsymbol{j} - \boldsymbol{k}$, evaluate
(a) $(\boldsymbol{a} \cdot \boldsymbol{c})\boldsymbol{b} - (\boldsymbol{b} \cdot \boldsymbol{c})\boldsymbol{a}$
(b) $(\boldsymbol{a} \times \boldsymbol{c}) \times \boldsymbol{c}$
Deduce that $(\boldsymbol{a} \cdot \boldsymbol{c})\boldsymbol{b} - (\boldsymbol{b} \cdot \boldsymbol{c})\boldsymbol{a} = (\boldsymbol{a} \times \boldsymbol{b}) \times \boldsymbol{c}$.

Solutions to exercises

1. $-3\boldsymbol{i} - 2\boldsymbol{j} - 13\boldsymbol{k}$

2. $-55\boldsymbol{k}$

3. $-5\boldsymbol{i} + 10\boldsymbol{j} - 5\boldsymbol{k}$

4. $5\boldsymbol{i} - 34\boldsymbol{j} + 6\boldsymbol{k}$

5. $-11\boldsymbol{i} + 9\boldsymbol{j} - \boldsymbol{k}, \dfrac{1}{\sqrt{203}}(-11\boldsymbol{i} + 9\boldsymbol{j} - \boldsymbol{k})$

6. $-\boldsymbol{i} + 2\boldsymbol{j} + 6\boldsymbol{k}$

7. $7\boldsymbol{i} - 17\boldsymbol{j} + 6\boldsymbol{k},\ -42\boldsymbol{i} - 46\boldsymbol{j} - 3\boldsymbol{k}$

8. $\dfrac{1}{\sqrt{26}}(33\boldsymbol{i} + 15\boldsymbol{j} - 21\boldsymbol{k}), \boldsymbol{0}$

9. $\frac{1}{2}\sqrt{1106}$

10. $-29\boldsymbol{i} - 10\boldsymbol{j} + \boldsymbol{k}$

End of block exercises

1. Find the vector product of $\boldsymbol{a} = 2\boldsymbol{i} + 4\boldsymbol{k}$ and $\boldsymbol{b} = \boldsymbol{i} - 7\boldsymbol{k}$.

2. If $\boldsymbol{a} = 3\boldsymbol{i} + 2\boldsymbol{j} + \boldsymbol{k}$ and $\boldsymbol{b} = -4\boldsymbol{i} + 6\boldsymbol{j} + 2\boldsymbol{k}$ find $\boldsymbol{a} \times \boldsymbol{b}$. Show that $\boldsymbol{a} \times \boldsymbol{b} \neq \boldsymbol{b} \times \boldsymbol{a}$.

3 Points A, B and C have coordinates (1, 3, 2), (4, 1, 3) and (0, 1, −1) respectively. Find the vector product $\overrightarrow{AB} \times \overrightarrow{AC}$.

4 Find a unit vector that is perpendicular to the plane containing $\boldsymbol{i} + 2\boldsymbol{k}$ and $2\boldsymbol{i} + \boldsymbol{j} + 7\boldsymbol{k}$.

5 For the vectors $\boldsymbol{a} = \boldsymbol{i} - 2\boldsymbol{j} + 3\boldsymbol{k}$, $\boldsymbol{b} = -3\boldsymbol{i} + \boldsymbol{k}$ and $\boldsymbol{c} = 2\boldsymbol{i} + \boldsymbol{j} + 4\boldsymbol{k}$, evaluate $\boldsymbol{a} \times (\boldsymbol{b} \times \boldsymbol{c})$ and $(\boldsymbol{a} \times \boldsymbol{b}) \times \boldsymbol{c}$.

6 A force of magnitude 4 units acts at the point with coordinates (4, 3, 2). The force is applied in the direction of the vector $\boldsymbol{i} - \boldsymbol{j}$. Find the moment of the force about O.

7 Find the area of the triangle with vertices at the points with coordinates (4, −3, 2), (5, 0, 5) and (1, 1, 1).

Solutions to exercises

1 $18\boldsymbol{j}$

2 $-2\boldsymbol{i} - 10\boldsymbol{j} + 26\boldsymbol{k}$

3 $8\boldsymbol{i} + 8\boldsymbol{j} - 8\boldsymbol{k}$

4 $\dfrac{1}{\sqrt{14}}(-2\boldsymbol{i} - 3\boldsymbol{j} + \boldsymbol{k})$

5 $-36\boldsymbol{i} + 12\boldsymbol{k}, -34\boldsymbol{i} - 4\boldsymbol{j} + 18\boldsymbol{k}$

6 $4\sqrt{2}\boldsymbol{i} + 4\sqrt{2}\boldsymbol{j} - 14\sqrt{2}\boldsymbol{k}$

7 $\frac{1}{2}\sqrt{458}$

BLOCK 5

The vector equation of a line and a plane

5.1 Introduction

Vectors are very convenient tools for analysing lines and planes in three dimensions. In this block you will learn how to formulate the vector equation of a line and the vector equation of a plane. Finding the equation of a plane relies heavily on an understanding of the scalar product, which should be revised if necessary.

5.2 The vector equation of a line

You will recall that in two dimensions a straight line has an equation of the form $y = mx + c$, such as $y = 3x - 2$. Values of x and y that satisfy this equation correspond to points that lie on the line. Lines in three dimensions are conveniently described using vectors. If we are given a point through which a line must pass, and if we can find a vector in the direction of the line, then the line can be described uniquely.

Consider the straight line APB shown in Figure 5.1.

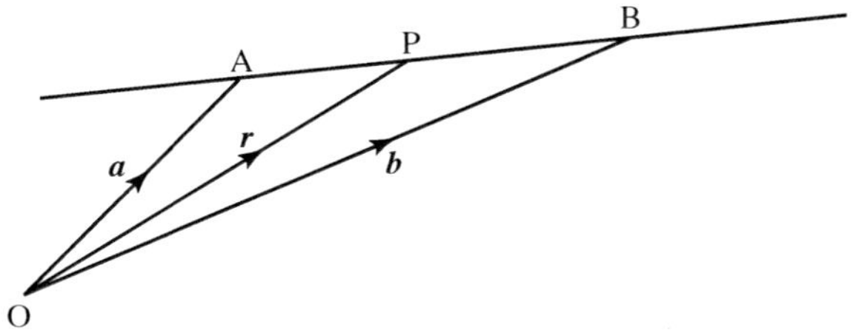

Figure 5.1 A straight line passing through points A and B.

Points A and B are fixed and known points on the line, and have position vectors $\boldsymbol{a}$ and $\boldsymbol{b}$ respectively. Point P is any other arbitrary and variable point on the line, and has position vector $\boldsymbol{r}$. Note that $\overrightarrow{AB}$ and $\overrightarrow{AP}$ are parallel. It is possible to express the position vector of the arbitrary point in terms of the vectors $\boldsymbol{a}$ and $\boldsymbol{b}$ in what is called the **vector equation of the line**. We shall develop this equation in stages.

Example 5.1

Refer to Figure 5.1. Using the triangle law of vector addition it is possible to write an expression for $\overrightarrow{AB}$ in terms of $\boldsymbol{a}$ and $\boldsymbol{b}$. Do this now.

Solution

$a + \overrightarrow{AB} = b$ so $\overrightarrow{AB} = b - a$

Example 5.2

Refer to Figure 5.1. Given $\overrightarrow{AB}$ and $\overrightarrow{AP}$ are parallel, write down a relationship between these vectors.

Solution

$\overrightarrow{AP} = k\overrightarrow{AB}$, for some scalar k

---

Using the triangle law of vector addition we can write

$$\overrightarrow{OP} = \overrightarrow{OA} + \overrightarrow{AP}$$

so that

$$\boldsymbol{r} = \boldsymbol{a} + k(\boldsymbol{b} - \boldsymbol{a})$$

This is the vector equation of the line.

Key point

$$\boldsymbol{r} = \boldsymbol{a} + k(\boldsymbol{b} - \boldsymbol{a})$$

is the **vector equation of the line** passing through the points with position vectors $\boldsymbol{a}$ and $\boldsymbol{b}$.

By varying the value of k we can move to any point on the line. For example, when

$$k = 0, \quad \boldsymbol{r} = \boldsymbol{a}, \quad \text{point A}$$
$$k = 1, \quad \boldsymbol{r} = \boldsymbol{b}, \quad \text{point B}$$

If k lies between 0 and 1, the point P lies on the line between A and B. If k is greater than 1, the point P lies on the line beyond B. If k is less than 0, the point P lies on the line beyond A on the opposite side.

Note that the vector $\boldsymbol{b} - \boldsymbol{a}$ is a vector in the direction of the line.

Example 5.3

Write down the vector equation of the line that passes through the points A and B with position vectors $\boldsymbol{a} = 3\boldsymbol{i} + 2\boldsymbol{j}$ and $\boldsymbol{b} = 7\boldsymbol{i} + 5\boldsymbol{j}$ respectively.

Solution

Note that

$$\begin{aligned}\boldsymbol{b} - \boldsymbol{a} &= (7\boldsymbol{i} + 5\boldsymbol{j}) - (3\boldsymbol{i} + 2\boldsymbol{j})\\ &= 4\boldsymbol{i} + 3\boldsymbol{j}\end{aligned}$$

The equation of the line is then

$$\begin{aligned}\boldsymbol{r} &= \boldsymbol{a} + k(\boldsymbol{b} - \boldsymbol{a})\\ &= (3\boldsymbol{i} + 2\boldsymbol{j}) + k(4\boldsymbol{i} + 3\boldsymbol{j})\end{aligned}$$

Alternatively, using column vector notation we could write the equation of the line as

$$\boldsymbol{r} = \begin{pmatrix} 3 \\ 2 \end{pmatrix} + k\begin{pmatrix} 4 \\ 3 \end{pmatrix}$$

This gives the position vector of any point on the line. Note that if $k = 0$ then

$$\boldsymbol{r} = \begin{pmatrix} 3 \\ 2 \end{pmatrix}$$

that is point A. If $k = 1$ then

$$\begin{aligned} \boldsymbol{r} &= \begin{pmatrix} 3 \\ 2 \end{pmatrix} + \begin{pmatrix} 4 \\ 3 \end{pmatrix} \\ &= \begin{pmatrix} 7 \\ 5 \end{pmatrix} \end{aligned}$$

which is point B. Any other value of k will give another point on the line. For example, if $k = 2$ we find

$$\boldsymbol{r} = \begin{pmatrix} 11 \\ 8 \end{pmatrix}$$

which is a point beyond B.

Example 5.4

Write down the vector equation of the line that passes through the points with position vectors $\boldsymbol{a} = 5\boldsymbol{i} - 2\boldsymbol{j} + 3\boldsymbol{k}$ and $\boldsymbol{b} = 2\boldsymbol{i} + \boldsymbol{j} - 4\boldsymbol{k}$.

Solution

Using column vector notation write down $\boldsymbol{b} - \boldsymbol{a}$.

$$\begin{pmatrix} 2 \\ 1 \\ -4 \end{pmatrix} - \begin{pmatrix} 5 \\ -2 \\ 3 \end{pmatrix} = \begin{pmatrix} -3 \\ 3 \\ -7 \end{pmatrix}$$

The equation of the line is then

$$\boldsymbol{r} = \boldsymbol{a} + k(\boldsymbol{b} - \boldsymbol{a}) = \begin{pmatrix} 5 \\ -2 \\ 3 \end{pmatrix} + k\begin{pmatrix} -3 \\ 3 \\ -7 \end{pmatrix}$$

Example 5.5

On a diagram mark two points M and N. Sketch a straight line through the points M and N, and show their respective position vectors $\boldsymbol{m}$ and $\boldsymbol{n}$. On your sketch mark an arbitrary point on the line, having position vector $\boldsymbol{r}$. Write down the vector equation of the line MN.

Solution

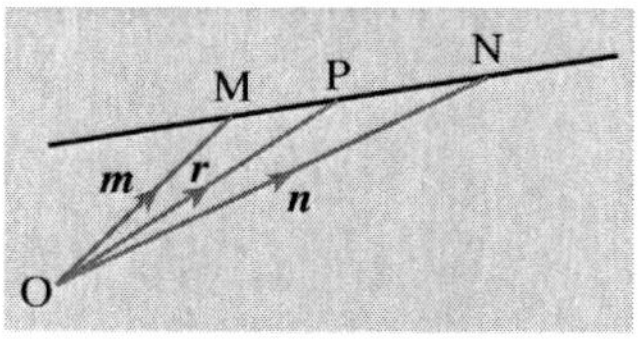

$$\boldsymbol{r} = \boldsymbol{m} + k(\boldsymbol{n} - \boldsymbol{m})$$

On occasions it is useful to convert the vector form of the equation of a straight line into cartesian form. Suppose we write

$$\boldsymbol{a} = \begin{pmatrix} a_1 \\ a_2 \\ a_3 \end{pmatrix}, \quad \boldsymbol{b} = \begin{pmatrix} b_1 \\ b_2 \\ b_3 \end{pmatrix}, \quad \text{and} \quad \boldsymbol{r} = \begin{pmatrix} x \\ y \\ z \end{pmatrix}$$

Then

$$\begin{aligned} \boldsymbol{r} &= \boldsymbol{a} + k(\boldsymbol{b} - \boldsymbol{a}) \\ \begin{pmatrix} x \\ y \\ z \end{pmatrix} &= \begin{pmatrix} a_1 \\ a_2 \\ a_3 \end{pmatrix} + k\begin{pmatrix} b_1 - a_1 \\ b_2 - a_2 \\ b_3 - a_3 \end{pmatrix} \\ &= \begin{pmatrix} a_1 + k(b_1 - a_1) \\ a_2 + k(b_2 - a_2) \\ a_3 + k(b_3 - a_3) \end{pmatrix} \end{aligned}$$

Equating the individual components we find

$$x = a_1 + k(b_1 - a_1), \quad \text{or equivalently } k = \frac{x - a_1}{b_1 - a_1}$$

$$y = a_2 + k(b_2 - a_2), \quad \text{or equivalently } k = \frac{y - a_2}{b_2 - a_2}$$

$$z = a_3 + k(b_3 - a_3), \quad \text{or equivalently } k = \frac{z - a_3}{b_3 - a_3}$$

Now, since each expression on the right is equal to k we can write

$$\frac{x - a_1}{b_1 - a_1} = \frac{y - a_2}{b_2 - a_2} = \frac{z - a_3}{b_3 - a_3}$$

This is the **cartesian form** of the equation of the straight line that passes through the points with coordinates (a_1, a_2, a_3) and (b_1, b_2, b_3).

Key point

$$\frac{x - a_1}{b_1 - a_1} = \frac{y - a_2}{b_2 - a_2} = \frac{z - a_3}{b_3 - a_3}$$

is the **cartesian form** of the equation of the straight line that passes through the points with coordinates (a_1, a_2, a_3) and (b_1, b_2, b_3).

Example 5.6

(a) Write down the cartesian form of the equation of the straight line that passes through the two points $(9, 3, -2)$ and $(4, 5, -1)$.

(b) State the equivalent vector equation.

Solution

(a)
$$\frac{x - 9}{4 - 9} = \frac{y - 3}{5 - 3} = \frac{z - (-2)}{-1 - (-2)}$$

that is

$$\frac{x - 9}{-5} = \frac{y - 3}{2} = \frac{z + 2}{1}$$

(b) The vector equation is

$$\begin{aligned} \boldsymbol{r} &= \boldsymbol{a} + k(\boldsymbol{b} - \boldsymbol{a}) \\ &= \begin{pmatrix} 9 \\ 3 \\ -2 \end{pmatrix} + k\left[\begin{pmatrix} 4 \\ 5 \\ -1 \end{pmatrix} - \begin{pmatrix} 9 \\ 3 \\ -2 \end{pmatrix}\right] = \begin{pmatrix} 9 \\ 3 \\ -2 \end{pmatrix} + k\begin{pmatrix} -5 \\ 2 \\ 1 \end{pmatrix} \end{aligned}$$

Exercises

1 (a) Write down the vector $\overrightarrow{AB}$ joining the points A and B with coordinates $(3, 2, 7)$ and $(-1, 2, 3)$ respectively.
(b) Find the equation of the straight line through A and B.

2 Write down the vector equation of the line passing through the points with position vectors

$$\boldsymbol{p} = 3\boldsymbol{i} + 7\boldsymbol{j} - 2\boldsymbol{k}$$
$$\boldsymbol{q} = -3\boldsymbol{i} + 2\boldsymbol{j} + 2\boldsymbol{k}$$

Find also the cartesian equation of this line.

3 Find the vector equation of the line passing through $(9, 1, 2)$ and which is parallel to the vector $(1, 1, 1)$.

4 Line I has equation

$$\boldsymbol{r}_1 = \begin{pmatrix} 2 \\ 3 \\ 5 \end{pmatrix} + k\begin{pmatrix} 1 \\ 2 \\ 4 \end{pmatrix}$$

Line II has equation

$$\boldsymbol{r}_2 = \begin{pmatrix} -5 \\ 8 \\ 1 \end{pmatrix} + l\begin{pmatrix} -6 \\ 7 \\ 0 \end{pmatrix}$$

Different values of k give different points on line I. Similarly, different values of l give different points on line II. If the two lines intersect then $\boldsymbol{r}_1 = \boldsymbol{r}_2$ at the point of intersection. If you can find values of k and l which satisfy this condition then the two lines intersect. Show the lines intersect by finding these values and hence find the point of intersection.

Solutions to exercises

1 (a) $-4\boldsymbol{i} - 4\boldsymbol{k}$ (b) $\boldsymbol{r} = \begin{pmatrix} 3 \\ 2 \\ 7 \end{pmatrix} + k\begin{pmatrix} -4 \\ 0 \\ -4 \end{pmatrix}$

2 $\boldsymbol{r} = \begin{pmatrix} 3 \\ 7 \\ -2 \end{pmatrix} + k\begin{pmatrix} -6 \\ -5 \\ 4 \end{pmatrix}$;

cartesian form $\dfrac{x-3}{-6} = \dfrac{y-7}{-5} = \dfrac{z+2}{4}$.

3 $\boldsymbol{r} = \begin{pmatrix} 9 \\ 1 \\ 2 \end{pmatrix} + k\begin{pmatrix} 1 \\ 1 \\ 1 \end{pmatrix}$

4 $k = l = -1$ and the point of intersection is $(1, 1, 1)$.

5.3 The vector equation of a plane

Consider the plane shown in Figure 5.2.

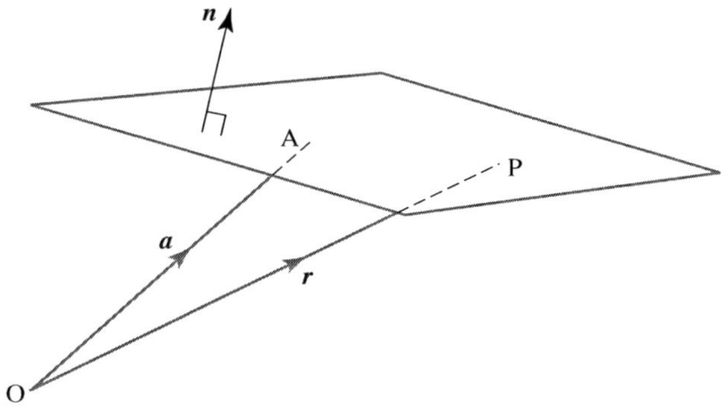

Figure 5.2
This plane passes through A and is perpendicular to $\boldsymbol{n}$.

Suppose that A is a known point in the plane and has position vector $\boldsymbol{a}$. Suppose that P is any other arbitrary point in the plane with position vector $\boldsymbol{r}$. Clearly the vector $\overrightarrow{AP}$ must lie in the plane. Note that

$$\overrightarrow{AP} = \boldsymbol{r} - \boldsymbol{a}$$

Also shown in Figure 5.2 is a vector that is perpendicular to the plane and denoted by $\boldsymbol{n}$. Now, because $\overrightarrow{AP}$ and $\boldsymbol{n}$ are perpendicular their scalar product must equal zero, that is

$$\overrightarrow{AP} \cdot \boldsymbol{n} = 0$$
$$(\boldsymbol{r} - \boldsymbol{a}) \cdot \boldsymbol{n} = 0$$

or alternatively, by removing the brackets and rearranging,

$$\boldsymbol{r} \cdot \boldsymbol{n} = \boldsymbol{a} \cdot \boldsymbol{n}$$

This is the equation of the plane passing through the point with position vector $\boldsymbol{a}$ and perpendicular to $\boldsymbol{n}$.

Key point

A plane passing through the point with position vector $\boldsymbol{a}$ and being perpendicular to the vector $\boldsymbol{n}$ is given by

$$\boldsymbol{r}\cdot\boldsymbol{n} = \boldsymbol{a}\cdot\boldsymbol{n}$$

The previous result is valid whether or not $\boldsymbol{n}$ is a unit vector. However, if $\hat{\boldsymbol{n}}$ is a unit vector then $\boldsymbol{a}\cdot\hat{\boldsymbol{n}}$ represents the perpendicular distance from the origin to the plane, which we usually denote by d. This was shown in Block 3. Hence we can write

$$\boldsymbol{r}\cdot\hat{\boldsymbol{n}} = d$$

This is the **vector equation of a plane** with unit normal $\hat{\boldsymbol{n}}$ and which is a perpendicular distance d from O.

Key point

A plane with unit normal $\hat{\boldsymbol{n}}$ and which is a perpendicular distance d from O is given by

$$\boldsymbol{r}\cdot\hat{\boldsymbol{n}} = d$$

The cartesian form of these equations is obtained by letting $\boldsymbol{r} = x\boldsymbol{i} + y\boldsymbol{j} + z\boldsymbol{k}$ and evaluating the scalar product.

Example 5.7

(a) Find the vector equation of the plane that passes through the point with position vector $3\boldsymbol{i} + 2\boldsymbol{j} + 5\boldsymbol{k}$ and which is perpendicular to $\boldsymbol{i} + \boldsymbol{k}$.

(b) Find the cartesian equation of this plane.

Solution

In this example, $\boldsymbol{a} = 3\boldsymbol{i} + 2\boldsymbol{j} + 5\boldsymbol{k}$ and the normal is $\boldsymbol{n} = \boldsymbol{i} + \boldsymbol{k}$.

(a) Using the previous results we can write down the equation

$$\begin{aligned}\boldsymbol{r}\cdot\boldsymbol{n} &= \boldsymbol{a}\cdot\boldsymbol{n}\\ \boldsymbol{r}\cdot(\boldsymbol{i}+\boldsymbol{k}) &= (3\boldsymbol{i} + 2\boldsymbol{j} + 5\boldsymbol{k})\cdot(\boldsymbol{i}+\boldsymbol{k})\\ &= 8\end{aligned}$$

(b) Writing $\boldsymbol{r}$ as $x\boldsymbol{i} + y\boldsymbol{j} + z\boldsymbol{k}$ we have the cartesian form

$$(x\boldsymbol{i} + y\boldsymbol{j} + z\boldsymbol{k})\cdot(\boldsymbol{i}+\boldsymbol{k}) = 8$$

so that

$$x + z = 8$$

Exercises

1 Find the equation of a plane that is normal to $8\boldsymbol{i} + 9\boldsymbol{j} + \boldsymbol{k}$ and which is a distance 1 from the origin.

2 Find the equation of a plane that passes through (8, 1, 0) and which is normal to the vector $\boldsymbol{i} + 2\boldsymbol{j} - 3\boldsymbol{k}$.

3 A plane passes through the points A, B and C with coordinates (1, 0, 1), (−2, 5, 0) and (3, 1, 1) respectively.

(a) Write down $\overrightarrow{AB}$ and $\overrightarrow{AC}$.

(b) Find the vector product $\overrightarrow{AB} \times \overrightarrow{AC}$.

(c) Comment upon the direction of $\overrightarrow{AB} \times \overrightarrow{AC}$ in relation to the plane through A, B and C.

(d) Find the vector and cartesian forms of the equation of the plane containing A, B and C.

Solutions to exercises

1 $\boldsymbol{r} \cdot \frac{1}{\sqrt{146}}\begin{pmatrix}8\\9\\1\end{pmatrix} = 1$, or

$8x + 9y + z = \sqrt{146}$

2 $\boldsymbol{r} \cdot \begin{pmatrix}1\\2\\-3\end{pmatrix} = \begin{pmatrix}8\\1\\0\end{pmatrix} \cdot \begin{pmatrix}1\\2\\-3\end{pmatrix}$, that is

$\boldsymbol{r} \cdot \begin{pmatrix}1\\2\\-3\end{pmatrix} = 10$

3 (a) $-3\boldsymbol{i} + 5\boldsymbol{j} - \boldsymbol{k}$, $2\boldsymbol{i} + \boldsymbol{j}$ (b) $\boldsymbol{i} - 2\boldsymbol{j} - 13\boldsymbol{k}$

(c) it is normal to the plane

(d) $\boldsymbol{r} \cdot \begin{pmatrix}1\\-2\\-13\end{pmatrix} = -12$,

$x - 2y - 13z = -12$

End of block exercises

1 (a) Write down the vector $\overrightarrow{AB}$ joining the points A and B with coordinates (−2, 1, 3) and (5, 2, 3) respectively.

(b) Find the equation of the straight line through A and B.

2 Write down the vector equation of the line passing through the points with position vectors

$$\boldsymbol{p} = 5\boldsymbol{i} + 3\boldsymbol{j} - 2\boldsymbol{k}$$
$$\boldsymbol{q} = 3\boldsymbol{i} + 7\boldsymbol{j} - \boldsymbol{k}$$

Find the cartesian equation of this line.

3 Find the vector equation of the line passing through (2, 1, 2) and which is parallel to the vector (1, 2, 3).

4 Find the vector equation of the line passing through (2, 1, 2) and which is parallel to the unit vector $\frac{1}{\sqrt{14}}(1, 2, 3)$.

5 Find the equation of a plane that passes through (2, −3, 1) and which is normal to the vector $3\boldsymbol{i} - 3\boldsymbol{j} - \boldsymbol{k}$.

6 Find the equation of a plane that passes through the origin and which is normal to the vector $5\boldsymbol{i} + \boldsymbol{j} - \boldsymbol{k}$.

7 What is the distance of the plane

$$\boldsymbol{r} \cdot \begin{pmatrix}3\\2\\1\end{pmatrix} = 5$$

from the origin?

8 (a) A plane Π is given by

$$\boldsymbol{r} \cdot \begin{pmatrix}1\\2\\1\end{pmatrix} = 6$$

Find the distance of this plane from the origin.

(b) A second plane passes through the point (3, 2, 1) and is parallel to the plane Π. Find its distance from the origin.

(c) Deduce the distance from the point (3, 2, 1) to the plane Π.

9 Write the plane $3x - 3y - z = 14$ in vector form.

Solutions to exercises

1 (a) $7\boldsymbol{i} + \boldsymbol{j}$ (b) $\boldsymbol{r} = \begin{pmatrix} -2 \\ 1 \\ 3 \end{pmatrix} + k\begin{pmatrix} 7 \\ 1 \\ 0 \end{pmatrix}$

2 $\boldsymbol{r} = \begin{pmatrix} 5 \\ 3 \\ -2 \end{pmatrix} + k\begin{pmatrix} -2 \\ 4 \\ 1 \end{pmatrix}$;

$$\frac{x-5}{-2} = \frac{y-3}{4} = \frac{z+2}{1}$$

3 $\boldsymbol{r} = \begin{pmatrix} 2 \\ 1 \\ 2 \end{pmatrix} + k\begin{pmatrix} 1 \\ 2 \\ 3 \end{pmatrix}$

4 same as 3

5 $\boldsymbol{r} \cdot \begin{pmatrix} 3 \\ -3 \\ -1 \end{pmatrix} = 14$

6 $\boldsymbol{r} \cdot \begin{pmatrix} 5 \\ 1 \\ -1 \end{pmatrix} = 0$

7 $\dfrac{5}{\sqrt{14}}$

8 (a) $\dfrac{6}{\sqrt{6}}$ (b) $\dfrac{8}{\sqrt{6}}$ (c) $\dfrac{2}{\sqrt{6}}$

9 $\boldsymbol{r} \cdot \begin{pmatrix} 3 \\ -3 \\ -1 \end{pmatrix} = 14$

End of chapter exercises

1 Show on a diagram three arbitrary vectors $\boldsymbol{p}$, $\boldsymbol{q}$ and $\boldsymbol{r}$. Using the triangle law of addition verify the associativity rule

$$\boldsymbol{p} + (\boldsymbol{q} + \boldsymbol{r}) = (\boldsymbol{p} + \boldsymbol{q}) + \boldsymbol{r}$$

2 A force of 23 newtons acts at an angle of 20° below the horizontal. Resolve this force into two components, one vertical and one horizontal.

3 On a diagram show the arbitrary vectors $\boldsymbol{p}$ and $\boldsymbol{q}$. Then show the following:
(a) $\boldsymbol{p} + \boldsymbol{q}$ (b) $\boldsymbol{p} - \boldsymbol{q}$ (c) $\boldsymbol{q} - \boldsymbol{p}$
(d) $4\boldsymbol{q}$ (e) $-2\boldsymbol{q}$

4 State the position vectors of the points with coordinates (9, 1, −1) and (−4, 0, 4).

5 If A has coordinates (4, 3, 0) and B has coordinates (−2, 1, 9) find $\overrightarrow{AB}$ and $|\overrightarrow{AB}|$.

6 Find the modulus of the vector

$$\boldsymbol{p} = 2\boldsymbol{i} - \boldsymbol{j} + 5\boldsymbol{k}$$

7 If A has coordinates (−4, 2, 1) and B has coordinates (2, 0, 2) find the direction ratio of the vector $\overrightarrow{AB}$. Find its direction cosines l, m and n and verify that $l^2 + m^2 + n^2 = 1$.

8 Find the angle between the vectors $12\boldsymbol{i} - \boldsymbol{j}$ and $2\boldsymbol{i} + \boldsymbol{j} + \boldsymbol{k}$.

9 Find the projection of the vector $6\boldsymbol{i} + \boldsymbol{j} + 5\boldsymbol{k}$ onto the vector $\boldsymbol{i} - \boldsymbol{j} + 2\boldsymbol{k}$.

10 Points A, B and C have position vectors (9, 1, 1), (8, 1, 1) and (9, 0, 2). Find
(a) the equation of the plane containing A, B and C
(b) the area of the triangle ABC.

11 Find the equation of the plane with normal $\boldsymbol{j}$ that is a distance 2 from the origin.

12 If $\boldsymbol{a} = 3\boldsymbol{i} + \boldsymbol{j} - 2\boldsymbol{k}$ and $\boldsymbol{b} = 13\boldsymbol{i} - \boldsymbol{j} - \boldsymbol{k}$ find (a) $\boldsymbol{a} + \boldsymbol{b}$ (b) $\boldsymbol{b} - 3\boldsymbol{a}$ (c) $|\boldsymbol{b}|$ (d) $\hat{\boldsymbol{a}}$ (e) $|\boldsymbol{b} - \boldsymbol{a}|$

13 Given that $\boldsymbol{p} = 2\boldsymbol{i} + 2\boldsymbol{j}$ and $\boldsymbol{q} = 7\boldsymbol{k}$ find $\boldsymbol{p} \cdot \boldsymbol{q}$ and interpret this result geometrically.

14 Find the work done by a force of magnitude 10 newtons acting in the direction of the vector $3\boldsymbol{i} + \boldsymbol{j} + 8\boldsymbol{k}$ if it moves a particle from the point (1, 1, 1) to the point (3, 1, 2).

15 Given three vectors $\boldsymbol{a}$, $\boldsymbol{b}$ and $\boldsymbol{c}$, their triple scalar product is defined to be $(\boldsymbol{a} \times \boldsymbol{b}) \cdot \boldsymbol{c}$. It can be shown that the modulus of this is the volume of the parallelepiped formed by the three vectors. Find the volume of the parallelepiped formed by the three vectors $\boldsymbol{a} = 3\boldsymbol{i} + \boldsymbol{j} - 2\boldsymbol{k}$, $\boldsymbol{b} = \boldsymbol{i} + 2\boldsymbol{j} - 2\boldsymbol{k}$ and $\boldsymbol{c} = 2\boldsymbol{i} + 5\boldsymbol{j} + \boldsymbol{k}$.

16 If the triple scalar product $(\boldsymbol{a} \times \boldsymbol{b}) \cdot \boldsymbol{c}$ is equal to zero, then
(i) $\boldsymbol{a} = \boldsymbol{0}$, or $\boldsymbol{b} = \boldsymbol{0}$, or $\boldsymbol{c} = \boldsymbol{0}$ or
(ii) two of the vectors are parallel, or
(iii) the three vectors lie in the same plane (they are said to be **coplanar**).

Show that the vectors
$2\boldsymbol{i} - \boldsymbol{j} + \boldsymbol{k}$, $3\boldsymbol{i} - 4\boldsymbol{j} + 5\boldsymbol{k}$, $\boldsymbol{i} + 2\boldsymbol{j} - 3\boldsymbol{k}$
are coplanar.

17 Given three vectors $\boldsymbol{a}$, $\boldsymbol{b}$ and $\boldsymbol{c}$, their triple vector product is defined to be $(\boldsymbol{a} \times \boldsymbol{b}) \times \boldsymbol{c}$. For the vectors $\boldsymbol{a} = 4\boldsymbol{i} + 2\boldsymbol{j} + \boldsymbol{k}$, $\boldsymbol{b} = 2\boldsymbol{i} - \boldsymbol{j} + 7\boldsymbol{k}$ and $\boldsymbol{c} = 2\boldsymbol{i} - 2\boldsymbol{j} + 3\boldsymbol{k}$ verify that

$$(\boldsymbol{a} \times \boldsymbol{b}) \times \boldsymbol{c} = (\boldsymbol{a} \cdot \boldsymbol{c})\boldsymbol{b} - (\boldsymbol{b} \cdot \boldsymbol{c})\boldsymbol{a}$$

18 Find the volume of the parallelepiped whose edges are represented by the vectors $12\boldsymbol{i} + \boldsymbol{j} + \boldsymbol{k}$, $2\boldsymbol{i}$ and $-2\boldsymbol{j} + \boldsymbol{k}$.

19 If

$$\boldsymbol{a} = \begin{pmatrix} 3 \\ 2 \\ 1 \end{pmatrix}, \quad \boldsymbol{b} = \begin{pmatrix} 4 \\ 3 \\ 4 \end{pmatrix} \quad \text{and} \quad \boldsymbol{c} = \begin{pmatrix} 8 \\ 1 \\ 0 \end{pmatrix}$$

show that $\boldsymbol{a} \cdot \boldsymbol{b} \times \boldsymbol{c} = 32$.

Solutions to exercises

2 21.6 N horiz., 7.9 N vert. downwards

4 $9\boldsymbol{i} + \boldsymbol{j} - \boldsymbol{k}$, $-4\boldsymbol{i} + 4\boldsymbol{k}$

5 $-6\boldsymbol{i} - 2\boldsymbol{j} + 9\boldsymbol{k}$, 11

6 $\sqrt{30}$

7 $6: -2:1, \dfrac{6}{\sqrt{41}}, -\dfrac{2}{\sqrt{41}}, \dfrac{1}{\sqrt{41}}$

8 38.8°

9 $\dfrac{15}{\sqrt{6}}$

10 (a) $r \cdot \begin{pmatrix} 0 \\ 1 \\ 1 \end{pmatrix} = 2$ (b) $\dfrac{\sqrt{2}}{2}$

11 $y = 2$

12 (a) $16\boldsymbol{i} - 3\boldsymbol{k}$ (b) $4\boldsymbol{i} - 4\boldsymbol{j} + 5\boldsymbol{k}$ (c) $3\sqrt{19}$
(d) $\dfrac{1}{\sqrt{14}}(3\boldsymbol{i} + \boldsymbol{j} - 2\boldsymbol{k})$ (e) $\sqrt{105}$

13 0, vectors are perpendicular

14 $\dfrac{140}{\sqrt{74}} = 16.3$

15 29

18 6

Differentiation

Chapter 15

Differentiation is one of the most important processes in engineering mathematics. It is the study of the way in which functions change. The function may represent pressure, stress, volume or some other physical variable. For example, the pressure of a vessel may depend upon temperature. As the temperature of the vessel increases, then so does the pressure. Engineers often need to know the rate at which such a variable changes.

Block 1 explains how to calculate the rate of change of a function, $y(x)$, across a range of values of the input variable, x. The rate of change of $y(x)$ at a single point is then developed. This requires the introduction of the idea of taking limits, which is also important in Chapter 18 on the applications of integration.

In practice, most people use a standard table to differentiate functions, and how this is done is explained in Block 2. The chapter closes with a study of repeated differentiation.

Chapter 15 contents

BLOCK 1 Interpretation of a derivative

1.1 Introduction

Engineers are often interested in the rate at which some variable is changing. For example, an engineer needs to know the rate at which the pressure in a vessel is changing, the rate at which the voltage across a capacitor is changing, or the rate at which the temperature is changing in a chemical reaction. Rapid rates of change of a variable may indicate that a system is not operating normally and is approaching critical values. Alarms may be triggered.

Rates of change may be positive, negative or zero. A positive rate of change means that the variable is increasing; a negative rate of change means that the variable is decreasing. A zero rate of change means that the variable is not changing.

Consider Figure 1.1, which illustrates a variable, $y(x)$.

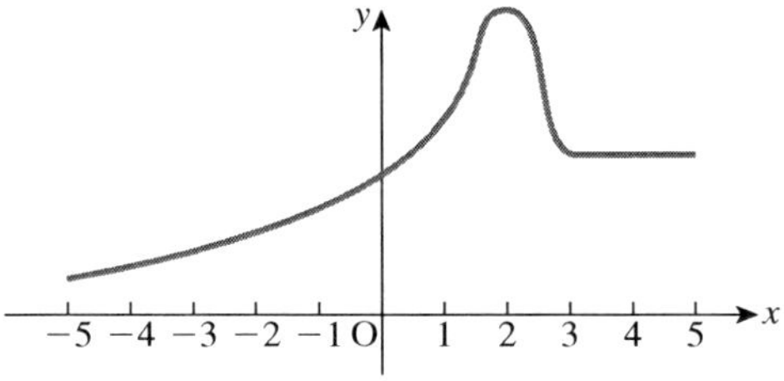

Figure 1.1 The function $y(x)$ changes at different rates for different values of x.

Between $x = -5$ and $x = -3$, y is increasing slowly. Across this interval the rate of change of y is small and positive. Between $x = -3$ and $x = 1$, y is increasing more rapidly; the rate of change of y is positive and fairly large. Between $x = 1$ and $x = 2$, y is increasing very rapidly and so the rate of change is positive and large. From $x = 2$ to $x = 3$, y decreases rapidly; the rate of change is large and negative. From $x = 3$ to $x = 5$, y is constant and so the rate of change on this interval is zero.

The technique for calculating rate of change is called **differentiation**. Often it is not sufficient to describe a rate of change as, for example, 'positive and large' or 'negative and quite small'. A precise value is needed. Use of differentiation provides a precise value or expression for the rate of change of a function.

1.2 Average rate of change across an interval

We see from Figure 1.1 that a function can have different rates of change at different points on its graph. We begin by defining and then calculating the **average rate of change** of a function across an interval. Figure 1.2 shows a function, $y(x)$, and values x_1, x_2, $y(x_1)$ and $y(x_2)$.

Consider x increasing from x_1 to x_2. The change in x is $x_2 - x_1$. As x increases from x_1 to x_2, then y increases from $y(x_1)$ to $y(x_2)$. The change in y is $y(x_2) - y(x_1)$. Then the average rate of change of y across the interval is

$$\frac{\text{change in } y}{\text{change in } x} = \frac{y(x_2) - y(x_1)}{x_2 - x_1} = \frac{\text{BC}}{\text{AC}}$$

From Figure 1.2 we see that $\frac{\text{BC}}{\text{AC}} = \tan\theta$, which is also the gradient of the straight line or **chord** AB. Hence we see that the average rate of change across an interval is identical to the gradient of the chord across that interval.

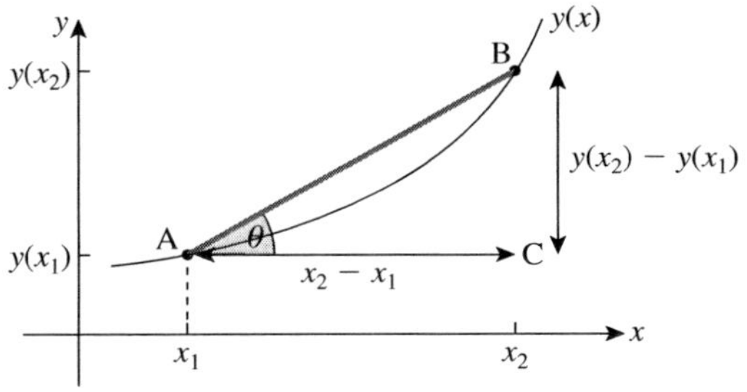

Figure 1.2 Average rate of change $= \dfrac{y(x_2) - y(x_1)}{x_2 - x_1}$.

Key point

$$\text{average rate of change of } y = \frac{\text{change in } y}{\text{change in } x} = \text{gradient of chord}$$

Example 1.1

Calculate the average rate of change of $y = x^2$ across the interval
(a) $x = 1$ to $x = 4$
(b) $x = -2$ to $x = 0$

Solution

(a) Change in $x = 4 - 1 = 3$.
When $x = 1$, $y = 1^2 = 1$. When $x = 4$, $y = 4^2 = 16$. Hence the change in y is $16 - 1 = 15$. So

$$\text{average rate of change across interval } [1, 4] = \frac{15}{3} = 5$$

This means that across the interval [1, 4], on average the y value increases by 5 for every 1 unit increase in x.

(b) Change in $x = 0 - (-2) = 2$. We have $y(-2) = 4$ and $y(0) = 0$ so the change in y is $0 - 4 = -4$. Hence

$$\begin{aligned}\text{average rate of change} &= \frac{-4}{2}\\ &= -2\end{aligned}$$

On average, across the interval $x = -2$ to $x = 0$, y decreases by 2 units for every 1 unit increase in x.

Example 1.2 Electrical Engineering – Voltage across a capacitor

The voltage, $v(t)$, across a capacitor varies with time, t, according to

$$v(t) = 3 + 2e^{-t}$$

Find the average rate of change of voltage as time varies

(a) from $t = 0$ to $t = 2$

(b) from $t = 1$ to $t = 3$

Solution

(a) Change in $t = 2 - 0 = 2$.

When $t = 0$, $v = 3 + 2e^0 = 5$.

When $t = 2$, $v =$ $3 + 2e^{-2} = 3.2707$

So

average rate of change of $v(t) =$

$$\frac{3.2707 - 5}{2} = -0.8647$$

(b) Change in $t =$ $3 - 1 = 2$

$$\begin{aligned}v(1) &= 3 + 2e^{-1}\\ &= 3.7358\end{aligned}$$

$v(3) =$ $3 + 2e^{-3} = 3.0996$

So

average rate of change of $v(t)$ across [1, 3] =

$$\frac{3.0996 - 3.7358}{2} = -0.3181$$

Across the interval from $t = 1$ to $t = 3$, the voltage is decreasing but at a slower rate than across the interval from $t = 0$ to $t = 2$.

Exercises

1 Calculate the average rate of change of $y = x^2 + 2x$ from $x = 1$ to $x = 4$.

2 Calculate the average rate of change of $h(t) = 2t^2 - 2t + 1$ from $t = 0$ to $t = 2$.

3 Calculate the average rate of change of $i(t) = 50 \sin t$ from $t = 0$ to $t = \pi$.

4 Calculate the average rate of change of

$$r(x) = \frac{1}{x + 1} \text{ from } x = -3 \text{ to } x = -2.$$

5 Calculate the average rate of change of $z(t) = 4 + 2t^2$ across (a) $t = 1$ to $t = 3$, (b) $t = -1$ to $t = 0$.

6 The temperature, T, of a vessel varies with time, t, according to

$$T(t) = 320 + \frac{65}{t^2}$$

Calculate the average rate of change of T from $t = 2$ to $t = 4$.

Solutions to exercises

1 7

2 2

3 0

4 −0.5

5 (a) 8 (b) −2

6 −6.094

1.3 Rate of change at a point

As mentioned earlier, we often need to know the rate of change of a function at a point, and not simply an average rate of change across an interval.

Refer again to Figure 1.2. Suppose we wish to find the rate of change of y at the point A. The average rate of change across the interval from $x = x_1$ to $x = x_2$ is given by the gradient of the chord AB. This provides an approximation to the rate of change at A.

Suppose the chord AB is extended on both sides, as shown in Figure 1.3. As B is moved closer to A, the gradient of the chord provides a better approximation to the rate of change at A.

Ultimately B is made coincident with A and then the chord AB becomes a tangent to the curve at A. The gradient of this tangent gives the rate of change of y at A:

Key point

rate of change at a point = gradient of tangent to the curve at that point

Calculating the rate of change of a function at a point by measuring the gradient of a tangent is usually not an accurate method. Consequently we develop an exact, algebraic way of finding rates of change.

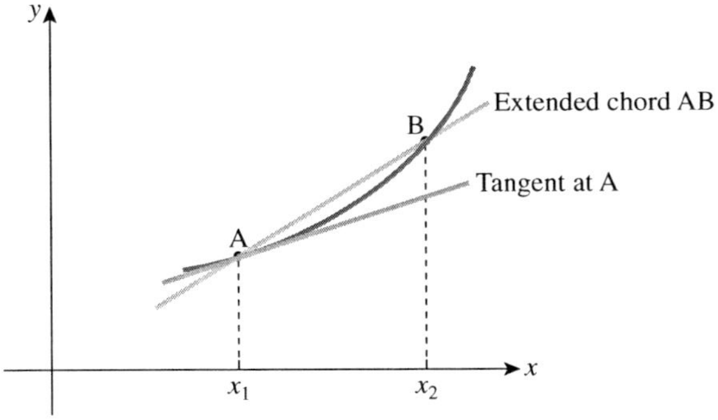

Figure 1.3
The extended chord ultimately becomes the tangent at A.

Consider the function $y(x)$ as shown in Figure 1.4.

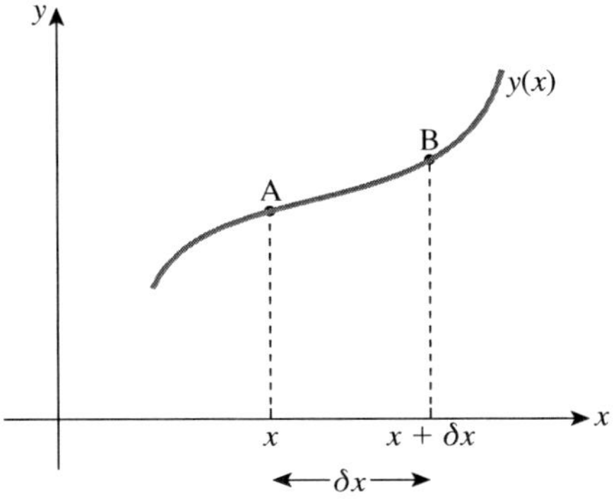

Figure 1.4
As B approaches A, $\delta x \rightarrow 0$.

Let A be a point on the curve with coordinates $(x, y(x))$. B is a point on the curve near to A. The x coordinate of B is $x + \delta x$. The term δx is pronounced 'delta x'. It represents a small change in the x direction. The y coordinate of B is $y(x + \delta x)$. We calculate the gradient of the chord AB:

$$\begin{aligned}\text{gradient of AB} &= \frac{\text{change in } y}{\text{change in } x} \\ &= \frac{y(x+\delta x) - y(x)}{x + \delta x - x} \\ &= \frac{y(x+\delta x) - y(x)}{\delta x}\end{aligned}$$

The change in y, that is $y(x + \delta x) - y(x)$, is also written as δy. So

$$\begin{aligned}\text{gradient of AB} &= \frac{y(x+\delta x) - y(x)}{\delta x} \\ &= \frac{\delta y}{\delta x}\end{aligned}$$

The gradient of AB gives the average rate of change of $y(x)$ across the small interval from x to $x + \delta x$. To calculate the rate of change of $y(x)$ at A we require the gradient of the tangent at A.

Consider A as a fixed point and let B move along the curve towards A. At each position of B we can calculate the gradient of the chord AB. As B gets closer to A, the chord AB approximates more closely to the tangent at A. Also, as B approaches A, the distance δx decreases. To find the gradient of the tangent at A we calculate the gradient of the chord AB and let δx get smaller and smaller. We say δx tends to zero and write this as $\delta x \to 0$.

As B approaches A, the x difference between A and B gets smaller, that is $\delta x \to 0$, and likewise the y difference, δy, also gets smaller, so $\delta y \to 0$. However, the gradient of AB, given by the ratio $\frac{\delta y}{\delta x}$, approaches a definite value, called a limit. So we seek the limit of $\frac{\delta y}{\delta x}$ as $\delta x \to 0$. We write this as

$$\lim_{\delta x \to 0} \frac{\delta y}{\delta x}$$

Note that 'limit' has been shortened to 'lim'.

In summary we have

Key point

$$\text{rate of change of } y = \text{gradient of tangent}$$
$$= \lim_{\delta x \to 0} \frac{\delta y}{\delta x}$$

Let us see this applied to an example.

Example 1.3

Find the rate of change of $y(x) = x^2$.

Solution

Suppose A is the fixed point with coordinates (x, x^2) as shown in Figure 1.5. B is a point on the curve near to A with coordinates $(x + \delta x, (x + \delta x)^2)$. We calculate the gradient of the chord AB.

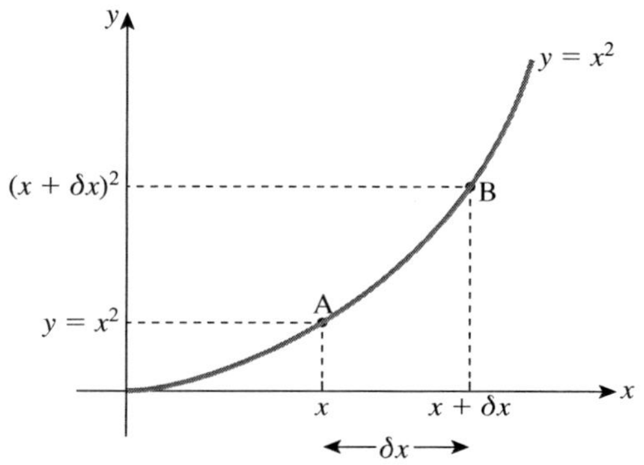

Figure 1.5
The gradient of the tangent at A is approximated by the gradient of the chord AB.

$$\text{change in } x = \delta x$$
$$\text{change in } y = \delta y$$
$$= (x + \delta x)^2 - x^2$$

$$
\begin{aligned}
&= x^2 + 2x\delta x + (\delta x)^2 - x^2 \\
&= 2x(\delta x) + (\delta x)^2 \\
\text{gradient of chord AB} &= \frac{\delta y}{\delta x} \\
&= \frac{2x(\delta x) + (\delta x)^2}{\delta x} \\
&= 2x + \delta x
\end{aligned}
$$

This is the average rate of change of $y(x)$ across the small interval from x to $x + \delta x$. To obtain the gradient of the tangent at A, we let $\delta x \rightarrow 0$.

$$
\begin{aligned}
\text{gradient of tangent at A} &= \lim_{\delta x \rightarrow 0} (2x + \delta x) \\
&= 2x
\end{aligned}
$$

Hence the rate of change of x^2 is $2x$.

For example, if $x = 3$, then A is the point (3, 9) and the rate of change of y at this point is 6. Similarly if $x = -1$, A is the point $(-1, 1)$ and the rate of change of $y = -2$.

Exercises

1 Find the rate of change of $y(x) = x^2 + 1$. Calculate the rate of change of y when x is (a) 6 (b) 3 (c) -2 (d) 0

2 Find the rate of change of $y(x) = x^2 + 2x$. Calculate the rate of change of y when x is (a) 6 (b) -5 (c) 0

Solutions to exercises

1 $2x$, (a) 12 (b) 6 (c) -4 (d) 0

2 $2x + 2$, (a) 14 (b) -8 (c) 2

1.4 Terminology and notation

The process of finding the rate of change of a given function is called **differentiation**. The function is said to be **differentiated**. If y is a function of the independent variable x, we say that y is differentiated with respect to (w.r.t.) x. The rate of change of a function is also known as the **derivative** of the function.

There is a notation for writing down the derivative of a function. If the function is $y(x)$, we denote the derivative of y by

$$\frac{\mathrm{d}y}{\mathrm{d}x}$$

pronounced ‘dee y by dee x’. Hence

Key point

$$\lim_{\delta x \to 0} \frac{\delta y}{\delta x} = \frac{dy}{dx}$$

Another notation for the derivative is simply y', pronounced y dash. Similarly if the function is $z(t)$ we write the derivative as $\frac{dz}{dt}$ or z'. When the independent variable is t, the derivative may also be denoted using the dot notation. Thus, for example, $\frac{dz}{dt}$ may be written as $\dot{z}$, pronounced 'z dot'. Sometimes, instead of writing y, a function is written in full: for example, to show the derivative of sin $5x$ we write

$$\frac{d(\sin 5x)}{dx}$$

Exercises

1 If x is a function of the independent variable t, write down two ways in which the derivative can be written.

2 If f is a function of x, write down two ways in which the derivative can be written.

Solutions

1 $\frac{dx}{dt}$ or $\dot{x}$

2 $\frac{df}{dx}$ or f'

End of block exercises

1 Calculate the average rate of change of $y = x^3 - 1$ from
(a) $x = 1$ to $x = 3$
(b) $x = 0$ to $x = 2$
(c) $x = -2$ to $x = 2$

2 The pressure, P atmospheres, in a vessel varies with temperature, T (degrees Celsius), according to

$$P(T) = 120 - 20e^{-T/20}$$

Calculate the average rate of change of pressure as T varies from 10°C to 100°C.

3 The current, $i(t)$, in a circuit decays exponentially with time, t, according to the equation

$$i(t) = 5 + 2e^{-t}$$

Calculate the average rate of change of current as t varies from 0 to 3.

4 Explain the meaning of the expression $\frac{dy}{dx}$.

5 (a) Calculate the rate of change of $y(x) = 5 - x^2$.
(b) Calculate the rate of change of y when $x = -4$.

6 (a) Calculate $\frac{dR}{dx}$ when $R(x) = 2x^2$.
(b) Calculate $\frac{dR}{dx}$ when $x = 0.5$.

Solutions to exercises

1 (a) 13 (b) 4 (c) 4

2 0.13

3 −0.63

5 (a) $-2x$ (b) 8

6 (a) $4x$ (b) 2

BLOCK 2 Using a table of derivatives

2.1 Introduction

Block 1 gave a brief introduction to the meaning of a derivative. A derivative is the rate of change of a function. Geometrically we saw that this is given by the gradient of a tangent. If we consider a typical function, as illustrated in Figure 2.1 it is clear that the gradient of a tangent depends upon where the tangent is drawn. For example, tangent A, drawn where x has a value x_1, has a different gradient from tangent B, drawn where x has a value x_2. In other words, the gradient of the tangent is itself a function of x. This was seen in Example 1.3 of Block 1, where the gradient was found to be $2x$.

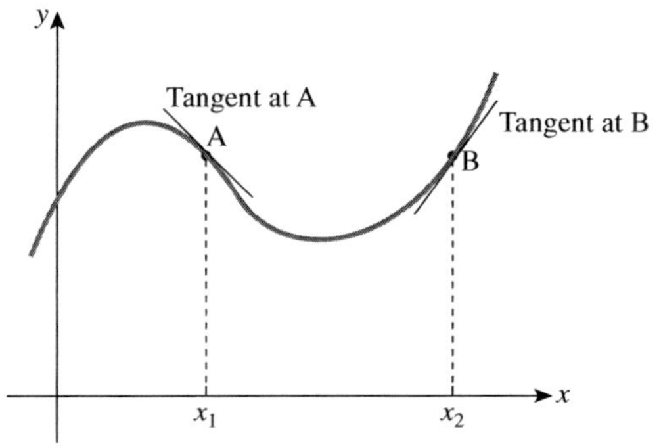

Figure 2.1 The gradient of a tangent varies along the curve.

Rather than calculate the derivative of a function as explained in Block 1, it is common practice to use a table of derivatives. This block shows how to use such a table.

2.2 Table of derivatives

Table 2.1 lists some of the common functions used in engineering and their corresponding derivatives.

Example 2.1

Use Table 2.1 to find $\frac{dy}{dx}$ when y is given by

(a) $3x$ (b) 3 (c) $3x^2$ (d) $4x^7$

Table 2.1
Common functions and their derivatives

Function	Derivative
constant	0
x	1
kx	k
x^n	nx^{n-1}
kx^n	knx^{n-1}
e^x	e^x
e^{kx}	ke^{kx}
$\ln x$	$\frac{1}{x}$
$\ln kx$	$\frac{1}{x}$
$\sin x$	$\cos x$
$\sin kx$	$k \cos kx$
$\sin(kx + \alpha)$	$k \cos(kx + \alpha)$
$\cos x$	$- \sin x$
$\cos kx$	$-k \sin kx$
$\cos(kx + \alpha)$	$-k \sin(kx + \alpha)$
$\tan x$	$\sec^2 x$
$\tan kx$	$k \sec^2 kx$
$\tan(kx + \alpha)$	$k \sec^2(kx + \alpha)$
$\sinh x$	$\cosh x$
$\sinh kx$	$k \cosh kx$
$\cosh x$	$\sinh x$
$\cosh kx$	$k \sinh kx$
$\tanh x$	$\mathrm{sech}^2 x$
$\tanh kx$	$k\, \mathrm{sech}^2 kx$
$\sin^{-1} x$	$\frac{1}{\sqrt{1 - x^2}}$
$\sin^{-1} kx$	$\frac{k}{\sqrt{1 - k^2x^2}}$
$\cos^{-1} x$	$\frac{-1}{\sqrt{1 - x^2}}$
$\cos^{-1} kx$	$\frac{-k}{\sqrt{1 - k^2x^2}}$
$\tan^{-1} x$	$\frac{1}{1 + x^2}$
$\tan^{-1} kx$	$\frac{k}{1 + k^2x^2}$

k, n and α are constants, and all angles are in radians

Solution

(a) We note that $3x$ is of the form kx where $k = 3$. Using Table 2.1 we then have $\dfrac{dy}{dx} = 3$.

(b) Noting that 3 is a constant we see that $\dfrac{dy}{dx} = 0$.

(c) We see that $3x^2$ is of the form kx^n, with $k = 3$ and $n = 2$. The derivative, knx^{n-1}, is then $6x^1$, or more simply, $6x$. So if $y = 3x^2$, then $\dfrac{dy}{dx} = 6x$.

(d) We see that $4x^7$ is of the form kx^n, with $k = 4$ and $n = 7$. Hence the derivative, $\dfrac{dy}{dx}$, is given by $28x^6$.

Example 2.2

Find $\dfrac{dy}{dx}$ when y is (a) $\sqrt{x}$, (b) $\dfrac{3}{x^2}$, (c) $\dfrac{2}{x}$.

Solution

(a) We write $\sqrt{x}$ as $x^{\frac{1}{2}}$, and use the result for x^n with $n = \frac{1}{2}$. So

$$\begin{aligned}\frac{dy}{dx} &= nx^{n-1}\\ &= \tfrac{1}{2}x^{\frac{1}{2}-1}\\ &= \tfrac{1}{2}x^{-\frac{1}{2}}\end{aligned}$$

This may be written as $\dfrac{1}{2\sqrt{x}}$.

(b) We write $\frac{3}{x^2}$ as $3x^{-2}$. Using the result of kx^n we see that

$$\begin{aligned}\frac{dy}{dx} &= knx^{n-1}\\ &= \qquad\qquad\end{aligned}$$

$3(-2)x^{-2-1} = -6x^{-3}$

(c) We write $\frac{2}{x}$ as $2x^{-1}$. Then we see that

$$\frac{dy}{dx} = \qquad\qquad$$

$2(-1)x^{-1-1} = -2x^{-2}$

Example 2.3

Use Table 2.1 to find $\dfrac{dz}{dt}$ given z is (a) e^t, (b) e^{3t}, (c) e^{-5t}.

Solution

Although Table 2.1 is written using x as the independent variable, it can be used for any variable.

(a) From Table 2.1, if $y = e^x$, then $\dfrac{dy}{dx} = e^x$. Hence if $z = e^t$ then $\dfrac{dz}{dt} = e^t$.

(b) From Table 2.1 we see that when $y = e^{3x}$ then

$\dfrac{dy}{dx} =$ — $3e^{3x}$

Hence $\dfrac{dz}{dt} =$ — $3e^{3t}$

(c) Using the result for e^{kx} in Table 2.1 we see that when $z = e^{-5t}$,

$\dfrac{dz}{dt} =$ — $-5e^{-5t}$

Example 2.4

Find the derivative, $\dfrac{dy}{dx}$, when y is (a) $\sin 3x$, (b) $\cos \dfrac{x}{2}$, (c) $\tan 2x$.

Solution

(a) Using the result for $\sin kx$, and taking $k = 3$, we see that

$$\frac{dy}{dx} = 3 \cos 3x$$

(b) From the result for $\cos kx$, and taking $k = \frac{1}{2}$ we see that

$\dfrac{dy}{dx} =$ — $-\dfrac{1}{2} \sin \dfrac{x}{2}$

(c) From the result for $\tan kx$, we see that

$\dfrac{dy}{dx} =$ — $2 \sec^2 2x$

Exercises

1 Find the derivative of the following functions:
(a) $9x$ (b) $4x$ (c) $6x^3$ (d) $-3x^2$ (e) $\ln 3t$

2 Find $\dfrac{dz}{dt}$ when z is given by

(a) $\dfrac{4}{t^3}$ (b) $\sqrt{t^3}$ (c) $5t^{-2}$ (d) $-\frac{3}{2}t^{3/2}$

3 Find the derivative of each of the following functions:
(a) $\sin 5x$ (b) $\cos 4t$ (c) $\tan 3r$ (d) e^{2v} (e) $\dfrac{1}{e^{3t}}$

4 Find the derivative of the following:
(a) $\cos \dfrac{2x}{3}$ (b) $\sin(-2x)$ (c) $\tan \pi x$ (d) $e^{x/2}$

Solutions to exercises

1 (a) 9 (b) 4 (c) $18x^2$ (d) $-6x$ (e) $\dfrac{1}{t}$

2 (a) $-12t^{-4}$ (b) $\frac{3}{2}t^{1/2}$ (c) $-10t^{-3}$ (d) $-\frac{9}{4}t^{1/2}$

3 (a) $5 \cos 5x$ (b) $-4 \sin 4t$ (c) $3 \sec^2 3r$
(d) $2e^{2v}$ (e) $-3e^{-3t}$

4 (a) $-\dfrac{2}{3} \sin \dfrac{2x}{3}$ (b) $-2 \cos(-2x)$ (c) $\pi \sec^2 \pi x$
(d) $\frac{1}{2}e^{x/2}$

2.3 Extending the table of derivatives

We introduce two simple rules that enable us to extend the range of functions that we can differentiate.

Key point

The derivative of $f(x) \pm g(x)$ is

$$\frac{df}{dx} \pm \frac{dg}{dx}$$

This rule says that to find the derivative of the sum (difference) of two functions, we simply calculate the sum (difference) of the derivatives of each function.

Key point

The derivative of $kf(x)$ is

$$k\frac{df}{dx}$$

This rule tells us that if a function is multiplied by a constant, k, then the derivative is likewise multiplied by the same constant, k.

Example 2.5

Find the derivative of each of the following functions:
(a) $y = 6 \sin 2x$ (b) $y = 6 \sin 2x + 3x^2$ (c) $y = 6 \sin 2x + 3x^2 - 5e^{3x}$

Solution

(a) From Table 2.1, the derivative of $\sin 2x$ is $2 \cos 2x$. Hence the derivative of $6 \sin 2x$ is $6(2 \cos 2x)$, that is $12 \cos 2x$.

$$y = 6 \sin 2x, \quad \frac{dy}{dx} = 6(2 \cos 2x) = 12 \cos 2x$$

(b) The function comprises two parts: $6 \sin 2x$ and $3x^2$. We have already differentiated $6 \sin 2x$ in part (a), so we consider the derivative of $3x^2$. The derivative of x^2 is $2x$ and so the derivative of $3x^2$ is $3(2x)$, that is $6x$. These derivatives are now summed.

$$y = 6 \sin 2x + 3x^2, \quad \frac{dy}{dx} = 12 \cos 2x + 6x$$

(c) We differentiate each part of the function in turn.

$$y = 6 \sin 2x + 3x^2 - 5e^{3x}$$

$$\frac{dy}{dx} = 6(2 \cos 2x) + 3(2x) - 5(3e^{3x}) = 12 \cos 2x + 6x - 15e^{3x}$$

Example 2.6

Find $\frac{dy}{dx}$ where y is defined by

(a) $\frac{x^6}{2} - 3e^{-2x}$ (b) $4 \cos \frac{x}{2} + 9 - 9x^3$

Solution

(a) The derivative of x^6 is $6x^5$. Hence the derivative of $\frac{x^6}{2}$ is $\frac{6x^5}{2} = 3x^5$

The derivative of e^{-2x} is $-2e^{-2x}$

Hence the derivative of $3e^{-2x}$ is

$3(-2)e^{-2x} = -6e^{-2x}$

So given

$$y = \frac{x^6}{2} - 3e^{-2x}$$

then

$$\frac{dy}{dx} = 3x^5 + 6e^{-2x}$$

(b) The derivative of $\cos \frac{x}{2}$ is

$-\frac{1}{2} \sin \frac{x}{2}$

The derivative of 9 is zero. The derivative of $9x^3$ is

$27x^2$

So given

$$y = 4 \cos \frac{x}{2} + 9 - 9x^3$$

then

$$\frac{dy}{dx} = -2 \sin \frac{x}{2} - 27x^2$$

Exercises

1 Find $\frac{dy}{dx}$ when y is given by

(a) $4x^6 + 8x^3$ (b) $-3x^4 + 2x^{1.5}$

(c) $\frac{9}{x^2} + \frac{14}{x} - 3x$ (d) $\frac{3 + 2x}{4}$ (e) $(2 + 3x)^2$

2 Find the derivative of each of the following functions:

(a) $z(t) = 5 \sin t + \sin 5t$

(b) $h(v) = 3 \cos 2v - 6 \sin \frac{v}{2}$

(c) $m(n) = 4e^{2n} + \frac{2}{e^{2n}} + \frac{n^2}{2}$

(d) $H(t) = \frac{e^{3t}}{2} + 2 \tan 2t$

(e) $S(r) = (r^2 + 1)^2 - 4e^{-2r}$

3 Differentiate the following functions:

(a) $A(t) = (3 + e^t)^2$

(b) $B(s) = \pi e^{2s} + \frac{1}{s} + 2 \sin \pi s$

(c) $V(r) = \left(1 + \frac{1}{r}\right)^2 + (r + 1)^2$

(d) $M(\theta) = 6 \sin 2\theta - 2 \cos \frac{\theta}{4} + 2\theta^2$

(e) $H(t) = 4 \tan 3t + 3 \sin 2t - 2 \cos 4t$

Solutions to exercises

1 (a) $24x^5 + 24x^2$ (b) $-12x^3 + 3x^{0.5}$ (c) $-\frac{18}{x^3} - \frac{14}{x^2} - 3$ (d) $\frac{1}{2}$ (e) $12 + 18x$

2 (a) $5 \cos t + 5 \cos 5t$ (b) $-6 \sin 2v - 3 \cos \frac{v}{2}$

(c) $8e^{2n} - 4e^{-2n} + n$ (d) $\frac{3e^{3t}}{2} + 4 \sec^2 2t$

(e) $4r^3 + 4r + 8e^{-2r}$

3 (a) $6e^t + 2e^{2t}$ (b) $2\pi e^{2s} - \frac{1}{s^2} + 2\pi \cos(\pi s)$

(c) $-\frac{2}{r^2} - \frac{2}{r^3} + 2r + 2$

(d) $12 \cos 2\theta + \frac{1}{2} \sin \frac{\theta}{4} + 4\theta$

(e) $12 \sec^2 3t + 6 \cos 2t + 8 \sin 4t$

2.4 Evaluating a derivative

Engineers may need to find the rate of change of a function at a particular point: that is, find the derivative of a function at a specific point. We do this by finding the derivative of the function, and then evaluating the derivative at the given value of x. When evaluating, all angles are in radians. Consider a function, $y(x)$. We use the notation $\frac{dy}{dx}(0.7)$ or $y'(0.7)$ to denote the derivative of y evaluated at $x = 0.7$.

Example 2.7

Find the value of the derivative of $y = 3x^2$ where $x = 4$. Interpret your result.

Solution

We have $y = 3x^2$ and so $\frac{dy}{dx} = 6x$. We now evaluate the derivative.

When $x = 4$, $\frac{dy}{dx} = 6(4) = 24$, that is

$$\frac{dy}{dx}(4) = 24$$

The derivative is positive when $x = 4$ and so y is increasing at this point. Thus when $x = 4$, y is increasing at a rate of 24 vertical units per horizontal unit.

Example 2.8 Electrical Engineering

Find the rate of change of current, $i(t)$, given by

$$i(t) = 3e^{-t} + 2 \quad t \geq 0$$

when $t = 0.7$ seconds.

Solution

The rate of change of a function is the same as the derivative of the function, that is $\frac{di}{dt}$.

$$\frac{di}{dt} = -3e^{-t}$$

When $t = 0.7$

$$\frac{di}{dt} = -3e^{-0.7} = -1.4898$$

The derivative is negative and so we know that $i(t)$ is decreasing when $t = 0.7$. Thus, when $t = 0.7$, the current is decreasing at a rate of 1.49 As^{-1}.

Exercises

1 Calculate the derivative of $y = 3x^2 + e^x$ when $x = 0.5$.

2 Calculate the rate of change of $i(t) = 4 \sin 2t + 3t$ when (a) $t = \frac{\pi}{3}$ (b) $t = 0.6$.

3 Evaluate the rate of change of $H(t) = 5 \sin t - 3 \cos 2t$ when (a) $t = 0$ (b) $t = 1.3$.

Solutions to exercises

1 4.6487

2 (a) -1 (b) 5.8989

3 (a) 5 (b) 4.4305

End of block exercises

1 Find $\frac{dy}{dx}$ when y is given by

(a) $7x^5 + 6x^{-2} + \sin 2x$

(b) $3 \cos 4x - 6 \sin 5x$

(c) $e^{3x} + e^{-3x} + 2e^x + 1$

(d) $4 \tan \frac{x}{2} + \frac{1}{\sqrt{x}}$

(e) $3\sqrt{x} + \frac{9}{x} + \frac{1}{2} \sin 6x + \ln x$

2 Find the rate of change of the following functions:
(a) $e^t + e^{-t}$ (b) $2 \sin 3t + \ln 2t$ (c) $-3 \cos x$
(d) $\sqrt{r} + 2r^2$ (e) $2e^{-0.5v} + v^3$

3 Find $\dot{x}$ when x is given by
(a) $2t^4 - 3t + 1 + 2 \ln t$
(b) $\sin \pi t - 2 \cos \pi t$
(c) $3 \tan 2t - e^t$ (d) $e^{2t} - e^{-2t} + t$
(e) $t^{3/2} - t^{2/3}$

4 Find the rate of change of each function when $t = 1.2$:
(a) $3t^2 - 2t^3$ (b) $\dfrac{e^{4t}}{2} + 3e^{-t}$
(c) $6 \sin\dfrac{t}{2} + 3 \cos\dfrac{t}{2}$
(d) $2 \tan t - \tan 2t$
(e) $\dfrac{4}{t} + 4 \ln t$

5 Find the derivative of the following:
(a) $e^{2t}(e^t + e^{-t})$ (b) $\dfrac{2t^2 + 1}{t}$
(c) $(2t + 1)(2t - 1)$
(d) $\sin^2 2x + \cos^2 2x + \sin 2x + \cos 2x$
(e) $\dfrac{1}{e^x}$ (f) $\dfrac{\sin x}{\cos x}$

Solutions to exercises

1 (a) $35x^4 - 12x^{-3} + 2 \cos 2x$
(b) $-12 \sin 4x - 30 \cos 5x$
(c) $3e^{3x} - 3e^{-3x} + 2e^x$
(d) $2 \sec^2 \dfrac{x}{2} - \dfrac{1}{2}x^{-3/2}$
(e) $\dfrac{3}{2}x^{-1/2} - \dfrac{9}{x^2} + 3 \cos 6x + \dfrac{1}{x}$

2 (a) $e^t - e^{-t}$ (b) $6 \cos 3t + \dfrac{1}{t}$ (c) $3 \sin x$
(d) $\dfrac{1}{2}r^{-1/2} + 4r$ (e) $-e^{-0.5v} + 3v^2$

3 (a) $8t^3 - 3 + \dfrac{2}{t}$ (b) $\pi \cos \pi t + 2\pi \sin \pi t$
(c) $6 \sec^2 2t - e^t$ (d) $2e^{2t} + 2e^{-2t} + 1$
(e) $\dfrac{3}{2}t^{1/2} - \dfrac{2}{3}t^{-1/3}$

4 (a) -1.44 (b) 242.12 (c) 1.6290 (d) 11.5538
(e) 0.5556

5 (a) $3e^{3t} + e^t$ (b) $2 - \dfrac{1}{t^2}$ (c) $8t$
(d) $2 \cos 2x - 2 \sin 2x$ (e) $-e^{-x}$ (f) $\sec^2 x$

BLOCK 3 Higher derivatives

3.1 Introduction

Block 2 showed how to calculate the derivative of a function using a table of derivatives. By differentiating the function, $y(x)$, we obtain the derivative, $\frac{dy}{dx}$.

The function, $\frac{dy}{dx}$, is more correctly called the **first derivative** of y. By differentiating the first derivative, we obtain the **second derivative**; by differentiating the second derivative we obtain the **third derivative** and so on. The second and subsequent derivatives are known as higher derivatives.

Example 3.1

Calculate the first, second and third derivatives of $y = e^{2x} + x^4$.

Solution

The first derivative is $\dfrac{dy}{dx}$.

$$\frac{dy}{dx} = 2e^{2x} + 4x^3$$

To obtain the second derivative we differentiate the first derivative:

$$\text{second derivative} = 4e^{2x} + 12x^2$$

The third derivative is found by differentiating the second derivative:

$$\text{third derivative} = 8e^{2x} + 24x$$

3.2 Notation

Just as there is a notation for the first derivative so there is a similar notation for higher derivatives.

Consider the function, $y(x)$. We know that the first derivative is denoted by $\frac{dy}{dx}$ or y'. The second derivative is calculated by differentiating the first derivative, that is

$$\text{second derivative} = \frac{d}{dx}\left(\frac{dy}{dx}\right)$$

So, the second derivative is denoted by $\dfrac{d^2y}{dx^2}$. This is often written more concisely as y''.

The third derivative is denoted by $\frac{d^3y}{dx^3}$ or y''' and so on. So, referring to Example 3.1 we could have written

$$\frac{dy}{dx} = 2e^{2x} + 4x^3$$

$$\frac{d^2y}{dx^2} = 4e^{2x} + 12x^2$$

$$\frac{d^3y}{dx^3} = 8e^{2x} + 24x$$

Key point

If $y = y(x)$

$$\text{first derivative} = \frac{dy}{dx}$$

$$\text{second derivative} = \frac{d^2y}{dx^2}$$

$$\text{third derivative} = \frac{d^3y}{dx^3}$$

Derivatives with respect to t are often indicated using a dot notation, so $\frac{dx}{dt}$ can be written as $\dot{x}$. Similarly, a second derivative with respect to t can be written as $\ddot{x}$, pronounced x double dot.

Example 3.2

Calculate $\frac{d^2y}{dt^2}$ and $\frac{d^3y}{dt^3}$ given $y = \sin t + \cos t$.

Solution

$$\frac{dy}{dt} = \cos t - \sin t$$

$$\frac{d^2y}{dt^2} = \qquad\qquad -\sin t - \cos t$$

$$\frac{d^3y}{dt^3} = \qquad\qquad -\cos t + \sin t$$

We could have used the dot notation and written $\dot{y} = \cos t - \sin t$, and $\ddot{y} = -\sin t - \cos t$.

We may need to evaluate higher derivatives at specific points. We use an obvious notation. The second derivative of $y(x)$, evaluated at, say, $x = 2$, is written as $\frac{d^2y}{dx^2}(2)$, or more simply as $y''(2)$. The third derivative evaluated at $x = -1$ is written as $\frac{d^3y}{dx^3}(-1)$ or $y'''(-1)$.

Example 3.3
Given

$$y(x) = 2\sin x + 3x^2$$

find (a) $y'(1)$ (b) $y''(-1)$ (c) $y'''(0)$

Solution
We have

$$y = 2\sin x + 3x^2$$

$$y' = 2\cos x + 6x$$

$$y'' = \qquad -2\sin x + 6$$

$$y''' = -2\cos x$$

(a) $y'(1) = 2\cos 1 + 6(1) = 7.0806.$

(b) $y''(-1) = \qquad -2\sin(-1) + 6 = 7.6829$

(c) $y'''(0) = -2\cos 0 = -2.$

Exercises

1 Find $\dfrac{d^2y}{dx^2}$ where $y(x)$ is defined by
(a) $3x^2 - e^{2x}$ (b) $\sin 3x + \cos x$ (c) $\sqrt{x}$
(d) $e^x + e^{-x}$ (e) $1 + x + x^2 + \ln x$

2 Find $\dfrac{d^3y}{dx^3}$ where y is given in question 1.

3 Calculate $y''(1)$ where $y(t)$ is given by
(a) $t(t^2 + 1)$ (b) $\sin(-2t)$ (c) $2e^t + e^{2t}$
(d) $\dfrac{1}{t}$ (e) $\cos\dfrac{t}{2}$

4 Calculate $y'''(-1)$ of the functions given in question 3.

Solutions to exercises

1 (a) $6 - 4e^{2x}$ (b) $-9\sin 3x - \cos x$
(c) $-\dfrac{1}{4}x^{-3/2}$ (d) $e^x + e^{-x}$ (e) $2 - \dfrac{1}{x^2}$

2 (a) $-8e^{2x}$ (b) $-27\cos 3x + \sin x$ (c) $\dfrac{3}{8}x^{-5/2}$
(d) $e^x - e^{-x}$ (e) $\dfrac{2}{x^3}$

3 (a) 6 (b) 3.6372 (c) 34.9928 (d) 2
(e) −0.2194

4 (a) 6 (b) −3.3292 (c) 1.8184 (d) −6
(e) −0.0599

End of block exercises

1 Calculate y'' where y is given by
(a) $\cos 2t - \sin 2t$ (b) $e^{2x} - e^x$ (c) $2x^6 - 3x^7$
(d) $-x^3 + 3x^2$ (e) $9 - \dfrac{9}{x}$

2 Find the fourth derivative of the following functions:
(a) e^{3t} (b) e^{kt}, k constant (c) $\sin 2t$ (d) $\sin kt$, k constant (e) $\cos kt$, k constant

3 Show that $y = e^x + 2x$ satisfies the equation

$$y'' - y' - y = -2 - 2x - e^x$$

4 Evaluate $y'''(0)$ where y is given by
(a) $\sin 3t + t^3$ (b) $2\cos t + \cos 2t$
(c) $e^{-x}(e^x + 1)$ (d) $3 - 3t^4$ (e) $\dfrac{e^{2x} + 1}{e^x}$

5 The function $y(x)$ is defined by

$$y(x) = x^4 - 3x^3 + 3x^2 + 1$$

Calculate the values of x where $y'' = 0$.

Solutions to exercises

1 (a) $-4\cos 2t + 4\sin 2t$ (b) $4e^{2x} - e^x$
(c) $60x^4 - 126x^5$ (d) $-6x + 6$ (e) $-18x^{-3}$

2 (a) $81e^{3t}$ (b) k^4e^{kt} (c) $16\sin 2t$ (d) $k^4 \sin kt$
(e) $k^4 \cos kt$

4 (a) -21 (b) 0 (c) -1 (d) 0 (e) 0

5 $\frac{1}{2}$, 1

End of chapter exercises

1 Calculate $\dfrac{dy}{dx}$ where y is given by
(a) $3x^4 - 2x + \ln x$ (b) $\sin 5x - 5\cos x$
(c) $(x + 1)^2$ (d) $e^{3x} + 2e^{-2x} + 1$
(e) $5 + 5x + \dfrac{5}{x} + 5\ln x$

2 Find the second derivatives of the functions in question 1.

3 Find $y'(1)$ of the functions in question 1.

4 Find $y''(1)$ of the functions in question 1.

5 Find the rate of change of the following functions:
(a) $\dfrac{3t^3 - t^2}{2t}$ (b) $\ln \sqrt{x}$ (c) $(t + 2)(2t - 1)$
(d) $e^{3v}(1 - e^v)$ (e) $\sqrt{x}(\sqrt{x} - 1)$

6 Find the third and fourth derivatives of y given the second derivative of y is
(a) $\dfrac{2}{e^{3x}}$ (b) $\dfrac{1 + x}{x^2}$ (c) $3\ln x^2$
(d) $\sin x + \sin(-2x)$ (e) $\dfrac{\cos^2 x + \cos x}{\cos x}$

7 Differentiate $(\sin x + \cos x)^2$. (Hint: use the trigonometrical identities on p. 345.)

8 Verify that
$y = A \sin kx + B \cos kx$ A, B, k constants
is a solution of

$$y'' + k^2y = 0$$

9 The function $y(x)$ is given by $y(x) = 1 - \cos x$. Find the values of x where (a) $y' = 0$, (b) $y'' = 0$.

10 The function $y(x)$ is given by $y(x) = x^3 - 3x$. Calculate the intervals on which y is (a) increasing, (b) decreasing.

11 The function $y(x)$ is given by

$$y(x) = 2x^3 - 9x^2 + 1$$

(a) Calculate the values of x for which $y' = 0$.
(b) Calculate the values of x for which $y'' = 0$.
(c) State the interval(s) on which y is increasing.
(d) State the interval(s) on which y is decreasing.
(e) State the interval(s) on which y' is increasing.
(f) State the interval(s) on which y' is decreasing.

Solutions to exercises

1 (a) $12x^3 - 2 + \frac{1}{x}$ (b) $5\cos 5x + 5\sin x$
(c) $2x + 2$ (d) $3e^{3x} - 4e^{-2x}$ (e) $5 - \frac{5}{x^2} + \frac{5}{x}$

2 (a) $36x^2 - \frac{1}{x^2}$ (b) $-25\sin 5x + 5\cos x$
(c) 2 (d) $9e^{3x} + 8e^{-2x}$ (e) $\frac{10}{x^3} - \frac{5}{x^2}$

3 (a) 11 (b) 5.6257 (c) 4 (d) 59.7153 (e) 5

4 (a) 35 (b) 26.6746 (c) 2 (d) 181.8525 (e) 5

5 (a) $3t - 0.5$ (b) $\frac{1}{2x}$ (c) $4t + 3$ (d) $3e^{3v} - 4e^{4v}$
(e) $1 - \frac{1}{2\sqrt{x}}$

6 (a) $-6e^{-3x}, 18e^{-3x}$
(b) $-2x^{-3} - x^{-1}, 6x^{-4} + x^{-2}$
(c) $\frac{6}{x}, \frac{-6}{x^2}$ (d) $\cos x - 2\cos(-2x)$,
$-\sin x - 4\sin(-2x)$ (e) $-\sin x, -\cos x$

7 $2\cos 2x$

9 (a) $\pm n\pi, n = 0, 1, 2, 3, \ldots$
(b) $\frac{\pi}{2} \pm n\pi, n = 0, 1, 2, 3, \ldots$

10 (a) $(-\infty, -1)$ and $(1, \infty)$ (b) $(-1, 1)$

11 (a) 0, 3 (b) 1.5 (c) $(-\infty, 0)$ and $(3, \infty)$
(d) $(0, 3)$ (e) $(1.5, \infty)$ (f) $(-\infty, 1.5)$

Techniques and applications of differentiation

Chapter **16**

This chapter continues the study of differentiation started in Chapter 15. The table of derivatives in Chapter 15, although useful, is limited. In this chapter several techniques for expanding the range of functions we can differentiate are introduced.

Methods for differentiating **products** and **quotients** of functions are explained in Block 1. Some functions can be differentiated when the function is written in terms of a new variable. This gives rise to the **chain rule** in Block 2.

Although we have focused on differentiating a function of x, say $y(x)$, it is not always possible to express y explicitly in terms of x. For example, it is impossible to rearrange the equation $e^x + e^y = x^2 + y^3$ to obtain y by itself on the left-hand side. However, by using **implicit differentiation** as explained in Block 3 it is still possible to find an expression for the derivative, $\frac{dy}{dx}$.

If a function is expressed **parametrically** the derivative is found by differentiating parametrically. This is covered in Block 4. The final technique, **logarithmic differentiation**, is useful for finding the derivative of products of functions involving many factors.

Blocks 6 and 7 turn to some applications of differentiation. The calculation of equations of **tangents and normals** is treated in Block 6. Finally, the important topic of **maximum and minimum values** of a function closes the chapter.

Chapter 16 contents

BLOCK 1

The product rule and the quotient rule

1.1 Introduction

Chapter 15 introduced the concept of differentiation and the use of a table of derivatives. Clearly every possible function cannot be listed in a table. We need a set of rules, used in conjunction with the table of derivatives, to extend the range of functions that we can differentiate. The product rule and the quotient rule are two such rules.

1.2 The product rule

As its name tells us, the product rule helps us to differentiate a product of functions. Consider the function $y(x)$, where $y(x)$ is the product of two functions, $u(x)$ and $v(x)$, that is

$$y(x) = u(x)v(x)$$

For example, if $y(x) = x^2 \sin x$ then $u(x) = x^2$ and $v(x) = \sin x$. The product rule states:

Key point

If

$$y(x) = u(x)v(x)$$

then

$$\begin{aligned}\frac{dy}{dx} &= \frac{du}{dx}v + u\frac{dv}{dx} \\ &= u'v + uv'\end{aligned}$$

Example 1.1

Find $\dfrac{dy}{dx}$ where $y = x^2 \sin x$.

Solution

We have

$$y = x^2 \sin x = uv$$

and so $u = x^2$ and $v = \sin x$. Hence

$$\frac{du}{dx} = 2x, \quad \frac{dv}{dx} = \cos x$$

Applying the product rule we have

$$\begin{aligned}\frac{dy}{dx} &= \frac{du}{dx}v + u\frac{dv}{dx} \\ &= 2x(\sin x) + x^2(\cos x) \\ &= x(2\sin x + x\cos x)\end{aligned}$$

Example 1.2

Find y' where $y = e^x \cos x$.

Solution

We have

$$y = e^x \cos x = uv$$

So

$u =$ ______, $v =$ ______ $\quad e^x, \cos x$

and hence

$\frac{du}{dx} =$ ______, $\frac{dv}{dx} =$ ______ $\quad e^x, -\sin x$

Applying the product rule yields:

$$\begin{aligned}\frac{dy}{dx} &= \frac{du}{dx}v + u\frac{dv}{dx} \\ &= e^x \cos x + \text{______} \qquad e^x(-\sin x) \\ &= e^x(\cos x - \sin x)\end{aligned}$$

Example 1.3

Find $\frac{d^2y}{dx^2}$ where $y = x^2 \ln x$.

Solution

We have

$$y = x^2 \ln x = uv$$

so

$$u = x^2, \quad v = \ln x$$

Then

$$\frac{du}{dx} = 2x, \quad \frac{dv}{dx} = \qquad \frac{1}{x}$$

Applying the product rule, we have

$$\frac{dy}{dx} = \frac{du}{dx}v + u\frac{dv}{dx}$$

$$= \qquad 2x \ln x + x$$

To obtain $\frac{d^2y}{dx^2}$ we differentiate $\frac{dy}{dx}$. Hence we need to find $\frac{d}{dx}(2x \ln x + x)$. The derivative of x is simply 1 so let us examine $\frac{d}{dx}(2x \ln x)$.

To find $\frac{d}{dx}(2x \ln x)$ we use the product rule, with $u = 2x, v = \ln x$. Then

$$\frac{du}{dx} = 2, \quad \frac{dv}{dx} = \frac{1}{x}$$

and so

$$\frac{d}{dx}(2x \ln x) = \frac{du}{dx}v + u\frac{dv}{dx}$$
$$= 2 \ln x + 2x\left(\frac{1}{x}\right)$$
$$= 2 \ln x + 2$$

Finally

$$\frac{d^2y}{dx^2} = \frac{d}{dx}(2x \ln x + x)$$

$$= \qquad 2 \ln x + 3$$

Exercises

1 Find $\frac{dy}{dx}$ where y is given by
(a) $x \cos x$ (b) xe^x (c) $\sin x \cos 2x$ (d) x^3e^{2x}
(e) $x^4 \sin 2x$
(c) $(e^x + e^{-2x})(3x^2 - 2x)$ (d) $\sqrt{x}e^x$
(e) $\frac{t^2 + 1}{e^t}$

2 Calculate y' where y is given by
(a) $(t^2 + 1)\sin 4t$ (b) $(3t + 7)e^{-2t}$

3 Find the second derivative of the functions in question 1.

Solutions to exercises

1 (a) $\cos x - x\sin x$ (b) $e^x(1+x)$
(c) $\cos x\cos 2x - 2\sin x\sin 2x$
(d) $x^2e^{2x}(3+2x)$ (e) $4x^3\sin 2x + 2x^4\cos 2x$
(d) $e^x\left(\dfrac{x^{-1/2}}{2} + x^{1/2}\right)$
(e) $-e^{-t}(t^2 - 2t + 1)$

2 (a) $2t\sin 4t + 4(t^2+1)(\cos 4t)$
(b) $-e^{-2t}(6t+11)$
(c) $(e^x - 2e^{-2x})(3x^2 - 2x) + (e^x + e^{-2x})(6x - 2)$, which may be written as $e^x(3x^2 + 4x - 2) - e^{-2x}(6x^2 - 10x + 2)$

3 (a) $-x\cos x - 2\sin x$ (b) $e^x(x+2)$
(c) $-5\sin x\cos 2x - 4\cos x\sin 2x$
(d) $2xe^{2x}(2x^2 + 6x + 3)$
(e) $16x^3\cos 2x - 4x^2(x^2 - 3)\sin 2x$

1.3 The quotient rule

The quotient rule shows us how to differentiate a quotient of functions, for example

$$\frac{\sin x}{x}, \quad \frac{t^2 - 1}{t^2 + 1}, \quad \frac{e^z + z}{\cos z}$$

The quotient rule may be stated thus:

Key point

If

$$y(x) = \frac{u(x)}{v(x)}$$

then

$$\frac{dy}{dx} = \frac{v\dfrac{du}{dx} - u\dfrac{dv}{dx}}{v^2} = \frac{vu' - uv'}{v^2}$$

Example 1.4

Find y' given $y = \dfrac{\sin x}{x}$.

Solution

We have

$$y = \frac{\sin x}{x} = \frac{u}{v}$$

so

$$u = \sin x, \quad v = x$$

and so

$$\frac{du}{dx} = \cos x, \quad \frac{dv}{dx} = 1$$

Applying the quotient rule gives

$$\begin{aligned}\frac{dy}{dx} &= \frac{vu' - uv'}{v^2} \\ &= \frac{x\cos x - \sin x\,(1)}{x^2} \\ &= \frac{x\cos x - \sin x}{x^2}\end{aligned}$$

Example 1.5

Find y' given $y = \dfrac{t^3}{t+1}$.

Solution

We have

$$y = \frac{t^3}{t+1} = \frac{u}{v}$$

and so

$$u = t^3, \quad v = t + 1, \quad u' = 3t^2, \quad v' = 1$$

Applying the quotient rule gives

$$\frac{dy}{dt} = \frac{vu' - uv'}{v^2}$$

$$= \qquad \frac{(t+1)\,3t^2 - t^3\,(1)}{(t+1)^2}$$

which can be simplified to

$$\frac{dy}{dt} = \qquad \frac{t^2(2t+3)}{(t+1)^2}$$

Exercises

1 Find $\dfrac{dy}{dx}$ where y is given by

(a) $\dfrac{e^x}{x}$ (b) $\dfrac{x}{e^x + 1}$ (c) $\dfrac{\cos x}{\sin x}$ (d) $\dfrac{1 - x}{1 + x}$

(e) $\dfrac{\ln x}{x^2}$

2 Find y' when y is given by

(a) $\dfrac{t^2 - 1}{t^2 + 1}$ (b) $\dfrac{e^{2t} + t}{e^t - 1}$ (c) $\dfrac{\sin 3t}{\cos t + t}$

(d) $\dfrac{z + \sin z}{z + \cos z}$ (e) $\dfrac{1 + x + x^2}{1 + x^3}$

Solutions to exercises

1 (a) $\dfrac{e^x(x-1)}{x^2}$ (b) $\dfrac{e^x+1-xe^x}{(e^x+1)^2}$

(c) $-\operatorname{cosec}^2 x$ (d) $\dfrac{-2}{(1+x)^2}$ (e) $\dfrac{1-2\ln x}{x^3}$

2 (a) $\dfrac{4t}{(t^2+1)^2}$

(b) $\dfrac{(e^t-1)(2e^{2t}+1)-(e^{2t}+t)e^t}{(e^t-1)^2}$

(c) $\dfrac{3(\cos t+t)\cos 3t-\sin 3t\,(-\sin t+1)}{(\cos t+t)^2}$

(d) $\dfrac{(z+1)\cos z+(z-1)\sin z+1}{(\cos z+z)^2}$

(e) $-\left(\dfrac{x^4+2x^3+3x^2-2x-1}{(x^3+1)^2}\right)$

End of block exercises

1 Find the derivative of each of the following:

(a) $(x-1)\sin 2x$ (b) $\dfrac{\sin 2x}{x-1}$ (c) $\dfrac{x-1}{\sin 2x}$

(d) $e^{2x}\sin 3x$ (e) $e^{-2x}\sin 3x$

2 Differentiate the following:

(a) $\dfrac{t^3-t^2}{t^2+1}$ (b) $3\sin 2x\cos x$ (c) $\dfrac{3\cos x}{\sin 2x}$

(d) $\dfrac{e^{3r}}{e^{2r}}$ (e) $(r+1)(r+\sin r)$

3 Find $\dfrac{dH}{dt}$ given

$$H = e^{2t}t^2\sin t$$

4 Find $\dfrac{dR}{dt}$ given

$$R = \frac{e^{2t}\sin t}{t^2}$$

Solutions to exercises

1 (a) $2(x-1)\cos 2x+\sin 2x$

(b) $\dfrac{2(x-1)\cos 2x-\sin 2x}{(x-1)^2}$

(c) $\dfrac{\sin 2x-2(x-1)\cos 2x}{\sin^2 2x}$

(d) $e^{2x}(3\cos 3x+2\sin 3x)$

(e) $e^{-2x}(3\cos 3x-2\sin 3x)$

2 (a) $\dfrac{t(t^3+3t-2)}{(t^2+1)^2}$

(b) $6\cos x\cos 2x-3\sin x\sin 2x$

(c) $-3\left(\dfrac{\sin 2x\sin x+2\cos x\cos 2x}{\sin^2 2x}\right)$

(d) e^r (e) $(r+1)\cos r+\sin r+2r+1$

3 $e^{2t}[t^2\cos t+2t(t+1)\sin t]$

4 $\dfrac{e^{2t}[2t\sin t+t\cos t-2\sin t]}{t^3}$

BLOCK 2

The chain rule

2.1 Introduction

In Block 1 we saw how to differentiate products and quotients of functions. This block introduces the chain rule, which allows us to differentiate an additional class of functions.

2.2 The chain rule

Suppose y is a function of z, that is $y = y(z)$, and that z is a function of x, that is $z = z(x)$. So

$$y = y(z) = y(z(x))$$

Hence y may be considered to be a function of x. For example, if $y(z) = 2z^2 + 3z$ and $z = \cos 2x$ then

$$y = 2(\cos 2x)^2 + 3(\cos 2x)$$

Since y can be considered as a function of x, then $\frac{dy}{dx}$ may be found. The chain rule helps us to find $\frac{dy}{dx}$. The chain rule states

Key point

If $y = y(z)$ and $z = z(x)$, then

$$\frac{dy}{dx} = \frac{dy}{dz} \times \frac{dz}{dx}$$

Example 2.1

Given $y = z^4$ and $z = 3x + 6$, find $\frac{dy}{dx}$.

Solution

We have

$$y = z^4 = (3x + 6)^4$$

and we seek $\frac{dy}{dx}$. Now

$$y = z^4, \quad z = 3x + 6$$

and so

$$\frac{dy}{dz} = 4z^3, \quad \frac{dz}{dx} = 3$$

Using the chain rule we have

$$\begin{aligned}\frac{dy}{dx} &= \frac{dy}{dz}\frac{dz}{dx}\\ &= 4z^3(3)\\ &= 12z^3\\ &= 12(3x + 6)^3\end{aligned}$$

Sometimes care must be taken to recognise the independent and dependent variables. Example 2.2 uses the chain rule, but it may look unfamiliar.

Example 2.2

Given $z(y) = y^3$ and $y(x) = 2x^2 - x$ find $\frac{dz}{dx}$.

Solution

We have

$$z(y) = y^3 \quad \text{so} \quad \frac{dz}{dy} = 3y^2$$

and

$$y(x) = 2x^2 - x \quad \text{so} \quad \frac{dy}{dx} = 4x - 1$$

The chain rule has the form

$$\begin{aligned}\frac{dz}{dx} &= \frac{dz}{dy}\frac{dy}{dx}\\ &= 3y^2(4x - 1)\\ &= 3(2x^2 - x)^2(4x - 1)\end{aligned}$$

Example 2.3

Given $y = (x^3 + x)^7$, find $\frac{dy}{dx}$.

Solution

We let $z = x^3 + x$ and so

$$y = (x^3 + x)^7 = z^7$$

Then $\frac{dy}{dz} = 7z^6$ and $\frac{dz}{dx} = 3x^2 + 1$. Applying the chain rule gives

$$\begin{aligned}\frac{dy}{dx} &= \frac{dy}{dz}\frac{dz}{dx}\\ &= (7z^6)(3x^2 + 1)\\ &= 7(3x^2 + 1)(x^3 + x)^6\end{aligned}$$

Example 2.4

Given $y = \sqrt{x^2 + 1}$ find $\dfrac{dy}{dx}$.

Solution

Let $z = x^2 + 1$ and then

$y = \sqrt{x^2 + 1} = \quad$ $\sqrt{z}$

Then

$\dfrac{dy}{dz} = \quad , \quad \dfrac{dz}{dx} = \quad$ $\dfrac{1}{2}z^{-1/2}, 2x$

and applying the chain rule gives

$$\frac{dy}{dx} = \frac{dy}{dz}\frac{dz}{dx}$$

$= \quad$ $\dfrac{1}{2}z^{-1/2}(2x)$

$$= \frac{x}{\sqrt{z}}$$

$= \quad$ $\dfrac{x}{\sqrt{x^2 + 1}}$

Example 2.5

Find $\dfrac{dy}{dx}$ given $y = \ln(x^2 + x + 1)$.

Solution

Let $z = x^2 + x + 1$ so that

$y = \ln(x^2 + x + 1) = \quad$ $\ln z$

Then

$\dfrac{dy}{dz} = \quad , \quad \dfrac{dz}{dx} = \quad$ $\dfrac{1}{z}, 2x + 1$

So

$$\frac{dy}{dx} = \frac{dy}{dz}\frac{dz}{dx}$$

$= \quad$ $\dfrac{2x + 1}{z}$

$$= \frac{2x + 1}{x^2 + x + 1}$$

We note that, in the final solution, the numerator is the derivative of the denominator. In general:

Key point

If $y = \ln f(x)$ then

$$\frac{dy}{dx} = \frac{f'}{f}$$

Example 2.6

Given $y = \ln(1 - x)$ find $\frac{dy}{dx}$.

Solution

Here $f(x) = 1 - x$ and $f'(x) = -1$. So

$$\frac{dy}{dx} = \frac{-1}{1 - x}$$

which may be simplified to

$$\frac{dy}{dx} = \frac{1}{x - 1}$$

Example 2.7

Given $y = 5\ \ln(2t - 1)$ find $\frac{dy}{dt}$.

Solution

Here $f(t) = 2t - 1$ and so $f'(t) = 2$. Hence

$$\begin{aligned}\frac{dy}{dt} &= 5\left(\frac{2}{2t - 1}\right)\\ &= \frac{10}{2t - 1}\end{aligned}$$

Example 2.8

Given $y = \ln(e^x + \sin x)$ find $\frac{dy}{dx}$.

Solution

We have

$$\begin{aligned}y &= \ln(e^x + \sin x)\\ &= \ln f(x) \quad \text{where } f(x) = e^x + \sin x\end{aligned}$$

So

$$\frac{dy}{dx} = \qquad \frac{f'}{f} = \frac{e^x + \cos x}{e^x + \sin x}$$

Exercises

1 Differentiate each of the following functions:
(a) $(x^3 + 2)^6$ (b) $\sqrt{\sin x}$ (c) $(e^x + 1)^7$
(d) $(\cos 2x)^5$ (e) $\ln(x + 1)$

2 Find $\frac{dy}{dt}$ where y is given by
(a) $e^{(3t^2)}$ (b) $3e^{t^2}$ (c) $e^{\sin 2t}$ (d) $e^{2 \sin t}$
(e) $2e^{\sin t}$

3 Find the rate of change of y at the specified point:
(a) $y = \ln(3t^2 + 5)$, $t = 1$
(b) $y = \sin(t^2)$, $t = 2$
(c) $y = \cos(t^3 + 1)$, $t = 1$
(d) $y = (t^3 - 1)^{2/3}$, $t = 2$
(e) $y = 4e^{\cos t}$, $t = \frac{\pi}{2}$

Solutions to exercises

1 (a) $18x^2(x^3 + 2)^5$ (b) $\frac{\cos x}{2\sqrt{\sin x}}$
(c) $7e^x(e^x + 1)^6$
(d) $-10 \sin 2x \cos^4 2x$ (e) $\frac{1}{x + 1}$

2 (a) $6te^{3t^2}$ (b) $6te^{t^2}$ (c) $2 \cos 2te^{\sin 2t}$
(d) $2 \cos te^{2 \sin t}$ (e) $2 \cos te^{\sin t}$

3 (a) 0.75 (b) −2.6146 (c) −2.7279
(d) 4.1821 (e) −4

End of block exercises

1 Use the chain rule to differentiate each of the following functions:
(a) $y = (6x^3 - x)^4$ (b) $h = (t^4 - 1)^{1/3}$
(c) $v = \sqrt{9 - 2t}$ (d) $i = \sin(y^3)$
(e) $R = \cos(\sqrt{r})$

2 Find the derivative of each function:
(a) $Y(t) = 5e^{\sin 2t}$ (b) $m(p) = 3 \ln(p^4 + 2)$
(c) $H(r) = 5 \sin(\pi r^2 + 1)$
(d) $x(t) = -3 \cos\left(\frac{1}{t}\right)$ (e) $Q(s) = \frac{1}{\ln s}$

3 Evaluate $\frac{dy}{dx}$ at the specified value of x.
(a) $y = \sqrt{x + \sin x}$, $x = 1$
(b) $y = \sin(x^2 + 1)$, $x = 0.5$
(c) $y = e^{\sqrt{x}}$, $x = 1$
(d) $y = 2 \cos\left(\frac{1}{x}\right)$, $x = 1$
(e) $y = \frac{1}{(3x^2 + 1)^4}$, $x = 0.5$

4 Differentiate the following functions where a, b and n are constants:
(a) $y = (at + b)^n$ (b) $y = e^{at+b}$
(c) $y = \sin(at + b)$
(d) $y = \cos(at + b)$ (e) $y = \ln(at + b)$

Solutions to exercises

1 (a) $4(18x^2 - 1)(6x^3 - x)^3$

(b) $\dfrac{4t^3\,(t^4 - 1)^{-2/3}}{3}$

(c) $-(9 - 2t)^{-1/2}$ (d) $3y^2 \cos(y^3)$

(e) $-\dfrac{1}{2}r^{-1/2}\sin\sqrt{r}$

2 (a) $10 \cos 2te^{\sin 2t}$ (b) $\dfrac{12p^3}{p^4 + 2}$

(c) $10\pi r \cos(\pi r^2 + 1)$

(d) $-\dfrac{3}{t^2}\sin\left(\dfrac{1}{t}\right)$ (e) $\dfrac{-1}{s\,(\ln s)^2}$

3 (a) 0.5675 (b) 0.3153
(c) 1.3591 (d) 1.6829
(e) −0.7311

4 (a) $an(at + b)^{n-1}$ (b) ae^{at+b}

(c) $a\cos(at + b)$ (d) $-a\sin(at + b)$

(e) $\dfrac{a}{at + b}$

BLOCK 3

Implicit differentiation

3.1 Introduction

So far we have met many functions of the form $y = f(x)$, for example $y = x^2 + 3$, $y = \sin 2x$ and $y = e^{3x} - 2x$. Whenever y is equated to an expression involving only x terms we say that y is expressed **explicitly** in terms of x.

Sometimes we have an equation connecting x and y but it is impossible to write it in the form $y = f(x)$. Examples of this include $x^2 - y^3 + \sin x - \cos y = 1$, $\sin(x + y) + e^x + e^{-y} = x^3 + y^3$. In these cases we say that y is expressed **implicitly** in terms of x.

Whether y is expressed explicitly or implicitly in terms of x we can still differentiate to find the derivative $\frac{dy}{dx}$. If y is expressed explicitly in terms of x then $\frac{dy}{dx}$ will also be expressed explicitly in terms of x. If y is expressed implicitly in terms of x then $\frac{dy}{dx}$ will be expressed in terms of x and y.

3.2 Differentiating $f(y)$ with respect to x

If y is expressed implicitly in terms of x and we wish to find $\frac{dy}{dx}$, then we frequently need to differentiate a function of y with respect to x: that is, find $\frac{d}{dx}(f(y))$. To do this we use the chain rule. The examples illustrate the technique.

Example 3.1

Find $\dfrac{d}{dx}(y^3)$.

Solution

We use the chain rule. Let $z = y^3$ so that we wish to find $\dfrac{dz}{dx}$. Using the chain rule (see Example 2.2 in Block 2)

$$\frac{dz}{dx} = \frac{dz}{dy}\frac{dy}{dx}$$

Now

$$z = y^3 \text{ and so } \frac{dz}{dy} = 3y^2$$

Hence

$$\frac{dz}{dx} = 3y^2\frac{dy}{dx}$$

Hence

$$\frac{d}{dx}(y^3) = 3y^2\frac{dy}{dx}$$

The result of Example 3.1 can easily be extended to

Key point

$$\frac{d}{dx}(y^n) = ny^{n-1}\frac{dy}{dx}$$

Example 3.2

Find $\frac{d}{dx}(\sin y)$.

Solution

Let $z = \sin y$ so that we wish to find $\frac{dz}{dx}$. We know from the chain rule that

$$\frac{dz}{dx} = \frac{dz}{dy}\frac{dy}{dx}$$

We have $z = \sin y$ so

$$\frac{dz}{dy} = \quad\quad \cos y$$

and

$$\frac{d}{dx}(\sin y) = \quad\quad \cos y\frac{dy}{dx}$$

Generalising the result of Example 3.2 we have

Key point

$$\frac{d}{dx}(f(y)) = \frac{df}{dy}\frac{dy}{dx}$$

Example 3.3

Find $\frac{d}{dt}(\ln y)$.

Solution

We use the previous result with $f(y) = \ln y$. Then

$$\begin{aligned}\frac{d}{dt}(\ln y) &= \frac{df}{dt}\\ &= \frac{df}{dy}\frac{dy}{dt}\\ &= \frac{1}{y}\frac{dy}{dt}\end{aligned}$$

Exercises

1 Differentiate the following functions of y with respect to x:
(a) y^2 (b) $3y^4$ (c) $2y^2 - 3y + 1$ (d) $\frac{1}{y}$
(e) $\sqrt{y}$

2 Differentiate the following functions of y with respect to x:
(a) $\sin 2y$ (b) $3\cos y - y$ (c) e^{2y}
(d) $2\cos 3y$ (e) $\sin^2 y$

3 Differentiate the following functions of y with respect to x:
(a) $(y + 3)^4$ (b) $(y^2 + 3)^4$

Solutions to exercises

1 (a) $2y\frac{dy}{dx}$ (b) $12y^3\frac{dy}{dx}$ (c) $4y\frac{dy}{dx} - 3\frac{dy}{dx}$
(d) $-\frac{1}{y^2}\frac{dy}{dx}$ (e) $\frac{1}{2\sqrt{y}}\frac{dy}{dx}$

2 (a) $2(\cos 2y)\frac{dy}{dx}$ (b) $-3(\sin y)\frac{dy}{dx} - \frac{dy}{dx}$
(c) $2e^{2y}\frac{dy}{dx}$ (d) $-6(\sin 3y)\frac{dy}{dx}$
(e) $2\sin y\cos y\frac{dy}{dx}$

3 (a) $4(y + 3)^3\frac{dy}{dx}$ (b) $8y(y^2 + 3)^3\frac{dy}{dx}$

3.3 Finding $\frac{dy}{dx}$ implicitly

We illustrate the technique.

Example 3.4

Find $\frac{dy}{dx}$ given $y^2 + x = x^3 + 3y$.

Solution

We differentiate each term w.r.t. x.

$$\frac{d}{dx}(y^2) = 2y\frac{dy}{dx}, \quad \frac{d}{dx}(x) = 1, \quad \frac{d}{dx}(x^3) = 3x^2, \quad \frac{d}{dx}(3y) = 3\frac{dy}{dx}$$

So

$$2y\frac{dy}{dx} + 1 = 3x^2 + 3\frac{dy}{dx}$$

Rearrangement yields

$$\frac{dy}{dx} = \frac{3x^2 - 1}{2y - 3}$$

Note that $\frac{dy}{dx}$ is given in terms of x and y.

Example 3.5

Find y' given

$$x^2y - 3xy^3 = y^2 + 7$$

Solution

We differentiate each term w.r.t. x.

To differentiate x^2y we use the product rule.

$$\frac{d}{dx}(x^2y) = 2xy + x^2\frac{dy}{dx}$$

To differentiate $3xy^3$ we again use the product rule.

$$\frac{d}{dx}(3xy^3) = \qquad\qquad 3y^3 + 9xy^2\frac{dy}{dx}$$

Finally we differentiate $y^2 + 7$.

$$\frac{d}{dx}(y^2 + 7) = \qquad\qquad 2y\frac{dy}{dx}$$

Hence

$$2xy + x^2\frac{dy}{dx} - 3y^3 - 9xy^2\frac{dy}{dx} = 2y\frac{dy}{dx}$$

Rearrangement yields

$$\frac{dy}{dx} = \frac{3y^3 - 2xy}{x^2 - 9xy^2 - 2y}$$

Example 3.6

Find $\frac{d^2y}{dx^2}$ if $5x + 3y^2 = 7$.

Solution

First, we calculate $\frac{dy}{dx}$. Differentiating each term of the equation w.r.t. x we find

$$5 + 6y\frac{dy}{dx} = 0$$

$$\text{so} \quad \frac{dy}{dx} = -\frac{5}{6y}$$

Now $\frac{d^2y}{dx^2}$ means $\frac{d}{dx}\left(\frac{dy}{dx}\right)$ so we must differentiate $-\frac{5}{6y}$ with respect to x, that is $\frac{d}{dx}\left(-\frac{5}{6y}\right)$. Here we are differentiating a function of y w.r.t. x. Using the result

$$\frac{d}{dx}(f(y)) = \frac{df}{dy}\frac{dy}{dx}$$

we have

$$\frac{d}{dx}\left(-\frac{5}{6y}\right) = \frac{d}{dy}\left(-\frac{5}{6y}\right)\frac{dy}{dx}$$
$$= \frac{5}{6y^2}\frac{dy}{dx}$$
$$= \frac{5}{6y^2}\left(-\frac{5}{6y}\right) = \frac{-25}{36\,y^3}$$

Exercises

1 Find $\frac{dy}{dx}$ given
(a) $x^2 + y^2 = 1$ (b) $3x - y^3 = 10$
(c) $x^2 + 2y^2 + 3x - 7y = 9$
(d) $x^3 - y^3 = x + y$ (e) $\sqrt{x} + \sqrt{y} = 10$

2 Find $\frac{dx}{dt}$ given
(a) $4 + \sin x = t$ (b) $3\cos 2x - t^2 = 20$
(c) $\tan x = \frac{1}{t}$ (d) $4\sin t - \cos 3x = \cos t$
(e) $\tan 2t - x^2 = \sin 2x$

3 Find $\frac{dy}{dx}$ given
(a) $2e^x + 3e^y = 10y$ (b) $e^{2x} - e^{3y} = x + 2y$
(c) $e^xe^y = x^2y^3$ (d) $e^{2x+3y} + 2x^3 - y^5 = 0$
(e) $2e^{y-x} = 3e^x + y^2$

4 Find $\frac{d^2y}{dx^2}$ given

$$x^2 + y^2 = 1$$

5 Find y'' given

$$\sin x + \cos y = 1$$

Solutions to exercises

1 (a) $-\frac{x}{y}$ (b) $\frac{1}{y^2}$ (c) $\frac{2x+3}{7-4y}$
(d) $\frac{3x^2-1}{3y^2+1}$ (e) $-\sqrt{\frac{y}{x}}$

2 (a) $\frac{1}{\cos x}$ (b) $-\frac{t}{3\sin 2x}$ (c) $-\frac{\cos^2 x}{t^2}$
(d) $\frac{-4\cos t - \sin t}{3\sin 3x}$ (e) $\frac{\sec^2 2t}{x + \cos 2x}$

3 (a) $\frac{2e^x}{10-3e^y}$ (b) $\frac{2e^{2x}-1}{3e^{3y}+2}$
(c) $\frac{2xy^3 - e^xe^y}{e^xe^y - 3x^2y^2}$
(d) $\frac{6x^2 + 2e^{2x+3y}}{5y^4 - 3e^{2x+3y}}$ (e) $\frac{3e^x + 2e^{y-x}}{2e^{y-x} - 2y}$

4 $-\frac{1}{y^3}$

5 $-\frac{\sin^2 y\sin x + \cos^2 x\cos y}{\sin^3 y}$

End of block exercises

1 In which of the following equations is y expressed implicitly in terms of x?

(a) $\sin x + \frac{x}{y} = 3$ (b) $\sin y + \frac{y}{x} = 3$

(c) $x^2 - y = 10$ (d) $x^2y + y^2x = \sqrt{y}$

(e) $\frac{x - y}{x + y} = e^x$

2 Find $\frac{dy}{dx}$ given

(a) $x^3 - y^4 = 1$

(b) $2x^2 - 3y^2 + 2x - 7y = 0$

(c) $x^3 - 2y^4 = x$

(d) $2x^2 + y^2 + 3x + 2y + 7 = 0$

(e) $x^3 - y^3 + 3x^2 - y = 0$

3 A circle, centre the origin, radius 5, has equation

$$x^2 + y^2 = 25$$

Find the equation of the tangent to the circle that passes through the point (3, 4).

4 Find $\frac{dx}{dt}$ given

(a) $2xt + x^2 - xt^2 = 0$ (b) $x^2t^2 - 3x^2t = t^3$

(c) $4(x + t)(x - t) - 3xt = 0$

(d) $\frac{x^2}{t^3} - \frac{t^2}{x^2} + x + t = 1$

(e) $\frac{x + t}{x - 2t} - \frac{3x}{t^2} = 0$

5 Find $\frac{dy}{dx}$:

(a) $e^x + e^y = x^3 + y^4$ (b) $x \sin y = y \cos x$

(c) $xe^y - 2ye^x = xy$ (d) $(x + 2y)e^{-y} = x^2y$

(e) $\sin 2x \cos 3y - 2 \sin y \cos x = 0$

6 Differentiate the following expressions w.r.t. x:
(a) $(x + y)^n$ (b) $(x^2 + y)^n$ (c) $(x^2 + y^2)^n$

Solutions to exercises

1 (b) and (d)

2 (a) $\frac{3x^2}{4y^3}$ (b) $\frac{4x + 2}{6y + 7}$ (c) $\frac{3x^2 - 1}{8y^3}$

(d) $-\frac{4x + 3}{2y + 2}$ (e) $\frac{3x^2 + 6x}{3y^2 + 1}$

3 $y = \frac{-3x + 25}{4}$

4 (a) $\frac{2x(t - 1)}{2t + 2x - t^2}$ (b) $\frac{3t^2 + 3x^2 - 2x^2t}{2xt^2 - 6xt}$

(c) $\frac{3x + 8t}{8x - 3t}$ (d) $\frac{3x^5 + 2xt^5 - x^3t^4}{2x^4t + 2t^6 + x^3t^4}$

(e) $\frac{2xt + 3t^2 + 6x}{6x - t^2 - 6t}$

5 (a) $\frac{3x^2 - e^x}{e^y - 4y^3}$ (b) $\frac{y \sin x + \sin y}{\cos x - x \cos y}$

(c) $\frac{y - e^y + 2ye^x}{xe^y - 2e^x - x}$ (d) $\frac{2xye^y - 1}{2 - x - 2y - x^2e^y}$

(e) $\frac{2 \cos 2x \cos 3y + 2 \sin y \sin x}{3 \sin 2x \sin 3y + 2 \cos y \cos x}$

6 (a) $n(x + y)^{n-1}\left(1 + \frac{dy}{dx}\right)$

(b) $n(x^2 + y)^{n-1}\left(2x + \frac{dy}{dx}\right)$

(c) $n(x^2 + y^2)^{n-1}\left(2x + 2y\frac{dy}{dx}\right)$

BLOCK 4

Parametric differentiation

4.1 Introduction

In some circumstances both x and y depend upon a third variable, usually denoted by t. This third variable is referred to as a **parameter**. By eliminating t, y can be determined in terms of x. For example, if $y = (3 + t)^2$ and $x = 2t$, then by eliminating t we have

$$y = (3 + t)^2$$
$$= \left(3 + \frac{x}{2}\right)^2$$

Hence we can consider y as a function of x and so the derivative $\frac{dy}{dx}$ can be found.

In some cases, elimination of t is difficult or even impossible. As an example consider $y = e^t + \sin t$, $x = t^3 + \ln t$. Here it is impossible to obtain y in terms of x, but the derivative $\frac{dy}{dx}$ can still be found using the chain rule.

Key point

$$\frac{dy}{dx} = \frac{dy}{dt}\frac{dt}{dx}$$
$$= \frac{dy/dt}{dx/dt}$$

Finding $\frac{dy}{dx}$ by this method is known as **parametric differentiation**.

4.2 Some examples of parametric differentiation

Example 4.1

Given $y = (3 + t)^2$ and $x = 2t$ find $\frac{dy}{dx}$.

Solution

We could eliminate t thus:

$$\begin{aligned} y &= (3 + t)^2 \\ &= \left(3 + \frac{x}{2}\right)^2 \\ &= 9 + 3x + \frac{x^2}{4} \end{aligned}$$

and then differentiate to obtain

$$\frac{dy}{dx} = 3 + \frac{x}{2}$$

Alternatively using parametric differentiation we have

$$\frac{dy}{dt} = 2(3 + t), \frac{dx}{dt} = 2$$

and so

$$\begin{aligned} \frac{dy}{dx} &= \frac{dy/dt}{dx/dt} \\ &= \frac{2(3 + t)}{2} \\ &= 3 + t \\ &= 3 + \frac{x}{2} \end{aligned}$$

Example 4.2

Find $\frac{dy}{dx}$ given $y = \sin t + t^2$, $x = e^t + t$.

Solution

In this case elimination of t is impossible. To find $\frac{dy}{dx}$ we must use parametric differentiation.

$$\frac{dy}{dt} = \cos t + 2t, \quad \frac{dx}{dt} = e^t + 1$$

and so

$$\begin{aligned} \frac{dy}{dx} &= \frac{dy/dt}{dx/dt} \\ &= \frac{\cos t + 2t}{e^t + 1} \end{aligned}$$

No further simplification is possible.

Example 4.3

(a) Find $\dfrac{dy}{dx}$ given $y = 2t - t^3$, $x = \sin t - \cos t$.

(b) Evaluate $\dfrac{dy}{dx}(t = 0)$.

Solution

(a) $\dfrac{dy}{dt} = \quad , \quad \dfrac{dx}{dt} = \quad$

$2 - 3t^2, \cos t + \sin t$

$$\frac{dy}{dx} = \frac{dy/dt}{dx/dt}$$

$$= \frac{2 - 3t^2}{\cos t + \sin t}$$

(b) $$\frac{dy}{dx}(t = 0) = \frac{2 - 3(0)^2}{\cos 0 + \sin 0}$$

$$= 2$$

Exercises

1 Use parametric differentiation to find $\dfrac{dy}{dx}$ given

(a) $x = 1 + t$, $y = 2 + 3t + t^2$

(b) $x = \sin t$, $y = \cos t$ (c) $x = t^2$, $y = t^3$

(d) $x = e^t$, $y = e^t + t$

(e) $x = \sqrt{t}$, $y = 1 + \ln t$

2 Find $\dfrac{dy}{dx}$ given

(a) $x = \sin(t^2)$, $y = t^3 + 1$

(b) $x = (1 + 2t)^4$, $y = (3 - 5t)^7$

(c) $x = 2\cos t$, $y = \cos 2t$

(d) $x = e^{\sin t}$, $y = 1 - t^2$

(e) $x = \ln(1 + 3t)$, $y = 1 + 2t$

Solutions to exercises

1 (a) $3 + 2t$ (b) $-\tan t$ (c) $\dfrac{3t}{2}$ (d) $1 + e^{-t}$

(e) $\dfrac{2}{\sqrt{t}}$

2 (a) $\dfrac{3t}{2\cos(t^2)}$ (b) $\dfrac{-35(3 - 5t)^6}{8(1 + 2t)^3}$ (c) $\dfrac{\sin 2t}{\sin t}$

(d) $\dfrac{-2t}{\cos t e^{\sin t}}$ (e) $\dfrac{2(1 + 3t)}{3}$

End of block exercises

1 Find y' given

(a) $x = 3 + 2t - t^2$, $y = 1 + 5t - t^3$

(b) $x = 1 + \dfrac{1}{t}$, $y = t + \dfrac{1}{t}$

(c) $x = 3\sin t$, $y = \sin t + 3t$

(d) $x = e^{2t}$, $y = e^{-t} + \cos t$

(e) $x = \tan 2t$, $y = e^{2t}$

2 Find $\frac{dy}{dx}$ given

(a) $x = \sqrt{1 + 2t},\ y = (t^2 + 1)^4$

(b) $x = \sin(t^2 + 1),\ y = \cos(2t - 3)$

(c) $x = r\sin t,\ y = r\cos(t^2)$, r constant

(d) $x = \frac{1}{1 + 2t},\ y = \frac{t}{1 + t}$

(e) $x = e^t \sin t,\ y = e^{-t}\cos t$

Solutions to exercises

1 (a) $\frac{5 - 3t^2}{2 - 2t}$ (b) $1 - t^2$ (c) $\frac{\cos t + 3}{3\cos t}$

(d) $\frac{-(e^{-t} + \sin t)}{2e^{2t}}$ (e) $e^{2t}\cos^2 2t$

2 (a) $8t\sqrt{1 + 2t}\,(t^2 + 1)^3$ (b) $\frac{-\sin(2t - 3)}{t\cos(t^2 + 1)}$

(c) $-\frac{2t\sin(t^2)}{\cos t}$ (d) $-\frac{(1 + 2t)^2}{2(1 + t)^2}$ (e) $-e^{-2t}$

BLOCK 5 Logarithmic differentiation

5.1 Introduction

The technique of **logarithmic differentiation** is useful when we need to differentiate a cumbersome product. The method involves taking the natural logarithm of the function to be differentiated.

5.2 Logarithmic differentiation

We gather together some important results that are commonly used in logarithmic differentiation.

1. $\frac{d}{dx}(\ln y) = \frac{1}{y}\frac{dy}{dx}$
2. $\frac{d}{dx}(\ln f(x)) = \frac{1}{f}\frac{df}{dx}$
3. $\ln(e^x) = x$
4. $\ln(e^{f(x)}) = f(x)$
5. $\ln AB = \ln A + \ln B$
6. $\ln \frac{A}{B} = \ln A - \ln B$
7. $\ln A^n = n \ln A$

The method of logarithmic differentiation is illustrated in the following examples.

Example 5.1

Given $y = t^2(1 + t)^3$ find $\frac{dy}{dt}$.

Solution

We could use the product rule to find $\frac{dy}{dt}$. However, we shall use logarithmic differentiation to illustrate the technique. Taking the natural logarithm of both sides of the given equation and applying the laws of logarithms yields

$$\begin{aligned}\ln y &= \ln (t^2 (1 + t)^3)\\ &= \ln t^2 + \ln (1 + t)^3\\ &= 2 \ln t + 3 \ln (1 + t)\end{aligned}$$

Now, both sides are differentiated w.r.t. t.

$$\frac{\mathrm{d}}{\mathrm{d}t}(\ln y) = \frac{\mathrm{d}}{\mathrm{d}t}(2\ln t) + \frac{\mathrm{d}}{\mathrm{d}t}(3\ln(1+t))$$

$$\frac{1}{y}\frac{\mathrm{d}y}{\mathrm{d}t} = 2\left(\frac{1}{t}\right) + 3\left(\frac{1}{1+t}\right)$$

$$\frac{\mathrm{d}y}{\mathrm{d}t} = y\left(\frac{2}{t} + \frac{3}{1+t}\right)$$

$$= t^2(1+t)^3\left(\frac{2}{t} + \frac{3}{1+t}\right)$$

Example 5.2

Given that

$$y = (t+1)^7(2t+3)^4(2t-1)^5$$

find $\frac{\mathrm{d}y}{\mathrm{d}t}$.

Solution

Taking the natural logarithm of both sides and applying the laws of logarithms yields

$$\ln y = \ln((t+1)^7(2t+3)^4(2t-1)^5)$$

$$= \ln(t+1)^7 + \ln(2t+3)^4 + \ln(2t-1)^5$$

$$= 7\ln(t+1) + 4\ln(2t+3) + 5\ln(2t-1)$$

We now differentiate both sides w.r.t. t.

$$\frac{\mathrm{d}}{\mathrm{d}t}(\ln y) = \frac{\mathrm{d}}{\mathrm{d}t}(7\ln(t+1)) + \frac{\mathrm{d}}{\mathrm{d}t}(4\ln(2t+3)) + \frac{\mathrm{d}}{\mathrm{d}t}(5\ln(2t-1))$$

$$\frac{1}{y}\frac{\mathrm{d}y}{\mathrm{d}t} = \frac{7}{t+1} + \frac{8}{2t+3} + \frac{10}{2t-1}$$

$$\frac{\mathrm{d}y}{\mathrm{d}t} = y\left(\frac{7}{t+1} + \frac{8}{2t+3} + \frac{10}{2t-1}\right)$$

$$\frac{\mathrm{d}y}{\mathrm{d}t} = (t+1)^7(2t+3)^4(2t-1)^5\left(\frac{7}{t+1} + \frac{8}{2t+3} + \frac{10}{2t-1}\right)$$

Example 5.3

Find $\frac{\mathrm{d}y}{\mathrm{d}x}$ given $y = \mathrm{e}^{2x}x^3(1-x)^4$.

Solution

Taking the natural logarithm of both sides and applying the laws of logarithms gives

$$\ln y = \ln(\mathrm{e}^{2x}x^3(1-x)^4)$$

$$= \ln \mathrm{e}^{2x} + \ln x^3 + \ln(1-x)^4$$

$$= \quad + \quad + \quad$$

$2x,\ 3\ln x,\ 4\ln(1-x)$

Differentiating w.r.t x gives

$$\frac{1}{y}\frac{\mathrm{d}y}{\mathrm{d}x} = $$

$$2 + \frac{3}{x} - \frac{4}{1-x}$$

and so

$$\frac{dy}{dx} = y\left(2 + \frac{3}{x} - \frac{4}{1 - x}\right)$$

$$\frac{dy}{dx} = e^{2x}x^3(1 - x)^4\left(2 + \frac{3}{x} - \frac{4}{1 - x}\right)$$

Example 5.4

Find $\frac{dz}{dt}$ given $z(t) = \sqrt{1 + t^2}\cos^4 t$.

Solution

Taking the natural logarithm of both sides gives

$$\ln z = \ln(\sqrt{1 + t^2}\cos^4 t)$$

$$= \ln\sqrt{1 + t^2} + \ln\cos^4 t$$

$$= \quad + $$

$$\frac{1}{2}\ln(1 + t^2) + 4\ln\cos t$$

Differentiating both sides w.r.t. t gives

$$\frac{1}{z}\frac{dz}{dt} = $$

$$\frac{t}{1 + t^2} - \frac{4\sin t}{\cos t}$$

So

$$\frac{dz}{dt} = z\left(\frac{t}{1 + t^2} - \frac{4\sin t}{\cos t}\right)$$

$$= \sqrt{1 + t^2}\cos^4 t\left(\frac{t}{1 + t^2} - 4\tan t\right)$$

Exercises

1. Find $\frac{dy}{dx}$ where y is given by
   (a) $x^5(3x + 7)^9$ (b) $x^8(5x - 1)^6$
   (c) $(3x + 2)^4(9x - 5)^7$
   (d) $(1 - 3x)^4(2 - 7x)^6$
   (e) $(5 + 2x)^4(5x + 2)^3$

2. Find the derivative of each of the following functions:
   (a) $z(t) = e^{3t}(2t - 5)^3(3t + 1)^4$
   (b) $h(t) = 3e^{-6t}t^7(t + 6)^3$
   (c) $M(p) = -p^4\sin^5 p$
   (d) $P(r) = 6(1 + r^2)^6\sqrt{3 + r^2}$
   (e) $y(x) = \dfrac{(7 - x)^3}{(3x^2 + 1)^2}$

3. Find the rate of change of
   $$q(t) = 2e^{-t/2}\cos 2t$$
   when $t = 1$.

4. Find the derivative of the following functions using logarithmic differentiation:
   (a) $a(t) = (1 + t^2)^3(1 - t^2)^4\sin^3 t$
   (b) $b(r) = e^{-r}\sin^5 2r\cos^4 3r$
   (c) $K(p) = 6p\sqrt{\sin p}\,(\cos 2p)^{1/3}$
   (d) $N(y) = \dfrac{(1 + \sqrt{y})^4(6 + 7y)^3}{\sqrt{1 + y}}$
   (e) $x(t) = \dfrac{6}{(2 + t)^3(1 - t)^4\cos^3 t}$

Solutions to exercises

1 (a) $7x^4(3x+7)^8(6x+5)$
(b) $2x^7(5x-1)^5(35x-4)$
(c) $33(3x+2)^3(9x-5)^6(9x+2)$
(d) $6(1-3x)^3(2-7x)^5(35x-11)$
(e) $7(2x+5)^3(5x+2)^2(10x+13)$

2 (a) $3e^{3t}(2t-5)^2(3t+1)^3(6t^2+t-23)$
(b) $-6t^6e^{-6t}(t+6)^2(3t^2+13t-21)$
(c) $-5p^4\sin^4 p\cos p - 4p^3\sin^5 p$
(d) $\dfrac{6r\,(r^2+1)^5\,(13r^2+37)}{\sqrt{r^2+3}}$
(e) $\dfrac{3(x-7)^2\,(x^2-28x-1)}{(3x^2+1)^3}$

3 -1.9537

4 (a) $a\left(\dfrac{6t}{1+t^2}-\dfrac{8t}{1-t^2}+3\cot t\right)$
(b) $b(-1+10\cot 2r-12\tan 3r)$
(c) $K\left(\dfrac{1}{p}+\dfrac{1}{2}\cot p-\dfrac{2}{3}\tan 2p\right)$
(d) $N\left(\dfrac{2}{\sqrt{y}+y}+\dfrac{21}{6+7y}-\dfrac{1}{2(1+y)}\right)$
(e) $x\left(\dfrac{-3}{2+t}+\dfrac{4}{1-t}+3\tan t\right)$

End of block exercises

1 Find $\dfrac{dy}{dx}$ where y is given by

(a) $x^3(3x-2)^4(5x-1)^6$
(b) $\sqrt{x}(x^2+1)^3(x^3+1)^2$
(c) $\dfrac{e^{2x}\sin^3 x}{x^4}$ (d) $\dfrac{4e^{-3x}\cos 3x}{(2-x)^3}$
(e) $\dfrac{3}{e^{2x}\sqrt{\sin x}\,(9+x^2)}$

2 Find the derivative of each of the following functions:

(a) $y(x)=3e^{(x^2)}x^2\sin x$
(b) $h(r)=\dfrac{(3r^2+2)^3}{\sqrt{4-r}\,(9+r^2)}$
(c) $m(p)=\dfrac{(\sqrt{p}+2)^2\,e^{-p^2}}{(1+p^2)^2}$
(d) $x(t)=\dfrac{2\,(t+e^{2t})^4\sqrt{t^2-2t^3}}{\sin^2 t}$
(e) $c(q)=e^q\sqrt{\dfrac{q^2-2}{3q^2+1}}$

Solutions to exercises

1 (a) $y\left(\dfrac{3}{x}+\dfrac{12}{3x-2}+\dfrac{30}{5x-1}\right)$
(b) $y\left(\dfrac{1}{2x}+\dfrac{6x}{x^2+1}+\dfrac{6x^2}{x^3+1}\right)$
(c) $y\left(2+3\cot x-\dfrac{4}{x}\right)$
(d) $y\left(-3-3\tan 3x+\dfrac{3}{2-x}\right)$
(e) $y\left(-2-\dfrac{1}{2}\cot x-\dfrac{2x}{9+x^2}\right)$

2 (a) $y\left(2x+\dfrac{2}{x}+\cot x\right)$
(b) $h\left(\dfrac{18r}{3r^2+2}+\dfrac{1}{2(4-r)}-\dfrac{2r}{9+r^2}\right)$
(c) $m\left(\dfrac{1}{p+2\sqrt{p}}-2p-\dfrac{4p}{1+p^2}\right)$
(d) $x\left[4\left(\dfrac{1+2e^{2t}}{t+e^{2t}}\right)+\left(\dfrac{1-3t}{t-2t^2}\right)-2\cot t\right]$
(e) $c\left(1+\dfrac{q}{q^2-2}-\dfrac{3q}{3q^2+1}\right)$

BLOCK 6

Tangents and normals

6.1 Introduction

The derivative gives the rate at which the function is changing. An alternative, but equally valid, interpretation of the derivative is that it represents the gradient of a tangent to the curve. We use this fact when calculating the equation of a tangent to a curve.

A normal is a line that is perpendicular to a tangent through the point of contact. Figure 6.1 illustrates a typical tangent and normal to $y(x)$.

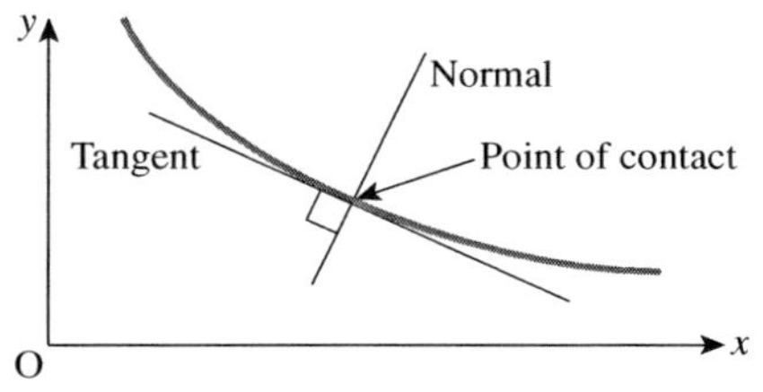

Figure 6.1
A tangent and normal to a curve, $y(x)$.

6.2 Calculating the equation of a tangent

Recall that a **tangent** is a straight line that touches a curve in one point only. This point is referred to as the **point of contact**. The derivative of a function can be interpreted as the gradient of a tangent to a curve.

When calculating the equation of a tangent we require its gradient and the coordinates of one point. Usually the coordinates of the point of contact are used.

Example 6.1
Find the equation of the tangent to $y = x^2$ at the point (2, 4).

Solution
Figure 6.2 illustrates the situation. The point of contact is (2, 4). To calculate the gradient of the tangent we find the derivative, $\frac{\mathrm{d}y}{\mathrm{d}x}$.

$$y = x^2 \quad \text{so} \quad \frac{\mathrm{d}y}{\mathrm{d}x} = 2x$$

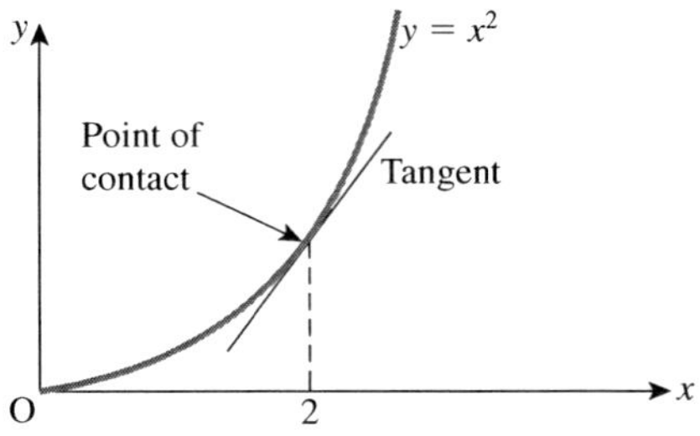

Figure 6.2 A tangent to $y = x^2$ at (2, 4)

When $x = 2$, $\dfrac{dy}{dx} = 4$. Hence the gradient of the tangent is 4. We are now ready to calculate the equation of the tangent. The tangent is a straight line and so has an equation of the form

$$y = mx + c$$

The gradient, m, is 4 and so

$$y = 4x + c$$

The point of contact, (2, 4), lies on the tangent, that is when $x = 2$, $y = 4$.

$$4 = 4(2) + c$$

$$c = -4$$

Hence the equation of the tangent is $y = 4x - 4$.

Example 6.2

Find the equation of the tangent to $y = 2e^x - x^3$ where $x = 1.5$.

Solution

When $x = 1.5$, $y =$ 5.5884

Thus the point of contact is (1.5, 5.5884).

The gradient of the tangent is now found.

$$\frac{dy}{dx} = 2e^x - 3x^2$$

When $x = 1.5$

$$\frac{dy}{dx} = 2e^{1.5} - 3(1.5)^2 = 2.2134$$

and so the gradient of the tangent is 2.2134. The equation of the tangent can now be found. The equation has the form $y = mx + c$ and using the gradient found we have

$$y = 2.2134x + c$$

Applying the point of contact given yields

$$5.5884 = 2.2134(1.5) + c$$

from which

$c =$ 2.2683

So the equation of the tangent is $y = 2.2134x + 2.2683$.

Exercises

1 Calculate the equation of the tangent to $y = 3x^2 - x + 9$ where $x = 2$.

2 Calculate the equation of the tangent to $y = \sin x$ where $x = \dfrac{\pi}{4}$.

3 The gradient of a tangent to $y = x^3 + x$ is 1. Calculate the equation of the tangent.

4 (a) Calculate the equation of the tangent to $y = e^{-x}$ where $x = 1.4$.
(b) Calculate where the tangent cuts the x axis.
(c) Calculate where the tangent cuts the y axis.

5 Calculate the equation of the tangents to $y = 9 - x^2$ at the points where y crosses the x axis.

Solutions to exercises

1 $y = 11x - 3$

2 $y = \dfrac{1}{\sqrt{2}}\left(x + 1 - \dfrac{\pi}{4}\right) = 0.7071x + 0.1517$

3 $y = x$

4 (a) $y = -0.2466x + 0.5918$
(b) (2.4, 0)
(c) (0, 0.5918)

5 $y = 6x + 18$, $y = -6x + 18$

6.3 The Newton–Raphson method

The Newton–Raphson method is a technique for generating a sequence of approximations to a solution, or root, of an equation $f(x) = 0$. The method uses differentiation because it relies upon knowledge of the equations of tangents to the graph of $y = f(x)$. It is known as a **numerical method** because it produces a numerical sequence of values that, under certain conditions, get closer and closer to the root. We say that this sequence of values converges. A more detailed discussion of convergence of sequences is given in Chapter 19.

Suppose we are interested in solving an equation that can be written in the form $f(x) = 0$. For example we may wish to solve equations such as

$$x^4 - 3x - 2 = 0 \quad \text{or} \quad e^{-x} - \sin x = 0$$

This problem is equivalent to finding values of x for which the graph of $y = f(x)$ intersects the horizontal axis, as illustrated in Figure 6.3. When x has the particular values x_1, x_2 or x_3 then y has the value of zero. In other words $f(x_1) = 0$, $f(x_2) = 0$ and $f(x_3) = 0$, and so the roots of $f(x) = 0$ are $x = x_1$, $x = x_2$ and $x = x_3$.

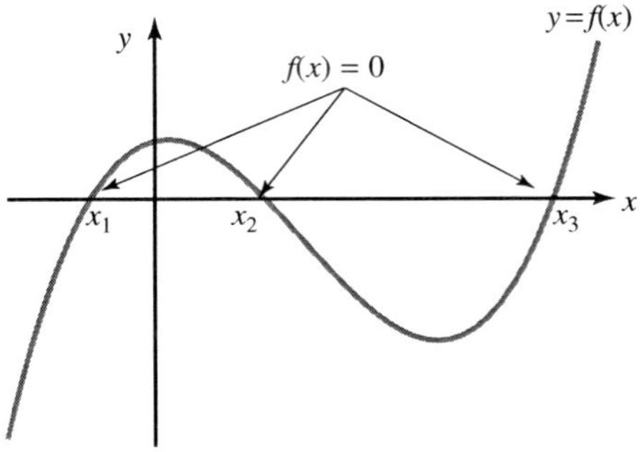

Figure 6.3 Solutions of $f(x) = 0$ can be located by finding values of x where the graph of $y = f(x)$ intersects the x axis.

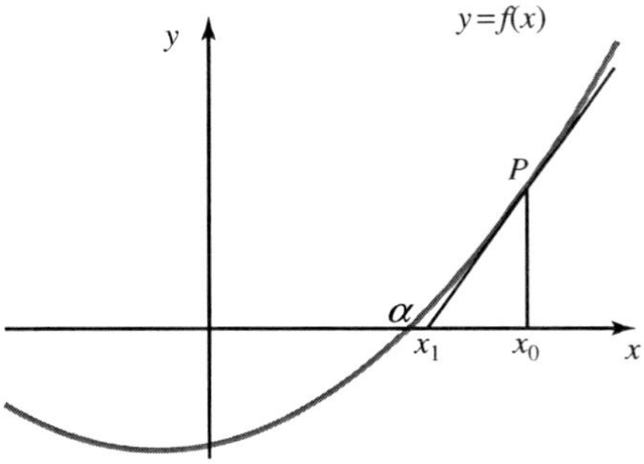

Figure 6.4 The tangent drawn at $P(x_0, f(x_0))$ intersects the x axis at x_1.

Suppose a root exists at some unknown value $x = \alpha$ as shown in Figure 6.4. Suppose we know or make an estimate of the root, $x = x_0$ say. We can draw a tangent to the curve $y = f(x)$ at the point $P(x_0, f(x_0))$, and use the value of x at the point where the tangent cuts the x axis, x_1 say, as a better estimate of the root.

First we obtain the equation of the tangent to $y = f(x)$ at $P(x_0, f(x_0))$. It will take the form $y = mx + c$. From section 6.2 we know that its gradient, m, will equal $\frac{dy}{dx}$ evaluated at x_0, which, in the context of the Newton–Raphson method, we write as $f'(x_0)$. So the equation becomes $y = f'(x_0)x + c$. We now find the constant c. The tangent passes through the point $(x_0, f(x_0))$, and so $f(x_0) = f'(x_0)x_0 + c$, from which $c = f(x_0) - f'(x_0)x_0$. Since x_0 is a known value we can calculate $f(x_0) - f'(x_0)x_0$, and so c can be evaluated. Finally, the equation of the tangent is

$$y = f'(x_0)x + f(x_0) - f'(x_0)x_0$$

From Figure 6.4 we see that this tangent will cut the horizontal axis when $y = 0$ and $x = x_1$, that is when

$$0 = f'(x_0)x_1 + f(x_0) - f'(x_0)x_0$$

Rearranging this formula to make x_1 the subject gives

$$x_1 = x_0 - \frac{f(x_0)}{f'(x_0)}$$

Recall that x_0 is our first approximation to the root. This formula enables us to calculate a better estimate of the root, denoted by x_1.

Example 6.3

Use the Newton–Raphson formula to find an improved estimate of a solution to the equation $x^4 - 3x - 2 = 0$ given that a first estimate is $x_0 = 1.5$.

Solution

Here $f(x) = x^4 - 3x - 2$ and so, differentiating,

$f'(x) =$ $\qquad$ $4x^3 - 3$

Then with a first estimate x_0 the Newton–Raphson formula is

$x_1 =$ $\qquad$ $x_0 - \dfrac{x_0^4 - 3x_0 - 2}{4x_0^3 - 3}$

Substitution of $x_0 = 1.5$ yields our new estimate x_1:

$x_1 =$

$$1.5 - \frac{1.5^4 - 3(1.5) - 2}{4(1.5)^3 - 3} = 1.636905$$

So 1.636905 is an improved estimate of the root.

In practice the formula is used repeatedly with each new estimate used to generate a further improvement. This leads to the following general formula.

Key point

If $x = x_n$ is an approximate root of $f(x) = 0$, then, under certain conditions, an improved estimate is given by

$$x_{n+1} = x_n - \frac{f(x_n)}{f'(x_n)}$$

Unfortunately the sequence of values produced does not always converge. For further details concerning the conditions for convergence and the rate of convergence consult a textbook on numerical methods for engineers.

The Newton–Raphson formula is easy to program in a loop structure. Exit from the loop is usually conditional upon $|x_{n+1} - x_n|$ being smaller than some prescribed very small value. This condition shows that successive approximate roots are very close to each other.

Example 6.4

Apply two more iterations of the Newton–Raphson method to the equation of Example 6.3.

Solution

With $x_1 = 1.636905$ we find

$$x_2 =$$

$$1.636905 - \frac{1.636905^4 - 3(1.636905) - 2}{4(1.636905)^3 - 3} = 1.618425$$

With $x_2 = 1.618425$ we find

$$x_3 =$$

$$1.618425 - \frac{1.618425^4 - 3(1.618425) - 2}{4(1.618425)^3 - 3} = 1.618034$$

We see that the numbers generated by this method appear to be getting closer to 1.618. In this example the method has performed well when we note that the true solution is 1.618034 (6 d.p.).

Exercises

1 Use the Newton–Raphson technique to find the value of a root of the following equations correct to two decimal places. An approximate root x_0 is given in each case.

(a) $x^2 - \cos x = 0$, $x_0 = 0.8$
(b) $3x^3 - 5x^2 + 7 = 0$, $x_0 = -0.9$
(c) $x^3 = e^{-x}$, $x_0 = 0.82$
(d) $e^x = \sin 2x$, $x_0 = -1.5$

Solutions to exercises

1 (a) 0.82 (b) -0.95 (c) 0.77 (d) -1.67

Computer and calculator exercise

Use a graphical calculator or computer package to plot a graph of $f(x) = x^3 - 8x^2 + 11x - 2$. Use your graph to estimate roots of the equation $x^3 - 8x^2 + 11x - 2 = 0$ and use your estimates together with the Newton–Raphson method to find improved estimates.

Solution to exercise

$x = 6.31, 1.48, 0.21$

6.4 Equation of a normal to a curve

A normal is a line that is perpendicular to a tangent and passes through the point of contact. (See Figure 6.1.)

It is useful to state an important result:

Key point

If two lines are perpendicular, the product of their gradients is -1.

Hence, if a tangent has gradient m_1 and the normal has gradient m_2, then $m_1 m_2 = -1$.

Example 6.5

Find the equation of the normal to $y = x^2$ at the point (2, 4).

Solution

We have found from Example 6.1 that the gradient of the tangent at (2, 4) is 4. Hence

$$\text{gradient of normal at } (2, 4) = \frac{1}{-4} = -\frac{1}{4}$$

Let the equation of the normal be $y = mx + c$. The gradient, m, has been found to be $-\frac{1}{4}$ and so

$$y = -\frac{x}{4} + c$$

The point of contact, (2, 4), is on the normal so

$$4 = -\frac{2}{4} + c$$

$$c = \frac{9}{2}$$

Hence the equation of the normal is

$$y = -\frac{x}{4} + \frac{9}{2}$$

Example 6.6

Find the equation of the normal to $y = 2x^4 - 3$ at $(1, -1)$.

Solution

We find $\frac{dy}{dx}$.

$\frac{dy}{dx} = $ ▢ $8x^3$

The tangent through (1, −1) has gradient

▢ 8

Hence the normal through (1, −1) has gradient

▢ $-\frac{1}{8}$

The equation of the normal is

$$y = mx + c$$
$$= -\frac{x}{8} + c$$

The normal passes through (1, −1) and so

$c = $ ▢ $-\frac{7}{8}$

Hence the equation of the normal is

$y = -\frac{x}{8} - \frac{7}{8}$

Exercises

1 Calculate the equation of the normal to
(a) $y = 3x^2 - x$ through (2, 10)
(b) $y = \sqrt{x}$ through (9, 3)
(c) $y = \frac{1}{x}$ through (0.5, 2)
(d) $y = 10 - x^4$ through (1, 9)
(e) $y = \frac{x}{2} - \frac{x^3}{6}$ through $\left(1, \frac{1}{3}\right)$

2 Calculate the equation of the normal to
(a) $y = xe^x$ where $x = 1$
(b) $y = 2\sin 3x$ where $x = \pi$
(c) $y = 2\ln x$ where $x = 1$
(d) $y = (2x + 1)^6$ where $x = 0$
(e) $y = \frac{e^x + 1}{x}$ where $x = 1$

Solutions to exercises

1 (a) $y = -\frac{x}{11} + \frac{112}{11}$
(b) $y = -6x + 57$
(c) $y = \frac{x}{4} + \frac{15}{8}$
(d) $y = \frac{x + 35}{4}$
(e) $x = 1$

2 (a) $y = \dfrac{-x + 2e^2 + 1}{2e}$
(b) $y = \dfrac{x - \pi}{6}$
(c) $y = \dfrac{1 - x}{2}$
(d) $y = -\dfrac{x}{12} + 1$
(e) $y = x + e$

End of block exercises

1 Calculate the equation of the tangent to
(a) $y = x^2 + 2$ at (1, 3)
(b) $y = 10 - 2x^2$ at (0, 10)
(c) $y = 2x^2 - x + 3$ at (2, 9)
(d) $y = x^3 + 1$ at (−1, 0)
(e) $y = x^3 + x^2 + x - 1$ at (1, 2)

2 Calculate the equation of the normal to
(a) $y = x^2 + 2x - 1$ at (0, −1)
(b) $y = 6 - x^2$ at (3, −3)
(c) $y = 3x^2 - 2x + 11$ at (1, 12)
(d) $y = 3x - x^3$ at (2, −2)
(e) $y = 2x^3 - 3x + 1$ at (0, 1)

3 Calculate the equation of the tangent to
(a) $y = 3\sin x - \cos x$ where $x = \pi$
(b) $y = 2\ln x$ where $x = e$
(c) $y = 3e^x + e^{-x}$ where $x = 0$
(d) $y = x^2 + e^{-2x}$ where $x = 0$
(e) $y = \sin 2x + 3\cos 2x$ where $x = \dfrac{\pi}{4}$

4 Calculate the equation of the normal to
(a) $y = 2\sin x + x$ where $x = 0$
(b) $y = 3e^{-x} + e^x$ where $x = 1$
(c) $y = 3x + 2\ln x$ where $x = 1$
(d) $y = 4\cos x + \sin x$ where $x = \pi$
(e) $y = 3\ln x + \cos 2x$ where $x = 0.5$

5 Calculate the equation of the tangent to
(a) $y = \sqrt{x + 1}$ where $x = 3$
(b) $y = \sin(2x + \pi)$ where $x = 0$
(c) $y = x^2e^{-x}$ where $x = 1$
(d) $y = \dfrac{2x + 1}{x + 2}$ where $x = 2$
(e) $y = \dfrac{x}{x^2 + 1}$ where $x = 1$

6 Calculate the equation of the normal to
(a) $y = \cos(x - \pi)$ where $x = \dfrac{\pi}{2}$
(b) $y = x^3 \ln x$ where $x = 1$
(c) $y = \sqrt{x^2 + 1}$ where $x = 2$
(d) $y = \dfrac{e^x}{x}$ where $x = -1$
(e) $y = \sin(x^2)$ where $x = 0.5$

7 Use the Newton–Raphson technique to find the value of a root of the following equations correct to two decimal places. An approximate root x_0 is given in each case.
(a) $x^5 - x^3 + 2 = 0$, $x_0 = -1.5$
(b) $2\sin x = \sin 2x$, $x_0 = 6.2$

8 Apply the Newton–Raphson method to the solution of $x - \tan x = 0$. Show that with an initial estimate of $x_0 = 4$ the sequence of values generated by the method fails to converge, but with an initial estimate $x_0 = 4.6$ the method converges to the root $x = 4.49$ (2 d.p.).

Solutions to exercises

1 (a) $y = 2x + 1$ (b) $y = 10$ (c) $y = 7x - 5$
(d) $y = 3x + 3$ (e) $y = 6x - 4$

2 (a) $y = -\dfrac{x}{2} - 1$ (b) $y = \dfrac{x}{6} - \dfrac{7}{2}$

(c) $y = \dfrac{49 - x}{4}$ (d) $y = \dfrac{x - 20}{9}$

(e) $y = \dfrac{x}{3} + 1$

3 (a) $y = -3x + 3\pi + 1$ (b) $y = \dfrac{2}{e}x$

(c) $y = 2x + 4$ (d) $y = -2x + 1$

(e) $y = -6x + \dfrac{3\pi}{2} + 1$

4 (a) $y = -\dfrac{x}{3}$ (b) $y = -0.6193x + 4.4412$

(c) $y = \dfrac{-x + 16}{5}$ (d) $y = x - 4 - \pi$

(e) $y = -0.2316x - 1.4233$

5 (a) $y = \dfrac{x + 5}{4}$ (b) $y = -2x$

(c) $y = \dfrac{x}{e}$ (d) $y = \dfrac{3x}{16} + \dfrac{7}{8}$

(e) $y = 0.5$

6 (a) $y = -x + \dfrac{\pi}{2}$ (b) $y = -x + 1$

(c) $y = \dfrac{-\sqrt{5}}{2}x + 2\sqrt{5}$

(d) $y = 1.3591x + 0.9913$

(e) $y = -1.0321x + 0.7634$

7 (a) $x = -1.35$ (b) $x = 6.28$

BLOCK 7

Maximum and minimum values of a function

7.1 Introduction

The maximum and minimum values of a function are often very important. For example, an engineer may need to know the value of the maximum power transferred from a voltage source to a load resistor. Maximum and minimum points are located by examining the derivative of a function, rather than the function itself.

Two tests are described that distinguish between maximum and minimum points. Finally, we explain what is meant by a point of inflexion and how such a point is located.

7.2 Maximum and minimum points

Consider Figures 7.1(a) and (b). The point A is a **local maximum**; the point B is a **local minimum**. Note that A is not the highest point on the graph. However, in the locality of A, A is the highest point. Use of the word 'local' stresses that A is a maximum only in its locality. Similarly B is a minimum in its locality but is not the lowest point on the entire graph.

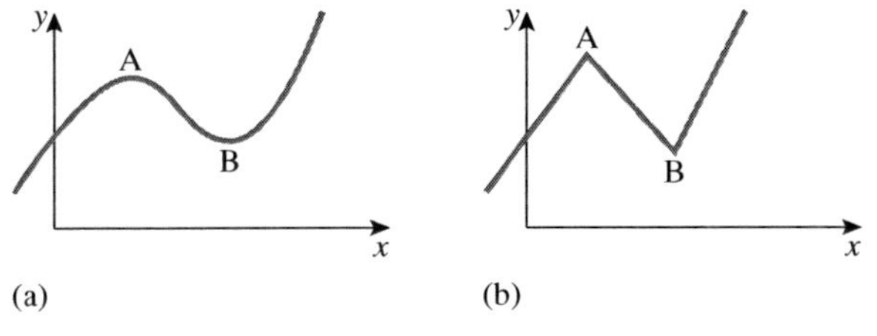

Figure 7.1
(a), (b) A is a local maximum, B is a local minimum.

When moving away from A along the function, both to the left and to the right, the value of y decreases; when moving away from B along the function, the value of y increases.

It is useful to be able to locate points such as A and B. This is done by referring to the gradient of the function, rather than the function itself.

7.3 Locating maximum and minimum points

Consider Figure 7.2, which shows the curve $y(x)$, together with some tangents. The tangents at A and B are parallel to the x axis, that is $\frac{dy}{dx} = 0$ at these points.

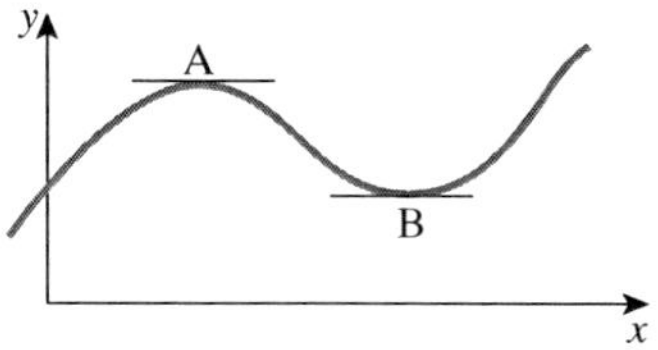

Figure 7.2
At A and B, $\frac{dy}{dx} = 0$.

We now consider Figure 7.1(b) again. At A and B it is impossible to draw tangents: that is, they do not exist. Hence at these points $\frac{dy}{dx}$ does not exist. In summary we have

Key point

At maximum and minimum points, $\dfrac{dy}{dx} = 0$ or $\dfrac{dy}{dx}$ does not exist.

So, maximum and minimum points are located by looking for points where $\frac{dy}{dx} = 0$ or $\frac{dy}{dx}$ does not exist.

7.4 The first-derivative test

When given any function, $y(x)$, we can limit our search for maximum and minimum points to those points where $\frac{dy}{dx} = 0$ or $\frac{dy}{dx}$ does not exist. We also need to distinguish between a maximum point and a minimum point. To do this we consider y' on either side of the point.

Immediately to the left of a maximum point, such as A in Figure 7.1, $y' > 0$, that is y is increasing. Immediately to the right of a maximum point, $y' < 0$, that is y is decreasing. Thus, in passing from left to right through a maximum point, y' changes from positive to negative.

Now consider a minimum point, such as B in Figure 7.1. Immediately to the left of such a point, $y' < 0$, that is y is decreasing. Immediately to the right, $y' > 0$, that is y is increasing. So, in passing from left to right through a minimum point, y' changes from negative to positive.

This information is contained in the **first-derivative test**.

Key point

- The first-derivative test distinguishes between maximum and minimum points.
- To the left of a maximum point, $\dfrac{dy}{dx}$ is positive; to the right $\dfrac{dy}{dx}$ is negative.
- To the left of a minimum point, $\dfrac{dy}{dx}$ is negative; to the right $\dfrac{dy}{dx}$ is positive.

Example 7.1

Determine the position of any maximum and minimum points of the function $y = x^2 + 1$.

Solution

By differentiation, $\frac{dy}{dx} = 2x$. The function $2x$ exists for all values of x. So, we need only look for maximum and minimum points by solving $y' = 0$. So

$$y' = 0$$
$$2x = 0$$

so

$$x = 0$$

At this stage, we know that the only place a maximum or a minimum point can be found is where $x = 0$. We now apply the first-derivative test.

To the left of $x = 0$, x is negative. So $2x$ is negative and hence y' is negative. To the right of $x = 0$, x is positive and so y' is positive. Since y' changes from negative to positive, there must be a minimum point at $x = 0$.

When $x = 0$, $y = 1$ so $(0, 1)$ is a minimum point. Figure 7.3 illustrates this.

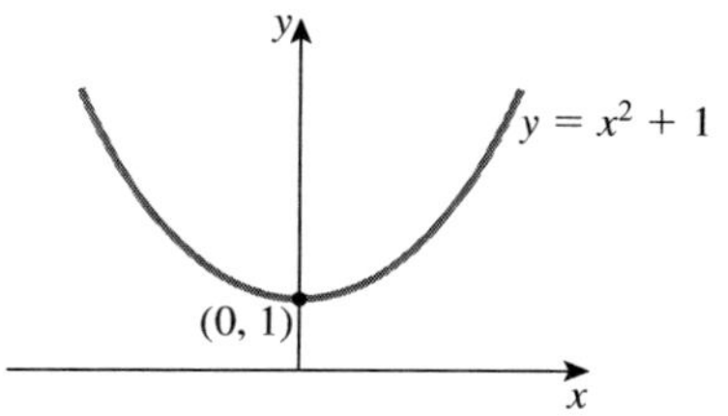

Figure 7.3 There is a minimum point at (0, 1).

Example 7.2

Determine the position of any maximum and minimum points of the function $y = 2x - x^2$.

Solution

We see that $\frac{dy}{dx} = 2 - 2x$, which exists for all x. We look for maximum and minimum points by solving $\frac{dy}{dx} = 0$.

$$\frac{dy}{dx} = 0$$
$$2 - 2x = 0$$
$$2 = 2x$$

so

$$x = 1$$

Thus we examine the point where $x = 1$.

We examine the sign of $\frac{dy}{dx}$ to the left and to the right of $x = 1$. To determine the sign of $2 - 2x$ to the left and to the right of $x = 1$ we can use one of two techniques. We can sketch a graph of $2 - 2x$ and note the sign on both sides of $x = 1$. Another method is to evaluate $2 - 2x$ just to the left of $x = 1$, say $x = 0.9$, and then evaluate $2 - 2x$ just to the right of $x = 1$, say at $x = 1.1$. When $x = 0.9$, the value of $2 - 2x$ is 0.2; when $x = 1.1$ the value of $2 - 2x$ is -0.2. Since y' changes from positive to negative there must be a maximum at $x = 1$.

When $x = 1$, $y = 1$ and so (1,1) is a maximum point. Figure 7.4 illustrates this.

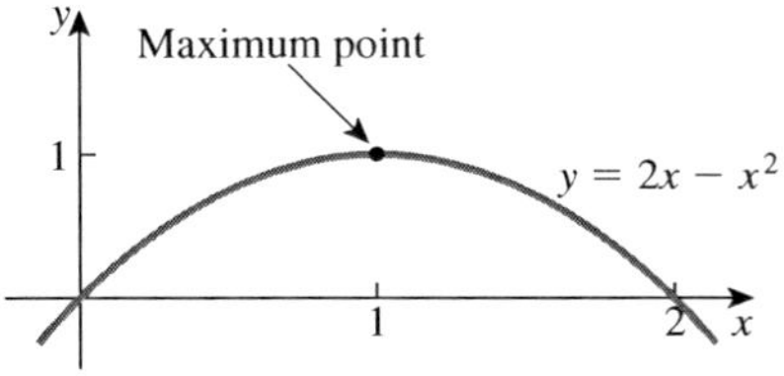

Figure 7.4 There is a maximum point at (1,1).

Example 7.3

Determine the position of any maximum and minimum points of the function $y = \frac{t^3}{3} - \frac{t^2}{2} - 2t + 3$.

Solution

We have

$$\frac{dy}{dt} = t^2 - t - 2$$

Clearly, $\frac{dy}{dt}$ exists for all values of t. Solving $\frac{dy}{dt} = 0$ yields

$$\begin{aligned} t^2 - t - 2 &= 0 \\ (t - 2)(t + 1) &= 0 \\ t &= -1, 2 \end{aligned}$$

We need to investigate the two points where $t = -1$ and $t = 2$.

$t = -1$

Consider a value just to the left of $t = -1$, say $t = -1.1$ Here

$$\begin{aligned} \frac{dy}{dt} &= (-1.1)^2 - (-1.1) - 2 \\ &= 0.31 \end{aligned}$$

So, at $t = -1.1$, $\frac{dy}{dt}$ is positive.

Just to the right of $t = -1$, say at $t = -0.9$,

$$\begin{aligned} \frac{dy}{dt} &= (-0.9)^2 - (-0.9) - 2 \\ &= -0.29 \end{aligned}$$

So, $\frac{dy}{dt}$ is negative. Since the derivative has changed from positive to negative there must be a maximum point at $t = -1$.

When $t = -1$, $y = \frac{25}{6}$ and so $(-1, \frac{25}{6})$ is a maximum point.

$t = 2$

By considering values just to the left and right of $t = 2$ we see that immediately to the left of $t = 2$, $\frac{dy}{dt}$ is negative; immediately to the right, $\frac{dy}{dt}$ is positive. Hence at $t = 2$ there is a minimum point.

When $t = 2$, $y = -\frac{1}{3}$ so $(2, -\frac{1}{3})$ is a minimum point. Figure 7.5 illustrates a graph of the function.

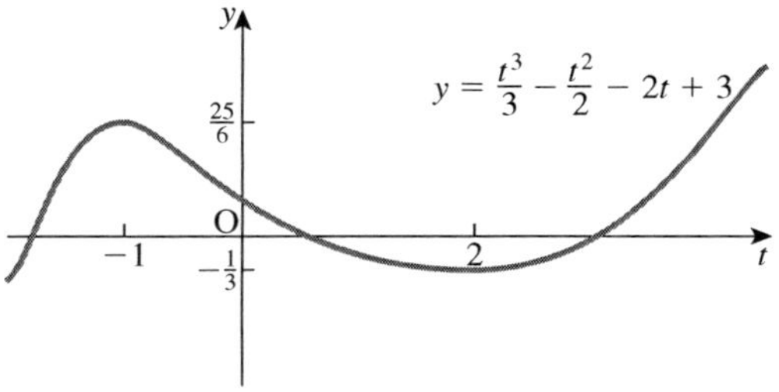

Figure 7.5 There is a maximum point at $(-1, \frac{25}{6})$ and a minimum point at $(2, -\frac{1}{3})$.

Example 7.4

Determine the position of any maximum and minimum points of the function $y = |t|$.

Solution

Recall that

$$y = |t| = \begin{cases} -t, & t < 0 \\ t, & t \geq 0 \end{cases}$$

A graph of $y = |t|$ is shown in Figure 8.5 of Chapter 6. Note that there is a corner at $t = 0$. Hence the derivative, $\frac{dy}{dt}$, does not exist at $t = 0$ and so this is a possible location of a maximum or minimum point. To the left of $t = 0$, $\frac{dy}{dt}$ is negative; to the right of $t = 0$, $\frac{dy}{dt}$ is positive and so there is a minimum at $t = 0$.

Example 7.5

Locate the maximum and minimum points of each of the following functions:

(a) $y = x^2 - 6x + 5$
(b) $y = x^3 - 3x$
(c) $y = x^{1/3}$

Solution

(a) Given $y = x^2 - 6x + 5$

$$\frac{dy}{dx} = \quad \square$$

$2x - 6$

Solving $\frac{dy}{dx} = 0$ yields

$$x = \quad \square$$

3

Immediately to the left of $x = 3$,

$\frac{dy}{dx}$ is ______ negative

Immediately to the right of $x = 3$,

$\frac{dy}{dx}$ is ______ positive

Hence at $x = 3$, there is a ______ minimum

When $x = 3$,

$y =$ ______ -4

Hence $(3, -4)$ is a minimum point.

(b) Given $y = x^3 - 3x$, here

$y' =$ ______ $3x^2 - 3$

Solving $y' = 0$, yields

$x =$ ______ $-1, 1$

Consider $x = -1$.

Immediately to the left of $x = -1$,

y' is ______ positive

Immediately to the right of $x = -1$,

y' is ______ negative

Hence at $x = -1$ there is a ______ maximum

When $x = -1$,

$y =$ ______ 2

So $(-1, 2)$ is a maximum point.

We now consider $x = 1$.

Immediately to the left of $x = 1$,

y' is ______ negative

Immediately to the right of $x = 1$,

y' is ______ positive

Hence at $x = 1$ there is a ______ minimum

When $x = 1$,

$y =$ ______ -2

So $(1, -2)$ is a minimum point.

(c) Given $y = x^{1/3}$ then by differentiation we have

$\frac{dy}{dx} =$ ______ $\frac{x^{-2/3}}{3} = \frac{1}{3x^{2/3}}$

Note that at $x = 0$ the function $\frac{1}{3x^{2/3}}$ does not exist so there is no derivative at $x = 0$.

To the left of $x = 0$,

y' is   positive

To the right of $x = 0$,

y' is   positive

Since y' does not change sign we conclude there is neither a maximum nor a minimum at $x = 0$.

Example 7.6 Electrical Engineering – Maximum power transfer

Consider the circuit of Figure 7.6 in which a non-ideal voltage source is connected to a variable load resistor with resistance R_L. The source voltage is V and its internal resistance is R_S. Calculate the value of R_L that results in the maximum power being transferred from the voltage source to the load resistor.

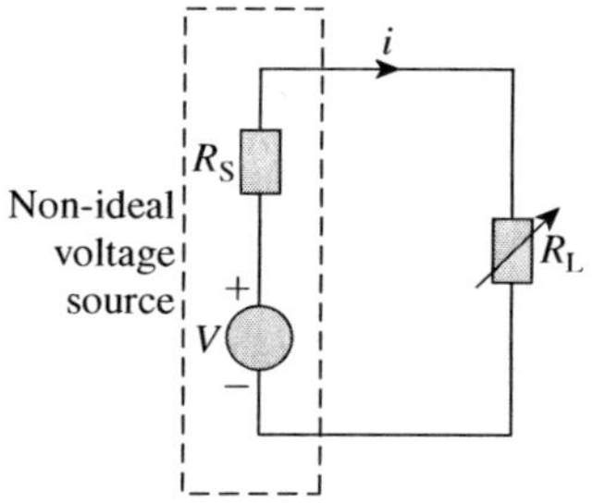

Figure 7.6 Maximum power transfer occurs when $R_L = R_S$.

Solution

Let i be the current flowing in the circuit. Using Kirchhoff's voltage law and Ohm's law gives

$$V = i(R_S + R_L)$$

Let P be the power developed in the load resistor. Then

$$P = i^2 R_L$$

$$= \frac{V^2 R_L}{(R_S + R_L)^2}$$

Clearly P depends on the value of R_L. Differentiating we obtain

$$\frac{dP}{dR_L} = V^2 \frac{1\,(R_S + R_L)^2 - R_L\;2\,(R_S + R_L)}{(R_S + R_L)^4}$$

$$= V^2 \frac{R_S - R_L}{(R_S + R_L)^3}$$

Equating $\frac{dP}{dR_L}$ to zero gives

$$V^2 \frac{R_S - R_L}{(R_S + R_L)^3} = 0$$

that is

$$R_L = R_S$$

We need to check whether this is a maximum point.

$$\frac{dP}{dR_L} = V^2 \frac{R_S - R_L}{(R_S + R_L)^3}$$

When R_L has a value just to the left of R_S, the derivative is positive. When R_L has a value just to the right of R_S, the derivative is negative. Hence there is a maximum when $R_L = R_S$. Therefore maximum power transfer occurs when the load resistance equals the source resistance.

Exercises

1 Determine the location of all maximum and minimum points of the following functions:
(a) $y = x^2 - 4x$
(b) $y = x^2 - 5x + 4$
(c) $y = 10 + 3x - x^2$
(d) $y = \frac{x^3}{3} - \frac{x^2}{2} + 1$
(e) $y = x^3 - 27x$

2 Determine the location of all maximum and minimum points of the following functions:
(a) $y = xe^x$
(b) $y = \frac{1}{1 + x^2}$
(c) $y = \frac{x^5}{5} - \frac{x^3}{3}$
(d) $y = \frac{x^4}{4} + x + 1$
(e) $y = (1 - \ln x)x$

Solutions to exercises

1 (a) $(2, -4)$ minimum
(b) $(\frac{5}{2}, -\frac{9}{4})$ minimum
(c) $(\frac{3}{2}, \frac{49}{4})$ maximum
(d) $(0, 1)$ maximum, $(1, \frac{5}{6})$ minimum
(e) $(-3, 54)$ maximum, $(3, -54)$ minimum

2 (a) $(-1, -0.3679)$ minimum
(b) $(0, 1)$ maximum
(c) $(-1, \frac{2}{15})$ maximum, $(1, -\frac{2}{15})$ minimum
(d) $(-1, \frac{1}{4})$ minimum
(e) $(1, 1)$ maximum

7.5 The second-derivative test

This is a test to distinguish between maximum and minimum points. Rather than examine the sign of y' on both sides of the points where $y' = 0$ we can instead consider the sign of the second derivative, y'', at these points.

On passing left to right through a maximum point, y' changes from positive to zero to negative. Hence, y' is decreasing and so the derivative of y' is negative, that is $y'' < 0$. Similarly, on passing left to right through a minimum point, y' changes from negative to zero to positive and so y' is increasing. Hence y'' is positive. The second-derivative test summarises this:

Key point

- If $y' = 0$ and $y'' < 0$ at a point, then the point is a maximum point.
- If $y' = 0$ and $y'' > 0$ at a point, then the point is a minimum point.
- If $y' = 0$ and $y'' = 0$ the second-derivative test fails and we must return to the first-derivative test.

Example 7.7

Use the second-derivative test to find all maximum and minimum points of

$$y = \frac{x^3}{3} - \frac{x^2}{2} - 6x + 2.$$

Solution

We see that

$$\begin{aligned} y' &= x^2 - x - 6 \\ &= (x + 2)(x - 3) \end{aligned}$$

Solving $y' = 0$ yields $x = -2, 3$. Now

$$y'' = 2x - 1$$

The sign of y'' is calculated at both $x = -2$ and $x = 3$.

When $x = -2$, $y'' = -5$. Since $y'' < 0$ then by the second-derivative test there is a maximum point at $x = -2$.

When $x = 3$, $y'' = -5$. Here $y'' > 0$ and so there is a minimum point at $x = 3$.

When $x = -2$, $y = \frac{28}{3}$. When $x = 3$, $y = -\frac{23}{2}$. So $(-2, \frac{28}{3})$ is a maximum point; $(3, -\frac{23}{2})$ is a minimum point.

Example 7.8

Determine the positions of all maximum and minimum points of $y = x^4$.

Solution

We have $y' = 4x^3$. Solving $y' = 0$ yields $x = 0$. Also we see

$$y'' = 12x^2$$

To apply the second-derivative test we evaluate y'' at $x = 0$. At $x = 0$, $y'' = 0$. Since $y'' = 0$ the second-derivative test fails. We return to the first-derivative test and examine the sign of y' to the left and to the right of $x = 0$.

Immediately to the left of $x = 0$, y' is negative. Immediately to the right of $x = 0$, y' is positive. Hence there is a minimum point at $x = 0$.

When $x = 0$, $y = 0$ and so $(0, 0)$ is a minimum point.

Example 7.9

Determine all maximum and minimum points of

$$y = \frac{x^5}{5} + \frac{x^2}{2} + 1$$

Solution

We have

$y' =$ ______ $x^4 + x$

Solving $y' = 0$, yields

$x =$ ______ $0, -1$

In order to use the second derivative test we calculate y''.

$y'' =$ ______ $4x^3 + 1$

The sign of y'' is calculated at each value of x.

When $x = -1$,

y'' is ______ negative

and so there is a ______ point at $x = -1$. maximum

When $x = 0$,

y'' is ______ positive

and so there is a ______ point at $x = 0$. minimum

When $x = -1$,

$y =$ ______ $\frac{13}{10}$

When $x = 0$,

$y =$ ______ 1

So $(-1, \frac{13}{10})$ is a maximum point; $(0, 1)$ is a minimum point.

Exercises

1 Determine the position of all maximum and minimum points using the second-derivative test.

(a) $y = \frac{x^2}{2} - x + 1$

(b) $y = 6 + 2x - \frac{3x^2}{2}$

(c) $y = \frac{x^3}{3} + \frac{3x^2}{2} - 1$

(d) $y = \frac{x^4}{4} - \frac{x^2}{2}$

Solutions to exercises

1 (a) $(1, \frac{1}{2})$, minimum

(b) $(\frac{2}{3}, \frac{20}{3})$, maximum

(c) $(0, -1)$, minimum; $(-3, \frac{7}{2})$, maximum

(d) $(0, 0)$, maximum; $(1, -\frac{1}{4})$, minimum; $(-1, -\frac{1}{4})$, minimum

7.6 Points of inflexion

Figure 7.7 show two curves. In both cases the gradient is increasing as we move along the curve from left to right, that is y' is increasing.

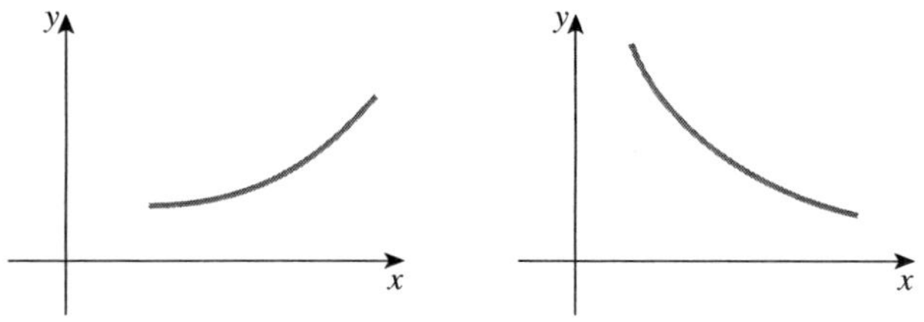

Figure 7.7
The gradient of both curves is increasing; the curves are concave up.

When y' is increasing, then y'' is positive, and the curve is described as **concave up**. Figure 7.8 shows two curves the gradients of which are decreasing as we move along the curve from left to right, that is y' is decreasing. When y' is decreasing, y'' is negative and the curve is said to be **concave down**.

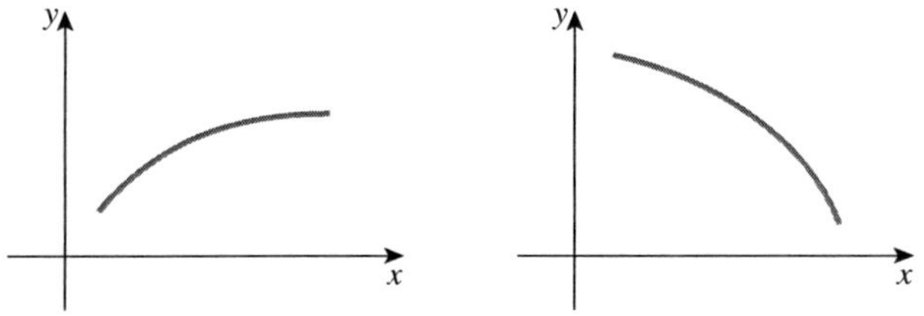

Figure 7.8
The gradient of both curves is decreasing; the curves are concave down.

A point at which the concavity changes from concave up to concave down, or vice versa, is called a **point of inflexion**. At such a point either $y'' = 0$ or y'' does not exist. Figure 7.9 illustrates some points of inflexion.

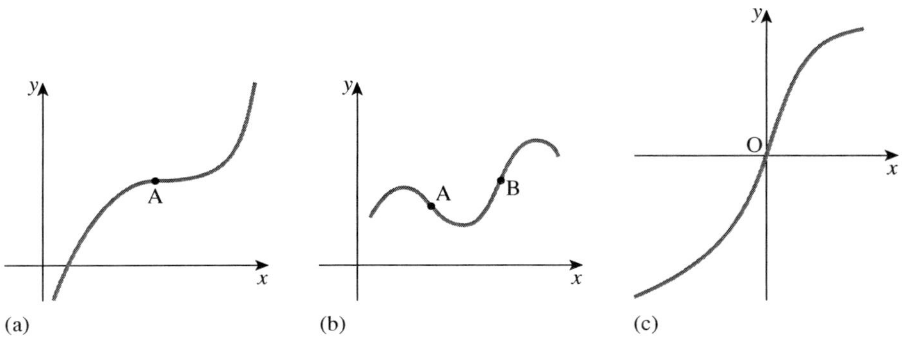

Figure 7.9
(a) There is a point of inflexion at A; (b) there are points of inflexion at A and B; (c) there is a point of inflexion at O.

Key point

A curve is **concave up** when $y'' > 0$, and **concave down** when $y'' < 0$. A **point of inflexion** is where the concavity changes.

Note that not all points where $y'' = 0$ or where y'' does not exist are points of inflexion. However, when searching for points of inflexion, we can limit our search to points where $y'' = 0$ or where y'' does not exist.

Example 7.10

Locate any points of inflexion of $y = x^3$.

Solution

We have

$$y' = 3x^2, \; y'' = 6x$$

A point of inflexion can occur only where either $y'' = 0$ or y'' does not exist. Clearly y'' exists for all values of x but $y'' = 0$ when $x = 0$.

We examine the concavity to the left and right of $x = 0$. To the left of $x = 0$, $6x$ is negative and so $y'' < 0$: that is, the function is concave down. To the right of $x = 0$, $6x$ is positive, and so $y'' > 0$: that is, the function is concave up. Hence the concavity changes at $x = 0$ and so there is a point of inflexion at $x = 0$.

When $x = 0$, $y = 0$ and so (0, 0) is a point of inflexion. Figure 7.10 illustrates $y = x^3$.

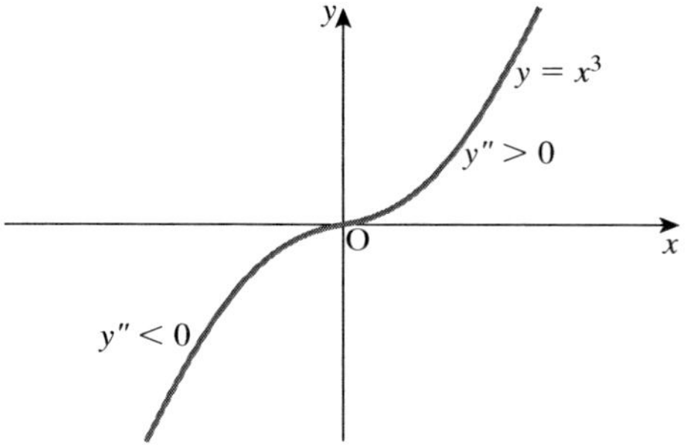

Figure 7.10
Since y'' changes sign at $x = 0$, there is a point of inflexion there.

Example 7.11

Determine all maximum points, minimum points and points of inflexion of

$$y = \frac{x^3}{6} - \frac{x^2}{2}$$

Solution

We have

$$y' = \frac{x^2}{2} - x, \qquad y'' = x - 1$$

To locate maximum and minimum points we solve $y' = 0$. This yields

$$\frac{x^2}{2} - x = 0$$

$$x\left(\frac{x}{2} - 1\right) = 0$$

$$x = 0, 2$$

To distinguish between maximum and minimum points we use the second-derivative test at $x = 0$ and at $x = 2$.

$y''(0) < 0$ and so there is a maximum point at $x = 0$.

$y''(2) > 0$ and so there is a minimum point at $x = 2$.

When $x = 0$, then $y = 0$. When $x = 2$, $y = -\frac{2}{3}$. So (0, 0) is a maximum point; $\left(2, -\frac{2}{3}\right)$ is a minimum point.

We now consider points of inflexion. We know that points of inflexion can occur only where $y'' = 0$ or where y'' does not exist. Clearly y'' exists for all values of x but $y'' = 0$ at $x = 1$. To check whether there is a point of inflexion at $x = 1$ we check the concavity to the left and right of $x = 1$.

Immediately to the left of $x = 1$, say at $x = 0.9$, $y'' < 0$. Immediately to the right of $x = 1$, say at 1.1, $y'' > 0$ and so the concavity changes at $x = 1$: that is, there is a point of inflexion at $x = 1$. When $x = 1$, $y = -\frac{1}{3}$, so $\left(1, -\frac{1}{3}\right)$ is a point of inflexion.

In summary we have: (0, 0) maximum point; $\left(2, -\frac{2}{3}\right)$ minimum point; $\left(1, -\frac{1}{3}\right)$ point of inflexion.

Example 7.12

Find all maximum points, minimum points and points of inflexion of

$$y = 1 + 12x + 3x^2 - 2x^3$$

Solution

We calculate y' and y''.

$y' =$ ______ $\quad$ $12 + 6x - 6x^2$

$y'' =$ ______ $\quad$ $6 - 12x$

Solving $y' = 0$ yields

$x =$ ______ $\quad$ $-1, 2$

We apply the second-derivative test to each value of x.

$y''(-1) =$ ______ $\quad$ 18

$y''(2) =$ ______ $\quad$ -18

Hence there is a ______ point at $x = -1$. $\quad$ minimum

There is a ______ point at $x = 2$. $\quad$ maximum

When $x = -1$, $y = -6$. When $x = 2$, $y = 21$.

We seek points of inflexion by considering y''. Solving $y'' = 0$ yields $x = 0.5$. Immediately to the left of $x = 0.5$, say at 0.4,

y'' is ______ $\quad$ positive

Immediately to the right of $x = 0.5$, say at 0.6,

y'' is **negative**

Hence the concavity changes and so there is a point of inflexion at $x = 0.5$.
When $x = 0.5$,

$y =$ **7.5**

In summary we have: $(-1,-6)$, minimum point; $(2, 21)$ maximum point; $(0.5, 7.5)$, point of inflexion.

Exercises

1 Determine the position of all points of inflexion of the following functions:

(a) $y = \frac{x^3}{6} - x^2$

(b) $y = 1 + 2x^2 - \frac{x^3}{6}$

(c) $y = \frac{x^4}{24} - \frac{x^3}{6} + x + 1$

(d) $y = \frac{x^4}{12} - \frac{x^2}{2} - x + 1$

(e) $y = x^4$

2 Locate all maximum points, minimum points and points of inflexion of the following functions:

(a) $y = \frac{x^3}{3} - 3x^2 + 5x + 1$

(b) $y = -x^5$

(c) $y = x^{1/3}$

Solutions to exercises

1 (a) $\left(2, -\frac{8}{3}\right)$ (b) $\left(4, \frac{67}{3}\right)$ (c) $(0, 1)$, $\left(2, \frac{7}{3}\right)$
(d) $\left(-1, \frac{19}{12}\right)$, $\left(1, -\frac{5}{12}\right)$
(e) no inflexion points

2 (a) $\left(1, \frac{10}{3}\right)$ maximum; $\left(5, -\frac{22}{3}\right)$ minimum; $(3,-2)$ inflexion
(b) $(0, 0)$ inflexion
(c) $(0, 0)$ inflexion

End of block exercises

1 State when each of the following functions are concave up and when they are concave down:

(a) $y = x^2$

(b) $y = x^3$

(c) $y = \frac{x^3}{6} - x^2$

(d) $y = \frac{x^2}{2} + \frac{x^3}{6}$

2 Find all maximum points, minimum points and points of inflexion of the following functions:

(a) $y = 1 + 4x - \frac{3x^2}{2}$

(b) $y = \frac{x^3}{3} + x^2 - 3x + 7$

(c) $y = \frac{2x^3}{3} - \frac{x^2}{2} - x + 6$

(d) $y = 1 + 4x - \frac{3x^2}{2} - \frac{x^3}{3}$

(e) $y = \frac{x^4}{4} - \frac{x^2}{2} + 2$

Solutions to exercises

1 (a) always concave up
(b) concave up on $(0, \infty)$; concave down on $(-\infty, 0)$
(c) concave down on $(-\infty, 2)$; concave up on $(2, \infty)$
(d) concave down on $(-\infty, -1)$; concave up on $(-1, \infty)$

2 (a) $\left(\frac{4}{3}, \frac{11}{3}\right)$ maximum
(b) $\left(1, \frac{16}{3}\right)$ minimum, $(-3, 16)$ maximum, $\left(-1, \frac{32}{3}\right)$ inflexion
(c) $\left(1, \frac{31}{6}\right)$ minimum, $\left(-\frac{1}{2}, \frac{151}{24}\right)$ maximum, $\left(\frac{1}{4}, \frac{275}{48}\right)$ inflexion
(d) $\left(-4, -\frac{53}{3}\right)$ minimum, $\left(1, \frac{19}{6}\right)$ maximum, $\left(-\frac{3}{2}, -\frac{29}{4}\right)$ inflexion
(e) $\left(1, \frac{7}{4}\right)$ minimum, $\left(-1, \frac{7}{4}\right)$ minimum, $(0, 2)$ maximum, $\left(-\frac{1}{\sqrt{3}}, \frac{67}{36}\right)$ inflexion, $\left(\frac{1}{3}, \frac{67}{36}\right)$ inflexion

End of chapter exercises

1 Find $\frac{dy}{dx}$ where y is given by
(a) x^3e^{2x} (b) $-3\sin 2x\cos 5x$ (c) $(x^2+1)\,e^{-x}$
(d) $\sin x\sin 2x\sin 3x$ (e) $x\tan 3x$

2 Find y' where y is given by
(a) $\dfrac{x^2+1}{2x+3}$ (b) $\dfrac{\cos 2t}{\sin 3t}$ (c) $\dfrac{r^3}{3e^{2r}}$
(d) $\dfrac{v+\sin v}{1+e^v}$ (e) $\dfrac{\sqrt{x}}{x+1}$

3 Find $\frac{dy}{dx}$ when $x = 1$ where y is defined by
(a) $\dfrac{x\cos x}{\sin x}$ (b) $\dfrac{x^2+1}{xe^x}$ (c) $\dfrac{\sin x\cos 2x}{x^2}$
(d) $\dfrac{1}{x\sin x}$ (e) $\dfrac{4\tan x}{e^x\sin x}$

4 Find the derivative of the following functions:
(a) $y = e^{2x}x^3\sin 3x\cos 2x$
(b) $y = (x+\sin x)^7$
(c) $H = \ln(t^2+3t-9)$
(d) $V(r) = \dfrac{1}{\ln r}$
(e) $M(b) = \ln b + \ln(b+1)$

5 Use logarithmic differentiation to differentiate

$$y = x^x$$

6 Find $\frac{dy}{dx}$ given
(a) $x(t) = t^2+3$, $y(t) = 2t^2+t+1$
(b) $x(t) = t^2$, $y(t) = t^3+k$, k constant
(c) $x(t) = \dfrac{1}{t}$, $y(t) = \sin t$
(d) $x(t) = 2e^t$, $y(t) = te^t$
(e) $x(t) = \sqrt{t}$, $y(t) = \sqrt{2t+1}$

7 Find $\frac{dy}{dx}$ given
(a) $x^2+x^3+y^2-y^3 = 1$
(b) $2x^2-y^2+3xy-7x-10y = 0$
(c) $xy^2+\dfrac{y}{x} = e^x$
(d) $\ln(xy)-\sqrt{x} = \sqrt{y}$
(e) $x\sin y + y^2\cos 2x = y$

8 Find $\frac{dy}{dx}$ given

$\ln(x+y) = k$, k constant.

9 Find y' given $(x^2-y^3)^6 = e^{xy}$.

10 Find $\frac{d^2y}{dx^2}$ given $y = e^{(x^2)}$.

11 Find the equation of the tangent to $y = 3x^3 - x$ where $x = 1$.

12 Find the equation of the normal to $y = \ln x$ where $x = 2$.

13 Find the equation of the tangent to $y = xe^x$ where $x = 1$.

14 Find the equation of the tangent to $y = \dfrac{1}{x^2}$ where $x = -1$.

15 State the range of values of x for which each of the following functions is (i) concave up (ii) concave down:

(a) $y = \dfrac{x^3}{6} - \dfrac{5x^2}{2} + 3x - 9$

(b) $y = 3 + x + \dfrac{x^2}{2} - \dfrac{x^4}{12}$

(c) $y = e^x - 100x - 100$

(d) $y = (x - 1)^4$

(e) $y = \dfrac{x^2}{2}\ln x - \dfrac{x^2}{4}$

16 Locate all maximum points, minimum points and points of inflexion of

$$y = \frac{2x^3}{3} - \frac{5x^2}{2} + 1$$

17 Locate all maximum points, minimum points and points of inflexion of

$$y = x^2e^x$$

Solutions to exercises

1 (a) $x^2e^{2x}(3 + 2x)$
(b) $15 \sin 2x \sin 5x - 6 \cos 2x \cos 5x$
(c) $-e^{-x}(x - 1)^2$
(d) $\cos x \sin 2x \sin 3x + 2 \sin x \cos 2x \sin 3x + 3 \sin x \sin 2x \cos 3x$
(e) $\tan 3x + 3x \sec^2 3x$

2 (a) $\dfrac{2x^2 + 6x - 2}{(2x + 3)^2}$

(b) $-\dfrac{(2 \sin 2t \sin 3t + 3 \cos 2t \cos 3t)}{\sin^2 3t}$

(c) $\dfrac{r^2}{3}\left(\dfrac{3 - 2r}{e^{2r}}\right)$

(d) $\dfrac{(1 + e^v)(1 + \cos v) - (v + \sin v)e^v}{(1 + e^v)^2}$

(e) $\dfrac{1}{2(x + 1)^2}\left(\dfrac{1 - x}{\sqrt{x}}\right)$

3 (a) -0.7702 (b) -0.7358 (c) -1.0548 (d) -1.9515 (e) 1.5181

4 (a) $x^2e^{2x}\,[2x \sin 3x \cos 2x + 3 \sin 3x \cos 2x + 3x \cos 3x \cos 2x - 2x \sin 3x \sin 2x]$

(b) $7(x + \sin x)^6(1 + \cos x)$

(c) $\dfrac{2t + 3}{t^2 + 3t - 9}$

(d) $-\dfrac{1}{r(\ln r)^2}$ (e) $\dfrac{1}{b} + \dfrac{1}{b + 1}$

5 $x^x(\ln x + 1)$

6 (a) $\dfrac{4t + 1}{2t}$ (b) $\dfrac{3t}{2}$ (c) $-t^2\cos t$

(d) $\dfrac{1 + t}{2}$ (e) $2\sqrt{\dfrac{t}{2t + 1}}$

7 (a) $\dfrac{2x + 3x^2}{3y^2 - 2y}$ (b) $\dfrac{4x + 3y - 7}{2y - 3x + 10}$

(c) $\dfrac{x^2e^x + y - x^2y^2}{x(2x^2y + 1)}$ (d) $\dfrac{y(\sqrt{x} - 2)}{x(2 - \sqrt{y})}$

(e) $\dfrac{2y^2 \sin 2x - \sin y}{x \cos y + 2y \cos 2x - 1}$

8 -1

9 $\dfrac{12x(x^2 - y^3)^5 - ye^{xy}}{18y^2(x^2 - y^3)^5 + xe^{xy}}$

10 $2e^{(x^2)}(1 + 2x^2)$

11 $y = 8x - 6$

12 $y = -2x + 4.6931$

13 $y = e(2x - 1)$

14 $y = 2x + 3$

15 (a) concave up on $x > 5$; concave down on $x < 5$
(b) concave up on $-1 < x < 1$; concave down on $x > 1$ and $x < -1$
(c) concave up for all values of x
(d) concave up for all values of x except $x = 1$
(e) concave up on $x > e^{-1}$; concave down on $x < e^{-1}$

16 (0, 1) maximum; $\left(\frac{5}{2}, -\frac{101}{24}\right)$ minimum; $\left(\frac{5}{4}, -\frac{77}{48}\right)$ point of inflexion

17 (0, 0) minimum; (−2, 0.5413) maximum; (−3.4142, 0.3835) and (−0.5858, 0.1910) points of inflexion

Integration

Chapter 17

When a function, $f(x)$, is known, we can differentiate it to obtain the derivative, $\frac{df}{dx}$. The reverse process is to obtain $f(x)$ from knowledge of its derivative. This process is called **integration.**

However, integration is much more than simply differentiation in reverse. It can be applied to finding areas bounded by curves. Such areas can have various physical interpretations. For example, the area underneath a graph of the velocity of an object against time represents the distance travelled by the object. The area under a graph of current flow into a capacitor against time represents the total charge stored by the capacitor. Clearly, there are many applications where it is required to calculate quantities like these, and this is why a knowledge of integration is important for the engineer.

It is also necessary to regard integration as a process of adding up, or *summation*. Often a physical quantity can be obtained by summing lots of small contributions or elements. For example, the position of the centre of mass of a solid body can be found by adding the contributions from all the small parts of which the body is composed. You will see how this is done using integration in Chapter 18.

In this chapter we lay the foundations, and explain a wide variety of techniques that are necessary to integrate the range of functions commonly met in engineering applications.

Modern software packages enable the easy integration of complicated functions. This is illustrated in Block 4.

Chapter 17 contents

BLOCK 1

Integration as differentiation in reverse

1.1 Introduction

The topic of **integration** can be approached in several different ways. Perhaps the simplest way of introducing it is to think of it as differentiation in reverse. In some applications we shall know the derivative of a function, but not the function from which it was derived. This is why we need knowledge of integration.

In this block we give a look-up table that you can use to integrate a wide range of functions, and we provide lots of opportunities for you to practise using it. Then rules are given that allow you to integrate a wider range of functions. In particular you will be able to integrate sums, differences and constant multiples of functions.

1.2 Differentiation in reverse

Suppose we differentiate the function $y = x^2$. We obtain $\frac{dy}{dx} = 2x$. Integration reverses this process, and we say that the integral of $2x$ is x^2. Pictorially we can regard this as shown in Figure 1.1.

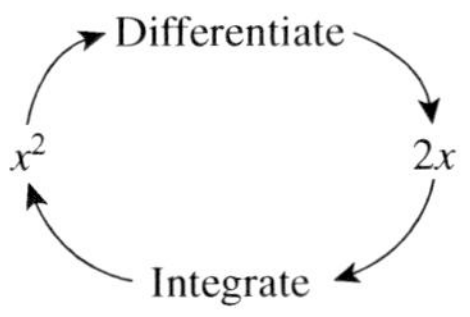

Figure 1.1 Integration can be thought of as differentiation in reverse.

The situation is just a little more complicated because there are lots of functions we can differentiate to give $2x$. Here are some of them:

$$x^2 + 4, \quad x^2 - 15, \quad x^2 + 0.5$$

Example 1.1

Write down some more functions that have derivative $2x$.

Solution

e.g. $x^2 - 7, x^2 + 0.1$

All these functions have the same derivative, $2x$, because when we differentiate the constant term we obtain zero. Consequently, when we reverse the process, we have no idea what the original constant term might have been. Because of this we include in our answer an unknown constant, c say, called the **constant of integration**. We state that the integral of $2x$ is $x^2 + c$. There is nothing special about the letter c. We might use K for example, but we avoid using letters from the end of the alphabet like x, y and z, which are used for variables.

The symbol for integration is $\int$, known as an **integral sign**. Formally we write,

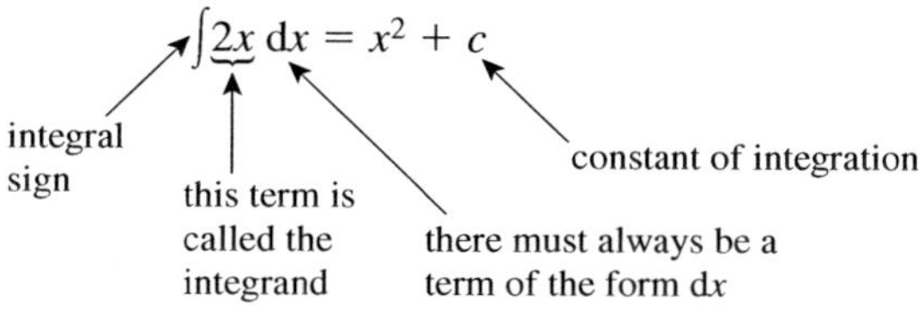

Note that along with the integral sign there is a term of the form dx, which must always be written, and which indicates the name of the variable involved, in this case x. The term dx must not be interpreted as a product of d and x. Rather it is a notation and as such you should think of dx as a single quantity.

We say that $2x$ is integrated *with respect to* x to give $x^2 + c$. The function being integrated is called the **integrand**. Technically, integrals of this sort are called **indefinite integrals**, to distinguish them from definite integrals, which are dealt with subsequently. When you find an indefinite integral your answer should always contain a constant of integration.

Exercises

1 (a) Write down the derivatives of each of

$$x^3, \quad x^3 + 17, \quad x^3 - 21$$

(b) Deduce that $\int 3x^2\,\mathrm{d}x = x^3 + c$.

2 Explain what is meant by the term 'integrand'.

3 Explain why, when finding indefinite integrals, a constant of integration is needed.

Solutions to exercises

1 (a) All have derivative $3x^2$.

1.3 A table of integrals

We could use a table of derivatives to find integrals, but the more common ones are usually found in a 'table of integrals' such as that shown in Table 1.1. You could check many of the entries in this table using your knowledge of differentiation. Try checking some of these for yourself.

When dealing with the trigonometrical functions the variable x must always be measured in radians and not degrees. Note that the fourth entry for integrating a power of x is valid whether n is positive, negative or fractional, but not when $n = -1$. If $n = -1$ use the fifth entry in the table. Various other conditions are detailed in the third column.

Example 1.2

(a) Use the table of integrals to find $\int x^7\,\mathrm{d}x$.
(b) Check the result by differentiating the answer.

Solution

(a) From the table note that

$$\int x^n\,\mathrm{d}x = \frac{x^{n+1}}{n+1} + c$$

In words, this states that to integrate a power of x, increase the power by one, and divide the result by the new power. You will find it helpful to remember this rule. With $n = 7$ we find

$$\int x^7\,\mathrm{d}x = \frac{x^8}{8} + c$$

(b) The answer can be differentiated as a check.

$$\begin{aligned}\frac{\mathrm{d}}{\mathrm{d}x}\left(\frac{x^8}{8} + c\right) &= \frac{1}{8}\frac{\mathrm{d}}{\mathrm{d}x}x^8\\ &= \frac{1}{8} \times 8x^7\\ &= x^7\end{aligned}$$

The answer has been verified.

Example 1.3

Find $\int \cos 5x\,\mathrm{d}x$.

Solution

From the table note that

$$\int \cos kx\,\mathrm{d}x = \frac{\sin kx}{k} + c$$

With $k = 5$ we find

$$\int \cos 5x\,\mathrm{d}x = \frac{\sin 5x}{5} + c$$

Check this result for yourself by differentiating it.

Table 1.1
Table of integrals.

Function $f(x)$	Indefinite integral $\int f(x)\,dx$	
constant, k	$kx + c$	
x	$\frac{x^2}{2} + c$	
x^2	$\frac{x^3}{3} + c$	
x^n	$\frac{x^{n+1}}{n+1} + c$	$n \neq -1$
$x^{-1} = \frac{1}{x}$	$\ln\lvert x\rvert + c$	
$\sin x$	$-\cos x + c$	
$\cos x$	$\sin x + c$	
$\sin kx$	$\frac{-\cos kx}{k} + c$	
$\cos kx$	$\frac{\sin kx}{k} + c$	
$\tan kx$	$\frac{1}{k}\ln\lvert\sec kx\rvert + c$	
$\sec kx$	$\frac{1}{k}\ln\lvert\sec kx + \tan kx\rvert + c$	
e^x	$e^x + c$	
e^{-x}	$-e^{-x} + c$	
e^{kx}	$\frac{e^{kx}}{k} + c$	
$\cosh kx$	$\frac{1}{k}\sinh kx + c$	
$\sinh kx$	$\frac{1}{k}\cosh kx + c$	
$\frac{1}{x^2 + a^2}$	$\frac{1}{a}\tan^{-1}\frac{x}{a} + c$	$a > 0$
$\frac{1}{x^2 - a^2}$	$\frac{1}{2a}\ln\frac{x-a}{x+a} + c$	$\lvert x\rvert > a > 0$
$\frac{1}{a^2 - x^2}$	$\frac{1}{2a}\ln\frac{a+x}{a-x} + c$	$\lvert x\rvert < a$
$\frac{1}{\sqrt{x^2 + a^2}}$	$\sinh^{-1}\left(\frac{x}{a}\right) + c$	$a > 0$
$\frac{1}{\sqrt{x^2 - a^2}}$	$\cosh^{-1}\left(\frac{x}{a}\right) + c$	$x \geq a > 0$
$\frac{1}{\sqrt{x^2 + k}}$	$\ln(x + \sqrt{x^2 + k}) + c$	
$\frac{1}{\sqrt{a^2 - x^2}}$	$\sin^{-1}\left(\frac{x}{a}\right) + c$	$-a \leq x \leq a$

In the table the independent variable is always given as x. However, with a little imagination you will be able to use it when other independent variables are involved.

Example 1.4

Find $\int \cos 5t \, dt$.

Solution

We integrated $\cos 5x$ in the previous example. Now the independent variable is t, so simply use the table and read every x as a t. With $k = 5$ we find

$$\int \cos 5t \, dt = \frac{\sin 5t}{5} + c$$

It follows immediately that, for example,

$$\int \cos 5\omega \, d\omega = \frac{\sin 5\omega}{5} + c, \quad \int \cos 5u \, du = \frac{\sin 5u}{5} + c$$

and so on.

Example 1.5

Find $\int \sin \frac{x}{2} \, dx$.

Solution

Note that $\frac{x}{2}$ is equivalent to $\frac{1}{2}x$. Use the table of integrals with $k = \frac{1}{2}$.

$$\int \sin \frac{x}{2} \, dx =$$

$$= -\frac{\cos \frac{x}{2}}{\frac{1}{2}} + c = -2\cos \frac{x}{2} + c$$

Example 1.6

Find $\int \sin \frac{2\pi t}{T} \, dt$ where T is a constant.

Solution

With respect to which variable is the integration being carried out?

t

The quantity $\frac{2\pi}{T}$ is a constant. Perform the integration:

$$\int \sin \frac{2\pi t}{T} \, dt =$$

$$= -\frac{\cos \frac{2\pi t}{T}}{\frac{2\pi}{T}} + c = -\frac{T}{2\pi} \cos \frac{2\pi t}{T} + c$$

Example 1.7

Find $\int 12\,\mathrm{d}x$.

Solution

In this example we are integrating a constant, 12. Using the table we find

$$\int 12\,\mathrm{d}x = 12x + c$$

Note that $\int 12\,\mathrm{d}t$ would be $12t + c$ and so on. This shows the importance of including the term $\mathrm{d}x$ or $\mathrm{d}t$ in the integral.

Example 1.8

Find $\int \mathrm{d}x$.

Solution

This example looks a little different from the earlier ones. But if we think of $\mathrm{d}x$ as $1\,\mathrm{d}x$ then we are integrating a constant, 1. Using the table we find

$$\int 1\,\mathrm{d}x = 1x + c \quad \text{or simply} \quad x + c$$

Note that $\int \mathrm{d}t$ would be $t + c$.

Example 1.9

Find $\int \mathrm{e}^{-3x}\,\mathrm{d}x$.

Solution

Use the appropriate entry in the table with $k = -3$:

$$\int \mathrm{e}^{-3x}\,\mathrm{d}x = \frac{\mathrm{e}^{-3x}}{-3} + c = -\frac{1}{3}\mathrm{e}^{-3x} + c$$

Example 1.10

Look for an entry in the table of integrals that will enable you to calculate

$$\int \frac{1}{\sqrt{9 - t^2}}\,\mathrm{d}t$$

Solution

Write down the appropriate entry.

$$\int \frac{1}{\sqrt{a^2 - x^2}}\,\mathrm{d}x = \sin^{-1}\left(\frac{x}{a}\right) + c$$

Select an appropriate value for the constant a and hence find the integral.

Take $a = 3$, so that $a^2 = 9$. $\displaystyle\int \frac{1}{\sqrt{9 - t^2}}\,\mathrm{d}t = \sin^{-1}\left(\frac{t}{3}\right) + c$

Exercises

1 Integrate each of the following functions with respect to x:
(a) x^9 (b) $x^{1/2}$ (c) x^{-3} (d) $\frac{1}{x^4}$ (e) 4 (f) $\sqrt{x}$
(g) e^{4x} (h) $\cos\frac{x}{2}$ (i) $\cos \pi x$

2 Find
(a) $\int t^2\,dt$ (b) $\int 6\,dt$ (c) $\int \sin 3t\,dt$
(d) $\int e^{7t}\,dt$ (e) $\int \cos\frac{2\pi t}{T}\,dt$ (f) $\int \frac{dz}{z}$

3 Find $\int e^t\,dt$.

4 Find
(a) $\int \frac{1}{x^2+25}\,dx$ (b) $\int \frac{1}{\sqrt{t^2-4}}\,dt$

5 Find
(a) $\int \sin\omega\,d\omega$
(b) $\int \cos 3t\,dt$
(c) $\int \tan\frac{1}{3}x\,dx$
(d) $\int \tan\frac{x}{3}dx$
(e) $\int \sinh 0.3x\,dx$
(f) $\int \cos 0.01\pi x\,dx$
(g) $\int \cosh 0.01t\,dt$
(h) $\int x^{7/2}\,dx$
(i) $\int \frac{1}{\sqrt[3]{x}}\,dx$
(j) $\int x^{1/4}\,dx$
(k) $\int \sqrt[5]{t}\,dt$
(l) $\int e^{-0.7t}\,dt$
(m) $\int \frac{1}{64-x^2}\,dx$
(n) $\int \frac{1}{\sqrt{64-x^2}}\,dx$
(o) $\int \frac{1}{\sqrt{x^2+8}}\,dx$

6 Find
(a) $\frac{1}{5}\int \cos\frac{n\pi t}{5}\,dt$, (b) $\frac{1}{5}\int \sin\frac{n\pi t}{5}\,dt$.

Solutions to exercises

1 (a) $\frac{x^{10}}{10}+c$ (b) $\frac{2x^{3/2}}{3}+c$ (c) $-\frac{1}{2}x^{-2}+c$
(d) $-\frac{1}{3}x^{-3}+c$ (e) $4x+c$ (f) same as (b)
(g) $\frac{e^{4x}}{4}+c$ (h) $2\sin\frac{x}{2}+c$ (i) $\frac{\sin\pi x}{\pi}+c$

2 (a) $\frac{t^3}{3}+c$ (b) $6t+c$ (c) $-\frac{\cos 3t}{3}+c$
(d) $\frac{e^{7t}}{7}+c$ (e) $\frac{T}{2\pi}\sin\frac{2\pi t}{T}+c$ (f) $\ln|z|+c$

3 e^t+c

4 (a) $\frac{1}{5}\tan^{-1}\left(\frac{x}{5}\right)+c$ (b) $\cosh^{-1}\left(\frac{t}{2}\right)+c$

5 (a) $-\cos\omega+c$ (b) $\frac{1}{3}\sin 3t+c$
(c) $3\ln|\sec\frac{x}{3}|+c$ (d) $3\ln|\sec\frac{x}{3}|+c$
(e) $\frac{10}{3}\cosh 0.3x+c$ (f) $\frac{100}{\pi}\sin 0.01\pi x+c$
(g) $100\sinh 0.01t+c$ (h) $\frac{2}{9}x^{9/2}+c$
(i) $\frac{3}{2}x^{2/3}+c$ (j) $\frac{4}{5}x^{5/4}+c$ (k) $\frac{5}{6}t^{6/5}+c$
(l) $-1.429e^{-0.7t}+c$ (m) $\frac{1}{16}\ln\frac{8+x}{8-x}+c$
(n) $\sin^{-1}\frac{x}{8}+c$ (o) $\ln(x+\sqrt{x^2+8})+c$

6 (a) $\frac{1}{n\pi}\sin\frac{n\pi t}{5}+c$ (b) $-\frac{1}{n\pi}\cos\frac{n\pi t}{5}+c$

1.4 Some rules of integration

To enable us to find integrals of a wider range of functions than those normally given in a table of integrals we can make use of the following rules.

The integral of $k\,f(x)$ where k is a constant

A constant factor in an integral can be moved outside the integral sign as follows

Key point

The integral of a constant multiple of a function

$$\int k\,f(x)\,\mathrm{d}x = k\int f(x)\,\mathrm{d}x$$

Example 1.11

Find $\int 11x^2\,\mathrm{d}x$.

Solution

$$\begin{aligned}\int 11x^2\,\mathrm{d}x &= 11\int x^2\,\mathrm{d}x\\ &= 11\left(\frac{x^3}{3}+c\right)\\ &= \frac{11x^3}{3}+K\end{aligned}$$

where K is a constant.

Example 1.12

Find $\int -5\cos x\,\mathrm{d}x$.

Solution

$$\begin{aligned}\int -5\cos x\,\mathrm{d}x &= -5\int \cos x\,\mathrm{d}x\\ &= -5\,(\sin x + c)\\ &= -5\sin x + K\end{aligned}$$

where K is a constant.

Example 1.13

Find $\displaystyle\int \frac{14}{1+s^2}\,\mathrm{d}s$.

Solution

Use the result in the previous key point to extract the constant factor 14. Then use the table to complete the solution.

$$\int \frac{14}{1+s^2}\,\mathrm{d}s =$$

$$14\int \frac{1}{1+s^2}\,\mathrm{d}s = 14\tan^{-1} s + c$$

Example 1.14
Find $\int 2\pi m r^3 \, \mathrm{d}r$.

Solution
In this example, integration is with respect to which variable?

r

The 2, π and m are all constant factors and can be written in front of the integral sign. Thus

$$\int 2\pi m r^3 \, \mathrm{d}r = 2\pi m \int r^3 \, \mathrm{d}r$$
$$= 2\pi m \left(\frac{r^4}{4}\right) + c$$
$$= \frac{\pi m r^4}{2} + c$$

The integral of $f(x) \pm g(x)$

When we wish to integrate the sum or difference of two functions, we integrate each term separately as follows:

Key point

The integral of a sum or difference of two functions

$$\int [f(x) \pm g(x)] \, \mathrm{d}x = \int f(x) \, \mathrm{d}x \pm \int g(x) \, \mathrm{d}x$$

Example 1.15
Find $\int (x^3 + \sin x) \, \mathrm{d}x$.

Solution

$$\int (x^3 + \sin x) \, \mathrm{d}x = \int x^3 \, \mathrm{d}x + \int \sin x \, \mathrm{d}x$$
$$= \frac{x^4}{4} - \cos x + c$$

Note that only a single constant of integration is needed.

Example 1.16
Find $\int 3t^4 + \sqrt{t} \, \mathrm{d}t$.

Solution
You will need to use both of the rules to deal with this integral.

$$\frac{3t^5}{5} + \frac{2t^{3/2}}{3} + c$$

Example 1.17

The hyperbolic sine and cosine functions, sinh x and cosh x, are defined as follows:

$$\sinh x = \frac{e^x - e^{-x}}{2} \qquad \cosh x = \frac{e^x + e^{-x}}{2}$$

Note that they are simply combinations of the exponential functions e^x and e^{-x}. Find $\int \sinh x\,dx$ and $\int \cosh x\,dx$.

Solution

$$\int \sinh x\,dx = \int \left(\frac{e^x - e^{-x}}{2}\right) dx$$

$$= \qquad\qquad = \frac{1}{2}(e^x + e^{-x}) + c = \cosh x + c$$

$$\int \cosh x\,dx = \int \left(\frac{e^x + e^{-x}}{2}\right) dx$$

$$= \qquad\qquad = \sinh x + c$$

Further rules for finding more complicated integrals are dealt with in subsequent blocks. However, it is important that you are aware at this stage that the integral of a product of two functions is not the product of two separate integrals:

$$\int f(x) \times g(x)\,dx \neq \int f(x)\,dx \times \int g(x)\,dx$$

You will learn how to integrate products in Block 5 on integration by parts.

Exercises

1. Find $\int 2x - e^x\,dx$.
2. Find $\int 3e^{2x}\,dx$.
3. Find $\displaystyle\int \frac{x + \cos 2x}{3}\,dx$.
4. Find $\int 7x^{-2}\,dx$.
5. Find $\int (x + 3)^2\,dx$ (be careful!).
6. Find $\int 3 \tan 2x + 2 \sin 3x\,dx$.
7. Find $\displaystyle\int \frac{8}{x^2 + 16}\,dx$.
8. Find $\int 3 \cos n\pi x\,dx$.
9. Find $\int 0.5 \sin n\pi x\,dx$.
10. Find $\displaystyle\int \frac{1}{2} \sin \frac{2\pi t}{T}\,dt$.
11. Find $\displaystyle\int \frac{\sin x + \cos x}{2}\,dx$.

Solutions to exercises

1 $x^2 - e^x + c$

2 $\frac{3e^{2x}}{2} + c$

3 $\frac{x^2}{6} + \frac{\sin 2x}{6} + c$

4 $-\frac{7}{x} + c$

5 $\frac{x^3}{3} + 3x^2 + 9x + c$

6 $\frac{3}{2}\ln|\sec 2x| - \frac{2}{3}\cos 3x + c$

7 $2\tan^{-1}\left(\frac{x}{4}\right) + c$

8 $\frac{3}{n\pi}\sin n\pi x + c$

9 $-\frac{0.5}{n\pi}\cos n\pi x + c$

10 $-\frac{T}{4\pi}\cos\frac{2\pi t}{T} + c$

11 $\frac{-\cos x + \sin x}{2} + c$

End of block exercises

1 Integrate each of the following functions with respect to x:
(a) x^2 (b) x^{17} (c) 6 (d) $\sin 4x$ (e) e^{8x}

2 Integrate each of the following functions with respect to t:
(a) t^3 (b) 7 (c) e^{-3t} (d) e^{-t} (e) $\frac{1}{t}$

3 Find the following integrals:
(a) $\int 3t\,dt$ (b) $\int 3t^2\,dt$ (c) $\int 2t^4\,dt$
(d) $\int t + t^2\,dt$

4 Find the following integrals:
(a) $\int x^2 + 4x + 8\,dx$ (b) $\int 2x^2 - 4x + 7\,dx$
(c) $\int 6x^2 - x + 2\,dx$

5 Find $\int \sqrt{t} + \frac{1}{t^2}\,dt$.

6 Find $\int e^{-st}\,dt$ where s is a number.

7 Find $\int \frac{1}{s^2 + 0.5}\,ds$.

8 Find $\int \frac{1}{\sqrt{4 + t^2}}\,dt$.

9 Find $\int \frac{1}{\sqrt{25 - x^2}}\,dx$.

10 Find $\int \tan\frac{x}{5}\,dx$.

11 Find $\int \sin 100\pi t + \cos 100\pi t\,dt$.

12 Find $\int \cos(m + n)t\,dt$.

13 Find $\int mbx^2\,dx$.

14 Find (a) $\int \frac{1}{2}\theta\,d\theta$, (b) $\int 4\cos\frac{\theta}{2}\,d\theta$,
(c) $\int \sqrt{2}\,d\theta$.

Solutions to exercises

1 (a) $\frac{x^3}{3} + c$ (b) $\frac{x^{18}}{18} + c$ (c) $6x + c$

(d) $-\frac{\cos 4x}{4} + c$ (e) $\frac{e^{8x}}{8} + c$

2 (a) $\frac{t^4}{4} + c$ (b) $7t + c$ (c) $-\frac{e^{-3t}}{3} + c$

(d) $-e^{-t} + c$ (e) $\ln|t| + c$

3 (a) $\frac{3t^2}{2} + c$ (b) $t^3 + c$

(c) $\frac{2t^5}{5} + c$ (d) $\frac{t^2}{2} + \frac{t^3}{3} + c$

4 (a) $\frac{x^3}{3} + 2x^2 + 8x + c$

(b) $\frac{2x^3}{3} - 2x^2 + 7x + c$

(c) $2x^3 - \frac{x^2}{2} + 2x + c$

5 $\frac{2t^{3/2}}{3} - \frac{1}{t} + c$

6 $-\frac{e^{-st}}{s} + c$

7 $\sqrt{2}\tan^{-1}(s\sqrt{2}) + c$

8 $\sinh^{-1}\left(\frac{t}{2}\right) + c$

9 $\sin^{-1}\left(\frac{x}{5}\right) + c$

10 $5\ln|\sec\frac{x}{5}| + c$

11 $-\frac{\cos 100\pi t}{100\pi} + \frac{\sin 100\pi t}{100\pi} + c$

12 $\frac{\sin(m+n)t}{(m+n)} + c$

13 $\frac{mbx^3}{3} + c$

14 (a) $\frac{\theta^2}{4} + c$ (b) $8\sin\frac{\theta}{2} + c$ (c) $\sqrt{2}\theta + c$

BLOCK 2 Definite integrals

2.1 Introduction

When integration was introduced as the reverse of differentiation in Block 1, the integrals you dealt with were *indefinite integrals*. The result of finding an indefinite integral is usually a function plus a constant of integration. In this block we introduce *definite integrals*, so called because the result will be a definite answer, usually a number, with no constant of integration. Definite integrals have many applications, for example in finding areas bounded by curves, and finding volumes of solids. Applications such as these will be described in later blocks.

2.2 Evaluating definite integrals

Definite integrals can be recognised by numbers written to the upper and lower right of the integral sign. The quantity

$$\int_a^b f(x)\,\mathrm{d}x$$

is called the definite integral of $f(x)$ from a to b. The numbers a and b are known as the **lower** and **upper limits** of the integral. When you evaluate a definite integral the result will usually be a number. To see how to evaluate a definite integral consider the following example.

Example 2.1

Find $\int_1^4 x^2\,\mathrm{d}x$.

Solution

First of all the integration of x^2 is performed in the normal way. However, to show we are dealing with a definite integral, the result is usually enclosed in square brackets and the limits of integration are written on the right bracket:

$$\int x^2\,\mathrm{d}x = \frac{x^3}{3} + c \quad \text{so that} \quad \int_1^4 x^2\,\mathrm{d}x = \left[\frac{x^3}{3} + c\right]_1^4$$

You should always use this convention. Then, the quantity in the square brackets is evaluated, first by letting x equal the value at the upper limit, then by letting x equal the value at the lower limit, and the difference between the resulting values is found:

$$\left[\frac{x^3}{3} + c\right]_1^4 = \text{(evaluate when } x \text{ equals upper limit)}$$

$$- \text{(evaluate when } x \text{ equals lower limit)}$$

$$= \left(\frac{4^3}{3} + c\right) - \left(\frac{1^3}{3} + c\right)$$

$$= \frac{64}{3} - \frac{1}{3}$$

$$= \frac{63}{3}$$

$$= 21$$

Note that the constants, c, cancel out. This will always happen, and so in future we can ignore them when we are evaluating definite integrals. So, the value of the definite integral $\int_1^4 x^2 \, dx$ is 21.

Example 2.2

Find $\int_0^{\pi/2} \cos x \, dx$.

Solution

Since $\int \cos x \, dx = \sin x + c$ then

$$\int_0^{\pi/2} \cos x \, dx = [\sin x]_0^{\pi/2}$$

$$= \sin\left(\frac{\pi}{2}\right) - \sin 0$$

$$= 1 - 0$$

$$= 1$$

Always remember that if you use a calculator to evaluate any trigonometrical functions, you must work in radian mode.

Example 2.3

Find $\int_1^2 (x^2 + 1) \, dx$.

Solution

First perform the integration:

$$\left[\frac{x^3}{3} + x\right]_1^2$$

Now insert the limits of integration, the upper limit first, and hence find the value of the integral.

$$\left(\frac{8}{3}+2\right)-\left(\frac{1}{3}+1\right)=\frac{10}{3} \text{ or } 3.333 \text{ (3 d.p.)}$$

Example 2.4

This exercise is very similar to the previous one. Note the limits of integration have been interchanged.

Find $\int_2^1 (x^2+1)\,\mathrm{d}x$.

Solution

$$-\frac{10}{3}$$

Note from these two exercises that interchanging the limits of integration changes the sign of the answer.

Key point

If you interchange the limits, you must introduce a minus sign.

$$\int_a^b f(x)\,\mathrm{d}x = -\int_b^a f(x)\,\mathrm{d}x$$

Example 2.5 The average value of a function

If a function $f(t)$ is defined on the interval $a \le t \le b$ then the **average value** of the function over the interval is defined to be

$$\text{average value} = \frac{\int_a^b f(t)\,\mathrm{d}t}{b-a}$$

The average value of a function is found by evaluating a definite integral.

Find the average value of the function $f(t) = t^2$ across the interval $2 \le t \le 5$.

Solution

Apply the formula for finding the average value:

$$\text{average value} = \frac{\int_2^5 t^2\,\mathrm{d}t}{5-2}$$

Complete the integration to find this average value.

$$\frac{1}{3}\left[\frac{t^3}{3}\right]_2^5 = 13$$

Exercises

1 Explain why a constant of integration is not needed when evaluating definite integrals.

2 Explain what happens to the value of a definite integral when the upper and lower limits are interchanged.

3 Evaluate

(a) $\int_0^1 x^2\,dx$ (b) $\int_2^3 \frac{1}{x^2}\,dx$

4 Evaluate $\int_1^2 e^x\,dx$.

5 Evaluate $\int_{-1}^1 (1 + t^2)\,dt$.

6 Find $\int_0^{\pi/3} \cos 2x\,dx$.

7 Find $\int_0^{\pi} \sin x\,dx$.

8 Find $\int_1^3 e^{2t}\,dt$.

9 Evaluate $\int_2^4 x^3\,dx$. Show that

$\int_2^4 x^3\,dx = -\int_4^2 x^3\,dx$.

10 Show that $\int_a^b \sin x\,dx = \int_a^b \sin t\,dt$.

11 Find $\int_0^k 2(kv^3 - v^4)\,dv$.

12 Find $\int_0^{0.001} 100\,dt$.

13 Find $100\int_0^{0.01} \sin 100\,n\pi t\,dt$.

14 Find the average value of the function $f(t) = \sin t$ across the interval $0 \le t \le \frac{\pi}{2}$.

15 Find $\int_0^1 \frac{1}{\sqrt{9 - 4t^2}}\,dt$.

16 Find $\int_0^a 2\pi m r^3\,dr$.

Solutions to exercises

3 (a) $\frac{1}{3}$ (b) $\frac{1}{6}$

4 $e^2 - e^1 = 4.671$

5 2.667

6 $\frac{\sqrt{3}}{4} = 0.4330$

7 2

8 198

9 60

11 $\frac{k^5}{10}$

12 0.1

13 $-\frac{1}{n\pi}(\cos n\pi - 1)$

14 $\frac{2}{\pi}$

15 0.365

16 $\frac{m\pi a^4}{2}$

2.3 Some integrals with infinite limits of integration

On occasions, and notably when dealing with Laplace and Fourier transforms, you will come across integrals in which one of the limits is infinite. We avoid a rigorous treatment of such cases here and instead give some commonly occurring examples.

Example 2.6

Find $\int_0^\infty \mathrm{e}^{-x}\,\mathrm{d}x$.

Solution

The integral is found in the normal way:

$$\int_0^\infty \mathrm{e}^{-x}\,\mathrm{d}x = \left[-\mathrm{e}^{-x}\right]_0^\infty$$

There is no difficulty in evaluating the square bracket at the lower limit. We obtain simply $-\mathrm{e}^{-0} = -1$. At the upper limit we must examine the behaviour of $-\mathrm{e}^{-x}$ as x gets infinitely large. This is where it is important that you are familiar with the graph of the exponential function. If you refer to the graph you will recognise that as x tends to infinity e^{-x} tends to zero. Consequently the contribution to the integral from the upper limit is zero. So

$$\begin{aligned}\int_0^\infty \mathrm{e}^{-x}\,\mathrm{d}x &= \left[-\mathrm{e}^{-x}\right]_0^\infty \\ &= (0) - (-\mathrm{e}^{-0}) \\ &= 1\end{aligned}$$

The value of $\int_0^\infty \mathrm{e}^{-x}\,\mathrm{d}x$ is 1.

Another way of achieving this result is as follows.

We change the infinite limit to a finite limit, b, say, and then examine the behaviour of the integral as b tends to infinity, written

$$\int_0^\infty \mathrm{e}^{-x}\,\mathrm{d}x = \lim_{b\to\infty} \int_0^b \mathrm{e}^{-x}\,\mathrm{d}x$$

So

$$\begin{aligned}\int_0^b \mathrm{e}^{-x}\,\mathrm{d}x &= \left[-\mathrm{e}^{-x}\right]_0^b \\ &= (-\mathrm{e}^{-b}) - (-\mathrm{e}^{-0}) \\ &= -\mathrm{e}^{-b} + 1\end{aligned}$$

Then as b tends to infinity $-\mathrm{e}^{-b}$ tends to zero, and the resulting integral has the value 1, as before.

Many integrals having infinite limits cannot be evaluated in a simple way like this, and many cannot be evaluated at all. Fortunately, most of the integrals you will meet will exhibit the sort of behaviour seen in the last example.

Exercises

1 Find $\int_1^{\infty} e^{-x}\,dx$.

2 Find $\int_0^{\infty} e^{-2x}\,dx$.

3 Find $\int_2^{\infty} e^{-3x}\,dx$.

4 Find $\int_{-\infty}^{0} e^{7x}\,dx$.

Solutions to exercises

1 e^{-1} or 0.368

2 $\frac{1}{2}$

3 $\frac{e^{-6}}{3} = 0.0008$ (4 d.p.)

4 $\frac{1}{7}$

End of block exercises

1 Find the value of the following integrals:
(a) $\int_1^2 x^2 + 1\,dx$ (b) $\int_3^4 x^2 + 1\,dx$
(c) $\int_0^{\pi/4} \sin x\,dx$ (d) $\int_{-1}^{1} \cos 2x\,dx$

2 Find the value of the following integrals:
(a) $\int_0^3 x^2 + 7x - 2\,dx$
(b) $\int_{-1}^{1} 2x^2 + x + 3\,dx$

3 Find $\int_1^3 e^t\,dt$.

4 Find $\displaystyle\int_a^b \frac{1}{r}\,dr$.

5 Show that $\int_a^b x^3\,dx = \int_a^b t^3\,dt$.

6 Find $\int_0^{0.1} 3 \tan 2x\,dx$.

7 Find $\int_{-1}^{0} e^{-2x} + e^{-3x}\,dx$.

8 Find $\int_{\omega_1}^{\omega_2} \sin \omega\,d\omega$.

9 Find $\displaystyle\frac{1}{\pi}\int_{-\pi}^{\pi} 1 + t\,dt$.

10 Find $\int_{-b/2}^{b/2} mbx^2\,dx$.

11 Find (a) $\displaystyle\int_0^{2\pi} \frac{\theta}{2}\,d\theta$, (b) $\displaystyle\int_0^{\pi/2} 4 \cos\frac{\theta}{2}\,d\theta$
(c) $\int_0^{\pi/2} \sqrt{2}\,d\theta$.

Solutions to exercises

1 (a) $\frac{10}{3}$ (b) $\frac{40}{3}$ (c) 0.293 (d) 0.909

2 (a) 34.5 (b) $\frac{22}{3}$

3 17.367

4 $\ln b - \ln a = \ln\left(\frac{b}{a}\right)$

6 0.030

7 9.556

8 $\cos\omega_1 - \cos\omega_2$

9 2

10 $\dfrac{b^4 m}{12}$

11 (a) π^2 (b) $4\sqrt{2}$ (c) $\dfrac{\pi\sqrt{2}}{2}$

BLOCK 3 The area bounded by a curve

3.1 Introduction

One of the important applications of integration is to find the area bounded by a curve. Often such an area can have a physical significance, such as the work done by a motor, or the distance travelled by a vehicle. In this block we explain how such an area is calculated.

3.2 The area bounded by a curve lying above the x axis

Consider the graph of the function $y(x)$ shown in Figure 3.1. Suppose we are interested in calculating the area underneath the graph and above the x axis, between the points where $x = a$ and $x = b$. When such an area lies entirely above the x axis, as is clearly the case in Figure 3.1, this area is given by the definite integral

$$\int_a^b y(x)\,\mathrm{d}x$$

Key point

The area under the curve $y(x)$, between $x = a$ and $x = b$, is given by

$$\text{area} = \int_a^b y(x)\,\mathrm{d}x$$

when the curve lies entirely above the x axis between a and b.

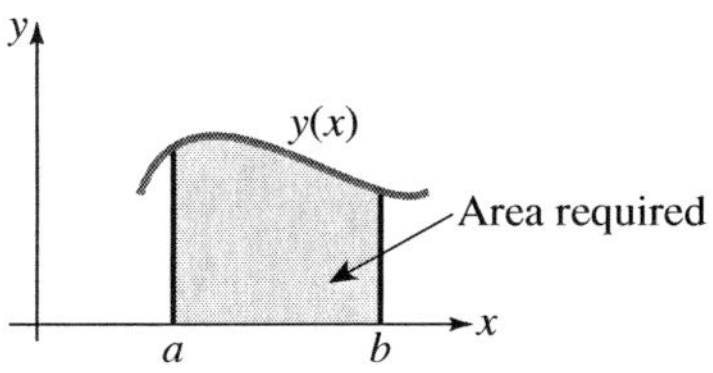

Figure 3.1
The area bounded by a graph is found by evaluating an integral.

Example 3.1

Calculate the area bounded by the curve $y = \dfrac{1}{x}$ and the x axis, between $x = 1$ and $x = 4$.

Solution

The graph of $y = \frac{1}{x}$, for x greater than 0, is shown in Figure 3.2. The area required is shaded. This area lies entirely above the x axis.

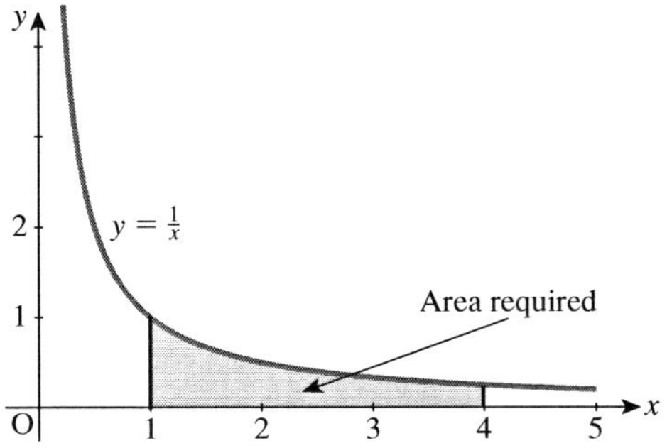

Figure 3.2
The required area lies entirely above the x axis.

The area is calculated as

$$\begin{aligned}\text{area} &= \int_1^4 \frac{1}{x}\,\mathrm{d}x \\ &= \left[\ln|x|\right]_1^4 \\ &= \ln 4 - \ln 1 \\ &= \ln 4 \quad \text{since } \ln 1 = 0 \\ &= 1.386 \text{ (3 d.p.)}\end{aligned}$$

Example 3.2

Find the area bounded by the curve $y = \sin x$ and the x axis between $x = 0$ and $x = \pi$.

Solution

The required area is shown in Figure 3.3. Note that it lies entirely above the x axis. Calculate the area

$$\int_0^{\pi} \sin x\,\mathrm{d}x = \left[-\cos x\right]_0^{\pi} = 2$$

Example 3.3

Find the area under $f(x) = e^{2x}$ from $x = 1$ to $x = 3$ given that the exponential function e^{2x} is always positive.

Solution

Because e^{2x} is positive, the area will lie above the x axis.

area =

$$\int_1^3 e^{2x}\,\mathrm{d}x = \left[\frac{e^{2x}}{2}\right]_1^3 = 198$$

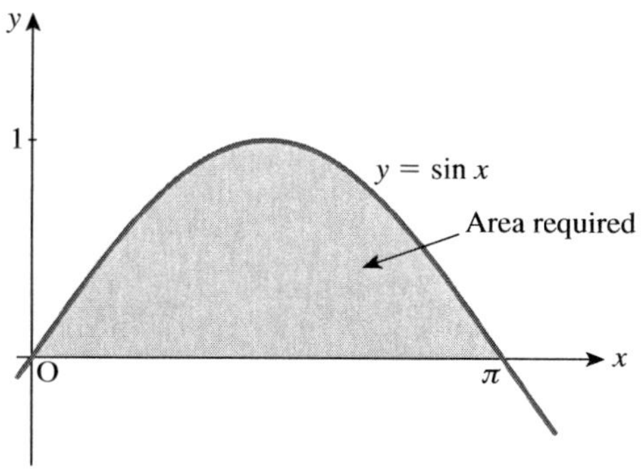

Figure 3.3
The area found in Example 3.2

Example 3.4

Figure 3.4 shows the graphs of $y = \sin x$ and $y = \cos x$ for $0 \leq x \leq \frac{\pi}{2}$. The two graphs intersect at the point where $x = \frac{\pi}{4}$. Find the area that is shaded in Figure 3.4.

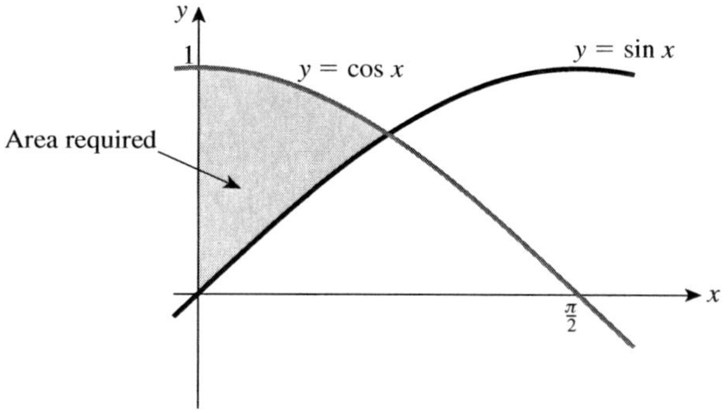

Figure 3.4
The required area is enclosed between two curves.

Solution

To find the shaded area we could calculate the area under the graph of $y = \sin x$ for x between 0 and $\frac{\pi}{4}$, and subtract this from the area under the graph of $y = \cos x$ between the same limits. Alternatively the two processes can be combined into one and we can write

$$\begin{aligned}\text{shaded area} &= \int_0^{\pi/4} \cos x - \sin x \, dx \\ &= [\sin x + \cos x]_0^{\pi/4} \\ &= \left(\sin\frac{\pi}{4} + \cos\frac{\pi}{4}\right) - (\sin 0 + \cos 0)\end{aligned}$$

If you are aware of the standard triangles you will know that $\sin\frac{\pi}{4} = \cos\frac{\pi}{4} = \frac{1}{\sqrt{2}}$, in which case the value of the integral is $\frac{2}{\sqrt{2}} - 1 = 0.414$. Alternatively you can use your calculator to obtain this result directly.

Example 3.5 The area under a velocity–time graph

Figure 3.5 shows a graph of the velocity, v, of an object plotted against time t. It can be shown that the area under such a graph between $t = a$ and $t = b$ represents the distance, s, travelled by the object between these times.

Suppose the velocity (m s^{-1}) of an object is given by the formula $v(t) = 3t^2 + 5$.

(a) State the velocity when $t = 1$ s.

(b) State the velocity when $t = 2$ s.

(c) Find the distance travelled between these times.

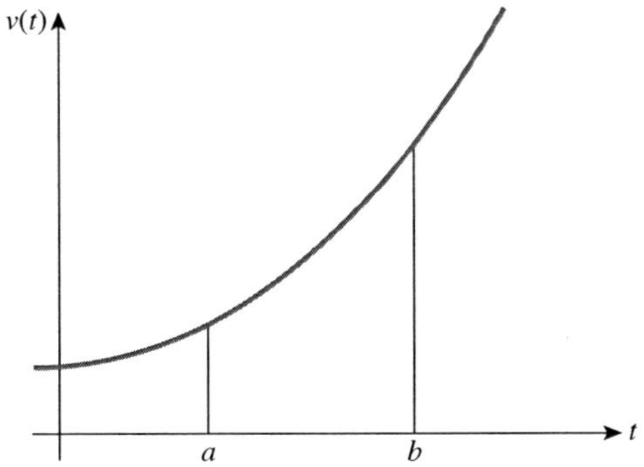

Figure 3.5 The area under a velocity–time graph represents distance travelled.

Solution

(a) When $t = 1$, $v =$ 8 m s^{-1}

(b) When $t = 2$, $v =$ 17 m s^{-1}

(c) The distance travelled is given by the area under the velocity–time graph.
Write down the required integral:

$$\int_1^2 (3t^2 + 5)\, dt$$

Finally, evaluate this integral to obtain the distance travelled.

$$[t^3 + 5t]_1^2 = 18 - 6 = 12 \text{ m}$$

We saw in Example 3.5 that the area under a velocity–time graph is interpreted as 'distance travelled'. Example 3.6 illustrates another interpretation of the area under a graph.

When the volume of a gas expands then work is done by the gas. If P denotes pressure, V denotes volume and W denotes work done then

$$W = \int_a^b P\,\mathrm{d}V$$

where a is the initial volume and b is the final volume. Note that the integral $\int_a^b P\,\mathrm{d}V$ is the area under a graph of P against V, as illustrated in Figure 3.6.

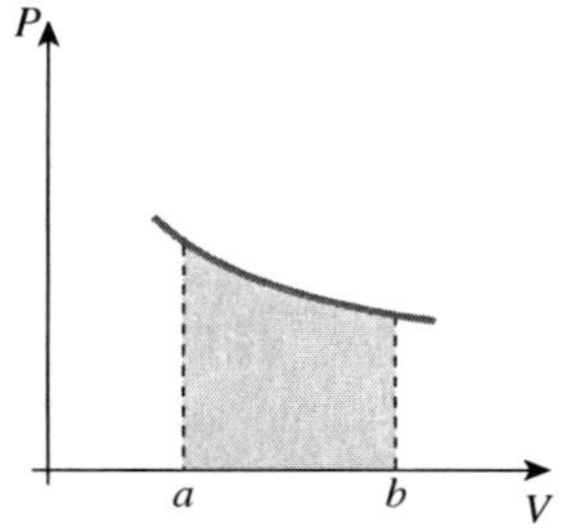

Figure 3.6 Shaded area is given by $\int_a^b P\,\mathrm{d}V$ which is the work done by the gas in expanding from volume a to volume b.

Example 3.6 Thermodynamics – Work done in expansion of a gas

Suppose that the volume, V, and pressure, P, of a gas are related by the equation

$$PV^{1.3} = K$$

where K is a constant. Calculate the work done in expanding from an initial volume of 3 cubic units to a final volume of 10 cubic units.

Solution

$$W = \int_3^{10} P\,\mathrm{d}V$$

From $PV^{1.3} = K$ then $P = KV^{-1.3}$ and so

$$\begin{aligned} W &= \int_3^{10} KV^{-1.3}\mathrm{d}V \\ &= K\left[\frac{V^{-0.3}}{-0.3}\right]_3^{10} \\ &= \frac{-K}{0.3}[10^{-0.3} - 3^{-0.3}] \\ &= 0.727K \end{aligned}$$

Exercises

In each question the required area lies entirely above the horizontal axis, although you should verify this fact for yourself independently.

1 Find the area bounded by the curve $y = x^3$ between $x = 0$ and $x = 2$.

2 Find the area bounded by the curve $y = 3t^2$ between $t = -3$ and $t = 3$.

3 Find the area under $y = \dfrac{1}{x^2}$ between $x = 1$ and $x = 10$.

4 **Mechanical Engineering – Area under a velocity–time graph.** The velocity, v (ms^{-1}) of an object varies with time, t, according to

$$v(t) = t^3 + 1$$

(a) Find the distance travelled by the object between $t = 0$ s and $t = 2$ s.
(b) Find the average velocity between $t = 0$ and $t = 2$.

5 **Thermodynamics – Expansion of a gas.** The pressure, P, and volume, V, of a gas are related by

$$PV^2 = 10$$

Calculate the work done when the gas expands from $V = 5$ cubic units to $V = 9$ cubic units.

Solutions to exercises

1 4

2 54

3 0.9

4 (a) 6 m (b) 3 ms^{-1}

5 $\frac{8}{9}$

3.3 The area bounded by a curve, parts of which lie below the x axis

Figure 3.7 shows a graph of $y = -x^2 + 1$. The shaded area is bounded by the x axis and the curve, but lies entirely below the x axis.

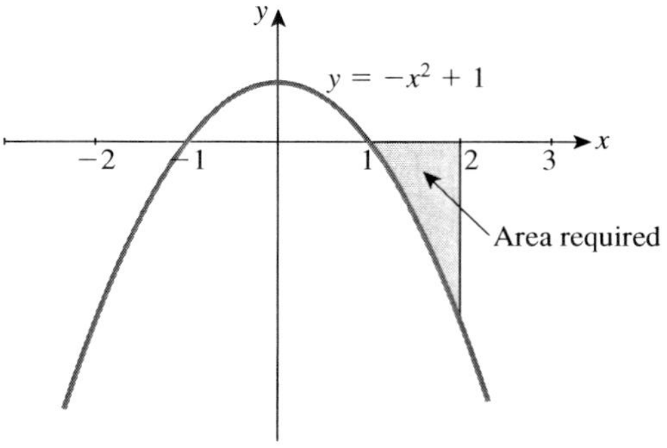

Figure 3.7 Areas lying below the x axis need special care.

Let us evaluate the integral $\int_1^2 -x^2 + 1\,dx$.

$$\int_1^2 -x^2 + 1\,dx = \left[-\frac{x^3}{3} + x\right]_1^2$$
$$= \left(-\frac{2^3}{3} + 2\right) - \left(-\frac{1^3}{3} + 1\right)$$
$$= -\frac{7}{3} + 1$$
$$= -\frac{4}{3}$$

The evaluation of the area yields a negative quantity. There is no such thing as a negative area. The area is actually $\frac{4}{3}$, and the negative sign is an indication that the area lies below the x axis.

If an area contains parts both above and below the horizontal axis, care must be taken when trying to calculate this area. It is necessary to determine which parts of the graph lie above the horizontal axis and which lie below. Separate integrals need to be calculated for each 'piece' of the graph. This idea is illustrated in the next example.

Example 3.7

Find the total area enclosed by the curve $y = x^3 - 5x^2 + 4x$ and the x axis between $x = 0$ and $x = 3$.

Solution

We need to determine which parts of the graph, if any, lie above and which lie below the x axis. To do this it is helpful to consider where the graph cuts the x axis. So we consider the function $x^3 - 5x^2 + 4x$ and look for its zeros.

$$\begin{aligned} x^3 - 5x^2 + 4x &= x(x^2 - 5x + 4) \\ &= x(x - 1)(x - 4) \end{aligned}$$

So the graph cuts the x axis when $x = 0$, $x = 1$ and $x = 4$. Also, when x is large and positive, y is large and positive since the term involving x^3 dominates. When x is large and negative, y is large and negative for the same reason. With this information we can sketch a graph showing the required area. If you have access to a graphics calculator or computer package this is a trivial matter. The graph is shown in Figure 3.8.

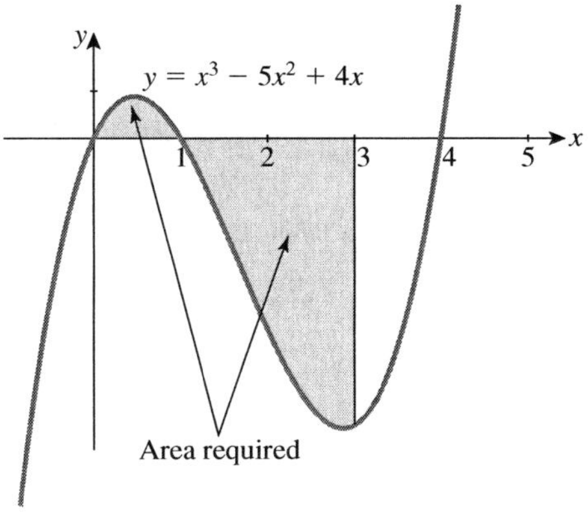

Figure 3.8 This area must be calculated in two parts.

From the graph we see that the required area lies partly above the x axis (when $0 \leq x \leq 1$) and partly below (when $1 \leq x \leq 3$). So we evaluate the integral in two parts.

First,

$$\begin{aligned}
\int_0^1 x^3 - 5x^2 + 4x \, dx &= \left[\frac{x^4}{4} - \frac{5x^3}{3} + \frac{4x^2}{2}\right]_0^1 \\
&= \left(\frac{1}{4} - \frac{5}{3} + 2\right) - (0) \\
&= \frac{7}{12}
\end{aligned}$$

This is the part of the required area that lies above the x axis.

Second,

$$\begin{aligned}
\int_1^3 x^3 - 5x^2 + 4x \, dx &= \left[\frac{x^4}{4} - \frac{5x^3}{3} + \frac{4x^2}{2}\right]_1^3 \\
&= \left(\frac{81}{4} - \frac{135}{3} + 18\right) - \left(\frac{1}{4} - \frac{5}{3} + 2\right) \\
&= -\frac{81}{12} - \frac{7}{12} \\
&= -\frac{88}{12} \\
&= -\frac{22}{3}
\end{aligned}$$

This represents the part of the required area that lies below the x axis. The actual area is $\frac{22}{3}$.

Combining the results of the two separate calculations we can find the total area bounded by the curve:

$$\begin{aligned}
\text{area} &= \frac{7}{12} + \frac{22}{3} \\
&= \frac{95}{12}
\end{aligned}$$

Example 3.8

(a) Sketch the graph of $y = \sin 2x$ for $0 \leq x \leq \pi$.

(b) Find the total area bounded by the curve and the x axis between $x = \dfrac{\pi}{3}$ and $x = \dfrac{3\pi}{4}$.

Solution

Sketch the graph and indicate the required area noting where the graph crosses the x axis.

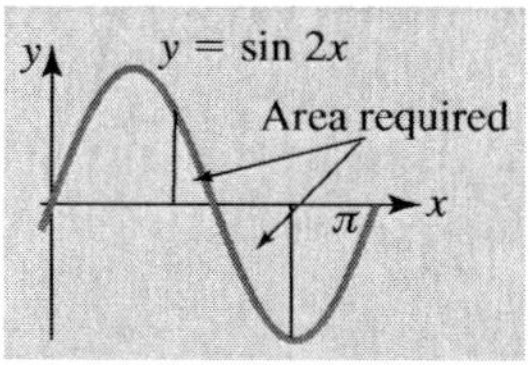

Perform the integration in two parts to obtain the required area.

For the area above the x axis evaluate the appropriate integral.

$$\int_{\pi/3}^{\pi/2} \sin 2x \, dx = \left[-\frac{\cos 2x}{2}\right]_{\pi/3}^{\pi/2} = \frac{1}{4}$$

Now evaluate the integral for finding the area below the x axis.

$$\int_{\pi/2}^{3\pi/4} \sin 2x \, dx = -\frac{1}{2}$$

Finally write down the total area required.

$$\frac{1}{4} + \frac{1}{2} = \frac{3}{4}$$

Exercises

1 Find the total area enclosed between the x axis and the curve $y = x^3$ between $x = -1$ and $x = 1$.

2 Find the area under $y = \cos 2t$ from $t = 0$ to $t = 0.5$.

3 Find the area enclosed by $y = 4 - x^2$ and the x axis from (a) $x = 0$ to $x = 2$, (b) $x = -2$ to $x = 1$, (c) $x = 1$ to $x = 3$.

4 Calculate the area enclosed by the curve $y = x^3$ and the line $y = x$.

5 Find the area bounded by $y = e^x$, the y axis, the x axis and the line $x = 2$.

6 Find the area enclosed between $y = x(x - 1)(x - 2)$ and the x axis.

7 Find the area enclosed by the graph of $y = \dfrac{1}{\sqrt{9 - 4t^2}}$ between $t = 0$ and $t = 1$.

Solutions to exercises

1. 0.5
2. 0.4207
3. (a) $\frac{16}{3}$ (b) 9 (c) 4
4. 0.5
5. $e^2 - 1$
6. $\frac{1}{2}$
7. 0.365

End of block exercises

1. Find the area enclosed by $y = 4t - t^2$ and the t axis between $t = 1$ and $t = 2$.
2. Find the area enclosed between the curves $y = x^2 - 2x$ and $y = 4 - x^2$.
3. Find the area enclosed by the curve $y = -x^2 + 6x - 5$ and the x axis.
4. Find the total area enclosed by the graph of the function $y = x^3 - 4x$ and the x axis.

Solutions to exercises

1. $3\frac{2}{3}$
2. 9
3. 10.667
4. 8

BLOCK 4 Computational approaches to integration

4.1 Introduction

Computer software packages are readily available that can integrate. The results that they produce fall into two categories, **symbolic** and **numerical**.

For many indefinite integrals, $\int f(x)\,dx$, it is possible for the computer to obtain a symbolic answer in terms of common functions such as exponential, trigonometrical or polynomial functions. Furthermore, the computer can evaluate *exactly* many definite integrals, $\int_a^b f(x)\,dx$, often by leaving an answer in the form of a fraction, or in surd form, or using common mathematical constants such as π and e. We shall illustrate such use of computer software.

For some integrals it is impossible to obtain a symbolic answer. However, there are techniques for approximating definite integrals. Such techniques are called **numerical methods**, and two of these, the trapezium rule and Simpson's rule, are explained here. Because such methods require substantial calculation they are very laborious to perform by hand. So, they are best implemented using a computer. We shall be content to illustrate the principles involved on simple examples, and then use software to tackle more substantial problems.

4.2 Use of symbolic algebra packages to find integrals exactly

Computer software designed for tackling mathematical problems invariably has the facility to integrate. This is certainly true of Matlab, Mathcad, Maple and Derive. You should work through the following examples using the package to which you have access. You may need to refer to local documentation. Some of the packages may require you to call, or load, an additional piece of software, e.g. a symbolic toolkit. You will note from the examples below that the particular commands and syntax required by the different packages vary, but often only slightly. Most packages provide extensive on-line help and examples to which you should refer for further details as required.

Example 4.1 Finding indefinite integrals exactly

Find $\int x \cos^2 x\,dx$.

Solution

Maple

In Maple the command to perform this integration is

```
int(x*cos(x)^2,x);
```

and Maple outputs

$$x\left(\frac{1}{2}\cos(x)\sin(x)+\frac{1}{2}x\right)+\frac{1}{4}\cos(x)^2-\frac{1}{4}x^2$$

Note that Maple can supply a symbolic answer, but gives no constant of integration – it is assumed that the user will remember to add this.

Matlab

In Matlab, to perform this calculation it is necessary first to declare that x is a symbol using the command

```
syms x
```

Then the command to integrate $x\cos^2 x$ is

```
int(x*cos(x)^2,x)
```

and Matlab outputs

```
ans=
x*(1/2*cos(x)*sin(x)+1/2*x)+1/4*cos(x)^2-1/4*x^2
```

This is equivalent to the answer produced by Maple although it is not set out in as friendly a form.

Mathcad

In Mathcad various 'toolbars' are available that contain clickable icons for commonly used mathematical operations. A 'calculus toolbar' contains icons $\boxed{\int}$ and $\boxed{\int_a^b}$ to perform indefinite or definite integration. Once clicked Mathcad produces a template within which the integrand, limits of integration and the variable of integration are typed. In this case, clicking $\boxed{\int}$ produces the template

$$\int * \, d*$$

and the user types in the missing quantities to obtain

$$\int x\cdot\cos(x)^2\,dx$$

To indicate that a symbolic answer is required it is necessary to click on the arrow icon $\boxed{\rightarrow}$ on the 'symbolic toolbar', followed by the ENTER key, and the output produced is the same as that produced by Maple.

Derive
In Derive the user must first 'author' the expression to be integrated. This is done by clicking the Author Expression tab, which produces a dialog box into which is typed

```
x*cos(x)^2
```

Pressing the ENTER key puts this expression into the active algebra window. Then clicking the button $\boxed{\int}$ brings up another dialog box from which various options can be selected, e.g. variable of integration, limits of integration if needed. Upon choosing the Simplify option Derive outputs

$$\frac{x\cdot\sin(x)\cdot\cos(x)}{2}-\frac{\sin(x)^2}{4}+\frac{x^2}{4}$$

Again, the user must supply the constant of integration. Note that this answer looks different from that provided by the other packages. In fact it is equivalent when constants of integration are included, but this is not obvious from a first inspection. A screenshot showing this use of Derive appears on page xxv.

Example 4.2 Finding definite integrals exactly

Find $\displaystyle\int_1^2 \frac{1}{t}\,dt$.

Solution

Maple
In Maple the command to perform this integration is

```
int(1/t,t=1..2);
```

and Maple outputs

$$\ln(2)$$

Note that, when possible, the output from the symbolic algebra package is an exact result, that is ln 2 as opposed to a decimal approximation.

Matlab
In Matlab, the symbol t must be declared before integrating:

```
syms t
int(1/t,1,2)
```

and Matlab outputs

```
ans = log(2)
```

Again, this answer is equivalent to that produced by Maple although given in a different form.

Mathcad

In Mathcad the icon $\boxed{\int_a^b}$ on the 'calculus toolbar' is used to perform exact definite integration. The integrand, limits of integration and variable of integration are typed into the placeholders on the template:

$$\int_*^* * \mathrm{d} *$$

giving

$$\int_1^2 \frac{1}{t}\,\mathrm{d}t$$

Again, to indicate that a symbolic answer is required it is necessary to click on the arrow icon $\boxed{\Rightarrow}$ on the 'symbolic toolbar', and press the ENTER key. The output produced is the same as that produced by Maple.

Derive

As before the required expression is entered into a dialog box. We enter

```
1/t
```

and press the ENTER key.

Then the button $\boxed{\int}$ is used to bring up the integration dialog box into which the variable and limits of integration are entered. Upon doing this and choosing the Simplify option Derive outputs

$$\ln(2)$$

Example 4.3

Find $\int_0^3 \sqrt{x}\,\mathrm{d}x$.

Solution

Maple

The command to perform this integration is

```
int(sqrt(x), x=0..3);
```

and Maple outputs

$$2\sqrt{3}$$

Once again, note the exact result produced by the package, rather than a decimal approximation. There is the facility in all packages to produce a decimal approximation if this is required.

Matlab

```
syms x
int(sqrt(x),0,3)
```

and the output is

```
ans = 2*3^(1/2)
```

Mathcad

The calculus toolbar is used as described above and the template is completed.

$$\int_0^3 \mathrm{sqrt}(x)\,\mathrm{d}x$$

Again, to indicate that a symbolic answer is required it is necessary to click on the arrow icon ⇒ on the 'symbolic toolbar', and the output produced is $2 \cdot 3^{1/2}$.

Derive

As before the required expression is entered into a dialog box. We enter

```
sqrt(x)
```

and press the ENTER key.

Then the button $\boxed{\int}$ is used to bring up the integration dialog box into which the variable and limits of integration are entered. Upon doing this and choosing the Simplify option Derive outputs

$$2 \cdot \sqrt{3}$$

Computer packages can find indefinite integrals when one or both limits is infinity. Consider the following example.

Example 4.4 Finding definite integrals with infinite limits of integration

Find $\int_{-\infty}^{\infty} \mathrm{e}^{-x^2}\,\mathrm{d}x$.

Solution

Maple

The Maple command to evaluate this integral is

```
int(exp(-x^2),x = -infinity..infinity);
```

and Maple outputs the exact solution

$$\sqrt{\pi}$$

Matlab

```
syms x
int(exp(-x^2),-inf,inf)
```

with output

```
ans = pi^(1/2)
```

Mathcad

As before, the template is completed

$$\int_{-\infty}^{\infty} \exp(-x\hat{\ }2)\, dx$$

The symbol ∞ is available on the Calculus toolbar. Again it is necessary to click on the arrow icon [→] on the 'symbolic toolbar'. Mathcad outputs the solution in the form

$$\pi^{1/2}$$

Derive

The required expression is entered into a dialog box. We enter

```
exp(-x^2)
```

and press the ENTER key.

Then the button [∫] is used to bring up the integration dialog box into which the variable and limits of integration are entered as -inf and inf. Upon doing this and choosing the Simplify option Derive outputs

$$\sqrt{\pi}$$

Although symbolic algebra packages are extremely powerful, there are nevertheless some integrals that are beyond their scope. In such cases you will either be warned that an explicit solution could not be found, or the expression you input may be returned to you unevaluated. For example, try to use a package to find $\int x^x\, dx$.

Computer and calculator exercises

Computer algebra packages are sophisticated products. Because they are designed for professionals their scope extends way beyond an introductory textbook like this one. Some of the computer output may well be given in terms of functions with which you are not familiar. This is normal, and when necessary you will need to explore these functions further.

Use a symbolic algebra package to find the following integrals exactly:

1 $\int_2^3 \frac{1}{\sqrt{x}}\,dx$

2 $\int x \sin^2 x\,dx$

3 $\int t e^{-st}\,dt$

4 $\int_0^1 \frac{\sin x}{x}\,dx$

5 $\int_{-1}^1 e^{-j\omega t}\,dt$ where j is the complex number with $j^2 = -1$.

Solutions to exercises

1 $2\sqrt{3} - 2\sqrt{2}$

2 $x\left(-\frac{1}{2}\cos(x)\sin(x) + \frac{1}{2}x\right) - \frac{1}{4}\cos(x)^2 - \frac{1}{4}x^2 + c$

3 $\frac{-ste^{-st} - e^{-st}}{s^2} + c$

4 Si(1). This result may be given in terms of a function you will probably not be familiar with, known as the sine integral. See if you can use the computer to evaluate a decimal approximation to this as 0.946 (3 d.p.).

5 $\frac{j(e^{-j\omega} - e^{j\omega})}{\omega}$ or the alternative form $\frac{2\sin\omega}{\omega}$.

4.3 The trapezium rule and Simpson's rule

We have seen the power of computer packages for performing some definite and indefinite integrals. We have also seen that not all functions can be integrated, and so not all integrals can be found exactly. However, techniques do exist for finding approximations to definite integrals. These techniques are called **numerical methods**.

Trapezium rule

We have seen in Block 3 that the definite integral $\int_a^b f(x)\,dx$ can be thought of as the area lying under the graph of $f(x)$ for $a \le x \le b$. This observation leads us to the following method for approximating the integral. We estimate the area lying under the graph and use this as an estimate of the integral. In the trapezium rule, the area under $f(x)$ between $x = a$ and $x = b$ is divided into several vertical strips, and the area of each strip is estimated by assuming that it has the shape of a trapezium. Consider Figure 4.1. Suppose that we divide the area under $y = f(x)$ from $x = a$ to $x = b$ into n strips. We denote the width of each strip by h. Note that since the distance from $x = a$ to $x = b$ is $b - a$, then the width of each strip is $\frac{b-a}{n}$. The lengths of the sides of the strips are denoted by $y_0, y_1, \ldots y_n$.

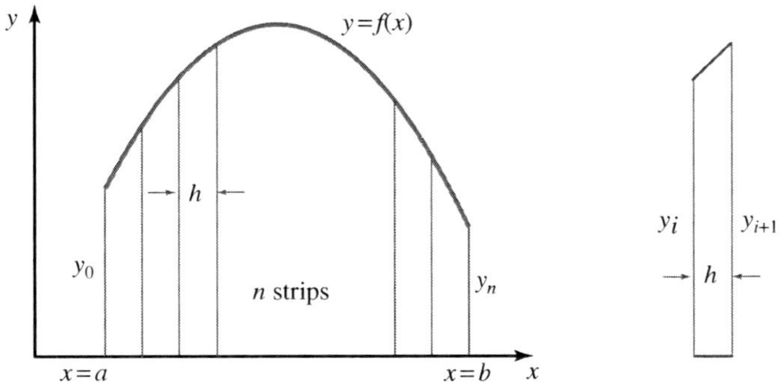

Figure 4.1 The area under $f(x)$ is divided into n strips, each of width h. The area of the typical strip shown is $\frac{h}{2}(y_i + y_{i+1})$.

Now the area of the first trapezium of width h, which has sides of heights y_0 and y_1, is $\frac{h}{2}(y_0 + y_1)$. Similarly the area of the second strip is $\frac{h}{2}(y_1 + y_2)$. We continue in this way until the areas of all the strips have been found. The area of the final strip is $\frac{h}{2}(y_{n-1} + y_n)$.

Consequently we can estimate the total area as

$$\text{area} \approx \frac{h}{2}(y_0 + y_1) + \frac{h}{2}(y_1 + y_2) + \frac{h}{2}(y_2 + y_3) + \ldots + \frac{h}{2}(y_{n-1} + y_n)$$

which can be simplified to

$$\text{area} \approx \frac{h}{2}(y_0 + 2y_1 + 2y_2 + \ldots + 2y_{n-1} + y_n)$$

Key point

Trapezium rule: with n strips, and $h = \dfrac{b-a}{n}$

$$\int_a^b f(x)\,dx \approx \frac{h}{2}(y_0 + 2y_1 + 2y_2 + \ldots + 2y_{n-1} + y_n)$$

Example 4.5

Use the trapezium rule with eight strips to estimate $\displaystyle\int_1^2 \frac{1}{x}\,dx$. Work throughout to six decimal places and quote your final result to four decimal places.

Solution

In this example $a = 1$, $b = 2$, and $n = 8$. We are dividing the area under the graph of $y = \dfrac{1}{x}$ from $x = 1$ to $x = 2$ into eight strips, and so the width of each strip will be $h = \dfrac{2-1}{8} = 0.125$. We must calculate the lengths of the sides of each of the strips, $y_0, y_1, \ldots y_8$. These are simply the respective y values calculated from $y = \dfrac{1}{x}$. It is helpful, and conventional, to set these out as in Table 4.1. The table has been laid out in the way shown because all y values other than the first and last will be multiplied by 2.

Table 4.1

x	$y = 1/x$	
1	$y_0 = 1.000000$	
1.125		$y_1 = 0.888889$
1.25		$y_2 = 0.800000$
1.375		$y_3 = 0.727273$
1.5		$y_4 = 0.666667$
1.625		$y_5 = 0.615385$
1.75		$y_6 = 0.571429$
1.875		$y_7 = 0.533333$
2	$y_8 = 0.500000$	
$y_0 + y_n$	1.500000	
$y_1 + y_2 + \ldots + y_{n-1}$		4.802976

Using the data in the table we can apply the trapezium rule formula:

$$\int_1^2 \frac{1}{x}\,dx \approx \frac{0.125}{2}(1.5000000 + 2(4.802976)) = 0.694122$$

So, to four decimal places we estimate the integral to be 0.6941. Compare this with the exact value $\ln 2 = 0.6931$ (4 d.p.).

Simpson's rule

Simpson's rule is a more sophisticated technique, which results in a more accurate estimate of the definite integral. It can be applied only when there is an even number of strips.

We state and use Simpson's rule without deriving it. For specific details refer to a textbook on numerical methods for engineers.

Key point

Simpson's rule: with n (even) strips, and $h = \dfrac{b-a}{n}$

$$\int_a^b f(x)\,dx \approx \frac{h}{3}(y_0 + 4y_1 + 2y_2 + 4y_3 + \ldots + 2y_{n-2} + 4y_{n-1} + y_n)$$

It can be helpful to remember this formula as

$$\int_a^b f(x)\,dx \approx \frac{h}{3}(\text{first} + \text{last} + 4(\text{odd numbered terms}) + 2(\text{even numbered terms}))$$

Example 4.6

Use Simpson's rule with eight strips to estimate $\displaystyle\int_1^2 \frac{1}{x}\,dx$.

As in the previous example it is helpful to set out the data as in Table 4.2. It has been laid out in this way because y_1, y_3 etc. will be multiplied by 4, whereas y_2, y_4 etc. will be multiplied by 2.

Table 4.2

x	$y = 1/x$		
1	$y_0 = 1.000000$		
1.125		$y_1 = 0.888889$	
1.25			$y_2 = 0.800000$
1.375		$y_3 = 0.727273$	
1.5			$y_4 = 0.666667$
1.625		$y_5 = 0.615385$	
1.75			$y_6 = 0.571429$
1.875		$y_7 = 0.533333$	
2	$y_8 = 0.500000$		
first + last, $y_0 + y_8$	1.500000		
sum of odd terms, $y_1 + y_3 + \ldots + y_7$		2.764880	
sum of even terms, $y_2 + y_4 + \ldots + y_6$			2.038096

Solution

Using the data in the table we can apply Simpson's rule:

$$\int_1^2 \frac{1}{x}\,\mathrm{d}x \approx \frac{0.125}{3}(1.500000 + 4(2.764880) + 2(2.038096)) = 0.693155$$

So, to four decimal places we can estimate the integral to be 0.6932. This compares well with the exact answer ln 2, which is 0.6931 to 4 d.p.

Computer algebra packages have the facility to carry out numerical integration, which means that the user can avoid lengthy and tedious arithmetical calculations.

Example 4.7 Using a computer package for numerical integration

Use a computer package to evaluate $\int_1^4 x^x\,\mathrm{d}x$.

Solution

We have seen previously that no symbolic expression exists for $\int x^x\,\mathrm{d}x$. However, computer packages can apply methods such as Simpson's rule.

Maple

The command to perform the required numerical evaluation is

```
evalf(int(x^x,x = 1..4));
```

and Maple outputs the result 113.3356 (4 d.p.).

Matlab

We need a command quad, which stands for quadrature, the technical name for numerical integration.

```
Q = quad('x.^x',1,4)
```

and Matlab calculates the value of the integral

$$\text{ans} = 113\ 3356$$

Mathcad

As before, the template is completed:

$$\int_*^* *\text{d}*$$

and the user types in the missing quantities to obtain

$$\int_1^4 x^x \, \text{d}x$$

Use of an = sign rather than → indicates that numerical as opposed to symbolic output is required. Mathcad outputs 113.336.

Derive

The expression to be integrated is entered into the dialog box:

```
x^x
```

and the ENTER key is pressed.

Pressing the integration button [∫] brings up the integration dialog box into which the limits of integration are typed. Upon selecting Simplify, Derive outputs

$$\int_1^4 x^x \, \text{d}x$$

because it cannot find an exact expression. However, by choosing option Simplify, Approximate, Derive outputs 113.3356.

Exercises

1 Use the trapezium rule with the number of strips specified to approximate the following definite integrals:

(a) $\int_0^1 \tan^2 x \, \text{d}x$, 4 strips

(b) $\displaystyle\int_1^{1.6} \frac{\text{e}^{2x}}{x^2} \, \text{d}x$, 3 strips

2 Use Simpson's rule with the number of strips specified to approximate the following definite integrals:

(a) $\int_0^{0.8} \tan^2 x \, \text{d}x$, 8 strips

(b) $\int_1^2 \sqrt{1 + x^3} \, \text{d}x$, 10 strips

Solutions to exercises

1 (a) 0.611069 (6 d.p.) (b) 4.906229 (6 d.p.)

2 (a) 0.229685 (6 d.p.) (b) 2.129862 (6 d.p.)

Computer and calculator exercises

1 Use software to evaluate

(a) $\int (\ln x)^2 \, \mathrm{d}x$ (b) $\int \sin^3 x \, \mathrm{d}x$ (c) $\int_0^1 \sin z^3 \, \mathrm{d}z$ (d) $\displaystyle\int_0^{0.1} \frac{x^3 + x}{\cos x} \, \mathrm{d}x$

Solutions to exercises

1 (a) $x(\ln x)^2 - 2x \ln x + 2x + c$

(b) $-\dfrac{1}{3} \sin^2 x \cos x - \dfrac{2}{3} \cos x + c$

(c) 0.23385 (5 d.p.) (d) 0.00504 (5 d.p.)

End of block exercises

1 Use a package to find an exact expression for the area bounded by $y = 5 - x^2$ and lying above the x axis.

Solutions to exercises

1 $\frac{20}{3} 5^{1/2}$

BLOCK 5

Integration by parts

5.1 Introduction

The technique known as **integration by parts** is used to integrate a product of two functions, for example

$$\int e^{2x} \sin 3x \, dx \quad \text{and} \quad \int_0^1 x^3 e^{-2x} \, dx$$

Note that in the first example the integrand is the product of the functions e^{2x} and $\sin 3x$, and in the second example the integrand is the product of the functions x^3 and e^{-2x}. Note also that we can change the order of the terms in the product if we wish and write

$$\int \sin 3x e^{2x} \, dx \quad \text{and} \quad \int_0^1 e^{-2x} x^3 \, dx$$

It is often possible to find integrals involving products using a method known as **integration by parts** – you can think of this as a *product rule* for integrals. This technique is described in the block.

5.2 The integration by parts formula

The integration by parts formula states:

Key point

For indefinite integrals:

$$\int u\left(\frac{dv}{dx}\right) dx = uv - \int v\left(\frac{du}{dx}\right) dx$$

For definite integrals:

$$\int_a^b u\left(\frac{dv}{dx}\right) dx = [uv]_a^b - \int_a^b v\left(\frac{du}{dx}\right) dx$$

Study the formula carefully and note the following observations:

- The formula replaces one integral, the one on the left, with a different integral, that on the right. The intention is that the latter is simpler to evaluate.

- The integrand on the left-hand side is the product of the terms u and $\frac{dv}{dx}$. To apply the formula to a particular example we must let one function in the product equal u. We must be able to differentiate this function to find $\frac{du}{dx}$. We let the other function in the product equal $\frac{dv}{dx}$. We must be able to integrate this function, to find v.

Consider the following example.

Example 5.1

Find $\int x \sin x \, dx$.

Solution

Compare the required integral with the formula for integration by parts: we see that it makes sense to choose

$$u = x \quad \text{and} \quad \frac{dv}{dx} = \sin x$$

It follows that

$$\frac{du}{dx} = 1 \quad \text{and} \quad v = \int \sin x \, dx = -\cos x$$

(When integrating $\frac{dv}{dx}$ to find v there is no need to worry about a constant of integration. When you become confident with the method, you may like to think about why this is the case.) Applying the formula we obtain

$$\begin{aligned}\int x \sin x \, dx &= uv - \int v \left(\frac{du}{dx}\right) dx \\ &= x(-\cos x) - \int (-\cos x) \cdot 1 \, dx \\ &= -x \cos x + \int \cos x \, dx \\ &= -x \cos x + \sin x + c\end{aligned}$$

Example 5.2

Find $\int (5x + 1) \cos 2x \, dx$.

Solution

Let $u = 5x + 1$ and $\frac{dv}{dx} = \cos 2x$. Now calculate $\frac{du}{dx}$ and v.

$$\frac{du}{dx} = 5 \quad \text{and} \quad v = \int \cos 2x \, dx = \frac{\sin 2x}{2}$$

Substitute these results into the formula for integration by parts:

$$\frac{(5x + 1) \sin 2x}{2} - \int \frac{\sin 2x}{2} 5 \, dx$$

Finish the problem by finding the final integral:

$$\frac{(5x + 1)\sin 2x}{2} + \frac{5}{4}\cos 2x + c$$

Example 5.3

Find $\int_0^2 xe^x \, dx$.

Solution

We let $u = x$ and $\frac{dv}{dx} = e^x$. Then $\frac{du}{dx} = 1$ and $v = e^x$. Using the formula for integration by parts we obtain

$$\begin{aligned}\int_0^2 xe^x \, dx &= [xe^x]_0^2 - \int_0^2 e^x \cdot 1 \, dx \\ &= 2e^2 - [e^x]_0^2 \\ &= 2e^2 - [e^2 - 1] \\ &= e^2 + 1 \text{ (or 8.389 to 3 d.p.)}\end{aligned}$$

Sometimes it is necessary to apply the formula more than once, as the next example shows.

Example 5.4

Find $\int_0^2 x^2e^x \, dx$.

Solution

We let

$$u = x^2 \quad \text{and} \quad \frac{dv}{dx} = e^x$$

Then

$$\frac{du}{dx} = 2x \quad \text{and} \quad v = e^x$$

Using the formula for integration by parts we find

$$\begin{aligned}\int_0^2 x^2e^x \, dx &= [x^2e^x]_0^2 - \int_0^2 2xe^x \, dx \\ &= 4e^2 - 2\int_0^2 xe^x \, dx\end{aligned}$$

The remaining integral must be integrated by parts also, but we have just done this in the previous example. So

$$\begin{aligned}\int_0^2 x^2e^x \, dx &= 4e^2 - 2[e^2 + 1] \\ &= 2e^2 - 2 \\ &= 12.778 \text{ (3 d.p.)}\end{aligned}$$

Example 5.5

Find $\int_0^{\pi/4} (4 - 3x) \sin x \, dx$.

Solution

Take $u = 4 - 3x$ and $\dfrac{dv}{dx} = \sin x$. State $\dfrac{du}{dx}$.

$$\frac{du}{dx} = -3$$

State v.

$$v = -\cos x$$

Now apply the formula.

$$\int_0^{\pi/4} (4 - 3x) \sin x \, dx =$$

$$[(4 - 3x)(-\cos x)]_0^{\pi/4} - 3\int_0^{\pi/4} \cos x \, dx$$

Perform the final integral and apply the limits:

$$[(4 - 3x)(-\cos x)]_0^{\pi/4} - 3[\sin x]_0^{\pi/4}$$

Evaluate this result:

$$0.716$$

Example 5.6

Let I stand for the integral

$$\int e^{-x} \sin x \, dx$$

Calculate this integral.

Solution

In this example you will find that it does not matter which term in the product is differentiated and which is integrated. Verify this for yourself later.

Take $u = e^{-x}$, and $\dfrac{dv}{dx} = \sin x$.

State $\dfrac{du}{dx}$.

$$\frac{du}{dx} = -e^{-x}$$

State v.

$$v = -\cos x$$

Apply the integration by parts formula.

$$I = \int e^{-x} \sin x \, dx =$$

$$e^{-x}(-\cos x) - \int (-\cos x)(-e^{-x}) \, dx$$

This simplifies to $I = -e^{-x} \cos x - \int e^{-x} \cos x \, dx$. This integral must now be evaluated by parts. Still with $u = e^{-x}$, and taking $\dfrac{dv}{dx} = \cos x$, perform the integration.

$$I = -e^{-x} \cos x - \left[e^{-x} \sin x + \int e^{-x} \sin x \, dx \right]$$

At this stage it looks as though we have gone round in a circle because the integral remaining is the same as the one we started with. However, writing this as I we find

$$I = -e^{-x} \cos x - e^{-x} \sin x - I$$

so that

$$2I = -e^{-x} \cos x - e^{-x} \sin x$$

from which

$$I = \frac{-e^{-x} \cos x - e^{-x} \sin x}{2}$$

We conclude that

$$I = \frac{-e^{-x} \cos x - e^{-x} \sin x}{2} + c$$

Exercises

In some questions it may be necessary to apply the formula more than once.

1. Find (a) $\int x \sin(2x) \, dx$, (b) $\int t e^{3t} \, dt$, (c) $\int x \cos x \, dx$.

2. Find $\int (x + 3) \sin x \, dx$.

3. By writing $\ln x$ as $1 \times \ln x$ find $\int \ln x \, dx$.

4. Find (a) $\int \tan^{-1} x \, dx$, (b) $\int -7x \cos 3x \, dx$, (c) $\int 5x^2 e^{3x} \, dx$, (d) $\int (x + 1)e^x \, dx$.

5. Find (a) $\int x \cos kx \, dx$, (b) $\int z^2 \cos kz \, dz$, where k is a constant.

6. Find $\int t e^{-st} \, dt$ where s is a constant.

7. Find $\int t^2 e^{-st} \, dt$ where s is a constant.

8 Evaluate the following definite integrals:

(a) $\int_0^1 x \cos 2x \, dx$ (b) $\int_0^{\pi/2} x \sin 2x \, dx$

(c) $\int_{-1}^1 te^{2t} \, dt$

9 Find $\displaystyle\int_1^2 (x + 2) \sin x \, dx$.

10 Find $\displaystyle\int_0^1 (x^2 - 3x + 1)e^x \, dx$.

11 Show that

$$\int e^{ax} \cos bx \, dx = \frac{e^{ax}(a \cos bx + b \sin bx)}{a^2 + b^2} + c$$

Solutions to exercises

1 (a) $\dfrac{\sin 2x}{4} - \dfrac{x \cos 2x}{2} + c$

(b) $e^{3t}\left(\dfrac{t}{3} - \dfrac{1}{9}\right) + c$

(c) $\cos x + x \sin x + c$

2 $-(x + 3) \cos x + \sin x + c$

3 $x \ln x - x + c$

4 (a) $x \tan^{-1} x - \dfrac{\ln(x^2 + 1)}{2} + c$

(b) $-\dfrac{7 \cos 3x}{9} - \dfrac{7x \sin 3x}{3} + c$

(c) $\dfrac{5e^{3x}(9x^2 - 6x + 2)}{27} + c$

(d) $xe^x + c$

5 (a) $\dfrac{\cos kx}{k^2} + \dfrac{x \sin kx}{k} + c$

(b) $\dfrac{2z \cos kz}{k^2} + \dfrac{z^2 \sin kz}{k} - \dfrac{2 \sin kz}{k^3} + c$

6 $\dfrac{-e^{-st}(st + 1)}{s^2} + c$

7 $\dfrac{-e^{-st}(s^2t^2 + 2st + 2)}{s^3} + c$

8 (a) 0.1006 (b) $\dfrac{\pi}{4} = 0.7854$ (c) 1.9488

9 3.3533

10 −0.5634

End of block exercises

1 Find the following integrals:

(a) $\int t \sin 4t \, dt$

(b) $\int te^{-5t} \, dt$

(c) $\int 3xe^{3x} \, dx$

(d) $\int (2 + 3x)e^x \, dx$

(e) $\int (7 - x)\sin x \, dx$

2 Evaluate the following definite integrals:

(a) $\int_0^1 2x^2e^x \, dx$

(b) $\int_{-1}^1 (x + 5)e^{5x} \, dx$

(c) $\int_0^{\pi} e^{-x} \sin x \, dx$

3 Let I_n stand for the integral $\int \sin^n x\,dx$, so for example I_4 means $\int \sin^4 x\,dx$. By writing $\sin^n x$ as $\sin^{n-1} x \sin x$ and using integration by parts show that

$$I_n = -\frac{1}{n}\sin^{n-1} x \cos x + \frac{n-1}{n} I_{n-2}$$

Such a formula is called a **reduction formula**. Used repeatedly it can be used to reduce an integral such as $\int \sin^4 x\,dx$ to one involving $\sin^2 x$ and then to one involving $\sin^0 x$ or simply 1. Use the reduction formula to find $\int \sin^6 x\,dx$.

4 Obtain a reduction formula for $\int \cos^n x\,dx$.

Solutions to exercises

1 (a) $\dfrac{\sin 4t}{16} - \dfrac{t\cos 4t}{4} + c$

(b) $-\dfrac{e^{-5t}(5t+1)}{25} + c$

(c) $\dfrac{e^{3x}(3x-1)}{3} + c$

(d) $e^x(3x-1) + c$

(e) $(x-7)\cos x - \sin x + c$

2 (a) 1.437 (b) 172.154 (c) 0.522

3 $I_6 = -\frac{1}{6}\sin^5 x\cos x - \frac{5}{24}\sin^3 x\cos x$

$-\frac{5}{16}\sin x\cos x + \frac{5x}{16} + c$

4 $I_n = \dfrac{1}{n}\cos^{n-1} x \sin x + \dfrac{n-1}{n} I_{n-2}$

BLOCK 6 Integration by substitution

6.1 Introduction

The technique described in this block involves making a substitution in order to simplify an integral or make it more amenable to integration. There are many different ways in which a substitution can be made. For example, we may let a new variable, u say, equal a more complicated part of the function we are trying to integrate. The choice of which substitution to make often relies upon experience: don't worry if at first you cannot see an appropriate substitution. This skill develops with practice. However, it is not simply a matter of changing the variable – care must be taken with the term dx, as we shall see.

Integrals of the form $\int \frac{f'(x)}{f(x)}\,\mathrm{d}x$ can be dealt with in a particularly simple way as we show in Section 6.4. In Section 6.5 we provide a table of suggested substitutions to be tried in some more difficult cases.

6.2 Making a substitution

The technique of integrating by substitution is illustrated in the following example.

Example 6.1

Find $\int (3x + 5)^6\,\mathrm{d}x$.

Solution

First, look at the function we are trying to integrate: $(3x + 5)^6$. It looks quite a complicated function to integrate. Suppose we introduce a new variable, u, such that $u = 3x + 5$. Doing this means that the function we must integrate becomes u^6. Would you not agree that this looks a much simpler function to integrate than $(3x + 5)^6$? There is a slight complication, however. The new function of u must be integrated with respect to u and not with respect to x. This means that we must take care of the term dx correctly. It is not simply a matter of changing the dx to du. From the substitution

$$u = 3x + 5$$

note, by differentiation, that

$$\frac{\mathrm{d}u}{\mathrm{d}x} = 3$$

It follows that we can write

$$dx = \frac{1}{3}\,du$$

This is the way in which the dx is changed into du.

The required integral then becomes

$$\int (3x + 5)^6\,dx = \int u^6 \frac{1}{3}\,du$$

The factor of $\frac{1}{3}$, being a constant, means that we can write

$$\begin{aligned}\int (3x + 5)^6\,dx &= \frac{1}{3}\int u^6\,du\\ &= \frac{1}{3}\frac{u^7}{7} + c\\ &= \frac{u^7}{21} + c\end{aligned}$$

To finish off we must rewrite this answer in terms of the original variable x and replace u by $3x + 5$:

$$\int (3x + 5)^6\,dx = \frac{(3x + 5)^7}{21} + c$$

Example 6.2

By making the substitution $u = 2x - 7$ find $\int \cos(2x - 7)\,dx$.

Solution

First differentiate the given substitution.

$$\frac{du}{dx} = \qquad\qquad 2$$

Hence write down an expression for dx.

$$dx = \frac{1}{2}\,du$$

Now the integral can be written entirely in terms of the variable u:

$$\int \cos(2x - 7)\,dx = \qquad\qquad \frac{1}{2}\int \cos u\,du$$

Complete the integration:

$$\frac{1}{2}\sin u + c = \frac{1}{2}\sin(2x - 7) + c$$

Example 6.3

By means of the substitution $u = 1 - x^2$, find the integral $\int x\sqrt{1 - x^2}\,dx$.

Solution

First differentiate $u = 1 - x^2$.

$$\frac{du}{dx} = \qquad -2x$$

This implies that $x\,dx = -\frac{1}{2}\,du$, so $\sqrt{1 - x^2} = \sqrt{u}$ and $x\,dx = -\dfrac{1}{2}\,du$.

Rewrite the integral in terms of u.

$$\int x\sqrt{1 - x^2}\,dx = \qquad -\frac{1}{2}\int \sqrt{u}\,du$$

Complete the integration:

$$-\frac{1}{2}\frac{u^{3/2}}{3/2} + c = -\frac{1}{3}u^{3/2} + c$$

Finally rewrite the answer in terms of the original variable, x.

$$-\frac{(1 - x^2)^{3/2}}{3} + c$$

Sometimes it may be possible to complete the square to obtain a recognisable standard form.

Example 6.4

Find $\displaystyle\int \frac{1}{s^2 + 6s + 18}\,ds$.

Solution

By completing the square in the denominator we can write the integral as

$$\int \frac{1}{(s + 3)^2 + 9}\,ds$$

Referring to the table of integrals on page 777 note that

$$\int \frac{1}{x^2 + a^2}\,dx = \frac{1}{a}\tan^{-1}\left(\frac{x}{a}\right) + c$$

This standard form suggests the substitution $x = s + 3$, $\frac{dx}{ds} = 1$ from which $dx = ds$. Write down and complete the resulting integral:

$$\int \frac{1}{x^2 + 3^2}\, dx$$

$$\frac{1}{3}\tan^{-1}\left(\frac{s+3}{3}\right) + c$$

Exercises

1. Use a substitution to find
(a) $\int (4x + 1)^7\, dx$ (b) $\int t^2 \sin(t^3 + 1)\, dt$ (hint: let $u = t^3 + 1$) (c) $\int \sin(3x - 1)\, dx$
(d) $\int e^{2x-3}\, dx$ (e) $\int x(2x^2 + 7)^4\, dx$
(f) $\int \sin^2 4t \cos 4t\, dt$

2. Find (a) $\int 3e^{-x-1}\, dx$, (b) $\int 4\sin(3x + 7)\, dx$.

3. By making the substitution $u = 3^x$, and using the laws of logarithms, find $\int 3^x\, dx$.

4. Find (a) $\int \frac{1}{(x+1)^2}\, dx$, (b) $\int \frac{1}{(2x+3)^3}\, dx$.

5. Find $\int \cos(1 - x)\, dx$.

6. By factorising the denominator and making a substitution find

$$\int \frac{1}{t^2 - 2t + 1}\, dt.$$

Solutions to exercises

1. (a) $\frac{(4x+1)^8}{32} + c$ (b) $-\frac{\cos(t^3+1)}{3} + c$
(c) $-\frac{\cos(3x-1)}{3} + c$ (d) $\frac{e^{2x-3}}{2} + c$
(e) $\frac{(2x^2+7)^5}{20} + c$ (f) $\frac{\sin^3 4t}{12} + c$

2. (a) $-3e^{-x-1} + c$ (b) $-\frac{4}{3}\cos(3x + 7) + c$

3. $\frac{1}{\ln 3}3^x + c$

4. (a) $-\frac{1}{x+1} + c$ (b) $-\frac{1}{4}\cdot\frac{1}{(2x+3)^2} + c$

5. $-\sin(1 - x) + c$

6. $-\frac{1}{t-1} + c$

6.3 Substitution and definite integrals

If you are dealing with definite integrals (ones with limits of integration) you must be particularly careful when you substitute. Consider the following example.

Example 6.5

Find $\int_2^3 t\sin(t^2)\, dt$ by making the substitution $u = t^2$.

Solution

Note that if $u = t^2$ then $\dfrac{du}{dt} = 2t$ so that $dt = \dfrac{du}{2t}$. We find

$$\int_{t=2}^{t=3} t\sin(t^2)\,dt = \int_{t=2}^{t=3} t\sin u\,\frac{du}{2t}$$

$$= \frac{1}{2}\int_{t=2}^{t=3} \sin u\,du$$

An important point to note is that the limits of integration are limits on the variable t, not on u. To emphasise this they have been written explicitly as $t = 2$ and $t = 3$. When we integrate with respect to the variable u, the limits must be written in terms of u too. From the substitution $u = t^2$, note that

when $t = 2$, $u = 4$ and when $t = 3$, $u = 9$

so the integral becomes

$$\frac{1}{2}\int_{u=4}^{u=9} \sin u\,du = \frac{1}{2}[-\cos u]_4^9$$

$$= \frac{1}{2}(-\cos 9 + \cos 4)$$

$$= 0.129$$

Example 6.6

By making the substitution $u = t + 1$ find $\int_1^4 t\sqrt{t+1}\,dt$.

Solution

State the corresponding limits on u: 2, 5

Make the substitution and obtain an integral in terms of u:

$$\int_2^5 (u-1)\sqrt{u}\,du$$

This integration can be performed by removing the brackets and integrating each term separately. Finish the solution:

$$\left[\frac{2}{5}u^{5/2} - \frac{2}{3}u^{3/2}\right]_2^5 = 14.530$$

Exercises

1 Use a substitution to find
(a) $\int_1^2 (2x+3)^7 dx$ (b) $\int_0^1 3t^2 e^{t^3} dt$

Solutions to exercises

1 (a) 3.3589×10^5 (b) 1.7183

6.4 Integrals of the form $\int \frac{f'(x)}{f(x)} dx$

Example 6.7

Find $\int \frac{(3x^2 + 1)\,dx}{x^3 + x + 2}$.

Solution

Let us consider what happens when we make the substitution $z = x^3 + x + 2$. Note that

$$\frac{dz}{dx} = 3x^2 + 1$$

so that we can write

$$dz = (3x^2 + 1)\,dx$$

Then

$$\begin{aligned}\int \frac{(3x^2 + 1)\,dx}{x^3 + x + 2} &= \int \frac{dz}{z} \\ &= \ln|z| + c \\ &= \ln|x^3 + x + 2| + c\end{aligned}$$

Note that, in the previous example, the numerator of the integrand is the derivative of the denominator. The result is the logarithm of the denominator. This is a special case of the following rule, which should be remembered:

Key point

$$\int \frac{df/dx}{f(x)}\,dx = \ln|f(x)| + c$$

Example 6.8

Write down, purely by inspection, the following integrals:

(a) $\int \frac{1}{x+1}\,dx$ (b) $\int \frac{2x}{x^2+8}\,dx$ (c) $\int \frac{1}{x-3}\,dx$

Solution

(a) $\ln|x + 1| + c$

(b) $\ln|x^2 + 8| + c$

(c) $\ln|x - 3| + c$

Example 6.9

Evaluate $\displaystyle\int_2^4 \frac{3t^2 + 2t}{t^3 + t^2 + 1}\,dt$ by inspection.

Solution

$$\left[\ln|t^3 + t^2 + 1|\right]_2^4 = \ln 81 - \ln 13 = 1.83$$

Sometimes it is necessary to make slight adjustments to the integrand to obtain a form for which the previous rule is suitable. Consider the next example.

Example 6.10

Find $\displaystyle\int \frac{x^2}{x^3 + 1}\,dx$.

Solution

In this example the derivative of the denominator is $3x^2$ whereas the numerator is just x^2. We adjust the numerator as follows:

$$\int \frac{x^2}{x^3 + 1}\,dx = \frac{1}{3}\int \frac{3x^2}{x^3 + 1}\,dx$$

Note that this sort of procedure is possible only because we can move constant factors through the integral sign. It would be wrong to try to move terms involving x in a similar way. Then

$$\frac{1}{3}\int \frac{3x^2}{x^3 + 1}\,dx = \frac{1}{3}\ln|x^3 + 1| + c$$

Example 6.11

Adjust the numerator of the integral $\displaystyle\int \frac{1}{1 - x}\,dx$ in order to find the integral.

Solution

$$\int \frac{1}{1 - x}\,dx = \qquad -\int \frac{-1}{1 - x}\,dx$$

Finish the calculation:

$$\int \frac{1}{1 - x}\,dx = \qquad -\ln|1 - x| + c$$

Exercises

1 Write down the result of finding the following integrals:

(a) $\int \frac{1}{x}\,\mathrm{d}x$ (b) $\int \frac{2t}{t^2+1}\,\mathrm{d}t$ (c) $\int \frac{1}{2x+5}\,\mathrm{d}x$ (d) $\int \frac{2}{3x-2}\,\mathrm{d}x$.

Solutions to exercises

1 (a) $\ln|x| + c$ (b) $\ln|t^2+1| + c$

(c) $\frac{1}{2}\ln|2x+5| + c$ (d) $\frac{2}{3}\ln|3x-2| + c$

6.5 Some harder examples of integration by substitution

The range of possible substitutions is so wide and varied that it is impossible to give examples of every type here. However, Table 6.1 provides some suggestions for evaluating $\int f(x)\,\mathrm{d}x$ when $f(x)$ takes particular forms.

Table 6.1

$f(x)$ contains	make the substitution:	
$\sqrt{a^2-x^2}$	$x = a\sin\theta$	$\frac{\mathrm{d}x}{\mathrm{d}\theta} = a\cos\theta$
	$x = a\tanh u$	$\frac{\mathrm{d}x}{\mathrm{d}u} = a\,\mathrm{sech}^2\,u$
$\sqrt{a^2+x^2}$	$x = a\sinh u$	$\frac{\mathrm{d}x}{\mathrm{d}u} = a\cosh u$
	$x = a\tan\theta$	$\frac{\mathrm{d}x}{\mathrm{d}\theta} = a\sec^2\theta$
$\sqrt{x^2-a^2}$	$x = a\cosh u$	$\frac{\mathrm{d}x}{\mathrm{d}u} = a\sinh u$
	$x = a\sec\theta$	$\frac{\mathrm{d}x}{\mathrm{d}\theta} = a\sec\theta\tan\theta$
$\sin x$, $\cos x$	$\sin x = \frac{2t}{1+t^2}$, $\cos x = \frac{1-t^2}{1+t^2}$, where $t = \tan\frac{x}{2}$	$\frac{\mathrm{d}x}{\mathrm{d}t} = \frac{2}{1+t^2}$
$\sin^2 x$, $\cos^2 x$	$\sin x = \frac{t}{\sqrt{1+t^2}}$, $\cos x = \frac{1}{\sqrt{1+t^2}}$, where $t = \tan x$	$\frac{\mathrm{d}x}{\mathrm{d}t} = \frac{1}{1+t^2}$

Example 6.12

By making a hyperbolic substitution, find $\int \sqrt{1 + x^2}\,dx$. You will also need to make use of the hyperbolic identities:

$$\cosh^2 u - \sinh^2 u = 1, \quad \cosh^2 u = \frac{1 + \cosh 2u}{2}$$

Solution

Study the form of the integrand and use Table 6.1 to select an appropriate substitution.

$$x = \sinh u$$

It follows that $\dfrac{dx}{du} = \cosh u$.

Make the substitution and use the first of the identities to obtain an integral in terms of u.

$$\int \sqrt{1 + \sinh^2 u}\,\cosh u\, du = \int \cosh^2 u\, du$$

The second of the identities allows us to rewrite the integral in the form

$$\int \frac{1 + \cosh 2u}{2}\, du$$

which can be integrated directly. Complete the calculation.

$$\frac{1}{2}u + \frac{\sinh 2u}{4} + c$$

From $x = \sinh u$ it follows that $u = \sinh^{-1} x$ and so in terms of the original variable, x, we have

$$\frac{1}{2}\sinh^{-1} x + \frac{1}{4}\sinh(2\sinh^{-1} x) + c$$

This integral arises when calculating the length of a quadratic curve as you will see in Chapter 18, Block 5.

Example 6.13

Find $\displaystyle\int \frac{dx}{1 + \cos x + \sin x}$.

Solution

By noting the form of the integrand and referring to Table 6.1 we let

$$\sin x = \frac{2t}{1 + t^2} \quad \text{and} \quad \cos x = \frac{1 - t^2}{1 + t^2}, \quad \text{where } t = \tan\frac{x}{2}$$

$$\frac{dx}{dt} = \frac{2}{1 + t^2}$$

Make these substitutions and simplify the result to obtain an integral in terms of t.

$$\int \frac{dt}{1 + t}$$

This can be integrated using the technique of Section 6.4.

$$\ln(1 + t) + c$$

Finally, reverting to the original variable x we have

$$\int \frac{dx}{1 + \cos x + \sin x} = \ln\left(1 + \tan\frac{1}{2}x\right) + c$$

Exercises

1 Find $\displaystyle\int \frac{x}{\sqrt{4 - x^2}}\,dx$.

2 Find $\int \sqrt{x^2 - 1}\,dx$.

3 Find $\displaystyle\int_0^{\pi/2} \frac{1}{2 + \cos x}\,dx$.

4 Refer to Figure 6.1 from which $\tan x = t$.

Show that (a) $\sin x = \dfrac{t}{\sqrt{1 + t^2}}$, (b) $\cos x = \dfrac{1}{\sqrt{1 + t^2}}$, (c) $\dfrac{dx}{dt} = \dfrac{1}{1 + t^2}$.

Figure 6.1

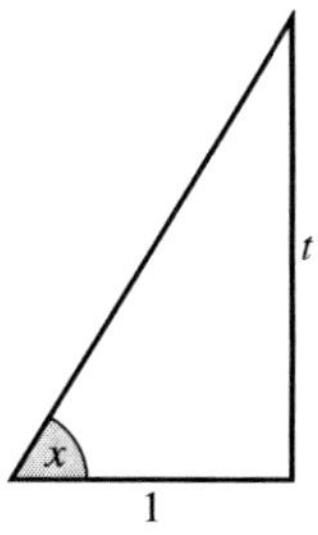

5 Refer to Figure 6.2 and use it to obtain the $t = \tan\frac{x}{2}$ substitution given in Table 6.1.

Figure 6.2

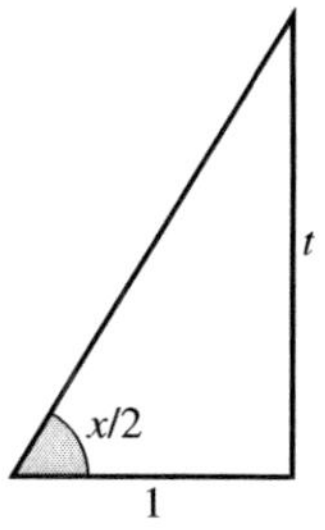

6 Show that

$$\int_0^{\pi/2} \frac{1}{3\cos x + 4\sin x}\,dx = \frac{1}{5}\ln 6.$$

Solutions to exercises

1 $-\sqrt{(4 - x^2)} + c$

2 $\dfrac{\sinh(2\cosh^{-1} x)}{4} - \dfrac{\cosh^{-1} x}{2} + c$

3 $\dfrac{\pi\sqrt{3}}{9}$

End of block exercises

1 Find $\displaystyle\int \frac{1}{4x - 3}\,dx$.

2 Find $\displaystyle\int_3^4 \frac{t}{\sqrt{t^2 - 3}}\,dt$.

3 Find $\displaystyle\int_0^{\pi/3} \cos^3 x \sin x\,dx$.

4 Find $\displaystyle\int \frac{3}{(x + 2)^2}\,dx$.

5 Find $\displaystyle\int \frac{7}{(2 - x)^3}\,dx$.

6 Find $\int (9 - 2t)^7\,dt$.

7 Find $\displaystyle\int \frac{1}{\sqrt{3 + y}}\,dy$.

8 Find $\displaystyle\int \frac{\ln x}{x}\,dx$ by making the substitution $z = \ln x$.

Solutions to exercises

1 $\frac{1}{4}\ln(4x - 3) + c$

2 1.156

3 0.234

4 $-\dfrac{3}{x + 2} + c$

5 $\dfrac{7}{2(2 - x)^2} + c$

6 $-\dfrac{(9 - 2t)^8}{16} + c$

7 $2(3 + y)^{1/2} + c$

8 $\dfrac{(\ln x)^2}{2} + c$

BLOCK 7

Integration using partial fractions

7.1 Introduction

Often the technique of partial fractions can be used to write an algebraic fraction as the sum of simpler fractions. On occasions this means that we can then integrate a complicated algebraic fraction. We shall explore this approach in this block. A thorough understanding of the various forms that partial fractions can take is an essential prerequisite.

7.2 Integration using partial fractions

Sometimes expressions which at first sight look impossible to integrate using the techniques already met may in fact be integrated by first expressing them as simpler partial fractions, and then using the techniques described earlier in this chapter. Consider the following example.

Example 7.1

By expressing the integrand as the sum of its partial fractions find

$$\int \frac{2x + 11}{(x + 7)^2} \, dx$$

Solution

The denominator of the integrand contains a repeated linear factor $(x + 7)^2$. The appropriate form of partial fractions is

$$\frac{2x + 11}{(x + 7)^2} = \frac{A}{x + 7} + \frac{B}{(x + 7)^2}$$

Then

$$2x + 11 = A(x + 7) + B$$

from which, by letting $x = -7$, we find $-3 = B$. Equating coefficients of x, for example, gives $A = 2$. The integral becomes

$$\int \frac{2}{x + 7} - \frac{3}{(x + 7)^2} \, dx$$

The first integral is of the form $\int \frac{f'(x)}{f(x)}\,\mathrm{d}x$ covered in Section 6.4. Thus

$$\int \frac{2}{x+7}\,\mathrm{d}x = 2\ln|x+7| + c$$

The second integral can be evaluated by making a substitution $u = x + 7$, $\frac{\mathrm{d}u}{\mathrm{d}x} = 1$, to give

$$\begin{aligned}\int \frac{3}{(x+7)^2}\,\mathrm{d}x &= \int \frac{3}{u^2}\,\mathrm{d}u \\ &= -\frac{3}{u} + c \\ &= -\frac{3}{x+7} + c\end{aligned}$$

Finally, putting both parts together we find

$$\int \frac{2x+11}{(x+7)^2}\,\mathrm{d}x = 2\ln|x+7| + \frac{3}{x+7} + K$$

Example 7.2
Express

$$\frac{23 - x}{(x-5)(x+4)}$$

as the sum of its partial fractions. Hence find

$$\int \frac{23 - x}{(x-5)(x+4)}\,\mathrm{d}x$$

Solution
First produce the partial fractions (hint: write the fraction in the form $\frac{A}{x-5} + \frac{B}{x+4}$):

$A = 2, B = -3$

Then integrate each term separately.

$2\ln|x-5| - 3\ln|x+4| + c$

Exercises

By expressing the following in partial fractions evaluate the given integral. Remember to select the correct form for the partial fractions.

1 $\int \frac{1}{x^3 + x}\,\mathrm{d}x$

2 $\int \frac{13x - 4}{6x^2 - x - 2}\,\mathrm{d}x$

3 $\displaystyle\int \frac{1}{(x+1)(x-5)}\,\mathrm{d}x$

4 $\displaystyle\int \frac{2x}{(x-1)^2(x+1)}\,\mathrm{d}x$

5 $\displaystyle\int \frac{1}{x^2-2x-1}\,\mathrm{d}x$

Solutions to exercises

1 $\ln|x| - \frac{1}{2}\ln|x^2+1| + c$

2 $\frac{3}{2}\ln|2x+1| + \frac{2}{3}\ln|3x-2| + c$

3 $\frac{1}{6}\ln|x-5| - \frac{1}{6}\ln|x+1| + c$

4 $-\frac{1}{2}\ln|x+1| + \frac{1}{2}\ln|x-1| - \dfrac{1}{x-1} + c$

5 $\dfrac{1}{2\sqrt{2}}\ln\left(\dfrac{x-1-\sqrt{2}}{x-1+\sqrt{2}}\right)$

End of block exercises

1 Find $\displaystyle\int \frac{3x-17}{x^2-2x-3}\,\mathrm{d}x$.

2 Find $\displaystyle\int \frac{x+3}{(x+1)^2}\,\mathrm{d}x$.

3 Find $\displaystyle\int \frac{t}{(t+3)(t-2)}\,\mathrm{d}t$.

4 Find $\displaystyle\int \frac{3-x}{(x-2)^2(x+1)}\,\mathrm{d}x$.

5 Find $\displaystyle\int \frac{15x-6}{(1-2x)(2-x)}\,\mathrm{d}x$.

6 Find $\displaystyle\int \frac{2\,\mathrm{d}t}{(1+t)(1+3t)}$.

7 Find $\displaystyle\int \frac{8-x}{(x-2)^2(x+1)}\,\mathrm{d}x$.

Solutions to exercises

1 $5\ln(x+1) - 2\ln(x-3) + c$

2 $\ln(x+1) - \dfrac{2}{x+1} + c$

3 $\dfrac{3}{5}\ln(t+3) + \dfrac{2}{5}\ln(t-2) + c$

4 $\dfrac{4}{9}\ln(x+1) - \dfrac{4}{9}\ln(x-2) - \dfrac{1}{3(x-2)} + c$

5 $8\ln(x-2) - \dfrac{\ln(2x-1)}{2} + c$

6 $\ln(3t+1) - \ln(t+1) + c$

7 $\ln\dfrac{x+1}{x-2} - \dfrac{2}{x-2} + c$

BLOCK 8 Integration of trigonometrical functions

8.1 Introduction

Integrals involving trigonometrical functions are commonplace in engineering mathematics. This is especially true when modelling waves, and alternating current circuits. When the root-mean-square (r.m.s.) value of a waveform or signal is to be calculated, you will often find this results in an integral of the form

$$\int \sin^2 t \, dt$$

In Fourier analysis it is necessary to find integrals such as

$$\int \sin mt \cos nt \, dt$$

In this block you will learn how such integrals can be evaluated.

Simple integrals involving trigonometrical functions have already been dealt with in Block 1. See what you can remember.

Example 8.1

Write down the following integrals:

(a) $\int \sin x \, dx$ (b) $\int \cos x \, dx$ (c) $\int \sin 2x \, dx$ (d) $\int \cos 2x \, dx$

Solution

(a) $-\cos x + c$

(b) $\sin x + c$

(c) $-\dfrac{\cos 2x}{2} + c$

(d) $\dfrac{\sin 2x}{2} + c$

The basic rules from which these results can be derived are summarised here:

Key point

$$\int \sin kx \, dx = -\frac{\cos kx}{k} + c \qquad \int \cos kx \, dx = \frac{\sin kx}{k} + c$$

8.2 The integration of more complicated trigonometrical functions

In engineering applications it is often necessary to integrate functions involving powers of the trigonometrical functions such as

$$\int \sin^2 x \, dx \quad \text{or} \quad \int \cos^2 \omega t \, dt$$

Note that these integrals cannot be obtained directly from the formulae in the key point above, which involve multiples of the variable x rather than powers of trigonometrical functions. However, by making use of trigonometrical identities the integrands can be rewritten in an alternative form. It is often not clear which identities are useful, and each case needs to be considered individually. Experience and practice are essential. Work through the following example.

Example 8.2

Use the trigonometrical identity

$$\sin^2 \theta = \tfrac{1}{2}(1 - \cos 2\theta)$$

to express the integral $\int \sin^2 x \, dx$ in an alternative form.

Solution

$\int \frac{1}{2}(1 - \cos 2x) \, dx$

Note from the last example that the trigonometrical identity was used to convert a power of $\sin x$ into a function involving $\cos 2x$, which can be integrated directly.

Example 8.3

Find the integral $\int \sin^2 x \, dx$.

Solution

$$\frac{1}{2}\left(x - \frac{\sin 2x}{2} + c\right) = \frac{1}{2}x - \frac{1}{4}\sin 2x + K \text{ where } K = \frac{c}{2}$$

Example 8.4

Use the trigonometrical identity $\sin 2x = 2 \sin x \cos x$ to find

$$\int \sin x \cos x \, dx$$

Solution

Use the identity to rewrite the integrand.

$$\int \frac{1}{2} \sin 2x \, dx$$

Complete the integration.

$$\int \frac{1}{2} \sin 2x \, dx = \qquad -\frac{1}{4} \cos 2x + c$$

Example 8.5

Find $\int 2 \sin 7x \cos 3x \, dx$.

Solution

In this example you will need to make use of the trigonometrical identity

$$2 \sin A \cos B = \sin(A + B) + \sin(A - B)$$

Use this identity to rewrite the integral:

$$\int \sin 10x + \sin 4x \, dx$$

Now complete the calculation:

$$-\frac{\cos 10x}{10} - \frac{\cos 4x}{4} + c$$

Example 8.6

Find $\int \sin^3 x \cos^3 x \, dx$.

Solution

To perform this calculation you will need to use a trigonometrical identity, and also use a substitution (see Block 6).

Make the substitution $u = \sin x$.

Write down $\dfrac{du}{dx}$.

$$\cos x$$

Write $\cos^3 x$ as $\cos^2 x \cos x$ and use the trigonometrical identity $\cos^2 x = 1 - \sin^2 x$.

Try to obtain an integral in terms of u.

$$\int u^3 - u^5 \, du$$

Complete the calculation: $\qquad \dfrac{\sin^4 x}{4} - \dfrac{\sin^6 x}{6} + c$

If you have worked through the previous examples you will have realised that there is no single approach for tackling such integrals. Sometimes it is appropriate to make a substitution; sometimes a trigonometrical substitution is appropriate. You may need to integrate by parts. When faced with a particular integral to evaluate you may need to have several attempts and try different methods. Carrying out a range of practice exercises will help build your confidence.

Exercises

You will need to refer to a table of trigonometrical identities to answer these questions.

1. Find $\int \cos^2 x \, dx$.

2. Find $\int_0^{\pi/2} \cos^2 t \, dt$.

3. Find $\int (\cos^2 \theta + \sin^2 \theta) \, d\theta$.

4. Use the identity $\sin(A + B) + \sin(A - B) = 2\sin A \cos B$ to find $\int \sin 3x \cos 2x \, dx$.

5. Find $\int (1 + \tan^2 x) \, dx$.

6. The mean square value of a function $f(t)$ over the interval $t = a$ to $t = b$ is defined to be

$$\frac{1}{b-a}\int_a^b (f(t))^2 \, dt$$

Find the mean square value of $f(t) = \sin t$ over the interval $t = 0$ to $t = 2\pi$.

7. Find $\int \sin mt \sin nt \, dt$ where m and n are constants and $m \neq n$.

8. Find $\int \frac{\sin^3 x}{\cos x} + \sin x \cos x \, dx$.

Solutions to exercises

1. $\frac{1}{2}x + \frac{1}{4}\sin 2x + c$

2. $\frac{\pi}{4}$

3. $\theta + c$

4. $-\frac{\cos 5x}{10} - \frac{\cos x}{2} + c$

5. $\tan x + c$

6. $\frac{1}{2}$

7. $\frac{1}{2}\left(\frac{\sin(m-n)t}{m-n} - \frac{\sin(m+n)t}{m+n}\right) + c$

8. $\int \tan x \, dx = \ln \sec x + c$

End of block exercises

1. Find $\int \sin^2 2x \, dx$.

2. Find $\int \sin 3x \cos 3x \, dx$.

3. Find $\int 5 \sin t \cos t \, dt$.

4. Find $\int \cos \omega t \sin \omega t \, dt$.

5 Find $\int_{-\pi}^{\pi} \sin^2 t \, dt$.

6 Find $\int_{-\pi}^{\pi} \cos^2 3t \, dt$.

7 Find $\int \cos 3x \cos 5x \, dx$.

8 Find $\int \sin t \sin 2t \, dt$.

9 Find $\int \sin^2 x + \cos^2 x \, dx$.

10 Find $\int \cos \pi \, dx$.

Solutions to exercises

1 $\dfrac{x}{2} - \dfrac{\sin 4x}{8} + c$

2 $-\dfrac{1}{12} \cos 6x + c$

3 $-\dfrac{5}{4} \cos 2t + c$

4 $-\dfrac{\cos 2\omega t}{4\omega} + c$

5 π

6 π

7 $\dfrac{\sin 8x}{16} + \dfrac{\sin 2x}{4} + c$

8 $\dfrac{\sin t}{2} - \dfrac{\sin 3t}{6} + c$

9 $x + c$

10 $(\cos \pi)x + c = -x + c$

End of chapter exercises

1 Find the following integrals using an appropriate technique selected from this chapter:

(a) $\displaystyle\int \frac{1}{4 + x^2} \, dx$

(b) $\int \cos^2 x \, dx$

(c) $\displaystyle\int \frac{1}{4 - t} \, dt$

(d) $\int_0^{\pi} \cos t \, dt$

(e) $\int_1^{1.2} \tan x \, dx$

(f) $\displaystyle\int \frac{2x^2 + x + 2}{x^3 + x} \, dx$

(g) $\int \sin 3t \cos 3t \, dt$

(h) $\displaystyle\int \frac{1}{16 - x^2} \, dx$

(i) $\displaystyle\int \frac{3}{\sqrt{t^2 + 0.25}} \, dt$

(j) $\int_{-1}^{1} \cosh 3t \, dt$

(k) $\displaystyle\int_1^3 \frac{1}{1 + x^2} \, dx$

(l) $\displaystyle\int \frac{1}{\sqrt{100 - 4x^2}} \, dx$

(m) $\displaystyle\int x \cos \frac{x}{2} \, dx$

(n) $\int 3^x \, dx$

(o) $\int \sec t \, dt$

(p) $\int \sin 5x \cos 2x \, dx$

(q) $\displaystyle\int \frac{1}{x(x - 3)} \, dx$

(r) $\int \frac{1}{t^2(t-1)}\,dt$

(s) $\int \frac{\ln x}{x}\,dx$

(t) $\int t\sqrt{3t-2}\,dt$

(u) $\int \frac{1}{5+4\cos x}\,dx$

(v) $\int_0^2 t^2 e^t\,dt$

(w) $\int \cos x\sqrt{\sin x}\,dx$

(x) $\int \frac{x^2}{x^3+1}\,dx$

(y) $\int \frac{8t+10}{4t^2+8t+3}\,dt$

(z) $\int \frac{7}{(e^t)^7}\,dt$

2 By making the substitution $u^2 = x$ find $\int \sin\sqrt{x}\,dx$.

3 Use the substitution $t = \frac{\pi}{4} - u$ to show that

$$\int_0^{\pi/4} \ln(1+\tan t)\,dt = \frac{1}{8}\pi \ln 2.$$

4 Find $\int_0^1 \frac{1+2x}{1+x^2}\,dx$.

5 Find $\int \frac{dx}{(1-x)\sqrt{x}}$.

6 By means of the substitution $x = \sin^2\theta$ find $\int \sqrt{\frac{x}{1-x}}\,dx$.

7 Find $\int \sqrt{\frac{x}{x-2}}\,dx$.

8 Find $\int_0^{\pi/4} \sin^2 t\,dt$.

9 Use the substitution $u = e^x - 1$ to find $\int \frac{e^{2x}}{e^x - 1}\,dx$.

10 Find $\int_0^{0.3} \frac{1}{x^2-3x+2}\,dx$.

11 Use integration by parts to find $\int \sec^3 x\,dx$.

12 If $I_n = \int x^n e^{2x}\,dx$ show that

$$I_n = \frac{x^n e^{2x}}{2} - \frac{n}{2} I_{n-1}.$$

13 Find $\int \frac{2x+7}{x^2+7x}\,dx$.

14 Find $\int \frac{\cos t - \sin t}{\sin t + \cos t}\,dt$.

15 Find $\int \frac{4}{3-x}\,dx$.

16 Find $\int \frac{1}{s^2-2s+5}\,ds$.

17 Find $\int_0^\infty e^{-2t}\,dt$.

18 Find $\int_0^\infty e^{-x}\cos x\,dx$.

19 Find $\int \frac{1}{x^2-4x+3}\,dx$.

20 **Mechanical Engineering – Distance travelled by a projectile.** The velocity, $v(t)$, in ms^{-1}, of a projectile is given by

$$v(t) = 10e^{-t} \qquad t \geq 0$$

(a) Calculate the distance travelled in the first 3 seconds.
(b) Calculate the average speed over the first 3 seconds.

21 **Thermodynamics.** The pressure, P, and volume, V, of a gas are connected by

$$PV^{0.9} = 10^6$$

Calculate the work done by the gas as it expands in volume from 100 to 1000.

Solutions to exercises

1 (a) $\frac{1}{2}\tan^{-1}\left(\frac{x}{2}\right) + c$

(b) $\frac{1}{2}\left(x + \frac{\sin 2x}{2}\right) + c$ (c) $-\ln(4 - t) + c$

(d) 0 (e) 0.4 (f) $\tan^{-1}x + 2\ln x + c$

(g) $-\frac{\cos 6t}{12} + c$ (h) $\frac{1}{8}\ln\frac{4 + x}{4 - x} + c$

(i) $3\sinh^{-1}2t + c$ (j) 6.679 (k) 0.464

(l) $\frac{1}{2}\sin^{-1}\frac{x}{5} + c$

(m) $2x\sin\left(\frac{x}{2}\right) + 4\cos\left(\frac{x}{2}\right) + c$

(n) $\frac{1}{\ln 3}3^x + c$ (o) $\ln|\sec x + \tan x| + c$

(p) $-\frac{\cos 7x}{14} - \frac{\cos 3x}{6} + c$

(q) $\frac{-1}{3}\ln x + \frac{1}{3}\ln(x - 3) + c$

(r) $\frac{1}{t} - \ln\frac{t}{t - 1} + c$ (s) $\frac{1}{2}(\ln x)^2 + c$

(t) $\frac{2(3t - 2)^{3/2}(9t + 4)}{135} + c$

(u) $\frac{2}{3}\tan^{-1}\left(\frac{\tan\left(\frac{x}{2}\right)}{3}\right) + c$

(v) 12.778 (w) $\frac{2}{3}(\sin x)^{3/2} + c$

(x) $\frac{1}{3}\ln(x^3 + 1) + c$

(y) $\frac{1}{2}\ln(2t + 3) + \frac{3}{2}\ln(2t + 1) + c$

(z) $-e^{-7t} + c$

2 $2\sin\sqrt{x} - 2\sqrt{x}\cos\sqrt{x} + c$

4 1.479

5 $-\ln\left(\frac{\sqrt{x} - 1}{\sqrt{x} + 1}\right) + c$

6 $(x - 1)\sqrt{\frac{x}{1 - x}} + \tan^{-1}\left(\sqrt{\frac{x}{1 - x}}\right) + c$

7 $\frac{2\sqrt{x - 2}\,(x + 4)}{3} + c$

8 $\frac{\pi}{8} - \frac{1}{4}$

9 $e^x + \ln(e^x - 1) + c$

10 0.194

11 $\frac{1}{2}\ln|\tan x + \sec x| + \frac{1}{2}\tan x\sec x + c$

13 $\ln(x^2 + 7x) + c$

14 $\ln(\sin t + \cos t) + c$

15 $-4\ln(3 - x) + c$

16 $\frac{1}{2}\tan^{-1}\left(\frac{s - 1}{2}\right) + c$

17 0.5

18 0.5

19 $\frac{1}{2}\ln(x - 3) - \frac{1}{2}\ln(x - 1) + c$

20 (a) 9.502 (b) 3.167

21 4.104×10^6

Applications of integration

Chapter 18

In the previous chapter integration was introduced, and you were shown a wide variety of techniques for obtaining integrals. In this chapter you will meet several important applications of those techniques.

The first block is particularly important for it introduces integration as the **limit of a sum.** This involves obtaining a physical quantity by considering it to be made up of contributions from lots of small parts. The sum of these contributions is calculated using integration. An understanding of Block 1 is essential if you want to be able to apply the techniques to a wider range of problems than those described here.

Chapter 18 contents

BLOCK 1 Integration as the limit of a sum

1.1 Introduction

In Chapter 17, integration was introduced as the reverse of differentiation. A more rigorous treatment would show that integration is a process of adding or 'summation'. By viewing integration from this perspective it is possible to apply the techniques of integration to finding areas, volumes, centres of gravity and many other important physical quantities.

The content of this block is important because it is here that integration is defined properly. A thorough understanding of the process involved is essential if you need to apply the techniques to practical problems.

1.2 The limit of a sum

Consider the graph of the positive function $y(x)$ shown in Figure 1.1. Suppose we are interested in finding the area under the graph between $x = a$ and $x = b$.

Figure 1.1
The area under a curve.

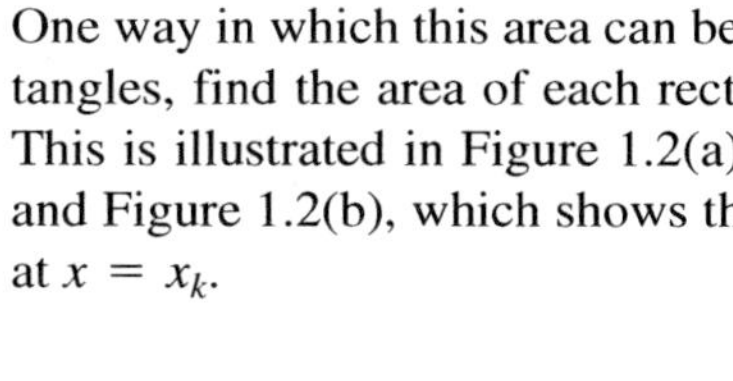

One way in which this area can be approximated is to divide it into a number of rectangles, find the area of each rectangle, and then add all these individual areas up. This is illustrated in Figure 1.2(a), which shows the area divided into n rectangles, and Figure 1.2(b), which shows the dimensions of a typical rectangle that is located at $x = x_k$.

Figure 1.2
(a) The area approximated by n rectangles; (b) a typical rectangle.

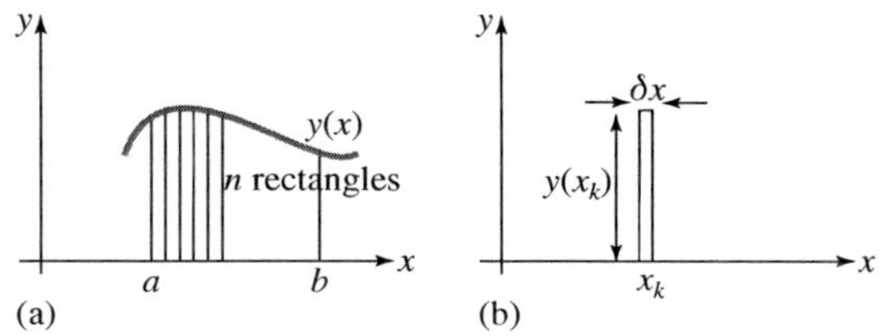

First, refer to Figure 1.2(a) and state the distance from a to b:

$b - a$

In Figure 1.2(a) the area has been divided into n rectangles. If n rectangles span the distance from a to b state the width of each rectangle:

$\frac{b-a}{n}$

It is conventional to label the width of each rectangle as δx. Suppose we label the x coordinates at the left-hand side of the rectangles as x_1, x_2 up to x_n. A typical rectangle, the kth rectangle, is shown in Figure 1.2(b). Note that its height is $y(x_k)$. Calculate its area:

$y(x_k) \times \delta x$

The sum of the areas is then

$$y(x_1)\delta x + y(x_2)\delta x + y(x_3)\delta x + \cdots + y(x_n)\delta x$$

which we write concisely using sigma notation (introduced in Chapter 5, Block 1) as

$$\sum_{k=1}^{n} y(x_k)\delta x$$

This, of course, gives us an estimate of the area under the curve, but it is not exact. To improve the estimate we must take a large number of very thin rectangles. So, what we want to find is the value of this sum when n tends to infinity and δx tends to zero. We write this as

$$\lim_{n\to\infty} \sum_{k=1}^{n} y(x_k)\delta x$$

The lower and upper limits on the sum correspond to the first and last rectangle where $x = a$ and $x = b$ respectively, and so we can write this limit in the equivalent form

$$\lim_{\delta x\to 0} \sum_{x=a}^{x=b} y(x)\delta x \qquad (1)$$

If this sum can actually be found, it is called the **definite integral** of $y(x)$, from $x = a$ to $x = b$, and it is written $\int_a^b y(x)\,dx$. You are already familiar with the mechanism for finding definite integrals, which were studied in Chapter 17, Block 2.

Therefore we have the following definition:

Key point

The definite integral

$$\int_a^b y(x)\,dx$$

is defined as

$$\lim_{\delta x\to 0} \sum_{x=a}^{x=b} y(x)\delta x$$

Note that the quantity δx represents the thickness of a small but finite rectangle. When we have taken the limit as δx tends to zero to obtain the integral, we write dx.

This process of dividing an area into very small regions, performing a calculation on each region, and then adding the results by means of an integral is very important. This will become apparent when finding volumes, centres of gravity, moments of inertia, etc., in the following blocks.

Example 1.1

The area under the graph of $y = x^2$ between $x = 0$ and $x = 1$ is to be found using the technique just described. If the required area is approximated by a large number of thin rectangles, the limit of the sum of their areas is given from equation (1) as

$$\lim_{\delta x \to 0} \sum_{x=0}^{x=1} y(x)\delta x$$

Write down the integral that this sum defines and evaluate it to obtain the area under the curve.

Solution

The limit of the sum defines the integral $\int_0^1 y(x)\,dx$. Here $y = x^2$ and so

$$\int_0^1 x^2\,dx = \left[\frac{x^3}{3}\right]_0^1 = \frac{1}{3}$$

To show that taking the limit of a sum actually works we have provided a detailed example for you to work through.

Example 1.2

Use the idea of the limit of a sum to find the area under the graph of $y = x^2$ between $x = 0$ and $x = 1$.

Solution

Refer to the graph in Figure 1.3 to help you answer the questions.

If the interval between $x = 0$ and $x = 1$ is divided into n rectangles what is the width of each rectangle?

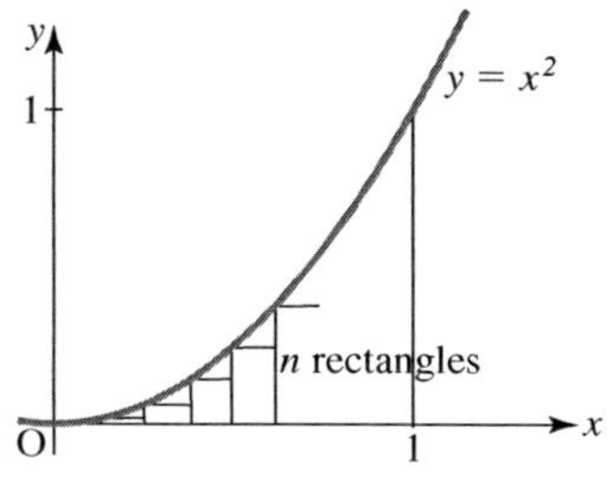

Figure 1.3 The area under $y = x^2$ is approximated by a number of thin rectangles.

$\frac{1}{n}$

Mark this on Figure 1.3.

What is the x coordinate at the left-hand side of the first rectangle?

0

What is the x coordinate at the left-hand side of the second rectangle?

$\frac{1}{n}$

What is the x coordinate at the left-hand side of the third rectangle?

$\frac{2}{n}$

Mark these coordinates on Figure 1.3.

What is the x coordinate at the left-hand side of the kth rectangle?

$\frac{k-1}{n}$

Given that $y = x^2$, what is the y coordinate at the left-hand side of the kth rectangle?

$\left(\frac{k-1}{n}\right)^2$

The area of the kth rectangle is its height $\times$ its width. Write down the area of the kth rectangle:

$\left(\frac{k-1}{n}\right)^2 \times \frac{1}{n} = \frac{(k-1)^2}{n^3}$

To find the total area of the n rectangles we must add up all these individual areas:

$$\text{total area of rectangles} = \sum_{k=1}^{n} \frac{(k-1)^2}{n^3}$$

This sum can be simplified and then calculated as follows. You will need to make use of the formulae for the sum of the first k integers, and the sum of the squares of the first k integers. Details of these will be given in Chapter 19, Block 2. For completeness we state the relevant formulae now:

$$\sum_{k=1}^{n} 1 = n, \quad \sum_{k=1}^{n} k = \frac{n}{2}(n+1), \quad \sum_{k=1}^{n} k^2 = \frac{n}{6}(n+1)(2n+1)$$

Then, the total area of the rectangles is given by

$$\begin{aligned}\sum_{k=1}^{n} \frac{(k-1)^2}{n^3} &= \frac{1}{n^3}\sum_{k=1}^{n} (k-1)^2 \\ &= \frac{1}{n^3}\sum_{k=1}^{n} k^2 - 2k + 1\end{aligned}$$

$$= \frac{1}{n^3}\left(\sum_{k=1}^{n} k^2 - 2\sum_{k=1}^{n} k + \sum_{k=1}^{n} 1\right)$$

$$= \frac{1}{n^3}\left(\frac{n}{6}(n+1)(2n+1) - 2\frac{n}{2}(n+1) + n\right)$$

$$= \frac{1}{n^2}\left(\frac{(n+1)(2n+1)}{6} - (n+1) + 1\right)$$

$$= \frac{1}{n^2}\left(\frac{(n+1)(2n+1)}{6} - n\right)$$

$$= \frac{1}{n^2}\left(\frac{(n+1)(2n+1)}{6} - \frac{6n}{6}\right)$$

$$= \frac{1}{6n^2}(2n^2 - 3n + 1)$$

$$= \frac{1}{3} - \frac{1}{2n} + \frac{1}{6n^2}$$

Note that this is a formula for the total area of the n rectangles. It is an estimate of the area under the graph of $y = x^2$. Now, as n gets larger, the terms $\frac{1}{2n}$ and $\frac{1}{6n^2}$ become small and will eventually tend to zero. If we now let n tend to infinity we obtain the exact answer:

$$\lim_{n\to\infty}\left(\frac{1}{3} - \frac{1}{2n} + \frac{1}{6n^2}\right) = \qquad \frac{1}{3}$$

The required area is $\frac{1}{3}$.

The area has been found as **the limit of a sum**.

In the calculations that follow in subsequent blocks the need to evaluate complicated limits like this is avoided by performing the integration using the techniques of Chapter 17. Nevertheless it will still be necessary to go through the process of dividing a region into small sections, performing a calculation on each section and then adding the results, in order to obtain the integral required.

Exercises

There are deliberately few exercises in this block because in practice integrals are evaluated using the techniques of Chapter 17 and not via taking the limits of sums explicitly. What is important though is an understanding of how the appropriate sum is formed.

1 Find the area under $y = x + 1$ from $x = 0$ to $x = 10$ using the limit of a sum.

2 Find the area under $y = 3x^2$ from $x = 0$ to $x = 2$ using the limit of a sum.

3 Write down, but do not evaluate, the integral defined by the limit as $\delta x \to 0$, or $\delta y \to 0$ of the following sums:

(a) $\sum_{x=0}^{x=1} x^3\,\delta x$ (b) $\sum_{x=0}^{x=4} 4\pi x^2\,\delta x$
(c) $\sum_{y=0}^{y=1} y^3\,\delta y$ (d) $\sum_{x=0}^{x=1} 6mx^2\,\delta x$

Solutions to exercises

1 60

2 8

3 (a) $\int_0^1 x^3\,dx$ (b) $4\pi\int_0^4 x^2\,dx$ (c) $\int_0^1 y^3\,dy$
(d) $\int_0^1 6mx^2\,dx$

End of block exercises

1 Use the method of the limit of a sum to find the area bounded by the curve $y = x^3$ and the x axis between $x = a$ and $x = b$. You may assume the result

$$\sum_{k=1}^{n} k^3 = \frac{n^2}{4}(n+1)^2$$

2 Write down, but do not evaluate, the integral defined by the limit as $\delta x \to 0$, $\delta y \to 0$, or $\delta s \to 0$ of the following sums:

(a) $\sum_{x=1}^{x=5} \pi x^3\,\delta x$ (b) $\sum_{x=0}^{x=a} \pi x^2\,\delta x$
(c) $\sum_{y=0}^{y=2} m(2-y)y\delta y$
(d) $\sum_{x=-b/2}^{x=b/2} mbx^2\,\delta x$
(e) $\sum_{s=0}^{s=1} s^2\,\delta s$

Solutions to exercises

1 $\dfrac{(b^4 - a^4)}{4}$

2 (a) $\int_1^5 \pi x^3\,dx$ (b) $\int_0^a \pi x^2\,dx$
(c) $\int_0^2 m(2-y)y\,dy$ (d) $\int_{-b/2}^{b/2} mbx^2\,dx$
(e) $\int_0^1 s^2\,ds$

BLOCK 2 Volumes of revolution

2.1 Introduction

In this block we show how the concept of integration as the limit of a sum can be used to find volumes of solids formed when areas are rotated around the x or y axes.

2.2 Volumes generated by rotating areas about the x axis

Figure 2.1 shows a graph of the function $y = 2x$ for x between 0 and 3.

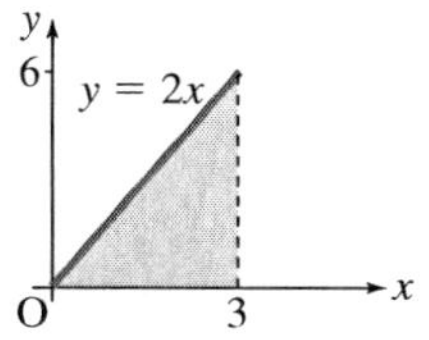

Figure 2.1 A graph of the function $y = 2x$, for $0 \le x \le 3$.

Imagine rotating the shaded area under $y = 2x$ a full revolution around the x axis. The body so formed is a cone as shown in Figure 2.2. Such a three-dimensional body is known as a **solid of revolution** or a **volume of revolution**.

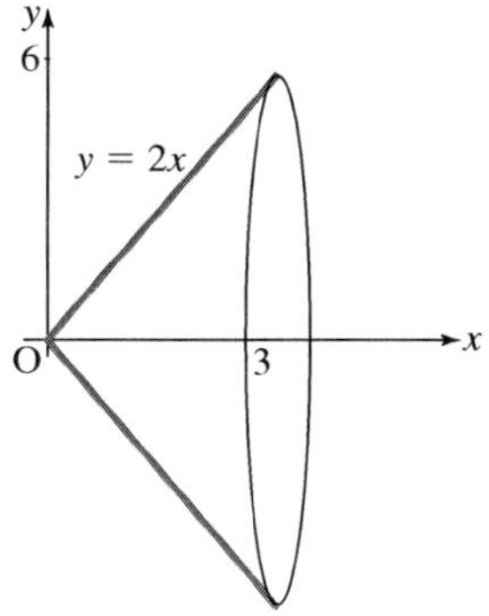

Figure 2.2 When the area under $y = 2x$ is rotated around the axis, a solid is generated.

Example 2.1

Find the volume of the cone generated by rotating the area under $y = 2x$, for $0 \le x \le 3$, around the x axis, as shown in Figure 2.2.

Solution

In order to find the volume of this solid we assume that it is composed of lots of thin circular discs all aligned perpendicular to the x axis, such as that shown in Figure 2.3. From Figure 2.3 we note that a typical disc has radius y, which in this example equals $2x$, and thickness δx.

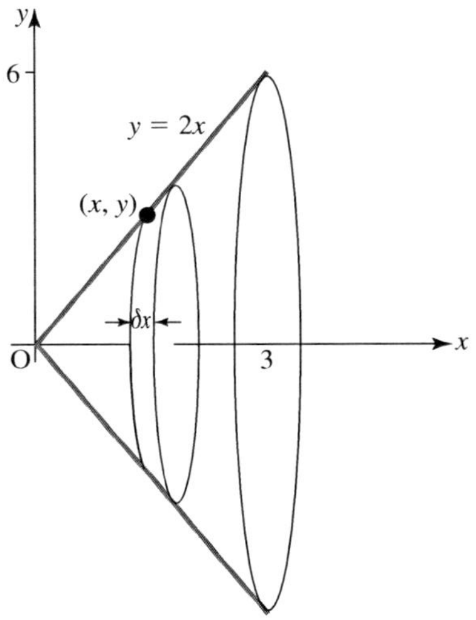

Figure 2.3 The cone is divided into a number of thin circular discs.

The volume of a circular disc is the circular area multiplied by the thickness. Write down an expression for the volume of this typical disc:

$$\pi(2x)^2\,\delta x = 4\pi x^2\,\delta x$$

To find the total volume we must sum the contributions from all discs and find the limit of this sum as the number of discs becomes infinite and δx becomes zero. That is,

$$\lim_{\delta x \to 0} \sum_{x=0}^{x=3} 4\pi x^2\,\delta x$$

This is the definition of a definite integral. Write down the corresponding integral.

$$\int_0^3 4\pi x^2\,dx$$

Find the required volume by performing the integration:

$$\left[\frac{4\pi x^3}{3}\right]_0^3 = 36\pi$$

Example 2.2

A graph of the function $y = x^2$ for x between 0 and 4 is shown in Figure 2.4. The area under the graph is rotated around the x axis to produce the solid shown. Find its volume.

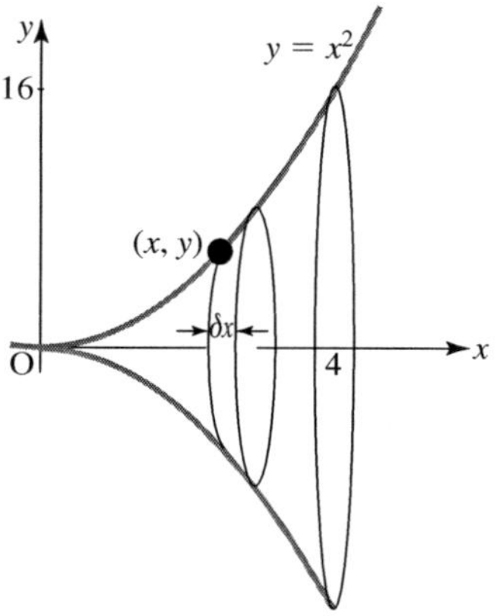

Figure 2.4 The solid of revolution is divided into a number of thin circular discs.

Solution

As in Example 2.1, the volume is considered to be composed of lots of circular discs of radius y, which in this example is equal to x^2, and thickness δx.

The volume of a circular disc is the circular area multiplied by the thickness.

Write down the volume of each disc:

$$\pi(x^2)^2\,\delta x = \pi x^4\,\delta x$$

Write down the expression that results by summing the volumes of all such discs:

$$\sum_{x=0}^{x=4} \pi x^4\,\delta x$$

Write down the integral that results from taking the limit of the sum as $\delta x \to 0$:

$$\int_0^4 \pi x^4\,dx$$

Perform the integration to find the volume of the solid:

$$\frac{4^5\,\pi}{5} = 204.8\pi$$

In general, suppose the area under the graph of $y(x)$ between $x = a$ and $x = b$ is rotated about the x axis, and the solid so formed is considered to be composed of lots of circular discs of thickness δx.

Write down an expression for the radius of a typical disc:

$$y$$

Write down an expression for the volume of a typical disc:

$\pi y^2\,\delta x$

The total volume is found by summing these individual volumes and taking the limit as δx becomes zero:

$$\lim_{\delta x \to 0} \sum_{x=a}^{x=b} \pi y^2\,\delta x$$

Write down the definite integral that this sum defines:

$\int_a^b \pi y^2\,\mathrm{d}x$

Key point

If the area under the graph of $y(x)$, between $x = a$ and $x = b$, is rotated about the x axis the volume of the solid formed is

$$\int_a^b \pi y^2\,\mathrm{d}x$$

Exercises

1. When the area under the graph of $y(x)$ between $x = a$ and $x = b$ is rotated around the x axis, show that the volume of the solid formed is $\int_a^b \pi y^2\,\mathrm{d}x$.

2. Find the volume of the solid formed when the area under $y = x^2$ between $x = 1$ and $x = 2$ is rotated about the x axis.

3. The area under the parabola $y^2 = 4x$ for $0 \leq x \leq 1$ is rotated around the x axis. Find the volume of the solid formed.

Solutions to exercises

2. $\dfrac{31\pi}{5}$

3. 2π

2.3 Volumes generated by rotating areas about the *y* axis

We can obtain a different solid of revolution by rotating an area around the y axis instead of around the x axis. In Figure 2.5 the area between the graph of $y(x)$ and the y axis has been rotated about the y axis.

To find the volume of this solid it is divided into a number of circular discs as before, but this time the discs are horizontal. The radius of a typical disc is x and

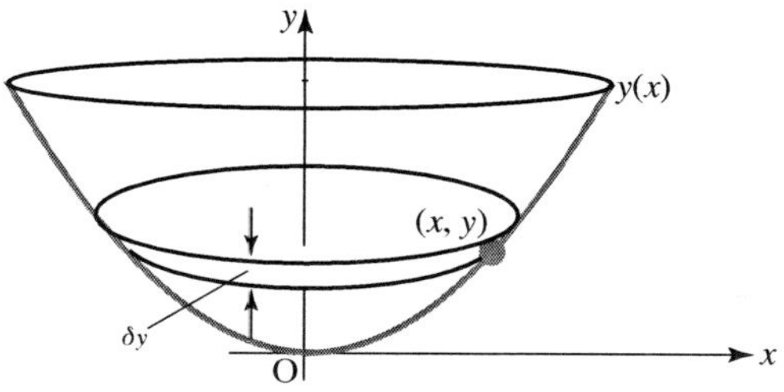

Figure 2.5
A solid can be generated by rotation around the y axis.

its thickness is δy. The volume of the disc will be $\pi x^2 \delta y$ where δy is the thickness of the disc.

The total volume is found by summing these individual volumes and taking the limit as $\delta y \to 0$. If the lower and upper limits on y are c and d, we find

$$\lim_{\delta y \to 0} \sum_{y=c}^{y=d} \pi x^2 \, \delta y$$

which is the definite integral

$$\int_c^d \pi x^2 \, \mathrm{d}y$$

Key point

If the area between the graph of $y(x)$ and the y axis between $y = c$ and $y = d$ is rotated about the y axis the volume of the solid formed is

$$\int_c^d \pi x^2 \, \mathrm{d}y$$

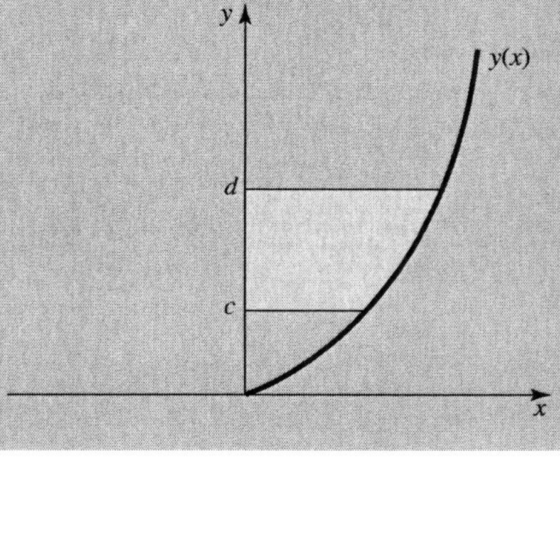

Figure 2.6
Rotating the shaded area about the y axis produces a volume of revolution.

Example 2.3
Find the volume generated when the area between $y = x^2$ and the y axis between $y = 0$ and $y = 1$ is rotated around the y axis.

Solution
Write down the required integral.

$$\int_0^1 \pi x^2 \, dy$$

Because $y = x^2$ this integral can be written entirely in terms of y. Do this now, and then evaluate the integral.

$$\int_0^1 \pi y \, dy = \left[\frac{\pi y^2}{2}\right]_0^1 = \frac{\pi}{2}$$

Exercises

1 The area between $y = x^2$ and the y axis between $y = 1$ and $y = 4$ is rotated about the y axis. Find the volume of the solid formed.

2 The area between $y = 2 - 2x$ and the y axis between $y = -2$ and $y = 2$ is rotated around the y axis. Find the volume of revolution.

Solutions to exercises

1 $\dfrac{15\pi}{2}$

2 $\dfrac{16\pi}{3}$

End of block exercises

1 The area between the parabola $y^2 = 4ax$ and the x axis for $0 < x < a$ is rotated around the x axis. Show that the volume of the solid formed is $2\pi a^3$.

2 The equation of a circle with centre the origin and radius a is $x^2 + y^2 = a^2$. By considering that portion of the circle that lies in the first quadrant, and rotating this around the x axis, show that the volume of a hemisphere of radius a is $\dfrac{2\pi a^3}{3}$.

3 Find the volume obtained when the area between $y = \sin x$ and the x axis for $0 < x < \pi$ is rotated around the x axis.

4 The area under $y = \frac{1}{x}$ between $x = 1$ and $x = 3$ is rotated about the x axis. Find the volume of revolution.

5 Consider the area bounded by the curve $y = x^2 - 1$ between $x = 1$ and $x = 2$ and the x axis. If this area is rotated around the y axis show that the volume of the solid generated is $\frac{9\pi}{2}$.

6 The area between $y = 1 - \frac{1}{2}x$ and the x axis for $0 \le x \le 2$ is rotated around the y axis. Find the volume of the solid generated.

Solutions to exercises

3 $\dfrac{\pi^2}{2}$

4 $\dfrac{2\pi}{3}$

6 $\dfrac{4\pi}{3}$

BLOCK 3 Calculating centres of mass

3.1 Introduction

In this block we show how the idea of integration as the limit of a sum can be used to find the centre of mass of an object such as a thin plate, like a sheet of metal. Such a plate is also known as a *lamina*. An understanding of a 'moment' is necessary, and so this concept is introduced as well.

3.2 The centre of mass of a collection of point masses

Suppose we have a collection of masses located at a number of known points. The **centre of mass** is the point where, for many purposes, all the mass can be assumed to be located.

For example, if two objects each of mass m are placed at the locations $x = 1$ and $x = 2$, as shown in Figure 3.1(a), then the total mass, $2m$, can be assumed to be located at $x = 1.5$ as shown in Figure 3.1(b). This is the point where we could imagine placing a pivot to achieve a perfectly balanced system.

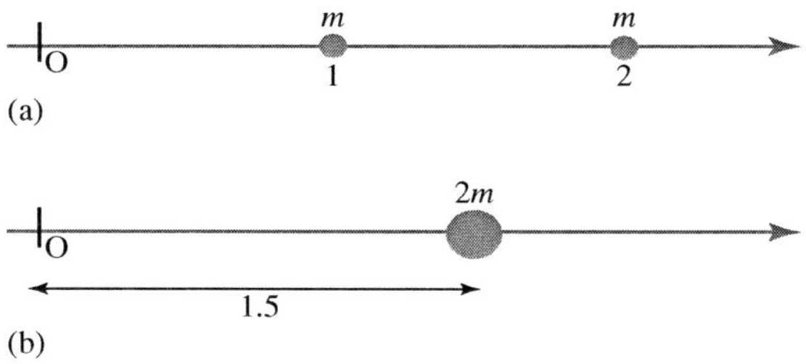

Figure 3.1
(b) The location of the centre of mass of the objects in (a).

To think of this another way, if a pivot is placed at the origin, as on a see-saw, then the two masses at $x = 1$ and $x = 2$ together have the same **turning effect** or **moment** as a single mass $2m$ located at $x = 1.5$. This is illustrated in Figure 3.2.

Before we can calculate the position of the centre of mass of a collection of masses it is important to define moment more precisely.

Given a mass M located a distance d from O, as shown in Figure 3.3, its moment about O is defined to be

$$\text{Moment} = Md$$

In words, the moment of the mass about O is the mass multiplied by its distance from O. The unit of moment will therefore be kg m when the mass is measured in kilograms and the distance is measured in metres.

Figure 3.2
The single object of mass $2m$ has the same turning effect as the two objects each of mass m.

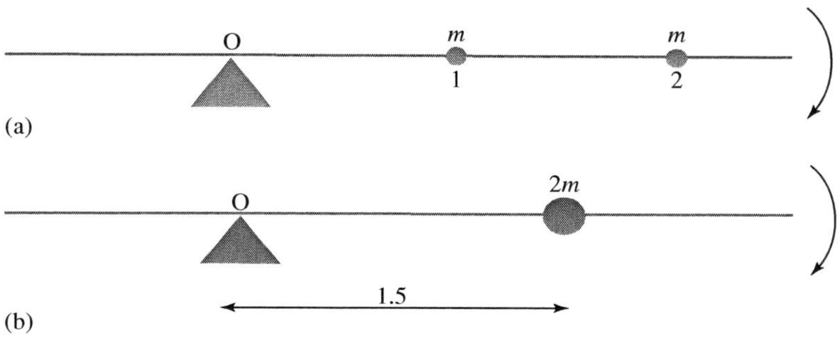

Figure 3.3
The moment of the mass M about O is Md.

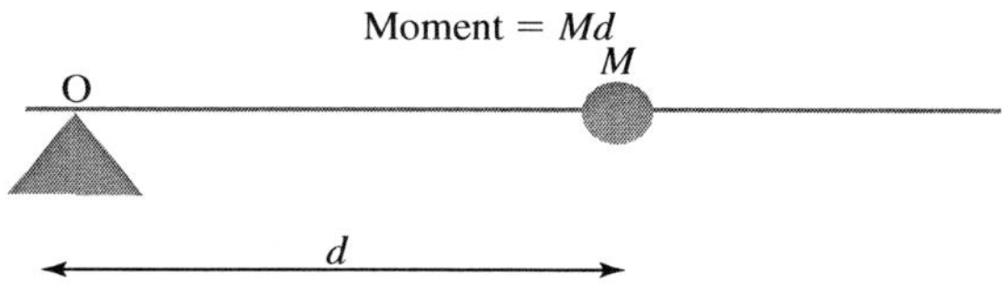

Example 3.1 Mechanical Engineering – Moments

Calculate the moment of the mass about O in each of the cases shown in Figures 3.4 and 3.5.

Figure 3.4

(a)

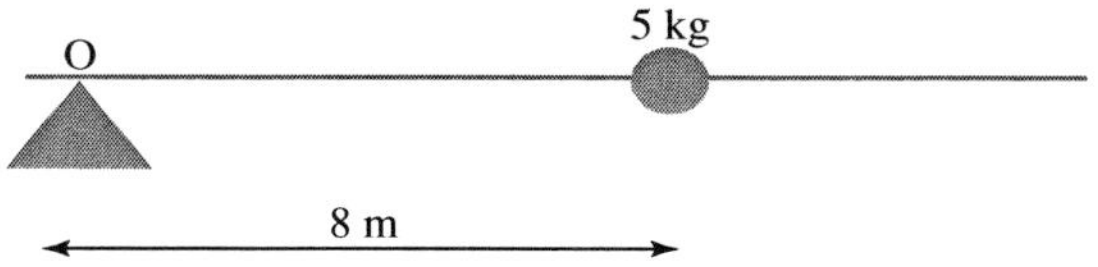

Figure 3.5

(b)

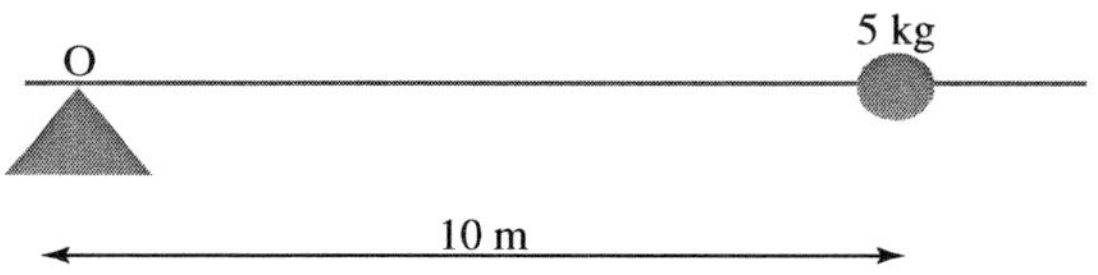

Solution

(a) 40 kg m

(b) 50 kg m

Intuition tells us that a large moment corresponds to a large turning effect. A mass placed 8 metres from the origin has a smaller turning effect than the same mass placed 10 metres from the origin. This is of course why it is easier to rock a see-saw by pushing it at a point further from the pivot.

For a collection of masses the moment of the total mass located at the centre of mass is equal to the sum of the moments of the individual masses. This result enables us to calculate the position of the centre of mass, as we shall see in the following examples. It is conventional to label the x coordinate of the centre of mass as $\bar{x}$, pronounced 'x bar'.

Key point

The moment of the total mass located at the centre of mass is equal to the sum of the moments of the individual masses.

Example 3.2 Mechanical Engineering – Centre of mass

Objects of mass m and $3m$ are placed at the locations shown in Figure 3.6. Find the distance $\bar{x}$ of the centre of mass from the origin O.

Figure 3.6

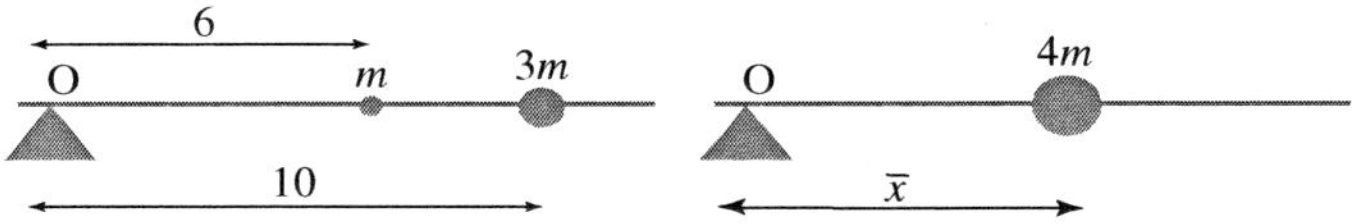

Solution

First calculate the sum of the individual moments:

$$6(m) + 10(3m) = 36m$$

The moment of the total mass about O is

$$(4m)\bar{x}$$

Now, the moment of the total mass is equal to the sum of the moments of the individual masses. Write down the equation satisfied by $\bar{x}$.

$$36m = 4m\bar{x}$$

Solve for $\bar{x}$.

$$\bar{x} = 9$$

So the centre of mass is located a distance 9 units along the x axis.

Example 3.3 Mechanical Engineering – Centre of mass

Obtain an equation for the location of the centre of mass of two objects of masses m_1 and m_2 located at $x = x_1$ and $x = x_2$ respectively, as shown in Figure 3.7.

Figure 3.7

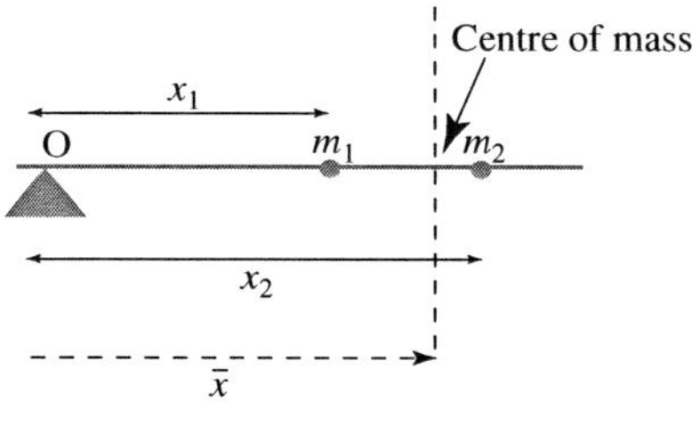

Solution

Referring to Figure 3.7, first write down an expression for the sum of the individual moments:

$$m_1x_1 + m_2x_2$$

Write down an expression for the total mass:

$$m_1 + m_2$$

Write down an expression for the moment of the total mass:

$$(m_1 + m_2)\bar{x}$$

The moment of the total mass is equal to the sum of the moments of the individual masses. Write down the equation satisfied by $\bar{x}$.

$$(m_1 + m_2)\bar{x} = m_1x_1 + m_2x_2$$

Finally write down an expression for $\bar{x}$.

$$\bar{x} = \frac{m_1x_1 + m_2x_2}{m_1 + m_2}$$

The formula obtained in the previous example can be generalised very easily to deal with the situation of n masses, $m_1, m_2, \ldots, m_n$, located at $x_1, x_2, \ldots, x_n$:

Key point

The centre of mass of $m_1, m_2, \ldots, m_n$ located at $x_1, x_2, \ldots, x_n$ is

$$\bar{x} = \frac{\sum_{i=1}^{n} m_i x_i}{\sum_{i=1}^{n} m_i}$$

Example 3.4 Mechanical Engineering – Centre of mass

Calculate the centre of mass of the four masses distributed as shown in Figure 3.8.

Figure 3.8

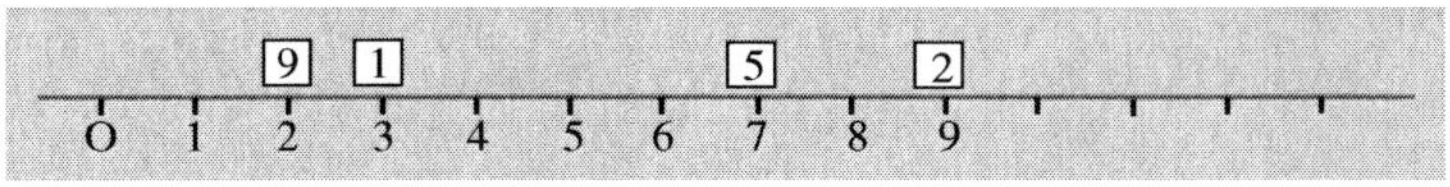

Solution

$$\bar{x} = \frac{\sum_{i=1}^{4} m_i x_i}{\sum_{i=1}^{4} m_i}$$

$$= \frac{(9)(2) + (1)(3) + (5)(7) + (2)(9)}{9 + 1 + 5 + 2}$$

$$= \frac{74}{17}$$

The centre of mass is located a distance $\frac{74}{17} \approx 4.35$ units along the x axis from O.

When n masses are distributed, not just along the x axis but anywhere in the xy plane (Figure 3.9), the coordinates of their centre of mass are given as follows:

Key point

The centre of mass of $m_1, m_2, \ldots, m_n$ located at $(x_1, y_1), (x_2, y_2), \ldots, (x_n, y_n)$ has coordinates

$$\bar{x} = \frac{\sum_{i=1}^{n} m_i x_i}{\sum_{i=1}^{n} m_i}, \bar{y} = \frac{\sum_{i=1}^{n} m_i y_i}{\sum_{i=1}^{n} m_i}$$

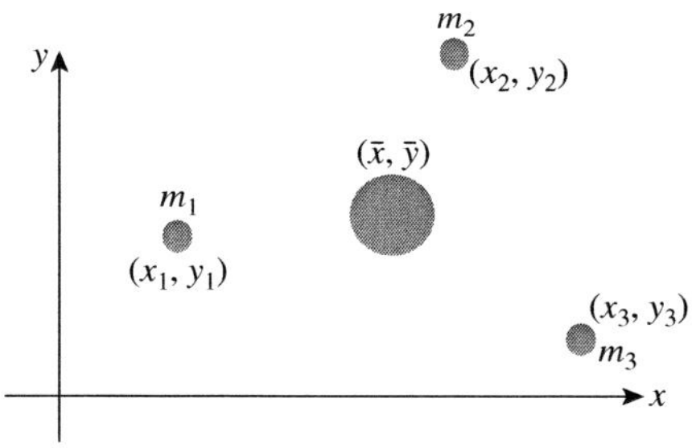

Figure 3.9 These masses are distributed throughout the xy plane.

Example 3.5 Mechanical Engineering – Centre of mass

Masses of 5 kg, 3 kg and 9 kg are located at the points with coordinates $(-1, 1)$, $(4, 3)$ and $(8, 7)$ respectively. Find the coordinates of their centre of mass.

Solution

(a) Here $n = 3$.

$$\bar{x} = \frac{\sum_{i=1}^{3} m_i x_i}{\sum_{i=1}^{3} m_i}$$

$$= \frac{5(-1) + 3(4) + 9(8)}{5 + 3 + 9}$$

$$= \frac{79}{17}$$

$$= 4.65$$

(b) $\bar{y} = \dfrac{5(1) + 3(3) + 9(7)}{17} = 4.53$

Hence the centre of mass is located at the point (4.65, 4.53).

Exercises

1 Explain what is meant by the centre of mass of a collection of point masses.

2 Find the x coordinate of the centre of mass of five identical masses placed at $x = 2$, $x = 5$, $x = 7$, $x = 9$, $x = 12$.

3 Derive the formula for $\bar{y}$ given in the previous key point.

4 **Mechanical Engineering – Centre of mass.** Calculate the position of the centre of mass of 2 kg placed at $x = 1$, 3 kg placed at $x = 4$, 1 kg placed at $x = 6$ and 6 kg placed at $x = -5$.

5 **Mechanical Engineering – Centre of mass.** Masses of 3 kg, 2 kg, 2 kg and 4 kg are located at points with coordinates (1, 3), (−2, 0), (4, −1) and (−3, 4), respectively. Calculate the coordinates of the centre of mass.

Solutions to exercises

2 $\bar{x} = 7$

4 $\bar{x} = -\frac{5}{6}$

5 $\bar{x} = -\frac{5}{11}$, $\bar{y} = \frac{23}{11}$

3.3 Finding the centre of mass of a plane uniform lamina

In the previous section you calculated the centre of mass of several individual point masses. Suppose we are interested in the centre of mass of a thin sheet of material, such as a plane sheet of metal. Such an object is called a **lamina**. The mass is not located at individual points. Rather, it is distributed continuously throughout the lamina. In what follows we assume that the mass is distributed uniformly throughout the lamina. In this section you will see how integration as the limit of a sum is used to find the centre of mass.

Figure 3.10 shows a lamina where the centre of mass has been marked at point G with coordinates $(\bar{x}, \bar{y})$. If the total mass of the lamina is M then the moments about

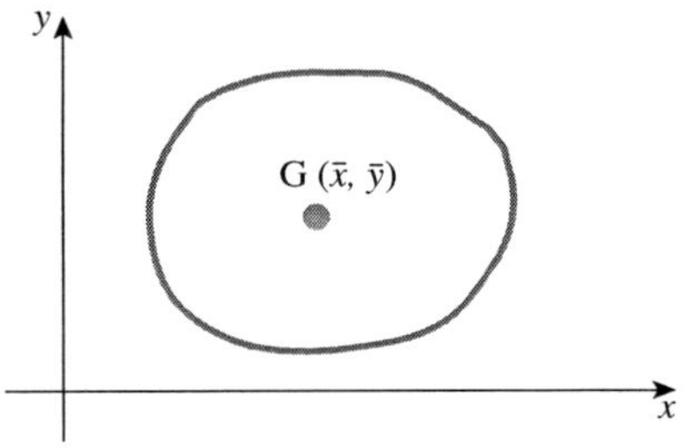

Figure 3.10 The centre of mass of the lamina is located at G$(\bar{x}, \bar{y})$.

the y and x axes are respectively $M\bar{x}$ and $M\bar{y}$. Our approach to locating the position of G is to divide the lamina into many small pieces, find the mass of each piece and the moment of each piece about the axes. The sum of the moments of the individual pieces about the y axis will be equal to $M\bar{x}$. The sum of the moments of the individual pieces about the x axis will be equal to $M\bar{y}$.

There are no formulae that can be memorised for finding the centre of mass of a lamina because of the wide variety of possible shapes. Instead you should be familiar with the technique for deriving the centre of mass.

An important preliminary concept is 'mass per unit area.'

Mass per unit area

Suppose we have a uniform lamina and suppose we select a piece of the lamina that has area equal to 1 unit. Let m stand for the mass of such a piece. Then m is called the **mass per unit area**. The mass of any other piece can be expressed in terms of m. For example, an area of 2 units must have mass $2m$. An area of 3 units must have mass $3m$, and so on. Any other portion of the lamina that has area A has mass mA.

Key point

If a lamina has mass per unit area m, then the mass of part of the lamina having area A is Am.

We shall illustrate the calculation of centre of mass in the following examples.

Example 3.6 Mechanical Engineering – Centre of mass of a lamina

Consider the plane sheet, or lamina, in Figure 3.11. Find the location of its centre of mass.

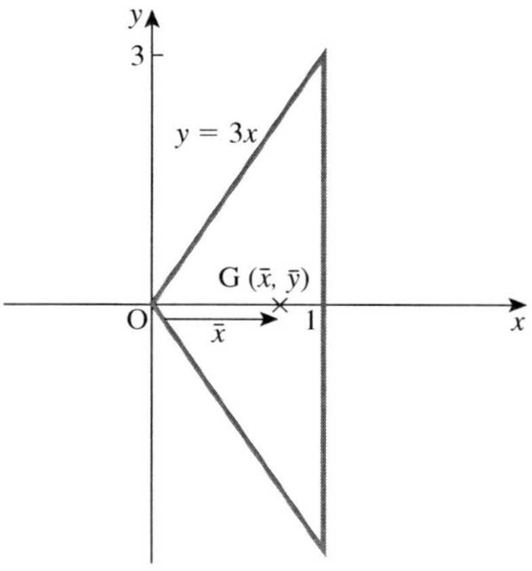

Figure 3.11 By symmetry the centre of mass of this lamina lies on the x axis.

Solution

First inspect the figure and note the symmetry of the lamina. Purely from the symmetry, what must be the y coordinate, $\bar{y}$, of the centre of mass?

$\bar{y} = 0$ since the centre of mass must lie on the x axis

Let m stand for the mass per unit area of the sheet. The total area is 3 units. The total mass is therefore $3m$. Its moment about the y axis is $3m\bar{x}$ where $\bar{x}$ is the x coordinate of the centre of mass.

To find $\bar{x}$ first divide the sheet into a large number of thin vertical slices. In Figure 3.12 a typical slice has been highlighted. Note that the slice has been drawn from the point P on the graph of $y = 3x$. The point P has coordinates (x, y). The thickness of the slice is δx. This notation is consistent with that introduced in Block 1.

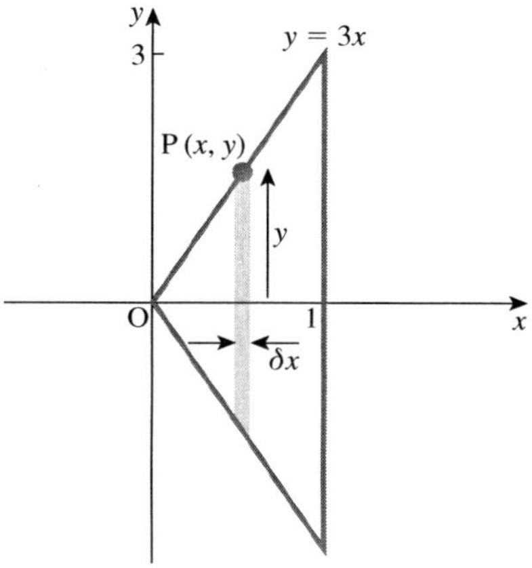

Figure 3.12 A typical slice of this sheet has been shaded.

Assuming that the slice is rectangular in shape, write down its area.

$2\,y\delta x$

Writing m as the mass per unit area, write down the mass of the slice.

$(2y\delta x)m$

The centre of mass of this slice lies on the x axis. So the slice can be assumed to be a point mass, $2ym\delta x$, located a distance x from O.

Write down the moment of the mass of the slice about the y axis:

$(2y\delta x)mx$

By adding up contributions from all such slices in the lamina we obtain the sum of the moments of the individual masses:

$$\sum_{x=0}^{x=1} 2mxy\delta x$$

The limits on the sum are chosen so that all slices are included.

Write down the integral defined by letting $\delta x \to 0$:

$$\int_{x=0}^{x=1} 2mxy\,dx$$

Note that this represents the sum of all the individual moments taken throughout the entire lamina. Noting that $y = 3x$ express the integral in terms of x and evaluate it:

$$\int_0^1 6mx^2\,dx = [2mx^3]_0^1 = 2m$$

This must equal the moment of the total mass acting at the centre of mass.

Hence

$$3m\bar{x} = 2m$$

from which

$$\bar{x} = \frac{2}{3}$$

Finally the coordinates of the centre of mass are $(\frac{2}{3}, 0)$.

Example 3.7 Mechanical Engineering – Centre of mass of a lamina

Find the centre of mass of the plane lamina shown in Figure 3.13.

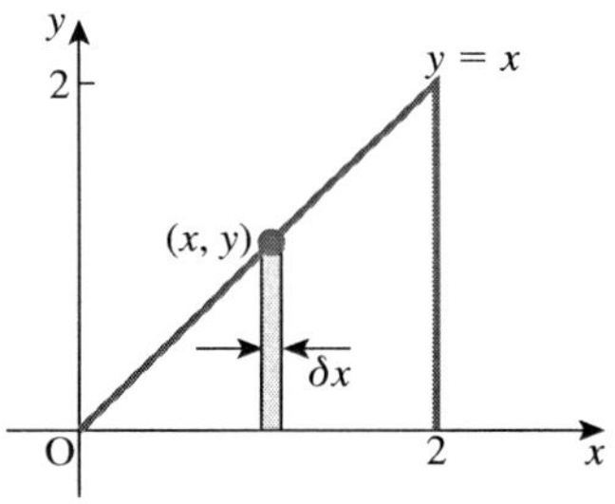

Figure 3.13 We assume that the shaded slice is rectangular.

Solution

The coordinates of $\bar{x}$ and $\bar{y}$ must be calculated separately.

To calculate $\bar{x}$

Let m equal the mass per unit area. Write down the total area, the total mass and its moment about the y axis:

$2, 2m, 2m\bar{x}$

To calculate $\bar{x}$ the lamina is divided into thin slices; a typical slice is shown in Figure 3.13. Assume that it is rectangular.

Write down the height of the typical strip shown in Figure 3.13.

y

Write down the area of the typical strip.

$y\delta x$

Write down the mass of the typical strip.

$(y\delta x)m$

Write down the moment about the y axis of the typical strip.

$(y\delta x)mx$

The sum of the moments of all strips is

$$\sum_{x=0}^{x=2} mxy\delta x$$

Write down the integral that follows as $\delta x \to 0$.

$$\int_0^2 mxy\,\mathrm{d}x$$

In this example, $y = x$. Substitute this for y in the integral, and evaluate it.

$$\int_0^2 mx^2\,\mathrm{d}x = \frac{8}{3}m$$

Equating the sum of individual moments and the total moment gives

$$2m\bar{x} = \frac{8}{3}m$$

from which

$$\bar{x} = \frac{4}{3}$$

To calculate $\bar{y}$
We will illustrate two alternative ways of calculating $\bar{y}$.

Referring to Figure 3.13, the centre of mass of the slice must lie half way along its length: that is, its y coordinate is $\frac{y}{2}$. Assume that all the mass of the slice, $ym\delta x$, acts at this point. Then its moment about the x axis is $ym\delta x\,\frac{y}{2}$. Adding contributions from all slices gives the sum

$$\sum_{x=0}^{x=2} \frac{y^2 m}{2}\delta x$$

Write down the integral which is defined as $\delta x \to 0$.

$$\int_{x=0}^{2} \frac{my^2}{2}\,\mathrm{d}x$$

which we can write as

$$m\int_{x=0}^{2} \frac{y^2}{2}\,\mathrm{d}x$$

In this example $y = x$, so the integral becomes

$$m\int_{x=0}^{2} \frac{x^2}{2}\,dx$$

which equals $\frac{4m}{3}$. This is the sum of the individual moments about the x axis and must equal the moment of the total mass about the x axis which is $2m\bar{y}$. Therefore

$$2m\bar{y} = \frac{4m}{3}$$

from which

$$\bar{y} = \frac{2}{3}$$

Finally, the coordinates of the centre of mass are $\left(\frac{4}{3}, \frac{2}{3}\right)$.

Consider now an alternative way of finding $\bar{y}$.

This time the lamina is divided into a number of horizontal slices; a typical slice is shown in Figure 3.14.

The length of the typical slice shown is $2 - x$.

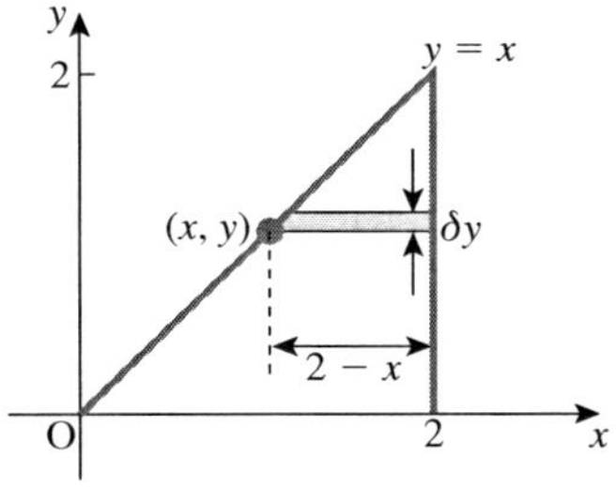

Figure 3.14
A typical horizontal slice is shaded.

Write down its area, its mass and its moment *about the x axis*

$(2 - x)\delta y,\ m(2 - x)\delta y,\ m(2 - x)y\delta y$

Write down the expression for the sum of all such moments and the corresponding integral as $\delta y \to 0$.

$\sum_{y=0}^{y=2} m(2 - x)y\delta y,\ \int_0^2 m(2 - x)y\,dy$

Now, since $y = x$ the integral can be written entirely in terms of y as

$$\int_0^2 m(2 - y)y\,dy$$

Evaluate the integral:

$\frac{4m}{3}$

As before the total mass is $2m$, and its moment about the x axis is $2m\overline{y}$. Hence

$$2m\overline{y} = \frac{4m}{3}$$

from which

$$\overline{y} = \frac{2}{3}$$

as before.

Example 3.8 Mechanical Engineering – Centre of mass of a lamina

Find the position of the centre of mass of a uniform semicircular lamina of radius a.

Solution

The lamina is shown in Figure 3.15. The equation of a circle with centre the origin, radius a, is $x^2 + y^2 = a^2$. By symmetry $\overline{x}$ must lie on the y axis. However, it is necessary to calculate $\overline{y}$.

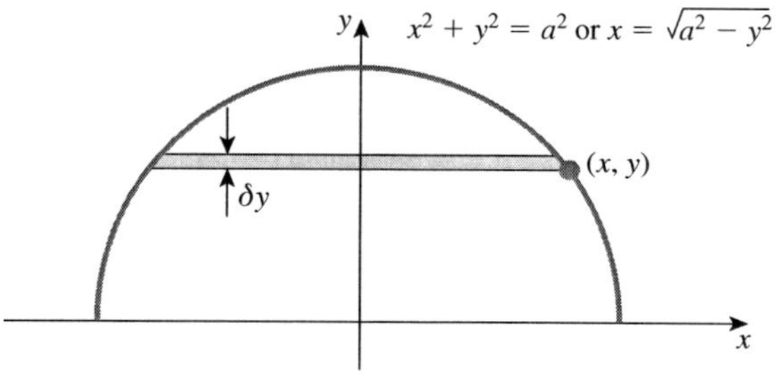

Figure 3.15 A typical horizontal strip is shaded.

The lamina is divided into a number of horizontal strips, and a typical strip is shown. Assume that each strip is rectangular. Writing the mass per unit area as m, identify the area and the mass of the strip:

$2x\delta y$, $2xm\delta y$

Write down the moment of the mass about the x axis:

$2xmy\delta y$

Write down the expression representing the sum of the moments of all strips and the corresponding integral obtained as $\delta y \to 0$.

$\sum_{y=0}^{y=a} 2xmy\delta y$, $\int_0^a 2xmy\,\mathrm{d}y$

Now since $x = \sqrt{a^2 - y^2}$ the integral becomes

$$\int_0^a 2my\sqrt{a^2 - y^2}\,\mathrm{d}y$$

Evaluate this integral by making the substitution $u^2 = a^2 - y^2$ to obtain the total moment.

$$\frac{2ma^3}{3}$$

The total area is half that of a circle of radius a, that is $\frac{1}{2}\pi a^2$. The total mass is $\frac{1}{2}\pi a^2 m$. Its moment is $\frac{1}{2}\pi a^2 m\bar{y}$.

Hence

$$\frac{1}{2}\pi a^2 m\bar{y} = \frac{2ma^3}{3}$$

from which

$$\bar{y} = \frac{4a}{3\pi}$$

Exercises

1 Find the centre of mass of a lamina bounded by $y^2 = 4x$, and $x = 9$.

Solutions to exercises

1 $\left(\frac{27}{5}, 0\right)$

End of block exercises

1 Find the position of the centre of mass of a lamina in the shape of a triangle formed by $y = 1 - x$, for $0 < x < 1$, and the x and y axes.

2 Show that the distance of the centre of mass of a uniform solid right circular cone, of height h, from its plane base is $\frac{h}{4}$. (Hint: you will need to introduce a mass per unit volume, or density, and divide the cone into a large number of discs.)

3 Show that the centre of mass of a uniform triangular lamina ABC is at a distance $\frac{1}{3}h$ from BC where h is the perpendicular distance from A to BC.

Solutions to exercises

1 $\left(\frac{1}{3}, \frac{1}{3}\right)$

BLOCK 4 Moment of inertia

4.1 Introduction

Figure 4.1 shows a lamina, or plane sheet, which is allowed to rotate about an axis perpendicular to the plane of the lamina and through O. The **moment of inertia** about this axis is a measure of how difficult it is to rotate the lamina. It plays the same role when dealing with rotating bodies as the mass of an object plays when dealing with motion in a line. An object with large mass needs a large force to achieve a given acceleration. Similarly, an object with large moment of inertia needs a large turning force to achieve a given angular acceleration. A knowledge of the moments of inertia of laminae, and also of solid bodies, is essential for understanding their rotational dynamics.

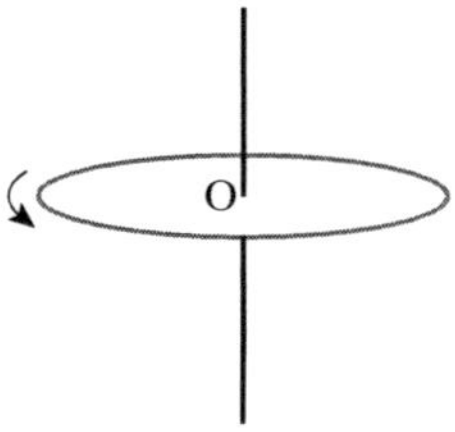

Figure 4.1 A lamina rotating about an axis through O.

In this block we show how the idea of integration as the limit of a sum can be used to find the moment of inertia of a lamina.

4.2 Calculating the moment of inertia

Suppose a lamina is divided into a large number of small pieces or *elements*. A typical piece is shown in Figure 4.2.

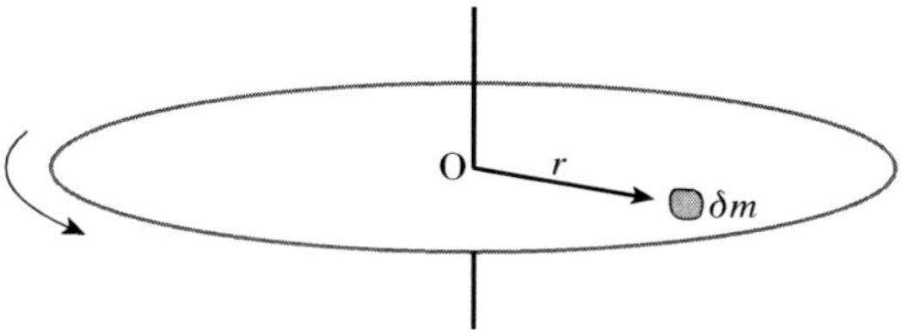

Figure 4.2 The moment of inertia of the small element is $\delta m r^2$.

It has mass δm, and is located a distance r from the axis O. The moment of inertia of this small piece is defined to be $\delta m r^2$, that is the mass multiplied by the square of its distance from the axis of rotation. To find the total moment of inertia we sum the individual contributions to give

$$\sum r^2 \delta m$$

where the sum must be taken in such a way that all parts of the lamina are included. As $\delta m \to 0$ we obtain the following integral as the definition of moment of inertia, I:

Key point

$$\text{moment of inertia } I = \int r^2 \, dm$$

where the limits of integration are chosen so that the entire lamina is included.

The unit of moment of inertia is kg m^2.

We shall illustrate how the moment of inertia is actually calculated in practice, in the following examples.

Example 4.1 Mechanical Engineering – Moment of inertia of a square

Calculate the moment of inertia about the y axis of the square lamina of mass M and width b, shown in Figure 4.3. The moment of inertia about the y axis is a measure of the resistance to rotation around this axis.

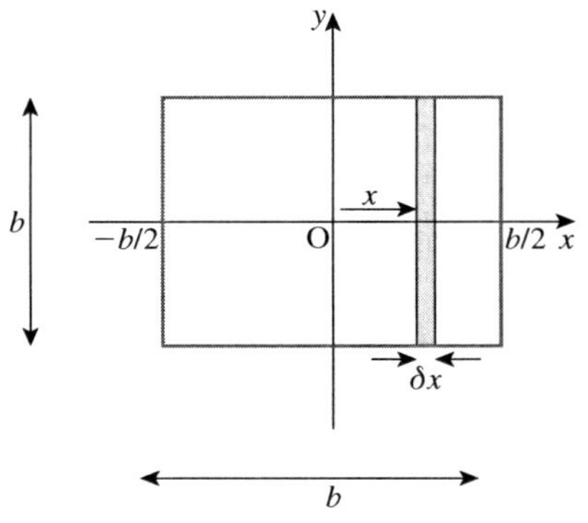

Figure 4.3
A square lamina rotating about the y axis.

Solution

Let the mass per unit area of the lamina be m. Then, because its total area is b^2, its total mass is $b^2 m$, which must equal the given mass, M.

Imagine that the lamina has been divided into a large number of thin vertical strips. A typical strip is shown in Figure 4.3. The strips are chosen in this way because each point on a particular strip is approximately the same distance from the axis of rotation (the y axis).

Referring to Figure 4.3 write down the width of each strip.

δx

Write down the area of the strip.

$b\delta x$

With m as the mass per unit area write down the mass of the strip.

$mb\delta x$

The distance of the strip from the y axis is x. Write down its moment of inertia.

$mbx^2\delta x$

Adding contributions from all strips gives the expression $\sum mbx^2\delta x$, where the sum must be such that the entire lamina is included. As $\delta x \to 0$ the sum defines an integral. Write down this integral.

$$I = \int_{-b/2}^{b/2} mbx^2 \, dx$$

Note that the limits on the integral have been chosen so that the whole lamina is included. Then

$$I = mb\int_{-b/2}^{b/2} x^2 \, dx$$

$$= mb\left[\frac{x^3}{3}\right]_{-b/2}^{b/2}$$

$$= \frac{mb^4}{12}$$

Noting that $M = b^2m$ then we can write I as $\dfrac{Mb^2}{12}$.

Example 4.2 Mechanical Engineering – Moment of inertia of a circular disc

Find the moment of inertia of a circular disc of mass M and radius a about an axis passing through its centre and perpendicular to the disc.

Solution

Figure 4.4 shows the disc lying in the plane of the paper. Imagine that the axis of rotation is coming out of the paper through O and is perpendicular to the disc. The disc can be considered to be spinning in the plane of the paper. Because of the circular symmetry the disc is divided into concentric rings of width δr. A typical ring is shown in Figure 4.5. Note that each point on the ring is approximately the same distance from the axis of rotation.

The ring has radius r and inner circumference $2\pi r$. Imagine cutting the ring and opening it up. Its area will be approximately that of a long thin rectangle of length $2\pi r$ and width δr. If m is the mass per unit area write down an expression for the mass of the ring.

$2\pi rm\delta r$

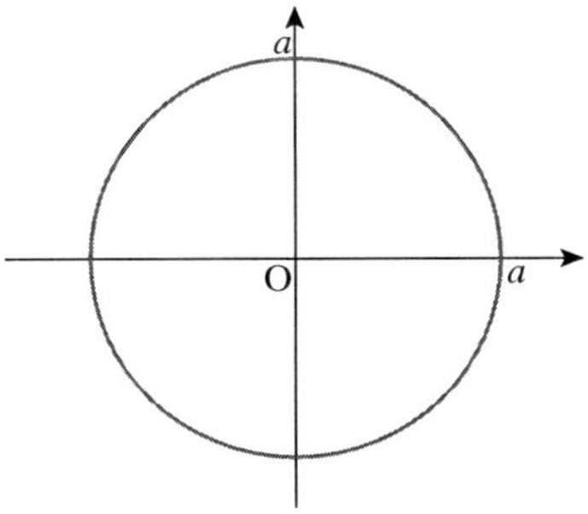

Figure 4.4
A circular disc rotating about an axis through O.

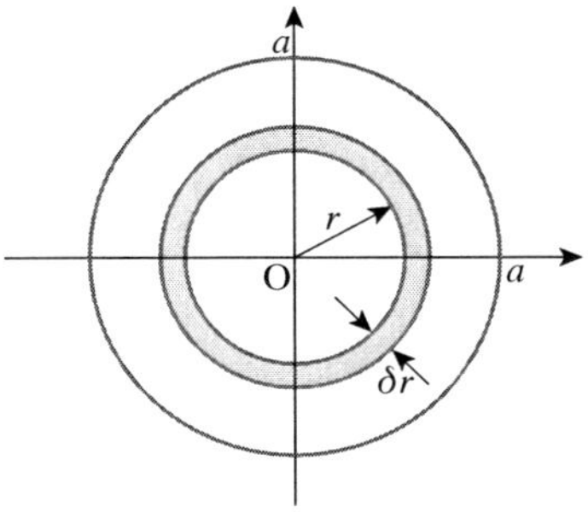

Figure 4.5
The lamina is divided into many circular rings.

The moment of inertia of the ring about O is its mass multiplied by the square of its distance from the axis of rotation. This is $(2\pi r m\delta r) \times r^2 = 2\pi r^3 m\delta r$.

The contribution from all rings must be summed. This gives rise to the sum

$$\sum_{r=0}^{r=a} 2\pi r^3 m\delta r$$

Note the way that the limits have been chosen so that all rings are included in the sum. As $\delta r \rightarrow 0$ the limit of the sum defines the integral

$$\int_0^a 2m\pi r^3 \, \mathrm{d}r$$

Evaluate this integral to give the moment of inertia I.

$$I = \left[\frac{2m\pi r^4}{4}\right]_0^a = \frac{m\pi a^4}{2}$$

Write down the radius and area of the whole disc.

$a, \pi a^2$

With m as the mass per unit area, write down the mass of the disc.

$\pi a^2 m$

But this total mass is M. Hence I can be written $\dfrac{Ma^2}{2}$.

Exercises

1 The moment of inertia about a diameter of a sphere of radius 1 m and mass 1 kg is found by evaluating the integral

$$\frac{3}{8}\int_{-1}^{1}(1 - x^2)^2\,dx$$

Show that the moment of inertia of the sphere is $\frac{2}{5}$ kg m^2.

2 Find the moment of inertia of the lamina in Figure 4.3 about one of its sides.

3 Calculate the moment of inertia of a uniform thin rod of mass M and length l about a perpendicular axis of rotation at its end.

4 Calculate the moment of inertia of the rod in question 3 about an axis through its centre and perpendicular to the rod.

5 The **parallel axis theorem** states that the moment of inertia about any axis is equal to the moment of inertia about a parallel axis through the centre of mass, plus the mass of the body $\times$ the square of the distance between the two axes. Verify this theorem for the rod in questions 3 and 4.

6 The **perpendicular axis theorem** applies to a lamina lying in the xy plane. It states that the moment of inertia of the lamina about the z axis is equal to the sum of the moments of inertia about the x and y axes. Suppose a thin circular disc of mass M and radius a lies in the xy plane and the z axis passes through its centre. The moment of inertia of the disc about this axis is $\frac{1}{2}Ma^2$.
(a) Use this theorem to find the moment of inertia of the disc about the x and y axes.
(b) Use the parallel axis theorem to find the moment of inertia of the disc about a tangential axis parallel to the plane of the disc.

Solutions to exercises

2 $\dfrac{Mb^2}{3}$

3 $\dfrac{1}{3}Ml^2$

4 $\dfrac{1}{12}Ml^2$

6 (a) The moments of inertia about the x and y axes must be the same by symmetry, and are equal to $\frac{1}{4}Ma^2$.

(b) $\dfrac{5Ma^2}{4}$

End of block exercises

1 A lamina of mass M has profile $y = 8 - x^2$ for $-2\sqrt{2} < x < 2\sqrt{2}$. Find the moment of inertia of the lamina about the y axis.

2 A uniform rectangular lamina of mass M is defined by the region $-a < x < a$ and $-b < y < b$. It is allowed to rotate about the y axis. Show that its moment of inertia is $\frac{1}{3}Ma^2$.

3 If the lamina in question 2 is allowed to rotate about the x axis, show that its moment of inertia is $\frac{1}{3}Mb^2$.

4 If the lamina in question 2 rotates about the line $x = -a$ show that the relevant moment of inertia is $\frac{4}{3}Ma^2$.

5 Prove that the moment of inertia of a uniform ring of mass M and radius a, about an axis through its centre and perpendicular to its plane, is Ma^2.

6 Use the parallel axis theorem given in the previous exercises to show that the moment of inertia of a thin circular disc of mass M and radius a, about an axis perpendicular to the plane of the disc and passing through a point on the circumference, is $\frac{3}{2}Ma^2$.

7 When a body rotates about a fixed axis with angular speed ω radians per second, its kinetic energy, KE, is given by $\text{KE} = \frac{1}{2}I\omega^2$, where I is the moment of inertia of the body about the fixed axis. Show that the kinetic energy of a rod of length l rotating about an axis through its midpoint is $\frac{1}{24}Ml^2\omega^2$.

8 A lamina has a profile in the first quadrant given by $y^2 = 4ax$, for $0 \leq x \leq b$.

(a) Show that the area of the lamina is $\frac{4}{3}a^{1/2}b^{3/2}$.

(b) Show that its moment of inertia about the y axis is $\frac{3}{7}Mb^2$.

(c) Show that its moment of inertia about the x axis is $\frac{4}{5}Mab$.

Solutions to exercises

1 $\dfrac{8M}{5}$

BLOCK 5 The length of a curve and the area of a surface of revolution

5.1 Introduction

Integration can be used to find the length of a curve and the area of the surface generated when a curve is rotated around an axis. In this block we state and use the formulae for doing this.

5.2 The length of a curve

Given a curve with equation $y = f(x)$, then the length of the curve between the points where $x = a$ and $x = b$ is given by the formula

Key point

$$\text{length of curve} = \int_a^b \sqrt{1 + \left(\frac{dy}{dx}\right)^2}\, dx$$

The proof of this formula is left as an exercise (question 1).

Because of the form of the integrand, and in particular the square root, integrals of this type are often difficult to calculate and, in practice, approximate rather than exact methods are needed to perform the integration. We shall illustrate the application of the formula by an example which could be calculated in a much simpler way, before looking at some harder examples.

Example 5.1

Find the length of the curve $y = 3x + 2$ between $x = 1$ and $x = 5$.

Solution

In this example, the curve is in fact a straight line, although we shall proceed as though it had been more complicated.

Notice from the formula in the key point that it is necessary to find $\frac{dy}{dx}$. Do this first.

$$\frac{dy}{dx} = 3$$

Applying the formula we find

$$\begin{aligned}
\text{length of curve} &= \int_1^5 \sqrt{1 + (3)^2}\,dx \\
&= \int_1^5 \sqrt{10}\,dx \\
&= \left[\sqrt{10}\,x\right]_1^5 \\
&= (5 - 1)\sqrt{10} \\
&= 4\sqrt{10} \\
&= 12.65
\end{aligned}$$

Thus the length of the curve $y = 3x + 2$ between the points where $x = 1$ and $x = 5$ is 12.65 units.

Example 5.2 Mechanical Engineering – Length of a curve
Find the length of the catenary $y = \cosh x$ between $x = 0$ and $x = 2$.

Solution

First find $\frac{dy}{dx}$.

$$\frac{dy}{dx} = \sinh x$$

Hence write down the required integral:

$$\int_0^2 \sqrt{1 + \sinh^2 x}\,dx$$

This integral can be evaluated by making use of the hyperbolic identity

$$\cosh^2 x - \sinh^2 x = 1$$

Write down the integral that results after applying this identity.

$$\int_0^2 \cosh x\,dx$$

Perform the integration for yourself to find the required length.

$$[\sinh x]_0^2 = 3.63$$

Thus the length of $y = \cosh x$ between $x = 0$ and $x = 2$ is 3.63 units.

The final example is more complicated still and requires the use of a hyperbolic substitution and knowledge of the hyperbolic identities.

Example 5.3

Find the length of the curve $y = x^2$ between $x = 0$ and $x = 3$.

Solution

Given $y = x^2$ then $\dfrac{dy}{dx} = 2x$. Apply the formula to obtain the integral required:

$$\int_0^3 \sqrt{1 + 4x^2}\, dx$$

Make the substitution $x = \dfrac{1}{2}\sinh u$, $\dfrac{dx}{du} = \dfrac{1}{2}\cosh u$, to obtain an integral in terms of u.

$$\int_0^{\sinh^{-1} 6} \sqrt{1 + \sinh^2 u}\, \frac{1}{2}\cosh u\, du$$

Use the hyperbolic identity $\cosh^2 u - \sinh^2 u = 1$ to rewrite this integral:

$$\frac{1}{2}\int_0^{\sinh^{-1} 6} \cosh^2 u\, du$$

Another hyperbolic identity is $\cosh^2 u = \dfrac{1}{2}(\cosh 2u + 1)$. Apply this identity to rewrite the integrand.

$$\frac{1}{4}\int_0^{\sinh^{-1} 6} \cosh 2u + 1\, du$$

Finally, performing the integration we can now complete the calculation:

$$\frac{1}{4}\int_0^{\sinh^{-1} 6} \cosh 2u + 1\, du = \frac{1}{4}\left[\frac{\sinh 2u}{2} + u\right]_0^{\sinh^{-1} 6}$$
$$= 9.75$$

Thus the length of the curve $y = x^2$ between $x = 0$ and $x = 3$ is 9.75 units.

Exercises

1 Figure 5.1 shows the portion of the curve $y(x)$ between $x = a$ and $x = b$. A small piece of this curve has been selected and can be considered as the hypotenuse of a triangle with base δx and height δy.

(a) Use Pythagoras's theorem to find the length of the hypotenuse.

(b) By summing all such contributions between $x = a$ and $x = b$, and letting $\delta x \to 0$, obtain the integral expression for the total length of the curve.

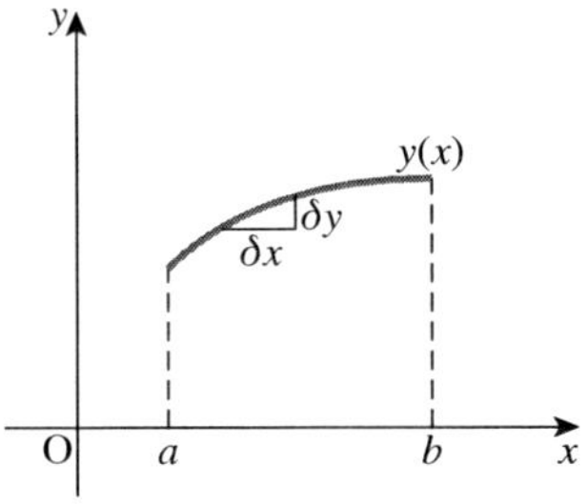

Figure 5.1

2 Find the length of the line $y = 2x + 7$ between $x = 1$ and $x = 3$ using the technique of this section. Verify your result from your knowledge of the straight line.

3 Find the length of $y = x^{3/2}$ between $x = 0$ and $x = 5$.

4 Calculate the length of the curve $y^2 = 4x^3$ between $x = 0$ and $x = 2$.

Solutions to exercises

1 (a) $\sqrt{(\delta x)^2 + (\delta y)^2}$

(b) $\sum_{x=a}^{x=b} \sqrt{(\delta x)^2 + (\delta y)^2}$ which by taking out a factor of $(\delta x)^2$ from under the square root, gives

$$\sum_{x=a}^{x=b} \sqrt{1 + \left(\frac{\delta y}{\delta x}\right)^2}\,\delta x$$

and then letting $\delta x \to 0$ defines the integral

$$\int_a^b \sqrt{1 + \left(\frac{\mathrm{d}y}{\mathrm{d}x}\right)^2}\,\mathrm{d}x$$

2 $2\sqrt{5} = 4.47$

3 12.41

4 6.06 (first quadrant only).

5.3 The area of a surface of revolution

Given a curve with equation $y = f(x)$, then the area of the surface generated by rotating that part of the curve between the points where $x = a$ and $x = b$ around the x axis is given by the formula

Key point

$$\text{area of surface} = \int_a^b 2\pi y\sqrt{1 + \left(\frac{\mathrm{d}y}{\mathrm{d}x}\right)^2}\,\mathrm{d}x$$

The proof of this formula is left as an exercise (question 1).

Example 5.4
Find the area of the surface generated when the part of the curve $y = x^3$ between $x = 0$ and $x = 4$ is rotated around the x axis.

Solution

The area of surface is given by

$$\text{area} = \int_a^b 2\pi y\sqrt{1 + \left(\frac{dy}{dx}\right)^2}\,dx$$
$$= \int_0^4 2\pi x^3\sqrt{1 + (3x^2)^2}\,dx$$
$$= \int_0^4 2\pi x^3\sqrt{1 + 9x^4}\,dx$$

This integral can be found by making a substitution $u = 1 + 9x^4$, $\frac{du}{dx} = 36x^3$ so that $x^3\,dx = \frac{du}{36}$. When $x = 0$, $u = 1$ and when $x = 4$, $u = 2305$.

Write down the corresponding integral in terms of u.

$$\frac{\pi}{18}\int_1^{2305}\sqrt{u}\,du$$

Perform the integration.

$$\frac{\pi}{18}\left[\frac{2}{3}u^{3/2}\right]_1^{2305}$$

Apply the limits of integration to find the area.

$$\frac{\pi}{27}[(2305)^{3/2} - 1]$$

Exercises

1 Figure 5.2 shows the portion of the curve $y(x)$ between $x = a$ and $x = b$, which is rotated around the x axis through 360°. A small disc of the solid of revolution has been selected. Its radius is y and so its circumference has length $2\pi y$. The surface area of this disc is then approximately $2\pi y\sqrt{(\delta x)^2 + (\delta y)^2}$. Obtain the formula for the total surface area.

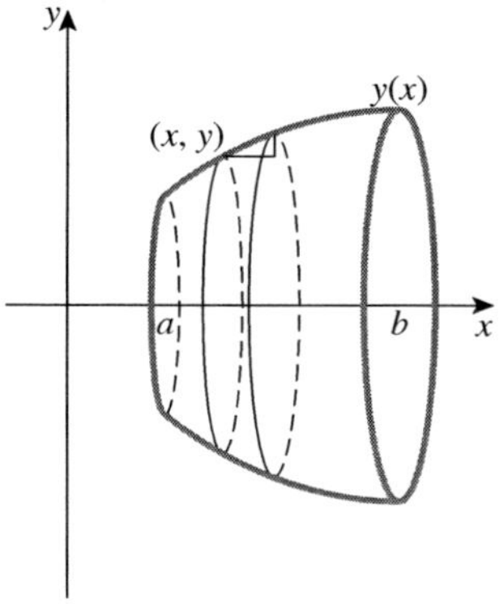

Figure 5.2

2 The line $y = x$ between $x = 0$ and $x = 1$ is rotated around the x axis.

(a) Find the area of the surface generated.

(b) Verify this result by finding the curved surface area of the corresponding cone. (The curved surface area of a cone of radius r and slant height l is $\pi r l$.)

3 Find the area of the surface generated when $y = \sqrt{x}$ for $1 \leq x \leq 2$ is rotated completely about the x axis.

Solutions to exercises

2 $\pi\sqrt{2}$

3 8.28

End of block exercises

1 Calculate the length of the curve $y^2 = 8x^3$ between $x = 1$ and $x = 3$.

2 When a curve is defined parametrically by $x = x(t)$, $y = y(t)$, show that

(a) the length of the curve between the points where $t = t_1$ and $t = t_2$ is

$$\int_{t_1}^{t_2} \sqrt{\left(\frac{dx}{dt}\right)^2 + \left(\frac{dy}{dt}\right)^2}\, dt$$

(b) the area of the surface of revolution is

$$\int_{t_1}^{t_2} 2\pi y \sqrt{\left(\frac{dx}{dt}\right)^2 + \left(\frac{dy}{dt}\right)^2}\, dt$$

3 Show that the area of the surface generated when $y = \frac{x^3}{9}$ between $x = 0$ and $x = 2$ is rotated around the x axis is $\frac{98\pi}{81}$.

4 The curve shown in Figure 5.3 is called a **cycloid**. It is the path traced out by a point on the rim of a wheel that rolls along the ground without slipping. This curve has parametric equations

$$x = \theta - \sin\theta, \quad y = 1 - \cos\theta$$

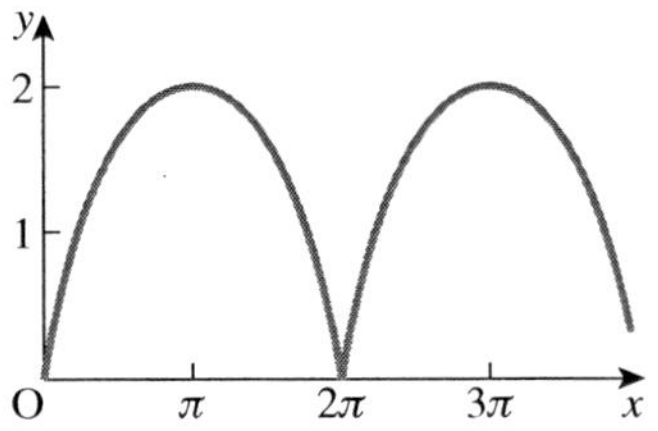

Figure 5.3
A cycloid.

and the graph shows the part of the curve generated when θ lies between 0 and 4π.

(a) Using the result from question 2(a) show that the length of one arch of this curve, that is $0 \leq \theta \leq 2\pi$, is 8. $\left(\text{Hint: to integrate } \sqrt{1 - \cos\theta} \text{ use the trigonometric identity } \sin^2 A = \frac{1 - \cos 2A}{2}.\right)$

(b) Using the result from question 2(b) show that the area of the surface generated when the arch between $0 \leq \theta \leq 2\pi$ is rotated completely around the x axis is $\frac{64\pi}{3}$.

Solutions to exercises

1 12.04

BLOCK 6 The mean value and root-mean-square value of a function

6.1 Introduction

Currents and voltages often vary with time. Engineers may wish to know the average value of such a current or voltage over some particular time interval. The average value of a time-varying function is defined in terms of an integral. An associated quantity is the root-mean-square (r.m.s.) value of a function. The r.m.s. value of a current is used in the calculation of the power dissipated by a resistor.

6.2 Average value of a function

Suppose a function $f(t)$ is defined on the interval $a \leq t \leq b$. The area, A, under the graph of $f(t)$ is given by the integral

$$A = \int_a^b f(t)\,\mathrm{d}t$$

This is illustrated in Figure 6.1.

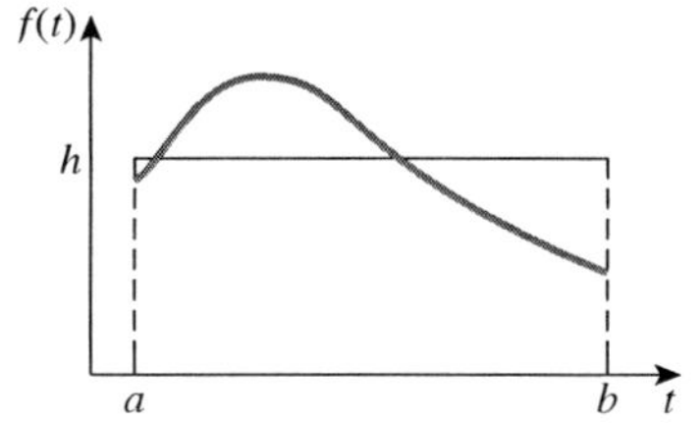

Figure 6.1
The area under the curve from $t = a$ to $t = b$ and the area of the rectangle are equal.

On Figure 6.1 we have also drawn a rectangle with base spanning the interval $a \leq t \leq b$ and which has the same area as that under the curve. Suppose the height of the rectangle is h. Then

$$\text{area of rectangle} = \text{area under curve}$$

$$h(b - a) = \int_a^b f(t)\,\mathrm{d}t$$

$$h = \frac{1}{b - a}\int_a^b f(t)\,\mathrm{d}t$$

The value of h is the **average value** of the function across the interval $a \leq t \leq b$.

Key point

$$\text{average value} = \frac{1}{b-a}\int_a^b f(t)\,\mathrm{d}t$$

The average value depends upon the interval chosen. If the values of a or b are changed, then the average value of the function across the interval from a to b will change as well. Note that the average value is also referred to as the **mean value**.

Example 6.1

Find the average value of $f(t) = t^2$ across the interval $1 \leq t \leq 3$.

Solution

Here $a = 1$ and $b = 3$.

$$\begin{aligned}
\text{average value} &= \frac{1}{b-a}\int_a^b f(t)\,\mathrm{d}t \\
&= \frac{1}{3-1}\int_1^3 t^2\,\mathrm{d}t \\
&= \frac{1}{2}\left[\frac{t^3}{3}\right]_1^3 \\
&= \frac{1}{2}\left(9 - \frac{1}{3}\right) \\
&= \frac{1}{2}\left(\frac{26}{3}\right) \\
&= \frac{13}{3}
\end{aligned}$$

Example 6.2

Find the average value of $f(t) = t^2$ across the interval $2 \leq t \leq 5$.

Solution

Here $a = 2$ and $b = 5$.

average value = $\frac{1}{5-2}\int_2^5 t^2\,\mathrm{d}t$

= 13

Example 6.3 Electrical Engineering – A thyristor-firing circuit

Figure 6.2 shows a simple circuit to control the voltage across a load resistor, R_L. This circuit has many uses, one of which is to adjust the level of lighting in a room. The circuit has an alternating current power supply with peak voltage, V_S. The main control element is the thyristor. This device is similar in many ways to a diode. It has a very high resistance when it is reverse biased and a low resistance when it is forward biased. However, unlike a diode, this low resistance depends on the thyristor being 'switched on' by the application of a gate current. The point at which the thyristor is switched on can be varied by varying the resistor, R_G. Figure 6.3 shows a typical waveform of the voltage, v_L, across the load resistor.

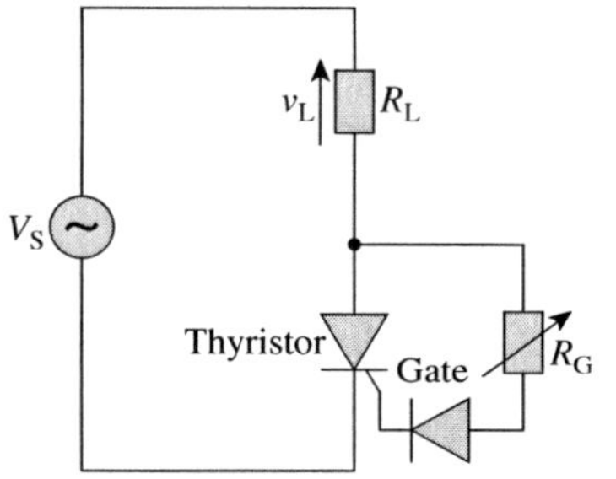

Figure 6.2 A thyristor firing circuit.

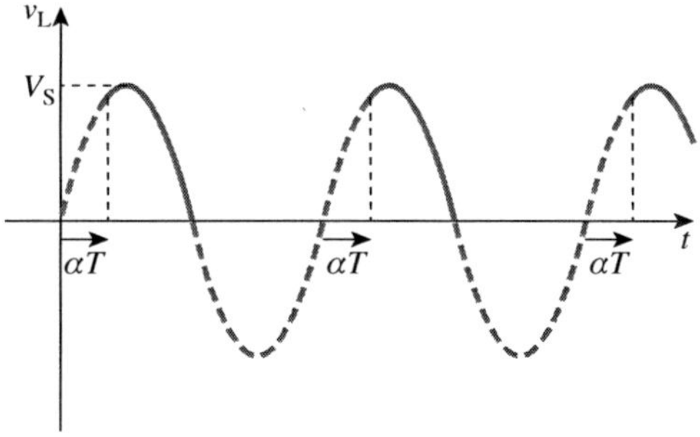

Figure 6.3 Load voltage waveform.

The point at which the thyristor is turned on in each cycle is characterised by the quantity αT, where $0 \leq \alpha \leq 0.25$ and T is the period of the waveform. This restriction on α reflects the fact that if the thyristor has not turned on when the supply voltage has peaked in the forward direction then it will never turn on.

Calculate the average value of the waveform over a period and comment on the result.

Solution

The average value of load voltage is

$$\frac{1}{T}\int_0^T v_L \,\mathrm{d}t = \frac{1}{T}\int_{\alpha T}^{T/2} V_S \sin\left(\frac{2\pi t}{T}\right)\mathrm{d}t$$

$$= \frac{V_S}{T}\frac{T}{2\pi}\left[-\cos\left(\frac{2\pi t}{T}\right)\right]_{\alpha T}^{T/2}$$

$$= \frac{V_S}{2\pi}(1 + \cos 2\pi\alpha)$$

If $\alpha = 0$, then the average value is $\frac{V_S}{\pi}$, the maximum value for this circuit. If $\alpha = 0.25$, then the average value is $\frac{V_S}{2\pi}$, which shows that delaying the turning on of the thyristor reduces the average value of the load voltage.

Exercises

1 Calculate the average value of the given functions across the specified interval:
(a) $f(t) = 1 + t$ across $[0, 2]$
(b) $f(x) = 2x - 1$ across $[-1, 1]$
(c) $f(t) = t^2$ across $[0, 1]$
(d) $f(t) = t^2$ across $[0, 2]$
(e) $f(z) = z^2 + z$ across $[1, 3]$

2 Calculate the average value of the given functions over the specified interval:
(a) $f(x) = x^3$ across $[1, 3]$
(b) $f(x) = \frac{1}{x}$ across $[1, 2]$
(c) $f(t) = \sqrt{t}$ across $[0, 2]$
(d) $f(z) = z^3 - 1$ across $[-1, 1]$
(e) $f(t) = \frac{1}{t^2}$ across $[-3, -2]$

3 Calculate the average value of the following:
(a) $f(t) = \sin t$ across $\left[0, \frac{\pi}{2}\right]$
(b) $f(t) = \sin t$ across $[0, \pi]$
(c) $f(t) = \sin \omega t$ across $[0, \pi]$
(d) $f(t) = \cos t$ across $\left[0, \frac{\pi}{2}\right]$
(e) $f(t) = \cos t$ across $[0, \pi]$
(f) $f(t) = \cos \omega t$ across $[0, \pi]$
(g) $f(t) = \sin \omega t + \cos \omega t$ across $[0, 1]$

4 Calculate the average value of the following functions:
(a) $f(t) = \sqrt{t + 1}$ across $[0, 3]$
(b) $f(t) = e^t$ across $[-1, 1]$
(c) $f(t) = 1 + e^t$ across $[-1, 1]$

Solutions to exercises

1 (a) 2 (b) −1 (c) $\frac{1}{3}$ (d) $\frac{4}{3}$ (e) $\frac{19}{3}$

2 (a) 10 (b) 0.6931 (c) 0.9428 (d) −1 (e) $\frac{1}{6}$

3 (a) $\frac{2}{\pi}$ (b) $\frac{2}{\pi}$ (c) $\frac{1}{\pi\omega}[1 - \cos(\pi\omega)]$ (d) $\frac{2}{\pi}$ (e) 0 (f) $\frac{\sin(\pi\omega)}{\pi\omega}$ (g) $\frac{1 + \sin\omega - \cos\omega}{\omega}$

4 (a) $\frac{14}{9}$ (b) 1.1752 (c) 2.1752

6.3 Root-mean-square value of a function

If $f(t)$ is defined on the interval $a \le t \le b$, the **root-mean-square** (r.m.s.) value is given by the following formula:

Key point

$$\text{r.m.s. value} = \sqrt{\frac{1}{b - a}\int_a^b [f(t)]^2\, dt}$$

The r.m.s. value depends upon the interval chosen. If the values of a or b are changed, then the r.m.s. value of the function across the interval from a to b will change as well. Note that when finding an r.m.s. value the function must be squared before it is integrated. The expression

$$\frac{1}{b-a}\int_a^b [f(t)]^2\,dt$$

is the mean value of $[f(t)]^2$ over the interval from a to b, that is the **mean-square value**.

Example 6.4

Find the r.m.s. value of $f(t) = t^2$ across the interval from $t = 1$ to $t = 3$.

Solution

$$\begin{aligned}
\text{r.m.s. value} &= \sqrt{\frac{1}{b-a}\int_a^b [f(t)]^2\,dt} \\
&= \sqrt{\frac{1}{3-1}\int_1^3 [t^2]^2\,dt} \\
&= \sqrt{\frac{1}{2}\int_1^3 t^4\,dt} \\
&= \sqrt{\frac{1}{2}\left[\frac{t^5}{5}\right]_1^3} \\
&= \sqrt{\frac{1}{2}\left(\frac{3^5}{5}-\frac{1}{5}\right)} \\
&= \sqrt{\frac{1}{2}\left(\frac{243}{5}-\frac{1}{5}\right)} \\
&= \sqrt{\frac{242}{10}} \\
&= 4.92
\end{aligned}$$

Example 6.5 Electrical Engineering – r.m.s. value of a sinusoidal current

The r.m.s. value is often used in the analysis of circuits. A sinusoidal current, $i(t)$, is given by

$$i(t) = \sin t$$

Calculate the r.m.s. value of $i(t)$ across the interval $t = 0$ to $t = 2\pi$.

Solution

Here $a = 0$ and $b = 2\pi$.

$$\text{r.m.s. value} = \sqrt{\frac{1}{2\pi}\int_0^{2\pi} \sin^2 t\,dt}$$

The integral of $\sin^2 t$ is performed by using trigonometrical identities to rewrite it in the alternative form $\frac{1}{2}(1 - \cos 2t)$. This technique was described in Chapter 17, Block 8.

$$\begin{aligned}
\text{r.m.s. value} &= \sqrt{\frac{1}{2\pi}\int_0^{2\pi} \frac{(1 - \cos 2t)}{2}\,\mathrm{d}t} \\
&= \sqrt{\frac{1}{4\pi}\int_0^{2\pi} (1 - \cos 2t)\,\mathrm{d}t} \\
&= \sqrt{\frac{1}{4\pi}\left[t - \frac{\sin 2t}{2}\right]_0^{2\pi}} \\
&= \sqrt{\frac{1}{4\pi}(2\pi)} \\
&= \sqrt{\frac{1}{2}} \\
&= 0.707
\end{aligned}$$

Thus the r.m.s. value is 0.707.

In the previous example the amplitude of the sine wave was 1, and the r.m.s. value was 0.707. In general, if the amplitude of a sine wave is A, its r.m.s. value is $0.707A$.

Key point

The r.m.s. value of any sinusoidal waveform taken across an interval equal to one period is $0.707 \times$ the amplitude of the waveform.

Exercises

1 Calculate the r.m.s. values of the functions in question 1 in the previous exercises.

2 Calculate the r.m.s. values of the functions in question 2 in the previous exercises.

3 Calculate the r.m.s. values of the functions in question 3 in the previous exercises.

4 Calculate the r.m.s. values of the functions in question 4 in the previous exercises.

Solutions to exercises

1 (a) 2.0817 (b) 1.5275 (c) 0.4472 (d) 1.7889 (e) 6.9666

2 (a) 12.4957 (b) 0.7071 (c) 1 (d) 1.0690 (e) 0.1712

3 (a) 0.7071 (b) 0.7071 (c) $\sqrt{\frac{1}{2} - \frac{\sin \pi\omega \cos \pi\omega}{2\pi\omega}}$ (d) 0.7071 (e) 0.7071 (f) $\sqrt{\frac{1}{2} + \frac{\sin \pi\omega \cos \pi\omega}{2\pi\omega}}$ (g) $\sqrt{1 + \frac{\sin^2 \omega}{\omega}}$

4 (a) 1.5811 (b) 1.3466 (c) 2.2724

End of block exercises

1 Find the average value of the following functions across the specified interval:
(a) $f(t) = 3 - t$ across [0, 4]
(b) $f(t) = t^2 - 2$ across [1, 3]
(c) $f(t) = t + \frac{1}{t}$ across [1, 4]
(d) $f(t) = \sqrt{t} + 1$ across [0, 4]
(e) $f(t) = t^{2/3}$ across [0, 1]

2 Calculate the average value of the following:
(a) $f(t) = 2\sin 2t$ across $\left[0, \frac{\pi}{2}\right]$
(b) $f(t) = A\sin 4t$ across $\left[0, \frac{\pi}{2}\right]$
(c) $f(t) = \sin t + \cos t$ across $[0, \pi]$
(d) $f(t) = \cos\left(\frac{t}{2}\right)$ across $\left[0, \frac{\pi}{2}\right]$
(e) $f(t) = \sin t \cos t$ across $[0, \pi]$

3 Calculate the average value of the following functions:
(a) $f(t) = Ae^{kt}$ across [0, 1]
(b) $f(t) = \frac{1}{e^{3t}}$ across [0, 2]
(c) $f(t) = 3 - e^{-t}$ across [1, 3]
(d) $f(t) = e^t + e^{-t}$ across [0, 2]
(e) $f(t) = t + e^t$ across [0, 2]

4 Find the average and r.m.s. values of $A\cos t + B\sin t$ across
(a) $[0, 2\pi]$
(b) $[0, \pi]$

5 Find the r.m.s. values of the functions in question 1.

6 Find the r.m.s. values of the functions in question 2.

7 Find the r.m.s. values of the functions in question 3.

Solutions to exercises

1 (a) 1 (b) $\frac{7}{3}$ (c) 2.9621 (d) $\frac{7}{3}$ (e) $\frac{3}{5}$

2 (a) $\frac{4}{\pi}$ (b) 0 (c) $\frac{2}{\pi}$ (d) 0.9003 (e) 0

3 (a) $A\left(\frac{e^k - 1}{k}\right)$ (b) 0.1663 (c) 2.8410
(d) 3.6269 (e) 4.1945

4 (a) average = 0, r.m.s. = $\sqrt{\frac{A^2 + B^2}{2}}$
(b) average = $\frac{2B}{\pi}$, r.m.s. = $\sqrt{\frac{A^2 + B^2}{2}}$

5 (a) 1.5275 (b) 3.2965 (c) 3.0414
(d) 2.3805 (e) 0.6547

6 (a) 1.4142 (b) $\frac{A}{\sqrt{2}}$ (c) 1 (d) 0.9046
(e) 0.3536

7 (a) $\sqrt{\frac{e^{2k} - 1}{2k}}$ (b) 0.2887 (c) 2.8423
(d) 3.9554 (e) 4.8085

End of chapter exercises

1 Find the mean value of each of the following functions across the interval stated:
(a) $f(t) = \sin t$, $[0, \pi]$
(b) $f(t) = t^3$, $[1, 5]$
(c) $f(t) = e^{3t}$, $[0, 2]$
(d) $f(t) = 20 + 2\sin \pi t$, $[0, 0.5]$.

2 Calculate the root-mean-square value of each of the following functions across the interval stated:
(a) $f(t) = t$, $[0, 10]$
(b) $f(t) = \cos 2t$, $[0, \pi]$
(c) $f(t) = \sin 2t$, $[0, \pi]$
(d) $f(t) = 10 \sin 50\pi t$, $[0, 0.01]$

3 The acceleration, a, of an object varies with time, t, according to the formula $a = t^2 + 3t$. Given that velocity v is given by $v = \int a(t)\,dt$, find the velocity after 5 seconds given that the object is at rest at $t = 0$.

4 Find the volume of the solid generated when the curve $y = 3x^2$ for $0 \le x \le 1$ is rotated around the y axis.

5 Find the volume of the solid generated when $y = \frac{1}{x}$ for $1 \le x \le 5$ is rotated about the x axis.

6 Consider the cycloid defined by $x = a(\theta - \sin\theta)$, $y = a(1 - \cos\theta)$ where a is a constant. Show that the length of this curve for values of the parameter θ between 0 and 2π is $8a$. (Hint: see Block 5, End of block exercises, question 4.)

7 Find the length of the curve $y = \cosh x$ for $-1 \le x \le 1$.

Solutions to exercises

1 (a) $\frac{2}{\pi}$ (b) 39 (c) 67.07 (d) $\frac{4}{\pi} + 20 = 21.2732$

2 (a) 5.7735 (b) $\frac{1}{\sqrt{2}}$ (c) $\frac{1}{\sqrt{2}}$

(d) $\sqrt{50} = 7.07106$

3 79.2

4 $\frac{3\pi}{2}$

5 $\frac{4\pi}{5}$

7 $2\sinh 1 = 2.35$

Sequences and series

Chapter 19

A **sequence** is a set of numbers written down in a specific order. If a continuous function or waveform is measured, or sampled, at periodic intervals we obtain a sequence of values. Sequences also arise when an attempt is made to find approximate solutions of equations that model physical phenomena. Such approximation is often necessary if a solution is to be obtained using a digital computer.

Sequences are important in engineering mathematics because they can be used to describe discrete time signals. These are signals that have a non-zero value only at certain specific instants of time. For example, in digital computers calculations are carried out at fixed intervals of time governed by an electronic clock.

A **series** is formed when the terms of a sequence are added. Series are important because the solutions of some mathematical problems can be expressed as series. Two notable groups of series are known as Taylor series and Maclaurin series. These are used extensively to provide approximations or estimates of function values.

In this chapter we discuss properties common to all sequences and series and look at some particular and important examples.

Chapter 19 contents

BLOCK 1 Sequences and series

1.1 Introduction

A **sequence** is a set of numbers written down in a specific order. For example, 1, 3, 5, 7, 9 and $-1, -2, -3, -4, -5$ are both sequences. Each number in the sequence is called a **term** of the sequence. Sometimes we use the symbol . . . to indicate that the sequence continues. For example, 1, 2, 3, . . . , 20 is the sequence of integers from 1 to 20 inclusive. The sequence 1, 3, 5, 7, 9, . . . can be assumed to continue indefinitely.

It is necessary to introduce a notation for handling sequences. Consider again the sequence of odd numbers 1, 3, 5, 7, 9, ... Suppose we let $x[1]$ stand for the first term, $x[2]$ stand for the second term and so on. Then

$$x[1] = 1, \quad x[2] = 3, \quad x[3] = 5 \text{ and so on}$$

Clearly $x[k]$ will stand for the kth term. Note that by inspection we can write down a formula for the kth term. It is $x[k] = 2k - 1$. Substitute some values of k for yourself to check this.

To denote the full sequence concisely we write

$$x[k] = 2k - 1 \text{ where } k = 1, 2, 3, \ldots$$

Some books use the alternative notation $x_1 = 1, x_2 = 3, x_3 = 5$ and $x_k = 2k - 1$.

Example 1.1

Consider the sequence of even numbers 2, 4, 6, 8, ... By inspection find a formula for the kth term of this sequence.

Solution

$x[k] = 2k$, where $k = 1, 2, 3, \ldots$

Example 1.2

Write down the first five terms of the sequence given by $x[k] = (-1)^{k+1}\frac{1}{k}$ where $k = 1, 2, 3, \ldots$.

Solution

$$x[1] = (-1)^2\tfrac{1}{1} = 1$$

$$x[2] = (-1)^3\tfrac{1}{2} = -\tfrac{1}{2}$$

Write down the third, fourth and fifth terms.

$\frac{1}{3}, -\frac{1}{4}, \frac{1}{5}$

A **series** is obtained when the terms of a sequence are added. For example, if we add the terms of the sequence 1, 3, 5, 7, 9 we obtain the series

$$1 + 3 + 5 + 7 + 9$$

We use **sigma notation**, first introduced in Chapter 5, Block 1, to write a series concisely. For example, the sum of the first 10 odd numbers can be written

$$\sum_{k=1}^{10} 2k - 1$$

where the lowermost and uppermost values of k are placed below and above the sigma sign respectively. Similarly, the sum of the first six even numbers can be written

$$\sum_{k=1}^{6} 2k$$

Example 1.3

Write out explicitly the terms of the series $\sum_{k=1}^{5} \frac{1}{k}$.

Solution

$$1 + \frac{1}{2} + \frac{1}{3} + \frac{1}{4} + \frac{1}{5}$$

In this block we start by discussing the behaviour of sequences and series that have an infinite number of terms. Then two particular types of sequence are described — the arithmetic sequence and the geometric sequence. These are particularly straightforward, and there are simple formulae for finding their sums.

Exercises

1 Explain carefully the distinction between a sequence and a series.

2 Write out fully the following sums:

(a) $\sum_{k=1}^{6} k$ (b) $\sum_{k=1}^{k=4} k^2$ (c) $\sum_{k=1}^{k=5} k^3$

3 A sequence is defined by

$$x[k] = \frac{k^2}{2} + k, \quad k = 0, 1, 2, 3, \ldots$$

State the first five terms.

4 A sequence is given by $5, \frac{5}{8}, \frac{5}{27}, \frac{5}{64}, \ldots$. Write down an expression to denote the full sequence.

5 Write out explicitly the series

$$\sum_{k=1}^{4} \frac{1}{(2k + 1)(2k + 3)}$$

Solutions to exercises

2 (a) $1 + 2 + 3 + 4 + 5 + 6$
(b) $1^2 + 2^2 + 3^2 + 4^2$
(c) $1^3 + 2^3 + 3^3 + 4^3 + 5^3$

3 $0, \frac{3}{2}, 4, \frac{15}{2}, 12$

4 $x[k] = \frac{5}{k^3}, k = 1, 2, 3, \ldots$, for example

5 $\frac{1}{(3)(5)} + \frac{1}{(5)(7)} + \frac{1}{(7)(9)} + \frac{1}{(9)(11)}$

1.2 The limit of an infinite sequence

Some sequences stop after a finite number of terms. These are called **finite sequences**. Others continue indefinitely, and these are called **infinite sequences**. Sometimes the terms of an infinite sequence get closer and closer to a fixed value. For example, the terms of the sequence $x[k] = \frac{1}{k}$, for $k = 1, 2, 3, \ldots$, are

$$1, \frac{1}{2}, \frac{1}{3}, \frac{1}{4}, \frac{1}{5}, \ldots$$

The terms appear to be getting smaller. What do you think will be the eventual behaviour of the sequence as k gets large?

terms approach the value 0

We say that 'as k tends to infinity, $x[k]$ tends to zero', or 'the **limit** of $x[k]$ as k tends to infinity is zero' and write this as

$$\lim_{k \to \infty} x[k] = 0$$

When a sequence possesses a limit as k tends to infinity, it is said to **converge**.

Example 1.4

Write down the first four terms of the sequence $x[k] = \frac{1}{k^2}$, for $k = 1, 2, 3, \ldots$. What is the behaviour of the sequence as k tends to infinity?

Solution

The first four terms are

$$1, \frac{1}{4}, \frac{1}{9}, \frac{1}{16}$$

As k tends to infinity, $\frac{1}{k^2}$ tends to zero.

Example 1.5

Explore the behaviour of the sequence $x[k] = \sqrt{2 + \frac{1}{k}}$, $k = 1, 2, 3, \ldots$ as $k \to \infty$.

Solution

Write down the first few terms of this sequence:

$$\sqrt{3}, \sqrt{2\tfrac{1}{2}}, \sqrt{2\tfrac{1}{3}}, \ldots$$

As k tends to infinity the term $\dfrac{1}{k}$ tends to zero. So $\lim_{k\to\infty} x[k] = \sqrt{2}$.

When a sequence does not possess a limit it is said to **diverge**. The sequence of odd numbers diverges because the terms of the sequence get larger and larger and so the sequence does not possess a limit. The oscillating sequence $-1, 1, -1, 1, -1, 1, \ldots$ is divergent because it does not possess a limit.

Example 1.6

(a) Write out the first four terms of the sequence $x[k] = \sqrt{k}$, $k = 1, 2, 3, \ldots$.
(b) Find $\lim_{k\to\infty} x[k]$.

Solution

(a) $1, \sqrt{2}, \sqrt{3}, \sqrt{4}$.
(b) The terms of this sequence increase indefinitely. The sequence therefore diverges.

Example 1.7

Find the limit of the sequence $x[k] = \dfrac{3k^2 + 2k - 7}{9k^2 - 7k}$ as $k \to \infty$.

Solution

The approach to tackling a problem like this is to rewrite $x[k]$ in a form in which we can sensibly let $k \to \infty$. Dividing both numerator and denominator by the highest power of k, that is k^2, gives

$$x[k] = \frac{3 + \dfrac{2}{k} - \dfrac{7}{k^2}}{9 - \dfrac{7}{k}}$$

Now because $\dfrac{1}{k}$ and $\dfrac{1}{k^2}$ both tend to zero as k tends to infinity it follows that

$$\begin{aligned}\lim_{k\to\infty} x[k] &= \lim_{k\to\infty} \frac{3 + \dfrac{2}{k} - \dfrac{7}{k^2}}{9 - \dfrac{7}{k}} \\ &= \frac{3}{9} \\ &= \frac{1}{3}\end{aligned}$$

Exercises

1 Find if possible the limit of each of the following sequences:

(a) $x[k] = \dfrac{1}{k+1}, k = 1, 2, 3, \ldots$

(b) $x[k] = k^2, k = 1, 2, 3, \ldots$

(c) $x[k] = \dfrac{k-1}{k+1}, k = 1, 2, 3, \ldots$

(d) $x[k] = \left(\dfrac{1}{3}\right)^k, k = 1, 2, 3, \ldots$

(e) $x[k] = \dfrac{2k+3}{4k+2}, k = 1, 2, 3, \ldots$

Solutions to exercises

1 (a) 0 (b) diverges (c) 1 (d) 0 (e) $\dfrac{1}{2}$

1.3 The sum of an infinite series

When the terms of an infinite sequence are added we obtain an **infinite series**. It may seem strange to try to add together an infinite number of terms but under some circumstances their sum is finite and can be found. For example, consider the infinite series formed from the sequence $x[k] = \dfrac{1}{2^k}, k = 0, 1, 2, \ldots$.

$$1 + \frac{1}{2} + \frac{1}{4} + \frac{1}{8} + \cdots$$

We can calculate the sum of n terms, S_n, for various values of n. For example, the sum of just the first term is

$$S_1 = 1$$

The sum of the first two terms is

$$\begin{aligned} S_2 &= 1 + \frac{1}{2} \\ &= 1.5 \end{aligned}$$

Similarly $S_3 = 1.75$, $S_4 = 1.875, \ldots, S_{10} = 1.9980$. The sequence $S_1, S_2, S_3, \ldots$ is called the **sequence of partial sums**. As we calculate S_n for larger and larger values of n, we note that S_n gets nearer and nearer to 2. We write S to stand for the sum of an infinite number of terms, so

$$\begin{aligned} S &= \sum_{k=0}^{\infty} \frac{1}{2^k} \\ &= 2 \end{aligned}$$

For any infinite series, say $\sum_{k=1}^{\infty} x[k]$, we can form the sequence of partial sums:

$$S_1 = x[1], S_2 = x[1] + x[2], S_3 = x[1] + x[2] + x[3], \ldots$$

If the sequence S_n converges to a limit S we say that the infinite series has sum S, or that it has converged to S.

In general it is difficult to determine whether or not an infinite series has a finite sum. It is possible to establish tests or **convergence criteria** to help decide whether or not a given series converges or diverges, but for these you must refer to a more advanced book.

Example 1.8

Calculate the first six partial sums of the series

$$\sum_{k=1}^{\infty} (-1)^{k+1} \frac{1}{k}$$

Solution

The first six terms of the series are

$$1 - \frac{1}{2} + \frac{1}{3} - \frac{1}{4} + \frac{1}{5} - \frac{1}{6}$$

Form the first six partial sums for yourself working to 4 d.p.

1, 0.5000, 0.8333, 0.5833, 0.7833, 0.6167

If you proceed to calculate many more terms you will see that the sequence of partial sums converges to 0.6931, which is in fact ln 2.

Exercises

1. Calculate the first four partial sums of the series $\sum_{k=0}^{\infty} \frac{1}{k!}$. (Recall $0! = 1$.)

2. Calculate the first four partial sums of the series $\sum_{k=0}^{\infty} (-1)^k \frac{1}{(2k)!}$.

Solutions to exercises

1. 1, 2, 2.5, 2.6667 (in fact this converges to e = 2.7183)

2. 1, 0.5, 0.5417, 0.5403 (this converges to cos 1 = 0.5403).

1.4 Arithmetic sequences

An **arithmetic sequence** is a sequence of numbers where each new term after the first is formed by adding a fixed amount called the **common difference** to the previous term in the sequence. For example, the sequence

$$3, 5, 7, 9, 11, \ldots$$

is an arithmetic sequence. Note that having chosen the first term to be 3, each new term is found by adding 2 to the previous term, so the common difference is 2.

The common difference can be negative: for example, the sequence

$$2, -1, -4, -7, \ldots$$

is an arithmetic sequence with first term 2 and common difference -3.

In general we can write an arithmetic sequence as follows:

Key point

Arithmetic sequence

$$a, a + d, a + 2d, a + 3d, \ldots$$

where the first term is a and the common difference is d. Some important results concerning arithmetic sequences now follow:

Key point

The nth term of an arithmetic sequence is given by

$$a + (n - 1)d$$

Key point

The sum of the first n terms of an arithmetic sequence is

$$S_n = \frac{n}{2}[2a + (n - 1)d]$$

The sum of the terms of an arithmetic sequence is known as an **arithmetic series**.

Example 1.9

Find the 17th term of an arithmetic sequence with first term 5 and common difference 2.

Solution

The nth term is $a + (n - 1)d$.

Hence

17th term =

$$5 + (17 - 1)2 = 5 + 32 = 37$$

Example 1.10

Find the sum of the first 23 terms of the arithmetic sequence

$$4, -3, 10, \ldots$$

Solution

First identify a and d.

$$a = 4, d = -7$$

Then, using $S_n = \frac{n}{2}[2a + (n - 1)d]$, find the sum of 23 terms:

$$\frac{23}{2}[2(4) + (23 - 1)(-7)] = -1679$$

Exercises

1 Find the 23rd term of an arithmetic sequence with first term 2 and common difference 7.

2 Find the sum of the first five terms of the arithmetic sequence with first term 3 and common difference 5.

3 Write down the 10th and 19th terms of the arithmetic sequence
(a) 8, 11, 14, . . . (b) 8, 5, 2, . . .

4 An arithmetic sequence is given by

$$b, \frac{2b}{3}, \frac{b}{3}, 0, \ldots$$

(a) State the sixth term.
(b) State the kth term.
(c) If the 20th term has a value of 15, find b.

Solutions to exercises

1 156

2 65

3 (a) 35, 62 (b) −19, −46

4 (a) $-\frac{2b}{3}$ (b) $\frac{b(4-k)}{3}$ (c) $-\frac{45}{16}$

1.5 Geometric sequences

A **geometric sequence** is a sequence of numbers where each term after the first is found by multiplying the previous term by a fixed number called the **common ratio**. For example, the sequence

$$1, 3, 9, 27, \ldots$$

is a geometric sequence with first term 1 and common ratio 3. Each term after the first is found by multiplying the preceding term by 3.

The common ratio could be a fraction and it might be negative.

Example 1.11

Write down the first few terms of the geometric sequence with first term 2 and common ratio $-\frac{1}{3}$.

Solution

$$2, -\frac{2}{3}, \frac{2}{9}, -\frac{2}{27}, \ldots$$

In general we can write a geometric sequence as follows:

Key point

Geometric sequence

$$a, ar, ar^2, ar^3, \ldots$$

where the first term is a and the common ratio is r.

Some important results concerning geometric sequences now follow:

Key point

The nth term of a geometric sequence is given by

$$ar^{(n-1)}$$

Key point

The sum of the first n terms of a geometric sequence is

$$S_n = \frac{a(1-r^n)}{1-r} \text{ (valid only if } r \neq 1)$$

The sum of the terms of a geometric sequence is known as a **geometric series**.

Example 1.12

Find the seventh term of the geometric sequence

$$2, -6, 18, \ldots$$

Solution

First identify a and the common ratio r.

$$a = 2, r = -3$$

Then, the nth term is ar^{n-1}, so the seventh term is

$$(2)(-3)^6 = 1458$$

If the common ratio in a geometric series is less than 1 in modulus (i.e. $-1 < r < 1$), the sum of an infinite number of terms converges and can be calculated. This is known as the **sum to infinity**, S_∞.

Key point

$$S_\infty = \frac{a}{1-r} \text{ provided } -1 < r < 1$$

Example 1.13

Find the sum to infinity of the geometric sequence with first term 3 and common ratio $\frac{1}{2}$.

Solution

$$S_\infty = \frac{a}{1-r}$$
$$= \quad \square$$

6

Exercises

1 Find the seventh term of a geometric sequence with first term 2 and common ratio 3.

2 Find the sum of the first five terms of the geometric sequence with first term 3 and common ratio 2.

3 Find the sum of the infinite geometric series with first term 2 and common ratio $\frac{1}{2}$.

4 A geometric sequence has first term 1. The ninth term exceeds the fifth term by 240. Find possible values for the eighth term.

5 The sum to infinity of a geometric sequence is four times the first term. Find the common ratio.

6 A geometric series has $S_3 = \frac{37}{8}$ and $S_6 = \frac{3367}{512}$. Find the first term and the common ratio.

7 A geometric sequence is given by $1, \frac{1}{2}, \frac{1}{4}, \ldots$. What is its common ratio?

Solutions to exercises

1 1458

2 93

3 4

4 ± 128

5 $\frac{3}{4}$

6 $2, \frac{3}{4}$

7 $\frac{1}{2}$

End of block exercises

1 State whether the following sequences are arithmetic, geometric or neither:
(a) $1, -1, -3, -5, \ldots$ (b) $4, 2, 1, 0.5, \ldots$
(c) $6, 7, 8, 9, \ldots$ (d) $4, 5, 7, 10, \ldots$
(e) $1, 0.1, 0.01, 0.001, \ldots$
(f) $1, -1, 1, -1, 1, \ldots$ (g) $1, 1, 1, 1, \ldots$

2 An arithmetic sequence has first term -3 and common difference 4. State (a) the 10th term, (b) the 300th term.

3 An arithmetic series has first term 4 and common difference $\frac{1}{2}$. Find (a) the sum of the first 20 terms, (b) the sum of the first 100 terms.

4 A geometric sequence has first term -2 and common ratio $-\frac{3}{4}$. State the 20th term.

5 A geometric series has first term equal to 3 and a common ratio of 1.5. Calculate the sum of (a) the first 10 terms, (b) the first 50 terms, (c) the 30th to the 49th terms inclusive.

6 Find the limit as $k \to \infty$, if it exists, of each of the following:
(a) $x[k] = k^5$ (b) $x[k] = \sin k$

(c) $x[k] = \dfrac{k^2 + k}{k^2 + k + 1}$

(d) $x[k] = \dfrac{3k^2 + k}{k^2 + k + 1}$

7 Show that the sum of the first n terms of an arithmetic sequence, S_n, can be expressed as

$$S_n = \frac{n}{2}(\text{first term} + \text{last term})$$

Solutions to exercises

1 (a) arithmetic (b) geometric (c) arithmetic (d) neither (e) geometric (f) geometric (g) arithmetic and geometric

2 (a) 33 (b) 1193

3 (a) 175 (b) 2875

4 8.4566×10^{-3}

5 (a) 339.99 (b) 3.8257×10^9 (c) 2.5497×10^9

6 (a) diverges (b) diverges (c) 1 (d) 3

BLOCK 2 Sums of whole numbers, their squares and cubes

2.1 Introduction

There are a number of series that arise in the solution of certain problems and it is useful to know their sums. In this block we give these series.

2.2 The sum of the first n positive integers

Key point

The sum of the first n positive integers is given by

$$\sum_{k=1}^{n} k = 1 + 2 + 3 + \cdots + n$$

$$= \frac{n}{2}(n + 1)$$

In fact this series is an arithmetic series with first term 1 and common difference 1, as discussed in Block 1.

Example 2.1

Find the sum of the first 100 integers, $1 + 2 + 3 + \cdots + 100$.

Solution

Use the formula with $n = 100$:

$$\frac{100}{2}(101) = 5050$$

2.3 The sum of the squares of the first n positive integers

Key point

The sum of the squares of the first n positive integers is given by

$$\sum_{k=1}^{n} k^2 = 1^2 + 2^2 + 3^2 + \cdots + n^2$$

$$= \frac{n}{6}(n + 1)(2n + 1)$$

Example 2.2
Find the sum of the squares of the first 10 integers, $1^2 + 2^2 + 3^2 + \cdots + 10^2$.

Solution
Use the formula with $n = 10$:

$$\frac{10}{6}(11)(21) = 385$$

2.4 The sum of the cubes of the first n positive integers

Key point

The sum of the cubes of the first n positive integers is given by

$$\sum_{k=1}^{n} k^3 = 1^3 + 2^3 + 3^3 + \cdots + n^3$$
$$= \left(\frac{n(n+1)}{2}\right)^2$$

Example 2.3
Find the sum of the cubes of the first 12 integers, $1^3 + 2^3 + 3^3 + \cdots + 12^3$.

Solution
Use the formula with $n = 12$:

$$\left(\frac{12(13)}{2}\right)^2 = 6084$$

Exercises

1. Find the sum of the first 20 positive integers.
2. Find the sum of the squares of the first 20 positive integers.
3. Find the sum of the cubes of the first six positive integers.
4. Find the sum of the first 40 positive integers.

Solutions to exercises

1. 210
2. 2870
3. 441
4. 820

End of block exercises

1 Find $\sum_{k=1}^{32} k^2$.

2 Find $\sum_{k=1}^{18} k$.

3 Find the sum of the integers from 18 to 96 inclusive.

4 Find the sum of the integers from -200 to -6 inclusive.

5 Find the sum of the integers from -50 to 24 inclusive.

6 Find $7^2 + 8^2 + \cdots + 21^2$.

Solutions to exercises

1 11440

2 171

3 4503

4 -20085

5 -975

6 3220

BLOCK 3 Pascal's triangle and the binomial theorem

3.1 Introduction

It is frequently necessary to expand expressions of the form $(a + b)^2$ or $(a + b)^3$. The expansion of an expression of the form $(a + b)^n$ is called a **binomial expansion**. When the power n is small it is possible to multiply out the brackets. If n is large this approach becomes tedious. An alternative and very simple approach is to use **Pascal's triangle**, which is described in the next section.

When n is very large, even Pascal's triangle is tedious, and the **binomial theorem** provides an alternative.

3.2 Pascal's triangle

Consider the triangle of numbers shown below. Every entry is obtained by adding the two entries on either side in the preceding row, always starting and finishing a row with a 1.

Key point

Pascal's triangle

1
1 1
1 2 1
1 3 3 1
1 4 6 4 1
1 5 10 10 5 1
⋮ ⋮ ⋮ ⋮ ⋮ ⋮ ⋮

Example 3.1
Complete the next two rows in the triangle. Add these rows to the triangle above.

1 6 15 20 15 6 1

1 7 21 35 35 21 7 1

Compare the third and fourth rows of the triangle with the expansions of $(a + b)^2$ and $(a + b)^3$.

$$(a + b)^2 = a^2 + 2ab + b^2, \quad (a + b)^3 = a^3 + 3a^2b + 3ab^2 + b^3$$

Note that Pascal's triangle gives the coefficients in the expansions. Furthermore, the terms in these expansions are composed of decreasing powers of a and increasing powers of b. If we want the expansion of $(a + b)^4$ the row in the triangle beginning 1, 4 will provide the coefficients. We simply insert the appropriate powers of a and b, starting with the highest power of a, namely a^4. Thus

$$(a + b)^4 = a^4 + 4a^3b + 6a^2b^2 + 4ab^3 + b^4$$

Example 3.2
Use Pascal's triangle to expand $(a + b)^5$.

Solution

$$a^5 + 5a^4b + 10a^3b^2 + 10a^2b^3 + 5ab^4 + b^5$$

Example 3.3
Find $(\cos x + \sin x)^3$.

Solution
The answer can be written down immediately:

$$(\cos x + \sin x)^3 = \cos^3 x + 3\cos^2 x \sin x + 3\cos x \sin^2 x + \sin^3 x$$

Exercises

1 Use Pascal's triangle to expand $(a + b)^7$.

2 Expand $(a + b)^4$. By letting $a = 1$ and $b = 3y$ expand $(1 + 3y)^4$.

Solutions to exercises

1 $a^7 + 7a^6b + 21a^5b^2 + 35a^4b^3 + 35a^3b^4 + 21a^2b^5 + 7ab^6 + b^7$

2 $1 + 12y + 54y^2 + 108y^3 + 81y^4$

3.3 The binomial theorem when n is a positive integer

The binomial theorem is concerned with the expansion of $(a + b)^n$. It is useful to separate the discussion into two cases, the first when n is a positive integer, and the second when n is negative or fractional. Section 3.4 will deal with the second case.

When n is a positive integer, the expansion of $(a + b)^n$ contains a finite number of terms. For example, we have seen in Example 3.2 that

$$(a + b)^5 = a^5 + 5a^4b + 10a^3b^2 + 10a^2b^3 + 5ab^4 + b^5$$

and so the expansion contains six terms. The binomial theorem is useful when we want to expand $(a + b)^n$ for large n. To use the theorem you will need to recall factorial notation first introduced in Chapter 5, Block 1.

$$2! = 2 \times 1, \quad 3! = 3 \times 2 \times 1, \quad 4! = 4 \times 3 \times 2 \times 1, \quad \text{and so on}$$

Key point

The binomial theorem states that when n is a positive integer

$$(a + b)^n = a^n + na^{n-1}b + \frac{n(n-1)}{2!}a^{n-2}b^2 + \frac{n(n-1)(n-2)}{3!}a^{n-3}b^3 + \cdots + b^n$$

This is a sum of a finite number of terms, that is the series stops. The last term is b^n.

Example 3.4

(a) Write out the first three terms of the expansion of $(a + b)^{21}$.
(b) What would be the last term?

Solution

(a) Using the theorem with $n = 21$ we can write down the first three terms:

$$(a + b)^{21} = a^{21} + 21a^{20}b + \frac{21(20)}{2!}a^{19}b^2 + \cdots$$

(b) The last term is b^{21}.

The theorem is often quoted for the particular case when $a = 1$ and $b = x$:

Key point

Binomial theorem (alternative form)

$$(1 + x)^n = 1 + nx + \frac{n(n-1)}{2!}x^2 + \frac{n(n-1)(n-2)}{3!}x^3 + \cdots + x^n$$

Example 3.5

Use the theorem to write down the expansion of $(1 + x)^4$.

Solution

Use the expansion with $n = 4$:

$$1 + 4x + 6x^2 + 4x^3 + x^4$$

Exercises

1 Use the binomial theorem to expand

(a) $(1 + x)^3$ (b) $\left(1 + \frac{x}{3}\right)^4$ (c) $\left(1 - \frac{x}{2}\right)^5$

2 Write down the first three terms in the expansion of $(x + 3y)^{12}$.

Solutions to exercises

1 (a) $1 + 3x + 3x^2 + x^3$

(b) $1 + \frac{4x}{3} + \frac{2x^2}{3} + \frac{4x^3}{27} + \frac{x^4}{81}$

(c) $1 - \frac{5x}{2} + \frac{5x^2}{2} - \frac{5x^3}{4} + \frac{5x^4}{16} - \frac{x^5}{32}$

2 $x^{12} + 36x^{11}y + 594x^{10}y^2 + \cdots$

3.4 The binomial theorem when *n* is not a positive integer

The theorem can be applied when n is not a positive integer provided that x lies between -1 and 1. However, when n is not a positive integer, the series is *infinite:*

Key point

The binomial theorem states that when n is not a positive integer

$$(1 + x)^n = 1 + nx + \frac{n(n-1)}{2!}x^2 + \frac{n(n-1)(n-2)}{3!}x^3 + \cdots$$

only for $-1 < x < 1$

This is an infinite series.

Example 3.6

Use the binomial theorem to write down the first four terms in the expansion of $(1 + x)^{1/2}$.

Solution

Use the theorem with $n = \frac{1}{2}$.

$$1 + \frac{1}{2}x + \frac{\left(\frac{1}{2}\right)\left(-\frac{1}{2}\right)}{2!}x^2 + \frac{\left(\frac{1}{2}\right)\left(-\frac{1}{2}\right)\left(-\frac{3}{2}\right)}{3!}x^3 + \cdots$$

Simplify your result:

$$1 + \frac{x}{2} - \frac{x^2}{8} + \frac{x^3}{16} + \cdots$$

Note that $(1 + x)^{1/2}$ and $1 + \dfrac{x}{2} - \dfrac{x^2}{8} + \dfrac{x^3}{16} + \cdots$ have the same numerical value only when x lies in the range -1 to 1. If x is outside this range the two expressions have different values.

Example 3.7

Expand $\dfrac{1}{1 + x}$ in ascending powers of x up to and including the term in x^3.

Solution

$\dfrac{1}{1 + x}$ can be written $(1 + x)^{-1}$. Use the binomial theorem with $n = -1$:

$$1 - x + x^2 - x^3 + \cdots$$

This expansion is valid provided $-1 < x < 1$.

Example 3.8

Obtain the first four terms in the expansion of $\dfrac{1}{(l - x)^2}$ in powers of $\dfrac{x}{l}$.

Solution

Note that we can rewrite $\dfrac{1}{(l - x)^2}$ in the following way:

$$\frac{1}{(l - x)^2} = \frac{1}{l^2\left(1 - \frac{x}{l}\right)^2}$$

$$= \frac{1}{l^2}\left(1 - \frac{x}{l}\right)^{-2}$$

The binomial theorem can then be used to expand $\left(1 - \dfrac{x}{l}\right)^{-2}$:

$$\left(1 - \frac{x}{l}\right)^{-2} = 1 + (-2)\left(-\frac{x}{l}\right) + \frac{(-2)(-3)}{2!}\left(-\frac{x}{l}\right)^2$$

$$+ \frac{(-2)(-3)(-4)}{3!}\left(-\frac{x}{l}\right)^3 + \cdots$$

$$= 1 + 2\left(\frac{x}{l}\right) + 3\left(\frac{x}{l}\right)^2 + 4\left(\frac{x}{l}\right)^3 + \cdots$$

Hence

$$\frac{1}{(l-x)^2} = \frac{1}{l^2}\left[1 + 2\left(\frac{x}{l}\right) + 3\left(\frac{x}{l}\right)^2 + 4\left(\frac{x}{l}\right)^3 + \cdots\right]$$

Exercises

1 Obtain the first five terms in the expansion of $(1+x)^{-2}$. State the range of values of x for which the expansion is valid.

2 Obtain a quadratic approximation to $(1-2x)^{1/2}$ using the binomial theorem. For what range of values of x is your expansion valid?

Solutions to exercises

1 $1 - 2x + 3x^2 - 4x^3 + 5x^4,\ -1 < x < 1$

2 $1 - x - \frac{1}{2}x^2 + \cdots,\ -\frac{1}{2} < x < \frac{1}{2}$

End of block exercises

1 (a) Use the binomial theorem to expand $(1+y)^5$.
(b) Use the result from part (a) to expand $(1+3y)^5$.

2 Expand (a) $(1-z)^3$, (b) $(2-z)^3$, (c) $(2+z)^3$, (d) $(1+2z)^3$, (e) $(z+3)^3$.

3 Expand $(\cos\theta + \mathrm{j}\sin\theta)^5$ where $\mathrm{j}^2 = -1$.

4 Write down the first two terms in the binomial expansion of

$$\left(1 + \frac{x}{5}\right)^{1/4}$$

5 Expand $\left(2 - \frac{1}{x}\right)^5$.

Solutions to exercises

1 (a) $1 + 5y + 10y^2 + 10y^3 + 5y^4 + y^5$
(b) $1 + 15y + 90y^2 + 270y^3 + 405y^4 + 243y^5$

2 (a) $1 - 3z + 3z^2 - z^3$
(b) $8 - 12z + 6z^2 - z^3$
(c) $8 + 12z + 6z^2 + z^3$
(d) $1 + 6z + 12z^2 + 8z^3$
(e) $z^3 + 9z^2 + 27z + 27$

3 $\cos^5\theta - 10\cos^3\theta\sin^2\theta + 5\cos\theta\sin^4\theta + \mathrm{j}(\sin^5\theta - 10\cos^2\theta\sin^3\theta + 5\cos^4\theta\sin\theta)$

4 $1 + \frac{x}{20}$

5 $32 - \frac{80}{x} + \frac{80}{x^2} - \frac{40}{x^3} + \frac{10}{x^4} - \frac{1}{x^5}$

BLOCK 4 Taylor series and Maclaurin series

4.1 Introduction

Suppose the value of a function and the value of its derivatives are known at a particular point. From this information it is possible to obtain values of the function around that point, using a series called a **Taylor series**.

When the particular point is the origin, it is possible to obtain function values at neighbouring points using a **Maclaurin series**. Thus the Maclaurin series is a special case of the Taylor series.

These two series are explored in this block.

4.2 Maclaurin series

Suppose we have a function $f(x)$ from which we find the value of the function when $x = 0$, that is $f(0)$. Suppose also that by successive differentiation we find the value of the derivatives of $f(x)$ at $x = 0$, that is $f'(0), f''(0)$, and so on.

The **Maclaurin series** formula enables us to find the value of the function at a point, x, close to the origin:

Key point

Maclaurin series

$$f(x) = f(0) + xf'(0) + \frac{x^2}{2!}f''(0) + \frac{x^3}{3!}f'''(0) + \cdots$$

This is an infinite series, although often we can approximate $f(x)$ by using just a finite number of the terms as we shall show.

Consider the following example.

Example 4.1

Obtain the Maclaurin series for $f(x) = e^x$.

Solution

Here $f(x) = e^x$. Evaluate $f(0)$:

$$f(0) = e^0 = 1$$

Differentiate $f(x)$ and so find $f'(0)$.

$$f'(x) = e^x, f'(0) = 1$$

We can continue in this way to show that

$$f''(0) = 1, f'''(0) = 1, \text{ and so on}$$

Applying the Maclaurin series formula,

$$f(x) = f(0) + xf'(0) + \frac{x^2}{2!}f''(0) + \frac{x^3}{3!}f'''(0) + \cdots$$

$$e^x = 1 + x + \frac{x^2}{2!} + \frac{x^3}{3!} + \cdots$$

This is an infinite series, which is equal to e^x for all values of x. We can write it concisely using sigma notation as

$$e^x = \sum_{n=0}^{\infty} \frac{x^n}{n!}$$

It is also known as the **power series expansion** of e^x about the origin.

We have shown in the previous example that

$$e^x = \sum_{n=0}^{\infty} \frac{x^n}{n!} = 1 + x + \frac{x^2}{2!} + \frac{x^3}{3!} + \cdots$$

By taking successive partial sums of this Maclaurin series we can obtain polynomials that are approximations to e^x, known as **Maclaurin polynomials**. Denoting these polynomials by $p_0(x)$, $p_1(x)$ and so on, we have

$p_0(x) = 1,$ by taking just the first term

$p_1(x) = 1 + x,$ by taking the first two terms

$p_2(x) = 1 + x + \frac{x^2}{2!},$ and so on

Each Maclaurin polynomial is a function that approximates the original function, in this case e^x. As more and more terms are included the approximation improves. To see this more clearly study the graphs in Figure 4.1. The first shows $f(x) = e^x$ together with the graph of $p_0 = 1$. The second and third graphs show $f(x) = e^x$ together with $p_1(x) = 1 + x$ and $p_2(x) = 1 + x + \frac{x^2}{2!}$. Notice that close to the origin you would expect p_1 and p_2 to give good approximate values of e^x, but the quality of the approximation will deteriorate as you move further from the origin.

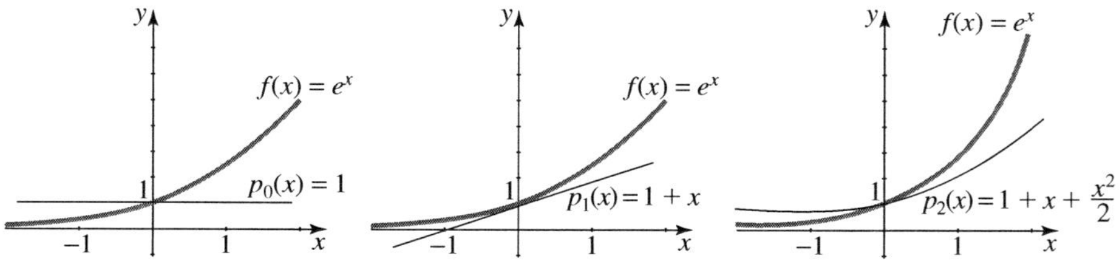

Figure 4.1 $f(x) = e^x$ together with a number of Maclaurin polynomials.

Example 4.2

(a) Find the Maclaurin series for $f(x) = \sin x$, where x is measured in radians.
(b) State a cubic approximation to $\sin x$.

Solution

(a) Obtain the successive derivatives of $f(x)$ and evaluate them when $x = 0$. Remember that, whenever it is necessary to differentiate trigonometrical functions, work must be carried out in radians and not in degrees.

$f(x) = \sin x, \quad f(0) =$ — 0

$f'(x) =$, $f'(0) =$ — $\cos x,\ 1$

$f''(x) =$, $f''(0) =$ — $-\sin x,\ 0$

$f'''(x) =$, $f'''(0) =$ — $-\cos x,\ -1$

Continuing in this way and then substituting into the Maclaurin series formula you will find

$$\sin x = x - \frac{x^3}{3!} + \frac{x^5}{5!} - \frac{x^7}{7!} + \cdots$$

This is the power series expansion of $\sin x$ about the origin.

(b) Taking the first two non-zero terms of the Maclaurin series gives the cubic polynomial

$$p_3(x) = x - \frac{x^3}{3!}$$

A useful exercise would be for you to use a computer package to draw graphs of $\sin x$ and the first few Maclaurin polynomials to see the way in which the approximation improves as the degree of the polynomial increases.

The power series expansions obtained in Examples 4.1 and 4.2 are valid for any x. This means that the value of the series and the value of the function used to generate it are equal for every value of x. However, some functions have a power series expansion that is valid only for a limited range of values of x. For example, the Maclaurin expansion of $f(x) = \frac{1}{1+x}$ is valid only when $-1 < x < 1$.

Some common power series expansions are shown in Table 4.1.

The small-angle approximations

The Maclaurin series for $\sin x$ and $\cos x$ can be used to approximate the trigonometrical ratios when x is small and measured in radians.

Key point

Small-angle approximations

If x is small and measured in radians:

$$\sin x \approx x \quad \text{and} \quad \cos x \approx 1 - \frac{x^2}{2}$$

Use your calculator to verify these approximations. For example, show that $\sin 0.3 \approx 0.3$.

Table 4.1
Some common power series expansions.

$$e^x = 1 + \frac{x}{1!} + \frac{x^2}{2!} + \frac{x^3}{3!} + \cdots \text{ for all } x$$

$$\sin x = x - \frac{x^3}{3!} + \frac{x^5}{5!} - \frac{x^7}{7!} + \cdots \text{ for all } x$$

$$\cos x = 1 - \frac{x^2}{2!} + \frac{x^4}{4!} - \frac{x^6}{6!} + \cdots \text{ for all } x$$

$$\log_e(1 + x) = x - \frac{x^2}{2} + \frac{x^3}{3} - \frac{x^4}{4} + \cdots \text{ for } -1 < x \leq 1$$

$$(1 + x)^p = 1 + px + \frac{p(p-1)}{2!}x^2 + \frac{p(p-1)(p-2)}{3!}x^3 + \cdots \text{ for } -1 < x < 1$$

$$\tan x = x + \frac{x^3}{3} + \frac{2x^5}{15} + \frac{17x^7}{315} + \cdots \text{ for } -\frac{\pi}{2} < x < \frac{\pi}{2}$$

$$\sinh x = x + \frac{x^3}{3!} + \frac{x^5}{5!} + \frac{x^7}{7!} + \cdots \text{ for all } x$$

$$\cosh x = 1 + \frac{x^2}{2!} + \frac{x^4}{4!} + \frac{x^6}{6!} + \cdots \text{ for all } x$$

Exercises

1 Derive the Maclaurin series for $f(x) = \cos x$.

2 Use the power series expansion of e^x to show that

$$e^{2x} = 1 + 2x + 2x^2 + \frac{4x^3}{3} + \cdots$$

3 Use the power series expansion of $\cos x$ to show that

$$\cos\frac{x}{2} = 1 - \frac{x^2}{8} + \frac{x^4}{384} - \frac{x^6}{46080} + \cdots$$

4 Determine the Maclaurin series expansion for $f(x) = \dfrac{1}{1+x}$.

5 Find the Maclaurin expansion for $\sin^2 x$. (Hint: use a trigonometrical identity and the series for $\sin x$.)

6 Obtain the Maclaurin series expansion for $f(x) = \cosh x$.

7 (a) Obtain a quadratic Maclaurin polynomial approximation, $p_2(x)$, to $f(x) = \cos 2x$.
(b) Compare the approximate value given by $p_2(1)$ with actual value $f(1)$.

Solutions to exercises

4 $1 - x + x^2 - x^3 + \cdots = \sum_{n=0}^{\infty} (-1)^n x^n$

5 $x^2 - \frac{1}{3}x^4 + \frac{2}{45}x^6 - \cdots$

6 $1 + \frac{x^2}{2!} + \frac{x^4}{4!} + \frac{x^6}{6!} + \cdots$

7 (a) $1 + 2x^2$ (b) $f(1) = 3.7622$, $p_2(1) = 3$

4.3 Taylor series

The Taylor series is very similar to the Maclaurin series. The only difference is that the expansion is now taken about any point, $x = a$ say, not necessarily the origin. So if we know the value of a function and its derivatives when $x = a$ we can use the Taylor series formula to find the value of the function at nearby points.

Key point

Taylor series

$$f(x) = f(a) + (x - a)f'(a) + \frac{(x-a)^2}{2!}f''(a) + \frac{(x-a)^3}{3!}f'''(a) + \cdots$$

Example 4.3

Find the Taylor series expansion of $f(x) = \sqrt{x}$ about the point $x = 4$.

Solution

Here, the known point is $x = 4$. We must evaluate $f(x)$ and its derivatives at this point:

$$f(4) = \sqrt{4} = 2$$

$f'(x) =$

$$\frac{1}{2}x^{-1/2} = \frac{1}{2\sqrt{x}}$$

and so $f'(4) = \dfrac{1}{2\sqrt{4}} = \dfrac{1}{4}$.

Now obtain the second and third derivatives of $f(x)$.

$$f''(x) = -\frac{1}{4(\sqrt{x})^3}, \quad f'''(x) = \frac{3}{8(\sqrt{x})^5}$$

Evaluate the second and third derivatives at $x = 4$.

$$f''(4) = -\frac{1}{32}, \quad f'''(4) = \frac{3}{256}$$

Substitute these values into the Taylor series formula:

$$f(x) = f(4) + (x - 4)f'(4) + \frac{(x-4)^2}{2!}f''(4) + \frac{(x-4)^3}{3!}f'''(4) + \cdots$$

$$\sqrt{x} = 2 + (x - 4)\frac{1}{4} + \frac{(x-4)^2}{2}\left(-\frac{1}{32}\right) + \frac{(x-4)^3}{6}\left(\frac{3}{256}\right) + \cdots$$

$$= 2 + \frac{1}{4}(x - 4) - \frac{1}{64}(x - 4)^2 + \frac{1}{512}(x - 4)^3 + \cdots$$

This is the Taylor series expansion of $\sqrt{x}$ about $x = 4$.

In the previous example we calculated the Taylor series of $\sqrt{x}$. By taking successive partial sums of this series we can obtain polynomials that are approximations to $\sqrt{x}$, known as **Taylor polynomials**. Denoting these polynomials by $p_0(x)$, $p_1(x)$ and so on, we have

$p_0(x) = 2,$ by taking just the first term

$p_1(x) = 2 + \frac{1}{4}(x - 4),$ by taking the first two terms

$p_2(x) = 2 + \frac{1}{4}(x - 4) - \frac{1}{64}(x - 4)^2,$ and so on

Each Taylor polynomial is a function that approximates the original function, in this case $\sqrt{x}$ when x is close to the expansion point, $x = 4$. As more and more terms are included the approximation improves.

The first graph in Figure 4.2 shows $f(x) = \sqrt{x}$ together with a graph of $p_0(x) = 2$. The second and third graphs show $f(x) = \sqrt{x}$ together with $p_1(x)$ and $p_2(x)$. Notice how the approximation improves as the degree of the polynomial increases.

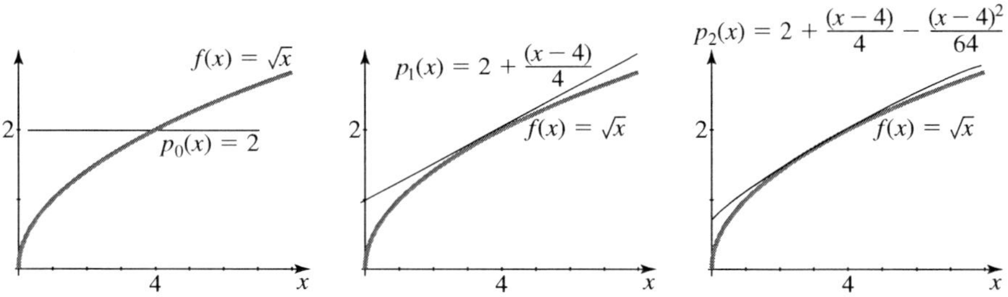

Figure 4.2 $f(x) = \sqrt{x}$ together with a number of Taylor polynomials.

Exercises

1 Show that the first four terms in the Taylor series expansion of $f(x) = \tan x$ about $x = \frac{\pi}{4}$ are

$$1 + 2\left(x - \frac{\pi}{4}\right) + 2\left(x - \frac{\pi}{4}\right)^2 + \frac{8}{3}\left(x - \frac{\pi}{4}\right)^3$$

2 Find the Taylor series for $f(x) = x + e^x$ about $x = 1$.

Solutions to exercises

2 $f(x) = (1 + e)x + e\left(\frac{(x-1)^2}{2!} + \frac{(x-1)^3}{3!} + \frac{(x-1)^4}{4!} + \cdots\right)$

Computer and calculator exercises

1 (a) Calculate the second-order Taylor polynomial, $p_2(x)$, generated by $y(x) = x^3$ about $x = 0$.
(b) Draw $y(x)$ and $p_2(x)$ for $-2 \le x \le 2$.

2 (a) Calculate the second-order Taylor polynomial, $p_2(x)$, generated by $y(x) = \sin x$ about $x = 0$.
(b) Draw $y(x)$ and $p_2(x)$ for $-2 \le x \le 2$.

3 (a) Calculate the second-order Taylor polynomial, $p_2(x)$, generated by

$$y(x) = \sin\left(\frac{1}{x}\right) \text{ about } x = 3.$$

(b) Draw $y(x)$ and $p_2(x)$ for $1 \le x \le 5$.

4 (a) Calculate the second-order Taylor polynomial, $p_2(x)$, generated by $y(x) = e^{\cos x}$ about $x = 0$.
(b) Draw $y(x)$ and $p_2(x)$ for $-2 \le x \le 2$.

5 Draw $y(x) = \frac{1}{x}$ for $1 \le x \le 8$. On the same axes draw the fourth-order Taylor polynomial generated by $y(x)$ about $x = 3$.

6 Draw $y = \tan x$ for $-1 \le x \le 1$. Using the same axes, draw the fifth-order Taylor polynomial generated by $y(x)$ about $x = 0$.

7 Draw $y(x) = \ln x$ for $0.5 \le x \le 10$. On the same axes, draw the third-, fourth- and fifth-order Taylor polynomials generated by $y(x)$ about $x = 1$.

End of block exercises

1 Use the Maclaurin expansion of e^x to find the value of e correct to 4 decimal places.

2 Obtain the Maclaurin series for $\ln(1 - 4x)$.

3 Obtain the Maclaurin series for $f(x) = \sinh x$.

4 Obtain a small-angle approximation for $\tan x$ and verify it by example.

5 Use the Maclaurin series for $\dfrac{1}{1 - x}$ to deduce that for $\dfrac{1}{1 - x^2}$.

Solutions to exercises

1 2.7183

2 $-4x - 8x^2 - \dfrac{64}{3}x^3 - \cdots$

4 $\tan x = x$

5 $1 + x^2 + x^4 + \cdots$

End of chapter exercises

1 Write out explicitly the first three non-zero terms of the series

$$\sum_{k=0}^{\infty} k(k + 1)(k + 3)$$

2 Use the binomial theorem to show that

$$\frac{1}{1 + x^2} = 1 - x^2 + x^4 - x^6 + \cdots$$

for $-1 < x < 1$

By integrating both sides of this expansion, assuming that this is permissible, show that $\tan^{-1} x$ has power series expansion

$$\tan^{-1} x = x - \frac{1}{3}x^3 + \frac{1}{5}x^5 - \frac{1}{7}x^7 + \cdots$$

for $-1 < x < 1$.

3 (a) If $y = \ln \cos x$ show that y satisfies the equation

$$y''' = -2\, y'' y'$$

(b) Hence obtain the Maclaurin expansion of $y = \ln \cos x$ as far as the term in x^5.

4 Find $10^3 + 11^3 + \cdots + 20^3$.

5 Expand $\left(3 - \frac{2}{x}\right)^5$.

6 Use the Maclaurin series for e^x to show that the sum of the infinite series

$$1 + \frac{1}{1!} + \frac{1}{2!} + \frac{1}{3!} + \cdots$$

is e.

7 Use the Maclaurin series for $\ln(1 + x)$ to show that the sum of the infinite series

$$1 - \frac{1}{2} + \frac{1}{3} - \frac{1}{4} + \cdots$$

is ln 2.

8 Find $\sum_{k=1}^{4} k^2$.

9 Expand $(1 - 2x)^4$.

10 By considering $x + x^2$ as a single term, expand $(1 + x + x^2)^3$.

11 Use the binomial theorem to expand $(9 + x^2)^{1/2}$.

12 By considering the Maclaurin expansions of $\sin kx$ and $\cos kx$ where k is a constant, evaluate, if possible,

(a) $\lim_{x\to 0} \frac{\sin kx}{x}$ (b) $\lim_{x\to 0} \frac{\cos kx - 1}{x}$

(c) $\lim_{x\to 0} \frac{\sin kx}{1 - \cos kx}$

Solutions to exercises

1 (1) (2) (4) + (2) (3) (5) + (3) (4) (6)

3 $-\frac{1}{2}x^2 - \frac{1}{12}x^4$

4 42075

5 $243 - \frac{810}{x} + \frac{1080}{x^2} - \frac{720}{x^3} + \frac{240}{x^4} - \frac{32}{x^5}$

8 30

9 $1 - 8x + 24x^2 - 32x^3 + 16x^4$

10 $1 + 3x + 6x^2 + 7x^3 + 6x^4 + 3x^5 + x^6$

11 $3 + \frac{x^2}{6} - \frac{x^4}{216} + \cdots$, valid for $-3 < x < 3$

12 (a) k (b) 0 (c) not defined

Differential equations

Chapter 20

The solution of problems concerning the motion of objects, the flow of charged particles, heat transport, etc., often involves discussion of relations of the form

$$\frac{dx}{dt} = f(x, t) \quad or \quad \frac{dq}{dt} = g(q, t)$$

In the first equation, x might represent distance. For this case $\frac{dx}{dt}$ is the rate of change of distance with respect to time, t, that is speed. In the second equation, q might be charge and $\frac{dq}{dt}$ the rate of flow of charge, that is current. These are examples of **differential equations**, so called because they are equations involving the derivatives of various quantities. Such equations arise out of situations in which change is occurring. To solve such a differential equation means to find the function $x(t)$ or $q(t)$ when we are given the differential equations. Solutions to these equations may be **analytical** in that we can write down an answer in terms of common elementary functions such as e^t, $\sin t$ and so on. Alternatively, the problem may be so difficult that only **numerical methods** are available, which produce approximate solutions. Modern software packages are available that can produce analytical and numerical solutions. We shall introduce some of these in Block 4.

In engineering, differential equations are most commonly used to model **dynamic systems**. These are systems that change with time. Examples include an electronic circuit with time-dependent currents and voltages, a chemical production line in which pressures, tank levels, flow rates, etc., vary with time, and a semiconductor device in which hole and electron densities change with time.

There are a wide variety of differential equations that occur in engineering applications, and consequently there are a wide variety of solution techniques available. In order to be able to apply an appropriate technique it is essential that you can identify the sort of equation you are dealing with. Block 1 gives details of the terminology associated with differential equations. Knowledge of this will help in the selection of an appropriate method. Later blocks describe these methods in detail.

Chapter 20 contents

BLOCK 1 Basic concepts of differential equations

1.1 Introduction

An equation is a mathematical expression that contains an unknown quantity that we try to find. A **differential equation** is an equation that contains the derivative of an unknown expression. For example, a very simple differential equation is

$$\frac{dy}{dx} = x^2$$

This equation contains the derivative of y, which represents the unknown expression that we seek. Clearly y is an expression that when differentiated gives x^2.

In order to solve a differential equation it is important to identify certain of its features. This is because there are different techniques applicable to different sorts of differential equations. In this block we introduce terminology associated with differential equations that then allows these features to be described.

1.2 Basic definitions

Dependent and independent variables

Recall that in a function such as $y = x^2 + 3x$ we say that x is the **independent variable** and y is the **dependent variable**, since the value of y depends upon the choice we have made for x. When solving a differential equation it is essential that you can identify the dependent and independent variables.

In the differential equation $\frac{dx}{dt} = x + t^2$, t is the independent variable and x is the dependent variable. In the equation $\frac{dy}{dx} = y + \sin x$, x is the independent variable and y is the dependent variable. Note that the dependent variable is always the variable being differentiated.

Example 1.1

For each of the following differential equations, state which variable is dependent and which is independent.

(a) $\dfrac{d^2y}{dx^2} + \dfrac{dy}{dx} = x$

(b) $\dfrac{dx}{dt} = (xt)^5$

(c) $RC\dfrac{dv_c}{dt} + v_c = V_S$; R, C, V_S are constants.

Solution

The dependent and independent variables are respectively:

(a) dep.: y; ind.: x

(b) dep.: x; ind.: t

(c) dep.: v_c; ind.: t

Order

A differential equation may contain derivatives of various orders, for example first derivatives, second derivatives, etc. The **order** of a differential equation is the order of its highest derivative. Thus in the equation

$$\frac{d^2y}{dx^2} + \frac{dy}{dx} = y$$

the highest derivative is the second derivative, $\frac{d^2y}{dx^2}$, so this equation is a **second-order differential equation**. In the equation

$$\frac{dv}{dt} + v^2 = 0$$

the highest derivative is the first derivative $\frac{dv}{dt}$, so this is a **first-order differential equation**.

Example 1.2

State the order of the following differential equations:

(a) $\dfrac{d^2y}{dx^2} + \left(\dfrac{dy}{dx}\right)^3 = x^7$

(b) $\dfrac{dx}{dt} = (xt)^5$

Solution

(a) Look for the term involving the highest derivative.

The order of $\dfrac{d^2y}{dx^2} + \left(\dfrac{dy}{dx}\right)^3 = x^7$ is

2

Note that although $\dfrac{dy}{dx}$ is raised to the power 3, it is not the highest derivative. The highest derivative is $\dfrac{d^2y}{dx^2}$.

(b) The order of $\frac{dx}{dt} = (xt)^5$ is

1

Linear

A differential equation is said to be **linear** if the dependent variable and its derivatives occur to the first power only and if there are no products involving the dependent variable and/or its derivatives. There should be no non-linear functions of the dependent variable, such as sine, exponential, etc. A differential equation that is not linear is said to be **non-linear**. The linearity of a differential equation is not determined or affected by the presence of non-linear terms involving the independent variable.

The equation

$$\frac{d^2y}{dx^2} - y = e^x$$

is linear, but the equations

$$\left(\frac{dy}{dx}\right)^2 = y \quad \text{and} \quad y\frac{dy}{dx} = x$$

are both non-linear, the former because the derivative of the dependent variable is raised to the power 2, and the latter because of the product $y\frac{dy}{dx}$.

The equation

$$\frac{dy}{dx} + y = e^y$$

is non-linear because it contains a non-linear function, e^y, of the dependent variable. However the equation

$$\frac{dy}{dx} + y = e^x$$

is linear.

It is particularly important to know whether an equation is linear or not, because in general non-linear equations can be much harder to solve than linear ones.

The solution of first-order linear equations is described in Block 3.

The solution of second-order linear equations is described in Blocks 5 and 6.

Example 1.3

Decide whether or not the following equations are linear:

(a) $\sin x \frac{dy}{dx} + y = x$

(b) $\sin y \frac{dy}{dx} + y = x$

(c) $\dfrac{d^2y}{dx^2} = -y^2$

(d) $\dfrac{dx}{dt} + x = t^3$

(e) $\dfrac{dy}{dx} + \sin y = 0$

Solution

(a) linear

(b) non-linear

(c) non-linear

(d) linear

(e) non-linear

Note in part (b) that the equation is non-linear because of the product term involving the dependent variable and its derivative $\left(\sin y \dfrac{dy}{dx}\right)$; however, it is also non-linear because of the non-linear function of the dependent variable, $\sin y$.

Constant-coefficient linear equations

A linear differential equation has **constant coefficients** if the coefficients of the dependent variable and its derivatives are constants.

So

$$5\frac{d^2y}{dx^2} - 3\frac{dy}{dx} + 8y = x^2$$

is constant coefficient. The coefficient of y is 8. The coefficients of the first and second derivatives of y are -3 and 5 respectively.

However,

$$x\frac{d^2y}{dx^2} + 7\frac{dy}{dx} + 4y = 0$$

is not constant coefficient since the coefficient of the second derivative of y is x (i.e. not constant).

Example 1.4 Chemical Engineering – A liquid system

Figure 1.1 shows a tank of liquid. The tank has a constant cross-sectional area A. The liquid can flow out from the tank through a valve near the base. As it does so, the height, or **head**, h, of liquid in the tank will reduce. Let q stand for the rate at which liquid flows out of the tank. Under certain conditions the rate of outflow is proportional to the head, so that $q = kh$ where k is a constant of proportionality. Situations like this one arise frequently in the chemical engineering industry. Obtain a differential equation for this system.

Solution

Refer to Figure 1.1 and write down an expression for the volume V of liquid in the tank at any time.

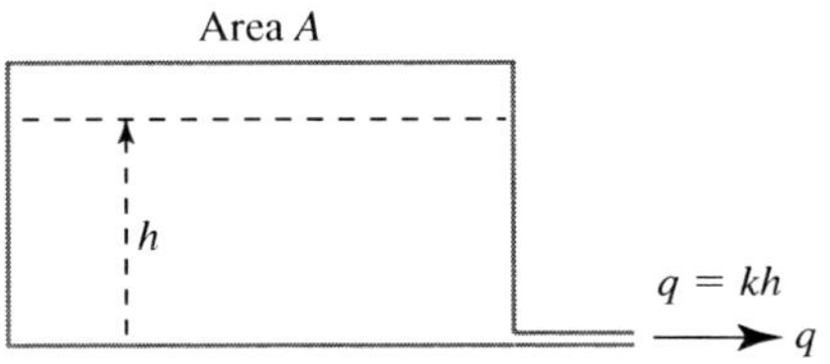

Figure 1.1 Modelling a liquid system can give rise to a constant-coefficient equation.

$$V = A \times h$$

Now, the volume of liquid in the tank changes because liquid is flowing out. Specifically

the rate at which this volume changes = rate of flow in − rate of flow out

This is the **law of conservation of mass**. The rate of change of volume is $\frac{dV}{dt}$. There is no flow into the tank and liquid flows out at a rate q. Hence

$$\frac{dV}{dt} = -q$$

But $V = Ah$ and A is constant, so the rate of change of volume is $A\frac{dh}{dt}$.
Therefore

$$A\frac{dh}{dt} = -q$$

We are also given that $q = kh$ and so

$$A\frac{dh}{dt} = -kh$$

This is a first-order differential equation with dependent variable h and independent variable t. It is linear and has constant coefficients. The unknown function that we seek is $h(t)$. You will see how this equation can be solved to find the head, h, at any time, t, in Block 2.

Example 1.5 Electrical Engineering – An *LCR* circuit

Figure 1.2 shows an *LCR* circuit. This is a circuit comprising an inductor of inductance L, a capacitor of capacitance C, and a resistor of resistance R placed in series.

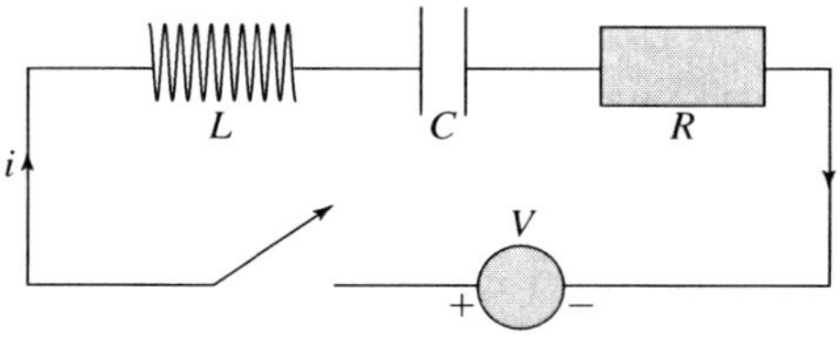

Figure 1.2 Modelling an *LCR* circuit can give rise to a constant-coefficient differential equation.

When a constant voltage source, V, is applied, it can be shown that the current, i, through the circuit satisfies the differential equation

$$L\frac{d^2i}{dt^2} + R\frac{di}{dt} + \frac{1}{C}i = 0$$

This equation can be derived using Kirchhoff's voltage law, and the individual laws for each component. Because L, R and C are constants, this is a constant-coefficient equation. Furthermore it is linear and second order. When you have learnt how to solve such equations you will be able to find the current in the circuit.

Exercises

1 Explain the distinction between a dependent variable and an independent variable.

2 In the differential equation

$$\frac{d\theta}{dt} + \theta = \sin t$$

state which is the dependent variable and which is the independent variable.

3 Explain what is meant by the order of a differential equation.

4 State the order of the equations

(a) $y'' + 2y' + 7y = 0$ (b) $\left(\frac{dx}{dt}\right)^3 + x = 0$

5 Explain what is meant by a linear differential equation.

6 Is the equation $\frac{d^2y}{dt^2} + y = \sin t$ linear?

Solutions to exercises

2 θ is the dependent variable and t is the independent variable.

4 (a) second (b) first

6 yes

1.3 The solution of a differential equation

Given a differential equation such as

$$\frac{dy}{dx} = y$$

a **solution** is found when we have obtained an expression for y in terms of x that can be substituted into the equation to make both sides equal. That is, a solution is an expression that **satisfies** the differential equation. Note that a solution is an expression of the dependent variable in terms of the independent variable.

Example 1.6

Show that $y = 5e^{2x}$ is a solution of the equation $\dfrac{d^2y}{dx^2} - \dfrac{dy}{dx} = 2y$.

Solution

We are given an expression for y in terms of x, namely $y = 5e^{2x}$. We need to substitute this into both sides of the given equation. To do this we need the derivatives $\dfrac{dy}{dx}$ and $\dfrac{d^2y}{dx^2}$.

Write expressions for $\dfrac{dy}{dx}$ and $\dfrac{d^2y}{dx^2}$.

$$\frac{dy}{dx} = 10e^{2x}$$

$$\frac{d^2y}{dx^2} = 20e^{2x}$$

Now substitute these expressions into the left-hand side of the given equation $\dfrac{d^2y}{dx^2} - \dfrac{dy}{dx}$:

$20e^{2x} - 10e^{2x}$ which equals $10e^{2x}$

Now substitute $y = 5e^{2x}$ into the right-hand side of the given equation, $2y$:

$$2y = 10e^{2x}$$

Note that both the left- and right-hand sides are the same and equal to $10e^{2x}$ when $y = 5e^{2x}$. We conclude that $y = 5e^{2x}$ is a solution of the equation.

Example 1.7

Show that $y = e^x$ is *not* a solution of $\dfrac{dy}{dx} = 2y$.

Solution

Differentiate the given expression and substitute into the left-hand side:

$$\frac{dy}{dx} = e^x$$

Substitute for y on the right-hand side:

$$2y = 2e^x$$

So the left-hand side is e^x and the right-hand side is $2e^x$. But e^x is not the same as $2e^x$ and so the given expression does not satisfy the equation and is therefore not a solution.

There are many different expressions that can satisfy a differential equation: that is, there are many solutions. A solution from which all possible solutions can be found is called the **general solution**.

The general solution of the equation $\frac{\mathrm{d}y}{\mathrm{d}x} = y$ is $y = C\mathrm{e}^x$, where C is any constant. C is called an **arbitrary constant**. By choosing different values of C, different solutions are obtained. Every solution of the equation can be obtained from this general solution.

Conditions

To determine a particular value for the constant C we need to be given more information in the form of a **condition**. For example, if we are told that at $x = 0$, $y = 4$ then from $y = C\mathrm{e}^x$ we have

$$\begin{aligned} 4 &= C\mathrm{e}^0 \\ &= C \end{aligned}$$

so that $C = 4$. Therefore $y = 4\mathrm{e}^x$ is the solution of the differential equation that additionally satisfies the condition $y(0) = 4$. This is called a **particular solution**.

When the solution of a differential equation is sought, and a condition is to be satisfied at the leftmost point of the interval of interest, such a condition is called an **initial condition**. The problem of solving a differential equation subject to an initial condition is often referred to as an **initial value problem**.

Example 1.8

Show that $x(t) = 2\mathrm{e}^{3t}$ is a solution of the initial value problem

$$\frac{\mathrm{d}x}{\mathrm{d}t} - 2x = 2\mathrm{e}^{3t}, \quad x(0) = 2$$

Solution

The solution requires us to do two things. First we must check that $x = 2\mathrm{e}^{3t}$ satisfies the differential equation, and second we must check that it satisfies the initial condition: that is, x must equal 2 when $t = 0$.

Differentiate $x(t) = 2\mathrm{e}^{3t}$.

$6\mathrm{e}^{3t}$

Substitute for $\frac{\mathrm{d}x}{\mathrm{d}t}$ and x in the left-hand side of the given equation.

$\frac{\mathrm{d}x}{\mathrm{d}t} - 2x =$

$6\mathrm{e}^{3t} - 2(2\mathrm{e}^{3t})$

which simplifies to $2\mathrm{e}^{3t}$, the same as the right-hand side. Thus $x = 2\mathrm{e}^{3t}$ is a solution of the differential equation.

We now check that the initial condition is satisfied. $x(0) = 2\mathrm{e}^0 = 2$ and so the condition is indeed satisfied.

Exercises

1 Verify that $y = 3\sin 2x$ is a solution of

$$\frac{d^2y}{dx^2} + 4y = 0$$

2 Verify that $3e^x$, Axe^x, $Axe^x + Be^x$, where A, B are constants, all satisfy the differential equation

$$\frac{d^2y}{dx^2} - 2\frac{dy}{dx} + y = 0$$

3 Verify that $x = t^2 + A\ln t + B$ is a solution of

$$t\frac{d^2x}{dt^2} + \frac{dx}{dt} = 4t$$

4 Verify that $y = A\cos x + B\sin x$ satisfies the differential equation

$$\frac{d^2y}{dx^2} + y = 0$$

Verify also that $y = A\cos x$ and $y = B\sin x$ each individually satisfy the equation.

5 The general solution of the equation

$$\frac{d^2x}{dt^2} - 3\frac{dx}{dt} + 2x = 0$$

is given by

$$x = Ae^t + Be^{2t}$$

Find the particular solution that satisfies $x = 3$ and $\frac{dx}{dt} = 5$ when $t = 0$.

6 The general solution of

$$\frac{d^2y}{dx^2} - 2\frac{dy}{dx} + y = 0$$

is $y = Axe^x + Be^x$. Find the particular solution satisfying $y(0) = 0$, $\frac{dy}{dx}(0) = 1$.

Solutions to exercises

5 $x = e^t + 2e^{2t}$

6 $y = xe^x$

1.4 Solving a differential equation by direct integration

When a differential equation has a particularly simple form it is easy to solve it by integration.

Suppose we have a first-order equation of the form

$$\frac{dy}{dx} = f(x)$$

Examples include $\frac{dy}{dx} = 3x^4$ and $\frac{dy}{dx} = 4\sin 2x + 3\cos 2x$. That is, $\frac{dy}{dx}$ is equal to a function of x only. Then y is given by

$$y = \int f(x)\,dx$$

Key point

$$\text{if} \quad \frac{dy}{dx} = f(x) \quad \text{then} \quad y = \int f(x)\, dx$$

Consider the following example.

Example 1.9
Obtain the general solution of the equation

$$\frac{dy}{dx} = \cos x + \sin x$$

Solution
Here, the right-hand side is a function of x only.

$$y = \int \cos x + \sin x \, dx$$

$$= \sin x - \cos x + c$$

This is the general solution. Notice that it contains one arbitrary constant.

The same method can be applied to second-order equations of the form

$$\frac{d^2y}{dx^2} = f(x)$$

Here again, the right-hand side is a function of x only.

Example 1.10
Obtain the general solution of the equation

$$\frac{d^2y}{dx^2} = 5e^{2x}$$

Solution
Integrating once gives

$$\frac{dy}{dx} = \int 5e^{2x}\, dx$$

$$\frac{dy}{dx} = \frac{5e^{2x}}{2} + A$$

where A is an arbitrary constant. This gives $\frac{dy}{dx}$. We must integrate again to find y.

$$y = \int \left(\frac{5e^{2x}}{2} + A \right) dx$$

$$= \frac{5e^{2x}}{4} + Ax + B$$

where B is another arbitrary constant.

This is the general solution. Notice that it contains two arbitary constants. This is because the differential equation is second order.

The technique described in this section is applicable only when the right-hand side is a function of the independent variable only. If the dependent variable appears on the right, such as in the equation

$$\frac{dy}{dx} = xy$$

you will need to apply other techniques such as those described in Blocks 2 and 3.

Example 1.11 Dynamics – The vertical motion of a projectile

When a projectile such as a ball is travelling vertically under the action of gravity its motion is described by the differential equation

$$\frac{d^2y}{dt^2} = -g$$

where g is a constant called the **acceleration due to gravity**. The dependent variable y is the vertical displacement of the projectile, and the independent variable is time t. This equation is a statement of Newton's second law of motion. Solving the equation gives y in terms of t, that is the displacement as a function of time.

(a) Integrate the differential equation twice, to obtain the general solution for y.

(b) Apply the following initial conditions: $y = 0$ at $t = 0$, $\frac{dy}{dt} = v_0$ at $t = 0$, in order to obtain a particular solution.

Solution

(a) Integrate once:

$$\frac{dy}{dt} = -gt + A$$

Integrate again:

$$y = -\frac{gt^2}{2} + At + B$$

This is the general solution.

(b) Apply the condition $y = 0$ when $t = 0$ to obtain a value for B.

$$B = 0$$

So $y = -\frac{gt^2}{2} + At$. If this is differentiated, $\frac{dy}{dt} = -gt + A$, which is a result already obtained. Applying the condition $\frac{dy}{dt} = v_0$ when $t = 0$ gives a value for A:

$$A = v_0$$

So the particular solution is $y = -\frac{gt^2}{2} + v_0 t$.

Exercises

1 Obtain the general solutions of the following differential equations:

(a) $\frac{dy}{dx} = 3x + 2$ (b) $\frac{dy}{dx} = e^{3x}$

(c) $\frac{d^2y}{dx^2} = k$, constant (d) $\frac{d^2y}{dx^2} = -\sin x$

2 Find the particular solution of

$$\frac{dx}{dt} = t^2$$

that satisfies the condition $x(3) = 0$.

Solutions to exercises

1 (a) $y = \frac{3x^2}{2} + 2x + c$ (b) $y = \frac{e^{3x}}{3} + c$

(c) $y = \frac{kx^2}{2} + Ax + B$

(d) $y = \sin x + Ax + B$

2 $x = \frac{t^3}{3} - 9$

End of block exercises

1 If $y = Ae^{2x}$ is the general solution of $\frac{dy}{dx} = 2y$, find the particular solution satisfying $y(0) = 3$. What is the particular solution satisfying $\frac{dy}{dx} = 2$ when $x = 0$?

2 Identify the dependent and independent variables of the following differential equations. Give the order of the equations and state which are linear.

(a) $\frac{dy}{dx} + 9y = 0$

(b) $\left(\frac{dy}{dx}\right)\left(\frac{d^2y}{dx^2}\right) + 3\frac{dy}{dx} = 0$

(c) $\frac{d^3x}{dt^3} + 5\frac{dx}{dt} = \sin x$

3 Show that $x(t) = 7\cos 3t - 2\sin 2t$ is a solution of

$$\frac{d^2x}{dt^2} + 2x = -49\cos 3t + 4\sin 2t$$

4 The general solution of

$$\frac{d^2x}{dt^2} = -\omega^2 x$$

is $x = Ae^{j\omega t} + Be^{-j\omega t}$, where $j^2 = -1$. Verify that this is indeed a solution. What is the particular solution satisfying $x(0) = 0$, $\frac{dx}{dt}(0) = 1$? Express the general solution and the particular solution in terms of trigonometric functions.

Solutions to exercises

1 $y(x) = 3e^{2x}$, $y(x) = e^{2x}$

2 (a) y is the dependent variable; x is the independent variable; first order, linear

(b) y is the dependent variable; x is the independent variable; second order, non-linear

(c) x is the dependent variable; t is the independent variable; third order, non-linear

4 particular solution: $\dfrac{\sin \omega t}{\omega}$ general solution:

$(A + B)\cos \omega t + (A - B)\mathrm{j}\sin \omega t$

BLOCK 2

Separation of variables

2.1 Introduction

Separation of variables is a technique commonly used to solve first-order differential equations. It is so called because we try to rearrange the equation to be solved in such a way that all terms involving the dependent variable (y say) appear on one side of the equation, and all terms involving the independent variable (x say) appear on the other. Then it is a matter of integration to complete the solution. It is not possible to rearrange all first-order equations in this way, so this technique is not always appropriate. Further, it is not always possible to perform the integration even if the variables are separable. In this block you will learn how to decide whether the method is appropriate, and how to apply it in such cases.

2.2 Separating the variables

In this section we consider differential equations that can be written in the form

$$\frac{\mathrm{d}y}{\mathrm{d}x} = f(x)g(y)$$

Note that the right-hand side is a product of a function of x and a function of y. Examples of such equations are

$$\frac{\mathrm{d}y}{\mathrm{d}x} = x^2y^3, \quad \frac{\mathrm{d}y}{\mathrm{d}x} = y^2 \sin x \quad \text{and} \quad \frac{\mathrm{d}y}{\mathrm{d}x} = (\ln x)(\sec y)$$

You may have to think carefully about some equations to recognise this form. For example, the equation

$$\frac{\mathrm{d}y}{\mathrm{d}x} = \frac{y}{x+1}$$

can be written as

$$\frac{\mathrm{d}y}{\mathrm{d}x} = \left(\frac{1}{x+1}\right)y$$

and so is of the form $\dfrac{\mathrm{d}y}{\mathrm{d}x} = f(x)g(y)$.

Not all first-order equations can be written in this form. For example, it is not possible to rewrite the equation

$$\frac{dy}{dx} = x^2 + y^3$$

in the form

$$\frac{dy}{dx} = f(x)g(y)$$

Example 2.1

Which of the following differential equations do you think can be written in the form $\frac{dy}{dx} = f(x)g(y)$?

If possible, rewrite each equation in this form.

(a) $\frac{dy}{dx} = \frac{x^2}{y^2}$ (b) $\frac{dy}{dx} = 4x^2 + 2y^2$ (b) $y\frac{dy}{dx} + 3x = 7$

Solution

(a) $\frac{dy}{dx} = x^2\left(\frac{1}{y^2}\right)$

(b) cannot be written in the stated form

(c) $\frac{dy}{dx} = (7 - 3x) \times \frac{1}{y}$

The variables involved need not be x and y. Other equations of this type are

$$\frac{dz}{dt} = te^z, \quad \frac{d\theta}{dt} = -\theta \quad \text{and} \quad \frac{dv}{dr} = \frac{v}{r^2}$$

Given a differential equation in the form $\frac{dy}{dx} = f(x)g(y)$ we can divide through by $g(y)$ to obtain

$$\frac{1}{g(y)}\frac{dy}{dx} = f(x)$$

Note that in this form terms involving y and $\frac{dy}{dx}$ have been placed on the left, and terms involving just x have been placed on the right.

If we now integrate both sides of this equation with respect to x we obtain

$$\int \frac{1}{g(y)}\frac{dy}{dx}\,dx = \int f(x)\,dx$$

that is

$$\int \frac{1}{g(y)}\,dy = \int f(x)\,dx$$

We have **separated the variables** because the left-hand side contains only the variable y, and the right-hand side contains only the variable x. We can now try to integrate each side separately. If we can actually perform the required integrations we shall obtain a relationship between y and x. Examples of this process are given in the next section.

Key point

Separation of variables
The solution of the equation

$$\frac{dy}{dx} = f(x)g(y)$$

is found from

$$\int \frac{1}{g(y)}\,dy = \int f(x)\,dx$$

2.3 Applying the method of separation of variables

The method is illustrated in the following example.

Example 2.2

Solve the first-order equation $\frac{dy}{dx} = 3ye^x$ by separation of variables.

Solution

Note that the right-hand side has the form $f(x)\,g(y)$, where $f(x) = e^x$ and $g(y) = 3y$. Dividing both sides by $g(y)$ we find

$$\frac{1}{3y}\frac{dy}{dx} = e^x$$

The left-hand side now contains terms involving only y and $\frac{dy}{dx}$. The right-hand side is a function of x. Integrating both sides with respect to x,

$$\int \frac{1}{3y}\frac{dy}{dx}\,dx = \int e^x\,dx$$

that is

$$\int \frac{1}{3y}\,dy = \int e^x\,dx$$

Performing the two integrations gives

$$\frac{1}{3}\ln y = e^x + c$$

You might think that there should be a constant of integration on the left too. You are quite right, but the two constants can be combined into a single constant and so we need write only one. We now have a relationship between y and x as required. This is the general solution. In this case it could be rearranged to give y explicitly if required.

Example 2.3

Use the method of separation of variables to solve the differential equation

$$\frac{dy}{dx} = \frac{3x^2}{y}$$

Solution

The equation already has the form $\frac{dy}{dx} = f(x)g(y)$ where $f(x) = 3x^2$ and $g(y) = \frac{1}{y}$. Dividing both sides by $g(y)$ we find

$$y\frac{dy}{dx} = 3x^2$$

Integrating both sides with respect to x gives

$$\int y\frac{dy}{dx}\,dx = \int 3x^2\,dx$$

that is

$$\int y\,dy = \int 3x^2\,dx$$

Note that the left-hand side is an integral involving just y; the right-hand side is an integral involving just x. After integrating we find

$$\frac{y^2}{2} = x^3 + c$$

where c is a constant of integration. We now have a relationship between y and x as required. This is the general solution. Often it is sufficient to leave your answer in this form but you may also be required to obtain an explicit relation for y in terms of x. In this particular case

$$y^2 = 2x^3 + 2c$$

so that

$$y = \pm\sqrt{2x^3 + D} \quad \text{where } D = 2c$$

Example 2.4

Use the method of separation of variables to solve the differential equation

$$\frac{dy}{dx} = \frac{\cos x}{\sin 2y}$$

Solution

Separate the variables so that terms involving y and $\frac{dy}{dx}$ appear on the left, and terms involving just x appear on the right:

$$\sin 2y\frac{dy}{dx} = \cos x$$

Then integrate both sides with respect to x to obtain

$$\int \sin 2y \frac{dy}{dx}\, dx = \int \cos x\, dx$$

that is

$$\int \sin 2y\, dy = \int \cos x\, dx$$

Now integrate both sides:

$$-\frac{\cos 2y}{2} = \sin x + c$$

Finally, rearrange, if possible, to obtain an expression for y in terms of x:

$$y = \frac{1}{2}\cos^{-1}(D - 2\sin x) \quad \text{where } D = -2c$$

This is the general solution.

Example 2.5 Mechanical Engineering – Simple harmonic motion

When an object such as a mass vibrating on a spring, or a pendulum oscillating under the action of gravity, moves in **simple harmonic motion** its velocity v satisfies a differential equation of the form

$$v\frac{dv}{dx} = -k^2 x$$

where x is displacement and k is a constant. Solve this equation.

Solution

The variables are already separated because v and $\frac{dv}{dx}$ are on the left, and the right-hand side is a function of x only.
Integrate both sides with respect to x.

$$\int v\frac{dv}{dx}\, dx = \int -k^2 x\, dx$$

This can be written

$$\int v\, dv = \int -k^2 x\, dx$$

Complete the integration to find v.

$$\frac{v^2}{2} = -k^2\frac{x^2}{2} + c$$

This is the general solution. If we wished to we could write v explicitly in terms of x.

Example 2.6 Chemical Engineering – A liquid system

In Block 1 the differential equation describing the head, h, of liquid in a tank was obtained:

$$A\frac{\mathrm{d}h}{\mathrm{d}t} = -kh$$

Solve this differential equation given that at $t = 0$ the head of liquid is h_0. A and k are constants.

Solution

Separate the variables h and t:

$$\frac{A}{h}\frac{\mathrm{d}h}{\mathrm{d}t} = -k$$

Both sides are then integrated.

$$A\int\frac{\mathrm{d}h}{h} = -k\int \mathrm{d}t$$

Perform the integration to obtain the general solution:

$$A \ln h = -kt + C$$

This is the general solution. By imposing the condition $h = h_0$ at $t = 0$ find the particular solution.

$$C = A \ln h_0$$

Thus

$$A \ln h = -kt + A \ln h_0$$

Rearranging and using the laws of logarithms to combine the two log terms,

$$\begin{aligned} A \ln h - A \ln h_0 &= A \ln \frac{h}{h_0} \\ &= -kt \end{aligned}$$

Rearrange this to obtain h:

$$h = h_0 \mathrm{e}^{-kt/A}$$

We interpret this result as saying that the head reduces exponentially from its initial value of h_0 to a final value of zero as we would expect on physical grounds.

Example 2.7 Manufacturing Engineering – Heat transfer during quenching

During the manufacture of steel components it is often necessary to quench them in a large bath of liquid in order to cool them down. This reduces the temperature of the component to the temperature of the liquid. If θ is the temperature of the component in excess of the liquid temperature it can be shown that the variation of θ with time, t, satisfies the first-order differential equation

$$\frac{\mathrm{d}\theta}{\mathrm{d}t} = -k\theta$$

where k is a constant that depends upon the volume and surface area of the component, its specific heat capacity, and the heat transfer coefficient between the component and the liquid. Solve this equation given the initial condition that at $t = 0$ the temperature excess is θ_0.

Solution

Separate the variables.

$$\frac{1}{\theta}\frac{d\theta}{dt} = -k$$

Integrate both sides with respect to t.

$$\ln \theta + C = -kt$$

Apply the initial condition.

$$\ln \theta_0 + C = 0 \text{ so } C = -\ln \theta_0$$

Hence

$$\ln \theta - \ln \theta_0 = -kt$$

from which

$$\ln\frac{\theta}{\theta_0} = -kt$$

Finally, obtain θ as a function of t.

$$\theta = \theta_0 e^{-kt}$$

This means that the temperature excess of the component decays exponentially from its initial value θ_0 to zero. When the temperature excess is zero, the component has cooled to the temperature of the bath.

Exercises

1 Solve the equation

$$\frac{dy}{dx} = \frac{e^{-x}}{y}$$

2 Solve the equation

$$\frac{dy}{dx} = 3x^2 e^{-y}$$

subject to the condition $y(0) = 1$.

3 Find the general solution of the following equations:

(a) $\dfrac{dy}{dx} = 3$ (b) $\dfrac{dy}{dx} = \dfrac{6 \sin x}{y}$

4 Find the general solution of the equation

$$\frac{dx}{dt} = t(x - 2)$$

Find the particular solution that satisfies the condition $x(0) = 5$.

5 Some equations that do not appear to be separable can be made so by means of a suitable substitution. In this exercise you will solve the equation

$$\frac{dy}{dx} = \frac{y^2}{x^2} + \frac{y}{x} + 1$$

by means of the substitution $z = \dfrac{y}{x}$.

(a) If $z = \frac{y}{x}$, then $y = zx$. Using the product rule for differentiation show that

$$\frac{dy}{dx} = z + x\frac{dz}{dx}$$

(b) Make the substitution to obtain an equation involving only z and x. Solve this by separation of variables. Hence obtain the solution of the given equation.

6 The equation

$$iR + L\frac{di}{dt} = E$$

where R, L and E are constants arises in electrical circuit theory. This equation can be solved by separation of variables. Find the solution that satisfies the condition $i(0) = 0$.

7 Solve the equation $\dot{x} = 4xt$.

Solutions to exercises

1 $y = \pm\sqrt{D - 2e^{-x}}$

2 $y = \ln(x^3 + e)$

3 (a) $y = 3x + C$ (b) $\frac{y^2}{2} = C - 6\cos x$

4 $x = 2 + Ae^{t^2/2}$, $x = 2 + 3e^{t^2/2}$

5 $z = \tan(\ln Dx)$ so that $y = x\tan(\ln Dx)$

6 $i = \frac{E}{R}(1 - e^{-t/\tau})$ where $\tau = L/R$

7 $x = Ae^{2t^2}$

End of block exercises

1 Find the general solution of the following equations:

(a) $\frac{dy}{dx} = kx$ (b) $\frac{dy}{dx} = -ky$ (c) $\frac{dy}{dx} = y^2$

(d) $y\frac{dy}{dx} = \sin x$ (e) $y\frac{dy}{dx} = x + 2$

(f) $x^2\frac{dy}{dx} = 2y^2 + yx$ (g) $\frac{dx}{dt} = \frac{t^4}{x^5}$

2 Find the general solution of the following:

(a) $\frac{dx}{dt} = xt$ (b) $\frac{dy}{dx} = \frac{x}{y}$

(c) $t\frac{dx}{dt} = \tan x$ (d) $\frac{dx}{dt} = \frac{x^2 - 1}{t}$

Solutions to exercises

1 (a) $\frac{kx^2}{2} + c$ (b) Ae^{-kx} (c) $-\frac{1}{x + c}$

(d) $y^2 = 2(C - \cos x)$ (e) $y^2 = x^2 + 4x + c$

(f) $\frac{x}{A - 2\ln x}$ (g) $\frac{x^6}{6} = \frac{t^5}{5} + c$

2 (a) $x = Ae^{t^2/2}$ (b) $y^2 = x^2 + C$

(c) $x = \sin^{-1}(kt)$ (d) $x = \frac{1 + At^2}{1 - At^2}$

BLOCK 3 Solving first-order linear equations using an integrating factor

3.1 Introduction

The standard form of a first-order linear differential equation is

$$\frac{dy}{dx} + P(x)y = Q(x) \qquad (1)$$

$P(x)$ and $Q(x)$ are given functions of x, which may be constants. All first-order linear equations can be written in this form. Note that the coefficient of $\frac{dy}{dx}$ is 1. An example is

$$\frac{dy}{dx} + x^2y = 3 + x$$

in which $P(x) = x^2$ and $Q(x) = 3 + x$.

Other variables will be used. For example,

$$\frac{dx}{dt} + x \sin t = t^2$$

is a first-order linear equation in standard form with dependent variable x and independent variable t. Here, $P(t) = \sin t$ and $Q(t) = t^2$.

Key point

All first-order linear differential equations can be written in standard form as

$$\frac{dy}{dx} + P(x)y = Q(x)$$

Equations of this type can always be solved by multiplying through by a function known as the **integrating factor** for the equation. In this block you will learn how to determine the integrating factor and how to obtain the solution of the original equation.

3.2 Writing equations in standard form

In order to use the technique described in this block you must write the equation in the standard form.

Example 3.1

Write $x^2\frac{dy}{dx} + 3xy = x^3$ in standard form. Identify $P(x)$ and $Q(x)$.

Solution

Note that this is a first-order equation. It is linear, and so the integrating factor method is appropriate. Study the standard form (1) of a first-order linear equation and note that the coefficient of the derivative term is 1. We divide the given equation through by x^2 to achieve this.

$$\frac{dy}{dx} + \frac{3}{x}y = x$$

Compare this with the standard form to identify $P(x)$ and $Q(x)$.

$P(x) =$ $\frac{3}{x}$

$Q(x) =$ x

Example 3.2

Compare the equation $\frac{dy}{dx} - 2y = x$ with the standard form and identify $P(x)$ and $Q(x)$.

Solution

The coefficient of the derivative term is already 1.

$P(x) =$ -2, in this case, a constant

$Q(x) =$ x

The equation is already written in standard form.

Example 3.3 Electrical Engineering – Current in a circuit

The equation $L\frac{di}{dt} + Ri = E \sin t$, where L, R and E are constants, models the current, $i(t)$, in a circuit. Write the equation in standard form. Identify P and Q.

Solution

Note that this is a first-order equation. It is linear, and so the integrating factor method is appropriate. Here the dependent variable is i and the independent variable is t. Study the standard form (1) and note that the coefficient of the derivative term is 1. Dividing the given equation through by L we can achieve this:

$$\frac{di}{dt} + \frac{R}{L}i = \frac{E \sin t}{L}$$

This is the standard form. Write down $P(t)$ and $Q(t)$.

$P(t) =$ $\frac{R}{L}$, which is constant

$Q(t) =$ $\frac{E \sin t}{L}$

Exercises

1 Write each of the following equations in standard form:

(a) $x\dfrac{dy}{dx} + 2xy = xe^{-2x}$

(b) $\dfrac{dy}{dx} + 3y - \sin x = 0$

(c) $iR + L\dfrac{di}{dt} = \sin \omega t$

Solutions to exercises

1 (a) $\dfrac{dy}{dx} + 2y = e^{-2x}$ (b) $\dfrac{dy}{dx} + 3y = \sin x$

(c) $\dfrac{di}{dt} + \dfrac{R}{L}i = \dfrac{1}{L}\sin \omega t.$

3.3 Finding an integrating factor

The idea behind the method is to multiply the equation

$$\frac{dy}{dx} + P(x)y = Q(x)$$

through by some function, as yet unknown, called an **integrating factor**. Let this integrating factor be μ. Then

$$\mu\frac{dy}{dx} + \mu P(x)y = \mu Q(x) \qquad (2)$$

Suppose we choose μ in a special way so that the left-hand side of this equation can be written more simply as

$$\frac{d}{dx}(\mu y)$$

This special way of choosing μ is described below. The equation becomes

$$\frac{d}{dx}(\mu y) = \mu Q(x)$$

In this form the equation is said to be **exact**. It follows immediately, by integrating both sides, that

$$\mu y = \int \mu Q(x)\, dx \qquad (3)$$

So by knowing $Q(x)$ and μ, and performing the integration on the right, and dividing through by μ, we can obtain y.

Choosing μ

We want to choose μ so that the left-hand side of (2) is equal to $\frac{d}{dx}(\mu y)$. That is,

$$\mu\frac{dy}{dx} + \mu P(x)y = \frac{d}{dx}(\mu y)$$

Using the product rule for differentiation we can expand the product on the right to give

$$\mu\frac{dy}{dx} + \mu P(x)y = \mu\frac{dy}{dx} + y\frac{d\mu}{dx}$$

Comparing the coefficients of y on both sides shows that we must choose μ to satisfy

$$\mu P(x) = \frac{d\mu}{dx}$$

This is a first-order equation for μ, which can be solved by separating the variables as follows:

$$\int\frac{d\mu}{\mu} = \int P(x)\,dx$$

from which

$$\ln\mu = \int P(x)\,dx$$

We have ignored the constant of integration. When you are experienced at this technique, try including a constant of integration and you will see that it makes no difference to the solution.

It follows that

$$\mu = e^{\int p(x)\,dx}$$

Thus knowing $P(x)$ we can use this formula to find the integrating factor. Once μ is known y can be determined from the key point.

Key point

The integrating factor method
If the linear differential equation is in the standard form

$$\frac{dy}{dx} + P(x)y = Q(x)$$

then the integrating factor is

$$\mu = e^{\int p(x)\,dx}$$

and y is given by

$$\mu y = \int \mu Q(x)\,dx$$

Example 3.4

Find the integrating factor for the equations

(a) $x\dfrac{dy}{dx} + 2xy = xe^{-2x}$ (b) $\dfrac{dy}{dx} - (\tan x)y = 1$

Solution

In each case write the equation in standard form and identify $P(x)$. The integrating factor is found from $\mu = e^{\int p(x)\,dx}$.

(a) $P(x) = 2;\ \mu = e^{2x}$

(b) $P(x) = -\tan x;\ \mu = e^{\ln \cos x} = \cos x$

Example 3.5

Use the integrating factors found in Example 3.4 to find the general solutions to the following differential equations.

(a) $x^2\dfrac{dy}{dx} + 2x^2y = x^2e^{-2x}$ (b) $\dfrac{dy}{dx} - (\tan x)y = 1$

Solution

(a) The standard form is $\dfrac{dy}{dx} + 2y = e^{-2x}$ for which the integrating factor is $\mu = e^{2x}$.
Note that $Q(x) = e^{-2x}$.
From the key point on p. 948 we have

$$\mu y = \int \mu Q(x)\,dx$$

so that

$$\begin{aligned} e^{2x}y &= \int e^{2x}e^{-2x}\,dx \\ &= \int 1\,dx \\ &= x + C \end{aligned}$$

Therefore

$$\begin{aligned} y &= \frac{(x + C)}{e^{2x}} \\ &= (x + C)e^{-2x} \end{aligned}$$

This is the general solution.

(b) The equation is in standard form. The integrating factor is $\mu = \cos x$ and $Q(x) = 1$. From the key point we have

$$\mu y = \int \mu\, Q(x)\,dx$$

so that

$$(\cos x)\, y = \int \cos x \, \mathrm{d}x$$
$$= \sin x + C$$

giving

$$y = \frac{\sin x}{\cos x} + \frac{C}{\cos x}$$
$$= \tan x + C \sec x$$

This is the general solution.

Example 3.6

(a) Use the integrating factor method to solve the equation $\frac{\mathrm{d}y}{\mathrm{d}x} + \frac{y}{x} = 1$.

(b) Find the particular solution where $y(1) = 3$.

Solution

(a) Refer to the standard form and identify $P(x)$ and $Q(x)$.

$P(x) =$ $\frac{1}{x}$

$Q(x) =$ 1

The integrating factor is found from the formula $\mu = \mathrm{e}^{\int p(x)\,\mathrm{d}x}$. Find the integrating factor:

$\mu = \mathrm{e}^{\int (1/x)\,\mathrm{d}x} = \mathrm{e}^{\ln x} = x$

Knowing the integrating factor y can be found using the key point on p. 948

$$\mu y = \int \mu Q(x)\, \mathrm{d}x$$
$$= \int x \times 1 \, \mathrm{d}x$$
$$= \frac{x^2}{2} + C$$

where C is the constant of integration. So

$$\mu y = xy = \frac{x^2}{2} + C$$

so that

$$y = \frac{x}{2} + \frac{C}{x}$$

is the general solution.

(b) We now apply the condition $y(1) = 3$ in order to find the constant C and thus obtain the particular solution.

We know that when $x = 1$, $y = 3$, and so

$$3 = \frac{1}{2} + \frac{C}{1}$$

that is $C = \frac{5}{2}$. Thus the particular solution is $y = \frac{x}{2} + \frac{5}{2x}$.

Exercises

1 Solve the equation

$$x^2 \frac{dy}{dx} + xy = 1$$

2 Find the solution of the equation

$$x \frac{dy}{dx} - y = x$$

subject to the condition $y(1) = 2$.

3 Find the general solution of the equation

$$\frac{dy}{dt} + (\tan t)\, y = \cos t$$

4 Solve the equation

$$\frac{dy}{dt} + (\cot t)\, y = \sin t$$

5 The temperature θ (measured in degrees) of a body immersed in an atmosphere of varying temperature is given by

$$\frac{d\theta}{dt} + 0.1\theta = 5 - 2.5t$$

Find the temperature at time t if $\theta = 60°$ when $t = 0$.

6 In an LR circuit with applied voltage $E = 10(1 - e^{-0.1t})$ the current i is given by

$$L\frac{di}{dt} + Ri = 10(1 - e^{-0.1t})$$

If the initial current is i_0 find i subsequently.

Solutions to exercises

1 $y = \frac{1}{x} \ln x + \frac{C}{x}$

2 $y = x \ln x + 2x$

3 $y = (t + C) \cos t$

4 $y = \left(\frac{1}{2}t - \frac{1}{4}\sin 2t + C\right)\operatorname{cosec} t$

5 $\theta = 300 - 25t - 240e^{-0.1t}$

6 $$i = \frac{10}{R} - \left(\frac{100}{10R - L}\right)e^{-0.1t} + \left(i_0 + \frac{10L}{R(10R - L)}\right)e^{-Rt/L}$$

End of block exercises

1 Find the general solution of the following equations:

(a) $\frac{dy}{dx} + y = 1$ (b) $\frac{dy}{dx} + 2y = 6$

(c) $\frac{dx}{dt} + 6x = 4$ (d) $\frac{dy}{dx} - 3y = 2$

(e) $\frac{dy}{dx} = 6y + 9$ (f) $\frac{dx}{dt} = 3x - 8$

2 Use an integrating factor to obtain the general solution of $iR + L\frac{di}{dt} = \sin \omega t$ where R, L and ω are constants.

Solutions to exercises

1 (a) $y = 1 + ce^{-x}$ (b) $y = 3 + ce^{-2x}$

(c) $x = \frac{2}{3} + ce^{-6t}$ (d) $y = ce^{3x} - \frac{2}{3}$

(e) $y = ce^{6x} - \frac{3}{2}$ (f) $x = \frac{8}{3} + ce^{3t}$

2 $\frac{L[(R/L)\sin \omega t - \omega \cos \omega t]}{R^2 + L^2\omega^2} + ce^{-Rt/L}$

BLOCK 4 Computational approaches to differential equations

4.1 Introduction

Computer software packages are readily available that can solve differential equations. You may recall that when using software to perform integration the results produced fall into two categories, **symbolic** and **numerical**. This is also true when we use computers to solve differential equations.

For many equations it is possible for the computer to obtain a symbolic answer in terms of common functions, and we shall illustrate this shortly. However, for many equations it is impossible to obtain a symbolic answer and so techniques, known as **numerical methods**, exist for obtaining approximate solutions. One technique for solving first-order equations is Euler's method. In general, numerical techniques are laborious to perform by hand and so are best implemented using a computer. We shall be content to illustrate Euler's method using simple examples, and then rely upon software to tackle more substantial problems.

4.2 Use of symbolic algebra packages to solve first-order differential equations exactly

Many software packages designed for tackling mathematical problems have the facility to solve first-order equations. You should enquire whether the package(s) to which you have access can solve differential equations symbolically. You may need to refer to local documentation. Some of the packages require additional software to be loaded. For example, the standard version of Matlab does not come with a symbolic processor, but requires a Symbolic Math Toolbox.

Example 4.1 Finding an exact, general solution

Use a computer algebra package to solve the differential equation $\frac{\mathrm{d}y}{\mathrm{d}x} - xy = 0$.

This is a first-order equation, which can be solved using the method of separation of variables.

Solution

Maple

In Maple the command **dsolve** can be used to find the general solution of a differential equation with dependent variable y and independent variable x. y must be input as $y(x)$, and the derivative term is input as diff ($y(x)$, x), which stands for the derivative of $y(x)$ with respect to x. So, to solve the equation $\frac{dy}{dx} - xy = 0$ the Maple command is

```
dsolve(diff(y(x),x)-x*y(x) = 0);
```

and Maple outputs

$$y(x) = \_C1e^{\left(\frac{1}{2}x^2\right)}$$

The output $\_C1$ is the arbitrary constant, and so we can interpret this general solution as simply $y = Ae^{\frac{1}{2}x^2}$.

Matlab

Assuming the Symbolic Math Toolbox is available, the function **dsolve** computes symbolic solutions to differential equations. In Matlab the symbol D is used to denote the derivative. The command

```
dsolve('Dy-x*y=0','x')
```

generates the result

```
C1*exp(1/2*x^2)
```

Note the requirement to put the differential equation and the independent variable between apostrophes. Clearly the output is not as user-friendly as that provided by Maple, although another Matlab command, **pretty**, can be applied to generate more familiar output.

Derive

When running Derive it is necessary to load a file called ode1.mth, which defines functions for finding exact solutions of differential equations. The command `separable_gen(p,q,x,y,c)` can be used to solve the separable equation $\frac{dy}{dx} = p(x)q(y)$. So, to solve $\frac{dy}{dx} = xy$ the command `separable_gen (x,y, x,y,c)` followed by the command `Simplify` produces the result

$$\ln(y) = \frac{x^2}{2} + c$$

Note that Derive gives the solution $y(x)$ implicitly rather than its explicit form given by Maple. Derive also contains commands for solving other sorts of first-order equations.

The power of software packages lies in their ability to handle symbolic constants in problems. Consider the following example.

Example 4.2 Electrical Engineering – *RL* circuit with sinusoidal input

On p. 952 the integrating factor method was used to solve the equation

$$iR + L\frac{\mathrm{d}i}{\mathrm{d}t} = \sin \omega t$$

where R, L and ω are constants, in order to find the current $i(t)$ in an RL circuit. Use a computer algebra package to obtain the general solution of this equation.

Solution

Maple

In Maple the relevant command is

```
dsolve(i(t)*R+L*diff(i(t),t) = sin(w*t));
```

and Maple produces the following output:

$$i(t) = \mathrm{e}^{\left(-\frac{Rt}{L}\right)}\_C1 + \frac{-L\,w\cos(wt) + R\sin(wt)}{R^2 + W^2L^2}$$

where $\_C1$ represents the arbitrary constant in the general solution. Compare this solution with the one stated analytically on p. 952.

Matlab

In Matlab the symbol i is used to denote $\sqrt{-1}$ and so should not be used here. Instead we use y as the dependent variable. The command

```
dsolve('y*R+L*Dy = sin(w*t)','t')
```

results in the output

```
(-L*w*cos(w*t) + R*sin(w*t) + exp(-1/L*R*t)*C1*R^2 +
exp(-1/L*R*t)*C1*w^2*L^2)/(R^2 + w^2*L^2)
```

This is equivalent to that produced by Maple, although the format is not so user-friendly.

Derive

After loading the file odel.mth, the command `Linear1_gen(p,q,x,y,c)` can be used to solve the first-order linear equation $\frac{\mathrm{d}y}{\mathrm{d}x} + p(x)y = q(x)$. So, dividing the given equation through by L, to solve $\frac{\mathrm{d}i}{\mathrm{d}t} + \frac{R}{L}i = \frac{1}{L}\sin \omega t$, the command `Linear1_gen (R/L,sin (wt) /L,t,i,c)` followed by the command `Simplify` produces the result

$$i = \frac{\mathrm{e}^{-R\cdot t/L}\cdot(C\cdot(L^2\cdot\omega^2 + R^2) - \mathrm{e}^{R\cdot t/L}\cdot(L\cdot\omega\cdot\cos(t\cdot\omega) - R\cdot\sin(t\cdot\omega)))}{L^2\cdot\omega^2 + R^2}$$

Example 4.3 Finding an exact, particular solution

Find the particular solution of $\dfrac{dy}{dx} - x^2y = 0$ that satisfies the initial condition $y(0) = 3$.

Solution

Software packages will have the facility to handle initial conditions.

Maple

In Maple the appropriate command is

```
dsolve({diff(y(x),x) - x^2*y(x) = 0,y(0) = 3});
```

and Maple outputs the particular solution

$$y(x) = 3e^{(\frac{1}{3}x^3)}$$

Matlab

The command

```
dsolve('Dy-x^2*y = 0','y(0) = 3','x')
```

results in the output

```
3*exp(1/3*x^3)
```

Derive

After loading ode1.mth the command `dsolve1(p, q, x, y, x0, y0)` can be used to solve $p(x, y) + q(x, y)\dfrac{dy}{dx} = 0$ subject to the condition $y(x_0) = y_0$. So, to solve $-x^2y + \dfrac{dy}{dx} = 0$ subject to $y(0) = 3$ we use `dsolve1(-x^2y,1,x,y,0,3)` which produces the result

$$3 \cdot \ln(y) - x^3 = 3 \cdot \ln(3)$$

Note that the solution is given implicitly.

Computer and calculator exercises

1 Use a computer algebra package to find the general solutions of the following differential equations:

(a) $\dfrac{dy}{dx} = \dfrac{xy}{x^2 + 1}$

(b) $m\dfrac{dv}{dt} = -v$ where m is a constant

2 Use a computer algebra package to find the exact, particular solution of the following equations:

(a) $\dfrac{d\theta}{dt} = -k\theta,\ \theta(0) = \theta_0$

(b) $iR + L\dfrac{di}{dt} = E,\ i(0) = 0$, where R, L and E are constants

Solutions

1 (a) $y(x) = C\sqrt{x^2 + 1}$
(b) $v(t) = Ce^{-t/m}$

2 (a) $\theta(t) = \theta_0 \, e^{-kt}$ (b) $i(t) = \dfrac{E}{R} - \dfrac{Ee^{(-Rt/L)}}{R}$

4.3 Euler's method

Although symbolic algebra packages are extremely powerful, there are nevertheless some differential equations that they cannot solve exactly. In such cases it may be possible to use the computer to obtain an approximate solution. There are many sophisticated techniques available for doing this, the details of which can be found in textbooks on numerical methods. The simplest technique is Euler's method, which we explain here.

Euler's method is a numerical technique for finding approximate solutions of differential equations having the form

$$\frac{dy}{dx} = f(x, y), \quad y(x_0) = y_0$$

Note that to use this method we need to be given an initial condition $y(x_0) = y_0$. When solving this equation numerically we use the fact that $\frac{dy}{dx}$ is the gradient of the tangent to $y(x)$. We know from the given equation that the point (x_0, y_0) lies on the graph of the solution. We also know that the gradient of the solution is $\frac{dy}{dx}$, that is $f(x, y)$. So, at the point (x_0, y_0) the graph of the solution has a tangent line with gradient $f(x_0, y_0)$. This is illustrated in Figure 4.1.

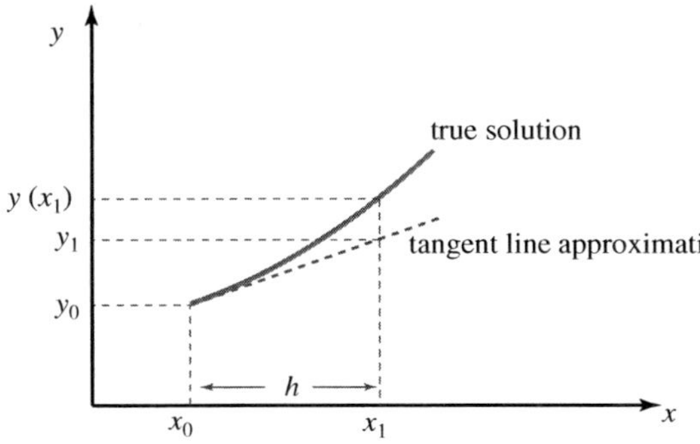

Figure 4.1 A tangent line is used to obtain an estimate of the true solution.

The point (x_0, y_0) lies both on the solution curve and on the tangent line. Consider moving to a nearby point on the tangent line. Let the nearby point be (x_1, y_1), where $x_1 = x_0 + h$. The value of h and hence x_1 is known. Then (x_1, y_1) is on the tangent line, but not on the solution curve. When $x = x_1$ the value of the solution is $y(x_1)$. We do not know the value of $y(x_1)$. We can, however, use y_1 as an approximation to $y(x_1)$.

Referring to Figure 4.1 we note that the gradient of the tangent line is $\dfrac{y_1 - y_0}{h}$, and so

$$\frac{y_1 - y_0}{h} = f(x_0, y_0)$$

It follows by rearrangement that $y_1 = y_0 + hf(x_0, y_0)$. So, knowing the values of x_0, y_0, the function $f(x, y)$, and the value of h we can calculate y_1. Note from Figure 4.1 that $y(x_1)$ is the true, but unknown, solution, whereas y_1 is now the known, but approximate solution.

We can use the point (x_1, y_1) as a new starting point to find the solution at $x_2 = x_1 + h$, and using an identical argument this is $y_2 = y_1 + hf(x_1, y_1)$.

The process is repeated using the general formula $y_{n+1} = y_n + hf(x_n, y_n)$. The result is a sequence of values, y_n, which approximates the true solution $y(x)$ at the points where $x = x_n$.

Key point

Euler's method

An approximate solution of $\frac{dy}{dx} = f(x, y)$, subject to the initial condition $y(x_0) = y_0$, is given by

$$y_{n+1} = y_n + hf(x_n, y_n), \quad y_0 = y(x_0)$$

where h is the step-size, or **increment**, in x.

Example 4.4

Use three steps of Euler's method to obtain an approximate solution of $\frac{dy}{dx} = \frac{x}{y}$, subject to the initial condition $y(1) = 2$, at the points where $x = 1.1$, 1.2 and 1.3. Compare the results with the exact solution.

Solution

We start from the given initial condition, $x_0 = 1$, $y_0 = y(x_0) = y(1) = 2$. Then applying Euler's method with $h = 0.1$, and $f(x, y) = \frac{x}{y}$ we find

$$\begin{aligned} y_1 &= y_0 + hf(x_0, y_0) \\ &= y_0 + h\left(\frac{x_0}{y_0}\right) \\ &= 2 + 0.1\left(\frac{1}{2}\right) \\ &= 2.05 \end{aligned}$$

So, at the point $x_1 = 1.1$ the solution is approximated by $y_1 = 2.05$. These values are recorded in Table 4.1.

Applying the formula again:

$$\begin{aligned} y_2 &= y_1 + hf(x_1, y_1) \\ &= y_1 + h\left(\frac{x_1}{y_1}\right) \end{aligned}$$

$$= 2.05 + 0.1\left(\frac{1.1}{2.05}\right)$$

$$= 2.103659 \text{ (6 d.p.)}$$

So, at the point $x_2 = 1.2$ the solution is approximated by $y_2 = 2.103659$. Applying the formula one more time:

$$y_3 = y_2 + hf(x_2, y_2) = y_2 + h\left(\frac{x_2}{y_2}\right) = \qquad\qquad 2.160702$$

These results and the true solutions, for comparison, are given in Table 4.1. Note that the true solution can be obtained by separation of variables and is $y = \sqrt{x^2 + 3}$.

Table 4.1
For Example 4.

x_n	y_n	true: $y(x_n)$ (to 6 d.p.)
$x_0 = 1$	$y_0 = 2$	2
$x_1 = 1.1$	$y_1 = 2.05$	2.051828
$x_2 = 1.2$	$y_2 = 2.103659$	2.107131
$x_3 = 1.3$	$y_3 = 2.160702$	2.165641

We note from Table 4.1 that our solution is correct to 2 decimal places. Clearly this rather crude approach can be improved by taking a smaller increment in x, but the price we pay is an increase in the number of calculations required.

We have provided details of the simplest numerical method for solving a first-order differential equation. More sophisticated formulae exist, but for a detailed treatment you should refer to a textbook on numerical methods for engineers.

Exercises

1. Use five steps of Euler's method to find an approximate solution of the initial value problem $\frac{dy}{dx} = x \sin y$, $y(0) = 2$ using $h = 0.2$, for $0 \le x \le 1$. Work throughout to 6 decimal places. Hence approximate $y(1)$.

2. Use five steps of Euler's method to find an approximate solution of the initial value problem $\frac{dx}{dt} = \frac{x + x^2}{t}$, $x(1) = -5$ using $h = 0.01$. Work throughout to 6 decimal places. Hence approximate $x(1.05)$.

Solutions to Exercises

1. $y(1) \approx 2.339282$

2. $x(1.05) \approx -4.169132$

4.4 Use of software to find numerical solutions of differential equations

As we stated in the previous section, symbolic algebra packages use sophisticated techniques to find accurate, approximate solutions of initial value problems. For full details of the underlying algorithms you will need to consult the documentation accompanying your package. We shall be content to illustrate their application in a simple example.

Example 4.5 Finding a numerical solution of a first-order equation

Find a numerical solution of the differential equation of Example 4.3, $\frac{\mathrm{d}y}{\mathrm{d}x} - x^2y = 0$, subject to the initial condition $y(0) = 3$.

Solution

A numerical solution produces a sequence of values of the dependent variable, at values of the independent variable specified by the user. For example, suppose we wish to know the value of y when $x = 0, 0.2, 0.4, 0.6, 0.8$ and 1.

Maple

```
dsolve({diff(y(x),x)-x^2*y(x)=0,y(0)=3},
type=numeric,output=array([0,0.2,0.4,0.6,0.8,1]));
```

and Maple outputs an array containing the x and y values:

[x	$y(x)$]
0	3.
.2	3.00801944725338
.4	3.06469041449842
.6	3.22396357678057
.8	3.55828609702334
1	4.18683969904184

You will find that producing a graph of the output using the software is straightforward.

Matlab

Using Matlab, it is first necessary to write, and save a file, known as an m.file, to store the right-hand side of the differential equation $\frac{\mathrm{d}y}{\mathrm{d}x} = f(x, y)$. The second line below represents the right-hand side of the equation $\frac{\mathrm{d}y}{\mathrm{d}x} = x^2\,y$.

```
function ode1=example1(x,y)
ode1=x^2*y
```

After saving this m.file the following command will obtain the numerical solution, subject to the initial condition $y(0) = 3$:

```
[x,y]=ode45('example1',[0,0.2,0.4,0.6,0.8,1],3)
```

resulting in

$$y = \begin{bmatrix} 3.0000 \\ 3.0080 \\ 3.0647 \\ 3.2240 \\ 3.5583 \\ 4.1868 \end{bmatrix}$$

Mathcad

Mathcad has the facility to obtain numerical solutions to differential equations. It will be necessary for you to refer to detailed documentation in the package manual. A differential equation 'solve block' must be created using the keyword **Given**. The differential equation and initial condition are typed in. Finally the command

```
y:=odesolve(x,1)
```

calculates the solution for $0 \leq x \leq 1$. It is then straightforward to display the solution at intermediate points and if necessary graph the solution. The whole process is shown in the screenshot on page xxiv.

Derive

Using Derive, it is necessary to load a file called ode_appr.mth, which defines functions for numerical solution of differential equations. Euler's method is then available, and the command

```
euler_ode(x^2y,x,y,0,3,0.2,5)
```

produces the required solution at 5 new points with step size $h = 0.2$:

$$y = \begin{bmatrix} 0 & 3.0000 \\ 0.2 & 3.0000 \\ 0.4 & 3.0240 \\ 0.6 & 3.1208 \\ 0.8 & 3.3455 \\ 1.0 & 3.7737 \end{bmatrix}$$

Euler's method is crude and yields inaccurate solutions. Derive has the facility to apply other methods that yield more accurate answers comparable with those obtained using the other packages.

Computer and calculator exercises

1 Use a computer algebra package to find an approximate numerical solution of the following initial value problems at the values of the independent variable specified:

(a) $\dfrac{dy}{dx} - \dfrac{1}{\ln y} = 0$, $y(0) = 2$,
at $x = 0, 0.1, 0.2, \ldots 0.5$.

(b) $\dfrac{dx}{dt} = \sin(x^2)$, $x(0) = 1$, at
$t = 0, 0.25, 0.5, 0.75, 1$.

Solutions

1

(a) $[x, y(x)]$

$$\begin{bmatrix} 0 & 2. \\ .1 & 2.13759470217855 \\ .2 & 2.26437308827318 \\ .3 & 2.38299104649312 \\ .4 & 2.49515771401761 \\ .5 & 2.60205536137248 \end{bmatrix}$$

(b) $[t, x(t)]$

$$\begin{bmatrix} 0 & 1. \\ .25 & 1.23412636541130 \\ .5 & 1.47072990280928 \\ .75 & 1.63173824177242 \\ 1 & 1.71208213688752 \end{bmatrix}$$

End of block exercises

1 Using software, obtain a symbolic solution of $L\frac{di}{dt} + Ri = 10\,(1 - e^{-0.1t})$ when $i(0) = i_0$.

2 Using software, obtain a symbolic solution of $iR + L\frac{di}{dt} = E$ where R, L and E are constants subject to the initial condition $i(0) = 0$.

3 Use a package to find the general solution of $\frac{dT}{d\theta} = \mu(T - K)$ where μ and K are constants.

4 Use Euler's method to find a numerical solution of $\frac{dy}{dx} = -2y$, $y(0) = 1$, for $0 \le x \le 0.5$. First take $h = 0.1$, then $h = 0.05$, and compare your answers at $x = 0.5$ with the exact solution obtained by separating the variables. Work throughout to 6 decimal places.

5 Use Euler's method to find a numerical solution of $\frac{dy}{dx} = \frac{xy}{x^2 + 2}$ subject to $y(1) = 3$. Take $h = 0.1$ and hence approximate $y(1.5)$. Obtain the true solution using the method of separation of variables. Work throughout to 6 decimal places.

Solutions

1 $$i(t) = \frac{10}{R} - \left(\frac{100}{10R - L}\right)e^{-0.1t} + \left(i_0 + \frac{10L}{R(10R - L)}\right)e^{-Rt/L}$$

2 $i(t) = \frac{E}{R}(1 - e^{-Rt/L})$

3 $T(\theta) = K + Ae^{\mu\theta}$

4 $h = 0.1$: $y(0.5) \approx 0.327680$.
$h = 0.05$: $y(0.5) \approx 0.348678$. True solution
$y = e^{-2x}$: $y(0.5) = 0.367879$

5 3, 3.1, 3.206231, 3.318076, 3.434973,
$y(1.5) \approx 3.556411$. True solution:
$y = \sqrt{3}(x^2 + 2)^{1/2}$, $y(1.5) = 3.570714$

BLOCK 5 Second-order linear constant-coefficient equations I

5.1 Introduction

In this block we start to learn how to solve second-order differential equations of a particular type – those that are linear and which have constant coefficients. Such equations are used widely in the modelling of physical phenomena – for example in the analysis of vibrating systems, and the analysis of electrical circuits.

The solution of these equations is achieved in stages. The first stage is to find what is called a **complementary function**, and is the subject of this block. The second stage is to find a **particular integral**. This is dealt with in the following block. Finally, the sum of the complementary function and the particular integral forms the general solution of a second-order linear differential equation. It is important that you understand and use this terminology. A knowledge of complex numbers, and particularly the exponential form, is essential.

Key point

Solving a second-order linear equation

1 Find the complementary function, y_{cf}.
2 Find a particular integral, y_{pi}.
3 The general solution is the sum of the complementary function and the particular integral:

$$y = y_{\text{cf}} + y_{\text{pi}}$$

5.2 Homogeneous equations and the complementary function, y_{cf}

The general form of a second-order linear equation that has constant coefficients is

$$a\frac{\mathrm{d}^2y}{\mathrm{d}x^2} + b\frac{\mathrm{d}y}{\mathrm{d}x} + cy = f(x) \qquad (1)$$

where a, b, c are constants. An example of such an equation is

$$3\frac{\mathrm{d}^2y}{\mathrm{d}x^2} - 2\frac{\mathrm{d}y}{\mathrm{d}x} + 4y = \mathrm{e}^{-x}\sin x$$

When $f(x)$ is not identically zero, the equation is said to be **inhomogeneous**. An important relative of this equation is found by replacing the function $f(x)$ with zero to give

$$a\frac{\mathrm{d}^2y}{\mathrm{d}x^2} + b\frac{\mathrm{d}y}{\mathrm{d}x} + cy = 0 \qquad (2)$$

This is the **homogeneous** form of equation (1). The homogeneous form is found by ignoring the term that is independent of y, or its derivatives.

To find the general solution of equation (1), it is first necessary to solve equation (2). The general solution of (2) is called the **complementary function** and will always contain two arbitrary constants. We shall denote this solution by y_{cf}.

The technique for finding the complementary function is described in this block.

Example 5.1

Which of the following are constant-coefficient equations? Which are homogeneous?

(a) $\dfrac{d^2y}{dx^2} + 4\dfrac{dy}{dx} + 3y = e^{-2x}$ (b) $x\dfrac{d^2y}{dx^2} + 2y = 0$

(c) $\dfrac{d^2x}{dt^2} + 3\dfrac{dx}{dt} + 7x = 0$ (d) $\dfrac{d^2y}{dx^2} + 4\dfrac{dy}{dx} + 4y = 0$

Solution

(a) const. coeff., not homogeneous

(b) not const. coeff., homogeneous

(c) const. coeff. and homogeneous

(d) const. coeff. and homogeneous

Example 5.2

What is a complementary function?

Solution

A complementary function is the general solution of a homogeneous, linear differential equation.

Example 5.3

The complementary function for the equation

$$\frac{d^2y}{dx^2} + y = 0$$

is $y = A\cos x + B\sin x$ for any constants A and B. Verify that this is indeed a solution.

Solution

The given equation is homogeneous, linear and constant coefficient. By differentiating $y = A\cos x + B\sin x$ twice and substituting into the equation it is easy to verify that this is a solution.

Find $\frac{dy}{dx}$ and $\frac{d^2y}{dx^2}$.

$y' = -A \sin x + B \cos x$, $y'' = -A \cos x - B \sin x$

Substitute the expressions for y and y'' into the left-hand side of the differential equation and simplify your answer.

$-A \cos x - B \sin x + A \cos x + B \sin x = 0$

So the left-hand side simplifies to zero. The right-hand side of the differential equation is zero. Hence $y = A \cos x + B \sin x$ is a solution.

Note that $y = A \cos x + B \sin x$ contains two arbitrary constants. It is the general solution and therefore the complementary function for this homogeneous equation.

Exercises

1 Write down the homogeneous form of the following equations:

(a) $\frac{d^2y}{dx^2} + 3\frac{dy}{dx} - 2y = \sin x$

(b) $\frac{d^2x}{dt^2} + 7x - e^t \cos t = 0$

(c) $\frac{d^2x}{dt^2} = -\omega^2 x$, where ω is a constant.

2 State what is meant by the term 'complementary function'.

Solutions to exercises

1 (a) $\frac{d^2y}{dx^2} + 3\frac{dy}{dx} - 2y = 0$ (b) $\frac{d^2x}{dt^2} + 7x = 0$ (c) is already homogeneous

5.3 Finding the complementary function

To find the complementary function we must make use of the following property.

If $y_1(x)$ and $y_2(x)$ are any two (linearly independent) solutions of a linear, homogeneous second-order differential equation then the general solution $y_{cf}(x)$ is

$$y_{cf}(x) = Ay_1(x) + By_2(x)$$

where A and B are constants.

We see that the second-order linear ordinary differential equation has two arbitrary constants in its general solution. The functions $y_1(x)$ and $y_2(x)$ are **linearly independent** if one is not simply a multiple of the other.

This property gives us a method for constructing the complementary function. If we can find two independent solutions of a homogeneous differential equation, we can form the complementary function by simply adding constant multiples of the two solutions.

Example 5.4

(a) Verify that $y_1 = e^{4x}$ and $y_2 = e^{2x}$ both satisfy the constant-coefficient homogeneous equation

$$\frac{d^2y}{dx^2} - 6\frac{dy}{dx} + 8y = 0 \tag{3}$$

(b) Write down the general solution of this equation and so form the complementary function.

Solution

(a) If $y_1 = e^{4x}$, differentiation yields

$$\frac{dy_1}{dx} = 4e^{4x}$$

and similarly,

$$\frac{d^2y_1}{dx^2} = 16e^{4x}$$

Substitution into the left-hand side of equation (3) gives

$$16e^{4x} - 6(4e^{4x}) + 8e^{4x}$$

which simplifies to zero. The right-hand side is zero. So $y_1 = e^{4x}$ is indeed a solution. Similarly if $y_2 = e^{2x}$, then

$$\frac{dy_2}{dx} = 2e^{2x} \quad \text{and} \quad \frac{d^2y_2}{dx^2} = 4e^{2x}$$

Substitution into the left-hand side of equation (3) gives

$$4e^{2x} - 6(2e^{2x}) + 8e^{2x}$$

which simplifies to zero, so $y_2 = e^{2x}$ is also a solution of equation (3).

(b) So we know two independent solutions of the equation: these are e^{2x} and e^{4x}. They are linearly independent because e^{2x} is not a multiple of e^{4x}. From the property stated above we have

$$y_{cf}(x) = Ae^{4x} + Be^{2x}$$

as the general solution of equation (3). This is the complementary function.

Key point

Finding a complementary function

If two independent solutions, y_1 and y_2, of a homogeneous second-order linear equation can be found, the complementary function is found by adding constant multiples of them:

$$y_{cf}(x) = Ay_1(x) + By_2(x)$$

where A and B are arbitrary constants.

Example 5.5

Substitute $y = \mathrm{e}^{kx}$, where k is a constant, into the equation

$$\frac{\mathrm{d}^2y}{\mathrm{d}x^2} - \frac{\mathrm{d}y}{\mathrm{d}x} - 6y = 0$$

in order to find the values of k that make $y = \mathrm{e}^{kx}$ a solution. Hence state the general solution.

Solution

As suggested we substitute $y = \mathrm{e}^{kx}$. Differentiating we find

$$\frac{\mathrm{d}y}{\mathrm{d}x} = k\mathrm{e}^{kx} \quad \text{and} \quad \frac{\mathrm{d}^2y}{\mathrm{d}x^2} = k^2\mathrm{e}^{kx}$$

Substitution into the given equation yields

$$k^2\mathrm{e}^{kx} - k\mathrm{e}^{kx} - 6\mathrm{e}^{kx} = 0$$

that is

$$(k^2 - k - 6)\mathrm{e}^{kx} = 0$$

Since the function e^{kx} can never be zero it follows that

$$k^2 - k - 6 = 0 \qquad (4)$$

that is

$$(k - 3)(k + 2) = 0$$

so that $k = 3$ or $k = -2$. That is to say, if $y = \mathrm{e}^{kx}$ is to be a solution of the differential equation k must be either 3 or -2. We therefore have found two solutions:

$$y_1(x) = \mathrm{e}^{3x} \quad \text{and} \quad y_2(x) = \mathrm{e}^{-2x}$$

These two functions are linearly independent because e^{-2x} is not a multiple of e^{3x}, and therefore the general solution is

$$y_{cf}(x) = A\mathrm{e}^{3x} + B\mathrm{e}^{-2x}$$

This is the complementary function for the given differential equation. Equation (4) for determining k is called the **auxiliary equation**.

Example 5.6

By substituting $y = e^{kx}$, find values of k so that y is a solution of

$$\frac{d^2y}{dx^2} - 3\frac{dy}{dx} + 2y = 0$$

Hence write down two solutions and the general solution of this equation. Hence state the complementary function.

Solution

By substituting $y = e^{kx}$ find the auxiliary equation:

$$k^2 - 3k + 2 = 0$$

This can be factorised:

$$(k - 1)(k - 2) = 0$$

So the required values of k are 1 and 2. Write down the two solutions:

$$y = e^x \quad \text{and} \quad y = e^{2x}$$

Finally write down the general solution:

$$y_{cf}(x) = Ae^x + Be^{2x}$$

The complementary function is therefore $y_{cf}(x) = Ae^x + Be^{2x}$.

Example 5.7

Find the auxiliary equation of the differential equation

$$a\frac{d^2y}{dx^2} + b\frac{dy}{dx} + cy = 0$$

where a, b and c are constants.

Solution

We try a solution of the form $y = e^{kx}$ so that

$$\frac{dy}{dx} = ke^{kx} \quad \text{and} \quad \frac{d^2y}{dx^2} = k^2e^{kx}$$

Substitution into the given differential equation yields

$$ak^2e^{kx} + bke^{kx} + ce^{kx} = 0$$

that is

$$(ak^2 + bk + c)e^{kx} = 0$$

Because e^{kx} cannot be zero it follows that

$$ak^2 + bk + c = 0$$

This is the required auxiliary equation.

Key point

The auxiliary equation of

$$a\frac{d^2y}{dx^2} + b\frac{dy}{dx} + cy = 0$$

is $ak^2 + bk + c = 0$. The solutions of the auxiliary equation give values of k that make $y = e^{kx}$ a solution of the differential equation.

Example 5.8

Write down, but do not solve, the auxiliary equations of the following differential equations:

(a) $\frac{d^2y}{dx^2} + \frac{dy}{dx} + y = 0$ (b) $2\frac{d^2y}{dx^2} + 7\frac{dy}{dx} - 3y = 0$

(c) $4\frac{d^2y}{dx^2} + 7y = 0$ (d) $\frac{d^2y}{dx^2} + \frac{dy}{dx} = 0$

Solution

(a) $k^2 + k + 1 = 0$

(b) $2k^2 + 7k - 3 = 0$

(c) $4k^2 + 7 = 0$

(d) $k^2 + k = 0$

Solution of the auxiliary equation gives the values of k that we seek. Note that the auxiliary equation is a quadratic equation and so has two roots. Clearly the nature of the roots will depend upon the values of a, b and c. If $b^2 > 4ac$ the roots will be real and distinct. The two values of k thus obtained, k_1 and k_2, will allow us to write down two independent solutions:

$$y_1(x) = e^{k_1x} \quad y_2(x) = e^{k_2x}$$

and so the general solution of the differential equation will be

$$y(x) = Ae^{k_1x} + Be^{k_2x}$$

Key point

If the auxiliary equation has real, distinct roots k_1 and k_2, the complementary function will be

$$y_{cf}(x) = Ae^{k_1x} + Be^{k_2x}$$

On the other hand, if $b^2 = 4ac$ the two roots of the auxiliary equation will be equal and this method will therefore yield only one independent solution. In this case, special treatment is required. If $b^2 < 4ac$ the two roots of the auxiliary equation will be complex: that is, k_1 and k_2 will be complex numbers. The procedure for dealing with such cases will become apparent in the following examples.

Example 5.9

Find the general solution of

$$\frac{d^2y}{dx^2} + 3\frac{dy}{dx} - 10y = 0$$

Solution

Write down the auxiliary equation:

$$k^2 + 3k - 10 = 0$$

Factorise to find the solutions:

$$(k - 2)(k + 5) = 0, k = 2 \text{ and } k = -5$$

Thus there exist two solutions $y_1 = e^{2x}$ and $y_2 = e^{-5x}$. We can write the general solution as

$$y(x) = Ae^{2x} + Be^{-5x}$$

This is the complementary function.

Example 5.10

Find the general solution of

$$\frac{d^2y}{dx^2} + 4y = 0$$

Solution

Write down the auxiliary equation:

$$k^2 + 4 = 0$$

It follows that

$$k^2 = -4$$

so that

$$k = \pm 2j$$

that is, we have complex roots. The two independent solutions of the equation are thus

$$y_1(x) = e^{2jx} \quad y_2(x) = e^{-2jx}$$

so that the general solution can be written in the form

$$y(x) = Ae^{2jx} + Be^{-2jx}$$

However, in cases such as this, it is usual to rewrite the solution in the following way. Recall that Euler's relations (Chapter 11, Block 3) give

$$e^{2jx} = \cos 2x + j\sin 2x \quad \text{and} \quad e^{-2jx} = \cos 2x - j\sin 2x$$

so that

$$y(x) = A(\cos 2x + \mathrm{j}\sin 2x) + B(\cos 2x - \mathrm{j}\sin 2x)$$
$$= (A + B)\cos 2x + (A\mathrm{j} - B\mathrm{j})\sin 2x$$

If we now relabel the constants such that

$$A + B = C \quad \text{and} \quad A\mathrm{j} - B\mathrm{j} = D$$

we can write the general solution in the form

$$y(x) = C\cos 2x + D\sin 2x$$

This is the complementary function.

Example 5.11

Given $a\dfrac{\mathrm{d}^2y}{\mathrm{d}x^2} + b\dfrac{\mathrm{d}y}{\mathrm{d}x} + cy = 0$, write down the auxiliary equation. If the roots of the auxiliary equation are complex (one root will always be the complex conjugate of the other) and are denoted by

$$k_1 = \alpha + \beta\mathrm{j} \qquad k_2 = \alpha - \beta\mathrm{j}$$

show that the general solution can be written as

$$y(x) = \mathrm{e}^{\alpha x}(C\cos\beta x + D\sin\beta x)$$

where C and D are arbitrary constants.

Solution

Write down the auxiliary equation:

$$ak^2 + bk + c = 0$$

If $k_1 = \alpha + \beta\mathrm{j}, k_2 = \alpha - \beta\mathrm{j}$ then the general solution is

$$y = A\mathrm{e}^{(\alpha+\beta\mathrm{j})x} + B\mathrm{e}^{(\alpha-\beta\mathrm{j})x}$$

where A and B are arbitrary constants. Using the laws of indices this is rewritten as

$$y = A\mathrm{e}^{\alpha x}\,\mathrm{e}^{\beta\mathrm{j}x} + B\mathrm{e}^{\alpha x}\,\mathrm{e}^{-\beta\mathrm{j}x}$$
$$= \mathrm{e}^{\alpha x}(A\mathrm{e}^{\beta\mathrm{j}x} + B\mathrm{e}^{-\beta\mathrm{j}x})$$

Then, using Euler's relations, we obtain

$$y = \mathrm{e}^{\alpha x}(A\cos\beta x + A\mathrm{j}\sin\beta x + B\cos\beta x - B\mathrm{j}\sin\beta x)$$
$$= \mathrm{e}^{\alpha x}[(A + B)\cos\beta x + (A\mathrm{j} - B\mathrm{j})\sin\beta x]$$

Writing $C = A + B$ and $D = A\mathrm{j} - B\mathrm{j}$, we find

$$y = \mathrm{e}^{\alpha x}(C\cos\beta x + D\sin\beta x)$$

This is the required solution.

Key point

If the auxiliary equation has complex roots, $\alpha + \beta\mathrm{j}$ and $\alpha - \beta\mathrm{j}$, then the complementary function is

$$y_{\mathrm{cf}} = \mathrm{e}^{\alpha x}(C\cos\beta x + D\sin\beta x)$$

Example 5.12
Find the general solution of $\frac{d^2y}{dx^2} + 2\frac{dy}{dx} + 4y = 0$.

Solution
The auxiliary equation is

$$k^2 + 2k + 4 = 0$$

This equation has complex roots. Find them.

$$k = -1 \pm \sqrt{3}j$$

Using the key point above with $\alpha = -1$ and $\beta = \sqrt{3}$ write down the general solution.

$$y = e^{-x}(C\cos\sqrt{3}\,x + D\sin\sqrt{3}\,x)$$

Example 5.13 Mechanical Engineering – Simple harmonic motion
The behaviour of a wide range of oscillating and vibrating mechanical and electrical systems is described by a differential equation of the form

$$\frac{d^2x}{dt^2} = -\omega^2 x$$

where ω is a constant. This is known as the **simple harmonic motion** equation. Find its general solution.

Solution
Writing the equation in the form $\frac{d^2x}{dt^2} + \omega^2 x = 0$ we recognise it as second order, constant coefficient and homogeneous. Write down the auxiliary equation.

$$k^2 + \omega^2 = 0$$

This has solutions $k = \pm\omega j$. So there are complex roots with real part zero and imaginary parts $\pm\omega$. From the previous key point write down the general solution.

$$x = C\cos\omega t + D\sin\omega t$$

The fact that the solution consists of a sine and a cosine wave is indicative of the fact that the differential equation describes an oscillating or vibrating system.

Key point

The simple harmonic motion equation and its solution are, respectively,

$$\frac{d^2x}{dt^2} = -\omega^2 x$$

and

$$x = C\cos\omega t + D\sin\omega t$$

It is often sufficient simply to quote this solution when faced with solving a simple harmonic motion problem.

When the auxiliary equation has equal roots special treatment is required. This is because the auxiliary equation provides only one independent solution, and we seek two to construct the general solution of any second-order differential equation. The second solution is found by multiplying the first by x, as shown in the following example.

Example 5.14

The auxiliary equation of $a\dfrac{d^2y}{dx^2} + b\dfrac{dy}{dx} + cy = 0$ is $ak^2 + bk + c = 0$. Suppose this equation has equal roots $k = k_1$. Verify that $y = xe^{k_1x}$ is a solution of the differential equation. Hence state the general solution.

Solution

We must check that $y = xe^{k_1x}$ is a solution. Using the product rule find $\dfrac{dy}{dx}$ and $\dfrac{d^2y}{dx^2}$.

$$\frac{dy}{dx} = \qquad e^{k_1x} + xk_1e^{k_1x} = e^{k_1x}(1 + k_1x)$$

$$\frac{d^2y}{dx^2} = \qquad (1 + k_1x)\,k_1e^{k_1x} + e^{k_1x}\,k_1 = e^{k_1x}(k_1^2x + 2k_1)$$

Substitution into the left-hand side of the differential equation yields

$$a(k_1^2\,x + 2k_1)e^{k_1x} + b(1 + k_1x)e^{k_1x} + cxe^{k_1x}$$

that is

$$e^{k_1x}[a(k_1^2\,x + 2k_1) + b(1 + k_1x) + cx]$$

which can be rewritten as

$$e^{k_1x}[(ak_1^2 + bk_1 + c)x + 2ak_1 + b] \tag{5}$$

But $ak_1^2 + bk_1 + c = 0$ since k_1 satisfies the auxiliary equation. Also,

$$k_1 = \frac{-b \pm \sqrt{b^2 - 4ac}}{2a}$$

but since the roots are equal, then $b^2 - 4ac = 0$ and hence $k_1 = -\dfrac{b}{2a}$. So $2ak_1 + b = 0$, and the expression (5) simplifies to zero. We conclude that $y = xe^{k_1x}$ is a solution of $a\dfrac{d^2y}{dx^2} + b\dfrac{dy}{dx} + cy = 0$ when the roots of the auxiliary equation are equal.

Since k_1 is a root of the auxiliary equation, $y = e^{k_1x}$ is a solution of the differential equation. The second independent solution is $y = xe^{k_1x}$. So the general solution is

$$\begin{aligned} y &= Ae^{k_1x} + Bxe^{k_1x} \\ &= (A + Bx)e^{k_1x} \end{aligned}$$

Key point

If the auxiliary equation has two equal roots, k_1, the complementary function is

$$y_{cf} = (A + Bx)e^{k_1x}$$

Example 5.15

Obtain the general solution of the equation

$$\frac{d^2y}{dx^2} + 8\frac{dy}{dx} + 16y = 0$$

Solution

As before, a trial solution of the form $y = e^{kx}$ yields an auxiliary equation

$$k^2 + 8k + 16 = 0$$

This equation factorises so that

$$(k + 4)(k + 4) = 0$$

and we obtain equal roots, that is $k = -4$ (twice). If we proceed as before, writing $y_1(x) = e^{-4x}$ and $y_2(x) = e^{-4x}$, it is clear that the two solutions are not independent. We need to find a second independent solution. Using the result of the previous example we conclude that, because the roots of the auxiliary equation are equal, the second independent solution is $y_2 = xe^{-4x}$. The general solution is then

$$y(x) = (A + Bx)e^{-4x}$$

This is the complementary function.

Key points

Summary

Second-order linear constant-coefficient homogeneous equation:

$$a\frac{d^2y}{dx^2} + b\frac{dy}{dx} + cy = 0$$

Auxiliary equation:

$$ak^2 + bk + c = 0$$

Roots of auxiliary equation	Complementary function
k_1, k_2, both real and different	$y = Ae^{k_1x} + Be^{k_2x}$
$\alpha \pm j\beta$, complex conjugate pair	$y = e^{\alpha x}(A\cos\beta x + B\sin\beta x)$
$k_1 = k_2 = k$, equal roots	$y = (A + Bx)e^{kx}$

Exercises

1 Obtain the general solutions, that is the complementary functions, of the following homogeneous equations:

(a) $\frac{d^2y}{dx^2} - 3\frac{dy}{dx} + 2y = 0$

(b) $\frac{d^2y}{dx^2} + 7\frac{dy}{dx} + 6y = 0$

(c) $\frac{d^2x}{dt^2} + 5\frac{dx}{dt} + 6x = 0$

(d) $\frac{d^2y}{dt^2} + 2\frac{dy}{dt} + y = 0$

(e) $\frac{d^2y}{dx^2} - 4\frac{dy}{dx} + 4y = 0$

(f) $\frac{d^2y}{dt^2} + \frac{dy}{dt} + 8y = 0$

2 Find the auxiliary equation for the differential equation

$$L\frac{d^2i}{dt^2} + R\frac{di}{dt} + \frac{1}{C}i = 0$$

Hence write down the complementary function.

3 Find the complementary function of the equation

$$\frac{d^2y}{dx^2} + \frac{dy}{dx} + y = 0$$

Solutions to exercises

1 (a) $y = Ae^x + Be^{2x}$ (b) $y = Ae^{-x} + Be^{-6x}$
(c) $x = Ae^{-2t} + Be^{-3t}$ (d) $y = Ae^{-t} + Bte^{-t}$
(e) $y = Ae^{2x} + Bxe^{2x}$
(f) $y = e^{-0.5t}(A\cos 2.78t + B\sin 2.78t)$

2 $Lk^2 + Rk + \dfrac{1}{C} = 0;$

$i(t) = Ae^{k_1 t} + Be^{k_2 t},$

$$k_1, k_2 = \frac{-R \pm \sqrt{\dfrac{R^2C - 4L}{C}}}{2L}$$

3 $e^{-x/2}\left(A\cos\dfrac{\sqrt{3}\,x}{2} + B\sin\dfrac{\sqrt{3}\,x}{2}\right)$

End of block exercises

1 Obtain the general solutions, that is the complementary functions, of the following homogeneous equations:

(a) $\dfrac{d^2y}{dx^2} - 2\dfrac{dy}{dx} + y = 0$

(b) $\dfrac{d^2y}{dt^2} + \dfrac{dy}{dt} + 5y = 0$

(c) $\dfrac{d^2y}{dx^2} + \dfrac{dy}{dx} - 2y = 0$

(d) $\dfrac{d^2y}{dx^2} + 9y = 0$

(e) $\dfrac{d^2y}{dx^2} - 2\dfrac{dy}{dx} = 0$

(f) $\dfrac{d^2x}{dt^2} - 16x = 0$

Solutions to exercises

1 (a) $y = Ae^x + Bxe^x$
(b) $x = e^{-0.5t}(A\cos 2.18t + B\sin 2.18t)$
(c) $y = Ae^{-2x} + Be^x$
(d) $y = A\cos 3x + B\sin 3x$
(e) $y = A + Be^{2x}$
(f) $x = Ae^{4t} + Be^{-4t}$

BLOCK 6 Second-order linear constant-coefficient equations II

6.1 Introduction

We stated in Block 5 that the general solution of an inhomogeneous equation is the sum of the complementary function and a particular integral. We have seen how to find the complementary function in the case of a constant-coefficient equation. We shall now deal with the problem of finding a particular integral.

The **particular integral** is *any* solution of the inhomogeneous equation. The remarkable thing is that we need only find any solution of the inhomogeneous equation, and from it, together with the complementary function, the general solution can be constructed.

There are a number of advanced techniques available for finding particular integrals but we shall adopt a simpler strategy. Since any solution will do we shall try to find one by a combination of educated guesswork and trial and error.

6.2 A particular integral

Given a second-order inhomogeneous differential equation

$$a\frac{d^2y}{dx^2} + b\frac{dy}{dx} + cy = f(x) \qquad (1)$$

a **particular integral** is any function, which we will denote by $y_{pi}(x)$, which satisfies the equation: that is, any function that, when substituted into the left-hand side and simplified, results in the function on the right.

Example 6.1

Show that $y = \sin 2x$ is a particular integral of

$$\frac{d^2y}{dx^2} + 7y = 3\sin 2x$$

Solution

We substitute $y = \sin 2x$ into the given equation to see whether it is a solution. First do the differentiation: if $y = \sin 2x$ then

$$\frac{dy}{dx} = \qquad\qquad 2\cos 2x$$

$$\frac{d^2y}{dx^2} = \qquad\qquad -4\sin 2x$$

Now substitute the expressions for y and $\dfrac{d^2y}{dx^2}$ into the left-hand side of the differential equation $\dfrac{d^2y}{dx^2} + 7y$, and simplify the result:

$$-4 \sin 2x + 7(\sin 2x) = 3 \sin 2x$$

which is the same as the right-hand side of the differential equation. So $y = \sin 2x$ is a solution of the inhomogeneous equation and so is a particular integral. We can write $y_{pi} = \sin 2x$.

Example 6.2
Show that

$$y = -\frac{1}{4}e^{2x}$$

is a particular integral of

$$\frac{d^2y}{dx^2} - \frac{dy}{dx} - 6y = e^{2x} \qquad (2)$$

Solution

Starting with $y = -\dfrac{1}{4}e^{2x}$, find $\dfrac{dy}{dx}$ and $\dfrac{d^2y}{dx^2}$:

$$\frac{dy}{dx} = -\frac{1}{2}e^{2x}, \quad \frac{d^2y}{dx^2} = -e^{2x}$$

Substitute the expressions for y, $\dfrac{dy}{dx}$ and $\dfrac{d^2y}{dx^2}$ into the left-hand side of (2) to show that y satisfies the inhomogeneous equation.

$$-e^{2x} - \left(-\frac{1}{2}e^{2x}\right) - 6\left(-\frac{1}{4}e^{2x}\right), \text{ which simplifies to } e^{2x}$$

Therefore $y = -\dfrac{1}{4}e^{2x}$ is a particular integral and we can write $y_{pi}(x) = -\dfrac{1}{4}e^{2x}$.

Example 6.3
What is a particular integral?

Solution

A particular integral is *any* solution of an inhomogeneous differential equation.

Exercises

1 Show that $y = 4$ is a particular integral of the equation $\dfrac{d^2y}{dx^2} - 5\dfrac{dy}{dx} + 6y = 24$.

2 Explain what is meant by a particular integral.

3 Show that $x = \dfrac{1}{15}e^{2t}$ is a particular integral of the equation $\ddot{x} + 4\dot{x} + 3x = e^{2t}$.

6.3 Finding a particular integral

In the previous section we explained what is meant by a particular integral. Now we look at how one is actually found. In fact our method is rather crude. It involves trial and error and educated guesswork. We try solutions that are of the same general form as the inhomogeneous term, $f(x)$, on the right-hand side. As a guide, use Table 6.1. The trial solutions all contain constants. These can be adjusted to force the trial solution to be an actual solution of the inhomogeneous equation.

Table 6.1 Trial solutions to find the particular integral.

Inhomogeneous term $f(x)$	Trial solution
Constant	Constant
$ax^r + \cdots + bx + c$	$\alpha x^r + \cdots + \beta x + \gamma$
$a \cos kx$	$\alpha \cos kx + \beta \sin kx$
$a \sin kx$	$\alpha \cos kx + \beta \sin kx$
ae^{kx}	αe^{kx}
$a \cosh kx$	$\alpha \cosh kx + \beta \sinh kx$
$a \sinh kx$	$\alpha \cosh kx + \beta \sinh kx$

Example 6.4

In each case you are given the inhomogeneous term $f(x)$. State the appropriate form of solution to try when finding a particular integral.

(a) $f(x) = 7e^{2x}$
(b) $f(x) = 5$
(c) $f(x) = 7x - 3$
(d) $f(x) = \cos 2x$

Solution

Use Table 6.1 to select an appropriate trial solution.

(a) $y = \alpha e^{2x}$

(b) $y = C$, constant

(c) $y = \alpha x + \beta$

(d) $y = \alpha \cos 2x + \beta \sin 2x$

Example 6.5

In each case you are given the inhomogeneous term $f(x)$. State the appropriate form of solution to try when finding a particular integral.

(a) $f(x) = x$
(b) $f(x) = e^{2x}$
(c) $f(x) = x + e^{2x}$

Solution

(a) $y = \alpha x + \beta$

(b) $y = \gamma e^{2x}$

(c) This time the inhomogeneous term is a combination of an exponential and a polynomial, so this is the form the trial solution should take.

$y = \gamma e^{2x} + \alpha x + \beta$

Example 6.6

Find a particular integral of the equation

$$\frac{d^2y}{dx^2} - \frac{dy}{dx} - 6y = e^{2x} \qquad (3)$$

Solution

We shall attempt to find a solution of the inhomogeneous problem by trying a function of the same form as that on the right-hand side. In particular, let us try $y(x) = \alpha e^{2x}$, where α is a constant that we shall now determine. If $y(x) = \alpha e^{2x}$ then

$$\frac{dy}{dx} = 2\alpha e^{2x} \quad \text{and} \quad \frac{d^2y}{dx^2} = 4\alpha e^{2x}$$

Substitution in equation (3) gives

$$4\alpha e^{2x} - 2\alpha e^{2x} - 6\alpha e^{2x} = e^{2x}$$

that is

$$-4\alpha e^{2x} = e^{2x}$$

so that y will be a solution if α is chosen so that $-4\alpha = 1$, that is $\alpha = -\frac{1}{4}$.

Therefore the particular integral is $y_{pi}(x) = -\frac{1}{4}e^{2x}$.

Example 6.7

By trying a solution of the form $y = \alpha e^{-x}$ find a particular integral of the equation

$$\frac{d^2y}{dx^2} + \frac{dy}{dx} - 2y = 3e^{-x}$$

Solution

If $y = \alpha e^{-x}$, write down expressions for $\frac{dy}{dx}$ and $\frac{d^2y}{dx^2}$.

$$\frac{dy}{dx} = -\alpha e^{-x}, \frac{d^2y}{dx^2} = \alpha e^{-x}$$

Substitute into the given equation to find α, and hence the particular integral.

$$-2\alpha = 3, \alpha = -\frac{3}{2}; y_{pi}(x) = -\frac{3}{2}e^{-x}$$

Example 6.8

Obtain a particular integral of the equation

$$\frac{d^2y}{dx^2} - 6\frac{dy}{dx} + 8y = x$$

Solution

In the last example, we found that a fruitful approach was to assume a solution in the same form as that on the right-hand side. Suppose we assume a solution $y(x) = \alpha x$ and proceed to determine α. This approach will actually fail, but let us see why. If $y(x) = \alpha x$ then $\frac{dy}{dx} = \alpha$ and $\frac{d^2y}{dx^2} = 0$. Substitution into the differential equation yields

$$0 - 6\alpha + 8\alpha x = x$$

and α ought now to be chosen so that this expression is true for all x. If we equate the coefficients of x we find $8\alpha = 1$ so that $\alpha = \frac{1}{8}$, but with this value of α the constant terms are inconsistent (i.e. $-\frac{6}{8}$ on the left, but zero on the right). Clearly a particular integral of the form αx is not possible. The problem arises because differentiation of the term αx produces constant terms that are unbalanced on the right-hand side. So, we try a solution of the form

$$y(x) = \alpha x + \beta$$

with α and β constants. This is consistent with the recommendation in Table 6.1. Proceeding as before, $\frac{dy}{dx} = \alpha$, $\frac{d^2y}{dx^2} = 0$. Substitution in the differential equation now gives

$$0 - 6\alpha + 8(\alpha x + \beta) = x$$

Equating coefficients of x we find

$$8\alpha = 1 \quad (4)$$

and equating constant terms we find

$$-6\alpha + 8\beta = 0 \quad (5)$$

From equation (4), $\alpha = \frac{1}{8}$ and then from equation (5)

$$-6\left(\frac{1}{8}\right) + 8\beta = 0$$

so that

$$8\beta = \frac{3}{4}$$

that is

$$\beta = \frac{3}{32}$$

The required particular integral is

$$y_{pi}(x) = \frac{x}{8} + \frac{3}{32}$$

Example 6.9

Find a particular integral for the equation

$$\frac{d^2y}{dx^2} - 6\frac{dy}{dx} + 8y = 3\cos x$$

Solution

First try to decide on an appropriate form for the trial solution. Refer to Table 6.1 if necessary.

$y = \alpha \cos x + \beta \sin x$

We shall try a solution of the form

$$y(x) = \alpha \cos x + \beta \sin x$$

Differentiating, we find

$$\frac{dy}{dx} = -\alpha \sin x + \beta \cos x, \quad \frac{d^2y}{dx^2} = -\alpha \cos x - \beta \sin x$$

Substitution into the differential equation gives

$$(-\alpha \cos x - \beta \sin x) - 6(-\alpha \sin x + \beta \cos x) + 8(\alpha \cos x + \beta \sin x) = 3 \cos x$$

which simplifies to

$$\quad \sin x + \quad \cos x = 3 \cos x$$

$7\beta + 6\alpha, 7\alpha - 6\beta$

Equating coefficients of sin x,

$7\beta + 6\alpha = 0$

and equating coefficients of cos x, we find

$7\alpha - 6\beta = 3$

Solve these simultaneously to find α and β, and hence the particular integral.

$$\alpha = \frac{21}{85}, \beta = -\frac{18}{85}$$

The particular integral is

$$y_{pi}(x) = \frac{21}{85}\cos x - \frac{18}{85}\sin x$$

Exercises

1 Find a particular integral for the equation

$$\frac{d^2x}{dt^2} - 3\frac{dx}{dt} + 2x = 5e^{3t}$$

2 Find a particular integral for the equation

$$\frac{d^2x}{dt^2} - x = 4e^{-2t}$$

3 Find a particular integral for $y'' + y' + y = 2 + x + \cos x$.

Solutions to exercises

1 $x_{pi} = 2.5e^{3t}$

2 $x_{pi} = \frac{4}{3}e^{-2t}$

3 $y_{pi} = 1 + x + \sin x$

6.4 Finding the general solution of a second-order inhomogeneous equation

The general solution of a second-order linear inhomogeneous equation is the sum of its complementary function and a particular integral. In Block 5 you learnt how to find a complementary function, and in the previous section you learnt how to find a particular integral. We now put these together to find the general solution.

Key point

The general solution of a constant-coefficient ordinary differential equation

$$a\frac{d^2y}{dx^2} + b\frac{dy}{dx} + cy = f(x)$$

is the sum of the particular integral and the complementary function:

$$y = y_{pi} + y_{cf}$$

y_{pi} contains no arbitrary constants; y_{cf} contains two arbitrary constants.

Example 6.10

Find the general solution of

$$\frac{d^2y}{dx^2} + 3\frac{dy}{dx} - 10y = 3x^2$$

Solution

The complementary function has already been found in Example 5.9 to be

$$y_{cf} = Ae^{2x} + Be^{-5x}$$

By noting that $3x^2$ is a polynomial of degree 2, the particular integral is found by trying a solution of the form

$$y = ax^2 + bx + c$$

Differentiate this trial solution twice:

$$\frac{dy}{dx} = 2ax + b, \frac{d^2y}{dx^2} = 2a$$

Substitute into the inhomogeneous equation and by equating coefficients of x^2, x and constants, write down the equations satisfied by a, b and c.

$$2a + 3(2ax + b) - 10(ax^2 + bx + c) = 3x^2$$

Equate coefficients of x^2:

$$-10a = 3$$

Equate coefficients of x:

$$6a - 10b = 0$$

Equate constants:

$$2a + 3b - 10c = 0$$

Solve these to find a, b and c.

$$a = -\frac{3}{10}, b = -\frac{9}{50}, c = -\frac{57}{500}$$

Hence write down the particular integral:

$$y_{pi}(x) = -\frac{3}{10}x^2 - \frac{9}{50}x - \frac{57}{500}$$

Thus the general solution is

$$\begin{aligned} y &= y_{pi}(x) + y_{cf}(x) \\ &= -\frac{3}{10}x^2 - \frac{9}{50}x - \frac{57}{500} + Ae^{2x} + Be^{-5x} \end{aligned}$$

Example 6.11

Find the particular solution of $y'' + y' - 12y = 4e^{2x}$ that satisfies $y(0) = 7$ and $y'(0) = 0$.

Solution

The solution must be found in three parts:

1 Solve the homogeneous equation to find the complementary function.
2 Find a particular integral of the inhomogeneous equation, and add this to the complementary function to find the general solution.
3 Apply the initial conditions to find the arbitrary constants.

First of all we find the complementary function. The homogeneous equation is $y'' + y' - 12y = 0$ and so the auxiliary equation is $k^2 + k - 12 = (k - 3)(k + 4) = 0$. Therefore $k = 3$ and $k = -4$ and so the complementary function is

$$y = Ae^{3x} + Be^{-4x}$$

The particular integral is found by trying a solution of the form $y = \alpha e^{2x}$.

If $y = \alpha e^{2x}$, $y' = 2\alpha e^{2x}$ and $y'' = 4\alpha e^{2x}$. Substitute these expressions into the differential equation

$$4\alpha e^{2x} + 2\alpha e^{2x} - 12\alpha e^{2x} = 4e^{2x}$$

so that

$$4\alpha + 2\alpha - 12\alpha = 4$$

from which $-6\alpha = 4$, that is $\alpha = -\frac{2}{3}$. The general solution is then

$$y = Ae^{3x} + Be^{-4x} - \frac{2}{3}e^{2x}$$

The particular solution is found by applying the initial conditions.

Apply the condition $y(0) = 7$.

$$7 = A + B - \frac{2}{3}$$

To apply the condition $y'(0) = 0$ we must differentiate the general solution:

$$\frac{dy}{dx} = \qquad 3Ae^{3x} - 4Be^{-4x} - \frac{4}{3}e^{2x}$$

Now apply the condition $y'(0) = 0$.

$$0 = 3A - 4B - \frac{4}{3}$$

Solve these simultaneous equations.

$$A = \frac{32}{7} \text{ and } B = \frac{65}{21}$$

Finally, the particular solution is

$$y = \frac{32}{7}e^{3x} + \frac{65}{21}e^{-4x} - \frac{2}{3}e^{2x}$$

Example 6.12 Electrical Engineering – An LC circuit with sinusoidal input

The differential equation governing the flow of current in the series LC circuit shown in Figure 6.1 when subject to an applied voltage $v(t) = V_0 \sin \omega t$ is

$$L\frac{d^2i}{dt^2} + \frac{1}{C}i = \omega V_0 \cos \omega t$$

Obtain its general solution.

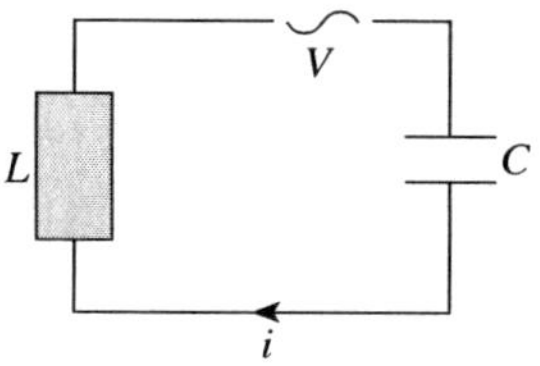

Figure 6.1
A series LC circuit.

Solution

The homogeneous equation is

$$L\frac{d^2i}{dt^2} + \frac{i}{C} = 0$$

Letting $i = e^{kt}$ we find the auxiliary equation is $Lk^2 + \frac{1}{C} = 0$ so that $k^2 = -\frac{1}{LC}$ and so $k = \pm\frac{j}{\sqrt{LC}}$. Therefore the complementary function is:

$$i_{cf} = A\cos\frac{t}{\sqrt{LC}} + B\sin\frac{t}{\sqrt{LC}}$$

where A and B are arbitrary constants. To find a particular integral, try $i = E\cos\omega t + F\sin\omega t$, where E and F are constants. We find

$$\frac{di}{dt} = -\omega E\sin\omega t + \omega F\cos\omega t$$

$$\frac{d^2i}{dt^2} = -\omega^2 E\cos\omega t - \omega^2 F\sin\omega t$$

Substitution into the inhomogeneous equation yields

$$L(-\omega^2 E\cos\omega t - \omega^2 F\sin\omega t) + \frac{1}{C}(E\cos\omega t + F\sin\omega t) = \omega V_0 \cos\omega t$$

which is simplified to

$$\qquad\qquad \sin\omega t + \qquad\qquad \cos\omega t = \omega V_0 \cos\omega t$$

$$-\omega^2 LF + \frac{F}{C},\ -\omega^2 LE + \frac{E}{C}$$

Equating coefficients of $\sin \omega t$ gives

$$-\omega^2 LF + \frac{F}{C} = 0$$

from which $F = 0$.
Equating coefficients of $\cos \omega t$ gives

$$-\omega^2 LE + \frac{E}{C} = \omega V_0$$

from which

$$E = \frac{CV_0\,\omega}{1 - \omega^2\,LC}$$

Hence the particular integral is

$$i_{\text{pi}} = \frac{CV_0\,\omega}{1 - \omega^2\,LC}\cos \omega t$$

Finally, the general solution is

$$\begin{aligned} i &= i_{\text{cf}} + i_{\text{pi}} \\ &= A\cos\frac{t}{\sqrt{LC}} + B\sin\frac{t}{\sqrt{LC}} + \frac{CV_0\omega}{1 - \omega^2 LC}\cos \omega t \end{aligned}$$

Exercises

1 Find the general solution of the following equations:

(a) $\dfrac{d^2x}{dt^2} - 2\dfrac{dx}{dt} - 3x = 6$

(b) $\dfrac{d^2y}{dx^2} + 5\dfrac{dy}{dx} + 4y = 8$

(c) $\dfrac{d^2y}{dt^2} + 5\dfrac{dy}{dt} + 6y = 2t$

(d) $\dfrac{d^2x}{dt^2} + 11\dfrac{dx}{dt} + 30x = 8t$

2 Obtain the general solution of

$$y'' - y' - 2y = 6$$

3 Obtain the general solution of the equation

$$\frac{d^2y}{dx^2} + 3\frac{dy}{dx} + 2y = 10\cos 2x$$

Find the particular solution satisfying

$$y(0) = 1, \quad \frac{dy}{dx}(0) = 0$$

Solutions to exercises

1 (a) $x = Ae^{-t} + Be^{3t} - 2$
(b) $y = Ae^{-x} + Be^{-4x} + 2$
(c) $y = Ae^{-2t} + Be^{-3t} + \dfrac{t}{3} - \dfrac{5}{18}$
(d) $x = Ae^{-6t} + Be^{-5t} + 0.267t - 0.0978$

2 $y = Ae^{2x} + Be^{-x} - 3$

3 $y = Ae^{-2x} + Be^{-x} + \frac{3}{2}\sin 2x - \frac{1}{2}\cos 2x$;
$\frac{3}{2}e^{-2x} + \frac{3}{2}\sin 2x - \frac{1}{2}\cos 2x$

6.5 Inhomogeneous term appears in the complementary function

Occasionally you will come across a differential equation

$$a\frac{d^2y}{dx^2} + b\frac{dy}{dx} + cy = f(x)$$

for which the inhomogeneous term, $f(x)$, forms part of the complementary function. One such example is the equation

$$\frac{d^2y}{dx^2} - \frac{dy}{dx} - 6y = e^{3x}$$

It is straightforward to check that the complementary function is $y_{cf} = Ae^{3x} + Be^{-2x}$. Note that the first of these terms has the same form as the inhomogeneous term, e^{3x}, on the right-hand side of the differential equation.

You should verify for yourself that trying a particular integral of the form $y(x) = \alpha e^{3x}$ will not work in a case like this. Can you see why?

Instead, try a particular integral of the form $y(x) = \alpha x e^{3x}$. Verify that

$$\frac{dy}{dx} = \alpha e^{3x}(3x + 1) \quad \text{and} \quad \frac{d^2y}{dx^2} = \alpha e^{3x}(9x + 6)$$

Substitute these expressions into the differential equation to find $\alpha = \frac{1}{5}$. Finally, the particular integral is $y_{pi}(x) = \frac{1}{5}xe^{3x}$ and so the general solution to the differential equation is

$$y = Ae^{3x} + Be^{-2x} + \frac{1}{5}xe^{3x}$$

In general, if $f(x)$ is part of the complementary function we try $y = \alpha x f(x)$ for the particular integral.

End of block exercises

1 Find the general solution of the following equations:

(a) $\frac{d^2y}{dx^2} + 2\frac{dy}{dx} + 3y = 2\sin 2x$

(b) $\frac{d^2y}{dt^2} + \frac{dy}{dt} + y = 4\cos 3t$

(c) $\frac{d^2y}{dx^2} + 9y = 4e^{8x}$

(d) $\frac{d^2x}{dt^2} - 16x = 9e^{6t}$

2 Find a particular integral for the equation

$$\frac{d^2y}{dx^2} + \frac{dy}{dx} + y = 1 + x$$

3 Find the general solution of

(a) $\frac{d^2x}{dt^2} - 6\frac{dx}{dt} + 5x = 3$

(b) $\frac{d^2x}{dt^2} - 2\frac{dx}{dt} + x = e^t$

Solutions to exercises

1 (a) $y = e^{-x}(A \sin \sqrt{2}x + B \cos \sqrt{2}x)$
$-\frac{8}{17} \cos 2x - \frac{2}{17} \sin 2x$

(b) $y = e^{-0.5t}(A \cos 0.866t + B \sin 0.866t)$
$-0.438 \cos 3t + 0.164 \sin 3t$

(c) $y = A \cos 3x + B \sin 3x + 0.0548e^{8x}$

(d) $x = Ae^{4t} + Be^{-4t} + \frac{9}{20}e^{6t}$

2 $y_{pi} = x$

3 (a) $x = Ae^{t} + Be^{5t} + \frac{3}{5}$

(b) $x = Ae^{t} + Bte^{t} + \frac{1}{2}t^2e^{t}$

End of chapter exercises

1 Give one example each of a first-order linear equation, first-order non-linear equation, second-order linear equation, second-order non-linear equation.

2 By integrating twice find the general solution of $y'' = 12x^2$.

3 Find a first-order equation satisfied by $x = Ae^{-2t}$.

4 Classify the following equations, specifying the order and type (linear or non-linear):

(a) $\frac{d^2y}{dx^2} - \frac{dy}{dx} = x^2$

(b) $\frac{dy}{dt} + \cos y = 0$

5 Find a second-order differential equation that is satisfied by

$$y = A \cosh 2x + B \sinh 2x$$

6 Integrate twice the differential equation

$$\frac{d^2y}{dx^2} = \frac{w}{2}(lx - x^2)$$

where w and l are constants, to find a general solution for y.

7 Integrate the equation $\frac{dy}{dx} = 3x^2$ subject to the condition $y(1) = 4$ in order to find the particular solution.

8 Two tanks containing a liquid are placed in series so that the first discharges into the second and the second discharges into a waste outlet. Let $q_1(t)$ and $q_2(t)$ be the flow rates out of the two tanks respectively, and let the height of liquid in each of the tanks be $h_1(t)$ and $h_2(t)$ respectively. The two tanks are identical and each has a constant cross-sectional area A. The outflow from each tank is proportional to the height of liquid in the tank. At $t = 0$ the height of liquid in the first tank is h_0 and the second tank is empty.

(a) Derive and solve the differential equation for $h_1(t)$.
(b) Hence find $q_1(t)$.
(c) Derive and solve the differential equation for $h_2(t)$.
(d) Hence find $q_2(t)$.

9 The charge, q, on a capacitor in an LCR series circuit satisfies the second-order differential equation

$$L\frac{d^2q}{dt^2} + R\frac{dq}{dt} + \frac{1}{C}q = E$$

where L, R, C and E are constants. Show that if $2L = CR^2$ the general solution of this equation is

$$q = e^{-t/(CR)}\left(A \cos \frac{1}{CR}t + B \sin \frac{1}{CR}t\right) + CE$$

If $i = \dfrac{dq}{dt} = 0$ and $q = 0$ when $t = 0$ show that the current in the circuit is

$$i = \frac{2E}{R} e^{-t/(CR)} \sin \frac{1}{CR} t$$

10 Obtain the general solution of the differential equation

$$\frac{dT}{d\theta} - \mu T = -\mu K$$

where μ and K are constants.

11 The equation governing the flow of current i in a series LR circuit with applied constant voltage E is

$$L \frac{di}{dt} + Ri = E$$

(a) Solve this equation subject to the condition $i(0) = 0$.
(b) State the final value of the current.
(c) Find the time taken for the current to reach 95% of its final value.

Solutions to exercises

2 $y = x^4 + Ax + B$

3 $x' = -2x$

4 (a) second-order linear
(b) first-order non-linear due to term cos y

5 $\dfrac{d^2y}{dx^2} = 4y$

6 $y = \dfrac{w}{2}\left(\dfrac{lx^3}{6} - \dfrac{x^4}{12}\right) + Ax + B$

7 $y = x^3 + 3$

8 (a) $h_1 = h_0 e^{-kt/A}$ (b) $q_1 = kh_0 e^{-kt/A}$
(c) $h_2 = \dfrac{kh_0 t}{A} e^{-kt/A}$ (d) $q_2 = \dfrac{k^2 h_0 t}{A} e^{-kt/A}$

10 $T = K + Ae^{\mu\theta}$

11 (a) $i = \dfrac{E}{R}\left(1 - e^{-Rt/L}\right)$ (b) $\dfrac{E}{R}$
(c) about $\dfrac{3L}{R}$

Functions of more than one variable and partial differentiation

In many engineering applications a physical quantity depends upon several other quantities that can vary independently. For example, the temperature at a point in a kiln will vary both with time and with the position of the point in the kiln. Such quantities are described mathematically using functions of more than one variable. In this chapter we explain the notation used to represent such functions. We go on to explain two ways in which these functions can be visualised. The techniques of calculus, previously applied to functions of one variable, are now extended to functions of several variables. Differentiation involving several variables is called **partial differentiation**. Finally we illustrate an application of partial differentiation to finding maximum, minimum and saddle points of a function of two variables.

Chapter 21 contents

BLOCK 1 Functions of two independent variables, and their graphs

1.1 Introduction

We have explained in Chapter 6 that a function is a mathematical rule that operates upon an input to produce a single output. We saw that the input is referred to as the independent variable because we are free, within reason, to choose its value. The output is called the dependent variable because its value *depends* upon the value of the input. Commonly we use the letter x to represent the input, y the output and f the function, in which case we write $y = f(x)$. Examples include $y = 5x^2$, $y = \frac{1}{x}$ and so on. In such cases, there is a single independent variable, x.

We now move on to consider examples in which there are two independent variables. This means that there will be two inputs to a function, each of which can be chosen independently. Once these values have been chosen, the function rule will be used to process them in order to produce a single output called the dependent variable. Notice that whilst there is now more than one input, there is still a *single* output.

We then illustrate how these functions can be visualised in the form of contour plots and three-dimensional graphs. User-friendly computer software can be used for such visualisation, and you should enquire about packages available for your use.

1.2 Functions of two variables

The block diagram in Figure 1.1 depicts the function $f(x, y) = 3x + 4y$. This function has two independent inputs, denoted by x and y. The function rule is 'multiply the input x by 3, multiply the input y by 4, and add the results'. There is a single output $3x + 4y$.

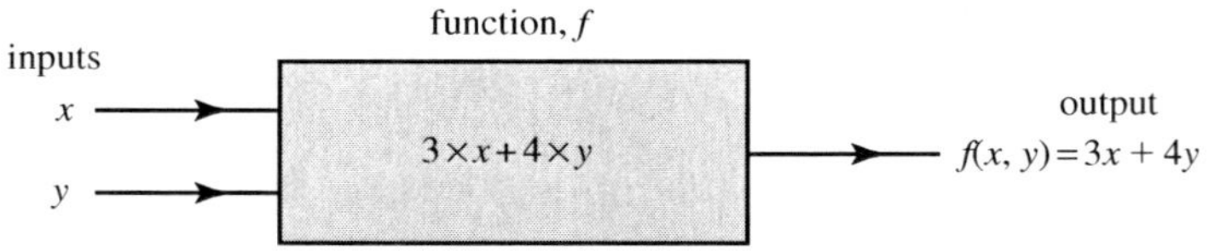

Figure 1.1 A block diagram of the function $f(x, y) = 3x + 4y$

The notation $f(x, y) = 3x + 4y$ indicates that, with inputs x and y, the function, f, produces an output of $3x + 4y$. The inputs to the function are placed in brackets, after the f. The expression $f(x, y)$ is read as 'f is a function of x and y'. As before, the inputs to a function are also known as the **arguments** of the function.

Key point

A function of two variables is a rule that produces a single output when values of two independent variables are chosen.

Example 1.1

A function f is defined by $f(x, y) = 3x + 4y$. Calculate the output when the input values are $x = 5$ and $y = 6$.

Solution

Refer to the block diagram in Figure 1.1. When the input x takes the value 5, and the input y takes the value 6, the output is $3 \times 5 + 4 \times 6 = 15 + 24 = 39$. We could write this as $f(5, 6) = 39$.

Example 1.2

A function f is defined by $f(x, y) = 11x^2 - 7y + 2$. Calculate the output when the inputs are $x = -2$ and $y = 3$.

Solution

In this example we are required to find $f(-2, 3)$. This can be calculated directly from the expression for $f(x, y)$, without reference to a block diagram. Substitution into the function rule produces

$$f(-2, 3) = 11 \times (-2)^2 - 7 \times (3) + 2 = 44 - 21 + 2 = 25.$$

Example 1.3

A function is defined by $f(x, y) = \frac{x}{y}$. Calculate the output when the inputs are $x = 12$ and $y = 3$.

Solution

$f(12, 3) =$

$\frac{12}{3} = 4$

Example 1.4

A function is defined by $f(x, y) = e^{x+y}$.

(a) Calculate the output when the inputs are $x = -1$ and $y = 2$.

(b) Show that this function can be written in the equivalent form $f(x, y) = e^x e^y$.

Solution

(a) $f(-1, 2) =$

$e^{-1+2} = e^1 = e = 2.718$ (3 d.p.)

(b) Using the first law of indices we can write e^{x+y} as $e^x e^y$.

Note that in the previous examples both x and y are independent variables. We can choose a value for y quite independently of the value we have chosen for x. This is quite different from the case of a function of a single variable when, for example, if we write $y = 5x^2$, choosing x automatically determines y.

It is common to introduce another symbol to stand for the output. So, in Example 1.1 we may write $z = f(x, y) = 3x + 4y$ or simply $z = 3x + 4y$. In Example 1.2 we can write simply $z = 11x^2 - 7y + 2$. Here the value of z depends upon the values chosen for x and y, and so z is referred to as the dependent variable.

Functions of two variables are introduced because they arise naturally in engineering applications. Consider the following example, which illustrates this.

Example 1.5

The volume V of the cylinder shown in Figure 1.2 is given by the formula $V = \pi r^2 h$, where r is the radius and h is the height of the cylinder. Suppose we choose a value for the radius, and a value for the height. Note that we can choose these values independently. We can then use the formula to determine the volume of the cylinder. We can regard V as depending upon the two independent variables r and h and write $V = f(r, h) = \pi r^2 h$. Here, the dependent variable is V since the value of the volume depends upon the values chosen for the radius and the height.

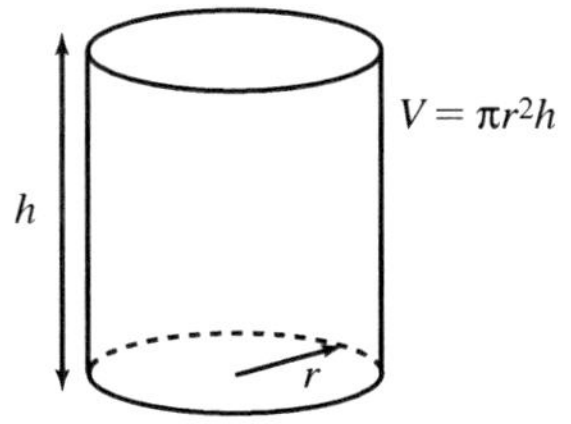

Figure 1.2 The volume, V, depends upon the two independent variables r and h, and is given by $V = \pi r^2 h$.

1.3 Contour plots of functions of two variables

By now you will be familiar with the way in which a function of one variable is represented graphically. For example, you have seen in Chapter 6 how the graph of the function $y = f(x)$ is drawn by plotting the independent variable x on the horizontal axis, and the dependent variable y on the vertical axis. Given a value of x, the function rule enables us to calculate a value for y, and the point with coordinates (x, y) is then plotted. Joining all such points produces a graph of the function.

When two independent variables are involved, as in $z = f(x, y)$, there are various ways in which we can represent this graphically. One way is to use a **contour plot**, as we shall show in Examples 1.6 and 1.7.

A contour plot is a two-dimensional visualisation of a function of two variables. You may already be familiar with contour plots in the context of maps. Contours are drawn on the map to show the location of points that are the same height above sea level. In the example that follows, contours show the location of points that have the same temperature. This is analogous to the plotting of isotherms on a weather map.

Example 1.6 Mechanical Engineering – Temperature distribution in a metal plate

There are many occasions in the engineering design process when it is necessary to analyse heat flow. For example an engineer may be interested in the effect of different insulation materials on heat losses through the roof of a building. In a nuclear reactor heat is generated in the fuel rods, which are then often cooled by water. It is critical to be able to calculate the rate of heat flow from the rods to the water if a life-threatening situation such as meltdown of the reactor is to be avoided. In applications like these an engineer will meet functions of more than one variable.

As an example consider a two-dimensional metal plate, defined by the region $0 \leq x \leq 1$, $0 \leq y \leq 1$, which contains no internal sources of heat. Suppose the temperature is maintained at 0 °C on three of the plate boundaries. Suppose it varies with x along the fourth boundary at $y = 1$ according to $T = \sin \pi x$, as shown in Figure 1.3.

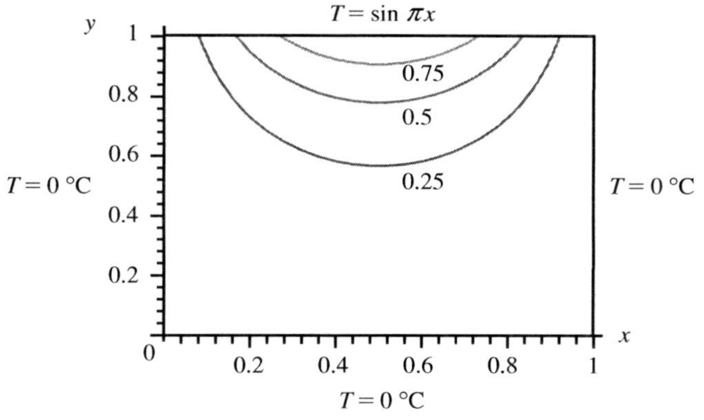

Figure 1.3 A metal plate with temperatures imposed on its boundaries.

A typical problem is to use this information to determine the temperature at any point in the plate. Knowing the equations for heat conduction, and some advanced techniques in calculus, it is possible to show that the temperature, T, at any point (x, y) is given by the function of two variables

$$T(x, y) = \frac{\sinh \pi y \sin \pi x}{\sinh \pi}$$

The function $\sinh \pi y$ is a hyperbolic function, detailed in Chapter 8 Block 1. It is straightforward, using a computer graphics package, to produce a contour plot from this function that shows curves of constant temperature. In Figure 1.3 we have plotted contours showing curves upon which the temperature is 0.25 °C, 0.5 °C, and 0.75 °C.

Example 1.7 Fluid Dynamics – Fluid flow around a corner

The analysis of the ways in which fluids flow around objects is essential in fields such as aeronautical and marine engineering, and the study of renewable energy systems. A useful quantity is the **streamfunction**, ψ. Under particular conditions ψ is a function of the two spatial variables x and y: that is, $\psi = \psi(x, y)$. Plotting curves upon which ψ is constant gives a useful visual representation because fluid flows along these curves.

For example, the streamfunction $\psi(x, y) = 4(x^2 - y^2)$ gives the streamlines for flow around a corner. Curves along which ψ is constant are illustrated in Figure 1.4.

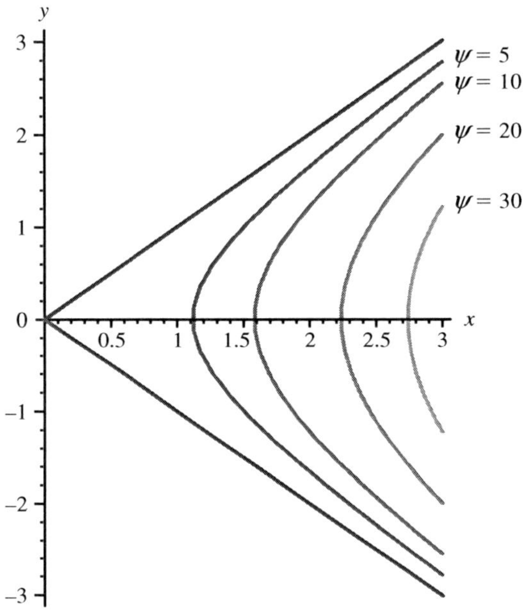

Figure 1.4 The streamlines of a flow around a corner are described by a function of two variables, $\psi = 4(x^2 - y^2)$.

Exercises

1. Given $z = f(x, y) = 7x + 2y$ find the output when $x = 8$ and $y = 2$.

2. If $z = f(x, y) = -11x + y$ find (a) $f(2, 3)$, (b) $f(11, 1)$.

3. If $z = f(x, y) = 3e^x - 2e^y + x^2y^3$ find $z(1, 1)$.

4. If $w = g(x, y) = 7 - xy$ find the value of the dependent variable w when $x = -3$ and $y = -9$.

5. If $z = f(x, y) = \sin(x + y)$ find $f(20°, 30°)$ where the inputs are angles measured in degrees.

6. If $f(x, t) = e^{2xt}$ find $f(0.5, 3)$.

7. Using the temperature distribution function $T(x, y) = \dfrac{\sinh \pi y \sin \pi x}{\sinh \pi}$ in Example 1.6, evaluate the temperature at the centre of the plate.

Solutions to exercises

1 60

2 (a) −19 (b) −120

3 $e^1 + 1 = 3.718$ (3 d.p.)

4 −20

5 0.766 (3 d.p.)

6 20.086 (3 d.p.)

7 0.199 °C (3 d.p.)

Computer and calculator exercises

1 Matlab code that can be used to generate the contour plot in Figure 1.3 is

```
[x, y] = meshgrid (0:0.1:1,
0:0.1:1);
z = sinh (pi*y) .*sin(pi*x) /
sinh (pi);
contour (x, y, z, [0.25, 0.5,
0.75]);
```

If you have access to Matlab, reproduce this figure and then modify the code to produce a contour plot of the function $\psi = 4(x^2 - y^2)$ shown in Figure 1.4. Note that x^2 will be coded as

```
x.^2
```

2 Maple code that can be used to generate Figure 1.4 is

```
with (plots):
contourplot (4*(x^2 − y^2),
x = 0..3, y = −3..3,
contours = [5, 10, 20, 30]);
```

If you have access to Maple, reproduce this figure and modify the code to produce the contour plot in Figure 1.3.

3 The function $\psi(x, y) = y\left(1 - \dfrac{1}{x^2 + y^2}\right)$ represents the streamline pattern of fluid flow past a cylinder. Investigate whether a computer graph-plotting package to which you have access can produce a contour plot of this flow.

1.4 Three-dimensional graphs

As an alternative to a contour plot, a graph can be drawn in three dimensions – a task that is difficult to do in the two-dimensional plane of the paper. We now need two axes for the independent variables and a third axis for the dependent variable. Computer software is readily available for plotting graphs in three dimensions, so rather than attempt this manually we shall be content with understanding the process involved in producing the graph, and illustrating this with several examples.

Three axes are drawn at right angles and these are labelled x, y and z as shown in Figure 1.5. There is more than one way of doing this, but the usual convention is shown here. When labelled in this way the axes are said to form a **right-handed set**. The axes intersect at the origin O.

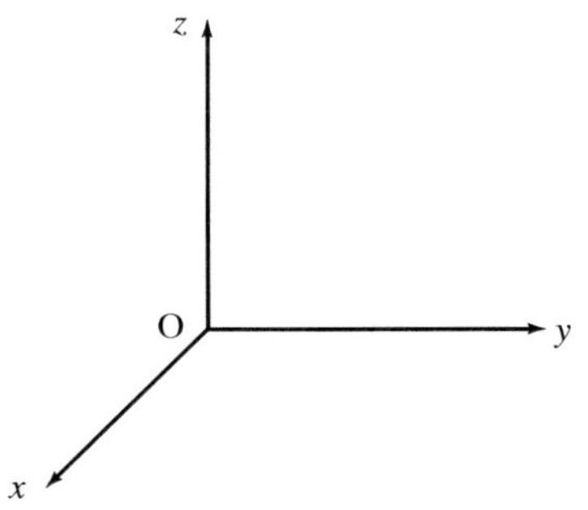

Figure 1.5
Three perpendicular axes, labelled x, y and z.

Example 1.8

Given the function of two variables $z = f(x, y) = 3x + 4y$ calculate the value of the function when x and y take the following values. Represent each point graphically.
(a) $x = 3,\ y = 2$ (b) $x = 5,\ y = 0$ (c) $x = 0,\ y = 5$

Solution

In each case we use the function rule $z = f(x, y) = 3x + 4y$ to calculate the corresponding value of z.
(a) $z = 3(3) + 4(2) = 17$ (b) $z = 3(5) + 4(0) = 15$ (c) $z = 3(0) + 4(5) = 20$
It is conventional to write the coordinates of the points in the form (x, y, z) so that the three points in this example are (3, 2, 17), (5, 0, 15) and (0, 5, 20).

Each of the points can then be drawn as shown in Figure 1.6, where they have been labelled A, B and C respectively. Notice that the z coordinate of point A, which is 17, gives the height of A above the point (3, 2) in the $x-y$ plane. Similar comments apply to points B and C.

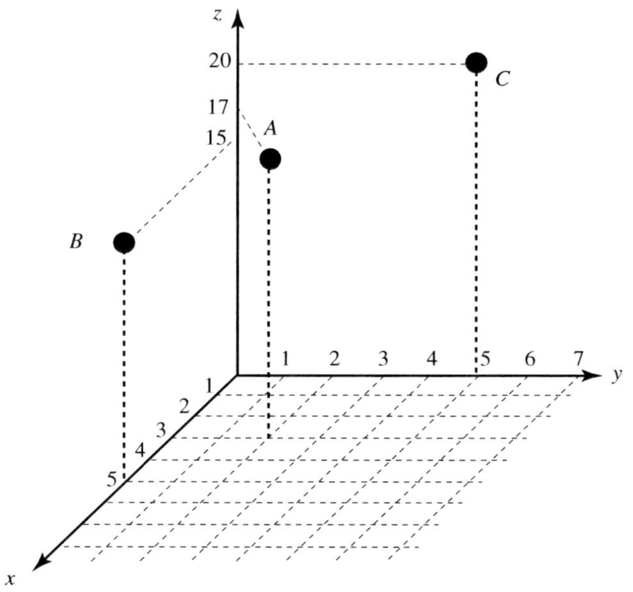

Figure 1.6
Three points in three-dimensional space with coordinates $A(3, 2, 17)$, $B(5, 0, 15)$ and $C(0, 5, 20)$.

If we were to continue selecting more points and plotting them we would find that all the points lie in a plane. This plane is shown in Figure 1.7. Notice that in each case the z coordinate is the height of the plane above the point (x, y) in the x–y plane.

For example, the point C is 20 units above the point (0, 5) in the x–y plane.

Figure 1.7
The plane
$z = 3x + 4y$.

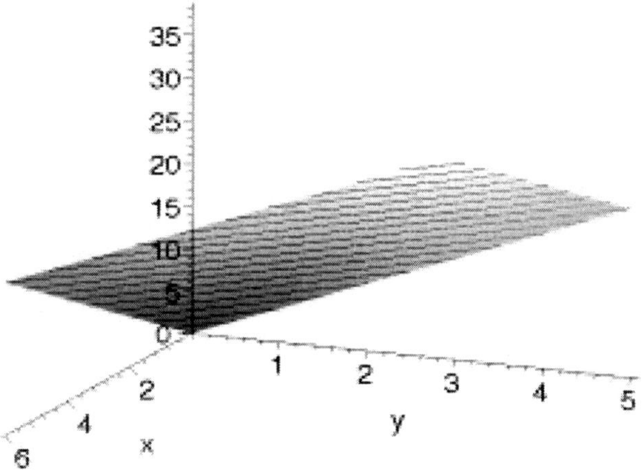

In the previous example we saw that when we drew a graph of the function of two variables $z = 3x + 4y$ we obtained a plane. In more general cases the graph of $z = f(x, y)$ will be a curved surface, and the z coordinate is the height of the surface above the point (x, y). Some more examples of functions of two variables and their graphs are shown in Figures 1.8 and 1.9. It would be a useful exercise for you to try to reproduce these graphs for yourself using computer software.

Figure 1.8
The function
$z = x^2 + y^2$.

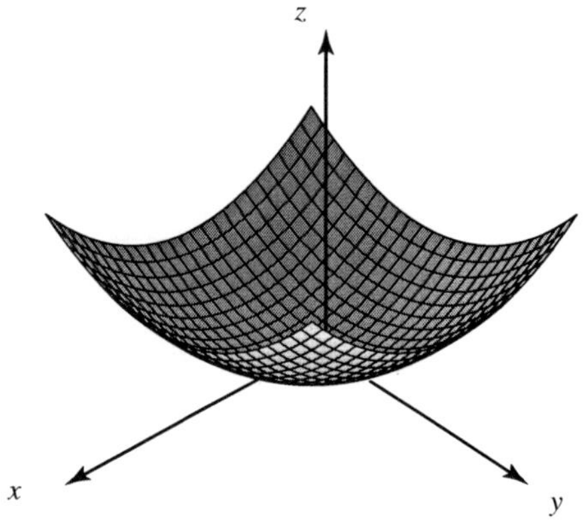

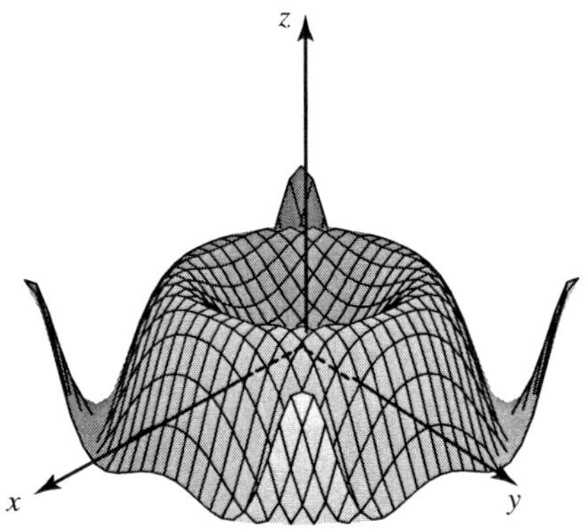

Figure 1.9
The function $z = \sin(x^2 + y^2)$.

Example 1.9 Mechanical Engineering – Temperature distribution in a metal plate

In Example 1.6 we saw that the function $T(x, y) = \dfrac{\sinh \pi y \sin \pi x}{\sinh \pi}$ represents the temperature distribution in a metal plate when three of its boundaries are maintained at 0 °C and the fourth has a temperature given by $T = \sin \pi x$. A graph of this function is shown in Figure 1.10. Observe the temperature distribution along the line $y = 1$, given by $T = \sin \pi x$.

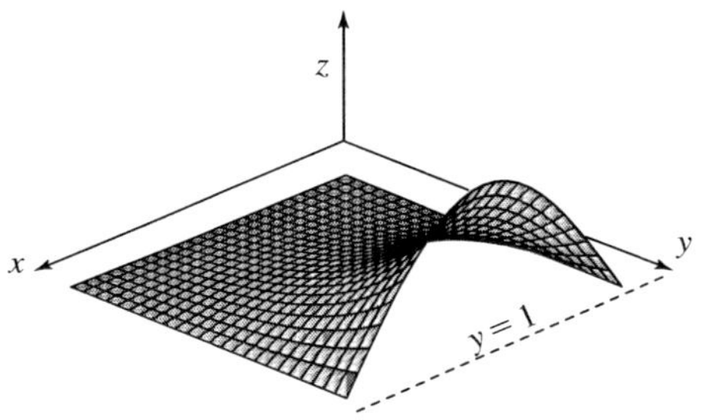

Figure 1.10
The function $T(x, y) = \frac{\sinh \pi y \sin \pi x}{\sinh \pi}$.

Exercises

1 Given the function $z = 3x - 6y$, find the z coordinate corresponding to each of the following points, which lie in the x–y plane: (a) (4, 4) (b) (0, 3) (c) (5, 0)

Plot the points on a three-dimensional graph.

Solutions to exercises

1 (a) −12 (b) −18 (c) 15

Computer and calculator exercises

1 The following Matlab code can be used to generate a three-dimensional plot as shown in Figure 1.10.

```
[x,y] = meshgrid (0:0.1:1,
0:0.1:1);
z = sinh(pi*y).*sin(pi*x)/
sinh(pi);
mesh(z);
```

If you have access to Matlab generate a plot for yourself. Plot a graph of the surface $z = \sin(x^2 + y^2)$ as shown in Figure 1.9.

2 The Maple code

```
plot3d(x^2+y^2,x =-3..3,
y =-3..3);
```

can be used to plot the graph of $z = x^2 + y^2$ as shown in Figure 1.8. Try to reproduce this graph for yourself.

End of block exercises

1 Find the value of the function $f(x, y) = \sqrt{x^2 + y^2}$ when $x = 2$ and $y = 6$.

2 If $f(x, y) = x^2 + 3xy$ find $f(2, 3)$.

3 If $V = \ln(x^2 + y^2)$ find the value of V when $x = 3$ and $y = 7$.

4 Functions of three (or more) independent variables can be defined in an analogous way to functions of two variables. Suppose $u(x, y, z)$ is a function of the three independent variables x, y and z, and is defined by

$$u = \frac{1}{\sqrt{x^2 + y^2 + z^2}}$$

Find u when $x = 1$, $y = 2$ and $z = 3$. Can the value of u be determined when $x = y = z = 0$?

Solutions to exercises

1 $\sqrt{40}$

2 22

3 $V = \ln 58 = 4.060$ (3 d.p.)

4 $u(1, 2, 3) = \frac{1}{\sqrt{14}}$. No, because division by zero is not allowed.

BLOCK 2 Partial differentiation

2.1 Introduction

Before attempting this section it is essential that you have a thorough understanding of differentiation of functions of one variable, and you should revise Chapters 15 and 16 if necessary. In particular, you may need to refer frequently to Table 2.1 on page 704, which gives the derivatives of some common functions.

In Chapter 15 we introduced differentiation of a function of a single variable and showed how the derivative of such a function can be calculated. Recall that this gives useful information about the gradient of the graph of the function at different points. In this section we explain how functions of two variables are differentiated.

In Chapter 15 we differentiated y, which was a function of x, to obtain the derivative $\frac{\mathrm{d}y}{\mathrm{d}x}$. Note that the dependent variable (in this case y) is differentiated with respect to the independent variable (in this case x).

Consider now z, which depends upon two variables x and y. Recall that z is then the dependent variable, and x and y are the independent variables. Hence z can be differentiated with respect to x to produce a derivative, and it can also be differentiated with respect to y to produce another, different, derivative. So for functions of two variables there are two derivatives: we can no longer talk about *the* derivative of z. This is a fundamental difference between functions of one variable and functions of two variables.

When differentiating functions of two variables we refer to this process as **partial differentiation**, and instead of using a normal letter d as in $\frac{\mathrm{d}y}{\mathrm{d}x}$, we use a curly d instead and write ∂. Do not be put off by this notation – you will soon get used to it. When we differentiate z with respect to (w.r.t) x we denote the resulting derivative by $\frac{\partial z}{\partial x}$. An alternative notation in common use is to write this derivative as z_x. When we differentiate z w.r.t y we denote the derivative produced by $\frac{\partial z}{\partial y}$. An alternative notation is to write this derivative as z_y.

Key point

If $z = f(x, y)$ then

the (first) partial derivative of z with respect to x is denoted $\dfrac{\partial z}{\partial x}$ or z_x,

the (first) partial derivative of z with respect to y is denoted $\dfrac{\partial z}{\partial y}$ or z_y.

We now explain how these derivatives are calculated.

2.2 Partial differentiation with respect to x

Suppose we have a function $z = 5x + 11$. You will recall that its derivative is $\frac{dz}{dx} = 5$. Note that the derivative of the constant 11 is zero. Similarly if $z = 6x + 12$, $\frac{dz}{dx} = 6$. Here the derivative of the constant 12 is zero. We are now ready to introduce partial differentiation with respect to x.

Consider the function $z = 5x + y$. When we differentiate with respect to x we treat any occurrence of the variable y *as though it were a constant*. Hence in this case the derivative of y is zero, and we write

$$\text{if } z = 5x + y \quad \text{then} \quad \frac{\partial z}{\partial x} = 5 + 0 = 5$$

Similarly,

$$\text{if } z = 7x^2 - y \quad \text{then} \quad \frac{\partial z}{\partial x} = 14x - 0 = 14x$$

If y is treated as a constant, then so too will be multiples of y, such as $7y$ and $-3y$. Furthermore, any functions of y, such as y^2 and e^y, will also be regarded as constants.

Example 2.1

Calculate $\frac{\partial z}{\partial x}$ when $z = 9x + 2$.

Solution

We must differentiate $z = 9x + 2$ with respect to x. This function is particularly simple because y does not appear at all. The derivative of $9x$ is 9, and the derivative of the constant 2 is zero. Hence $\frac{\partial z}{\partial x} = 9$.

Example 2.2

Calculate $\frac{\partial z}{\partial x}$ when $z = 9x + y$.

Solution

To find $\frac{\partial z}{\partial x}$ we treat y as though it were a constant. Imagine it were just a number like the '2' in the previous example. Then $\frac{\partial z}{\partial x} = 9$.

Example 2.3

Calculate $\frac{\partial z}{\partial x}$ when $z = y - 19x$.

Solution

Treat y as though it were a constant.

$$\frac{\partial z}{\partial x} = \qquad\qquad -19$$

Example 2.4

Calculate $\frac{\partial z}{\partial x}$ when $z = 3x + 4y + 11$.

Solution

In this case 11 is a constant and we treat y, and hence $4y$, as a constant.

$\frac{\partial z}{\partial x} =$ 3

Example 2.5

Calculate $\frac{\partial z}{\partial x}$ when $z = 4x^2 - 3y$.

Solution

$\frac{\partial z}{\partial x} = 8x - 0 = 8x$. The quantity $-3y$ is treated as a constant.

Example 2.6

Calculate $\frac{\partial z}{\partial x}$ when $z = x^2 - y^2$.

Solution

y, and hence y^2, is treated as a constant. When $-y^2$ is differentiated with respect to x the result will be zero. Hence if $z = x^2 - y^2$ then $\frac{\partial z}{\partial x} = 2x$.

Example 2.7

Calculate $\frac{\partial z}{\partial x}$ when $z = 5y^3 - x^4$.

Solution

y, and hence $5y^3$, is treated as a constant.

$\frac{\partial z}{\partial x} =$ $-4x^3$

Example 2.8

Calculate $\frac{\partial z}{\partial x}$ when $z = 3x - 4y^3$.

Solution

If $z = 3x - 4y^3$, then $\frac{\partial z}{\partial x} = 3$.

Recall that

- if $4x$ is differentiated with respect to x the result is 4,
- if $5x$ is differentiated with respect to x the result is 5.

Extending this to the following function of two variables:

- if $z = yx$ is differentiated with respect to x the result is y.

We see that because y is treated as if it were a constant then $\dfrac{\partial z}{\partial x} = y$.

Example 2.9

Calculate $\dfrac{\partial z}{\partial x}$ when $z = yx^2$.

Solution

To find $\dfrac{\partial z}{\partial x}$ imagine that you were trying to differentiate $3x^2$ say. The result would be $3(2x) = 6x$. Hence if $z = yx^2$ then $\dfrac{\partial z}{\partial x} = y(2x)$ or simply $2xy$.

Example 2.10

Calculate $\dfrac{\partial z}{\partial x}$ when $z = 3yx^2$.

Solution

Treating y as a constant we see that this function is of the form constant $\times$ x^2 and so

$$\frac{\partial z}{\partial x} = (3y)(2x) = 6xy.$$

Example 2.11

(a) Calculate $\dfrac{\partial z}{\partial x}$ when $z = 3x^2 + 4xy + 11$.

(b) Evaluate $\dfrac{\partial z}{\partial x}$ at the point $(x, y) = (-2, 5)$.

(c) Evaluate $\dfrac{\partial z}{\partial x}$ at the point $(x, y) = (9, -3)$.

Solution

(a) $\dfrac{\partial z}{\partial x} =$ ______ $6x + 4y$

(b) When $x = -2$ and $y = 5$, $\dfrac{\partial z}{\partial x} = 6(-2) + 4(5) = 8$.

(c) When $x = 9$ and $y = -3$

$\dfrac{\partial z}{\partial x} =$ ______ 42

Example 2.12

Calculate $\dfrac{\partial z}{\partial x}$ when (a) $z = x^2 e^y$, (b) $z = x^2 + e^y$, (c) $z = 3x^2 \cos y$, (d) $z = 3x^2 + \cos y$, (e) $z = 3x^2 + 4x \sin y$.

Solution

(a) y and hence e^y are treated as a constant. Then $\frac{\partial z}{\partial x} = 2xe^y$.

(b) $\frac{\partial z}{\partial x} = 2x$

(c) y and hence $\cos y$ are treated as a constant. Then $\frac{\partial z}{\partial x} = 6x \cos y$.

(d) $\frac{\partial z}{\partial x} = 6x$

(e) $\frac{\partial z}{\partial x} = 6x + 4 \sin y$

Example 2.13

Calculate $\frac{\partial z}{\partial x}$ when (a) $z = \sin 3x$, (b) $z = \sin yx$.

Solution

(a) If $z = \sin 3x$ then $\frac{\partial z}{\partial x} = 3 \cos 3x$.

(b) If $z = \sin yx$ then $\frac{\partial z}{\partial x} = y \cos yx$ because y is treated as a constant. Compare this result with that in part (a).

Key point

The (first) partial derivative with respect to x of a function $z = f(x, y)$ is denoted by $\frac{\partial z}{\partial x}$ and is calculated by differentiating the function with respect to x and treating y as though it were a constant.

2.3 Partial differentiation with respect to y

When we differentiate a function $f(x, y)$ with respect to y we treat any occurrence of the variable x *as though it were a constant*. The partial derivative with respect to y of a function $z = f(x, y)$ is denoted by $\frac{\partial z}{\partial y}$. Consider the following examples.

Example 2.14

Find $\frac{\partial z}{\partial y}$ when $z = 3y^4 + 4x^2 + 8$.

Solution

When calculating $\frac{\partial z}{\partial y}$ we treat any occurrence of x as if it were a constant. So the term $4x^2$ is treated as a constant and its partial derivative with respect to y is zero. That is

$$\text{if} \quad z = 3y^4 + 4x^2 + 8 \quad \text{then} \quad \frac{\partial z}{\partial y} = 12y^3 + 0 + 0 = 12y^3$$

Example 2.15

Find $\frac{\partial z}{\partial y}$ when $z = 3x^2y$.

Solution

Because x is treated as a constant, we are dealing with a function of the form $z = \text{constant} \times y$. The derivative with respect to y will be simply the constant factor. That is

$$\text{if} \quad z = 3x^2 y \quad \text{then} \quad \frac{\partial z}{\partial y} = 3x^2$$

Example 2.16

(a) Find $\frac{\partial z}{\partial y}$ when $z = 4xy^3$.

(b) Evaluate $\frac{\partial z}{\partial y}$ when $(x, y) = (6, 11)$.

Solution

(a) Because $4x$ is treated as a constant, we are dealing with a function of the form $z = \text{constant} \times y^3$.

$\frac{\partial z}{\partial y} =$ $4x \times (3y^2) = 12xy^2$

(b) When $x = 6$ and $y = 11$, $\frac{\partial z}{\partial y} =$ $12(6)(11^2) = 8712$

Key point

The (first) partial derivative with respect to y of a function $z = f(x, y)$ is denoted by $\frac{\partial z}{\partial y}$ and is calculated by differentiating the function with respect to y and treating x as though it were a constant.

It will be necessary to work with symbols other than z, x and y. Consider the following example.

Example 2.17

Consider the function $w = f(p, t)$. Find $\frac{\partial w}{\partial p}$ and $\frac{\partial w}{\partial t}$ when $w = 3t^7 + 4pt + p^2$.

Solution

When differentiating with respect to p, any occurrence of t is treated as if it were a constant. So $\frac{\partial w}{\partial p} = 4t + 2p$.

When differentiating with respect to t, any occurrence of p is treated as if it were a constant. So $\frac{\partial w}{\partial t} = 21t^6 + 4p$.

Exercises

1. In each case, given $z = f(x, y)$, find $\frac{\partial z}{\partial x}$ and $\frac{\partial z}{\partial y}$.
   (a) $z = 5x + 11y$ (b) $z = -7y - 14x$
   (c) $z = 8x$ (d) $z = -5y$
   (e) $z = 3x + 8y - 2$ (f) $z = 17 - 3x + 2y$
   (g) $z = 8$ (h) $z = 8 - 3y$
   (i) $z = 2x^2 - 7y$ (j) $z = 9 - 3y^3 + 7x$
   (k) $z = 9 - 9(x - y)$ (l) $z = 9(x + y + 3)$

2. In each case, given $z = f(x, y)$ find z_x and z_y.
   (a) $z = xy$ (b) $z = 3xy$ (c) $z = -9yx$
   (d) $z = x^2y$ (e) $z = 9x^2y$ (f) $z = 8xy^2$

3. If $z = 9x + y^2$ evaluate $\frac{\partial z}{\partial x}$ and $\frac{\partial z}{\partial y}$ at the point $(4, -2)$.

4. Find $\frac{\partial z}{\partial x}$ and $\frac{\partial z}{\partial y}$ when
   (a) $z = e^{2x}$ (b) $z = e^{5y}$ (c) $z = e^{xy}$
   (d) $z = 4e^{2y}$

5. If $y = x \sin t$ find $\frac{\partial y}{\partial x}$ and $\frac{\partial y}{\partial t}$.

Solutions to exercises

1. (a) $\frac{\partial z}{\partial x} = 5, \frac{\partial z}{\partial y} = 11$ (b) $-14, -7$
   (c) $8, 0$ (d) $0, -5$ (e) $3, 8$ (f) $-3, 2$
   (g) $0, 0$ (h) $0, -3$ (i) $4x, -7$
   (j) $7, -9y^2$ (k) $-9, 9$ (l) $9, 9$

2. (a) $z_x = y$, $z_y = x$ (b) $3y, 3x$ (c) $-9y, -9x$
   (d) $2xy, x^2$ (e) $18xy, 9x^2$ (f) $8y^2, 16xy$

3. $9, -4$

4. (a) $\frac{\partial z}{\partial x} = 2e^{2x}, \frac{\partial z}{\partial y} = 0$ (b) $0, 5e^{5y}$
   (c) ye^{xy}, xe^{xy} (d) $0, 8e^{2y}$

5. $\frac{\partial y}{\partial x} = \sin t, \frac{\partial y}{\partial t} = x \cos t$

2.4 Partial derivatives requiring the product or quotient rules

Consider the following more demanding examples, which use the rules developed in Chapter 16.

Example 2.18

Find $\frac{\partial z}{\partial x}$ and $\frac{\partial z}{\partial y}$ when $z = yxe^{2x}$.

Solution

To find $\frac{\partial z}{\partial x}$ we treat y as constant. We are dealing with a function of the form constant $\times\, xe^{2x}$. Note that this function itself contains a product of the functions x and e^{2x} and so we must use the product rule for differentiation. The derivative of xe^{2x} is $e^{2x}(1) + x(2e^{2x}) = e^{2x}(1 + 2x)$. Hence

$$\text{if} \quad z = yxe^{2x} \quad \text{then} \quad \frac{\partial z}{\partial x} = y(e^{2x}(1 + 2x)) = ye^{2x}(1 + 2x)$$

To find $\frac{\partial z}{\partial y}$ we treat x as constant. In turn, this means that xe^{2x} is constant too. This time the calculation is much simpler because we are dealing with a function of the form z = constant $\times\, y$. So,

$$\text{if} \quad z = yxe^{2x} \quad \text{then} \quad \frac{\partial z}{\partial y} = xe^{2x}$$

Example 2.19

Find $\frac{\partial z}{\partial x}$ and $\frac{\partial z}{\partial y}$ when $z = \frac{ye^x}{x}$.

Solution

To find $\frac{\partial z}{\partial x}$ we treat y as constant. We are dealing with a function of the form constant $\times\, \frac{e^x}{x}$. Note that this function itself contains a quotient of the functions e^x and x and so we must use the quotient rule for differentiation. The derivative of $\frac{e^x}{x}$ is $\frac{e^x x - e^x(1)}{x^2} = \frac{e^x(x - 1)}{x^2}$. Hence

$$\text{if} \quad z = \frac{ye^x}{x} \quad \text{then} \quad \frac{\partial z}{\partial x} = \frac{ye^x(x - 1)}{x^2}$$

To find $\frac{\partial z}{\partial y}$ we treat x as constant. In turn, this means that $\frac{e^x}{x}$ is constant too. This calculation is simple because we are dealing with a function of the form z = constant $\times\, y$. So,

$$\text{if} \quad z = \frac{ye^x}{x} \quad \text{then} \quad \frac{\partial z}{\partial y} = \frac{e^x}{x}$$

Exercises

1 Find $\frac{\partial z}{\partial x}$ and $\frac{\partial z}{\partial y}$ when
(a) $z = yxe^x$ (b) $z = xye^y$ (c) $z = xe^{xy}$
(d) $z = ye^{xy}$ (e) $z = x^2 \sin(xy)$
(f) $z = y \cos(xy)$ (g) $z = x \ln(xy)$
(h) $z = 3xy^3e^x$

2 Find the first partial derivatives of $u = \frac{1}{x^2 + y^2}$

3 Find the first partial derivatives of $u = \frac{x}{x^2 + y^2}$

Solutions to exercises

1 (a) $ye^x(x + 1)$, xe^x (b) ye^y, $xe^y(y + 1)$
(c) $e^{xy}(xy + 1)$, x^2e^{xy} (d) y^2e^{xy}, $e^{xy}(xy + 1)$
(e) $x^2y \cos(xy) + 2x \sin(xy)$, $x^3 \cos(xy)$
(f) $-y^2 \sin(xy)$, $-yx \sin(xy) + \cos(xy)$
(g) $1 + \ln(xy), \frac{x}{y}$ (h) $3e^xy^3(x + 1)$, $9xy^2e^x$

2 $-\frac{2x}{(x^2 + y^2)^2}, -\frac{2y}{(x^2 + y^2)^2}$

3 $\frac{y^2 - x^2}{(x^2 + y^2)^2}, \frac{-2xy}{(x^2 + y^2)^2}$

End of block exercises

1 The derivative of $f(x)$ with respect to x is defined as $\frac{df}{dx} = \lim_{\delta x \to 0} \frac{f(x + \delta x) - f(x)}{\delta x}$ (see Chapter 15 Block 1). In an analogous manner we define the partial derivatives of $f(x, y)$ by

$$\frac{\partial f}{\partial x} = \lim_{\delta x \to 0} \frac{f(x + \delta x, y) - f(x, y)}{\delta x}$$

$$\frac{\partial f}{\partial y} = \lim_{\delta y \to 0} \frac{f(x, y + \delta y) - f(x, y)}{\delta y}$$

Use these definitions to find the first partial derivatives of (a) $f(x, y) = x^2y$, (b) $f(x, y) = x^2 + 3xy$, from first principles.

2 If $r = \sqrt{x^2 + y^2}$ find $\frac{\partial r}{\partial x}$ and $\frac{\partial r}{\partial y}$.

3 The derivative of $f(x) = \tan^{-1} kx$ is $\frac{k}{1 + k^2x^2}$.

If $\phi = \tan^{-1} \frac{y}{x}$ find $\frac{\partial \phi}{\partial y}$.

Solutions to exercises

1 (a) $2xy$, x^2 (b) $2x + 3y$, $3x$

2 $\frac{x}{(x^2 + y^2)^{1/2}}, \frac{y}{(x^2 + y^2)^{1/2}}$

3 $\frac{1/x}{1 + (1/x)^2y^2} = \frac{x}{x^2 + y^2}$

BLOCK 3

Higher-order derivatives

3.1 Introduction

Just as a function of one variable has a second derivative found by differentiating the first derivative, so too does a function of two variables. If $z = f(x, y)$ the first partial derivatives are $\frac{\partial z}{\partial z}$ and $\frac{\partial z}{\partial y}$. The second partial derivatives are found by differentiating the first partial derivatives. We can do this in various ways, as we show in the next section.

3.2 Finding higher derivatives

We can differentiate either first partial derivatives with respect to x or with respect to y to obtain various second partial derivatives, as summarised in the next key point.

Key point

$$\text{differentiating } \frac{\partial z}{\partial x} \text{ w.r.t. } x \text{ produces } \frac{\partial}{\partial x}\left(\frac{\partial z}{\partial x}\right) = \frac{\partial^2 z}{\partial x^2}$$

$$\text{differentiating } \frac{\partial z}{\partial x} \text{ w.r.t. } y \text{ produces } \frac{\partial}{\partial y}\left(\frac{\partial z}{\partial x}\right) = \frac{\partial^2 z}{\partial y \partial x}$$

$$\text{differentiating } \frac{\partial z}{\partial y} \text{ w.r.t. } x \text{ produces } \frac{\partial}{\partial x}\left(\frac{\partial z}{\partial y}\right) = \frac{\partial^2 z}{\partial x \partial y}$$

$$\text{differentiating } \frac{\partial z}{\partial y} \text{ w.r.t. } y \text{ produces } \frac{\partial}{\partial y}\left(\frac{\partial z}{\partial y}\right) = \frac{\partial^2 z}{\partial y^2}$$

The **second partial derivatives** of z are

$$\frac{\partial^2 z}{\partial x^2}, \quad \frac{\partial^2 z}{\partial y \partial x}, \quad \frac{\partial^2 z}{\partial x \partial y}, \quad \frac{\partial^2 z}{\partial y^2}$$

These are sometimes written in the alternative, briefer form

$$z_{xx}, \quad z_{xy}, \quad z_{yx}, \quad z_{yy}$$

respectively.

Example 3.1

Given $z = 3xy^3 - 2xy$ find all the second partial derivatives of z.

Solution

First of all the first partial derivatives must be found.

$$\frac{\partial z}{\partial x} = 3y^3 - 2y, \quad \frac{\partial z}{\partial y} = 9xy^2 - 2x$$

Then each of these is differentiated with respect to x:

$$\frac{\partial}{\partial x}\left(\frac{\partial z}{\partial x}\right) = \frac{\partial}{\partial x}(3y^3 - 2y) = 0. \text{ Thus } \frac{\partial^2 z}{\partial x^2} = 0.$$

$$\frac{\partial}{\partial x}\left(\frac{\partial z}{\partial y}\right) = \frac{\partial}{\partial x}(9xy^2 - 2x) = 9y^2 - 2. \text{ Thus } \frac{\partial^2 z}{\partial x \partial y} = 9y^2 - 2.$$

Now, each of the first partial derivatives must be differentiated with respect to y.

$$\frac{\partial}{\partial y}\left(\frac{\partial z}{\partial x}\right) = \frac{\partial}{\partial y}(3y^3 - 2y) = 9y^2 - 2. \text{ Thus } \frac{\partial^2 z}{\partial y \partial x} = 9y^2 - 2.$$

$$\frac{\partial}{\partial y}\left(\frac{\partial z}{\partial y}\right) = \frac{\partial}{\partial y}(9xy^2 - 2x) = 18xy. \text{ Thus } \frac{\partial^2 z}{\partial y^2} = 18xy.$$

Note that $\frac{\partial^2 z}{\partial y \partial x} = \frac{\partial^2 z}{\partial x \partial y}$. It is usually the case that the result is the same either way.

Example 3.2

Find all second partial derivatives of $z = \sin(xy)$.

Solution

First of all the first partial derivatives are found.

$$\frac{\partial z}{\partial x} = y\cos(xy), \quad \frac{\partial z}{\partial y} = x\cos(xy)$$

Then each of these is differentiated with respect to x:

$$\frac{\partial^2 z}{\partial x^2} = \frac{\partial}{\partial x}\left(\frac{\partial z}{\partial x}\right) = -y^2 \sin(xy)$$

$$\frac{\partial^2 z}{\partial x \partial y} = \frac{\partial}{\partial x}\left(\frac{\partial z}{\partial y}\right) = -xy\sin(xy) + \cos(xy)$$

Note here the need to use the product rule to differentiate $x\cos(xy)$ with respect to x. Now, each of the first partial derivatives must be differentiated with respect to y.

$$\frac{\partial^2 z}{\partial y \partial x} = \frac{\partial}{\partial y}\left(\frac{\partial z}{\partial x}\right) = -xy\sin(xy) + \cos(xy)$$

$$\frac{\partial^2 z}{\partial y^2} = \frac{\partial}{\partial y}\left(\frac{\partial z}{\partial y}\right) = -x^2 \sin(xy)$$

Example 3.3

Consider the function $\phi(x, y) = 2xy$.

(a) Find $\dfrac{\partial \phi}{\partial x}$, $\dfrac{\partial \phi}{\partial y}$, $\dfrac{\partial^2 \phi}{\partial x^2}$ and $\dfrac{\partial^2 \phi}{\partial y^2}$.

(b) Using the result of part (a) evaluate $\dfrac{\partial^2 \phi}{\partial x^2} + \dfrac{\partial^2 \phi}{\partial y^2}$

Solution

(a) $\dfrac{\partial \phi}{\partial x} = \square$, $\dfrac{\partial \phi}{\partial y} = \square$ — $2y$ $2x$

$\dfrac{\partial^2 \phi}{\partial x^2} = \square$, $\dfrac{\partial^2 \phi}{\partial y^2} = \square$ — $0, 0$

(b) $\dfrac{\partial^2 \phi}{\partial x^2} + \dfrac{\partial^2 \phi}{\partial y^2} = \square$ — 0

Note from the last result that $\phi = 2xy$ satisfies the equation $\frac{\partial^2 \phi}{\partial x^2} + \frac{\partial^2 \phi}{\partial y^2} = 0$. This equation is a **partial differential equation**. It occurs in the modelling of heat conduction, fluid flow and electrostatics problems, and is known as **Laplace's equation**.

Exercises

1 Find all the second partial derivatives in each of the following cases:
(a) $z = xy$ (b) $z = 7xy$
(c) $z = 8x + 9y + 10$
(d) $z = 8y^2x + 11$ (e) $z = -2y^3x^2$
(f) $z = x + y$

2 Find all the second partial derivatives in each of the following cases:
(a) $z = \frac{1}{x}$ (b) $z = \frac{y}{x}$ (c) $z = \frac{x}{y}$ (d) $z = \frac{1}{x} + \frac{1}{y}$

3 Find all the second partial derivatives in each of the following cases:
(a) $z = x \sin y$ (b) $z = y \cos x$
(c) $z = ye^{2x}$ (d) $z = ye^{-x}$

4 Find all the second partial derivatives in each of the following cases:
(a) $z = 8e^{xy}$ (b) $z = -3e^x \sin y$
(c) $z = 4e^y \cos x$

5 Find all the second partial derivatives in each of the following cases:
(a) $z = \ln x$ (b) $z = \ln y$ (c) $z = \ln xy$
(d) $z = x \ln y$ (e) $z = y \ln x$

Solutions to exercises

1 (a) $\dfrac{\partial^2 z}{\partial x^2} = 0$, $\dfrac{\partial^2 z}{\partial x \partial y} = \dfrac{\partial^2 z}{\partial y \partial x} = 1$, $\dfrac{\partial^2 z}{\partial y^2} = 0$
(b) 0, 7, 0 (c) 0, 0, 0 (d) 0, $16y$, $16x$
(e) $-4y^3$, $-12y^2x$, $-12yx^2$ (f) 0, 0, 0

2 (a) $\dfrac{2}{x^3}$, 0, 0 (b) $\dfrac{2y}{x^3}$, $-\dfrac{1}{x^2}$, 0 (c) 0, $-\dfrac{1}{y^2}$, $\dfrac{2x}{y^3}$
(d) $\dfrac{2}{x^3}$, 0, $\dfrac{2}{y^3}$

3 (a) $0, \cos y, -x \sin y$ (b) $-y \cos x, -\sin x, 0$ (c) $4ye^{2x}, 2e^{2x}, 0$ (d) $ye^{-x}, -e^{-x}, 0$

4 (a) $8y^2e^{xy}, 8e^{xy}(xy + 1), 8x^2e^{xy}$ (b) $-3e^x \sin y, -3e^x \cos y, 3e^x \sin y$ (c) $-4e^y \cos x, -4e^y \sin x, 4e^y \cos x$

5 (a) $-\dfrac{1}{x^2}, 0, 0$ (b) $0, 0, -\dfrac{1}{y^2}$ (c) $-\dfrac{1}{x^2}, 0, -\dfrac{1}{y^2}$ (d) $0, \dfrac{1}{y}, -\dfrac{x}{y^2}$ (e) $-\dfrac{y}{x^2}, \dfrac{1}{x}, 0$

End of block exercises

1 If $u(x, t) = e^{-2t} \cos x$ find $\dfrac{\partial u}{\partial t}$ and $\dfrac{\partial^2 u}{\partial x^2}$. Verify that $\dfrac{\partial u}{\partial t} = 2\dfrac{\partial^2 u}{\partial x^2}$: that is, verify that u satisfies this partial differential equation, called the **heat equation**.

2 Verify that $u = x^2 + 4t^2$ satisfies the **wave equation** $\dfrac{\partial^2 u}{\partial t^2} = 4\dfrac{\partial^2 u}{\partial x^2}$.

BLOCK 4

Stationary values of a function of two variables

4.1 Introduction

When studying functions of a single variable we used differentiation to locate the positions of maximum and minimum points. We now extend this technique to functions of two variables.

4.2 Maxima, minima and saddle points

Figure 4.1 shows a graph of the function $z = f(x, y) = -x^2 - y^2$. The point labelled A is called a **maximum point**. If we were to move away from the maximum point in any direction but remain on the surface, the value of the function would decrease.

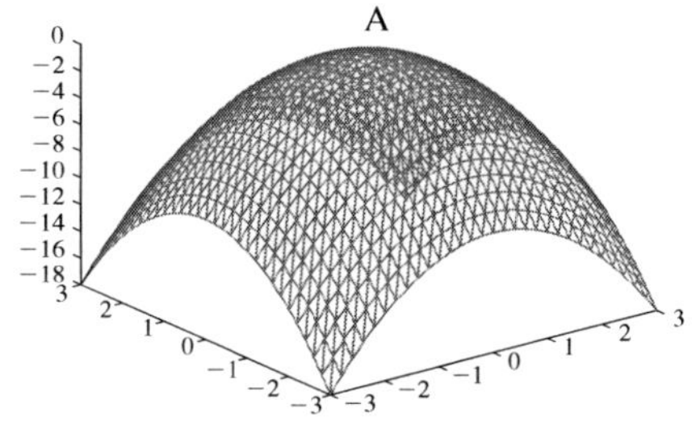

Figure 4.1 Point A is a maximum point. It is the highest point in its locality.

Figure 4.2 shows a graph of the function $z = f(x, y) = x^2 + y^2$. The point labelled B is called a **minimum point**. If we were to move away from the minimum point in any direction but remain on the surface, the value of the function would increase.

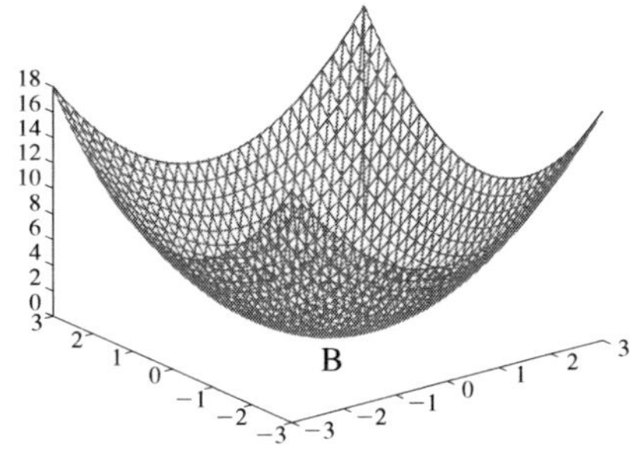

Figure 4.2 Point B is a minimum point. It is the lowest point in its locality.

Figure 4.3 shows a graph of the function $z = f(x, y) = 3xy + x + y$. The point labelled C is called a **saddle point**. When leaving a saddle point in one direction the function increases; when leaving in the perpendicular direction the function decreases.

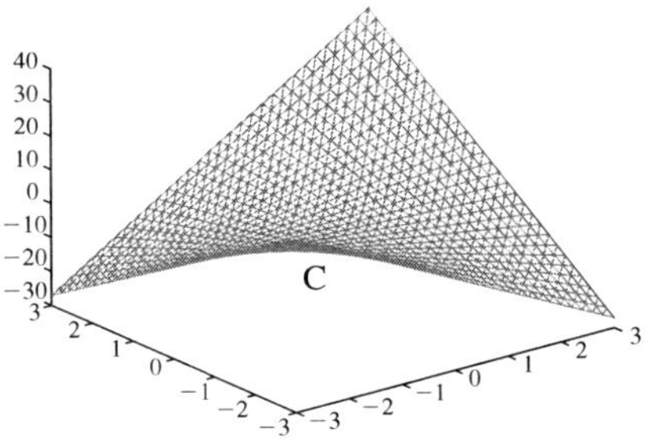

Figure 4.3
Point C is a saddle point.

Collectively, maximum points, minimum points and saddle points are known as **stationary points** of the function f.

4.3 Finding the location of stationary points

To locate stationary points both first partial derivatives are equated to zero: that is, we solve

$$\frac{\partial f}{\partial x} = 0 \quad \text{and} \quad \frac{\partial f}{\partial y} = 0$$

Key point

Stationary points are located by solving

$$\frac{\partial f}{\partial x} = 0 \quad \text{and} \quad \frac{\partial f}{\partial y} = 0$$

Example 4.1

Find the coordinates of any stationary points of the function $f(x, y) = x^2 + y^2$.

Solution

We begin by noting that stationary points are located by solving $\frac{\partial f}{\partial x} = 0$ and $\frac{\partial f}{\partial y} = 0$ and so we find the first partial derivatives of f. If $f = x^2 + y^2$ then $\frac{\partial f}{\partial x} = 2x$ and $\frac{\partial f}{\partial y} = 2y$. Equating these to zero produces two simultaneous equations: $2x = 0$ and $2y = 0$. Solving these we find $x = 0$ and $y = 0$. These are the x and y coordinates of the stationary point. The z coordinate is obtained using $z = x^2 + y^2$ and so $z = 0$ also. The graph of this function is shown in Figure 4.2, from which we note that the stationary point is a minimum.

Example 4.2

Find the coordinates of any stationary points of the function $f(x, y) = x^2 + xy - 7y$.

Solution

First of all find the partial derivatives of f and equate both of these derivatives to zero:

$\frac{\partial f}{\partial x} =$ $2x + y = 0$

$\frac{\partial f}{\partial y} =$ $x - 7 = 0$

Solve the resulting simultaneous equations. From the second equation

$x =$ 7

Substitution in the first equation gives $y = -14$.
Therefore a stationary point occurs at $(7, -14)$. The z coordinate is found from $z = x^2 + xy - 7y$.

$z =$ 49

Example 4.3

Find the coordinates of any stationary points of $f(x, y) = 2x^2 + 3xy - y^2 - 2x$.

Solution

First of all find the partial derivatives of f and equate these to zero.

$\frac{\partial f}{\partial x} = 0$ $4x + 3y - 2 = 0$

$\frac{\partial f}{\partial y} = 0$ $3x - 2y = 0$

Solving the simultaneous equations gives

$x =$, $y =$ $\frac{4}{17}, \frac{6}{17}$

Therefore a stationary point occurs at $\left(\frac{4}{17}, \frac{6}{17}\right)$. The z coordinate is found from $z = 2x^2 + 3xy - y^2 - 2x$.

$z =$ $-4/17$

Exercises

Locate the position of any stationary points of the following functions:

1 $f(x, y) = x^2 + y^3 - 3y$

2 $f(x, y) = 4xy - 2x^2y$

3 $f(x, y) = -x - y^3$

4 $f(x, y) = \frac{x^3}{3} + 3x^2 + xy + \frac{y^2}{2} + 6y$

Solutions to exercises

1 (0, 1) and (0, −1)

2 (0, 0) and (2, 0)

3 none

4 (1, −7) and (−6, 0)

4.4 The nature of stationary points

Equating the first partial derivatives to zero locates the stationary points but does not identify them as maximum points, minimum points or points of inflexion. To distinguish between such points we can make use of a test that involves second partial derivatives.

We consider the expression

$$\frac{\partial^2 f}{\partial x^2}\frac{\partial^2 f}{\partial y^2} - \left(\frac{\partial^2 f}{\partial x \partial y}\right)^2$$

We evaluate this expression at each of the stationary points.

- If the result is negative the stationary point is a saddle point.
- If the result is positive and if $\frac{\partial^2 f}{\partial x^2}$ is positive we have a minimum point.
- If the result is positive and if $\frac{\partial^2 f}{\partial x^2}$ is negative we have a maximum point.
- If the result is zero, this test fails and further tests are required that are beyond the scope of this book.

In summary:

Key point

The nature of a stationary point is determined using the following test:

$$\frac{\partial^2 f}{\partial x^2}\frac{\partial^2 f}{\partial y^2} - \left(\frac{\partial^2 f}{\partial x \partial y}\right)^2 < 0 \quad \text{saddle point}$$

$$\frac{\partial^2 f}{\partial x^2}\frac{\partial^2 f}{\partial y^2} - \left(\frac{\partial^2 f}{\partial x \partial y}\right)^2 > 0 \quad \text{and} \quad \frac{\partial^2 f}{\partial x^2} > 0 \quad \text{minimum point}$$

$$\frac{\partial^2 f}{\partial x^2}\frac{\partial^2 f}{\partial y^2} - \left(\frac{\partial^2 f}{\partial x \partial y}\right)^2 > 0 \quad \text{and} \quad \frac{\partial^2 f}{\partial x^2} < 0 \quad \text{maximum point}$$

Example 4.4

Locate and identify the nature of the stationary values of

$$f(x, y) = x^2 + xy - 7y$$

Solution

This function has been discussed already in Example 4.2. We found that a stationary point was located at (7, −14).

We now determine its nature. For this we need to calculate the second derivatives. Recall that $\frac{\partial f}{\partial x} = 2x + y$ and $\frac{\partial f}{\partial y} = x - 7$.

$$\frac{\partial^2 f}{\partial x^2} = \square$$ 2

$$\frac{\partial^2 f}{\partial y^2} = \square$$ 0

$$\frac{\partial^2 f}{\partial x \partial y} = \square$$ 1

We then consider the quantity $\frac{\partial^2 f}{\partial x^2}\frac{\partial^2 f}{\partial y^2} - \left(\frac{\partial^2 f}{\partial x \partial y}\right)^2$. In this case we have

$$\frac{\partial^2 f}{\partial x^2}\frac{\partial^2 f}{\partial y^2} - \left(\frac{\partial^2 f}{\partial x \partial y}\right)^2 = (2)(0) - (1)^2 = -1$$

Then, from the key point on page 1018 we deduce that this stationary point is a

saddle point

Exercises

Determine the position and nature of the stationary points of the following functions:

1. $f(x, y) = 3xy + x + y$
2. $f(x, y) = x^2 + y^2 - 3y$
3. $f(x, y) = x^2 + y^2 - 3xy$
4. $f(x, y) = \frac{1}{x} + \frac{1}{y} - \frac{3}{xy}$
5. $f(x, y) = e^{xy}$

Solutions to exercises

1. Saddle at $(-1/3, -1/3)$
2. Minimum at $(0, 3/2)$
3. Saddle at $(0, 0)$
4. Saddle at $(3, 3)$
5. Saddle at $(0, 0)$

End of block exercises

Determine the position and nature of the stationary points of the following functions:

1. $f(x, y) = xy + x + y^2$
2. $f(x, y) = -x^2 - y^2 - 3y$

3 $f(x, y) = 7x - 2y^2 - xy$

4 $f(x, y) = \frac{1}{x} + \frac{1}{y} + \frac{1}{xy}$

5 $f(x, y) = e^{-x(y-1)}$

Solutions to exercises

1 Saddle at $(2, -1)$

2 Maximum at $(0, -3/2)$

3 Saddle at $(-28, 7)$

4 Saddle at $(-1, -1)$

5 Saddle at $(0, 1)$

End of chapter exercises

1 If $z = 14x - 13y$ state $\dfrac{\partial z}{\partial x}$ and $\dfrac{\partial z}{\partial y}$.

2 If $w = 5y - 2x$ state $\dfrac{\partial^2 w}{\partial x^2}$ and $\dfrac{\partial^2 w}{\partial y^2}$.

3 If $z = 3x^2 + 7xy - y^2$ find $\dfrac{\partial^2 z}{\partial y \partial x}$ and $\dfrac{\partial^2 z}{\partial x \partial y}$.

4 If $z = 14 - 4xy$ evaluate $\dfrac{\partial z}{\partial x}$ and $\dfrac{\partial z}{\partial y}$ at the point $(1, 2)$.

5 If $z = 4e^{5xy}$ find $\dfrac{\partial z}{\partial x}$ and $\dfrac{\partial z}{\partial y}$.

6 If $y = x \cos t$ find $\dfrac{\partial y}{\partial x}$ and $\dfrac{\partial y}{\partial t}$.

7 If $w = 3xy^2 + 2yz^2$ find all first partial derivatives of w at the point with coordinates $(1, 2, 3)$.

8 If $V = D^{1/4}T^{-5/6}$ find $\dfrac{\partial V}{\partial T}$ and $\dfrac{\partial V}{\partial D}$.

9 If $p = \dfrac{RT}{V}$ where R is a constant, find $\dfrac{\partial p}{\partial V}$ and $\dfrac{\partial p}{\partial T}$.

10 Find $\dfrac{\partial f}{\partial x}, \dfrac{\partial f}{\partial y}, \dfrac{\partial^2 f}{\partial x^2}, \dfrac{\partial^2 f}{\partial y^2}$ and $\dfrac{\partial^2 f}{\partial x \partial y}$ if $f = (x - y)^2$.

11 Calculate $\dfrac{\partial z}{\partial x}$ when (a) $z = \dfrac{y}{x^2} - \dfrac{x}{y^2}$, (b) $z = e^{x^2 - 4xy}$.

12 Calculate $\dfrac{\partial z}{\partial y}$ when $z = \dfrac{x^2 - 3y^2}{x^2 + y^2}$.

13 If $T = \dfrac{\pi \mu \Omega h D^3}{4c}$ find $\dfrac{\partial T}{\partial D}$ and $\dfrac{\partial T}{\partial c}$.

14 Given $f(x, y) = \sin 4x \cos 3y$ find $\dfrac{\partial^2 f}{\partial x^2}, \dfrac{\partial^2 f}{\partial y^2}$ and $\dfrac{\partial^2 f}{\partial x \partial y}$.

15 Determine the stationary points of $f(x, y) = 2x^2 + 3y^2 + 5x + 12y + 19$.

16 Consider the function $f(x, y) = 5x^2y$.
(a) Evaluate this function and its first partial derivatives at the point A(2, 3).
(b) Suppose we consider point A. Suppose small changes, δx, δy, are made in the values of x and y so that we move to a nearby point B. It is possible to show that the corresponding change in f is given approximately by $\delta f \approx \dfrac{\partial f}{\partial x}\delta x + \dfrac{\partial f}{\partial y}\delta y$, where the partial derivatives are evaluated at the original point A. Use this result to find the approximate change in the value of f if x is increased to 2.1 and y is increased to 3.2.
(c) Compare your answer in (b) to the value of f at (2.1, 3.2).

Solutions to exercises

1 14, −13

2 0, 0

3 7, 7

4 −8, −4

5 $20ye^{5xy}$, $20xe^{5xy}$

6 $\cos t$, $-x \sin t$

7 12, 30, 24

8 $-\frac{5}{6}D^{1/4}T^{-11/6}, \frac{1}{4}D^{-3/4}T^{-5/6}$

9 $-\dfrac{RT}{V^2}, \dfrac{R}{V}$

10 $2(x-y), -2(x-y), 2, 2, -2$

11 (a) $-\dfrac{2y}{x^3} - \dfrac{1}{y^2}$ (b) $(2x - 4y)e^{x^2-4xy}$

12 $-\dfrac{8yx^2}{(x^2+y^2)^2}$

13 $\dfrac{3\pi\mu\Omega h D^2}{4c}, -\dfrac{\pi\mu\Omega h D^3}{4c^2}$

14 $-16 \sin 4x \cos 3y, -9 \sin 4x \cos 3y, -12 \cos 4x \sin 3y$

15 Minimum at $(-5/4, -2)$

16 (a) 60, 60, 20
(b) $\partial f = (60)(0.1) + (20)(0.2) = 10$
(c) From part (b) the approximate value of f at the new point is $60 + 10 = 70$. The exact value is $f(2.1, 3.2) = 70.56$.

Computer and calculator exercises

1 Investigate how to find the first partial derivatives of the function $f(x, y) = \tan^{-1}xy$ using a computer algebra package.

2 Use a computer algebra package to find $\dfrac{\partial^2 u}{\partial x^2}, \dfrac{\partial^2 u}{\partial y^2}, \dfrac{\partial u}{\partial z}$ when $u(x, y, z) = \dfrac{1}{z}e^{-\frac{x^2+y^2}{4z}}$

From your results show that u is a solution of the equation

$$\frac{\partial^2 u}{\partial x^2} + \frac{\partial^2 u}{\partial y^2} = \frac{\partial u}{\partial z}$$

Solutions to exercises

1 $\dfrac{y}{1+x^2y^2}, \dfrac{x}{1+x^2y^2}$.

2
$$\frac{\partial^2 u}{\partial x^2} = -\frac{e^{\left(-\frac{x^2+y^2}{4z}\right)}}{2z^2} + \frac{x^2 e^{\left(-\frac{x^2+y^2}{4z}\right)}}{4z^3},$$

$$\frac{\partial^2 u}{\partial y^2} = -\frac{e^{\left(-\frac{x^2+y^2}{4z}\right)}}{2z^2} + \frac{y^2 e^{\left(-\frac{x^2+y^2}{4z}\right)}}{4z^3},$$

$$\frac{\partial u}{\partial z} = -\frac{e^{\left(-\frac{x^2+y^2}{4z}\right)}}{z^2} + \frac{(x^2+y^2)e^{\left(-\frac{x^2+y^2}{4z}\right)}}{4z^3}$$

The Laplace transform

Chapter 22

The **Laplace transform** is an integral transform: that is, it is defined by an integral. Given a function, $f(t)$, the Laplace transform of $f(t)$ is a function $F(s)$ defined by

$$F(s) = \int_0^\infty e^{-st} f(t)\,dt$$

The original function, $f(t)$, has been transformed into a new function, $F(s)$.

As with differentiation and integration, most Laplace transforms are calculated from a table of standard functions. This is covered in Block 1. Block 2 deals with the **inverse Laplace transform**. Here we know the transformed function, $F(s)$, and we seek the original function, $f(t)$.

The chapter closes with Block 3, which illustrates the application of the transform to the solution of **differential equations**. Both first- and second-order linear constant-coefficient equations can be solved using the Laplace transform. This method has the advantage that initial conditions are automatically incorporated into the solution.

Chapter 22 contents

BLOCK 1 The Laplace transform

1.1 Introduction

In mathematics the word 'transform' has the same meaning as in everyday language. The Laplace transform is one of a number of integral transforms used by engineers.

The Laplace transform can be used to solve a linear constant-coefficient differential equation by transforming it into an algebraic equation. The resulting algebraic equation is solved and then the transform is reversed to find the solution of the differential equation in terms of the original variable.

The Laplace transform can also be used to calculate transfer functions. These functions describe the elements of an engineering system and are particularly important in the design of control systems.

1.2 Definition of the Laplace transform

Let $f(t)$ be a function of time, t. In many engineering problems t has only non-negative values, that is $t \geq 0$. Hence $f(t)$ will be given for $t \geq 0$, and for $t < 0$, $f(t)$ is assumed to be zero.

Key point

The **Laplace transform** of $f(t)$ is $F(s)$ and is defined by

$$F(s) = \int_0^\infty e^{-st} f(t)\, dt$$

So, to find the Laplace transform of a function $f(t)$, we multiply it by e^{-st} and then integrate between the limits 0 and ∞. Because of the infinite limit of integration, restrictions sometimes need to be placed on s to ensure that the integral exists. Throughout this chapter it is assumed that s has a value such that this condition is satisfied.

Note that although f is a function of t, the Laplace transform is a function of a new variable, s. It is conventional to use a lower-case letter for the function of t, as in $f(t)$, but an upper-case letter for the function of s, as in $F(s)$. In addition, we often write $\mathcal{L}\{f(t)\}$ to denote the Laplace transform of the function $f(t)$.

Example 1.1
Calculate the Laplace transform of $f(t) = 3$.

Solution

$$\begin{aligned} F(s) &= \int_0^{\infty} e^{-st}\, 3\, dt \\ &= 3\int_0^{\infty} e^{-st}\, dt \\ &= 3\left[\frac{e^{-st}}{-s}\right]_0^{\infty} \\ &= 3\left[0 + \frac{1}{s}\right] \\ &= \frac{3}{s} \end{aligned}$$

Hence we may write $\mathcal{L}\{3\} = \dfrac{3}{s}$.

Exercises

1 Write down the definition of the Laplace transform of a function $f(t)$.

2 Given a function $f(t)$, write two ways in which its Laplace transform might be expressed.

3 If x is a function of t, that is $x(t)$, how would you write its Laplace transform?

4 If y is a function of t, that is $y(t)$, how would you write its Laplace transform?

5 Use integration by parts to show that the Laplace transform of $f(t) = t$ is $\dfrac{1}{s^2}$.

6 Show that $\mathcal{L}\{e^t\} = \dfrac{1}{s-1}$.
(Hint: write $e^t e^{-st}$ as $e^{(1-s)t}$.)

Solutions to exercises

2 $\mathcal{L}\{f(t)\}$ or $F(s)$

3 $\mathcal{L}\{x(t)\}$ or $X(s)$

4 $\mathcal{L}\{y(t)\}$ or $Y(s)$

1.3 Using a table of Laplace transforms

Although the Laplace transforms of most functions can be calculated from the definition, most engineers use a table. Table 1.1 lists some common functions and their Laplace transforms.

Table 1.1

Function, $f(t)$	Laplace transform, $\mathcal{L}\{f(t)\} = F(s)$	Function, $f(t)$	Laplace transform, $\mathcal{L}\{f(t)\} = F(s)$
1	$\frac{1}{s}$	$\sinh bt$	$\frac{b}{s^2 - b^2}$
t	$\frac{1}{s^2}$	$\cosh bt$	$\frac{s}{s^2 - b^2}$
t^2	$\frac{2}{s^3}$	$e^{-at} \sinh bt$	$\frac{b}{(s + a)^2 - b^2}$
t^n	$\frac{n!}{s^{n+1}}$	$e^{-at} \cosh bt$	$\frac{s + a}{(s + a)^2 - b^2}$
e^{at}	$\frac{1}{s - a}$	$t \sin bt$	$\frac{2bs}{(s^2 + b^2)^2}$
e^{-at}	$\frac{1}{s + a}$	$t \cos bt$	$\frac{s^2 - b^2}{(s^2 + b^2)^2}$
$t^n e^{-at}$	$\frac{n!}{(s + a)^{n+1}}$	$u(t)$, unit step	$\frac{1}{s}$
$\sin bt$	$\frac{b}{s^2 + b^2}$	$u(t - d)$	$\frac{e^{-sd}}{s}$
$\cos bt$	$\frac{s}{s^2 + b^2}$	$\delta(t)$	1
$e^{-at} \sin bt$	$\frac{b}{(s + a)^2 + b^2}$	$\delta(t - d)$	e^{-sd}
$e^{-at} \cos bt$	$\frac{s + a}{(s + a)^2 + b^2}$		

Example 1.2

Use Table 1.1 to find the Laplace transform of each of the following functions:
(a) t^4 (b) e^{2t} (c) e^{-3t} (d) $t^2 e^{3t}$ (e) $\sin 2t$ (f) $\cos 5t$ (g) $e^{-t} \sin t$

Solution

(a) We use the result for $f(t) = t^n$ and put $n = 4$. The required Laplace transform is then

$$F(s) = \frac{4!}{s^{4+1}}$$

$$= \frac{4!}{s^5}$$

$$= \frac{24}{s^5}$$

We may write

$$\mathcal{L}\{t^4\} = \frac{24}{s^5}$$

(b) Using the result for e^{at} with $a = 2$ we find

$$\mathcal{L}\{e^{2t}\} = \qquad\qquad \frac{1}{s-2}$$

(c) Using the result for e^{-at} with $a = 3$ we have

$$\mathcal{L}\{e^{-3t}\} = \frac{1}{s+3}$$

(d) We use the result for $t^n e^{-at}$ when $n = 2$ and $a = -3$ to obtain

$$\mathcal{L}\{t^2 e^{3t}\} = \qquad\qquad \frac{2!}{(s-3)^3} = \frac{2}{(s-3)^3}$$

(e) $\mathcal{L}\{\sin 2t\} = \dfrac{2}{s^2+4}$

(f) $\mathcal{L}\{\cos 5t\} =$ $\qquad\qquad$ $\dfrac{s}{s^2+25}$

(g) $\mathcal{L}\{e^{-t}\sin t\} = \dfrac{1}{(s+1)^2+1}$

Example 1.3

Find the Laplace transform of each of the following functions:
(a) $e^{t/2}$ (b) $e^{2t}\cos t$ (c) $t^3 e^{2t}$

Solution

(a) We use the result for e^{at} and take $a = \frac{1}{2}$.

$$\mathcal{L}\{e^{t/2}\} = \qquad\qquad \frac{1}{s-\frac{1}{2}}$$

(b) We use the result for $e^{-at}\cos bt$. We take

$a =$ $\qquad$, $b =$ $\qquad\qquad$ -2, 1

so

$$\mathcal{L}\{e^{2t}\cos t\} = \qquad \frac{s-2}{(s-2)^2+1}$$

(c) We use the result for $\quad t^n e^{-at}$

We take

$n = \quad , \quad a = \qquad 3, \; -2$

Hence

$$\mathcal{L}\{t^3 e^{2t}\} = \qquad \frac{6}{(s-2)^4}$$

Exercises

1 Use Table 1.1 to find the Laplace transform of the following:
(a) t^5 (b) $\cos 4t$ (c) e^{9t} (d) e^{-6t} (e) $\sin 5t$

2 Find the Laplace transform of each of the following:
(a) $e^{-3t}\sin 5t$ (b) $e^{3t}\cos 2t$
(c) $t\sin 4t$ (d) $t\cos\frac{t}{2}$ (e) t^2e^{-5t}

3 Find the Laplace transform of each of the following:
(a) $e^{2t/3}$ (b) $\frac{t^2}{e^{4t}}$ (c) $\frac{\sin 5t}{e^{6t}}$ (d) $e^{t/2}\cos\frac{t}{2}$
(e) $e^{4t}\sin\frac{2t}{3}$

Solutions to exercises

1 (a) $\frac{5!}{s^6}$ (b) $\frac{s}{s^2+16}$ (c) $\frac{1}{s-9}$ (d) $\frac{1}{s+6}$
(e) $\frac{5}{s^2+25}$

2 (a) $\frac{5}{(s+3)^2+25}$ (b) $\frac{s-3}{(s-3)^2+4}$
(c) $\frac{8s}{(s^2+16)^2}$ (d) $\frac{s^2-0.25}{(s^2+0.25)^2}$
(e) $\frac{2!}{(s+5)^3}$

3 (a) $\frac{3}{3s-2}$ (b) $\frac{2}{(s+4)^3}$ (c) $\frac{5}{(s+6)^2+25}$
(d) $\frac{s-0.5}{(s-0.5)^2+0.25}$ (e) $\frac{6}{9(s-4)^2+4}$

1.4 Properties of the Laplace transform

Since the Laplace transform is defined in terms of an integral it comes as no surprise that some of the properties of integrals are also properties of the Laplace transform. We note two of these properties.

Key point

$$\mathcal{L}\{f + g\} = \mathcal{L}\{f\} + \mathcal{L}\{g\}$$

$$\mathcal{L}\{kf\} = k\mathcal{L}\{f\} \quad \text{if } k \text{ is a constant}$$

The first property states that to find the Laplace transform of two functions added together we simply find the transform of each individual function and then add together these transforms.

The second property states that when a function, f, is multiplied by a constant, k, the corresponding transform is also multiplied by the same constant.

Together, these properties mean that the Laplace transform is what is known as a **linear transform**.

Example 1.4

Find the Laplace transform of each of the following functions:
(a) 3 (b) $3 + 2t$ (c) $3 + 2t - 5t^2$

Solution

(a) We think of 3 as 3(1). From Table 1.1

$$\mathcal{L}\{1\} = \frac{1}{s}$$

and so, by property 2,

$$\mathcal{L}\{3\} = 3\left(\frac{1}{s}\right) = \frac{3}{s}$$

(b) We note that

$$\mathcal{L}\{t\} = \frac{1}{s^2}$$

and so, using property 2,

$\mathcal{L}\{2t\} =$

$\frac{2}{s^2}$

Finally, using property 1,

$$\mathcal{L}\{3 + 2t\} = \mathcal{L}\{3\} + \mathcal{L}\{2t\} = \frac{3}{s} + \frac{2}{s^2}$$

(c) $\mathcal{L}\{3 + 2t - 5t^2\} = \mathcal{L}\{3\} + \mathcal{L}\{2t\} - \mathcal{L}\{5t^2\}$

$$= \qquad \frac{3}{s} + \frac{2}{s^2} - \frac{10}{s^3}$$

Example 1.5

Find the Laplace transform of (a) $\dfrac{e^{3t}}{2} - 6\sin 2t$, (b) $\dfrac{1}{3}\cos 6t - 2e^{-t}\sin t$.

Solution

(a) From Table 1.1

$$L\{e^{3t}\} = \frac{1}{s-3}$$

and so

$$\mathcal{L}\left\{\frac{e^{3t}}{2}\right\} = \qquad \frac{1}{2(s-3)}$$

Similarly

$$\mathcal{L}\{\sin 2t\} = \qquad \frac{2}{s^2+4}$$

and so

$$\mathcal{L}\{6\sin 2t\} = \qquad \frac{12}{s^2+4}$$

Finally

$$\mathcal{L}\left\{\frac{e^{3t}}{2} - 6\sin 2t\right\} = \frac{1}{2(s-3)} - \frac{12}{s^2+4}$$

(b) We know from Table 1.1 that

$$\mathcal{L}\{\cos 6t\} = \qquad \frac{s}{s^2+36}$$

and hence

$$\mathcal{L}\left\{\frac{1}{3}\cos 6t\right\} = \qquad \frac{s}{3(s^2+36)}$$

Similarly

$$\mathcal{L}\{e^{-t}\sin t\} = \qquad \frac{1}{(s+1)^2+1}$$

and so

$$\mathcal{L}\{2e^{-t}\sin t\} = \qquad \frac{2}{(s+1)^2+1}$$

So

$$\mathcal{L}\left\{\frac{1}{3}\cos 6t - 2e^{-t}\sin t\right\} = \frac{s}{3(s^2+36)} - \frac{2}{(s+1)^2+1}$$

Exercises

1. Explain what is meant by stating that the Laplace transform is a linear transform. Write down the two linearity properties.

2. Find the Laplace transform of
(a) $2 + 3t$ (b) $2t^2 - 3$ (c) $\frac{t^2}{2} - 6$
(d) $2t^3 - 3t^2 + 5t - 6$ (e) $2 - 4t^3 + 5t^5$

3. Find the Laplace transform of
(a) $4e^{2t} + 3e^{-2t}$ (b) $\frac{e^{3t}}{2} + 4e^t - 5e^{-t}$
(c) $1 - 3e^{-t} + \frac{2e^t}{3}$ (d) $2te^t - 3t^2e^{-t}$
(e) $2t - 3te^{-t} + 4$

4. Find the Laplace transform of each of the following:
(a) $3\sin 2t - 4t\sin 3t$
(b) $5\cos 3t + 3\sin 3t$
(c) $2 - 3\cos\frac{2t}{3} + 2t\cos 2t$
(d) $2e^t\cos 2t - 4e^t\sin 2t$
(e) $3e^{-2t}\sin 3t - 2e^{-2t}\cos 3t$

Solutions to exercises

1. $\mathcal{L}\{f+g\} = \mathcal{L}\{f\} + \mathcal{L}\{g\}$, $\mathcal{L}\{kf\} = k\mathcal{L}\{f\}$ if k is a constant.

2. (a) $\frac{2}{s} + \frac{3}{s^2}$ (b) $\frac{4}{s^3} - \frac{3}{s}$ (c) $\frac{1}{s^3} - \frac{6}{s}$
(d) $\frac{12}{s^4} - \frac{6}{s^3} + \frac{5}{s^2} - \frac{6}{s}$ (e) $\frac{2}{s} - \frac{24}{s^4} + \frac{600}{s^6}$

3. (a) $\frac{4}{s-2} + \frac{3}{s+2}$
(b) $\frac{1}{2(s-3)} + \frac{4}{s-1} - \frac{5}{s+1}$
(c) $\frac{1}{s} - \frac{3}{s+1} + \frac{2}{3(s-1)}$
(d) $\frac{2}{(s-1)^2} - \frac{6}{(s+1)^3}$
(e) $\frac{2}{s^2} - \frac{3}{(s+1)^2} + \frac{4}{s}$

4. (a) $\frac{6}{s^2+4} - \frac{24s}{(s^2+9)^2}$ (b) $\frac{5s}{s^2+9} + \frac{9}{s^2+9}$
(c) $\frac{2}{s} - \frac{3s}{s^2+\frac{4}{9}} + \frac{2(s^2-4)}{(s^2+4)^2}$
(d) $\frac{2(s-1)}{(s-1)^2+4} - \frac{8}{(s-1)^2+4}$
(e) $\frac{9}{(s+2)^2+9} - \frac{2(s+2)}{(s+2)^2+9}$

End of block exercises

1 Find the Laplace transform of each of the following:
(a) 7 (b) $\frac{2}{3}$ (c) -0.25 (d) $t-2$ (e) $\frac{2t-1}{3}$

2 Find the Laplace transform of the following:
(a) $0.6t$ (b) $6-6t$ (c) $2(t+1)$
(d) $(t+1)(t-1)$ (e) $3t^4-2$

3 Find the Laplace transform of the following:
(a) $2-3t^2e^{-3t}$ (b) $t(2-3t+4e^t)$
(c) $2t(\sin 3t-2\cos 3t)$ (d) $3e^{2t}(1-t+e^t)$
(e) $\cos 2t(e^{-t}+t-2)$

Solutions to exercises

1 (a) $\frac{7}{s}$ (b) $\frac{2}{3s}$ (c) $-\frac{1}{4s}$ (d) $\frac{1}{s^2}-\frac{2}{s}$
(e) $\frac{2}{3s^2}-\frac{1}{3s}$

2 (a) $\frac{0.6}{s^2}$ (b) $\frac{6}{s}-\frac{6}{s^2}$ (c) $2\left(\frac{1}{s^2}+\frac{1}{s}\right)$
(d) $\frac{2}{s^3}-\frac{1}{s}$ (e) $\frac{72}{s^5}-\frac{2}{s}$

3 (a) $\frac{2}{s}-\frac{6}{(s+3)^3}$ (b) $\frac{2}{s^2}-\frac{6}{s^3}+\frac{4}{(s-1)^2}$
(c) $2\left(\frac{6s}{(s^2+9)^2}-2\frac{(s^2-9)}{(s^2+9)^2}\right)$
(d) $3\left(\frac{1}{s-2}-\frac{1}{(s-2)^2}+\frac{1}{s-3}\right)$
(e) $\frac{s+1}{(s+1)^2+4}+\frac{s^2-4}{(s^2+4)^2}-\frac{2s}{s^2+4}$

and so

$$\mathcal{L}\{2e^{-t}\sin t\} = \frac{2}{(s+1)^2+1}$$

So

$$\mathcal{L}\left\{\frac{1}{3}\cos 6t - 2e^{-t}\sin t\right\} = \frac{s}{3(s^2+36)} - \frac{2}{(s+1)^2+1}$$

Exercises

1 Explain what is meant by stating that the Laplace transform is a linear transform. Write down the two linearity properties.

2 Find the Laplace transform of

(a) $2 + 3t$ (b) $2t^2 - 3$ (c) $\frac{t^2}{2} - 6$

(d) $2t^3 - 3t^2 + 5t - 6$ (e) $2 - 4t^3 + 5t^5$

3 Find the Laplace transform of

(a) $4e^{2t} + 3e^{-2t}$ (b) $\frac{e^{3t}}{2} + 4e^{t} - 5e^{-t}$

(c) $1 - 3e^{-t} + \frac{2e^{t}}{3}$ (d) $2te^{t} - 3t^2e^{-t}$

(e) $2t - 3te^{-t} + 4$

4 Find the Laplace transform of each of the following:

(a) $3\sin 2t - 4t\sin 3t$

(b) $5\cos 3t + 3\sin 3t$

(c) $2 - 3\cos\frac{2t}{3} + 2t\cos 2t$

(d) $2e^{t}\cos 2t - 4e^{t}\sin 2t$

(e) $3e^{-2t}\sin 3t - 2e^{-2t}\cos 3t$

Solutions to exercises

1 $\mathcal{L}\{f+g\} = \mathcal{L}\{f\} + \mathcal{L}\{g\}$, $\mathcal{L}\{kf\} = k\mathcal{L}\{f\}$ if k is a constant.

2 (a) $\frac{2}{s} + \frac{3}{s^2}$ (b) $\frac{4}{s^3} - \frac{3}{s}$ (c) $\frac{1}{s^3} - \frac{6}{s}$

(d) $\frac{12}{s^4} - \frac{6}{s^3} + \frac{5}{s^2} - \frac{6}{s}$ (e) $\frac{2}{s} - \frac{24}{s^4} + \frac{600}{s^6}$

3 (a) $\frac{4}{s-2} + \frac{3}{s+2}$

(b) $\frac{1}{2(s-3)} + \frac{4}{s-1} - \frac{5}{s+1}$

(c) $\frac{1}{s} - \frac{3}{s+1} + \frac{2}{3(s-1)}$

(d) $\frac{2}{(s-1)^2} - \frac{6}{(s+1)^3}$

(e) $\frac{2}{s^2} - \frac{3}{(s+1)^2} + \frac{4}{s}$

4 (a) $\frac{6}{s^2+4} - \frac{24s}{(s^2+9)^2}$ (b) $\frac{5s}{s^2+9} + \frac{9}{s^2+9}$

(c) $\frac{2}{s} - \frac{3s}{s^2+\frac{4}{9}} + \frac{2(s^2-4)}{(s^2+4)^2}$

(d) $\frac{2(s-1)}{(s-1)^2+4} - \frac{8}{(s-1)^2+4}$

(e) $\frac{9}{(s+2)^2+9} - \frac{2(s+2)}{(s+2)^2+9}$

BLOCK 2

The inverse Laplace transform

2.1 Introduction

In Block 1 we saw how to use Table 1.1 to find the Laplace transform of a variety of functions. Often, however, we know the Laplace transform of a function without knowing the actual function. In such cases we need to calculate the original function from knowledge of its Laplace transform: that is, we seek the **inverse Laplace transform**. This is the subject of this block.

2.2 Using Table 1.1 to find inverse Laplace transforms

To find the inverse Laplace transform we use Table 1.1 in Block 1. We write any given Laplace transform as the sum of standard expressions given in Table 1.1 and then find the inverse from the table. We use the notation $\mathcal{L}^{-1}$ to denote an inverse Laplace transform, so that

$$\text{if } \mathcal{L}\{f(t)\} = F(s), \quad \text{then } \mathcal{L}^{-1}\{F(s)\} = f(t)$$

In addition we shall make use of the following linearity properties:

Key point

$$\mathcal{L}^{-1}\{F + G\} = \mathcal{L}^{-1}\{F\} + \mathcal{L}^{-1}\{G\}$$

$$\mathcal{L}^{-1}\{kF\} = k\mathcal{L}^{-1}\{F\} \text{ if } k \text{ is a constant}$$

The first property states that to find the inverse Laplace transform of two functions added together we simply find the inverse transform of each individual function and then add together these inverse transforms.

The second property states that when a function, $F(s)$, is multiplied by a constant, k, the corresponding inverse transform is also multiplied by the same constant.

The technique is illustrated by examples.

Example 2.1

Find the inverse Laplace transform of

(a) $\frac{1}{s}$ (b) $\frac{4}{s}$ (c) $\frac{1}{2s}$

Solution

(a) From Table 1.1 we note that

$$\mathcal{L}\{1\} = \frac{1}{s}$$

Hence the inverse Laplace transform of $\frac{1}{s}$ is 1. We may write this compactly as

$$\mathcal{L}^{-1}\left\{\frac{1}{s}\right\} = 1$$

Thus the function, $f(t)$, whose Laplace transform is $\frac{1}{s}$, is $f(t) = 1$.

(b) We write $\frac{4}{s}$ as $4\left(\frac{1}{s}\right)$. From (a) we know $\mathcal{L}^{-1}\left\{\frac{1}{s}\right\} = 1$ and so

$$\begin{aligned}\mathcal{L}^{-1}\left\{\frac{4}{s}\right\} &= 4\mathcal{L}^{-1}\left\{\frac{1}{s}\right\}\\ &= 4(1)\\ &= 4\end{aligned}$$

Here we have made use of the second linearity property.

(c) We write $\frac{1}{2s}$ as $\frac{1}{2}\left(\frac{1}{s}\right)$ and so

$$\mathcal{L}^{-1}\left\{\frac{1}{2s}\right\} = \frac{1}{2}$$

Example 2.2

Find the inverse Laplace transform of

(a) $\frac{1}{s^2}$ (b) $\frac{3}{s^2}$ (c) $\frac{3}{s^2} - \frac{7}{s}$

Solution

(a) From Table 1.1 we note that $\mathcal{L}\{t\} = \frac{1}{s^2}$ and so

$$\mathcal{L}^{-1}\left\{\frac{1}{s^2}\right\} = t$$

The inverse Laplace transform of $\frac{1}{s^2}$ is t.

(b)

$$\begin{aligned}\mathcal{L}^{-1}\left\{\frac{3}{s^2}\right\} &= 3\mathcal{L}^{-1}\left\{\frac{1}{s^2}\right\}\\ &= 3t\end{aligned}$$

(c) First note that $\mathcal{L}^{-1}\left\{\frac{7}{s}\right\} = 7$. Then using the first linearity property we can write

$$\begin{aligned}\mathcal{L}^{-1}\left\{\frac{3}{s^2} - \frac{7}{s}\right\} &= \mathcal{L}^{-1}\left\{\frac{3}{s^2}\right\} - \mathcal{L}^{-1}\left\{\frac{7}{s}\right\}\\ &= 3t - 7\end{aligned}$$

Example 2.3

Find the inverse Laplace transform of

(a) $\dfrac{2}{s+1} - \dfrac{4}{s-2}$ (b) $\dfrac{3}{(s+1)^6}$

Solution

(a) Using Table 1.1 we see that

$$\mathcal{L}^{-1}\left\{\frac{1}{s+1}\right\} = e^{-t}$$

and so

$$\mathcal{L}^{-1}\left\{\frac{2}{s+1}\right\} = \quad\quad 2e^{-t}$$

Similarly

$$\mathcal{L}^{-1}\left\{\frac{4}{s-2}\right\} = \quad\quad 4e^{2t}$$

Hence

$$\mathcal{L}^{-1}\left\{\frac{2}{s+1} - \frac{4}{s-2}\right\} = \quad\quad 2e^{-t} - 4e^{2t}$$

(b) We note that

$$\mathcal{L}^{-1}\left\{\frac{5!}{(s+1)^6}\right\} = \quad\quad t^5e^{-t}$$

Noting that $5! = 120$, then

$$\mathcal{L}^{-1}\left\{\frac{3}{(s+1)^6}\right\} = \quad\quad \frac{t^5e^{-t}}{40}$$

Sometimes it is necessary to carry out some preliminary rewriting of a transform in order to be able to use Table 1.1. The best way to proceed is not always obvious, but doing plenty of practice exercises will help. Consider Example 2.4

Example 2.4

Find the inverse Laplace transform of

(a) $\dfrac{5}{(s+2)^2+9}$ (b) $\dfrac{s+2}{(s+2)^2+9}$ (c) $\dfrac{s+7}{(s+2)^2+9}$

Solution

(a) From Table 1.1 we see that

$$\mathcal{L}\{e^{-2t}\sin 3t\} = \quad\quad \frac{3}{(s+2)^2+9}$$

so that

$$\mathcal{L}^{-1}\left\{\frac{3}{(s+2)^2+9}\right\} = e^{-2t}\sin 3t$$

Hence

$$\mathcal{L}^{-1}\left\{\frac{5}{(s+2)^2+9}\right\} = \frac{5}{3}e^{-2t}\sin 3t$$

(b) $$\mathcal{L}^{-1}\left\{\frac{s+2}{(s+2)^2+9}\right\} = e^{-2t}\cos 3t$$

(c) We think of $\dfrac{s+7}{(s+2)^2+9}$ as

$$\frac{5}{(s+2)^2+9} + \frac{s+2}{(s+2)^2+9}$$

So

$$\mathcal{L}^{-1}\left\{\frac{s+7}{(s+2)^2+9}\right\} = \frac{5}{3}e^{-2t}\sin 3t + e^{-2t}\cos 3t$$

Exercises

1 Find the inverse Laplace transform of each of the following:

(a) $\dfrac{4}{s^2}$ (b) $-\dfrac{3}{s}$ (c) $\dfrac{5}{s^3}$ (d) $\dfrac{3}{s^5} - \dfrac{2}{s^4}$

(e) $\dfrac{1}{3s^5} - \dfrac{2}{3s^2}$

2 Find the inverse Laplace transform of

(a) $\dfrac{3}{s+2}$ (b) $\dfrac{-2}{s-1}$ (c) $\dfrac{2}{(s+2)^3}$

(d) $\dfrac{1}{s} + \dfrac{1}{s+1}$ (e) $\dfrac{1}{(s-3)^2} + \dfrac{1}{(s-3)^3}$

3 Find the inverse Laplace transform of

(a) $\dfrac{1}{2(s+3)}$ (b) $\dfrac{1}{2s+3}$ (c) $\dfrac{3s}{s^2+1}$

(d) $\dfrac{-6}{s^2+9}$ (e) $\dfrac{s+2}{s^2+4}$

4 Find the inverse Laplace transform of

(a) $\dfrac{s-1}{(s-1)^2+36}$ (b) $\dfrac{3}{(s+2)^2+9}$

(c) $\dfrac{-1}{(s-1)^2+4}$ (d) $\dfrac{s+5}{(s+2)^2+9}$

(e) $\dfrac{s+5}{(s+3)^2+4}$

Solutions to exercises

1 (a) $4t$ (b) -3 (c) $\dfrac{5t^2}{2}$ (d) $\dfrac{t^4}{8} - \dfrac{t^3}{3}$

(e) $\dfrac{t^4}{72} - \dfrac{2t}{3}$

2 (a) $3e^{-2t}$ (b) $-2e^t$ (c) t^2e^{-2t} (d) $1 + e^{-t}$

(e) $te^{3t} + \dfrac{t^2e^{3t}}{2}$

3 (a) $\dfrac{e^{-3t}}{2}$ (b) $\dfrac{e^{-1.5t}}{2}$ (c) $3\cos t$ (d) $-2\sin 3t$

(e) $\cos 2t + \sin 2t$

4 (a) $e^t\cos 6t$ (b) $e^{-2t}\sin 3t$ (c) $-\dfrac{e^t\sin 2t}{2}$

(d) $e^{-2t}\cos 3t + e^{-2t}\sin 3t$

(e) $e^{-3t}\cos 2t + e^{-3t}\sin 2t$

2.3 Inversions requiring completing the square

The technique of completing the square, which was described in Chapter 7, Block 2 is often used to rewrite Laplace transforms in alternative forms so that they can be inverted. Consider the following examples.

Example 2.5

Find the inverse Laplace transform of $\dfrac{1}{s^2 - 2s + 5}$.

Solution

By completing the square we write $s^2 - 2s + 5$ as $(s - 1)^2 + 4$, which is the same as $(s - 1)^2 + 2^2$. From Table 1.1

$$\mathcal{L}\{e^t \sin 2t\} = \frac{2}{(s-1)^2 + 2^2}$$

and so

$$\mathcal{L}^{-1}\left\{\frac{1}{(s-1)^2 + 2^2}\right\} = \frac{1}{2} e^t \sin 2t$$

Example 2.6

Find the inverse Laplace transform of $\dfrac{2s - 1}{s^2 + 6s + 10}$.

Solution

By completing the square we see that

$$s^2 + 6s + 10 = (s + 3)^2 + 1^2$$

From Table 1.1, the results with $(s + 3)^2 + 1^2$ in the denominator are

$$\mathcal{L}\{e^{-3t} \sin t\} = \frac{1}{(s+3)^2 + 1^2}, \quad \mathcal{L}\{e^{-3t} \cos t\} = \frac{s+3}{(s+3)^2 + 1^2}$$

We need to rewrite the given transform in terms of these two results.

$$\begin{aligned}
\frac{2s - 1}{s^2 + 6s + 10} &= \frac{2s - 1}{(s+3)^2 + 1^2} \\
&= \frac{2s + 6 - 7}{(s+3)^2 + 1^2} \\
&= \frac{2s + 6}{(s+3)^2 + 1^2} - \frac{7}{(s+3)^2 + 1^2} \\
&= 2\frac{s + 3}{(s+3)^2 + 1^2} - 7\frac{1}{(s+3)^2 + 1^2}
\end{aligned}$$

Now

$$\mathcal{L}^{-1}\left\{2\frac{s+3}{(s+3)^2 + 1^2}\right\} = 2e^{-3t}\cos t, \quad \mathcal{L}^{-1}\left\{7\frac{1}{(s+3)^2 + 1^2}\right\} = 7e^{-3t}\sin t$$

and so

$$\mathcal{L}^{-1}\left\{\frac{2s - 1}{s^2 + 6s + 10}\right\} = 2e^{-3t}\cos t - 7e^{-3t}\sin t$$

Example 2.7

Find the inverse Laplace transform of $\dfrac{9 - 4s}{2s^2 + 8s + 40}$.

Solution

We write $2s^2 + 8s + 40$ as $2(s^2 + 4s + 20)$ and then complete the square to obtain

$2(s^2 + 4s + 20) =$ $2[(s + 2)^2 + 4^2]$

The relevant parts of Table 1.1 are

$\mathcal{L}\{e^{-2t}\sin 4t\} =$ $\dfrac{4}{(s + 2)^2 + 4^2}$

$\mathcal{L}\{e^{-2t}\cos 4t\} =$ $\dfrac{s + 2}{(s + 2)^2 + 4^2}$

The given transform is rewritten so that these results can be used.

$$\begin{aligned}\frac{9 - 4s}{2s^2 + 8s + 40} &= \frac{9 - 4s}{2[(s + 2)^2 + 4^2]}\\ &= \frac{17 - 4(s + 2)}{2[(s + 2)^2 + 4^2]}\\ &= \frac{8.5 - 2(s + 2)}{(s + 2)^2 + 4^2}\\ &= \frac{8.5}{(s + 2)^2 + 4^2} - 2\frac{s + 2}{(s + 2)^2 + 4^2}\end{aligned}$$

Now

$\mathcal{L}^{-1}\left\{\dfrac{8.5}{(s + 2)^2 + 4^2}\right\} =$ $2.125e^{-2t}\sin 4t$

and

$\mathcal{L}^{-1}\left\{2\dfrac{s + 2}{(s + 2)^2 + 4^2}\right\} =$ $2e^{-2t}\cos 4t$

Hence

$$\mathcal{L}^{-1}\left\{\frac{9 - 4s}{2s^2 + 8s + 40}\right\} = 2.125e^{-2t}\sin 4t - 2e^{-2t}\cos 4t$$

Exercises

1. Find the inverse Laplace transform of each of the following:
(a) $\dfrac{1}{s^2+4s+5}$ (b) $\dfrac{3s-5}{s^2+1}$ (c) $\dfrac{3-2s}{s^2-4s+8}$
(d) $\dfrac{1-2s}{s^2+4}$ (e) $\dfrac{1}{s^2-6s+9}$

2. Find the inverse Laplace transform of
(a) $\dfrac{6+s}{2s^2-4s+4}$ (b) $\dfrac{s}{2s^2+0.5}$ (c) $\dfrac{1+s}{s^2}$
(d) $\dfrac{3s+7}{9+3s^2}$ (e) $\dfrac{2s-5}{s^2+4s+13}$

Solutions to exercises

1. (a) $e^{-2t}\sin t$ (b) $3\cos t-5\sin t$
(c) $-2e^{2t}\cos 2t-\dfrac{1}{2}e^{2t}\sin 2t$
(d) $\dfrac{1}{2}\sin 2t-2\cos 2t$ (e) te^{3t}

2. (a) $\frac{1}{2}e^t\cos t+\frac{7}{2}e^t\sin t$ (b) $\frac{1}{2}\cos\frac{t}{2}$ (c) $t+1$
(d) $\cos\sqrt{3}t+\dfrac{7}{3\sqrt{3}}\sin\sqrt{3}t$
(e) $2e^{-2t}\cos 3t-3e^{-2t}\sin 3t$

2.4 Using partial fractions to find an inverse Laplace transform

The method of partial fractions was met in Chapter 7. It is a technique for expressing an algebraic fraction as a sum of simpler fractions. It is also used as an intermediate step when finding the inverse Laplace transform.

Example 2.8

Find the inverse Laplace transform of $\dfrac{5s+4}{s^2+2s}$.

Solution

The algebraic fraction is expressed as a sum of partial fractions.

$$\frac{5s+4}{s^2+2s}=\frac{2}{s}+\frac{3}{s+2}$$

The inverse Laplace transform of each partial fraction is found.

$$\mathcal{L}^{-1}\left\{\frac{2}{s}\right\}=2,\quad \mathcal{L}^{-1}\left\{\frac{3}{s+2}\right\}=3e^{-2t}$$

and so

$$\mathcal{L}^{-1}\left\{\frac{5s+4}{s^2+2s}\right\}=2+3e^{-2t}$$

Example 2.9

Find the inverse Laplace transform of

$$\frac{s+7}{s^2+4s+3}$$

Solution

The algebraic fraction is expressed as its partial fractions.

$$\frac{s+7}{s^2+4s+3} = \frac{3}{s+1} - \frac{2}{s+3}$$

The inverse Laplace transform of each partial fraction can now be found.

$$\mathcal{L}^{-1}\left\{\frac{3}{s+1}\right\} = 3e^{-t}, \quad \mathcal{L}^{-1}\left\{\frac{2}{s+3}\right\} = 2e^{-3t}$$

and so

$$\mathcal{L}^{-1}\left\{\frac{s+7}{s^2+4s+3}\right\} = 3e^{-t} - 2e^{-3t}$$

Example 2.10

Find the inverse Laplace transform of

$$\frac{s^2+6s+1}{s^3+2s^2+s}$$

Solution

The fraction is expressed as its partial fractions.

$$\frac{s^2+6s+1}{s^3+2s^2+s} = \qquad \qquad \frac{1}{s} + \frac{4}{(s+1)^2}$$

The inverse Laplace transform of each partial fraction is found.

$$\mathcal{L}^{-1}\left\{\frac{1}{s}\right\} = \quad , \quad \mathcal{L}^{-1}\left\{\frac{4}{(s+1)^2}\right\} = \quad , \qquad 1, 4te^{-t}$$

and so

$$\mathcal{L}^{-1}\left\{\frac{s^2+6s+1}{s^3+2s^2+s}\right\} = \qquad 1 + 4te^{-t}$$

Exercises

1 Find the inverse Laplace transform of the following:

(a) $\dfrac{3s+1}{s^2-1}$ (b) $\dfrac{7s+11}{s^2+s-6}$ (c) $\dfrac{3s+2}{s^2}$

(d) $\dfrac{s+4}{s^2+4s+4}$ (e) $\dfrac{3s^2+2s+5}{(s+1)(s^2+1)}$

2 Find the inverse Laplace transform of each of the following:

(a) $\dfrac{2s^2-3s+1}{(s-3)(s^2+1)}$ (b) $\dfrac{-(s+6)}{2(s^2+6s+8)}$

(c) $\dfrac{-8s-2}{s^3-s^2-2s}$ (d) $\dfrac{s^2+3s+2}{s^3+2s^2+2s}$

(e) $\dfrac{5s^2-1}{s^4-1}$

Solutions to exercises

1 (a) $2e^t + e^{-t}$ (b) $5e^{2t} + 2e^{-3t}$ (c) $3 + 2t$ (d) $e^{-2t} + 2te^{-2t}$ (e) $2\sin t + 3e^{-t}$

2 (a) $e^{3t} + \cos t$ (b) $\frac{1}{2}e^{-4t} - e^{-2t}$ (c) $1 + 2e^{-t} - 3e^{2t}$ (d) $1 + e^{-t}\sin t$ (e) $2\sinh t + 3\sin t$

End of block exercises

1 Find the inverse Laplace transform of the following:

(a) $\dfrac{3}{s^2} - \dfrac{4}{s}$ (b) $\dfrac{2}{s^3} + \dfrac{1}{s^2} - \dfrac{2}{s}$ (c) $\dfrac{12}{s^4} - \dfrac{6}{s^3}$

(d) $\dfrac{1}{5}\left(\dfrac{18}{s^4} - \dfrac{8}{s^3} + \dfrac{2}{s}\right)$

(e) $\dfrac{6\alpha}{s^4} - \dfrac{2\beta}{s^3} + \dfrac{\gamma}{s^2}$, α, β, γ constants

2 Find the inverse Laplace transform of the following:

(a) $\dfrac{3}{s+1} + \dfrac{5}{s+2}$

(b) $\dfrac{1}{s-1} + \dfrac{1}{s-2} - \dfrac{1}{s-3}$

(c) $\dfrac{4}{(s+1)^3} + \dfrac{1}{(s+2)^2}$

(d) $\dfrac{2}{(s-2)^4} + \dfrac{1}{(s+2)^3}$

(e) $\dfrac{1}{s} + \dfrac{1}{s+1} - \dfrac{2}{s+2}$

3 Find the inverse Laplace transform of the following:

(a) $\dfrac{6}{s^2+9} - \dfrac{s}{2(s^2+9)}$ (b) $\dfrac{2}{(s+4)^2+4}$

(c) $\dfrac{3}{(s+1)^2+9} - \dfrac{2(s+1)}{(s+1)^2+9}$

(d) $\dfrac{1}{2[(s+2)^2+0.25]} + \dfrac{2}{s^3}$

(e) $\dfrac{s-2}{(s-2)^2+16}$

4 Find the inverse Laplace transform of the following:

(a) $\dfrac{3s-3}{s^2-s-2}$ (b) $\dfrac{5s+6}{s^2+9}$ (c) $\dfrac{3s+5}{s^2+2s+5}$

(d) $\dfrac{4s^2+7s+6}{2s^3+4s^2}$ (e) $\dfrac{4s+5}{2s^2+5s+2}$

Solutions to exercises

1 (a) $3t - 4$ (b) $t^2 + t - 2$ (c) $2t^3 - 3t^2$ (d) $\dfrac{3t^3 - 4t^2 + 2}{5}$ (e) $\alpha t^3 - \beta t^2 + \gamma t$

2 (a) $3e^{-t} + 5e^{-2t}$ (b) $e^t + e^{2t} - e^{3t}$ (c) $2t^2e^{-t} + te^{-2t}$ (d) $\dfrac{t^3e^{2t}}{3} + \dfrac{t^2e^{-2t}}{2}$ (e) $1 + e^{-t} - 2e^{-2t}$

3 (a) $2\sin 3t - \dfrac{\cos 3t}{2}$ (b) $e^{-4t}\sin 2t$ (c) $e^{-t}\sin 3t - 2e^{-t}\cos 3t$ (d) $e^{-2t}\sin\dfrac{t}{2} + t^2$ (e) $e^{2t}\cos 4t$

4 (a) $e^{2t} + 2e^{-t}$ (b) $2\sin 3t + 5\cos 3t$ (c) $e^{-t}(\sin 2t + 3\cos 2t)$ (d) $1 + \dfrac{3t}{2} + e^{-2t}$ (e) $e^{-t/2} + e^{-2t}$

BLOCK 3 Solving differential equations using the Laplace transform

3.1 Introduction

In Blocks 1 and 2 we have seen how to find the Laplace transform and its inverse. These techniques are now applied to finding the solution to differential equations.

Linear constant-coefficient differential equations may be solved using the Laplace transform. By applying the transform, the differential equation is converted into an algebraic equation. This algebraic equation is solved and then the inverse Laplace transform is applied to yield the solution to the differential equation. One advantage of using the Laplace transform is that initial conditions are automatically incorporated into the solution.

3.2 The Laplace transform of a derivative

Let $f(t)$ be a function of t and let $F(s)$ be the Laplace transform of f. The value of f and its derivatives when $t = 0$ are denoted by $f(0), f'(0), f''(0)$ and so on. The nth derivative of f is denoted by $f^{(n)}(t)$. Then it can be shown that the Laplace transform of $f^{(n)}(t)$ is given by

Key point

$$\mathcal{L}\{f^{(n)}(t)\} = s^n F(s) - s^{n-1} f(0) - s^{n-2} f'(0) - \cdots - f^{(n-1)}(0)$$

Two common cases are given when $n = 1$ and $n = 2$. In these cases

Key point

$$\mathcal{L}\{f'(t)\} = sF(s) - f(0)$$
$$\mathcal{L}\{f''(t)\} = s^2 F(s) - sf(0) - f'(0)$$

Example 3.1

The Laplace transform of $f(t)$ is $F(s)$. Given $f(0) = 3$ and $f''(0) = -2$ write expressions for the Laplace transform of
(a) $f'(t)$ (b) $f''(t)$ (c) $2f'' - 3f' + f$

Solution

(a)
$$\mathcal{L}\{f'(t)\} = sF(s) - f(0) = sF(s) - 3$$

(b)
$$\mathcal{L}\{f''(t)\} = s^2 F(s) - sf(0) - f'(0) = s^2 F(s) - 3s + 2$$

(c)
$$\begin{aligned}\mathcal{L}\{2f'' - 3f' + f\} &= 2\mathcal{L}\{f''\} - 3\mathcal{L}\{f'\} + \mathcal{L}\{f\}\\ &= 2[s^2F(s) - 3s + 2] - 3[sF(s) - 3] + F(s)\\ &= (2s^2 - 3s + 1)\,F(s) - 6s + 13\end{aligned}$$

Example 3.2

Obtain an expression for the Laplace transform of $3x''(t) + 2x'(t) - 2x(t)$ where $\mathcal{L}\{x(t)\} = X(s)$, $x(0) = -4$ and $x'(0) = 3$.

Solution

$\mathcal{L}\{x'(t)\} =$

$sX(s) + 4$

$\mathcal{L}\{x''(t)\} =$

$s^2X(s) + 4s - 3$

so

$$\begin{aligned}\mathcal{L}\{3x'' + 2x' - 2x\} &= 3\mathcal{L}\{x''\} + 2\mathcal{L}\{x'\} - 2\mathcal{L}\{x\}\\ &= 3(s^2X + 4s - 3) + 2(sX + 4) - 2X\\ &=\end{aligned}$$

$(3s^2 + 2s - 2)\,X + 12s - 1$

Exercises

1 The Laplace transform of $y(t)$ is $Y(s)$, $y(0) = 2$ and $y'(0) = -1$. Find the Laplace transform of the following expressions:
(a) y' (b) y'' (c) $2y'' - y' + 3y$
(d) $-y'' + 4y' - 6y$
(e) $\dfrac{y''}{2} + 3y' - y$

2 The Laplace transform of $x(t)$ is $X(s)$, $x(0) = 2$, $x'(0) = 3$, $x''(0) = -1$. Find the Laplace transform of
(a) $2x' - 3x$ (b) $x'' - 2x' + 3x$ (c) x'''
(d) $x''' + 2x'' + 3x' - 4x$
(e) $2x''' - 3x'' - 7x' + 6x$

3 From the definition of the Laplace transform, and using integration by parts, show that

$$\mathcal{L}\{f'(t)\} = sF(s) - f(0)$$

4 From the definition of the Laplace transform, and using integration by parts, show that

$$\mathcal{L}\{f''(t)\} = s^2F(s) - sf(0) - f'(0)$$

Solutions to exercises

1 (a) $sY-2$

(b) $s^2Y - 2s + 1$

(c) $(2s^2 - s + 3)Y - 4s + 4$

(d) $(-s^2 + 4s - 6)Y + 2s - 9$

(e) $\left(\dfrac{s^2}{2} + 3s - 1\right)Y - s - \dfrac{11}{2}$

2 (a) $(2s - 3)X - 4$

(b) $(s^2 - 2s + 3)X - 2s + 1$

(c) $s^3X - 2s^2 - 3s + 1$

(d) $(s^3 + 2s^2 + 3s - 4)X - 2s^2 - 7s - 11$

(e) $(2s^3 - 3s^2 - 7s + 6)X - 4s^2 + 25$

3.3 Solving differential equations

We are now in a position to solve linear constant-coefficient differential equations using the Laplace transform method. The method consists of three distinct phases:

1 Take the Laplace transform of the given differential equation.
2 Make the transformed variable (usually X or Y) the subject.
3 Apply the inverse Laplace transform to find $x(t)$ (or $y(t)$).

Example 3.3
Solve

$$\frac{dx}{dt} - 2x = 2e^{3t}, \quad x(0) = 2$$

Solution
The Laplace transform of every term is found, noting that the transform of $x(t)$ is $X(s)$. In what follows we write $X(s)$ as simply X in the knowledge that X is a function of s.

$$\begin{aligned}\mathcal{L}\left\{\frac{dx}{dt}\right\} &= sX - x(0)\\ &= sX - 2\\ \mathcal{L}\{2x\} &= 2X\\ \mathcal{L}\{2e^{3t}\} &= \frac{2}{s-3}\end{aligned}$$

So, by taking the Laplace transform of each term, the differential equation becomes

$$sX - 2 - 2X = \frac{2}{s-3}$$

Note that this is no longer a differential equation but an algebraic equation for X. This equation is rearranged so that X is made the subject.

$$\begin{aligned}(s-2)X - 2 &= \frac{2}{s-3}\\ (s-2)X &= \frac{2}{s-3} + 2\\ X &= \frac{2}{(s-3)(s-2)} + \frac{2}{s-2}\\ &= \frac{2 + 2(s-3)}{(s-3)(s-2)}\\ &= \frac{2s-4}{(s-3)(s-2)}\\ &= \frac{2}{s-3}\end{aligned}$$

The inverse Laplace transform is now found.

$$\mathcal{L}^{-1}\left\{\frac{2}{s-3}\right\} = 2e^{3t}$$

so

$$x(t) = 2e^{3t}$$

Thus $x(t) = 2e^{3t}$ is the solution to the given differential equation. Note that the initial condition, $x(0) = 2$, is automatically incorporated into the solution.

Example 3.4 Dynamics – Change in pressure

The pressure, p, of a gas varies with altitude, x, according to

$$\frac{dp}{dx} = -Kp$$

where K is a constant. The pressure at ground level (i.e. $x = 0$) is known to be p_0. Solve the equation to find p in terms of x.

Note that in this example, the independent variable is x; the dependent variable is p.

Solution

We are given

$$\frac{dp}{dx} = -Kp \qquad p(0) = p_0$$

Let the Laplace transform of p be $P(s)$.

Taking the Laplace transform of $\frac{dp}{dx}$:

$$\mathcal{L}\left(\frac{dp}{dx}\right) = sP - p(0)$$
$$= sP - p_0$$

Taking the Laplace transform of Kp:

$$\mathcal{L}(Kp) = K\mathcal{L}(p) = KP$$

So taking the Laplace transform of the entire equation gives:

$$sP - p_0 = -KP$$

This equation is rearranged to make P the subject.

$$sP + KP = p_0$$
$$P(s + K) = p_0$$
$$P = \frac{p_0}{s + K}$$

We now apply the inverse Laplace transform to find $p(x)$.

$$\mathcal{L}^{-1}(P) = \mathcal{L}^{-1}\left(\frac{p_0}{s + K}\right)$$
$$p(x) = p_0\mathcal{L}\left(\frac{1}{s + K}\right)$$
$$= p_0 e^{-Kx}$$

The pressure exhibits an exponential decay as height, x, is increased.

Note that the differential equation has the same form as those in Examples 2.6 and 2.7 in Chapter 20 (Differential Equations) which were solved using a separation of variables method. They could equally well have been solved using the Laplace transform method.

Example 3.5

Solve

$$\frac{d^2y}{dt^2} - y = 2, \quad y(0) = y'(0) = 0$$

Solution

Write $\mathcal{L}\{y\} = Y(s)$ and take the Laplace transform of each term. We write $Y(s)$ concisely as Y.

$$\mathcal{L}\left\{\frac{d^2y}{dt^2}\right\} = \qquad s^2\,Y$$

$$\mathcal{L}\{y\} = \qquad Y$$

$$\mathcal{L}\{2\} = \qquad \frac{2}{s}$$

The differential equation then becomes

$$(s^2 - 1)\,Y = \frac{2}{s}$$

from which

$$Y = \qquad \frac{2}{s(s^2-1)} = \frac{2}{s(s+1)(s-1)}$$

Expressing Y as partial fractions yields

$$Y = \qquad \frac{1}{s-1} + \frac{1}{s+1} - \frac{2}{s}$$

Taking the inverse Laplace transform produces

$$y(t) = \qquad e^t + e^{-t} - 2$$

Example 3.6

Solve

$$y'' - y' + y = t, \quad y(0) = y'(0) = 1$$

Solution

We take the Laplace transform of all the terms.

$\mathcal{L}\{y\} = Y$

$\mathcal{L}\{y'\} =$ $sY - 1$

$\mathcal{L}\{y''\} =$ $s^2Y - s - 1$

$\mathcal{L}\{t\} =$ $\frac{1}{s^2}$

Hence the equation becomes

$$s^2Y - s - 1 - (sY - 1) + Y = \frac{1}{s^2}$$

$$Y(s^2 - s + 1) = s + \frac{1}{s^2}$$

$$= \frac{s^3 + 1}{s^2}$$

$$Y(s^2 - s + 1) = \frac{(s + 1)(s^2 - s + 1)}{s^2}$$

So, cancelling $(s^2 - s + 1)$ from both sides we obtain

$$Y = \frac{s + 1}{s^2}$$

Written as partial fractions we have

$Y =$ $\frac{1}{s} + \frac{1}{s^2}$

from which

$y(t) =$ $1 + t$

Example 3.7 Electrical Engineering – Current in a circuit

The current, $i(t)$, in a circuit is given by

$$L\frac{di}{dt} + Ri = E \sin t$$

where L, R and E are constants and the initial current is 0, i.e. $i(0) = 0$. Find $i(t)$.

Solution

Taking the Laplace transform of each component of the equation gives:

$$\mathcal{L}\left(L\frac{di}{dt}\right) = L\mathcal{L}\left(\frac{di}{dt}\right) = L(sI - i(0)) = LsI$$

$$\mathcal{L}(Ri) = RI$$

$$\mathcal{L}(E \sin t) = E\mathcal{L}(\sin t) = E\left(\frac{1}{s^2 + 1}\right) = \frac{E}{s^2 + 1}$$

So

$$LsI + RI = \frac{E}{s^2 + 1}$$

Rearranging for I yields:

$$I(Ls + R) = \frac{E}{s^2 + 1}$$

$$I = \frac{E}{(s^2 + 1)(Ls + R)}$$

The right-hand side of this equation must now be written, using partial fractions, in a form suitable for taking the inverse Laplace transform.

$$\frac{E}{(s^2 + 1)(Ls + R)} = \frac{E}{L}\left(\frac{1}{(s^2 + 1)(s + R/L)}\right)$$

$$= \frac{E}{L}\left(\frac{As + B}{s^2 + 1} + \frac{C}{s + R/L}\right)$$

The constants A, B and C can be found to be:

$$A = \frac{-L^2}{R^2 + L^2}, \quad B = \frac{RL}{R^2 + L^2}, \quad C = \frac{L^2}{R^2 + L^2}$$

The expression is further written in a form suitable for inversion.

$$I = \frac{E}{L}\left(\frac{As + B}{s^2 + 1} + \frac{C}{s + R/L}\right)$$

$$= \frac{E}{L}\left(\frac{As}{s^2 + 1} + \frac{B}{s^2 + 1} + \frac{C}{s + R/L}\right)$$

$$= \frac{EA}{L}\left(\frac{s}{s^2 + 1}\right) + \frac{EB}{L}\left(\frac{1}{s^2 + 1}\right) + \frac{EC}{L}\left(\frac{1}{s + R/L}\right)$$

Note that the inverse Laplace transform of each expression in brackets can be found using Table 1.1 on p. 1026. Taking the inverse Laplace transform yields:

$$i(t) = \frac{EA}{L}\cos t + \frac{EB}{L}\sin t + \frac{EC}{L}\mathrm{e}^{-Rt/L}$$

With the previously calculated values of A, B and C, $i(t)$ could also be written as:

$$i(t) = \frac{E}{R^2 + L^2}\left(R\sin t - L\cos t + L\mathrm{e}^{-Rt/L}\right)$$

Example 3.8

Solve

$$\frac{\mathrm{d}^2x}{\mathrm{d}t^2} - \frac{\mathrm{d}x}{\mathrm{d}t} + 2x = \cos 3t - 17\sin 3t, \quad x(0) = -1, \quad x'(0) = 6$$

Solution

$$\mathcal{L}\{x\} = X$$

$$\mathcal{L}\left\{\frac{\mathrm{d}x}{\mathrm{d}t}\right\} = \qquad\qquad sX + 1$$

$$\mathcal{L}\left\{\frac{\mathrm{d}^2x}{\mathrm{d}t^2}\right\} = \qquad\qquad s^2X + s - 6$$

$$\mathcal{L}\left\{\frac{\mathrm{d}^2x}{\mathrm{d}t^2} - \frac{\mathrm{d}x}{\mathrm{d}t} + 2x\right\} = \qquad\qquad (s^2 - s + 2)X + s - 7$$

$$\mathcal{L}\{\cos 3t - 17\sin 3t\} = \frac{s}{s^2 + 9} - \frac{51}{s^2 + 9}$$

$$= \frac{s - 51}{s^2 + 9}$$

Hence on taking the Laplace transform of the differential equation we have

$$(s^2 - s + 2)X + s - 7 = \frac{s - 51}{s^2 + 9}$$

$$(s^2 - s + 2)X = \frac{s - 51}{s^2 + 9} - s + 7$$

$$= \frac{\qquad}{s^2 + 9} \qquad\qquad -s^3 + 7s^2 - 8s + 12$$

$$= \frac{(s^2 - s + 2)(6 - s)}{s^2 + 9}$$

So, on cancelling $(s^2 - s + 2)$ we obtain

$$X = \frac{6 - s}{s^2 + 9}$$

$$= \frac{6}{s^2 + 9} - \frac{s}{s^2 + 9}$$

Hence

$$x(t) = \qquad\qquad 2\sin 3t - \cos 3t$$

Exercises

1 Solve the following differential equations using the Laplace transform technique:

(a) $y' - y = 0, \quad y(0) = 3$

(b) $y' + y = 2e^t, \quad y(0) = 2$

(c) $y' + 4y = 3e^{2t}, \quad y(0) = 0.5$

(d) $y' + y = 2\cos t, \quad y(0) = 1$

(e) $y' - y = 2 - t^2, \quad y(0) = 0$

2 Solve the following equations using the Laplace transform method:
(a) $x'' + 3x' - 4x = 5e^t$, $x(0) = 0$, $x'(0) = 1$
(b) $x'' - 4x' + 5x = 0$, $x(0) = 0$, $x'(0) = 1$
(c) $y'' + y' + 4y = 4t^2 + 2t + 2 + 2\cos 2t$, $y(0) = 0$, $y'(0) = 2$
(d) $y'' + 2y' + 9y = 2(3\cos 3t + \sin 3t + 3t\cos 3t)$, $y(0) = y'(0) = 0$
(e) $x'' + 2x' + x = 2e^{-t}$, $x(0) = x'(0) = 0$

Solutions to exercises

1 (a) $y = 3e^t$ (b) $y = e^t + e^{-t}$ (c) $y = 0.5e^{2t}$
(d) $y = \sin t + \cos t$ (e) $y = 2t + t^2$

2 (a) $x = te^t$ (b) $x = e^{2t}\sin t$ (c) $y = t^2 + \sin 2t$
(d) $y = t\sin 3t$ (e) $x = t^2e^{-t}$

End of block exercises

1 Given $\mathcal{L}\{y\} = Y$, $y(0) = 2$, $y'(0) = -3$ write expressions for the Laplace transform of the following:
(a) y' (b) y'' (c) $y'' + y'$ (d) $y'' + 3y' - 2y$
(e) $2y'' - y' + 3y$

2 Given $\mathcal{L}\{y\} = X$, $x(0) = x'(0) = 2$, $x''(0) = -1$ write down the Laplace transform of the following expressions:
(a) x' (b) x'' (c) x''' (d) $2x''' + 3x'' - x' + 2x$
(e) $-x''' - 2x'' + 3x' + 7x$

3 Use the Laplace transform technique to solve
(a) $x' - 2x = 1 - 2t^2$, $x(0) = (0)$
(b) $x' + x = 1 + t + 2\cos t$, $x(0) = 1$
(c) $4x'' + x = 3$, $x(0) = 3$, $x'(0) = -0.5$
(d) $x'' + 4x = 0$, $x(0) = 2$, $x'(0) = 0$
(e) $x'' + x' - 2x = \cos t - 3\sin t$, $x(0) = 2$, $x'(0) = -3$

4 Solve using the Laplace transform method:
(a) $y'' + y = 2\cos t$, $y(0) = 0$, $y'(0) = 1$
(b) $y'' - 2y' = 2e^{2t}$, $y(0) = 0$, $y'(0) = 1$
(c) $y''' + y'' + y' + y = 1 + t$, $y(0) = 1$, $y'(0) = 0$, $y''(0) = 1$
(d) $y'' + y = 2(\cos t - \sin t)$, $y(0) = 0$, $y'(0) = 1$
(e) $y'' + 2y' + 5y = 0$, $y(0) = 1$, $y'(0) = -1$

Solutions to exercises

1 (a) $sY - 2$
(b) $s^2Y - 2s + 3$
(c) $(s^2 + s)Y - 2s + 1$
(d) $(s^2 + 3s - 2)Y - 2s - 3$
(e) $(2s^2 - s + 3)Y - 4s + 8$

2 (a) $sX - 2$ (b) $s^2X - 2s - 2$
(c) $s^3X - 2s^2 - 2s + 1$
(d) $(2s^3 + 3s^2 - s + 2)X - 4s^2 - 10s - 2$
(e) $(-s^3 - 2s^2 + 3s + 7)X + 2s^2 + 6s - 3$

3 (a) $t^2 + t$ (b) $t + \sin t + \cos t$ (c) $3 - \sin\frac{t}{2}$
(d) $2\cos 2t$ (e) $2e^{-2t} + \sin t$

4 (a) $\sin t + t\sin t$ (b) te^{2t} (c) $e^{-t} + t$
(d) $t\cos t + t\sin t$ (e) $e^{-t}\cos 2t$

End of chapter exercises

1 Find the Laplace transform of each of the following expressions:
(a) $t - 3$ (b) $2t^3 + 5t$ (c) $7 - 3t^4$
(d) $\sin 2t + 2\sin t$ (e) $\cos t + t$

2 Find the Laplace transform of each of the following expressions:
(a) $2te^{2t}$ (b) $1 - t^3e^{3t}$
(c) $e^t(1 + \sin t)$ (d) $e^{-2t}(\sin 3t + 2\cos 3t)$
(e) $t(\cos 2t - 3\sin 2t)$

3 Find the Laplace transform of each of the following expressions:
(a) $(t + 1)^2$ (b) $(e^t + t)^2$ (c) $\dfrac{\sin 4t}{2e^{3t}}$
(d) $2 \sin t \cos t$ (e) $\dfrac{2t^2}{3e^{2t}}$

4 The **first shift theorem** states that if $\mathcal{L}\{f(t)\} = F(s)$, then

$$\mathcal{L}\{e^{-at} f(t)\} = F(s + a)$$

where a is a constant.
(a) From the definition of the Laplace transform show that

$$\mathcal{L}\{e^{-at} f(t)\} = \int_0^\infty e^{-(s+a)t} f(t)\, dt$$

and hence prove the first shift theorem.
(b) Use Table 1.1 in Block 1 and the first shift theorem to find $\mathcal{L}\{u(t-3)e^{-7t}\}$ where $u(t)$ is the unit step function.

5 Given

$$\mathcal{L}\{g(t)\} = \frac{s + 6}{s^2 + 3}$$

use the result from question 4 to find the Laplace transform of
(a) $e^{-t}g(t)$ (b) $2e^{-2t}g(t)$ (c) $e^{2t}g(t)$

6 The **second shift theorem** states that if $\mathcal{L}\{f(t)\} = F(s)$ then

$$\mathcal{L}\{u(t-d)f(t-d)\} = e^{-sd}F(s), \quad d > 0$$

where $u(t)$ is the unit step function.
(a) Prove this theorem.
(b) Find the Laplace transform of $u(t-3)(t-3)^5$.
(c) Find the inverse Laplace transform of

$$\frac{e^{-4s}\, 4!}{s^5}$$

7 Find the inverse Laplace transform of each of the following expressions:

(a) $\dfrac{3}{s} - \dfrac{2}{s^2}$ (b) $\dfrac{16}{s^4}$ (c) $\dfrac{3s}{s^2 + 9}$

(d) $\dfrac{s + 3}{(s + 3)^2 + 1}$ (e) $\dfrac{10}{(s + 2^3)}$

8 Find the inverse Laplace transform of each of the following expressions:
(a) $\dfrac{4}{s^2 + 4s + 5}$ (b) $\dfrac{s + 5}{s^2 + 10s + 29}$
(c) $\dfrac{2s - 3}{s^2 + 6s + 10}$ (d) $\dfrac{s^2 + 6s - 4}{(s^2 + 4)^2}$
(e) $\dfrac{1}{4s^2 + 4s + 1}$

9 Find the inverse Laplace transform of the following expressions:
(a) $\dfrac{3s + 5}{s^2 + 4s + 3}$ (b) $\dfrac{s + 2}{s^2 + s}$
(c) $\dfrac{s^2 - s + 4}{(s - 1)(s^2 - 2s + 5)}$
(d) $\dfrac{2s^3 - 3s^2 + 8s - 3}{(s^2 + 1)(s^2 + 4)}$
(e) $\dfrac{6s^2 - 12s + 2}{(s^2 - 4s + 13)(s^2 + 1)}$

10 Given $\mathcal{L}\{x\} = X$, $x(0) = 2$, $x'(0) = 3$ find the Laplace transform of each of the following expressions:
(a) x' (b) x'' (c) $2x' - x$ (d) $3x'' + 2x' - x$
(e) $-2x'' + x' + 3x$

11 Given $\mathcal{L}\{y\} = Y$, $y(0) = 1$, $y'(0) = 0$, $y''(0) = -1$, $y'''(0) = 2$ write an expression for $\mathcal{L}\{y^{(4)}(t)\}$.

12 Solve the following differential equations using the Laplace transform method:
(a) $x' - x = e^t$, $x(0) = 0$
(b) $x'' + x' + 2x = 4\cos 2t$, $x(0) = -1$, $x'(0) = 2$
(c) $x'' + x' - 6x = 1 + 7t - 6t^3$, $x(0) = x'(0) = 0$
(d) $x'' - 4x = 4t$, $x(0) = x'(0) = 1$
(e) $x'' + x = 2\sin t$, $x(0) = x'(0) = 0$

Solutions to exercises

1 (a) $\frac{1}{s^2} - \frac{3}{s}$ (b) $\frac{12}{s^4} + \frac{5}{s^2}$ (c) $\frac{7}{s} - \frac{72}{s^5}$

(d) $\frac{2}{s^2+4} + \frac{2}{s^2+1}$ (e) $\frac{s}{s^2+1} + \frac{1}{s^2}$

2 (a) $\frac{2}{(s-2)^2}$ (b) $\frac{1}{s} - \frac{6}{(s-3)^4}$

(c) $\frac{1}{s-1} + \frac{1}{(s-1)^2+1}$ (d) $\frac{2s+7}{(s+2)^2+9}$

(e) $\frac{s^2 - 12s - 4}{(s^2+4)^2}$

3 (a) $\frac{2}{s^3} + \frac{2}{s^2} + \frac{1}{s}$ (b) $\frac{1}{s-2} + \frac{2}{(s-1)^2} + \frac{2}{s^3}$

(c) $\frac{2}{(s+3)^2+16}$ (d) $\frac{2}{s^2+4}$ (e) $\frac{4}{3(s+2)^3}$

4 (b) $\frac{e^{-3(s+7)}}{s+7}$

5 (a) $\frac{s+7}{(s+1)^2+3}$ (b) $\frac{2(s+8)}{(s+2)^2+3}$

(c) $\frac{s+4}{(s-2)^2+3}$

6 (b) $\frac{e^{-3s}\,5!}{s^6}$ (c) $u(t-4)(t-4)^4$

7 (a) $3 - 2t$ (b) $\frac{8t^3}{3}$ (c) $3\cos 3t$ (d) $e^{-3t}\cos t$

(e) $5t^2e^{-2t}$

8 (a) $4e^{-2t}\sin t$ (b) $e^{-5t}\cos 2t$

(c) $2e^{-3t}\cos t - 9e^{-3t}\sin t$

(d) $t\cos 2t + 1.5t\sin 2t$ (e) $0.25te^{-0.5t}$

9 (a) $e^{-t} + 2e^{-3t}$ (b) $2 - e^{-t}$ (c) $0.5e^{t}\sin 2t + e^{t}$

(d) $2\cos t - 1.5\sin 2t$

(e) $e^{2t}\cos 3t + \frac{4}{3}e^{2t}\sin 3t - \cos t$

10 (a) $sX - 2$ (b) $s^2X - 2s - 3$

(c) $(2s-1)X - 4$

(d) $(3s^2 + 2s - 1)X - 6s - 13$

(e) $(-2s^2 + s + 3)X + 4s + 4$

11 $s^4X - s^3 + s - 2$

12 (a) $x = te^{t}$ (b) $x = \sin 2t - \cos 2t$

(c) $x = \frac{t^2}{2} + t^3$ (d) $x = e^{2t} - t$

(e) $x = \sin t - t\cos t$

Statistics and probability

Most experimental work in engineering involves the use of statistics and probability. When an experiment is carried out, **data** are collected and analysed. Data may be classified as either **discrete** or **continuous**. This distinction is explained in Block 1. Two key parameters, the centre and the variation, are useful in describing a set of data, and comparing it with other sets. Various ways in which these parameters can be calculated are covered in Blocks 2 and 3.

The second part of the chapter focuses on **probability**. The probability of an event is the likelihood of it occurring, measured on a scale from 0 to 1, where 0 represents impossibility and 1 represents certainty. In any particular trial or experiment there are usually several possible outcomes, each with a different probability. It is useful to think of the total probability, that is 1, being spread out or distributed amongst the various possibilities. This idea gives rise to probability distributions for discrete data and probability density functions for continuous data. The common probability distributions and density functions – binomial, Poisson and normal – are covered in Blocks 7, 8 and 9.

Chapter 23 contents

BLOCK 1 Data

1.1 Introduction

When a new engineering component is developed, there will be extensive testing at each stage. Much data will be gathered and analysed. It is useful to classify data as either **discrete** or **continuous**.

1.2 Discrete data

Sometimes a variable must take on a value from a specific set of numbers and no other values are possible. Such a variable is then called a **discrete variable**. Consider a quality control engineer who selects five silicon chips at random and tests each one to see whether it works or not. The engineer is interested in the number of chips that work. Let this variable be n. Then n must be a number from the set $\{0, 1, 2, 3, 4, 5\}$. It is impossible for n to have any other values.

As another example, consider the number of people living in a household. This could be 0, 1, 2, 3, . . . and so on. It is impossible to have 2.3 or 1.7 people living in a household.

These are just two examples of variables that are discrete. When a discrete variable is measured several times, the data so generated are called **discrete data**. Discrete data can have only a limited number of values. Other examples of discrete data are

- the number of cars produced in a factory in a week
- the shoe sizes of people in an office block
- the number of times a machine breaks down in 1 year.

1.3 Continuous data

Sometimes a variable can take on any value within a specified range. Such a variable is called **continuous**. For example, consider the weight of a pack of butter produced in a factory. A pack could have any weight between, say, 230 g and 270 g. The weight will be recorded to a particular accuracy, which depends upon the measuring device and the use to which the data will be put. However, the actual weight could be any value in the given range. When a continuous variable is measured several times the data generated are **continuous data**.

Examples of continuous data are

- the diameters of pistons produced in a factory
- the volume of gas produced in a chemical reaction
- the current in a branch of a circuit.

Exercises

1 Explain what is meant by (a) discrete data, (b) continuous data.

2 Give two examples of (a) discrete data, (b) continuous data.

3 Classify the following variables as discrete or continuous:
(a) the number of times a machine breaks down in 12 months
(b) the time between breakdowns of a machine
(c) the capacitance of a capacitor
(d) the amount of money in your pocket
(e) the number of hairs on your head.

Solutions to exercises

2 (a) number of employees of a firm, the number of cars passing a given point in 12 hours;
(b) the length of a metal bar, the volume of petrol used on a journey.

3 (a) discrete (b) continuous (c) continuous (d) discrete (e) discrete

End of block exercises

1 Classify the following variables as discrete or continuous:
(a) the distance travelled before a set of tyres needs replacing
(b) the intensity of light in a room
(c) the force needed to extend a spring by a set amount
(d) the number of bearings in a machine
(e) the percentage mark obtained in an examination.

2 Classify each of the following as discrete or continuous:
(a) the number of pages in a book
(b) the weight of a book
(c) the area of paper needed to make the pages of a book
(d) the price of a book
(e) the number of copies of a book that are sold.

Solutions to exercises

1 (a) continuous (b) continuous (c) continuous (d) discrete (e) discrete

2 (a) discrete (b) continuous (c) continuous (d) discrete (e) discrete

BLOCK 2

Data averages

2.1 Introduction

We are often presented with a large amount of data. It may be useful if we can look at a single number that typifies the data. For example, we measure the force at which a certain gauge of wire breaks. If this experiment is repeated many times the force required for breaking will vary: some values will be low, some will be high, and of course there will be some in between. We aim to find a single force that in some way summarises or typifies the measurements that we have made.

A value that typifies a set of data is called an **average**. In statistics there are three important averages: the arithmetic mean, the median and the mode.

2.2 The arithmetic mean

The arithmetic mean is also referred to simply as the **mean**. The mean is found by adding up all the data values and then dividing this total by the number of values:

Key point

$$\text{mean} = \frac{\text{sum of values}}{\text{number of values}}$$

Example 2.1 Mechanical Engineering – Breaking force

The force, in newtons, needed to break a wire was measured and the experiment repeated 10 times. The breaking forces are

26 19 17 23 25 20 23 18 20 21

Find the mean breaking force.

Solution

The sum of the values is 212. The number of values is 10. Thus

$$\begin{aligned}\text{mean} &= \frac{\text{sum of values}}{\text{number of values}} \\ &= \frac{212}{10} \\ &= 21.2\end{aligned}$$

To the nearest whole number, the mean breaking force is 21 newtons.

Example 2.2

The temperature, in °C, at which a liquid boils is measured several times. The results are

93.7 91.4 95.3 94.9 92.3 95.8

Find the mean temperature.

Solution

Sum of values = 563.4

Number of values = 6

$$\text{Mean temperature} = \frac{563.4}{6} = 93.9$$

A special notation is often used when calculating a mean. Suppose we have n values and we label these $x_1, x_2, x_3, \ldots, x_n$. The sum of these values is denoted by $\sum_{i=1}^{n} x_i$, or more simply as Σx. The mean is denoted by $\bar{x}$, pronounced 'x bar'. Hence

Key point

$$\text{mean} = \bar{x} = \frac{\sum_{i=1}^{n} x_i}{n}$$

Exercises

1 The diameters in mm of some ball bearings were measured; the results are

5.1 4.9 5.0 5.2 5.1 4.8 5.2

Calculate the mean diameter, giving your answer to 1 d.p.

2 The current, in amps, in a wire was measured several times and the results noted as follows:

13.1 12.9 13.1 12.8 12.7 12.6 13.2 13.1

Calculate the mean current, giving your answer to 1 d.p.

3 The temperature, in °C, at which a liquid froze was recorded several times. The results are

−7 −4 −1 −6 −3 −2 −3 −4

Calculate the mean temperature at which the liquid freezes. Give your answer to the nearest integer.

Solution to exercises

1 5.0 mm

2 12.9 amps

3 −4°C

2.3 Calculating the mean of a frequency distribution

The **frequency** of a value is the number of times it occurs. A set of numbers, together with their frequency, is called a **frequency distribution**. For example, suppose the force, in newtons, needed to break a wire is measured and the experiment repeated several times. The results are recorded in Table 2.1.

Table 2.1

Force (N)	Frequency, f
17	3
18	4
19	9
20	11
21	6
22	2

Thus a force of 17 N was recorded three times, a force of 18 N was recorded four times, and so on. Table 2.1 is an example of a frequency distribution. Note that the sum of the frequencies gives the total number of measurements made.

When data are presented in the form of a frequency distribution, the mean can still be calculated. Example 2.3 illustrates the method.

Example 2.3

Table 2.2 is a frequency distribution for the variable x.

Table 2.2

x	frequency, f
5	2
6	3
7	4
8	2
9	1

Calculate the mean of x: that is, $\bar{x}$.

Solution

The value 5 occurs twice and so contributes 5×2 to the sum of the x values. The value 6 occurs three times and so this contributes 6×3 to the sum of the x values. The remaining contributions are 7×4, 8×2 and 9×1. Hence

$$\begin{aligned} \text{sum of values} &= (5 \times 2) + (6 \times 3) + (7 \times 4) + (8 \times 2) + (9 \times 1) \\ &= 10 + 18 + 28 + 16 + 9 \\ &= 81 \end{aligned}$$

The number of values is 2 + 3 + 4 + 2 + 1 = 12, that is the sum of the frequencies. Finally

$$\text{mean} = \bar{x} = \frac{\text{sum of values}}{\text{number of values}}$$
$$= \frac{81}{12}$$
$$= 6.75$$

The mean of the frequency distribution is 6.75.

By referring to Example 2.3 we see that the sum of the values is found by adding the products $x \times f$. The number of values is found by adding up all the frequencies. If the values are denoted by $x_1, x_2, \ldots, x_n$ and the corresponding frequencies by $f_1, f_2, \ldots, f_n$ then we see that

$$\text{Sum of values} = \sum_{i=1}^{n} x_i f_i$$
$$\text{Number of values} = \sum_{i=1}^{n} f_i$$

These are often written respectively in the more compact form as Σxf and Σf, where the limits are assumed.

The mean can now be stated:

Key point

$$\text{mean} = \frac{\sum_{i=1}^{n} x_i f_i}{\sum_{i=1}^{n} f_i} = \frac{\sum xf}{\sum f}$$

When calculating the mean of the frequency distribution as given in Table 2.2 usually we would extend the table as follows:

x	f	xf
5	2	10
6	3	18
7	4	28
8	2	16
9	1	9
	$\Sigma f = 12$	$\Sigma xf = 81$

Example 2.4

Find the mean of the data given in Table 2.1.

Solution

The table is extended.

Force, x (N)	Frequency, f	xf
17	3	51
18	4	72
19	9	171
20	11	220
21	6	126
22	2	44
	$\Sigma f = 35$	$\Sigma xf = 684$

$$\text{mean} = \bar{x} = \frac{\Sigma xf}{\Sigma f} = \frac{684}{35} = 19.54$$

Exercises

1 Calculate the mean of the frequency distribution

x	f
17	4
18	11
19	14
20	9
21	5

2 The resistance, in ohms, of a certain type of resistor is measured many times. The results are

Resistance (Ω)	Frequency
4.7	6
4.8	11
4.9	4
5.0	8
5.1	3
5.2	7

Calculate the mean value of the resistance, giving your answer to 1 d.p.

3 The lifetimes of a set of components are measured to the nearest 100 hours. The results are

Lifetime (h)	Frequency
0	1
100	1
200	4
300	10
400	17
500	3
600	2
700	10

Calculate the mean lifetime.

4 The temperature of ignition of a certain mixture of gases is recorded to the nearest 10°C as follows:

Temperature (°C)	Frequency
170	2
180	11
190	10
200	6
210	1
220	2
230	1

Calculate the mean temperature of ignition.

Solutions to exercises

1 19

2 4.9 ohms

3 425 hours

4 190°C to the nearest 10°C

2.4 The median

The **median** of a set of numbers is found by listing all the numbers in ascending order and selecting the number that is half way along the list.

Example 2.5

Find the median of the numbers

$$6\ 8\ 3\ 11\ 10\ 12\ 7\ 9\ 7$$

Solution

The numbers are arranged in ascending order.

$$3\ 6\ 7\ 7\ 8\ 9\ 10\ 11\ 12$$

There are nine numbers in the list. The middle number is the fifth one, that is 8. Therefore, the median is 8.

When there is an even number of values in the list, the median is the mean of the two middle values.

Example 2.6

Find the median of the following temperatures:

$$49\ 50\ 40\ 38\ 41\ 57\ 56\ 52$$

Solution

The numbers are arranged in ascending order:

$$38\ 40\ 41\ 49\ 50\ 52\ 56\ 57$$

There are eight numbers in the list. The middle two values are 49 and 50. The mean of these is $\frac{49 + 50}{2} = 49.5$ and so the median temperature is 49.5.

Exercises

1 Calculate the median of each of the following sets of numbers:
(a) 63 47 51 59 56 50 61 55 58 61
(b) 10 12 16 11 14 11 10 7 13
(c) −4 0 −1 2 3 2 −3 −1
(d) 76 79 81 70 64 62 75 70 71 63 69

Solutions to exercises

1 (a) 57 (b) 11 (c) −0.5 (d) 70

2.5 The mode

The **mode** of a set of values is the value that occurs most often.

Example 2.7

Find the mode of the set of numbers

2 3 3 4 5 5 6 6 6 8 11

Solution

The number 6 occurs three times; this is more than any other number. Hence the mode is 6.

Example 2.8

Find the mode of the set of numbers

2 2 2 3 3 5 6 11 14 14 14 16

Solution

In this example there is no single number that occurs most frequently. The numbers 2 and 14 both occur three times. There are two modes. The data are said to be **bimodal**.

Exercises

1 State the mode of each of the following sets of data:
(a) 5 5 5 6 6 7 7 7 7 9 9 9 11 11
(b) 4 1 3 6 4 5 1 4 5 3 2
(c) 4 0 1 3 2 0 2 0 1 3 0 2

Solution to exercises

1 (a) 7 (b) 4 (c) 0

End of block exercises

1 Find the mean, median and mode of each of the following sets of values:
(a) 6 9 5 7 6 8 10
(b) 0 −3 0 −2 1 2 −2 −1 −2 0
(c) 2 3 1 5 2 5 1 4 3 1 6

2 The resistance of several resistors was measured. The results are

Resistance (Ω)	Frequency
5.0	3
5.5	4
6.0	9
6.5	17
7.0	11
7.5	1

(a) Calculate the mean resistance.
(b) Calculate the median.
(c) Calculate the mode.

3 The mean of the set of values

$$5 \quad 3 \quad X \quad 10 \quad 2 \quad 11$$

is 8.3. Find X.

4 Find the mean of the data set

2 2 2 2 2 2 2 20

Explain why the mean does not represent the data adequately. Which average would have been more appropriate to use?

5 The force needed to buckle a support beam is measured several times. The results are tabulated thus

Force ($\times 10^3$ N)	Frequency
2.00	4
2.25	1
2.50	2
2.75	5
3.00	2
3.25	2

Calculate the mean buckling force.

Solutions to exercises

1 (a) 7.29, 7, 6 (b) −0.7, −0.5, −2 and 0 (bimodal) (c) 3, 3, 1

2 (a) 6.36 Ω (b) 6.5 Ω (c) 6.5 Ω

3 18.8

4 Mean = 4.57. Mode would be more appropriate.

5 2.59×10^3 N

BLOCK 3 Variation of data

3.1 Introduction

Block 2 illustrated different ways of describing the central location of a data set. We now look at the variation in a data set.

Consider the mean of the two sets of data: 4 4 4 and 1 3 8. The means are

$$\frac{4+4+4}{3} = 4 \text{ and } \frac{1+3+8}{3} = 4$$

Both data sets have the same mean although the values in the first data set are all the same whereas those in the second set are spread widely. Clearly the mean value does not reflect the variability of the values in a data set. We need additional parameters to describe variability of data. These additional parameters are the **variance** and the **standard deviation**.

3.2 Variance and standard deviation

Both the variance and the standard deviation quantify the variation of a set of data values.

Suppose we have a set of n values: $x_1, x_2, x_3, \ldots, x_n$. The mean of these values is found and labelled as $\bar{x}$. Then the variance is given by

Key point

$$\text{variance} = \frac{\sum_{i=1}^{n}(x_i - \bar{x})^2}{n}$$

Example 3.1

Find the variance of

(a) 4 4 4

(b) 1 3 8

Solution

(a) We have $x_1 = 4, x_2 = 4, x_3 = 4$. The mean, $\bar{x}$, is calculated to be 4. So

$$x_1 - \bar{x} = 0, \quad x_2 - \bar{x} = 0, \quad x_3 - \bar{x} = 0$$

and so

$$\text{variance} = \frac{\sum_{i=1}^{3}(x_i - \bar{x})^2}{3}$$

$$= \frac{0^2 + 0^2 + 0^2}{3}$$
$$= 0$$

The variance is zero. Since there is no variation in the data values it is not surprising that the variance is zero.

(b) Here we have $x_1 = 1, x_2 = 3, x_3 = 8$ and $\bar{x} = 4$. Then

$$x_1 - \bar{x} = -3, \quad x_2 - \bar{x} = -1, \quad x_3 - \bar{x} = 4$$

and so

$$\begin{aligned} \text{variance} &= \frac{\sum_{i=1}^{3}(x_i - \bar{x})^2}{3} \\ &= \frac{(-3)^2 + (-1)^2 + 4^2}{3} \\ &= \frac{26}{3} \\ &= 8.67 \end{aligned}$$

The variance is 8.67.

The **standard deviation** is found from

Key point

$$\text{standard deviation} = \sqrt{\text{variance}}$$

Note that the standard deviation has the same units as the given data, and as such is a useful measure of variation.

From Example 3.1 we see that the standard deviation of 4, 4, 4 is $\sqrt{0} = 0$. The standard deviation of 1, 3, 8 is $\sqrt{8.67} = 2.94$.

Example 3.2

Calculate the variance and standard deviation of

11 6 9.6 10.2

Solution

$$\begin{aligned} \text{mean} &= \frac{11 + 6 + 9.6 + 10.2}{4} \\ &= 9.2 \end{aligned}$$

The calculation of the variance is given in Table 3.1.

Table 3.1

x_i	$x_i - \bar{x}$	$(x_i - \bar{x})^2$
11	$11 - 9.2 = 1.8$	$(1.8)^2 = 3.24$
6	$6 - 9.2 = -3.2$	$(-3.2)^2 = 10.24$
9.6	$9.6 - 9.2 = 0.4$	$(0.4)^2 = 0.16$
10.2	$10.2 - 9.2 = 1.0$	$1.0^2 = 1.00$
		$\Sigma(x_i - \bar{x})^2 = 14.64$

$$\text{variance} = \frac{\Sigma(x_i - \bar{x})^2}{n} = \frac{14.64}{4} = 3.66$$

$$\text{standard deviation} = \sqrt{\text{variance}} = \sqrt{3.66} = 1.91$$

Example 3.3

Calculate the variance and standard deviation of

0 2 3 6 6 10

Solution

mean = 4.5

Complete the calculation started in Table 3.2.

Table 3.2

x_i	$x_i - \bar{x}$	$(x_i - \bar{x})^2$
0		
2		
3		
6		
6		
10		

−4.5,	20.25
−2.5,	6.25
−1.5,	2.25
1.5,	2.25
1.5,	2.25
5.5,	30.25

$\Sigma(x_i - \bar{x})^2 =$ 63.5

variance = $\frac{63.5}{6} = 10.58$

standard deviation = $\sqrt{10.58} = 3.25$

When data are presented in the form of a frequency distribution the variance and standard deviation can still be found. Example 3.4 illustrates this.

Example 3.4

The number of hardware faults for each computer in a laboratory containing 30 computers is recorded over a 12 month period. The results, in the form of a frequency distribution, are given in Table 3.3.

Table 3.3

Number of faults, x	Frequency, f
0	11
1	4
2	3
3	7
4	5

So 11 of the computers had no faults during the 12 month period, 4 had one fault, 3 had two faults and so on. Note that the sum of the frequencies gives the total number of computers, that is 30.

Calculate the variance and standard deviation.

Solution

The mean, $\bar{x}$, is found to be 1.7. The remainder of the calculation is set out in Table 3.4.

Table 3.4

x_i	f_i	$x_i - \bar{x}$	$(x_i - \bar{x})^2$	$f_i(x_i - \bar{x})^2$
0	11	−1.7	2.89	31.79
1	4	−0.7	0.49	1.96
2	3	0.3	0.09	0.27
3	7	1.3	1.69	11.83
4	5	2.3	5.29	26.45
	$\Sigma f_i = 30$			$\Sigma f_i(x_i - \bar{x})^2 = 72.3$

Then

$$\text{variance} = \frac{\Sigma f_i (x_i - \bar{x})^2}{n} = \frac{72.3}{30} = 2.41$$

and

$$\text{standard deviation} = \sqrt{\text{variance}} = 1.55$$

Example 3.4 illustrates the formula for calculating the variance of a frequency distribution.

Key point

$$\text{variance} = \frac{\Sigma f_i (x_i - \bar{x})^2}{n}$$

End of block exercises

1 Find the variance and standard deviation of the following sets of data:
(a) 6 11 10 9 7 8 9
(b) 5.3 7.2 9.1 8.6 5.9 7.3
(c) −6 −6 −5 −1 0 2 1 0 −2
Which set has the greatest variation?

2 Find the variance and standard deviation of the following frequency distribution:

x	f
6	7
7	3
8	2
9	4
10	2

3 The resistances of 50 resistors are measured and the results recorded as follows:

Resistance (Ω)	Frequency
5.0	17
5.5	12
6.0	10
6.5	6
7.0	5

Calculate the standard deviation of the measurements.

4 The standard deviation of the values $x_1, x_2, x_3, \ldots, x_n$ is σ. Calculate the standard deviation of the values $kx_1, kx_2, kx_3, \ldots, kx_n$ where k is a constant.

5 Calculate the variance and standard deviation of the values

$$-6 \ -11 \ 4 \ 0 \ 1 \ -5 \ 6 \ 3$$

Solutions to exercises

1 (a) variance = 2.53, standard deviation = 1.59 (b) 1.81, 1.35 (c) 8.32, 2.88. Set (c) has the greatest variation.

2 variance = 2.14, standard deviation = 1.46

3 variance = 0.44, standard deviation = 0.66

4 $k\sigma$

5 variance = 29.50, standard deviation = 5.43

BLOCK 4 Elementary probability

4.1 Introduction

When an event is impossible we say the probability of it happening is 0. When an event is certain, we say the probability of it happening is 1. For example, it is impossible to live without oxygen and so the probability of doing this is 0. It is certain that a metal bar will sink when placed in water and so the probability of this happening is 1.

Most events are neither impossible nor certain. They have varying degrees of likelihood. The probability of such events lies between 0 and 1. Events that are likely to happen have probabilities close to 1; events that are unlikely to happen have probabilities close to 0. An event that is as likely to happen as not has a probability of 0.5. For example, the probability of throwing a head with a fair coin is 0.5.

4.2 Experimental and theoretical probabilities

We introduce the notation used in probability theory and calculations.

We let E denote an event and $P(E)$ denote the probability of the event E happening. For example, suppose E is the event 'A 4 is obtained on throwing a die'. The probability of this is $\frac{1}{6}$. We would write this as $P(E) = \frac{1}{6}$.

Since all probabilities lie between 0 and 1 we know that for any event, E, $0 \leq P(E) \leq 1$.

Key point

For any event, E

$$0 \leq P(E) \leq 1$$

There are two ways in which we ascertain the probability of a particular event: theoretically and experimentally.

To calculate a theoretical probability we need to have knowledge of the event. For example, suppose we toss a fair coin and let H be the event that it lands with the head facing uppermost. Clearly $P(H) = 0.5$. Similarly suppose we roll a fair die and E is the event that a 4 is obtained; then $P(E) = \frac{1}{6}$. These probabilities have been calculated from knowledge of the physical situation. When any experiment is carried out there are usually several possible outcomes, or **events** as we call them. For example, when throwing a coin there are two possible events: the coin lands with the tail uppermost or lands with the head uppermost. Often the possible events have equal probabilities. In the case of throwing a coin, there are two equally likely events. So if

H: the coin lands with the head uppermost
T: the coin lands with the tail uppermost

then clearly

$$P(H) = P(T) = 0.5$$

Example 4.1

A die is rolled. Calculate the probability that a 4 is uppermost.

Solution

When a die is rolled there are six possible events: a 1 is uppermost, a 2 is uppermost and so on. Each of the six events is equally likely to happen and so the probability of each event is $\frac{1}{6}$. In particular, the probability that a 4 is uppermost is $\frac{1}{6}$.

In some circumstances we do not have sufficient information to calculate a theoretical probability. We know that if a coin is unbiased the probability of obtaining a head is $\frac{1}{2}$. However, suppose the coin is biased so that it is more likely to land with the head uppermost than with its tail uppermost. We can experiment by tossing the coin a large number of times and counting the number of heads obtained. Suppose we toss the coin 1000 times and obtain 650 heads. We can estimate the probability of obtaining a head as $\frac{650}{1000} = 0.65$. Such a probability is known as an **experimental probability**. It is accurate only if a large number of experiments have been performed.

Example 4.2

A biased die is thrown 1000 times and a 6 is obtained on 330 occasions. Calculate the probability of obtaining a 6 on a single throw of the die.

Solution

$$\text{probability of throwing a 6} = \frac{330}{1000} = 0.33$$

Exercises

1 A company manufactures precision bearings. On an inspection three batches out of 500 were rejected. Calculate the probability that a batch is rejected.

2 A pack of 52 cards is shuffled and a single card is drawn. Calculate the probability that it is the queen of hearts.

3 A television manufacturer sold 36 000 TV sets of which 297 were returned within 12 months with faults.
(a) Calculate the probability that a TV set, chosen at random, is returned within 12 months.
(b) A store buys 500 TV sets from the manufacturer. How many can be expected to develop faults within 12 months?

Solutions to exercises

1 0.006

2 $\frac{1}{52}$

3 (a) 0.00825 (b) 4.125, that is four sets.

4.3 Compound events

Suppose we roll a fair die and we wish to calculate the probability that the number showing is 3 or higher. To obtain a score of 3 or more, we could throw a 3, 4, 5 or 6: that is, there are four ways of obtaining such a score. When the die is rolled there are six possible outcomes, of which four result in a score of 3 or more. So

$$\begin{aligned} P\,(\text{obtaining a score of 3 or more}) &= \frac{4}{6} \\ &= \frac{2}{3} \end{aligned}$$

An event such as 'score 3 or higher' is an example of a **compound event**. When all the outcomes of an experiment are equally likely then we can calculate the probability of a compound event, E, using

Key point

$$P(E) = \frac{\text{number of ways that } E \text{ can happen}}{\text{total number of possible outcomes}}$$

Example 4.3

A fair die is rolled. Calculate the probability of obtaining an odd score.

Solution

The chosen event is throwing an odd score: that is, a 1, 3 or 5. Thus there are three ways in which the chosen event can occur out of a total of six equally likely outcomes. So

$$\begin{aligned} P\,(\text{odd score}) &= \frac{3}{6} \\ &= \frac{1}{2} \end{aligned}$$

Example 4.4

Two fair coins are tossed.

(a) Write down all the possible outcomes.

(b) Calculate the probability of obtaining one or more heads.

Solution

(a) Letting H stand for head and T for tail, the possible outcomes are

HH HT TH TT

All outcomes are equally likely.

(b)

number of ways of obtaining one or more heads = 3

total number of possible outcomes = 4

probability of obtaining one or more heads = $\frac{3}{4}$

Exercises

1 A pack of 52 cards is shuffled and a card is selected. Calculate the probability that the card is
(a) black
(b) red
(c) a club
(d) a jack
(e) a red queen

2 Three fair coins are tossed.
(a) List the eight possible outcomes.
(b) Calculate the probability of obtaining (i) exactly two heads, (ii) at least two heads, (iii) no heads.

3 A fair die is rolled. Calculate the probability that the number showing is
(a) odd
(b) 2 or more
(c) less than 4

4 Two fair dice are thrown. Calculate the probability that the total is
(a) 6 (b) 8 (c) more than 10

Solutions to exercises

1 (a) $\frac{1}{2}$ (b) $\frac{1}{2}$ (c) $\frac{1}{4}$ (d) $\frac{1}{13}$ (e) $\frac{1}{26}$

2 (a) HHH, HHT, HTH, HTT, THH, THT, TTH, TTT

(b) (i) $\frac{3}{8}$ (ii) $\frac{1}{2}$ (iii) $\frac{1}{8}$

3 (a) $\frac{1}{2}$ (b) $\frac{5}{6}$ (c) $\frac{1}{2}$

4 (a) $\frac{5}{36}$ (b) $\frac{5}{36}$ (c) $\frac{1}{12}$

4.4 Complementary events

Consider the following situation. A component is tested. Either it works or it does not work, so there are two possible events. When the component is tested one of these events must happen. In addition, each event excludes the other. We say that the two events are **complementary**.

In general, two events are complementary if one of them must happen and, when it does, the other event cannot happen. If A is an event, then the corresponding complementary event is denoted by $\overline{A}$. The sum of probabilities of two complementary events is always one. For example, if the probability that the component works is 0.92, then the probability that it does not work is $1 - 0.92 = 0.08$.

Example 4.5

The events A and B are defined by

A: a score of 5 is rolled with a fair die
B: the box contains more than 10 components

State the complementary events, $\overline{A}$ and $\overline{B}$.

Solution

$\overline{A}$ is the event: a score other than 5 is obtained when the die is rolled.
$\overline{B}$ is the event: the box contains 10 or fewer components.

Exercises

1 State the complement of the following events:
(a) the component is reliable
(b) the digit is greater than 7
(c) the volume is less than or equal to 1 litre
(d) the machine is not working
(e) all components have been tested
(f) at least four components from the batch are unreliable.

Solutions to exercises

1 (a) the component is not reliable
(b) the digit is 7 or less
(c) the volume is more than 1 litre
(d) the machine is working
(e) some components have not been tested
(f) three or fewer components from the batch are unreliable.

4.5 Use of tree diagrams to calculate probabilities

When a problem involving probabilities is complex, it is sometimes useful to introduce a **tree diagram**. Tree diagrams enable information to be presented in a clear way and aid understanding.

Example 4.6 Reliability Engineering

Machines A and B make components. Of those made by machine A, 95% are reliable; of those made by machine B, 92% are reliable. Machine A makes 70% of the components with machine B making the rest. Calculate the probability that a component picked at random is

(a) made by machine B
(b) made by machine A and is reliable
(c) made by machine B and is unreliable
(d) reliable.

Solution

(a) Since machine A makes 70% of the components then machine B makes the remaining 30%. Hence the probability that a component is made by machine B is 0.3.

To answer (b), (c) and (d) we introduce the tree diagram.

Consider 100 components: 70 are made by machine A and 30 are made by machine B. This is represented as in Figure 4.1.

Consider the 70 components made by machine A: 95% of these are reliable and so 5% are unreliable. Now 95% of 70 = 66.5, 5% of 70 = 3.5, and this information is represented by Figure 4.2.

Similarly, of the 30 components made by machine B, 92% are reliable and so 8% are unreliable. We know that 92% of 30 = 27.6 and 8% of 30 = 2.4. This information is represented by Figure 4.3.

Putting together Figures 4.1, 4.2, and 4.3 we obtain the tree diagram shown in Figure 4.4.

We use Figure 4.4 to answer (b), (c) and (d).

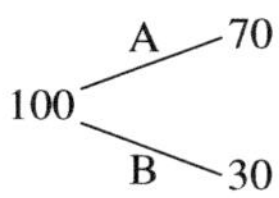

Figure 4.1

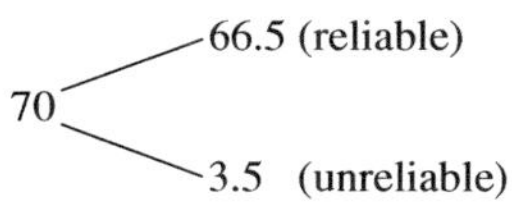

Figure 4.2

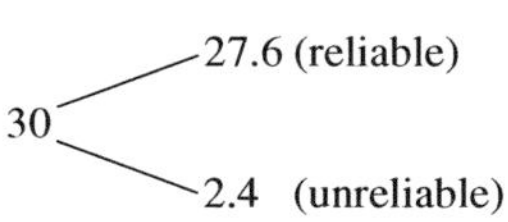

Figure 4.3

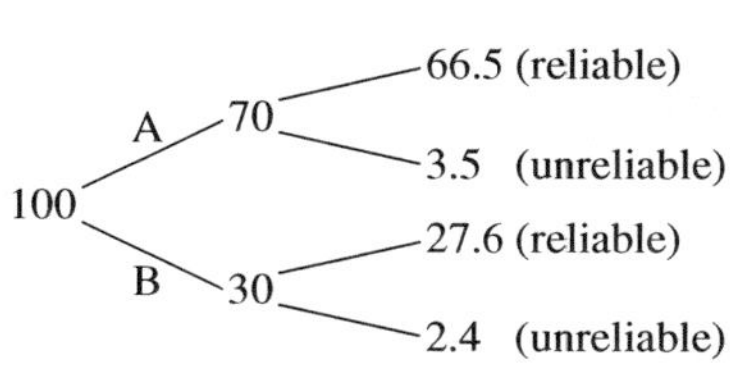

Figure 4.4

(b) We see that there are 66.5 components made by machine A that are reliable from the original 100 components. So

$$\begin{aligned} P(\text{component is made by A and is reliable}) &= \frac{66.5}{100} \\ &= 0.665 \end{aligned}$$

(c) We see from Figure 4.4 that there are 2.4 components made by machine B that are unreliable.

$$\begin{aligned} P(\text{component made by B and is unreliable}) &= \frac{2.4}{100} \\ &= 0.024 \end{aligned}$$

(d) There are $66.5 + 27.6 = 94.1$ reliable components from the original 100. So

$$\begin{aligned} P(\text{component is reliable}) &= \frac{94.1}{100} \\ &= 0.941 \end{aligned}$$

Example 4.7 Reliability Engineering

Machines A, B and C make components. Machine A makes 30% of the components, machine B makes 50% of the components, and machine C makes the remainder. Of those components made by machine A, 93% are reliable, of those made by machine B, 89% are reliable, and of those made by machine C, 96% are reliable.

A component is picked at random. Calculate the probability that it is

(a) made by machine C
(b) made by machine B and is unreliable
(c) made by either machine A or machine B
(d) reliable.

Solution

Consider 100 components. A tree diagram that illustrates the information is shown in Figure 4.5.

Figure 4.5

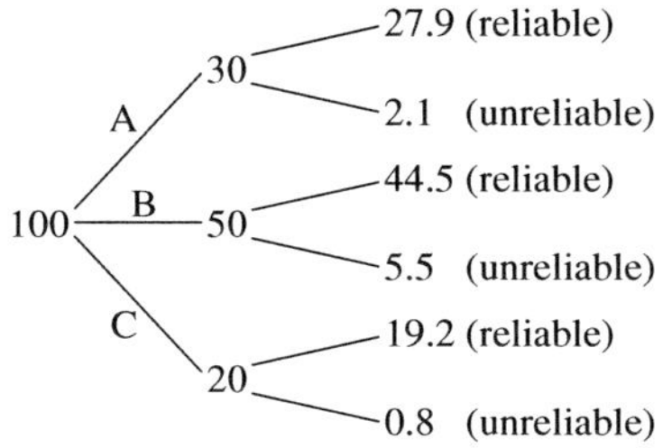

(a) Machine A makes 30% of the components, machine B makes 50% of the components and so machine C makes $(100 - 30 - 50)\% = 20\%$ of the components. So

$$P(\text{component is made by machine C}) = 0.20$$

(b) From Figure 4.5, the number of components made by machine B that are unreliable is

5.5

So

$$P(\text{component is made by B and is unreliable}) = \frac{5.5}{100} = 0.055$$

(c) Out of 100 components, machine A makes 30 and machine B makes 50. So

$$P(\text{component is made by either A or B}) = \frac{30 + 50}{100} = 0.8$$

(d) Out of 100 components there are reliable ones. 91.6

So

$$P(\text{component is reliable}) = \frac{91.6}{100} = 0.916$$

Exercises

1 Components are made by machines A and B. Machine A makes twice as many components as machine B. When made by machine A, 3% of the components are faulty; when made by machine B, 5% are faulty. Calculate the probability that a component picked at random is
(a) made by machine B
(b) made by machine A and is faulty
(c) made by machine B and is not faulty
(d) faulty.

2 Silicon chips are manufactured by four machines, A, B, C and D. Machines A, B, C and D manufacture 20%, 25%, 35% and 20% of the components respectively. Of those silicon chips manufactured by machine A, 2.1% are faulty. The respective figures for machines B, C and D are 3%, 1.6% and 2.5%. A silicon chip is selected at random. Calculate the probability that it is
(a) made by machine C and is faulty
(b) made by machine A and is not faulty
(c) faulty.

3 Precision components are made by machines A, B and C. Machines A and C each make 30% of the components with machine B making the rest. The probability that a component is acceptable is 0.91 when made by machine A, 0.95 when made by machine B and 0.88 when made by machine C.
(a) Calculate the probability that a component selected at random is acceptable.
(b) A batch of 2000 components is examined. Calculate the number of components you expect are not acceptable.

Solutions to exercises

1 (a) 0.3333 (b) 0.02 (c) 0.3167 (d) 0.0367

2 (a) 0.0056 (b) 0.1958 (c) 0.0223

3 (a) 0.917 (b) 166

End of block exercises

1 Which of the following numbers cannot represent probabilities?

$$\frac{2}{3}, \frac{1}{11}, -\frac{2}{3}, \frac{3}{7}, \frac{9}{7}, \frac{7}{9},$$
$$0.000, 1.010, 1$$

2 A company manufactures resistors. During a quality control check, 36 out of 2500 resistors failed to perform to the required standard.
(a) Calculate the probability that a resistor picked at random will fail to perform to the required standard.
(b) In a batch of 700 resistors how many would you expect to fail?

3 Resistors are manufactured by machines A and B. Machine A makes 60% of the resistors with machine B making the rest. When made by machine A, 3% of the resistors are faulty; when made by machine B, 7% are faulty.
A resistor is picked at random. Calculate the probability it is
(a) made by machine B
(b) made by machine A and is not faulty
(c) made by machine B and is faulty
(d) faulty.

4 The probability of throwing a '6' with a fair die is $\frac{1}{6}$. A student makes the following argument.
If I throw the die once, the probability of obtaining a '6' is $\frac{1}{6}$. So if I throw the die twice, then the probability of throwing a '6' must be $2 \times \frac{1}{6} = \frac{1}{3}$. If I throw the die three times then the probability of throwing a '6' must be $3 \times \frac{1}{6} = \frac{1}{2}$ and so on.
Is the argument sound? If not, why not?

5 Components are made by machines A, B and C. Machines A and B each make 36% of the components with machine C making the rest. For machine A, 2% of the components made are faulty, for machine B, 6% are faulty, and for machine C, 7% are faulty.
A component is picked at random. Calculate the probability that it is
(a) faulty and made by machine C
(b) not faulty.

6 State the complement of the events:
(a) the machine is ready
(b) the assignment was delivered on time
(c) both printers are working
(d) at least one person is absent today.

Solutions to exercises

1 $-\frac{2}{3}, \frac{9}{7},$ 1.010

2 (a) 0.0144 (b) 10

3 (a) 0.4 (b) 0.582 (c) 0.028 (d) 0.046

4 The argument is unsound. Using this argument, when the die is thrown seven times, the probability of throwing a '6' is $7 \times \frac{1}{6} = \frac{7}{6}$, which is clearly nonsense.

5 (a) 0.0196 (b) 0.9516

6 (a) the machine is not ready
(b) the assignment was not delivered on time
(c) at least one of the printers is not working
(d) no one is absent today.

BLOCK 5 Laws of probability

5.1 Introduction

In this block we extend the knowledge of probability gained in Block 4. The concept of **mutually exclusive events** leads naturally to the **addition law of probability**. The probability of an event happening depends upon the conditions that prevail at the time. This gives rise to the idea of **conditional probability**. Finally, once we understand the meaning of **independent events** we can see when to apply the **multiplication law of probability**.

5.2 Mutually exclusive events

The quality control department of a manufacturing unit examines components and places them into one of three categories:

A: acceptable quality
B: substandard quality
C: reject quality

A component can be placed in only one category. If it is placed in A then this excludes the possibility of it being placed anywhere else. Similarly, if it is placed in B, it cannot possibly belong to A or C. We say the categories are **mutually exclusive**. The events 'The component is placed in category A', 'The component is placed in category B' and 'The component is placed in category C' are **mutually exclusive events**.

After examining many components, the quality control manager calculates the experimental probabilities of a component belonging in category A, B or C as 0.85, 0.10 and 0.05 respectively. Since a component must be placed in one of the three categories, then the three probabilities must add to one.

If $E_1, E_2, \ldots, E_n$ are n mutually exclusive events then the occurrence of any one of these events excludes the occurrence of all other events.

Example 5.1

A fair die is rolled. Events E_1, E_2, E_3, E_4, E_5 are defined by

E_1: the score is even
E_2: the score is more than 3
E_3: the score is odd
E_4: the score is 1
E_5: the score is 3

Which events are mutually exclusive?

Solution

E_1 and E_3 are mutually exclusive.
E_1, E_4 and E_5 are mutually exclusive.
E_2, E_4 and E_5 are mutually exclusive.

Exercises

1 Two fair coins are tossed. State the events that are mutually exclusive.

E_1: both show heads
E_2: both show tails
E_3: there is one head and one tail
E_4: there is at least one tail

2 A fair die is rolled. The events E_1, E_2, E_3 and E_4 are given by

E_1: the score is less than 2
E_2: the score is divisible by 3
E_3: the score is even
E_4: the score is 5

State which events are mutually exclusive.

Solutions to exercises

1 E_1, E_2 and E_3 are mutually exclusive. E_1 and E_4 are mutually exclusive.

2 E_1, E_2 and E_4 are mutually exclusive. E_1, E_3 and E_4 are also mutually exclusive.

5.3 Addition law of probability

Suppose E_1 and E_2 are mutually exclusive events with probabilities $P(E_1)$ and $P(E_2)$. We consider the event 'E_1 or E_2'.

Key point

The addition law of probability states

$$P(E_1 \text{ or } E_2) = P(E_1) + P(E_2)$$

This idea can be generalised.

Key point

Suppose $E_1, E_2, \ldots, E_n$ are n mutually exclusive events. Then the addition law of probability states

$$P(E_1 \text{ or } E_2 \text{ or} \ldots \text{or } E_n) = P(E_1) + P(E_2) + \cdots + P(E_n)$$

Example 5.2 Reliability Engineering

A machine makes chips that are then classified as one of the following: top quality, standard quality or substandard. An examination of 3000 chips showed 2700 were top quality, 240 were standard quality and 60 were substandard. A chip is selected at random. Calculate the experimental probability that it is

(a) (i) top quality, (ii) standard quality, (iii) substandard
(b) top quality or standard quality
(c) standard quality or substandard

Solution

Let the events E_1, E_2 and E_3 be given by

E_1: the chip selected is top quality
E_2: the chip selected is standard quality
E_3: the chip selected is substandard

These events are mutually exclusive.

(a) (i) $$\text{probability chip is top quality} = P(E_1) = \frac{2700}{3000} = 0.9$$

(ii) $$\text{probability chip is standard quality} = P(E_2) = \frac{240}{3000} = 0.08$$

(iii) $$\text{probability chip is substandard} = P(E_3) = \frac{60}{3000} = 0.02$$

(b) The events are mutually exclusive and so the addition law of probability can be applied.

$$\begin{aligned}\text{probability chip is top or standard quality} &= P(E_1 \text{ or } E_2)\\ &= P(E_1) + P(E_2)\\ &= 0.90 + 0.08\\ &= 0.98\end{aligned}$$

(c) $$\begin{aligned}\text{probability chip is standard quality or substandard} &= P(E_2 \text{ or } E_3)\\ &= P(E_2) + P(E_3)\\ &= 0.08 + 0.02\\ &= 0.10\end{aligned}$$

Example 5.3 Reliability Engineering

The lifespan, L, of each of 4000 motors was measured and is given in Table 5.1. A motor is randomly selected. Calculate the probability that it had a lifespan of

(a) between 1000 and 2000 hours
(b) between 2000 and 3000 hours
(c) between 1000 and 3000 hours
(d) less than or equal to 4000 hours.

Table 5.1
The lifespan of 4000 motors.

Lifespan of motor (h)	Number
$L \le 1000$	20
$1000 < L \le 2000$	75
$2000 < L \le 3000$	100
$3000 < L \le 4000$	420
$4000 < L \le 5000$	585
$L > 2000$	2800

Solution

Let E_1 and E_2 be the events:

E_1: the lifespan is between 1000 and 2000 hours
E_2: the lifespan is between 2000 and 3000 hours

(a) $P(E_1) =$

$$\frac{75}{4000} = 0.01875$$

(b) $P(E_2) =$

$$\frac{100}{4000} = 0.025$$

(c) The events E_1 and E_2 are mutually exclusive and so the addition law of probability can be applied.

$$P(1000 < L \le 3000) = P(E_1 \text{ or } E_2)$$

$$=$$

$$= P(E_1) + P(E_2) = 0.04375$$

(d) If the lifespan, L, is less than or equal to 4000 hours then L lies between 3000 and 4000 hours, or between 2000 and 3000 hours, or between 1000 and 2000 hours, or is less than 1000 hours. So

$$P(L \le 4000) = P(3000 < L \le 4000) + P(2000 < L \le 3000) + P(1000 < L \le 2000) + P(L \le 1000)$$

$$=$$

$$\frac{420}{4000} + \frac{100}{4000} + \frac{75}{4000} + \frac{20}{4000}$$

$$= 0.1538$$

Exercises

1 Components are made by machines A, B, C and D. Machine A makes 30% of the components, machine B makes 17%, machine C makes 21% and machine D makes the rest. Calculate the probability that a component is made by
(a) machine A or machine B
(b) machine B or machine D
(c) machine A or machine B or machine D.

2 Components are made by machines A and B. Machine A makes 75% of the components with machine B making the rest. When made by machine A, 6% of the components are substandard, 2% are standard and the rest are superior. When made by machine B, 3% are substandard, 1% are standard and the rest are superior. A component is picked at random. Calculate the probability it is
(a) substandard
(b) standard
(c) substandard or standard
(d) standard or superior.

Solutions to exercises

1 (a) 0.47 (b) 0.49 (c) 0.79

2 (a) 0.0525 (b) 0.0175 (c) 0.07 (d) 0.9475

5.4 Conditional probability

Consider components that are manufactured by two machines X and Y. When made by machine X, 93% of the components are acceptable; when made by machine Y, 89% are acceptable. Let the event E be

E: a component is acceptable

If all the components are made by machine X then $P(E) = 0.93$. If all the components are made by machine Y then $P(E) = 0.89$. Clearly the probability of the event depends upon the prevailing conditions. This is intuitive and leads to the idea of **conditional probability**.

Let the events A and B be

A: the component is manufactured by machine X
B: the component is manufactured by machine Y

There is a notation for writing conditional probabilities. The probability that the component is acceptable given it is manufactured by machine X is written $P(E|A)$. Similarly, $P(E|B)$ is the probability that the component is acceptable given it is manufactured by machine Y: that, is the probability of event E happening given that event B has already happened.

In general

Key point

$P(R|S)$ is the probability of event R happening given that event S has already happened. $P(R|S)$ is the conditional probability of R given S.

Example 5.4 Reliability Engineering

Machines X and Y manufacture components. Machine X makes 65% of the components and machine Y makes the rest. When made by machine X, 95% of the components are acceptable; when made by machine Y, 91% are acceptable. A component is picked at random. Calculate the probability that it is

(a) acceptable, given that it is made by machine Y
(b) acceptable
(c) not acceptable, given that it is made by machine X
(d) made by machine X, given that it is acceptable.

Solution

Consider 100 components. The tree diagram in Figure 5.1 illustrates the given information.

Let the events A, B, E and $\overline{E}$ be defined by

A: the component is made by machine X
B: the component is made by machine Y
E: the component is acceptable
$\overline{E}$: the component is not acceptable

Figure 5.1

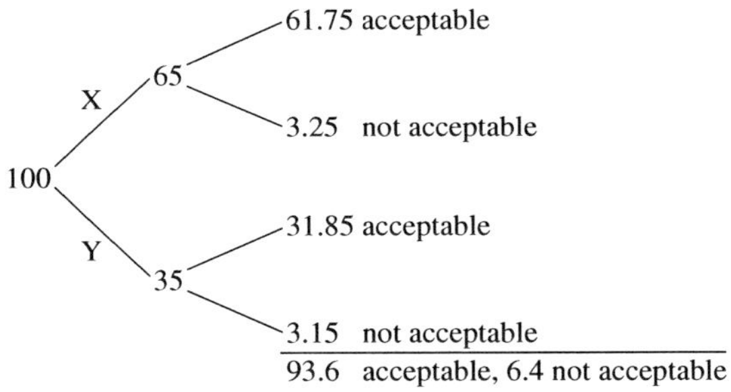

(a) When made by machine Y, 91% of the components are acceptable. So

$$P(E|B) = 0.91$$

(b) From Figure 5.1 we see that there are 93.6 acceptable components from the original 100. So

$$P(E) = 0.936$$

(c) When made by machine X, 95% of the components are acceptable and so 5% are not acceptable. Hence

$$P(\overline{E}|A) = 0.05$$

(d) From Figure 5.1 there are 93.6 acceptable components, of which 61.75 are made by machine X. So

$$\begin{aligned} P(\text{component is made by machine X given that it is acceptable}) &= P(A|E) \\ &= \frac{61.75}{93.6} \\ &= 0.6597 \end{aligned}$$

Example 5.5 Reliability Engineering

A quality control manager records the lifespan, L, of 1000 components of a particular kind. The results are shown in Table 5.2.

Table 5.2 Lifespan of 1000 components (hours).

Lifespan (h)	Number of components
$L < 1000$	69
$1000 \le L < 2000$	113
$2000 \le L < 3000$	516
$3000 \le L < 4000$	201
$L \ge 4000$	101

A component is picked at random. Calculate the probability that it has

(a) a lifespan between 2000 and 3000 hours

(b) a lifespan of 3000 to 4000 hours, given that it is still working after 2000 hours.

Solution

A tree diagram representing the information is shown in Figure 5.2.

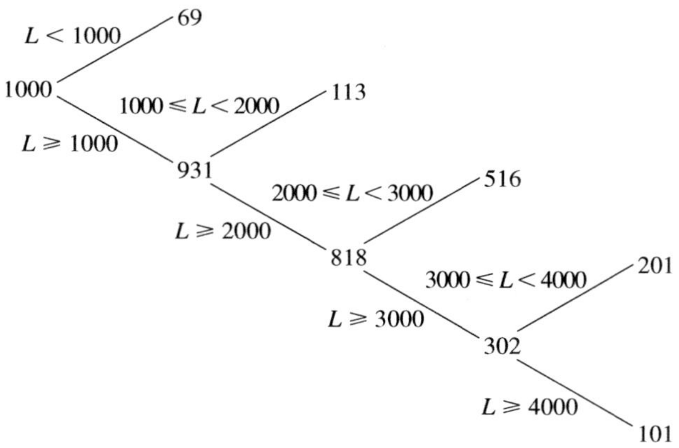

Figure 5.2 Tree diagram representing the information of Example 5.5.

(a) Out of 1000 components, 516 have a lifespan of between 2000 and 3000 hours. So

$$P(2000 \le L < 3000) = \qquad \frac{516}{1000} = 0.516$$

(b) There are components still working after 2000 hours.

$$516 + 201 + 101 = 818$$

Of these, have a lifespan of between 3000 and 4000 hours. 201

The probability that the lifespan is between 3000 and 4000 hours, given that the component is still working after 2000 hours, is $\frac{201}{818} = 0.2457$

Exercises

1 Table 5.3 shows the lifespan, L, of 3958 car batteries.

Table 5.3

Lifespan (months)	Number of batteries
$L < 12$	56
$12 \le L < 24$	219
$24 \le L < 36$	436
$36 \le L < 48$	1621
$48 \le L < 60$	1319
$L \ge 60$	307

Calculate the probability that a battery picked at random
(a) has a lifespan of between 24 and 36 months
(b) has a lifespan of between 12 and 48 months
(c) fails to work more than 48 months
(d) has a lifespan of between 36 and 48 months given it is working after 24 months
(e) has a lifespan greater than 60 months given it is working after 48 months
(f) fails to last more than 48 months given it has lasted 36 months.

2 Resistors are manufactured by machines A, B and C. Machine A manufactures 32% of the production, machine B manufactures 28% of the production and machine C makes the rest. When made by machine A, 3% of the resistors are faulty, when made by machine B, 4.5% are faulty, and when made by machine C, 2.7% are faulty. A resistor is picked at random. Calculate the probability that it is
(a) made by machine C
(b) made by machine A or machine C
(c) faulty
(d) faulty, given it is made by machine B
(e) made by machine B, given it is faulty
(f) made by machine A, given it is not faulty
(g) not made by machine B given it is not faulty.

3 The lifespan, L, of 3000 components is shown in Table 5.4.

Table 5.4

Lifespan (weeks)	Frequency
$0 \le L < 50$	93
$50 \le L < 100$	317
$100 \le L < 150$	1102
$150 \le L < 200$	1376
$200 \le L < 250$	112

A component is chosen at random. Calculate the probability that its lifespan is
(a) between 50 and 200 weeks
(b) more than 100 weeks
(c) less than 150 weeks
(d) between 150 and 200 weeks given it is still working after 50 weeks
(e) more than 200 weeks given it is still working after 100 weeks.

4 Components are manufactured by machines A, B, C and D in equal numbers. When made by machine A, 2% of the components are faulty. The figures for machines B, C and D are 3%, 2.5% and 3.5%, respectively. A component is picked at random. Calculate the probability that it is
(a) faulty and made by machine C or faulty and made by machine D
(b) faulty
(c) made by machine A given it is faulty
(d) faulty given it is made by machine C
(e) made by machine B given it is not faulty.

Solutions to exercises

1. (a) 0.1102 (b) 0.5750 (c) 0.5892 (d) 0.4401 (e) 0.1888 (f) 0.4992

2. (a) 0.4 (b) 0.72 (c) 0.033 (d) 0.045 (e) 0.3818 (f) 0.3210 (g) 0.7235

3. (a) 0.9317 (b) 0.8633 (c) 0.504 (d) 0.4733 (e) 0.0432

4. (a) 0.015 (b) 0.0275 (c) 0.1818 (d) 0.025 (e) 0.2494

5.5 Independent events

Key point

Two events are independent if the occurrence of either event does not change the probability of the other event occurring.

For independent events we can apply the **multiplication law of probability**.

Key point

The multiplication law of probability
If E_1 and E_2 are two independent events then

$$P(E_1 \text{ and } E_2) = P(E_1)\,P(E_2)$$

The multiplication law states that when E_1 and E_2 are independent, then the probability of both events happening is the product of the individual probabilities.

The law can be extended to three or more independent events. For example, if E_1, E_2 and E_3 are independent events then

$$P(E_1 \text{ and } E_2 \text{ and } E_3) = P(E_1)\,P(E_2)\,P(E_3)$$

Example 5.6 Reliability Engineering

A machine manufactures components, 90% of which are not faulty and 10% of which are faulty. Two components are picked at random. Calculate the probability that

(a) both components are not faulty
(b) both components are faulty.

Solution

Let the events E_1 and E_2 be

E_1: the first component is not faulty
E_2: the second component is not faulty

Note that $P(E_1) = P(E_2) = 0.9$. The events are independent.

(a) For both components to be not faulty we require E_1 and E_2 to happen. These events are independent: that is, whether or not E_1 happens does not change the probability of E_2 happening and vice versa. Hence the multiplication law can be applied.

$$\begin{aligned} P(\text{both components are not faulty}) &= P(E_1 \text{ and } E_2) \\ &= P(E_1)\,P(E_2) \\ &= (0.9)(0.9) \\ &= 0.81 \end{aligned}$$

(b) The events that are complementary to E_1 and E_2 are

$\overline{E}_1$: the first component is faulty

$\overline{E}_2$: the second component is faulty

Note that $P(\overline{E}_1) = P(\overline{E}_2) = 0.1$.

$$\begin{aligned} P(\text{both components are faulty}) &= P(\overline{E}_1 \text{ and } \overline{E}_2) \\ &= P(\overline{E}_1)\,P(\overline{E}_2) \\ &= (0.1)(0.1) \\ &= 0.01 \end{aligned}$$

Example 5.7 Reliability Engineering

The probability that a component is faulty is 0.05. Two components are picked at random. Calculate the probability that

(a) both are faulty
(b) both are not faulty
(c) one of the components is not faulty
(d) at least one component is faulty.

Solution

We define events E_1 and E_2 to be

E_1: the first component is faulty

E_2: the second component is faulty

The events are independent and $P(E_1) = P(E_2) = 0.05$.

The complementary events, $\overline{E}_1$ and $\overline{E}_2$, are given by

$\overline{E}_1$ the first component is not faulty

$\overline{E}_2$ the second component is not faulty

Then $P(\overline{E}_1) = P(\overline{E}_2) =$ $1 - 0.05 = 0.95$

(a) $P(E_1 \text{ and } E_2) =$ $(0.05)(0.05) = 0.0025$

(b) $P(\overline{E}_1 \text{ and } \overline{E}_2) =$ $(0.95)(0.95) = 0.9025$

(c) If one component is not faulty, then the other component must be faulty. So we have either 'E_1 and $\overline{E}_2$' or '$\overline{E}_1$ and E_2'.

$P(E_1 \text{ and } \overline{E}_2)$ $(0.05)(0.95) = 0.0475$

$P(\overline{E}_1 \text{ and } E_2)$ $(0.95)(0.05) = 0.0475$

Now the events 'E_1 and $\overline{E}_2$' and '$\overline{E}_1$ and E_2' are mutually exclusive and so the addition law of probability can be used.

$$\begin{aligned} P(\text{'}E_1 \text{ and } \overline{E}_2\text{' or '}\overline{E}_1 \text{ and } E_2\text{'}) &= P(\text{'}E_1 \text{ and } \overline{E}_2\text{'}) + P(\text{'}\overline{E}_1 \text{ and } E_2\text{'}) \\ &= 0.0475 + 0.0475 \\ &= 0.095 \end{aligned}$$

An alternative way to view this is as follows. We can consider three possible outcomes, X_1, X_2 and X_3 as follows:

X_1: two components are not faulty
X_2: one component is not faulty
X_3: there are no components that are not faulty

The probability of X_1 has been calculated in (b), that is $P(X_1) = 0.9025$.
The event X_3 may be reworded to

X_3: both components are faulty

and so, by (a), $P(X_3) = 0.0025$.
Now, since X_1, X_2 and X_3 together cover every possible outcome, we know that

$$P(X_1) + P(X_2) + P(X_3) = 1$$

and so

$$\begin{aligned} P(X_2) &= 1 - P(X_1) - P(X_3) \\ &= 1 - 0.9025 - 0.0025 \\ &= 0.095 \end{aligned}$$

(d) 'At least one component is faulty' means that either 'one component is faulty' or 'both components are faulty'. Now

$$P(\text{one component is faulty}) = 0.095$$
$$P(\text{both components are faulty}) = 0.0025$$

and these events are mutually exclusive. So

$P(\text{at least one component is faulty}) =$

$0.095 + 0.0025 = 0.0975$

Example 5.8
Three coins are tossed. Calculate the probability that all the coins show heads.

Solution
Let the events E_1, E_2 and E_3 be

E_1: first coin shows a head
E_2: second coin shows a head
E_3: third coin shows a head

Clearly, $P(E_1) = P(E_2) = P(E_3) = 0.5$ and all the events are independent. So

$$\begin{aligned} P(E_1 \text{ and } E_2 \text{ and } E_3) &= P(E_1)\,P(E_2)\,P(E_3) \\ &= (0.5)\,(0.5)\,(0.5) \\ &= 0.125 \end{aligned}$$

Exercises

1 A and B are independent events with $P(A) = 0.75$ and $P(B) = 0.9$. The compound event 'A occurs, then A occurs, then B occurs' is denoted by AAB. Other compound events are denoted in a similar way. Calculate the probability of the following compound events occurring:
(a) AAB (b) BBA (c) $AABB$

2 A fair die is thrown three times. Calculate the probability of obtaining
(a) three 6s
(b) three 1s
(c) two 6s given the first number is a 1
(d) two 6s given the first number is a 6.

3 Components are made by machines A, B and C. Machine A makes 35% of the components, machine B makes 25% and machine C makes the rest. Two components are picked at random. Calculate the probability that
(a) both are made by machine C
(b) one is made by machine A and one is made by machine B
(c) exactly one is made by machine A
(d) at least one is made by machine B
(e) both are made by the same machine.

4 A machine makes resistors of which 96% are acceptable and 4% are unacceptable. Three resistors are picked at random. Calculate the probability that
(a) all are acceptable
(b) all are unacceptable
(c) at least one is unacceptable.

Solutions to exercises

1 (a) 0.5063 (b) 0.6075 (c) 0.4556

2 (a) 0.0046 (b) 0.0046 (c) 0.0278 (d) 0.2778

3 (a) 0.16 (b) 0.175 (c) 0.455 (d) 0.4375 (e) 0.345

4 (a) 0.8847 (b) 0.000064 (c) 0.1153

End of block exercises

1 The probability that a component is reliable is 0.89. Four components are picked at random. Calculate the probability that
(a) all are reliable
(b) all are unreliable
(c) at least one is unreliable
(d) at least one is reliable.

2 A machine makes three components, A, B and C. For every 1000 components made, 400 are component A, 250 are component B and the rest are component C. Three components are picked at random. Calculate the probability that
(a) all are component B
(b) all are of the same type

(c) all are of a different type
(d) two of the components are of type A.

3 Three machines A, B and C manufacture a component. Machine A makes 30% of the components, machine B makes 35% of the components and machine C makes the rest. Components are classified as either acceptable or faulty: 3% of those made by machine A are faulty, 4% of those made by machine B are faulty, and 3.5% of those made by machine C are faulty.
(a) Find the probability that a component is made either by machine A or by machine C.
(b) Find the probability that it is made by machine B given that it is faulty.
(c) Find the probability that it is not made by machine B given that it is not faulty.
(d) Two components are picked at random. Calculate the probability that exactly one of them is made by machine A.
(e) Three components are picked at random. Calculate the probability that they are made by different machines.
(f) Three components are picked at random. Calculate the probability that they are all acceptable.

4 The lifespans, L, of 807 components were measured and the results recorded in Table 5.5.

Table 5.5
Lifespans of 807 components.

Lifespan (days)	Number
$0 \le L < 200$	19
$200 \le L < 300$	86
$300 \le L < 400$	417
$400 \le L < 500$	210
$L \ge 500$	75

(a) Calculate the probability that a component has a lifespan of at least 400 days given that it is still working after 200 days.
(b) Calculate the probability of a component failing before reaching 500 days given that it is still working after 300 days.
(c) Calculate the probability of a component failing between 300 and 500 days given that it is still working after 200 days.

5 A box contains 10 red, 12 blue and 8 yellow blocks.
(a) A block is picked at random. Calculate the probability that it is blue.
(b) A block is picked at random, its colour is noted and then it is replaced. This is repeated. Calculate the probability that
(i) both blocks are yellow
(ii) one block is yellow and one is red
(iii) both blocks are the same colour
(iv) the blocks have different colours.

6 A simple circuit is shown in Figure 5.3.

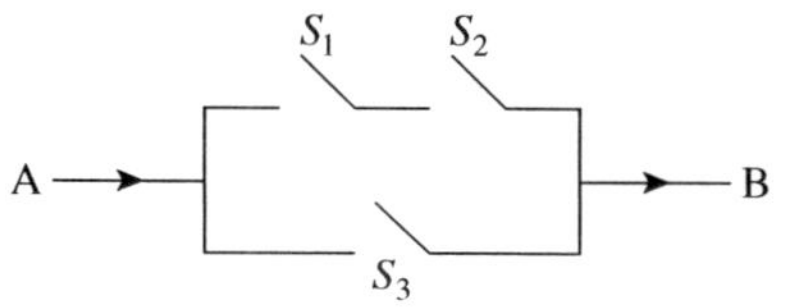

Figure 5.3

S_1, S_2 and S_3 are switches. The probabilities that S_1, S_2 and S_3 are closed are 0.86, 0.91 and 0.70 respectively. The switches open and close independently.
(a) Calculate the probability that S_1 and S_2 are both closed.
(b) Calculate the probability that a current can flow from A to B.

7 Two machines A and B manufacture components, with machine A making 55% and machine B making the rest. Of those made by machine A, 7% are defective; of those made by machine B, 5% are defective.
(a) A component is picked at random. Calculate the probability that it is made by machine A given that it is defective.
(b) Two components are picked at random. Calculate the probability that neither is defective.
(c) Two components are picked at random. Calculate the probability that they are made by different machines.

8 An aeroplane has four engines that all work independently of each other. The probability of an engine failing during a flight is 3×10^{-6}. If the plane can fly on two engines, calculate the probability that the plane is unable to fly.

Solutions to exercises

1 (a) 0.6274 (b) 0.0001 (c) 0.3726 (d) 0.9999

2 (a) 0.0156 (b) 0.1225 (c) 0.21 (d) 0.288

3 (a) 0.65 (b) 0.3972 (c) 0.6517 (d) 0.42 (e) 0.2205 (f) 0.8979

4 (a) 0.3617 (b) 0.8932 (c) 0.7957

5 (a) 0.4 (b) (i) 0.0711 (ii) 0.1778 (iii) 0.3422 (iv) 0.6578

6 (a) 0.7826 (b) 0.9348

7 (a) 0.6311 (b) 0.8817 (c) 0.495

8 1.08×10^{-16}

BLOCK 6 Probability distributions

6.1 Introduction

There are usually several possible outcomes for any given experiment. For example, when a component is tested it may be classified as substandard, satisfactory or first class. Here there are three possible outcomes. The outcome is a discrete variable. As another example, consider measuring the diameter of a piston. It may be 10.101 cm, 10.093 cm, 10.102 cm and so on. Here the outcome is a continuous variable, which can have any value within a specified range.

Probability distributions are used to assign probabilities to the various possible outcomes of an experiment. If the variable is discrete we use a probability distribution; if the variable is continuous we use a modified form of a distribution, called a **probability density function** (p.d.f.).

6.2 Probability distributions

Key point

The probability distribution of a discrete variable, X, gives the probabilities of all the possible values of X.

Example 6.1

Components produced in a factory are graded as substandard, satisfactory or first class. The percentage of each is 10%, 85% and 5% respectively. Thus the probability distribution is as follows:

Component description	Probability
Substandard	0.10
Satisfactory	0.85
First class	0.05

Example 6.2

A service engineer records the number of calls received in an 8 hour period for 300 similar periods. The results are given as:

Number of calls	Frequency
0	2
1	7
2	26
3	97
4	101
5	53
6	14

Construct a probability distribution for the number of calls.

Solution

Let X be the number of calls received. Note that X is a discrete variable that takes on values 0, 1, 2, . . . , 6. The probability of each different value of X occurring is calculated.

$$P(X = 0) = \frac{2}{300}$$
$$= 0.0067$$

$$P(X = 1) = \frac{7}{300}$$
$$= 0.0233$$

$P(X = 2) =$ $\qquad$ $\frac{26}{300} = 0.0867$

$P(X = 3) =$ $\qquad$ $\frac{97}{300} = 0.3233$

$P(X = 4) =$ $\qquad$ $\frac{101}{300} = 0.3367$

$P(X = 5) =$ $\qquad$ $\frac{53}{300} = 0.1767$

$P(X = 6) =$ $\qquad$ $\frac{4}{300} = 0.0467$

The probability distribution is

Number of calls, X	Probability
0	0.0067
1	0.0233
2	0.0867
3	0.3233
4	0.3367
5	0.1767
6	0.0467

A probability distribution may be represented graphically in the form of a **bar chart**. Figure 6.1 is a bar chart that represents the probability distribution of Example 6.2.

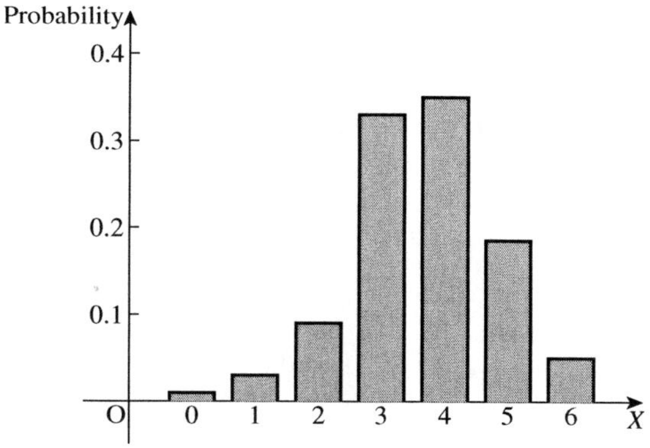

Figure 6.1 Bar chart for probability distribution of Example 6.2.

Note that when all the possible values of a variable have been considered, then the sum of the probabilities is 1.

To find the probability of several outcomes, the individual probabilities are added. Example 6.3 illustrates this.

Example 6.3

Using the data from Example 6.2, calculate the probability that the service engineer receives five or six calls in an 8 hour period.

Solution

The individual probabilities are noted: $P(X = 5) = 0.1767$, $P(X = 6) = 0.0467$.

So adding the probabilities we find the probability of receiving five or six calls.

$$\begin{aligned} P(X = 5 \text{ or } 6) &= P(X = 5) + P(X = 6) \\ &= 0.1767 + 0.0467 \\ &= 0.2234 \end{aligned}$$

Exercises

1 Explain what is meant by a probability distribution.

2 The number of employees absent each day in a particular firm is recorded over a 200 day period. The results are as follows:

Number absent	Frequency
2	12
3	36
4	81
5	10
6	15
7	46

(a) Calculate the corresponding probability distribution.
(b) Calculate the probability there are five or more absent employees on a day chosen at random.

Solutions to exercises

2 (a)

Number absent	Probability
2	0.06
3	0.18
4	0.405
5	0.05
6	0.075
7	0.23

(b) 0.355.

6.3 Probability density functions

Consider a continuous variable, X, which can take on any value between some prescribed limits. The probability that X lies somewhere between values, say, a and b is found from a **probability density function (p.d.f.)**, $f(x)$.

Key point

The probability that the continuous variable, X, lies between a and b, that is $P(a < X < b)$, is given by

$$P(a < X < b) = \int_a^b f(x)\,\mathrm{d}x$$

where $f(x)$ is the probability density function of X.

Thus the area under the p.d.f. between $x = a$ and $x = b$ gives the probability that the variable X lies between a and b. Figure 6.2 illustrates this.

Figure 6.2
$P(a < X < b) = \int_a^b f(x)\,dx$

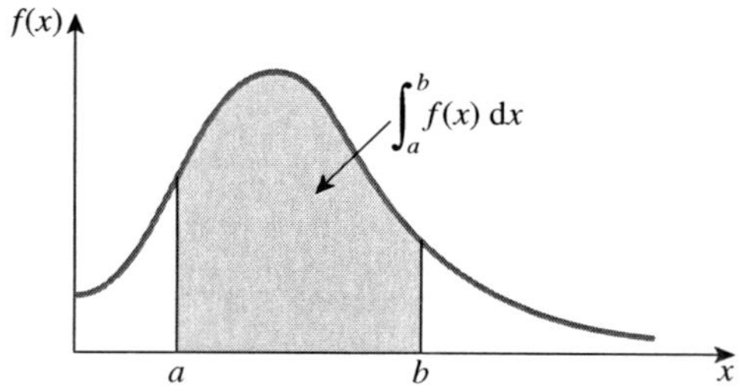

For a function to be a valid p.d.f. it must

1 never be negative
2 have a total area under the curve of 1, representing total probability.

Example 6.4

Given that X is a continuous variable, interpret the following expressions.

(a) $P(15 < X < 20)$
(b) $P(X < 1.7)$
(c) $P(X > 9.6)$
(d) $P(X = 2.6)$

Solution

(a) This represents the probability that X lies between 15 and 20.
(b) This is the probability that X is less than 1.7.
(c) This is the probability that X is greater that 9.6.
(d) $P(X = 2.6)$ is not a valid statement for a continuous variable. Probability statements for continuous variables must always be in terms of intervals. We could calculate $P(2.59 < X < 2.61)$ for example, but not $P(X = 2.6)$.

Example 6.5

A p.d.f. for the continuous variable X is given by

$$f(x) = 2x \quad 0 < x < 1$$

(a) Check that $f(x)$ is a valid p.d.f.
(b) Calculate $P(0.1 < X < 0.7)$.

Solution

(a) The function, $f(x)$, is defined only on the interval $0 < x < 1$ and on this interval it is never negative. Also

$$\begin{aligned}\int_0^1 f(x)\,dx &= \int_0^1 2x\,dx\\ &= [x^2]_0^1\\ &= 1\end{aligned}$$

and so the total area under $f(x)$ is 1. Hence $f(x)$ is a valid p.d.f.

$$\text{(b) } P(0.1 < X < 0.7) = \int_{0.1}^{0.7} 2x \, dx$$
$$= [x^2]_{0.1}^{0.7}$$
$$= 0.48$$

The probability that X lies between 0.1 and 0.7 is 0.48.

Example 6.6

A p.d.f., $f(x)$, for a continuous variable X is given by

$$f(x) = \frac{3}{16}(4 - x^2) \quad 0 < x < 2$$

Calculate
(a) $P(0.5 < X < 1.5)$ (b) $P(X < 1)$ (c) $P(X = 1.6)$

Solution

(a) $P(0.5 < X < 1.5) =$

$$\frac{3}{16}\int_{0.5}^{1.5} 4 - x^2 \, dx = 0.5469$$

(b) $P(X < 1) =$

$$\frac{3}{16}\int_{0}^{1} 4 - x^2 \, dx = 0.6875$$

(c) $P(X = 1.6)$ is not a meaningful statement for a continuous variable.

Exercises

1 Explain what is meant by a probability density function.

2 State two properties that a function must have in order to be a probability density function.

3 A p.d.f., $f(x)$, for a continuous variable X is given by

$$f(x) = \frac{3}{10}(x^2 + 1) \quad 1 < x < 2$$

(a) Verify that $f(x)$ can be a p.d.f.
(b) Find $P(1.7 < X < 2)$.
(c) Find $P(X < 1.5)$.
(d) Find $P(X > 1.25)$.

4 A p.d.f. for a continuous variable X is given by

$$f(x) = e^x \quad x < 0$$

Calculate
(a) $P(-1 < X < 0)$
(b) $P(-3.5 < X < -3)$
(c) $P(X < -1)$
(d) $P(X > -2)$

5 A p.d.f. for the continuous variable X is given by

$$f(x) = e^{-x} \quad x > 0$$

If $P(0 < X < \alpha) = 0.5$, find α.

Solutions to exercises

3 (b) 0.3987 (c) 0.3875 (d) 0.8297

4 (a) 0.6321 (b) 0.0196 (c) 0.3679 (d) 0.8647

5 0.6931

End of block exercises

1 A p.d.f., $f(x)$, has the form

$$f(x) = \alpha(x + 1) \quad 0 < x < 1$$

Calculate α.

2 Table 6.1 is a probability distribution.

Table 6.1

x	$P(x)$
6.0	0.13
6.5	0.10
7.0	0.09
7.5	0.02
8.0	0.23
8.5	0.43

Find
(a) $P(x \geq 7.0)$ (b) $P(x > 7.5)$
(c) $P(x \leq 8.0)$ (d) $P(x < 7.5)$
(e) $P(6.5 < x \leq 8.0)$

3 The number of reject components in each of 700 boxes is counted and recorded in Table 6.2.
(a) Construct a frequency distribution from the given data.
(b) Calculate the probability that the number of reject components is between 1 and 4 inclusive.

Table 6.2

Number of rejects per box	Frequency
0	117
1	123
2	236
3	147
4	63
5	14

4 A p.d.f. for the continuous variable X is given by

$$f(x) = \frac{x^2}{21} \quad 1 < x < 4$$

Calculate
(a) $P(2 < X < 3)$ (b) $P(X > 2.5)$
(c) $P(X < 3.5)$

5 A p.d.f. for the continuous variable X is given by

$$f(x) = 2e^{-2x} \quad x > 0$$

Calculate
(a) $P(1 < X < 5)$
(b) $P(X > 1)$
(c) $P(X < 2)$
(d) the value of α such that 90% of the X values are less than α.

Solutions to exercises

1 $\frac{2}{3}$

2 (a) 0.77 (b) 0.66 (c) 0.57 (d) 0.32 (e) 0.34

3 (a)

Number of rejects per box	$P(x)$
0	0.1671
1	0.1757
2	0.3371
3	0.2100
4	0.0900
5	0.0200

(b) 0.813

4 (a) 0.3016 (b) 0.7679 (c) 0.6647

5 (a) 0.1353 (b) 0.1353 (c) 0.9871 (d) 1.1513

BLOCK 7 The binomial distribution

7.1 Introduction

Consider an experiment in which a particular result may or may not occur. For example, a component is tested and it may be acceptable or not be acceptable, a circuit may work or not work. Such outcomes are complementary, and so their probabilities sum to 1. In general, we consider an experiment with possible outcomes of A and its complement $\overline{A}$. We let $P(A) = p$ and $P(\overline{A}) = q$ where clearly $p + q = 1$.

Suppose the experiment is repeated n times. We wish to calculate the probability of A occurring k times and $\overline{A}$ occurring $n - k$ times. For example, in testing a sample of 10 components, a quality control engineer may wish to know the probability of finding eight working components and two non-working components. The calculation of probabilities such as these uses the binomial distribution.

7.2 The binomial distribution

We consider an experiment, or **trial** as it is sometimes known, that is repeated n times. On each occasion the event A may occur with probability p, or its complement, $\overline{A}$, may occur with probability $q = 1 - p$. We assume that p and q are constants. If A occurs k times then $\overline{A}$ must occur $n - k$ times.

We can calculate the probability of no occurrences of A and n occurrences of $\overline{A}$, of one occurrence of A and $n - 1$ occurrences of $\overline{A}$, of two occurrences of A and $n - 2$ occurrences of $\overline{A}$ and so on. Thus we can calculate a probability corresponding to every possible outcome. These probabilities are known as a **binomial distribution**. The number of occurrences of A is known as a **binomial random variable**.

Example 7.1 Reliability Engineering

A machine manufactures components, 90% of which are acceptable. Three components are picked. Calculate the probability that the number of acceptable components is

(a) 0 (b) 1 (c) 2 (d) 3

Solution

We define A and $\overline{A}$ by

A: the component is acceptable

$\overline{A}$: the component is not acceptable

Then clearly, $P(A) = 0.9$ and $P(\overline{A}) = 0.1$.

(a) If there are no acceptable components then all three components are not acceptable. We denote this by $\bar{A}\,\bar{A}\,\bar{A}$. Since the events are independent the multiplication law can be applied.

$$\begin{aligned} P(\bar{A}\,\bar{A}\,\bar{A}) &= P(\bar{A})\,P(\bar{A})\,P(\bar{A}) \\ &= (0.1)(0.1)(0.1) \\ &= 0.001 \end{aligned}$$

(b) Here one of the three components is acceptable. We denote by $A\bar{A}\,\bar{A}$ the event: the first component is acceptable, the second is not acceptable, the third is not acceptable. Events $\bar{A}A\bar{A}$ and $\bar{A}\,\bar{A}A$ have obvious meanings.

If one component is acceptable, then $A\bar{A}\,\bar{A}$ or $\bar{A}A\bar{A}$ or $\bar{A}\,\bar{A}A$ occurs. These compound events are mutually exclusive and so the addition law can be applied.

$$\begin{aligned} P(\text{one component is acceptable}) &= P(A\bar{A}\,\bar{A} \text{ or } \bar{A}A\bar{A} \text{ or } \bar{A}\,\bar{A}A) \\ &= P(A\bar{A}\,\bar{A}) + P(\bar{A}A\bar{A}) + P(\bar{A}\,\bar{A}A) \\ &= (0.9)(0.1)(0.1) + (0.1)(0.9)(0.1) \\ &\quad + (0.1)(0.1)(0.9) \\ &= 0.027 \end{aligned}$$

(c) Two of the three components are acceptable. The various possibilities are

$$AA\bar{A}, \quad A\bar{A}A, \quad \bar{A}AA$$

These compound events are mutually exclusive.

$$\begin{aligned} P(AA\bar{A} \text{ or } A\bar{A}A \text{ or } \bar{A}AA) &= P(AA\bar{A}) + P(A\bar{A}A) + P(\bar{A}AA) \\ &= (0.9)(0.9)(0.1) + (0.9)(0.1)(0.9) \\ &\quad + (0.1)(0.9)(0.9) \\ &= 0.243 \end{aligned}$$

(d) All three components are acceptable. In this case there is only one possibility, AAA.

$$\begin{aligned} P(AAA) &= (0.9)^3 \\ &= 0.729 \end{aligned}$$

The results of Example 7.1 are summarised in Table 7.1.

Table 7.1

Number of acceptable components	Probability
0	0.001
1	0.027
2	0.243
3	0.729
	1.000

Since all possibilities have been covered the probabilities sum to 1. Let the number of acceptable components be x. Clearly x is a variable that can have values 0, 1, 2 and 3 with varying likelihood. Table 7.1 shows how the total probability, 1, is distributed between the various possible values of x. It is known as a **probability distribution** of the variable x. Since there are two possible outcomes for each event the distribution is referred to as a binomial distribution.

Exercises

1 The probability that a component is acceptable is 0.95. Four components are picked at random. Calculate the probability that
(a) all four are acceptable
(b) exactly three are acceptable
(c) all four are unacceptable.

2 The probability that a silicon chip works is 0.97. Five such chips are tested. Calculate the probability that
(a) all five chips work
(b) one chip does not work.

Solutions to exercises

1 (a) 0.8145 (b) 0.1715 (c) 6.25×10^{-6}

2 (a) 0.8587 (b) 0.1328

7.3 Combination notation

Before we can make progress and study a general binomial distribution we need to introduce combination notation.

Recall the factorial notation: $2! = 2 \times 1, 3! = 3 \times 2 \times 1, 4! = 4 \times 3 \times 2 \times 1$ and so on. We define the combination notation as follows:

Key point

$$\binom{n}{r} = \frac{n!}{r!(n-r)!}$$

For example, with $n = 5$, $r = 3$ we have

$$\binom{5}{3} = \frac{5!}{3!(5-3)!} = \frac{5!}{3!2!} = 10$$

The quantity $\binom{n}{r}$ is the number of ways of selecting r objects from n distinct objects, with the order of selection being unimportant.

Example 7.2
Calculate the number of ways of selecting three digits from 10 digits.

Solution

There are $\binom{10}{3}$ ways of making the selection.

$$\binom{10}{3} = \frac{10!}{3!7!} = 120$$

Exercises

1 Evaluate

(a) $\binom{10}{5}$ (b) $\binom{8}{7}$ (c) $\binom{9}{9}$

2 Calculate the number of ways of choosing seven objects from 26 distinct objects.

3 A nuclear power station is to be built. There are 15 possible sites. A team of engineers is commissioned to select a shortlist of the three sites. Calculate the number of ways this may be done.

4 Prove that

$$\binom{n}{r} = \binom{n}{n-r}$$

Solutions to exercises

1 (a) 252 (b) 8 (c) 1

2 657800

3 455

7.4 Probability of k occurrences from n trials

We are now able to consider the problem posed in Section 7.1.

An experiment, or trial, has two possible outcomes, A and $\overline{A}$, with respective probabilities of p and q where $p + q = 1$. The trial is repeated n times.

Key point

The binomial distribution
The probability of k occurrences of A and $n - k$ occurrences of $\overline{A}$ in a sequence of n independent trials is

$$\binom{n}{k} p^k q^{n-k}$$

where $P(A) = p$, $P(\overline{A}) = q = 1 - p$.

Example 7.3 Reliability Engineering

The probability that a component is acceptable is 0.97. Ten components are picked at random. Calculate the probability that

(a) nine are acceptable
(b) three are unacceptable.

Solution

Let A and $\bar{A}$ be defined:

A: the component is acceptable
$\bar{A}$: the component is unacceptable

Then $P(A) = p = 0.97$, $P(\bar{A}) = q = 1 - 0.97 = 0.03$. Ten components are examined, that is $n = 10$.

(a)
$$
\begin{aligned}
P(\text{nine acceptable components}) &= \binom{10}{9} p^9 q^{10-9} \\
&= \binom{10}{9}(0.97)^9(0.03)^1 \\
&= 10(0.97)^9(0.03) \\
&= 0.2281
\end{aligned}
$$

(b) if three components are unacceptable, then seven are acceptable.

$$
\begin{aligned}
P(\text{three unacceptable}) = P(\text{seven acceptable}) &= \binom{10}{7} p^7 q^3 \\
&= 120(0.97)^7(0.03)^3 \\
&= 0.0026
\end{aligned}
$$

Example 7.4 Reliability Engineering

The probability that a component is acceptable is 0.91. Twelve components are selected at random. Calculate the probability that at least 10 are acceptable.

Solution

At least 10 components being acceptable means that 10 or 11 or 12 components are acceptable. These three compound events are mutually exclusive. We calculate the probability of each.

We have $p =$ ____, $q =$ ____, $n =$ ____ 0.91, 0.09, 12

$P(10 \text{ acceptable components}) =$ ____ $\binom{12}{10}(0.91)^{10}(0.09)^2$

$= 0.2082$

$P(11 \text{ acceptable components}) =$ ____ $\binom{12}{11}(0.91)^{11}(0.09)$

$= 0.3827$

$$P(12 \text{ acceptable components}) = \binom{12}{12}(0.91)^{12}(0.09)^0$$

$$= 0.3225$$

Since the events are mutually exclusive, the addition law is used.

$$P(10 \text{ or more acceptable components}) = 0.2082 + 0.3827 + 0.3225$$

$$= 0.9134$$

There is a 91.34% chance that the 12 components contain 10 or more acceptable ones.

Exercises

1 The probability that a car will not develop a major fault within the first 3 years of its life is 0.997. Calculate the probability that of 20 cars selected at random
(a) 19 will not develop any major faults in the first 3 years
(b) 19 or more will not develop any major faults in the first 3 years.

2 The probability that a machine has a lifespan of more than 7 years is 0.85. Twelve machines are chosen at random. Calculate the probability that
(a) 10 have a lifespan of more than 7 years
(b) 11 have a lifespan of more than 7 years
(c) 10 or more have a lifespan of more than 7 years.

3 A machine needs all five of its micro-chips to be functional in order to work correctly. The probability that a micro-chip works is 0.99. Calculate the probability that the machine works.

4 The probability that a bearing meets a specification is 0.92. Six bearings are picked at random. Calculate the probability that
(a) all six meet the specification
(b) more than four meet the specification
(c) one or none meets the specification
(d) exactly four meet the specification.

5 The probability of passing a module on the first attempt is 0.9. A student takes six modules. Calculate the probability that the student
(a) passes five modules
(b) passes all modules
(c) is required to take two or more resits.

Solutions to exercises

1 (a) 0.0567 (b) 0.9984

2 (a) 0.2924 (b) 0.3012 (c) 0.7358

3 0.9510

4 (a) 0.6064 (b) 0.9227 (c) 1.835×10^{-5} (d) 6.877×10^{-2}

5 (a) 0.3543 (b) 0.5314 (c) 0.1143

7.5 Mean and variance

Key point

The mean and variance of a binomial random variable, X, are given by

$$\text{mean} = \mu = np$$

$$\text{variance} = \sigma^2 = np(1 - p)$$

where n is the number of trials and p is the probability of an occurrence of X in a single trial.

Example 7.5 Reliability Engineering

The probability that a component is acceptable is 0.96. Fifty components are tested. The number of acceptable components is X. Calculate (a) the mean, (b) the variance of X.

Solution

Here $n = 50$ and $p = 0.96$.
(a) Mean $= np = 50(0.96) = 48$.
(b) Variance $= np(1 - p) = 1.92$.

End of block exercises

1 Evaluate

(a) $\binom{10}{7}$ (b) $\binom{10}{1}$ (c) $\binom{12}{9}$ (d) $\binom{100}{99}$

2 Write a simple expression for

(a) $\binom{n}{1}$ (b) $\binom{n}{n}$ (c) $\binom{n}{n-1}$

3 The probability that a component is acceptable is 0.92. Ten components are selected at random. Calculate the probability that
(a) all 10 are acceptable
(b) eight are acceptable
(c) one is unacceptable
(d) eight or more are acceptable.

4 The probability that a component has a lifespan of more than 6 years is 0.85. Out of 10 components calculate the probability that
(a) nine have a lifespan of more than 6 years
(b) two have a lifespan of less than 6 years.

5 A fair die is thrown eight times. Calculate the probability that
(a) a 6 occurs six times
(b) a 6 never occurs
(c) an odd number of 6s is thrown.

6 A fair coin is tossed five times. Calculate the probability that
(a) five heads are obtained
(b) four heads are obtained
(c) three heads are obtained
(d) two heads are obtained
(e) one head is obtained.

7 A batch of 1500 components is examined and 1411 are found to be acceptable. Five components are picked at random from the production line. Calculate the probability that
(a) all are acceptable
(b) four are acceptable
(c) two are unacceptable.

8 The probability that a component is reliable is 0.92. An engineer wants to collect a number of

components to be at least 95% certain that there are at least seven components that are reliable. Calculate the number of components the engineer should collect.

9 The probability that a component is acceptable is 0.93. An engineer picks 200 components at random. If X is the number of acceptable components calculate (a) the mean, (b) the variance of X.

Solutions to exercises

1 (a) 120 (b) 10 (c) 220 (d) 100

2 (a) n (b) 1 (c) n

3 (a) 0.4344 (b) 0.1478 (c) 0.3777 (d) 0.9599

4 (a) 0.3474 (b) 0.2759

5 (a) 4.1676×10^{-4} (b) 0.2326 (c) 0.4805

6 (a) 0.03125 (b) 0.15625 (c) 0.3125 (d) 0.3125 (e) 0.15625

7 (a) 0.7365 (b) 0.2323 (c) 0.0293

8 9

9 (a) 186 (b) 13.02

BLOCK 8

The Poisson distribution

8.1 Introduction

We consider a fixed time interval, during which an event may happen 0, 1, 2, 3, . . . times. For example, during a 12 hour period, a fire department may receive 0, 1, 2, 3 or more calls. The department will know from experience that it is likely to receive, say, two or three calls, but on some days it may receive only one, or even none. On other days it will receive four or more calls. It would be useful to the fire department if it knew how likely it was to receive various numbers of calls. The Poisson distribution serves this purpose.

8.2 The Poisson distribution

The Poisson distribution models the number of occurrences of an event in a given time interval. It allows us to calculate the probability of the number of occurrences being 0, 1, 2, 3 and so on. Note that in the Poisson distribution the number of occurrences can be infinite. In contrast, the number of occurrences in a binomial distribution is limited to the number of trials.

The number of occurrences of an event, E, in a given time interval is a discrete variable, which we denote by X. If E does not occur then $X = 0$, if E occurs once then $X = 1$, if E occurs twice then $X = 2$ and so on. If the occurrence of E in any time interval is not affected by its occurrence in any preceding interval, then the probability of X having a particular value can be modelled using the Poisson distribution.

Suppose the number of occurrences, X, in the given time interval is measured many times. The mean of X can then be found; we denote this mean by λ. The probability that X has a value r is given by the Poisson distribution.

Key point

Poisson distribution

$$P(X = r) = \frac{e^{-\lambda}\lambda^r}{r!} \qquad r = 0, 1, 2, 3, \ldots$$

where λ is the mean of the distribution.

Example 8.1
In a particular Poisson distribution $\lambda = 2$. Calculate the probability that (a) $X = 1$, (b) $X = 2$, (c) $X = 3$.

Solution
We are given $\lambda = 2$ and so the distribution is

$$P(X = r) = \frac{e^{-2}2^r}{r!}$$

(a) We evaluate the probability expression with $r = 1$.

$$P(X = 1) = \frac{e^{-2}2^1}{1!} = 0.2707$$

(b)
$$P(X = 2) = \frac{e^{-2}2^2}{2!} = 0.2707$$

(c)
$$P(X = 3) = \frac{e^{-2}2^3}{3!} = 0.1804$$

Example 8.2 Reliability Engineering
A service engineer receives four emergency calls per day on average. Calculate the probability that on a particular day the engineer will receive (a) no calls, (b) one call, (c) two calls, (d) two or fewer calls, (e) more than four calls.

Solution
The average number of calls per day is four, that is $\lambda = 4$. Let X be the number of emergency calls received in 1 day. Then X is a variable with a Poisson distribution given by

$$P(X = r) = \frac{e^{-4}4^r}{r!}$$

(a)
$$P(X = 0) = \frac{e^{-4}4^0}{0!} = 0.0183$$

Thus there will be no calls on less than 2 days in 100.

(b)
$$P(X = 1) = \frac{e^{-4}4^1}{1!} = 0.0733$$

There will be one call per day in just over 7 days in a 100.

(c)
$$P(X = 2) = \frac{e^{-4}4^2}{2!} = 0.1465$$

(d) 'Two or fewer calls' means that the engineer receives two calls, one call or no calls. These events are mutually exclusive and so the addition law can be used.

$$\begin{aligned} P(X = 0 \text{ or } X = 1 \text{ or } X = 2) &= P(X = 0) + P(X = 1) + P(X = 2) \\ &= 0.0183 + 0.0733 + 0.1465 \\ &= 0.2381 \end{aligned}$$

(e) Let E be the event

E: the engineer receives more than four calls in a day

Then the complement of E is $\overline{E}$ given by

$\overline{E}$: the engineer receives four or fewer calls in a day

We calculate $P(\overline{E})$.

$$\begin{aligned} P(\overline{E}) &= P(X \leq 4) \\ &= P(X = 0) + P(X = 1) + P(X = 2) + P(X = 3) + P(X = 4) \\ &= \frac{e^{-4}4^0}{0!} + \frac{e^{-4}4^1}{1!} + \frac{e^{-4}4^2}{2!} + \frac{e^{-4}4^3}{3!} + \frac{e^{-4}4^4}{4!} \\ &= 0.6288 \end{aligned}$$

Since E and $\overline{E}$ are complementary events then

$$P(E) + P(\overline{E}) = 1$$

and so

$$\begin{aligned} P(E) &= 1 - P(\overline{E}) \\ &= 1 - 0.6288 \\ &= 0.3712 \end{aligned}$$

Example 8.3 Reliability Engineering

A service engineer mends washing machines. In a typical week, five machines will break down. Calculate the probability that in a week

(a) three machines break down
(b) six machines break down
(c) less than three machines break down
(d) more than three machines break down.

Solution

On average, five machines break down in a week, that is $\lambda = 5$. Let X be the number of machines that break down in a week. Then X follows a Poisson distribution given by

$$P(X = r) = \frac{e^{-5}5^r}{r!}$$

(a)
$$P(X = 3) = \frac{e^{-5}5^3}{3!} = 0.1404$$

(b) $P(X = 6) =$ $\qquad$ $\dfrac{e^{-5}5^6}{6!}$

$= 0.1462$

(c) 'Less than three breakdowns' means that $X = 0$ or $X = 1$ or $X = 2$. Since these events are mutually exclusive we can use the addition law of probability. Hence

$P(X < 3) = P(X = 0 \text{ or } X = 1 \text{ or } X = 2)$

$=$

$P(X = 0) + P(X = 1) + P(X = 2)$

$=$ $\qquad$ $\dfrac{e^{-5}5^0}{0!} + \dfrac{e^{-5}5^1}{1!} + \dfrac{e^{-5}5^2}{2!}$

$= 0.1247$

(d) Let E be the event

E: more than three machines break down

The complementary event, $\overline{E}$, is

$\overline{E} =$

three or fewer machines break down

We calculate $P(\overline{E})$.

$$
\begin{aligned}
P(\overline{E}) &= P(X \leq 3) \\
&= P(X = 0) + P(X = 1) + P(X = 2) + P(X = 3) \\
&= 0.1247 + P(X = 3) \quad \text{using(c)} \\
&=
\end{aligned}
$$

0.2651

Now

$$
\begin{aligned}
P(E) &= 1 - P(\overline{E}) \\
&= 0.7349
\end{aligned}
$$

So far we have looked at the probability of a number of occurrences during a time period. Sometimes, however, we consider the probability of a number of occurrences over a length as Example 8.4 illustrates.

Example 8.4 Reliability Engineering

A machine manufactures high-quality pipes. Experience has shown that on average there are three faults per 100 m of pipe. Calculate the probability that in 100 m of pipe there will be (a) no faults, (b) three faults.

Solution

The average number of faults per 100 m is three, that is $\lambda = 3$. Let X be the number of faults per 100 m of pipe. Then X has a Poisson distribution given by

$$P(X = r) = \frac{e^{-3}3^r}{r!}$$

(a)

$$P(X = 0) = \frac{e^{-3}3^0}{0!} = 0.0498$$

(b)

$$P(X = 3) = \frac{e^{-3}3^3}{3!} = 0.2240$$

Exercises

1 In a computer laboratory, on average three drives malfunction every month. Calculate the probability that in a particular month
(a) two drives malfunction
(b) one drive malfunctions
(c) more than three drives malfunction.

2 A firm has on average seven people absent due to illness per day. Calculate the probability that on a particular day there are
(a) five people absent
(b) eight people absent
(c) more than three people absent.

3 A Poisson distribution is given by

$$P(X = r) = \frac{e^{-3}3^r}{r!}$$

Calculate
(a) $P(X = 2)$ (b) $P(X < 2)$ (c) $P(X \geq 2)$

4 An engineer receives, on average, five emergency calls in an 8 hour period. Calculate the probability that in an 8 hour period the engineer receives
(a) exactly five calls
(b) less than three calls
(c) more than four calls.

Solutions to exercises

1 (a) 0.2240 (b) 0.1494 (c) 0.3528

2 (a) 0.1277 (b) 0.1304 (c) 0.9182

3 (a) 0.2240 (b) 0.1991 (c) 0.8009

4 (a) 0.1755 (b) 0.1247 (c) 0.5595

8.3 Poisson approximation to the binomial distribution

The Poisson and binomial distributions are related. Consider a binomial distribution in which n trials take place. Note that n is fixed. Suppose the probability of an event A occurring on a single trial is p. Let X be the number of occurrences of A in n trials. Also consider a Poisson distribution with mean λ.

If n is large and p is small and $\lambda = np$ then the Poisson and binomial distributions are very similar. Table 8.1 lists the probabilities for both distributions where $n = 20$, $p = 0.05$ and $\lambda = 20(0.05) = 1$.

Table 8.1 Probabilities for binomial and Poisson distributions.

	Binomial $P(X = r); n = 20, p = 0.05$	Poisson $P(X = r), \lambda = 1$
$r = 0$	0.3585	0.3679
$r = 1$	0.3774	0.3679
$r = 2$	0.1887	0.1839
$r = 3$	0.0596	0.0613
$r = 4$	0.0133	0.0153
$r = 5$	0.0022	0.0031

Example 8.5 Reliability Engineering

A computer room contains 100 PCs. The probability that a PC breaks down in a week is 0.005. Calculate the probability that in a week
(a) one machine breaks down
(b) no machine breaks down.

Solution

We solve the problem with both the binomial and the Poisson distribution.
Binomial distribution

E: the machine breaks down in a week
n = number of trials = 100
p = probability that E occurs in a single trial = 0.005
X = number of occurrences of E

The binomial distribution is then

$$P(X = r) = \binom{100}{r}(0.005)^r\,(0.995)^{n-r}$$

(a)
$$P(X = 1) = \binom{100}{1}(0.005)^1\,(0.995)^{99} = 0.3044$$

(b)
$$P(X = 0) = \binom{100}{0}(0.005)^0\,(0.995)^{100} = 0.6058$$

Poisson distribution
Strictly speaking, to calculate the probabilities we should use the binomial distribution because the number of occurrences is finite. However, since n, the number of trials, is large, 100, and the probability of breakdown small, 0.005, then a Poisson

distribution can approximate closely to the binomial distribution. The mean of the Poisson distribution is λ where $\lambda = np = 0.5$. The Poisson distribution is then

$$P(X = r) = \frac{e^{-0.5}\,(0.5)^r}{r!}$$

(a)

$$P(X = 1) = \frac{e^{-0.5}\,(0.5)^1}{1!} = 0.3033$$

(b)

$$P(X = 0) = \frac{e^{-0.5}\,(0.5)^0}{0!} = 0.6065$$

Example 8.6 Reliability Engineering

The probability that a disk drive fails in any month is 0.004. An engineer is responsible for 500 drives. Calculate the probability that in a month the number of drives failing is (a) none, (b) one, (c) more than two.

Use the Poisson approximation to the binomial distribution.

Solution

Number of drives $= n = 500$
Probability of failure $= p = 0.004$

$\lambda =$ $np = 2$

The Poisson distribution we use is

$P(X = r) =$ $\dfrac{e^{-2}\,2^r}{r!}$

(a) $P(X = 0) =$ $\dfrac{e^{-2}2^0}{0!}$

$= 0.1353$

(b) $P(X = 1) =$ $\dfrac{e^{-2}2^1}{1!}$

$= 0.2707$

(c) $P(X > 2) = 1 - [P(X = 0) + P(X = 1) + P(X = 2)]$

$=$ 0.3233

Exercises

1 On any day, the probability that a person is absent due to illness is 0.001. In a workforce of 600 people, calculate the probability that on any day the number of people absent is (a) none, (b) one, (c) more than one, (d) less than three.

2 The probability that a component fails within a month is 0.009. If 800 components are examined calculate the probability that the number failing within a month is (a) nine, (b) five, (c) less than three, (d) four or more.

3 A machine manufactures 350 micro-chips per hour. The probability that a chip is faulty is 0.012. Calculate the probability that in a particular hour there are (a) one, (b) three, (c) more than three faulty chips manufactured.

Solutions to exercises

1 (a) 0.5488 (b) 0.3293 (c) 0.1219 (d) 0.9769

2 (a) 0.1070 (b) 0.1204 (c) 0.0255 (d) 0.9281

3 (a) 0.0630 (b) 0.1852 (c) 0.6046

End of block exercises

1 A Poisson distribution is given by

$$P(X = r) = \frac{e^{-4}\,4^r}{r!}$$

(a) State the mean value of X.
(b) Calculate the probability that $X = 5$.
(c) Calculate the probability that $X = 2$.
(d) Calculate the probability that $X \geq 2$.

2 In a computer laboratory, a technician replaces, on average, four drives per month. Calculate the probability that in a particular month the technician replaces
(a) four drives
(b) more than four drives
(c) less than four drives.

3 A service engineer receives on average six call-outs in an 8 hour period. Calculate the probability that in an 8 hour period the engineer receives
(a) four call-outs
(b) seven call-outs
(c) between three and five call-outs inclusive.

4 A medium-sized firm has, on average, five people absent on any day. Calculate the probability that on a particular day there are
(a) four people absent
(b) more than four people absent.

5 A Poisson distribution is given by

$$P(X = r) = \frac{e^{-4}\,4^r}{r!}$$

Calculate
(a) $P(X < 3)$ (b) $P(X \leq 3)$ (c) $P(X \geq 3)$

6 A workforce comprises 750 people. During any week the probability that a person is absent is 0.01. Use the Poisson approximation to the binomial distribution to calculate the probability that there are
(a) seven absent people
(b) five absent people
(c) more than four absent people.

7 The probability that a component fails within 2 weeks is 0.0075. If 500 components are examined calculate the probability that the number failing within 2 weeks is (a) three, (b) four, (c) less than three.

Solutions to exercises

1 (a) 4 (b) 0.1563 (c) 0.1465 (d) 0.9084

2 (a) 0.1954 (b) 0.3712 (c) 0.4335

3 (a) 0.1339 (b) 0.1377 (c) 0.3837

4 (a) 0.1755 (b) 0.5595

5 (a) 0.2381 (b) 0.4335 (c) 0.7619

6 (a) 0.1465 (b) 0.1094 (c) 0.8679

7 (a) 0.2067 (b) 0.1938 (c) 0.2771

BLOCK 9 The normal distribution

9.1 Introduction

A variable that can take on any value within a given range is called a **continuous variable**. Examples of continuous variables include the weights of packets of sugar produced in a factory, the diameter of ball bearings and the heights of people. The **normal distribution** allows us to calculate the probability of a continuous variable falling within a particular range of values. Many variables such as weight, volume and density have been found to be modelled by a normal distribution, which is the reason why it has become one of the most important distributions needed by engineers.

In this block we describe the normal distribution and show how it is used to calculate probabilities. An understanding of probability density functions is essential; these were introduced in Block 6 of this chapter.

9.2 The normal probability density function

Suppose a factory produces pistons for a particular model of car. The diameters of the pistons must lie within a given range of values to be acceptable. The quality control manager measures the diameter of several hundred pistons. From these measurements the mean and standard deviation can be calculated.

For a normal distribution we denote the mean by μ and the standard deviation by σ. It is these two values that characterise a normal distribution. Suppose x is a variable, such as length or weight. Then the **normal probability density function**, $N(x)$, is a bell-shaped curve, illustrated in Figure 9.1. Note that $N(x)$ is symmetrical about

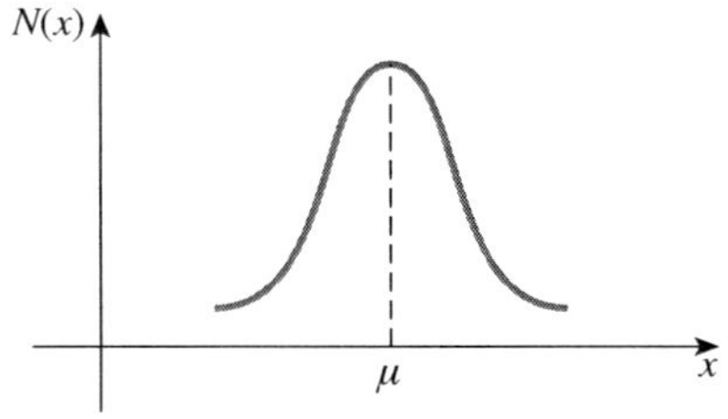

Figure 9.1 A typical normal probability density function.

a vertical line placed at $x = \mu$, the mean of the distribution. This means that a variable that is normally distributed is as likely to lie above as below the mean. Furthermore, it is more likely to have a value close to the mean than further from the mean. The symmetry of the normal distribution will be very important when we come to calculate probabilities.

A formula for the normal probability density function $N(x)$ is as follows.

Key point

Normal probability density function

$$N(x) = \frac{1}{\sigma\sqrt{2\pi}} e^{-(x-\mu)^2/2\sigma^2} \quad -\infty < x < \infty$$

Note that the expression for $N(x)$ involves both μ and σ.

As the values of μ and σ change, the curve, $N(x)$, changes but still retains the bell-shaped feature and the symmetry about $x = \mu$. Figure 9.2 shows two graphs of $N(x)$, both with the same value of σ but with different values of μ.

As μ increases the effect on $N(x)$ is to 'move' it to the right, along the x axis.

Figure 9.3 shows two graphs of $N(x)$, with the same value of μ, but different values of σ.

In Figure 9.3, σ_2 is greater than σ_1. Clearly the spread of the distribution increases as σ increases.

In summary, the value of μ, the mean, determines where the centre of the distribution lies. The value of σ, the standard deviation, determines how far spread out the distribution is.

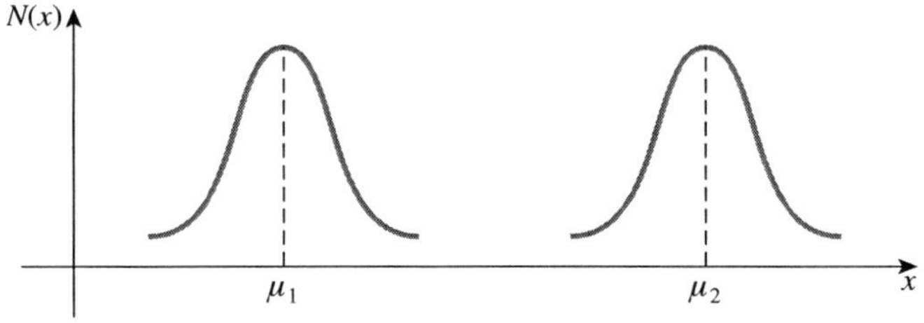

Figure 9.2
As μ increases, the curve moves to the right.

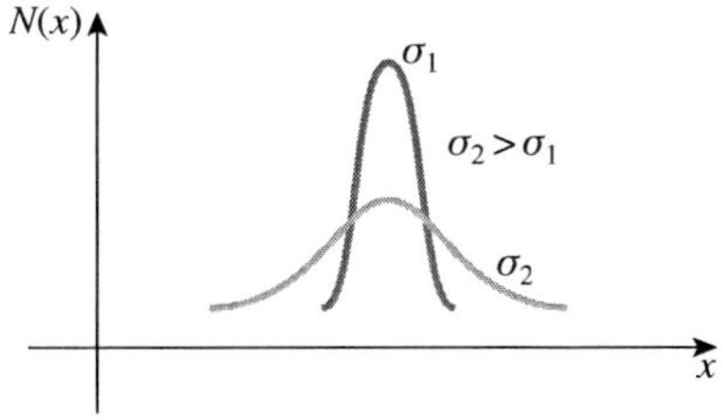

Figure 9.3
As σ increases, the spread of the normal distribution increases.

Exercises

1 Figure 9.4 shows two normal distributions, A and B.

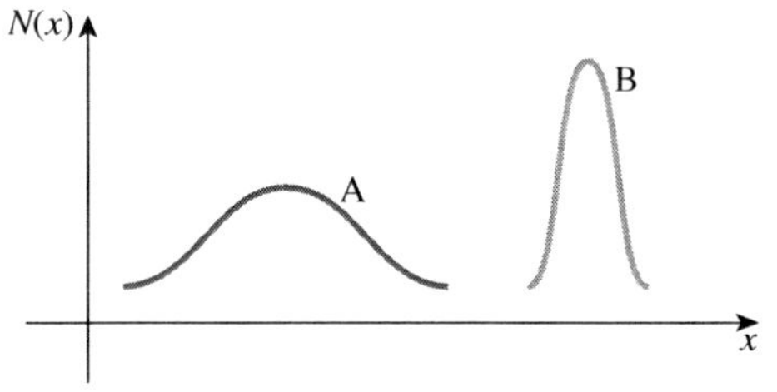

Figure 9.4

(a) Which distribution has the higher mean?
(b) Which distribution has the higher standard deviation?

2 Figure 9.5 shows two normal distributions, A and B.

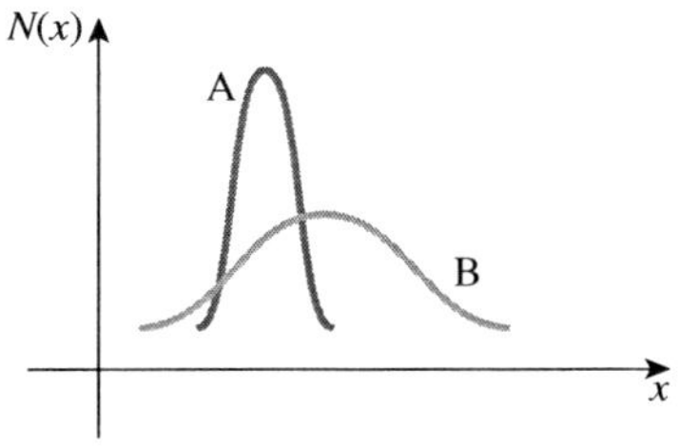

Figure 9.5

(a) Which distribution has the higher mean?
(b) Which distribution has the higher standard deviation?

Solutions to exercises

1 (a) B (b) A

2 (a) B (b) B

9.3 The standard normal distribution

We have seen how a normal distribution, $N(x)$, depends upon the mean, μ, and the standard deviation, σ. We now look at a particular normal distribution with mean 0 and standard deviation 1. Such a distribution is called a **standard normal distribution**. Its probability density function is $N(x) = \frac{1}{\sqrt{2\pi}}e^{-x^2/2}$.

Key point

The **standard normal distribution** has a mean of 0 and a standard deviation of 1.

Suppose we have a continuous variable, x, which has a standard normal distribution. Since x is continuous, it can take on any value. We can calculate the probability that x will lie within a given interval, say (a, b).

Key point

If x has a standard normal distribution, $N(x)$, then the probability that x lies within the interval (a, b) is

$$P(a < x < b) = \int_a^b N(x)\,dx$$

The quantity $\int_a^b N(x)\,dx$ is illustrated in Figure 9.6.

Figure 9.6
The shaded area represents the probability that x lies in the interval (a, b).

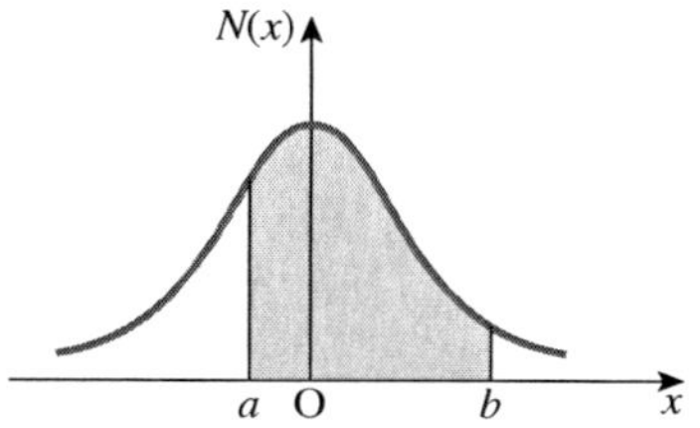

Because $N(x)$ is a probability density function it can be shown that the total area under $N(x)$ is 1, that is

$$\int_{-\infty}^{\infty} N(x)\,dx = 1$$

This represents total probability.

However, we are immediately presented with a problem because $N(x)$ cannot be integrated exactly.

To make numerical calculations easier we introduce a new function $A(z)$ defined by

$$A(z) = P(x < z)$$

Thus $A(z)$ is the probability that x is less than z. Being a probability, $A(z)$ must lie between 0 and 1. In terms of an integral we have

$$A(z) = P(x < z) = \int_{-\infty}^{z} N(x)\,dx$$

The shaded area in Figure 9.7 represents $A(z)$, so it will be helpful to think of $A(z)$ as the area under the graph of $N(x)$ up to the point where $x = z$.

Figure 9.7
The shaded area represents the value of $A(z)$.

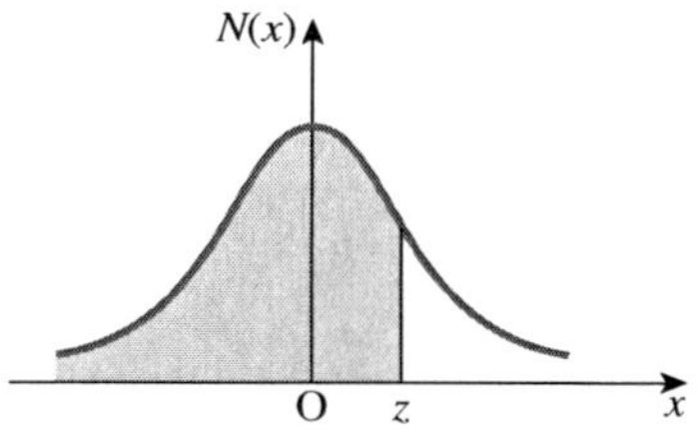

Consider the case where $z = 0$. Then $A(z = 0)$ is illustrated in Figure 9.8.

Recall that $N(x)$ is symmetrical about the mean, which for a standard normal is 0. The total area under the curve is 1. Hence the shaded area in Figure 9.8 is 0.5, that is, $A(z = 0) = 0.5$.

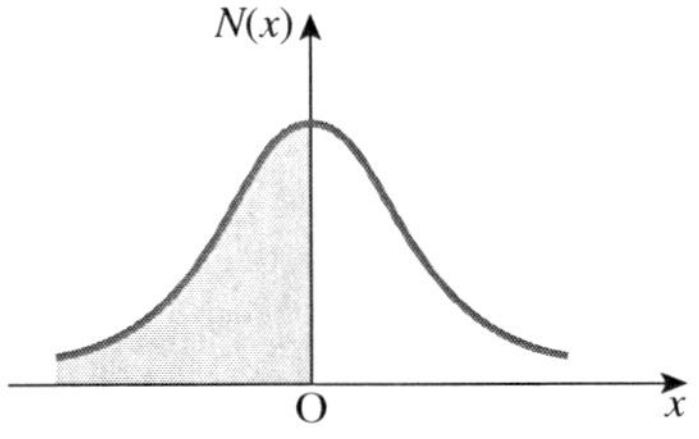

Figure 9.8 Owing to symmetry $A(z = 0) = 0.5$.

Values of $A(z)$ for other values of z cannot be found by simply inspecting the graph. $A(z)$ must be found by evaluating the integral $\int_{-\infty}^{z} N(x)\,dx$. This is difficult and must be done numerically. Fortunately tables of $A(z)$ are commonly available so that integration is not necessary. Values of $A(z)$ for various values of z are given in Table 9.1 on page 1124.

Using Table 9.1 we are able to calculate the probability that x lies within a given interval.

9.4 Calculating probabilities using Table 9.1

Table 9.1 can be used to calculate the probability that x lies within a given interval. Recall that x follows a standard normal distribution: that is, it has a mean of 0 and a standard deviation of 1. The values of $A(z)$ in Table 9.1 give the probability that x is less than z, that is

$$A(z) = P(x < z)$$

Example 9.1

The continuous variable, x, has a standard normal distribution. Calculate the probability that

(a) $x < 0.86$ (b) $x > 0.86$ (c) $x < -0.86$ (d) $x > -0.86$

Solution

(a) This case is illustrated in Figure 9.9.

$$P(x < 0.86) = A(0.86)$$

From Table 9.1, $A(0.86) = 0.8051$. Hence

$$P(x < 0.86) = 0.8051$$

There is a probability of 0.8051 that the variable x is less than 0.86.

Figure 9.9
$P(x < 0.86) = 0.8051$.

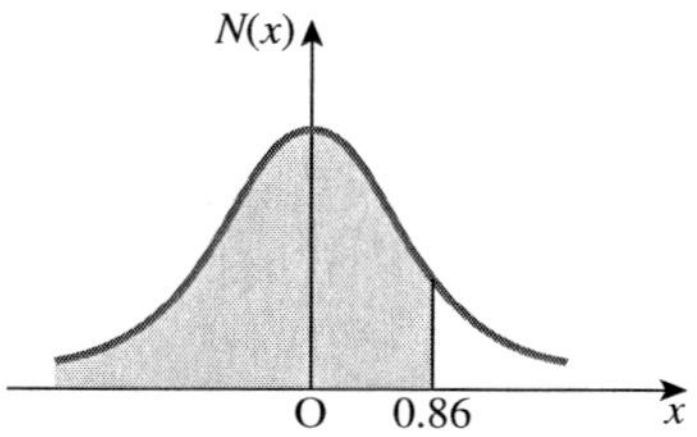

(b) This case is illustrated in Figure 9.10. Since the total area under the curve is 1, we have

$$\begin{aligned} P(x > 0.86) &= 1 - P(x < 0.86) \\ &= 1 - 0.8051 \\ &= 0.1949 \end{aligned}$$

Figure 9.10
$P(x > 0.86) = 1 - 0.8051 = 0.1949$.

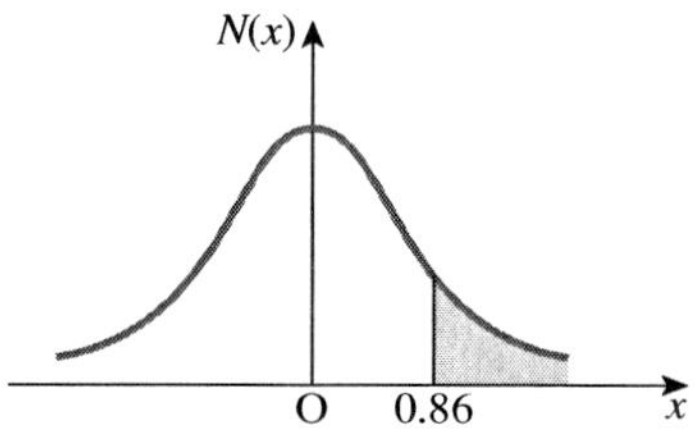

(c) Figure 9.11 illustrates the required area.

Figure 9.11
By symmetry $P(x < -0.86) = P(x > 0.86)$.

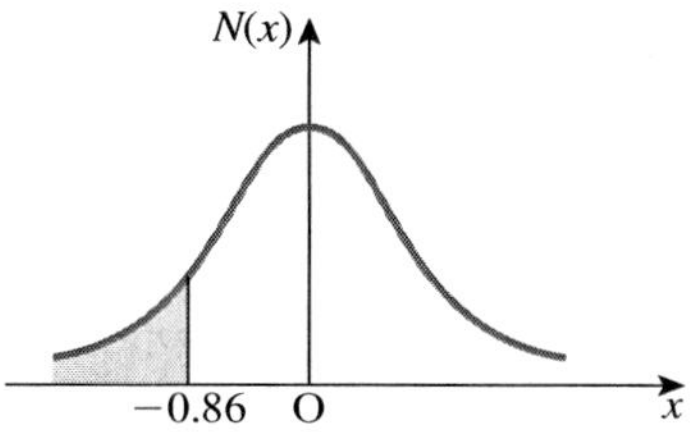

Using the symmetry of the normal distribution we see that

$$\begin{aligned} P(x < -0.86) &= P(x > 0.86) \\ &= 1 - P(x < 0.86) \\ &= 0.1949 \end{aligned}$$

(d) Figure 9.12 illustrates the area.
Again by the symmetry we see that

$$P(x > -0.86) = P(x < 0.86)$$

and so

$$P(x > -0.86) = 0.8051$$

Table 9.1 Cumulative normal probabilities.

z	$A(z)$	z	$A(z)$	z	$A(z)$	z	$A(z)$	z	$A(z)$	z	$A(z)$
0.00	0.5000000	0.30	0.6179114	0.60	0.7257469	0.90	0.8159399	1.20	0.8849303	1.50	0.9331928
0.01	0.5039894	0.31	0.6217195	0.61	0.7290691	0.91	0.8185887	1.21	0.8868606	1.51	0.9344783
0.02	0.5079783	0.32	0.6255158	0.62	0.7323711	0.92	0.8212136	1.22	0.8887676	1.52	0.9357445
0.03	0.5119665	0.33	0.6293000	0.63	0.7356527	0.93	0.8238145	1.23	0.8906514	1.53	0.9369916
0.04	0.5159534	0.34	0.6330717	0.64	0.7389137	0.94	0.8263912	1.24	0.8925123	1.54	0.9382198
0.05	0.5199388	0.35	0.6368307	0.65	0.7421539	0.95	0.8289439	1.25	0.8943502	1.55	0.9394292
0.06	0.5239222	0.36	0.6405764	0.66	0.7453731	0.96	0.8314724	1.26	0.8961653	1.56	0.9406201
0.07	0.5279032	0.37	0.6443088	0.67	0.7485711	0.97	0.8339768	1.27	0.8979577	1.57	0.9417924
0.08	0.5318814	0.38	0.6480273	0.68	0.7517478	0.98	0.8364569	1.28	0.8997274	1.58	0.9429466
0.09	0.5358564	0.39	0.6517317	0.69	0.7549029	0.99	0.8389129	1.29	0.9014747	1.59	0.9440826
0.10	0.5398278	0.40	0.6554217	0.70	0.7580363	1.00	0.8413447	1.30	0.9031995	1.60	0.9452007
0.11	0.5437953	0.41	0.6590970	0.71	0.7611479	1.01	0.8437524	1.31	0.9049021	1.61	0.9463011
0.12	0.5477584	0.42	0.6627573	0.72	0.7642375	1.02	0.8461358	1.32	0.9065825	1.62	0.9473839
0.13	0.5517168	0.43	0.6664022	0.73	0.7673049	1.03	0.8484950	1.33	0.9082409	1.63	0.9484493
0.14	0.5556700	0.44	0.6700314	0.74	0.7703500	1.04	0.8508300	1.34	0.9098773	1.64	0.9494974
0.15	0.5596177	0.45	0.6736448	0.75	0.7733726	1.05	0.8531409	1.35	0.9114920	1.65	0.9505285
0.16	0.5635595	0.46	0.6772419	0.76	0.7763727	1.06	0.8554277	1.36	0.9130850	1.66	0.9515428
0.17	0.5674949	0.47	0.6808225	0.77	0.7793501	1.07	0.8576903	1.37	0.9146565	1.67	0.9525403
0.18	0.5714237	0.48	0.6843863	0.78	0.7823046	1.08	0.8599289	1.38	0.9162067	1.68	0.9535213
0.19	0.5753454	0.49	0.6879331	0.79	0.7852361	1.09	0.8621434	1.39	0.9177356	1.69	0.9544860
0.20	0.5792597	0.50	0.6914625	0.80	0.7881446	1.10	0.8643339	1.40	0.9192433	1.70	0.9554345
0.21	0.5831662	0.51	0.6949743	0.81	0.7910299	1.11	0.8665005	1.41	0.9207302	1.71	0.9563671
0.22	0.5870604	0.52	0.6984682	0.82	0.7938919	1.12	0.8686431	1.42	0.9221962	1.72	0.9572838
0.23	0.5909541	0.53	0.7019440	0.83	0.7967306	1.13	0.8707619	1.43	0.9236415	1.73	0.9581849
0.24	0.5948349	0.54	0.7054015	0.84	0.7995458	1.14	0.8728568	1.44	0.9250663	1.74	0.9590705
0.25	0.5987063	0.55	0.7088403	0.85	0.8023375	1.15	0.8749281	1.45	0.9264707	1.75	0.9599408
0.26	0.6025681	0.56	0.7122603	0.86	0.8051055	1.16	0.8769756	1.46	0.9278550	1.76	0.9607961
0.27	0.6064199	0.57	0.7156612	0.87	0.8078498	1.17	0.8789995	1.47	0.9292191	1.77	0.9616364
0.28	0.6102612	0.58	0.7190427	0.88	0.8105703	1.18	0.8809999	1.48	0.9305634	1.78	0.9624620
0.29	0.6140919	0.59	0.7224047	0.89	0.8132671	1.19	0.8829768	1.49	0.9318879	1.79	0.9632730

1.80	0.9640697	1.95	0.9744119	2.10	0.9821356	2.25	0.9877755	2.40	0.9918025	2.55	0.9946139
1.81	0.9648521	1.96	0.9750021	2.11	0.9825708	2.26	0.9880894	2.41	0.9920237	2.56	0.9947664
1.82	0.9656205	1.97	0.9755808	2.12	0.9829970	2.27	0.9883962	2.42	0.9922397	2.57	0.9949151
1.83	0.9663750	1.98	0.9761482	2.13	0.9834142	2.28	0.9886962	2.43	0.9924506	2.58	0.9950600
1.84	0.9671159	1.99	0.9767045	2.14	0.9838226	2.29	0.9889893	2.44	0.9926564	2.59	0.9952012
1.85	0.9678432	2.00	0.9772499	2.15	0.9842224	2.30	0.9892759	2.45	0.9928572	2.60	0.9953383
1.86	0.9685572	2.01	0.9777844	2.16	0.9846137	2.31	0.9895559	2.46	0.9930531	2.70	0.9965330
1.87	0.9692581	2.02	0.9783083	2.17	0.9849966	2.32	0.9898296	2.47	0.9932443	2.80	0.9974449
1.88	0.9699460	2.03	0.9788217	2.18	0.9853713	2.33	0.9900969	2.48	0.9934309	2.90	0.9981342
1.89	0.9706210	2.04	0.9793248	2.19	0.9857379	2.34	0.9903581	2.49	0.9936128	3.00	0.9986501
1.90	0.9712834	2.05	0.9798178	2.20	0.9860966	2.35	0.9906133	2.50	0.9937903	3.20	0.9993129
1.91	0.9719334	2.06	0.9803007	2.21	0.9864474	2.36	0.9908625	2.51	0.9939634	3.40	0.9996631
1.92	0.9725711	2.07	0.9807738	2.22	0.9867906	2.37	0.9911060	2.52	0.9941323	3.60	0.9998409
1.93	0.9731966	2.08	0.9812372	2.23	0.9871263	2.38	0.9913437	2.53	0.9942966	3.80	0.9999277
1.94	0.9738102	2.09	0.9816911	2.24	0.9874545	2.39	0.9915758	2.54	0.9944574	4.00	0.9999683
										4.50	0.9999966
										5.00	0.9999997
										5.50	0.9999999

Source: This table was originally printed as Table 1 in *Biometrika Tables for Statisticians*, Vol. 1 (1st ed.), edited by E. S. Pearson and H. O. Hartley, 1970. Shown here is the condensed version which was printed in *Statistics: Probability, Inference and Decision*, Vol. 1 & 2 (1st ed.) by Hays, W. L. and Winkler, R. L., 1970. The table is reproduced with kind permission from Oxford University Press and Brooke/Cole, a division of Thomson Learning.

Figure 9.12
$P(x > -0.86) = P(x < 0.86)$.

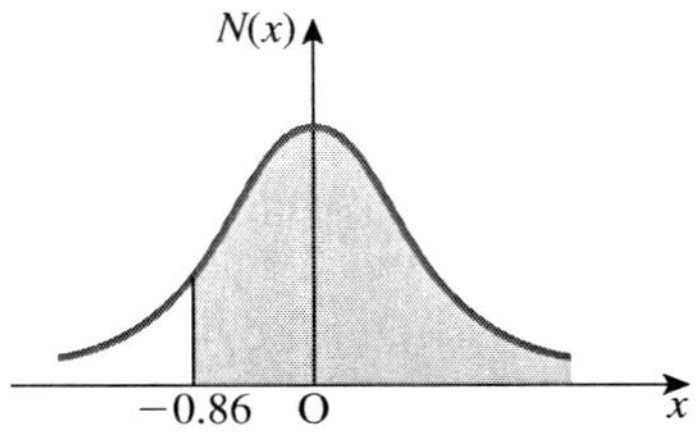

Example 9.2

The variable x has a standard normal distribution. Calculate the probability that (a) $x < 2.06$ (b) $x < -1.17$ (c) $x > 0.5$ (d) $x > -0.75$

Solution

(a) Figure 9.13 illustrates the area.

Figure 9.13
The shaded area represents $P(x < 2.06)$.

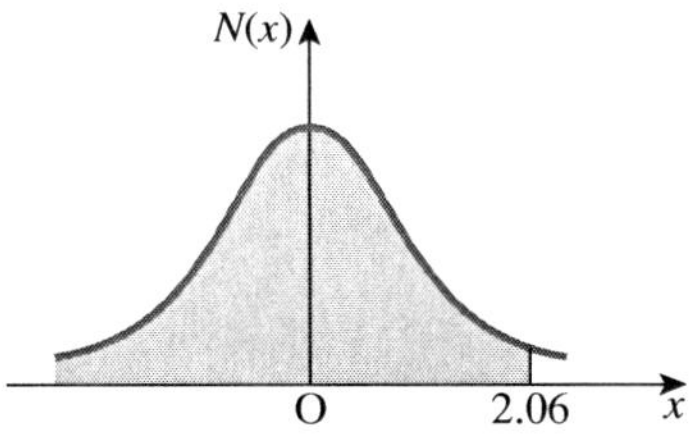

Using Table 9.1 we see

$P(x < 2.06) =$ ______ 0.9803

(b) Figure 9.14 illustrates the area.

Figure 9.14
The shaded area represents $P(x < -1.17)$.

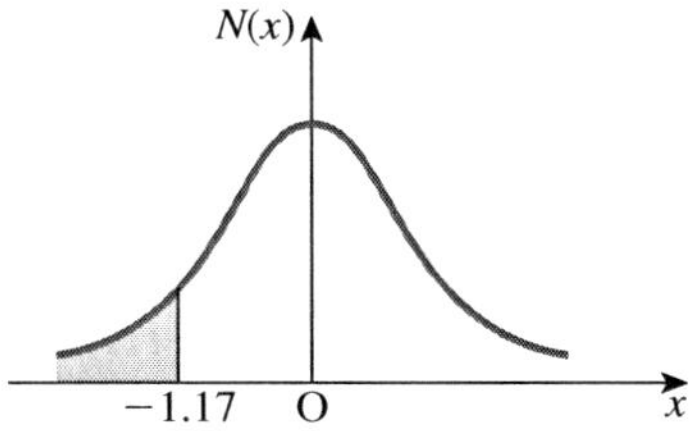

Using the symmetry of the distribution we have

$P(x < -1.17) =$ ______ $P(x > 1.17)$

$= 1 -$ ______ $P(x < 1.17)$

$=$ ______ $1 - 0.8790 = 0.1210$

(c) Figure 9.15 illustrates the area.

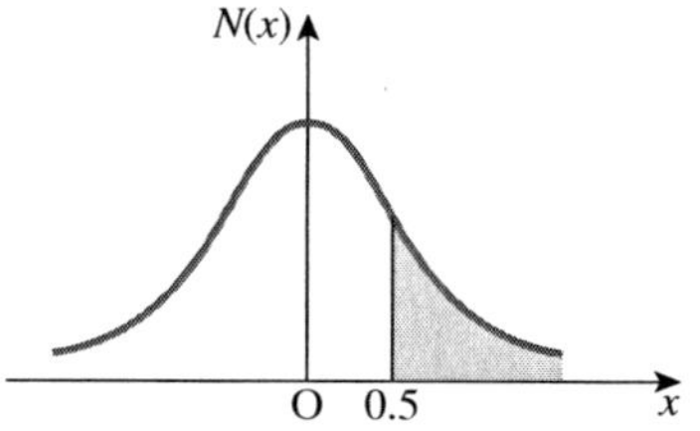

Figure 9.15 The shaded area represents $P(x > 0.5)$.

$$P(x > 0.5) = 1 - P(x < 0.5)$$
$$= 1 - 0.6915 = 0.3085$$

(d) Figure 9.16 illustrates the required area.

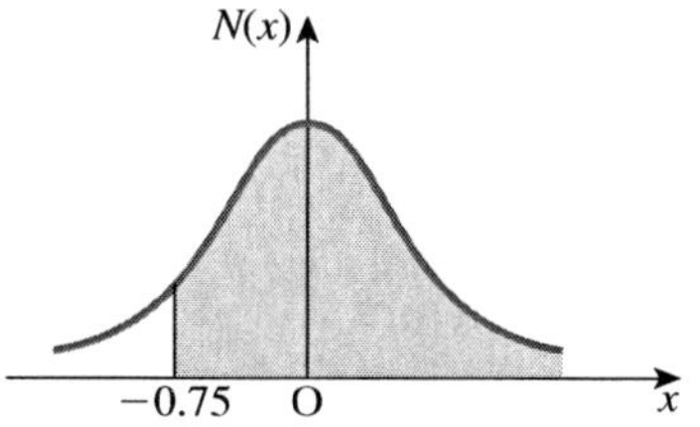

Figure 9.16 The shaded area represents $P(x > -0.75)$.

$$P(x > -0.75) = P(x < 0.75)$$
$$= 0.7734$$

Example 9.3

A variable, x, has a normal distribution with a mean of 0 and a standard deviation of 1: that is, it has a standard normal distribution. Calculate
(a) $P(0.6 < x < 1.9)$ (b) $P(-0.86 < x < 0.3)$ (c) $P(-1.5 < x < -0.7)$

Solution

(a) Figure 9.17 illustrates the required area.

Recall that Table 9.1 gives values of $A(z)$ where

$$A(z) = P(x < z)$$

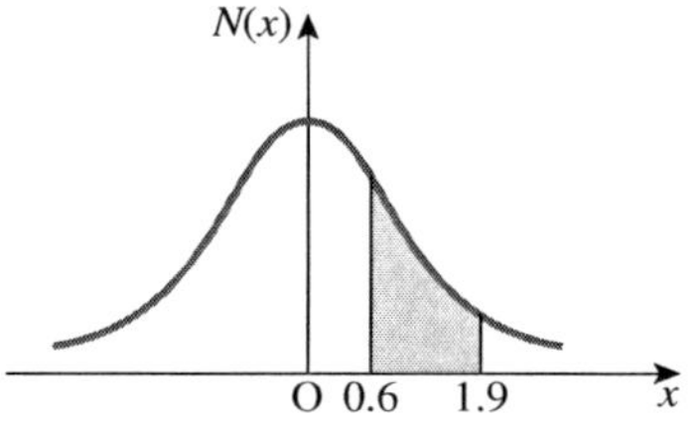

Figure 9.17 The shaded area represents $P(0.6 < x < 1.9)$.

that is, the probability that x is less than some specified value, z. We can view the shaded area in Figure 9.17 as $A(1.9) - A(0.6)$. Figure 9.18 illustrates this.

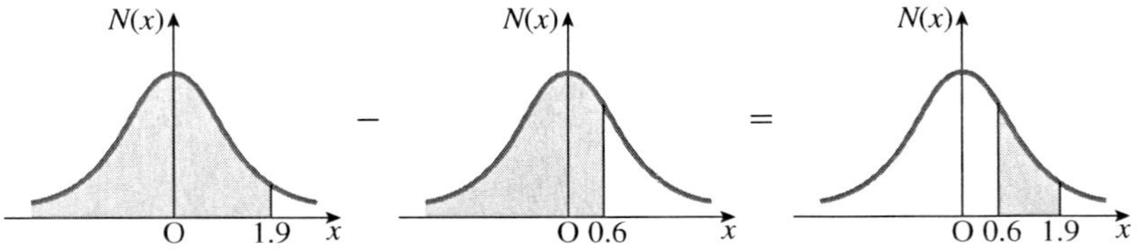

Figure 9.18 $A(1.9) - A(0.6)$ gives the area between $x = 0.6$ and $x = 1.9$.

So

$$\begin{aligned} P(0.6 < x < 1.9) &= P(x < 1.9) - P(x < 0.6) \\ &= A(1.9) - A(0.6) \\ &= 0.9713 - 0.7257 \\ &= 0.2456 \end{aligned}$$

There is a probability of 0.2456 that x lies between 0.6 and 1.9.

(b) Using the same reasoning as in (a) we have

$$P(-0.86 < x < 0.3) = P(x < 0.3) - P(x < -0.86)$$

Now

$$\begin{aligned} P(x < -0.86) &= P(x > 0.86) \\ &= 1 - P(x < 0.86) \\ &= 0.1949 \end{aligned}$$

So

$$\begin{aligned} P(-0.86 < x < 0.3) &= P(x < 0.3) - P(x < -0.86) \\ &= 0.6179 - 0.1949 \\ &= 0.4230 \end{aligned}$$

(c)

$$\begin{aligned} P(-1.5 < x < -0.7) &= P(x < -0.7) - P(x < -1.5) \\ &= [1 - P(x < 0.7)] - [1 - P(x < 1.5)] \\ &= P(x < 1.5) - P(x < 0.7) \\ &= 0.9332 - 0.7580 \\ &= 0.1752 \end{aligned}$$

Example 9.4

Given that x has a standard normal distribution calculate

(a) $P(1 < x < 2)$ (b) $P(-1.5 < x < 1)$ (c) $P(-1.2 < x < -0.5)$

Solution

(a) $P(1 < x < 2) = P(x < 2) - \square$ $\quad$ $P(x < 1)$

$= \square - \square$ $\quad$ 0.9772, 0.8413

$= 0.1359$

(b) $P(-1.5 < x < 1) = P(x < 1) - P(x < -1.5)$

$= P(x < 1) - (1 - \square)$ $\quad$ $P(x < 1.5)$

$= 0.8413 - \square$ $\quad$ 0.0668

$= 0.7745$

(c) $P(-1.2 < x < -0.5) = P(x < -0.5) - P(x < -1.2)$

$= (1 - \square) - (1 - \square)$

$P(x < 0.5)$, $P(x < 1.2)$

$= \square - \square$ $\quad$ 0.3085, 0.1151

$= 0.1934$

Exercises

1 Given that y has a standard normal distribution calculate
(a) $P(y < 1.36)$ (b) $P(y > 1.36)$
(c) $P(y < -0.9)$ (d) $P(y > -0.57)$
(e) $P(0.56 < y < 1.82)$
(f) $P(-0.15 < y < 0)$
(g) $P(-2.1 < y < -1.7)$

2 Given that x has a standard normal distribution calculate
(a) $P(1 < x < 2)$ (b) $P(-1.2 < x < 1.2)$
(c) $P(x < 0)$ (d) $P(-1.75 < x < -0.75)$
(e) $P(x > 0)$ (f) $P(|x| < 1)$
(g) $P(|x| > 1.5)$

3 Given that z has a standard normal distribution calculate the probability that
(a) z lies within two standard deviations of the mean
(b) z lies more than one standard deviation from the mean.

4 The temperature in a fridge follows a normal distribution with a mean of 0° and a standard deviation of 1°. Calculate the probability that the temperature is (a) more than 2°, (b) less than 1°, (c) between −2° and 1°.

Solutions to exercises

1 (a) 0.9131 (b) 0.0869 (c) 0.1841 (d) 0.7157 (e) 0.2534 (f) 0.0596 (g) 0.0267

2 (a) 0.1359 (b) 0.7699 (c) 0.5 (d) 0.1866 (e) 0.5 (f) 0.6827 (g) 0.1336

3 (a) 0.9545 (b) 0.3173

4 (a) 0.02275 (b) 0.8413 (c) 0.8186

9.5 Non-standard normal distribution

So far we have calculated probabilities for a standard normal distribution. We now consider non-standard normal distributions. In a non-standard normal distribution, the mean is non-zero and/or the standard deviation is not 1.

Recall that Table 9.1 lists probabilities for a standard normal distribution. In order to use Table 9.1 for problems involving non-standard normal distributions we introduce a way of 'standardizing' a variable.

Key point

Suppose a variable, x, has a normal distribution with mean μ and standard deviation σ. We standardise x to Z using the formula

$$Z = \frac{x - \mu}{\sigma}$$

The variable $Z = \frac{x - \mu}{\sigma}$ now has a standard normal distribution and so Table 9.1 can be used.

Example 9.5

A variable, x, has a normal distribution with mean 5 and standard deviation 2. Calculate the probability that

(a) $x < 7$ (b) $x > 4$ (c) $2 < x < 6$

Solution

(a) We standardise 7 to

$$\begin{aligned} Z &= \frac{7 - \mu}{\sigma} \\ &= \frac{7 - 5}{2} \\ &= 1 \end{aligned}$$

So $x < 7$ has the same probability as $Z < 7$ where Z follows a standard normal distribution.

$$P(x < 7) = P(Z < 1) = 0.8413$$

(b) Applying the standardisation to 4 gives

$$Z = \frac{4 - 5}{2} = -0.5$$

So $x > 4$ has the same probability as $Z > -0.5$:

$$\begin{aligned} P(x > 4) &= P(Z > -0.5) \\ &= P(Z < 0.5) \\ &= 0.6915 \end{aligned}$$

(c) Both 2 and 6 are standardised.

$$Z = \frac{2 - 5}{2} = -1.5, \quad Z = \frac{6 - 5}{2} = 0.5$$

So

$$\begin{aligned} P(2 < x < 6) &= P(-1.5 < Z < 0.5) \\ &= P(Z < 0.5) - P(Z < -1.5) \\ &= P(Z < 0.5) - [1 - P(Z < 1.5)] \\ &= P(Z < 0.5) + P(Z < 1.5) - 1 \\ &= 0.6247 \end{aligned}$$

Example 9.6

The number of miles travelled on 5 litres of petrol by a particular model of car follows a normal distribution with mean 47 and standard deviation 4.3. Calculate the probability that on 5 litres of petrol a car can travel

(a) more than 50 miles
(b) between 45 and 55 miles.

Solution

We let M be the number of miles travelled on 5 litres of petrol. Then M has a normal distribution with mean 47 miles and standard deviation 4.3 miles.

(a) We require the probability that $M > 50$. Using the standardisation we have

$Z =$

$$\frac{50 - 47}{4.3} = 0.70$$

So

$P(M > 50) = P(Z > 0.70) =$

$1 - P(Z < 0.70) = 0.2420$

(b) We standardise 45 and 55.

$Z =$, $Z =$

$-0.47, 1.86$

So

$$P(45 < M < 55) = P(-0.47 < Z < 1.86)$$
$$= P(Z < 1.86) + P(Z < 0.47) - 1$$
$$= 0.6494$$

Exercises

1. A variable, x, has a normal distribution with mean 6 and standard deviation 1.5. Calculate the probability that
   (a) $x < 7.5$ (b) $x < 5$ (c) $x > 7$ (d) $x > 5.5$
   (e) $5 < x < 8$
   (f) x lies within one standard deviation of the mean
   (g) x lies more than two standard deviations from the mean.

2. The temperature, T °C, of a freezer follows a normal distribution with mean −6°C and standard deviation of 2°C. Calculate the probability that
   (a) $T > -5$ (b) $T < -7$ (c) $-6 < T < -3$

3. Studies of a particular type of car tyre show that the mileage for which it can be used legally follows a normal distribution with mean 38000 miles and standard deviation 2500 miles. The manufacturers claim that '9 out of 10 of our tyres last more than 35000 miles'. Is the claim justified?

4. The diameters of ball bearings produced in a factory follow a normal distribution with mean 6 mm and standard deviation 0.04 mm. Calculate the probability that a diameter is (a) more than 6.05 mm, (b) less than 5.96 mm, (c) between 5.98 and 6.01 mm.

5. A normally distributed variable has mean 2 and standard deviation 2.5. Calculate the probability that the variable is negative.

Solutions to exercises

1. (a) 0.8413 (b) 0.2514 (c) 0.2514 (d) 0.6293 (e) 0.6568 (f) 0.6829 (g) 0.0455

2. (a) 0.3085 (b) 0.3085 (c) 0.4332

3. Only 88.49% of tyres last more than 35000 miles and so the claim is unjustified.

4. (a) 0.1056 (b) 0.1587 (c) 0.2902

5. 0.2119

End of block exercises

1. The variable, z, has a standard normal distribution. Calculate the probability that
   (a) $z < 1.42$ (b) $z < -0.75$ (c) $z > 0.55$
   (d) $z > -1.36$ (e) $0.52 < z < 1.42$
   (f) $-1.38 < z < 0.75$
   (g) $-1.06 < z < 0.08$

2. The variable, x, has a standard normal distribution. Calculate the probability that
   (a) x is within 1.5 standard deviations of the mean
   (b) x is more than 1.75 standard deviations from the mean.

3 The variable, X, has a normal distribution with a mean of 5 and a standard deviation of 3. Calculate the probability that
(a) $X > 10$ (b) $X > 0$ (c) $X < 2$
(d) $X < 1.75$ (e) $1 < X < 9$

4 The lifespan of bulbs has a normal distribution with mean of 10000 hours and a standard deviation of 1200 hours. Calculate
(a) the percentage of bulbs that last more than 11000 hours
(b) the probability that the lifespan of a bulb is between 8000 and 11000 hours
(c) the percentage of bulbs that fail before 8000 hours.

5 The lifespan of car batteries follows a normal distribution with a mean of 5 years and a standard deviation of 10 months. Calculate
(a) the probability that a car battery lasts more than 6 years
(b) the percentage of batteries that fail before they are 3 years old.

6 The scores from IQ tests have a normal distribution with a mean of 100 and a standard deviation of 15.
(a) Calculate the probability that a person has an IQ of more than 120.
(b) Calculate the probability that a person has an IQ of more than 130.
(c) What should a person score in order to be described as being in the top 10% of the population?

7 A factory produces metal bars used in the steering columns of cars. The car manufacturer requires that the bars are 60 ± 0.2 cm long. The lengths of the bars produced in the factory follow a normal distribution with mean 60.2 cm and standard deviation 0.2 cm. What percentage of bars produced by the factory are acceptable to the car manufacturer?

8 A normally distributed variable, Y, has a mean of 30 and a standard deviation of 4. Calculate
(a) $P(Y > 31.6)$ (b) $P(Y < 28.2)$
(c) $P(31 < Y < 35)$ (d) $P(25 < Y < 29)$
(e) $P(Y$ is more than 1.25 standard deviations from the mean).

9 The random variable, x, has a normal distribution. How many standard deviations above the mean must the point P be placed if the tail-end is to represent (a) 10%, (b) 5%, (c) 1% of the total area? (See Figure 9.19.)

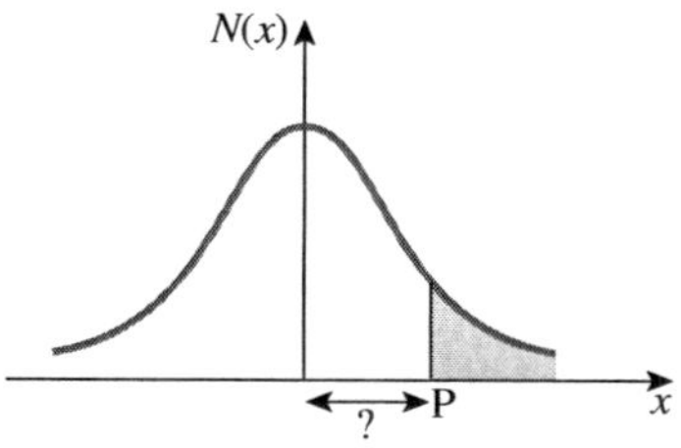

Figure 9.19

10 Consider Figure 9.20.

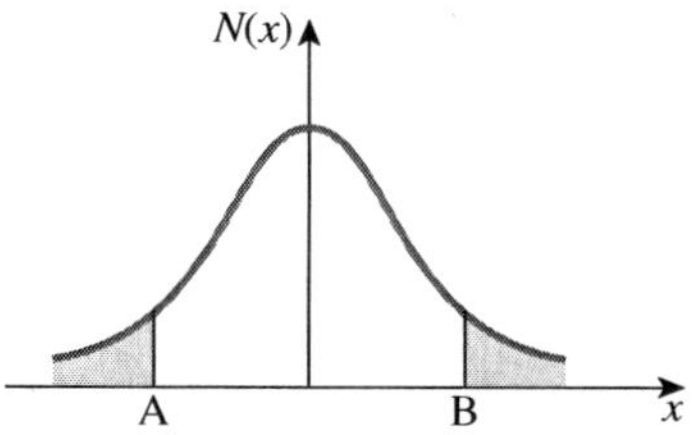

Figure 9.20

The two tail-ends have equal area. How many standard deviations from the mean must A and B be placed if the tail-ends are (a) 10%, (b) 5%, (c) 1% of the total area?

Solutions to exercises

1 (a) 0.9222 (b) 0.2266 (c) 0.2912 (d) 0.9131 (e) 0.2237 (f) 0.6896 (g) 0.3873

2 (a) 0.8664 (b) 0.0801

3 (a) 0.0475 (b) 0.9525 (c) 0.1587 (d) 0.1401 (e) 0.8165

4 (a) 20.33% (b) 0.7493 (c) 4.75%

5 (a) 11.51% (b) 0.82%

6 (a) 0.0918 (b) 0.0228 (c) 119

7 47.72%

8 (a) 0.3446 (b) 0.3264 (c) 0.2956 (d) 0.2956 (e) 0.2113

9 (a) 1.28 (b) 1.64 (c) 2.33

10 (a) 1.64 (b) 1.96 (c) 2.57

End of chapter exercises

1 Calculate (a) the mean and (b) the standard deviation of the data set

17, 26, 31, 19, 25, 20, 19, 29, 11, 27

2 State (a) the median and (b) the mode of the data in question 1.

3 Two identical data points are added to the data set of question 1. The mean of the new data set is 29. Calculate the value of the additional data points.

4 Table 1 shows the results of measuring the petrol consumption of a car over 90 trials.

Table 1

Miles per gallon	Frequency
42	17
43	18
44	12
45	20
46	23

(a) Calculate the mean consumption.
(b) Calculate the standard deviation.

5 State (a) the median and (b) the mode of the distribution of question 4.

6 The data set $A = \{x_1, x_2, x_3, \ldots, x_n\}$ has a mean of $\bar{x}$ and a standard deviation of σ. The data set B is $\{kx_1, kx_2, kx_3, \ldots, kx_n\}$, the data set C is $\{x_1 + k, x_2 + k, x_3 + k, \ldots, x_n + k\}$ where k is a constant.
(a) State the mean of set B.
(b) State the mean of set C.
(c) State the standard deviation of set B.
(d) State the standard deviation of set C.

7 Out of 6000 components, 39 fail within 12 months of manufacture.
(a) Calculate the probability that a component picked at random fails within 12 months of manufacture.
(b) A batch contains 2000 components. How many of these would you expect to fail within 12 months?

8 A fair die is rolled. Calculate the probability that the score is
(a) 4 (b) 4 or more (c) more than 4 (d) not 4

9 Two fair dice are thrown. Calculate the probability that the total is
(a) 9 (b) 13 (c) more than 9

10 State the complement of the following statements.
(a) the score is more than 4
(b) all of the components are working
(c) at least two of the machines are not working
(d) none of the machines are switched on.

11 Components are manufactured by machines A and B. Machine A makes 55% of the components. Of those components made by machine A, 7% are unacceptable; of those made by machine B, 5% are unacceptable. A component is picked at random. Calculate the probability that it is
(a) made by machine B
(b) acceptable
(c) acceptable and made by machine A
(d) unacceptable given it is made by machine B
(e) made by machine A given it is unacceptable.

12 Components are manufactured by three machines, A, B and C. Machine A makes 30% of the components, machine B makes 25% of the components and machine C makes the rest. Of those components made by machine A, 6% are substandard; when made by machine B, 3% are substandard; and when made by machine C, 5% are substandard. A component is picked at random. Calculate the probability that it is
(a) substandard
(b) made by machine B given it is substandard
(c) made by either machine A or machine B
(d) substandard and made by machine B
(e) substandard, given it is made by machine A
(f) made by machine A or is substandard.

13 The lifespans, L, of 2500 components were monitored and recorded in Table 2.

Table 2

Lifespan, L (hours)	Frequency
$0 \le L \le 5000$	16
$5000 < L \le 8000$	132
$8000 < L \le 9000$	219
$9000 < L \le 10000$	496
$10000 < L \le 11000$	1012
$11000 < L \le 12000$	480
$L > 12000$	145

Calculate the probability that a component picked at random has a lifespan
(a) of between 8000 and 11000 hours
(b) of more than 11000 hours
(c) of more than 10000 hours given that it has already lasted for at least 8000 hours
(d) of between 11000 and 12000 hours given that it has already lasted for at least 9000 hours.

14 The probability that a component is acceptable is 0.91. Ten components are picked at random. Calculate the probability that
(a) eight are acceptable
(b) more than eight are acceptable
(c) three are not acceptable.

15 The probability that a motor will malfunction within 5 years of manufacture is 0.03. Out of eight motors calculate the probability that within 5 years of manufacture
(a) all eight will malfunction
(b) six will malfunction
(c) none will malfunction.

16 The probability that a component works is 0.92. An engineer wants to be at least 99% certain of carrying six working components. Calculate the minimum number of components that the engineer needs to carry.

17 A service engineer receives on average seven calls in a 24 hour period. Calculate the probability that in a 24 hour period the engineer receives
(a) seven calls (b) eight calls (c) six calls
(d) fewer than three calls

18 A firm has 1400 employees. The probability that an employee is absent on any day is 0.006. Use the Poisson approximation to the binomial distribution to calculate the probability that the number of absent employees is
(a) eight (b) nine

19 The lengths of components have a normal distribution, with a mean of 7 cm and a standard deviation of 0.03 cm. Calculate the probability that a component chosen at random has a length
(a) between 6.95 cm and 7.02 cm
(b) more than 7.05 cm
(c) less than 6.96 cm
(d) between 6.95 cm and 6.99 cm.

20 The diameters of bearings have a normal distribution with a mean of 8 mm and a standard deviation of 0.04 mm. In a batch of 6000 bearings how many would you expect to have a diameter of
(a) more than 8.03 mm
(b) less than 7.95 mm
(c) between 8.01 mm and 8.06 mm
(d) more than 2.5 standard deviations from the mean?

Solutions to exercises

1 (a) 22.4 (b) 5.886

2 (a) 22.5 (b) 19

3 62

4 (a) 44.2 (b) 1.475

5 (a) 44 (b) 46

6 (a) $k\bar{x}$ (b) $\bar{x} + k$ (c) $k\sigma$ (d) σ

7 (a) 0.0065 (b) 13

8 (a) $\frac{1}{6}$ (b) $\frac{1}{2}$ (c) $\frac{1}{3}$ (d) $\frac{5}{6}$

9 (a) $\frac{1}{9}$ (b) 0 (c) $\frac{1}{6}$

10 (a) the score is 4 or less
(b) at least one of the components is not working
(c) fewer than two of the machines are not working
(d) some of the machines are switched on.

11 (a) 0.45 (b) 0.939 (c) 0.5115 (d) 0.05 (e) 0.6311

12 (a) 0.048 (b) 0.1563 (c) 0.55 (d) 0.0075 (e) 0.06 (f) 0.33

13 (a) 0.6908 (b) 0.25 (c) 0.6960 (d) 0.2250

14 (a) 0.1714 (b) 0.7746 (c) 0.0452

15 (a) 6.561×10^{-13} (b) 1.921×10^{-8} (c) 0.7837

16 12

17 (a) 0.1490 (b) 0.1304 (c) 0.1490 (d) 0.0296

18 (a) 0.1382 (b) 0.1290

19 (a) 0.7011 (b) 0.0475 (c) 0.0918 (d) 0.3232

20 (a) 1360 (b) 634 (c) 2007 (d) 75

An introduction to Fourier series and the Fourier transform

Chapter 24

The ability to analyse waveforms of various types is an important engineering skill. Fourier analysis provides a set of mathematical tools that enable the engineer to break down a wave into its various frequency components. It is then possible to predict the effect that a particular waveform may have from knowledge of the effects of its individual frequency components. Often an engineer finds it useful to think of a signal in terms of its frequency components rather than in terms of its time-domain representation. This alternative view is called a frequency-domain representation. It is particularly useful when trying to understand the effect of a filter on a signal. Filters are used extensively in many areas of engineering. In particular, communication engineers use them in signal reception equipment for filtering out unwanted frequencies in the received signal.

When a signal or waveform is periodic, it is possible to represent it as a sum of sine and/or cosine functions of different frequencies and amplitudes. Such a frequency-domain representation is called a **Fourier series.** Calculating a Fourier series is essentially an exercise in integration, in particular the integration of trigonometrical functions. In Block 1 of this chapter you will have the opportunity to calculate several Fourier series. When a signal is not periodic the equivalent frequency-domain representation is found by using a **Fourier transform**. In Block 2, this important transform will be introduced.

This chapter is intended to provide an introduction to these topics rather than give a thorough and rigorous treatment.

Chapter 24 contents

BLOCK 1 Periodic waveforms and their Fourier representation

1.1 Introduction

Suppose we have a periodic function $f(t)$. Under certain conditions, which will be given at the end of this block, it can be expressed as the sum of an infinite number of sine and/or cosine functions. This infinite sum is known as a **Fourier series**.

For example, Figure 1.1(a) shows a graph of the function $2 \sin t$. Figure 1.1(b) shows a graph of $2 \sin t - \sin 2t$. Notice that we have now included a second sine function that has twice the frequency of the first and a different amplitude.

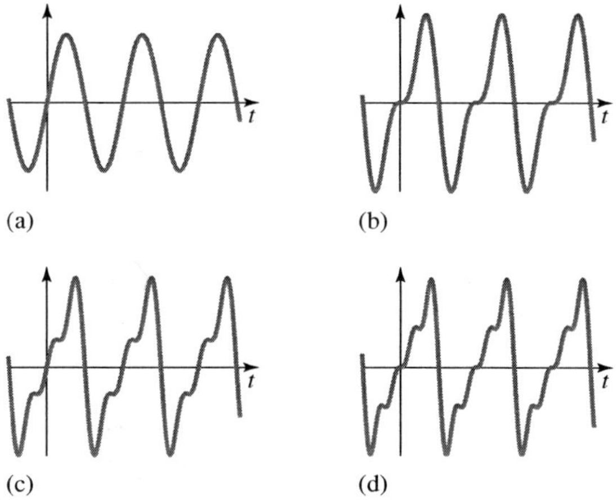

Figure 1.1

Figures 1.1(c) and 1.1(d) show graphs of $2 \sin t - \sin 2t + \frac{2}{3} \sin 3t$ and $2 \sin t - \sin 2t + \frac{2}{3} \sin 3t - \frac{1}{2} \sin 4t$

As more and more sine terms are included the graph appears to resemble more and more closely the periodic saw-tooth waveform shown in Figure 1.2.

By using an infinite series of sine functions it can be shown that the saw-tooth waveform of Figure 1.2 can be represented exactly.

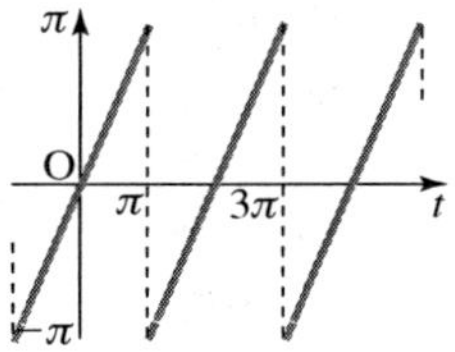

Figure 1.2 A periodic saw-tooth waveform.

The infinite series of sine functions is the Fourier series of the saw-tooth waveform. You will notice that the Fourier series is built up of sine functions of increasing frequencies, and with decreasing amplitudes. In this block you will learn how to calculate the appropriate frequencies and amplitudes for yourself, so that, given any periodic function, you will be able to calculate its corresponding Fourier series.

In the example above it was necessary only to include sine functions to construct the Fourier series, but in general you will need both sine and cosine functions, unless the periodic function under consideration takes rather special forms.

Exercises

1 The Fourier series of the saw-tooth waveform can be expressed concisely in the form

$$f(t) = \sum_{n=1}^{\infty} \left(\frac{-2 \cos n\pi}{n} \right) \sin nt$$

Noting that $\cos \pi = -1$, $\cos 2\pi = 1$, $\cos 3\pi = -1$, and so on, use this form to write out the first few terms in the infinite series explicitly.

2 A Fourier series is given by

$$f(t) = \frac{1}{2} + \sum_{n=1}^{\infty} \frac{2}{(2n - 1)\pi} \sin (2n - 1)t$$

Write out the first four terms of this infinite series.

Solutions to exercises

1 $f(t) = 2 \sin t - \sin 2t + \frac{2}{3} \sin 3t - \frac{1}{2} \sin 4t + \cdots$

2 $\frac{1}{2} + \frac{2}{\pi} \sin t + \frac{2}{3\pi} \sin 3t + \frac{2}{5\pi} \sin 5t + \cdots$

1.2 Calculating a Fourier series

To find a Fourier series for yourself you will make use of several formulae that involve the integration of trigonometrical functions. You will also need the technique of integration by parts. You may wish to revise these topics before proceeding.

Given a periodic function $f(t)$, with period T, calculate the quantities a_0, a_n and b_n from the following formulae. These quantities are known as **Fourier coefficients**:

Key point

Fourier coefficients

$$a_0 = \frac{2}{T} \int_0^T f(t)\, \mathrm{d}t$$

$$a_n = \frac{2}{T} \int_0^T f(t) \cos \frac{2n\pi t}{T}\, \mathrm{d}t, \quad n = 1, 2, 3, \ldots$$

$$b_n = \frac{2}{T} \int_0^T f(t) \sin \frac{2n\pi t}{T}\, \mathrm{d}t, \quad n = 1, 2, 3, \ldots$$

When these quantities have been calculated the Fourier series is given by the following:

Key point

Fourier series

$$f(t) = \frac{a_0}{2} + \sum_{n=1}^{\infty} \left(a_n \cos \frac{2n\pi t}{T} + b_n \sin \frac{2n\pi t}{T} \right)$$

If we write out the first few terms of the infinite series explicitly we find

$$f(t) = \frac{a_0}{2} + a_1 \cos \frac{2\pi t}{T} + b_1 \sin \frac{2\pi t}{T} + a_2 \cos \frac{4\pi t}{T} + b_2 \sin \frac{4\pi t}{T} + \cdots$$

In this form we see that the Fourier coefficients a_n are the amplitudes of the cosine terms in the series, and the b_n are the amplitudes of the sine terms in the series.

These formulae can look quite intimidating when first met, but we shall lead you carefully through the various stages of the calculation in order that you develop confidence in their use. However, you should always sketch a graph of the periodic function before doing anything else.

Example 1.1

Sketch a graph of the periodic function

$$f(t) = \begin{cases} 0 & -5 < t < 0 \\ 1 & 0 < t < 5 \end{cases}$$

of period $T = 10$, from $t = -10$ to $t = 15$.

Solution

Sketch the function for yourself.

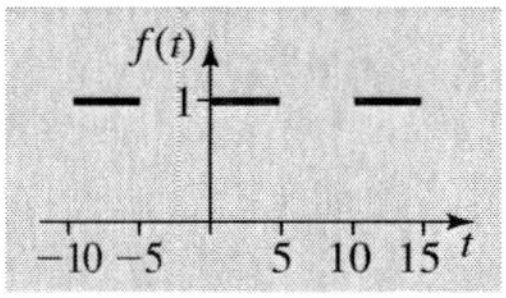

Example 1.2

For the function

$$f(t) = \begin{cases} 0 & -5 < t < 0 \\ 1 & 0 < t < 5 \end{cases}$$

of period $T = 10$, in Example 1.1, evaluate $\frac{2}{T}\int_0^T f(t)\,dt$: that is, calculate the Fourier coefficient a_0.

Solution

First identify the period, T.

$T =$ 10

We need to find $\frac{2}{10}\int_0^{10} f(t)\,dt$. We are required to integrate $f(t)$ between $t = 0$ and $t = 10$. However, by studying the graph of $f(t)$ you will see that $f(t)$ is zero for t between 5 and 10, and so we only need integrate between 0 and 5, and over this interval the function takes the value 1. Now write down the required integral:

$a_0 =$

$$\frac{2}{10}\int_0^5 1\,dt$$

Perform the integration to find a_0.

$$\frac{1}{5}[t]_0^5 = 1$$

We conclude that the Fourier coefficient, a_0, is equal to 1.

Example 1.3

For the function

$$f(t) = \begin{cases} 0 & -5 < t < 0 \\ 1 & 0 < t < 5 \end{cases}$$

of period $T = 10$, in Example 1.1, evaluate $\frac{2}{T}\int_0^T f(t)\cos\frac{2n\pi t}{T}\,dt$: that is, calculate the Fourier coefficients a_n.

Solution

As in Example 1.2, because $f(t)$ is zero between $t = 5$ and $t = 10$ we need only perform the integration over the interval $t = 0$ to $t = 5$.

Write down the required integral:

$a_n =$

$$\frac{2}{10}\int_0^5 1\cos\frac{2n\pi t}{10}\,dt$$

Perform the integration and complete the calculation:

$a_n =$

$$\frac{1}{5}\left[\frac{\sin\frac{n\pi t}{5}}{\frac{n\pi}{5}}\right]_0^5$$

If you substitute the limits of integration you will find that all terms are zero since $\sin n\pi = 0$ for all integers n. Hence $a_n = 0$. You have found that all the Fourier coefficients, a_n, are zero. This means that there will be no cosine terms in the Fourier series.

Example 1.4

For the function

$$f(t) = \begin{cases} 0 & -5 < t < 0 \\ 1 & 0 < t < 5 \end{cases}$$

of period $T = 10$, in Example 1.1, evaluate $\frac{2}{T}\int_0^T f(t)\sin\frac{2n\pi t}{T}\,dt$: that is, calculate the Fourier coefficients b_n.

Solution

As in Examples 1.2 and 1.3, because $f(t)$ is zero between $t = 5$ and $t = 10$ we need only perform the integration over the interval $t = 0$ to $t = 5$.

$$b_n = \frac{2}{10}\int_0^5 1 \sin\frac{2n\pi t}{10}\,dt$$

Perform the integration:

$$b_n = \frac{1}{5}\left[-\frac{\cos\frac{n\pi t}{5}}{\frac{n\pi}{5}}\right]_0^5$$

Insert the limits of integration and so complete the calculation of b_n:

$$-\frac{1}{n\pi}(\cos n\pi - 1)$$

This result gives us a formula for calculating each Fourier coefficient, b_n. Evaluate the formula when $n = 1$, $n = 2$, and so on:

When $n = 1$, $b_1 =$ $-\frac{1}{\pi}(\cos\pi - 1) = \frac{2}{\pi}$

When $n = 2$, $b_2 =$ $-\frac{1}{2\pi}(\cos 2\pi - 1) = 0$

When $n = 3$, $b_3 =$ $\frac{2}{3\pi}$

Continuing in this way you will find $b_4 = 0$, $b_5 = \frac{2}{5\pi}$ and so on. These are the Fourier coefficients, b_n.

Example 1.5

Combine the results of Examples 1.2, 1.3 and 1.4 to write down the Fourier series for

$$f(t) = \begin{cases} 0 & -5 < t < 0 \\ 1 & 0 < t < 5 \end{cases}$$

of period 10.

Solution

Using the key point on p. 1141 the Fourier series is given by

$$f(t) = \frac{a_0}{2} + \sum_{n=1}^{\infty}\left(a_n \cos\frac{2n\pi t}{T} + b_n \sin\frac{2n\pi t}{T}\right)$$

In this example $a_n = 0$ and $T = 10$ so the series reduces to

$$f(t) = \frac{a_0}{2} + \sum_{n=1}^{\infty} b_n \sin\frac{n\pi t}{5}$$

where the numbers a_0 and b_n are those obtained in Examples 1.2 and 1.4. If we write the series out explicitly we find

$$f(t) = \frac{1}{2} + \frac{2}{\pi}\sin\frac{\pi t}{5} + \frac{2}{3\pi}\sin\frac{3\pi t}{5} + \frac{2}{5\pi}\sin\frac{5\pi t}{5} + \cdots$$

A graph of the first four terms in this series is shown in Figure 1.3. Notice how closely, even with only four terms, it resembles the original graph obtained in Example 1.1.

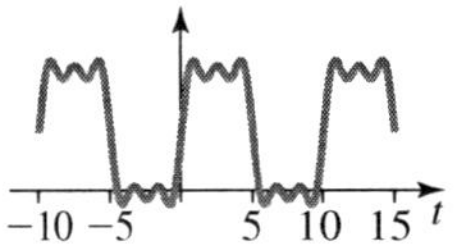

Figure 1.3 The first four terms in the Fourier series of $f(t)$.

The Fourier series of $f(t)$ has now been found.

Integration over any convenient period

Although the integrals given in the formulae for the Fourier coefficients have limits 0 and T, they can in fact be performed over any complete period. On occasions it may be more convenient to integrate over a different interval, say from $-\frac{T}{2}$ to $\frac{T}{2}$. This is the case in the following example.

Example 1.6

(a) Sketch a graph of the function

$$f(t) = \begin{cases} -t & -\pi < t < 0 \\ 0 & 0 < t < \pi \end{cases}$$

of period 2π, over the interval from -3π to 3π.

(b) Find the Fourier series for $f(t)$.

Solution

(a) First draw the required graph over the interval stated.

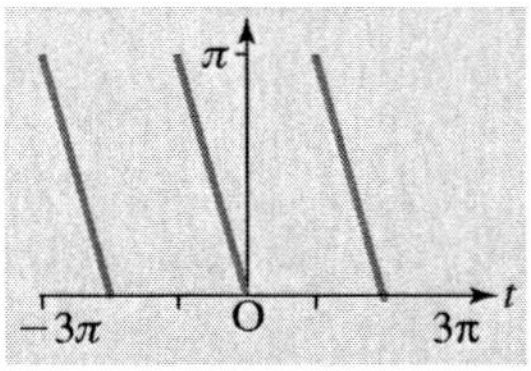

(b) State the value of T:

$T = 2\pi$

Because the period is 2π the Fourier series formulae simplify somewhat. For example, terms like $\sin\dfrac{2n\pi t}{T}$ become simply $\sin nt$.

Because the function $f(t)$ is given over the interval from $-\pi$ to π it is convenient to use this complete period in the Fourier coefficient integrals. Noting that $f(t) = 0$ between 0 and π write down the required integrals:

$a_0 =$

$$\frac{1}{\pi}\int_{-\pi}^{0} -t\,dt$$

$a_n =$

$$\frac{1}{\pi}\int_{-\pi}^{0} -t\cos nt\,dt$$

$b_n =$

$$\frac{1}{\pi}\int_{-\pi}^{0} -t\sin nt\,dt$$

Now evaluate a_0:

$a_0 =$

$$\frac{1}{\pi}\left[-\frac{t^2}{2}\right]_{-\pi}^{0} = \frac{\pi}{2}$$

To find a_n we note that the integrand is a product and we use integration by parts:

$$\begin{aligned} a_n &= \frac{1}{\pi}\int_{-\pi}^{0} -t\cos nt\,dt = \frac{1}{\pi}\left\{\left[-t\frac{\sin nt}{n}\right]_{-\pi}^{0} + \int_{-\pi}^{0}\frac{\sin nt}{n}\,dt\right\} \\ &= \frac{1}{\pi}\left[-\frac{\cos nt}{n^2}\right]_{-\pi}^{0} \\ &= \frac{1}{\pi}\left(\frac{\cos n\pi}{n^2} - \frac{1}{n^2}\right) \end{aligned}$$

To achieve this result we have made use of the following facts: $\sin 0 = 0$, $\sin(-n\pi) = 0$ for all n, and $\cos(-n\pi) = \cos n\pi$ since the cosine function is even.

Use this result to find a_1, a_2 and a_3 explicitly:

$a_1 =$

$$-\frac{2}{\pi}$$

$a_2 =$

$$0$$

$a_3 =$

$$-\frac{2}{9\pi}$$

To find b_n note that the integrand is a product and use integration by parts in the same way as we did when finding a_n:

$b_n =$

$$\frac{1}{\pi}\int_{-\pi}^{0} -t\sin nt\,dt = \frac{1}{\pi}\left\{\left[(-t)\left(-\frac{\cos nt}{n}\right)\right]_{-\pi}^{0} - \int_{-\pi}^{0} -\frac{\cos nt}{n}(-1)\,dt\right\}$$

Simplify this.

$$b_n = \qquad \frac{1}{\pi}\left\{\left[\frac{t\cos nt}{n}\right]_{-\pi}^{0} - \int_{-\pi}^{0}\frac{\cos nt}{n}\,dt\right\}$$

The remaining integral is $\int_{-\pi}^{0}\frac{\cos nt}{n}\,dt = \left[\frac{\sin nt}{n^2}\right]_{-\pi}^{0}$, which vanishes.

Complete the calculation:

$$b_n = \qquad \frac{1}{\pi}\left\{0 - \frac{-\pi\cos(-n\pi)}{n}\right\} = \frac{1}{n}\cos n\pi$$

Explicitly, $b_1 = -1$, $b_2 = \frac{1}{2}$, $b_3 = -\frac{1}{3}$ and so on.

Putting all these results together we can write the first few terms in the Fourier series as

$$f(t) = \frac{\pi}{4} - \frac{2}{\pi}\cos t - \sin t + \frac{1}{2}\sin 2t - \frac{2}{9\pi}\cos 3t - \frac{1}{3}\sin 3t + \cdots$$

A graph of these first few terms is shown in Figure 1.4.

Figure 1.4

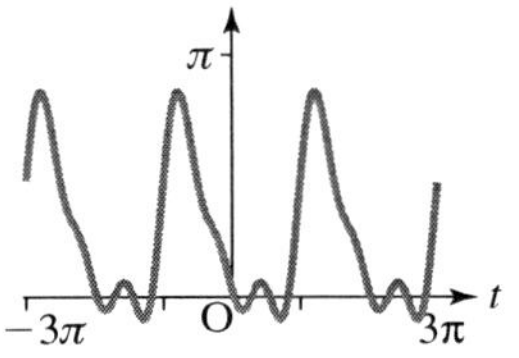

Fourier series of odd functions and even functions

When a function is odd, its Fourier series will contain no cosine or constant terms. Consequently $a_n = 0$ for all n.

When a function is even, its Fourier series will contain no sine terms. Consequently $b_n = 0$ for all n.

These facts will enable you to save considerable effort during the calculation of a Fourier series.

Convergence of the Fourier series

There are certain conditions that must be satisfied before we can be sure that a Fourier series truly represents the function $f(t)$. These conditions, which are called the **Dirichlet conditions**, state that the integral $\int |f(t)|\,dt$ over a complete period must be finite, and $f(t)$ may have no more than a finite number of discontinuities in any finite interval. Fortunately, most functions of interest to engineers satisfy these conditions. At any point where $f(t)$ is continuous, the Fourier series converges to $f(t)$. At any point where $f(t)$ is discontinuous, the Fourier series converges to the average of the two function values at either side of the discontinuity. So, referring to the graph shown in Example 1.1, the Fourier series converges to the value 1 when $x = 2$ say, because $f(t)$ is continuous there and equal to 1, but converges to the value $\frac{1}{2}$ when $x = 5$, the point of discontinuity, and $\frac{1}{2}$ is the average of the function values on either side of $x = 5$.

Exercises

1 (a) Sketch a graph of the function with period 2π defined by

$$f(t) = \begin{cases} 0 & -\pi < t < -\frac{\pi}{2} \\ 4 & -\frac{\pi}{2} \le t \le \frac{\pi}{2} \\ 0 & \frac{\pi}{2} < t < \pi \end{cases}$$

(b) Find the Fourier series for this function.

2 Find the Fourier series representation of the function

$$f(t) = \begin{cases} -4 & -\pi < t \le 0 \\ 4 & 0 < t < \pi \end{cases}$$

of period 2π.

3 Find the Fourier series representation of the function

$$f(t) = \begin{cases} 2(1+t) & -1 \le t \le 0 \\ 0 & 0 < t < 1 \end{cases}$$

of period 2.

Solutions to exercises

1 (b) $a_0 = 4$, $a_n = \dfrac{8}{n\pi}\sin\dfrac{n\pi}{2}$, $b_n = 0$

$$f(t) = 2 + \frac{8}{\pi}\cos t - \frac{8}{3\pi}\cos 3t + \frac{8}{5\pi}\cos 5t \cdots$$

2 $\dfrac{8}{\pi}\left(2\sin t + \dfrac{2}{3}\sin 3t + \dfrac{2}{5}\sin 5t + \cdots\right)$

3 $$\frac{1}{2} + \frac{2}{\pi}\left(\frac{2}{\pi}\cos \pi t - \sin \pi t - \frac{1}{2}\sin 2\pi t + \frac{2}{9\pi}\cos 3\pi t - \frac{1}{3}\sin 3\pi t \cdots\right)$$

End of block exercises

1 Find the Fourier series representation of the function $f(t) = t^2$, $0 < t \le 2\pi$, of period 2π.

2 Find the Fourier series representation of $f(t) = \dfrac{t}{2}$, $0 < t < 2\pi$, of period 2π.

3 Find the first four non-zero terms in the Fourier series representation of

$$f(t) = \begin{cases} 0 & -\pi < t < -\frac{\pi}{2} \\ 1 & -\frac{\pi}{2} < t < \frac{\pi}{2} \\ 0 & \frac{\pi}{2} < t < \pi \end{cases}$$

of period 2π.

4 Show that the Fourier series representation of $f(x) = x$, $-\pi < x < \pi$, of period 2π, can be written

$$2\sum_{n=1}^{\infty} \frac{(-1)^{n+1}}{n} \sin nx$$

5 (a) Find the Fourier series expansion of

$$f(t) = \begin{cases} 0 & -\pi < t < 0 \\ t^2 & 0 < t < \pi \end{cases}$$

of period 2π.

(b) Use the series to show that

$$\sum_{n=1}^{\infty} \frac{1}{n^2} = \frac{\pi^2}{6}$$

(Hint: let $t = \pi$ and read the comments concerning convergence at the end of this block.)

(c) Use the series to show that

$$\sum_{n=1}^{\infty} (-1)^{n+1} \frac{1}{n^2} = \frac{\pi^2}{12}$$

(Hint: let $t = 0$.)

Solutions to exercises

1 $a_0 = \dfrac{8\pi^2}{3}$, $a_n = \dfrac{4}{n^2}$, $b_n = -\dfrac{4\pi}{n}$

2 $a_0 = \pi$, $a_n = 0$, $n \geq 1$, $b_n = \dfrac{-1}{n}$

3 $$f(t) = \frac{1}{2} + \frac{2}{\pi}\left(\cos t - \frac{1}{3}\cos 3t + \frac{1}{5}\cos 5t - \cdots\right)$$

5 (a) $a_0 = \dfrac{\pi^2}{3}$, $a_n = \dfrac{2\cos n\pi}{n^2}$,

$$b_n = -\frac{\pi}{n}\cos n\pi + \frac{2}{\pi n^3}(\cos n\pi - 1)$$

BLOCK 2

Introducing the Fourier transform

2.1 Introduction

Many practical signals are not periodic. Examples are pulse signals, such as that shown in Figure 2.1, and noise signals. Under certain conditions it can be shown that a non-periodic function $f(t)$ can be expressed not as a sum of sine and cosine waves but as an integral. This idea gives rise to the Fourier transform, which is described in this block.

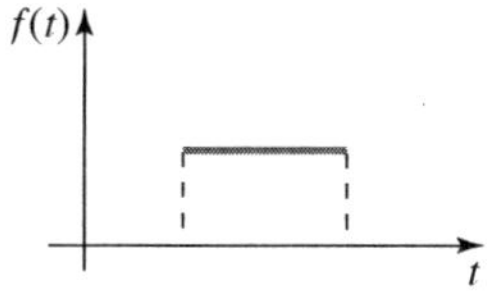

Figure 2.1
A pulse signal.

2.2 Calculating a Fourier transform

The Fourier transform of a function $f(t)$ is a function of a new variable ω, which is found from the following formula.

Key point

The Fourier transform of $f(t)$ is a function $F(\omega)$ defined by

$$\mathcal{F}\{f(t)\} = F(\omega) = \int_{-\infty}^{\infty} f(t)e^{-j\omega t}\,dt$$

Some authors use alternative definitions of the Fourier transform, but the one used here is widely accepted. However, when consulting other texts be aware of possible variations.

It is frequently the case that when a Fourier transform is calculated the result is a complex function, as you will see in the examples below.

Example 2.1
Find the Fourier transform of the function defined by

$$f(t) = \begin{cases} 3 & -1 < t < 1 \\ 0 & \text{otherwise} \end{cases}$$

Solution
A graph of $f(t)$ is shown in Figure 2.2.

Figure 2.2
A pulse signal.

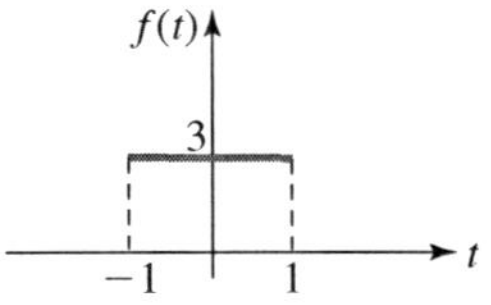

We apply the formula for finding the Fourier transform:

$$\mathcal{F}\{f(t)\} = F(\omega) = \int_{-\infty}^{\infty} f(t)e^{-j\omega t}\,dt$$

Note that in this example $f(t)$ is defined to be zero outside the interval $-1 < t < 1$, and so the integral reduces to

$$\begin{aligned}\mathcal{F}\{f(t)\} = F(\omega) &= \int_{-1}^{1} 3e^{-j\omega t}\,dt \\ &= \left[\frac{3e^{-j\omega t}}{-j\omega}\right]_{-1}^{1} \\ &= \frac{3e^{-j\omega}}{-j\omega} - \frac{3e^{j\omega}}{-j\omega} \\ &= \frac{3e^{j\omega} - 3e^{-j\omega}}{j\omega}\end{aligned}$$

This can be written as $F(\omega) = 6\dfrac{\sin\omega}{\omega}$, by making use of Euler's relations (Chapter 11, Block 3). Its graph is shown in Figure 2.3. The function $\dfrac{\sin\omega}{\omega}$ occurs frequently and is often referred to as the **sinc function**.

Figure 2.3
A sinc function.

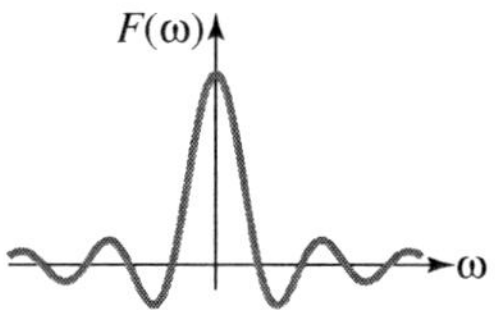

Example 2.2
Find the Fourier transform of the function $f(t) = u(t)e^{-t}$ where $u(t)$ is the unit step function.

Solution
A graph of this function is shown in Figure 2.4. Notice that it is zero when t is negative.

Figure 2.4

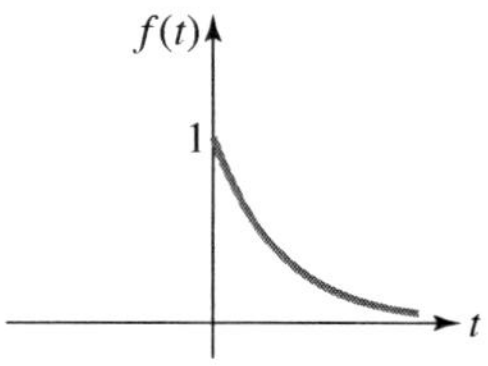

The Fourier transform is

$$F(\omega) = \int_{-\infty}^{\infty} u(t)\mathrm{e}^{-t}\,\mathrm{e}^{-\mathrm{j}\omega t}\,\mathrm{d}t$$

Because $u(t)\mathrm{e}^{-t}$ is zero when t is negative, the limits of integration can be altered as follows:

$$F(\omega) = \int_{0}^{\infty} u(t)\mathrm{e}^{-t}\,\mathrm{e}^{-\mathrm{j}\omega t}\,\mathrm{d}t$$

Further, since $u(t) = 1$ when $t \geq 0$ the integral becomes

$$F(\omega) = \int_{0}^{\infty} \mathrm{e}^{-t}\,\mathrm{e}^{-\mathrm{j}\omega t}\,\mathrm{d}t$$

Carry out this integration by combining the two exponential terms into a single term:

$$F(\omega) = \qquad \int_{0}^{\infty} \mathrm{e}^{-(1+\mathrm{j}\omega)t}\,\mathrm{d}t = \left[\frac{\mathrm{e}^{-(1+\mathrm{j}\omega)t}}{-(1+\mathrm{j}\omega)}\right]_{0}^{\infty}$$

Complete the integration by noting that the contribution from the upper limit is zero, because e^{-t} tends to zero as t tends to infinity.

$$F(\omega) = \qquad \frac{1}{1+\mathrm{j}\omega}$$

This is the required Fourier transform. Unlike the function in Example 2.1 this is complex.

Because the Fourier transform in Example 2.2 is a complex function we cannot immediately plot its graph. However, it is possible to find its modulus and argument, and plot graphs of these against ω. Such plots are called **amplitude spectra** and **phase spectra** respectively.

The amplitude spectrum of $f(t) = u(t)\mathrm{e}^{-t}$ is the modulus of $\dfrac{1}{1+\mathrm{j}\omega}$ which equals $\dfrac{1}{\sqrt{1+\omega^2}}$. A graph of this function is shown in Figure 2.5.

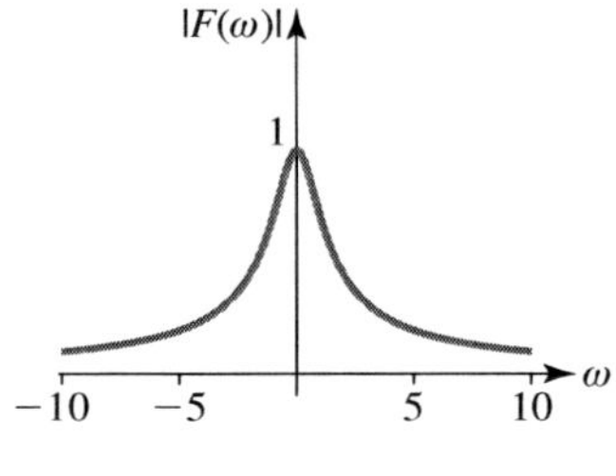

Figure 2.5 The amplitude spectrum of $f(t) = u(t)\mathrm{e}^{-t}$.

It is usual practice to make use of tables of transforms such as those shown in Table 2.1.

Table 2.1
Table of common Fourier transforms.

$f(t)$	$F(\omega)$
$Au(t)e^{-\alpha t}, \alpha > 0$	$\dfrac{A}{\alpha + j\omega}$
$\begin{cases} 1 & -\alpha \le t \le \alpha \\ 0 & \text{otherwise} \end{cases}$	$\dfrac{2 \sin \omega\alpha}{\omega}$
A, constant	$2\pi A\delta(\omega)$
$Au(t)$	$A\left(\pi\delta(\omega) - \dfrac{j}{\omega}\right)$
$\delta(t)$	1
$\delta(t - a)$	$e^{-j\omega a}$
$\cos at$	$\pi[\delta(\omega + a) + \delta(\omega - a)]$
$\sin at$	$\dfrac{\pi}{j}[\delta(\omega - a) - \delta(\omega + a)]$
$e^{-\alpha\|t\|}, \alpha > 0$	$\dfrac{2\alpha}{\alpha^2 + \omega^2}$

Example 2.3 Electronic Engineering – Fourier analysis and digital audio

The mechanism by which sounds can be heard is as follows. A source of sound, for example a singer or a musical instrument, causes the air pressure in its vicinity to rise and fall rapidly. This in turn causes a sound wave to travel through the air until it reaches the ears of a listener, or maybe a microphone. The number of times that the air pressure rises and falls each second is the **frequency** of the sound wave, measured in cycles per second, or Hertz.

If a sound wave has a frequency of 440 Hz then a listener will hear a single note, A. If the frequency is higher than this, the pitch of the note will be higher too. If the frequency is lower, then a lower-pitched note will be produced. Musical pieces and songs will be made up from sounds at many different frequencies. Most human beings can hear frequencies only in the range 20 Hz up to 20 000 Hz. Sounds with frequencies outside this range will not be heard by humans, although they may be heard by other creatures.

When a sound wave arrives at a microphone it causes a thin diaphragm to vibrate at the same frequency. This motion is converted into an electrical voltage within the microphone. This electrical voltage is a time-domain signal. The voltage will vary with time just as the frequency of the sound varies as the musical pitch is changed during the course of a song or piece of music. To store this continuous voltage signal on a digital computer or CD we take samples of it and store these instead. To obtain a high-quality recording we need to take a large number of samples every second. Then, by taking the Fourier transform we can determine which sound frequencies are being sung or played. A form of Fourier transform especially adapted to deal with sampled signals is known as the **discrete Fourier transform**, or DFT.

For a good introduction to the mathematics underlying the DFT the reader is referred to *Engineering Mathematics: A Foundation for Electronic, Electrical, Communications and Systems Engineers*, 3rd edn by Croft, Davison and Hargreaves.

One of the technical difficulties associated with storing digital audio is the enormous volume of data that has to be stored. If some of this data can be discarded then this problem can be reduced. One way this can be achieved is to ignore any sounds having frequencies greater than 22 000 Hz. An important result in digital audio theory is called the **Nyquist sampling theorem**. This states that a signal needs to be sampled at a rate that is twice the highest signal we want to record. Hence if we want to record a signal as high as 22 kHz we need to sample at 44 kHz. It is for this reason that, for CD purposes, an audio signal is sampled at 44 100 times each second. We have already shown in Chapter 5, Section 2.8 that with 16 bit technology, and at this sampling rate, we need around 10 megabytes to store a 1 minute stereo recording.

An extremely important modern application of mathematics is to find ways in which these large files can be reduced in size or **compressed**. PC users will know that there are techniques for compressing binary data files. Some of these techniques are known as **loss-less**. This means that none of the original information is lost in the compression process. Audio .wav files are produced by loss-less compression. Unfortunately such files are still enormous. The key to achieving substantial savings in file size is to introduce so-called **lossy** compression. The most widely known lossy compression technique is MP3. This technique works by dividing the frequency range into a large number of different bands. Within each band some of the frequency components are discarded. This is possible because of the way the human ear works. For example, suppose two very close frequencies are being sounded, one played loudly and one played quietly. The quieter sound is masked by the louder one and so its corresponding frequency component can be discarded without a noticeable effect on the sound heard.

To understand compression techniques such as MP3 thoroughly requires not only a knowledge of the physiology of the human ear but also a good understanding of the Fourier transform and related techniques.

Exercises

1 Find, using Table 2.1, the Fourier transform of

$$f(t) = \begin{cases} 1 & -1 \leq t \leq 1 \\ 0 & \text{otherwise} \end{cases}$$

2 Find, by direct integration, the Fourier transform of

$$f(t) = \begin{cases} e^{-t} & t \geq 0 \\ e^{t} & t \leq 0 \end{cases}$$

3 Find, using Table 2.1, the Fourier transform of $f(t) = 4$.

4 Find, using Table 2.1, the Fourier transform of $f(t) = e^{-3t}$ if $t > 0$ and 0 otherwise.

Solutions to exercises

1 $\dfrac{2 \sin \omega}{\omega}$

2 $\dfrac{2}{1 + \omega^2}$

3 $8\pi\delta(\omega)$

4 $\dfrac{1}{3 + j\omega}$

2.3 The frequency-domain representation of a non-periodic function

Under certain conditions a non-periodic function $f(t)$ can be expressed in the following form:

$$f(t) = \frac{1}{2\pi}\int_{-\infty}^{\infty} F(\omega)\,e^{j\omega t}\,d\omega$$

where $F(\omega)$ is the Fourier transform of $f(t)$. Such a representation is called a **Fourier integral representation**.

Example 2.4

Find the Fourier integral representation of the function $f(t)$ given in Example 2.1.

Solution

In Example 2.1 the pulse function was shown to have Fourier transform $F(\omega) = \dfrac{6 \sin \omega}{\omega}$. Hence the Fourier integral representation of the pulse is

$$f(t) = \frac{1}{2\pi}\int_{-\infty}^{\infty} \frac{6 \sin \omega}{\omega}\,e^{j\omega t}\,d\omega$$

2.4 Linearity of the Fourier transform

The Fourier transform possesses a property known as **linearity**, which can be used to find transforms of a wider range of functions than those already discussed.

Key point

The Fourier transform is a linear transform. This means that if k is a constant:

$$\mathcal{F}\{f(t) + g(t)\} = \mathcal{F}\{f(t)\} + \mathcal{F}\{g(t)\}$$

$$\mathcal{F}\{kf(t)\} = k\mathcal{F}\{f(t)\}$$

Example 2.5

Use the linearity properties and the table of transforms to find the Fourier transform of $u(t)e^{-t} + u(t)e^{-2t}$.

Solution

The transforms of $u(t)e^{-t}$ and $u(t)e^{-2t}$ can be obtained separately from the table.

$$\mathcal{F}\{u(t)e^{-t}\} = \qquad \frac{1}{1 + j\omega}$$

$$\mathcal{F}\{u(t)e^{-2t}\} = \qquad \frac{1}{2 + j\omega}$$

Now write down the required Fourier transform:

$$\frac{1}{1 + j\omega} + \frac{1}{2 + j\omega}$$

Exercises

1 Find the Fourier transform of $3u(t) - 7u(t)e^{-3t}$.

Solutions to exercises

1 $3\left(\pi\delta(\omega) - \frac{j}{\omega}\right) - \frac{7}{3 + j\omega}$.

End of block exercises

1 Find the Fourier transform of $6u(t)e^{-3t}$.

2 Find the Fourier transform of $f(t) = 5$ for $-2 \le t \le 2$, and 0 otherwise.

3 Find the function $f(t)$ that has Fourier transform

$$F(\omega) = \frac{3}{2 + j\omega} - \frac{7}{1 + j\omega}$$

4 The **first shift theorem** states that if $F(\omega)$ is the Fourier transform of $f(t)$ then

$$\mathcal{F}\{e^{jat} f(t)\} = F(\omega - a)$$

where a is a constant. Use this theorem to find the Fourier transform of

$$g(t) = \begin{cases} e^{2jt} & -3 \le t \le 3 \\ 0 & \text{otherwise} \end{cases}$$

5 The **second shift theorem** states that if $F(\omega)$ is the Fourier transform of $f(t)$ then

$$\mathcal{F}\{f(t - \alpha)\} = e^{-j\alpha\omega} F(\omega)$$

(a) Prove this theorem from the definition of the Fourier transform.

(b) Given that

$$\mathcal{F}\{u(t)e^{-t}\} = \frac{1}{1 + j\omega}$$

use the second shift theorem to find

$$\mathcal{F}\{u(t+4)e^{-(t+4)}\}$$

(c) Verify the result in (b) by direct integration.

6 Find the Fourier transform of $f(t) = 7$ for $-3 \le t \le 3$, and 0 otherwise.

Solutions to exercises

1 $\dfrac{6}{3 + j\omega}$

2 $\dfrac{10 \sin 2\omega}{\omega}$

3 $3u(t)e^{-2t} - 7u(t)e^{-t}$

4 $\dfrac{2 \sin 3(\omega - 2)}{\omega - 2}$

5 (b) $\dfrac{e^{4j\omega}}{1 + j\omega}$

6 $\dfrac{14 \sin 3\omega}{\omega}$

End of chapter exercises

1 (a) Sketch a graph of the function $f(t) = e^{-|t|}$.
(b) Show from the definition of the Fourier transform that

$$\mathcal{F}\{f(t)\} = F(\omega) = \frac{2}{1 + \omega^2}$$

(c) Show that the Fourier transform of $f(t)$ is an even function of ω.

2 Sketch a graph of $f(t) = e^{-|3t|}$ and find its Fourier transform.

3 (a) Sketch a graph of

$$f(t) = \begin{cases} e^{-2t} & t > 0 \\ -e^{2t} & t < 0 \end{cases}$$

(b) Find the Fourier transform of $f(t)$.
(c) Show that this Fourier transform is purely imaginary.

4 (a) Sketch a graph of $u(-t)$ where $u(t)$ is the unit step function.
(b) Sketch a graph of $f(t) = 7e^{2t}u(-t)$.
(c) Find the Fourier transform of $f(t)$.

5 (a) Sketch a graph of three cycles of the function with period 2π given by

$$f(t) = 1 - \frac{|t|}{\pi}, \qquad -\pi \le t < \pi$$

(b) Find its Fourier series representation.

6 Find the Fourier series representation of the function with period 2 given by

$$f(t) = \begin{cases} 3t & 0 < t < 1 \\ 3 & 1 < t < 2 \end{cases}$$

7 Find the Fourier series representation of the function with period 0.02 defined by

$$f(t) = \begin{cases} 1 & 0 \le t < 0.01 \\ 0 & 0.01 \le t < 0.02 \end{cases}$$

8 Find the Fourier series representation of the function with period 1 given by

$$f(t) = \begin{cases} t & 0 < t < \frac{1}{2} \\ 0 & \frac{1}{2} < t < 1 \end{cases}$$

9 From the definition of the Fourier transform find $F(\omega)$ when $f(t) = u(t)te^{-3t}$.

Solutions to exercises

2 $\dfrac{6}{9 + \omega^2}$

3 (b) $\dfrac{-2j\omega}{4 + \omega^2}$

4 (c) $\dfrac{7}{2 - j\omega}$

5 (b) $b_n = 0$, $a_0 = 1$, $a_n = \dfrac{4}{n^2\pi^2}$ if n is odd and zero if n is even.

6 $a_0 = \frac{9}{2}$, $a_n = \dfrac{3}{n^2\pi^2}(\cos n\pi - 1)$, $b_n = -\dfrac{3}{n\pi}$

7 $a_0 = 1$, $a_n = 0$, for $n \geq 1$, $b_n = \dfrac{1}{n\pi}[1 - (-1)^n]$

8 $a_0 = \frac{1}{4}$, $a_n = \dfrac{1}{2\pi^2 n^2}[(-1)^n - 1]$, $b_n = \dfrac{(-1)^{n+1}}{2\pi n}$

9 $\dfrac{1}{(3 + j\omega)^2}$

7 Vector Calculus

Chapter 7 Contents

7.1 Introduction

In many applications we use functions of the space variable $\boldsymbol{r} = x\boldsymbol{i} + y\boldsymbol{j} + z\boldsymbol{k}$ as models for quantities that vary from point to point in three-dimensional space. There are two types of such functions. There are **scalar point functions**, which model scalar quantities like the temperature at a point in a body, and **vector point functions**, which model vector quantities like the velocity of the flow at a point in a liquid. We can express this more formally in the following way. For each scalar point function f we have a **rule**, $u = f(\boldsymbol{r})$, which assigns to each point with coordinate $\boldsymbol{r}$ in the **domain** of the function a unique real number u. For vector point functions the rule $\boldsymbol{v} = \boldsymbol{F}(\boldsymbol{r})$ assigns to each $\boldsymbol{r}$ a unique vector $\boldsymbol{v}$ in the range of the function. Vector calculus was designed to measure the variation of such functions with respect to the space variable $\boldsymbol{r}$. That development made use of the ideas about vectors (components, addition, subtraction, scalar and vector products) described in Chapter 4 of *Modern Engineering Mathematics* and summarized here in Figure 7.1.

Figure 7.1 Elementary vector algebra.

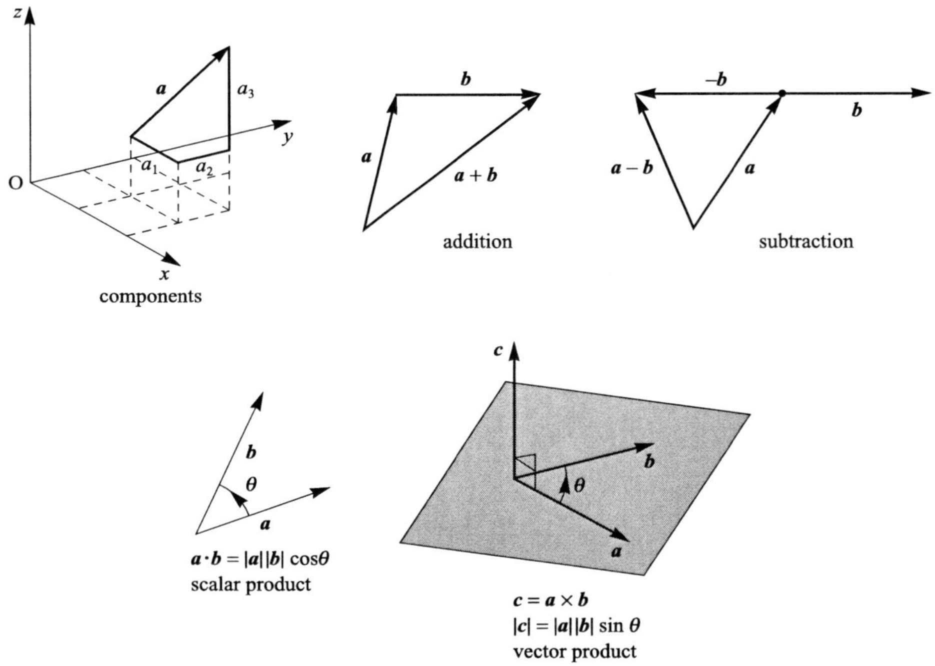

In component form if $\boldsymbol{a} = (a_1, a_2, a_3)$ and $\boldsymbol{b} = (b_1, b_2, b_3)$ then

$$\boldsymbol{a} \pm \boldsymbol{b} = (a_1 \pm b_1,\ a_2 \pm b_2,\ a_3 \pm b_3)$$

$$\boldsymbol{a} \cdot \boldsymbol{b} = (a_1b_1 + a_2b_2 + a_3b_3) = \boldsymbol{b} \cdot \boldsymbol{a}$$

$$\boldsymbol{a} \times \boldsymbol{b} = \begin{vmatrix} \boldsymbol{i} & \boldsymbol{j} & \boldsymbol{k} \\ a_1 & a_2 & a_3 \\ b_1 & b_2 & b_3 \end{vmatrix} = -\boldsymbol{b} \times \boldsymbol{a}$$

$$= (a_2b_3 - b_2a_3,\ b_1a_3 - a_1b_3,\ a_1b_2 - b_1a_2)$$

The recent development of computer packages for the modelling of engineering problems involving vector quantities has relieved designers of much tedious analysis and computation. To be able to use those packages effectively, however, designers need a good understanding of the mathematical tools they bring to their tasks. It is on that basic understanding that this chapter focuses.

7.1.1 Basic concepts

We can picture a scalar point function $f(\boldsymbol{r})$ by means of its level surfaces $f(\boldsymbol{r}) =$ constant. For example, the level surfaces of $f(\boldsymbol{r}) = 2x + 2y - z$ are planes parallel to the plane $z = 2x + 2y$, as shown in Figure 7.2. On the level surface the function value does not change, so the rate of change of the function will be zero along any line drawn on the level surface. An alternative name for a scalar point function is **scalar field**. This is in contrast to the vector point function (or **vector field**). We picture a vector field by its field (or flow) lines. A field line is a curve in space represented by the position vector $\boldsymbol{r}(t)$ such that at each point of the curve its tangent is parallel to the vector field. Thus the field lines of $\boldsymbol{F}(\boldsymbol{r})$ are given by the differential equation

$$\frac{\mathrm{d}\boldsymbol{r}}{\mathrm{d}t} = \boldsymbol{F}(\boldsymbol{r}), \quad \text{where } \boldsymbol{r}(t_0) = \boldsymbol{r}_0$$

and $\boldsymbol{r}_0$ is the point on the line corresponding to $t = t_0$. This vector equation represents the three simultaneous ordinary differential equations

$$\frac{\mathrm{d}x}{\mathrm{d}t} = P(x, y, z),$$

$$\frac{\mathrm{d}y}{\mathrm{d}t} = Q(x, y, z),$$

$$\frac{\mathrm{d}z}{\mathrm{d}t} = R(x, y, z)$$

where $\boldsymbol{F} = (P, Q, R)$.

Modern computer algebra packages make it easier to draw both the level surfaces of scalar functions and the field lines of vector functions, but to underline the basic ideas we shall consider two simple examples.

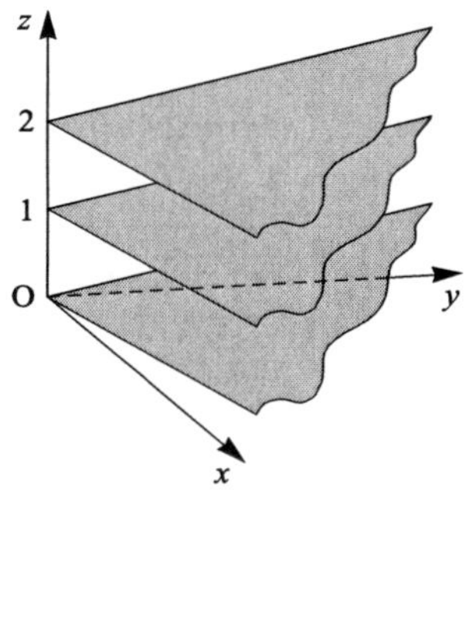

Figure 7.2 Level surfaces of $f(\boldsymbol{r}) = (2, 2, -1) \cdot \boldsymbol{r} = 2x + 2y - z$.

Example 7.1 Sketch

(a) the level surfaces of the scalar point function $f(\mathbf{r}) = z\,\mathrm{e}^{-xy}$;

(b) the field lines of the vector point function $\mathbf{F}(\mathbf{r}) = (y, -x, 1)$.

Solution (a) Consider the level surface given by $f(\mathbf{r}) = c$, where c is a number. Then $z\,\mathrm{e}^{-xy} = c$ and so $z = c\,\mathrm{e}^{xy}$. For c, x and y all positive we can easily sketch part of the surface as shown in Figure 7.3(a), from which we can deduce the appearance of the whole family of level surfaces.

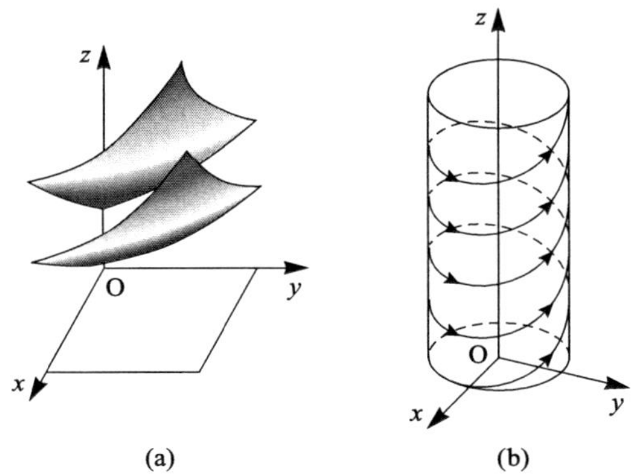

Figure 7.3 (a) Level surfaces of $f(\mathbf{r}) = z\,\mathrm{e}^{-xy}$; (b) field lines of $\mathbf{F}(\mathbf{r}) = (y, -x, 1)$.

(b) For the function $\mathbf{F}(\mathbf{r}) = (y, -x, 1)$ the field lines are given by

$$\frac{\mathrm{d}\mathbf{r}}{\mathrm{d}t} = (y, -x, 1)$$

that is, by the simultaneous differential equations

$$\frac{\mathrm{d}x}{\mathrm{d}t} = y, \quad \frac{\mathrm{d}y}{\mathrm{d}t} = -x, \quad \frac{\mathrm{d}z}{\mathrm{d}t} = 1$$

The general solution of these simultaneous equations is

$$x(t) = A\cos t + B\sin t, \quad y(t) = B\cos t - A\sin t, \quad z(t) = t + C$$

where A, B and C are arbitrary constants. Considering, in particular, the field line that passes through (1, 0, 0), we determine the parametric equation

$$(x(t), y(t), z(t)) = (\cos t, -\sin t, t)$$

This represents a circular helix as shown in Figure 7.3(b), from which we can deduce the appearance of the whole family of flow lines.

To investigate the properties of scalar and vector fields further we need to use the calculus of several variables. Here we shall describe the basic ideas and definitions needed for vector calculus. A fuller treatment is given in Chapter 9 of *Modern Engineering Mathematics*.

Given a function $f(x)$ of a single variable x, we measure its rate of change (or gradient) by its derivative with respect to x. This is

$$\frac{df}{dx} = f'(x) = \lim_{\Delta x \to 0} \frac{f(x+\Delta x) - f(x)}{\Delta x}$$

However, a function $f(x, y, z)$ of three independent variables x, y and z does not have a unique rate of change. The value of the latter depends on the direction in which it is measured. The rate of change of the function $f(x, y, z)$ in the x direction is given by its **partial derivative** with respect to x, namely

$$\frac{\partial f}{\partial x} = \lim_{\Delta x \to 0} \frac{f(x+\Delta x, y, z) - f(x, y, z)}{\Delta x}$$

This measures the rate of change of $f(x, y, z)$ with respect to x when y and z are held constant. We can calculate such partial derivatives by differentiating $f(x, y, z)$ with respect to x, treating y and z as constants. Similarly,

$$\frac{\partial f}{\partial y} = \lim_{\Delta y \to 0} \frac{f(x, y+\Delta y, z) - f(x, y, z)}{\Delta y}$$

and

$$\frac{\partial f}{\partial z} = \lim_{\Delta z \to 0} \frac{f(x, y, z+\Delta z) - f(x, y, z)}{\Delta z}$$

define the partial derivatives of $f(x, y, z)$ with respect to y and z respectively.

For conciseness we sometimes use a suffix notation to denote partial derivatives, for example writing f_x for $\partial f/\partial x$. The rules for partial differentiation are essentially the same as for ordinary differentiation, but it must always be remembered which variables are being held constant.

Higher-order partial derivatives may be defined in a similar manner, with, for example,

$$\frac{\partial^2 f}{\partial x^2} = \frac{\partial}{\partial x}\left(\frac{\partial f}{\partial x}\right) = f_{xx}$$

$$\frac{\partial^2 f}{\partial y \partial x} = \frac{\partial}{\partial y}\left(\frac{\partial f}{\partial x}\right) = f_{xy}$$

$$\frac{\partial^3 f}{\partial z \partial y \partial x} = \frac{\partial}{\partial z}\left(\frac{\partial^2 f}{\partial y \partial x}\right) = f_{xyz}$$

Example 7.2

Find the first partial derivatives of the functions $f(x, y, z)$ with formula (a) $x + 2y + z^3$, (b) $x^2(y + 2z)$ and (c) $(x + y)/(z^3 + x)$.

Solution

(a) $f(x, y, z) = x + 2y + z^3$. To obtain f_x, we differentiate $f(x, y, z)$ with respect to x, keeping y and z constant. Thus $f_x = 1$, since the derivative of a constant $(2y + z^3)$ with respect to x is zero. Similarly, $f_y = 2$ and $f_z = 3z^2$.

(b) $f(x, y, z) = x^2(y + 2z)$. Here we use the same idea: when we differentiate with respect to one variable, we treat the other two as constants. Thus

$$\frac{\partial}{\partial x}[x^2(y+2z)] = (y+2z)\frac{\partial}{\partial x}(x^2) = 2x(y+2z)$$

$$\frac{\partial}{\partial y}[x^2(y+2z)] = x^2\frac{\partial}{\partial y}(y+2z) = x^2(1) = x^2$$

$$\frac{\partial}{\partial z}[x^2(y+2z)] = x^2\frac{\partial}{\partial z}(y+2z) = x^2(2) = 2x^2$$

(c) $f(x, y, z) = (x+y)/(z^3+x)$. Here we use the same idea, together with basic rules from ordinary differentiation:

$$\frac{\partial f}{\partial x} = \frac{(1)(z^3+x)-(x+y)(1)}{(z^3+x)^2} \quad \text{(quotient rule)}$$

$$= \frac{z^3-y}{(z^3+x)^2}$$

$$\frac{\partial f}{\partial y} = \frac{1}{z^3+x}$$

$$\frac{\partial f}{\partial z} = \frac{-3z^2(x+y)}{(z^3+x)^2} \quad \text{(chain rule)}$$

In Example 7.2 we used the **chain** (or **composite-function**) **rule** of ordinary differentiation

$$\frac{\mathrm{d}f}{\mathrm{d}x} = \frac{\mathrm{d}f}{\mathrm{d}u}\frac{\mathrm{d}u}{\mathrm{d}x}$$

to obtain the partial derivative $\partial f/\partial z$. The multivariable calculus form of the chain rule is a little more complicated. If the variables u, v and w are defined in terms of x, y and z then the partial derivative of $f(u, v, w)$ with respect to x is

$$\frac{\partial f}{\partial x} = \frac{\partial f}{\partial u}\frac{\partial u}{\partial x} + \frac{\partial f}{\partial v}\frac{\partial v}{\partial x} + \frac{\partial f}{\partial w}\frac{\partial w}{\partial x}$$

with similar expressions for $\partial f/\partial y$ and $\partial f/\partial z$.

Example 7.3 Find $\partial T/\partial r$ and $\partial T/\partial\theta$ when

$$T(x, y) = x^3 - xy + y^3$$

and

$$x = r\cos\theta \quad \text{and} \quad y = r\sin\theta$$

Solution By the chain rule,

$$\frac{\partial T}{\partial r} = \frac{\partial T}{\partial x}\frac{\partial x}{\partial r} + \frac{\partial T}{\partial y}\frac{\partial y}{\partial r}$$

In this example

$$\frac{\partial T}{\partial x} = 3x^2 - y \quad \text{and} \quad \frac{\partial T}{\partial y} = -x + 3y^2$$

and

$$\frac{\partial x}{\partial r} = \cos\theta \quad \text{and} \quad \frac{\partial y}{\partial r} = \sin\theta$$

so that

$$\frac{\partial T}{\partial r} = (3x^2 - y)\cos\theta + (-x + 3y^2)\sin\theta$$

Substituting for x and y in terms of r and θ gives

$$\frac{\partial T}{\partial r} = 3r^2(\cos^3\theta + \sin^3\theta) - 2r\cos\theta\sin\theta$$

Similarly,

$$\begin{aligned}\frac{\partial T}{\partial \theta} &= (3x^2 - y)(-r\sin\theta) + (-x + 3y^2)r\cos\theta \\ &= 3r^3(\sin\theta - \cos\theta)\cos\theta\sin\theta + r^2(\sin^2\theta - \cos^2\theta)\end{aligned}$$

Example 7.4

Find $\mathrm{d}H/\mathrm{d}t$ when

$$H(t) = \sin(3x - y)$$

and

$$x = 2t^2 - 3 \quad \text{and} \quad y = \tfrac{1}{2}t^2 - 5t + 1$$

Solution

We note that x and y are functions of t only, so that the chain rule becomes

$$\frac{\mathrm{d}H}{\mathrm{d}t} = \frac{\partial H}{\partial x}\frac{\mathrm{d}x}{\mathrm{d}t} + \frac{\partial H}{\partial y}\frac{\mathrm{d}y}{\mathrm{d}t}$$

Note the mixture of partial and ordinary derivatives. H is a function of the one variable t, but its dependence is expressed through the two variables x and y.

Substituting for the derivatives involved, we have

$$\begin{aligned}\frac{\mathrm{d}H}{\mathrm{d}t} &= 3[\cos(3x - y)]4t - [\cos(3x - y)](t - 5) \\ &= (11t + 5)\cos(3x - y) \\ &= (11t + 5)\cos(\tfrac{11}{2}t^2 + 5t - 10)\end{aligned}$$

Example 7.5

A scalar point function $f(\boldsymbol{r})$ can be expressed in terms of rectangular cartesian coordinates (x, y, z) or in terms of spherical polar coordinates (r, θ, ϕ), where

$$x = r\sin\theta\cos\phi, \quad y = r\sin\theta\sin\phi, \quad z = r\cos\theta$$

as shown in Figure 7.4. Find $\partial f/\partial x$ in terms of the partial derivatives of the function with respect to r, θ and ϕ.

Solution Using the chain rule, we have

$$\frac{\partial f}{\partial x} = \frac{\partial f}{\partial r}\frac{\partial r}{\partial x} + \frac{\partial f}{\partial \theta}\frac{\partial \theta}{\partial x} + \frac{\partial f}{\partial \phi}\frac{\partial \phi}{\partial x}$$

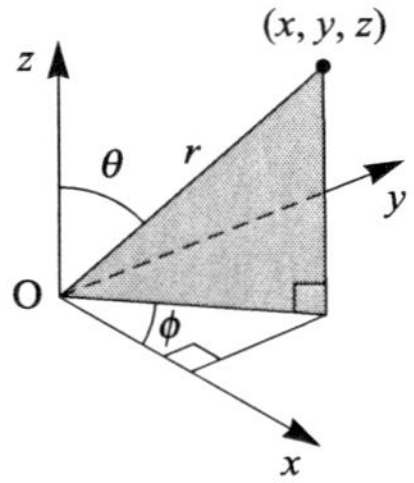

Figure 7.4 Spherical polar coordinates.

From Figure 7.4, $r^2 = x^2 + y^2 + z^2$, $\tan\phi = y/x$ and $\tan\theta = (x^2 + y^2)^{1/2}/z$, so that

$$\frac{\partial r}{\partial x} = \frac{x}{r} = \sin\theta\cos\phi$$

$$\frac{\partial \phi}{\partial x} = \frac{\partial}{\partial x}\left(\tan^{-1}\frac{y}{x}\right) = -\frac{y}{x^2 + y^2} = -\frac{\sin\phi}{r\sin\theta}$$

$$\frac{\partial \theta}{\partial x} = \frac{\partial}{\partial x}\left\{\tan^{-1}\left[\frac{(x^2 + y^2)^{1/2}}{z}\right]\right\} = \frac{xz}{(x^2 + y^2 + z^2)(x^2 + y^2)^{1/2}}$$

$$= \frac{\cos\phi\cos\theta}{r}$$

Thus

$$\frac{\partial f}{\partial x} = \sin\theta\cos\phi\frac{\partial f}{\partial r} - \frac{\sin\phi}{r\sin\theta}\frac{\partial f}{\partial \phi} + \frac{\cos\phi\cos\theta}{r}\frac{\partial f}{\partial \theta}$$

7.1.2 Exercises

1. Sketch the contours (in two dimensions) of the scalar functions

   (a) $f(x, y) = \ln(x^2 + y^2 - 1)$

   (b) $f(x, y) = \tan^{-1}[y/(1 + x)]$

2. Sketch the flow lines (in two dimensions) of the vector functions

   (a) $\boldsymbol{F}(x, y) = y\boldsymbol{i} + (6x^2 - 4x)\boldsymbol{j}$

   (b) $\boldsymbol{F}(x, y) = y\boldsymbol{i} + (\frac{1}{6}x^3 - x)\boldsymbol{j}$

   where $\boldsymbol{i}$ and $\boldsymbol{j}$ are unit vectors in the direction of the x and y axes respectively.

3. Sketch the level surfaces of the functions

   (a) $f(\boldsymbol{r}) = z - xy$ (b) $f(\boldsymbol{r}) = z - e^{-xy}$

4. Sketch the field lines of the functions

   (a) $\boldsymbol{F}(\boldsymbol{r}) = (xy, y^2 + 1, z)$

   (b) $\boldsymbol{F}(\boldsymbol{r}) = (yz, zx, xy)$

5. Find all the first and second partial derivatives of the functions

   (a) $f(\boldsymbol{r}) = xyz - x^2 + y - z$ (b) $f(\boldsymbol{r}) = x^2yz^3$

   (c) $f(\boldsymbol{r}) = z\tan^{-1}(y/x)$

6. Find $\mathrm{d}f/\mathrm{d}t$, where

   (a) $f(\boldsymbol{r}) = x^2 + y^2 - z$, and $x = t^3 - 1$, $y = 2t$, $z = 1/(t - 1)$

   (b) $f(\boldsymbol{r}) = xyz$, and $x = e^{-t}\sin t$, $y = e^{-t}\cos t$, $z = t$

7. Find $\partial f/\partial y$ and $\partial f/\partial z$ in terms of the partial derivatives of f with respect to spherical polar coordinates (r, θ, ϕ) (see Example 7.5).

8. Show that if $u(\boldsymbol{r}) = f(r)$, where $r^2 = x^2 + y^2 + z^2$, as usual, and

$$\frac{\partial^2 u}{\partial x^2} + \frac{\partial^2 u}{\partial y^2} + \frac{\partial^2 u}{\partial z^2} = 0$$

then

$$\frac{d^2f}{dr^2} + \frac{2}{r}\frac{df}{dr} = 0$$

Hence find the general form for $f(r)$.

9 Show that

$$V(x, y, z) = \frac{1}{z}\exp\left(-\frac{x^2+y^2}{4z}\right)$$

satisfies the differential equation

$$\frac{\partial^2 V}{\partial x^2} + \frac{\partial^2 V}{\partial y^2} = \frac{\partial V}{\partial z}$$

10 Verify that $V(x, y, z) = \sin 3x \cos 4y \cosh 5z$ satisfies the differential equation

$$\frac{\partial^2 V}{\partial x^2} + \frac{\partial^2 V}{\partial y^2} + \frac{\partial^2 V}{\partial z^2} = 0$$

7.1.3 Transformations

Example 7.3 may be viewed as an example of *transformation of coordinates*. For example, consider the transformation or mapping from the (x, y) plane to the (s, t) plane defined by

$$s = s(x, y), \qquad t = t(x, y) \tag{7.1}$$

Then a function $u = f(x, y)$ of x and y becomes a function $u = F(s, t)$ of s and t under the transformation, and the partial derivatives are related by

$$\left.\begin{aligned} \frac{\partial u}{\partial x} &= \frac{\partial u}{\partial s}\frac{\partial s}{\partial x} + \frac{\partial u}{\partial t}\frac{\partial t}{\partial x} \\ \frac{\partial u}{\partial y} &= \frac{\partial u}{\partial s}\frac{\partial s}{\partial y} + \frac{\partial u}{\partial t}\frac{\partial t}{\partial y} \end{aligned}\right\} \tag{7.2}$$

In matrix notation this becomes

$$\begin{bmatrix} \dfrac{\partial u}{\partial x} \\ \dfrac{\partial u}{\partial y} \end{bmatrix} = \begin{bmatrix} \dfrac{\partial s}{\partial x} & \dfrac{\partial t}{\partial x} \\ \dfrac{\partial s}{\partial y} & \dfrac{\partial t}{\partial y} \end{bmatrix} \begin{bmatrix} \dfrac{\partial u}{\partial s} \\ \dfrac{\partial u}{\partial t} \end{bmatrix} \tag{7.3}$$

The determinant of the matrix of the transformation is called the **Jacobian** of the transformation defined by (7.1) and is abbreviated to

$$\frac{\partial(s, t)}{\partial(x, y)} \quad \text{or simply to} \quad J$$

so that

$$J = \frac{\partial(s, t)}{\partial(x, y)} = \begin{vmatrix} \dfrac{\partial s}{\partial x} & \dfrac{\partial t}{\partial x} \\ \dfrac{\partial s}{\partial y} & \dfrac{\partial t}{\partial y} \end{vmatrix} = \begin{vmatrix} s_x & t_x \\ s_y & t_y \end{vmatrix} \tag{7.4}$$

The matrix itself is referred to as the **Jacobian matrix**. The Jacobian plays an important role in various applications of mathematics in engineering, particularly in implementing changes in variables in multiple integrals, as considered later in this chapter.

As indicated earlier, (7.1) define a transformation of the (x, y) plane to the (s, t) plane and give the coordinates of a point in the (s, t) plane corresponding to a point in the (x, y) plane. If we solve (7.1) for x and y, we obtain

$$x = X(s, t), \qquad y = Y(s, t) \tag{7.5}$$

which represent a transformation of the (s, t) plane into the (x, y) plane. This is called the inverse transformation of the transformation defined by (7.1), and, analogously to (7.2), we can relate the partial derivatives by

$$\left.\begin{aligned} \frac{\partial u}{\partial s} &= \frac{\partial u}{\partial x}\frac{\partial x}{\partial s} + \frac{\partial u}{\partial y}\frac{\partial y}{\partial s} \\ \frac{\partial u}{\partial t} &= \frac{\partial u}{\partial x}\frac{\partial x}{\partial t} + \frac{\partial u}{\partial y}\frac{\partial y}{\partial t} \end{aligned}\right\} \tag{7.6}$$

The Jacobian of the inverse transformation (7.5) is

$$J_1 = \frac{\partial(x, y)}{\partial(s, t)} = \begin{vmatrix} x_s & y_s \\ x_t & y_t \end{vmatrix}$$

and, provided $J \neq 0$, it is always true that $J_1 = J^{-1}$ or

$$\frac{\partial(x, y)}{\partial(s, t)}\frac{\partial(s, t)}{\partial(x, y)} = 1$$

If $J = 0$ then the variables s and t defined by (7.1) are functionally dependent; that is, a relationship of the form $f(s, t) = 0$ exists. This implies a non-unique correspondence between points in the (x, y) and (s, t) planes.

Example 7.6

(a) Obtain the Jacobian J of the transformation

$$s = 2x + y, \qquad t = x - 2y$$

(b) Determine the inverse transformation of the above transformation and obtain its Jacobian J_1. Confirm that $J_1 = J^{-1}$.

Solution

(a) Using (7.4), the Jacobian of the transformation is

$$J = \frac{\partial(s, t)}{\partial(x, y)} = \begin{vmatrix} 2 & 1 \\ 1 & -2 \end{vmatrix} = -5$$

(b) Solving the pair of equations in the transformation for x and y gives the inverse transformation as

$$x = \tfrac{1}{5}(2s + t), \qquad y = \tfrac{1}{5}(s - 2t)$$

The Jacobian of this inverse transformation is

$$J_1 = \frac{\partial(x, y)}{\partial(s, t)} = \begin{vmatrix} \frac{2}{5} & \frac{1}{5} \\ \frac{1}{5} & -\frac{2}{5} \end{vmatrix} = -\tfrac{1}{5}$$

confirming that $J_1 = J^{-1}$.

Example 7.7 Show that the variables x and y given by

$$x = \frac{s+t}{s}, \qquad y = \frac{s+t}{t} \tag{7.7}$$

are functionally dependent, and obtain the relationship $f(x, y) = 0$.

Solution The Jacobian of the transformation (7.7) is

$$J = \frac{\partial(x, y)}{\partial(s, t)} = \begin{vmatrix} x_s & y_s \\ x_t & y_t \end{vmatrix} = \begin{vmatrix} -\frac{t}{s^2} & \frac{1}{t} \\ \frac{1}{s} & -\frac{s}{t^2} \end{vmatrix} = \frac{1}{st} - \frac{1}{st} = 0$$

Since $J = 0$, the variables x and y are functionally related.

Rearranging (7.7), we have

$$x = 1 + \frac{t}{s}, \qquad y = \frac{s}{t} + 1$$

so that

$$(x-1)(y-1) = \frac{t}{s}\frac{s}{t} = 1$$

giving the functional relationship as

$$xy - (x + y) = 0$$

The definition of a Jacobian is not restricted to functions of two variables, and it is readily extendable to functions of many variables. For example, for functions of three variables, if

$$u = U(x, y, z), \qquad v = V(x, y, z), \qquad w = W(x, y, z) \tag{7.8}$$

represents a transformation in three dimensions from the variables x, y, z to the variables u, v, w then the corresponding Jacobian is

$$J = \frac{\partial(u, v, w)}{\partial(x, y, z)} = \begin{vmatrix} u_x & v_x & w_x \\ u_y & v_y & w_y \\ u_z & v_z & w_z \end{vmatrix}$$

Again, if $J = 0$, it follows that there exists a functional relationship $f(u, v, w) = 0$ between the variables u, v and w defined by (7.8).

7.1.4 Exercises

11 Show that if $x + y = u$ and $y = uv$, then

$$\frac{\partial(x, y)}{\partial(u, v)} = u$$

12 Show that, if $x + y + z = u$, $y + z = uv$ and $z = uvw$, then

$$\frac{\partial(x, y, z)}{\partial(u, v, w)} = u^2 v$$

13 If $x = e^u \cos v$ and $y = e^u \sin v$, obtain the two Jacobians

$$\frac{\partial(x, y)}{\partial(u, v)} \quad \text{and} \quad \frac{\partial(u, v)}{\partial(x, y)}$$

and verify that they are mutual inverses.

14 Find the values of the constant parameter λ for which the functions

$$u = \cos x \cos y - \lambda \sin x \sin y$$

$$v = \sin x \cos y + \lambda \cos x \sin y$$

are functionally dependent.

15 Find the value of the constant K for which

$$u = Kx^2 + 4y^2 + z^2$$
$$v = 3x + 2y + z$$
$$w = 2yz + 3zx + 6xy$$

are functionally related, and obtain the corresponding relation.

16 Show that, if $u = g(x, y)$ and $v = h(x, y)$, then

$$\frac{\partial x}{\partial u} = \frac{\partial v}{\partial y}\Big/ J \qquad \frac{\partial x}{\partial v} = -\frac{\partial u}{\partial y}\Big/ J$$
$$\frac{\partial y}{\partial u} = -\frac{\partial v}{\partial x}\Big/ J \qquad \frac{\partial y}{\partial v} = \frac{\partial u}{\partial x}\Big/ J$$

where in each case

$$J = \frac{\partial(u, v)}{\partial(x, y)}$$

17 Use the results of Exercise 16 to obtain the partial derivatives

$$\frac{\partial x}{\partial u}, \quad \frac{\partial x}{\partial v}, \quad \frac{\partial y}{\partial u}, \quad \frac{\partial y}{\partial v}$$

where

$$u = e^x \cos y \quad \text{and} \quad v = e^{-x} \sin y$$

7.1.5 The total differential

Consider a function $u = f(x, y)$ of two variables x and y. Let Δx and Δy be increments in the values of x and y. Then the corresponding increment in u is given by

$$\Delta u = f(x + \Delta x, y + \Delta y) - f(x, y)$$

We rewrite this as two terms: one showing the change in u due to the change in x, and the other showing the change in u due to the change in y. Thus

$$\Delta u = [f(x + \Delta x, y + \Delta y) - f(x, y + \Delta y)] + [f(x, y + \Delta y) - f(x, y)]$$

Dividing the first bracketed term by Δx and the second by Δy gives

$$\Delta u = \frac{f(x + \Delta x, y + \Delta y) - f(x, y + \Delta x)}{\Delta x}\Delta x + \frac{f(x, y + \Delta y) - f(x, y)}{\Delta y}\Delta y$$

From the definition of the partial derivative, we may approximate this expression by

$$\Delta u \approx \frac{\partial f}{\partial x}\Delta x + \frac{\partial f}{\partial y}\Delta y$$

We define the **differential** du by the equation

$$\mathrm{d}u = \frac{\partial f}{\partial x}\Delta x + \frac{\partial f}{\partial y}\Delta y \tag{7.9}$$

By setting $f(x, y) = f_1(x, y) = x$ and $f(x, y) = f_2(x, y) = y$ in turn in (7.9), we see that

$$\mathrm{d}x = \frac{\partial f_1}{\partial x}\Delta x + \frac{\partial f_1}{\partial y}\Delta y = \Delta x \quad \text{and} \quad \mathrm{d}y = \Delta y$$

so that for the independent variables increments and differentials are equal. For the dependent variable we have

$$\mathrm{d}u = \frac{\partial f}{\partial x}\mathrm{d}x + \frac{\partial f}{\partial y}\mathrm{d}y \tag{7.10}$$

We see that the differential du is an approximation to the change Δu in $u = f(x, y)$ resulting from small changes Δx and Δy in the independent variables x and y; that is,

$$\Delta u \approx \mathrm{d}u = \frac{\partial f}{\partial x}\mathrm{d}x + \frac{\partial f}{\partial y}\mathrm{d}y = \frac{\partial f}{\partial x}\Delta x + \frac{\partial f}{\partial y}\Delta y \tag{7.11}$$

a result illustrated in Figure 7.5.

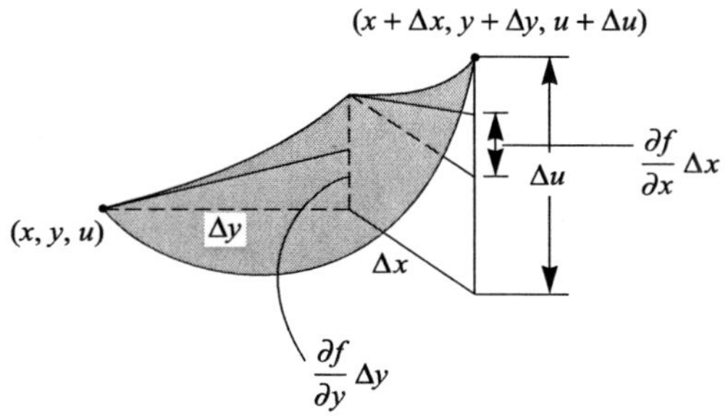

Figure 7.5
Illustration of result (7.11).

This extends to functions of as many variables as we please, provided that the partial derivatives exist. For example, for a function of three variables (x, y, z) defined by $u = f(x, y, z)$ we have

$$\begin{aligned}\Delta u \approx \mathrm{d}u &= \frac{\partial f}{\partial x}\mathrm{d}x + \frac{\partial f}{\partial y}\mathrm{d}y + \frac{\partial f}{\partial z}\mathrm{d}z \\ &= \frac{\partial f}{\partial x}\Delta x + \frac{\partial f}{\partial y}\Delta y + \frac{\partial f}{\partial z}\Delta z\end{aligned}$$

The differential of a function of several variables is often called a **total differential**, emphasizing that it shows the variation of the function with respect to small changes in *all* the independent variables.

Example 7.8 Find the total differential of $u(x, y) = x^y$.

Solution Taking partial derivatives we have

$$\frac{\partial u}{\partial x} = yx^{y-1} \quad \text{and} \quad \frac{\partial u}{\partial y} = x^y \ln x$$

Hence, using (7.10),

$$\mathrm{d}u = yx^{y-1}\,\mathrm{d}x + x^y \ln x\,\mathrm{d}y$$

Differentials sometimes arise naturally when modelling practical problems. When this occurs, it is often possible to analyse the problem further by testing to see if the expression in which the differentials occur is a total differential. Consider the equation

$$P(x, y)\,\mathrm{d}x + Q(x, y)\,\mathrm{d}y = 0$$

connecting x, y and their differentials. The left-hand side of this equation is said to be an **exact differential** if there is a function $f(x, y)$ such that

$$\mathrm{d}f = P(x, y)\,\mathrm{d}x + Q(x, y)\,\mathrm{d}y$$

Now we know that

$$\mathrm{d}f = \frac{\partial f}{\partial x}\,\mathrm{d}x + \frac{\partial f}{\partial y}\,\mathrm{d}y$$

so if $f(x, y)$ exists then

$$P(x, y) = \frac{\partial f}{\partial x} \quad \text{and} \quad Q(x, y) = \frac{\partial f}{\partial y}$$

For functions with continuous second derivatives we have

$$\frac{\partial^2 f}{\partial x \partial y} = \frac{\partial^2 f}{\partial y \partial x}$$

Thus if $f(x, y)$ exists then

$$\frac{\partial P}{\partial y} = \frac{\partial Q}{\partial x} \qquad \textbf{(7.12)}$$

This gives us a test for the existence of $f(x, y)$, but does not tell us how to find it! The technique for finding $f(x, y)$ is shown in Example 7.9.

Example 7.9 Show that

$$(6x + 9y + 11)\,\mathrm{d}x + (9x - 4y + 3)\,\mathrm{d}y$$

is an exact differential and find the relationship between y and x given

$$\frac{\mathrm{d}y}{\mathrm{d}x} = -\frac{6x + 9y + 11}{9x - 4y + 3}$$

and the condition $y = 1$ when $x = 0$.

Solution In this example

$$P(x, y) = 6x + 9y + 11 \quad \text{and} \quad Q(x, y) = 9x - 4y + 3$$

First we test whether the expression is an exact differential. In this example

$$\frac{\partial P}{\partial y} = 9 \quad \text{and} \quad \frac{\partial Q}{\partial x} = 9$$

so from (7.12), we have an exact differential. Thus we know that there is a function $f(x, y)$ such that

$$\frac{\partial f}{\partial x} = 6x + 9y + 11 \quad \text{and} \quad \frac{\partial f}{\partial y} = 9x - 4y + 3 \tag{7.13a, b}$$

Integrating (7.13a) with respect to x, keeping y constant (that is, reversing the partial differentiation process), we have

$$f(x, y) = 3x^2 + 9xy + 11x + g(y) \tag{7.14}$$

Note that the 'constant' of integration is a function of y. You can check that this expression for $f(x, y)$ is correct by differentiating it partially with respect to x. But we also know from (7.13b) the partial derivative of $f(x, y)$ with respect to y, and this enables us to find $g'(y)$. Differentiating (7.14) partially with respect to y and equating it to (7.13b), we have

$$\frac{\partial f}{\partial y} = 9x + \frac{\mathrm{d}g}{\mathrm{d}y} = 9x - 4y + 3$$

(Note that since g is a function of y only we use $\mathrm{d}g/\mathrm{d}y$ rather than $\partial g/\partial y$.) Thus

$$\frac{\mathrm{d}g}{\mathrm{d}y} = -4y + 3$$

so, on integrating,

$$g(y) = -2y^2 + 3y + C$$

Substituting back into (7.13b) gives

$$f(x, y) = 3x^2 + 9xy + 11x - 2y^2 + 3y + C$$

Now we are given that

$$\frac{\mathrm{d}y}{\mathrm{d}x} = -\frac{6x + 9y + 11}{9x - 4y + 3}$$

which implies that

$$(6x + 9y + 11)\mathrm{d}x + (9x - 4y + 3)\mathrm{d}y = 0$$

which in turn implies that

$$3x^2 + 9xy + 11x - 2y^2 + 3y + C = 0$$

The arbitrary constant C is fixed by applying the given condition $y = 1$ when $x = 0$, giving $C = -1$. Thus x and y satisfy the equation

$$3x^2 + 9xy + 11x - 2y^2 + 3y = 1$$

7.1.6 Exercises

18 Determine which of the following are exact differentials of a function, and find, where appropriate, the corresponding function.

(a) $(y^2 + 2xy + 1)\,dx + (2xy + x^2)\,dy$

(b) $(2xy^2 + 3y\cos 3x)\,dx + (2x^2y + \sin 3x)\,dy$

(c) $(6xy - y^2)\,dx + (2x\,e^y - x^2)\,dy$

(d) $(z^3 - 3y)\,dx + (12y^2 - 3x)\,dy + 3xz^2\,dz$

19 Find the value of the constant λ such that

$$(y\cos x + \lambda\cos y)\,dx + (x\sin y + \sin x + y)\,dy$$

is the exact differential of a function $f(x, y)$. Find the corresponding function $f(x, y)$ that also satisfies the condition $f(0, 1) = 0$.

20 Show that the differential

$$g(x, y) = (10x^2 + 6xy + 6y^2)\,dx + (9x^2 + 4xy + 15y^2)\,dy$$

is not exact, but that a constant m can be chosen so that

$$(2x + 3y)^m g(x, y)$$

is equal to dz, the exact differential of a function $z = f(x, y)$. Find $f(x, y)$.

7.2 Derivatives of a scalar point function

In many practical problems it is necessary to measure the rate of change of a scalar point function. For example, in heat transfer problems we need to know the rate of change of temperature from point to point, because that determines the rate at which heat flows. Similarly, if we are investigating the electric field due to static charges, we need to know the variation of the electric potential from point to point. To determine such information, the ideas of calculus were extended to vector quantities. The first development of this was the concept of the gradient of a scalar point function.

7.2.1 The gradient of a scalar point function

We described in Section 7.1.1 how the gradient of a scalar field depended on the direction along which its rate of change was measured. We now explore this idea further. Consider the rate of change of the function $f(\boldsymbol{r})$ at the point (x, y, z) in the direction of the unit vector (l, m, n). To find this, we need to evaluate the limit

$$\lim_{\Delta r \to 0} \frac{f(\boldsymbol{r} + \Delta\boldsymbol{r}) - f(\boldsymbol{r})}{\Delta r}$$

where $\Delta\boldsymbol{r}$ is in the direction of (l, m, n). In terms of coordinates, this means

$$\begin{aligned}\boldsymbol{r} + \Delta\boldsymbol{r} &= \boldsymbol{r} + \Delta r(l, m, n)\\ &= (x + \Delta x,\ y + \Delta y,\ z + \Delta z)\end{aligned}$$

so that

$$\Delta x = l\Delta r, \qquad \Delta y = m\Delta r, \qquad \Delta z = n\Delta r$$

Thus we have to consider the limit

$$\lim_{\Delta r \to 0} \frac{f(x + l\Delta r,\ y + m\Delta r,\ z + n\Delta r) - f(x, y, z)}{\Delta r}$$

We can rewrite this as

$$\lim_{\Delta r\to 0}\left[\frac{f(x+l\Delta r,\ y+m\Delta r,\ z+n\Delta r)-f(x,\ y+m\Delta r,\ z+n\Delta r)}{l\Delta r}\right]l$$

$$+\lim_{\Delta r\to 0}\left[\frac{f(x,\ y+m\Delta r,\ z+n\Delta r)-f(x,\ y,\ z+n\Delta r)}{m\Delta r}\right]m$$

$$+\lim_{\Delta r\to 0}\left[\frac{f(x,\ y,\ z+n\Delta r)-f(x,\ y,\ z)}{n\Delta r}\right]n$$

Evaluating the limits, remembering that $\Delta x = l\Delta r$ and so on, we find that the rate of change of $f(\boldsymbol{r})$ in the direction of the unit vector (l, m, n) is

$$\frac{\partial f}{\partial x}l + \frac{\partial f}{\partial y}m + \frac{\partial f}{\partial z}n = \left(\frac{\partial f}{\partial x}, \frac{\partial f}{\partial y}, \frac{\partial f}{\partial z}\right)\cdot(l,\ m,\ n)$$

The vector

$$\left(\frac{\partial f}{\partial x}, \frac{\partial f}{\partial y}, \frac{\partial f}{\partial z}\right)$$

is called the **gradient** of the scalar point function $f(x, y, z)$, and is denoted by grad f or by $\boldsymbol{\nabla} f$, where $\boldsymbol{\nabla}$ is the vector operator

$$\boldsymbol{\nabla} = \boldsymbol{i}\frac{\partial}{\partial x} + \boldsymbol{j}\frac{\partial}{\partial y} + \boldsymbol{k}\frac{\partial}{\partial z}$$

where $\boldsymbol{i}, \boldsymbol{j}$ and $\boldsymbol{k}$ are the usual triad of unit vectors.

The symbol $\boldsymbol{\nabla}$ is called 'del' or sometimes 'nabla'. Then

$$\text{grad}\, f = \boldsymbol{\nabla} f = \frac{\partial f}{\partial x}\boldsymbol{i} + \frac{\partial f}{\partial y}\boldsymbol{j} + \frac{\partial f}{\partial z}\boldsymbol{k} \equiv \left(\frac{\partial f}{\partial x}, \frac{\partial f}{\partial y}, \frac{\partial f}{\partial z}\right) \qquad \textbf{(7.15)}$$

Thus we can calculate the rate of change of $f(x, y, z)$ along any direction we please. If $\hat{\boldsymbol{u}}$ is the unit vector in that direction then

$$(\text{grad}\, f)\cdot\hat{\boldsymbol{u}}$$

gives the required **directional derivative**, that is the rate of change of $f(x, y, z)$ in the direction of $\hat{\boldsymbol{u}}$. Remembering that $\boldsymbol{a}\cdot\boldsymbol{b} = |a||b|\cos\theta$, where θ is the angle between the two vectors, it follows that the rate of change of $f(x, y, z)$ is zero along directions perpendicular to grad f and is maximum along the direction parallel to grad f. Furthermore, grad f acts along the normal direction to the level surface of $f(x, y, z)$. We can see this by considering the level surfaces of the function corresponding to c and $c + \Delta c$, as shown in Figure 7.6(a). In going from P on the surface $f(\boldsymbol{r}) = c$ to any point Q on $f(\boldsymbol{r}) = c + \Delta c$, the increase in f is the same whatever point Q is chosen, but the distance PQ will be smallest, and hence the rate of change of $f(x, y, z)$ greatest, when Q lies on the normal $\hat{\boldsymbol{n}}$ to the surface at P. Thus grad f at P is in the direction of the outward normal $\hat{\boldsymbol{n}}$ to the surface $f(\boldsymbol{r}) = u$, and represents in magnitude and direction the greatest rate of increase of $f(x, y, z)$ with distance (Figure 7.6(b)). It is frequently written as

$$\text{grad}\, f = \frac{\partial f}{\partial n}\hat{\boldsymbol{n}}$$

where $\partial f/\partial n$ is referred to as the normal derivative to the surface $f(\boldsymbol{r}) = c$.

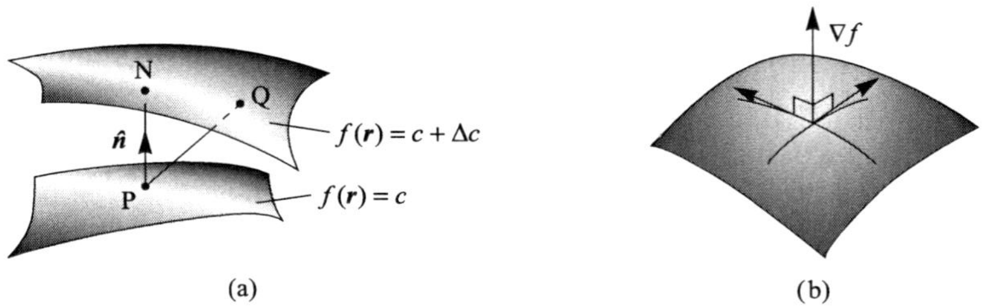

Figure 7.6 (a) Adjacent level surfaces of $f(\boldsymbol{r})$; (b) grad f acts normally to the surface $f(\boldsymbol{r}) = c$.

Example 7.10 Find grad f for $f(\boldsymbol{r}) = 3x^2 + 2y^2 + z^2$ at the point (1, 2, 3). Hence calculate

(a) the directional derivative of $f(\boldsymbol{r})$ at (1, 2, 3) in the direction of the unit vector $\frac{1}{3}(2, 2, 1)$;

(b) the maximum rate of change of the function at (1, 2, 3) and its direction.

Solution (a) Since $\partial f/\partial x = 6x$, $\partial f/\partial y = 4y$ and $\partial f/\partial z = 2z$, we have from (7.15) that

$$\text{grad}\, f = \boldsymbol{\nabla} f = 6x\boldsymbol{i} + 4y\boldsymbol{j} + 2z\boldsymbol{k}$$

At the point (1, 2, 3)

$$\text{grad}\, f = 6\boldsymbol{i} + 8\boldsymbol{j} + 6\boldsymbol{k}$$

Thus the directional derivative of $f(\boldsymbol{r})$ at (1, 2, 3) in the direction of the unit vector $(\frac{2}{3}, \frac{2}{3}, \frac{1}{3})$ is

$$(6\boldsymbol{i} + 8\boldsymbol{j} + 6\boldsymbol{k}) \cdot (\tfrac{2}{3}\boldsymbol{i} + \tfrac{2}{3}\boldsymbol{j} + \tfrac{1}{3}\boldsymbol{k}) = \tfrac{34}{3}$$

(b) The maximum rate of change of $f(\boldsymbol{r})$ at (1, 2, 3) occurs along the direction parallel to grad f at (1, 2, 3); that is, parallel to (6, 8, 6). The unit vector in that direction is $(3, 4, 3)/\sqrt{34}$ and the maximum rate of change of $f(\boldsymbol{r})$ is $|\text{grad}\, f| = 2\sqrt{34}$.

If a surface in three dimensions is specified by the equation $f(x, y, z) = c$, or equivalently $f(\boldsymbol{r}) = c$, then grad f is a vector perpendicular to that surface. This enables us to calculate the normal vector at any point on the surface, and consequently to find the equation of the tangent plane at that point.

Example 7.11 A paraboloid of revolution has equation $2z = x^2 + y^2$. Find the unit normal vector to the surface at the point (1, 3, 5). Hence obtain the equation of the normal and the tangent plane to the surface at that point.

Solution A vector normal to the surface $2z = x^2 + y^2$ is given by

$$\text{grad}\,(x^2 + y^2 - 2z) = 2x\boldsymbol{i} + 2y\boldsymbol{j} - 2\boldsymbol{k}$$

At the point (1, 3, 5) the vector has the value $2\boldsymbol{i} + 6\boldsymbol{j} - 2\boldsymbol{k}$. Thus the normal unit vector at the point (1, 3, 5) is $(\boldsymbol{i} + 3\boldsymbol{j} - \boldsymbol{k})/\sqrt{11}$. The equation of the line through (1, 3, 5) in the direction of this normal is

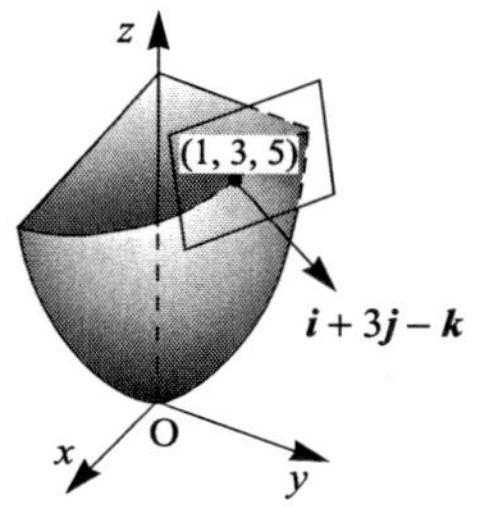

Figure 7.7 Tangent plane at (1, 3, 5) to the paraboloid $2z = x^2 + y^2$.

$$\frac{x-1}{1} = \frac{y-3}{3} = \frac{z-5}{-1}$$

and the equation of the tangent plane is

$$(1)(x-1) + (3)(y-3) + (-1)(z-5) = 0$$

which simplifies to $x + 3y - z = 5$ (see Figure 7.7).

The concept of the gradient of a scalar field occurs in many applications. The simplest, perhaps, is when $f(\boldsymbol{r})$ represents the potential in an electric field due to static charges. Then the electric force is in the direction of the greatest decrease of the potential. Its magnitude is equal to that rate of decrease, so that the force is given by $-\text{grad} f$.

7.2.2 Exercises

21 Find grad f for $f(\boldsymbol{r}) = x^2yz^2$ at the point (1, 2, 3). Hence calculate

(a) the directional derivative of $f(\boldsymbol{r})$ at (1, 2, 3) in the direction of the vector (−2, 3, −6);
(b) the maximum rate of change of the function at (1, 2, 3) and its direction.

22 Find ∇f where $f(\boldsymbol{r})$ is

(a) $x^2 + y^2 - z$ (b) $z \tan^{-1}(y/x)$
(c) $e^{-x-y+z}/\sqrt{(x^3 + y^2)}$
(d) $xyz \sin\{\pi(x + y + z)\}$

23 Find the directional derivative of $f(\boldsymbol{r}) = x^2 + y^2 - z$ at the point (1, 1, 2) in the direction of the vector (4, 4, −2).

24 Find a unit normal to the surface $xy^2 - 3xz = -5$ at the point (1, −2, 3).

25 If $\boldsymbol{r}$ is the usual position vector $\boldsymbol{r} = x\boldsymbol{i} + y\boldsymbol{j} + z\boldsymbol{k}$, with $|\boldsymbol{r}| = r$, evaluate

(a) ∇r (b) $\nabla\left(\frac{1}{r}\right)$

26 If $\nabla\phi = (2xy + z^2)\boldsymbol{i} + (x^2 + z)\boldsymbol{j} + (y + 2xz)\boldsymbol{k}$, find a possible value for ϕ.

27 Given the scalar function of position

$$\phi(x, y, z) = x^2y - 3xyz + z^3$$

find the value of grad ϕ at the point (3, 1, 2). Also find the directional derivative of ϕ at this point in the direction of the vector (3, −2, 6); that is, in the direction $3\boldsymbol{i} - 2\boldsymbol{j} + 6\boldsymbol{k}$.

28 Find the angle between the surfaces $x^2 + y^2 + z^2 = 9$ and $z = x^2 + y^2 - 3$ at the point (2, −1, 2).

29 Find the equations of the tangent plane and normal line to the surfaces

(a) $x^2 + 2y^2 + 3z^2 = 6$ at (1, 1, 1)
(b) $2x^2 + y^2 - z^2 = -3$ at (1, 2, 3)
(c) $x^2 + y^2 - z = 1$ at (1, 2, 4).

30 (Spherical polar coordinates) When a function $f(\boldsymbol{r})$ is specified in polar coordinates, it is usual to express grad f in terms of the partial derivatives of f with respect to r, θ and ϕ and the unit vectors $\boldsymbol{u}_r$, $\boldsymbol{u}_\theta$ and $\boldsymbol{u}_\phi$ in the directions of increasing r, θ and ϕ as shown in Figure 7.8. Working from first principles, show that

$$\nabla f = \text{grad} f = \frac{\partial f}{\partial r}\boldsymbol{u}_r + \frac{1}{r}\frac{\partial f}{\partial \theta}\boldsymbol{u}_\theta + \frac{1}{r \sin\theta}\frac{\partial f}{\partial \phi}\boldsymbol{u}_\phi$$

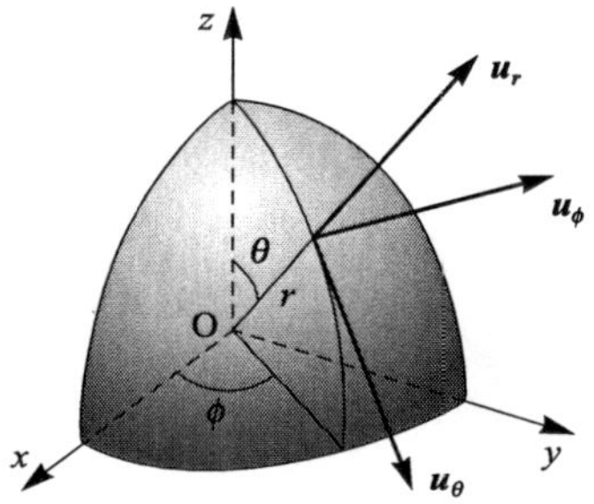

Figure 7.8 Unit vectors associated with spherical polar coordinates.

7.3 Derivatives of a vector point function

When we come to consider the rate of change of a vector point function $\boldsymbol{F}(\boldsymbol{r})$, we see that there are two ways of combining the vector operator ∇ with the vector $\boldsymbol{F}$. Thus we have two cases to consider, namely

$$\nabla \cdot \boldsymbol{F} \quad \text{and} \quad \nabla \times \boldsymbol{F}$$

that is, the scalar product and vector product respectively. Both of these 'derivatives' have physical meanings, as we shall discover in the following sections. Roughly, if we picture a vector field as a fluid flow then at every point in the flow we need to measure the rate at which the field is flowing away from that point and also the amount of spin possessed by the particles of the fluid at that point. The two 'derivatives' given formally above provide these measures.

7.3.1 Divergence of a vector field

Consider the steady motion of a fluid in a region R such that a particle of fluid instantaneously at the point $\boldsymbol{r}$ with coordinates (x, y, z) has a velocity $\boldsymbol{v}(\boldsymbol{r})$ that is independent of time. To measure the flow away from this point in the fluid, we surround the point by an 'elementary' cuboid of side $(2\Delta x) \times (2\Delta y) \times (2\Delta z)$, as shown in Figure 7.9, and calculate the average flow out of the cuboid per unit volume.

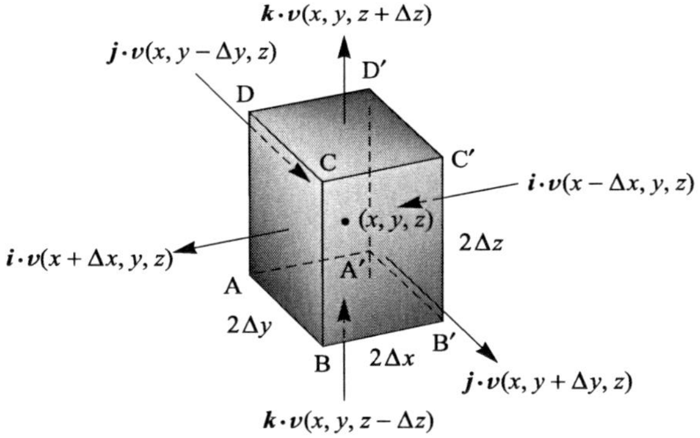

Figure 7.9 Flow out of a cuboid.

The flow out of the cuboid is the sum of the flows across each of its six faces. Representing the velocity of the fluid at (x, y, z) by $\boldsymbol{v}$, the flow out of the face ABCD is given approximately by

$$\boldsymbol{i} \cdot \boldsymbol{v}(x + \Delta x, y, z)(4\Delta y \Delta z)$$

The flow out of the face A′B′C′D′ is given approximately by

$$-\boldsymbol{i} \cdot \boldsymbol{v}(x - \Delta x, y, z)(4\Delta y \Delta z)$$

There are similar expressions for the remaining four faces of the cuboid, so that the total flow out of the latter is

$$\begin{aligned} &\boldsymbol{i} \cdot [\boldsymbol{v}(x + \Delta x, y, z) - \boldsymbol{v}(x - \Delta x, y, z)](4\Delta y \Delta z) \\ &\quad + \boldsymbol{j} \cdot [\boldsymbol{v}(x, y + \Delta y, z) - \boldsymbol{v}(x, y - \Delta y, z)](4\Delta x \Delta z) \\ &\quad + \boldsymbol{k} \cdot [\boldsymbol{v}(x, y, z + \Delta z) - \boldsymbol{v}(x, y, z - \Delta z)](4\Delta x \Delta y) \end{aligned}$$

Dividing by the volume $8\Delta x\Delta y\Delta z$, and proceeding to the limit as Δx, Δy, $\Delta z \to 0$, we see that the flow away from the point (x, y, z) per unit time is given by

$$\boldsymbol{i}\cdot\frac{\partial \boldsymbol{v}}{\partial x}+\boldsymbol{j}\cdot\frac{\partial \boldsymbol{v}}{\partial y}+\boldsymbol{k}\cdot\frac{\partial \boldsymbol{v}}{\partial z}$$

This may be rewritten as

$$\left(\boldsymbol{i}\frac{\partial}{\partial x}+\boldsymbol{j}\frac{\partial}{\partial y}+\boldsymbol{k}\frac{\partial}{\partial z}\right)\cdot\boldsymbol{v}$$

or simply as $\nabla\cdot\boldsymbol{v}$. Thus we see that the flow away from this point is given by the scalar product of the vector operator ∇ with the velocity vector $\boldsymbol{v}$. This is called the **divergence** of the vector $\boldsymbol{v}$, and is written as $\text{div}\,\boldsymbol{v}$. In terms of components,

$$\begin{aligned}\text{div}\,\boldsymbol{v} = \nabla\cdot\boldsymbol{v} &= \left(\boldsymbol{i}\frac{\partial}{\partial x}+\boldsymbol{j}\frac{\partial}{\partial y}+\boldsymbol{k}\frac{\partial}{\partial z}\right)\cdot(\boldsymbol{i}v_1+\boldsymbol{j}v_2+\boldsymbol{k}v_3)\\ &= \frac{\partial v_1}{\partial x}+\frac{\partial v_2}{\partial y}+\frac{\partial v_3}{\partial z}\end{aligned} \qquad \textbf{(7.16)}$$

When $\boldsymbol{v}$ is specified in this way, it is easy to compute its divergence. Note that the divergence of a vector field is a scalar quantity.

Example 7.12 Find the divergence of the vector $\boldsymbol{v} = (2x - y^2, 3z + x^2, 4y - z^2)$ at the point (1, 2, 3).

Solution Here $v_1 = 2x - y^2$, $v_2 = 3z + x^2$ and $v_3 = 4y - z^2$, so that

$$\frac{\partial v_1}{\partial x} = 2, \qquad \frac{\partial v_2}{\partial y} = 0, \qquad \frac{\partial v_3}{\partial z} = -2z$$

Thus from (7.16), at a general point (x, y, z),

$$\text{div}\,\boldsymbol{v} = \nabla\cdot\boldsymbol{v} = 2 - 2z$$

so that at the point (1, 2, 3)

$$\nabla\cdot\boldsymbol{v} = -4$$

A more general way of defining the divergence of a vector field $\boldsymbol{F}(\boldsymbol{r})$ at the point $\boldsymbol{r}$ is to enclose the point in an elementary volume ΔV and find the flow or flux out of ΔV per unit volume. Thus

$$\text{div}\,\boldsymbol{F} = \nabla\cdot\boldsymbol{F} = \lim_{\Delta V\to 0}\frac{\text{flow out of }\Delta V}{\Delta V}$$

A non-zero divergence at a point in a fluid measures the rate, per unit volume, at which the fluid is flowing away from or towards that point. That implies that either the density of the fluid is changing at the point or there is a source or sink of fluid there. In the case of a non-material vector field, for example temperature gradient in heat transfer, a non-zero divergence indicates a point of generation or absorption. When the divergence is everywhere zero, the flow entering any element of the space is exactly balanced by the outflow. This implies that the lines of flow of the field $\boldsymbol{F}(\boldsymbol{r})$ where $\operatorname{div} \boldsymbol{F} = 0$ must either form closed curves or finish at boundaries or extend to infinity. Vectors satisfying this condition are sometimes termed **solenoidal**.

7.3.2 Exercises

31 Find $\operatorname{div} \boldsymbol{v}$ where

(a) $\boldsymbol{v}(\boldsymbol{r}) = 3x^2y\boldsymbol{i} + z\boldsymbol{j} + x^2\boldsymbol{k}$

(b) $\boldsymbol{v}(\boldsymbol{r}) = (3x + y)\boldsymbol{i} + (2z + x)\boldsymbol{j} + (z - 2y)\boldsymbol{k}$

32 If $\boldsymbol{F} = (2xy^2 + z^2)\boldsymbol{i} + (3x^2z^2 - y^2z^3)\boldsymbol{j} + (yz^2 - xz^3)\boldsymbol{k}$, calculate $\operatorname{div} \boldsymbol{f}$ at the point $(-1, 2, 3)$.

33 Find $\nabla(\boldsymbol{a} \cdot \boldsymbol{r})$, $(\boldsymbol{a} \cdot \nabla)\boldsymbol{r}$ and $\boldsymbol{a}(\nabla \cdot \boldsymbol{r})$, where $\boldsymbol{a}$ is a constant vector and, as usual, $\boldsymbol{r}$ is the position vector $\boldsymbol{r} = (x, y, z)$.

34 The vector $\boldsymbol{v}$ is defined by $\boldsymbol{v} = \boldsymbol{r}r^{-1}$, where $\boldsymbol{r} = (x, y, z)$ and $r = |\boldsymbol{r}|$. Show that

$$\nabla(\nabla \cdot \boldsymbol{v}) \equiv \operatorname{grad} \operatorname{div} \boldsymbol{v} = -\frac{2}{r^3}\boldsymbol{r}$$

35 Find the value of the constant λ such that the vector field defined by

$$\boldsymbol{F} = (2x^2y^2 + z^2)\boldsymbol{i} + (3xy^3 - x^2z)\boldsymbol{j} + (\lambda xy^2z + xy)\boldsymbol{k}$$

is solenoidal.

36 (Spherical polar coordinates) Using the notation introduced in Exercise 30, show, working from first principles, that

$$\nabla \cdot \boldsymbol{v} = \operatorname{div} \boldsymbol{v} = \frac{1}{r^2}\frac{\partial}{\partial r}(r^2 v_r) + \frac{1}{r \sin\theta}\frac{\partial}{\partial \theta}(v_\theta \sin\theta) + \frac{1}{r \sin\theta}\frac{\partial}{\partial \phi}(v_\phi)$$

where $\boldsymbol{v} = v_r\boldsymbol{u}_r + v_\theta\boldsymbol{u}_\theta + v_\phi\boldsymbol{u}_\phi$.

37 A force field $\boldsymbol{F}$, defined by the inverse square law, is given by

$$\boldsymbol{F} = \boldsymbol{r}/r^3$$

Show that $\nabla \cdot \boldsymbol{F} = 0$.

7.3.3 Curl of a vector field

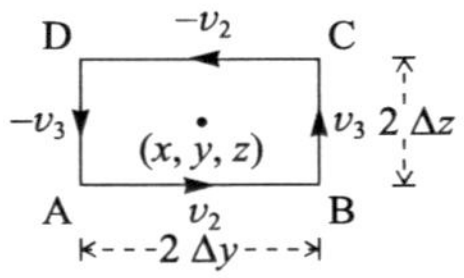

Figure 7.10 Flow around a rectangle.

It is clear from observations (for example, by watching the movements of marked corks on water) that many fluid flows involve rotational motion of the fluid particles. Complete determination of this motion requires knowledge of the axis of rotation, the rate of rotation and its sense (clockwise or anticlockwise). The measure of rotation is thus a vector quantity, which we shall find by calculating its x, y and z components separately. Consider the vector field $\boldsymbol{v}(\boldsymbol{r})$. To find the flow around an axis in the x direction at the point $\boldsymbol{r}$, we take an elementary rectangle surrounding $\boldsymbol{r}$ perpendicular to the x direction, as shown in Figure 7.10.

To measure the circulation around the point $\boldsymbol{r}$ about an axis parallel to the x direction, we calculate the flow around the elementary rectangle ABCD and divide by its area, giving

$$[v_2(x, y^*, z - \Delta z)(2\Delta y) + v_3(x, y + \Delta y, z^*)(2\Delta z)$$
$$- v_2(x, \tilde{y}, z + \Delta z)(2\Delta y) - v_3(x, y - \Delta y, \tilde{z})(2\Delta z)]/(4\Delta y \Delta z)$$

where $y^*, \tilde{y} \in (y - \Delta y, y + \Delta y)$, $z^*, \tilde{z} \in (z - \Delta z, z + \Delta z)$ and $\boldsymbol{v} = v_1\boldsymbol{i} + v_2\boldsymbol{j} + v_3\boldsymbol{k}$. Rearranging, we obtain

$$-[v_2(x, \tilde{y}, z + \Delta z) - v_2(x, y^*, z - \Delta z)]/(2\Delta z)$$
$$+ [v_3(x, y + \Delta y, z^*) - v_3(x, y - \Delta y, \tilde{z})]/(2\Delta y)$$

Proceeding to the limit as $\Delta y \Delta z \to 0$, we obtain the x component of this vector as

$$\frac{\partial v_3}{\partial y} - \frac{\partial v_2}{\partial z}$$

By similar arguments, we obtain the y and z components as

$$\frac{\partial v_1}{\partial z} - \frac{\partial v_3}{\partial x}, \qquad \frac{\partial v_2}{\partial x} - \frac{\partial v_1}{\partial y}$$

respectively.

The vector measuring the rotation about a point in the fluid is called the **curl** of $\boldsymbol{v}$:

$$\text{curl } \boldsymbol{v} = \left(\frac{\partial v_3}{\partial y} - \frac{\partial v_2}{\partial z}\right)\boldsymbol{i} + \left(\frac{\partial v_1}{\partial z} - \frac{\partial v_3}{\partial x}\right)\boldsymbol{j} + \left(\frac{\partial v_2}{\partial x} - \frac{\partial v_1}{\partial y}\right)\boldsymbol{k}$$

$$= \left(\frac{\partial v_3}{\partial y} - \frac{\partial v_2}{\partial z}, \frac{\partial v_1}{\partial z} - \frac{\partial v_3}{\partial x}, \frac{\partial v_2}{\partial x} - \frac{\partial v_1}{\partial y}\right) \tag{7.17}$$

It may be written formally as

$$\text{curl } \boldsymbol{v} = \begin{vmatrix} \boldsymbol{i} & \boldsymbol{j} & \boldsymbol{k} \\ \dfrac{\partial}{\partial x} & \dfrac{\partial}{\partial y} & \dfrac{\partial}{\partial z} \\ v_1 & v_2 & v_3 \end{vmatrix} \tag{7.18}$$

or more compactly as

$$\text{curl } \boldsymbol{v} = \nabla \times \boldsymbol{v}$$

Example 7.13 Find the curl of the vector $\boldsymbol{v} = (2x - y^2, 3z + x^2, 4y - z^2)$ at the point (1, 2, 3).

Solution Here $v_1 = 2x - y^2$, $v_2 = 3z + x^2$, $v_3 = 4y - z^2$, so that

$$\text{curl } \boldsymbol{v} = \begin{vmatrix} \boldsymbol{i} & \boldsymbol{j} & \boldsymbol{k} \\ \dfrac{\partial}{\partial x} & \dfrac{\partial}{\partial y} & \dfrac{\partial}{\partial z} \\ 2x - y^2 & 3z + x^2 & 4y - z^2 \end{vmatrix}$$

$$= \boldsymbol{i}\left[\frac{\partial}{\partial y}(4y - z^2) - \frac{\partial}{\partial z}(3z + x^2)\right]$$

$$- \boldsymbol{j}\left[\frac{\partial}{\partial x}(4y - z^2) - \frac{\partial}{\partial z}(2x - y^2)\right]$$

$$+ \boldsymbol{k}\left[\frac{\partial}{\partial x}(3z + x^2) - \frac{\partial}{\partial y}(2x - y^2)\right]$$

$$= \boldsymbol{i}(4 - 3) - \boldsymbol{j}(0 - 0) + \boldsymbol{k}(2x + 2y) = \boldsymbol{i} + 2(x + y)\boldsymbol{k}$$

Thus, at the point (1, 2, 3), $\nabla \times \boldsymbol{v} = (1, 0, 6)$.

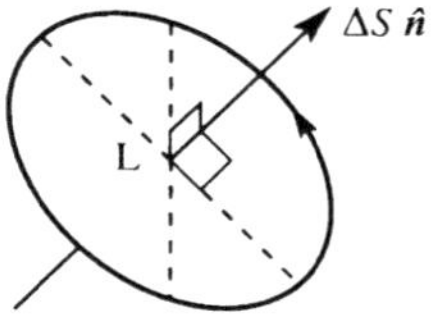

Figure 7.11 Circulation around the element ΔS.

More generally, the component of the curl of a vector field $\boldsymbol{F}(\boldsymbol{r})$ in the direction of the unit vector $\hat{\boldsymbol{n}}$ at a point L is found by enclosing L by an elementary area ΔS that is perpendicular to $\hat{\boldsymbol{n}}$, as in Figure 7.11, and calculating the flow around ΔS per unit area. Thus

$$(\text{curl}\,\boldsymbol{F})\cdot\hat{\boldsymbol{n}} = \lim_{\Delta S\to 0}\frac{\text{flow round }\Delta S}{\Delta S}$$

Another way of visualizing the meaning of the curl of a vector is to consider the motion of a rigid body. We can describe such motion by specifying the angular velocity $\boldsymbol{\omega}$ of the body about an axis OA, where O is a fixed point in the body, together with the translational (linear) velocity $\boldsymbol{v}$ of O itself. Then at any point P in the body the velocity $\boldsymbol{u}$ is given by

$$\boldsymbol{u} = \boldsymbol{v} + \boldsymbol{\omega}\times\boldsymbol{r}$$

as shown in Figure 7.12. Here $\boldsymbol{v}$ and $\boldsymbol{\omega}$ are independent of (x, y, z). Thus

$$\text{curl}\,\boldsymbol{u} = \text{curl}\,\boldsymbol{v} + \text{curl}\,(\boldsymbol{\omega}\times\boldsymbol{r}) = 0 + \text{curl}\,(\boldsymbol{\omega}\times\boldsymbol{r})$$

The vector $\boldsymbol{\omega}\times\boldsymbol{r}$ is given by

$$\begin{aligned}\boldsymbol{\omega}\times\boldsymbol{r} &= (\omega_1, \omega_2, \omega_3)\times(x, y, z)\\ &= (\omega_2 z - \omega_3 y)\boldsymbol{i} + (\omega_3 x - \omega_1 z)\boldsymbol{j} + (\omega_1 y - \omega_2 x)\boldsymbol{k}\end{aligned}$$

and

$$\begin{aligned}\text{curl}(\boldsymbol{\omega}\times\boldsymbol{r}) &= \begin{vmatrix}\boldsymbol{i} & \boldsymbol{j} & \boldsymbol{k}\\ \dfrac{\partial}{\partial x} & \dfrac{\partial}{\partial y} & \dfrac{\partial}{\partial z}\\ \omega_2 z - \omega_3 y & \omega_3 x - \omega_1 z & \omega_1 y - \omega_2 x\end{vmatrix}\\ &= 2\omega_1\boldsymbol{i} + 2\omega_2\boldsymbol{j} + 2\omega_3\boldsymbol{k} = 2\boldsymbol{\omega}\end{aligned}$$

Thus

$$\text{curl}\,\boldsymbol{u} = 2\boldsymbol{\omega}$$

that is,

$$\boldsymbol{\omega} = \tfrac{1}{2}\,\text{curl}\,\boldsymbol{u}$$

Figure 7.12 Rotation of a rigid body.

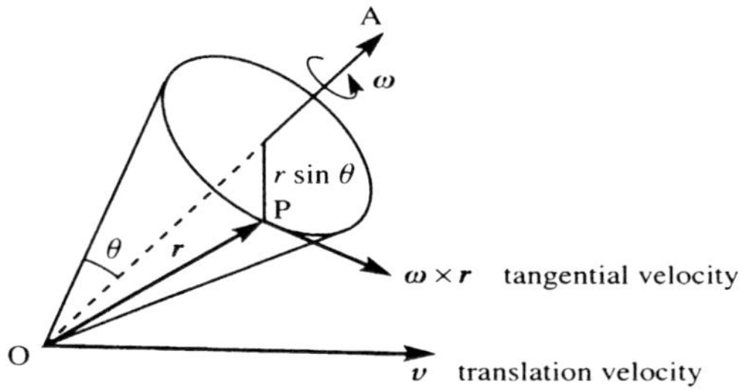

Hence when any rigid body is in motion, the curl of its linear velocity at any point is twice its angular velocity in magnitude and has the same direction.

Applying this result to the motion of a fluid, we can see by regarding particles of the fluid as miniature bodies that when the curl of the velocity is zero there is no rotation of the particle, and the motion is said to be **curl-free** or **irrotational**. When the curl is non-zero, the motion is **rotational**.

7.3.4 Exercises

38 Find $\boldsymbol{u} = \text{curl}\, \boldsymbol{v}$ when $\boldsymbol{v} = (3xz^2, -yz, x + 2z)$.

39 A vector field is defined by $\boldsymbol{v} = (yz, xz, xy)$. Show that $\text{curl}\, \boldsymbol{v} = 0$.

40 Show that if $\boldsymbol{v} = (2x + yz, 2y + zx, 2z + xy)$ then $\text{curl}\, \boldsymbol{v} = 0$, and find $f(\boldsymbol{r})$ such that $\boldsymbol{v} = \text{grad}\, f$.

41 By evaluating each term separately, verify the identity

$$\nabla \times (f\boldsymbol{v}) = f(\nabla \times \boldsymbol{v}) + (\nabla f) \times \boldsymbol{v}$$

for $f(\boldsymbol{r}) = x^3 - y$ and $\boldsymbol{v}(\boldsymbol{r}) = (z, 0, -x)$.

42 Find constants a, b and c such that the vector field defined by

$$\boldsymbol{F} = (4xy + az^3)\boldsymbol{i} + (bx^2 + 3z)\boldsymbol{j} + (6xz^2 + cy)\boldsymbol{k}$$

is irrotational. With these values of a, b and c, determine a scalar function $\phi(x, y, z)$ such that $\boldsymbol{F} = \nabla\phi$.

43 If $\boldsymbol{v} = -y\boldsymbol{i} + x\boldsymbol{j} + xyz\boldsymbol{k}$ is the velocity vector of a fluid, find the local value of the angular velocity at the point (1, 3, 2).

44 If the velocity of a fluid at the point (x, y, z) is given by

$$\boldsymbol{v} = (ax + by)\boldsymbol{i} + (cx + dy)\boldsymbol{j}$$

find the conditions on the constants a, b, c and d in order that

$$\text{div}\, \boldsymbol{v} = 0, \qquad \text{curl}\, \boldsymbol{v} = \boldsymbol{0}$$

Verify that in this case

$$\boldsymbol{v} = \tfrac{1}{2}\,\text{grad}\,(ax^2 + 2bxy - ay^2)$$

45 (Spherical polar coordinates) Using the notation introduced in Exercise 30, show that

$$\nabla \times \boldsymbol{v} = \text{curl}\ \boldsymbol{v}$$

$$= \frac{1}{r^2 \sin\theta}\begin{vmatrix} \boldsymbol{u}_r & r\boldsymbol{u}_\theta & r\sin \boldsymbol{u}_\phi \\ \dfrac{\partial}{\partial r} & \dfrac{\partial}{\partial \theta} & \dfrac{\partial}{\partial \phi} \\ v_r & rv_\theta & r\sin v_\phi \end{vmatrix}$$

7.3.5 Further properties of the vector operator ∇

So far we have used the vector operator in three ways:

$$\nabla f = \text{grad}\, f = \frac{\partial f}{\partial x}\boldsymbol{i} + \frac{\partial f}{\partial y}\boldsymbol{j} + \frac{\partial f}{\partial z}\boldsymbol{k}, \qquad f(\boldsymbol{r}) \text{ a scalar field}$$

$$\nabla \cdot \boldsymbol{F} = \text{div}\, \boldsymbol{F} = \frac{\partial f_1}{\partial x} + \frac{\partial f_2}{\partial y} + \frac{\partial f_3}{\partial z}, \qquad \boldsymbol{F}(\boldsymbol{r}) \text{ a vector field}$$

$$\nabla \times \boldsymbol{F} = \text{curl}\, \boldsymbol{F}$$

$$= \left(\frac{\partial f_3}{\partial y} - \frac{\partial f_2}{\partial z}\right)\boldsymbol{i} + \left(\frac{\partial f_1}{\partial z} - \frac{\partial f_3}{\partial x}\right)\boldsymbol{j} + \left(\frac{\partial f_2}{\partial x} - \frac{\partial f_1}{\partial y}\right)\boldsymbol{k}, \qquad \boldsymbol{F}(\boldsymbol{r}) \text{ a vector field}$$

A further application is in determining the directional derivative of a vector field:

$$\boldsymbol{a}\cdot\nabla\boldsymbol{F} = \left(a_1\frac{\partial}{\partial x}+a_2\frac{\partial}{\partial y}+a_3\frac{\partial}{\partial z}\right)\boldsymbol{F}$$

$$= \left(a_1\frac{\partial f_1}{\partial x}+a_2\frac{\partial f_1}{\partial y}+a_3\frac{\partial f_1}{\partial z}\right)\boldsymbol{i}+\left(a_1\frac{\partial f_2}{\partial x}+a_2\frac{\partial f_2}{\partial y}+a_3\frac{\partial f_2}{\partial z}\right)\boldsymbol{j}$$

$$+\left(a_1\frac{\partial f_3}{\partial x}+a_2\frac{\partial f_3}{\partial y}+a_3\frac{\partial f_3}{\partial z}\right)\boldsymbol{k}$$

The ordinary rules of differentiation carry over to this vector differential operator, but they have to be applied with care, using the rules of vector algebra. For non-orthogonal coordinate systems a specialist textbook should be consulted. Thus for scalar fields $f(\boldsymbol{r})$, $g(\boldsymbol{r})$ and vector fields $\boldsymbol{u}(\boldsymbol{r})$, $\boldsymbol{v}(\boldsymbol{r})$ we have

$$\nabla[f(g(\boldsymbol{r}))] = \frac{\mathrm{d}f}{\mathrm{d}g}\nabla g \quad \textbf{(7.19a)}$$

$$\nabla[f(\boldsymbol{r})g(\boldsymbol{r})] = g(\boldsymbol{r})\nabla f(\boldsymbol{r})+f(\boldsymbol{r})\nabla g(\boldsymbol{r}) \quad \textbf{(7.19b)}$$

$$\nabla[\boldsymbol{u}(\boldsymbol{r})\cdot\boldsymbol{v}(\boldsymbol{r})] = \boldsymbol{v}\times(\nabla\times\boldsymbol{u})+\boldsymbol{u}\times(\nabla\times\boldsymbol{v})+(\boldsymbol{v}\cdot\nabla)\boldsymbol{u}+(\boldsymbol{u}\cdot\nabla)\boldsymbol{v} \quad \textbf{(7.19c)}$$

$$\nabla\cdot[f(\boldsymbol{r})\boldsymbol{u}(\boldsymbol{r})] = \boldsymbol{u}\cdot\nabla f+f\nabla\cdot\boldsymbol{u} \quad \textbf{(7.19d)}$$

$$\nabla\times[f(\boldsymbol{r})\boldsymbol{u}(\boldsymbol{r})] = (\nabla f)\times\boldsymbol{u}+f\nabla\times\boldsymbol{u} \quad \textbf{(7.19e)}$$

$$\nabla\cdot[\boldsymbol{u}(\boldsymbol{r})\times\boldsymbol{v}(\boldsymbol{r})] = \boldsymbol{v}\cdot(\nabla\times\boldsymbol{u})-\boldsymbol{u}\cdot(\nabla\times\boldsymbol{v}) \quad \textbf{(7.19f)}$$

$$\nabla\times[\boldsymbol{u}(\boldsymbol{r})\times\boldsymbol{v}(\boldsymbol{r})] = (\boldsymbol{v}\cdot\nabla)\boldsymbol{u}-\boldsymbol{v}(\nabla\cdot\boldsymbol{u})-(\boldsymbol{u}\cdot\nabla)\boldsymbol{v}+\boldsymbol{u}(\nabla\cdot\boldsymbol{v}) \quad \textbf{(7.19g)}$$

Higher-order derivatives can also be formed, giving the following:

$$\text{div}\,[\text{grad}\,f(\boldsymbol{r})] = \nabla\cdot\nabla f = \frac{\partial^2 f}{\partial x^2}+\frac{\partial^2 f}{\partial y^2}+\frac{\partial^2 f}{\partial z^2} = \nabla^2 f \quad \textbf{(7.20)}$$

where ∇^2 is called the **Laplacian operator** (sometimes denoted by $\triangle$);

$$\text{curl}\,[\text{grad}\,f(\boldsymbol{r})] = \nabla\times\nabla f(\boldsymbol{r}) \equiv 0 \quad \textbf{(7.21)}$$

since

$$\nabla\times\nabla f = \left(\frac{\partial^2 f}{\partial y\partial z}-\frac{\partial^2 f}{\partial z\partial y}\right)\boldsymbol{i}+\left(\frac{\partial^2 f}{\partial z\partial x}-\frac{\partial^2 f}{\partial x\partial z}\right)\boldsymbol{j}+\left(\frac{\partial^2 f}{\partial x\partial y}-\frac{\partial^2 f}{\partial y\partial x}\right)\boldsymbol{k}$$

$$= 0$$

when all second-order derivatives of $f(\boldsymbol{r})$ are continuous;

$$\text{div}[\text{curl}\,\boldsymbol{v}(\boldsymbol{r})] = \nabla\cdot(\nabla\times\boldsymbol{v}) \equiv 0 \quad \textbf{(7.22)}$$

since

$$\frac{\partial}{\partial x}\left(\frac{\partial v_3}{\partial y}-\frac{\partial v_2}{\partial z}\right)+\frac{\partial}{\partial y}\left(\frac{\partial v_1}{\partial z}-\frac{\partial v_3}{\partial x}\right)+\frac{\partial}{\partial z}\left(\frac{\partial v_2}{\partial x}-\frac{\partial v_1}{\partial y}\right) = 0$$

$$\text{grad}\,(\text{div}\,\boldsymbol{v}) = \nabla(\nabla\cdot\boldsymbol{v}) = \left(\boldsymbol{i}\frac{\partial}{\partial x}+\boldsymbol{j}\frac{\partial}{\partial y}+\boldsymbol{k}\frac{\partial}{\partial z}\right)\left(\frac{\partial v_1}{\partial x}+\frac{\partial v_2}{\partial y}+\frac{\partial v_3}{\partial z}\right) \tag{7.23}$$

$$\nabla^2\boldsymbol{v} = \left(\frac{\partial^2}{\partial x^2}+\frac{\partial^2}{\partial y^2}+\frac{\partial^2}{\partial z^2}\right)(v_1\boldsymbol{i}+v_2\boldsymbol{j}+v_3\boldsymbol{k}) \tag{7.24}$$

$$\text{curl}\,[\text{curl}\,\boldsymbol{v}(\boldsymbol{r})] = \nabla\times(\nabla\times\boldsymbol{v}) = \nabla(\nabla\cdot\boldsymbol{v}) - \nabla^2\boldsymbol{v} \tag{7.25}$$

Example 7.14

Verify that $\nabla\times(\nabla\times\boldsymbol{v}) = \nabla(\nabla\cdot\boldsymbol{v}) - \nabla^2\boldsymbol{v}$ for the vector field $\boldsymbol{v} = (3xz^2, -yz, x+2z)$.

Solution

$$\nabla\times\boldsymbol{v} = \begin{vmatrix} \boldsymbol{i} & \boldsymbol{j} & \boldsymbol{k} \\ \dfrac{\partial}{\partial x} & \dfrac{\partial}{\partial y} & \dfrac{\partial}{\partial z} \\ 3xz^2 & -yz & x+2z \end{vmatrix} = (y,\ 6xz-1,\ 0)$$

$$\nabla\times(\nabla\times\boldsymbol{v}) = \begin{vmatrix} \boldsymbol{i} & \boldsymbol{j} & \boldsymbol{k} \\ \dfrac{\partial}{\partial x} & \dfrac{\partial}{\partial y} & \dfrac{\partial}{\partial z} \\ y & 6xz-1 & 0 \end{vmatrix} = (-6x,\ 0,\ 6z-1)$$

$$\begin{aligned}\nabla\cdot\boldsymbol{v} &= \frac{\partial}{\partial x}(3xz^2) + \frac{\partial}{\partial y}(-yz) + \frac{\partial}{\partial z}(x+2z) \\ &= 3z^2 - z + 2 \\ \nabla(\nabla\cdot\boldsymbol{v}) &= (0, 0, 6z-1) \\ \nabla^2\boldsymbol{v} &= (\nabla^2(3xz^2), \nabla^2(-yz), \nabla^2(x+2z)) \\ &= (6x, 0, 0)\end{aligned}$$

Thus

$$\begin{aligned}\nabla(\nabla\cdot\boldsymbol{v}) - \nabla^2\boldsymbol{v} &= (-6x, 0, 6z-1) \\ &= \nabla\times(\nabla\times\boldsymbol{v})\end{aligned}$$

Similar verifications for other identities are suggested in Exercises 7.3.6.

Example 7.15

Maxwell's equations in free space may be written, in Gaussian units, as

(a) $\text{div}\,\boldsymbol{H} = 0$, (b) $\text{div}\,\boldsymbol{E} = 0$

(c) $\text{curl}\,\boldsymbol{H} = \nabla\times\boldsymbol{H} = \dfrac{1}{c}\dfrac{\partial\boldsymbol{E}}{\partial t}$, (d) $\text{curl}\,\boldsymbol{E} = \nabla\times\boldsymbol{E} = -\dfrac{1}{c}\dfrac{\partial\boldsymbol{H}}{\partial t}$

where c is the velocity of light (assumed constant). Show that these equations are satisfied by

$$\boldsymbol{H} = \frac{1}{c}\frac{\partial}{\partial t}\,\text{grad}\,\phi\times\boldsymbol{k}, \qquad \boldsymbol{E} = -\boldsymbol{k}\frac{1}{c^2}\frac{\partial^2\phi}{\partial t^2} + \frac{\partial}{\partial z}\,\text{grad}\,\phi$$

where ϕ satisfies

$$\nabla^2\phi = \frac{1}{c^2}\frac{\partial^2\phi}{\partial t^2}$$

and $\boldsymbol{k}$ is a unit vector along the z axis.

Solution (a) $$\boldsymbol{H} = \frac{1}{c}\frac{\partial}{\partial t}\,\text{grad}\,\phi \times \boldsymbol{k}$$

gives

$$\text{div}\,\boldsymbol{H} = \frac{1}{c}\frac{\partial}{\partial t}\,\text{div}\,(\text{grad}\,\phi \times \boldsymbol{k})$$

$$= \frac{1}{c}\frac{\partial}{\partial t}[\boldsymbol{k}\cdot\text{curl}\,(\text{grad}\,\phi) - (\text{grad}\,\phi)\cdot\text{curl}\,\boldsymbol{k}], \quad \text{from (7.19f)}$$

By (7.21), curl (grad ϕ) = 0, and since $\boldsymbol{k}$ is a constant vector, curl $\boldsymbol{k} = 0$, so that

$$\text{div}\,\boldsymbol{H} = 0$$

(b) $$\boldsymbol{E} = -\frac{\boldsymbol{k}}{c^2}\frac{\partial^2\phi}{\partial t^2} + \frac{\partial}{\partial z}\,\text{grad}\,\phi$$

gives

$$\text{div}\,\boldsymbol{E} = -\frac{1}{c^2}\,\text{div}\left(\boldsymbol{k}\frac{\partial^2\phi}{\partial t^2}\right) + \frac{\partial}{\partial z}\,\text{div grad}\,\phi$$

$$= -\frac{1}{c^2}\frac{\partial}{\partial z}\left(\frac{\partial^2\phi}{\partial t^2}\right) + \frac{\partial}{\partial z}(\nabla^2\phi), \quad \text{by (7.20)}$$

$$= \frac{\partial}{\partial z}\left(\nabla^2\phi - \frac{1}{c^2}\frac{\partial^2\phi}{\partial t^2}\right)$$

and since $\nabla^2\phi = (1/c^2)\partial^2\phi/\partial t^2$, we have

$$\text{div}\,\boldsymbol{E} = 0$$

(c) $$\text{curl}\,\boldsymbol{H} = \frac{1}{c}\frac{\partial}{\partial t}\,\text{curl}\,(\text{grad}\,\phi \times \boldsymbol{k})$$

$$= \frac{1}{c}\frac{\partial}{\partial t}[(\boldsymbol{k}\cdot\boldsymbol{\nabla})\,\text{grad}\,\phi$$

$$- \boldsymbol{k}\,(\text{div grad}\,\phi) - (\text{grad}\,\phi\cdot\boldsymbol{\nabla})\boldsymbol{k} + \text{grad}\,\phi(\boldsymbol{\nabla}\cdot\boldsymbol{k})], \quad \text{from (7.19g)}$$

$$= \frac{1}{c}\frac{\partial}{\partial t}\left(\frac{\partial}{\partial z}\text{grad}\,\phi - \boldsymbol{k}\nabla^2\phi\right), \quad \text{since } \boldsymbol{k} \text{ is a constant vector}$$

$$= \frac{1}{c}\frac{\partial \boldsymbol{E}}{\partial t}$$

(d) $$\text{curl}\,\boldsymbol{E} = -\frac{1}{c^2}\text{curl}\left(\boldsymbol{k}\frac{\partial^2\phi}{\partial t^2}\right) + \frac{\partial}{\partial z}\text{curl grad}\,\phi$$

$$= -\frac{1}{c^2}\begin{bmatrix} \boldsymbol{i} & \boldsymbol{j} & \boldsymbol{k} \\ \frac{\partial}{\partial x} & \frac{\partial}{\partial y} & \frac{\partial}{\partial z} \\ 0 & 0 & \frac{\partial^2\phi}{\partial t^2} \end{bmatrix}, \quad \text{since curl grad}\,\phi = 0 \text{ by (7.21)}$$

$$= -\frac{1}{c^2}\left(\boldsymbol{i}\frac{\partial^3\phi}{\partial y\partial t^2} - \boldsymbol{j}\frac{\partial^3\phi}{\partial x\partial t^2}\right)$$

Also,

$$\frac{\partial \boldsymbol{H}}{\partial t} = \frac{1}{c}\frac{\partial^2}{\partial t^2}\text{grad}\,\phi \times \boldsymbol{k}$$

$$= \frac{1}{c}\frac{\partial^2}{\partial t^2}(\text{grad}\,\phi \times \boldsymbol{k}), \quad \text{since } \boldsymbol{k} \text{ is a constant vector}$$

$$= \frac{1}{c}\frac{\partial^2}{\partial t^2}\left[\left(\frac{\partial\phi}{\partial x}\boldsymbol{i} + \frac{\partial\phi}{\partial y}\boldsymbol{j} + \frac{\partial\phi}{\partial z}\boldsymbol{k}\right) \times \boldsymbol{k}\right]$$

$$= \frac{1}{c}\frac{\partial^2}{\partial t^2}\left(\boldsymbol{i}\frac{\partial\phi}{\partial y} - \boldsymbol{j}\frac{\partial\phi}{\partial x}\right) = \frac{1}{c}\left(\boldsymbol{i}\frac{\partial^3\phi}{\partial y\partial t^2} - \boldsymbol{j}\frac{\partial^3\phi}{\partial x\partial t^2}\right)$$

so that we have

$$\nabla \times \boldsymbol{E} = -\frac{1}{c}\frac{\partial \boldsymbol{H}}{\partial t}$$

7.3.6 Exercises

46 Show that if g is a function of $\boldsymbol{r} = (x, y, z)$ then

$$\text{grad}\, g = \frac{1}{r}\frac{dg}{dr}\boldsymbol{r}$$

Deduce that if $\boldsymbol{u}$ is a vector field then

$$\text{div}\,[(\boldsymbol{u} \times \boldsymbol{r})g] = (\boldsymbol{r} \cdot \text{curl}\,\boldsymbol{u})g$$

47 For $\phi(x, y, z) = x^2y^2z^3$ and $\boldsymbol{F}(x, y, z) = x^2y\boldsymbol{i} + xy^2z\boldsymbol{j} - yz^2\boldsymbol{k}$ determine

(a) $\nabla^2\phi$ (b) grad div $\boldsymbol{F}$ (c) curl curl $\boldsymbol{F}$

48 Show that if $\boldsymbol{a}$ is a constant vector and $\boldsymbol{r}$ is the position vector $\boldsymbol{r} = (x, y, z)$ then

$$\text{div}\,\{\text{grad}\,[(\boldsymbol{r} \cdot \boldsymbol{r})(\boldsymbol{r} \cdot \boldsymbol{a})]\} = 10(\boldsymbol{r} \cdot \boldsymbol{a})$$

49 Verify the identity

$$\nabla^2\boldsymbol{v} = \text{grad div}\,\boldsymbol{v} - \text{curl curl}\,\boldsymbol{v}$$

for the vector field $\boldsymbol{v} = x^2y(x\boldsymbol{i} + y\boldsymbol{j} + z\boldsymbol{k})$.

50 Verify, by calculating each term separately, the identities

$$\text{div}\,(\boldsymbol{u} \times \boldsymbol{v}) = \boldsymbol{v} \cdot \text{curl}\,\boldsymbol{u} - \boldsymbol{u} \cdot \text{curl}\,\boldsymbol{v}$$

$$\text{curl}\,(\boldsymbol{u} \times \boldsymbol{v}) = \boldsymbol{u}\,\text{div}\,\boldsymbol{v} - \boldsymbol{v}\,\text{div}\,\boldsymbol{u} + (\boldsymbol{v} \cdot \nabla)\boldsymbol{u} - (\boldsymbol{u} \cdot \nabla)\boldsymbol{v}$$

when $\boldsymbol{u} = xy\boldsymbol{j} + xz\boldsymbol{k}$ and $\boldsymbol{v} = xy\boldsymbol{i} + yz\boldsymbol{k}$.

51 If $\boldsymbol{r}$ is the usual position vector $\boldsymbol{r} = (x, y, z)$, show that

(a) $\operatorname{div}\operatorname{grad}\left(\frac{1}{r}\right) = 0$

(b) $\operatorname{curl}\left[\boldsymbol{k} \times \operatorname{grad}\left(\frac{1}{r}\right)\right] + \operatorname{grad}\left[\boldsymbol{k} \cdot \operatorname{grad}\left(\frac{1}{r}\right)\right] = 0$

52 If $\boldsymbol{A}$ is a constant vector and $\boldsymbol{r}$ is the position vector $\boldsymbol{r} = (x, y, z)$, show that

(a) $\operatorname{grad}\left(\frac{\boldsymbol{A}\cdot\boldsymbol{r}}{r^3}\right) = \frac{\boldsymbol{A}}{r^3} - 3\frac{(\boldsymbol{A}\cdot\boldsymbol{r})}{r^5}\boldsymbol{r}$

(b) $\operatorname{curl}\left(\frac{\boldsymbol{A}\times\boldsymbol{r}}{r^3}\right) = \frac{2\boldsymbol{A}}{r^3} + \frac{3}{r^5}(\boldsymbol{A}\times\boldsymbol{r})\times\boldsymbol{r}$

53 If $\boldsymbol{r}$ is the position vector $\boldsymbol{r} = (x, y, z)$, and $\boldsymbol{a}$ and $\boldsymbol{b}$ are constant vectors, show that

(a) $\nabla \times \boldsymbol{r} = 0$

(b) $(\boldsymbol{a}\cdot\nabla)\boldsymbol{r} = \boldsymbol{a}$

(c) $\nabla \times [(\boldsymbol{a}\cdot\boldsymbol{r})\boldsymbol{b} - (\boldsymbol{b}\cdot\boldsymbol{r})\boldsymbol{a}] = 2(\boldsymbol{a}\times\boldsymbol{b})$

(d) $\nabla \cdot [(\boldsymbol{a}\cdot\boldsymbol{r})\boldsymbol{b} - (\boldsymbol{b}\cdot\boldsymbol{r})\boldsymbol{a}] = 0$

54 By evaluating $\nabla\cdot(\nabla f)$, show that the Laplacian in spherical polar coordinates (see Exercise 30) is given by

$$\nabla^2 f = \frac{1}{r^2}\frac{\partial}{\partial r}\left(r^2\frac{\partial f}{\partial r}\right) + \frac{1}{r^2\sin\theta}\frac{\partial}{\partial\theta}\left(\sin\theta\frac{\partial f}{\partial\theta}\right) + \frac{1}{r^2\sin^2\theta}\frac{\partial^2 f}{\partial\phi^2}$$

55 Show that Maxwell's equations in free space, namely

$$\operatorname{div}\boldsymbol{H} = 0, \qquad \operatorname{div}\boldsymbol{E} = 0$$

$$\nabla\times\boldsymbol{H} = \frac{1}{c}\frac{\partial\boldsymbol{E}}{\partial t}, \qquad \nabla\times\boldsymbol{E} = -\frac{1}{c}\frac{\partial\boldsymbol{H}}{\partial t}$$

are satisfied by

$$\boldsymbol{H} = \frac{1}{c}\operatorname{curl}\frac{\partial\boldsymbol{Z}}{\partial t}$$

$$\boldsymbol{E} = \operatorname{curl}\operatorname{curl}\boldsymbol{Z}$$

where the Hertzian vector $\boldsymbol{Z}$ satisfies

$$\nabla^2\boldsymbol{Z} = \frac{1}{c}\frac{\partial^2\boldsymbol{Z}}{\partial t^2}$$

7.4 Topics in integration

In the previous sections we saw how the idea of the differentiation of a function of a single variable is generalized to include scalar and vector point functions. We now turn to the inverse process of integration. The fundamental idea of an integral is that of summing all the constituent parts that make a whole. More formally, we define the integral of a function $f(x)$ by

$$\int_a^b f(x)\,\mathrm{d}x = \lim_{\substack{n\to\infty \\ \text{all } \Delta x_i \to 0}} \sum_{i=1}^{n} f(\tilde{x}_i)\Delta x_i$$

where $a = x_0 < x_1 < x_2 < \ldots < x_{n-1} < x_n = b$, $\Delta x_i = x_i - x_{i-1}$ and $x_{i-1} \leqslant \tilde{x}_i \leqslant x_i$. Geometrically, we can interpret this integral as the area between the graph $y = f(x)$, the x axis and the lines $x = a$ and $x = b$, as illustrated in Figure 7.13.

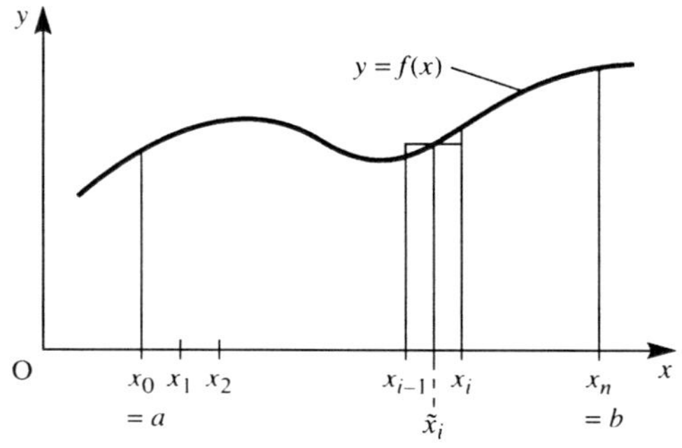

Figure 7.13 Definite integral as an area.

7.4.1 Line integrals

Consider the integral

$$\int_b^a f(x, y)\,dx, \quad \text{where } y = g(x)$$

This can be evaluated in the usual way by first substituting for y in terms of x in the integrand and then performing the integration

$$\int_a^b f(x, g(x))\,dx$$

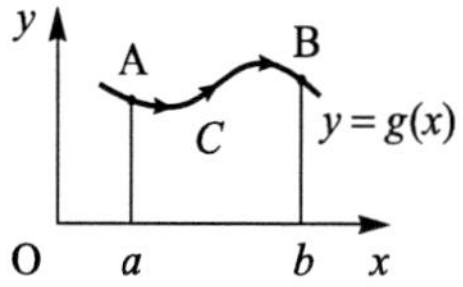

Figure 7.14 Integral along a curve.

Clearly the value of the integral will, in general, depend on the function $y = g(x)$. It may be interpreted as evaluating the integral $\int_a^b f(x, y)\,dx$ along the curve $y = g(x)$, as shown in Figure 7.14. Note, however, that the integral is *not* represented in this case by the area under the curve. This type of integral is called a **line integral**.

There are many different types of such integrals, for example

$$\int_{A\atop C}^{B} f(x, y)\,dx, \quad \int_{A\atop C}^{B} f(x, y)\,ds, \quad \int_{t_1\atop C}^{t_2} f(x, y)\,dt, \quad \int_{A\atop C}^{B} [f_1(x, y)\,dx + f_2(x, y)\,dy]$$

Here the letter under the integral sign indicates that the integral is evaluated along the curve (or **path**) C. This path is not restricted to two dimensions, and may be in as many dimensions as we please. It is normal to omit the points A and B, since they are usually implicit in the specification of C.

Example 7.16

Evaluate $\int_C xy\,dx$ from A(1, 0) to B(0, 1) along the curve C that is the portion of $x^2 + y^2 = 1$ in the first quadrant.

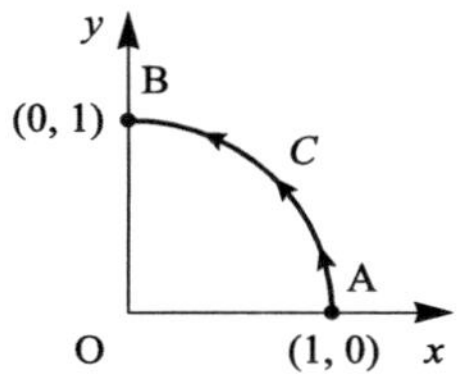

Figure 7.15 Portion of circle.

Solution

The curve C is the first quadrant of the unit circle as shown in Figure 7.15. On the curve, $y = \sqrt{(1 - x^2)}$, so that

$$\int_C xy\,dx = \int_1^0 x\sqrt{(1 - x^2)}\,dx = [-\tfrac{1}{2}\tfrac{2}{3}(1 - x^2)^{3/2}]_1^0 = -\tfrac{1}{3}$$

Example 7.17

Evaluate the integral

$$I = \int_C [(x^2 + 2y)\,dx + (x + y^2)\,dy]$$

from A(0, 1) to B(2, 3) along the curve C defined by $y = x + 1$.

Solution The curve C is the straight line $y = x + 1$ from the point A(0, 1) to the point B(2, 3). In this case we can eliminate either x or y. Using

$$y = x + 1 \quad \text{and} \quad dy = dx$$

we have, on eliminating y,

$$I = \int_{x=0}^{x=2} \{[x^2 + 2(x+1)]\,dx + [x + (x+1)^2]\,dx\}$$

$$= \int_0^2 (2x^2 + 5x + 3)\,dx = [\tfrac{2}{3}x^3 + \tfrac{5}{2}x^2 + 3x]_0^2 = \tfrac{64}{3}$$

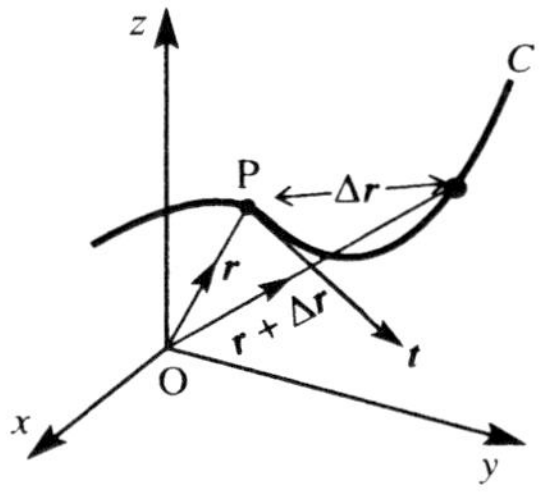

Figure 7.16
Element of arclength.

In many practical problems line integrals involving vectors occur. Let $P(\boldsymbol{r})$ be a point on a curve C in three dimensions, and let $\boldsymbol{t}$ be the unit tangent vector at P in the sense of the integration (that is, in the sense of increasing arclength s), as indicated in Figure 7.16. Then $\boldsymbol{t}\,ds$ is the vector element of arc at P, and

$$\boldsymbol{t}\,ds = \left[\frac{dx}{ds}\boldsymbol{i} + \frac{dy}{ds}\boldsymbol{j} + \frac{dz}{ds}\boldsymbol{k}\right] ds = dx\,\boldsymbol{i} + dy\boldsymbol{j} + dz\,\boldsymbol{k} = d\boldsymbol{r}$$

If $f_1(x, y, z)$, $f_2(x, y, z)$ and $f_3(x, y, z)$ are the scalar components of a vector field $\boldsymbol{F}(\boldsymbol{r})$ then

$$\int_C [f_1(x, y, z)\,dx + f_2(x, y, z)\,dy + f_3(x, y, z)\,dz]$$

$$= \int_C \left[f_1(x, y, z)\frac{dx}{ds}\,ds + f_2(x, y, z)\frac{dy}{ds}\,ds + f_3(x, y, z)\frac{dz}{ds}\,ds\right]$$

$$= \int_C \boldsymbol{F}\cdot\boldsymbol{t}\,ds$$

$$= \int_C \boldsymbol{F}\cdot d\boldsymbol{r}$$

Thus, given a vector field $\boldsymbol{F}(\boldsymbol{r})$, we can evaluate line integrals of the form $\int_C \boldsymbol{F}\cdot d\boldsymbol{r}$. In order to make it clear that we are integrating along a curve, the line integral is sometimes written as $\int_C \boldsymbol{F}\cdot d\boldsymbol{s}$, where $d\boldsymbol{s} = d\boldsymbol{r}$ (some authors use $d\boldsymbol{l}$ instead of $d\boldsymbol{s}$ in order to avoid confusion with $\mathrm{d}\boldsymbol{S}$, the element of surface area). In a similar manner we can evaluate line integrals of the form $\int_C \boldsymbol{F} \times \mathrm{d}\boldsymbol{r}$.

Example 7.18

Calculate (a) $\int_C \boldsymbol{F} \cdot \mathrm{d}\boldsymbol{r}$ and (b) $\int_C \boldsymbol{F} \times \mathrm{d}\boldsymbol{r}$, where C is the part of the spiral $\boldsymbol{r} = (a\cos\theta, a\sin\theta, a\theta)$ corresponding to $0 \leqslant \theta \leqslant \frac{1}{2}\pi$, and $\boldsymbol{F} = r^2\boldsymbol{i}$.

Solution

The curve C is illustrated in Figure 7.17.

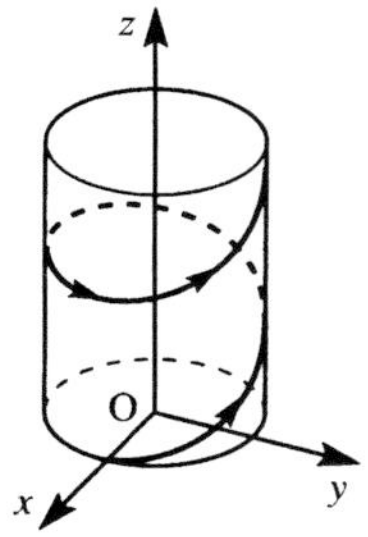

Figure 7.17 The spiral $\boldsymbol{r} = (a\cos\theta, a\sin\theta, a\theta)$.

(a) Since $\boldsymbol{r} = a\cos\theta\boldsymbol{i} + a\sin\theta\boldsymbol{j} + a\theta\boldsymbol{k}$,

$$\mathrm{d}\boldsymbol{r} = -a\sin\theta\,\mathrm{d}\theta\boldsymbol{i} + a\cos\theta\,\mathrm{d}\theta\boldsymbol{j} + a\,\mathrm{d}\theta\boldsymbol{k}$$

so that

$$\begin{aligned}\boldsymbol{F}\cdot\mathrm{d}\boldsymbol{r} &= r^2\boldsymbol{i}\cdot(-a\sin\theta\,\mathrm{d}\theta\boldsymbol{i} + a\cos\theta\,\mathrm{d}\theta\boldsymbol{j} + a\,\mathrm{d}\theta\boldsymbol{k})\\ &= -ar^2\sin\theta\,\mathrm{d}\theta\\ &= -a^3(\cos^2\theta + \sin^2\theta + \theta^2)\sin\theta\,\mathrm{d}\theta = -a^3(1+\theta^2)\sin\theta\,\mathrm{d}\theta\end{aligned}$$

since $r = |\boldsymbol{r}| = \sqrt{(a^2\cos^2\theta + a^2\sin^2\theta + a^2\theta^2)}$. Thus,

$$\begin{aligned}\int_C \boldsymbol{F}\cdot\mathrm{d}\boldsymbol{r} &= -a^3\int_0^{\pi/2}(1+\theta^2)\sin\theta\,\mathrm{d}\theta\\ &= -a^3[\cos\theta + 2\theta\sin\theta - \theta^2\cos\theta]_0^{\pi/2}, \text{ using integration by parts}\\ &= -a^3(\pi - 1)\end{aligned}$$

(b)
$$\begin{aligned}\boldsymbol{F}\times\mathrm{d}\boldsymbol{r} &= \begin{vmatrix}\boldsymbol{i} & \boldsymbol{j} & \boldsymbol{k}\\ r^2 & 0 & 0\\ -a\sin\theta\,\mathrm{d}\theta & a\cos\theta\,\mathrm{d}\theta & a\,\mathrm{d}\theta\end{vmatrix}\\ &= -ar^2\,\mathrm{d}\theta\boldsymbol{j} + ar^2\cos\theta\,\mathrm{d}\theta\boldsymbol{k}\\ &= -a^3(1+\theta^2)\,\mathrm{d}\theta\boldsymbol{j} + a^3(1+\theta^2)\cos\theta\,\mathrm{d}\theta\boldsymbol{k}\end{aligned}$$

so that

$$\begin{aligned}\int_C \boldsymbol{F}\times\mathrm{d}\boldsymbol{r} &= -\boldsymbol{j}a^3\int_0^{\pi/2}(1+\theta^2)\,\mathrm{d}\theta + \boldsymbol{k}a^3\int_0^{\pi/2}(1+\theta^2)\cos\theta\,\mathrm{d}\theta\\ &= -\frac{\pi a^3}{24}(12+\pi^2)\boldsymbol{j} + \frac{a^3}{4}(\pi^2 - 4)\boldsymbol{k}\end{aligned}$$

The work done as the point of application of a force $\boldsymbol{F}$ moves along a given path C as illustrated in Figure 7.18 can be expressed as a line integral. The work done as the point of application moves from $\mathrm{P}(\boldsymbol{r})$ to $\mathrm{P}'(\boldsymbol{r} + \mathrm{d}\boldsymbol{r})$, where $\overrightarrow{\mathrm{PP}'} = \mathrm{d}\boldsymbol{r}$, is $\mathrm{d}W = |\mathrm{d}\boldsymbol{r}||\boldsymbol{F}|\cos\theta = \boldsymbol{F}\cdot\mathrm{d}\boldsymbol{r}$. Hence the total work done as P goes from A to B is

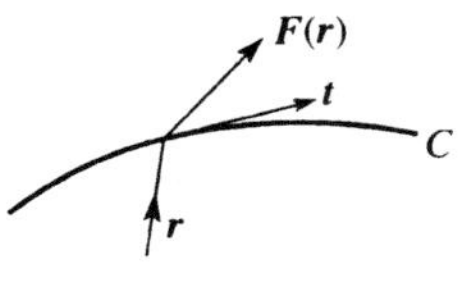

Figure 7.18 Work done by a force $\boldsymbol{F}$.

$$W = \int_C \boldsymbol{F}\cdot\mathrm{d}\boldsymbol{r}$$

In general, W depends on the path chosen. If, however, $\boldsymbol{F}(\boldsymbol{r})$ is such that $\boldsymbol{F}(\boldsymbol{r})\cdot\mathrm{d}\boldsymbol{r}$ is an exact differential, say $-\mathrm{d}U$, then $W = \int_C -\mathrm{d}U = U_A - U_B$, which depends only on A and B and is the same for all paths C joining A and B. Such a force is a **conservative** force, and $U(\boldsymbol{r})$ is its potential energy, with $\boldsymbol{F}(\boldsymbol{r}) = -\mathrm{grad}\, U$. Forces that do not have this property are said to be **dissipative** or **non-conservative**.

Similarly, if $\boldsymbol{v}(\boldsymbol{r})$ represents the velocity field of a fluid then $\oint_C \boldsymbol{v}\cdot\mathrm{d}\boldsymbol{r}$ is the flow around the closed curve C in unit time. This is sometimes termed the **net circulation integral** of $\boldsymbol{v}$. If $\oint_C \boldsymbol{v}\cdot\mathrm{d}\boldsymbol{r} = 0$ then the fluid is curl-free or irrotational, and in this case $\boldsymbol{v}$ has a potential function $\phi(\boldsymbol{r})$ such that $\boldsymbol{v} = -\mathrm{grad}\,\phi$.

7.4.2 Exercises

56 Evaluate $\int y\,\mathrm{d}s$ along the parabola $y = 2\sqrt{x}$ from A$(3, 2\sqrt{3})$ to B$(24, 4\sqrt{6})$. [Recall: $\left(\frac{\mathrm{d}s}{\mathrm{d}y}\right)^2 = 1 + \left(\frac{\mathrm{d}x}{\mathrm{d}y}\right)^2$.]

57 Evaluate $\int_A^B [2xy\,\mathrm{d}x + (x^2 - y^2)\,\mathrm{d}y]$ along the arc of the circle $x^2 + y^2 = 1$ in the first quadrant from A(1, 0) to B(0, 1).

58 Evaluate the integral $\int_C \boldsymbol{V}\cdot\mathrm{d}\boldsymbol{r}$, where $\boldsymbol{V} = (2yz + 3x^2, y^2 + 4xz, 2z^2 + 6xy)$, and C is the curve with parametric equations $x = t^3$, $y = t^2$, $z = t$ joining the points (0, 0, 0) and (1, 1, 1).

59 If $\boldsymbol{A} = (2y + 3)\boldsymbol{i} + xz\boldsymbol{j} + (yz - x)\boldsymbol{k}$, evaluate $\int_C \boldsymbol{A}\cdot\mathrm{d}\boldsymbol{r}$ along the following paths C:

(a) $x = 2t^2$, $y = t$, $z = t^3$ from $t = 0$ to $t = 1$;
(b) the straight lines from (0, 0, 0) to (0, 0, 1), then to (0, 1, 1) and then to (2, 1, 1);
(c) the straight line joining (0, 0, 0) to (2, 1, 1).

60 Prove that $\boldsymbol{F} = (y^2\cos x + z^3)\boldsymbol{i} + (2y\sin x - 4)\boldsymbol{j} + (3xz^2 + z)\boldsymbol{k}$ is a conservative force field. Hence find the work done in moving an object in this field from (0, 1, −1) to (π/2, −1, 2).

61 Find the work done in moving a particle in the force field $\boldsymbol{F} = 3x^2\boldsymbol{i} + (2xz - y)\boldsymbol{j} + z\boldsymbol{k}$ along

(a) the curve defined by $x^2 = 4y$, $3x^3 = 8z$ from $x = 0$ to $x = 2$;
(b) the straight line from (0, 0, 0) to (2, 1, 3).

Does this mean that $\boldsymbol{F}$ is a conservative force? Give reasons for your answer.

62 Prove that the vector field $\boldsymbol{F} = (3x^2 - y, 2yz^2 - x, 2y^2z)$ is conservative, but not solenoidal. Hence evaluate the scalar line integral $\int_C \boldsymbol{F}\cdot\mathrm{d}\boldsymbol{r}$ along any curve C joining the point (0, 0, 0) to the point (1, 2, 3).

63 If $\boldsymbol{F} = xy\boldsymbol{i} - z\boldsymbol{j} + x^2\boldsymbol{k}$ and C is the curve $x = t^2$, $y = 2t$, $z = t^3$ from $t = 0$ to $t = 1$, evaluate the vector line integral $\int_C \boldsymbol{F}\times\mathrm{d}\boldsymbol{r}$.

64 If $\boldsymbol{A} = (3x + y, -x, y - z)$ and $\boldsymbol{B} = (2, -3, 1)$ evaluate the line integral $\oint_C (\boldsymbol{A}\times\boldsymbol{B})\times\mathrm{d}\boldsymbol{r}$ around the circle in the (x, y) plane having centre at the origin and radius 2, traversed in the positive direction.

7.4.3 Double integrals

In the introduction to Section 7.4 we defined the definite integral of a function $f(x)$ of one variable by the limit

$$\int_a^b f(x)\,\mathrm{d}x = \lim_{\substack{n\to\infty \\ \text{all } \Delta x_i \to 0}} \sum_{i=1}^{n} f(\tilde{x}_i)\,\Delta x_i$$

where $a = x_0 < x_1 < x_2 < \ldots < x_n = b$, $\Delta x_i = x_i - x_{i-1}$ and $x_{i-1} \leqslant \tilde{x}_i \leqslant x_i$. This integral is represented by the area between the curve $y = f(x)$ and the x axis and between $x = a$ and $x = b$, as shown in Figure 7.13.

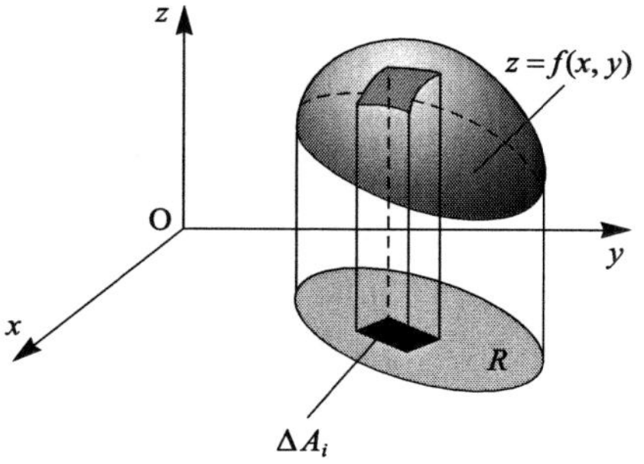

Figure 7.19 Volume as an integral.

Now consider $z = f(x, y)$ and a region R of the (x, y) plane, as shown in Figure 7.19. Define the integral of $f(x, y)$ over the region R by the limit

$$\iint_R f(x, y)\,\mathrm{d}A = \lim_{\substack{n\to\infty \\ \text{all } \Delta A_i \to 0}} \sum_{i=1}^{n} f(\tilde{x}_i, \tilde{y}_i)\,\Delta A_i$$

where ΔA_i $(i = 1, \ldots, n)$ is a partition of R into n elements of area ΔA_i and $(\tilde{x}_i, \tilde{y}_i)$ is a point in ΔA_i. Now $z = f(x, y)$ represents a surface, and so $f(\tilde{x}_i, \tilde{y}_i)\,\Delta A_i = \tilde{z}_i \Delta A_i$ is the volume between $z = 0$ and $z = \tilde{z}_i$ on the base ΔA_i. The integral $\iint_R f(x, y)\,\mathrm{d}A$ is the limit of the sum of all such volumes, and so it is the volume under the surface $z = f(x, y)$ above the region R.

The partition of R into elementary areas can be achieved using grid lines parallel to the x and y axes as shown in Figure 7.20. Then $\Delta A_i = \Delta x_i \Delta y_i$, and we can write

$$\iint_R f(x, y)\,\mathrm{d}A = \iint_R f(x, y)\,\mathrm{d}x\,\mathrm{d}y = \lim_{n\to\infty} \sum_{i=1}^{n} f(\tilde{x}_i, \tilde{y}_i)\,\Delta x_i\,\Delta y_i$$

Other partitions may be chosen, for example a polar grid as in Figure 7.21. Then the element of area is $(r_i \Delta\theta_i)\,\Delta r_i = \Delta A_i$ and

$$\iint_R f(x, y)\,\mathrm{d}A = \iint_R f(r\cos\theta, r\sin\theta) r\,\mathrm{d}r\,\mathrm{d}\theta \qquad \textbf{(7.26)}$$

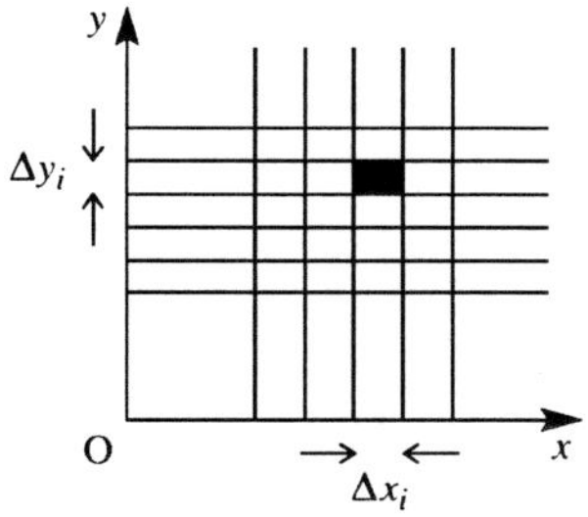

Figure 7.20 A possible grid for the partition of R (rectangular cartesian).

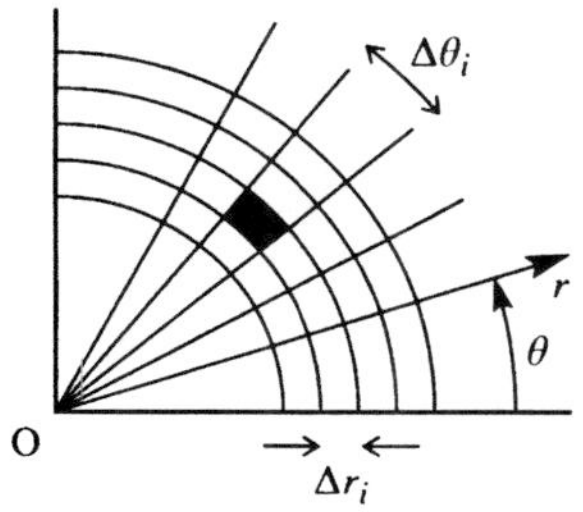

Figure 7.21 Another possible grid for the partition of R (polar).

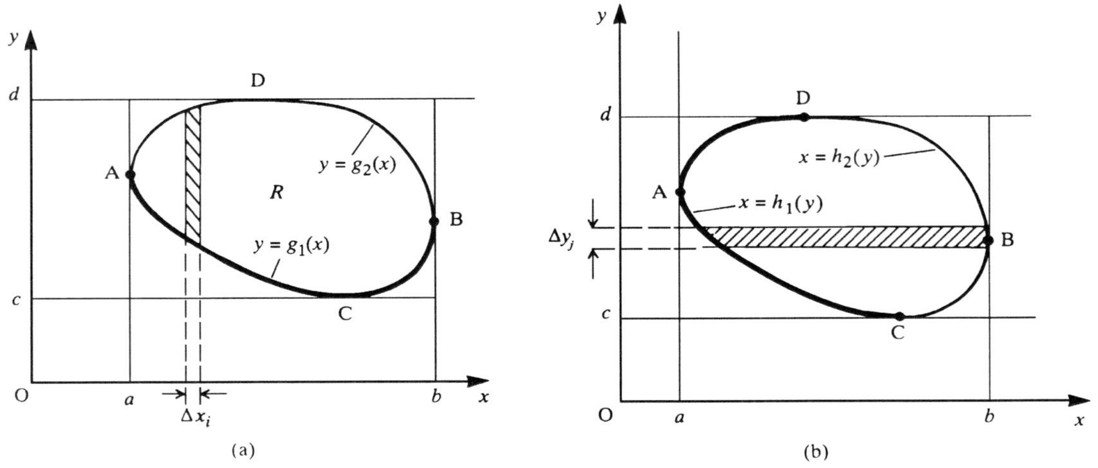

Figure 7.22 The region R.

The expression for ΔA is more complicated when the grid lines do not intersect at right angles; we shall discuss this case in Section 7.4.5.

We can evaluate integrals of the type $\iint_R f(x, y)\,\mathrm{d}x\,\mathrm{d}y$ as repeated single integrals in x and y. Consequently, they are usually called **double integrals**.

Consider the region R shown in Figure 7.22, with boundary ACBD. Let the curve ACB be given by $y = g_1(x)$ and the curve ADB by $y = g_2(x)$. Then we can evaluate $\iint_R f(x, y)\,\mathrm{d}x\,\mathrm{d}y$ by summing for y first over the Δy_i, holding x constant ($x = \tilde{x}_i$, say), from $y = g_1(x_i)$ to $y = g_2(x_i)$, and then summing all such strips from A to B; that is, from $x = a$ to $x = b$. Thus we may write

$$\iint_R f(x, y)\,\mathrm{d}A = \lim_{\substack{n\to\infty \\ \text{all } \Delta x_i,\, \Delta y_j \to 0}} \sum_{i=1}^{n_2}\left[\sum_{j=1}^{n_1} f(\tilde{x}_i, y_j)\Delta y_j\right]\Delta x_i \quad (n = \min(n_1, n_2))$$

$$= \int_a^b \left[\int_{y=g_1(x)}^{y=g_2(x)} f(x, y)\,\mathrm{d}y\right]\mathrm{d}x$$

Here the integral inside the brackets is evaluated first, integrating with respect to y, keeping the value of x fixed, and then the result of this integration is integrated with respect to x.

Alternatively, we can sum for x first and then y. If the curve CAD is represented by $x = h_1(y)$ and the curve CBD by $x = h_2(y)$, we can write the integral as

$$\iint_R f(x, y)\,\mathrm{d}A = \lim_{\substack{n\to\infty \\ \text{all } \Delta y_j,\, \Delta x_i \to 0}} \sum_{j=1}^{n_1}\left[\sum_{i=1}^{n_2} f(x_i, \tilde{y}_j)\,\Delta x_i\right]\Delta y_j \quad (n = \min(n_1, n_2))$$

$$= \int_c^d \left[\int_{x=h_1(y)}^{x=h_2(y)} f(x, y)\,\mathrm{d}x\right]\mathrm{d}y$$

If the double integral exists then these two results are equal, and in going from one to the other we have changed the order of integration. Notice that the limits of integration are also changed in the process. Often, when evaluating an integral analytically, it is easier to perform the evaluation one way rather than the other.

Example 7.19 Evaluate $\iint_R (x^2 + y^2)\,\mathrm{d}A$ over the triangle with vertices at (0, 0), (2, 0) and (1, 1).

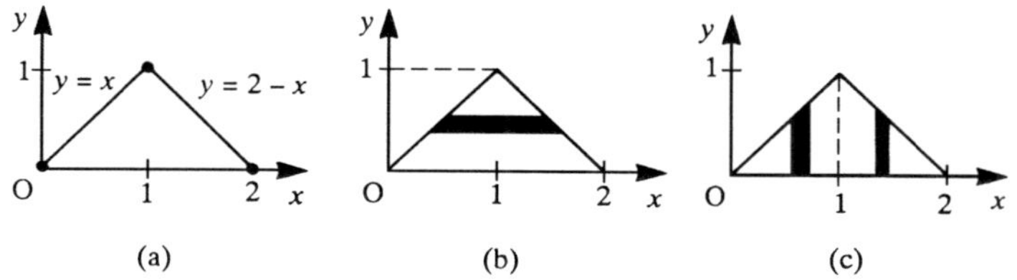

Figure 7.23 Domain of integration for Example 7.19.

Solution The domain of integration is shown in Figure 7.23(a). The triangle is bounded by the lines $y = 0$, $y = x$ and $y = 2 - x$.

(a) Integrating with respect to x first, as indicated in Figure 7.23(b), gives

$$\iint_R (x^2 + y^2)\,\mathrm{d}A = \int_0^1 \int_{x=y}^{x=2-y} (x^2 + y^2)\,\mathrm{d}x\,\mathrm{d}y$$

$$= \int_0^1 [\tfrac{1}{3}x^3 + y^2x]_{x=y}^{x=2-y}\,\mathrm{d}y$$

$$= \int_0^1 [\tfrac{8}{3} - 4y + 4y^2 - \tfrac{8}{3}y^3]\,\mathrm{d}y = \tfrac{4}{3}$$

(b) Integrating with respect to y first, as indicated in Figure 7.23(c), gives

$$\iint_R (x^2 + y^2)\,\mathrm{d}A = \int_0^1 \int_{y=0}^{y=x} (x^2 + y^2)\,\mathrm{d}y\,\mathrm{d}x + \int_1^2 \int_{y=0}^{y=2-x} (x^2 + y^2)\,\mathrm{d}y\,\mathrm{d}x$$

Note that because the upper boundary of the region R has different equations for it along different parts, the integral has to be split up into convenient subintegrals. Evaluating the integrals we have

$$\int_0^1 \int_{y=0}^{y=x} (x^2 + y^2)\,\mathrm{d}y\,\mathrm{d}x = \int_0^1 [x^2y + \tfrac{1}{3}y^3]_{y=0}^{y=x}\,\mathrm{d}x = \int_0^1 \tfrac{4}{3}x^3\,\mathrm{d}x = \tfrac{1}{3}$$

$$\int_1^2 \int_{y=0}^{y=2-x} (x^2 + y^2)\,\mathrm{d}y\,\mathrm{d}x = \int_1^2 [x^2y + \tfrac{1}{3}y^3]_{y=0}^{y=2-x}\,\mathrm{d}x$$

$$= \int_1^2 (\tfrac{8}{3} - 4x + 4x^2 - \tfrac{4}{3}x^3)\,\mathrm{d}x = 1$$

Thus

$$\iint_R (x^2 + y^2)\,\mathrm{d}A = \tfrac{1}{3} + 1 = \tfrac{4}{3}, \quad \text{as before}$$

Clearly, in this example it is easier to integrate with respect to x first.

Example 7.20 Evaluate $\iint_R (x + 2y)^{-1/2}\,\mathrm{d}A$ over the region $x - 2y \leqslant 1$ and $x \geqslant y^2 + 1$.

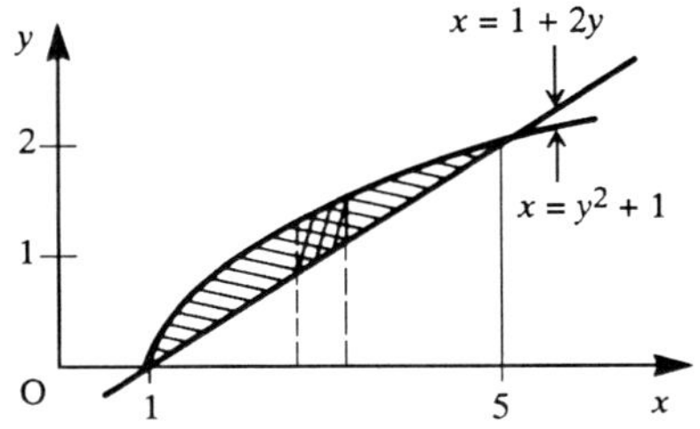

Figure 7.24 Domain of integration for Example 7.20.

Solution The bounding curves intersect where $2y + 1 = y^2 + 1$, which gives $y = 0$ (with $x = 1$) and $y = 2$ (with $x = 5$). The region R is shown in Figure 7.24. In this example we choose to take x first because the formula for the boundary is easier to deal with: $x = y^2 + 1$ rather than $y = (x - 1)^{1/2}$. Thus we obtain

$$\iint_R (x+2y)^{-1/2}\,\mathrm{d}A = \int_0^2 \int_{y^2+1}^{2y+1} (x+2y)^{-1/2}\,\mathrm{d}x\,\mathrm{d}y$$

$$= \int_0^2 [2(x+2y)^{1/2}]_{x=y^2+1}^{x=2y+1}\,\mathrm{d}y$$

$$= \int_0^2 [2(4y+1)^{1/2} - 2(y+1)]\,\mathrm{d}y$$

$$= [\tfrac{1}{3}(4y+1)^{3/2} - y^2 - 2y]_0^2 = \tfrac{2}{3}$$

As indicated earlier, the evaluation of integrals over a domain R is not restricted to the use of rectangular cartesian coordinates (x, y). Example 7.21 shows how polar coordinates can be used in some cases to simplify the analytical process.

Example 7.21 Evaluate $\iint_R x^2 y\,\mathrm{d}A$, where R is the region $x^2 + y^2 \leqslant 1$.

Solution The fact that the domain of integration is a circle suggests that polar coordinates are a natural choice for the integration process. Then, from (7.26), $x = r\cos\theta$, $y = r\sin\theta$ and $\mathrm{d}A = r\,\mathrm{d}\theta\,\mathrm{d}r$, and the integral becomes

$$\iint_R x^2 y\,\mathrm{d}A = \int_{r=0}^{1} \int_{\theta=0}^{2\pi} r^2\cos^2\theta\; r\sin\theta\; r\,\mathrm{d}\theta\,\mathrm{d}r$$

$$= \int_{r=0}^{1} \int_{\theta=0}^{2\pi} r^4\cos^2\theta\sin\theta\,\mathrm{d}\theta\,\mathrm{d}r$$

Note that in this example the integration is such that we can separate the variables r and θ and write

$$\iint_R x^2y\,dA = \int_{r=0}^{1} r^4 \int_{\theta=0}^{2\pi} \cos^2\theta \sin\theta\, d\theta\, dr$$

Furthermore, since the limits of integration with respect to θ do not involve r, we can write

$$\iint_R x^2y\,dA = \int_{r=0}^{1} r^4\,dr \int_{\theta=0}^{2\pi} \cos^2\theta \sin\theta\, d\theta$$

and the double integral in this case reduces to a product of integrals. Thus we obtain

$$\iint_R x^2y\,dA = [\tfrac{1}{5}r^5]_0^1[-\tfrac{1}{3}\cos^2\theta]_0^{2\pi} = 0$$

7.4.4 Exercises

65 Evaluate the following:

(a) $\int_0^3\int_1^2 xy(x+y)\,dy\,dx$ (b) $\int_2^3\int_1^5 x^2y\,dy\,dx$

(c) $\int_{-1}^{1}\int_{-2}^{2} (2x^2+y^2)\,dy\,dx$

66 Evaluate

$$\iint \frac{x^2}{y}\,dx\,dy$$

over the rectangle bounded by the lines $x = 0$, $x = 2$, $y = 1$ and $y = 2$.

67 Evaluate $\iint (x^2+y^2)\,dx\,dy$ over the region for which $x \geqslant 0$, $y \geqslant 0$ and $x + y \leqslant 1$.

68 Sketch the domain of integration and evaluate

(a) $\int_1^2 dx \int_x^{2x} \frac{dy}{x^2+y^2}$ (b) $\int_0^1 dx \int_0^{1-x} (x+y)\,dy$

(c) $\int_0^1 dx \int_{\sqrt{(x-x^2)}}^{\sqrt{(1-x^2)}} \frac{1}{\sqrt{(1-x^2-y^2)}}\,dy$

69 Evaluate $\iint \sin\frac{1}{2}\pi(x+y)\,dx\,dy$ over the triangle whose vertices are (0, 0), (2, 1), (1, 2).

70 Sketch the domains of integration of the double integrals

(a) $\int_0^1 dx \int_x^1 \frac{xy\,dy}{\sqrt{(1+y^4)}}$

(b) $\int_0^{\pi/2} dy \int_0^y (\cos 2y)\sqrt{(1-k^2\sin^2 x)}\,dx$

Change the order of integration, and hence evaluate the integrals.

71 Evaluate

$$\int_0^1 dy \int_{\sqrt{y}}^1 \frac{dx}{\sqrt{[y(1+x^2)]}}$$

72 Sketch the domain of integration of the double integral

$$\int_0^1\int_0^{\sqrt{(x-x^2)}} \frac{x}{\sqrt{(x^2+y^2)}}\,dy\,dx$$

Express the integral in polar coordinates, and hence show that its value is $\frac{1}{3}$.

73 Sketch the domain of integration of the double integral

$$\int_0^1 \mathrm{d}x \int_0^{\sqrt{(1-x^2)}} \frac{x+y}{\sqrt{(x^2+y^2)}}\,\mathrm{d}y$$

and evaluate the integral.

74 Evaluate

$$\iint \frac{x+y}{x^2+y^2+a^2}\,\mathrm{d}x\,\mathrm{d}y$$

over the portion of the first quadrant lying inside the circle $x^2+y^2=a^2$.

75 By using polar coordinates, evaluate the double integral

$$\iint \frac{x^2-y^2}{x^2+y^2}\,\mathrm{d}x\,\mathrm{d}y$$

over the region in the first quadrant bounded by the arc of the parabola $y^2=4(1-x)$ and the coordinate axes.

76 By transforming to polar coordinates, show that the double integral

$$\iint \frac{(x^2+y^2)^2}{(xy)^2}\,\mathrm{d}x\,\mathrm{d}y$$

taken over the area common to the two circles $x^2+y^2=ax$ and $x^2+y^2=by$ is ab.

7.4.5 Green's theorem in a plane

This theorem shows the relationship between line integrals and double integrals, and will also provide a justification for the general change of variables in a double integral.

Consider a simple closed curve, C, enclosing the region A as shown in Figure 7.25. If $P(x, y)$ and $Q(x, y)$ are continuous functions with continuous partial derivatives then

$$\oint_C (P\,\mathrm{d}x+Q\,\mathrm{d}y)=\iint_A \left(\frac{\partial Q}{\partial x}-\frac{\partial P}{\partial y}\right)\mathrm{d}x\,\mathrm{d}y \tag{7.27}$$

where C is traversed in the positive sense (that is, so that the bounded area is always on the left). This result is called **Green's theorem** in a plane.

The proof of this result is straightforward. Consider the first term on the right-hand side. Then, with reference to Figure 7.25,

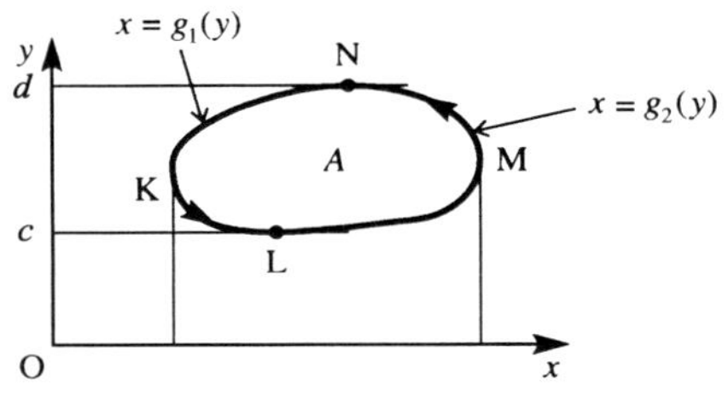

Figure 7.25 Green's theorem.

$$\iint_R \frac{\partial Q}{\partial x}\,dx\,dy = \int_c^d \left[\int_{g_1(y)}^{g_2(y)} \frac{\partial Q}{\partial x}\,dx\right] dy$$

$$= \int_c^d [Q(g_2(y), y) - Q(g_1(y), y)]\,dy$$

$$= \int_{LMN} Q(x, y)\,dy - \int_{LKN} Q(x, y)\,dy$$

$$= \int_{LMNKL} Q(x, y)\,dy = \oint_C Q(x, y)\,dy$$

Similarly,

$$-\iint_A \frac{\partial P}{\partial y}\,dx\,dy = \oint_C P(x, y)\,dx$$

and hence

$$\iint_A \left(\frac{\partial Q}{\partial x} - \frac{\partial P}{\partial y}\right) dx\,dy = \oint_C [P(x, y)\,dx + Q(x, y)\,dy]$$

An elementary application is shown in Example 7.22.

Example 7.22

Evaluate $\oint [2x(x + y)\,dx + (x^2 + xy + y^2)\,dy]$ around the square with vertices at (0, 0), (1, 0), (1, 1) and (0, 1) illustrated in Figure 7.26.

Solution

Here $P(x, y) = 2x(x + y)$ and $Q(x, y) = x^2 + xy + y^2$, so that $\partial P/\partial y = 2x$, $\partial Q/\partial x = 2x + y$ and $\partial Q/\partial x - \partial P/\partial y = y$. Thus the line integral transforms into an easy double integral

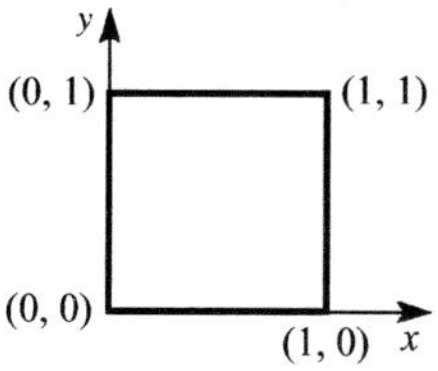

Figure 7.26 Path of integration for Example 7.22.

$$\oint_C [2x(x + y)\,dx + (x^2 + xy + y^2)\,dy] = \iint_A y\,dx\,dy$$

$$= \int_0^1 \int_0^1 y\,dx\,dy$$

$$= \int_0^1 y\,dy \int_0^1 dx = \tfrac{1}{2}$$

It follows immediately from Green's theorem (7.27) that the area A enclosed by the closed curve C is given by

$$A = \oint_C x\,\mathrm{d}y \equiv \iint_A 1\,\mathrm{d}x\,\mathrm{d}y = -\oint_C y\,\mathrm{d}x \equiv \iint_A 1\,\mathrm{d}x\,\mathrm{d}y = \tfrac{1}{2}\oint_C (-y\,\mathrm{d}x + x\,\mathrm{d}y)$$

Suppose that under a transformation of coordinates $x = x(u, v)$ and $y = y(u, v)$, the curve becomes C', enclosing an area A'. Then

$$A' = \oint_{C'} u\,\mathrm{d}v \equiv \iint_{A'} \mathrm{d}u\,\mathrm{d}v = \oint_C u\left(\frac{\partial v}{\partial x}\mathrm{d}x + \frac{\partial v}{\partial y}\mathrm{d}y\right)$$

$$= \iint_A \left[\frac{\partial}{\partial x}\left(u\frac{\partial v}{\partial y}\right) - \frac{\partial}{\partial y}\left(u\frac{\partial v}{\partial x}\right)\right]\mathrm{d}x\,\mathrm{d}y = \iint_A \left(\frac{\partial u}{\partial x}\frac{\partial v}{\partial y} - \frac{\partial u}{\partial y}\frac{\partial v}{\partial x}\right)\mathrm{d}x\,\mathrm{d}y$$

This implies that the element of area $\mathrm{d}u\,\mathrm{d}v$ is equivalent to the element

$$\left|\left(\frac{\partial u}{\partial x}\frac{\partial v}{\partial y} - \frac{\partial u}{\partial y}\frac{\partial v}{\partial x}\right)\right|\mathrm{d}x\,\mathrm{d}y$$

Here the modulus sign is introduced to preserve the orientation of the curve under the mapping. Similarly, we may prove that

$$\mathrm{d}x\,\mathrm{d}y = \left|\frac{\partial(x, y)}{\partial(u, v)}\right|\mathrm{d}u\,\mathrm{d}v \quad \textbf{(7.28)}$$

where $\partial(x, y)/\partial(u, v)$ is the **Jacobian**

$$\frac{\partial x}{\partial u}\frac{\partial y}{\partial v} - \frac{\partial x}{\partial v}\frac{\partial y}{\partial u} = J(x, y)$$

This enables us to make a general change of coordinates in a double integral:

$$\iint_A f(x, y)\,\mathrm{d}x\,\mathrm{d}y = \iint_{A'} f(x(u, v), y(u, v))|J|\,\mathrm{d}u\,\mathrm{d}v \quad \textbf{(7.29)}$$

where A' is the region in the (u, v) plane corresponding to A in the (x, y) plane.

Note that the above discussion confirms the result

$$\frac{\partial(u, v)}{\partial(x, y)} = \left[\frac{\partial(x, y)}{\partial(u, v)}\right]^{-1}$$

as shown in Section 7.1.3. Using (7.29), the result (7.26) when using polar coordinates is readily confirmed.

Example 7.23 Evaluate $\iint xy\,\mathrm{d}x\,\mathrm{d}y$ over the region in $x \geqslant 0$, $y \geqslant 0$ bounded by $y = x^2 + 4$, $y = x^2$, $y = 6 - x^2$ and $y = 12 - x^2$.

Solution The domain of integration is shown in Figure 7.27(a). The bounding curves can be rewritten as $y - x^2 = 4$, $y - x^2 = 0$, $y + x^2 = 6$ and $y + x^2 = 12$, so that a natural change of coordinates is to set

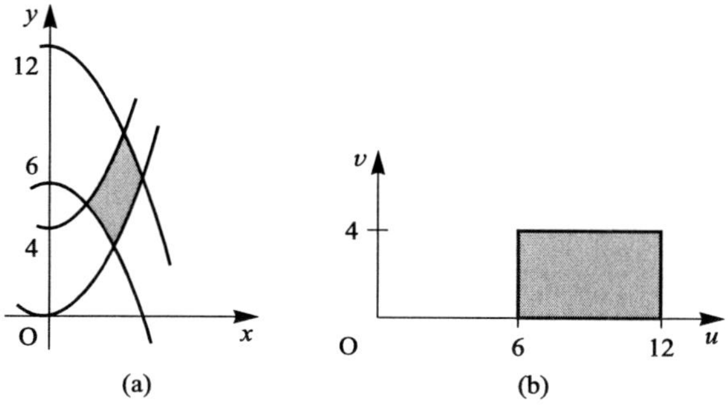

Figure 7.27 Domain of integration for Example 7.23: (a) in the (x, y) plane; (b) in the (u, v) plane.

$$u = y + x^2, \qquad v = y - x^2$$

Under this transformation, the region of integration becomes the rectangle $6 \leqslant u \leqslant 12$, $0 \leqslant v \leqslant 4$, as shown in Figure 7.27(b). Thus since

$$J(x, y) = \frac{\partial(x, y)}{\partial(u, v)} = \left[\frac{\partial(u, v)}{\partial(x, y)}\right]^{-1} = \frac{1}{4x}$$

the integral simplifies to

$$\iint_A xy \,\mathrm{d}x\,\mathrm{d}y = \iint_{A'} xy \frac{1}{4x} \,\mathrm{d}u\,\mathrm{d}v$$

Hence

$$\iint_A xy \,\mathrm{d}x\,\mathrm{d}y = \tfrac{1}{4}\iint_{A'} y \,\mathrm{d}u\,\mathrm{d}v = \tfrac{1}{8}\iint_{A'} (u + v) \,\mathrm{d}u\,\mathrm{d}v, \qquad \text{since } y = (u + v)/2$$

$$= \tfrac{1}{8}\int_0^4 \mathrm{d}v \int_6^{12} (u + v)\,\mathrm{d}u = 33$$

We remark in passing that Green's theorem in a plane may be generalized to three dimensions. Note that the result (7.27) may be written as

$$\oint_C (P, Q, 0) \cdot \mathrm{d}\boldsymbol{r} = \iint_A \operatorname{curl}\,[(P, Q, 0)] \cdot \boldsymbol{k}\,\mathrm{d}x\,\mathrm{d}y$$

For a general surface S with bounding curve C as shown in Figure 7.28 this identity becomes

$$\oint_C \boldsymbol{F}(\boldsymbol{r}) \cdot \mathrm{d}\boldsymbol{r} = \iint_S \operatorname{curl} \boldsymbol{F}(\boldsymbol{r}) \cdot \mathrm{d}\boldsymbol{S}$$

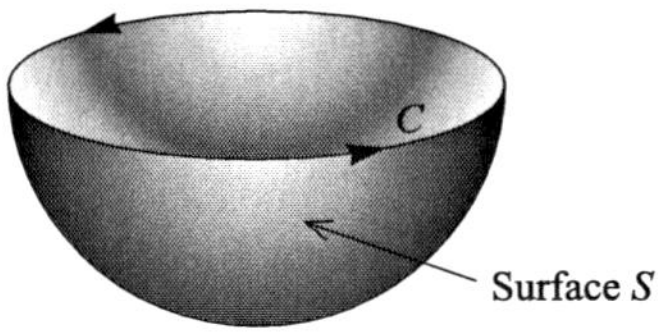

Figure 7.28 Three-dimensional generalization of Green's theorem.

where $\mathrm{d}\boldsymbol{S} = \hat{\boldsymbol{n}}\,\mathrm{d}S$ is the vector element of surface area and $\hat{\boldsymbol{n}}$ is a unit vector along the normal. This generalization is called Stokes' theorem, and will be discussed in Section 7.4.12 after we have formally introduced the concept of a surface integral.

7.4.6 Exercises

77 Evaluate the line integral

$$\oint_C [\sin y\,\mathrm{d}x + (x - \cos y)\,\mathrm{d}y]$$

taken in the anticlockwise sense, where C is the perimeter of the triangle formed by the lines

$$y = \tfrac{1}{2}\pi x, \qquad y = \tfrac{1}{2}\pi, \qquad x = 0$$

Verify your answer using Green's theorem in a plane.

78 Use Green's theorem in a plane to evaluate

$$\oint_C [(xy^2 - y)\,\mathrm{d}x + (x + y^2)\,\mathrm{d}y]$$

as a double integral, where C is the triangle with vertices at (0, 0), (2, 0) and (2, 2) and is traversed in the anticlockwise direction.

79 Evaluate the line integral

$$I = \oint_C (xy\,\mathrm{d}x + x\,\mathrm{d}y)$$

where C is the closed curve consisting of $y = x^2$ from $x = 0$ to $x = 1$ and $y = \sqrt{x}$ from $x = 1$ to $x = 0$. Confirm your answer by applying Green's theorem in the plane and evaluating I as a double integral.

80 Use Green's theorem in a plane to evaluate the line integral

$$\oint_C [(\mathrm{e}^x - 3y^2)\,\mathrm{d}x + (\mathrm{e}^y + 4x^2)\,\mathrm{d}y]$$

where C is the circle $x^2 + y^2 = 4$. (*Hint*: use polar coordinates to evaluate the double integral.)

81 Evaluate

$$\int_0^a \mathrm{d}x \int_x^{2a-x} \frac{y - x}{4a^2 + (y + x)^2}\,\mathrm{d}y$$

using the transformation of coordinates $u = x + y$, $v = x - y$.

82 Using the transformation

$$x + y = u, \qquad \frac{y}{x} = v$$

show that

$$\int_0^1 \mathrm{d}y \int_y^{2-y} \frac{x + y}{x^2}\,\mathrm{e}^{x+y}\,\mathrm{d}x = \int_0^2 \mathrm{d}u \int_0^1 \mathrm{e}^u\,\mathrm{d}v = \mathrm{e}^2 - 1$$

7.4.7 Surface integrals

The extensions of the idea of an integral to line and double integrals are not the only generalizations that can be made. We can also extend the idea to integration over a general surface S. Two types of such integrals occur:

(a) $$\iint_S f(x, y, z)\,\mathrm{d}S$$

(b) $$\iint_S \boldsymbol{F}(\boldsymbol{r}) \cdot \hat{\boldsymbol{n}}\,\mathrm{d}S = \iint_S \boldsymbol{F}(\boldsymbol{r}) \cdot \mathrm{d}\boldsymbol{S}$$

In case (a) we have a scalar field $f(\boldsymbol{r})$ and in case (b) a vector field $\boldsymbol{F}(\boldsymbol{r})$. Note that $\mathrm{d}\boldsymbol{S} = \hat{\boldsymbol{n}}\,\mathrm{d}S$ is the vector element of area, where $\hat{\boldsymbol{n}}$ is the unit outward-drawn normal vector to the element $\mathrm{d}S$.

In general, the surface S can be described in terms of two parameters, u and v say, so that on S

$$\boldsymbol{r} = \boldsymbol{r}(u, v) = (x(u, v), y(u, v), z(u, v))$$

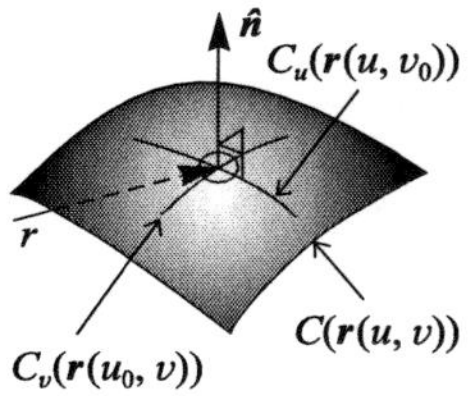

Figure 7.29 Parametric curves on a surface.

The surface S can be specified by a scalar point function $C(\boldsymbol{r}) = c$, where c is a constant. Curves may be drawn on that surface, and in particular if we fix the value of one of the two parameters u and v then we obtain two families of curves. On one, $C_u(\boldsymbol{r}(u, v_0))$, the value of u varies while v is fixed, and on the other, $C_v(\boldsymbol{r}(u_0, v))$, the value of v varies while u is fixed, as shown in Figure 7.29. Then as indicated in Figure 7.29, the vector element of area $\mathrm{d}\boldsymbol{S}$ is given by

$$\mathrm{d}\boldsymbol{S} = \frac{\partial \boldsymbol{r}}{\partial u}\,\mathrm{d}u \times \frac{\partial \boldsymbol{r}}{\partial v}\,\mathrm{d}v = \frac{\partial \boldsymbol{r}}{\partial u} \times \frac{\partial \boldsymbol{r}}{\partial v}\,\mathrm{d}u\,\mathrm{d}v$$

$$= \left(\frac{\partial x}{\partial u}, \frac{\partial y}{\partial u}, \frac{\partial z}{\partial u}\right) \times \left(\frac{\partial x}{\partial v}, \frac{\partial y}{\partial v}, \frac{\partial z}{\partial v}\right) \mathrm{d}u\,\mathrm{d}v = (J_1\boldsymbol{i} + J_2\boldsymbol{j} + J_3\boldsymbol{k})\,\mathrm{d}u\,\mathrm{d}v$$

where

$$J_1 = \frac{\partial y}{\partial u}\frac{\partial z}{\partial v} - \frac{\partial y}{\partial v}\frac{\partial z}{\partial u}, \qquad J_2 = \frac{\partial z}{\partial u}\frac{\partial x}{\partial v} - \frac{\partial z}{\partial v}\frac{\partial x}{\partial u}, \qquad J_3 = \frac{\partial x}{\partial u}\frac{\partial y}{\partial v} - \frac{\partial x}{\partial v}\frac{\partial y}{\partial u} \tag{7.30}$$

Hence

$$\iint_S \boldsymbol{F}(\boldsymbol{r}) \cdot \mathrm{d}\boldsymbol{S} = \iint_A (PJ_1 + QJ_2 + RJ_3)\,\mathrm{d}u\,\mathrm{d}v$$

$$\iint_S f(x, y, z)\,\mathrm{d}S = \iint_A f(u, v)\sqrt{(J_1^2 + J_2^2 + J_3^2)}\,\mathrm{d}u\,\mathrm{d}v$$

where $\boldsymbol{F}(\boldsymbol{r}) = (P, Q, R)$ and A is the region of the (u, v) plane corresponding to S. Here, of course, the terms in the integrands have to be expressed in terms of u and v.

In particular, u and v can be chosen as any two of x, y and z. For example, if $z = z(x, y)$ describes a surface as in Figure 7.30 then

$$\boldsymbol{r} = (x, y, z(x, y))$$

with x and y as independent variables. This gives

$$J_1 = -\frac{\partial z}{\partial x}, \qquad J_2 = -\frac{\partial z}{\partial y}, \qquad J_3 = 1$$

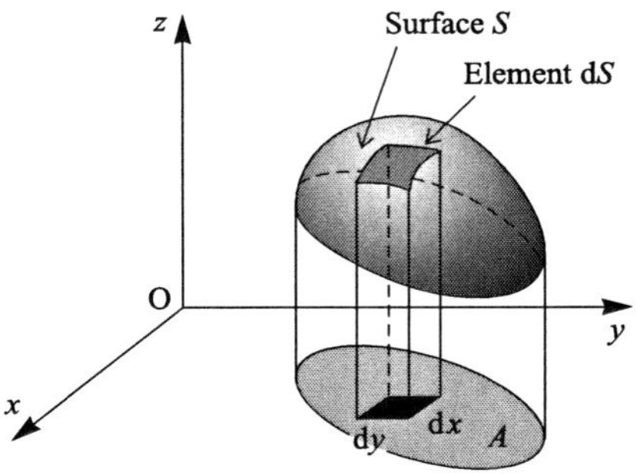

Figure 7.30 A surface described by $z = z(x, y)$.

and

$$\iint_S \boldsymbol{F}(\boldsymbol{r}) \cdot \mathrm{d}\boldsymbol{S} = \iint_A \left(-P\frac{\partial z}{\partial x} - Q\frac{\partial z}{\partial y} + R\right) \mathrm{d}x\,\mathrm{d}y \tag{7.31a}$$

$$\iint_S f(x, y, z)\,\mathrm{d}S = \iint_A f(x, y, z(x, y)) \sqrt{\left[1 + \left(\frac{\partial z}{\partial x}\right)^2 + \left(\frac{\partial z}{\partial y}\right)^2\right]}\,\mathrm{d}x\,\mathrm{d}y \tag{7.31b}$$

Example 7.24 Evaluate the surface integral

$$\iint_S (x + y + z)\,\mathrm{d}S$$

where S is the portion of the sphere $x^2 + y^2 + z^2 = 1$ that lies in the first quadrant.

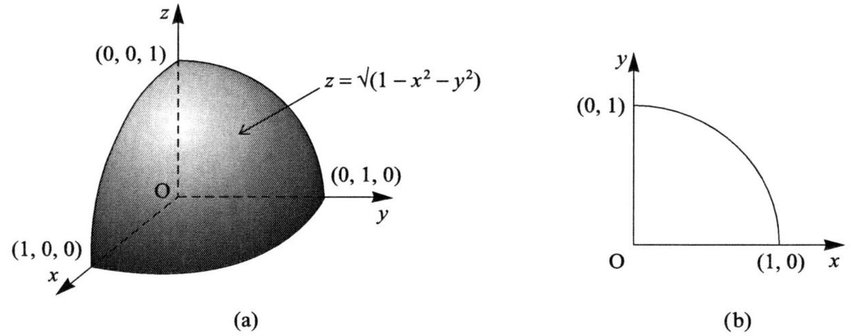

Figure 7.31 (a) Surface S for Example 7.24; (b) quadrant of a circle in the (x, y) plane.

Solution The surface S is illustrated in Figure 7.31(a). Taking

$$z = \sqrt{(1 - x^2 - y^2)}$$

we have

$$\frac{\partial z}{\partial x} = \frac{-x}{\sqrt{(1 - x^2 - y^2)}}, \qquad \frac{\partial z}{\partial y} = \frac{-y}{\sqrt{(1 - x^2 - y^2)}}$$

giving

$$\sqrt{\left[1+\left(\frac{\partial z}{\partial x}\right)^2+\left(\frac{\partial z}{\partial y}\right)^2\right]}=\sqrt{\left[\frac{x^2+y^2+(1-x^2-y^2)}{(1-x^2-y^2)}\right]}=\frac{1}{\sqrt{(1-x^2-y^2)}}$$

Using (7.17) then gives

$$\iint_S (x+y+z)\,\mathrm{d}S=\iint_A [x+y+\sqrt{(1-x^2-y^2)}\,]\frac{1}{\sqrt{(1-x^2-y^2)}}\,\mathrm{d}x\,\mathrm{d}y$$

where A is the quadrant of a circle in the (x, y) plane illustrated in Figure 7.31(b).

Transforming to polar coordinates

$$x=r\cos\theta,\qquad y=r\sin\theta,\qquad \mathrm{d}x\,\mathrm{d}y=r\,\mathrm{d}r\,\mathrm{d}\theta$$

gives

$$\begin{aligned}\iint_S (x+y+z)\,\mathrm{d}S &= \int_0^{\pi/2}\int_0^1\left[\frac{r(\sin\theta+\cos\theta)}{\sqrt{(1-r^2)}}+1\right]r\,\mathrm{d}r\,\mathrm{d}\theta\\ &= \int_0^1\left[\frac{r^2(-\cos\theta+\sin\theta)}{\sqrt{(1-r^2)}}+r\right]_0^{\pi/2}\mathrm{d}r\\ &= \int_0^1\left[\frac{2r^2}{\sqrt{(1-r^2)}}+\tfrac{1}{2}r\pi\right]\mathrm{d}r\\ &= \int_0^1\left[-2\sqrt{(1-r^2)}+\frac{2}{\sqrt{(1-r^2)}}+\tfrac{1}{2}r\pi\right]\mathrm{d}r\\ &= [-r\sqrt{(1-r^2)}-\sin^{-1}r+2\sin^{-1}r+\tfrac{1}{4}r^2\pi\,]_0^1\\ &= \tfrac{3}{4}\pi\end{aligned}$$

An alternative approach to evaluating the surface integral in Example 7.24 is to evaluate it directly over the surface of the sphere using spherical polar coordinates. As illustrated in Figure 7.32, on the surface of a sphere of radius a we have

Figure 7.32 Surface element in spherical polar coordinates.

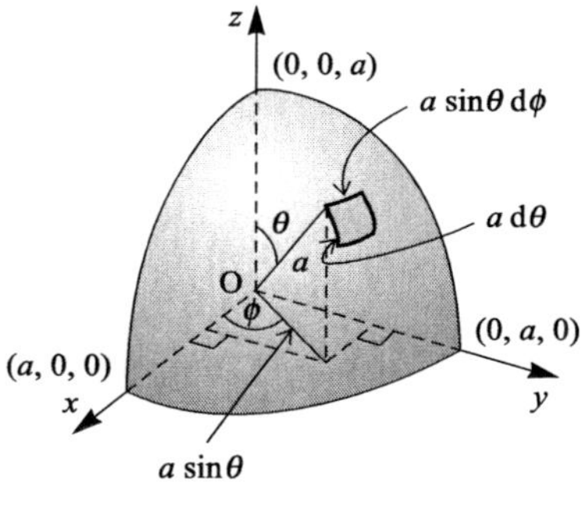

$$x = a\sin\theta\cos\phi, \qquad y = a\sin\theta\sin\phi$$
$$z = a\cos\theta, \qquad dS = a^2\sin\theta\, d\theta\, d\phi$$

In the sphere of Example 7.24 the radius $a = 1$, so that

$$\iint_S (x+y+z)\,dS = \int_0^{\pi/2}\int_0^{\pi/2} (\sin\theta\cos\phi + \sin\theta\sin\phi + \cos\theta)\sin\theta\, d\theta\, d\phi$$

$$= \int_0^{\pi/2} [\tfrac{1}{4}\pi\cos\phi + \tfrac{1}{4}\pi\sin\phi + \tfrac{1}{2}]\, d\phi = \tfrac{3}{4}\pi$$

In a similar manner, when evaluating surface integrals over the surface of a cylinder of radius a, we have, as illustrated in Figure 7.33,

$$x = a\cos\phi, \qquad y = a\sin\phi, \qquad z = z, \qquad dS = a\, dz\, d\phi$$

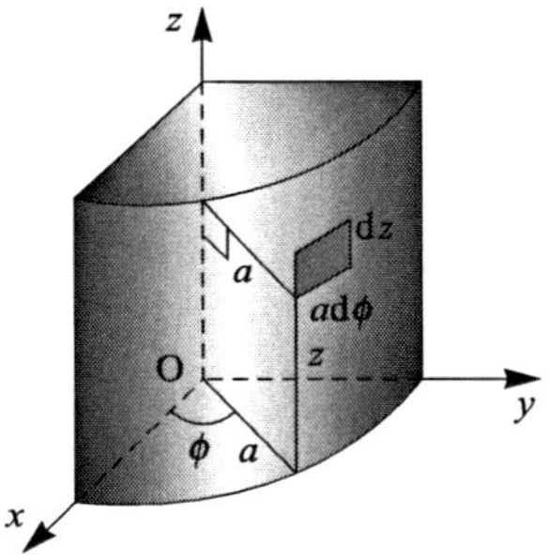

Figure 7.33 Surface element in cylindrical polar coordinates.

Example 7.25 Find the surface area of the torus shown in Figure 7.34(a) formed by rotating a circle of radius b about an axis distance a from its centre.

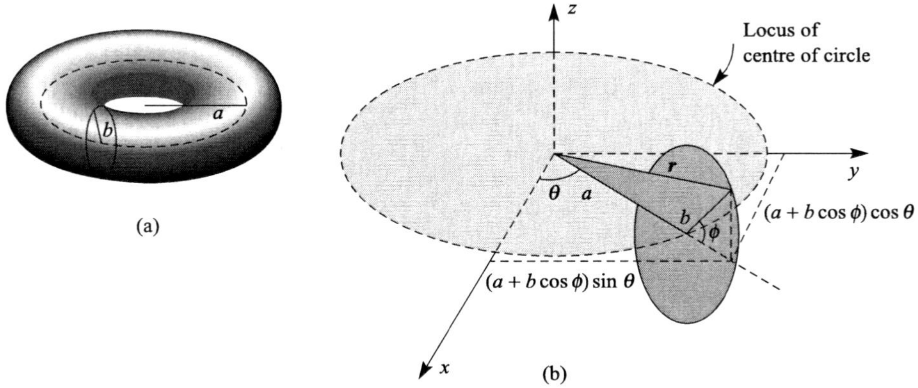

Figure 7.34 (a) Torus of Example 7.25; (b) position vector of a point on the surface of the torus.

Solution From Figure 7.34(b), the position vector $\boldsymbol{r}$ of a point on the surface is given by

$$\boldsymbol{r} = (a + b\cos\phi)\cos\theta\boldsymbol{i} + (a + b\cos\phi)\sin\theta\boldsymbol{j} + b\sin\phi\boldsymbol{k}$$

(Notice that θ and ϕ are not the angles used for spherical polar coordinates.) Thus using 7.16,

$$J_1 = (a + b\cos\phi)\cos\theta(b\cos\phi) - (-b\sin\phi\sin\theta)(0)$$

$$J_2 = (0)(-b\sin\phi\cos\theta) - (b\cos\phi)(a + b\cos\phi)(-\sin\theta)$$

$$J_3 = -(a + b\cos\phi)\sin\theta(-b\sin\phi\sin\theta) - (-b\sin\phi\cos\theta)(a + b\cos\phi)\cos\theta$$

Simplifying, we obtain

$$J_1 = b(a + b\cos\phi)\cos\theta\cos\phi$$

$$J_2 = b(a + b\cos\phi)\sin\theta\cos\phi$$

$$J_3 = b(a + b\cos\phi)\sin\phi$$

and the surface area is given by

$$\begin{aligned} S &= \int_0^{2\pi}\int_0^{2\pi} \sqrt{(J_1^2 + J_2^2 + J_3^2)}\,\mathrm{d}\theta\,\mathrm{d}\phi \\ &= \int_0^{2\pi}\int_0^{2\pi} b(a + b\cos\phi)\,\mathrm{d}\theta\,\mathrm{d}\phi \\ &= 4\pi^2 ab \end{aligned}$$

Thus the surface area of the torus is the product of the circumferences of the two circles that generate it.

Example 7.26 Evaluate $\iint_S \boldsymbol{V}\cdot \mathrm{d}\boldsymbol{S}$, where $\boldsymbol{V} = z\boldsymbol{i} + x\boldsymbol{j} - 3y^2z\boldsymbol{k}$ and S is the surface of the cylinder $x^2 + y^2 = 16$ in the first octant between $z = 0$ and $z = 5$.

Solution The surface S is illustrated in Figure 7.35. From Section 7.2.1, the outward normal to the surface is in the direction of the vector

$$\boldsymbol{n} = \text{grad}\,(x^2 + y^2 - 16) = 2x\boldsymbol{i} + 2y\boldsymbol{j}$$

so that the unit outward normal $\hat{\boldsymbol{n}}$ is given by

$$\hat{\boldsymbol{n}} = \frac{2x\boldsymbol{i} + 2y\boldsymbol{j}}{2\sqrt{(x^2 + y^2)}}$$

Hence on the surface $x^2 + y^2 = 16$,

$$\hat{\boldsymbol{n}} = \tfrac{1}{4}(x\boldsymbol{i} + y\boldsymbol{j})$$

giving

$$\mathrm{d}\boldsymbol{S} = \mathrm{d}S\hat{\boldsymbol{n}} = \tfrac{1}{4}\,\mathrm{d}S(x\boldsymbol{i} + y\boldsymbol{j})$$

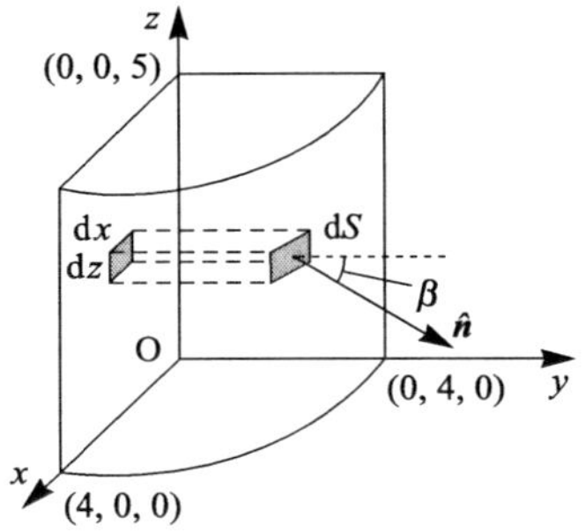

Figure 7.35 Surface S for Example 7.26.

Projecting the element of surface $\mathrm{d}S$ onto the (x, z) plane as illustrated in Figure 7.35, the area $\mathrm{d}x\,\mathrm{d}z$ of the projected element is given by

$$\mathrm{d}x\,\mathrm{d}z = \mathrm{d}S\cos\beta$$

where β is the angle between the normal $\hat{\boldsymbol{n}}$ to the surface element and the normal $\boldsymbol{j}$ to the (x, z) plane. Thus

$$\mathrm{d}x\,\mathrm{d}z = \mathrm{d}S|\hat{\boldsymbol{n}}\cdot\boldsymbol{j}| = \tfrac{1}{4}\mathrm{d}S\,|(x\boldsymbol{i}+y\boldsymbol{j})\cdot\boldsymbol{j}| = \tfrac{1}{4}\mathrm{d}S\,y$$

giving

$$\mathrm{d}S = \frac{4}{y}\,\mathrm{d}x\,\mathrm{d}z$$

Also,

$$\boldsymbol{V}\cdot\mathrm{d}\boldsymbol{S} = \boldsymbol{V}\cdot\hat{\boldsymbol{n}}\,\mathrm{d}S = (z\boldsymbol{i}+x\boldsymbol{j}-3y^2z\boldsymbol{k})\cdot\left(\frac{x\boldsymbol{i}+y\boldsymbol{j}}{4}\right)\frac{4}{y}\,\mathrm{d}x\,\mathrm{d}z = \frac{xz+xy}{y}\,\mathrm{d}x\,\mathrm{d}z$$

so that

$$\iint_S \boldsymbol{V}\cdot\mathrm{d}\boldsymbol{S} = \iint_A \frac{xz+xy}{y}\,\mathrm{d}x\,\mathrm{d}z$$

where A is the rectangular region in the (x, z) plane bounded by $0 \leqslant x \leqslant 4$, $0 \leqslant z \leqslant 5$. Noting that the integrand is still evaluated on the surface, we can write $y = \sqrt{(16-x^2)}$, so that

$$\iint_S \boldsymbol{V}\cdot\mathrm{d}\boldsymbol{S} = \int_0^4\int_0^5\left[x+\frac{xz}{\sqrt{(16-x^2)}}\right]\mathrm{d}z\,\mathrm{d}x$$

$$= \int_0^4\left[xz+\frac{xz^2}{2\sqrt{(16-x^2)}}\right]_0^5\mathrm{d}x = \int_0^4\left[5x+\frac{25x}{2\sqrt{(16-x^2)}}\right]\mathrm{d}x$$

$$= [\tfrac{5}{2}x^2 - \tfrac{25}{2}\sqrt{(16-x^2)}]_0^4 = 90$$

An alternative approach in this case is to evaluate $\frac{1}{4}\iint_S (xz + xy)\,\mathrm{d}S$ directly over the surface using cylindrical polar coordinates. This is left as Exercise 90 below.

7.4.8 Exercises

83 Evaluate the area of the surface $z = 2 - x^2 - y^2$ lying above the (x, y) plane. (*Hint*: Use polar coordinates to evaluate the double integral.)

84 Evaluate

(a) $\iint_S (x^2 + y^2)\,dS$, where S is the surface area of the plane $2x + y + 2z = 6$ cut off by the planes $z = 0$, $z = 2$, $y = 0$, $y = 3$;
(b) $\iint_S z\,dS$, where S is the surface area of the hemisphere $x^2 + y^2 + z^2 = 1$ $(z > 0)$ cut off by the cylinder $x^2 - x + y^2 = 0$.

85 Evaluate $\iint_S \boldsymbol{v} \cdot d\boldsymbol{S}$, where

(a) $\boldsymbol{v} = (xy, -x^2, x + z)$ and S is the part of the plane $2x + 2y + z = 6$ included in the first octant;
(b) $\boldsymbol{v} = (3y, 2x^2, z^3)$ and S is the surface of the cylinder $x^2 + y^2 = 1$, $0 < z < 1$.

86 Show that $\iint_S z^2\,dS = \frac{1}{2}\pi$, where S is the surface of the sphere $x^2 + y^2 + z^2 = 1$, $z \geqslant 0$.

87 Evaluate the surface integral $\iint_S U(x, y, z)\,dS$, where S is the surface of the paraboloid $z = 2 - (x^2 + y^2)$ above the (x, y) plane and $U(x, y, z)$ is given by

(a) 1 (b) $x^2 + y^2$ (c) z

Give a physical interpretation in each case.

88 Determine the surface area of the plane $2x + y + 2z = 16$ cut off by $x = 0$, $y = 0$ and $x^2 + y^2 = 64$.

89 Show that the area of that portion of the surface of the paraboloid $x^2 + y^2 = 4z$ included between the planes $z = 1$ and $z = 3$ is $\frac{16}{3}\pi(4 - \sqrt{2})$.

90 Evaluate the surface integral in Example 7.26 using cylindrical polar coordinates.

91 If $\boldsymbol{F} = y\boldsymbol{i} + (x - 2xz)\boldsymbol{j} - xy\boldsymbol{k}$, evaluate the surface integral $\iint_S (\text{curl}\,\boldsymbol{F}) \cdot d\boldsymbol{S}$, where S is the surface of the sphere $x^2 + y^2 + z^2 = a^2$, $z \geqslant 0$.

7.4.9 Volume integrals

In Section 7.4.7 we defined the integral of a function over a curved surface in three dimensions. This idea can be extended to define the integral of a function of three variables through a region T of three-dimensional space by the limit

$$\iiint_T f(x, y, z)\,dV = \lim_{\substack{n \to \infty \\ \text{all } \Delta V_i \to 0}} \sum_{i=1}^{n} f(\tilde{x}_i, \tilde{y}_i, \tilde{z}_i)\Delta V_i$$

where ΔV_i $(i = 1, \ldots, n)$ is a partition of T into n elements of volume, and $(\tilde{x}_i, \tilde{y}_i, \tilde{z}_i)$ is a point in ΔV_i as illustrated in Figure 7.36.

In terms of rectangular cartesian coordinates the triple integral can, as illustrated in Figure 7.37, be written as

$$\iiint_T f(x, y, z)\,dV = \int_a^b dx \int_{g_1(x)}^{g_2(x)} dy \int_{h_1(x, y)}^{h_2(x, y)} f(x, y, z)\,dz \tag{7.32}$$

Note that there are six different orders in which the integration in (7.32) can be carried out.

As we saw for double integrals in (7.28), the expression for the element of volume $dV = dx\,dy\,dz$ under the transformation $x = x(u, v, w)$, $y = y(u, v, w)$, $z = z(u, v, w)$ may be obtained using the Jacobian

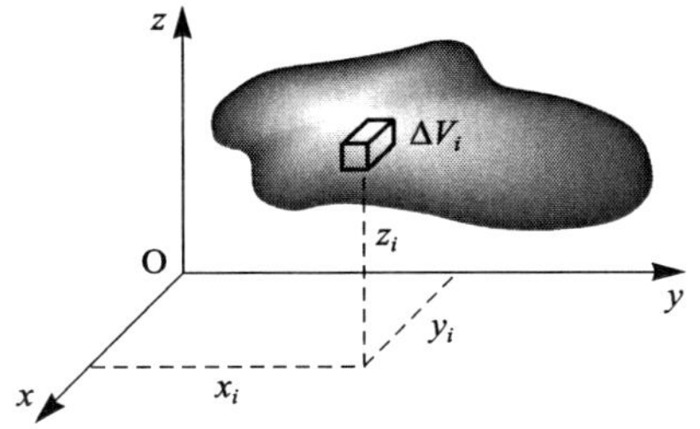

Figure 7.36 Partition of region T into volume elements ΔV_i.

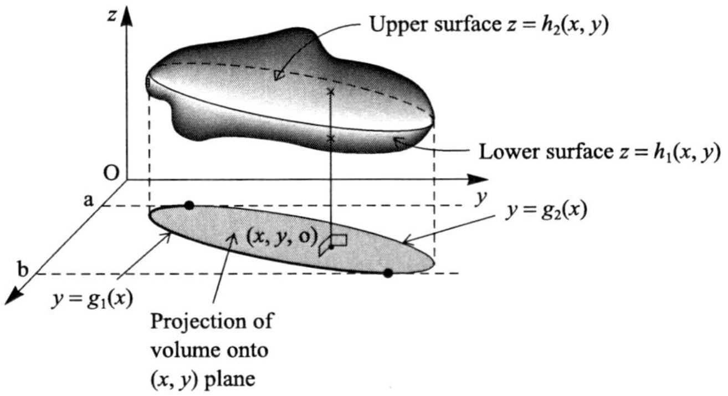

Figure 7.37 The volume integral in terms of rectangular cartesian coordinates.

$$J = \frac{\partial(x, y, z)}{\partial(u, v, w)} = \begin{vmatrix} \frac{\partial x}{\partial u} & \frac{\partial y}{\partial u} & \frac{\partial z}{\partial u} \\ \frac{\partial x}{\partial v} & \frac{\partial y}{\partial v} & \frac{\partial z}{\partial v} \\ \frac{\partial x}{\partial w} & \frac{\partial y}{\partial w} & \frac{\partial z}{\partial w} \end{vmatrix}$$

as

$$\mathrm{d}V = \mathrm{d}x\,\mathrm{d}y\,\mathrm{d}z = |J|\mathrm{d}u\,\mathrm{d}v\,\mathrm{d}w \tag{7.33}$$

For example, in the case of cylindrical polar coordinates

$$x = \rho\cos\phi, \qquad y = \rho\sin\phi, \qquad z = z$$

$$J = \rho\begin{vmatrix} \cos\phi & \sin\phi & 0 \\ -\sin\phi & \cos\phi & 0 \\ 0 & 0 & 1 \end{vmatrix} = \rho$$

so that

$$\mathrm{d}V = \rho\,\mathrm{d}\rho\,\mathrm{d}\phi\,\mathrm{d}z \tag{7.34}$$

a result illustrated in Figure 7.38.

Similarly, for spherical polar coordinates (r, θ, ϕ)

$$x = r\sin\theta\cos\phi, \qquad y = r\sin\theta\sin\phi, \qquad z = r\cos\theta$$

$$J = \begin{vmatrix} \sin\theta\cos\phi & \sin\theta\sin\phi & \cos\theta \\ r\cos\theta\cos\phi & r\cos\theta\sin\phi & -r\sin\theta \\ -r\sin\theta\sin\phi & r\sin\theta\cos\phi & 0 \end{vmatrix} = r^2\sin\theta$$

so that

$$\mathrm{d}V = r^2\sin\theta\,\mathrm{d}r\,\mathrm{d}\theta\,\mathrm{d}\phi \tag{7.35}$$

a result illustrated in Figure 7.39.

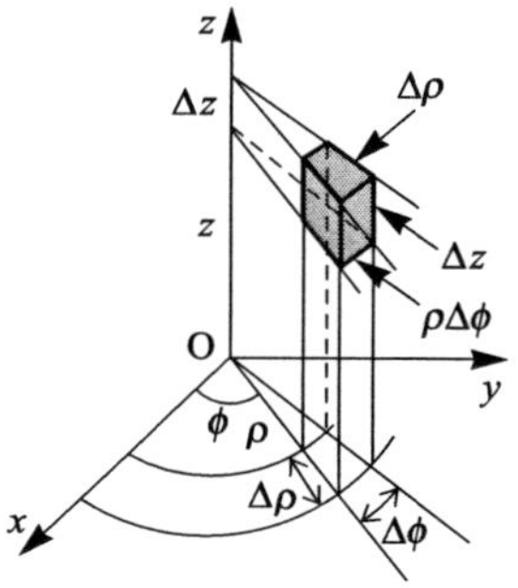

Figure 7.38 Volume element in cylindrical polar coordinates.

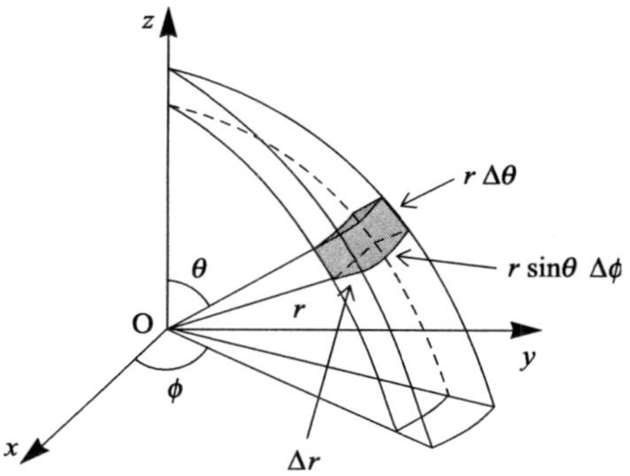

Figure 7.39 Volume element in spherical polar coordinates.

Example 7.27 Find the volume and the coordinates of the centroid of the tetrahedron defined by $x \geqslant 0$, $y \geqslant 0$, $z \geqslant 0$ and $x + y + z \leqslant 1$.

Solution The tetrahedron is shown in Figure 7.40. Its volume is

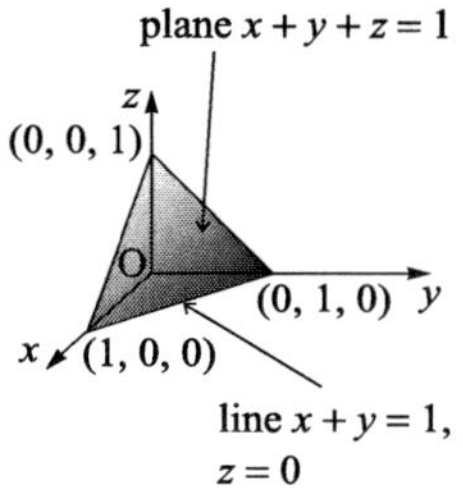

Figure 7.40 Tetrahedron for Example 7.27.

$$V = \iiint\limits_{\text{tetrahedron}} \mathrm{d}x\,\mathrm{d}y\,\mathrm{d}z = \int_{x=0}^{x=1} \mathrm{d}x \int_{y=0}^{y=1-x} \mathrm{d}y \int_{z=0}^{z=1-x-y} \mathrm{d}z$$

$$= \int_0^1 \mathrm{d}x \int_0^{1-x} (1 - x - y)\,\mathrm{d}y = \int_0^1 \tfrac{1}{2}(1 - x)^2\,\mathrm{d}x = \tfrac{1}{6}$$

Let the coordinates of the centroid be $(\bar{x}, \bar{y}, \bar{z})$; then, taking moments,

$$\bar{x}V = \iiint\limits_{\text{tetrahedron}} x\,\mathrm{d}V = \iiint\limits_{\text{tetrahedron}} x\,\mathrm{d}x\,\mathrm{d}y\,\mathrm{d}z$$

$$= \int_0^1 \mathrm{d}x \int_0^{1-x} \mathrm{d}y \int_0^{1-x-y} x\,\mathrm{d}z = \int_0^1 \tfrac{1}{2}x(1 - x)^2\,\mathrm{d}x = \tfrac{1}{24}$$

Hence $\bar{x} = \frac{1}{4}$, and by symmetry $\bar{y} = \bar{z} = \frac{1}{4}$.

Example 7.28 Find the moment of inertia of a uniform sphere of mass M and radius a about a diameter.

Solution A sphere of radius a has volume $4\pi a^3/3$, so that its density is $3M/4\pi a^3$. Then the moment of inertia of the sphere about the z axis is

$$I = \frac{3M}{4\pi a^3} \iiint\limits_{\text{sphere}} (x^2 + y^2)\,\mathrm{d}x\,\mathrm{d}y\,\mathrm{d}z$$

In this example it is natural to use spherical polar coordinates, so that

$$I = \frac{3M}{4\pi a^3} \iiint_{\text{sphere}} (r^2 \sin^2\theta)\, r^2 \sin\theta \, dr \, d\theta \, d\phi$$

$$= \frac{3M}{4\pi a^3} \int_0^a r^4 \, dr \int_0^\pi \sin^3\theta \, d\theta \int_0^{2\pi} d\phi = \frac{3M}{4\pi a^3} (\tfrac{1}{5}a^5)(\tfrac{4}{3})(2\pi)$$

$$= \tfrac{2}{5} Ma^2$$

7.4.10 Exercises

92 Evaluate the triple integrals

(a) $\displaystyle\int_0^1 dx \int_0^2 dy \int_1^3 x^2 yz \, dz$

(b) $\displaystyle\int_0^2 \int_1^3 \int_2^4 xyz^2 \, dz \, dy \, dx$

93 Show that

$$\int_{-1}^1 dz \int_0^z dx \int_{x-z}^{x+z} (x + y + z) \, dy = 0$$

94 Evaluate $\iiint \sin(x + y + z) \, dx \, dy \, dz$ over the portion of the positive octant cut off by the plane $x + y + z = \pi$.

95 Evaluate $\iiint_V xyz \, dx \, dy \, dz$, where V is the region bounded by the planes $x = 0$, $y = 0$, $z = 0$ and $x + y + z = 1$.

96 Sketch the region contained between the parabolic cylinders $y = x^2$ and $x = y^2$ and the planes $z = 0$ and $x + y + z = 2$. Show that the volume of the region may be expressed as the triple integral

$$\int_0^1 \int_{x^2}^{\sqrt{x}} \int_0^{2-x-y} dz \, dy \, dx$$

and evaluate it.

97 Use spherical polar coordinates to evaluate

$$\iiint_V x(x^2 + y^2 + z^2) \, dx \, dy \, dz$$

where V is the region in the first octant lying within the sphere $x^2 + y^2 + z^2 = 1$.

98 Evaluate $\iiint x^2y^2z^2(x + y + z) \, dx \, dy \, dz$ throughout the region defined by $x + y + z \leqslant 1$, $x \geqslant 0$, $y \geqslant 0$, $z \geqslant 0$.

99 Show that if $x + y + z = u$, $y + z = uv$ and $z = uvw$ then

$$\frac{\partial(x, y, z)}{\partial(u, v, w)} = u^2 v$$

Hence evaluate the triple integral

$$\iiint_V \exp[-(x + y + z)^3] \, dx \, dy \, dz$$

where V is the volume of the tetrahedron bounded by the planes $x = 0$, $y = 0$, $z = 0$ and $x + y + z = 1$.

100 Evaluate $\iiint_V yz \, dx \, dy \, dz$ taken throughout the prism with sides parallel to the z axis, whose base is the triangle with vertices at (0, 0, 0), (1, 0, 0), (0, 1, 0) and whose top is the triangle with vertices at (0, 0, 2), (1, 0, 1), (0, 1, 1). Find also the position of the centroid of this prism.

101 Evaluate $\iiint z \, dx \, dy \, dz$ throughout the region defined by $x^2 + y^2 \leqslant z^2$, $x^2 + y^2 + z^2 \leqslant 1$, $z > 0$.

102 Using spherical polar coordinates, evaluate $\iiint x \, dx \, dy \, dz$ throughout the positive octant of the sphere $x^2 + y^2 + z^2 = a^2$.

7.4.11 Gauss's divergence theorem

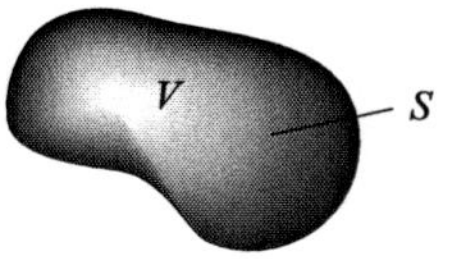

Figure 7.41 Closed volume V with surface S.

In the same way that Green's theorem relates surface and line integrals, Gauss's theorem relates surface and volume integrals.

Consider the closed volume V with surface area S shown in Figure 7.41. The surface integral $\iint_S \boldsymbol{F} \cdot \mathrm{d}\boldsymbol{S}$ may be interpreted as the flow of a liquid with velocity field $\boldsymbol{F}(\boldsymbol{r})$ out of the volume V. In Section 7.3.1 we saw that the divergence of $\boldsymbol{F}$ could be expressed as

$$\operatorname{div} \boldsymbol{F} = \nabla \cdot \boldsymbol{F} = \lim_{\Delta V \to 0} \frac{\text{flow out of } \Delta V}{\Delta V}$$

In terms of differentials, this may be written

$$\operatorname{div} \boldsymbol{F}\, \mathrm{d}V = \text{flow out of } \mathrm{d}V$$

Consider now a partition of the volume V given by ΔV_i $(i = 1, \ldots, n)$. Then the total flow out of V is the sum of the flows out of each ΔV_i. That is,

$$\iint_S \boldsymbol{F} \cdot \mathrm{d}\boldsymbol{S} = \lim_{n\to\infty} \sum_{i=1}^{n} (\text{flow out of } \Delta V_i) = \lim_{n\to\infty} \sum_{i=1}^{n} (\operatorname{div} \boldsymbol{F} \Delta V_i)$$

giving

$$\iint_S \boldsymbol{F} \cdot \mathrm{d}\boldsymbol{S} = \iiint_V \operatorname{div} \boldsymbol{F}\, \mathrm{d}V \tag{7.36}$$

This result is known as the **divergence theorem** or **Gauss's theorem**. It enables us to convert surface integrals into volume integrals, and often simplifies their evaluation.

Example 7.29

A vector field $\boldsymbol{F}(\boldsymbol{r})$ is given by

$$\boldsymbol{F}(\boldsymbol{r}) = x^3 y \boldsymbol{i} + x^2 y^2 \boldsymbol{j} + x^2 yz \boldsymbol{k}$$

Find $\iint_S \boldsymbol{F} \cdot \mathrm{d}\boldsymbol{S}$, where S is the surface of the region in the first octant for which $x + y + z \leqslant 1$.

Solution

We begin by sketching the region V enclosed by S, as shown in Figure 7.42. It is clear that evaluating the surface integral directly will be rather clumsy, involving four separate integrals (one over each of the four surfaces). It is simpler in this case to transform it into a volume integral using the divergence theorem (7.36):

Figure 7.42 Region V and surface S for Example 7.29.

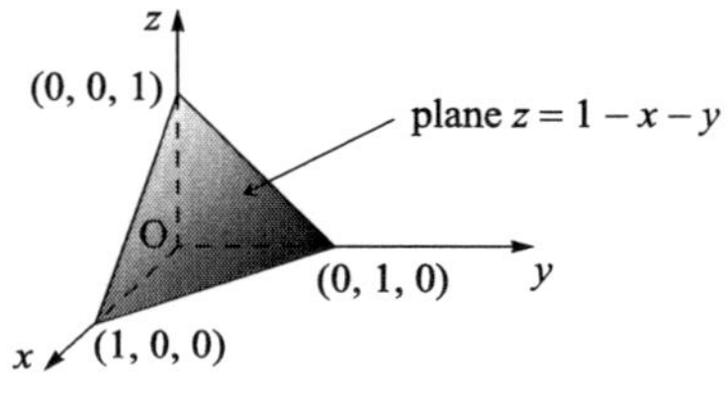

$$\iint_S \boldsymbol{F} \cdot \mathrm{d}\boldsymbol{S} = \iiint_V \operatorname{div} \boldsymbol{F} \, \mathrm{d}V$$

Here

$$\operatorname{div} \boldsymbol{F} = 3x^2y + 2x^2y + x^2y = 6x^2y$$

and we obtain

$$\iint_S \boldsymbol{F} \cdot \mathrm{d}\boldsymbol{S} = \int_0^1 \mathrm{d}x \int_0^{1-x} \mathrm{d}y \int_0^{1-x-y} 6x^2y \, \mathrm{d}z$$

$$= 6 \int_0^1 x^2 \, \mathrm{d}x \int_0^{1-x} y \, \mathrm{d}y \int_0^{1-x-y} \mathrm{d}z \qquad \text{(see Example 7.27)}$$

$$= 6 \int_0^1 x^2 \, \mathrm{d}x \int_0^{1-x} [(1-x)y - y^2] \, \mathrm{d}y$$

$$= \int_0^1 x^2(1-x)^3 \, \mathrm{d}x = \tfrac{1}{60}$$

Example 7.30 Verify the divergence theorem

$$\iint_S \boldsymbol{F} \cdot \mathrm{d}\boldsymbol{S} = \iiint_V \operatorname{div} \boldsymbol{F} \, \mathrm{d}V$$

when $\boldsymbol{F} = 2xz\boldsymbol{i} + yz\boldsymbol{j} + z^2\boldsymbol{k}$ and V is the volume enclosed by the upper hemisphere $x^2 + y^2 + z^2 = a^2$, $z \geqslant 0$.

Solution The volume V and surface S of the hemisphere are illustrated in Figure 7.43. Note that since the theorem relates to a closed volume, the surface S consists of the flat circular base in the (x, y) plane as well as the hemispherical surface. In this case

$$\operatorname{div} \boldsymbol{F} = 2z + z + 2z = 5z$$

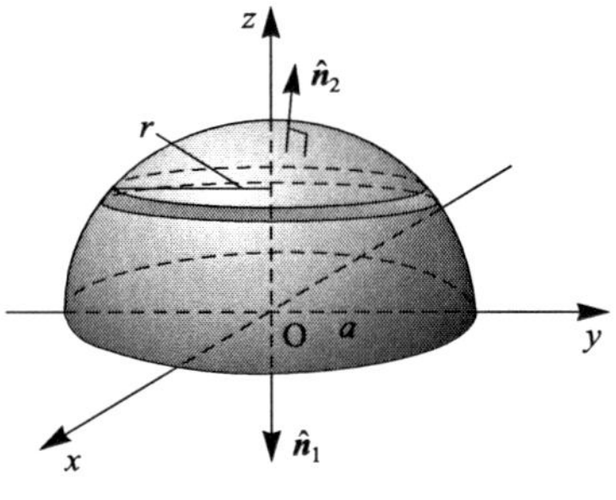

Figure 7.43 Hemisphere for Example 7.30.

so that the volume integral is readily evaluated as

$$\iiint_V 5z\,\mathrm{d}x\,\mathrm{d}y\,\mathrm{d}z = \int_0^a 5z\pi r^2\,\mathrm{d}z = \int_0^a 5\pi z(a^2 - z^2)\mathrm{d}z = \tfrac{5}{4}\pi a^4$$

Considering the surface integral

$$\iint_S \boldsymbol{F}\cdot \mathrm{d}\boldsymbol{S} = \iint_{\text{circular base}} \boldsymbol{F}\cdot\hat{\boldsymbol{n}}_1\,\mathrm{d}S + \iint_{\text{hemisphere}} \boldsymbol{F}\cdot\hat{\boldsymbol{n}}_2\,\mathrm{d}S$$

The unit normal to the base is clearly $\hat{\boldsymbol{n}}_1 = -\boldsymbol{k}$, so

$$\boldsymbol{F}\cdot\hat{\boldsymbol{n}}_1 = -z^2$$

giving

$$\iint_{\text{circular base}} \boldsymbol{F}\cdot\hat{\boldsymbol{n}}_1\,\mathrm{d}S = 0$$

since $z = 0$ on this surface.

The hemispherical surface is given by

$$f(x, y, z) = x^2 + y^2 + z^2 - a^2 = 0$$

so the outward unit normal $\hat{\boldsymbol{n}}_2$ is

$$\hat{\boldsymbol{n}}_2 = \frac{\nabla f}{|\nabla f|} = \frac{2x\boldsymbol{i} + 2y\boldsymbol{j} + 2z\boldsymbol{k}}{2\sqrt{(x^2 + y^2 + z^2)}}$$

Since $x^2 + y^2 + z^2 = a^2$ on the surface,

$$\hat{\boldsymbol{n}}_2 = \frac{x}{a}\boldsymbol{i} + \frac{y}{a}\boldsymbol{j} + \frac{z}{a}\boldsymbol{k}$$

giving

$$\boldsymbol{F}\cdot\hat{\boldsymbol{n}}_2 = \frac{2x^2z}{a} + \frac{y^2z}{a} + \frac{z^3}{a} = \frac{x^2z}{a} + \frac{z}{a}(x^2 + y^2 + z^2)$$

Hence

$$\iint_{\text{hemisphere}} \boldsymbol{F}\cdot\hat{\boldsymbol{n}}_2\,\mathrm{d}S = \iint_{\text{hemisphere}} \frac{z}{a}(x^2 + a^2)\,\mathrm{d}S$$

since $x^2 + y^2 + z^2 = a^2$ on the surface. Transforming to spherical polar coordinates,

$$x = a\sin\theta\cos\phi, \qquad z = a\cos\theta, \qquad \mathrm{d}S = a^2\sin\theta\,\mathrm{d}\theta\,\mathrm{d}\phi$$

the surface integral becomes

$$\iint_{\text{hemisphere}} \boldsymbol{F} \cdot \hat{\boldsymbol{n}}_2 \, \mathrm{d}S = a^4 \int_0^{2\pi} \int_0^{\pi/2} (\sin\theta \cos\theta + \sin^3\theta \cos\theta \cos^2\phi) \, \mathrm{d}\theta \, \mathrm{d}\phi$$

$$= a^4 \int_0^{2\pi} [\tfrac{1}{2} \sin^2\theta + \tfrac{1}{4} \sin^4\theta \cos^2\phi]_0^{\pi/2} \, \mathrm{d}\phi$$

$$= a^4 \int_0^{2\pi} [\tfrac{1}{2} + \tfrac{1}{4} \cos^2\phi] \, \mathrm{d}\phi = \tfrac{5}{4}\pi a^4$$

thus confirming that

$$\iint_S \boldsymbol{F} \cdot \mathrm{d}\boldsymbol{S} = \iiint_V \operatorname{div} \boldsymbol{F} \, \mathrm{d}V$$

7.4.12 Stokes' theorem

Stokes' theorem is the generalization of Green's theorem, and relates line integrals in three dimensions with surface integrals. At the end of Section 7.3.3 we saw that the curl of the vector $\boldsymbol{F}$ could be expressed in the form

$$\operatorname{curl} \boldsymbol{F} \cdot \hat{\boldsymbol{n}} = \lim_{\Delta S \to 0} \frac{\text{flow round } \Delta S}{\Delta S}$$

In terms of differentials, this becomes

$$\operatorname{curl} \boldsymbol{F} \cdot \mathrm{d}\boldsymbol{S} = \text{flow round } \mathrm{d}S$$

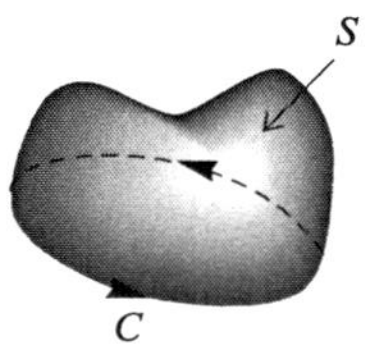

Figure 7.44 Surface S bounded by curve C.

Consider the surface S shown in Figure 7.44, bounded by the curve C. Then the line integral $\oint_C \boldsymbol{F} \cdot \mathrm{d}\boldsymbol{r}$ can be interpreted as the total flow of a fluid with velocity field $\boldsymbol{F}$ around the curve C. Partitioning the surface S into elements ΔS_i ($i = 1, \ldots, n$), we can write

$$\oint_C \boldsymbol{F} \cdot \mathrm{d}\boldsymbol{r} = \lim_{n \to \infty} \sum_{i=1}^{n} (\text{flow round } \Delta S_i) = \lim_{n \to \infty} \sum_{i=1}^{n} (\operatorname{curl} \boldsymbol{F} \cdot \Delta \boldsymbol{S}_i)$$

so that

$$\oint_C \boldsymbol{F} \cdot \mathrm{d}\boldsymbol{r} = \iint_S (\operatorname{curl} \boldsymbol{F}) \cdot \mathrm{d}\boldsymbol{S} \qquad \textbf{(7.37)}$$

This result is known as **Stokes' theorem**. It provides a condition for a line integral to be independent of its path of integration. For, if the integral $\int_A^B \boldsymbol{F} \cdot \mathrm{d}\boldsymbol{r}$ is independent of the path of integration then

$$\int_{C_1} \boldsymbol{F} \cdot \mathrm{d}\boldsymbol{r} = \int_{C_2} \boldsymbol{F} \cdot \mathrm{d}\boldsymbol{r}$$

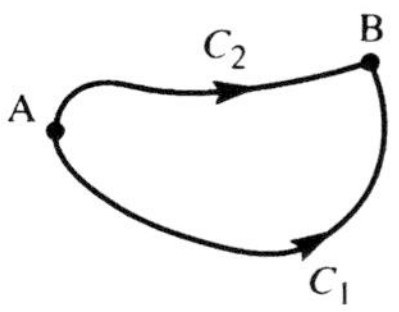

Figure 7.45 Two paths, C_1 and C_2, joining points A and B.

where C_1 and C_2 are two different paths joining A and B as shown in Figure 7.45. Since

$$\int_{C_1} \boldsymbol{F} \cdot \mathrm{d}\boldsymbol{r} = -\int_{-C_2} \boldsymbol{F} \cdot \mathrm{d}\boldsymbol{r}$$

where $-C_2$ is the path C_2 traversed in the opposite direction, we have

$$\int_{C_1} \boldsymbol{F} \cdot \mathrm{d}\boldsymbol{r} + \int_{-C_2} \boldsymbol{F} \cdot \mathrm{d}\boldsymbol{r} = 0$$

That is,

$$\oint_C \boldsymbol{F} \cdot \mathrm{d}\boldsymbol{r} = 0$$

where C is the combined, closed curve formed from C_1 and $-C_2$. Stokes' theorem implies that if $\oint_C \boldsymbol{F} \cdot \mathrm{d}\boldsymbol{r} = 0$ then

$$\iint_S (\text{curl } \boldsymbol{F}) \cdot \mathrm{d}\boldsymbol{S} = 0$$

for any surface S bounded by C. Since this is true for all surfaces bounded by C, we deduce that the integrand must be zero, that is curl $\boldsymbol{F} = \boldsymbol{0}$. Writing $\boldsymbol{F} = (F_1, F_2, F_3)$, we then have that

$$\boldsymbol{F} \cdot \mathrm{d}\boldsymbol{r} = F_1\,\mathrm{d}x + F_2\,\mathrm{d}y + F_3\,\mathrm{d}z$$

is an exact differential if curl $\boldsymbol{F} = \boldsymbol{0}$; that is, if

$$\frac{\partial F_1}{\partial z} = \frac{\partial F_3}{\partial x}, \qquad \frac{\partial F_1}{\partial y} = \frac{\partial F_2}{\partial x}, \qquad \frac{\partial F_2}{\partial z} = \frac{\partial F_3}{\partial y}$$

Thus there is a function $f(x, y, z) = f(\boldsymbol{r})$ such that

$$F_1 = \frac{\partial f}{\partial x}, \qquad F_2 = \frac{\partial f}{\partial y}, \qquad F_3 = \frac{\partial f}{\partial z}$$

that is, such that $\boldsymbol{F}(\boldsymbol{r}) = \text{grad} f$.

When $\boldsymbol{F}(\boldsymbol{r})$ represents a field of force, the field is said to be **conservative** (since it conserves rather than dissipates energy). When $\boldsymbol{F}(\boldsymbol{r})$ represents a velocity field for a fluid, the field is said to be curl-free or **irrotational**.

Example 7.31 Verify Stokes' theorem for $\boldsymbol{F} = (2x - y)\boldsymbol{i} - yz^2\boldsymbol{j} - y^2z\boldsymbol{k}$, where S is the upper half of the sphere $x^2 + y^2 + z^2 = 1$ and C is its boundary.

Solution The surface and boundary involved are illustrated in Figure 7.46. We are required to show that

$$\oint_C \boldsymbol{F} \cdot \mathrm{d}\boldsymbol{r} = \iint_S \text{curl } \boldsymbol{F} \cdot \mathrm{d}\boldsymbol{S}$$

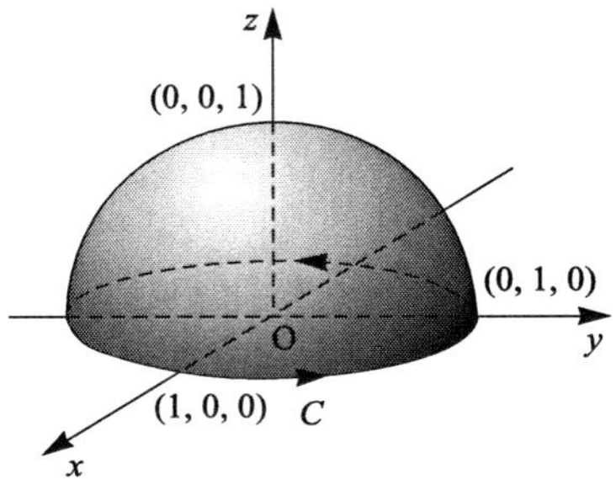

Figure 7.46 Hemispherical surface and boundary for Example 7.31.

Since C is a circle of unit radius in the (x, y) plane, to evaluate $\oint_C \boldsymbol{F}\cdot \mathrm{d}\boldsymbol{r}$, we take

$$x = \cos\phi, \qquad y = \sin\phi$$

so that

$$\boldsymbol{r} = \cos\phi\boldsymbol{i} + \sin\phi\boldsymbol{j}$$

giving

$$\mathrm{d}\boldsymbol{r} = -\sin\phi\,\mathrm{d}\phi\boldsymbol{i} + \cos\phi\,\mathrm{d}\phi\boldsymbol{j}$$

Also, on the boundary C, $z = 0$, so that

$$\boldsymbol{F} = (2x - y)\boldsymbol{i} = (2\cos\phi - \sin\phi)\boldsymbol{i}$$

Thus

$$\oint_C \boldsymbol{F}\cdot \mathrm{d}\boldsymbol{r} = \int_0^{2\pi} (2\cos\phi - \sin\phi)\boldsymbol{i}\cdot(-\sin\phi\boldsymbol{i} + \cos\phi\boldsymbol{j})\,\mathrm{d}\phi$$

$$= \int_0^{2\pi} (-2\sin\phi\cos\phi + \sin^2\phi)\,\mathrm{d}\phi$$

$$= \int_0^{2\pi} [-\sin 2\phi + \tfrac{1}{2}(1 + \cos 2\phi)]\,\mathrm{d}\phi = \pi$$

$$\text{curl}\,\boldsymbol{F} = \begin{vmatrix} \boldsymbol{i} & \boldsymbol{j} & \boldsymbol{k} \\ \dfrac{\partial}{\partial x} & \dfrac{\partial}{\partial y} & \dfrac{\partial}{\partial z} \\ 2x - y & -yz^2 & -y^2z \end{vmatrix} = \boldsymbol{k}$$

The unit outward-drawn normal at a point (x, y, z) on the hemisphere is given by $(x\boldsymbol{i} + y\boldsymbol{j} + z\boldsymbol{k})$, since $x^2 + y^2 + z^2 = 1$. Thus

$$\iint_S \text{curl}\,\boldsymbol{F}\cdot \mathrm{d}\boldsymbol{S} = \iint_S \boldsymbol{k}\cdot(x\boldsymbol{i} + y\boldsymbol{j} + z\boldsymbol{k})\,\mathrm{d}S = \iint_S z\,\mathrm{d}S$$

$$= \int_0^{2\pi}\int_0^{\pi/2} \cos\theta\sin\theta\,\mathrm{d}\theta\,\mathrm{d}\phi = 2\pi[\tfrac{1}{2}\sin^2\theta]_0^{\pi/2} = \pi$$

Hence $\oint_C \boldsymbol{F}\cdot\mathrm{d}\boldsymbol{r} = \iint_S(\text{curl}\,\boldsymbol{F})\cdot\mathrm{d}\boldsymbol{S}$, and Stokes' theorem is verified.

7.4.13 Exercises

103 Evaluate $\iint_S \boldsymbol{F}\cdot d\boldsymbol{S}$, where $\boldsymbol{F} = (4xz, -y^2, yz)$ and S is the surface of the cube bounded by the planes $x = 0$, $x = 1$, $y = 0$, $y = 1$, $z = 0$ and $z = 1$.

104 Use the divergence theorem to evaluate the surface integral $\iint_S \boldsymbol{F}\cdot d\boldsymbol{S}$, where $\boldsymbol{F} = xz\boldsymbol{i} + yz\boldsymbol{j} + z^2\boldsymbol{k}$ and S is the closed surface of the hemisphere $x^2 + y^2 + z^2 = 4$, $z > 0$. (Note that you are not required to verify the theorem.)

105 Verify the divergence theorem

$$\iint_S \boldsymbol{F}\cdot d\boldsymbol{S} = \iiint_V \text{div}\,\boldsymbol{F}\,dV$$

for $\boldsymbol{F} = 4x\boldsymbol{i} - 2y^2\boldsymbol{j} + z^2\boldsymbol{k}$ over the region bounded by $x^2 + y^2 = 4$, $z = 0$ and $z = 3$.

106 Prove that

$$\iiint_V (\text{grad}\,\phi)\cdot(\text{curl}\,\boldsymbol{F})\,dV = \iint_S (\boldsymbol{F}\times\text{grad}\,\phi)\cdot d\boldsymbol{S}$$

107 Verify the divergence theorem for $\boldsymbol{F} = (xy + y^2)\boldsymbol{i} + x^2y\boldsymbol{j}$ and the volume V in the first octant bounded by $x = 0$, $y = 0$, $z = 0$, $z = 1$ and $x^2 + y^2 = 4$.

108 Use Stokes' theorem to show that the value of the line integral $\int_A^B \boldsymbol{F}\cdot d\boldsymbol{r}$ for

$$\boldsymbol{F} = (36xz + 6y\cos x,\ 3 + 6\sin x + z\sin y,\ 18x^2 - \cos y)$$

is independent of the path joining the points A and B.

109 Use Stokes' theorem to evaluate the line integral $\oint_C \boldsymbol{A}\cdot d\boldsymbol{r}$, where $\boldsymbol{A} = -y\boldsymbol{i} + x\boldsymbol{j}$ and C is the boundary of the ellipse $x^2/a^2 + y^2/b^2 = 1$, $z = 0$.

110 Verify Stokes' theorem by evaluating both sides of

$$\iint_S (\text{curl}\,\boldsymbol{F})\cdot d\boldsymbol{S} = \oint_C \boldsymbol{F}\cdot d\boldsymbol{r}$$

where $\boldsymbol{F} = (2x - y)\boldsymbol{i} - yz^2\boldsymbol{j} - y^2z\boldsymbol{k}$ and S is the curved surface of the hemisphere $x^2 + y^2 + z^2 = 16$, $z \geqslant 0$.

111 By applying Stokes' theorem to the function $\boldsymbol{a}f(\boldsymbol{r})$, where $\boldsymbol{a}$ is a constant, deduce that

$$\iint_S (\boldsymbol{n}\times\text{grad}\,f)\,dS = \int_C f(\boldsymbol{r})\,d\boldsymbol{r}$$

Verify this result for the function $f(\boldsymbol{r}) = 3xy^2$ and the rectangle in the plane $z = 0$ bounded by the lines $x = 0$, $x = 1$, $y = 0$ and $y = 2$.

112 Verify Stokes' theorem for $\boldsymbol{F} = (2y + z, x - z, y - x)$ for the part of $x^2 + y^2 + z^2 = 1$ lying in the positive octant.

7.5 Engineering application: streamlines in fluid dynamics

As we mentioned in Section 7.1.5, differentials often occur in mathematical modelling of practical problems. An example occurs in fluid dynamics. Consider the case of steady-state incompressible fluid flow in two dimensions. Using rectangular cartesian coordinates (x, y) to describe a point in the fluid, let u and v be the velocities of the fluid in the x and y directions respectively. Then by considering the flow in and flow out of a small rectangle, as shown in Figure 7.47, per unit time, we obtain a differential relationship between $u(x, y)$ and $v(x, y)$ that models the fact that no fluid is lost or gained in the rectangle; that is, the fluid is conserved.

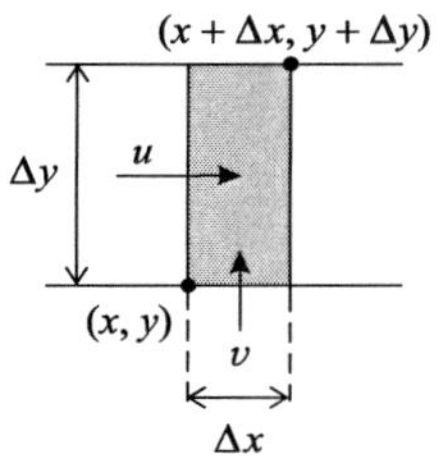

Figure 7.47

The velocity of the fluid $\boldsymbol{q}$ is a vector point function. The values of its components u and v depend on the spatial coordinates x and y. The flow into the small rectangle in unit time is

$$u(x, \bar{y})\Delta y + v(\bar{x}, y)\Delta x$$

where $\bar{x}$ lies between x and $x + \Delta x$, and $\bar{y}$ lies between y and $y + \Delta y$. Similarly, the flow out of the rectangle is

$$u(x + \Delta x, \tilde{y})\Delta y + v(\tilde{x}, y + \Delta y)\Delta x$$

where $\tilde{x}$ lies between x and $x + \Delta x$ and $\tilde{y}$ lies between y and $y + \Delta y$. Because no fluid is created or destroyed within the rectangle, we may equate these two expressions, giving

$$u(x, \bar{y})\Delta y + v(\bar{x}, y)\Delta x = u(x + \Delta x, \tilde{y})\Delta y + v(\tilde{x}, y + \Delta y)\Delta x$$

Rearranging, we have

$$\frac{u(x + \Delta x, \tilde{y}) - u(x, \bar{y})}{\Delta x} + \frac{v(\tilde{x}, y + \Delta y) - v(\bar{x}, y)}{\Delta y} = 0$$

Letting $\Delta x \to 0$ and $\Delta y \to 0$ gives the **continuity equation**

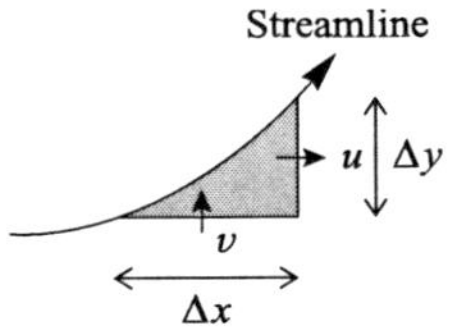

Figure 7.48
Streamline.

$$\frac{\partial u}{\partial x} + \frac{\partial v}{\partial y} = 0$$

The fluid actually flows along paths called **streamlines** so that there is no flow across a streamline. Thus from Figure 7.48 we deduce that

$$v\,\Delta x = u\,\Delta y$$

and hence

$$v\,dx - u\,dy = 0$$

The condition for this expression to be an exact differential is

$$\frac{\partial}{\partial y}(v) = \frac{\partial}{\partial x}(-u)$$

or

$$\frac{\partial u}{\partial x} + \frac{\partial v}{\partial y} = 0$$

This is satisfied for incompressible flow since it is just the continuity equation, so that we deduce that there is a function $\psi(x, y)$, called the **stream function**, such that

$$v = \frac{\partial \psi}{\partial x} \quad \text{and} \quad u = -\frac{\partial \psi}{\partial y}$$

It follows that if we are given u and v, as functions of x and y, that satisfy the continuity equation then we can find the equations of the streamlines given by $\psi(x, y) = \text{constant}$.

Example 7.32 Find the stream function $\psi(x, y)$ for the incompressible flow that is such that the velocity $\boldsymbol{q}$ at the point (x, y) is

$$(-y/(x^2 + y^2), x/(x^2 + y^2))$$

Solution From the definition of the stream function, we have

$$u(x, y) = -\frac{\partial \psi}{\partial y} \quad \text{and} \quad v(x, y) = \frac{\partial \psi}{\partial x}$$

provided that

$$\frac{\partial u}{\partial x} + \frac{\partial v}{\partial y} = 0$$

Here we have

$$u = \frac{-y}{x^2 + y^2} \quad \text{and} \quad v = \frac{x}{x^2 + y^2}$$

so that

$$\frac{\partial u}{\partial x} = \frac{2xy}{(x^2 + y^2)^2} \quad \text{and} \quad \frac{\partial v}{\partial y} = -\frac{2yx}{(x^2 + y^2)^2}$$

confirming that

$$\frac{\partial u}{\partial x} + \frac{\partial v}{\partial y} = 0$$

Integrating

$$\frac{\partial \psi}{\partial y} = -u(x, y) = \frac{y}{x^2 + y^2}$$

with respect to y, keeping x constant, gives

$$\psi(x, y) = \tfrac{1}{2}\ln(x^2 + y^2) + g(x)$$

Differentiating partially with respect to x gives

$$\frac{\partial \psi}{\partial x} = \frac{x}{x^2 + y^2} + \frac{dg}{dx}$$

Since it is known that

$$\frac{\partial \psi}{\partial x} = v(x, y) = \frac{x}{x^2 + y^2}$$

we have

$$\frac{dg}{dx} = 0$$

which on integrating gives

$$g(x) = C$$

where C is a constant. Substituting back into the expression obtained for $\psi(x, y)$, we have

$$\psi(x, y) = \tfrac{1}{2}\ln(x^2 + y^2) + C$$

A streamline of the flow is given by the equation $\psi(x, y) = k$, where k is a constant. After a little manipulation this gives

$$x^2 + y^2 = a^2 \quad \text{and} \quad \ln a = k - C$$

and the corresponding streamlines are shown in Figure 7.49. This is an example of a **vortex**.

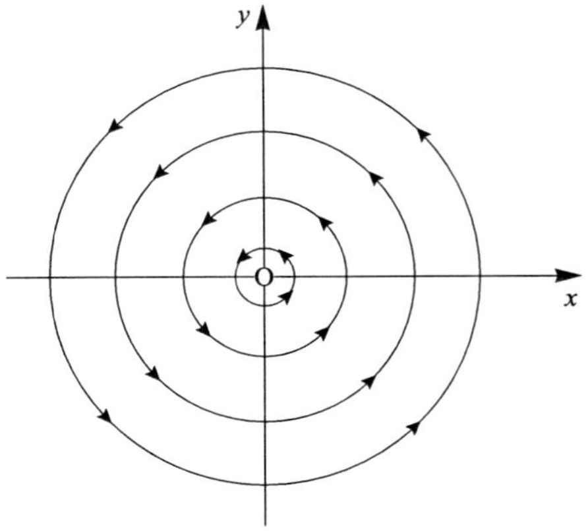

Figure 7.49
Streamline illustrating a vortex.

7.6 Engineering application: heat transfer

In modelling heat transfer problems we make use of three experimental laws.

(1) Heat flows from hot regions to cold regions of a body.

(2) The rate at which heat flows through a plane section drawn in a body is proportional to its area and to the temperature gradient normal to the section.

(3) The quantity of heat in a body is proportional to its mass and to its temperature.

In the simplest case we consider heat transfer in a medium for which the constants of proportionality in the above laws are independent of direction. Such a medium is called **thermally isentropic**. For any arbitrary region within such a medium we can obtain an equation that models such heat flows. The total amount $Q(t)$ of heat within the region V is

$$Q(t) = \iiint_V c\rho u(\boldsymbol{r}, t)\,\mathrm{d}V$$

where c is the specific heat of the medium, ρ is the density and $u(\boldsymbol{r}, t)$ is the temperature at the point $\boldsymbol{r}$ at time t. Heat flows out of the region through its bounding surface S. The experimental laws (1) and (2) above imply that the rate at which heat flows across an element $\Delta\boldsymbol{S}$ of that surface is $-k\nabla u \cdot \Delta\boldsymbol{S}$, where k is the thermal conductivity of the medium. (The minus sign indicates that heat flows from hot regions to cold.) Thus the rate at which heat flows across the whole surface of the region is given by

$$\iint_S (-k\nabla u)\cdot \mathrm{d}\boldsymbol{S} = -k \iint_S \nabla u \cdot \mathrm{d}\boldsymbol{S}$$

Using Gauss's theorem, we deduce that the rate at which heat flows out of the region is

$$-k \iiint_V \nabla^2 u\,\mathrm{d}V$$

If there are no sources or sinks of heat within the region, this must equal the rate at which the region loses heat, $-\mathrm{d}Q/\mathrm{d}t$. Therefore

$$-\frac{\mathrm{d}}{\mathrm{d}t}\left[\iiint_V c\rho u(\boldsymbol{r}, t)\,\mathrm{d}V\right] = -k\iiint_V \nabla^2 u\,\mathrm{d}V$$

Since

$$\frac{\mathrm{d}}{\mathrm{d}t}\iiint_V u(\boldsymbol{r}, t)\,\mathrm{d}V = \iiint_V \frac{\partial u}{\partial t}\,\mathrm{d}V$$

this implies that

$$\iiint_V \left(k\nabla^2 u - c\rho\frac{\partial u}{\partial t}\right)\mathrm{d}V = 0$$

This models the situation for any arbitrarily chosen region V. The arbitrariness in the choice of V implies that the value of the integral is independent of V and that the integrand is equal to zero. Thus

$$\nabla^2 u = \frac{c\rho}{k}\frac{\partial u}{\partial t}$$

The quantity $k/c\rho$ is termed the **thermal diffusivity** of the medium and is usually denoted by the Greek letter kappa, κ. The differential equation models heat flow within a medium. Its solution depends on the initial temperature distribution $u(\boldsymbol{r}, 0)$ and on the conditions pertaining at the boundary of the region. Methods for solving this equation are discussed in Chapter 9. This differential equation also occurs as a model for water percolation through a dam, for neutron transport in reactors and in charge transfer within charge-coupled devices. We shall now proceed to obtain its solution in a very special case.

Example 7.33 A large slab of material has an initial temperature distribution such that one half is at $-u_0$ and the other at $+u_0$. Obtain a mathematical model for this situation and solve it, stating explicitly the assumptions that are made.

Solution When a problem is stated in such vague terms, it is difficult to know what approximations and simplifications may be reasonably made. Since we are dealing with heat transfer, we know that for an isentropic medium the temperature distribution satisfies the equation

$$\nabla^2 u = \frac{1}{\kappa}\frac{\partial u}{\partial t}$$

throughout the medium. We know that the region we are studying is divided so that at $t = 0$ the temperature in one part is $-u_0$ while that in the other is $+u_0$, as illustrated in Figure 7.50. We can deduce from this figure that the subsequent temperature at a point in the medium depends only on the perpendicular distance of the point from the

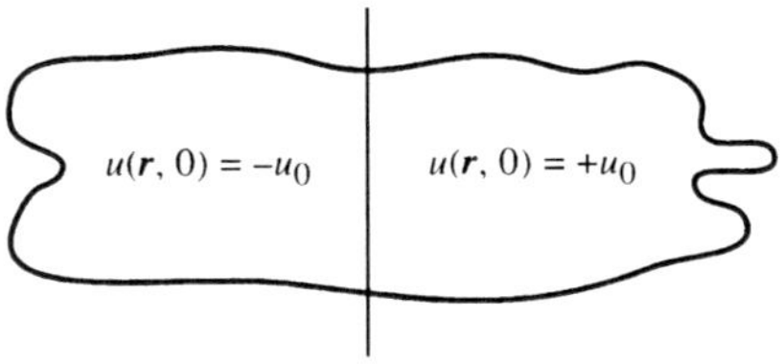

Figure 7.50 Region for Example 7.33.

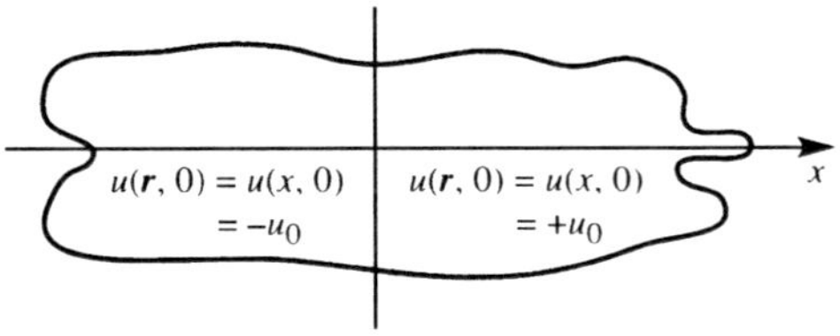

Figure 7.51 Coordinate system for Example 7.33.

dividing plane. We choose a coordinate system so that its origin lies on the dividing plane and the x axis is perpendicular to it, as shown in Figure 7.51. Then the differential equation simplifies, since $u(\boldsymbol{r}, t)$ is independent of y and z, and we have

$$\frac{\partial^2 u}{\partial x^2} = \frac{1}{\kappa}\frac{\partial u}{\partial t} \quad \text{with} \quad u(x, 0) = \begin{cases} -u_0 & (x < 0) \\ +u_0 & (x \geqslant 0) \end{cases}$$

Thinking about the physical problem also provides us with some further information. The heat flows from the hot region to the cold until (eventually) the temperature is uniform throughout the medium. In this case that terminal temperature is zero, since initially half the medium is at temperature $+u_0$ and the other half at $-u_0$. So we know that $u(x, t) \to 0$ as $t \to \infty$. We also deduce from the initial temperature distribution that $-u_0 \leqslant u(x, t) \leqslant u_0$ for all x and t, since there are no extra sources or sinks of heat in the medium. Summarizing, we have

$$\frac{\partial^2 u}{\partial x^2} = \frac{1}{\kappa}\frac{\partial u}{\partial t} \quad (-\infty < x < \infty, t \geqslant 0) \quad \text{with} \quad \begin{aligned} & u(x, 0) = \begin{cases} -u_0 & (x < 0) \\ +u_0 & (x \geqslant 0) \end{cases} \\ & u(x, t) \quad \text{bounded for all } x \\ & u(x, t) \to 0 \quad \text{as} \quad t \to \infty \end{aligned}$$

There are many approaches to solving this problem (see Chapter 9). One is to investigate the effect of changing the scale of the independent variables x and t. Setting $x = \lambda X$ and $t = \mu T$, where λ and μ are positive constants, the problem becomes

$$\mu \frac{\partial^2 U}{\partial X^2} = \frac{\lambda^2}{\kappa}\frac{\partial U}{\partial T}$$

with $U(X, T) = u(x, t)$ and $U(X, 0) = u_0 \operatorname{sgn} X$. Choosing $\mu = \lambda^2$, we see that

$$\frac{\partial^2 U}{\partial X^2} = \frac{1}{\kappa}\frac{\partial U}{\partial T}, \quad \text{with} \quad U(X, 0) = u_0 \operatorname{sgn} X$$

which implies that the solution $u(x, t)$ of the original equation is also a solution of the scaled equation. Thus

$$u(x, t) = u(\lambda x, \lambda^2 t)$$

which suggests that we should look for a solution expressed in terms of a new variable s that is proportional to the ratio of x to $\sqrt{t}$. Setting $s = ax/\sqrt{t}$, we seek a solution as a function of s:

$$u(x, t) = u_0 f(s)$$

This reduces the partial differential equation for u to an ordinary differential equation for f, since

$$\frac{\partial u}{\partial x} = \frac{au_0}{\sqrt{t}}\frac{\mathrm{d}f}{\mathrm{d}s}, \qquad \frac{\partial^2 u}{\partial x^2} = \frac{a^2 u_0}{t}\frac{\mathrm{d}^2 f}{\mathrm{d}s^2}, \qquad \frac{\partial u}{\partial t} = -\frac{1}{2}\frac{axu_0}{t\sqrt{t}}\frac{\mathrm{d}f}{\mathrm{d}s}$$

Thus the differential equation is transformed into

$$\frac{a^2}{t}\frac{\mathrm{d}^2 f}{\mathrm{d}s^2} = -\frac{ax}{2\kappa t\sqrt{t}}\frac{\mathrm{d}f}{\mathrm{d}s}$$

giving

$$a^2\frac{\mathrm{d}^2 f}{\mathrm{d}s^2} = -\frac{s}{2\kappa}\frac{\mathrm{d}f}{\mathrm{d}s}$$

Choosing the constant a such that $a^2 = 1/(4\kappa)$ reduces this to the equation

$$\frac{\mathrm{d}^2 f}{\mathrm{d}s^2} = -2s\frac{\mathrm{d}f}{\mathrm{d}s}$$

The initial condition is transformed into two conditions, since for $x < 0$, $s \to -\infty$ as $t \to 0$ and for $x > 0$, $s \to +\infty$ as $t \to 0$. So we have

$$f(s) \to 1 \quad \text{as} \quad s \to \infty$$

$$f(s) \to -1 \quad \text{as} \quad s \to -\infty$$

Integrating the differential equation once gives

$$\frac{\mathrm{d}f}{\mathrm{d}s} = A\,\mathrm{e}^{-s^2}, \qquad \text{where } A \text{ is a constant}$$

and integrating a second time gives

$$f(s) = B + A\int \mathrm{e}^{-s^2}\,\mathrm{d}s$$

The integral occurring here is one that frequently arises in heat transfer problems, and is given a special name. We define the **error function**, erf(x), by the integral

$$\operatorname{erf}(x) = \frac{2}{\sqrt{\pi}}\int_0^x \mathrm{e}^{-z^2}\,\mathrm{d}z$$

Its name derives from the fact that it is associated with the normal distribution, which is a common model for the distribution of experimental errors. This is a well-tabulated function, and has the property that $\operatorname{erf}(x) \to 1$ as $x \to \infty$.

Writing the solution obtained above in terms of the error function, we have

$$f(s) = A\operatorname{erf}(s) + B$$

Letting $s \to \infty$ and $s \to -\infty$ gives two equations for A and B:

$$1 = A + B$$

$$-1 = -A + B$$

from which we deduce $A = 1$ and $B = 0$. Thus

$$f(s) = \operatorname{erf}(s)$$

so that

$$u(x, t) = u_0 \operatorname{erf}\left(\frac{x}{2\sqrt{t}}\right) = \frac{2u_0}{\sqrt{\pi}} \int_0^{x/2\sqrt{t}} e^{-z^2}\,dz$$

7.7 Review exercises (1–20)

1 Show that $u(x, y) = x^n f(t)$, $t = y/x$, satisfies the differential equations

(a) $x\dfrac{\partial u}{\partial x} + y\dfrac{\partial u}{\partial y} = nu$

(b) $x^2\dfrac{\partial^2 u}{\partial x^2} + 2xy\dfrac{\partial^2 u}{\partial x \partial y} + y^2\dfrac{\partial^2 u}{\partial y^2} = n(n-1)u$

Verify these results for the function $u(x, y) = x^4 + y^4 + 16x^2y^2$.

2 Find the values of the numbers a and b such that the change of variables $u = x + ay$, $v = x + by$ transforms the differential equation

$$9\frac{\partial^2 f}{\partial x^2} - 9\frac{\partial^2 f}{\partial x \partial y} + 2\frac{\partial^2 f}{\partial y^2} = 0$$

into

$$\frac{\partial^2 f}{\partial u \partial v} = 0$$

Hence deduce that the general solution of the equation is given by

$$u(x, y) = f(x + 3y) + g(x + \tfrac{3}{2}y)$$

where f and g are arbitrary functions.

Find the solution of the differential equation that satisfies the conditions

$$u(x, 0) = \sin x, \qquad \frac{\partial u(x, 0)}{\partial y} = 3\cos x$$

3 A differential $P(x, y, z)\,dx + Q(x, y, z)\,dy + R(x, y, z)\,dz$ is exact if there is a function $f(x, y, z)$ such that

$$P(x, y, z)\,dx + Q(x, y, z)\,dy + R(x, y, z)\,dz = \nabla f \cdot (dx, dy, dz)$$

Show that this implies $\nabla \times (P, Q, R) = 0$. Deduce that curl grad $f = 0$.

4 Find grad f, plot some level curves $f =$ constant and indicate grad f by arrows at some points on the level curves for $f(\boldsymbol{r})$ given by

(a) xy (b) $x/(x^2 + y^2)$

5 Show that if $\boldsymbol{\omega}$ is a constant vector then

(a) grad $(\boldsymbol{\omega} \cdot \boldsymbol{r}) = \boldsymbol{\omega}$

(b) curl $(\boldsymbol{\omega} \times \boldsymbol{r}) = 2\boldsymbol{\omega}$

6 (a) Prove that if $f(\boldsymbol{r})$ is a scalar point function then

curl grad $f = 0$

(b) Prove that if $\boldsymbol{v} = \text{grad}\,[zf(\boldsymbol{r})] + \alpha f(\boldsymbol{r})\boldsymbol{k}$ and $\nabla^2 f = 0$, where α is a constant and f is a scalar point function, then

$$\text{div}\,\boldsymbol{v} = (2 + \alpha)\frac{\partial f}{\partial z}, \qquad \nabla^2 \boldsymbol{v} = \text{grad}\left(2\frac{\partial f}{\partial z}\right)$$

7 Show that if $\boldsymbol{F} = (x^2 - y^2 + x)\boldsymbol{i} - (2xy + y)\boldsymbol{j}$, then curl $\boldsymbol{F} = 0$, and find $f(\boldsymbol{r})$ such that $\boldsymbol{F} = \text{grad}\, f$.

Verify that

$$\int_{(1,2)}^{(2,1)} \boldsymbol{F} \cdot d\boldsymbol{r} = [f(\boldsymbol{r})]_{(1,2)}^{(2,1)}$$

8 A force $\boldsymbol{F}$ acts on a particle that is moving in two dimensions along the semicircle $x = 1 - \cos\theta$, $y = \sin\theta$ $(0 \leqslant \theta \leqslant \pi)$. Find the work done when

(a) $\boldsymbol{F} = \sqrt{(x^2 + y^2)}\boldsymbol{i}$

(b) $\boldsymbol{F} = \sqrt{(x^2 + y^2)}\hat{\boldsymbol{n}}$

$\hat{\boldsymbol{n}}$ being the unit vector *tangential* to the path.

9 A force $\boldsymbol{F} = (xy, -y, 1)$ acts on a particle as it moves along the straight line from (0, 0, 0) to (1, 1, 1). Calculate the work done.

10 The force $\boldsymbol{F}$ per unit length of a conducting wire carrying a current $\boldsymbol{I}$ in a magnetic field $\boldsymbol{B}$ is $\boldsymbol{F} = \boldsymbol{I} \times \boldsymbol{B}$. Find the force acting on a circuit whose shape is given by $x = \sin\theta$, $y = \cos\theta$, $z = \sin\frac{1}{2}\theta$, when current I flows in it and when it lies in a magnetic field $\boldsymbol{B} = x\boldsymbol{i} - y\boldsymbol{j} + \boldsymbol{k}$.

11 The velocity $\boldsymbol{v}$ at the point (x, y) in a two-dimensional fluid flow is given by $\boldsymbol{v} = (y\boldsymbol{i} - x\boldsymbol{j})/(x^2 + y^2)$. Find the net circulation around the square $x = \pm 1$, $y = \pm 1$.

12 A metal plate has its boundary defined by $x = 0$, $y = x^2/c$ and $y = c$. The density at the point (x, y) is kxy (per unit area). Find the moment of inertia of the plate about an axis through (0, 0) and perpendicular to the plate.

13 A right circular cone of height h and base radius a is cut into two pieces along a plane parallel to and distance c from the axis of the cone. Find the volume of the smaller piece.

14 The axes of two circular cylinders of radius a intersect at right angles. Show that the volume common to both cylinders may be expressed as the triple integral

$$8\int_0^a \mathrm{d}y \int_0^{\sqrt{(a^2-y^2)}} \mathrm{d}x \int_0^{\sqrt{(a^2-y^2)}} \mathrm{d}z$$

and hence evaluate it.

15 The elastic energy of a volume V of material is $q^2V/(2EI)$, where q is its stress and E and I are constants. Find the elastic energy of a cylindrical volume of radius r and length l in which the stress varies directly as the distance from its axis, being zero at the axis and q_0 at the outer surface.

16 The velocity of a fluid at the point (x, y, z) has components $(3x^2y, xy^2, 0)$. Find the flow rate out of the triangular prism bounded by $z = 0$, $z = 1$, $x = 0$, $y = 0$ and $x + y = 1$.

17 An electrostatic field has components $(2xy, -y^2, x + y)$ at the point (x, y, z). Find the total flux out of the sphere $x^2 + y^2 + z^2 = a^2$.

18 Verify Stokes' theorem

$$\oint_C \boldsymbol{F}\cdot \mathrm{d}\boldsymbol{r} = \iint_S (\mathrm{curl}\,\boldsymbol{F})\cdot \mathrm{d}\boldsymbol{S}$$

where $\boldsymbol{F} = (x^2 + y - 4, 3xy, 2xz + z^2)$ and S is the surface of the hemisphere $x^2 + y^2 + z^2 = 16$ above the (x, y) plane.

19 Use the divergence theorem to evaluate the surface integral

$$\iint_S \boldsymbol{a}\cdot \mathrm{d}\boldsymbol{S}$$

where $\boldsymbol{a} = x\boldsymbol{i} + y\boldsymbol{j} - 2z\boldsymbol{k}$ and S is the surface of the sphere $x^2 + y^2 + z^2 = a^2$ *above* the (x, y) plane.

20 Evaluate the volume integral

$$\iiint_V xyz\,\mathrm{d}V$$

where V denotes the wedge-shaped region bounded in the positive octant by the four planes $x = 0$, $y = 0$, $y = 1 - x$ and $z = 2 - x$.